Organizational Behavior and Management

Ninth Edition

John M. Ivancevich

*Hugh Roy and Lillie Cranz Cullen Chair
and Professor of Organizational Behavior
and Management, C. T. Bauer College of
Business, University of Houston*

Robert Konopaske

*Associate Professor of Management,
McCoy College of Business
Administration, Texas State University*

Michael T. Matteson

*Professor Emeritus Organizational
Behavior and Management, C. T. Bauer
College of Business, University of Houston*

This book is dedicated to the students who inspire and challenge us.

ORGANIZATIONAL BEHAVIOR AND MANAGEMENT, NINTH EDITION

Published by McGraw-Hill, a business unit of The McGraw-Hill Companies, Inc., 1221 Avenue of the Americas, New York, NY 10020. Copyright © 2011 by The McGraw-Hill Companies, Inc. All rights reserved. Previous editions © 2008, 2005, 2002. No part of this publication may be reproduced or distributed in any form or by any means, or stored in a database or retrieval system, without the prior written consent of The McGraw-Hill Companies, Inc., including, but not limited to, in any network or other electronic storage or transmission, or broadcast for distance learning.

Some ancillaries, including electronic and print components, may not be available to customers outside the United States.

⊛ This book is printed on recycled, acid-free paper containing 10% postconsumer waste.

2 3 4 5 6 7 8 9 0 QDB/QDB 1 0 9 8 7 6 5 4 3 2 1

ISBN 978-0-07-353050-5
MHID 0-07-353050-6

Vice President & Editor-in-Chief: *Brent Gordon*
Vice President EDP/Central Publishing Services: *Kimberly Meriwether David*
Publisher: *Paul Ducham*
Sponsoring Editor: *Laura Spell*
Editorial Coordinator: *Jane Beck*
Marketing Manager: *Jaime Halteman*
Senior Project Manager: *Lisa Bruflodt*
Design Coordinator: *Brenda Rolwes*
Cover Designer: *Studio Montage, St. Louis, Missouri*
Photo Research: *Lori Kramer*
Cover Image Credit: © Digital Vision/Getty Images
Production Supervisor: *Nicole Baumgartner*
Media Project Manager: *Babu Suresh*
Compositor: *Aptara®, Inc.*
Typeface: *Times New Roman*
Printer: *Quad/Graphics*

Photo credits: RF/Corbis, pages 3, 35; Ryan McVay/Getty, pages 67, 93, 119, 149, 179, 215, 241; © Fancy Photographer/Veer, pages 277, 309, 339; Digital Vision/Getty, pages 371, 407, 439; © Image 100/Corbis, pages 481, 513.

Library of Congress Cataloging-in-Publication Data

Ivancevich, John M.
    Organizational behavior and management / John M.
Ivancevich, Robert Konopaske, Michael T. Matteson.—9th ed.
      p. cm.
    Includes bibliographical references and index.
    ISBN-13: 978-0-07-353050-5 (acid-free paper)
    ISBN-10: 0-07-353050-6 (acid-free paper)
    1. Organizational behavior. I. Konopaske, Robert. II. Matteson, Michael T. III. Title.
HD58.7.I89 2011
658.4—dc21

                2009053310

www.mhhe.com

About the Authors

John (Jack) M. Ivancevich (August 16, 1939–October 26, 2009): **In Memoriam.**

Hugh Roy and Lillie Cranz Cullen Chair and Professor of Organizational Behavior and Management, C. T. Bauer College of Business, University of Houston; B.S. from Purdue University, and MBA and DBA from the University of Maryland.

Never one to miss a deadline, Jack submitted his last revisions for this textbook during the summer of 2009. A few months later, he passed away with quiet dignity surrounded by loved ones. On that day, the management discipline lost a passionate and award-winning educator, and an influential leader with an incomparable work ethic and sense of integrity. Jack led by example, and those of us who were fortunate enough to know him, were inspired to work harder and reach higher than we ever thought possible.

Jack was committed to higher education and the creation and dissemination of management knowledge. He was comfortable in the classroom and would encourage students to think critically about and apply the concepts and theories of organizational behavior and management to their lives. Jack had an "open door" policy, and spent countless hours helping students and answering their questions. His reputation as a tough teacher was softened by his appreciation for the need of many students to balance a desire for education with a full-time job and family demands. Among Jack's most valued honors was the *Ester Farfel Award for Research, Teaching, and Service Excellence,* the highest honor bestowed to a University of Houston faculty member.

Complementing his passion for teaching, Jack loved to write books. He tried to write at least 300 days a year, averaging about 1,200 words per day. Over a 40-year period, Jack reached well over a million students by authoring or co-authoring 88 books about various aspects of management and organizational behavior. In 1987, the first edition of *Organizational Behavior and Management* (with Michael T. Matteson) was published. Preceding this textbook were several others like the award-winning and popular textbook *Organizations: Behavior, Structure, Processes* (co-authored with James L. Gibson and James H. Donnelly); which was first published in 1973 and is currently in its 13th edition. In 2005, *Organizations* (11th edition) received the McGuffey Longevity Award from the Text and Academic Authors Association. This award recognizes textbooks and learning materials whose excellence has been demonstrated over time. A sample of Jack's other textbooks include: *Human Resource Management, Global Management and Organizational Behavior* (co-authored with Robert Konopaske), *Management and Organizational Behavior Classics* (co-authored with Michael T. Matteson), *Fundamentals of Management: Functions, Behavior, Models* (co-authored with James L. Gibson and James H. Donnelly), and *Management: Quality and Competitiveness* (co-authored with Peter Lorenzi, Steven Skinner, and Philip Crosby).

Jack was not only an accomplished educator and book author but also a prolific and highly respected researcher. Well known for his highly disciplined work ethic, Jack authored or co-authored some 160 research articles, which were published in such journals as *Academy of Management Journal, Academy of Management Review, Administrative Science Quarterly, Journal of Applied Psychology,* and *Harvard Business Review*. His research was highly influential and explored a range of management and organizational behavior topics, including job stress, white-collar crime, diversity management, global assignments, job loss, absenteeism, job satisfaction, goal setting, job performance, training method effectiveness, and organizational climate. The diversity of Jack's research reflected the complex and interrelated nature of management issues in organizations. In 2000, in recognition of publishing a substantial number of refereed articles in Academy of Management journals, Jack was inducted into the Academy of Management's *Journals Hall of Fame* as one of the first thirty-three Charter Members. This is an impressive achievement when considering that in 2000, the Academy of Management had approximately 13,500 members.

In addition to teaching, writing books and conducting research, Jack applied his knowledge of organizational behavior and management to the several leadership positions he held since joining the University of Houston faculty in 1974. In 1975, he was named Chair of the Department of Organizational Behavior and Management, and in the following year, Jack became the Associate Dean of Research for the College of Business Administration at UH. In 1979, Jack was awarded the *Hugh Roy and Lillie Cranz Cullen Chair of Organizational Behavior and Management,* among the most prestigious positions at the University of Houston. From 1988–1995, he served as Dean of the UH College of Business Administration. In 1995, Jack was named UH Executive Vice President for Academic Affairs and Provost, a position he held for two years. Through visionary, performance-driven, and principled leadership, Jack left a lasting and meaningful imprint on the entire University of Houston community, including internal constituents like fellow administrators, Deans, program directors, faculty, staff, and students, as well as external stakeholders like legislators, donors, alumni, and area company executives. His accomplishments were even more extraordinary, given the fact that Jack continued to teach classes, write books, and publish research articles while holding these myriad leadership positions.

Jack made innumerable contributions to all facets of higher education, all of which will be felt for years to come. Perhaps one of Jack's greatest and longest lasting legacies will be from the many individuals he mentored during his 45 years in higher education. As busy as he was throughout his entire career, Jack was extremely generous with his time and made it a priority to mentor a large number of individuals, including current and former students, junior faculty, colleagues from the publishing industry, and many others. He wanted people to succeed and would do everything he could to help them accomplish their goals. Jack would often invite younger faculty members to collaborate with him on research projects. As a member of 80 doctoral and master's committees, Jack relished his role as mentor and would spend hours with graduate students, helping and guiding them through the process of conducting original research for their theses or dissertations. Jack was always willing to make phone calls and write detailed letters of recommendation on behalf of his students to help them get hired or, later in their careers, get promoted or be awarded tenure. He invested heavily in these individuals and expected hard work and commitment to excellence in return. Many of these former graduate students are professors at universities and colleges throughout the United States and now find themselves mentoring and inspiring their own students.

On a personal note, Jack was my mentor, colleague, and friend. Words cannot capture how grateful and honored I feel to have worked so closely with him on several organizational behavior textbooks and research projects over the past 10 years. We became acquainted in 1999, after Jack agreed to be my dissertation chair at the University of Houston. Given Jack's stature and commanding presence, I was a little intimidated by him in the beginning but quickly realized he was a "gentle giant" who could switch rapidly between discussions of research, books, academic careers, teaching, and the importance of being a good family man and father, and achieving balance in one's life. Jack was a great story teller and especially liked relating tales of his early years in the south side of Chicago. Like me, he was proud of the fact that he grew up in a multiethnic environment where one's parents, extended family, and family friends were always around to keep an eye on the kids in the neighborhood, while always ready to offer them a delicious home-cooked meal. Jack taught me many things; some lessons were passed along during thoughtful conversations, but most came by observing him in action. Jack taught me to take life "head on" with a strong, positive, and can-do attitude while never losing sight of the importance of being a loving and committed husband and father. He will be sorely missed by all of us who were fortunate to have been touched by his warm friendship and guided by his generous spirit.

Jack is survived by his wife of 37 years, Margaret (Pegi) Karsner Ivancevich; son Daniel and wife Susan; daughter Jill and husband David Zacha, Jr.; and grandchildren Kathryn Diane and Amanda Dana Ivancevich, and Hunter David Michael, Hailey Dana, and Hannah Marie Zacha. Jack was preceded in death by his beloved daughter Dana and by his first wife, Diane Frances Murphy Ivancevich.

Robert Konopaske
December 28, 2009

Robert Konopaske is Associate Professor of Management at the McCoy College of Business Administration, Texas State University. He earned his Doctoral Degree in management from the University of Houston, a Master's Degree in international business studies from the University of South Carolina, and an undergraduate degree at Rutgers College, Rutgers University. His teaching and research interests focus on international management, organizational behavior, and human resource management issues.

Rob has co-authored *Organizations: Behavior, Structure, Processes* (11th, 12th, and 13th editions), *Organizational Behavior and Management* (7th through 9th editions), and *Global Management and Organizational Behavior.* He has published numerous academic articles in *Journal of Applied Psychology, Academy of Management Executive, Journal of Management Education, Journal of Business Research, Work and Stress, Human Resource Management Review, Management International Review,* and *International Journal of Human Resource Management.* He is on the editorial boards of two international management journals, and has held multiple national leadership positions for the Academy of Management's Human Resource Division. Rob has worked in the private, nonprofit, and education sectors, and has conducted research-based consulting for such global companies as Credit Suisse, PricewaterhouseCoopers, and KPMG.

Michael T. Matteson is an Emeritus Professor of Management at the University of Houston. After receiving his Ph.D. in industrial psychology from the University of Houston, Mike taught graduate and undergraduate courses in the C. T. Bauer College of Business for over three decades. He also served as Associate Dean and Department Chairperson at the University of Houston. Mike has published numerous research and theory-based articles on occupational stress, managing stress, preventive health, work-site health promotion, intervention programs, and research methods. He has consulted with and provided training programs for organizations in numerous industries. He is the co-author or co-editor of a number of textbooks and trade books including *Stress and Work: A Managerial Perspective, Management and Organizational Behavior Classics,* and *Controlling Work Stress.*

Brief Contents

Contents

Preface

Revising and updating this textbook is always an exciting and challenging job. In completing this ninth edition of *Organizational Behavior and Management* we reviewed the most current theories, research, and organizational applications for possible inclusion. We retained the classic, crucial, and long-standing work in organizational behavior. Chapter by chapter, we made a concerted effort to add several more company and other real-world examples to make the content more relevant and interesting for students. Our own teaching of organizational behavior and many excellent suggestions from the reviewers of the previous edition were factored into each phase of the revision.

The major task of the author team was to produce a user-friendly, accurate, clear, and meaningful revision that will result in enhanced student learning. The student and the instructor were always in mind as we carefully revised the book.

We have reviewed and considered numerous suggestions and notes from current instructors and students who use *Organizational Behavior and Management,* as well as from colleagues, managers, and previous users of the text. The themes and tone of these excellent ideas was to keep this book relevant, add more company examples than in previous editions, and help users apply the content to their own lives and job situations. The basic structure has been kept much as it was originally, but we have significantly updated, streamlined, and/or expanded the content of each chapter. We have, in each new edition, added more comprehensive treatment of the content base. The content in this revision has been related to events, activities, and decisions made in organizational life. We have updated all information that needed to be refreshed. Our intention in making these changes has been to offer an intensive treatment of organizational behavior that helps instructors teach easily and effectively. As dedicated teachers, we revise with fellow teachers and the student population in mind. This book was not written as a research message or as a new theoretical model. Like its predecessors, the ninth edition of *Organizational Behavior and Management* contains knowledge that applies both inside and outside the classroom.

Can the serious theory and research basis of organizational behavior be presented to students in an exciting, fun, and challenging way? We believe it can. Thus, we expanded the theory, research, and applications of the subject matter in the revision of the book. The ninth edition of *Organizational Behavior and Management* differs from the previous editions in these ways:

1. Over a hundred domestic and global organizational examples have been added to help students relate theory and research to actual organizations and current events. Here is a sample of the real-world organizations and events that we added to this revision: Bernard Madoff scandal, Lehman Brothers, Simply Splendid Donuts and Ice Cream Shops, United Auto Workers union, the Chinese government, Facebook, LinkedIn, National Football League, Starbucks, Twitter, Apple, Walt Disney, Frito-Lay, *Saturday Night Live,* H1N1 virus, Best Buy, Google, eBay, the Green Berets, and Verizon Communications.

2. Expanded coverage of topics that is relevant to managers today, including: social corporate responsibility, the impact of the current economic recession on employee stress and wellness, the explosion of social network sites, servant leadership, different

types of organizational justice, skills needed by the 21st century workforce, rapid growth in employee diversity, workplace spirituality, positive attitude and cultures, organizational socialization, Gen Y employees' characteristics, work–life balance and alternative work arrangements, breach in psychological contracts, pay equity for women, violence and uncivil behavior at work, "love contracts," different types of sexual harassment, and impression management tactics.

3. Fundamental themes were woven throughout the book, including globalization, managing diversity and demographic changes, technological changes, total quality, and ethics and social responsibility. These themes are consistent with the recommendations for balanced subject matter coverage made by the American Assembly of Collegiate Schools of Business/International Association for Management Education. This internationally acclaimed accrediting body establishes the boundaries for appropriate topic coverage.

4. Several of the end-of-chapter cases have been revised. New cases have replaced some of the previously used cases. A sample of the new cases includes: "Conflict at Walt Disney World: A Distant Memory?"; "The Power and Politics of Privacy on Social Networking Sites"; and "The Race for a Top-Selling Electric Car: Will Upstart Company Detroit Electric Beat Ford?"

5. Many of the book's elements—Reality Check, Global OB, Organizational Encounter, You Be the Judge, and Management Pointers—have been updated or replaced with current examples and issues relevant to managers. The elements included in the final array were considered to be relevant, teachable, and complete.

6. The complete set of materials—text, exercises, elements, and cases—stimulates students to think about how they would respond if they were in the situation being discussed or displayed.

Reading the ninth edition of *Organizational Behavior and Management,* students become involved participants in learning about behavior and management within work settings. We have designed the book with instructional flexibility in mind. The book combines text, self-learning exercises, group participation exercises, and cases. These elements are directed at students interested in understanding, interpreting, and attempting to predict the behavior of people working in organizations.

Organizational functioning is complex. No single theory or model of organizational behavior has emerged as the best or most practical. Thus, managers must be able to probe and diagnose organizational situations when they attempt to understand, interpret, and predict behavior. The ninth edition of the text devotes considerable attention to encouraging the development of these probing and diagnostic skills. The first step in this development is for each reader to increase his or her own self-awareness. Before a person can diagnose why another person (a friend, subordinate, or competitor) is behaving in a particular way, he or she should conduct a self-analysis. This introspective first step is built into each chapter's content and into the learning elements found at the end of chapters. The content and these elements encourage the students to relate their own knowledge and experience to the text, exercises, and cases in the book.

Framework of the Book

Organizational Behavior and Management is organized into five parts containing a total of 17 chapters, one appendix, and a comprehensive glossary. The framework highlights behavior, structure, and processes that are part of life in profit and non-profit organizations. The five parts are as follows:

Part One: The Field of Organizational Behavior

The first chapter, "Introduction to Organizational Behavior," introduces the field of organizational behavior and explores the how, what, why, and when of organizational behavior as viewed and practiced by managers. Chapter 2, "Organizational Culture," covers such issues as internal culture, cultural diversity, and cross-cultural research.

Part Two: Understanding and Managing Individual Behavior

These seven chapters focus on the individual, including topics such as "Individual Differences and Work Behavior" (Chapter 3), "Perceptions, Attributions, and Emotions," (Chapter 4), "Motivation" (Chapter 5), "Job Design, Work, and Motivation" (Chapter 6) "Evaluation, Feedback, and Rewards (Chapter 7), "Managing Misbehavior" (Chapter 8), and "Managing Individual Stress" (Chapter 9).

Part Three: Group Behavior and Interpersonal Influence

These two topics are explored in a three-chapter sequence: Chapter 10, "Groups and Teams"; Chapter 11, "Managing Conflict and Negotiations"; and Chapter 12, "Power, Politics, and Empowerment."

Part Four: Organizational Processes

Part Four includes three chapters: Chapter 13, "Communication"; Chapter 14, "Decision Making"; and Chapter 15, "Leadership."

Part Five: Organizational Design, Change, and Innovation

Two chapters make up the final part: Chapter 16, "Organizational Structure and Design," and Chapter 17, "Managing Organizational Change and Innovation."

Features of the Ninth Edition

The new "Reality Check" and "You Be the Judge" elements start and end each chapter and are helpful for reflective analysis and debate individually or in small in-class groups.

Second, this edition includes many other teaching and discussion "elements." We define a text element as a specific, content-based story, case, or example that is associated with and illustrates the chapter's objectives and themes. The end-of-chapter elements include exercises and cases that were selected because of their relevance to the chapter content and because of feedback from adopters.

Third, we have purposefully woven global events, situations, and examples throughout the book's content, elements, and end-of-chapter material. Globalization is such a vital concern today that it must be presented and covered throughout the book.

Fourth, managing diversity in the workplace is presented and discussed through the text.

Fifth, ethical behavior and social corporate responsibility are topics of major concern throughout the world, especially in the wake of recent U.S. scandals. Examples, incidents, and debates that present ethical dilemmas are integrated into the book.

Sixth, the text emphasizes realism and relevance. Hundreds of real-world examples of decisions, business situations, problem solving, successes, and failures are presented. Fortune 1000 companies do not dominate this book. Smaller and medium-size firms that students may not be familiar with are also used to illustrate organizational behavior and management activities. Finally, we have taken the time and space to explain the concepts, frameworks, and studies presented in the text. It was not our intention to be an encyclopedia of terms and references, but instead to use the ideas, work, and concepts of colleagues only when they add learning value to the chapter content. The goal of each presentation is to present something of value. A "cookbook" list of terms, names, historical points of reference, or empirical studies often becomes pedantic and boring. Comments on previous editions of this text suggest that *Organizational Behavior and Management* is readable and teachable. We believe this is so as we actively teach using this book.

The learning and knowledge enrichment elements, the Reality Checks, Organizational Encounters, Global OB examples, Management Pointers, You Be the Judge features, exercises, and cases, can be used by instructors in any combination that fits the course objectives, teaching style, and classroom situation.

Organizational Encounters

Organizational Encounter features are interspersed throughout the text. They focus on ethical issues, global examples, and general organizational behavior and management activities. The encounters bring the concepts to life by presenting meaningful examples of activities that tie in with the chapter content.

Global OB

Global OB features focus specifically on global issues, problems, solutions, and programs. These are based on a variety of individual, group, or organizational situations.

Management Pointers

Management Pointers appear throughout the text—with at least one in each chapter. This element explains, in straightforward terms, principles of how to manage and how to lead. These principles are easy to understand and use and are based on experience, theory, and empirical research.

You Be the Judge

The "You Be the Judge" scenarios in each chapter present a particular problem, dilemma, or issue and require the student to make a decision and solve the dilemma, problem, or situation. These action-oriented elements are intended to increase student involvement. Our "Comment" on the dilemmas is found at the end of each chapter.

Exercises

Organizational Behavior and Management also includes self-learning and group exercises. Some of the exercises allow the individual student to participate in a way that enhances self-knowledge. These self-learning exercises illustrate how to gather and use feedback properly and emphasize the uniqueness of perception, values, personality, and communication abilities. In addition, a number of exercises apply theories and principles from the text in group activities. Working in groups is a part of organizational life, so these exercises introduce a touch of reality. Group interaction can generate debates, lively discussions, testing of personal ideas, and sharing of information.

Furthermore, the exercises are designed to involve the instructor in the learning process. Student participation allows for trying out techniques and patterns of behavior and integrating exercise materials with the text. None of the exercises requires advance preparation for the instructor, although some require returning to a particular section or model in the chapter for information. The main objective is to get the reader involved.

Cases

The chapters end with full-length cases. These cases reflect a blend of old- and new-economy examples, principles, and lessons. Lessons can and are still being learned from older situations, recent examples, and current front-page news incidents. These realistic, dynamic cases link theory, research, and practice. They provide an inside view of various organizational settings and dynamics. The cases, like the real world, do not have one "right" solution. Instead, each case challenges students to analyze the complexity of the work environment as if they were general managers. The cases also are an invaluable teaching tool. They encourage the individual student to probe, diagnose, and creatively solve real problems. Group participation and learning are encouraged through in-class discussion and debate. The questions at the end of each case may be used to guide the discussion. A case analysis should follow the following format:

1. Read the case quickly.
2. Reread the case using the following model:
   a. Define the major problem in the case in organizational behavior and management terms.
   b. If information is incomplete, which it is likely to be, make realistic assumptions.
   c. Outline the probable causes of the problem.
   d. Consider the costs and benefits of each possible solution.
   e. Choose a solution and describe how you would implement it.
   f. Go over the case again. Make sure the questions at the end of the case are answered, and make sure your solution is efficient, feasible, ethical, legally defensible, and can be defended in classroom debate.

Other Learning Devices

Learning objectives begin each chapter to help the reader anticipate the chapter's concepts, practices, and concerns.

An important part of any course is vocabulary building. Thus, the book provides a thorough glossary of key terms at the end of the book. Before a quiz or test, students can use the glossary to pick out terms that they will be expected to know and use.

We were determined to help the reader prepare his or her own portrait of organizational behavior and management. We hope the text, exercises, cases, and other learning and knowledge enrichment elements help each student become an adventurous explorer of how organizational behavior and management occurs within organizations.

Supplementary Materials

The ninth edition includes a variety of supplementary materials, all designed to provide additional classroom support for instructors. These materials are as follows:

McGraw-Hill Internet Support Site → www.mhhe.com/ivancevichob9e

The *Organizational Behavior and Management* website provides supplemental support materials for instructors and student. Instructor materials include the instructor's manual, PowerPoint slides, and test bank. Student materials include practice quizzes and chapter review material, as well as the following premium content: Self-Assessments, Test Your Knowledge exercises, and Manager's Hot Seat interactive video exercises.

The Instructor's Manual is organized to follow each chapter in the text. It includes chapter objectives, chapter synopses, chapter outlines with tips and ideas, and project and class speaker ideas. Organizational encounter discussion questions and suggested answers, as well as exercise and case notes, are also provided to help you incorporate these dynamic features into your lecture presentations.

The test bank has been updated to complement the ninth edition of the text. This testing resource contains approximately 80 true/false, multiple choice, and essay questions per chapter. Each question is classified according to level of difficulty and contains a page reference to the text.

Video DVD

The Organizational Behavior Video DVD offers a selection of videos illustrating various key concepts from the book and exploring current trends in today's workplace.

Contributors

The authors wish to acknowledge the many scholars, managers, reviewers, and researchers who contributed to every edition of *Organizational Behavior and Management*. In particular, we would like to thank the following reviewers of the Eighth Edition, whose valuable feedback helped guide this revision of the book: Bret Becton, University of Southern Mississippi; Lee Grubb, East Carolina University; Dan Morrell, Middle Tennessee State University; Michelle Ross, National University, San Diego; and Pat Scescke, National Louise University, Lisle. We are indebted to those individuals who granted permission for the use of exercises and cases. In addition, adopters of former editions have made invaluable suggestions, offered materials to incorporate, and informed us about what worked well. These adopters are too numerous to list, but we appreciate the votes of confidence, the willingness to help us improve the book, and the obvious dedication each of you have to teaching.

Michael Dutch, associate professor and chair of the Department of Business Administration and Economics at Greensboro College, contributed significantly to the development of chapters, pedagogy, and revision work on this ninth edition. He made suggestions, introduced relevant research and organizational examples, and discussed with the authors ways to improve the student and instructor friendliness of the book. Michael is an insightful and conscientious colleague who made a meaningful and timely contribution to this revision.

In addition, sections of the book were shaped significantly by two colleagues, James Donnelly, Jr., and James Gibson at the University of Kentucky. These two colleagues have shared and put into practice a common belief that teaching and learning about organizational behavior and management can be an exhilarating and worthwhile experience. Roger Blakeney, Dick DeFrank, Bob Keller, Tim McMahon, Dale Rude, and Jim Phillips, all at the University of Houston; Dave Schweiger at the University of South Carolina; and Art Jago at the University of Missouri have exchanged materials, ideas, and opinions with the authors over the years, and these are reflected in these pages.

Finally, the book is dedicated to our current and former organizational behavior and management students at Texas State University, the University of Maryland, the University of Kentucky, the University of North Carolina at Wilmington, Florida Atlantic University, and the University of Houston. We also dedicate this textbook to the students who are becoming the managers and leaders so vital to the improvement of the overall quality of life in society in the 21st century.

John M. Ivancevich
Robert Konopaske
Michael T. Matteson

The Field of Organizational Behavior

What really binds men together is their culture, the ideas and the standards they have in common.

Ruth Benedict, Patterns of Culture *(1934)*

CHAPTER ONE

Introduction to Organizational Behavior

Learning Objectives

After completing Chapter 1, you should be able to:

- **Define** in applied terms *organizational behavior* (OB).
- **Describe** the disciplines that have contributed to the field of organizational behavior.
- **Discuss** the importance of understanding behavior in organizations.
- **Explain** the time dimension model of measuring effectiveness.
- **Explain** the relationship between quality and organizational effectiveness.

Imagine going to work in an office, plant, medical facility, or store and finding co-workers who are excited about their jobs, managers who listen carefully to workers' comments about the job, and a general atmosphere that is vibrant. In this pleasant setting, people want to work hard, have pride in the job they are doing, trust each other, and share ideas on how to improve performance—groups work together, solve problems, set high quality standards, and enjoy the diversity of each co-worker's family, ethnic, and religious background.

Is this just an illusion or a dream of an ideal work setting? Any manager would cherish, enjoy, and strive to maintain such a work setting. It is a picture of the kind of workplace that managers should use as a target to achieve. This is the workplace that will have to be created if a firm, entrepreneur, or institution is to survive in the coming years.

Jack Welch, former chief executive officer of General Electric and once known as a traditional hard-edge authoritarian manager, became a more human resource–oriented manager during his years at the helm. In his earlier days, Welch had a reputation for eliminating entire layers of employees. He was referred to as "Neutron Jack." People were eliminated, but the firm's buildings remained intact. Eventually, Welch learned that the human being is essential and the key to an organization's success:

> The talents of our people are greatly underestimated and their skills are underutilized. Our biggest task is to fundamentally redesign our relationship with our employees. The objective is to build a place where people have the freedom to be creative, where they feel a sense of accomplishment—a place that brings out the best in everybody.[1]

How much do you know about organizations?

1. True or false: Eighteen of the top 25 largest (in market value) global companies are from the United States.
   a. True
   b. False
2. The first comprehensive general theory of management applied to organizations was offered by _____.
   a. Henry Ford
   b. Thomas Watson
   c. Henri Fayol
   d. Thomas Edison
3. An American icon who emphasized the importance of quality production and products was _____.
   a. W. Edwards Deming
   b. Walt Disney
   c. Sam Walton
   d. Mark Stine
4. The most publicized study of organizations is called the _____.
   a. Los Alamos Experiment
   b. Tavistock Studies
   c. Hawthorne Studies
   d. Dell Analysis
5. Organizational behavior as a field is considered to be _____.
   a. outdated
   b. the same as management
   c. multidisciplinary-anchored
   d. only applicable in developed countries

The key to managing people in ways that lead to profits, productivity, innovation, and real organizational learning ultimately lies in the manager's perspective. Pfeffer captured the importance of people as assets by posing a number of questions and issues:

> When managers look at their people, do they see costs to be reduced? Do they see reluctant employees prone to opportunism, shirking, and free riding, who can't be trusted and who need to be closely controlled through monitoring, rewards, and sanctions? . . . Or do they see intelligent, motivated, trustworthy individuals—the most critical and valuable strategy assets their organizations can have? . . . With the right perspective, anything is possible. With the wrong one, change efforts and new programs become gimmicks, and no amount of consultations, seminars, and slogans will help.[2]

Welch's and Pfeffer's views about people are likely to be significant well into the 21st century. In addition to being people-sensitive and astute, managers and leaders will need other skills and competencies. The next generation of leaders will need the charm of a debutante, the flexibility of a gymnast, and the quickness and agility of a cheetah. Foreign language ability, an international business perspective, and a working knowledge of technology and the law will also help. Since change is so widespread and constant, managers will have to be entrepreneurial. Waiting to be instructed on what to do and how to work with people will not be tolerated. The core qualities

MANAGING AND WORKING TODAY AND IN THE FUTURE

The general opinion is that managers must become agile and flexible to help their firms develop and sustain an advantage in an increasingly competitive globalized world. They will need to harness the powers of information technology and human capital to be successful.

The competitive forces facing managers are led by technological changes and increasing globalization. These driving forces are characterized by greater knowledge intensity and the use of information, the liberalization of developing economies (e.g., Brazil, Russia, India, and China), and new economic alliances and rules.

A good way to acquire a perspective on how fast the environment and competitive forces change is to examine the computer industry. In the mid-1980s, two of the hottest firms were IBM and Apple Computer. These two were fighting fiercely for market share in personal computers and software. Today, both of these firms have lost ground to firms such as Dell (personal computers), Microsoft (software), and Google (search technology). Looking to the future, who will be in the front of the pack of the computer industry?

Markets are becoming borderless and global. Mergers, acquisitions, and start-ups are changing how global markets operate. Strategic alliances have been formed in many industries. The key to competing globally is human capital. To attract, retain, and develop human capital, organizations will have to make available continuous learning. Organizations must identify knowledge, transfer it to employees, and update it continuously. Knowledge is required on the job, working in teams, interacting with external stakeholders (e.g., suppliers), and tapping competitors. Walmart managers systematically shop at competitors' stores to examine how they operate, how products and services are delivered, and how they are marketed.

Knowledge sharing is another important aspect of remaining competitive. Ericsson, a Swedish electronics firm, encourages knowledge sharing through information technology. Ericsson employees and their families have free Internet access. An internal Web site focuses on competence development. Discussion groups, chat rooms, and specialty forums are used by many employees to create communities of practice (e.g., informed groups bound together by shared expertise, interest, and values for a concept, idea, or activity).

Sources: Adapted from Stefan Stern, "Your Attention, Please, I Need You to Focus on This Now," *Financial Times*, January 6, 2009; Thomas H. Davenport and Laurence Prusak, *What's the Big Idea? Creating and Capitalizing on the Best Management Thinking* (Boston: Harvard Business School Press, 2003); T. Hellstrom, "Knowledge and Competence Management at Ericsson: Decentralization and Organizational Fit," *Journal of Knowledge Management*, 2000, pp. 4–10; and Michael A. Hitt, "The New Frontier: Transformation of Management for the New Millennium," *Organizational Dynamics* 28 (Winter 2000), pp. 7–16.

needed to create the ideal work atmosphere begin with intelligence, passion, a strong work ethic, a team orientation, and a genuine concern for people.[3]

Working and managing today and in the future is discussed in the above Organizational Encounter. This Encounter captures some major drivers of change that managers must address to be effective.

Environmental Forces Reshaping Management Practice

power
The ability to get things done in the way one wants them to be done.

globalism
The interdependency of transportation, distribution, communication, and economic networks across international borders.

A number of forces are reshaping the nature of managing within organizations. Organizations that have recognized these forces are working to channel their managerial talents to accomplish goals by using their knowledge about each of six major forces.[4]

The first force at work is the **power** of human resources. The way people (managers, technicians, and staff specialists) work, think, and behave dictates the direction and success of a firm. Unfortunately, companies face a shrinking pool of skilled job candidates and a shortage of technically skilled workers. Managing human resources as valuable assets to be maintained and improved is more important than ever.

To compete effectively in the 21st century, **globalism** must be understood and leveraged. Global competition characterized by networks that bring together countries, institutions, and people is beginning to dominate the global economy. Of the largest 25 global corporations in terms of market value, 11 are from the United States, 5 from China, 2 from the U.K., 2 from Switzerland, and one each from the Netherlands, Australia, Japan, France, and Brazil.[5] As a result of global integration, the growth

THE GLOBALIZATION INDEX

Several events during the past few years demonstrate how global the world has become. For example, thousands of Chinese-manufactured toys containing lead were shipped around the world, a U.S.-led financial crisis sent several other economies into recession, and the H1N1 virus infected people in several different countries.

Attempting to make sense of a "borderless" world, A.T. Kearney and *Foreign Policy* magazine developed the Globalization Index to attempt to measure how fast or far globalization has occurred. How extensive is globalization? Which countries are the most globalized? The least? The index employs indicators spanning information technology, finance, trade, politics, travel, and personal communication to evaluate levels of global integration. It attempts to measure the dense web of cross-border relationships and activities that occur each year.

With few exceptions the countries scoring the highest on the Globalization Index, calculated for 62 nations representing 85 percent of the world's population, enjoyed greater political freedom as measured by the annual Freedom House survey of civil liberties and political rights.

Singapore, Hong Kong, and the Netherlands lead the list as the most globalized nations in the world. Although each of these countries is relatively small in size compared with the United States, these countries compensate for their lack of size, natural resources, and small domestic markets by opening their economies to foreign investment and trade.

Based on data collected in 2005 by A.T. Kearney and *Foreign Policy,* the United States ranks seventh among nations with regard to globalization because of its strength in the technology area. For example, the United States is the leader in the amount of international cyber-traffic it handles; it has so much capacity that it also handles most of the e-mail traffic between Europe and Latin America. The top 20 globalized countries in rank order (1 being most globalized) are:

1. Singapore	11. Sweden
2. Hong Kong	12. United Kingdom
3. Netherlands	13. Australia
4. Switzerland	14. Austria
5. Ireland	15. Belgium
6. Denmark	16. New Zealand
7. United States	17. Norway
8. Canada	18. Finland
9. Jordan	19. Czech Republic
10. Estonia	20. Slovenia

Source: "The Globalization Index," *Foreign Policy,* November/December 2007, pp. 68–76.

rate of world trade has increased faster than that of world gross domestic product. That is, the trading of goods and services among nations has been increasing faster than the actual world production of goods. To survive the fast-paced changes in the global world, firms must make not only capital investments but also investments in people. How well a firm recruits, selects, retains, and motivates a skilled workforce will have a major impact on its ability to compete in the more globally interdependent world.

The above Global OB describes the Globalization Index, a ranking of the globalization integration and activities of 62 nations. This index provides a broad indicator of the global integration rates achieved by the transactions and activities within and between nations. Singapore stands out as the most globally integrated nation according to the Globalization Index.

cultural diversity
The vast array of differences created by cultural phenomena such as history, economic conditions, personality characteristics, language, norms, and mores.

A **culturally diverse** workforce is becoming a reality in the United States. As the complexion of America's workforce changes, managers and co-workers need to learn more about each other so that a receptive work culture is created. While Japan and China are basically homogeneous societies in terms of race, the United States is racially diverse and has been rapidly increasing its workforce diversity since the 1970s. Not only are racial and ethnic diversity growing, but also more women, older workers, and people with disabilities are entering the workforce in increasing numbers. The workforce in March 2009 was quite diverse with 48 percent being female, 13.9 percent Hispanic, and 12 percent African-American.[6]

African-Americans, Hispanics, and Asians are now the fastest-growing groups in the U.S. employee mix. About 28 percent of the U.S. workforce is likely to be non-white by the year 2012.[7] Increased minority and female participation raises a number of issues managers must address to remain competitive globally. Are minorities and women ready to take over high-paying, higher-status jobs? Unless they properly train and prepare minorities and women for significant jobs, organizations are not going to be competitive.

rapidity of change
The speed at which change occurs. Rapid change is found in many areas such as technology, demographics, globalism, and new products and services.

The **rapidity of change** is another crucial force to recognize. The fax machine, Internet, genetic engineering, microchips, and more demanding consumers who want better-quality products and services at a lower price and on time are some of the changes sweeping the world. Understanding, accommodating, and using change are now a part of a manager's job requirement.

The elements of change include almost instantaneous communication and computation.[8] Technological connectivity is putting everything online, which has resulted in the shrinking of space and distance. Intangible value of all kinds, such as service and information, is growing at a rapid speed. The modern manager is going to have to be adaptable to such rapid change. Those who fail to understand speed and resist how fast adaptation must come about will have problems.

psychological contract
An unwritten agreement between an employee and the organization that specifies what each expects to give to and receive from the other.

The worker–employer **psychological contract** is another force. From the employer's view, employees do not have lifetime jobs, guaranteed advancement or raises, and assurance that their work roles will be fixed. However, the most admired employers believe that openness, integrity, providing opportunities, and supporting the growth and development of their employees are top priorities. They believe this is an unwritten contract they have with their people. Employees believe that employers must be honest, open, and fair and also be willing to give workers a larger say in their jobs. Employees also want organizations to pay more attention to their family situations and their physical and mental health. Employees want employers to appreciate the humanness of workers. Employees view their role in the contract with employers as important for their psychological fitness and health.

technology
An important concept that can have many definitions in specific instances but that generally refers to actions, physical and mental, that an individual performs upon some object, person, or problem to change it in some way.

Another major force influencing management is **technology.** In a general sense, technology is the processes that convert raw materials or intellectual capital into products or services. Technology is more than just machinery. It also encompasses the design of practices that can be used to service customers, treat patients, and manufacture high-quality products. The technology of an organization influences the work flow, structure, systems, and philosophy of the organization to a significant degree. Today, computer technology is so pervasive and powerful that it needs to be well understood to be used effectively.[9]

The semiconductor pioneer Gordon Moore predicted in 1965 that chip density—and all kinds of computer power—would double every two years. (Some claim he said 18 months, but he denies the shorter cycle.) It is common to cite Moore's law to refer to the rapidly advancing computing power-per-unit cost. His prediction has been right on target. Moore's law highlights the speed-up in the general technological pace.

In the agricultural era, land was the core factor in achieving competitive advantage. Landowners were dominant in shaping markets, policies, and legislation. In the present information age, we use computer technology and human assets to operate, maintain, and invent new computer systems that are more powerful than the previous computer generation. Organizations, in their quest for competitive advantage, must attract, retain, and recognize crucial human assets to continue advancing.

Google, Goldman Sachs, and Walt Disney's Pixar are sought out by talented, technology-savvy job candidates. In examining the programs, practices, and approaches

THE U.S. WORKFORCE IN THE 21ST CENTURY: HIGH-PAID KNOWLEDGE WORKERS OR LOW-PAID SERVICE WORKERS?

In 2007, the National Institutes of Health and the Russell Sage Foundation asked the National Academies' Center for Education to bring researchers together from multiple disciplines—psychology, sociology, political science, and business—to present their research regarding which skills will be necessary for work in the 21st century. One important conclusion from the workshop was that the U.S. economy would continue to evolve into a "barbell" economy with most jobs falling into one of two categories: either high-paid, high-skill professional or low-wage, low-skill service jobs. According to the U.S. Bureau of Labor Statistics, between 2006 and 2016, the fastest-growing occupational clusters of jobs will be the "professional and related" (16.7 percent growth) and "service" (16.7 percent growth) clusters. The "professional and related" category includes health care practitioners and technicians, and education, training, and library professionals, all of which require certifications and bachelor degrees or higher. The "service" cluster, including food preparation and health care support roles, often require only a high school diploma.

Another important finding that emerged from the future skills workshop is that two important trends will affect the future labor demand and supply in the United States. First, the pending retirements of baby boomers (those born between 1946 and 1964) over the next 10 to 20 years will create skills shortages. Second, the majority of the population growth of the U.S. work force will come from immigrants and their U.S.-born offspring. Research suggests that the education attainment of the immigrant labor force in the United States also follows a barbell shape, with half of this group being highly educated and the other half being without much formal education.

Many skills will be needed for these knowledge-based and service-oriented jobs. The future of knowledge work will not only rely on strong scientific, engineering, and IT skills, but also on social and interpersonal skills as many knowledge workers occupy "techno-serve" jobs; such jobs require workers to combine their high-tech skill set with the softer skills (e.g., interpersonal, communication, and empathy) needed for service. Although some of these high-tech jobs (e.g., IT and software development) will continue to be outsourced to countries such as India and China, many will remain in the United States. However, more jobs will require Americans to collaborate with individuals from many different countries via virtual teams and online collaboration.

Skills requirements for low-paid service jobs are more demanding than conventional wisdom would suggest. Many customer-intensive service jobs require good communication, technical, emotional, and time management skills. When problems occur, these employees are expected to quickly adapt to the situation and solve the customer's problem in a creative manner. Service providers also need to convey to customers or clients that they care and want them to have a positive experience.

In sum, the U.S. economy will increasingly consist of either high-paid knowledge and professional-type individuals like scientists, professors, lawyers, researchers, accountants, and so on or low-paid service workers such as nursing aids, janitorial staff, and restaurant servers. This barbell-shaped economy combined with the upcoming large number of baby boomer retirements and increase in immigration present substantial challenges and opportunities for future managers and leaders as they figure out how best to recruit, train, develop, and retain the critical human resources needed to compete successfully in the 21st century.

Sources: Adapted from Margaret Hilton, "Skills for Work in the 21st Century: What Does the Research Tell Us?" *Academy of Management Perspectives,* 22, no. 4 (November 2008), pp. 63–78; J. Passel and D. Cohn, *Immigration to Play Key Role in Future U.S. Growth* (Washington, DC: Pew Research Center, 2008), retrieved September 10, 2008, from http://pewresearch.org/pubs/729/united-states-populationprojections; U.S. Bureau of Labor Statistics, "Table 4: Employment by Major Occupational Group: 2006–2016," www.bls.gov/news.release/ecopro.t04.htm, accessed July 5, 2009; and I. Hampson and A. Junor, "Invisible Work, Invisible Skills: Interactive Customer Service as Articulation Work," *New Technology, Work and Employment* 20 (2005), pp. 166–81.

used by these and other firms, it is obvious that valuing those who have knowledge about how to use technology is a priority. Technology can yield competitive advantages only when it is utilized effectively.

For years W. Edwards Deming, the father of continuous quality improvement, had trouble convincing U.S. auto manufacturers to implement quality-improvement programs. He recommended improved information, training to improve quality, and delegating more authority to operating employees. Inspired by Deming, others have talked about putting more accurate, timely, and relevant information in the hands of all employees.[10]

The introduction of computer technology has fostered an era of information technology (IT). The IT era, combined with improved selection, training, and a positive and strong organizational culture, provides the potential for using information and technology in a more knowledgeable and effective way. The right information is a precious commodity that, when applied effectively, can result in higher growth and productivity.[11] The Organizational Encounter on page 8 discusses how jobs in the U.S. economy can be categorized as either high-paid knowledge (e.g., IT manager) or low-paid service (e.g., nursing aid) jobs.

Information technology has changed the way managers act and perform. Before the IT era, subordinates gathered data and information and provided it up the chain of command.[12] The manager (up the chain) analyzed what was provided, made a decision, and informed the subordinates to carry out the decision. This method had a high potential for errors of omission, plodding along, and miscommunication. IT today provides easier access to information (e.g., computer databases) and provides managers an opportunity to share, delegate, or oversee decision making by their team or unit. This enhanced access to information helped U.S. businesses respond faster to weaker demand for their products and services caused by the economic recession.[13] Managers acted on accurate IT reports on sales and spending by cutting payrolls, capital expenditures, and inventories. The effect of these steps led to an increase in national-level productivity of 3.2 percent (annualized rate) in 2009 and to better-positioned businesses for when the economic recovery occurs.[14]

The six forces reshaping management practice—the *power* of human resources, *globalism, cultural diversity,* the *rapidity of change,* a new worker–employer *psychological contract,* and *technology*—offer challenges to managers. Resisting the reality of these forces will likely lead to unnecessary conflict, reduced managerial and non-managerial performance, and lost opportunities. In managerial terms, failing to cope and deal with these forces will likely result in job dissatisfaction, poor morale, reduced commitment, lower work quality, burnout, poor judgment, and a host of unhealthy consequences.

The purpose of this book is to help you learn how to manage and lead individuals and groups in organizations. These human resources are operating in a world impacted by powerful forces. Organizations are essential to the way our society operates in the world. In industry, education, health care, and defense, organizations have created impressive gains for the standard of living and prestige of entire nations. The size of the organizations with which you deal daily should illustrate the tremendous political, economic, and social powers they separately possess. If a large firm announced that it was closing its plant in your community, the resulting impact might be devastating economically. On the other hand, if Dell announced it was opening a computer assembly plant in your community, the effect probably would be very positive.

Organizations are much more than only a means for providing goods and services.[15] They create the settings in which most of us spend our lives. In this respect, they have profound influence on employee behavior. However, because large-scale organizations have developed only in recent times, we are just now beginning to recognize the necessity for studying them. Researchers have just begun the process of developing ways to study the behavior of people in organizations of all sizes.

The Origins of Management

The formal and modern study of management started around 1900.[16] However, the management process probably first began in the family organization, later expanded to the tribe, and finally pervaded the formalized political units such as those found in early Babylonia (5000 B.C.). The Egyptians, Chinese, Greeks, and Romans were all noted in history for major managerial feats such as the building of the pyramids, organizing governments, planning military maneuvers, operating trading companies that traversed the world, and controlling a geographically dispersed empire.

A Brief History Lesson

A review of the early history of management dating back over 7,000 years ago suggests that management as a process was based on trial and error, with little or no theory and virtually no sharing of ideas and practices. This lack of sharing slowed the influence of management practices throughout the world. Management for thousands of years was based on trying an approach that seemed to be suited for accomplishing a particular goal. There was no common body of knowledge or theoretical basis for managing the Roman Empire or building the Great Pyramid of Cheops.

The period between 1700 and 1785 is referred to as the Industrial Revolution in England.[17] As a nation, England changed dramatically from a rural society to the workshop of the world. It was the first nation to successfully make the transition from a rural-agrarian society to an industrial-commercial society.[18] Management of the workshops of England was characterized by an emphasis on efficiency, strict controls, and rigid rules and procedures.

Industrialization   A new industrial era began in the United States around the time of the Civil War. There was a dramatic expansion of mechanical industries such as the railroad. In addition, large industrial manufacturing complexes grew in importance. Attempts to better plan, organize, and control the work of these complexes led managers to discuss their situations and present papers at meetings. The first modern management publications were published in engineering journals.

In 1881, a new way to study management started with a $100,000 gift by Joseph Wharton to the University of Pennsylvania to establish a management department in a college. The management curriculum at that time covered such topics as strikes, business law, the nature of stocks and bonds, and principles of work cooperation.

Scientific Management

scientific management
A body of literature that emerged during the period 1890–1930 and that reports the ideas and theories of engineers concerned with such problems as job definition, incentive systems, and selection and training.

In 1886, an engineer named Frederick W. Taylor presented a paper titled "The Engineer as an Economist" at a national meeting of engineers. This paper and others prepared by Taylor expressed his philosophy of **scientific management**.[19] Taylor's major thesis was that maximum good for society can come only through the cooperation of management and labor in the application of scientific methods. He stated that the principles of management were to:

- Develop a science for each element of an employee's work, which replaces the old rule-of-thumb method.
- Scientifically select and then train, teach, and develop the worker, whereas in the past a worker chose the work to do and was self-trained.
- Heartily cooperate with each other to ensure that all work was done in accordance with the principles of science.
- Strive for an almost equal division of work and responsibility between management and nonmanagers.

These four principles constituted Taylor's concept of scientific management. Some regard him as the father of all present-day management. Even if this is considered an exaggerated viewpoint, Taylor was a key figure in the promotion of the role of management in organizations. He has had a lasting impact on a unified, coherent way to improve the way managers perform their jobs.

Functions of Management

Henri Fayol, a French industrialist, presented what is considered the first comprehensive statement of a general theory of management. First published in France in 1916,[20] Fayol's *Administration Industrielle et Générale* was largely ignored in the United States until it was translated into English in 1949.

Fayol attributed his success in managing a large mining firm to his system of management, which he believed could be taught and learned. He emphasized the importance of carefully practicing efficient planning, organizing, commanding, coordinating, and controlling.

Fayol's approach was a significant contribution in that it presented three important developments that have had a lasting impact on the field.

1. Management is a separate body of knowledge that can be applied in any type of organization.
2. A theory of management can be learned and taught.
3. There is a need for teaching management in colleges.

The Importance of Studying Organizational Behavior

organizational behavior
The study of human behavior, attitudes, and performance within an organizational setting; drawing on theory, methods, and principles from such disciplines as psychology, sociology, and cultural anthropology to learn about *individual* perceptions, values, learning capacities, and actions while working in *groups* and within the total *organization;* analyzing the external environment's effect on the organization and its human resources, missions, objectives, and strategies.

Why do employees behave as they do in organizations? Why is one individual or group more productive than another? Why do managers continually seek ways to design jobs and delegate authority? These and similar questions are important to the relatively new field of study known as **organizational behavior.** Understanding the behavior of people in organizations has become increasingly important as management concerns—such as employee productivity, the quality of work life, job stress, and career progression—continue to make front-page news.

Clearly understanding that organizational behavior (OB) has evolved from multiple disciplines, we will use the following definition of OB throughout this book:

> The study of human behavior, attitudes, and performance within an organizational setting; drawing on theory, methods, and principles from such disciplines as psychology, sociology, political science, and cultural anthropology to learn about individuals, groups, structure, and processes.

This multidisciplinary view of organizational behavior illustrates a number of points. First, OB is a *way of thinking.* Behavior is viewed as operating at individual, group, and organizational levels. This approach suggests that when studying OB, we must identify clearly the level of analysis being used—individual, group, and/or organizational. Second, OB is *multidisciplinary.* This means that it utilizes principles, models, theories, and methods from other disciplines. The study of OB is not a discipline or a generally accepted science with an established theoretical foundation. It is a field that only now is beginning to grow and develop in stature and impact. Third, there is a distinctly *humanistic orientation* within organizational behavior. People and their attitudes, perceptions, learning capacities, feelings, and goals are of major importance to the organization. Fourth, the field of OB is *performance-oriented.* Why is performance low or high? How can performance be improved? Can training enhance on-the-job performance? Practicing managers face these important issues. Fifth, since the field of OB relies heavily on recognized disciplines, the role of the *scientific method* is deemed important in studying variables and relationships. As the scientific method has been used in conducting research on organizational behavior, a set of principles and guidelines on what constitutes good research has emerged.[21] Finally, the field has a distinctive *applications orientation;* it is concerned with providing useful answers to questions that arise in the context of managing organizations.[22]

Exhibit 1.1 offers a framework and overview of the multiple disciplines that have contributed to the study of OB and the application of OB principles in organizational settings.

EXHIBIT 1.1

Contributions to the Study of Organizational Behavior

Source: Adapted from Stephen P. Robbins, *Organizational Behavior* (Upper Saddle River, NJ: Prentice Hall, 2003), p. 11.

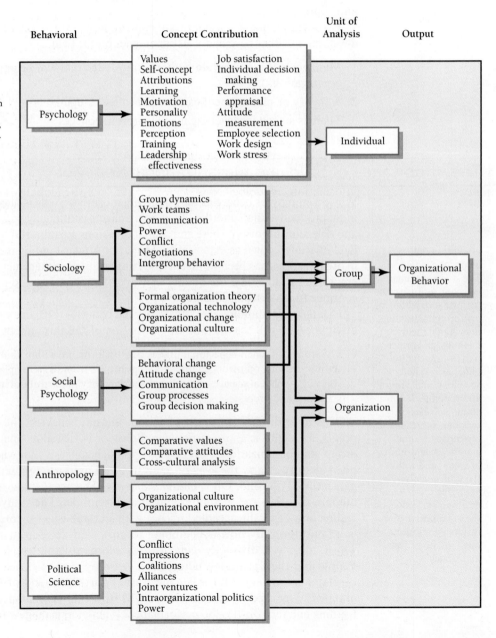

Leaders and Organizational Behavior

Changes occurring within and outside of institutions challenge leaders of workers, managers, and administrators in organizations. Terms such as *social responsibility, cultural diversity, ethics, global competitiveness, social networking,* and *reengineering* are used freely by experts and nonexperts. Each of these concepts points out that leaders are being asked to perform effectively in a changing world.

In addition to the changing makeup and diversity of the workforce is the increased emphasis that consumers are placing on *value*.[23] The trend among consumers is to consider the total value of a product or service. Today, more than ever, customers expect organizations to be responsive to their needs, to provide prompt service and delivery, and to produce top quality goods or services at the best price possible.

Along with an increasingly diverse workforce and demanding customers, leaders must contend with changes in both domestic and global markets and competition. Today, richer, more educated, and more demanding customers exist in every competitive country. The global market wants a world of easy access to products and services. Leaders must assure customers that their high-quality goods or services will be available when the consumer wants them and at a competitive price. Leaders are being asked to establish the work team, department, or organization that can respond, compete, and negotiate globally.

For over three decades, the development of the integrated circuit has permitted an increasing amount of information to be processed or stored on a single microchip. The leaders within organizations are asked to efficiently use and manage the available information technology so that the firm can compete globally. The Internet is an example of an electronic information sharing system. A national web of high-speed networks links business, state, university, and regional computer systems. Information is passed from one network to another. The dramatic growth of the Internet has resulted in managers from around the world sharing data and ideas with like-minded peers. The length of time it takes an idea to circulate or a problem to be considered by peers across the ocean has dropped from weeks to hours. The potential for using information technology and other technologies in managing workers, motivating an individual, or altering the structure of an organization is endless.

Everything facing a leader in an organization is in motion and churning. Properly aligning the human resources of the organization with the changing conditions requires an understanding of such phenomena as the organization's environment, individual characteristics, group behavior, organizational structure and design, decision making, and organizational change processes. The modern-day impetus of aligning human resources with organizational factors was initiated with the Hawthorne studies.

The Hawthorne Studies

From 1900 to 1930, Taylor's concept of scientific management dominated thought about management. His approach focused on maximizing worker output. However, Taylor's emphasis on output and efficiency didn't address employees' needs. Trade unions rebelled against Taylor's focus on scientific management principles.

Mary Parker Follett was opposed to Taylor's lack of specific attention on human needs and relationships in the workplace. She was one of the first management theorists to promote participatory decision making and decentralization. Her view emphasized individual and group needs. The human element was the focus of Follett's view about how to manage. However, she failed to produce empirical evidence to support her views. Industry leaders wanted concrete evidence that focusing on human resources would result in higher productivity. Some concrete evidence became available from data collected in the Hawthorne studies.

A team of Harvard University researchers was asked to study the activities of work groups at Western Electric's Hawthorne plant outside of Chicago (Cicero, Illinois).[24] Before the team arrived, an initial study at the plant examined the effects of illumination on worker output. It was proposed that "illumination" would affect the work group's output. One group of female workers completed its job tasks in a test room where the illumination level remained constant. The other study group was placed in a test room where the amount of illumination was changed (increased and decreased).

In the test room where illumination was varied, worker output increased when illumination increased. This, of course, was an expected result. However, output also increased when illumination was decreased. In addition, productivity increased in the control-group test room, even though illumination remained constant throughout the study.

The Harvard team was called in to solve the mystery. The team concluded that something more than pay incentives was improving worker output within the work groups. The researchers conducted additional studies on the impact of rest pauses, shorter working days, incentives, and type of supervision on output. They also uncovered what is referred to as the "Hawthorne effect" operating within the study groups.[25] That is, the workers felt important because someone was observing and studying them at work. Thus, they produced more because of being observed and studied.

Elton Mayo, Fritz Roethlisberger, and William Dickson, leaders of the Harvard study team, continued their work at the Hawthorne plant from 1924 to 1932. Eight years of study included over 20,000 Western Electric employees.

The Harvard researchers found that individual behaviors were modified within and by work groups. In a study referred to as the "bank wiring room," the Harvard researchers again faced perplexing results. The study group completed only two terminals per worker daily. This was considered to be a low level of output.

The bank wiring room workers appeared to be restricting output. The work group members were friendly, got along well on and off the job, and helped each other. There appeared to be a practice of protecting the slower workers. The fast producers did not want to outperform the slowest producers. The slow producers were part of the team, and fast workers were instructed to "slow it down." The group formed an informal production norm of only two completed boards per day.

The Harvard researchers learned that economic rewards did not totally explain worker behavior. Workers were observant, complied with norms, and respected the informal social structure of their group. The researchers also learned that social pressures could restrict output.

Interviews conducted years after the Hawthorne studies with a small number of actual study participants and a reanalysis of data raised doubts about a number of the original conclusions.[26] The conclusion that supportive managers helped boost productivity is considered incorrect by critics. Instead, the fear of job loss during the Great Depression and managerial discipline, not the practices of supportive managers, are considered responsible for the higher rate of productivity in the relay assembly test room experiments. Despite the criticism, the Hawthorne studies are still considered the major impetus behind the emphasis on understanding and dealing with human resources.

Since the 1930s, the Hawthorne studies are perhaps the most-cited research in the applied behavioral science area, though they are not referred to as the most rigorous series of studies. Nonetheless, the Hawthorne studies did point out that workers are more complex than the economic theories of the time proposed. Workers respond to group norms, social pressures, and observation. In 1924 to 1932, these were important revelations that changed the way management viewed workers.

Framing the Study of Organizational Behavior

The text frames in Exhibit 1.2 illustrate the flow of chapters in this book as well as create a perspective on how to study organizations. The study of the environment, individual and interpersonal influence, and group, common structure, and design processes is presented with the concept of effectiveness in mind. The effectiveness of the organization is the major task faced by managers and leaders. Unless effectiveness is achieved over time, an enterprise's very existence can be in jeopardy.

The Organization's Environment

Organizations exist in societies and are created by societies. Within a society many factors impinge upon the effectiveness of an organization, and management must be responsive to them. Every organization must respond to the needs of its customers or clients, to legal and political constraints, and to economic and technological changes and developments. The model proposes environmental forces interacting within the organization; throughout our discussion of each aspect of the model, the relevant environmental factors will be identified and examined.

Managers constantly receive information, ideas, reports, gossip, and so forth from the external environment. When Dell is working on a new computer, Hewlett-Packard and Apple managers are hearing about what is occurring. The environmental "sound bites" provide managers with a picture of what they are facing in terms of competition, new products, regulations, and a host of other environmental forces. Eventually, the manager must pause and ask: "How should I respond to the environmental stimuli?" Answering this and similar questions is difficult, but the environment demands it.

The Individual in the Organization

Individual performance is the foundation of organization performance. Understanding individual behavior, therefore, is critical for effective management, as illustrated in this account:

> Miguel Avila has been a field representative for a major drug manufacturer since he graduated from college seven years ago. He makes daily calls on physicians, hospitals, clinics, and pharmacies as a representative of the many drugs his firm manufactures. During his time in the field, prescription rates and sales for all of his firm's major drugs have increased, and he has won three national sales awards given by the firm. Yesterday, Miguel was promoted to sales manager for a seven-state region. He no longer will be selling but instead will be managing 15 other representatives. Miguel accepted the promotion because he believes he knows how to motivate and lead salespeople. He commented: "I know the personality profile of the successful salesperson. They are special people. I know what it takes to get them to perform. Remember that I am one. I know their values and attitudes and what it takes to motivate them. I know I can motivate a sales force."

In his new job, Miguel Avila will be trying to maximize the individual performance of 15 sales representatives. Most of his interactions will be pleasant, but he is aware of

EXHIBIT 1.2
Topics in Studying and Understanding Organizational Behavior

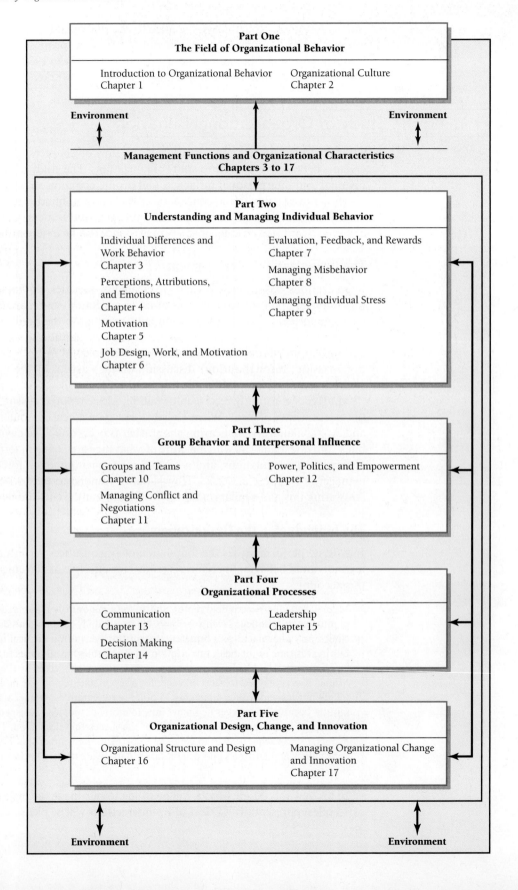

Part One
The Field of Organizational Behavior

Introduction to Organizational Behavior
Chapter 1

Organizational Culture
Chapter 2

Environment

Environment

Management Functions and Organizational Characteristics
Chapters 3 to 17

Part Two
Understanding and Managing Individual Behavior

Individual Differences and Work Behavior
Chapter 3

Perceptions, Attributions, and Emotions
Chapter 4

Motivation
Chapter 5

Job Design, Work, and Motivation
Chapter 6

Evaluation, Feedback, and Rewards
Chapter 7

Managing Misbehavior
Chapter 8

Managing Individual Stress
Chapter 9

Part Three
Group Behavior and Interpersonal Influence

Groups and Teams
Chapter 10

Managing Conflict and Negotiations
Chapter 11

Power, Politics, and Empowerment
Chapter 12

Part Four
Organizational Processes

Communication
Chapter 13

Decision Making
Chapter 14

Leadership
Chapter 15

Part Five
Organizational Design, Change, and Innovation

Organizational Structure and Design
Chapter 16

Managing Organizational Change and Innovation
Chapter 17

Environment

Environment

WORKING SMARTER

The economic data churned out by the government every month doesn't identify whether workers are working harder or smarter. But some part of productivity gains may be attributed to technology and working smarter.

When a Raleigh, North Carolina, Internet start-up downsized Forsyth's job, she was not too upset. She had developed an aversion to the 50- and 60-hour workweeks, the chaotic working conditions, and the lack of a job description. The mother of two now works in publishing, finds her current employer more "family friendly," and enjoys keeping to a 40-hour workweek.

Jeff, an early member of the Netscape management team, left his position thanks to a nice nest egg generated from the sale of Netscape to America Online. Today, he works part-time as an investor and advisor to small Internet start-ups. He is able to play with his three children, make them lunch, and even tag along on school field trips. After his 18-hour days at Netscape, Jeff's time with his children "seems like mundane stuff, but when you finally get a chance to do it, you appreciate it."

Despite the fact that Americans have always placed great stock in hard work, there is growing evidence that "working hard" may not mean "working long." According to the U.S. Bureau of Labor Statistics, the proportion of Americans working 49 hours or more a week has remained steady in recent years, after rising in the late 1980s and early 1990s to approximately 29.5 percent. But in the past several years, the percentage of managers and professionals working 49 hours or more a week has begun to fall, reaching 27.9 percent.

It appears that America's work ethic is changing from working hard to working smart. It is more than simply a work/life balance issue, however, in that a basic American social value of more hard work is being transformed into "work smart but don't forget your other life obligations." How will this change the workplace? Will hourly workers decline overtime opportunities more consistently? Will they move to ensure (through their union) that their workweek remains consistent and does not include continual overtime requests? Will the 40-hour workweek be challenged (as it has in some European countries)? How will this change the pace of productivity? Will face time at the office continue to be important? Will HR professionals promote the firm's use of flextime and telecommuting to attract and retain workers?

Sources: Adapted from R. Burke, "Working to Live or Living to Work: Should Individuals and Organizations Care?" *Journal of Business Ethics* 84 (2009), pp. 167–72; Jason Desena, "While America Is Sleeping, Europe Is Catching Up," *Financial Times*, July 17, 2007, p. 36; Eric Clarke, "Working Smarter, Not Harder," *Accounting Technology,* April 2006, pp. 20–22; John W. Schoen, "Are We Working Smarter or Harder?" MSNBC, August 28, 2003, www.msnbc.com/news/954222.asp; and Shel Leonard, "Is America's Work Ethic Changing?" *HR Magazine*, April 2000, p. 224.

some expense account padding that he intends to stop. As a manager, Miguel will be dealing with several facets of individual behavior. Our model includes three important influences on individual behavior and motivation in organizations: individual characteristics, individual motivation, and rewards.

Individual Characteristics

Because organizational performance depends on individual performance, managers such as Miguel Avila must have more than a passing knowledge of the determinants of individual performance. Social psychology and psychology contribute a great deal of relevant knowledge about the relationships among attitudes, perceptions, emotions, personality, values, and individual performance. Managers cannot ignore the necessity for acquiring and acting on knowledge of the individual characteristics of both their subordinates and themselves.

Individual Motivation

Motivation and ability to work interact to determine performance. Motivation theory attempts to explain and predict how the behavior of individuals is aroused, started, sustained, and stopped. Unlike Miguel Avila, not all managers and behavioral scientists agree on what is the "best" theory of motivation. In fact, motivation is so complex that it may be impossible to have an all-encompassing theory of how it occurs. However, managers must still try to understand it. They must be knowledgeable about motivation because they are concerned with performance.

Rewards

One of the most powerful influences on individual performance is an organization's reward system. Management can use rewards (or punishment) to increase performance by present employees. Management also can use rewards to attract skilled employees to join the organization. Paychecks, raises, and stock options are important aspects of the reward system, but they are not the only aspects. Miguel Avila makes this point very clear when he states: "I know what it takes to get them to perform." Performance of the work or job itself can provide employees with rewards, particularly if job performance leads to a sense of personal responsibility, autonomy, and meaningfulness.

Stress

Stress is an important result of the interaction between the job and the individual. Stress in this context is a state of imbalance within an individual that often manifests itself in such symptoms as insomnia, excessive perspiration, nervousness, and irritability. Whether stress is positive or negative depends on the individual's tolerance level. People react differently to situations that outwardly would seem to induce the same physiological and psychological demands. Some individuals respond positively through increased motivation and commitment to finish the job. Other individuals respond less desirably by turning to such outlets as alcoholism and drug abuse. Hopefully, Miguel Avila will respond positively to the stresses of his new job as sales manager.

Handling the expense account padding misbehavior of one of his employees will produce a form of stress that Miguel didn't experience as a field representative. Management's responsibility in managing stress has not been clearly defined, but there is growing evidence that organizations are devising programs to deal with work-induced stress.

Group Behavior and Interpersonal Influence

Interpersonal influence and group behavior are also powerful forces affecting organizational performance. The effects of these forces are illustrated in the following account:

> Kelly Davis spent two and a half years as a teller in the busiest branch of First National Bank. During that time she developed close personal friendships among her co-workers. These friendships extended off the job as well. Kelly and her friends were the top team in the bank bowling league.
>
> Two months ago Kelly was promoted to branch manager. She was excited about the new challenge but was a little surprised that she received the promotion since some other likely candidates in the branch had been with the bank longer. She began the job with a great deal of optimism and believed her friends would be genuinely happy for her and supportive of her efforts. However, since she became branch manager, things haven't seemed quite the same. Kelly can't spend nearly as much time with her friends because she is often away from the branch attending management meetings at the main office. A computer training course she must attend two evenings a week has caused her to miss the last two wine-and-cheese club meetings, and she senses that some of her friends have been acting a little differently toward her lately.
>
> Recently, Kelly said, "I didn't know that being part of the management team could make that much difference. Frankly, I never really thought about it. I guess I was naïve. I'm seeing a totally different perspective on the business and have to deal with problems I never knew about."

Kelly Davis's promotion has made her a member of more than one group. In addition to being a member of her old group of friends at the branch, she also is a member of the management team. She is finding out that group behavior and expectations have a strong impact on individual behavior and interpersonal influence. Our model includes a number of important aspects of group and interpersonal influence on organization behavior: leadership, group behavior, intergroup behavior and conflict, and organizational power and politics.

Group Behavior

Groups form because of managerial action, and also because of individual efforts. Managers create work groups to carry out assigned jobs and tasks. Such groups, created by managerial decisions, are termed *formal groups*. The group that Kelly Davis manages at her branch is a formal group.

Groups also form as a consequence of employees' actions. Such groups, termed *informal groups,* develop around common interests and friendships. The wine-and-cheese club at Kelly Davis's branch is an informal group. Though not sanctioned by management, groups of this kind can affect organizational and individual performance. The effect can be positive or negative, depending on the intention of the group's members. If the group at Kelly's branch decided informally to slow the work pace, this norm would exert pressure on individuals who wanted to remain a part of the group. Effective managers recognize the consequences of the individual's need for affiliation.

Intergroup Behavior and Conflict

As groups function and interact with other groups, they develop their own unique set of characteristics, including structure, cohesiveness, roles, norms, and processes. As a result, groups may cooperate or compete with other groups, and intergroup competition can lead to conflict. If the management of Kelly's bank instituted an incentive program with cash bonuses to the branch bringing in the most new customers, this might lead to competition and conflict among the branches. While conflict among groups can have beneficial results for an organization, too much or the wrong kinds of intergroup conflict can have very negative results. Thus, managing intergroup conflict is an important aspect of managing organizational behavior.

Power and Politics

Power is the ability to get someone to do something you want done or to make things happen in the way you want them to happen. Many people in our society are very uncomfortable with the concept of power, and some are very offended by it. This is because the essence of power is control over others. To many Americans, control over others is an offensive thought. However, power is a reality in organizations. Managers derive power from both organizational and individual sources. Kelly Davis has power by virtue of her position in the formal hierarchy of the bank. She controls performance evaluations and salary increases. However, she also may have power because her co-workers respect and admire the abilities and expertise she possesses. Managers, therefore, must understand the concept of power as a reality in organizations and managerial roles.

Organizational Processes

Certain behavioral processes give life to an organization. When these processes do not function well, unfortunate problems can arise, as illustrated in this account:

> When she began to major in marketing as a junior in college, Debra Chin knew that some day she would work in that field. Once she completed her MBA, she was more positive than ever that marketing would be her life's work. Because of her excellent academic record, she received several outstanding job offers. She decided to accept the job offer she received from one of the nation's largest consulting firms. She believed

this job would allow her to gain experience in several areas of marketing and to engage in a variety of exciting work. On her last day on campus, she told her favorite professor: "This has got to be one of the happiest days of my life, getting such a great career opportunity."

Recently, while visiting the college placement office, the professor was surprised to hear that Debra had told the placement director that she was looking for another job. Since she had been with the consulting company less than a year, the professor was somewhat surprised. He decided to call Debra to find out why she wanted to change jobs. This is what she told him: "I guess you can say my first experience with the real world was 'reality shock.' Since being with this company, I have done nothing but gather data on phone surveys. All day long I sit and talk on the phone, asking questions and checking off the answers. In graduate school I was trained to be a manager, but here I am doing what any high school graduate can do. I talked to my boss, and he said that all employees have to pay their dues. Well, why didn't they tell me this while they were recruiting me? To say there was a conflict between the recruiting information and the real world would be a gross understatement. I'm an adult—why didn't they provide me with realistic job information, then let me decide if I want it? A little bit of accurate communication would have gone a long way."

This book includes discussion of a number of processes that contribute to effective organizational performance: communication, decision making, and leadership.

Communication Process

Organizational survival is related to the ability of management to receive, transmit, and act on information. The communication process links the people within the organization. Information integrates the activities of the organization with the demands of the environment. But information also integrates the internal activities of the organization. Debra Chin's problem arose because the information that flowed *from* the organization was different from the information that flowed *within* the organization.

The accompanying You Be the Judge explains an unusual method of communication at New Hope Natural Media. This method can be used to acquire a sense of what employees are thinking, which can then be valuable to a manager in modifying the compensation system.

Decision-Making Process

The quality of decision making in an organization depends on selecting proper goals and identifying means for achieving them. With good integration of behavioral and structural factors, management can increase the probability that high-quality decisions will be made. Debra Chin's experience illustrates inconsistent decision making by different organizational units (personnel and marketing) in the hiring of new employees. Organizations rely on individual decisions as well as group decisions, and effective management requires knowledge of both types of decisions.

The power of managers is clearly evidenced in making decisions about employees' well-being, distributing organizational resources, and designing and implementing rules and policies. In Debra Chin's case, she claims the consulting firm didn't provide a realistic job preview. She is making a statement that suggests unethical behavior on the part of the individuals who interviewed her for the consulting firm job. Was this the right thing for the company to do? Debra suggests that it was not the right thing or the ethical way to conduct an interview. Ethical dilemmas will be discussed throughout the book because managers and workers must make decisions every day that have an ethical component.[27]

YOU BE THE JUDGE

RECEIVING FEEDBACK REGULARLY

At New Hope Natural Media in Boulder, Colorado, a questionnaire is included in every paycheck asking for feedback in four key areas: the employees' feelings about their financial package, their feelings toward other employees, their feelings about the skills they are developing, and their overall feelings about their job. What is the company's objective of receiving feedback in these four areas? How can this feedback be used?

Communication and feedback are considered the "breakfast of champions" at New Hope Natural Media. You be the judge. Do you think this is a good management approach? Why? These days it is common to read about managerial decisions that are considered unethical. It is now accepted that most decisions made in an organization are permeated by ethical implications. Managers are powerful, and, where power exists, there is potential for good and evil. Headlines emphasize the ethical nature of decision making: "Ponzi Victims Find Little Solace in Guilty Plea"; "Merrill's $3.6bn Bonuses under Fire"; "Top Pain Scientist Fabricated Data in Studies, Hospital Says"; "Crisis on Wall Street: Ex-AIG Executive Is Sentenced to 4 Years"; and "Siemens to Pay €1bn Fines in Effort to Close Bribery Scandal."

Sources: J. Rosanas, "Beyond Economic Criteria: A Humanistic Approach to Organizational Survival," *Journal of Business Ethics* 78, no. 3 (2008), pp. 447–62; John L. Akula, "Business Crime: What to Do When the Law Pursues You," *Sloan Management Review,* Spring 2000, pp. 29–42; Vita Bekker, Joanna Chung, Brooke Masters, Megan Murphy, and Alan Rappeport, "Ponzi Victims Find Little Solace in Guilty Plea," *Financial Times,* March 12, 2009, p. 16; Sarah O'Connor, "Merrill's $3.6bn Bonuses under Fire," *Financial Times,* March 31, 2009, p. 2; Keith J. Winstein and David Armstrong, "Top Pain Scientist Fabricated Data in Studies, Hospital Says," *The Wall Street Journal,* March 11, 2009, p. A12; Amir Efrati, "Crisis on Wall Street: Ex-AIG Executive Is Sentenced to 4 Years," *The Wall Street Journal,* January 28, 2009, p. C3; and Daniel Schäfer, "Siemens to Pay €1bn Fines in Effort to Close Bribery Scandal," *Financial Times,* December 16, 2008, p. 17.

Leadership Process

Leaders exist within all organizations. Like the bank's Kelly Davis, they may be found in formal groups, but they also may be found in informal groups. Leaders may be managers or nonmanagers. The importance of effective leadership for obtaining individual, group, and organizational performance is so critical that it has stimulated a great deal of effort to determine the causes of such leadership. Some people believe that effective leadership depends on traits and certain behaviors—separately and in combination. Other people believe that one leadership style is effective in all situations. Still others believe that each situation requires a specific leadership style. Are managers always leaders? Unfortunately, the answer is *no,* as will be found throughout this book.

Organizational Structure

To work effectively in organizations, managers must have a clear understanding of the organizational structure. Viewing an organization chart on a piece of paper or framed on a wall, one sees only a configuration of positions, job duties, and lines of authority among the parts of an organization. However, organizational structures can be far more complex than that, as illustrated in the following account:

> Dr. John Rice recently was appointed dean of the business school at a major university. Before arriving on campus, John spent several weeks studying the funding, programs, faculty, students, and organizational structure of the business school. He was trying to develop a list of priorities for things he believed would require immediate attention during his first year as dean. The president of the university had requested that he have such a list of priorities available when he arrived on campus.

During his first official meeting with the president, John was asked the question he fully expected to be asked: "What will be your No. 1 priority?" Rice replied: "Although money is always a problem, I believe the most urgent need is to reorganize the business school. At present, students can major in only one of two departments—accounting and business administration. The accounting department has 20 faculty members. The business administration department has 43 faculty members, including 15 in marketing, 16 in management, and 12 in finance. I foresee a college with four departments—accounting, management, marketing, and finance—each with its own chairperson. First, I believe such a structure will enable us to better meet the needs of our students. Specifically, it will facilitate the development of major programs in each of the four areas. Students must be able to major in one of the four functional areas if they are going to be prepared adequately for the job market. Finally, I believe such an organizational structure will enable us to more easily recruit faculty since they will be joining a group with interests similar to their own."

As this account indicates, an organization's structure is the formal pattern of activities and interrelationships among the various subunits of the organization.

Organizational Change and Innovation Processes

Managers sometimes must consider the possibility that effective organizational functioning can be improved by making significant changes in the total organization. Organizational change and development represent planned attempts to improve overall individual, group, and organizational performance. Debra Chin might well have been spared the disappointment she experienced had an organizational development effort uncovered and corrected the inconsistent communication and decision making that brought about Debra's unhappiness. Concerted, planned, and evaluative efforts to improve organizational functioning have great potential for success.

Change and innovation are so vital to an organization's success that managers must be prepared for reactions to them from employees. Change and innovation typically disrupt normal routines and patterns of behavior. When routines are disrupted, reactions can range from enthusiastic acceptance to covert sabotage.

Effectiveness in Organizations

For centuries, economists, philosophers, engineers, military generals, government leaders, and managers have attempted to define, measure, analyze, and capture the essence of effectiveness. Adam Smith wrote in *The Wealth of Nations* over two centuries ago that efficiency of operations could be achieved most easily through high degrees of specialization.

Whether and how managers can influence effectiveness is difficult to determine. There is still confusion about how to manage within organizations so that organizational effectiveness is the final result. Problems of definition, criteria identification, and finding the best model to guide research and practice continue to hinder, block, and discourage practitioners and researchers. Instead of simply ignoring effectiveness because of underlying confusion, we believe important insights can be found by attempting to clarify various perspectives.

The field of organizational behavior focuses on three levels of analysis as presented earlier in Exhibit 1.2: (1) individual, (2) group, and (3) organizational. Theorists and researchers in organizational behavior have accumulated a vast amount of information about each of these levels. These three levels of analysis also coincide with the three levels of managerial responsibility. That is, managers are responsible for the effectiveness of individuals, groups of individuals, and organizations themselves.

During California's frenzied gold rush in 1853, Levi Strauss, a Bavarian immigrant, arrived in San Francisco aboard a clipper ship.[28] He quickly discovered that the prospectors wanted sturdy pants that could survive the rigors of digging for gold, so he created the world's first jeans. Word of the quality of the pants spread like wildfire and the Levi's legend was born. Today the firm has annual sales of approximately $4.4 billion.[29]

Levi Strauss has emphasized quality, being socially responsible, and using the most talented people the firm can recruit to work for the firm. The value of each individual, the effective leadership of work groups, and the success of the enterprise has been the emphasis at Levi Strauss since its founding. Long before a stream of firms paid attention to flatter hierarchies, cultural diversity, empowerment, quality, and globalization, Levi Strauss was leading the way. Levi Strauss embraced the view that every organizational decision should be grounded ethically in what is right.[30]

In its values-based philosophy, Levi Strauss emphasizes what it aspires to be in terms of effectiveness. The firm believes that if specific values are practiced, effectiveness within the firm and in competitive markets will result.[31] Some of Levi Strauss's value principles are:

Empathy. Empathy focuses on listening and "paying close attention to the world around us . . . understanding, appreciating and meeting the needs of those we serve, including consumers, retail customers, shareholders and each other as employees."

Integrity. "Ethical conduct and social responsibility characterize our way of doing business. We are honest and trustworthy. We do what we say we are going to do."

Behaviors. Management must exemplify "directness, openness to influence, commitment to the success of others, and willingness to acknowledge our own contributions to problems."

Diversity. Levi Strauss "values a diverse work force (age, sex, ethnic group, etc.) at all levels of the organization. . . . Differing points of view will be sought; diversity will be valued and honestly rewarded, not suppressed."

Recognition. Levi's "will provide greater recognition—both financial and public—for individuals and teams that contribute to our success."

Ethical Practices. Management should epitomize "the stated standards of ethical behavior. We must provide clarity about our expectations and must enforce these standards throughout the corporation."

Empowerment. Management must "increase the authority and responsibility of those closest to our products and customers. By actively pushing the responsibility, trust, and recognition into the organization, we can harness and release the capabilities of our people."

Levi Strauss is not offered here as a perfect company. Like every firm, there are problems, including the well-founded criticism of being slow to adopt new fashion trends. The company is struggling with a generation gap problem. It announced in September 2003 the closing of its final plant in the United States after deciding to focus on manufacturing outside the United States because of cheaper labor costs. Levi Strauss has had particularly strong growth in the Asia Pacific region with its Levi Signature brand.

The clothing company is attempting to attract teenagers without turning off older people. As the Levi brand plodded along, fashion shifted to big-pocketed cargo pants, and Levi Strauss seemed to sit and watch.[32] The loss of the youth market posed problems for the future of Levi Strauss. The company's managers regrouped and developed strategies and programs to remain in business.

The approach that Levi's has taken to remain an effective and viable organization is not the only way to do so. Systems theory provides managers with another perspective on how organizations can survive over time.

Systems Theory and the Time Dimension of Effectiveness

Systems theory enables managers to describe the behavior of organizations both internally and externally. Internally, you can see how and why people within organizations perform their individual and group tasks. Externally, you can relate the transactions of organizations with other organizations and institutions. All organizations acquire resources from the outside environment of which they are a part and, in turn, provide goods and services demanded by the larger environment. Managers must deal simultaneously with the internal and external aspects of organizational behavior. This essentially complex process can be simplified, for analytical purposes, by employing the basic concepts of systems theory.

In systems theory, the organizations are seen as one element of a number of elements that act interdependently. The flow of inputs and outputs is the basic starting point in describing the organization. In the simplest terms, the organization takes resources (inputs) from the larger system (environment), processes these resources, and returns them in changed form (output). Exhibit 1.3 displays the fundamental elements of the organization as a system.

The concept of organizational effectiveness presented in this book relies on systems theory, but we believe another concept, the dimension of time, is important. Two main conclusions suggested by systems theory are: (1) effectiveness criteria must reflect the entire input-process-output cycle, not simply output, and (2) effectiveness criteria must reflect the interrelationships between the organization and its outside environment. Thus:

> Organizational effectiveness is an all-encompassing concept about how products or services are produced or provided.

Much additional research is needed to develop knowledge about the components of effectiveness. There is little consensus about these relevant components, about the interrelationships among them, and about the effects of managerial action on them.[33] In this textbook we attempt to provide the basis for asking questions about what constitutes effectiveness and how the qualities that characterize effectiveness interact.

EXHIBIT 1.3
The Basic Elements of a System

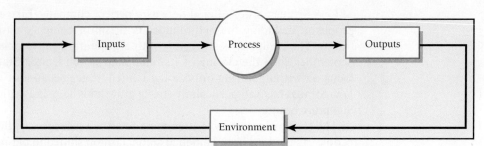

According to systems theory, an organization is an element of a larger system, the environment. With the passage of time, every organization takes, processes, and returns resources to the environment. The ultimate criterion of organizational effectiveness is whether the organization survives in the environment. Survival requires adaptation, and adaptation often involves predictable sequences. As the organization ages, it probably will pass through different phases. It forms, develops, matures, and declines in relation to environmental circumstances. Organizations and entire industries rise and fall. Today, the personal computer industry is on the rise, and the steel industry is declining. Marketing experts acknowledge the existence of product–market life cycles. Organizations also seem to have life cycles. Consequently, the criteria of effectiveness must reflect the stage of the organization's life cycle.[34]

Managers and others with interests in the organization must have indicators that assess the probability of the organization's survival. In actual practice, managers use a number of short-run indicators of long-run survival. Among these indicators are measurements of productivity, efficiency, accidents, turnover, absenteeism, quality, rate of return, morale, and employee satisfaction.[35] The overarching criterion that cuts across each time dimension is *quality*. Unless quality is perceived by customers, there will be no survival. Any of these criteria can be relevant for particular purposes. For simplicity, we will use four criteria of short-run effectiveness as representatives of all such criteria. They are quality, productivity, efficiency, and satisfaction.

Three intermediate criteria in the time dimension model are quality, adaptiveness, and development. The final two long-run criteria are quality and survival. Exhibit 1.4 shows the relationships between these criteria and the time dimension.

EXHIBIT 1.4
Time Dimension Model of Effectiveness

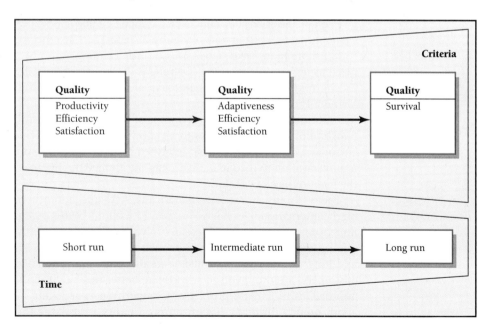

Time-Based Criteria

Introducing time-based criteria of effectiveness suggests such terms as short run, intermediate run, and long run. Short-run criteria are those referring to the results of actions concluded in a year or less. Intermediate-run criteria are applicable when you judge the effectiveness of an individual, group, or organization for a longer time period, perhaps five years. Long-run criteria are those for which the indefinite future is applicable. We will discuss six general categories of effectiveness criteria, beginning with those of a short-run nature.

Quality

J. M. Juran and W. Edwards Deming, in 1950, were prophets without honor in their own country, the United States. These two Americans emphasized the importance of quality. The belief now is that to survive, organizations must design products, make products, and treat customers in a close-to-perfection way, meaning that quality is now an imperative.[36]

More than any other single event, the 1980 NBC-TV White Paper, "If Japan Can . . . Why Can't We?" introduced the importance of quality to the public. The television program showed how, from 1950 to 1980, the Japanese had risen from the ashes of World War II to become an economic giant with products of superior quality. Japanese organizational effectiveness centered on the notion of quality. The Japanese interpret quality as it relates to the customer's perception. Customers compare the actual performance of the product or evaluate the service being provided to their own set of expectations. The product or service either passes or fails. Thus, quality has nothing to do with how shiny or good looking something is or with how much it costs. Quality is defined as meeting customers' needs and expectations.

In today's competitive global world, the effective company is typically the one that provides customers with quality products or services. Retailers, bankers, manufacturers, lawyers, doctors, airlines, and others are finding out that, to stay in business (survival in effectiveness terms), the customer must be kept happy and satisfied.

Each of the criteria of effectiveness discussed above is significant. However, the one element that executives now recognize as being perhaps the most crucial is quality.

For more than five decades, W. Edwards Deming and J. M. Juran have been recognized as pioneers of quality.[37] Deming is the most recognized guru of statistical quality control (SQC). He is the namesake of Japan's most prestigious quality award, the Deming Prize, created in 1951.

Juran is best known for his concept of total quality control (TQC). This is the application of quality principles to all company programs, including satisfying internal customers. In 1954 Juran first described his method in Japan. He became an important inspiration to the Japanese because he applied quality to everyone from the top of the firm to the clerical staff.

Today Asians, Europeans, Americans, Africans, and others who want to compete on the international level have learned a lot about Deming's, Juran's, and other quality improvement methods. Managers have learned that simply paying lip service to quality and what it means is not enough. If managers are to be effective over the short and long run, they must translate quality improvement into results: more satisfied customers, a more involved workforce, better designed products, and more creative approaches to solving problems. Competition is sparking a long overdue concern about quality. In many organizations, quality is now the top priority in the short, intermediate, and long run.[38]

Mercedes-Benz has worked hard for years to restore its image once tarnished by recalls, defects, and failure. Once the highest-rated luxury automobile, Mercedes-Benz's quality and reputation problems included high-tech braking systems that failed and were too complex to use, and transmission glitches. The ability to win back a reputation is difficult for any automaker. Defects and recalls indicate quality issues that sour consumers for a long time, even as improvements are brought on line. Mercedes-Benz dropped to 14th in quality ratings of luxury cars. Major television and newspaper advertising campaigns have attempted to polish the Mercedes-Benz image. The concerted effort to improve has begun to show results; according to a recent J.D. Power and Associates Initial Quality Survey, the 2008 Mercedes-Benz E-Class tied for first place in the midsize premium car segment, and the 2008 S-Class ranked second in the large premium car segment.[39]

Productivity

As used here, *productivity* reflects the relationship between inputs (e.g., hours of work, effort, use of equipment) and output (e.g., personal computers produced, customer complaints handled, trucks loaded). The concept excludes any consideration of efficiency, which is defined below. The measures of productivity, such as profit, sales, market share, students graduated, patients released, documents processed, clients serviced, and the like, depend upon the type of industry or institution that is being discussed. Every institution has outputs and inputs that need to be in alignment with the organization's mission and goals. These measures relate directly to the output consumed by the organization's customers and clients.

Efficiency

Efficiency is defined as the ratio of outputs to inputs. The short-run criterion focuses attention on the entire input-process-output cycle, yet it emphasizes the input and process elements. Among the measures of efficiency are rate of return on capital or assets, unit cost, scrap and waste, downtime, occupancy rates, and cost per patient, per student, or per client. Measures of efficiency inevitably must be in ratio terms; the ratios of benefit to cost or to time are the general forms of these measures.

Satisfaction

The idea of the organization as a social system requires that some consideration be given to the benefits received by its participants as well as by its customers and clients. Satisfaction and morale are similar terms referring to the extent to which the organization meets the needs of employees. We use the term *satisfaction* to refer to this criterion. Measures of satisfaction include employee attitudes, turnover, absenteeism, tardiness, and grievances.

Adaptiveness

Adaptiveness is the extent to which the organization can and does respond to internal and external changes. Adaptiveness in this context refers to management's ability to sense changes in the environment as well as changes within the organization itself. Ineffectiveness in achieving production, efficiency, and satisfaction can signal the need to adapt managerial practices and policies. Or the environment may demand different outputs or provide different inputs, thus necessitating change. To the extent that the organization cannot or does not adapt, its survival is jeopardized.

Development

This criterion measures the ability of the organization to increase its capacity to deal with environmental demands. An organization must invest in itself to increase its chances of

YOU BE THE JUDGE COMMENT

RECEIVING FEEDBACK REGULARLY

Receiving feedback from employees about their jobs, feelings, attitudes, preferences, and impressions is invaluable. The feedback can be used to make specific modifications in financial packages, social and interpersonal opportunities, skill development, and job characteristics. Feedback from trusted sources can result in noticeable changes and improvement.

survival in the long run. The usual development efforts are training programs for managerial and nonmanagerial personnel. More recently the range of organizational development has expanded to include a number of psychological and sociological approaches.

Time considerations enable you to evaluate effectiveness in the short, intermediate, and long run. For example, you could evaluate a particular organization as effective in terms of production, satisfaction, and efficiency criteria but as ineffective in terms of adaptiveness and development. A manufacturer of buggy whips may be optimally effective because it can produce buggy whips better and faster than any other producer in the short run but still have little chance of survival because no one wants to buy its products. Thus, maintaining optimal balance means, in part, balancing the organization's performance over time.

Introducing the time dimension into a discussion of effectiveness enables us to understand the work of managers in organizations. The basic job of managers is to identify and influence the causes of individual, group, and organizational effectiveness in the short, intermediate, and long run. Reviewing, evaluating, and modifying a manager's roles and responsibilities with time, effectiveness, and a systems perspective is how the book will evolve.

Summary of Key Points

- The key to an organization's success is the institution's human resources. Organizations need human resources that work hard, think creatively, and perform excellently. Rewarding, encouraging, and nurturing the human resources in a timely and meaningful manner is required.

- A number of contributing disciplines stand out such as psychology, sociology, and cultural anthropology.

- The behavior of employees is the key to achieving effectiveness. People behave in many predictable and unpredictable ways. Each person has a unique behavioral pattern. Managers must observe, respond to, and cope with the array of behavior patterns displayed by employees.

- The "effect" is the behavior or reaction of a person who is being observed. Individuals who are being observed are likely to react in a nonroutine way because they are being watched or are a part of an experiment.

- Employers and employees enter into psychological contracts. The employer believes that no worker is guaranteed a lifelong job or pay raise. If the worker's performance is good and profit is earned, then employment continues and pay raises are provided. Employees today believe that employers should be honest, concerned about their families, and interested in their overall health. These assumptions are the basis of what is called the *new* psychological agreement.

- Systems theory is used to integrate organizational effectiveness and time. Two main conclusions of systems theory are: (1) effectiveness criteria (e.g., productivity, quality, adaptiveness) must reflect the entire input-process-output cycle; and (2) effectiveness criteria must reflect the interrelationships between the organization and its outside environment. The organization is simply an element or part of a larger system, the environment.

Review and Discussion Questions

1. Why are managers so necessary in organizations?

2. Some of the value principles of Levi Strauss are based on *diversity, ethical practices,* and *empowerment*. How does management expect them to be demonstrated on the job?

3. What knowledge about human behavior in the workplace was discovered during the Hawthorne studies?

4. How is the increasing globalization of organizations impacting the study of applied organizational behavior?

5. How would you determine whether a large public hospital in your city (community or regional) is effective?

6. In today's fast-paced, global, and technological environment, it is important for an organization of any size to be adaptive. How do firms such as Facebook, Google, and Apple adapt?

7. What abilities will managers need to be successful in the 21st century? Which of these abilities do you have now? How do you plan to acquire the others?

8. The psychological contract between workers and employers specifies what each expects to give and receive from the other. What can you offer an employer, and what do you expect in return?

9. As a manager, what type of quality improvement results should you strive for to achieve success over both the short and long run?

10. What are five things that you, as a manager, can do to lead the way to higher levels of effectiveness?

Exercise

Exercise 1.1: *Initial View of Organizational Behavior*

Now that you have completed Chapter 1, which sets the tone for the book *Organizational Behavior and Management,* complete the following exercise. This should be used as your beginning baseline assumptions, opinions, and understanding of organizational behavior. Once you have completed the course (book), we will take another look at your assumptions, opinions, and understanding.

This exercise contains 20 pairs of statements about organizational behavior. For each pair, circle the letter preceding the statement that you think is most accurate. Circle only *one* letter in each pair.

Now how much do you know about organizations?

6. Deming and Juran are considered world-class experts on _____.
   a. organizations
   b. quality
   c. mathematics
   d. business planning

7. Psychology has made a major contribution to organizational behavior, especially at what level of analysis?
   a. System
   b. Team
   c. Individual
   d. Organization

8. A crucial time-based, long-run criteria of effectiveness is _____.
   a. efficiency
   b. satisfaction
   c. costs
   d. survival

9. The field of organizational behavior considers _____ to be crucial for conducting research.
   a. cost factors
   b. scientific method
   c. board of examiners
   d. forensic accounting

10. Who first expressed a philosophy of the scientific manager?
    a. Joseph Juran
    b. Henri Fayol
    c. Frederick W. Taylor
    d. Joseph Wharton

REALITY CHECK ANSWERS

Before	After
1. *b* 2. *c* 3. *a* 4. *c* 5. *c*	6. *b* 7. *c* 8. *d* 9. *b* 10. *c*
Number Correct	Number Correct
_____	_____

After you have circled the letter, indicate how certain you are of your choice by writing 1, 2, 3, or 4 on the line following each item according to the following procedure.

- Place a "1" if you are *very uncertain* that your choice is correct.
- Place a "2" if you are *somewhat uncertain* that your choice is correct.
- Place a "3" if you are *somewhat certain* that your choice is correct.
- Place a "4" if you are *very certain* that your choice is correct.

Do not skip any pairs.

1. a. A supervisor is well advised to treat, as much as possible, all members of his/her group exactly the same way.
   b. A supervisor is well advised to adjust his/her behavior according to the unique characteristics of the members of his/her group. _____

2. *a.* Generally speaking, individual motivation is greatest if the person has set goals for himself/herself that are *difficult* to achieve.

   b. Generally speaking, individual motivation is greatest if the person has set goals for himself/herself that are *easy* to achieve. _____

3. *a.* A major reason organizations are not as productive as they could be these days is that managers are too concerned with managing the work group rather than the individual.

   b. A major reason organizations are not as productive as they could be these days is that managers are too concerned with managing the individual rather than the work group. _____

4. *a.* Supervisors who, sometime before becoming a supervisor, have performed the job of the people they are currently supervising are apt to be more effective supervisors than those who have never performed that particular job.

   b. Supervisors who, sometime before becoming a supervisor, have performed the job of the people they are currently supervising are apt to be less effective supervisors than those who have never performed that particular job. _____

5. *a.* On almost every matter relevant to the work, managers are well advised to be completely honest and open with their subordinates.

   b. There are very few matters in the workplace where managers are well advised to be completely honest and open with their subordinates. _____

6. *a.* One's need for power is a better predictor of managerial advancement than one's motivation to do the work well.

   b. One's motivation to do the work well is a better predictor of managerial advancement than one's need for power. _____

7. *a.* When people fail at something, they try harder the next time.

   b. When people fail at something, they quit trying. _____

8. *a.* Performing well as a manager depends most on how much education you have.

   b. Performing well as a manager depends most on how much experience you have. _____

9. *a.* The most effective leaders are those who give more emphasis to getting the work done than they do to relating to people.

   b. The most effective leaders are those who give more emphasis to relating to people than they do to getting the work done. _____

10. *a.* It is very important for a leader to "stick to his/her guns."

    b. It is *not* very important for a leader to "stick to his/her guns." _____

11. *a.* Pay is the most important factor in determining how hard people work.

    b. The nature of the task people are doing is the most important factor in determining how hard people work. _____

12. *a.* Pay is the most important factor in determining how satisfied people are at work.

    b. The nature of the task people are doing is the most important factor in determining how satisfied people are at work. _____

13. *a.* Generally speaking, it is correct to say that a person's attitudes cause his/her behavior.

    b. Generally speaking, it is correct to say that a person's attitudes are primarily rationalizations for his/her behavior. _____

14. *a.* Satisfied workers produce more than workers who are not satisfied.

    b. Satisfied workers produce no more than workers who are not satisfied. _____

15. *a.* The notion that most semiskilled workers desire work that is interesting and meaningful is most likely incorrect.

    b. The notion that most semiskilled workers desire work that is interesting and meaningful is most likely correct. _____

16. *a.* People welcome change for the better.

    b. Even if change is for the better, people will resist it. _____

17. *a.* Leaders are born, not made.

    b. Leaders are made, not born. _____

18. *a.* Groups make better decisions than individuals.

    b. Individuals make better decisions than groups. _____

19. *a.* The statement, "A manager's authority needs to be commensurate with his/her responsibility" is, practically speaking, a very meaningful statement.

b. The statement, "A manager's authority needs to be commensurate with his/her responsibility" is, practically speaking, a very meaningless statement. _____

20. *a.* A major reason for the relative decline in North American productivity is that the division of labor and job specialization have gone too far.

b. A major reason for the relative decline in North American productivity is that the division of labor and job specialization have not been carried far enough. _____

Source: Adapted from Robert Weinberg and Walter Nord, "Coping with 'It's All Common Sense'," *Exchange: The Organizational Behavior Teaching Journal* 7, no. 2 (1982), pp. 29–32. Used with permission.

Case

Case 1.1: *Drexler's World Famous Bar-B-Que*

Change seems to be a fact of life, yet in Texas some things remain the same, such as people's love for Texas-style barbecue. As you drive from Houston to Waco, for example, you will see many roadside stands asking you to stop by and sample different forms of bbq or bar-b-q (the tastes vary as much as the spellings, and both are often inspired). In the cities, there are many restaurants, several of them large chains that compete with smaller, neighborhood businesses for the barbecue portion of individuals' dining out budgets.

Survival can sometimes depend on the restaurant's ability to identify and capitalize on "windows of opportunity." Small businesses are presumed to be more flexible, having the ability to react more quickly to changes when they occur, but the risk is also greater for them than for large organizations, which can more easily absorb losses. Although there may be differences in scale, an important question for all organizations is whether they have the willingness and the ability to take advantage of opportunities as they arise.

Drexler's World Famous Bar-B-Que is located in an area of Houston called the Third Ward—an economically disadvantaged neighborhood not far from downtown—and has been in the family "almost forever." The restaurant relocated in 2003 to a 13,000-square-foot location. It now features its traditional fare and more healthy menu items.

Source: Edits, additions, and updates were provided by the authors of this text. Case was originally written by Forrest F. Aven, Jr., University of Houston–Downtown and V. Jean Ramsey, Texas Southern University.

The restaurant's history began in the late 1940s, when a great-uncle of the present owners operated the establishment as Burney's BBQ. He died in the late 1950s, and an uncle of the present owners took the restaurant over and, because of a leasing arrangement with another popular barbecue restaurant in southwest Houston, changed the name of the restaurant to Green's Barbecue. In the 1970s, 12-year-old James Drexler began working with his uncle and learned the secrets of the old family recipes for the barbecue beef, chicken, and sausage. He learned the business "from the ground up." In 1982, when his uncle died, James and his mother took over the business, ended the leasing arrangement, and, in 1985, renamed it Drexler's Bar-B-Que.

Drexler's continues to be a "family affair," but there has been increased specialization in tasks as the business has grown. James Drexler continues to do all the meat preparation; his mother, Eunice Scott, handles the other food preparation (the "standard fare" is potato salad, coleslaw, barbecue beans, and slices of white bread); and his sister, Virginia Scott, manages the "front operations"—customer orders and the cash register. There are only two or three other full-time employees, although sometimes during the summer a couple of nephews work part-time.

Drexler's is a family business with strong underlying values. It is in the neighborhood and is of the neighborhood. Despite the success of the business and the increased patronage of individuals from other parts of the city (many of whom previously had few occasions to do more than drive through the Third Ward), the Drexlers have never considered moving from their original location. The current head of the family, Mrs. Scott, influences the culture of the organization, and the values underpinning it. Her values of honesty, hard work, and treating people fairly and with respect—and her faith in God—permeate the atmosphere and operations of Drexler's. She moves through the restaurant inquiring about individual needs—equally for longtime customers and new ones—and always with a smile and warm greeting for all. She is there every day the restaurant is open and holds the same set of high standards for herself as she does for others who work in the restaurant.

Values also get played out in the way in which Drexler's Bar-B-Que "gives back to" the surrounding African-American community. For many years, Drexler's has sponsored a softball team and a local Boy Scout troop. Youths from the neighborhood have opportunities to go camping and visit a local amusement park because the family believes that a business is obligated to aggressively seek out opportunities to help others.

In some ways it would appear that Drexler's is not very flexible or adaptable. The restaurant closes at 6:00 p.m., and is not open Sundays and Mondays. The menu has remained the same for many years. Drexler's has always been well known in Houston's African-American community, especially in the southwest portion of the city. Regular customers have frequented the restaurant for many years, and a successful catering business has also developed. Business has improved every year. During the early 1990s, the business had grown to a point where the

small, somewhat ramshackle, restaurant could no longer meet the demand—there simply were not enough tables or space. So the decision was made in 1994 to close the business for six months, raze the building, and rebuild a new and modern restaurant (with additional space attached for future expansion into related, and unrelated, businesses by other family members). It was a good decision—upon re-opening, business doubled.

Eunice Scott has two sons, James and Clyde Drexler. James is the co-owner of the restaurant, and Clyde is an ex-NBA player. Clyde was popular in the city, having played collegiate basketball at the University of Houston. He had been a very successful member of the Portland and Houston NBA teams, playing on several all-star teams, in two NBA championships, and on the original Dream Team that sent NBA players to the 1992 Summer Olympics.

Since his retirement from basketball, Clyde has become more involved in the day-to-day operations of the restaurant. The restaurant is adorned with memorabilia from his playing days with the University of Houston Cougars, the Portland Trailblazers, and the Houston Rockets.

Questions

1. What role do values play in how Drexler's Bar-B-Que interacts with its neighbors and customers?
2. Is Drexler's an effective organization? Why?
3. Apply the systems model to illustrate how Drexler's Bar-B-Que operates within its environment.

CHAPTER TWO

Organizational Culture

Learning Objectives

After completing Chapter 2, you should be able to:

- **Define** the terms *organizational culture, socialization,* and *career.*
- **Explain** why it is too simplistic to assume that managers can state that they are creating a firm's culture.

- **Describe** the relationship between a society's culture and organizational culture.
- **Explain** why valuing diversity has become an important leadership requirement.
- **Identify** specific practices and programs used by organizations to facilitate socialization.

national culture
The sum total of the beliefs, rituals, rules, customs, artifacts, and institutions that characterize the population of the nation.

Society is composed of people and their culture. Anthropologists often use the term *sociocultural.* They propose that a national culture is learned, it is shared, and it defines the boundaries of different groups and various aspects of national culture (e.g., aesthetics, religion, attitudes, legal factors, language, and education) that are interrelated.[1] Thus, a **national culture** is the sum total of the beliefs, rituals, rules, customs, artifacts, and institutions that characterize the population of the nation.

Nation states such as Canada, Russia, the United States, and India are created politically. They usually contain more than one culture. For example, Canada's population is comprised of several cultures—Anglo, Quebecers (French-speaking), Asian, African, Arab, and Amerindian. Iraq consists of Kurds and Arab cultural groups—Shiites and Sunnis (different sects of the Islam religion).[2]

The values, norms, customs, and rituals of cultures do not simply appear. They take an evolutionary course and are influenced by politics, religion, language, and other cultural aspects. Individuals and groups in the society play a role in the course that a culture takes over time.

A nation's culture and subcultures (less dominant) affect how organizational transactions are conducted (e.g., marketing, hiring practices, reward programs, supervisor–employee interactions, use of technology). Knowledge, respect, and flexibility for coping with national culture differences have become important factors for managers to consider in their plans. Learning to operate in a world influenced by national culture differences is becoming a mandatory requirement for effective management. It is important for managers to understand both the national culture and various organizational culture characteristics.[3]

When a person moves from one firm to another or even from one department to another in the same firm, he or she senses and experiences differences between the environments. Attempting to adjust to these different environments involves learning new values, processing information in new ways, and working within an established set of norms, customs, and rituals. The adaptation to new environments is becoming a common occurrence and is likely to remain so well into the 21st century. Although adaptation is difficult, it can be better understood by learning about organizational culture.[4]

Culture and Societal Value Systems

values
The guidelines and beliefs that a person uses when confronted with a situation in which a choice must be made.

Organizations are able to operate efficiently only when shared values exist among the employees. **Values** are the conscious, affective desires or wants of people that guide behavior. An individual's personal values guide behavior on and off the job. If a person's set of values is important, it will guide the person and also enable the person to behave consistently across situations.

Values are a society's ideas about what is right or wrong, such as the belief that hurting someone physically is immoral. Values are passed from one generation to the next and are communicated through education systems, religion, families, communities, and organizations.[5]

One useful framework for understanding the importance of values in organizational behavior is provided by Hofstede. The result of his research on 116,000 people in 50 countries has been a four–value dimension framework.[6] From this initial research, Hofstede identified four value dimensions by which cultures can differ: (1) power distance, (2) uncertainty avoidance, (3) individualism, and (4) masculinity. A fifth dimension, long-term orientation, was added as a result of subsequent research.

Power distance is the level of acceptance by a society of the unequal distribution of power in organizations. The extent to which unequal power is accepted by subordinates in organizations differs across countries. In countries in which people display high power distance (e.g., Malaysia), employees acknowledge the boss's authority and typically follow the chain of command. This respectful response results, predictably, in more centralized authority and structure. In countries where people display low power distance (e.g., Denmark), superiors and subordinates are likely to regard one another as equal in power, resulting in a more decentralized and less rigid management structure and style.

The concept of *uncertainty avoidance* refers to the extent to which people in a society feel threatened by ambiguous situations. Countries with a high level of uncertainty avoidance (e.g., Japan) tend to have specific rules, laws, and procedures. Managers in these countries tend to have a propensity for low-risk decision making, and employees exhibit little aggressiveness. In countries with lower levels of uncertainty avoidance (e.g, Great Britain), organizational activities are less formal, more risk taking occurs, and there is high job mobility.

Individualism refers to the tendency of people to fend for themselves and their family. In countries that value individualism (e.g., the United States), individual initiative and achievement are highly valued and the relationship of the individual with organizations is one of independence.

In countries such as Pakistan, where low individualism exists, one finds tight social frameworks and emotional dependence on belonging to the organization. These countries emphasize collectivism. Japan is a collectivist country in which the will of the group rather than the individual predominates. Collectivist societies value harmony, whereas individualistic cultures value self-respect and autonomy.

Masculinity refers to the presence of traditionally "masculine" values—assertiveness and materialism. In comparison, *femininity* emphasizes "feminine" values—a concern for relationships and the quality of life. In highly masculine societies (e.g., Austria), one finds considerable job stress and conflict between the job and family roles. In countries with low masculinity (e.g., Switzerland), one finds less conflict and stress.

Several years after Hofstede's original research was conducted, Chinese scholars identified a fifth cultural dimension. They administered the Chinese Value Survey (CVS) to Chinese students in 22 countries across five continents. *Long-term orientation,* the dimension identified, is defined as the degree to which members of a given culture value persistence, thrift (savings), and order in relationships.[7] It has been argued that cultures with a long-term orientation are more likely to experience stronger economic growth and entrepreneurial activity. The opposite pole of this dimension, *short-term orientation,* is when a culture values respect for tradition, the exchange of favors and gifts, protecting one's "face" (i.e., avoiding shame), and steadiness and stability.[8] Both poles of this dimension can be traced to the teachings of the Chinese philosopher, Confucius; however, this dimension also applies to non-Confucian-influenced countries.[9]

The results of Hofstede's research are shown in what he calls maps of the world. The maps reveal at a glance the similarities and differences in work values across nations. Exhibit 2.1 presents a sample of Hofstede's research findings. The five cultural value dimensions are interdependent and complex.[10] Consequently, the effects of values on workplace productivity, attitudes, and effectiveness are difficult to determine. Managers must be cautious about grossly overgeneralizing. For example, not all Americans value individualism, masculinity, a low power distance, and moderate uncertainty avoidance.

EXHIBIT 2.1 **Sample of Hofstede's Research on Cultural Values**

Sources: Adapted from www.geert-hofstede.com/hofstede_dimensions.php (accessed July 8, 2009); and Geert Hofstede and Michael Harris Bond, "The Confucius Connection: From Cultural Roots to Economic Growth," *Organizational Dynamics* 16, no. 4 (1988), pp. 4–21.

Hofstede Dimension	High	Medium	Low
Individualism	United States	Austria	Indonesia
Power distance	Malaysia	Italy	Israel
Uncertainty avoidance	Argentina	Australia	Hong Kong
Masculinity	Japan	Brazil	Sweden
Long-term orientation	China	Netherlands	Philippines

A society's values have an impact on organizational values because of the interactive nature of work, leisure, family, and community.[11] American culture has historically given work a central place in the constellation of values. Work remains a source of self-respect and material reward in the United States. Work also serves as a place to achieve personal growth and fulfillment. As the demographics and makeup of the workforce become more culturally diverse, it will become extremely important for managers to learn about the value system and orientations of the changing workforce.[12] Does the value mix change or is it different for African-Americans, Mexican-Americans, immigrants, physically challenged workers, and others who are increasing in numbers in the society and in the workforce? This is a question that Hofstede's research, new research, and extensive analysis and debate will need to cover more thoroughly in the next few decades. Hofstede's research has inspired other major international research projects. One project in particular has provided additional insight into how culture influences work values, leadership, and behavior in organizations around the world.

GLOBE project
A large international research project that analyzed data on 62 cultures to identify and understand managers' perceptions of cultural practices and values from their home countries.

The **Global Leadership and Organizational Behavior Effectiveness (GLOBE) project**, conceived by Robert House of the University of Pennsylvania, is a large international research project involving 150 researchers who have collected data from more than 17,000 managers from 62 cultures.[13] One of the goals of this large-scale study is to identify and understand managers' perceptions of cultural practices and values in their respective countries. In other words, the research aims at understanding which cultural variables influence leaders and organizational cultures in different countries.[14] Most of the researchers involved are from the host countries in which data are collected, so they have expertise in the culture, language(s), and so on. Also, the GLOBE project is ongoing in that researchers continue to collect data and publish interesting research findings.

As can be seen in Exhibit 2.1, the Globe project classified cultures based on their scores on the following nine cultural dimensions:[15]

1. *Uncertainty avoidance*: The degree to which members of a society or organization use rules, regulations, and social norms to avoid uncertainty or unpredictable future events.

2. *Power distance*: The extent to which a society accepts unequal distribution of power.

3. *Societal collectivism*: The extent to which an organization encourages and rewards group outcomes as opposed to employees pursuing individual goals.

4. *In-group collectivism*: The degree to which individuals express loyalty, pride, and cohesiveness in their organizations and families.

EXHIBIT 2.2 **Cultural Comparisons of Three Country Clusters from the GLOBE Project**

Sources: Adapted from Mansour Javidan, Peter W. Dorfman, Mary Sully de Luque, and Robert J. House, "In the Eye of the Beholder: Cross Cultural Lessons in Leadership from Project GLOBE," *The Academy of Management Perspectives* 20, no. 1 (2006), pp. 67–90; Mansour Javidan, Gunter K. Stahl, Felix Brodbeck, and Celeste P.M. Wilderom, "Cross-Border Transfer of Knowledge: Cultural Lessons from Project GLOBE," *Academy of Management Executive* 19, no. 2 (2005), pp. 59–76; and Robert J. House, Paul J. Hanges, Mansour Javidan, Peter W. Dorfman, and Vipin Gupta, eds., *Culture, Leadership, and Organizations: The GLOBE Study of 62 Societies* (Thousand Oaks, CA: Sage, 2004).

Cultural Dimensions	Anglo Cluster*	Confucian Cluster[†]	Latin European Cluster[‡]
Power distance	Medium-high	High	High
In-group collectivism	Medium	High	Medium-high
Institutional collectivism	Medium	Medium-high	Medium
Uncertainty avoidance	Medium	Medium	Medium
Future orientation	Medium	Medium	Medium
Gender egalitarianism	Medium-low	Medium-low	Medium-low
Assertiveness	Medium	Medium	Medium
Humane orientation	Medium	Medium	Medium
Performance orientation	Medium	Medium-high	Medium

*Anglo cluster: Australia, Canada, Ireland, New Zealand, South Africa, United States, and United Kingdom.
[†]Confucian cluster: China, Hong Kong, Japan, Korea, Singapore, and Taiwan.
[‡]Latin European cluster: France, Switzerland, Israel, Italy, Portugal, and Spain.

5. *Gender egalitarianism*: The extent to which an organization avoids gender discrimination and role inequities.

6. *Assertiveness*: The degree to which members of organizations are aggressive and confrontational in social relationships.

7. *Future orientation*: The extent to which members of a society plan, invest in the future, and delay immediate gratification.

8. *Performance orientation*: The degree to which individuals in a society are rewarded for performance improvement and excellence.

9. *Humane orientation*: The degree to which individuals in an organization are rewarded for being friendly, altruistic, fair, caring, and kind to others.

Based on the data, countries receive an average score on each of the aforementioned nine cultural dimensions. For example, Russia scored high on power distance, Singapore scored low on humane orientation, and China scored high on gender differentiation and in-group collectivism.[16] Managers can also use the GLOBE data to cluster countries based on similar cultural values. Exhibit 2.2 compares the scores of three clusters of countries—Anglo, Confucian, and Latin European—on the nine cultural values in the GLOBE project. This gives expatriates who are not familiar with these cultures a research-based "starting point" on how members from these cultural clusters are likely to behave. The GLOBE project, although still a work in progress, is a comprehensive and valid resource for improving our understanding of the similarities and differences between cultures around the world.

Based on their studies and review of the literature, scholars such as Hofstede and House and colleagues believe that managers' national origin significantly affects their views and style of managing. Just as there's an American bias in some managerial approaches, there's a Brazilian, Japanese, or Indian bias in other management practices. No nation, group of managers, or set of researchers is perfectly free of any bias or ethnocentric tendencies. Cross-cultural understanding will come about only if managers and researchers are willing to increase their global perspectives and knowledge bases about diverse groups of employees. Global approaches to managing organizational behavior will eventually become a top priority around the world. The era of domestically bound approaches to managing what occurs in organizations is ending.

Organizational Culture

When people walk into the Broadmoor Hotel in Colorado Springs, the Breakers Hotel in West Palm Beach, or the Four Seasons Resort in Carlsbad, they sense a certain atmosphere, feeling, and style. These hotels have a personality, a charm, a feel. They have a cultural anchor that influences the way employees interact with guests and how these guests respond to the treatment they receive. Although culture can't be seen, it can be sensed or felt through employees' attitudes, emotions, and perceptions.

McDonald's, for instance, gives off a powerful cultural message.[17] The 13,000 restaurants in the McDonald's network all pay attention to quality, service, and cleanliness. Ray Kroc, the founder, instilled these cultural anchors at McDonald's. He had a significant influence on what McDonald's stands for throughout the world from Tokyo to Chicago to Moscow. Kroc projected his vision and his openness about what McDonald's would be to customers. He gave McDonald's a purpose, goals, and a cultural base from which to operate.

So whether the discussion focuses on a grand hotel that exudes luxury or a McDonald's restaurant that projects its founder's vision of the business, culture is a part of organizational life that influences the behavior, attitudes, and overall effectiveness of employees.

Organizational Culture Defined

Despite being an important concept, organizational culture as a perspective to understand the behavior of individuals and groups within organizations has its limitations. First, it is not the only way to view organizations. We have already discussed the systems view without even mentioning culture. Second, like so many concepts, organizational culture is not defined the same way by any two popular theorists or researchers. Some of the definitions of culture are as follows:

- Symbols, language, ideologies, rituals, and myths.[18]
- Organizational scripts derived from the personal scripts of the organization's founder(s) or dominant leader(s).
- Is a product; is historical; is based upon symbols; and is an abstraction from behavior and the products of behavior.[19]

Organizational culture is what the employees perceive and how this perception creates a pattern of beliefs, values, and expectations. Edgar Schein defined organization culture as:

> A pattern of basic assumptions—invented, discovered, or developed by a given group as it learns to cope with the problems of external adaptation and internal integration—that has worked well enough to be considered valid and, therefore, to be taught to new members as the correct way to perceive, think, and feel in relation to those problems.[20]

The Schein definition points out that culture involves assumptions, adaptations, perceptions, and learning. He further contends that an organization's culture such as that of the Walt Disney Co., JCPenney, or IBM has three layers. Layer one includes artifacts and creations that are visible but often not interpretable. An annual report, a

EXHIBIT 2.3
Schein's Three-Layer Organizational Model

Sources: Adapted from E.H. Schein, *Organizational Culture and Leadership,* 3rd ed. (San Francisco: Jossey-Bass, 2004); and E.H. Schein, "Does Japanese Management Style Have a Message for American Managers?" *Sloan Management Review,* Fall 1981, p. 64.

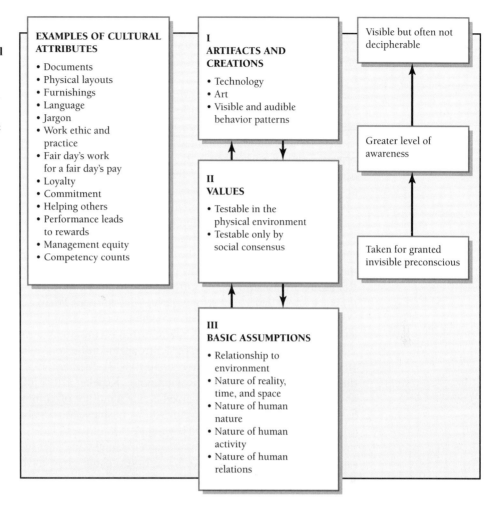

EXAMPLES OF CULTURAL ATTRIBUTES

- Documents
- Physical layouts
- Furnishings
- Language
- Jargon
- Work ethic and practice
- Fair day's work for a fair day's pay
- Loyalty
- Commitment
- Helping others
- Performance leads to rewards
- Management equity
- Competency counts

I ARTIFACTS AND CREATIONS

- Technology
- Art
- Visible and audible behavior patterns

Visible but often not decipherable

II VALUES

- Testable in the physical environment
- Testable only by social consensus

Greater level of awareness

III BASIC ASSUMPTIONS

- Relationship to environment
- Nature of reality, time, and space
- Nature of human nature
- Nature of human activity
- Nature of human relations

Taken for granted invisible preconscious

newsletter, wall dividers between workers, and furnishings are examples of artifacts and creations. At layer two are values or the things that are important to people. Values are conscious, affective desires or wants. In layer three are the basic assumptions people make that guide their behavior. Included in this layer are assumptions that tell individuals how to perceive, think about, and feel about work, performance goals, human relationships, and the performance of colleagues. Exhibit 2.3 presents the Schein three-layer model of organizational culture.

Asking Twitter or IKEA employees about their firm's organizational culture is not likely to reveal much. A person's feelings and perceptions are usually kept at the subconscious level. The feelings one has about a stay at Motel 6 or a stay at the Breakers Hotel are often difficult to express. The culture of a firm can be inferred by looking at those aspects that are perceptible. For example, four specific manifestations of culture at Disney are shared things (wearing the Disney uniform to fit the attraction), shared sayings (a "Mickey" is a compliment for doing a good job), shared behavior (smiling at customers and being polite), and shared feelings (taking pride in working at Disney). Such a pervasive culture is even more impressive when considering that Disney World in Florida employs over 58,000 workers with an annual payroll of $1.1 billion; making it the "largest single-site employer in America."[21]

Organizational Culture and Its Effects

Since organizational culture involves shared expectations, values, and attitudes, it exerts influence on individuals, groups, and organizational processes. For example, members are influenced to be good citizens and to go along. Thus, if quality customer service is important in the culture, then individuals are expected to adopt this behavior, and if adhering to a specific set of procedures in dealing with customers is the norm, then this type of behavior would be expected, recognized, and rewarded.

Researchers who have studied the impact of culture on employees indicate that it provides and encourages a form of stability.[22] Organizational identity provided by an organization's culture instills a feeling of stability. Disney is able to attract, develop, and retain top-quality employees because of the firm's stability and the pride of identity that go with being a part of the Disney team.

It has become useful to differentiate between strong and weak cultures.[23] A strong culture is characterized by employees sharing core values and agreeing to the way things should be done within the organization. The more employees share and accept the core values, the stronger the culture is and the more influential it is on behavior. Religious organizations and cults may be said to have strong cultures. Toyota and other Japanese firms have strong, influential cultures. Weak cultures are those in which members of the organization do not share a core set of values, and as such, they are less likely to perform tasks in a manner that is consistent across the organization.

An American firm with a famously strong and influential culture is Southwest Airlines. Herb Kelleher, one of the founders and now the former CEO, is largely responsible for the strong culture. Along with Roland King, Kelleher rather impulsively decided to start an airline in 1971.[24] Kelleher helped create a culture of commitment by pitching in to help employees as he traveled around doing business. Stories about Kelleher's pitching in are, even after his departure, still legendary at Southwest. One story tells of how Kelleher sat next to mail-room employees through one night and later into the morning doing the same work they did. He would often get off a plane, go to the baggage center, and pitch in handling bags. The day before Thanksgiving one year, which is the busiest airline travel day, Kelleher worked in baggage all day despite a pouring rain.[25] At Southwest today, employees are hired if they possess the company's core values, known as the "Southwest Way." These values consist of three important elements:[26]

1. The warrior spirit—that which a person needs to achieve excellence;
2. A servant's heart—the tendency to put others' needs before one's own; and,
3. A fun-loving attitude—the ability to enjoy one's work and maintain balance in life.

Once the right people are hired, Southwest will train them how to do their jobs; this approach is captured in the company's motto: "Hire for attitude and train for skill."[27]

The closeness of the employees at Southwest is expressed as having fun and working hard. One researcher who studied the airline concluded:

> The atmosphere at Southwest Airlines shows that having fun is a value that pervades every part of the organization. Joking, cajoling, and prank-pulling at Southwest Airlines are representative of the special relationships that exist among the employees in the company.[28]

At Southwest, fun involves flight attendants singing the safety instructions to passengers and pilots telling jokes over the PA system. On some flights, attendants don masks of cartoon characters and entertain the children and parents on flights.

CREDOS OF THREE FIRMS

Johnson & Johnson, Our Credo

We believe our first responsibility is to the doctors, nurses, and patients, to mothers and fathers and all others who use our products and services. In meeting their needs, everything we do must be of high quality. We must constantly strive to reduce our cost in order to maintain reasonable prices. Customers' orders must be serviced promptly and accurately. Our suppliers and distributors must have an opportunity to make a fair profit.

We are responsible to our employees, the men and women who work with us throughout the world. Everyone must be considered as an individual. We must respect their dignity and recognize their merit. They must have a sense of security in their jobs. Compensation must be fair and adequate, and working conditions clean, orderly, and safe. We must be mindful of ways to help other employees fulfill their family responsibilities. Employees must feel free to make suggestions and complaints. There must be equal opportunity for employment, development, and advancement for those qualified. We must provide competent management, and their actions must be just and ethical.

The Body Shop

Against Animal Testing:

We have never, and will never, test our cosmetic products on animals.

Support Community Trade:

We believe that all people have a right to a fair wage and to be treated with respect.

Activate Self-Esteem:

To us, beauty is a feeling, a natural way of being where character, self-esteem and humor are freely expressed and celebrated.

Defend Human Rights:

We've always seen ourselves as a lot more than just a beauty company. For years, we've campaigned against injustices, stood up for the vulnerable and spoken out for those without a voice of their own.

Protect Our Planet:

We are continually seeking out renewable resources, sustainable raw ingredients, and better ways of protecting rainforests and preserving the natural balance of the world that we live in.

Medtronic, Our Mission

To contribute to human welfare by application of biomedical engineering in the research, design, manufacture and sale of instruments or appliances that alleviate pain, restore health, and extend life.

To direct our growth in the areas of biomedical engineering where we display maximum strength and ability; to gather people and facilities that tend to augment these areas; to continuously build on these areas through education and knowledge assimilation; to avoid participation in areas where we cannot make unique and worthy contributions.

To strive without reserve for the greatest possible reliability and quality in our products; to be recognized as a company of dedication, honesty, integrity, and service.

To make a fair profit on current operations to meet our obligations, sustain our growth, and reach our goals.

To recognize the personal worth of employees by providing an employment framework that allows personal satisfaction in work accomplished, security, advancement opportunity, and means to share in the company's success.

To maintain good citizenship as a company.

Sources: See www.jnj.com, www.thebodyshop.com, and www.medtronic.com (accessed July 8, 2009). Also see Raymond E. Miles, Charles C. Snow, John A. Mathews, Grant Miles, and Henry J. Coleman, Jr., "Organizing in the Knowledge Age: Anticipating the Cellular Form," *The Academy of Management Executive,* November 1997, pp. 42–45.

Making customers feel comfortable and helping them laugh are considered important at Southwest Airlines.[29] The strong culture created by the founder has evolved at Southwest Airlines and is perpetuated today by the employees. They make it a distinct culture that influences everyone within the firm.

Popular best-selling books provide anecdotal evidence about the powerful influence of culture on individuals, groups, and processes. Heroes and stories about firms are interestingly portrayed.[30] However, theoretically based and empirically valid research on culture and its impact is still quite sketchy. Questions remain about the measures used to assess culture, and definitional problems have not been resolved. Researchers have also been unable to show that a specific culture contributes to positive effectiveness in comparison to less effective firms with another cultural profile. Comparative cultural studies are needed to better understand how culture impacts behavior.

Creating Organizational Culture

Can a culture be created that influences behavior in the direction management desires? This is an intriguing question. An attempt and an experiment to create a positive, productive culture were conducted in a California electronics firm.[31] Top managers regularly met to establish the core values of the firm. A document was developed to express the core values as: "paying attention to detail," "doing it right the first time," "delivering defect-free products," and "using open communications." The document of core values was circulated to middle-level managers who refined the statements. Then the refined document was circulated to all employees as the set of guiding principles of the firm.

An anthropologist was in the firm at the time working as a software trainer. He insightfully analyzed what actually occurred. There was a gap between the management-stated culture and the firm's actual working conditions and practices. Quality problems existed throughout the firm. There was also a strictly enforced chain of command and a top-down-only communication system. The culture-creation experiment was too artificial and was not taken seriously by employees.

The consequences of creating a culture in the California electronics firm included decreased morale, increased turnover, and a poorer financial performance. Ultimately, the firm filed for bankruptcy and closed its doors.

The California electronics firm case points out that artificially imposing a culture may be an exercise in futility and even counterproductive. Imposing a culture is often met with resistance. It is difficult to simply create core values. Also, when a disparity exists between reality and a stated set of values, employees become confused, irritated, and skeptical. They also usually lack enthusiasm and respect when a false image is portrayed. Creating a culture apparently doesn't happen just because a group of intelligent, well-intentioned managers meet and prepare a document.

Despite the inability of the managers of the California electronics firm to create a productive culture, many leaders and founders of organizations believe they can create specific types of organizational cultures, including those focusing on customer service, ethical, and diversity cultures. Here are some examples of each type of specific culture:

Customer-Service Culture

Founded in 1901 by John W. Nordstrom, a Swedish immigrant who settled in Seattle, Nordstrom's 100-year-old store culture rests on the principle that the customer should be offered the best possible service, selection, quality, and value.[32] The company relies on experienced, acculturated "Nordies" to direct new employees on how to provide superb customer service.[33]

Nordstrom's unique approach to customer service is legendary in the retail industry:

- One customer fell in love with a particular pair of pleated burgundy slacks that were on sale at the Nordstrom downtown Seattle store. Unfortunately, the store was out of her size. The sales associate got cash from her department manager, went to a competitor's store across the street, bought the slacks at full price, brought them back, and sold them to the customer at Nordstrom's lower sales price.

- A Nordstrom customer inadvertently left her airline ticket on a counter. The sales associate tried to get the lost ticket problem solved by calling the airline. No luck. She then hailed a cab, headed for the airport, and made a personal delivery to the customer.

The founder started Nordstrom's commitment to customers, and today's employees carry on this dedication. The Nordstrom Handbook for employees lists rules as follows:

> Rule #1:
> Use your good judgment in all situations.
> There will be no additional rules.

At Nordstrom the culture has evolved over time and is now embedded in the cultural fabric of the firm. Rituals, history, humor, and common sense have resulted in Nordstrom's being recognized as a leader in how to treat customers. The culture reinforces this leadership role every single day.

Ethical Culture

Companies such as Johnson & Johnson, The Body Shop, and Medtronic have established credos or missions based on values and ethical principles that serve to project to others what they believe and to guide behavior. Research suggests that when ethics codes such as these are developed and enforced within an organization, they have a positive impact on job satisfaction, esprit de corps, and organizational commitment.[34] The Tylenol incident and Johnson & Johnson's proactive, ethical response often serve as a guide for other leaders and organizations that confront crises or difficult business decisions that have ethical implications. The Organizational Encounter on page 43 presents excerpts of the credos of these three firms.

Diversity Culture

One organization that is consistently in the Top 50 Best Companies to Work for Minorities is PepsiCo. Indra Nooyi, chief executive officer since 2006, leads this global food and beverage company with over 198,000 employees in 200 countries and 2008 sales of $43 billion.[35] Given that the firm markets products to a widely diverse set of customers, PepsiCo believes its commitment to diversity makes it more competitive and successful: "Diversity isn't just the right thing to do. It's the right thing to do for our business. We've made it our commitment to make diversity and inclusion a way of life at PepsiCo." The company supports over 1,000 community organizations that promote diversity initiatives, develops long-term relationships with minority and female suppliers, and creates an internal environment of inclusion for its minority and female employees. The following is a sample of the current diversity initiatives underway at PepsiCo:[36]

* Executives are dedicated to managing diversity within operating divisions.
* Multiyear strategic plans and goals are aimed at diverse recruitment, improved retention, and fostering a more inclusive culture.
* Annual performance reviews rate managers on inclusion-related goals.
* External diversity advisory boards advise senior management at PepsiCo on diversity issues.
* Training is provided for employees to work in an inclusive environment.
* Networks are used to mentor and support diverse employees.

Cultures seem to evolve over time, as they have at McDonald's, Disney, Nordstrom, Johnson & Johnson, The Body Shop, Medtronic, and PepsiCo. Schein describes this evolution as follows:

> The culture that eventually evolves in a particular organization is … a complex outcome of external pressures, internal potentials, responses to critical events, and, probably, to some unknown degree, chance factors that could not be predicted from a knowledge of either the environment or the members.[37]

There are also times when leaders attempt to create or maintain a positive culture with the goal of increasing teamwork, information sharing, and employee morale.[38] For example, Hewlett-Packard employees at the company's Great Lake division reported that they were experiencing "excessive pressure" and stress from their jobs. The effects of this stress suppressed morale and contributed to a high turnover rate of 20 percent annually. The company decided to create a more positive and lower-stress culture by encouraging employees to set three business and three personal goals each year. When employees accomplished a personal goal (e.g., spending time with children), fellow employees were asked to "cheer them on" and give them positive feedback for taking the time to do things that are important on a personal level. This change in culture from "all work" to "work hard, but stay balanced" seems to be helping. Just two years into the program, productivity had been maintained (even though employees worked fewer hours) and the turnover rate had decreased.[39]

supportive organizational climate
The amount of perceived support employees receive from their co-workers, supervisor, and other departments that helps them successfully perform their job duties.

Related to the concept of a positive culture is that of a **supportive organizational climate** (SOC). SOC can be defined as the amount of perceived support employees receive from their co-workers, supervisor, and other departments that helps them successfully perform their job duties.[40] Although research has not consistently found a direct link between SOC and individual performance, other research has reported that organizations with an SOC are more likely to have employees that are satisfied with their jobs and committed to the organization.[41]

Influencing Culture Change

Only a limited amount of research has been done on cultural change. The research themes that discuss how to bring about significant change are these:

- Cultures are so elusive and hidden that they cannot be adequately diagnosed, managed, or changed.
- Many leaders believe they can have a major impact on an already-established organizational culture, but such cultural change requires a major commitment of resources and an influential and powerful leader.
- Because it takes difficult techniques, rare skills, and considerable time to understand a culture and then additional time to change it, deliberate attempts at culture change are not really practical.
- Cultures sustain people throughout periods of difficulty and serve to ward off anxiety. One of the ways they do this is by providing continuity and stability. Thus, people will naturally resist change to a new culture.[42]

These four views suggest that managers who are interested in producing cultural changes face a daunting challenge. However, courageous managers can and do intervene and alter their organization's culture. Exhibit 2.4 presents a view of five intervention points for managers to consider.[43]

EXHIBIT 2.4
Changing Culture Intervention Points

Source: Lisa A. Mainiero and Cheryl L. Tromley, *Developing Managerial Skills in Organizational Behavior* (Englewood Cliffs, NJ: Prentice Hall, 1989), p. 403.

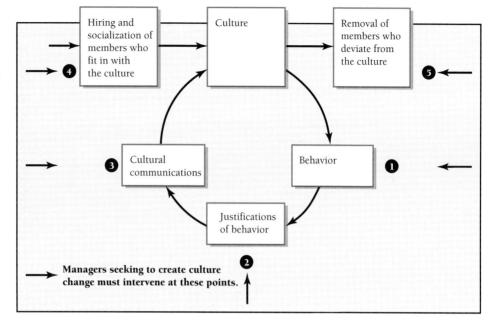

A considerable body of knowledge suggests that one of the most effective ways of changing people's beliefs and values is to first change their behavior (intervention 1).[44] However, behavior change does not necessarily produce culture change unless supported by *justification.* The California electronics example clearly illustrates this point. Behavioral compliance does not mean cultural commitment. Managers must get employees to see the inherent worth in behaving in a new way, that is, justify the new behavior (intervention 2). Typically, managers use communications (intervention 3) to motivate and justify the new behaviors. Cultural communications can include announcements, memos, rituals, stories, dress, and various other forms of communications.

Another set of interventions includes the socialization of new members (intervention 4) and the removal of existing members who deviate from the culture (intervention 5). Each of these interventions must be done after performing careful diagnoses. Although some individuals may not perfectly fit the firm's culture, they may possess exceptional skills and talents. Weeding out cultural misfits might be necessary, but it should be done only after weighing the costs and benefits of losing talented performers who deviate from the core cultural value system.

socialization processes
The activities by which an individual comes to appreciate the values, abilities, expected behaviors, and social knowledge essential for assuming an organizational role and for participating as an organization member.

Sustaining the Culture

person–organization fit
The extent to which a person's values and personality are perceived to fit the culture of the organization.

Socialization is the process by which organizations bring new employees into their culture. There is a transmittal of values, assumptions, and attitudes from the older to the new employees. Intervention 4 in Exhibit 2.4 emphasizes the compatibility or fit between the new employees and the culture. Referred to as **person–organization (PO) fit**, an analysis of 25 research studies on the topic found that employees who fit well with an organizational culture were more likely to be satisfied with their jobs, co-workers, and supervisors; be more committed to the organization; and be less likely to quit.[45] Socialization attempts to make this "fit" more comfortable by reducing incoming employees' uncertainty about their new jobs and roles for the benefit of both employees and the firm.

EXHIBIT 2.5   A Model of the Process of Organizational Socialization

Sources: Adapted from Talya N. Bauer, Todd Bodner, Berrin Erdogan, Donald M. Truxillo, and Jennifer S. Tucker, "Newcomer Adjustment during Organizational Socialization: A Meta-analytic Review of Antecedents, Outcomes, and Methods," *Journal of Applied Psychology* 92, no. 3 (2007), pp. 707–21; Blake E. Ashforth, David M. Sluss, and Alan M. Saks, "Socialization Tactics, Proactive Behavior, and Newcomer Learning: Integrating Socialization Models," *Journal of Vocational Behavior* 70, no. 3 (2007), pp. 447–62; Alan M. Saks, Krista L. Uggerslev, and Neil E. Fassina,"Socialization Tactics and Newcomer Adjustment: A Meta-analytic Review and Test of a Model," *Journal of Vocational Behavior* 70, no. 3 (2007), pp. 413–46; and Blake E. Ashforth and Alan M. Saks, "Socialization Tactics: Longitudinal Effects on Newcomer Adjustment," *Academy of Management Journal* 39, no. 1 (1996), pp. 149–78.

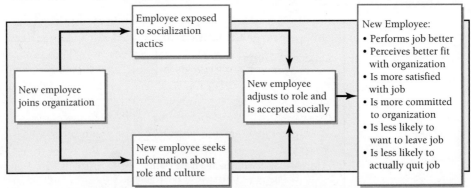

Two ways of analyzing how socialization works in organizations are the process and career stage models. The process model of organizational socialization presented in Exhibit 2.5 illustrates how a new employee, through a combination of seeking information and experiencing socialization tactics from the organization, can adjust to his or her role and gain social acceptance. Once adjustment and acceptance are achieved, the new employee may experience a variety of positive outcomes such as better job performance and perceived fit with the organization, high commitment and job satisfaction, and lower intentions to leave the organization.

As the model in Exhibit 2.5 suggests, employees are more likely to adjust to the new job and be accepted socially if they take a proactive approach to learning about how things work, who makes the decisions, what the organization values, and so on. Also, new employees benefit from a well-organized company-sponsored socialization program. Originally proposed by Van Maanen and Schein,[46] six ways in which organizations can structure the socialization process for new employees include:

- *Collective socialization*: This occurs when all of the new employees are grouped together and exposed to a common set of experiences (e.g., luncheons, orientations, speakers, facility tours, etc.).
- *Formal socialization*: The company keeps the newcomers separated from the experienced employees for a defined socialization period.
- *Sequential socialization*: The new employee must follow a fixed sequence of steps before actually starting the new job.
- *Fixed socialization*: A specific timetable is set before the new employee can begin the new job.
- *Serial socialization*: The new employee is assigned to an experienced employee who acts like a role model or mentor for the newcomer.
- *Investiture*: This approach confirms and accepts the identity of the incoming employee and does not attempt to strip that person of his or her personal identity.

The opposite approach to socializing new employees is much less structured and informal, whereby a new employee assumes the new job without meeting other new employees, attending social events, or being assigned to a mentor who can show him or her the ropes. This "sink or swim" approach may work but often results in poorly adjusted new employees who may end up being mentored by the "wrong employee," getting frustrated, or quitting the organization in six months. Such turnover has a negative effect on both the employee and organization, and it can often be prevented by a well-organized socialization program that helps new employees adjust successfully.

Not only for newcomers, the socialization process also goes on throughout an individual's career. As the needs of the organization change, for example, its employees must adapt to those new needs; that is, they must continue to be socialized. But even as we recognize that socialization is ongoing, we must also recognize that it is more important at some times than at others. For example, socialization is most important when an individual first takes a job or takes a different job in the same organization. The socialization process occurs throughout various career stages, but individuals are more aware of it when they change jobs or organizations.[47]

Newcomers at Nordstrom encounter the culture norms at the initial employee orientation meeting. They are given a five-by-eight-inch card that reads:[48]

> Welcome to Nordstrom: We're glad to have you with our company. Our number-one goal is to provide outstanding customer service. Set both your personal and professional goals high. We have great confidence in your ability to achieve them.

The career stage model of socialization coincides generally with the stages of a career. Although researchers have proposed various descriptions of the stages of socialization,[49] three stages sufficiently describe it: (1) anticipatory socialization, (2) accommodation, and (3) role management.[50] Each stage involves specific activities that, if undertaken properly, increase the individual's chances of having an effective career. Moreover, these stages occur continuously and often simultaneously.

Anticipatory Socialization

The first stage involves all those activities the individual undertakes before entering the organization or taking a different job in the same organization. The primary purpose of these activities is to acquire information about the new organization and/or new job.

People are vitally interested in two kinds of information before entering a new job or organization. First, they want to know as much as they can about what working for the organization is really like. This form of learning is actually attempting to assess the firm's culture. Second, they want to know whether they are suited to the jobs available in the organization. Individuals seek out this information with considerable effort when they are faced with the decision to take a job, whether it is their first one or one that comes along by way of transfer or promotion. At these times, the information is specific to the job or the organization. People also form impressions about jobs and organizations in less formal ways. For example, friends and relatives talk of their experiences. Parents impart both positive and negative information to their offspring regarding the world of work. Although people continually receive information about this or that job or organization, they are more receptive to such information when faced with the necessity to make a decision.

Accommodation

The second stage of socialization occurs after the individual becomes a member of the organization. During this stage, the individual sees the organization and the job for what they actually are. Through a variety of activities, the individual attempts to become an active participant in the organization and a competent performer. This breaking-in period is ordinarily stressful for the individual because of anxiety created by the uncertainties inherent in any new and different situation. Apparently, individuals who experience realism and congruence during the anticipatory stage have a less stressful accommodation stage. Nevertheless, the demands on the individual do create situations that induce stress.

Four major activities comprise the accommodation stage: All individuals, to a degree, must engage in (1) establishing new interpersonal relationships with both co-workers and supervisors, (2) learning the tasks required to perform the job, (3) clarifying their role in the organization and in the formal and informal groups relevant to that role, and (4) evaluating the progress they are making toward satisfying the demands of the job and the role. Readers who have been through the accommodation stage probably recognize these four activities and recall more or less favorable reactions to them. If all goes well in this stage, the individual feels a sense of acceptance by co-workers and supervisors and experiences competence in performing job tasks.

Role Management

In contrast to the accommodation stage, which requires the individual to adjust to demands and expectations of the immediate work group, the role management stage takes on a broader set of issues and problems. Specifically, during the third stage, conflicts arise. One conflict is between the individual's work and home lives. Employees unable to resolve work/life conflict are often forced to leave the organization or to perform at an ineffective level. In either case, the individual and the organization are not well served by unresolved conflict between work and family.

The second source of conflict during the role management stage is between the individual's work group and other work groups in the organization. This source of conflict can be more apparent for some employees than for others. For example, as an individual moves up in the organization's hierarchy, he or she is required to interact with various groups both inside and outside the organization. Each group can and often does place different demands on the individual, and to the extent that these demands are beyond the individual's ability to meet them, stress results. Tolerance for the level of stress induced by these conflicting and irreconcilable demands varies among individuals. Generally, the existence of unmanaged stress works to the disadvantage of the individual and the organization.

Characteristics of Effective Socialization

Organizational socialization processes vary in form and content from organization to organization. Even within the same organization, various individuals experience different socialization processes. For example, the accommodation stage for a college-trained management recruit is quite different from that of a person in the lowest-paid occupation in the organization. As John Van Maanen has pointed out, socialization

EXHIBIT 2.6
A Checklist of Effective Socialization Practices

Socialization Stage Practices	
Anticipatory socialization	1. Recruitment using realistic job previews 2. Selection and placement using realistic career paths 3. Provide detailed information about the organization: history, founders, milestones, success stories
Accommodation socialization	1. Tailor-made and individualized orientation programs 2. Social as well as social skills training 3. Supportive and accurate feedback 4. Challenging work assignments 5. Demanding but fair supervisors
Role management socialization	1. Provision of professional counseling 2. Adaptive and flexible work assignments

processes are not only extremely important in shaping the individuals who enter an organization, but they are also remarkably different from situation to situation.[51] This variation reflects either lack of attention by management to an important process or the uniqueness of the process as related to organizations and individuals. Either explanation permits the suggestion that, while uniqueness is apparent, some general principles can be implemented in the socialization process.

Exhibit 2.6 provides examples to foster and sustain effective anticipatory, accommodation, and role management socialization. These are only a few suggestions and practices that can be used by managers.

Management Pointer

MENTORING GUIDELINES

A number of guidelines that can be useful in mentoring programs include:

1. Do not dictate mentoring relationships, but encourage leaders/managers to serve as mentors.
2. Train mentors in how to be effective.
3. Include in the firm's newsletter or in other forms of mass communication (print and electronic) an occasional story of mentoring as reported by a current top-level executive. He or she will explain how a mentor helped them succeed.
4. Inform employees about the benefits and difficulties of mentor relationships with individuals of different gender and race.
5. Make sure there is diversity among the mentors. All mentors should be trained in dealing with diversity.

Mentoring

The concept of mentoring covers many areas.[52] Interns in the medical field learn proper procedures and behavior from established physicians; Ph.D. graduate students learn how to conduct organizational research from professors who have conducted studies; a "big sister" helps a "little sister" learn better study habits. What about the process of learning or working with a senior person, called a *mentor,* in work settings? From Greek mythology, we get the designation *mentor* for a trusted and experienced advisor. Odysseus, absent from home because of the Trojan War, charged his servant Mentor with the task of educating and guiding his son. In work organizations, a mentor can provide coaching, friendship, sponsorship, and role modeling to a younger, less-experienced protégé. In working with younger or new employees, a mentor can satisfy his or her need to have an influence on another employee's career. Some organizations use mentoring as a means of developing leaders. The Organizational Encounter on page 52 discusses eight applied principles of mentoring that can work on the job or in the community.

Research has indicated that a majority of managers report having had at least one mentoring relationship during

EIGHT WAYS TO BE A GREAT MENTOR

Mentoring is a set of skills for a special relationship, sometimes more honest and more intense than a marriage. To learn more about mentoring principles, Frank Horton is a good place to start. Frank works at a unique nonprofit employment training program called STRIVE (Support and Training Results in Valuable Employment), based in Harlem in New York City. Frank has mentored thousands of women and men—many of whom have never held a job. Frank's unique methods have been widely celebrated by *The New York Times, The Wall Street Journal,* and two profiles on CBS-TV's "60 Minutes." Here are Frank's tips on how to have one of the greatest relationships in life: mentoring.

1. *The most valuable technique?* It's to understand how much fear the person has. What are they afraid of? Authority figures? Their own inadequacy? That they don't wear the right clothes or have the right background? I determine who they are by what they fear. Then I work on what their fear is.

2. *Don't be afraid to be honest.* People don't really like you unless you challenge them. I look for people's sensitivities, stuff they thought they'd hidden, and I tell people exactly what I see in them. "Oh, you don't do what you're told," I tell them. "Probably because you don't know how to say no, because you grew up thinking that good people don't question authority, they just don't show up and/or they turn passive."

3. *Get a mentor yourself.* The best way to learn how to mentor is to be mentored. My mentor is my boss.

4. *Get your mentees to agree with your style of intervention.* What are the shortfalls in their skills or in their behavior? Then devise a plan, with or without their assistance, to move them forward. And they've got to buy into the plan. I tell my mentees, "This is what we're going to do with you." Make it precise. Don't say, "We're going to meet twice a week and talk." Say, "We're gonna meet twice a week, and we're gonna talk about _____."

5. *Don't keep your feelings bottled up.* I don't keep any of it inside. I talk. All the STRIVE mentors do; we dump it all out. I understand that initially I have to provide the energy. I'm the source. I plug in and get them going.

6. *Understand that mentoring is a very important relationship, not just for the mentee but for you.* Sometimes the mentoring relationship is like a marriage. You think with a spouse you share everything? Never. You give people different parts of you. You're different with your wife or your husband than you are with your friends or your family. So there are parts of people you are married to you'll never get to know.

7. *Work at building trust and at feeling it yourself.* I didn't trust people for years because as a child it seemed as if no one was there to help me. I was an angry individual. Coming into STRIVE has helped me channel that anger into what I do. People see it as passion, which it is, but initially it was just anger at the shortcomings of the world.

8. *Recognize this is a process that's going to change both of you.* A mentor needs to understand that in the process of mentoring she's going to change as much as the person she's mentoring. You can't come in with this notion of, "Oh, I'm just going to mentor today. It's not going to affect me." It's going to affect you—in a lot of different ways.

Frank Horton and other key people at STRIVE understand how powerful mentoring can be. Along with their international affiliates in the United Kingdom and Israel, STRIVE is mentoring and placing more than 3,000 individuals into meaningful jobs and careers each year. Remember, mentoring is not just work. It's a relationship. With any real relationship, you'll want to put all of yourself into it.

Source: Adapted from www.village.com/workingdiva/mentoring/mentor, October 1, 2000; www.strivenewyork.org/ (accessed July 11, 2009).

their careers.[53] Companies also see the value in mentoring, evidenced by the fact that 71 percent of Fortune 500 companies report they have mentoring programs.[54] Allen and Eby define mentoring as a unique, reciprocal, learning partnership between two people that involves psychosocial and career support.[55] Kram identified the career support functions as sponsorship, exposure and visibility, coaching, production, and challenging assignments and the psychological and social functions as role modeling, acceptance and confirmation, counseling, and friendship.[56]

Although mentoring functions can be important in socializing a person, it is not clear that a single individual must play all of these roles. New employees can obtain valuable career and psychosocial influences from a variety of individuals—managers, peers, trainers, and personal friends. At KPMG, for example, each new employee is assigned a "transitional coach" to help him or her adjust to working at the company.

EXHIBIT 2.7   **Phases of the Mentor Relationship**

Source: Kathy E. Kram, "Phases of the Mentor Relationship," *Academy of Management Journal*, December 1983, p. 622. Used with permission.

Phase	Definition	Turning Points*
Initiation	A period of six months to a year during which time the relationship gets started and begins to have importance for both managers.	Fantasies become concrete expectations. Expectations are met; senior manager provides coaching, challenging work, visibility; junior manager provides technical assistance, respect, and desire to be coached. There are opportunities for interaction around work tasks.
Cultivation	A period of two to five years during which time the range of career and psychosocial functions provided expands to a maximum.	Both individuals continue to benefit from the relationship. Opportunities for meaningful and more frequent interaction increase. Emotional bond deepens and intimacy increases.
Separation	A period of six months to two years after a significant change in the structural role relationship and/or in the emotional experience of the relationship.	Junior manager no longer wants guidance but rather the opportunity to work more autonomously. Senior manager faces midlife crisis and is less available to provide mentoring functions. Job rotation or promotion limits opportunities for continued interaction; career and psychosocial functions can no longer be provided. Blocked opportunity creates resentment and hostility that disrupt positive interaction.
Redefinition	An indefinite period after the separation phase, during which time the relationship is ended or takes on significantly different characteristics, making it a more peerlike friendship.	Stresses of separation diminish and new relationships are formed. The mentor relationship is no longer needed in its previous form. Resentment and anger diminish; gratitude and appreciation increase. Peer status is achieved.

* Examples of the most frequently observed psychological and organizational factors that cause movement into the current relationship phase.

To reinforce the importance of mentoring at KPMG, mentors and mentees receive training, being a mentor becomes part of performance reviews, and the best mentors are recognized formally by senior managers at an awards dinner.[57] Currently, there are 13,000 mentoring relationships out of a total of 23,000 employees in the United States. The mentoring program is paying off; in 2008, turnover for employees with mentor partners was 50 percent lower than the turnover of those employees without mentors.[58]

Most mentor–mentee relationships develop over time. There appear to be several distinct phases of mentor–mentee relationships. Exhibit 2.7 presents a four-phase model proposed by Kram. The reasons that cause movement in the relationship are described as turning points. Initiation, cultivation, separation, and redefinition cover general time periods of six months to more than five years.

The benefits that result from mentoring can extend beyond the individuals involved. Mentoring can contribute to employee motivation, retention, and the cohesiveness of the organization.[59] The organization's culture can be strengthened by passing the core values from one generation to the next.

The increasing diversity of the workforce adds a new dimension to the mentor–mentee matching process.[60] People are attracted to mentors who talk, look, act, and communicate like them. Gender, race, ethnicity, and religion can all play a role in matching. If mentor–mentee matching is left to occur naturally, women, blacks, Hispanics, and Asians may be left out.[61] The underrepresentation of these groups in management-level positions needs to be evaluated in each firm that considers using mentor–mentee matching. One study showed that cross-gender mentor relationships can be beneficial. The results of 32 mentor–mentee pairings (14 male–female; 18 female–female) found that male–female mentor matching can be successful.[62]

Cultural Diversity

According to the U.S. Census Bureau, the nation's society will become older and more diverse over the next 40 years.[63] Minorities, which now comprise about one-third of the U.S. population, will become the majority by 2050. The minority population (everyone except for non-Hispanic whites) is projected to reach 53.7 percent of the population. In contrast, non-Hispanic whites are expected to decrease from 66 percent in 2008 to 46 percent of the U.S. population in 2050. The Hispanic or Latino population will grow rapidly from 15 percent to reach 30 percent of the U.S. population over the same time frame. The African-American population is expected to have modest growth from 14 percent in 2008 to 15 percent of the U.S. population by 2050. The Asian-American population is projected to increase from 5.1 to 9.2 percent of the nation's population by midcentury.

In terms of age, the number of people aged 65 and over is expected to increase from 38.7 million in 2008 to 88.5 million in 2050. Also, the 85 and older population is expected to more than triple between 2008 and 2050 from 5.4 million to 19 million. This means that approximately 108 million (or an estimated 24.6 percent) Americans are projected to be 65 or older by midcentury.[64]

Diversity in the workplace is much more than understanding population projections based on age, race, and ethnicity. We hear a lot about diversity, but what it means is sometimes confusing.[65] Diversity is not a synonym for equal employment opportunity (EEO). Nor is it another word for affirmative action. Diversity is the vast array of physical and cultural differences that constitute the spectrum of human differences. Six core dimensions of diversity exist: age, ethnicity, gender, physical attributes, race, and sexual/affectional orientation. These are the core elements of diversity that have a lifelong impact on behavior and attitudes. Organizations that commit to diversity and create a culture of inclusiveness can gain several important benefits, including:[66]

1. *Enhanced decision quality*. Diverse board members, executives, managers, and employees bring a wide variety of experiences, frames of reference, perspectives, professional contacts, and information networks to bear on complex problems.
2. *Better connection with customers*. As the U.S. population becomes increasingly diverse, this means an organization's customers (as well as other key stakeholders such as vendors, regulators, investors, etc.) are also becoming more diverse. In 2009, Hispanics, African-Americans, Asian-Americans, and Native Americans' combined buying power in the United States exceeded $1.5 trillion.[67] This helps explain why DuPont Merck experienced a large increase in the sales of its anticoagulant drug to

the Hispanic market. Sales increased after a Hispanic employee suggested that the drug should be labeled not only in English, but also Spanish.[68]

3. *More creative innovation.* Organizations that are diverse can "tap the creative, cultural, and communicative skills of a variety of employees and use those skills to improve company policies, products, and customer experiences." At Frito-Lay, the Latino Employee Network provided feedback on the taste and packaging of Doritos' guacamole-flavored tortilla chips before the product was launched into the U.S. market. Their goal was to make the product "authentic" in the eyes of Latino customers. This input helped make these Doritos one of the most successful product launches at Frito-Lay, with first-year sales exceeding $100 million.[69]

In addition to these important benefits, organizations with a strong commitment to diversity may also enjoy higher financial performance. A study that compared the DiversityInc Top 50 Companies with companies not on the list found that the top 50 companies (all strongly committed to diversity) outperformed their peers on average on several financial measures.[70] The authors suggested that other firms can increase their organizationwide commitment to diversity by: linking diversity to the business strategy; encouraging line managers to own the diversity strategy of the firm; setting clear targets and specific action plans; treating human capital as a source of competitive advantage; being proactive in recruiting diverse employees; connecting with diverse consumer markets; cultivating diverse groups of suppliers; and emphasizing fairness of the diversity program to decrease any potential negative reactions from majority groups.[71]

Microsoft, based in Redmond, Washington, places a premium on diversity and has created a culture that reflects the value of differences across people. Microsoft has grown from a small start-up to the largest software firm in the world in a short time. Microsoft management believes that its growth is made possible by having a proactive diversity program. A Microsoft philosophy is to make people—"customers and employees"—feel welcome. A diversity staff implements diversity training programs, updates benefits policies, and investigates any allegations of discrimination and harassment.[72]

Microsoft's diversity advisory council includes representatives from employee groups of persons with disabilities, women, gay persons, African-Americans, Hispanics, Native Americans, Jewish Americans, and Asian-Indian-Americans, and it continually expands to embrace new groups. The council helps Microsoft formulate policy, identify problems, and create a supportive work atmosphere.[73]

Microsoft believes that people from different backgrounds and with a range of talents add to the cultural fabric and the effectiveness of the firm. Microsoft's philosophy is:

> We must make our products accessible to all types of consumers, and therefore we must market them differently to each group. A diverse company is better able to sell to a diverse world.

Secondary forms of diversity can be changed. These are differences that people acquire, discard, or modify throughout their lives. Secondary dimensions of diversity include educational background, marital status, religious belief, and work experience.

Valuing diversity from an organizational and leadership perspective means understanding and valuing core and secondary diversity differences between oneself and others. An increasingly important goal in a changing society is to understand that all individuals are different and to appreciate these differences.[74]

Management's Ability to Capitalize on Diversity

Due to the changing demographics in the United States, differences in the employee pool will continue to increase over the next few decades. Managers will have to study socialization much more closely and intervene so that the maximum benefits result from hiring an increasingly diverse workforce. Studying the ethnic background and national cultures of these workers will have to be taken seriously. The managerial challenge will be to identify ways to integrate the increasing mix of people from diverse national cultures into the workplace. Some obvious issues for managers of ethnically diverse workforces to consider are these:

- Coping with employees' unfamiliarity with the English language.
- Increased training for service jobs that require verbal skills.
- Cultural (national) awareness training for the current workforce.
- Learning which rewards are valued by different ethnic groups.
- Developing career development programs that fit the skills, needs, and values of the ethnic group.
- Rewarding managers for effectively recruiting, hiring, and integrating a diverse workforce.
- Spending time not only focusing on ethnic diversity, but also learning more about age, gender, and workers with disability.

Socializing an ethnically diverse workforce is a two-way proposition. Not only must the manager learn about the employees' cultural background, but also the employee must learn about the rituals, customs, and values of the firm or the work unit.[75] Awareness workshops and orientation sessions are becoming more popular every day. Merck uses an educational program to raise its employees' awareness and attitudes about women and minorities.[76] The program emphasizes how policies and systems can be tailored to meet changes in the demographics of the workplace. Procter & Gamble has stressed the value of diversity. The firm uses multicultural advisory teams, minority and women's networking conferences, and "on-boarding" programs to help new women and minority employees become acclimated and productive as quickly as possible. Ortho Pharmaceutical initiated a program to "manage diversity" that is designed to foster a process of cultural transition within the firm. Northeastern Products Company established an on-site English as a second language (ESL) program to meet the needs of Hispanic and Asian employees. A buddy system has been established at Ore-Ida. A buddy (English speaker) is assigned to a new employee (first language is not English) to assist him or her with communication problems.

Global competition, like changing domestic demographics, is placing a new requirement on managers to learn about unfamiliar cultures from which new employees are coming. The emphasis on open expression of diversity in the workforce is paralleled by a social movement toward the retention of ethnic roots. The "new ethnicity," a renewed awareness of and pride in cultural heritage, can become an advantage of American firms operating in foreign countries.[77] Using the multicultural workforce to better compete, penetrate, and succeed in foreign cultures is one potential benefit of managing diversity effectively.

Certainly, claiming that having employees from different cultural backgrounds provides only benefits is misleading. Ethnic and cultural diversity creates some potential problems in communications, understanding, and responding to authority. The managers involved in this socialization process need to clearly recognize the benefits and the potential problems of working with a more diverse workforce. In the You Be the Judge illustration, there appears to be a problem regarding the status of Asian-Americans and the income they earn.

YOU BE THE JUDGE

STEREOTYPES AND ASIAN-AMERICANS

Asian-Americans (Chinese, Filipino, Japanese, Korean, Asian-Indian, Southeast Asian, and others) must deal with many stereotypes and myths. They have been dealing with overt prejudice since Chinese immigrants first came to the United States more than 150 years ago. Today, third- and fourth-generation Asian-Americans tend to be very Americanized. As a group, they have higher educational achievement than average. Asian-Americans also hold higher-status jobs than average, yet make less income. Why? You be the judge!

Spirituality and Culture

A steadily growing number of organizations such as Chick-fil-A, Tom's of Maine, the YMCA, Kingston Technology, Ben & Jerry's, and Southwest Airlines have embraced workplace spirituality. Some people are using the term *spirituality* to describe a firm's cultural characteristics, while others are confused or freeze up and think the term means religion at work.[78] Workplace spirituality is not the same as religion. Religion is a system of thought, a set of doctrines and beliefs, a prescribed code of conduct, and the product of a time and place. Spirituality is a personal and private path, contains elements of many religions, and grows from a person's self-inquiry. *Spirituality* means that people (employees) have a personal or inner life that nourishes and is nourished by performing relevant, meaningful, and challenging work.[79]

The story of Cirque du Soleil is an example of spiritual nourishment as practiced by the performers and delivered to audiences around the world. Cirque du Soleil is entertainment that is worth experiencing to acquire a firsthand impression of the creative spirit of employees. (See the Global OB on page 58.)

The Person and Spirituality

Over the past decade, theory and research in organizational behavior and ethics have begun to pay more attention to workplace spirituality. Although spirituality has been described as "soft" or "nonstrategic" by many academics,[80] there is growing interest among many researchers and practitioners to explain, study, and analyze the role of spirituality in organizations.[81]

There is a long tradition in the United States of keeping religion and government separate. From this traditional separation it is a logical step to keeping religion and nongovernment organizations separate too. Although workplace spirituality is certainly not a religion, many observers use the terms synonymously and loosely.

Research on Spirituality and Work Dimensions

The Academy of Management has recognized spirituality at work as a field of study.[82] In addition, the academy created the Management, Spirituality and Religion Interest Group, which describes itself as follows:

> The study of the relationship and relevance of spirituality and religion in management and organizations. Major topics include: theoretical advances or empirical evidence about the effectiveness of spiritual or religious principles and practices in management, from approaches represented in the literature including religious ethics, spirituality and work, and spiritual leadership, as well as applications of particular religions, and secular spiritualities to work, management/leadership, organization, and the business system; and evaluation studies of the effectiveness of management approaches that nurture the human spirit in private, non-public or public institutions.[83]

CIRQUE DU SOLEIL: ENTERTAINING AUDIENCES AROUND THE WORLD

"Awe inspiring" are words that are often applied to Cirque du Soleil ("circus of the sun"), a business that exudes spirituality as we use the term in organizational behavior. The business was started by about 20 Quebec street performers in 1984 who formed a touring company. The performances combine acrobats, clowns, music, and dance with a go-for-broke spirit that stretches to the limits human ability, creativity, and style. Drummers descend from the ceiling seemingly suspended in midair; acrobats execute unbelievable moves with precision, power, and grace; while clowns perform tricks that make audiences around the world erupt in laughter.

Cirque du Soleil is an experience that has been seen by over 90 million people in 200 cities around the world. The performers are constantly working on moves that exceed their wildest expectations. Their pride, concern about the audience, and feelings of performing at the highest level possible have a spiritual aura and tone. To become a performer in Cirque du Soleil represents an honor, a fulfillment, and membership in a family. There are no prima donnas, only "family" members helping and sharing with others.

Cirque du Soleil is a privately owned company. Although, its success has attracted overtures from many investors, the company prefers to remain independent. The independence seems to perpetuate a feeling of being able to take risks, try new routines, and make decisions that the "family" feels good about.

Every year the audiences grow larger, the supply of potential new performers increases, and the morale of performers stays high. The creative spirit of Cirque du Soleil is a powerful force that cannot be measured, but its presence is obvious to the performers and audiences that have so much fun being together for a few hours.

Sources: Bernard Simon, "Steady Footing on Cirque's High Wire: The Leaders of the International Circus Act Have Ensured That Creativity Remains at Its Core, Even When It Comes to Management," *Financial Times*, July 1, 2008; www.cirquedusoleil.com/en/about/faq/faq.asp (accessed July 12, 2009); and www.circusnet.info/cirque/circarte/soleil.htm (accessed December 12, 2003).

This recognition from the Academy of Management is an important step in gaining exposure and creating more research interest in the role that spirituality plays in work settings.

Research on workplace spirituality is still in its infancy, but some interesting findings have been reported to date. One study of the spirituality of medical units within a hospital system found that work units' spirituality was associated with the unit's performance, and unit leaders impacted the degree to which unit members expressed workplace spirituality.[84] Another study reported that organizational spirituality was positively related to employee job involvement, organizational identification, and work rewards satisfaction.[85]

Researchers such as Mitroff and Denton report that many organizations are convinced that spirituality and workplace performance are linked.[86] They studied spiritual beliefs and practices among managers and executives, interviewing more than 80 managers. They also conducted field surveys, and the researchers propose that the sensitivity of the subject and the length of the survey resulted in the low return rate of less than 7 percent. Despite the research design limitations, the Mitroff and Denton study provided some interesting results. They found that:

- Employees who are more spiritually involved achieve better results.
- There was near-unanimous agreement about the meaning of *spirituality*: "the desire to find ultimate meaning and purpose in one's life and to live an integrated life."
- Few respondents feel they can act on their spirituality in the workplace.
- Employees do not want to fragment their lives. They want to be acknowledged as whole persons in the workplace.
- People differentiate strongly between religion and spirituality.

The results of the Mitroff and Denton research led them to identify a number of distinct models that describe how workplace spirituality can be practiced: recovery

YOU BE THE JUDGE COMMENT

STEREOTYPES AND ASIAN-AMERICANS

This is a puzzling issue. The personality or style of Asian-Americans may mean they do not use an assertive approach to secure what is fair or based on performance. Because Asian-Americans do not promote themselves or attempt to secure an explanation for rewards or performance information, they may not share in benefits in proportion to their achievement. Being humble and remaining in the background for many Asians is something they have been taught since childhood.

(e.g., Alcoholics Anonymous), evolutionary (evolved from religious to more ecumenical, e.g., YMCA), socially responsible (e.g., Ben & Jerry's), values-based (e.g., Kingston Technology), and religion-based (e.g., Mormon-owned Ag Reserves, Inc.).[87]

These five models representing different kinds of spirituality in organizations suggest that spirituality can be productive, encouraging trust, work/life balance, empathy and compassion about others, the valuing of human assets, the full development and self-actualization of people, and ethical behavior.

Other researchers have examined the relationship of spirituality and work attitudes.[88] One study examined dimensions of spirituality (e.g., meaningful work, community, and alignment with organizational values) and the relationship to such attitudinal variables as commitment, intentions to quit, and intrinsic work satisfaction.[89] The results were supportive of the hypothesized relationships between spirituality and the work attitudes studied.

Although the results of the limited number of research studies is encouraging, there is still much work to accomplish.[90] There is a lack of rigor, critical thinking, and theoretical foundations in the area of spirituality inquiry. However, this can be said about most new, nontraditional concepts studied by researchers. Most of the now accepted concepts in organizational behavior such as team building, negotiations, and leadership began to have a presence slowly.

Spirituality researchers need to develop research methods, designs, and processes that are acceptable in terms of reliability, validity, and response rates.[91] Research must also include more consideration of moderating and mediating variables. What role does the manager, culture, or organizational system play?

There may also be a negative or dark side to workplace spirituality. Someone who is promoting and prodding others to show or be more spiritual may disrupt the work performance of colleagues. Is there a dark side of spirituality that should be considered? This and other questions need theoretical and research attention.

Summary of Key Points

- *Organizational culture* is a pattern of assumptions and values that are invented, discovered, or developed to cope with organizational life. *Socialization* is the process by which organizations bring new employees into the culture.

- Simply declaring that "this will be the culture" is not realistic. Culture evolves over time. Organizational cultures can be influenced by powerful individuals such as Ray Kroc at McDonald's, Walt Disney, or John Nordstrom. Typically, an organizational culture evolves and becomes real when people interact and work together to create one.

- Organizations can achieve effectiveness only when employees share values. The values of an increasingly diverse workforce are shaped long before a person enters an organization. Thus, it is important to recruit, select, and retain employees whose values best fit those of the firm.
- Spirituality in the workplace is beginning to be empirically studied and discussed. By *spirituality* most practitioners and researchers mean that employees have a personal concept or inner life that can be strengthened and nourished at work. Currently, most studies of spirituality use surveys and research designs that are being improved, but much work needs to be done in this area.

Review and Discussion Questions

1. Organizational culture is a difficult concept to diagnose. How would you diagnose the culture of an office or a manufacturing plant?
2. A growing number of Americans work for foreign-owned firms in the United States. Do you think that these American employees are being influenced by the approach to management and the culture of the country that owns the firm? Explain.
3. Identify the three socialization stages. Which of these stages is most important for developing high-performing employees? Explain.
4. Can spirituality be measured validly and reliably? How?
5. How can a leader or founder help create a strong culture in an organization? Can a leader eliminate culture? Explain.
6. Hofstede's research indicates that national cultures exist. Do you believe that in a heterogeneous nation, such as the United States, a national culture that is shared by society does exist?
7. What should managers of diverse workforces know about differences in values and spirituality among individuals?
8. Point out three assumptions about the culture of the last (or present) firm at which you were employed.
9. What can a leader do to promote cultural change that helps improve the overall effectiveness of an organization?
10. Why is culture so difficult to measure or assess?

Exercise

Exercise 2.1: *Assessing and Considering Organizational Culture*

Listed below are what two researchers refer to as specific manifestations of organizational culture. Enterprises over a period of time illustrate or use these cultural factors to strengthen and perpetuate the culture. Some of the widely publicized firms such as Harley-Davidson, Merck, Nike, Compaq Computer, Intel, Amazon.com, Oracle, Honda, Nestlé, Hershey, and Coca-Cola have distinct and strongly influential cultures.

- *Rite*—A relatively elaborate, dramatic planned set of activities that combines various forms of cultural expressions and that often has both practical and expressive consequences.

Now how much do you know about culture?

6. True or false: The Academy of Management has not yet recognized the increasing interest its members have in workplace spirituality.
   a. True
   b. False

7. A society's concepts of what is right or wrong are reflected in what are called _____.
   a. values
   b. needs
   c. preferences
   d. fulfillment

8. The first stage of socialization is identified as _____.
   a. accommodation
   b. preview
   c. anticipatory
   d. uniform

9. The more intense awareness of the socialization process occurs when an individual _____.
   a. retires
   b. changes jobs
   c. receives job feedback
   d. is involved in training

10. The Walt Disney Company is considered to have a _____.
    a. strong culture
    b. weak culture
    c. unstable culture
    d. single-layer culture

REALITY CHECK ANSWERS

Before	After
1. *c* 2. *d* 3. *b* 4. *b* 5. *c*	6. *b* 7. *a* 8. *c* 9. *b* 10. *a*
Number Correct	Number Correct
_____	_____

- *Ritual*—A standardized, detailed set of techniques and behaviors that manages anxieties but seldom produces intended, practical consequences of any importance.
- *Myth*—A dramatic narrative of imagined events, usually used to explain origins or transformations of something; also, an unquestioned belief about the practical benefits of certain techniques and behaviors that is not supported by demonstrated facts.
- *Saga*—A historical narrative of some wonderful event that has a historical basis but has been embellished with fictional details.
- *Folktale*—A completely fictional narrative.
- *Symbol*—Any object, act, event, quality, or relation that serves as a vehicle for conveying meaning, usually by representing another thing.
- *Language*—A particular manner in which members of a group use vocal sounds and written signs to convey meanings to each other.
- *Gesture*—Movements of parts of the body used to express meanings.
- *Physical setting*—Those things that physically surround people and provide them with immediate sensory stimuli as they carry out culturally expressive activities.

- *Artifact*—Material objects manufactured by people to facilitate culturally expressive activities.

The instructor will divide the class into groups of five or six to discuss each of the manifestations in terms of: (1) a firm the students have worked in, and (2) a popular firm such as the widely publicized enterprises listed above. The groups should also discuss the following:

1. How managers can influence the cultural factors listed above.

2. Which of the factors listed apply to the school/university they are now attending.

3. Why culture can influence the morale of employees.

The exercise can be completed in one or two classes (45–90 minutes). After the group discusses the questions and issues in the first class, a second class can be used to review each of the group's considerations and findings.

Exercise

Exercise 2.2: *Determining Your Diversity Quotient (DQ)*

Lee Gardenswartz and Anita Rowe are well-known and highly regarded diversity management trainers and advocates. They have developed a number of interesting approaches to managing diverse work groups. Listed below is a short, nine-item diversity quotient scale. Take the short questionnaire and score your own answers. The DQ could be used by the instructor as a discussion starter in class.

Diversity Questionnaire

Directions

Indicate your views by placing a T (true) next to any of these nine statements you believe is true.

1. I know about the rules and customs of several different cultures. _____

2. I know that I hold stereotypes about other groups. _____

3. I feel comfortable with people who are different from me. _____

4. I associate with people who are different from me. _____

5. I find working on a multicultural team satisfying. _____

6. I find change stimulating and exciting. _____

7. I enjoy learning about other cultures. _____

8. When dealing with someone whose English is limited, I show patience and understanding. _____

9. I find that spending time building relationships with others is useful because more gets done. _____

Interpretation

The more true responses you have the more adaptable and open you are to diversity.

If you have five or more true responses, you probably are someone who finds value in cross-cultural experiences.

If you have fewer than five true responses, you may be resistant to interacting with people who are different from you. If that is the case, you may find that your interactions with others are sometimes blocked.

Case

Case 2.1: *Organizational Culture: Life or Death*

Anyone working for a company, a project, a joint venture, or in a group that's been together even for a few months is working in a cultural system. Human beings can't work around each other for very long without repetitive activities, strategies, and rituals appearing. How things are accomplished has a cultural rhythm and flow.

Studies suggest that a key feature of employee success is how closely an individual's work habits match the culture in which he or she is employed.

Success in this research is defined as both productivity and longevity. A sound understanding of culture is important in making the best hiring, assignment, and retention decisions.

In an interesting study involving hospitals, success has a life and death aspect. The rapid, efficient, and top-quality treatment of heart attacks is important and crucial for survival. A research study in the Yale School of Medicine journal, *Circulation: Journal of the American Heart Association,* points out the role that culture plays in survival.

Eleven hospitals consistently delivered therapy to restore blood flow to heart attack patients in 90 minutes or less. The researchers studied how staff at these hospitals, including Yale–New Haven Hospital, regularly delivered such speedy treatment, which can save lives.

The authors write that many of the nation's hospitals do not respond as quickly as national guidelines suggest, even though speed is important in restoring blood flow to reduce the amount of damage to heart muscle. Faster "door-to-balloon" time—time elapsed from a patient's arrival to treatment with angioplasty—translates into better survival and less disability.

The researchers visited each of the 11 hospitals and conducted extensive interviews with staff—from the top administrators to technical support staff—and identified a set of common themes.

"We found that success involved much more than skilled individual doctors and nurses," said lead author Elizabeth Bradley, associate professor in the Department of Epidemiology and Public Health at Yale. "What distinguished these hospitals was how well they were organized, how teams functioned together, how the culture rewarded quality improvement and how they dealt with setbacks."

Bradley added, "The themes also reflect the ability of the top performing hospitals to pursue simultaneously contrasting approaches and balance the tensions between them. For example, having standardized protocol but retaining flexibility to refine them continuously, or having intense and individualized data feedback but a no-blame culture. The ability to balance these paradoxes may be a critical aspect of bouncing back from the speed bumps in the process of improvement."

"All of these top hospitals share eight common characteristics that drive their ability to deliver fast, effective treatment to patients with ST-elevation acute myocardial infarction (STEMI)," said senior author Harlan M. Krumholz, M.D., the Harold H. Hines, Jr., Professor of Medicine. "This study has direct and important information for hospitals around the country."

Each of the hospitals had explicit commitment to reduce delays throughout the process; senior management support for quality improvement efforts; innovative protocols and flexibility in refining those protocols; collaborative teams across nursing, cardiology and emergency services,; real-time data feedback to measure success; and an organizational culture that made hospitals resilient to setback.

Questions

1. What values appear to be driving the doctors and nurses in the hospitals to treat heart attack patients?
2. Why must a person's work habits match the team culture in the hospitals depicted above?
3. What types of events could change or alter the strong team culture in the hospitals depicted above?

Source: Adapted from Elizabeth H. Bradley, et al., "Achieving Rapid Door-to-Balloon Times: How Top Hospitals Improve Complex Clinical Systems," *Circulation,* February 2006, pp. 1079–85.

Understanding and Managing Individual Behavior

Be what you are. This is the first step toward becoming better than you are.

Julius Charles Hare and Augustus William Hare, Guesses at Truth *(1827)*

CHAPTER THREE

Individual Differences and Work Behavior

Learning Objectives

After completing Chapter 3, you should be able to:

- **Identify** the major individual variables that influence work behavior.
- **Understand** how diversity is influencing the workplace.
- **Explain** what an attitude is and identify its three components.

- **Discuss** the relationship between job satisfaction and performance.
- **Describe** the major forces influencing personality.
- **Identify** the Big Five personality dimensions.
- **Discuss** several important personality factors.

Why Individual Differences Are Important

Individual differences are important in studying organizational behavior and management for a very important reason. Individual differences have a direct effect on behavior. Every person is unique because of their background, individual characteristics, needs, and how they perceive the world and other individuals. People who perceive things differently behave differently. People with different personalities interact differently with bosses, co-workers, subordinates, and customers. In a multitude of different ways individual differences shape organizational behavior and, consequently, individual and organizational success. Individual differences, for example, help explain why some people embrace change and others are fearful of it. Or why some employees will be productive only if they are closely supervised, while others will be productive only if they are not. Or why some workers learn new tasks more effectively than others. There is virtually no area of organizational activity that is not affected by individual differences.

attraction-selection-attrition (ASA) framework
The concept that attraction to an organization, selection by it, and attrition from it result in particular kinds of people being in the organization. These people, in turn, determine organizational behavior.

A helpful way to think about the importance of individual differences in influencing work behavior is through the use of the **attraction-selection-attrition (ASA) framework.**[1] According to ASA, attraction to an organization, selection by it, and attrition from it result in particular kinds of people being in the organization. These people, in turn, determine organizational behavior.

The ASA cycle works something like this: Different people are *attracted* to different careers and organizations as a function of their own abilities, interests, and personalities. Similarly, organizations *select* employees on the basis of the needs the organization has. *Needs* refers not only to skills and abilities, but also to individual attributes such as values and personality. Not all attraction decisions and selection decisions work out, however. *Attrition* occurs when individuals discover they do not like being part of the organization and elect to resign, or when the organization determines an individual is not succeeding and elects to terminate. Each phase of this ASA cycle is significantly influenced by the characteristics—individual differences—of each person.

In a very real sense, the essence of any organization is defined by the people who work there. For example, the energy trading firm Enron Corporation was once heralded as a role model for 21st century companies, both from an economic and an ethical perspective. The company's success and reputation were built by its leaders and employees who constantly pushed the limits to achieve higher levels of performance. Unfortunately, the needs and actions of its leaders changed over time, leading to a number of unethical and illegal business practices. This behavior led the organization and its thousands of employees to a tragic demise—the largest bankruptcy in U.S. history. The people who worked at Enron, as well as those who did not, were both a part of the ASA cycle.[2] Since the ASA cycle is strongly influenced by individual differences, it is not an overstatement to describe individual variables like those discussed in the remainder of this chapter as critical building blocks in the success or failure of any organization.

Each individual is different from every other individual in many respects. A manager needs to ask how such differences influence the behavior and performance of employees. This chapter highlights some of the important individual differences that can help explain why one person is a significantly better or poorer performer than another person. Differences among people require forms of adjustments for both the individual and those for whom she or he will work. Managers who ignore such differences often become involved in practices that hinder achieving organizational and personal goals.

The Basis for Understanding Work Behavior

Demographic factors such as age, race, and gender influence individual differences. In addition, a person's genetics influence such individual differences as temperament. Another set of factors from a person's environmental background (e.g., urban versus rural; single parent versus dual parent; poor, middle class, or wealthy) impact a person's personality and behavior. For example, a middle-class Caucasian child from Chicago is likely to respond, behave, and even talk differently than an African-American child born and raised in Athens, Georgia.

To understand individual differences, heredity and personal environment need to be weighed and considered. Even when these factors are understood, it is still difficult to accurately predict behavior. A person's behavior at work, in school, or in the home is a complex interaction of the variables depicted in Exhibit 3.1. This graphical portrayal of individual differences is only a starting point and shows some of the large number of variables that influence behavior.

Exhibit 3.1 suggests that effective managerial practice requires that individual behavior differences be recognized and, when feasible, considered while managing organizational behavior. To understand *individual differences,* a manager must (1) observe and recognize the differences and (2) study relationships among variables that influence individual behavior. For example, a manager is in a better position to make optimal decisions if he or she knows what the attitudes, perceptions, and mental abilities of employees are as well as how these and other variables are related. Being able to

EXHIBIT 3.1
Individual Differences in the Workplace

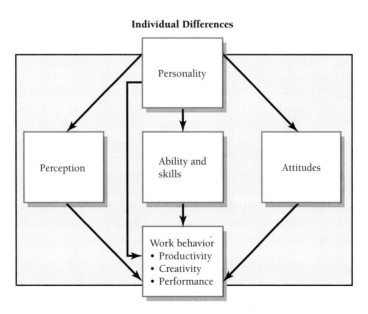

observe differences, understand relationships, and predict linkages can facilitate managerial attempts to improve performance.

Work behavior is anything a person does in the work environment. Talking to a manager, listening to a co-worker, creating a new method of following up on a sale, learning new computer software, typing a memo, researching a question using an Internet search engine, placing a completed unit in inventory, and learning how to use the firm's accounting system are all work behaviors. However, so are daydreaming about being on the golf course, socializing with friends around the water cooler, and sabotaging a new piece of equipment. Some of these behaviors contribute to productivity; others are nonproductive or even counterproductive.

Individual Differences Influencing Work Behavior

The individual variables presented in Exhibit 3.1 are classified as heredity and diversity factors, personality, ability and skills, perception, and attitudes. These variables all impact key work behaviors such as employee productivity, creativity, and performance.

Heredity Factors

Heredity provides a genetic explanation of some aspects of human variability. Included in discussions of heredity are debates about gender, race, and ethnic background. Psychological, mental, and moral differences are influenced by genetic inheritance. However, the genetic basis of individual differences is complicated and controversial. The debate as to whether human behavior is determined largely by heredity or by environment has been going on for a long time. It lies at the center of such controversies as the reasons for differences between men and women, why people have higher and lower IQs, and the extent to which twins raised in separate environments are alike or different. For example, studies suggest that identical twins raised apart are more similar to each other (behaviorally) than to other adoptive family members.[3]

Perhaps the foremost heredity difference is gender. Possible gender-related differences have received particular attention in regard to professional and managerial careers. It has been argued, for example, that men make better managers because they are more assertive, women are less committed to organizational careers because of family considerations, or men are less sensitive to the feelings of others and thus are better able to make tough decisions. While it is true that some evidence supporting each of these generalizations can be found, one also can find evidence that refutes them. Indeed, research suggests that most of the stereotypical differences frequently used to describe males and females in organizations are simply not valid.[4]

diversity
Refers to those attributes that make people different from one another. Primary dimensions of diversity include age, ethnicity, gender, physical attributes, race, and sexual/affectional orientation.

Related to the concept of heredity, **diversity** refers to those attributes that make people different from one another. The six primary (and stable) dimensions include age, ethnicity, gender, physical attributes, race, and sexual/affectional orientation. Secondary (and changeable) dimensions include educational background, marital status, religious beliefs, health, and work experience.[5]

In terms of employee diversity, the workforce is rapidly becoming much more diverse than in the past. The following trends in the U.S. labor force are expected from 2006 to 2016:

- The labor force will continue to grow more diverse.
- Dramatic growth in "older workers" (i.e., people aged 55 and older) will occur.

YOU BE THE JUDGE

CAN JOBS BE GENDER STEREOTYPED?

One of the most important—and interesting—individual difference variables is gender. While many gender distinctions are more imagined than actual, there are some real differences. Men tend to be taller than women and women tend to live longer than men, to mention just a couple. It is also true that there are some real differences in the proportion of males and females in certain jobs. A significant majority of nurses are female, for example. Similarly, most electricians are male. There are, however, no true gender differences that would dictate that nurses had to be women, or that electricians had to be men. Still, many people believe that some jobs are "female" and others are "male."

Such a person was a male manager for a Washington DC company. When a receptionist position became available in his office, he instructed one of his female employees to fill the vacant position with a woman. The notion of having a male receptionist simply did not fit his stereotype of this category. In a number of different ways he made it clear that "men are not receptionists." Clearly upset by this kind of thinking, the female employee who had been instructed to fill this position with a woman sued her employer for sex discrimination.

How would you have ruled in this case? Is this sex discrimination? Do you think any laws were broken here? If not, should there be a law against such behavior?

- There will be 76.5 million women in the labor force by 2016, 6.3 million more than in 2006.
- White (non-Hispanic) workers' participation in the workforce will decrease to about 65 percent.
- The majority of the 22.4 million disabled individuals will be looking for jobs and careers.
- Hispanic- and Asian-Americans will continue to enter the workforce at a rapid rate.
- More African-American women than men will enter the workforce.[6]

The proliferation of gender, racial, age, and ethnic diversity in the workplace brings onto center stage differences in values, work ethics, and norms of behaviors. Miscommunication, insensitivity, ignorance, and hostility are likely to become major managerial concerns. For example, the U.S. Equal Employment Opportunity Commission (EEOC) settled a racial harassment lawsuit in 2008 for $1,650,000 against four companies on behalf of African-American employees who were subjected to the following extreme racist behaviors at a construction site in the United States: life-size nooses hanging in African-American employees' work areas; racist graffiti (e.g., "If u not white u not right") in the portable toilets; and regular use of verbally offensive language (e.g., the "N-word").[7] Employees who are isolated and harassed for their uniqueness and diversity will not only suffer, but due to resentment, fear, and anger, will be less likely to be enthusiastic contributors to the organization.[8]

A number of companies are taking active steps to manage this dramatic shift in employee diversity. For example, IBM's board of directors and its Worldwide Executive Council (WEC) are 57 percent and 40 percent (respectively) female and multicultural, or not-U.S. born. The WEC is responsible for overseeing the company's worldwide diversity initiatives, including recruiting, retaining, and promoting talent, and linking diversity initiatives to the global marketplace.[9]

In another example, Deloitte Touche has undertaken several initiatives to help its female employees break the "glass ceiling" including: decreasing the level of travel for employees to allow them to better balance their work and personal lives; enhancing career opportunities for women; and making diversity management a key priority for the organization.[10] Leaders at Deloitte Touche understand the long-term benefits of retaining diverse employees. Although research shows that women comprise less than 15% percent of corporate board members in the United States and many European countries, evidence shows that Fortune 500 firms with a higher percentage of female directors and managers performed better financially.[11]

Understanding diversity in the global marketplace is equally as important as understanding it in the United States. As the Global OB on page 73 illustrates, global managers must develop a keen understanding of differences among cultures to be successful in their international business endeavors.

In addition to understanding the impact of racial, ethnic, and gender differences at the workplace, managers also need to be aware of these other ways that employee diversity can manifest itself:

- *Generational diversity*: Gen Y or Millennials (those who are in their 20s and younger) are different in key ways when compared to Gen X (those in their 30s to low 40s) and baby boomers (those who are in their mid-40s and older). Gen X and baby boomers, as managers, need to realize that Millennials can be used to leverage their skills at online social networking to collaborations and teamwork on virtual team projects. Millennials tend to require more praise and short-term rewards than do Gen X and baby boomers, but they will put their own careers first and will look for organizations that provide meaningful training and projects to build their résumés. Managers need to assign mentors to help match organizational opportunities with Millennial employees' career goals and to help Millennials understand the company culture, dress policies, office politics, and so on.[12]

- *Disability diversity*: The Americans with Disabilities Act (ADA) of 1990 prohibits discrimination against qualified individuals with disabilities. A disabled person is someone who has a physical or mental impairment that substantially limits one or more of his or her major life activities. Given that the ADA requires that organizations make reasonable accommodations for disabled individuals, managers may be called upon to make one or more of the following accommodations:[13]

  - Make existing facilities accessible. A manager may be asked to assist in the planning and budgeting for a wheelchair ramp to be added to the front of the building.

  - Restructure jobs. A manager may purchase voice interface software so that a blind customer service representative can relate information from a PC to customers who call in with questions and problems. Basically, the PC speaks to the blind employee who then communicates that information to the customer.

  - Modify work schedules. Some ill individuals have set days/times when they need to receive treatment (e.g., kidney dialysis, etc.) from medical providers. A manager may need to accommodate the employee by scheduling work around these medical visits.

  - Reassign employees. A police officer, after being wounded in the line of duty, may need to be reassigned to a desk job for a certain period until able to assume full responsibilities again.

GUIDELINES FOR EXPATRIATES WHEN MANAGING IN ANOTHER CULTURE

When a manager is managing in another culture, a number of crucial cultural characteristics must be considered. A few pointers that apply to specific cultures could prove to be invaluable.

China

- Mandarin is spoken by over 70 percent of the population.
- Although the government encourages atheism, Buddhism, Islam, and Christianity also are practiced in China. Confucianism, although not a religion, has a great influence on Chinese society.
- As a collectivist society, individual rights and needs are subordinate to collective rights and needs.
- Harmony and family must be respected.
- Although women are purported to be equal to men, economic and work-related inequities exist.

India

- Hinduism and Islamic religions play a major role in the lives of most Indians.
- The caste system exerts a strong influence over Indian society.

- A moderately collective culture exists. Thus, a friendship may be more important than work or technical expertise.
- Punctuality is not a priority.
- Being passive is considered a virtue.
- Women have few privileges and male chauvinism is strong.

Russia

- Literacy is almost 100 percent. Information is processed subjectively and outsider-initiated communication is viewed suspiciously.
- Specialists with technical expertise are respected.
- Sexual harassment is excessive in business organizations and in the government.
- Compromise is viewed as a sign of personal weakness.

Mexico

- Good impressions are made when foreign nationals are familiar with the nation's history, customs, and arts.
- General suspicion is directed at foreign nationals.
- Time is a flexible concept.
- Personal friendships and long-term relationships are very important.
- Conversations occur at close physical distances.

What are the implications of heredity and diversity differences in the global and domestic workplace? It is important to understand that even the perception that these differences exist influences the behavior of men, women, and minorities in the workplace. A male manager, for example, who assumes a female employee is less committed to the organization because of family responsibilities is likely—perhaps unconsciously—to behave differently toward her than he otherwise would. In turn, the female employee's behavior will likely be influenced—again, perhaps unconsciously—by the manager's behavior.

Abilities and Skills

ability
A person's talent to perform a mental or physical task.

mental ability
Refers to one's level of intelligence and can be divided into subcategories, including verbal fluency and comprehension, inductive and deductive reasoning, associative memory, and spatial orientation.

Some employees, though highly motivated, simply do not have the abilities or skills to perform well. Abilities and skills play a major role in individual behavior and performance.[14] **Ability** is a person's talent to perform a mental or physical task. *Skill* is a learned talent that a person has acquired to perform a task. A person's ability is generally stable over time. Skills change as one's training or experience occurs. A person can be trained and consequently acquire new skills.

The following abilities have been identified as important factors in helping to differentiate between higher- and lower-performing employees: *mental ability, emotional intelligence,* and *tacit knowledge*. When selecting candidates for a particular position, one of the better predictors of training proficiency and job success is **mental ability**. Often referred to as intelligence, mental ability can be divided into several subcategories: verbal fluency and comprehension, inductive and deductive reasoning, associative memory, and spatial orientation.[15]

One of the more popular cognitive ability tests is the Wonderlic Personnel Test.[16] Organizations from the National Football League to American Residential Services (a home maintenance and repair company) give this 12-minute, 50-question test to aspiring recruits and job applicants to assess their mental ability. At American Residential Services candidates scoring in the lowest 10 to 15 percent are not hired. The company claims that this enhances the quality of new employees, ultimately improving customer service and cutting turnover.[17]

Another important ability is emotional intelligence. Discussed in greater detail in Chapter 4, **emotional intelligence (EI)** refers to a person's ability to be self-aware of feelings, to manage emotions, to motivate oneself, to express empathy, and to handle relationships with others.[18] The topic of emotional intelligence has spawned a great deal of interest among researchers and managers, as evidenced by the countless number of books and research studies published on the topic. Though not conclusive, research findings are increasingly showing that people high in emotional intelligence are more successful in certain ways on the job.[19] For example, one study found that employees low in EI reacted more negatively to job insecurity and were more likely to adopt negative coping strategies.[20]

Tacit knowledge refers to work-related practical know-how that employees acquire through observation and direct experience.[21] By gaining hands-on work experience, successful employees learn the ins and outs of their jobs, the norms of their work teams, and the values of the organizational culture. For example, a customer service representative from a large cable television company learned over the years that it's best not to interrupt irate customers while they are upset and venting their problems. By showing the customer genuine concern and a willingness to listen, the representative could help the customer feel better, ultimately retaining his or her business. This skill was not learned from a manual or training session; it was developed by the representative through trial and error and experience with hundreds of irate customers.

According to Robert J. Sternberg, people who develop and use tacit knowledge will increase their chances of success within organizations.[22] He believes that *practically* intelligent leaders and managers tend to:

- Capitalize on their own strengths and overcome their weaknesses.
- Realize they are not good at everything.
- Overcome negative expectations set by others around them.
- Learn from their positive and negative experiences.
- Have can-do attitudes.

Although far from conclusive, research supports such claims about the virtues of practical intelligence. For example, in a study of the leadership effectiveness of 562 military leaders, those with higher levels of tacit knowledge were perceived as more effective than those with lower amounts of practical, experience-based knowledge.[23]

The presence or absence of various abilities and skills has an obvious relationship to job performance. Managers must attempt to match a person's abilities and skills to the job requirements. This matching process is important since no amount of leadership, motivation, or organizational resources can make up for deficiencies in abilities or skills (although clearly, some skills can be improved with practice and training). Job analysis is a widely used technique that takes some of the guesswork out of matching.

emotional intelligence (EI)
The handling of relationships and interactions with others.

tacit knowledge
The work-related practical know-how that employees acquire through observation and direct experience on the job.

Job analysis is the process of defining and studying a job in terms of tasks or behaviors and specifying the responsibilities, education, and training needed to perform the job successfully. Job analysis will be discussed in more detail in Chapter 6.

Attitudes

attitudes
Mental states of readiness for need arousal.

Attitudes are determinants of behavior because they are linked with perception, personality, feelings, and motivation. An **attitude** is a mental state of readiness learned and organized through experience, exerting a specific influence on a person's response to people, objects, and situations with which it is related. Each person has attitudes on numerous topics—computers, jogging, restaurants, friends, jobs, religion, the government, elder care, crime, education, income taxes, and so on.

This definition of attitude has certain implications for the manager. First, attitudes are learned. Second, attitudes define one's predispositions toward given aspects of the world. Third, attitudes provide the emotional basis of one's interpersonal relations and identification with others. And fourth, attitudes are organized and are close to the core of personality. Some attitudes are persistent and enduring. Yet, like each of the psychological variables, attitudes are subject to change.[24]

cognition
This is basically what individuals know about themselves and their environment. Cognition implies a conscious process of acquiring knowledge.

Attitudes are intrinsic parts of a person's personality. A number of theories attempt to account for the formation and change of attitudes. One such theory proposes that people "seek a congruence between their beliefs and feelings toward objects" and suggests that the modification of attitudes depends on changing either the feelings or the beliefs.[25] The theory proposes that cognition, affect, and behavior determine attitudes, and that attitudes, in turn, determine cognition, affect, and behavior. The **cognitive** component of an attitude consists of the person's perceptions, opinions, and beliefs. It refers to the thought processes with special emphasis on rationality and logic. An important element of cognition is the evaluative beliefs held by a person. Evaluative beliefs are manifested in the form of favorable or unfavorable impressions that a person holds toward an object or person.

affect
The emotional component of an attitude; often learned from parents, teachers, and peer group members.

Affect is the emotional component of an attitude and is often learned from parents, teachers, and peer group members. It is the part of an attitude that is associated with "feeling" a certain way about a person, group, or situation. The *behavioral* component of an attitude refers to the tendency of a person to act in a certain way toward someone or something. A person may act in a warm, friendly, aggressive, hostile, teasing, or apathetic way, or in any number of other ways. Such actions could be measured to examine the behavioral component of attitudes.

cognitive dissonance
A mental state of anxiety that occurs when there is a conflict among an individual's various cognitions (for example, attitudes and beliefs) after a decision has been made.

Sometimes there may be discrepancies between attitudes and behaviors. This kind of discrepancy is called **cognitive dissonance.** An individual who has the attitude that smoking is bad for one's health but who continues to smoke anyway would probably experience cognitive dissonance. Such an inconsistency between beliefs and behavior is thought to create discomfort and a desire on the part of the individual to eliminate or reduce the inconsistency.

In terms of the smoker, this could mean changing beliefs about the negative health consequences ("I'm in good health—smoking isn't as bad as they say") or modifying the behavior (quitting, cutting back, switching to a "lower-tar" brand). The concept of cognitive dissonance is developed further in Chapter 14.

Exhibit 3.2 illustrates how a work environment factor (e.g., managers' style) can influence the three components of attitudes. This stimulus triggers cognitive (thought), affective (emotional), and behavior responses. In essence, the stimulus results in the formation of attitudes, which then lead to one or more responses.

EXHIBIT 3.2
The Three Components of Attitudes: Cognition, Affect, and Behavior

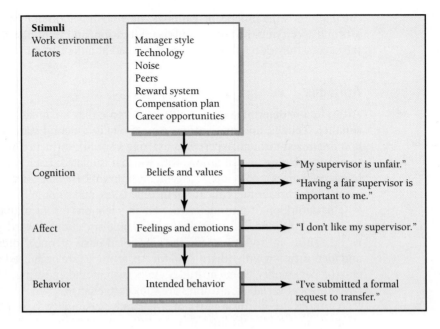

The theory of cognitive, affective, and behavioral components as determinants of attitudes has a significant implication for managers. The theory implies that the manager must be able to demonstrate that the positive aspects of contributing to the organization outweigh any negative aspects of a situation. It is through attempts to develop generally favorable attitudes toward the organization and the job among employees that many managers achieve effectiveness.

Changing Attitudes

Managers often face the task of changing their employees' attitudes to get them to work harder and achieve higher job performance. Although many variables affect attitude change, the process depends on three general factors: the communicator, the message itself, and the situation.[26] For this discussion, it is assumed that the communicator is the manager of several employees of a five-star hotel. The employees work in a variety of positions, including the front desk, sales, banquets, cleaning, laundry, concierge services, and the hotel restaurant.

The Communicator The employees are more likely to change their attitudes (e.g., like the job more and try to provide higher levels of customer service) if they trust the manager, like the manager, and perceive the manager as having prestige. If the manager is not trusted, then his or her efforts at changing attitudes will fall short because the employees will not believe or accept the manager's message. Calls for better customer service will likely be perceived as self-serving for the manager in terms of his or her annual performance and pay raises (as opposed to a sincere effort to make customers feel better about staying at the hotel). Liking the manager can lead to attitude change because employees try to identify with a liked communicator and tend to adopt attitudes and behaviors of the liked individual. In addition, perceiving the manager as having prestige can lead employees to be more receptive to changing their attitudes. If a manager with little prestige is not shown respect by peers and superiors, this makes the job of changing the employees' attitudes very difficult.

The Message Even if the manager is trusted, liked, and seen as having prestige, the message needs to be clear, understandable, and convincing. The manager attempts to change attitudes by delivering persuasive messages. As will be discussed in Chapter 13, managers send both intentional and unintentional messages through verbal and non-verbal communication. For example, if a manager says verbally that he or she supports the new vice president of the hotel but then misses several of the new VP's meetings, the manager is sending a powerful nonverbal message to employees (i.e., I do not support the new VP). To be more effective at changing employees' attitudes, managers need to develop and deliver consistent and persuasive verbal and nonverbal messages.

The Situation Managers' ability to change employees' attitudes depends partly on the situation in which the effort takes place. Assume the manager wants the cleaning staff to clean rooms 20 percent faster than they currently are doing. Knowing that a persuasive message can be more effective when accompanied by a distraction, the manager first announces that each member of the cleaning staff is going to receive a year-end bonus for their hard work and commitment. After making that announcement, the manager then asks the employees to make an even greater effort over the next 12 months by cleaning rooms much faster. Research indicates that if people are distracted while they are listening to a message, they will show more attitude change because the distraction interferes with silent counterarguing.[27] In other words, the employees are more likely to listen to and respond to the manager's plea to work faster because they don't have time to come up with strong internal arguments against this request.

Distraction is just one of many factors that can increase persuasion. Another factor that makes people more susceptible to attempts to change attitudes is pleasant surroundings. The pleasant surroundings may be associated with the attempt to change the attitude.

Attitudes and Job Satisfaction

Job satisfaction is an attitude people have about their jobs. It results from their perception of their jobs and the degree to which there is a good fit between them as individuals and the organization.[28] A number of factors have been associated with job satisfaction. Among the more important ones are these:

Pay—the amount of pay received and the perceived fairness of that pay.

Work itself—the extent to which job tasks are considered interesting and provide opportunities for learning and accepting responsibility.

Promotion opportunities—the availability of opportunities for advancement.

Supervision—the technical competence and the interpersonal skills of one's immediate boss.

Co-workers—the extent to which co-workers are friendly, competent, and supportive.

Working conditions—the extent to which the physical work environment is comfortable and supportive of productivity.

Job security—the belief that one's position is relatively secure and continued employment with the organization is a reasonable expectation.

Many organizations recognize the importance of the potential link between job satisfaction and a number of desirable organizational outcomes. Ben & Jerry's Homemade, Inc., for example, is very proactive in providing a work environment it believes increases satisfaction and, consequently, productivity. This multimillion-dollar ice cream maker has established an employee-run Joy Committee. The sole purpose of this committee is to suggest and implement activities that make Ben & Jerry's a fun place to work. Among other innovations, the committee has sponsored an official tacky dress-up day in which employees are encouraged to wear their most outlandish and stylistically incorrect outfits. On one occasion the company hired masseuses to reduce stress during the busiest season. Employees could take a break for a half hour and have a massage. Through these and other personnel policies, Ben & Jerry's is committed to increasing employee satisfaction.[29]

Another company committed to building and maintaining high levels of job satisfaction is SAS Institute Inc., a North Carolina–based software maker with more than 10,000 employees in 522 offices around the world. The SAS Institute offers a generous family-friendly package of benefits aimed to boost employee morale on the job. To help keep their stress levels under control, employees can work out in a state-of-the-art gym, drop their children at the company-run day care facility, receive on-site health care, and take advantage of flex hours to meet family obligations.[30]

Satisfaction and Job Performance

One of the most widely debated and controversial issues in the study of job satisfaction is its relationship to job performance or effectiveness.[31] Three general views of this relationship have been advanced: (1) job satisfaction causes job performance; (2) job performance causes job satisfaction; and (3) the job satisfaction–job performance relationship is moderated by other variables such as rewards. Exhibit 3.3 shows each of these viewpoints.

The first two views have mixed, but generally weak, research support. Most studies dealing with the performance–satisfaction relationship have found low association

EXHIBIT 3.3
Satisfaction–Performance Relationships: Three Views

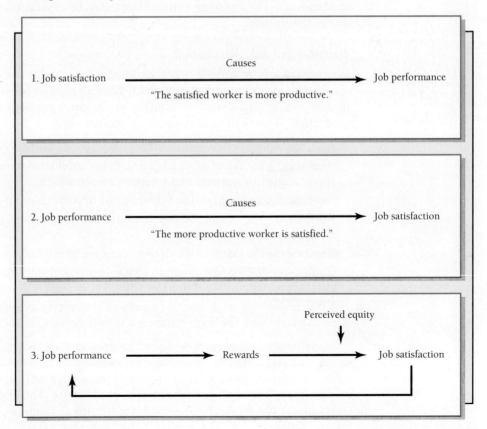

ARE U.S. WORKERS SATISFIED WITH ANYTHING AT WORK?

A study conducted by The Conference Board of a representative sample of 5,000 U.S. households provides interesting results on job satisfaction. The study found that more than 50 percent of Americans are not happy with their jobs. A decline in job satisfaction has been occurring over the past 20 years and isn't showing any signs of reversing itself.

The survey found interesting differences among respondents. Younger workers (some of whom work part-time) and middle-aged employees from the Mid-Atlantic states are the least satisfied with their jobs. Older workers who make better salaries and who live in the Mountain states are more satisfied with their jobs.

Worker discontentment did not stop with age, income, or geographic location. For example, less than 23 percent were satisfied with their companies' bonus plans and promotion policies; less than 30 percent were content with their firm's training programs, recognition and performance review process; and less than 36 percent were happy with their workload, work/life balance, communication channels and potential for growth.

Were there any aspects of work with which the majority of respondents were satisfied? Yes, 56 percent expressed interest in their work and said they were satisfied with their commute and co-workers.

Source: Adapted from "U.S. Job Satisfaction Declines, The Conference Board Reports," February 23, 2007, www.conference-board.org/utilities/pressDetail.cfm?press_ID = 3075 (accessed April 6, 2009); and Nancy H. Woodward, "Uplifting Employees," *HR Magazine* 52, no. 8 (August 2007), pp. 81–85.

Less satisfied with job	More satisfied with job
Younger workers less than 25 years old	Older workers aged 55 to 64
Workers aged 45 to 55 years old	Older workers aged 65 and over
Workers earning $15,000 or less per year	Workers earning $50,000 or more
Workers who live in the Mid-Atlantic states (New Jersey, Pennsylvania, and New York)	Workers in the Mountain states (Montana, Idaho, Wyoming, Nevada, Utah, Colorado, Arizona, and New Mexico)

between performance and satisfaction. The evidence is rather convincing that a satisfied employee is not necessarily a high performer. Managerial attempts to make everyone satisfied will not necessarily yield high levels of productivity. Likewise, the assumption that a high-performing employee is likely to be satisfied is not well supported.

The third view suggests that satisfaction and performance are related only under certain conditions. A number of other factors, such as employee participation, have been suggested as affecting the relationship.[32] Most attention, however, has focused on rewards as influencing the relationship. Generally, this view suggests that the rewards one receives as a consequence of good performance, and the degree to which these rewards are perceived as reasonable or equitable, affect both the extent to which satisfaction results from performance and the extent to which performance is affected by satisfaction. This means that if an employee is rewarded for good performance and if the reward is deemed fair by the employee, job satisfaction will increase (or remain high). This in turn will have a positive effect on performance, leading to additional rewards and continued higher levels of job satisfaction.

There is a great deal we do not yet understand regarding the role of job satisfaction. It is clear, however, that it can affect a number of important performance variables. Absenteeism and turnover, for example, have been frequently associated with satisfaction, although the relationship is not strong.[33] Increasing job performance and employee productivity will continue to be a major management focus in the 21st century. As long as this remains the case, it is unlikely that interest in job satisfaction will diminish among either organizational researchers or managers.

The Organizational Encounter on job satisfaction on page 79 provides managers with suggestions. The feedback from the employees studied indicates managers should examine their promotion policies, training programs, and engagement opportunities.

Personality

The relationship between behavior and personality is perhaps one of the most complex matters that managers have to understand. When we speak about an individual's personality we are referring to *a relatively stable set of feelings and behaviors that have been significantly formed by genetic and environmental factors.* Although many aspects of personality formation, development, and expression are not perfectly understood, certain principles are generally accepted as being true. For example, personality:

1. Appears to be organized into patterns that are, to some degree, observable and measurable.
2. Has superficial aspects, such as attitudes toward being a team leader, and a deeper core, such as sentiments about authority or a strong work ethic.
3. Involves both common and unique characteristics. Every person is different from every other person in some respects and similar to other persons in other respects.

Your own personality did not just suddenly or randomly happen. It is the product of a number of forces that together have helped shape the unique individual that you are. Exhibit 3.4 presents some of these major forces.

Personality is a product of both nature and nurture. Nature refers to the hereditary forces in Exhibit 3.4. The genetic makeup you inherited from your mother and father has partially determined the personality you have today. While scientists have yet to identify specific "personality" genes, it is clear heredity is an important determiner of personality. Research on identical twins who have been reared apart suggests that hereditary factors may account for as much as half of the variation in different personalities.[34] Heredity is not a constant factor in personality, however.

EXHIBIT 3.4
Some Major Forces Influencing Personality

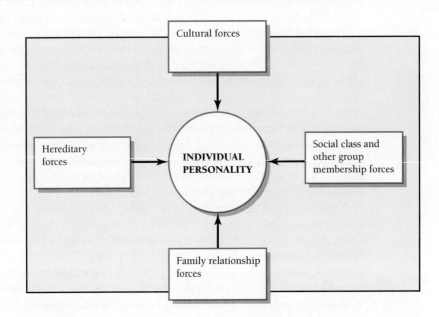

The importance of heredity varies from one personality trait to another. For example, heredity generally is more important in determining a person's temperament than values and ideals.

The remaining forces depicted in Exhibit 3.4 are part of the nurture side of the personality equation. *Nurture* refers to the pattern of life experiences you have. *Family relationship* forces are an important part of nurture. This includes the experiences you had with parents, siblings, and other family members. How your parents expressed their feelings, how strict or permissive they were, how many siblings you had, where you were in the birth order (whether you were an only child or the first, middle, or last child, etc.), the role grandparents played in your upbringing—all are examples of family relationship forces that played a role in shaping what your personality is today.

The degree to which every person is molded by *culture* is significant. We frequently do not comprehend the impact of culture in shaping our personalities. It happens gradually, and usually there is no alternative but to accept the culture. The stable functioning of a society requires that there be shared patterns of behavior among its members and that there be some basis for knowing how to behave in certain situations. To ensure this, the society institutionalizes various patterns of behavior. The institutionalization of some patterns of behavior means that most members of a culture will have many common personality characteristics. At the same time, however, there is a great deal of cultural diversity within our society. The effective management of such diversity, and the differences that may exist within an organization's workforce because of it, is a critical and challenging task.

Increasingly in today's world, business operations are global in scope. This means they are frequently multicultural as well. Thus, while most members of a culture will share similar personality characteristics, there may be significant differences across cultures. One of the challenges of doing business in a global economy is understanding and respecting cultural differences, particularly as they may affect personality and behavior.

Social class also is important in shaping personality. The various neighborhoods of cities and towns tend to be populated by different social classes, each with its own mores. The neighborhood or community where a child grows up is the setting in which he or she learns about life. Social class influences the person's self-perception, perception of others, and perceptions of work, authority, and money. In terms of such pressing organizational problems as adjustment, quality of work life, and dissatisfaction, the manager attempting to understand employees must give attention to social class factors.

A review of each of the major forces that shapes personality indicates that managers have little control over these determinants. However, no manager should conclude that personality is therefore an unimportant factor for them to consider in workplace behavior. Employee behavior cannot be understood without considering the concept of personality. In fact, personality is so interrelated with perception, attitudes, learning, and motivation that any analysis of behavior is grossly incomplete unless personality is considered.

Personality and Behavior in Organizations

In the years following World War II, many researchers and managers believed that measures of personality could predict job performance and other behaviors at work. It was common for companies to administer psychological inventories to job applicants to see if they were well suited to work in certain jobs and the organization's culture. By the 1960s, however, the validity or accuracy of such personality tests was questioned.[35] One of the main reasons for this concern was the fear that such personality tests would lead to the unfair treatment of minority groups commonly discriminated against in the past.

Despite the concern over the potential misuse of personality tests, more researchers continued to ask the question, "Does an individual's personality affect his or her behavior at work?" To many, the answer was "yes." In addition, many companies today use personality testing to help make selection, career planning, training, and team assignment decisions. For example, one popular personality test, the Myers-Briggs Inventory (MBTI), is used by many companies to assist in team building, management development, decision making, leadership, and career development. For example, Southwest Airlines uses the MBTI as a diagnostic tool to help its employees and work teams communicate and work together more effectively.[36] It has been reported that over 3 million individuals complete the MBTI each year.[37] Although the validity of some of the uses of MBTI has been questioned,[38] the large number of companies and people using this personality test is indicative of the increasing popularity of personality tests in general.

This renewed interest and focus on personality as a key to understanding organizational behavior led to research in the following areas: the "Big Five" personality dimensions, locus of control, self-efficacy, and creativity. The following sections will discuss the research and managerial implications of each of these personality domains.

The Big Five Personality Dimensions

Personality is a term used to describe a great many feelings and behaviors. Literally hundreds of personality dimensions or traits have been identified by psychologists over the last 100 years. However, within the past 25 years or so, a consensus has emerged that, for the most part, the human personality can be described by five dimensions or factors.[39] The Big Five personality dimensions include: extroversion, emotional stability, agreeableness, conscientiousness, and openness to experience.[40] Each of the five factors is briefly described below. As you read the descriptions, ask yourself the following question, "To what extent does this factor describe my personality?"

extroversion
One of the Big Five personality dimensions; it is a trait that indicates a person's outgoing, sociable behavior.

Extroversion refers to the tendency to be sociable, gregarious, assertive, talkative, and active. People high in extroversion tend to enjoy talking and interaction with coworkers, and they gravitate toward jobs that have a good deal of social interaction. Research indicates that extroverted people tend to perform well in sales and managerial jobs, tend to do better in training programs, and tend to have higher levels of overall job satisfaction.[41] This suggests that organizations such as Avon and The Sharper Image, both of which rely heavily on the successful training and performance of their salespeople, would benefit from using a valid personality test to measure extroversion as part of an overall selection program.

emotional stability
One of the Big Five personality dimensions; it is the ability to be calm, serene, relaxed, and secure.

Emotional stability is the tendency to experience positive emotional states, such as feeling psychologically secure, calm, and relaxed. Anxiety, depression, anger, and embarrassment are characteristics of low emotional stability. The low-stability individual is more likely to experience job-related stress, a topic discussed in detail in Chapter 9. Although the link between emotional stability and job performance does not appear to be a strong one, some interesting research findings relate to other important work behaviors. For example, a meta-analysis (a large research study that analyzes results from several previous studies) found that low levels of emotional stability were associated with low levels of employee motivation.[42]

agreeableness
One of the Big Five personality dimensions; it is the tendency to be courteous, forgiving, tolerant, trusting, and softhearted.

Being courteous, forgiving, tolerant, trusting, and softhearted are traits associated with **agreeableness**. The employee described as "someone who gets along with others" is high on agreeableness. It is a dimension that can help make someone an effective team player and can pay off in jobs where developing and maintaining good interpersonal relationships and helping fellow employees is important.[43] Individuals low on agreeableness are often described as rude, cold, uncaring, unsympathetic, and antagonistic. Jobs and professions that require individuals high in agreeableness include customer service, sales, auditing, nursing, teaching, and social work.

conscientiousness
One of the Big Five personality dimensions; it is the tendency to be dependable, organized, thorough, and responsible.

Conscientiousness is exhibited by those who are described as dependable, organized, thorough, and responsible. Individuals who are conscientious also tend to persevere, work hard, and enjoy achieving and accomplishing things. It is not hard to understand why this trait is highly valued by all organizations. Employees who are low in conscientiousness tend to be sloppy, inefficient, careless, and even lazy. From a research perspective, conscientiousness is the most closely linked dimension to job performance. Put succinctly, conscientious employees perform better across a wide variety of occupations. Emerging research also indicates that conscientious individuals tend to exhibit higher levels of motivation and job satisfaction,[44] as well as other important work behaviors (retention, attendance, and fewer counterproductive behaviors).

openness to experience
One of the Big Five personality dimensions; it reflects the extent to which an individual is broad-minded, creative, curious, and intelligent.

The final personality dimension is **openness to experience.** This dimension reflects the extent to which an individual has broad interests and is willing to take risks. Specific traits include curiosity, broad-mindedness, creativity, imagination, and intelligence. People high in openness to experience tend to thrive in occupations where change is continuous and where innovation is critical. For example, people who create spectacular special effects for large-budget action films need to possess high levels of this personality dimension. This holds true for employees of Cyberware, the special effects firm that created many of the cutting-edge special effects in the movie *Terminator II*. Individuals low in openness to experience (i.e., unimaginative, conventional, and habit-bound) would not fit in well at Cyberware, where change and innovation are critical for organizational survival.

As Exhibit 3.5 indicates, research on the Big Five personality dimensions is promising due to the evidence that shows personality does influence important work behaviors such as job performance, training proficiency, and job satisfaction. This personality model also has implications for global management and organizational behavior. The five factors have been obtained in different cultures and using different languages.[45] So, it is not surprising that relationships among the Big Five dimensions and job performance also apply across country borders. The existence of very similar relationships has been demonstrated in Great Britain, Germany, France, the Netherlands, Norway, and Spain.[46]

A review of the personality research suggests that even with the Big Five, not one trait or group of traits predicts with precision how well someone will perform on a particular project or in a specific job. In addition to assessing one's personality, firms should use a variety of selection tools to try to match a person's interests and skills with a particular job. These can include a structured interview, a cognitive ability test, and a work performance test. The individual job candidate or employee applying for an internal promotion also should be attempting to find the best fit for himself or herself in the job and organization. Using only the scores on a personality test will often lead to misalignment and poor person–job (and person–organization) fit. Once into a job, individuals who work hard at the "fit" are likely to experience higher levels of job satisfaction, more positive attitudes, and better relationships among peers.

EXHIBIT 3.5   The Big Five Personality Dimensions: A Summary

Dimension	Associated with These Work Behaviors	Managerial Implications
High extroversion	Job performance of managers and salespersons; training proficiency	Use personality assessment to identify extroverted individuals for jobs requiring large amounts of social interaction.
High emotional stability	Overall job satisfaction; motivation	Managers can only do so much to increase job satisfaction and to motivate employees; employees low in emotional stability will be more difficult to influence in these areas.
High agreeableness	Peer ratings of team members; interpersonal skills	Managers should try to include on teams individuals who are agreeable because they help the team to function more smoothly by using their good interpersonal skills to keep communication channels open and to work out intragroup problems.
High conscientiousness	Job performance across most occupations; motivation; job satisfaction; retention; attendance; and fewer counterproductive behaviors.	Personality assessments should be used to select individuals with high levels of conscientiousness. Selections should include new hires and current employees applying for internal promotions.
Openness to experience	Training proficiency	Personality assessment should be used to identify employees for key training opportunities.

In addition to assessing applicants and employees on certain dimensions of the Big Five, organizations often choose a few relevant personality traits that they believe are closely linked to performance in certain jobs and in their organization. We now will look at three such personality traits of interest to many organizations: locus of control, self-efficacy, and creativity.

Locus of Control

locus of control
Specifies a person's belief that he or she does or does not master his or her fate.

The **locus of control** of individuals determines the degree to which they believe their behaviors influence what happens to them.[47] Some people believe they are autonomous—that they are masters of their own fate and have personal responsibility for what happens to them. When they perform well, they believe it is because of their effort or skill. They are called *internals*. Others view themselves as helpless pawns of fate, controlled by outside forces over which they have little, if any, influence. When they perform well, they believe it is due to luck or because it was an easy task. They are *externals*. Some research suggests that externals score low on the Big Five dimensions of extroversion and emotional stability.[48] If you believe that the grades you typically receive in school are due to the particular classes you take, the characteristics of your professors, or the type of tests given, you are probably an external. On the other hand, if you think your grades typically reflect the amount of time and effort you devote to a particular class and your knowledge of the subject matter, you are most likely an internal.

GEN Y EMPLOYEES: HOW ARE THEY DIFFERENT?

Research suggests that Gen Y employees (also known as Millennials) who were born in the 1980s and 1990s are different in many substantive ways compared with members of other generations (i.e., Gen X, baby boomers, etc.). In general, Gen Y workers are thought to be very comfortable with technology, prefer jobs that are defined by task, not by time, and are more individualistic and focused on their own interests and lifestyles. However, there may be deeper psychological traits that differentiate this segment of the workforce from the older generations. Research suggests that the following psychological traits are common among Gen Y workers:

Less need for social approval.

- Implications: casual dress and tone with supervisors, customers, etc.
- Organizational response: dress codes and mentoring.

Higher self-esteem.

- Implications: high need for praise; less ethical behaviors.
- Organizational response: encourage managers to praise and provide ethics training.

External locus of control.

- Implications: not taking responsibility for success or failures.
- Organizational response: more work in teams; add accountability for performance.

Higher anxiety and depression.

- Implications: stressed-out and less productive workers; absenteeism and turnover.

- Organizational response: stress management training and mental health services.

Women more assertive.

- Implications: more women in powerful positions.
- Organizational response: provide flextime, child care; gender equality.

How can Gen Y workers use the above information about the shared personality traits of their generation? They can look for jobs and careers that fit well with these and their individual personality traits. For example, Gen Y workers may want to work for organizations that value work–life balance and a casual work environment, offer meaningful work assignments, have supportive managers who give a lot of feedback, and offer ongoing training and career enhancement opportunities. There are many jobs and careers from which Gen Y workers can choose; a better fit will generally lead to high job and life satisfaction in the long run.

Sources: Adapted from Jean M. Twenge and Stacy M. Campbell, "Generational Differences in Psychological Traits and Their Impact on the Workplace," *Journal of Managerial Psychology* 23, no. 8 (2008), pp. 862–77; Tamara J. Erickson, "Task, Not Time: Profile of Gen Y Job," *Harvard Business Review* 86, no. 2 (2008), p. 19; Karen Auby, "A Boomer's Guide to Communicating with Gen X and Gen Y," *BusinessWeek,* August 25, 2008, pp. 63–64; and Elisabeth Kelan, "Generational and Gender Transformations," *Personnel Today,* September 16, 2008, pp. 38–40.

In organizational settings, internals usually do not require as much supervision as do externals because they are more likely to believe their own work behavior will influence outcomes such as performance, promotions, and pay. Some research suggests locus of control is related to moral behavior, with internals doing what they think is right and being willing to suffer the consequences for doing so.[49] The Organizational Encounter above demonstrates a possible relationship between locus of control and ethical behavior.

Self-Efficacy

self-efficacy
Designates a person's belief that he or she has the competency to complete a job successfully.

Self-efficacy relates to personal beliefs regarding competencies and abilities. Specifically, it refers to one's belief in one's ability to successfully complete a task. Individuals with a high degree of self-efficacy firmly believe in their performance capabilities. The concept of self-efficacy includes three dimensions: magnitude, strength, and generality.

Magnitude refers to the level of task difficulty that individuals believe they can attain. For example, Jim may believe he can put an arrow in the archery range target six times in 10 attempts. Sara may feel she can hit the target eight times; thus Sara has a higher magnitude of self-efficacy regarding this task than Jim. *Strength*

CAN LOCUS OF CONTROL PREDICT UNETHICAL BEHAVIOR?

Throughout history, the media have reported wrongdoing and unethical behavior in business, government, and education. Leaders and managers at Enron, Arthur Andersen, WorldCom, Parmalat, and Tyco are but a few of the individuals who have made headlines. Are personality factors related to choices individuals make to behave ethically or unethically? Recent research on ethical decision making sheds some light on this question. A partial description of a portion of this research follows.

In this study individuals with an average of five years' work experience participated in an in-basket exercise in which they played the role of Pat Sneed, a national sales manager for an electronics firm. Among the dozen or so items in the in-basket were two that required decisions involving ethical concerns. In one, a regional sales director informs Sneed that one of his sales representatives is paying kickbacks. Sneed must decide whether to put an end to the kickbacks. In the second situation, Sneed receives a memo from the vice president of production that indicates the vice president has decided to change the material used in a product to save production costs. The memo advises that customers should not be informed of this change despite problems it might create. Sneed must decide what, if anything, to do. Responses by study participants to these two situations were judged on the basis of preestablished criteria to be either ethical or unethical.

Internal locus of control participants demonstrated more ethical behavior than their *external* counterparts. In fact, locus of control showed nearly twice as much effect on ethical decision making as did the combination of all other variables that were included. The researchers suggest organizations may wish to assess locus of control when selecting managers for positions involving ethical decision making. Other research studies support this conclusion.

Sources: Gregory G. Manley, Juan Benavidez, and Kristen Dunn, "Development of a Personality Biodata Measure to Predict Ethical Decision Making," *Journal of Managerial Psychology* 22, no. 7 (2007), pp. 664–82; Marc Street and Vera L. Street, "The Effects of Escalating Commitment on Ethical Decision-Making," *Journal of Business Ethics* 64 (2006), pp. 343–56; Susan Key, "Perceived Managerial Discretion: An Analysis of Individual Ethical Intentions," *Journal of Managerial Issues* 14, no. 2 (Summer 2002), pp. 218–34; and L.K. Trevino and S.A. Youngblood, "Bad Apples in Bad Barrels: A Causal Analysis of Ethical Decision-Making Behavior," *Journal of Applied Psychology*, August 1990, pp. 378–86.

refers to whether the belief regarding magnitude is strong or weak. If in the previous example Jim is moderately certain he can hit the target six times, while Sara is positive she can achieve eight hits, Sara is displaying greater strength of belief in her ability than is Jim. Finally, *generality* indicates how generalized across different situations the belief in capability is. If Jim thinks he can hit the target equally well with a pistol and rifle and Sara does not think she can, Jim is displaying greater generality than is Sara.

Beliefs regarding self-efficacy are learned. The most important factor in the development of positive self-efficacy appears to be past experience. If over a period of time we attempt a task and are increasingly successful in our performance, we are likely to develop self-confidence and an increasing belief in our ability to perform the task successfully; conversely, if we repeatedly fail in our attempts to perform a task well, we are not as likely to develop strong feelings of self-efficacy. Self-efficacy tends to be task specific; that is, a belief that we can perform very well in one job does not necessarily suggest a corresponding belief in our ability to excel in other jobs.

According to an analysis of self-efficacy by Gist and Mitchell,[50] research on self-efficacy has led to several consistent findings. They indicated that self-efficacy is associated with work-related performance, career choice, learning and achievement, and adaptability to new technology, and they noted that certain training methods could enhance self-efficacy in individual trainees. A related large-scale research study found that individuals high in self-efficacy tended to perform at a higher level.[51] Also supporting these conclusions is the research by Bandura and Locke, who found that, when combined with goal setting, individuals with high levels of self-efficacy tend to display higher levels of motivation and performance.[52]

Thus, feelings of self-efficacy have a number of managerial and organizational implications:

- *Selection decisions*—Organizations should select individuals who have a strong sense of self-efficacy. These individuals will be motivated to engage in the behaviors that will help them perform well. A measure of self-efficacy can be administered during the hiring/promotion process.
- *Training programs*—Organizations should consider employee levels of self-efficacy when choosing among candidates for training programs. If the training budget is limited, then more return (i.e., performance) on training investment can be realized by sending only those employees high in self-efficacy. These individuals will tend to learn more from the training and, ultimately, will be more likely to use that learning to enhance their job performance.
- *Goal setting and performance*—Organizations can encourage higher performance goals from employees who have high levels of self-efficacy. This will lead to higher levels of performance from employees, which is critical for many organizations in this era of hypercompetition.

Creativity

Creativity is a personality trait that involves the ability to break away from habit-bound thinking and produce novel and useful ideas. Creativity produces innovation, and innovation is the lifeblood of a growing number of corporations. The 3M Company is famous for its creativity and product innovations. Rubbermaid introduces one new product a day. These companies and others, such as Hewlett-Packard, Walt Disney Company, Home Depot, and Apple Computer, are well known for their efforts to stimulate creativity.

Creativity is a personality trait that can be encouraged and developed within organizations by giving people opportunity and freedom to think in unconventional ways.[53] For example, one major impediment to increasing creativity in work settings is the fear of failure. If an organization is intolerant of mistakes and failure, it should not expect employees to take the risks often inherent in creative approaches to problems. At Heinz's highly successful frozen foods subsidiary, Ore-Ida, management is aware that creative behavior will sometimes result in mistakes. They have defined what they call the "perfect failure" and have arranged for a cannon to be shot off in celebration every time one occurs. The cannon symbolizes that a failure has occurred, been learned from, and been forgotten. Because failures are openly discussed and treated positively, the creative risk-taking behavior that management attempts to nourish is continued.[54]

Each of the individual difference variables discussed here—heredity and diversity factors, abilities and skills, perception, attitudes, and personality—impact organizational effectiveness and efficiency. Managers who ignore the importance of these variables do themselves, their employees, and their organizations a disservice. As we proceed through the next six chapters focusing on individual-level behavior, keep in mind how these individual differences help shape the behavior and performance of employees.

Management Pointer

HOW TO DEVELOP EMPLOYEE CREATIVITY

1. Encourage everyone to view old problems from new perspectives.
2. Make certain people know that it is OK to make mistakes.
3. Provide as many people with as many new work experiences as you can.
4. Set an example in your own approach to dealing with problems and opportunities.

YOU BE THE JUDGE COMMENT

CAN JOBS BE GENDER STEREOTYPED?

Unless the male manager can show empirical evidence that a man couldn't perform the job, the woman who sued would win the case. Yes, it is sex discrimination unless empirical evidence shows otherwise. The male manager has applied a stereotype to the position. Can he support his thinking? Probably not for this type of job.

- The Big Five personality model suggests that five dimensions are central to describing personality. These five dimensions are extroversion, emotional stability, agreeableness, conscientiousness, and openness to experience. Every individual's personality reflects differing degrees of these five factors.

- Numerous personality factors operate to influence behavior. Three that are frequently identified as important in explaining behavior and performance are locus of control, self-efficacy, and creativity.

Summary of Key Points

- Major individual variables that influence work behavior include demographic factors (e.g., age, sex, race), abilities and skills, perception, attitudes, and personality. These combine with various organizational variables (resources, leadership, rewards, job design, structure) to shape productive, nonproductive, and counterproductive work behaviors.

- Attributions we make about why an event occurs influence our behavior. The process involves analyzing why something has happened (attributing a cause to the event) and fitting that explanation into a general framework that provides a basis for subsequent behavior. Thus, our behavior is shaped by our perception of why certain things happen.

- Stereotyping is a process employed to assist us in dealing more efficiently with massive information demands. It can be a useful, even necessary, perceptual process. A prejudice is a particular form of stereotyping that resists change even in the face of contrary information.

- An attitude is a learned predisposition to respond favorably or unfavorably to people, objects, and situations with which it is related. An attitude consists of a cognitive component (beliefs), an affect component (feelings), and a behavioral component, which consists of the individual's behavioral intentions.

- Although the job satisfaction–job performance relationship is a complex one that is not fully understood, it seems clear that these two variables are related under certain conditions. One current view is that the rewards one receives as a consequence of good performance, and the degree to which these rewards are perceived as reasonable, affect both the extent to which satisfaction results from performance and the extent to which performance is affected by satisfaction.

- Major forces influencing the nature of an individual's personality include (1) heredity factors, (2) parent–child and family relationships, (3) social class and other group membership forces, and (4) cultural factors. The latter is particularly critical as cross-cultural interactions increase in today's global business environment.

Review and Discussion Questions

1. So many factors influence an individual's behavior that it is impossible to accurately predict what that behavior will be in all situations. Why then should managers take time to understand individual differences?

2. In what ways can stereotyping be a helpful process? Can a stereotype be useful even if it is not entirely accurate? Are we better off by getting rid of our stereotypes or by making them more accurate?

3. Have you ever had a "bad attitude" toward a situation, a certain course that you didn't like, or an unattractive job assignment? How did that attitude affect your behavior (i.e., performance, attendance, and so on)? How did you attempt to improve your attitude?

4. Think of an important attitude you have regarding a career. Identify the three components of that attitude and indicate what each outcome response would be.

5. As the U.S. workforce becomes much more diverse over the next 10 years, what implications will that have for managers as they attempt to create and maintain a work environment that allows all types of employees to contribute to the organization? How should employees' individual differences be treated: accepted/valued or assimilated into the organization culture?

6. The text identified job satisfaction as an important attitude. What other attitudes might be important in work settings?

7. Are you an internal or an external? Would you rather have a boss who is an internal or an external? Why?

8. Of the Big Five personality dimensions, conscientiousness is the most important factor in predicting job performance across most occupations. How can a person develop a greater amount of conscientiousness in his or her work? What steps can you as a manager take to encourage employees to be more conscientious?

9. As a manager, how might you increase a subordinate's feelings of self-efficacy regarding a job assignment? How might you attempt to increase the creativity of your subordinate?

10. "If everyone were alike, the task of managing organizations would be much easier." Do you agree or disagree with this statement? Explain.

Exercise

Exercise 3.1: *Personality Insights*

The following 27 statements are designed to provide some insights regarding how you see yourself. In the blank space next to each of these statements, write the number that best describes how strongly you agree or disagree with the statement, or how true or false the statement is as it applies to you. The numbers represent the following:

5 = Strongly Agree, or Definitely True

4 = Generally Agree, or Mostly True

3 = Neither Agree nor Disagree, Neither True nor False

2 = Generally Disagree, or Mostly False

1 = Strongly Disagree, or Definitely False

Reality Check

Now how much do you know about individual differences?

6. _____ is a personality trait displayed by an employee who is dependable, organized, responsible, and thorough.
   a. Conscientiousness
   b. Agreeableness
   c. Open
   d. Extroverted

7. The most important factor in developing positive self-efficacy is _____.
   a. intelligence
   b. past experience
   c. attitude
   d. self-concept

8. True or false: The SAS Institute offers a generous family-friendly package of benefits aimed to boost employee morale on the job. _____
   a. True
   b. False

9. Attitudes consist of three components. Two of these are behavior and affect. What is the third component?
   a. Style
   b. Response
   c. Cognition
   d. Impression

10. _____ is a learned talent that an employee has acquired to complete and perform a task as expected.
    a. Ability
    b. Personality
    c. Mental trait
    d. Skill

REALITY CHECK ANSWERS

Before	After
1. c 2. c 3. d 4. a 5. b	6. a 7. b 8. a 9. c 10. d
Number Correct	Number Correct
_____	_____

Example:

__2__   You enjoy playing "bridge."

(The "2" in the space next to the statement indicates that you generally disagree: you are more negative than neutral about enjoying "bridge.")

_____ 1. In some circumstance in the past you have taken the lead.

_____ 2. Everyone should place trust in a supernatural force whose decisions he or she always obeys.

_____ 3. You like to perform activities involving selling or salesmanship.

_____ 4. As a rule you assess your previous actions closely.

_____ 5. You often observe those around you to see how your words and actions affect them.

_____ 6. What you earn depends on what you know and how hard you work.

_____ 7. Generally, those in authority do their share of the unpleasant jobs without passing them on to others.

_____ 8. The remedy for social problems depends on eliminating dishonest, immoral, and mentally inferior people.

_____ 9. Most people today earn their pay by their own work.

_____ 10. The lowest type of person is the one who does not love and respect his parents.

_____ 11. There are two kinds of people: the weak and the strong.

_____ 12. You are the kind of person who tends to look into and analyze himself or herself.

_____ 13. Your promotions depend more on whom you know than on how well you do your work.

_____ 14. All children should be taught obedience and respect for authority.

_____ 15. Those who are in public offices usually put their own interest ahead of the public interest.

_____ 16. Many bosses actually deserve lower pay than their employees.

_____ 17. Taking on important responsibilities like starting your own company is something you would like to do.

_____ 18. An insult to your good name should never go unpunished.

_____ 19. In a meeting you will speak up when you disagree with someone you are convinced is wrong.

_____ 20. Thinking about complex problems is enjoyable to you.

_____ 21. Generally, people are well paid for their contributions to society.

_____ 22. It is better to work for a good boss than for yourself.

_____ 23. Many times you would like to know the real reasons some people behave as they do.

_____ 24. In the long run, we each get what we deserve.

_____ 25. Most organizations believe in paying a fair day's wages for a fair day's work.

_____ 26. Getting ahead is based more on your performance than your politics.

_____ 27. You can't expect to be treated fairly by those above you unless you insist on it.

Enter your answers to the questions above in the appropriate spaces below. In those cases where there is an asterisk before the number, use *reverse scoring* by subtracting your score from six, that is, a 1 becomes a 5, a 4 becomes a 2, and so forth.

Group 1	Group 2	Group 3	Group 4
6. _____	1. _____	*2. _____	4. _____
7. _____	3. _____	*8. _____	5. _____
9. _____	17. _____	*10. _____	12. _____
*13. _____	19. _____	*11. _____	20. _____
*15. _____	*22. _____	*14. _____	23. _____
*16. _____	Total _____	*18. _____	Total _____
21. _____		Total _____	
24. _____			
25. _____			
26. _____			
*27. _____			
Total _____			

Now take each of your totals and divide by the number of answers to obtain your average responses, that is, 2.3, 3.2, 4.1, and so forth. On a scale of 1–5, this measures how you see yourself in each of these four areas.

Average Score

The four areas, represented by Groups 1–4, respectively, are:

_____ 1. Fair—this score measures the extent to which you see the world as treating you fairly.

_____ 2. Assertive—this score measures the extent to which you see yourself as aggressive.

_____ 3. Equalitarian—this score measures the extent to which you see yourself as nonauthoritarian.

_____ 4. Introspective—this score measures the extent to which you see yourself as thinking about things that go on around you and trying to determine why they occur.

Source: This self-feedback experiential exercise is reprinted with permission from the *Subordinates' Management Style Survey* by Bernard M. Bass, Enzo R. Valenzi, and Larry D. Eldridge.

Case

Case 3.1: *Personality Testing: Yes or No?*

Mark, a project leader in Austin, Texas, needed a new software engineer for his eight-person team. He used his network, reviewed résumés, and invited 15 candidates for interviews. In addition he had the top three candidates complete the 16-Personality Factors Test. This was a general test that he believed would reveal personality characteristics that were important to know before making a job offer.

Personality testing is a relatively inexpensive method that helps managers make important hiring decisions. Tom, a member of Mark's team, warned everyone about putting too much confidence into personality test results, however. Tom had read that personality tests were not reliable and could be faked.

Another team member, Mary, believed Tom to be correct and incorrect at the same time. Some tests are poor, while others have helped employers make good selection decisions, she said. She emphasized "helped." Tests by themselves shouldn't be the sole factor in hiring top performers. They are just one tool, she said. She had heard about other firms using different kinds of tests to assess emotions, intelligence, and interpersonal style.

In fact, studies do indicate that good personality tests are more reliable predictions of performance than interviews and résumés. However, they are still controversial. Some employers have had to face lawsuits because personality tests were used inappropriately. For example, Rent-A-Center, Inc., used a personality test to fill management positions. The U.S. Court of Appeals for the Seventh Circuit in Chicago ruled that the test qualified as a medical exam. The Americans with Disabilities Act prohibits requiring medical examinations before making a job offer.

Court rulings on and controversy about personality testing has not stopped employers from using such tests. In an effort to match the best-qualified person with the position, personality testing, although controversial, can be beneficial.

Employers are very interested in what differentiates one person from another in terms of behavior and performance. Personality testing attempts to provide quantifiable data that can make the differentiation easier. Such differentiation is still difficult. Some personality researchers suggest there are regional differences in personality. That is, a New York candidate for Mark's position would be different from an Oregon candidate.

Mark, after considering all the issues surrounding personality testing, decided he would not conduct or use such tests in the future.

Questions

1. Is Mark making a good decision to drop the use of personality testing? Why?
2. The better-quality personality tests are difficult to fake. Other than attempting to land the job, why would a job candidate fake a personality test?
3. Could personality testing be used for management decisions other than hiring? Explain.

Source: Adapted from Patrick D. Converse, Frederick L. Oswald, Anna Imus, Cynthia Hedricks, and Radha Roy, "Comparing Personality Test Formats and Warnings: Effects on Criterion-Related Validity and Test-Taker Reactions," *International Journal of Selection and Assessment* 16, no. 2 (June 2008), pp. 155–69; Victoria Knight, "Personality Tests as Hiring Tools," *The Wall Street Journal,* March 15, 2006, p. B3A; and "The Big Five Personality Test," www.outofservice.com/bigfive/info (accessed April 6, 2009).

CHAPTER FOUR

Perceptions, Attributions, and Emotions

Learning Objectives

After completing Chapter 4, you should be able to:

- **Explain** how primary emotions can be observed or determined.
- **Discuss** the potential problems one faces when using stereotypes to make judgments.
- **Describe** the role that perception plays in organizing stimuli.

- **Explain** why and where impression management tactics are used.
- **Discuss** why emotional intelligence has potential for managerial use, but should be treated cautiously.
- **Describe** how attribution can be used in evaluating individual and group performance.

Perceptions, attributions, and emotions play a role in workplace settings and situations. Managers must cope with their own and their employees' perceptions, attributions, and emotions. Understanding these individual characteristics helps managers and nonmanagers perform their roles and jobs more efficiently and more effectively.

The Perceptual Process

Perception, attribution, and emotion are not concepts a manager can directly access or fix in others, but a manager needs to understand how these factors impact a person's view of the work environment. The "view" is the difficult part to pin down or to be confident about. In attempting to learn about employees, managers are in a continual battle to consider the views of others. What would it be like to have your vision restored after a lifetime of blindness? In reality, a first look at the world would likely be confusing, disappointing, and not impressive. A newly sighted person would have to learn to identify shapes, read clocks, recognize danger, judge distances, and find a way to navigate across busy intersections.

One researcher describes a cataract patient as Mr. B, a 52-year-old, who had been blind since birth.[1] After a delicate operation his sight was restored, but Mr. B struggled to use his new vision. One day Mr. B was found crawling out of a hospital window to get a closer look at the traffic on the street. His curiosity and unfamiliarity with judging distance created a dangerous problem. He left his fourth-floor room to get a closer look. Mr. B wasn't familiar with judging distance. He had a size constancy perception

How much do you know about perceptions, attributions, and emotions?

1. Perception is based on _____.
   a. current events
   b. attitudes
   c. prior experience
   d. archival data

2. The mildest form of emotions is called _____.
   a. fear
   b. surprise
   c. moods
   d. preferences

3. _____ has proposed a view that considers intelligence to include multiple branches—verbal, mathematical, spatial, musical, interpersonal, and intrapersonal.
   a. Grayson
   b. Gardner
   c. Heider
   d. Pygmalion

4. _____ is concerned with the process by which individuals interpret events around them as being caused by a relatively stable portion of their environment.
   a. Perception theory
   b. Stereotyping
   c. Consistency
   d. Attribution theory

5. When a person (e.g., manager) allows one important or noticeable characteristic of another person to bias the evaluation, perception, or impression of that person, it is called the _____ effect.
   a. angel
   b. halo
   c. error
   d. evaluative

perception
The process by which an individual gives meaning to the environment. It involves organizing and interpreting various stimuli into a psychological experience.

problem. The perceived size of the cars remained the same, despite changes in their image as it was processed through the retina.

Perception is empirical in that it is based on prior experience. Mr. B had never before experienced seeing cars at a distance of four floors. **Perception** is defined as the cognitive process by which an individual selects, organizes, and gives meaning to environmental stimuli.[2] Through perception, individuals (e.g., Mr. B) attempt to make sense of their environment and the objects, people, and events in it. Because each person gives his or her own meaning to stimuli, different individuals will "perceive" the same thing in different ways. When we comment to a classmate, "This course is exciting," what we really mean is, "This class excites me." While we think we are describing some objective reality, we are in fact describing our subjective reactions to that reality.[3]

Peter Drucker, who has been referred to as the father of modern management, remains prominent in the business literature even after his death.[4] Through his many writings, he offered his subjective perceptions about a number of economic issues; some of which are presented in the Global OB on page 95. An interesting cautionary perception of Drucker's is that China has a small proportion of educated people, which could limit the country's long-term economic future.

DRUCKER'S VIEWPOINT ON SOME SIGNIFICANT ISSUES

Peter F. Drucker is considered one of the most influential forces that shaped current thought on management, work, and globalization. Practicing into his 90s, he was considered a management "guru" who viewed the world in unique and interesting ways. As stated in this chapter, perception is an individual phenomenon. How one person views the environment, people, trends, or objects is often quite different than someone else's perceptions.

A few of Drucker's perceptions differed from other experts in a number of ways.

Drucker on the U.S. Economy

The United States imports twice or three times as many jobs as are exported. He is referring to the jobs created by foreign companies coming into the United States. For example, the German company Siemens has 69,000 U.S. employees. The United States is exporting low-skill, low-paying jobs and importing high-skill, high-paying jobs.

Drucker on U.S. Unemployment Problems

The United States has the lowest long-term unemployment rate among industrialized nations (e.g., Germany, Japan, Italy). Most of the nation's unemployment is short term.

Drucker on the United States Setting the Tone for the World Economy

The dominance of the United States is over. What has emerged is a world economy of blocks—the North American Free Trade Agreement, the European Union, the Association of Southeast Asian Nations. India is becoming a world powerhouse fast. The greatest weakness of China is its incredibly small proportion of educated people. China has only 20 million college students out of a total population of over 1.3 billion.

These examples recount a few of Drucker's perceptions and opinions. They differ widely from those of a number of other experts. Each person's perception is subjective, offering a view of reality as seen through his or her own cognitive filtering process.

Sources: Adapted from B. Schlender, "Peter Drucker Sets Us Straight," *Fortune*, January 12, 2004, pp. 114–18; "Welcome to the Siemens USA Corporate Web Site," *Siemens USA-Corporate Home*, 2008, http://www.usa.siemens.com/en/; and Amelia Newcomb, "China Goes to College—in a Big Way," *Christian Science Monitor*, July 25, 2005, www.csmonitor.com/2005/0729/p01s01-woap.html.

Individuals are constantly bombarded by environmental stimuli that impact their senses of sight, hearing, smell, taste, and touch. Exactly which stimuli a person focuses on is determined by what he or she chooses to pay attention to at a particular moment. For example, an irate manager screaming out a directive may cause a subordinate to ignore an alarm bell signaling the identification of a defective part. The subordinate is shutting out the noisy alarm to focus on the words, body language, and overall behavior of the manager.

Exhibit 4.1 illustrates the basic framework and elements of perception operating as a cognitive process. Each person makes personal/individual choices and responds differently. Learning about perceptual interpretation helps managers understand why individual differences must be considered at work. People see the world around them in their own unique way and behave and respond according to their interpretation.

EXHIBIT 4.1   The Perceptual Process: An Individual Interpretation

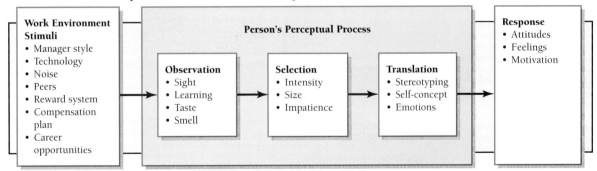

Individuals try to make sense of environmental stimuli by observation, selection, and translation. Each of these three activities is influenced by the factors displayed in Exhibit 4.1. Perceptual *selection* is the process of focusing on the stimuli that are important, large, or intense.

In general, people perceive stimuli that satisfy needs, emotions, attitudes, or their self-concept. This is the *translation* portion of Exhibit 4.1. If a person has a need to receive positive feedback on performance, then the positive statements made by her boss will be remembered more clearly and accurately than the negative statements she received. Again, the notions of observing, selecting, and translating are linked to form the perceptual process, which precedes any response. Exhibit 4.1 shows three internal responses—attitudes, feelings, and motivation.

There is always the possibility that a person's perception is inaccurate. Misinterpreting stimuli can and often does result in perceptual errors. The research literature on interviewing suggests that interviewers rate candidates who are similar to themselves in appearance, background, and interests higher than candidates who are dissimilar.[5] This is referred to as the "similar-to-me perception error." Interviewers also tend to make quick first impression errors based on the first few minutes of an interview. Unfortunately, making first impression errors can eliminate many good job candidates, which is detrimental to a firm.[6] Pause for a moment and think about the last time someone was introduced to you. Did you shake the person's hand? Did the firmness of the handshake suggest something about the person's personality? While a firm handshake has been associated with an outgoing personality,[7] could it have been due to other causes, and is such an instant assessment valid? Once formed, how long did you maintain this initial impression of this person, and after getting to know the person better was the initial impression accurate?

Each person selects various cues that influence his or her perception of people, objects, and symbols. Because of these factors and their potential for imbalance, people often misperceive another person, group, or object. To a considerable extent, people interpret the behavior of others in the context in which they find themselves. A classic study reported by Rensis Likert clearly illustrates this. He examined the perceptions of superiors and subordinates to determine the amounts and types of recognition that subordinates received for good performance. Both supervisors and subordinates were asked how often superiors provided rewards for good work. Exhibit 4.2 presents the results.

The two groups perceived significant differences. Each group viewed the type of recognition being given at a different level. The subordinates in most cases reported that very little recognition was provided by their supervisors and that rewards were provided infrequently. The superiors, on the other hand, saw themselves as giving a wide variety of rewards for good performance. The two groups were looking at the

EXHIBIT 4.2

The Perceptual Gap between Supervisor and Subordinates

Source: Adapted from Rensis Likert, *New Patterns in Management* (New York: McGraw-Hill, 1961), p. 91.

Types of Recognition	Frequency with Which Supervisors Say They Give Various Types of Recognition for Good Performance	Frequency with Which Subordinates Say Supervisors Give Various Types of Recognition for Good Performance
Gives privileges	52%	14%
Gives more responsibility	48	10
Gives a pat on the back	82	13
Gives sincere and thorough praise	80	14
Trains for better jobs	64	9
Gives more interesting work	51	3

THE PYGMALION AND GOLEM EFFECTS

Perceptions do influence reality. This is the notion behind what is called the self-fulfilling prophecy or the tendency for someone's expectations about another to cause the individual to behave in a manner consistent with those expectations. These expectations can be positive or negative. The positive case is called the **Pygmalion effect**. A parent who expects her child to behave properly can subtly influence the child's behavior so that the mother's expectations are met.

Researchers have also found that the self-fulfilling prophecy can be negative—low expectations of success lead to poor performance. This is known as the **Golem effect.**

Both of these effects seem to follow a four-stage sequence:

The positive result of the four-stage process is the *Pygmalion outcome*, while the negative result is the *Golem outcome.* The lesson for managers is that the Pygmalion path is the one to take, practice, and refine. The excitement expressed by managers who expect good results is picked up by employees. Because of their pride, they strive to meet those expectations and they hope for good results as well.

Sources: For more in-depth discussion, see D. Eden, "Self-Fulfilling Prophecies in Organizations," in *Organizational Behavior: The State of the Science*, ed. J. Greenberg (Mahwah, NJ: Lawrence Erlbaum, 2003); O.B. Davidson and D. Eden, "Remedial Self-Fulfilling Prophecy: Two Field Experiments to Prevent Golem Effects among Disadvantaged Women," *Journal of Applied Psychology* 79 (2000), pp. 744–54; and G. Natanovich and D. Eden, "Pygmalion Effects among Outreach Supervisors and Tutors: Extending Sex Generalizability," *Journal of Applied Psychology* 96, no. 6 (November 2008), pp. 1382–89.

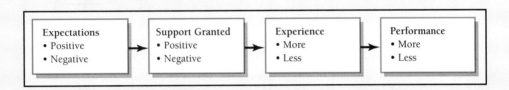

same objective reality and very honestly reaching quite different conclusions. The situation was the same, but their interpretations of the situation were markedly different.

Managers and their employees "view" the world, stimuli, and organizational programs differently and from various perspectives. Understanding that subjective perceptions are going to differ must be tolerated and coped with in work environments. The manager has a responsibility to manage within a framework that permits and respects perceptual differences to be voiced without fear or impatience. The above Organizational Encounter illustrates how a manager's expectations can impact the behaviors and performance of employees.

Perceptual Grouping

Pygmalion effect
A self-fulfilling prophecy that causes a person to behave in a positive manner to meet expectations.

Golem effect
A self-fulfilling prophecy that causes a person to behave in a negative manner to meet low expectations.

Once relevant stimuli are selected, individuals categorize and group them so that they will make sense. The brain receives stimuli and seeks to recognize common patterns.[8] This is a way of organizing sensations and applies to perceptions of people, objects, or events. Exhibit 4.3 presents the laws of perceptual grouping.

- The law of *nearness*—all other things being equal, stimuli that are near each other tend to be grouped together.
- The law of *similarity*—stimuli that are similar in size, color, shape, or form tend to be grouped together.
- The law of *closure*—the tendency to complete a figure, so that it has a consistent overall form.
- The law of *figure and ground*—the tendency to group sensations into figures and backgrounds.

EXHIBIT 4.3   Perceptual Grouping

Law of Nearness

Groups of six objects can be perceptually organized depending on spacing.

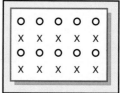

Law of Similarity

Group similar items. Do you see alternating rows of Os and Xs or columns of alternating Os and Xs?

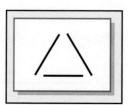

Law of Closure

Fill in the gaps in incomplete stimuli. Do you see a triangle or three lines?

Law of Figure and Ground

Organize sensations into figures and backgrounds.

A person who creates faulty groupings faces a number of different types of perceptual inaccuracies or distortions.

Individuals engaging in grouping also use what are referred to as schemas. A *schema* is a framework embodying descriptions of people, situations, or objects. Like everyone, managers use schemas to make better sense of information. A number of useful schemas for managers are:[9]

Person-based. Managers employ a profile schema of the characteristics of good, poor, and outstanding employees. The schema is used to compare present employees and job candidates.

Role-based. These are judgments about the roles people play or can play. For example, some managers may perceive that an older employee doesn't have enough energy to travel around the world overseeing various projects. This perception may be erroneous and biased. Certainly not all old people have low energy levels.

Self-based. Individuals generalize about their own prowess, competencies, and preferences based on a current or previous experience.

Events-based. Managers develop a script or story about the events they are facing. For example, the creation of a script for conducting a difficult performance feedback session would help the manager prepare for the meeting.

Managers can use schemas to examine a situation or to prepare for a situation. The schema allows a person the chance to think, organize, and compare before acting. Unfortunately, the process of perceiving, grouping, and creating schemas is open to the potential for inaccuracies and distortions, such as prejudice resulting from inaccurate stereotyping; selective attention; the halo effect; similar-to-me errors; and others.

Stereotyping

stereotyping
A translation step in the perceptual process that people use to classify or categorize events, people, or situations.

Stereotyping is a translation step in the perceptual process employed to assist individuals in dealing with massive information-processing demands. It represents a useful, even essential, way of categorizing individuals (or events, organizations, etc.) on the basis of limited information or observation. Stereotyping may occur not only as a result of direct interaction with an individual, but may also be the result of a reaction to a label or name. For example, a recent study found that work associated with names stereotypically connected with a particular race was evaluated differently from work associated with more general names.[10] The process of forming stereotypes and placing individuals in certain categories on a shorthand basis of such stereotypes can be productive if we recognize its dangers and limitations. When we speak of the Germans as efficient or the French as outstanding cooks, we are engaging in nationality stereotyping. Since many stereotypes relate to ethnic group membership, it is important to distinguish between a stereotype and a prejudice. A **prejudice** is a stereotype that refuses to change when presented with information indicating the stereotype is inaccurate. Stereotypes can be helpful; prejudice is never helpful.

prejudice
A stereotype that doesn't change even when information disputing it is presented.

An extreme form of prejudice is *scapegoating* (blaming a person or a group for the actions of others or for conditions not of their making). Thus, scapegoating is a type of displaced aggression in which hostilities triggered by frustration are redirected at safe targets. The 2009 H1N1 flu outbreak provided a modern and vivid example of scapegoating. With little information beyond the facts that the initial flu clusters originated in Mexico and the initial naming of the flu strain (i.e., swine flu), there were calls to ban Mexican pork from the United States and turn Mexican migrant workers away from U.S. hospitals.[11] Some elements of the public, frightened and lacking information about the flu outbreak, lashed out in a prejudicial manner and used Mexican nationals as a scapegoat.

At times, the development of prejudice can be traced to direct experiences with members of the rejected group.[12] An employee who is repeatedly belittled and embarrassed by members of a particular work unit might develop a dislike for all members of the unit. Once the prejudice is formed, positive experiences with the persons, group, or unit usually do not reverse the prejudice. Such contrasting information will produce what has been termed cognitive dissonance, a topic presented in Chapter 14.

Allport concluded that there are two sources of prejudice.[13] *Personal* prejudice occurs when members of another group (e.g., work group, race, age cohort) are perceived as a threat to one's own interest. *Group* prejudice occurs when a person conforms to norms of a group she belongs to. For example, key members of a work unit dislike managers. You may have no personal reason for disliking managers; however, your group expects you to follow the group's position and you may go along.

Although it is often assumed that stereotyping is inherently bad or wrong, this is not always the case. Stereotyping can be a useful process in that it can greatly increase our efficiency in making sense out of our environment. Nonetheless, stereotyping can and does lead to perceptual inaccuracies and their negative consequences.[14] To the extent that stereotypes create social injustice, result in poorer decision making, stifle innovation, or cause underutilization of human resources, they contribute to ineffectiveness and inefficiency. For example, employers' stereotypes regarding disabled workers may be an important source of the employment problems these workers frequently experience. Inaccurate stereotypes include beliefs that disabled workers lack job-related abilities, have lower performance levels, and have higher absenteeism and turnover rates. Objective data, on the other hand, consistently reveal that these stereotypes are false.[15]

Stereotypes can be problematic when talented, qualified people are held back or are unfairly considered unqualified. A study of African-American and Caucasian managers indicated that African-Americans were granted less positive support and slower rates of promotion.[16] Another study of female and male executives found that women reported more barriers to overcome for promotion and more assignments with limited authority than men.[17]

Selective and Divided Attention

Selective attention refers to the fact that people give some messages priority and put others on hold. Psychologists refer to selective attentiveness as a bottleneck or narrowing in the information channel linking the senses to perception.[18] When one message enters the bottleneck zone, it seems to prevent others from passing through. This may be why it is difficult to listen to two or more colleagues talking at once. *Divided attention* occurs when a person must divide his or her mental efforts among tasks, each of which requires some amount of attention (multitasking). Research suggests that when individuals are distracted by multiple demands, they will be more likely to engage in stereotypes.[19]

Managers learn that some stimuli (e.g., employees) require more attention than others. Employees who make forceful requests, are superior performers, or are more respected capture the manager's attention more quickly. An employee who keeps making a request for a transfer also receives more attention. This is because of the repetition of the request.[20] Obviously the potential for error in selecting which stimuli to attend to is always present.

Halo Effect

halo effect
In perception it occurs when a person allows one important factor or characteristic to bias his or her view, impression, or evaluation.

The **halo effect** occurs when a person (e.g., manager) allows one important or noticeable characteristic of another person to bias the evaluation, perception, or impression of that person.[21] An employee who is always at work before everyone else arrives or after they leave may be assumed to be productive and hard working. On the other hand, an employee with multiple body piercings may be considered wild and not reliable. Both of these judgments made by a manager utilize the halo effect and may be erroneous.

Thus, a manager's judgment of a worker based on a single, obvious characteristic has to be cautiously reviewed. One trait or characteristic can't possibly predict with accuracy a person's performance. To think so should raise an alarm in the mind of a manager. Research has found an individual's attractiveness (e.g., beauty, looks, and shape) can significantly influence managerial decisions. Attractiveness increased the evaluations, pay raises, and promotion for women in nonmanagerial positions. However, attractive women in management received lower performance reviews and pay raises, as well as a decreased number of promotion opportunities.[22] Both of these outcomes stem from the halo effect. The halo effect isn't limited to perceptions of people. Think of the last purchase you made; did you evaluate the product favorably because of a single attribute like a low price, attractive color, or established brand name? The halo effect can be a powerful force in the marketing of products.[23]

Similar-to-Me Errors

similar-to-me errors
Using yourself as a benchmark against which others are judged.

People frequently use themselves as benchmarks in perceiving others. This can give rise to **similar-to-me errors**. One's own characteristics may affect the characteristics identified as present or lacking in others. Research suggests that knowing oneself well makes it easier to see others accurately. Also, persons who accept themselves are more likely to see the favorable aspects of other people.[24]

Basically, these conclusions suggest that if managers understand that their own traits and values influence their perception of others, they probably can perform a more accurate evaluation of their subordinates. A manager who is a perfectionist tends to look for perfection in subordinates, while a manager who is quick in responding to technical requirements looks for this ability in subordinates. This may not be appropriate to the situation.

Situational Factors

The press of time, the attitudes of the people a manager is working with, and other situational factors all influence perceptual accuracy. If a manager is pressed for time and has to immediately fill an order, then her perceptions will be influenced by these time constraints. The press of time literally will force the manager to overlook some details, to rush certain activities, and to ignore certain stimuli such as requests from other managers or from superiors.

Needs and Desires

Perceptions are influenced significantly by needs and desires. In other words, the employee, the manager, the vice president, and the director see what they want to see. Like the mirrors in the fun house at the amusement park, the work can be distorted; the distortion is related to needs and desires.

The influence of needs in shaping perceptions has been studied in laboratory settings. For instance, subjects at various stages of hunger were asked to report what they saw in ambiguous drawings flashed before them. It was found that as hunger increased up to a certain point, the subjects saw more and more of the ambiguous drawings as articles of food. The hungry subjects saw steaks, salads, and sandwiches, while the subjects who recently had eaten saw nonfood images in the same drawings.[25]

Attribution Theory

attribution theory
A process by which individuals attempt to explain the reasons for events.

It is often said that perception is reality. That is, what an employee perceives to be real is in fact real for that employee. Since behavior is greatly influenced by our personal interpretation of reality, it is easy to understand why our perceptual processes are potent determinants of behavior. One approach that provides a basis for understanding the relationship between perception and behavior is *attribution theory*. Attribution theory attempts to explain the *why* of behavior as based on people's attributions of causes to events that happen to them. **Attribution theory** views the process by which individuals interpret events around them as being caused by (attributed to) a relatively stable portion of their environment.[26] Exhibit 4.4 displays the attribution process.

According to attribution theory, it is the perceived causes of events, not the actual events themselves, that influence people's behavior.[27] More specifically, individuals attempt to analyze why certain events have occurred, and the results of that analysis influence their behavior in the future. As the example in Exhibit 4.4 indicates, an employee

EXHIBIT 4.4   The Attribution Process

Source: Adapted from Abraham Korman, *Organizational Behavior* (Englewood Cliffs, NJ: Prentice Hall, 1977), p. 273.

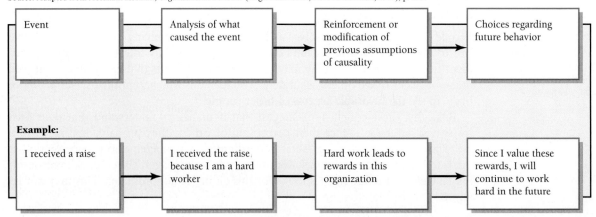

distinctiveness
In attribution theory the degree to which a person behaves similarly in different situations.

consistency
In attribution theory the degree to which a person engages in the same behaviors at different times.

consensus
In attribution theory the degree to which other people are engaging in the same behavior.

who receives a raise will attempt to attribute the raise to some underlying cause. If the employee perceives the explanation for the raise to be the fact that she is a hard worker and consequently concludes that working hard leads to rewards in her organization, she will decide to continue working hard in the future. Another employee, however, may attribute his raise to the fact that he participates in the company's bowling team and decide it makes sense to continue bowling for that reason. Thus, in both cases the two employees have made decisions affecting their future behaviors on the basis of their *attributions* of the causes of events. Then, subsequent events will be further interpreted by these two employees based on their attributions of why *these* events happened, and their attributions will be either reinforced or modified depending on the future events.

The attribution process can be important in understanding the behavior of others. The behavior of others can be examined on the basis of its *distinctiveness, consistency,* and *consensus*. **Distinctiveness** is the degree to which a person behaves similarly in different situations. **Consistency** is the degree to which a person engages in the same behaviors at different times. **Consensus** is the degree to which other people are engaging in the same behavior. Knowing the extent to which a person's behavior exhibits these qualities can be very useful in helping us better understand that behavior.

Exhibit 4.5 casts these qualities in the form of questions, the answers to which can lead us to some conclusions about the behavior in question. Let's look at an example.

EXHIBIT 4.5
Internal and External Attributions

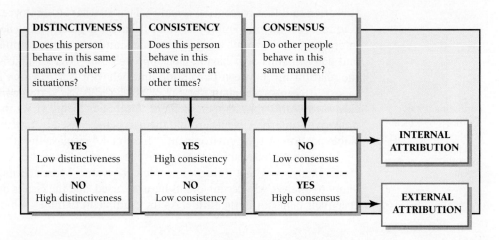

Caroline has done poorly on a test in her organizational behavior class and has expressed her concern to her professor. Her professor, in trying to understand the possible reasons for her behavior (doing poorly on the test) tries to determine its degree of distinctiveness, consistency, and consensus. If Caroline tends to also do poorly on tests in other courses (low distinctiveness), has performed poorly on earlier tests in the course (high consistency), and if no other students did poorly on the test (low consensus), the professor might make an *internal* attribution regarding Caroline's behavior. That is, the explanation for the poor test is to be found within Caroline herself (lack of motivation, poor study habits, etc.). On the other hand, if Caroline does well on tests in other courses (high distinctiveness), the professor might make an *external* attribution about the behavior. That is, the explanation for the poor test result may be found in factors outside Caroline herself (the professor put together a poor test, used the wrong answer key, etc.). The important point here is that the attributions made regarding why events occur have important implications for dealing with a problem.

Not all attributions, of course, are correct. Another important contribution made by attribution theory is the identification of systematic errors or biases that distort attributions. One such error is called the *fundamental attribution error*. The fundamental attribution error is a tendency to underestimate the importance of external factors and overestimate the importance of internal factors when making attributions about the behavior of others. An example might be that of a shop floor supervisor who attributes a high injury rate to employee carelessness (a cause internal to the employees), instead of considering the possibility the equipment is old and in poor repair (a cause external to the employees). Another frequent error is the *self-serving bias*. This is reflected in the tendency people have to take credit for successful work and deny responsibility for poor work. The self-serving bias leads us to conclude that when we succeed it is a result of our outstanding efforts, while when we fail it is because of factors beyond our control.

The managerial implications of an attributional approach to understanding work behavior are important. To influence employee behavior, the manager must understand the attributions employees make. Further, a manager must be aware that his own attributions may be different from employees'. For example, if a manager perceives employees' poor performance to be the result of lack of effort, she may attempt to increase motivation levels. On the other hand, if employees perceive performance problems to be attributable to lack of managerial guidance, the efforts made by the manager are not likely to have the desired effect on performance. Managers cannot assume that their attributions will be the same as their employees'. Neither can they assume their own attributions are error-free. Knowing this, coupled with an effort to understand what attributions employees make, can greatly enhance the manager's ability to have a positive effect on employee behavior.

Impression Management

impression management
The attempt to influence others' perception of you.

Through actions, body language, and manner of speaking, individuals attempt to influence the perceptions that others have of them. The attempt to influence others' perceptions of oneself has been called **impression management**.[28] Managers manage impressions of themselves by how they talk, their overall style, their office location and furniture, and even by the individuals they select as employees. The range of managers' techniques for creating and sustaining a particular impression of themselves is very wide.

Nearly everybody practices impression management. Managers, employees, job candidates, and external stakeholders (e.g., supply chain members) engage in impression management. While most people try to present themselves in a favorable light, candidates who use excessive impression management techniques may decrease the effectiveness of employee selection decisions. A recent study found that job candidates could be coached to present a specific personality profile and score favorably on a variety of tests used for selection. The coaching allowed applicants to present an ideal impression and score higher than noncoached (but perhaps better-qualified) applicants.[29]

An Interpersonal Process

Goffman proposed that impression management is a kind of theater—a dramaturgical process.[30] When a person is in the presence of others, there is a reason to mobilize resources, style, and creativity to make a positive impression. The process occurs at first contact, but also over the course of a long-term relationship.

Individuals (managers and nonmanagers) engage in impression management for numerous reasons. First, to interact socially, impression management allows the person to communicate a desired identity. Once the identity is established, the individual tries to remain congruent with the impression—or face cognitive dissonance. The audience (manager, colleagues, stakeholders) respects the desired identity and attempts to comply with the impression being conveyed.

Some situations (e.g., performance feedback meeting, a meeting to discuss the theft of company property) elicit significantly different behaviors than others (e.g., a company softball game). Some have defined norms while others are more ambiguous, presenting a challenge. Despite these differences all interpersonal meetings are "theater" that involves actors, audience, stage, and script. Organizations that interact heavily with the public always engage in impression management. For example, impression management is a stated policy at Disney World. All "cast members" are on stage performing for audiences and they use a script. The scripts are practiced and delivered to audiences.[31] This is why the term *dramatizing* is used to describe impression management situations.

A Model and Impression Management in Practice

Organizational researchers have proposed various impression management frameworks.[32] The one framework that has been carefully examined empirically is offered by Jones and Pittman. According to Jones and Pittman, individuals engage in five impression management tactics:

1. *Ingratiation:* They seek to be viewed positively by flattering others or offering to do favors for them.
2. *Self-promotion:* They tout their abilities and competence.
3. *Exemplification:* They seek to be viewed as dedicated by going above and beyond the call of duty.
4. *Supplication:* They seek to be viewed as needing help because of limitations.
5. *Intimidation:* They seek to be viewed as powerful and threatening.

This model suggests a number of impression management tactics. However, not everyone practices impression management the same way. Some people are not accurate self-monitors of the impressions they make. They do not pay a lot of attention to what they say, how they dress, and how they interact with others.

Research on impression management suggests that men and women often seek to create impressions in different ways.[33] Females engage in less aggressive behaviors and use a more passive approach. Also, women in comparison to men are less likely to use impression management tactics.

EXHIBIT 4.6   What Job Applicants Say to Generate a Positive Impression of Themselves

Source: Adapted from C.K. Stevens and A.L. Kristof, "Making the Right Impression: A Field Study of Applicant Impression Management during Job Interviews," *Journal of Applied Psychology* 80 (1995), pp. 587–606.

Impression Management	Description	Frequency Using Technique (%)
Self-promotion	Positively describing oneself (e.g., "I work hard every day").	100%
Personal stories	Describing the past in a puffed-up way (e.g., "I solved the most difficult problems").	96
Opinion conformity	Expressing beliefs that are assumed to be held by another person (e.g., "I agree with your statement").	54
Entitlements	Claiming responsibility for successful past events (e.g., "My work led to the securing of the contract").	50
Enhancement of another	Making comments that compliment another person (e.g., "I've been so impressed with your work accomplishments").	46
Overcoming obstacles	Describing success despite obstacles that should have lowered performance (e.g., "I won the award even though I had to work three different jobs").	33
Justifications	Accepting some responsibility, but denying the negative implications (e.g., "We lost over 30 percent of the market, but the economy went sour for everyone").	17
Excuses	Designating responsibility for one's actions (e.g., "I missed the deadline because two of my team members had the flu").	13

Studies show that some employees attempt to create a bad impression.[34] These individuals create bad impressions to exercise power; to make someone look bad, get fired, or get suspended; to obtain a transfer; or to avoid additional work or job stress. Tactics to create a bad impression include withdrawing from work, losing one's temper, communicating a lack of skills, and pretending to lack knowledge.

Generating a positive or a good impression is the preferred goal and strategy of most people. One opportune place for creating a favorable impression is during the employment interview. Exhibit 4.6 lists some popular impression management tactics used by job candidates. Note that self-promotion is the most common tactic used. In fact, every job candidate promotes his or her skills, background, experience, and competence. Organizations also engage in and encourage impression management in their employees. Stereotypically, IT workers have been viewed as introverted, messy, and moody. This stereotype is captured in the *Saturday Night Live* skit starring Jimmy Fallon: "Nick Burns, Your Company's Computer Guy." Customers can find such personalities hard to approach. To overcome this stereotype, Best Buy has engaged in impression management by presenting its IT professionals, the Geek Squad, as friendly, fun, and approachable.[35]

emotions
A state of physiological arousal and changes in facial expressions, gestures, posture, and subjective feelings.

Emotions

One thing common to all people is that they have emotions. A person's **emotions** are a state of physiological arousal accompanied by changes in facial expressions, gestures, posture, and subjective feelings.[36] In the past, emotions were largely ignored in the study of organizational behavior and management. The work setting was considered a rational and fairly stable place where emotions existed but were not a top priority to understand. This has changed in the past few decades as discussions of emotions, studies of the role emotion plays in work performance, and experiments with how managers can modify and better manage emotions have appeared in the literature.[37]

Examining Emotions

The root of the word *emotion* means "to move." The body is physically aroused during the exertion of an emotion.[38] Such bodily reactions are what cause people to say they were moved by an inspirational speech or by being recognized by their peers as the best friend in the unit. Also, people are moved to take action by emotions such as fear, anger, or joy. Many sought-after work goals make workers "feel" good. The activities that employees try to avoid make them "feel" bad.

Underlying an examination of emotions is the link between emotions and basic adaptive behaviors, such as helping others, retreating, seeking a comfortable work area, or verbally attacking someone for starting an erroneous rumor.[39] Adaptive behavior aids a person's attempts to adjust to changes. It is also apparent, however, that emotions can have a negative effect. Disgust and fear can disrupt behavior and relationships.

A faster-pounding heart, a "gurgling" stomach, sweat, and nervous tics are bodily reactions initiated by fear, anger, disgust, joy, and awe. Most of these changes in activity are caused by adrenaline, a hormone produced by the adrenal glands. Adrenaline enters the bloodstream when the sympathetic nervous system is activated.[40]

Emotional expressions are visible or audible signs of what a person is feeling. For example, when a person is very upset and frustrated his or her face contorts, hands and legs move and jerk, voice modulation changes, and posture becomes more rigid.

Primary Emotions

Based on research studies, eight primary emotions have been determined to exist: fear, surprise, sadness, joy, disgust, anger, anticipation, and acceptance. These eight primary emotions vary in intensity.[41] Sadness, for example, may range from a mild sadness to a deep sorrow that makes a person immobile.

mood
A long-lasting state of emotion.

The mildest forms of emotions are called moods. A **mood** is a low-intensity, long-lasting emotional state.[42] Moods act as subtle emotional factors that affect day-to-day behavior. Emotions generally last for short time frames, minutes or hours. Moods often last for longer periods, hours to days. For example, when a co-worker is in an irritable mood, he may react angrily to any request made to pitch in on a specific job task. When the same person is in a good mood he can handle any request.

In addition to primary emotions are broader emotions such as aggression, love, awe, remorse, contempt, optimism, and disappointment. There are also mixtures of emotions. For example, an employee may experience joy and fear simultaneously upon hearing that a co-worker he doesn't like was downsized, glad to see him go but anticipating that the employee himself may be next in line to be let go.

Expressions

The most basic emotional expressions appear to be fairly common. Individuals who are born blind have little opportunity to learn emotional expressions by observing others.[43] Despite being blind, they use the same facial expressions as others to show joy, sadness, anger, disgust, and so on.

YOU BE THE JUDGE

CHOOSING A CEO: DO EMOTIONS MATTER?

What factors would you consider in hiring the next CEO for a major organization? Perhaps you'd select an internal candidate who has had a particularly successful record of accomplishment, or you'd go outside the organization to find an individual with the skills and vision needed to move the organization forward. Regardless of whether candidates are internal or external, what specific attributes must they have for you to deem them suitable? In the recent article "When Bad People Rise to the Top," author Terry Leap characterizes "bad" CEOs as ones who are self-centered and have "deplorable" interpersonal skills. These bad CEOs may bully subordinates, refuse counsel, and take unwarranted credit for success. They have poor emotional control. Leap states that although bad CEOs may have been able to manage these faults at lower levels of an organization, the stress of the top position causes them to be revealed.

While few would argue that general intelligence is an important attribute for CEOs to possess, how important is it for them to understand their own and others' emotions? Is the ability to effectively interact with others as important as or even more important than raw intelligence?

Source: Terry Leap, "When Bad People Rise to the Top," *MIT Sloan Management Review* 49, no. 2 (Winter 2008), pp. 23–27.

Some facial expressions are influenced by learning and are unique to a national culture.[44] In China, sticking out the tongue is a gesture of surprise; sticking out the tongue is a sign of disrespect in the United States. It is important in working with people from different cultures to remember that expressions need to be evaluated carefully.

Despite some cultural differences, facial expressions of fear, anger, happiness, and sadness are similar around the world. A difference, however, is how often these expressions occur daily in various cultures. For example, some degree of anger is a commonly displayed emotion in Western cultures,[45] perhaps because independence and the right to freely display emotions are highly valued in Western cultures.

In many Asian cultures, by contrast, group harmony is very important.[46] Expressing anger publicly is not a natural facial expression. Showing anger is not conducive to bringing about group harmony, so seeing it is uncommon.

Some suggest that women are more emotional than men. Research in Western cultures has found that women do tend to be more emotionally expressive.[47] Research has also suggested that the pathways, or transitions, between emotions are typically different between men and women, indicating that women characteristically encounter more intervening steps and have additional difficulty in moving between emotions.[48] It has been suggested that the difference between genders in the expression of emotion is the result of learning. Boys learn to suppress their emotions during childhood. Girls are allowed to express their emotions as children.

Body Language: Mimicking

kinesics
The study of communication through body movement, postures, gestures, and facial expressions.

The study of communication through body movement, posture, gestures, and facial expressions is called **kinesics**.[49] We commonly call these body language. Chapter 13 covers in more detail nonverbal body language.

Psychologists Bargh and Chartrand identified an aspect of body language they call the "chameleon effect."[50] People often unconsciously mimic the postures, mannerisms, and facial expressions of other people included in the interaction. Bargh and Chartrand found that if another person copies your gestures and physical postures, you are more inclined to like the person. Further research on mimicking has indicated it also has an impact on the mimicker. Those who mimic have been shown to be more empathetic to their subjects.[51]

Facial Feedback

According to researchers, emotional activity causes innately programmed changes in facial expression. Our understanding of these changes has grown to the extent that computers can now be programmed to read facial expressions. One such program examines 27 facial features and their movements and has been able to identify even subtle expressions with an accuracy of 88 percent.[52] But our expressions may do more than communicate our feelings to the external world. Sensations from the face provide a signal to the brain that helps us determine what specific emotion we are feeling. This is called the facial feedback hypothesis.[53] This hypothesis suggests that having facial expressions and becoming aware of them will lead to emotional experience.

Ekman believes that "making faces" can actually cause emotion. In one study participants were guided muscle by muscle how to arrange their facial expressions to show surprise, disgust, anger, fear, and happiness. While facial expressions were being taught, the participants' bodily reactions were monitored.[54]

The muscle-by-muscle arrangements and monitoring showed that "making faces" brought about changes in the person's autonomic nervous system (e.g., heart rate, skin temperature).[55] An angry face raised heart rate, while disgust lowered heart rate. This study suggests that not only do emotions influence expressions, but also expressions may influence emotions.

Emotional Labor

emotional labor
The effort and work to manage your emotions to keep them under control.

Managing emotions for compensation is called emotional labor.[56] In organizations **emotional labor** may involve enhancing, faking, or suppressing emotions to modify the emotional expression. The rules or norms regarding expectations about emotional expression may be acquired by observing colleagues or they may be stated in selection or training material.[57] For example, an employee working in customer service may be encouraged to smile, listen attentively, and show respect to even the most belligerent customers. On the other hand, a person attempting to collect an accounts receivable payment may be instructed to be firm, somewhat angry, but polite in attempting to secure the overdue payment. In these cases the employee is managing and modifying the emotions that the organization believes are most effective. While emotional labor results from modifying emotional expression in an interaction, this labor is also experienced through empathy. Employees observing co-workers being treated unfairly showed increased emotional labor even though they themselves were being treated fairly.[58]

Although emotional labor may be organizationally effective, employees may pay a price. Some researchers have found that managing emotions (e.g., emotional labor) is stressful and may result in burnout. The assumption is that managing emotions requires effort, time, and energy. Organizations that attempt to orchestrate emotions, something very personal, have found resistance, skepticism, and discomfort among the employees.[59]

Individuals can manage their emotions in two ways: through what is called *surface acting,* where one regulates his or her emotional expressions, and through *deep acting,* where one modifies feelings in order to express a desired emotion. In both surface and deep acting, a conscious effort is being made.[60]

More emotional labor is likely in work settings that have a high frequency of negative events. And the more emotional labor, the more stress and burnout. The amount of emotional labor relates to increased stress because of the physiological demands for managing emotions.

Managers who are aware of the possible negative effects (e.g., withdrawal, poor attitudes, depression) of emotional labor are better prepared to provide necessary support, coaching, training, and guidance. Emotional labor is still a relatively new area of study, but it is already known that emotions play a significant role in an organization's life.[61]

Emotional Intelligence

emotional intelligence (EI)
The handling of relationships and interactions with others.

The Greek philosopher Aristotle believed he knew how to handle relationships correctly. He claimed you had to be angry with the right person, to the right degree, at the right time, for the right purpose, and in the right way. Salovey and Mayer called the capacity for handling relationships with others **emotional intelligence.**[62] Exhibit 4.7 portrays their detailed definition of emotional intelligence. Summarizing Exhibit 4.7 yields a definition of emotional intelligence as a combination of skills and abilities such as self-awareness, self-control, empathy toward others, and sensitivity to the feelings of others. President Abraham Lincoln is an example of a leader who had high levels of emotional intelligence. He is said to have learned from mistakes, shared responsibility for the mistakes of others, and did not begrudge those who made those mistakes.[63]

EXHIBIT 4.7   Emotional Intelligence (as Defined by Mayer and Salovey)

Source: P. Salovey, B.T. Bedell, J.B. Detweiler, and J.D. Mayer, "Current Directions in Emotional Intelligence Research," in *Handbook of Emotions,* eds. M. Lewis and J.M. Haviland-Jones (New York: Guilford Press, 2003).

Perception, Appraisal, and Expression of Emotion

Ability to:
• Identify emotion in one's physical and psychological states.
• Identify emotion in other people and objects.
• Express emotions accurately, and express needs related to those feelings.
• Discriminate between accurate and inaccurate, or honest and dishonest, expressions of feelings.

Emotional Facilitation of Thinking

Ability to:
• Redirect and prioritize one's thinking based on the feelings associated with objects, events, and other people.
• Generate or emulate vivid emotions to facilitate judgments and memories concerning feelings.
• Capitalize on mood swings to take multiple points of view; ability to integrate these mood-induced perspectives.
• Use emotional states to facilitate problem solving and creativity.

Understanding and Analyzing Emotional Information; Employing Emotional Knowledge

Ability to:
• Understand how different emotions are related.
• Perceive the cause and consequences of feelings.
• Interpret complex feelings, such as emotional blends and contradictory feeling states.
• Understand and predict likely transitions between emotions.

Regulation of Emotion

Ability to:
• Be open to feelings, both those that are pleasant and those that are unpleasant.
• Monitor and reflect on emotions.
• Engage, prolong, or detach from an emotional state, depending upon its judged informativeness or utility.
• Manage emotion in oneself or others.

BE POSITIVE, STAY EMPLOYED!

Is a positive outlook good for your career? While most would agree it's more pleasant to be around those with positive emotions, anecdotal evidence suggests that being positive may save your job. In a recent article on "fireproofing" your job in a time of layoffs, a positive attitude was listed as one of the best ways to be retained. The logic is simple: If you had to choose one of two comparable employees to lay off, would you keep the complainer or the employee with a positive attitude? The article also stated that socializing with those exhibiting negative attitudes could lead to your being labeled with that same attitude. It suggests that if you find yourself in a negative conversation about low salaries, layoffs, poor supervision, and so on, break it off while trying to maintain a positive connection with the complainer(s). A similar article observes that while managers must maintain the bottom line, they also have a strong desire to maintain morale and don't want people around that may cause trouble. Make it known that you are willing to make a positive contribution to the organization. These articles suggest that the employee perspective "the glass is half full" (versus "the glass is half empty") may become a self-fulfilling prophecy when it comes to staying employed during tough times.

Other than potentially making the workplace more pleasant, does a positive attitude impact business outcomes? Studies have found that a smile can lead to favorable interactions with customers. While the research on the impact of smiles has focused on retail, one could expect similar outcomes with internal customers and maybe even a supervisor within an organization.

Sources: Donna Rosato, "Smart Job Strategies to Avoid Layoffs," *CNN Money.com*, January 15, 2009, http://money.cnn.com/2009/01/14/news/economy/avoid_layoffs.moneymag/index.htm?postversion = 2009031606; Tyler Cowen, "Strategies for Keeping Your Job," *CNN Money.com*, May 5, 2009, http://money.cnn.com/2009/05/04/pf/avoid_layoffs.moneymag/; Clive Muir, "Smiling with Customers," *Business Communication Quarterly* 71, no. 2 (June 2008), pp. 241–46.

An Elusive Construct

The growing interest in emotional intelligence (EI) has been stimulated by thinking about intelligence in nontraditional ways.[64] Some suggest that EI can be viewed as a form of intelligence that is still not fully developed as a construct.[65]

Most theories of intelligence have posited that the central factor is general ability, called *g*, at the top of a hierarchical model.[66] The *g* factor is proposed as primary mental ability. Lower strata of intelligence suggest more specific mental abilities. Despite different theories, there is a common belief that intelligence is a goal-directed mental activity that is marked by efficient problem solving, critical thinking, and abstract reasoning.

Gardner has argued for a new view of nonhierarchically arrayed mental abilities that he calls *multiple intelligence*.[67] He contends there are many ways to be intelligent: verbal, mathematical, spatial, musical, interpersonal, and intrapersonal. The interpersonal and intrapersonal types of intelligence coincide with EI as a type of intelligence.

A major weakness with EI as a concept is the lack of scientifically sound, objective measures of the still elusive EI construct.[68] Theorists and researchers are not in agreement as to whether EI is an actual, scientifically grounded construct or a fad. This weakness does not mean that EI may not prove eventually to be a valid and useful construct. Rather, it means that work must still be done. However, the fact that the public and many managers show an interest in learning more about EI suggests that it has validity.

Goleman's Theory of Emotional Intelligence

The publication of Goleman's best-selling book, *Emotional Intelligence,* popularized the notion that emotions are a domain of intelligence.[69] His engaging and authoritative style is very persuasive. It is, however, very broad and nonscientifically based.

Goleman argues that we have two brains, two minds, and two different kinds of intelligence: rational and emotional. How we do in life is determined by both. His thesis is that the balance and management of emotions determine how intelligently a person acts and how successful he or she will be in life.[70]

The book has prompted the organizational community to learn about emotions, the role they play at work, and how managers can better understand and manage them, and it has started a debate among managers regarding EI.

Another concept that, like EI, is in its development phase but is generating interest in the public is "happiness," the idea that this positive emotion can be increased or introduced in work settings. Also, there is recent anecdotal evidence that suggests that employees who are positive and upbeat at work may have a better chance of keeping their jobs during layoffs. See the Organizational Encounter on page 110.

The Salovey and Mayer Theme

Salovey and Mayer coined the term *emotional intelligence*.[71] Their work and writing is not as exciting as Goleman's or as easy for managers to understand, but it is well structured, systematic, and scientifically anchored. They propose that EI emphasizes four cognitive components: a capacity to perceive emotion, to integrate emotion in thought, to understand emotion, and to manage emotion effectively. Salovey and Mayer acknowledge that neither the theory of EI nor research supports a *g* type of model of emotional intelligence. They believe it is more important that EI fit within the domain of conceptual definitions of intelligence. They propose that the ability to process affective information is an intellectual aptitude or type of intelligence.

The theoretical and research work of Salovey and Mayer uses a variety of self-report measures of EI.[72] They develop their own scales and borrow from the work of Bar-On,[73] Bernet,[74] and Roger and Najarian.[75] Unfortunately, presently the Salovey and Mayer scales, such as the MEIS, are cumbersome for respondents and take significant time to complete.

The debates about domain, measurement, and implications of EI are likely to continue indefinitely. The different conceptualizations and measurements of EI indicate that the construct will remain controversial.

Success in Careers

A major reason EI interests people is that it has been proposed to be important for career success. Salovey and Mayer temper any claims about the link between EI and career success. They dispute the claim that "if intelligence predicts 20 percent of success, EI can fill in the 80 percent gap."[76]

Even if EI is important for career success, it works in conjunction with other factors: integrity, persistence, passion, general intelligence. Over the course of a career, EI seems to increase. Learning about emotional skills and how to apply them is an exciting idea. It suggests a maturation process: A person starting a career with moderate or poor EI can learn to improve his or her emotional management skills. Over time, better EI may indeed mean more career success. There is a caution regarding EI and career progression. While increasing EI has been associated with increasing rank through middle management, EI has also been shown to decrease as one moves from middle to senior management. The drop does not mean EI is less important to senior management but may indicate that the stress and prestige of senior positions has led some executives to forget its importance.[77]

The Next Generation of EI

Gardner's view of multiple intelligences inspired others to consider his concept of interpersonal and intrapersonal abilities.[78] Goleman, Salovey, and Mayer renamed Gardner's two types of intelligence EI. Then unsupported claims about EI were

YOU BE THE JUDGE COMMENT

CHOOSING A CEO: DO EMOTIONS MATTER?

While CEOs almost always have the technical competence to do the job, can they enjoy long-term success without a high degree of emotional intelligence (EI)? Would you be inspired to follow a leader who could not manage his or her own emotions or did not show empathy toward yours? The stress and perhaps the prestige of their position may lead CEOs to forget the EI skills that allowed them to rise to the pinnacle of their organizations. How can boards of directors do a better job of screening future CEOs for EI?

- Individuals through action, body language, and manner of speaking attempt to create a particular impression of themselves in the perceptions of others. Job candidates, for instance, often attempt to foster a positive impression. This is called impression management.

- A few widely used impression management tactics are ingratiation, self-promotion, exemplification, supplication, and intimidation.

- Emotions are important in understanding the behavior and attitudes of people.

- Research has identified a number of universal primary emotions: fear, surprise, sadness, disgust, anger, joy, anticipation, and acceptance. But what is not universal is the degree to which people in various cultures express emotion.

- Emotional labor is the work, time, and effort used to manage emotions.

- Emotional intelligence (EI) is a combination of skills and abilities such as self-awareness, self-control, empathy, and sensitivity to the feelings of others.

- There is debate over whether EI is really a form of intelligence. Until it is measured more precisely, EI is likely to remain a topic of interest to managers but one of questionable value to organizational researchers.

offered as solutions to many problems. However, problems with the EI construct caused some to question the soundness of the notion of this kind of intelligence.

The next generation of work on EI needs to (1) conceptualize EI in a manner that is concise and meaningful, (2) develop more precise and concise multimethods of EI measures, and (3) determine if there is practical value in the EI concept for managers.

Clearly, the historical background illustrates that emotion has not been included in the study of intelligence. Some of the more rigorous theoretical research on EI indicates that understanding behavior in the workplace or in any setting may be incomplete without examining emotions. EI is an interesting topic that deserves further refinement and clarification.

Summary of Key Points

- Perception is a process that involves selection, organization, and interpretation of environmental factors, from shapes to people and other stimuli. Through the perceptual process, individuals attempt to make sense of the stimuli they receive.

- Once stimuli are selected they are categorized into groups according to a number of laws: nearness, similarity, closure, simplicity, and figure and ground. Grouping makes the interpretation and sense-making process easier. It doesn't, however, eliminate inaccuracies or distortions.

- Stereotyping can help a person organize perceptions. However, if it contributes to prejudice, bias, or discrimination it can be problematic.

- Some of the distortions in perception occur because of selective and divided attention, the halo effect, similar-to-me errors, and situational factors.

- Attribution theory attempts to explain the relationship between perception and behavior by investigating how people attribute events to causes.

Review and Discussion Questions

1. Assume that an employee is generally performing above expected levels. How would a manager utilize the attribution process to make a judgment about a sudden decrease in the employee's performance?

2. Why are the perceptions you have of your skills usually different from the perceptions that others have of your skills?

3. Why is impression management practiced?

4. How can stereotyping result in inaccuracies and distortions?

5. How would a manager utilize knowledge about facial expressions to learn how an employee feels about some workplace practice or process?

6. Emotional intelligence is an intriguing construct. Do you believe that EI is a form of intelligence? Why?

7. If you were in a managerial position and believed that emotions play a role in behavior and performance, how would you assess the emotions of your work team?

8. How can managers use "schemas" to reduce perceptual inaccuracies?

9. What is the Golem effect? What should managers do to decrease the chance a Golem perspective may impact the performance of their team?

10. How should emotional intelligence be measured so that critics would be satisfied with the measurement? Explain.

Exercise

Exercise 4.1: *Your Impressions of Others*

Stereotypes are one-dimensional portrayals of people—usually based on sex, race, religion, profession, or age. To attempt to make sense of the world, all people engage in some level of stereotyping. The way individuals interact with others is to some extent affected by stereotypes.

Directions

Use the rating scale below to provide a rating of the following categories of people based on your opinions of them and experience of working or interacting with them.

None/Not = 1

Somewhat = 2

Average = 3

Above Average/Very = 4

Significant/Highly = 5

Recent college graduate who is beginning a career

Knowledgeable _2_

Intelligent _2_

Sensitive _2_

Open _3_

Conscientious _3_

Emotional _2_

Arrogant _2_

Boring _2_

Internal Revenue Service accountant

Knowledgeable _3_

Intelligent _3_

Sensitive _2_

Open _3_

Conscientious _4_

Now how much do you know about perceptions, attributions, and emotions?

6. The term "emotional intelligence" was a term first used by _____.
   a. Goleman
   b. Gardner
   c. Salovey and Mayer
   d. Drucker

7. True or false: Selective attention refers to the fact that people give some messages no priority at all and emphasize selected ones.
   a. True
   b. False

8. A positive self-fulfilling prophecy is called the _____ effect.
   a. bias
   b. stereotype
   c. Pygmalion
   d. Golem

9. The attempt to influence others' perception of oneself is called _____.
   a. impression management
   b. assimilation
   c. integration
   d. attitude change

10. The ability of people to understand and manage their personal feelings and emotions as well as their emotions toward other individuals, events, and objects is called _____.
    a. general intelligence
    b. emotional intelligence
    c. behavioral intelligence
    d. emotional control

REALITY CHECK ANSWERS

Before	After
1. c 2. c 3. b 4. d 5. b	6. c 7. b 8. b 9. a 10. b
Number Correct	Number Correct
_____	_____

Emotional	2	Emotional	2
Arrogant	5	Arrogant	2
Boring	4	Boring	2

Service mechanic in car dealership

		Elected politician	
Knowledgeable	4	Knowledgeable	5
Intelligent	3	Intelligent	4
Sensitive	3	Sensitive	2
Open	4	Open	3
Conscientious	3	Conscientious	3
		Emotional	2

Arrogant   3

Boring   3

Experienced contract lawyer

Knowledgeable   4

Intelligent   4

Sensitive   3

Open   3

Conscientious   4

Emotional   2

Arrogant   3

Boring   2

Emergency room nurse

Knowledgeable   3

Intelligent   2

Sensitive   3

Open   2

Conscientious   3

Emotional   3

Arrogant   1

Boring   1

Police officer

Knowledgeable   _____

Intelligent   _____

Sensitive   _____

Open   _____

Conscientious   _____

Emotional   _____

Arrogant   _____

Boring   _____

Discussion Questions

1. Which category of persons received your most favorable and which received your least favorable ratings? Why?

2. Do your ratings show any type of stereotyping pattern? What sort? Why?

3. Have you had any experiences with any of these types of individuals that could be classified as having been influenced by management style, philosophy, or practices? When?

4. What other descriptors (other than the eight used in this exercise) would you add for these individuals? Add at least *one* per category of person.

Exercise

Exercise 4.2: *Applying Attribution Theory*

Objectives

1. To examine the causes of a person's behavior.
2. To develop an approach that's best suited to improve unacceptable behavior.

Related Topics

The concept of perception plays a role in how each of us views other people. Making attributions in terms of dispositional or situational factors is based on how a person views the event, the behaviors of another person, and previous experience.

Starting the Exercise

Carefully read the situation facing a manager. If you were this manager, what would you conclude about causes and how would you proceed? Why?

The Loss of Quality

Don Dubose has worked for Maybrooke Manufacturing since its beginning 10 years ago. He has won four top performer awards during his tenure in the firm. The last award he won was presented to him with a $15,000 bonus check about three years ago. But in the past 18 months, Don's relations with co-workers have become strained. He has never been talkative, but on occasion he has ordered co-workers out of his work area. Don has made it clear that tools have been missing, and he wants to protect his area. His work's quality has also suffered. Until about a year ago, Don's work producing generators was at the "zero-defect" level. Error-free, top-quality generators came from Don again and again. Today when random sample checks are made, Don occasionally produces generators that must be reworked less than 3 percent of the time. He has gone from zero defects to 3 out of 100 defects. His co-workers average about 1.5 defects out of 100 for reworking.

What could be causing Don's behavior changes? They could be caused by:

	Not Very Likely	Very Likely
1. Low motivation	1 2 3 4	5 6 7
2. Low self-efficacy	1 2 3 4	5 6 7
3. Physical health problems	1 2 3 4	5 6 7
4. Family problems	1 2 3 4	5 6 7
5. Poor management	1 2 3 4	5 6 7
6. Lack of creativity	1 2 3 4	5 6 7

Comment on each of your ratings:

1. _____
2. _____
3. _____
4. _____
5. _____
6. _____

Don's behavior has become a topic of concern within the organization. An outstanding worker has become average. What actions would you take as the manager?

	Yes	No	Why?
Transfer Don to a new job.	____	____	____
Fire Don.	____	____	____

continued

	Yes	No	Why?
Call Don in to discuss your observations.	____	____	____
Suspend Don after informing him about your concerns.	____	____	____
Ask Don's co-workers why they believe his performance isn't up to previous norms.	____	____	____
Leave the situation alone for another six months.	____	____	____
Contact Don's wife to see if there's a personal reason for the performance problem.	____	____	____
Examine your own behavior (as manager) in working with Don.	____	____	____
Send Don to a human resource management counselor to discuss his attitudes about the job.	____	____	____
Promote Dan since he has been in the present job for over six years.	____	____	____
Other courses of action:			

_____
_____
_____

In Class

After you've analyzed this situation, meet with classmates to discuss their reactions. What did you learn about your attribution process? Are your reactions different from your classmates'?

Case

Case 4.1: *A Management Style That Made an Impression*

Chairs? There is not much that can be said about chairs, right? Some are comfortable, some are not; some are cushy, some are firm. Since that is just about the whole story on the subject, I never thought I'd ever consider a column on chairs.

Then Bill died.

When I heard the news, I knew I eventually had to write something about the chairs.

I'd known Bill for years, admired his inquiring mind, his wit, his management style, and his record of achievements, which was lengthy. He was a CEO with a considerable reputation for his successes, yet every time I saw him over a period of many years, I never focused on his triumphs. My first thought was always of the chairs.

I guess you could rightly conclude those chairs made a big impression on me. There were two of them in Bill's office, utilitarian metal armchairs, chairs with an upholstered seat and back, the kind that are advertised in most office furniture catalogs. I have two of them in my own office.

Over a varied career, I've been in many offices, the offices of buyers and sellers, the offices of top managers and middle managers, the offices of editors and publishers, the offices of CEOs and human resource specialists. Usually the chairs for visitors are comfortable, but just ordinary, and not very memorable.

There was that one legendary chair in the office of that famous Buffalo editor. It was legendary because it was bolted to the floor, thus preventing any visitor from attempting to move any closer to the editor. All discussions in his office were held at a prescribed and safe distance. I sat in that chair once, when he invited me over and offered me a job, which I eventually declined. But I did test the chair, attempting to edge in slightly when he was distracted by a phone call, and it surely was fastened securely in position. The man wanted nobody invading his space. He sat protected, barricaded behind his oversize desk.

Desks are not just for working upon and storing papers. They do perform that insulating function. They separate the host from the visitor, forming a definite barrier, a barrier that sends a message that says, "This is my room and I am in charge here."

It was different with Bill, and that is why I always associated him with those chairs.

He had the big desk. He had the comfortable leather swivel chair that accompanied the office of the CEO. He called me one day and asked me to come and see him to discuss a problem that he thought I could help him solve. I had known him, but I had never been to his office.

When I arrived, he rose from his chair, greeted me with a handshake, and politely directed me to have a seat in one of the pair of chairs facing the desk and reserved for visitors. Then he sat down in the other chair, forsaking the status and the security of the big chair behind the big desk.

This was nonverbal communication, behavior that I'd never seen before and I instantly recognized what was transpiring. He was telling me to relax, that we were both on the same level in his office, conferring to solve a problem.

That was a first for me. I'd always had to talk to the person behind a desk. No one had ever before vacated that traditional position and joined me at midfield. It gave me a good feeling. I said nothing to Bill about it that day, or ever, but I always remembered it and chalked it up to experience.

I also went back to my own office and rearranged the furniture and modified my style. I had a desk and a chair behind it, plus two chairs for visitors. I had always stayed behind the desk, but I changed forever that day. It wasn't a big change, I suppose, but it was a significant one that I remember planning and executing. Some people noticed, including the owner of the company, whose office was down the hall, and who rarely strayed from behind his desk, one of the biggest in the catalog.

"How come you're always walking around and sitting over here?" he asked me one day.

I never told him. I was evasive. I figured if he had to ask, he would never understand.

Questions

1. Why do you think the legendary chair in the editor's office was bolted to the floor? Is the reason cited in the case the only reason for the bolts?

2. What impression is being portrayed by the case writer?

3. What other type of office layouts and flows could be used to create an impression?

Source: Prepared by Dick Hirsch, "His Management Style Made an Impression," *Buffalo Business First,* July 9, 2001.

CHAPTER FIVE

Motivation

Learning Objectives

After completing Chapter 5, you should be able to:

- **Describe** the three determinants of job performance.
- **Identify** the need levels in Maslow's hierarchy.
- **Explain** Alderfer's ERG theory.
- **Compare** motivators with hygiene factors.
- **Discuss** the factors that reflect a high need for achievement.

- **Define** the key terms in expectancy theory.
- **Distinguish** between inputs and outputs in equity theory.
- **Understand** the different types of organizational justice.
- **Identify** the key steps in goal setting.
- **Describe** the concept of the psychological contract.

One story about the culture of IBM concerns a situation involving company founder Thomas Watson. One of his top senior managers made a very costly mistake costing IBM about $3 million. The manager started to clean out his desk to be ready for the inevitable "pink slip" firing. When Watson came to his office to talk, the manager started, "I know why you're here. I'll offer my resignation and leave." Watson looked at the manager and warmly replied: "You don't think I would let you go after I just spent $3 million to train you." Watson valued the manager, knew the individual wanted to do well, but had failed.[1]

Although, the manager's performance goal in this case was not achieved, he exerted every effort to do the job. Watson wanted to provide a positive motivation atmosphere at IBM. This IBM story has become part of the firm's cultural history concerning motivation. The manager was an important part of IBM and despite his failure in this case, the leader of the firm was there to support the manager's willingness to perform.

No one questions the central role motivation plays in shaping behavior and, specifically, in influencing work performance in organizations.[2] Nonetheless, as important as motivation is, it is not the only factor that determines performance. Over the years, a variety of other variables thought to play an important role in performance have been suggested. These include ability, instinct, and aspiration level as well as personal factors such as age, education, and family background.

One way of conceptualizing the various determinants of performance is illustrated in Exhibit 5.1. As can be seen from this exhibit, job performance may be viewed as a function of the *capacity* to perform, the *opportunity* to perform, and the *willingness* to perform. The capacity to perform relates to the degree to which an individual possesses task-relevant skills, abilities, knowledge, and experiences. Unless an employee knows what is supposed to be done and how to do it, high levels of job performance are not possible. Having the opportunity to perform is also a critical ingredient in the performance recipe. A researcher for a pharmaceutical drug company whose lab equipment is constantly breaking is unable to perform at the same level as a researcher

How much do you know about motivation?

1. True or false: The most important factor in achieving high job performance is an employee's willingness to perform at that level.
   a. True
   b. False

2. There are many steps in the motivational process. Which step follows after identification of need deficiencies and searching for ways to satisfy those needs?
   a. Goal-directed behavior
   b. Performance
   c. Rewards or punishments
   d. Need deficiencies reassessed

3. Maslow's needs hierarchy, Alderfer's ERG, and McClelland's learned needs theories can be classified as _____.
   a. process theories
   b. content theories
   c. learning theories
   d. both *a* and *c* are correct

4. Herzberg referred to such components as salary, job security, and working conditions as _____ and reasoned that these conditions were needed to keep employees from becoming dissatisfied.
   a. satisfiers
   b. motivating factors
   c. hygiene factors
   d. core benefits

5. _____ is when an employee feels that the organization has failed to fulfill an unwritten exchange agreement between the individual and the organization.
   a. Expectancy contract violation
   b. Organizational justice retraction
   c. Judicial contract disturbance
   d. Psychological contract breach

EXHIBIT 5.1

Determinants of Job Performance

Source: Adapted from M. Blumberg and C. Pringle, "The Missing Opportunity in Organizational Research: Some Implications for a Theory of Work Performance," *Academy of Management Review,* October 1982, p. 565.

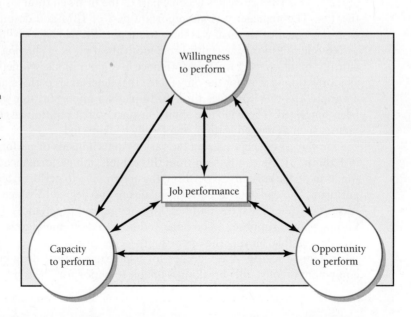

who does not encounter those difficulties. Sometimes employees may lack the opportunity to perform not because of poor equipment or outdated technology, but because of poor decisions and outdated attitudes.

The third factor, willingness to perform, relates to the degree to which an individual both desires and is willing to exert effort toward attaining job performance. It is, in other words, motivation, and it is what this chapter is about. No combination of capacity and opportunity will result in high performance in the absence of some level of motivation or willingness to perform.

From a managerial perspective, it is important to realize that the presence of motivation per se, coupled with a capacity and opportunity to perform, does not ensure high performance levels. It is a rare manager who has not at some point concluded that performance would be much higher "if I could just get my people motivated." In all likelihood, those individuals are already motivated; what that manager really wants is motivation that results in more or different kinds of behaviors. To understand this distinction it is helpful to think of motivation as being made up of at least three distinct components: direction, intensity, and persistence.

Direction relates to what an individual chooses to do when presented with a number of possible alternatives. When faced with the task of completing a report requested by management, for example, an employee may choose to direct effort toward completing the report or toward surfing the Internet (or any number of other possible activities). Regardless of which option is selected, the employee is motivated. If the employee selects the first alternative, the direction of his or her motivation is consistent with that desired by management. If the employee chooses the second alternative, the direction is counter to that desired by management, but the employee is nonetheless motivated.

The *intensity* component of motivation refers to the strength of the response once the choice (direction) is made. Using the previous example, the employee may choose the proper direction (working on the report) but respond with very little intensity. Intensity, in this sense, is synonymous with effort. Two people may focus their behavior in the same direction, but one may perform better because he or she exerts more effort and intensity than the other.

Finally, *persistence* is an important component of motivation. Persistence refers to the staying power of behavior or how long a person will continue to devote effort. Some people will focus their behavior in the appropriate direction and do so with a high degree of intensity but only for a short time period. Individuals who tackle a task enthusiastically but quickly tire of it, or burn out and seldom complete it, lack this critical attribute in their motivated behavior. Thus, the manager's real challenge is not so much one of increasing motivation per se but of creating an environment wherein employee motivation is channeled in the right direction at an appropriate level of intensity and continues over time.

The Starting Point: The Individual

Most managers must motivate a diverse and, in many respects, unpredictable group of people. The diversity results in different behavioral patterns that are in some manner related to needs and goals. This type of diversity makes the manager's motivational work very challenging.

As can be seen in Exhibit 5.2, **needs** refer to deficiencies an individual experiences at a particular time. The deficiencies may be physiological (e.g., a need for food), psychological (e.g., a need for self-esteem), or sociological (e.g., a need for social interaction). Needs are viewed as energizers or triggers of behavioral responses. The implication is

needs
The deficiencies that an individual experiences at a particular point in time.

EXHIBIT 5.2
The Motivational Process: A General Model

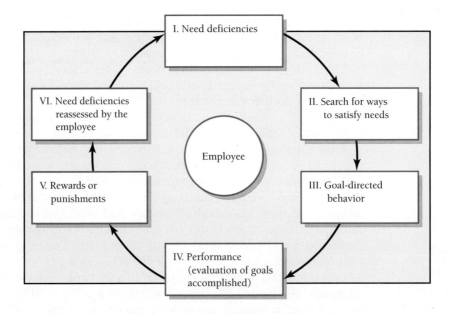

that when need deficiencies are present, the individual is more susceptible to a manager's motivational efforts.

A study of about 4,000 employees found three main areas that affect employee motivation: *organizational issues* such as compensation, benefits, career opportunities, and company reputation; *job issues* including work schedules, opportunities to learn new skills, and challenging work; and *leader issues* such as whether their leaders/supervisors are trustworthy, good motivators and coaches, and flexible in solving problems.[3]

People seek to reduce various need deficiencies. Need deficiencies trigger a search process for ways to reduce the tension caused by the deficiencies. A course of action is selected, and goal-directed (outcome-directed) behavior occurs. After a period, managers assess that behavior, and the performance evaluation results in some type of reward or punishment. Such outcomes are weighed by the person, and the need deficiencies are reassessed. This, in turn, triggers the process, and the circular pattern starts again.

The importance of goals in any discussion of motivation is apparent. The motivational process, as interpreted by most theorists, is goal-directed. The goals, or outcomes, that an employee seeks are viewed as forces that attract the person. The accomplishment of desirable goals can result in a significant reduction in need deficiencies.

Each person is attracted to some set of goals. If a manager is to predict behavior with any accuracy, he or she must know something about an employee's goals and about the actions the employee will take to achieve them. There is no shortage of motivation theories and research findings that attempt to provide explanations of the behavior–outcome relationship. Individual theories can be classified as representing either a *content* or a *process* approach to motivation. Content approaches focus on identifying specific motivation factors. Process approaches focus on describing how behavior is motivated. Exhibit 5.3 summarizes the basic characteristics of content and process theories of motivation from a managerial perspective.

Both categories of theories have important implications for managers, who are—by the nature of their jobs—involved with the motivational process. We will examine several examples of both types, beginning with the content approaches.

EXHIBIT 5.3 **Managerial Perspective of Content and Process Theories of Motivation**

Theoretical Base	Theoretical Explanation	Founders of the Theories	Managerial Application
Content	Focuses on factors within the person that energize, direct, sustain, and stop behavior. These factors can only be inferred.	Maslow—five-level need hierarchy Alderfer—three-level hierarchy (ERG) Herzberg—two major factors called hygiene factors and motivators McClelland—three learned needs acquired from the culture: achievement, affiliation, and power	Managers need to be aware of differences in needs, desires, and goals because each individual is unique in many ways.
Process	Describes, explains, and analyzes how behavior is energized, directed, sustained, and stopped.	Vroom—an expectancy theory of choices Adams—equity theory based on comparisons that individuals make Locke—goal-setting theory that conscious goals and intentions are the determinants of behavior	Managers need to understand the process of motivation and how individuals make choices based on preferences, rewards, and accomplishments.

Content Approaches

The content theories of motivation focus on the factors within the person that energize, direct, sustain, and stop behavior. They attempt to determine the specific needs that motivate people. Four important content approaches to motivation are: (1) Maslow's need hierarchy, (2) Alderfer's ERG theory, (3) Herzberg's two-factor theory, and (4) McClelland's learned needs theory. Each of these four theories has had an impact on managerial practices and will be considered in the paragraphs that follow.

Maslow's Need Hierarchy

The crux of Maslow's theory is that needs are arranged in a hierarchy.[4] The lowest-level needs are the physiological needs, and the highest-level needs are the self-actualization needs. These needs are defined to mean the following:

1. *Physiological.* The need for food, drink, shelter, and relief from pain.
2. *Safety and security.* The need for freedom from threat, that is, security from threatening events or surroundings.
3. *Belongingness, social, and love.* The need for friendship, affiliation, interaction, and love.
4. *Esteem.* The need for self-esteem and for esteem from others.
5. *Self-actualization.* The need to fulfill oneself by making maximum use of abilities, skills, and potential.

Exhibit 5.4 shows the hierarchical nature of Maslow's theory. For each of the five need levels, the exhibit provides examples of work-related factors that might be associated with need satisfaction.

EXHIBIT 5.4
Maslow's Need Hierarchy Related to the Job

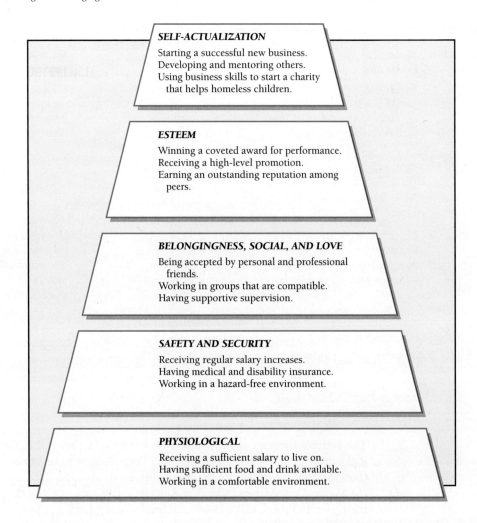

SELF-ACTUALIZATION
Starting a successful new business.
Developing and mentoring others.
Using business skills to start a charity
    that helps homeless children.

ESTEEM
Winning a coveted award for performance.
Receiving a high-level promotion.
Earning an outstanding reputation among
    peers.

BELONGINGNESS, SOCIAL, AND LOVE
Being accepted by personal and professional
    friends.
Working in groups that are compatible.
Having supportive supervision.

SAFETY AND SECURITY
Receiving regular salary increases.
Having medical and disability insurance.
Working in a hazard-free environment.

PHYSIOLOGICAL
Receiving a sufficient salary to live on.
Having sufficient food and drink available.
Working in a comfortable environment.

Maslow's theory assumes that a person attempts to satisfy the more basic needs (physiological) before directing behavior toward satisfying upper-level needs. Several other crucial points in Maslow's thinking are important to understanding the need-hierarchy approach.

1. A satisfied need ceases to motivate. For example, when a person decides that he or she is earning enough pay for contributing to the organization, money loses its power to motivate. Large multinational corporations such as Wal-Mart are trying to prevent such problems by offering **cafeteria-style benefits plans**.[5] Similarly, many small and medium-sized enterprises are also offering flexible benefits.[6] By allowing employees to choose and change benefits over time, these firms let employees meet their changing needs.[7]

2. Unsatisfied needs can cause frustration, conflict, and stress. From a managerial perspective, unsatisfied needs are dangerous because they may lead to undesirable performance outcomes.

3. Maslow assumes that people have a need to grow and develop and, consequently, will strive constantly to move up the hierarchy in terms of need satisfaction. This assumption may be true for some employees but not others.

cafeteria-style benefits plans
Plans that allow employees to choose benefits that suit them and to make adjustments to meet their changing needs.

Mary Kay, Inc., uses the full range of Maslow's need hierarchy to motivate its 1.8 million beauty consultants in 35 markets worldwide. The company is still best known for its reward of the Mary Kay Pink Cadillac for outstanding sales and team building. Consultants report that they are motivated by commissions and incentives (pay), being a part of a team (belongingness and social), recognition (esteem), and the privilege to help others (self-actualization). Mary Kay management appears to understand motivation and needs. Pay, incentives, recognition, autonomy, and helping others succeed are a combination of factors that the consultants seek.[8]

Several research studies have attempted to test the need-hierarchy theory. The first field-reported research that tested a modified version of Maslow's need hierarchy was performed by Porter.[9] At the time of the initial studies, Porter assumed that physiological needs were being adequately satisfied for managers, so he substituted a higher-order need called *autonomy,* defined as the person's satisfaction with opportunities to make independent decisions, set goals, and work without close supervision.

Research studies have reported:

1. Managers higher in the organization chain of command place greater emphasis on self-actualization and autonomy.[10]
2. Managers at lower organizational levels in small firms (less than 500 employees) are more satisfied than their counterpart managers in large firms (more than 5,000 employees); however, managers at upper levels in large companies are more satisfied than their counterparts in small companies.[11]
3. American managers overseas are more satisfied with autonomy opportunities than are their counterparts working in the United States.[12]

Despite these findings, a number of issues remain regarding the need-hierarchy theory. First, data from managers in two different companies provided little support that a hierarchy of needs exists.[13] The data suggested that only two levels of needs exist: one is the physiological level, and the other is a level that includes all other needs. Further evidence also disputes the hierarchy notions.[14] Researchers have found that as managers advance in an organization, their needs for security decrease, with a corresponding increase in their needs for social interaction, achievement, and self-actualization.

Alderfer's ERG Theory

Alderfer agrees with Maslow that individual needs are arranged in a hierarchy. However, his proposed need hierarchy involves only three sets of needs:[15]

1. *Existence.* Needs satisfied by such factors as food, air, water, pay, and working conditions.
2. *Relatedness.* Needs satisfied by meaningful social and interpersonal relationships.
3. *Growth.* Needs satisfied by an individual making creative or productive contributions.

Alderfer's three needs—existence (E), relatedness (R), and growth (G), or ERG—correspond to Maslow's in that the existence needs are similar to Maslow's physiological and safety categories; the relatedness needs are similar to the belongingness, social, and love category; and the growth needs are similar to the esteem and self-actualization categories.

In addition to a difference in the number of categories, Alderfer's ERG theory and Maslow's need hierarchy differ on how people move through the sets of needs. Maslow proposed that unfulfilled needs are predominant and that the next-higher level of needs isn't activated or triggered until the predominant need is adequately satisfied. Thus, a person only progresses up the need hierarchy once a lower-level need is adequately satisfied. In contrast, Alderfer's ERG theory suggests that, in addition to the satisfaction-progression process that Maslow proposed, a frustration-regression process is also at work. That is, if a person is continually frustrated in attempts to satisfy growth needs, relatedness needs reemerge as a major motivating force, causing the individual to redirect efforts toward satisfying a lower-order need category.

Alderfer's ERG explanation of motivation provides an interesting suggestion to managers about behavior. If a subordinate's higher-order needs (for example, growth) are being blocked, perhaps because of a company policy or lack of resources, then it's in the manager's best interest to attempt to redirect the subordinate's efforts toward relatedness or existence needs by assigning him or her to projects with desired coworkers. The ERG theory implies that individuals are motivated to engage in behavior to satisfy one of the three sets of needs.

The ERG theory hasn't stimulated a great deal of research, so no empirical verification can be claimed. Salancik and Pfeffer proposed that need models such as Maslow's and Alderfer's have become popular because they are consistent with other theories of rational choice and because they attribute freedom to individuals. The idea that individuals shape their actions to satisfy unfulfilled needs gives purpose and direction to individual activity. Furthermore, need explanations are also popular, despite little research verification, because they are simple and easily expressed views of human behavior.[16]

Herzberg's Two-Factor Theory

Herzberg developed a content theory known as the two-factor theory of motivation.[17] The two factors are called the dissatisfiers–satisfiers or the hygiene motivators or the extrinsic–intrinsic factors, depending on the discussant of the theory. The original research that led to the theory gave rise to two specific conclusions. First, there is a set of *extrinsic* conditions, the job context, which results in dissatisfaction among employees when the conditions are not present. If these conditions are present, this does not necessarily motivate employees. These conditions are the *dissatisfiers* or *hygiene* factors, since they are needed to maintain at least a level of "no dissatisfaction." They include salary, job security, working conditions, status, company procedures, quality of technical supervision, and quality of interpersonal relations among peers, superiors, and subordinates.

Second, a set of *intrinsic* conditions—the job content—when present, builds strong levels of motivation that can result in good job performance. If these conditions are not present, jobs do not prove highly satisfying. The factors in this set are called the *satisfiers* or *motivators* and include achievement, recognition, responsibility, advancement, the work itself, and the possibility of growth.

These motivators are directly related to the nature of the job or task itself. When present, they contribute to satisfaction. This, in turn, can result in intrinsic task motivation.[18] Referring to Exhibit 5.5, several important managerial implications of Herzberg's two-factor theory include:

1. ***No job dissatisfaction, high job satisfaction.*** An employee who is paid well, has job security, has good relationships with co-workers and the supervisor (hygiene factors are present = no job dissatisfaction), and is given challenging duties for which he is accountable will be motivated.

   Managers should continue to assign challenging tasks and transfer accountability to high-performing subordinates. Pay raises, job security, and good supervision need to be continued.

EXHIBIT 5.5
Traditional versus Herzberg View of Job Satisfaction

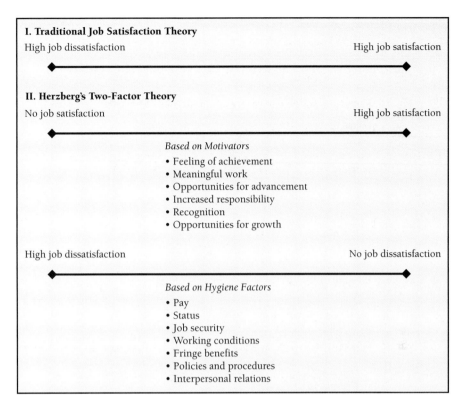

I. Traditional Job Satisfaction Theory

High job dissatisfaction ◆——————————————————————————◆ High job satisfaction

II. Herzberg's Two-Factor Theory

No job satisfaction ◆——————————————————————————◆ High job satisfaction

Based on Motivators
- Feeling of achievement
- Meaningful work
- Opportunities for advancement
- Increased responsibility
- Recognition
- Opportunities for growth

High job dissatisfaction ◆——————————————————————————◆ No job dissatisfaction

Based on Hygiene Factors
- Pay
- Status
- Job security
- Working conditions
- Fringe benefits
- Policies and procedures
- Interpersonal relations

2. ***No job dissatisfaction, no job satisfaction.*** An employee who is paid well, has job security, and has good relationships with co-workers and the supervisor (hygiene factors are present = no job dissatisfaction), but is not given any challenging assignments and is very bored with her job (motivators are absent = no job satisfaction) will not be motivated.

   Managers should reevaluate subordinate's job description and enlarge it by providing more challenging and interesting assignments. Pay raises, job security, and good supervision need to be continued.

3. ***High job dissatisfaction, no job satisfaction.*** An employee who is not paid well, has little job security, has poor relationships with co-workers and the supervisor (hygiene factors are not present = high job dissatisfaction), and is not given any challenging assignments and is very bored with his job (motivators are absent = no job satisfaction) will not be motivated.

   To prevent low performance, absenteeism, and turnover, managers should make drastic changes by adding hygiene factors and motivators.

Herzberg suggests that motivators (intrinsic conditions) and hygiene factors can be applied to understanding factory (extrinsic conditions) workers in most countries and cultures. The Global OB on page 128, which combines the research and reports of a number of researchers, supports the application of Herzberg's two-factor explanation across diverse cultures. For example, in Italy 60 percent of the workers indicated that motivators accounted for job satisfaction, while 90 percent of workers in Finland reported that motivators accounted for job satisfaction.[19] A related study of employees in Turkey, Cyprus, Nigeria, and Great Britain reported general support for Herzberg's two-factor theory. Factors associated with the work attitudes of employees from these nations could be

MOTIVATORS AND HYGIENE FACTORS ACROSS CULTURES

Motivators	Satisfying Job Events	Dissatisfying Job Events
United States	80%	20%
Japan	82	40
Finland	90	18
Hungary	78	30
Italy	60	35
Hygiene Factors		
United States	20%	75%
Japan	10	65
Finland	10	80
Hungary	22	78
Italy	30	70

Source: Adapted from S.A. Snell, C.C. Snow, S. Canney Davison, and D.C. Hambrick, "Designing and Supporting Transnational Teams: The Human Resource Agenda," *Human Resource Management* 37 (1998), pp. 147–58; and F. Herzberg, "Workers' Needs: The Same around the World," *Industry Week* 234, no. 6 (September 21, 1987), pp. 29–32.

separated into two distinct categories: motivators and hygiene factors.[20] Other recent research studies in Japan and Brazil are also generally supportive of Herzberg's theory.[21]

Herzberg's model basically assumes that job satisfaction is not a unidimensional concept. His research leads to the conclusion that two continua are needed to correctly interpret job satisfaction. Exhibit 5.5 presents two different views of job satisfaction. Before Herzberg's work, those studying motivation viewed job satisfaction as a unidimensional concept; that is, they placed job satisfaction at one end of a continuum and job dissatisfaction at the other end. This meant that if a job condition caused job satisfaction, removing it would cause job dissatisfaction. Similarly, if a job condition caused job dissatisfaction, removing it would cause job satisfaction.

One appealing aspect of Herzberg's explanation of motivation is that the terminology is work-oriented. There is no need to translate psychological terminology into everyday language. Despite this important feature, Herzberg's work has been criticized for a number of reasons. For example, some researchers believe that Herzberg's work oversimplifies the nature of job satisfaction. Other critics focus on Herzberg's methodology, which requires people to look at themselves retrospectively. Still other critics charge that Herzberg has directed little attention toward testing the motivational and performance consequences of the theory. In his original study, only self-reports of performance were used, and in most cases, the respondents described job activities that had occurred over a long period of time.

job enrichment
Increases motivation by building challenge, responsibility, recognition, and growth opportunities into a person's job.

Although the list of criticisms for Herzberg's model is long, the impact of the theory on practicing managers should not be underestimated. For example, one concept that emerged from Herzberg's work is that of **job enrichment**. Job enrichment is defined as the process of building personal achievement, recognition, challenge, responsibility, and growth opportunities into a person's job. This has the effect of increasing the individual's motivation by providing her with more discretion and accountability

GOING THE EXTRA MILE

A passenger on a Southwest Airlines flight was very nervous about flying. Sara, one of the flight attendants, noticed the passenger was nervous while taking her drink order. Sara immediately reassured the passenger that everything was going to be OK, but she didn't stop there. Sara told two of her fellow flight attendants, Jody and Judy, about the passenger's anxiousness. During the long flight from Philadelphia to Los Angeles, the three flight attendants went out of their way to make sure the passenger was comfortable. They even explained the different normal noises a plane makes during takeoff, flight, and landing to put the customer at ease. Following the flight, the grateful passenger wrote a letter to the company describing how the three flight attendants were amazing and incredible. As a result of "going the extra mile" to help a nervous flyer, these three Southwest employees received commendations from their co-workers and recognition from Chairman and CEO Gary Kelly.

The idea of expecting employees to go the extra mile has become more common as service organizations continue to dominate the economy. Employees from airlines, retail stores, hotels, banks, and other service organizations who deal with customers are expected to do more than expected several times a day. This type of "super service" can help earn an organization an edge relative to its competitors.

These extra activities are called organizational citizenship behaviors (OCBs) and are important because research suggests that when employees engage in these extra helping behaviors, organizations achieve higher customer satisfaction, productivity, and reduced costs. At the individual employee level, OCBs are linked to higher ratings on employee performance and reward allocation decisions. When employees decrease or stop engaging in OCBs, then it is more likely they will miss work and quit the organization.

There are several types of OCBs, including:

Altruism: Sara and other the flight attendants were dedicated to the passenger's welfare.

Courtesy: The flight attendants treated the passenger with consideration.

Compliance: The flight attendants complied with Southwest Airlines' norms of customer service.

Civic virtue: Co-workers of the flight attendants took the time to honor their colleagues for going the extra mile for the nervous passenger.

Sportsmanship: Instead of acting too busy or ignoring the passenger's discomfort, these three flight attendants worked together to provide exceptional customer service.

An important question for managers in service organizations is, "Why do employees engage in OCBs, and what can be done to encourage them?" Research has provided some explanations.

First, no clear relationships with most personality characteristics have been found. But a higher frequency of OCBs has been found among those employees with a higher collectivist orientation than among those who have a more individualistic perspective.

Second, certain situational factors seem to be related to OCBs. One of these factors relates to what employees and managers define as part of the job and what is "out-of-role." Employees will often define their jobs quite broadly and will include activities as part of their duties that their managers perceive as "extra." These OCBs also are likely to influence managerial evaluations of employees, but sometimes they may be interpreted as attempts to influence these evaluations rather than efforts to do something good for the company and the customer.

Finally, a major influence on OCBs is the leadership that employees receive from their managers. Specifically, trust between an employee and a manager and a management style that encourages the development of leadership skills among employees have been found to encourage the expression of OCBs.

Sources: www.southwest.com/about_swa (accessed April 18, 2009); Nathan P. Podsakoff, Steven W. Whiting, Philip M. Podsakoff, and Brian D. Blume, "Individual- and Organizational-Level Consequences of Organizational Citizenship Behaviors: A Meta-Analysis," *Journal of Applied Psychology* 94, no. 1 (2009), pp. 122–41; Philip M. Podsakoff, Scott B. MacKenzie, Julie Beth Paine, and Daniel G. Bachrach, "Organizational Citizenship Behaviors: A Critical Review of the Theoretical and Empirical Literature and Suggestions for Future Research," *Journal of Management* 26, no. 3, pp. 513–63; Bradley J. Alge, Gary A. Ballinger, Subrahmaniam Tangirala, and James L. Oakley, "Information Privacy in Organizations: Empowering Creative and Extrarole Performance," *Journal of Applied Psychology* 91, no. 1 (January 2006), pp. 221–32; Suzanne S. Masterson and Christina L. Stamper, "Perceived Organizational Membership: An Aggregate Framework Representing the Employee-Organization Relationship," *Journal of Organizational Behavior* 24, no. 5 (August 2003), pp. 473–87; Dennis W. Organ, "Personality and Organizational Citizenship Behavior," *Journal of Management*, Summer 1994, pp. 465–78; and Mary A. Konovsky and S. Douglas Pugh, "Citizenship Behavior and Social Exchange," *Academy of Management Journal*, June 1994, pp. 656–69.

when performing challenging work. Herzberg believed that job enlargement would improve task efficiency and human satisfaction.

Many managers feel very comfortable about many of the things Herzberg includes in his two-factor discussion. From a scientific vantage point, this satisfaction presents some dangers of misuse, but this hasn't stopped the theory from being implemented in numerous organizations. Hewlett-Packard, for example, has restructured many of its operations along the lines described by Herzberg. The company relies on both motivators and hygiene factors to increase satisfaction and decrease the likelihood of dissatisfaction. Examples at Hewlett-Packard include providing resources (time, money, and space) to work on ideas for improving products and processes; instituting flextime-time scheduling to increase employee job discretion; and using a profit-sharing plan that may increase satisfaction by providing a source of both achievement and recognition. With the amount of discretion increasing in many jobs, the opportunity also exists for employees to do more than what is expected. The Organizational Encounter on page 129 examines this pleasant situation.

McClelland's Learned Needs Theory

McClelland has proposed a theory of motivation that is closely associated with learning concepts. He believes that many needs are acquired from the culture.[22] Three of these learned needs are the need for achievement (n Ach), the need for affiliation (n Aff), and the need for power (n Pow).

McClelland contends that when a need is strong in a person, its effect is to motivate the person to use behavior that leads to its satisfaction. For example, having a high n Ach encourages an individual to set challenging goals, to work hard to achieve the goals, and to use the skills and abilities needed to achieve them.

Based on research results, McClelland developed a descriptive set of factors that reflect a high need for achievement. These are:

1. The person likes to take responsibility for solving problems.
2. The person tends to set moderate achievement goals and is inclined to take calculated risks.
3. The person desires feedback on performance.

The need for affiliation reflects a desire to interact socially with people. A person with a high need for affiliation is concerned about the quality of important personal relationships, and thus, social relationships take precedence over task accomplishment. A person with a high need for power, meanwhile, concentrates on obtaining and exercising power and authority. He or she is concerned with influencing others and winning arguments. Power has two possible orientations according to McClelland. It can be negative in that the person exercising it emphasizes dominance and submission. Or power can be positive in that it reflects persuasive and inspirational behavior.

The main theme of McClelland's theory is that these needs are learned through coping with one's environment. Since needs are learned, behavior that is rewarded tends to recur at a higher frequency. Managers who are rewarded for achievement behavior learn to take moderate risks and to achieve goals. Similarly, a high need for affiliation or power can be traced to a history of receiving rewards for sociable, dominant, or inspirational behavior. As a result of the learning process, individuals develop unique configurations of needs that affect their behavior and performance.

McClelland's theory faces a number of criticisms. Not the least of these criticisms is that most of the available evidence supporting the theory has been provided by McClelland or his associates. McClelland's use of projective psychological personality tests has been questioned as being unscientific. Furthermore, McClelland's claim that n Ach can be learned runs counter to a large body of literature that argues the acquisition of motives normally occurs in childhood and is very difficult to alter in adulthood. Finally, McClelland's theory is questioned on grounds of whether the needs are permanently acquired. Research is needed to determine whether acquired needs last.

EXHIBIT 5.6 **A Graphic Comparison of Four Content Approaches to Motivation**

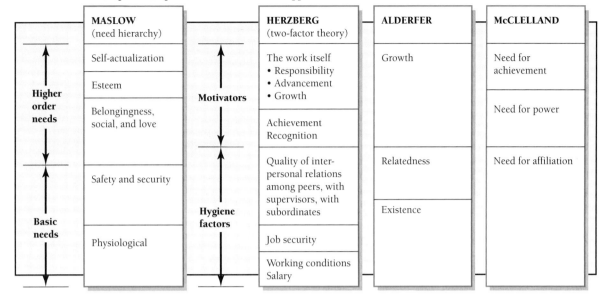

Can something learned in a training-and-development program be sustained on the job? This is an issue that McClelland and others have not been able to clarify.

A Synopsis of the Four Content Theories

Each of the four content theories attempts to explain behavior from a slightly different perspective. None of the theories has been accepted as the sole basis for explaining motivation. Although some critics are skeptical, it appears that people have innate and learned needs and that various job factors result in a degree of satisfaction. Thus, each of the theories provides the manager with some understanding of behavior and performance.

Exhibit 5.6 compares the four approaches. McClelland proposed no lower-order needs. Moreover, his needs for achievement and power aren't identical with Herzberg's motivators, Maslow's higher-order needs, or Alderfer's growth needs, although there are some similarities. A major difference between the four content theories is McClelland's emphasis on socially acquired needs. Also, the Maslow theory offers a static need-hierarchy system; Alderfer presents a flexible, three-need classification approach; and Herzberg discusses intrinsic and extrinsic job factors.

Each of the content approaches purports to present the clearest, most meaningful, and most accurate explanation of motivation. In reality, each has strengths and limitations that practicing managers need to consider; none is clearly inferior or superior to the others, especially in today's diverse workplace. Smart managers will look to all of these approaches to provide insights that can be applied to specific challenges and problems.

Process Approaches

The content theories we have examined focus mainly on the needs and incentives that cause behavior. They are concerned primarily about which specific things motivate people. The process theories of motivation are concerned with answering the questions of how individual behavior is energized, directed, maintained, and stopped. This section examines three process theories: expectancy theory, equity theory, and goal-setting theory. In discussing each of these in the paragraphs that follow, we will show how the motivational process works in organizational settings.

Expectancy Theory

expectancy theory
A theory of motivation that suggests employees are more likely to be motivated when they perceive their efforts will result in successful performance and, ultimately, desired rewards and outcomes.

One of the more popular explanations of motivation was developed by Victor Vroom.[23] Numerous studies have been done to test the accuracy of **expectancy theory** in predicting employee behavior, and direct tests have been generally supportive.[24] In addition, a research study that rated the overall importance, scientific validity, and practical usefulness of 73 organizational behavior theories reported that expectancy theory has high levels of importance, validity, and usefulness.[25] Vroom defines *motivation* as a process governing choices among alternative forms of voluntary activity. In his view, most behaviors are considered to be under the voluntary control of the person and consequently are motivated. To understand expectancy theory, it is necessary to define the terms of the theory and explain how they operate. The four most important terms are: *first-* and *second-level outcomes, instrumentality, valence,* and *expectancy.*

First-Level and Second-Level Outcomes

First-level outcomes resulting from behavior are those associated with doing the job itself and include productivity, absenteeism, turnover, and quality of productivity. The second-level outcomes are those events (rewards or punishments) that the first-level outcomes are likely to produce, such as merit pay increases, group acceptance or rejection, promotion, and termination.

The individual in the expectancy theory approach is saying, "If I work hard, I can accomplish a specific performance level (assuming the person has the ability and skill and that the performance is recognized). Then the individual asks, "If my performance is acknowledged (e.g., managers make comments, performance appraisal rating is high), will it lead to rewards (e.g., recognition, pay, opportunities, time off)?"

Instrumentality

Instrumentality is the perception by an individual that first-level outcomes (performance) are associated with second-level outcomes (rewards). It refers to the strength of a person's belief that attainment of a particular outcome will lead to (be instrumental in) attaining one or more second-level outcomes. Instrumentality can be negative, suggesting that attaining a second-level outcome is less likely if a first-level outcome has occurred, or positive, suggesting that the second-level outcome is more likely if the first-level outcome has been attained.

Valence

Valence refers to the preferences for outcomes as seen by the individual. For example, a person may prefer a 10 percent merit raise over a relocation to a new facility. An outcome is positively valent when it is preferred and negatively valent when it is not preferred or is avoided. An outcome has a valence of zero when the individual is indifferent to attaining or not attaining it. The valence concept applies to both first- and second-level outcomes. Thus, a person may prefer to be a high-performing employee (first-level outcome) because she believes this will lead to a desired merit raise in pay (second-level outcome).

Expectancy

Expectancy refers to the individual's belief regarding the likelihood or subjective probability that a particular behavior will be followed by a particular outcome, and it is most easily thought of as a single-probability statement. That is, it refers to a perceived chance of something occurring because of the behavior. Expectancy can take values ranging from 0, indicating no chance that an outcome will occur after the behavior or act, to +1, indicating perceived certainty that a particular outcome will follow a behavior or act.

In the work setting, individuals hold an effort-performance expectancy. This expectancy represents the individual's perception of how hard it will be to achieve a particular behavior (say, completing the budget on time) and the probability of achieving that behavior. There is also a performance-outcome expectancy. In the individual's mind, every behavior is associated with outcomes (rewards or punishments). For example, an individual may have an expectancy that if the budget is completed on time, he or she will receive a day off next week. Exhibit 5.7 presents the general expectancy model and includes the two expectancy points (E→P and P→O).

Managers also need to implement fair, meaningful, and easy-to-understand performance review and evaluation systems. It is important in applying expectancy theory to be able to recognize and use performance. At Frito-Lay Processing and Packaging Division in Lubbock, Texas, an incentive program has achieved excellent results. Machine operators were involved in reducing the amount of "give-away" in each bag of chips. Frito-Lay strives to maintain .4 grams of give-away in each bag of chips. If too

EXHIBIT 5.7
Expectancy Theory

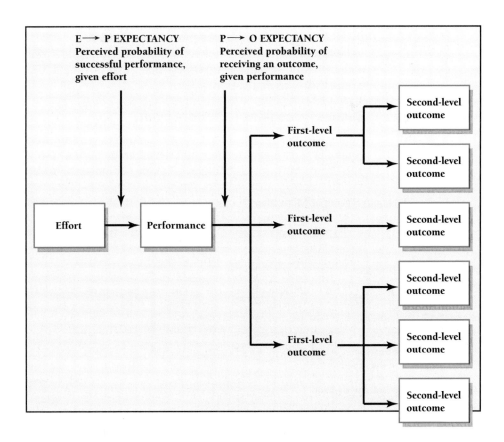

much is given away, profit margins are reduced. The exact weight of each bag is calculated to the gram. The operator's performance can be specifically pinpointed. Each week the operator who is the best in reducing the give-away waste wins a gift certificate. Since the gift certificate prize is one that operators prefer, this type of reward is significant enough for the operators to be fully involved in trying to win the contest and has significantly reduced waste and improved morale among operators.[26]

Equity Theory

equity theory
A theory of motivation that examines how a person might respond to perceived discrepancies between her input/outcome ratio and that of a reference person.

Equity theory explains how people's perceptions of how fairly they are treated in social exchanges at work (e.g., amount of the pay raise this year, how well the supervisor treats them, etc.) can influence their motivation. The essence of *equity* (which also means "fairness") theory is that employees compare their efforts and rewards with those of others in similar work situations. This theory of motivation is based on the assumption that individuals are motivated by a desire to be equitably treated at work. The individual works in exchange for rewards from the organization.

Four important terms in this theory are:

1. *Person.* The individual for whom equity or inequity is perceived.
2. *Comparison other.* Any group or persons used by Person as a referent regarding the ratio of inputs and outcomes.
3. *Inputs.* The individual characteristics brought by Person to the job. These may be achieved (e.g., skills, experience, learning) or ascribed (e.g., age, sex, race).
4. *Outcomes.* What Person received from the job (e.g., recognition, fringe benefits, pay).

Equity exists when employees perceive that the ratios of their inputs (efforts) to their outcomes (rewards) are equivalent to the ratios of other employees. Inequity exists when these ratios are not equivalent; an individual's own ratio of inputs to outcomes could be greater than, or less than, that of others.[27] Exhibit 5.8 illustrates the equity theory of motivation.

Change Procedures to Restore Equity

Equity theory suggests a number of alternative ways to restore a feeling or sense of equity. Let's assume you and your co-worker are both working as sales associates for a popular sporting goods company. You put in longer hours and have more sales than

EXHIBIT 5.8 **The Equity Theory of Motivation**

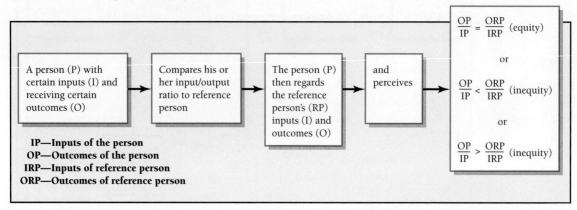

A person (P) with certain inputs (I) and receiving certain outcomes (O) → Compares his or her input/output ratio to reference person → The person (P) then regards the reference person's (RP) inputs (I) and outcomes (O) → and perceives →

$$\frac{OP}{IP} = \frac{ORP}{IRP} \text{ (equity)}$$

or

$$\frac{OP}{IP} < \frac{ORP}{IRP} \text{ (inequity)}$$

or

$$\frac{OP}{IP} > \frac{ORP}{IRP} \text{ (inequity)}$$

IP—Inputs of the person
OP—Outcomes of the person
IRP—Inputs of reference person
ORP—Outcomes of reference person

your colleague. To your shock and surprise, you have just found out that your colleague received a $10,000 raise (compared to your $3,000 raise). Not only do you feel angry and frustrated, but you also feel unfairly treated.

In response to this underrewarded condition, equity theory suggests a number of alternative methods to restore a feeling or sense of equity vis-à-vis your treatment (as compared to that of your colleague). Some examples of restoring equity are:

1. *Changing inputs.* You may decide to put less time or effort into the job.
2. *Changing outcomes.* You may decide to negotiate for a much larger pay raise (e.g., to get at least $10,000 total).
3. *Changing attitudes.* Instead of changing inputs or outcomes, you may simply change your attitude by convincing yourself that the money is less important than other outcomes (e.g., nice place to work, job security, etc.).
4. *Changing the reference person.* In this example, you can change the reference person to someone who received a raise that was similar to the one you received. This might allow you to restore equity by comparing your outcomes/input ratio to someone with a similar ratio.
5. *Changing the inputs or outcomes of the reference person.* Since the original reference person is a co-worker, you might encourage the individual to work longer hours and work harder to justify the larger pay increase (i.e., increase inputs).
6. *Leaving the field.* Due to the frustration and perceived unfairness of the situation, you may decide to simply quit your job.

Research on Equity

Most of the research on equity theory has focused on pay as the basic outcome.[28] The failure to incorporate other relevant outcomes limits the impact of the theory in work situations. A review of the studies also reveals that the reference person is not always clarified. A typical research procedure is to ask a person to compare his or her inputs and outcomes with those of a specific person. In most work situations, an employee selects the reference person after working for some time in the organization. Two issues to consider are whether comparison persons are within the organization and whether reference persons change during a person's work career.

Several individuals have questioned the extent to which inequity that results from overpayment (rewards) leads to perceived inequity. Locke argues that employees seldom are told they are overpaid. He believes that individuals are likely to adjust their idea of what constitutes an equitable payment to justify their pay.[29] Campbell and Pritchard point out that employer–employee exchange relationships are highly impersonal when compared to exchanges between friends.[30] Perceived overpayment inequity may be more likely when friends are involved. Thus, an individual probably will react to overpayment inequity only when that individual believes that his or her actions have led to a friend's being treated unfairly. The individual receives few signals from the organization that he or she is being treated unfairly.

Despite limitations, equity theory provides a relatively insightful model to help explain and predict employee attitudes about pay. The theory also emphasizes the importance of comparisons in the work situation. The identification of reference persons seems to have some potential value when attempting to restructure a reward program. The theory has been shown to be a useful framework for examining the growing number of two-tier wage structures.[31] Equity theory also raises the issue of methods for resolving inequity, which can cause problems with morale, turnover, and absenteeism.

Organizational Justice

In the 1980s and 1990s, equity theory inspired new streams of research to explain employee attitudes and behavior.[32] The concept of **organizational justice,** or the degree to which individuals feel fairly treated at the workplace, attracted a considerable amount of research attention. The four components of this research domain are: distributive, procedural, interpersonal, and informational justice.[33] **Distributive justice** is the perceived fairness of how resources and rewards are distributed throughout an organization. This concept often deals with compensation and is closely related to the previous discussion of equity theory. However, researchers have applied the concept of distributive justice to a wide variety of workplace situations, including organizational politics, university tenure and promotion decisions, antismoking policies, mentoring, teams, and satisfaction with benefit levels.[34]

Related to distributive justice is the notion of procedural justice. **Procedural justice** refers to the perceived equity or fairness of the organization's processes and procedures used to make resource and allocation decisions.[35] That is, employees are concerned with the fairness of decision making in all areas of work, including decisions related to compensation, performance appraisal, training, and work group assignments.

Procedural justice has been shown to have a positive impact on a number of affective and behavioral reactions.[36] These reactions include:

- Organizational commitment.
- Intrinsic motivation.
- Intent to stay with organization.
- Organizational citizenship.
- Trust in supervisor.
- Satisfaction with decision outcome.
- Work effort.
- Task performance.

Positive consequences of procedural justice have been found in important organizational decision contexts, including pay allocation, personnel selection, and performance appraisal. Since procedural justice can provide benefits to organizations, an important issue involves the types of decision-making procedures that people consider to be fair. People are more inclined to interpret decisions to be fair when they have a voice in the decision, there is consistency in decision making, and the process and procedures conform to ethical and moral values.

Two explanations have emerged regarding why procedural justice works. Self-interest theory proposes that people want fair procedures because such fairness enables them to obtain desired extrinsic outcomes. Although a manager may decide not to promote a person, if the process has been fair it will be accepted[37] and the employee will be more likely to remain committed to the organization.[38]

Group value theory suggests that people value fairness as a means of realizing such desired intrinsic outcomes as self-esteem. People have a strong sense of affiliation with groups to which they belong. Fair group procedures are considered to be a sign of respect and an indication that they are valued members of the group. This results in a higher sense of self-esteem.

---

organizational justice
An area of organizational science research that focuses on perceptions and judgments by employees regarding the fairness of their organizations' procedures and decisions.

distributive justice
The perceived fairness of how resources and rewards are distributed throughout an organization. For example, employees make judgments about the fairness of the amount of their pay raises.

procedural justice
The perceived fairness of the processes used by the organization to arrive at decisions such as who receives promotions, how pay raises are established, and how bonus payouts are allocated.

Treating employees and customers fairly, respectfully, and in a timely manner is a worthy managerial approach. First, managers must understand the importance of procedural justice. Second, managers can achieve good performance results when procedural justice is widely practiced for decision making. Finally, employee perceptions are extremely critical in identifying procedural justice. Determining these perceptions requires strong interpersonal and observation skills on the part of managers.[39]

interpersonal justice
Judgments made by employees about the perceived fairness of the treatment received by employees from authorities.

Related to procedural justice is the concept of **interpersonal justice,** which refers to judgments made by employees about whether they feel fairly treated by their supervisors and other authorities in the organization.[40] Perceptions of interpersonal justice are higher when authorities are seen as treating employees in a dignified and respectful manner. However, interpersonal injustice can occur if employees perceive that the authorities treat them in an insulting, embarrassing, humiliating manner in front of others or label the employees as racist or sexist.[41]

Unfortunately, poor treatment by authorities in organizations appears to be a common occurrence. In a random telephone survey of 1,000 working adults in the United States, about 45 percent of respondents reported that they work or have worked for an abusive supervisor.[42] The researchers defined abusive behavior as verbal abuse, intimidation, and threatening gestures. Other researchers analyzed 110 research studies to compare the effects of sexual harassment and workplace bullying on employees.[43] They defined workplace aggression as any behavior that included:

- Persistently criticizing employees' work.
- Yelling.
- Spreading gossip or lies.
- Reminding employees of their mistakes.
- Excluding or ignoring workers.
- Insulting workers' habits, attitudes, or personal lives.

The study found that employees who experienced bullying and incivility at work were more likely to quit their jobs and have lower levels of well-being and job satisfaction. Indeed, research suggests that abusive treatment from authorities and supervisors is associated with lower job and life satisfaction, lower organizational commitment, conflict between work and family, and psychological distress.[44]

informational justice
An area of organizational science research that focuses on the perceived fairness of the communication provided to employees from authorities.

A final form of organizational justice, **informational justice,** focuses on whether employees perceive that decisions and other communication from authorities are explained in a fair manner.[45] When important decisions are being communicated to employees, do authorities take time to explain their decisions in a thorough and reasonable manner? Or, do they send out a brief e-mail or memo that announces major changes without adequate justification? The former approach will build a sense of informational justice among employees whereas the latter approach will erode it. For example, layoffs are a fact of life for many organizations. Unfortunately, evidence shows that companies that engage in layoffs may find that many "survivors" of the layoffs end up voluntarily leaving the company as well. Layoffs, combined with the loss of "good employees," may leave the firm understaffed for when the economy picks up again. What can managers of a company do to lessen the negative impact of layoffs on those employees who survive the personnel cuts? One approach is to overcommunicate and tell the truth when communicating with employees. Managers should keep many channels of communication open and provide information about the organization's financial condition and current/additional layoffs on a frequent basis. Here are some approaches that managers can take to promote high levels of informational justice during turbulent times:[46]

- Informal "chats" by top managers (via e-mail, in person, or by videoconference).
- Don't sugarcoat bad news; employees will sense this and lose confidence in decision makers.
- Establish a human resources hotline or "800" number for employees to call for updates.
- Create a Web page that is updated on a daily basis.

In addition, some CEOs are communicating with their employees via blogs. Bill Marriott, chairman and CEO of Marriott International, has a blog called "On the Move," while Mike Critelli, executive chairman of Pitney Bowes, keeps employees up to date with his blog "Open Mike." These blogs and the other communication channels listed above are meant to convey a sense of trust and inclusiveness while decreasing secrecy and dishonesty when authorities communicate with employees.[47]

In sum, the organizational justice literature suggests that if authorities treat employees in what's perceived to be a fair manner, then employees are more likely to trust their supervisors and organizations.

Goal Setting

goal
A specific target that an individual is trying to achieve; a goal is the target (object) of an action.

Interest in applying goal setting to organizational problems and issues has been growing since Locke presented what is now considered a classic paper in 1968.[48] A **goal** is a result that a person, team, or group is attempting to accomplish through behavior and actions. Locke proposed that goal setting is a cognitive process of some practical utility. His view is that an individual's conscious goals and intentions are the primary determinants of behavior.[49] It has been noted that "one of the commonly observed characteristics of intentional behavior is that it tends to keep going until it reaches completion."[50] That is, once a person starts something (e.g., a job, a new project), he or she pushes on until a goal is achieved. Also, goal-setting theory emphasizes the importance of conscious goals in explaining motivated behavior. Locke has used the notion of intentions and conscious goals to propose and provide research support for the thesis that difficult and specific conscious goals will result in higher levels of performance if these goals are accepted by the individual.[51]

Descriptions of Goal Setting

goal specificity
The degree of quantitative precision of the goal.

goal difficulty
The degree of proficiency or the level of goal performance that is being sought.

goal intensity
The process of setting a goal or of determining how to reach it.

goal commitment
The amount of effort that is actually used to achieve a goal.

Some examples of goal setting at work include: developing a new software program within 4 to 6 months to detect malicious viruses on the Internet; landing five new customers or increasing sales of existing customers by 10 percent over the next 12 months; and decreasing waste in the manufacturing process by 20 percent over the next three years. Setting such goals is a process that includes the attributes or the mental (cognitive) processes of goal setting. The attributes Locke highlights are goal specificity, goal difficulty, and goal intensity.

Goal specificity is the degree of quantitative precision (clarity) of the goal. **Goal difficulty** is the degree of proficiency or the level of performance that is sought. **Goal intensity** pertains to the process of setting the goal or of determining how to reach it. To date, goal intensity has not been widely studied, although a related concept, **goal commitment,** has been considered in a number of studies. Goal commitment is the amount of effort used to achieve a goal.

YOU BE THE JUDGE

THE ETHICAL WAY TO MANAGE?

Employee participation has become an integral feature of quality work life, quality circles, employee stock option plans, and workplace design. When used properly, participative management has been effective in improving performance, productivity, and job satisfaction. Employees—as members of a manager–employee team or as part of a group of co-workers—participate in decision making, goal setting, salary determination, and changing the organization's structure.

Some believe that participative management is an ethical imperative. Their argument is that research clearly demonstrates the effectiveness of participative management because it satisfies a basic human need.

Others argue, however, that job satisfaction is not an employee right and that an organization is not duty-bound to provide it. Is participative management the ethical way to manage? You be the judge.

Sources: Richard L. Daft, "Theory Z: Opening the Corporate Door for Participative Management," *Academy of Management Executive* 8, no. 4 (November 2004), pp. 117–21. The "ethical imperative" idea was introduced by Marshall Saskin, "Participative Management Is an Ethical Imperative," *Organizational Dynamics,* Spring 1984, pp. 5–22, and elaborated on in "Participative Management Remains an Ethical Imperative," *Organizational Dynamics,* Spring 1986, pp. 62–75. Arguments opposing the ethical imperative view can be found in Edwin A. Locke, David M. Schweiger, and Gary Latham, "Participation in Decision Making: When Should It Be Used?" *Organizational Dynamics,* Winter 1986, pp. 65–79.

Exhibit 5.9 presents a model of individual goal setting using available theoretical research, but illustrating a practical framework that managers can apply. The goal-setting model emphasizes that a goal serves as a motivator. It is important for any goal to be clear, meaningful, and challenging. When goals are not accomplished, an individual faces a sense of dissatisfaction. Whether there is a relationship between goals and job performance is moderated by a number of factors, including ability, commitment, and feedback.

A person's ability can limit his or her efforts to accomplish goals. If a manager sets a difficult goal and a person lacks the ability to accomplish it, there will not be accomplishment.

A person who is committed to a goal has a drive, intensity, and persistence to work hard. Commitment creates a desire to reach the goal and overcome problems or barriers.

EXHIBIT 5.9
Goal Setting Applied to Organizations

Source: Modified and based on Edwin A. Locke and Gary P. Locke, *A Theory of Goal Setting and Task Performance* (Englewood Cliffs, NJ: Prentice-Hall, 1990).

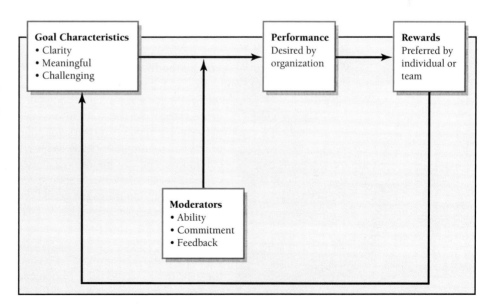

Feedback provides data, information, and facts about progress in goal accomplishment. A person can use feedback to gauge where adjustments in effort need to be made. Without feedback a person operates without guidance or information to make corrections so that goals are accomplished on time and at budgeted levels.

As goals are accomplished and this performance is evaluated, rewards are distributed. If the rewards are preferred, as discussed in expectancy theory, employees are likely to be satisfied and motivated.

Goal-Setting Research

Between 1968 and 2009, the amount of research on goal setting increased considerably. Locke's 1968 paper certainly contributed to the increase in laboratory and field research on goal setting. Another force behind the increase in interest and research was the demand of managers for practical and specific techniques that they could apply in their organizations. Goal setting offered such a technique for some managers, and it thus became an important management tool for enhancing work performance.[52]

Empirical research findings from a variety of managerial and student samples have provided support for the theory that conscious goals regulate behavior. Yet a number of important issues concerning goal setting still must be examined more thoroughly. One area of debate concerns the issue of how much subordinate participation in goal setting is optimal. A field experiment conducted by skilled technicians compared three levels of subordinate participation: full (the subordinates were totally involved); limited (the subordinates made some suggestions about the goals the superior set); and none.[53] Measures of performance and satisfaction were taken over a 12-month period. The groups with full- or limited-participant involvement in goal setting showed significantly more performance and satisfaction improvements than did the group that did not participate in goal setting. Interestingly, these improvements began to dissipate six to nine months after the program was started. Some research, however, has failed to find significant relationships between performance and participation in the goal-setting process.[54] Not surprisingly, the necessity for and effectiveness of participatory management styles in any area of management is a much debated topic. This chapter's You Be the Judge box briefly describes the issue.

Research has found that specific goals lead to higher output than do vague goals such as "do your best." Field experiments using clerical workers, maintenance technicians, marketing personnel, engineers, typists, manufacturing employees, and others have compared specific versus do-your-best goal-setting conditions. The vast majority of these studies support—partly or totally—the hypothesis that specific goals lead to better performance than do vague goals. The Weyerhaeuser Corporation, for example, used specific goals to improve an important aspect of the performance of its logging trucks. Traditionally, logging truckers had been operating under the instruction to "do their best" in terms of judging weight loads for their trucks in the field. Management decided that 94 percent of weight capacity was a difficult, yet attainable, specific

---

Management Pointer

IS GOAL SETTING FOR YOU?

Many successful managers and other successful professionals claim to be goal-setters and believe that it is a key to their success. They continually write down goals and keep track of how they are doing. Is goal setting for you? Here are some questions that, once answered, can be converted into specific goals.

1. Is my knowledge of my job progressing?

2. How developed are my people skills?

3. Have I improved and increased my network of contacts?

4. What other skills should I be working on (e.g., problem solving, managing time, negotiation)?

5. How does this period's performance match up with similar periods of past performance?

6. Out of everything I've done at work in the past three months, of which three things am I the most proud? Least proud?

goal for the drivers. This specific goal worked and became an effective motivator; in less than a full year, the company saved over $250,000.

Certain aspects of goal setting need to be subjected to scientific examination. One such area centers on individual differences and their impact on the success of goal-setting programs. Such factors as personality, career progression, training background, and personal health are important individual differences that should be considered when implementing goal-setting programs. Goal-setting programs also should be subjected to ongoing examination to monitor attitudinal and performance consequences. Some research has demonstrated that goal-setting programs tend to lose their potency over time, so there is a need to discover why this phenomenon occurs in organizations. Sound evaluation programs assist management in identifying success, problems, and needs.

Goal setting can be a very powerful technique for motivating employees. When used correctly, carefully monitored, and actively supported by managers, goal setting can improve performance. However, neither goal setting nor any other technique can be used to correct every problem. Is goal setting for you? The Management Pointer "Is Goal Setting for You?" provides you with some questions to ask and answer.

Motivation and the Psychological Contract

A conceptual framework that provides a useful perspective for viewing the topic of motivation is *exchange theory*.[55] In a very general sense, exchange theory suggests that members of an organization engage in reasonably predictable give-and-take relationships (exchanges) with each other. For example, an employee gives time and effort in exchange for pay; management provides pleasant working conditions in exchange for employee loyalty. Schein suggests that the degree to which employees are willing to exert effort, commit to organizational goals, and derive satisfaction from their work depends on two conditions:[56]

1. The extent to which employee expectations of what the organization will give them and what they owe the organization in return matches the organization's expectations of what it will give and receive.

2. Assuming there is agreement on these expectations, the specific nature of what is exchanged (effort for pay, for example).

psychological contract
An unwritten agreement between an employee and the organization that specifies what each expects to give to and receive from the other.

These mutual expectations regarding exchanges constitute part of the psychological contract.[57] The **psychological contract** is an unwritten agreement between the individual and the organization that specifies what each expects to give to and receive from the other. While some aspects of an employment relationship, such as pay, may be explicitly stated, many others are not. These implicit agreements, which may focus on exchanges involving satisfaction, challenging work, fair treatment, loyalty, and opportunity to be creative, may take precedence over written agreements.

psychological contract breach
Employee perception that the organization has failed to fulfill an unwritten exchange agreement.

In the ideal psychological contract, those contributions the individual was willing to give would correspond perfectly to what the organization wanted to receive; similarly, what the organization wanted to give would correspond totally with what the individual wished to receive. In reality, however, this seldom occurs. Additionally, psychological contracts are not static; either party's expectations can change as can either party's ability or willingness to continue meeting expectations. In more extreme cases, an organization may take actions (e.g., layoffs) that lead employees to perceive that a **psychological contract breach** has occurred. Such a violation in the psychological contract can lead to decreased job satisfaction and citizenship behavior.[58]

When there are few or a decreasing number of matches between what each party expects to give and receive in the contract, work motivation suffers. The psychological contract provides a perspective for why this is true. Looking at motivation from a content theory approach, the psychological contract suggests that in return for time, effort, and other considerations, individuals desire to receive need gratification. Using Maslow's need hierarchy as an example, if an employee is operating at the self-actualization level and fails to receive a challenging job that allows for the application of all the capabilities that employee has, motivation will suffer. In other words, the satisfaction of needs is part of the contract; when the expectation of need satisfaction is not matched with the opportunity to achieve such satisfaction, the contract is violated and motivation is negatively affected.

The perspective on motivation provided by the concept of the psychological contract is not limited to content approaches to motivation, however; it is equally applicable to process explanations as well. Adam's equity theory is, in fact, a form of exchange theory. The notion of inputs and outcomes within equity theory is very similar to expectations of giving and receiving in the psychological contract. In the context of an expectancy approach to motivation, performance-outcome expectancies relate directly to the exchange of performance for pay, advancement, satisfaction, or other outcomes in the psychological contract; likewise, the desire to receive certain considerations in the context of the contract is analogous to positively valent outcomes in expectancy theory.

Managing the psychological contract successfully is one of the more important and challenging aspects of most managers' jobs.[59] The more attuned the manager is to the needs and expectations of subordinates, the greater the number of matches that are likely to exist and be maintained in the psychological contract. This, in turn, can positively impact the direction, intensity, and persistence of motivation in the organization.

Reviewing Motivation

In this chapter, a number of popular theories of motivation are portrayed. The theories typically are pitted against one another in the literature. This is unfortunate, since each approach can help managers better understand workplace motivation. Each approach attempts to organize, in a meaningful manner, major variables associated with explaining motivation in work settings. The content theories are individual-oriented in that they place primary emphasis on the characteristics of people. Each of the process theories has a specific orientation. Expectancy theory places emphasis on individual, job, and environmental variables. It recognizes differences in needs, perceptions, and beliefs. Equity theory primarily addresses the relationship between attitudes toward inputs and outputs and reward practices. Goal-setting theory emphasizes the cognitive processes and the role of intentional behavior in motivation.

This chapter suggests that instead of ignoring motivation, managers must take an active role in motivating their employees. Four specific conclusions are offered here:

1. Managers can influence the motivation state of employees. If performance needs to be improved, then managers must intervene and help create an atmosphere that encourages, supports, and sustains improvement.

2. Managers should be sensitive to variations in employees' needs, abilities, and goals. Managers also must consider differences in preferences (valences) for rewards.

YOU BE THE JUDGE COMMENT

THE ETHICAL WAY TO MANAGE?
The strongest argument for participation is that it's natural for people to want to participate in those matters (e.g., goals for the department, salary increases, etc.) that impact them. When managers and supervisors make decisions without such input, employees often feel frustrated and powerless at the workplace, and in our opinion, this is an ethically undesirable situation. Those who argue against employee participation in decision making point out that decades of research do not indicate that participation leads to improved employee morale and job satisfaction in all situations. In fact, they point out that in many cases authoritative methods lead to similar improvements in productivity. That being said, we still believe that participation is a "net positive" that has many beneficial effects not only for the employees but also for their organizations.

3. Continual monitoring of needs, abilities, goals, and preferences of employees is each individual manager's responsibility and is not the domain of personnel/human resource managers only.

4. Managers need to work on providing employees with jobs that offer task challenge, diversity, and a variety of opportunities for need satisfaction.

In simple terms, the theme of our discussion of motivation is that the *manager needs to be actively involved.* If motivation is to be energized, sustained, and directed, managers must know about needs, intentions, preferences, goals, and comparisons, and they must act on that knowledge. Failure to do so will result in many missed opportunities to help motivate employees in a positive manner.

Summary of Key Points

- Motivation is made up of at least three distinct components. *Direction* refers to what an individual chooses to do when presented with a number of possible alternative courses of action. *Intensity* relates to the strength of the individual's response once the choice (direction) is made. Finally, *persistence* refers to the staying power of behavior, or how long a person will continue to devote effort.

- Maslow's theory of motivation suggests that individuals' needs are arranged in a hierarchical order of importance and that people will attempt to satisfy the more basic (lower-level) needs before directing behavior toward satisfying higher-level needs. Maslow's five need levels, from lowest to highest, are (1) physiological, (2) safety and security, (3) belongingness, social, and love, (4) esteem, and (5) self-actualization.

- Alderfer's ERG theory is a need hierarchy comprised of three sets of needs: *existence, relatedness,* and *growth.* In addition to the satisfaction-progression process Maslow describes, Alderfer suggests that if a person is continually frustrated in trying to satisfy one level of need, he or she may regress to the next lowest level need.

- Herzberg's research suggests that there are two important sets of factors. *Motivators* are intrinsic conditions and include achievement, recognition, and responsibility. *Hygiene factors* are extrinsic conditions and include salary, working conditions, and job security. In Herzberg's view, it is only the motivators that contribute to satisfaction and thus have the power to provide motivation.

- McClelland has developed a descriptive set of factors that reflect a high need for achievement. These are: (1) the person likes to take responsibility for solving problems; (2) the person tends to set moderate achievement goals and is inclined to take calculated risks; and (3) the person desires feedback on performance.

- Key terms in expectancy theory include instrumentality, valence, and expectancy. *Instrumentality* refers to the strength of a person's belief that achieving a specific result or outcome will lead to attaining a secondary outcome. *Valence* refers to a person's preference for attaining or avoiding a particular outcome. *Expectancy* refers to a person's belief regarding the likelihood or subjective probability that a particular behavior will be followed by a particular outcome.

- The essence of equity theory is that employees compare their job inputs and outputs with those of others in similar work situations. *Inputs* are what an individual brings to the job and include skills, experiences, and effort, among others. *Outcomes* are what a person receives from a job and include recognition, pay, fringe benefits, and satisfaction, among others.

- The key steps in applying goal setting are: (1) diagnosis for readiness; (2) preparing employees via increased interpersonal interaction, communication, training, and action plans for goal setting; (3) emphasizing the attributes of goals that should be understood by a manager and subordinates; (4) conducting intermediate reviews to make necessary adjustments in established goals; and (5) performing a final review to check the goals set, modified, and accomplished.

- Employee expectations of what the organization will give them, what they owe the organization, and the organization's expectation of what it will give to and receive from employees constitute the psychological contract. A *psychological contract* is an unwritten agreement between the individual and the organization that specifies what each expects to give to and receive from the other.

Review and Discussion Questions

1. Why is it important for a manager to consider the various components of motivation when diagnosing motivation problems? Is any one of the components more or less important than any of the others? Explain.

2. Which of the content theories discussed in the chapter do you believe offers the best explanation of motivation? Which of the process theories? Overall, do you feel the content approach or the process approach best explains motivation?

3. Motivation is just one of several factors that influence productivity. What other factors were discussed in this chapter? What is the relationship between these factors and motivation?

4. What implications does Herzberg's two-factor theory have for the design of organizational reward systems? How can the theory be used to explain differences in the three components of motivation?

5. Assume you are a global manager responsible for an international subsidiary that has employees from many parts of the world—China, India, Morocco, Brazil, and Spain. How will you go about learning how to motivate these individuals to perform their jobs well? Which of the motivation theories discussed in this chapter can help you to understand their work attitudes and behaviors?

6. As a manager, would you prefer the people for whom you are responsible to be extrinsically or intrinsically motivated? Explain.

7. Think about a challenging work or school project that you have had to undertake. How did you motivate yourself to tackle the project? Were there times when you felt the project was too difficult? Maybe you even wanted to give up? What factors

(internal and external) kept you motivated so that you could successfully complete the project?

8. How important a role does perception play in determining whether an employee is receiving equitable treatment? What kinds of things might a manager do to influence those perceptions?

9. Goal setting can be a difficult system to implement effectively. What kinds of problems might be encountered in attempting to install a goal-setting program in an organization? As a manager, what would you do to minimize the likelihood you would encounter these problems?

10. Is there a psychological contract between the students enrolled in this course and the instructor? What are some of the specifics of this contract? How was the contract determined?

Exercise

Exercise 5.1: *Goal Setting—How to Do It*

Each person is to work alone for at least 30 minutes with this exercise. After sufficient time has elapsed for each person to work through the exercise, the instructor will go over each goal and ask for comments from the class or group. The discussion should display the understanding of goals that each participant has and what will be needed to improve his or her goal-writing skills.

Writing and evaluating goals seem simple, but they are often not done well in organizations. The press of time, previous habits, and little concern about the attributes of a goal statement are reasons goals are often poorly constructed. Actually, a number of guidelines should be followed in preparing goals.

1. A well-presented goal statement contains four elements:
   a. An action or accomplishment verb.
   b. A single and measurable result.
   c. A date of completion.
   d. A cost in terms of effort, resources, or money, or some combination of these factors.
2. A well-presented goal statement is short; it is not a paragraph, but should be presented in a sentence.
3. A well-presented goal statement specifies only what and when and doesn't get into how or why.
4. A well-presented goal statement is challenging and attainable. It should cause the person to stretch his or her skills, abilities, and efforts.

5. A well-presented goal statement is meaningful and important. It should be a priority item.
6. A well-presented goal statement must be acceptable to you so that you will try hard to accomplish the goal. The goal statement model should be:

To (action or accomplishment verb) (single result) by (a date—keep it realistic) at (effort, use of what resource, cost).

An example for a production operation:

To reduce the production cost per unit of mint toothpaste by at least 3 percent by March 1, at a changeover of equipment expense not to exceed $45,000.

Examine the next four statements that are presented as goal statements. Below each goal, write a critique of the statement. Is it a good goal statement? Why? Discuss your viewpoints in the class group discussion.

1. To reduce my blood pressure to an acceptable level.
2. To make financial investments with a guaranteed minimum return of at least 16 percent.
3. To spend a minimum of 45 minutes a day on a doctor-approved exercise plan, starting Monday, lasting for six months, at no expense.
4. To spend more time reading nonwork-related novels and books during the next year.

Now how much do you know about motivation?

6. _____ motivational theories describe, explain, and analyze how behavior is energized, directed, sustained, and stopped.
   a. Current
   b. Process
   c. Developmental
   d. Content

7. True or false: According to Maslow, "safety and security" needs are higher in the need hierarchy than "esteem" needs.
   a. True
   b. False

8. _____ is an area of organizational science research that focuses on the perceived fairness of the communication provided to employees from authorities.
   a. Procedural justice
   b. Informational justice
   c. Interpersonal justice
   d. None of these (a–c) are correct.

9. True or false: McClelland's learned needs theory states that motivation is closely linked to learning concepts, and the three learned needs that individuals can possess are the need for achievement, affiliation, and power.
   a. True
   b. False

10. According to equity theory, if an employee feels that she or he is not being treated fairly (e.g., paid less than a co-worker who does not perform well), then this person will try to restore equity by _____.
   a. sabotaging the work of the co-worker who receives a higher salary
   b. changing outcomes (e.g., asking the supervisor for a pay raise)
   c. changing inputs (e.g., putting less time in at work)
   d. Both b and c are correct.

REALITY CHECK ANSWERS

Before	After
1. b 2. a 3. b 4. c 5. d	6. b 7. b 8. b 9. a 10. d
Number Correct	Number Correct
_____	_____

Case 5.1: *Comparing Co-Workers against Each Other: Does This Motivate Employees?*

Rigid rankings hinder the teamwork and risk-taking necessary for innovation. But what combination of methods works best?

Holiday shopping, year-end deadlines, and emotional family dramas aren't the only stresses in December. 'Tis the season for companies to embark on that dreaded annual rite, the often bureaucratic and always time-consuming performance review. The process can be brutal: As many as one-third of U.S. corporations evaluate employees based on systems that pit them against their colleagues, and some even lead to the firing of low performers.

Fans say such "forced ranking" systems ensure that managers take a cold look at performance. But the practice increasingly is coming under fire. Following a string of discrimination lawsuits from employees who believe they were ranked and yanked based on age and not merely their performance, fewer companies are adopting the controversial management tool. Critics charge that it unfairly penalizes groups made up of stars and hinders collaboration and risk-taking, a growing concern for companies that are trying to innovate their way to growth. And a new study calls into question the long-term value of forced rankings. "It creates a zero-sum game, and so it tends to discourage cooperation," says Steve Kerr, a managing director at Goldman Sachs Group Inc., who heads the firm's leadership training program.

Even General Electric Co., the most famous proponent of the practice, is trying to inject more flexibility into its system. Former Chief Executive Jack Welch required managers to divide talent into three groups—a top 20 percent, a middle 70 percent, and a bottom 10 percent, many of whom were shown the door. More than a year ago, GE launched a proactive campaign to remind managers to use more common sense in assigning rankings. "People in some locations take [distributions] so literally that judgment comes out of the practice," says Susan P. Peters, GE's vice president for executive development.

Striking that balance between strict yardsticks and managerial judgment is something every company, from GE to Yahoo! to American Airlines, is grappling with today. But finding a substitute for a rigid grading system is not an easy task. It drives truth into a process frequently eroded by grade inflation and helps leaders identify managers who are good at finding top talent.

That's one reason GE isn't abandoning its system. But it has removed all references to the 20/70/10 split from its online performance management tool and now presents the curve as a set of guidelines. The company's 200,000 professional employees tend to fall into Welch's categories anyway, but individual groups are freer to have a somewhat higher number of "A" players or even, says Peters, no "bottom 10s." Even those low achievers are getting kinder treatment, from a new appellation—the "less effectives"—to more specific coaching and intervention than in the past.

The changes are key for a company trying to evolve its culture from a Six Sigma powerhouse to one that also values innovation. Tempering such rigid performance metrics, says Peters, "enables individuals and organizations to be more comfortable with risk-taking and with failure." To drive that point home, the company's top 5,000 managers were evaluated for the first time this year on five traits, such as imagination and external focus, that represent the company's strategic goals.

Separating stars from slackers remains a long-standing part of GE's performance-driven culture. But for most companies, especially those without such cultures, the benefits of adopting a forced ranking system are likely to dissipate over the long term.

A recent study lends hard data to that theory. Steve Scullen, an associate professor of management at Drake University in Des Moines, Iowa, found that forced ranking, including the firing of the bottom 5 percent or 10 percent, results in an impressive 16 percent productivity improvement—but only over the first couple of years. After that, Scullen says, the gains drop off, from 6 percent climbs in the third and fourth years to basically zero by year 10. "It's a terrific idea for companies in trouble, done over one or two years, but to do it as a long-term solution is not going to work," says Dave Ulrich, a business professor at the University of Michigan at Ann Arbor. "Over time it gets people focused on competing with each other rather than collaborating."

Yahoo!, too, was looking for better dialogue and less demoralizing labels when it substantially changed its rating system, which compared employees' performance to an absolute standard rather than to each other. Libby Sartain, Yahoo!'s senior vice president for human resources, knew that review discussions at the Sunnyvale, California, tech leader frequently included the wink-wink "I wanted to put you here, but I was forced by human resources to do something different" comment that discredits so many appraisals. Yahoo! stripped away its performance labels, partly in hopes that reviews would center more on substance and less on explaining away a grade.

But that doesn't mean Yahoo! went all Pollyanna on its employees. To do a better job of finding and showering top performers with the rewards necessary to keep them from jumping ship in talent-tight Silicon Valley, the company also instituted a "stack-ranking" system to determine how compensation increases are distributed. It asks managers to rank employees within each unit—a group of 20 people would be ranked 1 through 20, for example—with raises and bonuses distributed accordingly. During reviews, employees are told how their increases generally compare to those of others.

Some Yahoo! managers are livid about the new system. "It's going to kill morale," laments one senior engineering manager who says he's getting a stronger message to cull his bottom performers. Yahoo! says its new program doesn't automatically weed out a bottom group and was designed specifically to reward its stars.

Indeed, what Yahoo! has introduced in place of its old system shows how hard it is for companies to find ways to foster merit-driven cultures that coddle standouts while staying tough on low performers. Whether a company calls it stack ranking, forced ranking, or differentiation, "there's no magic process," says Sartain. "We just want to make sure we're making our bets and that we're investing in the people we most want to keep. That's what this is all about."

Best-Practice Ideas

Review season is here, with all the time-consuming bureaucracy and stress that come with it. Here are five ideas to help put performance back into the process:

Meet More Often

Time-strapped managers may sound a collective groan, but year-end reviews on their own are hardly enough. The best managers meet at least three times a year, if not four—once to set goals, once or twice for an update, and finally, to review—with many informal check-ins in between. In this quickly shifting economy, goals may change, and fewer surprises will surface at year-end.

Make Room for Risk

As innovation trumps efficiency, some companies—including GE—are putting some wiggle room into their rankings and ratings. But more flexible guidelines have to have teeth, too: Low-performing units shouldn't get more than their share of top grades, for example. Exceptions should go to people who set aggressive goals and come close to achieving them.

Adjust Goals along with Grades

While many companies use "calibration" sessions to check that performance assessments level out among different managers, less than 10 percent fine-tune up-front goals across groups, according to Hewitt Associates.

Choose Words Wisely

Whether or not you strip the labels off your performance reviews entirely, as Yahoo! has, faint-praise terms such as "fully satisfies" make essential B-players feel like also-rans. Try "strong" or "successful" to drive home their value.

Build Trust

With so much focus on the tools and tricks of performance management, it's easy to lose sight of what really matters: the conversation. The University of Michigan's Dave Ulrich suggests putting three simple words—"help me understand"—in front of difficult feedback.

Questions

1. What's your opinion regarding forced ranking performance appraisals? Do they motivate employees? Explain.
2. How would equity theory explain some employees' negative reactions to forced rankings? Explain.
3. Based on Chapter 5, if you decided not to use forced rankings at your company, how would you motivate employees?

Source: Adapted from Sarah Boehle, "Keep Forced Ranking Out of Court," *Training* 45, no. 5 (June 2008), pp. 44–46; Paul Falcone, "Big-Picture Performance Appraisal," *HR Magazine* 52, no. 8 (August 2007), pp. 99–100; and Jena McGregor, "The Struggle to Measure Performance," *BusinessWeek*, January 9, 2006, pp. 26–27.

CHAPTER SIX

Job Design, Work, and Motivation

Learning Objectives

After completing Chapter 6, you should be able to:

- **Describe** the relationship between job design and quality of work life.
- **Identify** the key elements linking job design and performance.
- **Define** the term *job analysis.*
- **Compare** the job design concepts of range and depth.

- **Describe** what is meant by perceived job content.
- **Identify** the different types of job performance outcomes.
- **Compare** job rotation with job enlargement.
- **Discuss** several approaches to job enrichment.

Earlier chapters have shown that a multitude of factors may affect job performance: Skills and abilities, perceptions, attitudes, and personality characteristics are all examples of previously discussed individual differences that play a role in shaping performance. Additionally, the direction, intensity, and persistence of an individual's motivation play a critical role, as does the evaluation and reward system that is used. In this chapter we will examine another critical variable: job design.

The jobs that people perform in organizations are the building blocks of all organization structures. The phrase *Let's get organized!* usually means that we need to clarify what job each individual should be doing. But we are also interested in understanding the causes of effective and ineffective job performance.

A major cause of effective job performance is job design, which refers to the process by which managers decide what job tasks and how much authority each employee will have. Apart from the very practical issues associated with job design (that is, issues that relate to effectiveness in economic, political, and monetary terms), we can appreciate its importance in social and psychological terms. Jobs can be sources of psychological stress and even mental and physical impairment. On a more positive note, jobs can provide income, meaningful life experiences, self-esteem, esteem from others, regulation of our lives, and association with others. Thus, the well-being of organizations and people relates to how well management designs jobs.

This chapter describes some of the many theories and practices that deal with job design and redesign. We must understand the implication of the term *job redesign* in the context of our discussion. It means that management has decided it's worthwhile to reconsider what employees are expected to do on the job. In some instances, the redesign effort may be nothing more than requiring the individual to use a smart phone rather than a desk phone to answer customer service inquiries. In other instances, the redesign effort may require the individual to work with other employees in a team effort rather than to work alone on the task. The contemporary trend in organizations is to redesign jobs that require individuals to work together in groups. In some instances, these are virtual groups whose members are located in different parts of the country and world. Whether Americans can work effectively in groups is the controversial issue.

job design
The process by which managers decide individual job tasks and authority.

In contrast to job redesign, **job design** refers to the first instance in which management creates a job by specifying its duties and responsibilities. But with the passage of time and the development of new tools and processes, management's expectations for that job will change (i.e., it will be redesigned). We should understand job design to be an ongoing, dynamic process. *Thus, we will use the term job design to refer to any and all managerial efforts to create jobs whether initially or subsequently.*

We begin the discussion of job design by introducing the issue of quality of work life. As is apparent to anyone who has ever worked, what we do on the job plays a major role in our social, health, and psychological statuses as well as our economic standing. After introducing the relationships between job design and quality of work life, we'll address the more technical aspects of job design.

Job Design and Quality of Work Life

quality of work life
Management philosophy and practice that enhance employee dignity, introduce cultural change, and provide opportunities for growth and development.

The concept of **quality of work life** (QWL) is widely used to refer to "a philosophy of management that enhances the dignity of all workers; introduces changes in an organization's culture; and improves the physical and emotional well-being of employees (e.g., providing opportunities for growth and development)."[1] Indicators of quality of work life include accident rates, sick leave usage, employee turnover, stress, and number of grievances filed.[2] In some organizations, QWL programs are intended to increase employee trust, involvement, and problem solving so as to increase both worker satisfaction and organizational effectiveness.[3] Thus, the concept and application of QWL are broad and involve more than jobs, but the jobs that people do are important sources of satisfaction. It is not surprising to find that the quality of work life concept embodies theories and ideas of the human relations movement of the 1950s and the job enrichment efforts of the '60s and '70s. It also has been partially responsible for inspiring research and interest in work–family conflict issues in the 1980s to today.[4]

The continuing challenge to management is to provide for quality of work life and to improve production, quality, and efficiency through revitalization of business and industry. At present, the trade-offs between the gains in human terms from improved quality of work life and the gains in economic terms from revitalization aren't fully known. Some believe that we must defer quality of work life efforts so as to make the American economy more productive and efficient.[5] Others observe that the sense of urgency to become more competitive in domestic and global trade presents opportunities to combine quality of life and reindustrialization efforts.[6] To those ends, job design can play a vital role.

Job design attempts (1) to identify the most important needs of employees and the organization and (2) to remove obstacles in the workplace that frustrate those needs. Managers hope that the results are jobs that fulfill important individual needs and contribute to individual, group, and organizational effectiveness. Managers are, in fact, designing jobs for teams and groups. Some studies have reported that employees who participate in teams get greater satisfaction from their jobs.[7] But other studies report contrary results.[8] So we're left with the uncomfortable, but realistic, conclusion that quality of work life improvements through job design cannot be ensured in specific instances. Obviously, designing jobs is complex. This chapter reviews the important theories, research, and practices of job design. As will be seen, contemporary management has at its disposal a wide range of techniques that facilitate the achievement of personal and organizational performance.

A Conceptual Model of Job Design

The conceptual model in Exhibit 6.1 is based upon extensive research and practical experience. The model includes the various terms and concepts appearing in the current literature. When linked together, these concepts describe the important determinants of job performance and organizational effectiveness. The model takes into account a number of sources of complexity. It recognizes that individuals react differently to jobs. While one person may derive positive satisfaction from a job, another may not. It also recognizes the difficult trade-offs between organizational and individual needs. For example, the technology of manufacturing (an environmental difference) may dictate that management adopt assembly-line mass production methods and low-skilled jobs to achieve optimal efficiency. Such jobs, however, may result in

EXHIBIT 6.1
Job Design and Job Performance

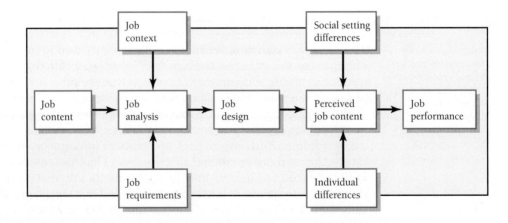

great unrest and worker discontent. Perhaps these costs could be avoided by carefully balancing organizational and individual needs.

The ideas reflected in Exhibit 6.1 are the bases for this chapter. We'll present each important cause or effect of job design, beginning with the end result of job design, *job performance.*

Job Performance Outcomes

Job performance includes a number of outcomes. In this section we'll discuss performance outcomes that have value to the organization and to the individual.

Objective Outcomes

Quantity and quality of output, absenteeism, tardiness, and turnover are objective outcomes that can be measured in quantitative terms. For each job, implicit or explicit standards exist for each of these objective outcomes. Industrial engineering studies establish standards for daily quantity, and quality control specialists establish tolerance limits for acceptable quality. These aspects of job performance account for characteristics of the product, client, or service for which the jobholder is responsible. But job performance includes other outcomes.

Personal Behavior Outcomes

The jobholder reacts to the work itself. She reacts by either attending regularly or being absent, by staying with the job or by quitting. Moreover, physiological and health-related problems can ensue as a consequence of job performance. Stress related to job performance can contribute to physical and mental impairment; accidents and occupation-related disease can also result.

Intrinsic and Extrinsic Outcomes

Job outcomes include intrinsic and extrinsic work outcomes. The distinction between intrinsic and extrinsic outcomes is important for understanding people's reactions to their jobs. In a general sense, an intrinsic outcome is an object or event that follows from the worker's own efforts and doesn't require the involvement of any other person. More simply, it's an outcome clearly related to action on the worker's part. Contemporary job design theory defines *intrinsic motivation* in terms of the employee's "empowerment" to achieve outcomes from the application of individual ability and talent.[9] Such outcomes typically are thought to be solely in the province of professional and technical jobs; yet all jobs potentially have opportunities for intrinsic outcomes. Such outcomes involve feelings of responsibility, challenge, and recognition; they result from such job characteristics as variety, autonomy, identity, and significance.[10] The Global OB on page 156 highlights the desire of many employees to have significant jobs that allow them to make a difference in other people's lives.

Extrinsic outcomes, however, are objects or events that follow from the workers' own efforts in conjunction with other factors or persons not directly involved in the job itself. Pay, working conditions, co-workers, and even supervision are objects in the workplace that are potentially job outcomes, but that aren't a fundamental part of the work. Dealing with others and friendship interactions are sources of extrinsic outcomes.

Most jobs provide opportunities for both intrinsic and extrinsic outcomes, so we must understand the relationship between the two. It's generally held that extrinsic rewards reinforce intrinsic rewards in a positive direction when the individual can attribute the source of the extrinsic reward to her own efforts. For example, a pay raise (extrinsic reward) increases feeling good about oneself if the cause of the raise is thought to be one's own efforts and competence and not favoritism by the boss. This line of reasoning explains why some individuals get no satisfaction out of sharing in the gains derived from group effort rather than individual effort.[11]

Job Satisfaction Outcomes

job satisfaction
An attitude that workers have about their jobs. It results from their perception of the jobs.

Job satisfaction depends on the levels of intrinsic and extrinsic outcomes and how the jobholder views those outcomes. These outcomes have different values for different people. For some people, responsible and challenging work may have neutral or even negative value depending upon their education and prior experience with work providing intrinsic outcomes.[12] For other people, such work outcomes may have high positive values. People differ in the importance they attach to job outcomes. Those differences alone would account for different levels of job satisfaction for essentially the same job tasks. For example, one company that has initiated management systems intended to provide employees with a great deal of opportunity for exercising judgment and making decisions has found many individuals unable or unwilling to work for it. The company, W. L. Gore & Associates, has been the subject of considerable interest among those who advocate employee empowerment.[13] W. L. Gore encourages employees to spend "dabble time" on projects that they believe are interesting and promising. Employees name their own project leaders, who then go through a review process to determine which new projects receive funding. This employee-driven approach led recently to the development of a high-tech guitar string (using the same polymer from Gore-Tex fabric); this string is outselling the competitive brand by two to one.[14]

Other important individual differences include job involvement and commitment to the organization.[15] People differ in the extent to which (1) work is a central life interest, (2) they actively participate in work, (3) they perceive work as central to self-esteem, and (4) they perceive work as consistent with self-concept. Persons who are not involved in their work or the organizations that employ them cannot be expected to realize the same satisfaction as those who are. This variable accounts for the fact that two workers could report different levels of satisfaction for the same performance levels.

A final individual difference is the perceived equity of the outcome in terms of what the jobholder considers a fair reward.[16] If outcomes are perceived to be unfair in relation to those of others in similar jobs requiring similar effort, the jobholder will experience dissatisfaction and seek means to restore the equity, either by seeking greater rewards (primarily extrinsic) or by reducing effort.

Thus, we see that job performance includes many potential outcomes. Some are of primary value to the organization—the objective outcomes, for example. Other outcomes (such as job satisfaction) are of primary importance to the individual. Job performance is a complex variable that depends upon the interplay of numerous factors. Managers can make some sense of the issue by understanding the motivational implications of jobs through the application of job analysis.[17]

Job Analysis

job analysis
The description of how one job differs from another in terms of the demands, activities, and skills required.

The purpose of **job analysis** is to provide an objective description of the job itself.[18] The result of a job analysis is a job description. Individuals who perform job analysis gather information about three aspects of all jobs: job content, job requirements, and job context. A major source of information about job content can be found on the O*NET, a comprehensive and flexible, Internet-accessible database created by the U.S. Department of Labor, that describes occupations.[19] Many different job analysis methods help managers accomplish this task. One study suggests that these methods can be classified into four categories (mechanistic, motivational, biological, and perceptual-motor) depending upon the primary focus and intent.[20] Here we'll be concerned only with understanding the three general aspects of all jobs.[21]

Job Content

job content
The factors that define the general nature of a job.

functional job analysis
A method of job analysis that focuses attention on the worker's specific job activities, methods, machines, and output. The method is used widely to analyze and classify jobs.

Job content refers to the activities required of the job. Depending upon the specific job analysis used, this description can be broad or narrow in scope. The description can vary from general statements of job activities down to highly detailed statements of each and every hand and body motion required to do the job. One widely used method, **functional job analysis (FJA)**, describes jobs in terms of:

1. What the worker does in relation to data, people, and jobs.
2. What methods and techniques the worker uses.
3. What machines, tools, and equipment the worker uses.
4. What materials, products, subject matter, or services the worker produces.

The first three aspects relate to job activities. The fourth aspect relates to job performance. FJA provides descriptions of jobs that can be the bases for classifying jobs according to any one of the four dimensions. In addition to defining what activities, methods, and machines make up the job, FJA also defines what the individual doing the job should produce. FJA can, therefore, be the basis for defining standards of performance. Research on this popular and widely used job analysis method suggests it is a valid approach to analyzing jobs.[22]

Job Requirements

Job requirements refer to education, experience, licenses, and other personal characteristics that are expected of an individual if he's to perform the job content. In recent years, the idea has emerged that job requirements should also identify skills,

position analysis questionnaire (PAQ)
A method of job analysis that takes into account the human, task, and technological factors of jobs and job classes.

job context
The physical environment and other working conditions, along with other factors considered to be intrinsic to a job.

abilities, knowledge, and other personal characteristics required to perform the job content in the particular setting. One widely used method, **position analysis questionnaire (PAQ),** takes into account these human factors through analysis of the following job aspects:

1. Information sources critical to job performance.
2. Information processing and decision making critical to job performance.
3. Physical activity and dexterity required by the job.
4. Interpersonal relationships required by the job.
5. Reactions of individuals to working conditions.[23]

The position analysis questionnaire can be adapted to jobs of all types, including managerial jobs.[24]

Management Pointer

ADVICE ON WHAT MANAGERS SHOULD DO FROM F.W. TAYLOR

F.W. Taylor stated that managers should undertake specific activities if they were to be effective. In fact, he noted four distinct principles they should adopt as follows:

First: Develop a science for each element of a man's work that replaces the old rule-of-thumb method (current application: perform a job analysis).

Second: Scientifically select and then train, teach, and develop the workman, whereas in the past he chose his own work and trained himself as best he could (current application: use valid selection and training methods).

Third: Heartily cooperate with the men so as to ensure that all of the work is done in accordance with the principles of the science that has been developed (current application: support and guide subordinates).

Fourth: There is almost an equal division of the work and the responsibility between management and workmen. Management takes over all work for which it's better fitted than workmen, while in the past, almost all of the work and the greater part of the responsibility were thrown upon workmen (current application: managers should manage).

These four principles express the theme of scientific management methods. Management should take into account task and technology to determine the best way for each job to be performed and then train people to do the job that way.

Job Context

Job context refers to factors such as the physical demands and working conditions of the job, the degree of accountability and responsibility, the extent of supervision required or exercised, and the consequences of error. Job context describes the environment within which the job is to be performed.

Numerous methods exist to perform job analysis. Different methods can give different answers to important questions such as, "How much is the job worth?"[25] Thus, selecting the method for performing job analysis isn't trivial—it's one of the most important decisions in job design.[26] Surveys of expert job analysts' opinions bear out the popularity of PAQ and FJA.[27]

Job Analysis in Different Settings

People perform their jobs in a variety of settings—too many to discuss them all. We'll instead discuss two significant job settings: the factory and the office. One has historical significance; the other has future significance.

Jobs in the Factory

Job analysis began in the factory. Industrialization created the setting in which individuals perform many hundreds of specialized jobs. The earliest attempts to do job analysis followed the ideas advanced by the proponents of scientific management. They were industrial engineers who, at the turn of the 20th century, began to devise ways to analyze industrial jobs. The major theme of scientific management is that objective analyses of facts and data collected in the workplace can provide the bases for determining the one best way to design work.[28] Even though Taylor was writing almost 100 years ago, his advice to managers still has considerable validity as noted in the Management Pointer.[29]

Scientific management produced many techniques in current use. Motion and time study, work simplification, and standard methods are at the core of job analysis in factory

MAKING A PROSOCIAL DIFFERENCE: IS IT MOTIVATIONAL?

Most would agree that firefighters, teachers, and doctors make a difference in the lives of others. What about managers and employees who work for businesses such as social networking Web sites, multinational banks, and global clothing manufacturers: Do they make a difference, too? Do they want to make a difference? Research suggests that many people want their efforts at work to make a positive difference in other people's lives. For example, managers often feel good about "protecting" their subordinates from unfair decisions (e.g., layoffs) made by higher-level administrators in the organization. In essence, these managers engage in prosocial behavior by helping others. Another example would be if an employee goes "beyond the call of duty" to help a customer. A retail sales associate, instead of pushing a customer to purchase a suit at full price, whispers to the customer that she heard the suit will be on sale during the following week. The sales associate learned that the customer has just graduated from college and doesn't have a job yet (and needs a suit for interviews). The salesperson feels like she "did the right thing" and helped out a customer who may not be able to afford the suit at full price.

How can jobs be designed so employees can help others? Jobs need to have task significance (or the amount an individual's work impacts the health and well-being of others) built into them. Research suggests task significance has a positive impact on job performance. In other words, employees who believe their work helps others are more likely to do their job well. Also, this relationship is stronger for employees with high levels of intrinsic motivation.

What can employees do to increase their motivation at work? They can think about their jobs from the perspective of "Who do I help by doing my job well?" By linking their work to the welfare of others—other employees, customers, their supervisor, and so on—employees are more likely to feel that they're making a difference in the lives of others. This prosocial behavior can help increase the employee's motivation and job performance.

Sources: Adapted from Adam M. Grant, "Does Intrinsic Motivation Fuel the Prosocial Fire? Motivational Synergy in Predicting Persistence, Performance, and Productivity," *Journal of Applied Psychology* 93, no. 1 (2008), p. 48; Adam M. Grant, "The Significance of Task Significance: Job Performance Effects, Relational Mechanisms, and Boundary Conditions," *Journal of Applied Psychology* 93, no. 1 (2008), p. 108; and Adam M. Grant, "Relational Job Design and the Motivation to Make a Prosocial Difference," *The Academy of Management Review* 32, no. 2 (2007), pp. 393–417.

settings. Although the mechanistic approach to job analysis is widespread, many service organizations as well as manufacturers are discovering some of the negative consequences of jobs that are overly routine.[30]

Consequently, many organizations are turning away from the idea of one person doing one specialized job. As we'll learn later in the chapter, many manufacturing firms now analyze jobs to determine the extent to which content and requirements can be increased to tap a larger portion of the individual's talents and abilities.

Jobs in the Service Economy

In the short space of time since the advent of scientific management, the American economy has shifted from being factory-oriented to being dominated by services and knowledge management. This new economy is characterized by rapidly changing business and employment conditions, often brought about by intense pressure from domestic and global competitors; cost containment; downsizing; and technological breakthroughs. Breakthroughs in automation, robotics, and computer-assisted manufacturing, coupled with U.S. companies' increased use of offshore manufacturing in countries with lower labor costs, have reduced the overall number of manufacturing jobs in the United States. Evidence of this shift from a manufacturing to service economy can be found in analyses conducted by the U.S. Bureau of Labor Statistics, which report that over a 20-year period (1996–2016), approximately 1.6 million manufacturing jobs in the United States will be lost. In contrast, more than 33.2 million jobs in service and professional areas are expected to be created during that same 20-year period.[31] The following service sectors are poised for above-average employment growth through 2016: professional and business services, health care and social assistance, leisure and hospitality, state and local government, and financial services.

What are the high growth jobs? According to the Bureau of Labor Statistics, the fastest-growing occupations (i.e., "hot jobs") between 2006 and 2016 include:[32]

- Five of the top 20 jobs are in health care (registered nurses, home care aides, home health aides, child care, and nursing aides/orderlies/attendants).

- Eight of the top 20 jobs are in business service (retail sales, customer service representatives, food preparation and service, waiting tables, office clerks, bookkeeping/accounting/auditing clerks, executive/administrative assistants, and receptionists).

- Two of the top 20 jobs are in education (college/university professors and elementary school teachers).

- Two of the top 20 jobs are professional jobs—computer software engineers (applications) and accountants/auditors.

- The remaining three of the top 20 jobs include janitors and cleaners, landscaping, and truck drivers.

In recent times, managers and researchers have found that human factors must be given special attention when analyzing jobs in the electronic office. PC users report that they suffer visual and postural problems such as headaches, burning eyes, and shoulder and backaches.[33] In particular, many intensive PC users (e.g., programmers, data entry clerks, etc.) are vulnerable to repetitive stress injuries that occur over time and affect the arms, shoulders, and back. Such cumulative trauma disorders can be the cause of costly medical bills, absenteeism, and decreased productivity.[34] The sources of these problems seem to be in the design of the workplace, particularly the interaction between the individual and the PC.

Job analysis in the office environment must pay particular attention to human factors. The tendency is to overemphasize the technological factor—in this case, the computer—and to analyze jobs only as extensions of the technology. As was true of job analysis in factories, it's simply easier to deal with the relatively fixed nature of tasks and technology than to deal with the variable of human nature.[35]

In the new economy, the reliance on job analysis and specific job descriptions may be altered significantly. Today an emphasis on speed, creativity, information processing, and the influence of computer technology has resulted in criticisms of passive job descriptions or broadly stated descriptions of what a person or team is expected to do to service customers, contribute to the firm's profit, and gain market share. In the new economy, knowledge workers will be expected to do what is needed. Adhering to a narrow job description is not going to be sufficient in a world pressed by constant change.[36]

William Bridges, author of *Job Shift,* described a shift from narrow job classifications and descriptions to a work environment in which "work" is emphasized.[37] He believes that a continuum exists, with work at one end that needs clear job descriptions (e.g., nuclear power plant technician). This type of work specifies a need to be crystal clear. On the other end of the continuum are whole industries (e.g., software, dot-com, consulting) in which job descriptions are stifling and irrelevant. Work gets done in cross-functional and/or virtual teams or parts of it are outsourced. The word *job* is too narrow.[38] Many industries in which technology is rendering place and time less important are moving away from "job" identities to "work," "project," or "team" entities.

Job Designs: The Results of Job Analysis

Job designs are the results of job analysis. They specify three characteristics of jobs: range, depth, and relationships.

Range and Depth

job range
The number of operations that a job occupant performs to complete a task.

job depth
The amount of control that an individual has to alter or influence the job and the surrounding environment.

Job range refers to the number of tasks a jobholder performs. The individual who performs eight tasks to complete a job has a wider job range than a person performing four tasks. In most instances, the greater the number of tasks performed, the longer it takes to complete the job.

A second characteristic is **job depth,** the amount of discretion an individual has to decide job activities and job outcomes. In many instances, job depth relates to personal influence as well as delegated authority. Thus, an employee with the same job title who's at the same organizational level as another employee may possess more, less, or the same amount of job depth because of personal influence.

Job range and depth distinguish one job from another not only within the same organization, but also among different organizations. To illustrate how jobs differ in range and depth, Exhibit 6.2 depicts the differences for selected jobs of firms, hospitals, and universities. For example, business research scientists, hospital chiefs of surgery, and university presidents generally have high job range and significant depth. Research scientists perform a large number of tasks and are usually not closely supervised. Chiefs of surgery have significant job range in that they oversee and counsel on many diverse surgical matters. In addition, they aren't supervised closely and they have the authority to influence hospital surgery policies and procedures.

University presidents have a large number of tasks to perform. They speak to alumni groups, politicians, community representatives, and students. They develop, with the consultation of others, policies on admissions, fund-raising, and adult education. They can alter the faculty recruitment philosophy and thus alter the course of the entire institution. The critical point is that university presidents have sufficient depth and range to alter the course of a university's direction.

Examples of jobs with high depth and low range are packaging machine mechanics, anesthesiologists, and faculty members. Mechanics perform the limited tasks that pertain to repairing and maintaining packaging machines. But they can decide how breakdowns on the packaging machine are to be repaired. The discretion means the mechanics have relatively high job depth.

EXHIBIT 6.2   Job Depth and Range

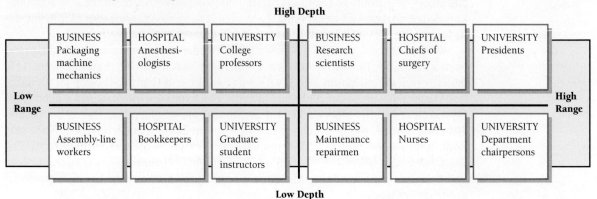

Anesthesiologists also perform a limited number of tasks. They are concerned with the rather restricted task of administering anesthetics to patients. However, they can decide the type of anesthetic to be administered in a particular situation, a decision indicative of high job depth. University professors specifically engaged in classroom instruction have relatively low job range. Teaching involves comparatively more tasks than the work of the anesthesiologist, yet fewer tasks than that of the business research scientist. However, professors' job depth is greater than graduate student instructors' since professors determine how they'll conduct the class, what materials will be presented, and the standards to be used in evaluating students. Graduate student instructors typically don't have complete freedom in the choice of class materials and procedures. Professors decide these matters for them.

Highly specialized jobs are those having few tasks to accomplish by prescribed means. Such jobs are quite routine; they also tend to be controlled by specified rules and procedures (low depth). A highly despecialized job (high range) has many tasks to accomplish within the framework of discretion over means and ends (high depth). Within an organization, there typically are great differences among jobs in both range and depth. Although there are no precise equations that managers can use to decide job range and depth, they can follow this guideline: Given the economic and technical requirements of the organization's mission, goals, and objectives, what is the optimal point along the continuum of range and depth for each job?

Job Relationships

Job relationships are determined by managers' decisions regarding departmentalization bases and spans of control. The resulting groups become the responsibility of a manager to coordinate toward organization purposes. These decisions also determine the nature and extent of jobholders' interpersonal relationships, individually and within groups. As we already have seen in the discussion of groups in organizations, group performance is affected in part by group cohesiveness. And the degree of group cohesiveness depends upon the quality and kind of interpersonal relationships of jobholders assigned to a task or command group.

The wider the span of control, the larger the group and consequently the more difficult it is to establish friendship and interest relationships. Simply, people in larger groups are less likely to communicate (and interact sufficiently to form interpersonal ties) than people in smaller groups. Without the opportunity to communicate, people will be unable to establish cohesive work groups. Thus, an important source of satisfaction may be lost for individuals who seek to fulfill social and esteem needs through relationships with co-workers.

The basis for departmentalization that management selects also has important implications for job relationships. The functional basis places jobs with similar depth and range in the same groups, while product, territory, and customer bases place jobs with dissimilar depth and range in different groups. Thus, in functional departments, people will be doing much the same specialty. Product, territory, and customer departments, however, are comprised of jobs that are quite different and heterogeneous. Individuals who work in heterogeneous departments experience feelings of dissatisfaction and stress more intensely than those in homogeneous, functional departments. People with homogeneous backgrounds, skills, and training have more common interests than those with heterogeneous ones. Thus, it's easier for them to establish social relationships that are satisfying with less stress, but also with less involvement in the department's activities.

Job designs describe the *objective* characteristics of jobs. That is, through job analysis techniques managers can design jobs in terms of required activities to produce a specified outcome. But yet another factor—perceived job content—must be considered before we can understand the relationship between jobs and performance.

The Way People Perceive Their Jobs

The way people do their jobs depends in part on how they perceive and think of their jobs. Even though Taylor proposed that the way to improve work (that is, to make it more efficient) is to determine (1) the "best way" to do a task (motion study) and (2) the standard time for completion of the task (time study), the actual performance of a job goes beyond its technical description.

The belief that job design can be based solely on technical data ignores the very large role played by the individual who performs the job. Individuals differ profoundly, as we noted in the chapter on individual differences. They come to work with different backgrounds, needs, and motivations. Once on the job, they experience the social setting in which the work is performed in unique ways. It's not surprising to find that different individuals perceive jobs differently.

Perceived job content refers to characteristics of a job that define its general nature as perceived by the jobholder. We must distinguish between a job's *objective properties* and its *subjective properties* as reflected in the perceptions of people who perform it.[39] Managers can't understand the causes of job performance without considering individual differences such as personality, needs, and span of attention.[40] Nor can managers understand the causes of job performance without considering the social setting in which the job is performed.[41] According to Exhibit 6.1, perceived job content precedes job performance. Thus, if managers desire to increase job performance by changing perceived job content, they can change job design, individual perceptions, or social settings—the causes of perceived job content.

If management is to understand perceived job content, some method for measuring it must exist.[42] In response to this need, organization behavior researchers have attempted to measure perceived job content in a variety of work settings. The methods that researchers use rely upon questionnaires that jobholders complete and that measure their perceptions of certain job characteristics.

Job Characteristics

The pioneering effort to measure perceived job content through employee responses to a questionnaire resulted in the identification of six characteristics: variety, autonomy, required interaction, optional interaction, knowledge and skill required, and responsibility.[43] The index of these six characteristics is termed the Requisite Task Attribute Index (RTAI). The original RTAI has been extensively reviewed and analyzed. One important development was the review by Hackman and Lawler, who revised the index to include six characteristics.[44]

Variety, task identity, and feedback are perceptions of job range. Autonomy is the perception of job depth; dealing with others and friendship opportunities reflect perceptions of job relationships. Employees sharing similar perceptions, job designs, and social settings should report similar job characteristics. Employees with different perceptions, however, report different job characteristics of the same job. For example, an individual with a high need for social belonging would perceive "friendship opportunities" differently than another individual with a low need for social belonging.

Individual Differences

Individual differences "provide filters such that different persons perceive the same objective stimuli in different manners."[45] Individual differences in need for strength, particularly the strength of growth needs, have been shown to influence the perception of task variety. Employees with relatively weak higher-order needs are less concerned with performing a variety of tasks than are employees with relatively strong growth needs. Thus, managers expecting higher performance to result from increased task variety would be disappointed if the jobholders did not have strong growth needs. Even individuals with strong growth needs cannot respond continuously to the opportunity to perform more and more tasks. At some point, performance turns down as these individuals reach the limits imposed by their abilities and time. The relationship between performance and task variety (even for individuals with high growth needs) is likely to be curvilinear.[46]

Social Setting Differences

Differences in social settings of work also affect perceptions of job content. Examples of social setting differences include leadership style[47] and what other people say about the job.[48] A.G. Lafley, CEO of Procter & Gamble until July 2009, revitalized the $50 billion global consumer goods corporation by creating an environment where top executives and employees of all levels perceive themselves as soldiers, ready to regain ground (i.e., market share) from competitors worldwide. Such a change in job perception helped this firm's stock price rebound after dropping precipitously (at one point, the firm had lost $85 billion in market capitalization) in the summer of 2000 shortly after Lafley was named CEO.[49] In addition, as more than one research study has pointed out, how one perceives a job is greatly affected by what other people say about it. Thus, if a worker's friends state their jobs are boring, he is likely to state that his job is also boring. If the individual perceives the job as boring, job performance will suffer. Job content, then, results from the interaction of many factors in the work situation.

The field of organization behavior has advanced a number of suggestions for improving the motivational properties of jobs. Invariably, the suggestions, termed *job design strategies,* attempt to improve job performance through changes in actual job characteristics.[50] The next section reviews the more significant of these strategies.

Designing Job Range: Job Rotation and Job Enlargement

The earliest attempts to design jobs date to the scientific management era. Efforts at that time emphasized efficiency criteria. In so doing, the individual tasks that comprise a job are limited, uniform, and repetitive. This practice leads to narrow job range and, consequently, reported high levels of job discontent, turnover, absenteeism, and dissatisfaction. Accordingly, strategies were devised that resulted in wider job range through increasing the requisite activities of jobs. Two of these approaches are job rotation and job enlargement.

Job Rotation

Managers of organizations such as General Electric, Tata Consultancy Services, Ford, and Deloitte Services LP have utilized different forms of the job rotation strategy.[51] This practice involves rotating managers and nonmanagers alike from one job to another. Given the increased need to develop global experience, many firms are rotating managers to one or more international postings.[52] In so doing, the individual is expected to complete more job activities since each job includes different tasks.[53] Job rotation involves increasing the range of jobs and the perception of variety in the job content. Increasing task variety should, according to recent studies, increase employee satisfaction, reduce mental overload, decrease the number of errors due to fatigue, improve production and efficiency,[54] and reduce on-the-job injuries.[55] However, job rotation doesn't change the basic characteristics of the assigned jobs. Some relatively small firms have successfully used job rotation.

Critics state that job rotation often involves nothing more than having people perform several boring and monotonous jobs rather than one. An alternative strategy is job enlargement.

Job Enlargement

The pioneering Walker and Guest study[56] was concerned with the social and psychological problems associated with mass production jobs in automobile assembly plants. They found that many workers were dissatisfied with their highly specialized jobs. In particular, they disliked mechanical pacing, repetitiveness of operations, and a lack of a sense of accomplishment. Walker and Guest also found a positive relationship between job range and job satisfaction. Findings of this research gave early support for motivation theories that predict that increases in job range will increase job satisfaction and other objective job outcomes. Job enlargement strategies focus upon the opposite of dividing work—they're a form of despecialization or increasing the number of tasks that an employee performs. For example, a job is designed such that the individual performs six tasks instead of three.

Although in many instances an enlarged job requires a longer training period, job satisfaction usually increases because boredom is reduced. The implication, of course, is that job enlargement will lead to improvement in other performance outcomes.

The concept and practice of job enlargement have become considerably more sophisticated. In recent years, effective job enlargement involves more than simply increasing task variety. In addition, it's necessary to design certain other aspects of job range, including providing worker-paced (rather than machine-paced) control.[57] Each of these changes involves balancing the gains and losses of varying degrees of division of labor. Contemporary applications of job enlargement involve training individuals to perform several different jobs, each requiring considerable skill, whether in manufacturing or service organizations.

Zao Noodle Bar uses job enlargement to increase employee ownership and overall profitability. Founded by Adam Willner, the first Zao Noodle Bar branch opened in 1996 near Stanford University and served fresh, made-to-order, Asian-style cuisine at an affordable price. Its operating philosophy is to "bring noodles to the people." As the chain expanded into other states, it became apparent that having two different managers—a general manager and a kitchen manager—contributed to a divided organizational culture. So the firm did away with the kitchen manager position and enlarged the role of the general manager. Cross-training the general managers to understand how to run a kitchen began with a six- to eight-week training course. This type of job enlargement increased the sense of ownership among the general managers while decreasing labor costs (i.e., paying one manager instead of two).[58]

Some employees can't cope with enlarged jobs because they can't comprehend complexity; moreover, they may not have a sufficiently long attention span to complete an enlarged set of tasks. However, if employees are amenable to job enlargement and have the requisite ability, then job enlargement should increase satisfaction and product quality and decrease absenteeism and turnover. These gains aren't without costs, including the likelihood that employees will demand larger salaries in exchange for

YOU BE THE JUDGE

JOB DESIGN AND ETHICS

Some jobs, even when properly designed, may still be inherently hazardous. For example, it may be impossible to completely eliminate exposure to toxic chemicals or hazardous substances even when jobs have been well designed. Such was the case at the battery manufacturing division of Johnson Controls, an automotive equipment supplier.

By its very nature, battery manufacturing entails possible exposure to high lead levels. Sufficiently high blood lead levels can be dangerous to anyone; even moderately elevated levels, however, can pose a particular risk for pregnant women and their unborn children. Thus, after having designed the manufacturing operation in a manner to minimize exposure, Johnson Controls instituted a policy to provide further safeguards for a particularly susceptible group: Women with childbearing capacity were essentially prohibited from working in high lead exposure positions in its battery facility. Fertile women already employed in such positions when the policy went into effect were permitted to stay as long as they maintained safe blood lead levels; otherwise they were transferred to another job with no loss of pay or benefits.

Most management students, when queried, indicate that this sounds like a reasonable policy, with many suggesting that it would be unethical (and perhaps should be illegal) for the company not to protect a particularly susceptible group of individuals—some of whom (unborn children) are powerless to protect themselves. At the same time, however, virtually all of these students agree that sex discrimination in hiring and employment decisions is clearly unethical (and also illegal). And sex discrimination is what Johnson Controls was charged with as a result of this policy. What do you think the court should decide?

Sources: See Johnson Controls's ethics policy at www. johnsoncontrols.com/corpvalues/ethics.htm (2003); Caryn L. Beck-Dudley and Edward J. Conry, "Legal Reasoning and Practical Reasonableness," *American Business Law Journal,* Fall 1995, pp. 91–130; Matthew F. Weil, "Protecting Employees' Fetuses from Workplace Hazards: Johnson Controls Narrows the Options," *Berkeley Journal of Employment and Labor Law* 14, no. 1 (1993); and G.P. Panaro, *Employment Law Manual* (Boston: Warren, Gorham & Lamont, 1991), pp. 29–30.

performing enlarged jobs. Yet these costs must be borne if management desires to implement the design strategy—job enrichment—that enlarges job depth. Job enlargement is a necessary precondition for job enrichment.

Redesigning jobs is not without ethical and legal implications, as suggested in this chapter's You Be the Judge feature.

Designing Job Depth: Job Enrichment

The impetus for designing job depth was provided by Herzberg's two-factor theory of motivation. The basis of his theory is that factors that meet individuals' need for psychological growth (especially responsibility, job challenge, and achievement) must be characteristic of their jobs. The application of his theory is termed *job enrichment.*

The implementation of job enrichment is realized through direct changes in job depth.[59] Managers can provide employees with greater opportunities to exercise discretion by making the following changes:

1. *Direct feedback.* The evaluation of performance should be timely and direct.
2. *New learning.* A good job enables people to feel that they are growing. All jobs should provide opportunities to learn.
3. *Scheduling.* People should be able to schedule some part of their own work.
4. *Uniqueness.* Each job should have some unique qualities or features.
5. *Control over resources.* Individuals should have some control over their job tasks.
6. *Personal accountability.* People should be provided with an opportunity to be accountable for the job.

As defined by the executive in charge of a pioneering job enrichment program at Texas Instruments (TI), job enrichment is a process that (1) encourages employees to behave like managers in managing their jobs and (2) designs the job to make such behavior feasible.[60]

As the theory and practice of job enrichment have evolved, managers have become aware that successful applications require numerous changes in how work is done. Important changes include giving workers greater authority to participate in decisions, to set their own goals, and to evaluate their (and their work groups') performance. Job enrichment also involves changing the nature and style of managers' behavior. Managers must be willing and able to delegate authority.[61] Given employees' ability to carry out enriched jobs and managers' willingness to delegate authority, gains in performance can be expected. These positive outcomes are the result of increasing employees' expectations that efforts lead to performance, that performance leads to intrinsic and extrinsic rewards, and that these rewards have power to satisfy needs. These significant changes in managerial jobs, when coupled with changes in nonmanagerial jobs, suggest that a supportive work environment is a prerequisite for successful job enrichment efforts.[62]

Jobs can be designed on the basis of range and significant depth (called *job specialization*), a moderate amount of range and depth (called *job enlargement*), or significant depth and generally low range.

Job enrichment and job enlargement aren't competing strategies. Job enlargement but not job enrichment may be compatible with the needs, values, and abilities of some individuals. Yet job enrichment, when appropriate, necessarily involves job enlargement. A promising new approach to job design that attempts to integrate the two approaches is the job characteristics model. Hackman, Oldham, Janson, and Purdy devised the approach, basing it on the job diagnostic survey cited in an earlier section.[63]

The model attempts to account for the interrelationships among (1) certain job characteristics; (2) psychological states associated with motivation, satisfaction, and performance; (3) job outcomes; and (4) growth needs strength. Exhibit 6.3 describes the relationships among these variables. Although variety, identity, significance, autonomy, and feedback don't completely describe perceived job content, according to this model they sufficiently describe those aspects that management can manipulate to bring about gains in productivity.

Steps that management can take to increase the core dimensions include:

1. Combining task elements.
2. Assigning whole pieces of work (i.e., work modules).
3. Allowing discretion in selection of work methods.
4. Permitting self-paced control.
5. Opening feedback channels.

These actions increase task variety, identity, and significance; consequently, the "experienced meaningfulness of work" psychological state is increased. By permitting employee participation and self-evaluation and by creating autonomous work groups, the feedback and autonomy dimensions are increased along with the psychological states "experienced responsibility" and "knowledge of actual results."

Implementing the job characteristics model in a particular situation begins with a study of existing job perceptions by means of the job diagnostic survey. Hackman and Oldham have reported numerous applications of the model in a variety of organizations.[64] They have also compiled normative data for a variety of job categories so that

EXHIBIT 6.3
The Job Characteristics Model

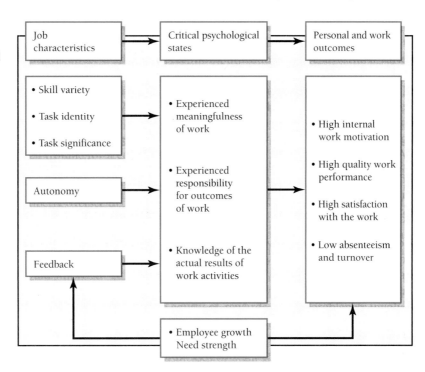

managers and practitioners can compare the responses of their own employees to those of a larger population.[65] Although the track record of job design efforts is generally positive, some caveats are warranted.

The positive benefits of these efforts are moderated by individual differences in the strength of employees' growth needs. That is, employees with a strong need for accomplishment, learning, and challenge will respond more positively than those with relatively weak growth needs. In more familiar terms, employees with a high need for self-esteem and self-actualization are the more likely candidates for job design.[66] Employees who are forced to participate in job design programs but who lack either the need strength or the ability to perform designed jobs may experience stress, anxiety, adjustment problems, erratic performance, turnover, and absenteeism.

The available research on the interrelationships between perceived job content and performance is meager. One survey of 30 applications of job design strategies confirms that failures are as frequent as successes.[67] It's apparent, however, that managers must cope with significant problems in matching employee needs with organizational needs.[68]

Problems associated with job design include:

1. Unless lower-level needs are satisfied, people will not respond to opportunities to satisfy upper-level needs. And even though our society has been rather successful in providing food and shelter, these needs regain importance when the economy moves through periods of recession and high inflation.

2. Job design programs are intended to satisfy needs typically not satisfied in the workplace. As workers are told to expect higher-order need satisfaction, they may raise their expectations beyond what's possible. Dissatisfaction with the program's unachievable aims may displace dissatisfaction with the jobs.

3. Job design may be resisted by labor unions that see the effort as an attempt to get more work for the same pay.

4. Job design efforts may not produce tangible performance improvements for some time after the beginning of the effort. One study indicated that significant improvements in effectiveness couldn't be seen until four years after the beginning of the job design program.[69]

Practical efforts by automobile companies such as Volvo to improve productivity and satisfaction through job design have emphasized autonomy and feedback. Relatively less emphasis has been placed on identity, significance, and variety.[70] Apparently, it's easier to provide individuals with greater responsibility for the total task and increased feedback than to change the essential nature of the task itself.

Two general conclusions can be reached when considering the experience of job design approaches. First, job design approaches are relatively successful in increasing quality of output. This conclusion pertains, however, only if the reward system already satisfies lower-level needs. If it presently doesn't satisfy lower-level needs, employees can't be expected to experience upper-level need satisfaction (intrinsic rewards) through enriched jobs. In particular, managers can't expect individuals with relatively low growth needs to respond as would those with relatively high growth needs.[71]

Successful efforts are the result of the circumstances that initiate the effort and the process undertaken to manage the effort. Organizations under external pressure to change have a better chance of successfully implementing job design than those not under such pressure. Moreover, successful efforts are accompanied by broad-scale participation of managers and employees alike. Since a primary source of organizational effectiveness is job performance, managers should design jobs according to the best available knowledge.[72]

Self-Managed Teams

One approach to job redesign that has emphasized factors such as task significance and identity is the use of self-managed teams. Self-managed teams (SMTs) represent a job enrichment approach to redesign at the group level. An SMT is a relatively small group of individuals who are empowered to perform certain activities based on procedures established and decisions made within the group, with minimum or no outside direction. SMTs can take many forms, including task forces, project teams, quality circles, and new venture teams.[73] Typically, SMTs determine their own work assignments within the team and are responsible for an entire process from inception to completion. It is not unusual for SMTs to select their own members and to evaluate their own performance, activities usually thought of as management functions.

The automotive industry has been particularly interested in the use of self-managed work groups. In an attempt to ward off growing competition from Toyota and Honda, General Motors launched a bold endeavor 25 years ago, the Saturn Corporation. An independent subsidiary of General Motors, Saturn used the team approach to producing new automobiles in its state-of-the-art plant in Spring Hill, Tennessee.[74] Before plant construction, a team of 99 Saturn workers visited 160 facilities around the world, traveling over 2 million miles to find what worked and what didn't.[75] The Saturn plant was organized around nearly 200 SMTs, each of which had the authority to decide how to do its job, including hiring team members. Most even had budgetary responsibilities and could make decisions to change suppliers. These initiatives have paid off: The Spring Hill plant has consistently achieved a high level of production quality previously unequaled by other domestic automobile manufacturers.

The difficulty of switching from a traditional hierarchical structure to one in which work teams assume responsibility for their own decisions is not easy. Two notable barriers to SMTs are resistance and misunderstanding. SMTs require not only a new workflow and set of processes, but also new attitudes and behaviors. Team members may not like being responsible for goals that others on the team have not helped to achieve. Managers often fear loss of control and status.[76]

The implementation of SMTs causes changes in thinking about "yourself," leadership, and organization. It is hard for employees to understand how SMTs apply to themselves. Also, managers are often not clear about what employees should be doing under an SMT arrangement.

Simply assuming that SMTs will work is not accurate since resistance and misunderstandings are obvious problems. Team leaders who strike a balance between too much involvement and not enough are needed. As SMTs evolve, each member needs to acquire and develop the qualities of a leader and move from "I" to "we" thinking and behavior.

Alternative Work Arrangements

Enriching the content of a job is not the only way to provide enrichment. Enrichment can also be achieved within the context of a job. One aspect of job context relates to when the job is performed, or the work schedule. Giving employees decision-making control over when they perform their work is an increasingly popular approach to job redesign. It has led to a variety of innovations we will collectively refer to as alternative work arrangements.

One of the earliest forms of alternative work arrangements was that of the compressed workweek. In its most popular form, employees are given an opportunity to work four 10-hour days rather than the more standard five 8-hour days. The 4–40 programs allow workers more leisure time, as well as permit them to travel to and from work during non-rush-hour traffic. While some employees may be able to opt for a compressed work schedule with others electing a standard one, typically everyone at the same location is on the same schedule.

An arrangement that provides employees even greater individual control over work scheduling is flextime. In a flextime arrangement, employees can determine, within some limits, when they work at the office and when they work from home or a coffee shop. Many companies, including Intel, PricewaterhouseCoopers, Prudential Financial, and Time Warner, offer their employees flexible work schedules.[77] As is shown in the two examples in Exhibit 6.4, employees are required to be present during the "common core" hours. They may make up the rest of their workday in any combination during flextime hours. In most flextime plans, employees may vary their

EXHIBIT 6.4
Two Possible Flextime Schedules

Flextime	Common Core	Flextime		
6 a.m. – 10 a.m.	10 a.m. – 4 p.m.	4 p.m. – 8 p.m.		

Flextime	Common Core	Flextime	Common Core	Flextime
6 a.m. – 9 a.m.	9 a.m. – 11 a.m.	11 a.m. – 2 p.m.	2 p.m. – 4 p.m.	4 p.m. – 7 p.m.

attendance day-to-day, provided they are at work a specific number of hours a week. Some flextime plans allow employees to accumulate extra hours worked and exchange them for an additional day off each month. Two factors enable the increased use of flextime, namely technology (e.g., BlackBerry and PDA phones) and a shift to focusing on results, not hours (or "face time") at work.[78]

Employees concerned about balancing personal and work life report that a flexible work schedule is high on the list of benefits that factor into job satisfaction. Aladdin Equipment of Sarasota, Florida, established a workweek of four nine-hour days and a half day on Friday. Its result has been a 50 percent increase in productivity. In a survey of 6,000 workers by Randstad, an Atlanta staffing firm, 51 percent said they would stay with the firm even without a pay raise if Randstad offered flexible work hours.[79] Some of the benefits of flextime schedules are presented in the Organizational Encounter on page 170.

Another approach that increases employee discretion is that of job sharing. In job sharing, two or more individuals share one job. One person might work from 8:00 a.m. until noon, and a second person may do the same job from 1:00 p.m. until 5:00 p.m. Or they might each work full, but alternate, days. Job sharing provides maximum flexibility for the employee. The payoff for the employer is being able to draw upon the talents of two individuals in one job. Job sharers Stephanie Kahn and Joan Girardi at American Express are typical examples. Stephanie works on Monday, Tuesday, and Thursday; Joan works Tuesday, Wednesday, and Friday. Their job is to enroll new cardholders. In addition to splitting days of the week, they also split the job by marketing channels. Joan handles direct mail, while Stephanie concentrates on telemarketing.[80]

Perhaps the ultimate in alternative work arrangements is telecommuting. Telecommuting involves working at home while being linked to the office via a computer and/or fax machine. While telecommuting emphasizes location rather than scheduling, most telecommuting jobs provide a high degree of flexible scheduling as well. Pacific Bell has been a pioneer in the use of telecommuting. In addition to experiencing increased productivity and improved employee morale, the company, with major offices in Los Angeles, has made significant contributions to reducing freeway congestion and smog.

Employees like alternative work arrangements because they give them the flexibility to balance their work–life demands. Companies, especially during an economic downturn, are increasingly experimenting with job sharing, reduced workweeks, sabbaticals, and telecommuting programs as a way to reduce costs and avoid layoffs that may lessen productivity and motivation.[81] An interesting twist is that although some companies are offering employees more flexible work options, some employees who engage in flextime and telecommuting are fearful of being "out of sight and out of mind" and, thus, easy targets for layoffs. As a result, employees are less likely to take advantage of these alternatives during hard times. For example, the number of telecommuters declined from 9.2 million in 2006 to 8.7 million during the recession year of 2009.[82]

virtual teams
A geographically distributed, functionally and/or culturally diverse group of individuals who rely on interactive technology such as e-mail, Webcasts, and videoconferencing to work together.

Virtual Teams

As organizations aggressively pursue ways in which to cut costs, decrease product cycle times, increase customer responsiveness, and integrate more fully with suppliers, many are creating and using **virtual teams** to help achieve those objectives. Other benefits of virtual teams include the ability to offer employees more flexible work arrangements (e.g., telecommuting), provide 24-hour-a-day, seven-day-a-week customer service for geographically dispersed customers in different time zones, and decrease the amount of travel time and expenses that team members have to incur.[83]

Defined as "a team that relies on interactive technology to work together when separated by physical distance,"[84] a virtual team can draw on a variety of interactive technology that includes traditional e-mail, instant messaging, teleconferencing, videoconferencing, Webcasts, meeting managers, white boards, and bulletin boards.[85] One company that uses virtual teams is Microsoft, which deploys virtual teams to provide sales and post-sales service to major global corporate customers.[86] General Electric provides a variety of real-time collaboration tools to its 340,000 employees and to several of its customers and suppliers.[87] Included in the virtual team rollout are tools that will allow employees to do the following:

- Engage in instant messaging and real-time conferencing and application sharing.
- Create shared Web workspaces among nontechnical users.
- Break down projects into tasks and track progress.
- Apply best practices from completed projects to new projects.

In addition, customers and suppliers have access to real-time data and internal processes within GE's intranet. Officials at GE argue that these features will help revolutionize the company.[88]

To successfully manage virtual teams, organizations may want to consider several factors. First, the technology should fit the purpose of the collaboration. If all members of the group need to receive the same information quickly, then a bulletin board or group e-mail is appropriate. If training needs to be done, then a Web conference with real-time white board and data sharing may be more suitable. Second, virtual team members must be carefully selected. Choosing members who have the necessary skills, experience, work ethic, and interpersonal skills is critical to effective team functioning. Third, trust between team members should be cultivated early in the process. Face-to-face meetings and/or team-building training exercises should be used during the initial periods of team formation to facilitate the development of trust. This trust will be critical later when problems, disagreements, and deadlines stress the relationships of members who can't just walk down the hallway to discuss and resolve these issues. Fourth, teams need to develop a sense of purpose and shared goals. Last, leaders must be able to set a vision for the team and help resolve conflicts between members as well as assist members in overcoming obstacles.[89]

Special care needs to be taken when managing virtual teams whose members are from countries with distinct cultures and languages. Such team members can find communicating and building trust more challenging.[90] Cultural nuances that might be detected in face-to-face meetings may go unnoticed during a teleconference or Webcast. As a result, virtual team members may experience misunderstandings and miscommunications while working on important projects. To decrease the risk of such problems, team members should be brought together for face-to-face meetings and cross-cultural training sessions in the early stages of the team-building process.

As companies such as GE, AT&T, Pfizer, Motorola, Shell Oil, and Sun Microsystems continue to experiment with and use virtual teams across their global businesses, such practices will become more and more common in organizations of all types and sizes.[91] To assist companies with their virtual collaboration needs, the company Huddle.net offers a virtual team workspace application for use in the social-networking site Facebook.[92] The use of various alternative work arrangements is increasing. As the needs of an increasingly diverse workforce grow, alternative arrangements can have a positive appeal to both employers and employees. While more and better research needs to be conducted to determine the effectiveness of such plans, job redesign

FLEXTIME AND WORK–LIFE BALANCE

Companies such as PricewaterhouseCoopers, Chubb Corporation, JCPenney, Booz Allen Hamilton, and Motorola are helping their employees achieve work–life balance by allowing them to use flexible scheduling. Often ranked as the most-desired benefit in job surveys, flexible scheduling comes in many shapes and forms. At the Chubb Corporation, employees can opt for working four longer shifts instead of five each week. At JCPenney's Plano, Texas, telemarketing operation, 5,000 employees punch in their scheduling preferences at a PC station/kiosk. This allows them to quickly add, drop, or trade shifts to accommodate their individual work–life balance needs. Nahan Printing Inc. in St. Cloud, Minnesota, offers an even more unusual flexible schedule. "We work three 12-hour shifts," explains Judy Wehking, HR manager. "But then we also rotate this schedule every three weeks."

What are the benefits of offering employees flexible scheduling? Companies can attract and retain talented employees. Most employees want to work at a company where they have some control over their schedules. This need will increase as employees increasingly try to juggle work and life priorities such as a second job, providing care for children, a disabled spouse, or elderly relatives, spending quality time with friends and loved ones, pursuing volunteer leadership opportunities, engaging in hobbies, and so on.

Companies have learned that they cannot just create a flexible scheduling program that allows employees to come and go as they please. Firms must create and manage a program that encourages employee flexibility while preserving accountability and cohesion among co-workers and supervisors. Here are some tips:

1. Survey employees to determine their scheduling needs.
2. Allow all employees to apply for flexible schedules.
3. Assign manageable workloads.
4. Encourage frequent face-to-face and virtual communication between the employee and his or her supervisor and co-workers.
5. Publish clear guidelines for developing flexible work arrangements.
6. Evaluate flexible arrangements on a quarterly to semiannual basis.
7. Assess job performance based on measured results, rather than hours worked.

Before implementing a flexible work schedule program, managers should research the specific state laws that may apply.

Sources: Adapted from Sabine A.E. Geurts, Debby G.J. Beckers, Toon W. Taris, Michiel A.J. Kompier, and Peter G.W. Smulders, "Worktime Demands and Work-Family Interference: Does Worktime Control Buffer the Adverse Effects of High Demands?" *Journal of Business Ethics* 84, pp. 229–41; Sue Shellenbarger, "Fairer Flextime: Employers Try New Policies for Alternative Schedules," *The Wall Street Journal,* November 17, 2005; Leah Carlson, "Work–Life Benefits Don't Guarantee Work–Life Balance," *Employee Benefit News,* August 1, 2005; Kenneth L. Schultz, John O. McClain, and L. Joseph Thomas, "Overcoming the Dark Side of Worker Flexibility," *Journal of Operations Management* 21, no. 1 (January 2003), pp. 81–87; and Nancy Hatch Woodward, "TGI Thursday," *HR Magazine,* July 2000, pp. 72–76.

strategies for the future no doubt will include a multitude of these flexible scheduling arrangements.

Job Embeddedness and Job Design

As discussed in the earlier section on job enrichment, job design can influence important workplace attitudes such as job satisfaction and intent to leave the job or organization. Emerging research in the area of "job embeddedness" adds an important new way of looking at such job design–work outcome relationships. **Job embeddedness** refers to an employee's links with other people and teams within the organization, perceptions of his fit with the job/organization/community, and sacrifices that would be made if he left the job. Job embeddedness is like a net or a web that can expand across an individual's work, home, and community activities and interests.[93] For example, an individual who works for PricewaterhouseCoopers in New York City may find that she enjoys the team members who make up her traveling auditor team, but she also volunteers for a soup kitchen every Thursday night, goes to the opera and theater several times a month, and has a spouse who has a good job five blocks away. Taken together, this person will be more embedded in her job and much less likely to want to leave the job or organization.

job embeddedness
Refers to an employee's connections with other employees within the organization, fit with the job/organization/community, and sacrifices that would be made if he or she were to leave the organization.

Managers can increase job embeddedness (and thus decrease turnover of key employees) by placing employees on teams with members who have compatible skill sets and, to the best possible degree, personalities. Employees who feel a connection to teammates are less likely to want to leave their job and organization. Also, managers can support the idea of flexible work scheduling to allow their employees to pursue some nonwork hobbies and volunteer leadership opportunities. This will encourage the employees to establish deeper roots within the community, which will likely increase the length of time the individual will remain in the job. As the U.S. economy approaches wide-scale retirements of the baby boomers in the next several years, managers of all types of organizations will need to combat critical skills shortages.

Total Quality Management and Job Design

total quality management
A philosophy and system of management that, using statistical process control and group problem-solving processes, places the greatest priority on attaining high standards for quality and continuous improvement.

Total quality management (TQM) refers to an organizational culture that is dedicated to continuous improvement and the production of high-quality products and services, ultimately resulting in higher levels of customer satisfaction.[94] TQM, according to those who espouse and practice it, combines technical knowledge and human knowledge. To deal with the inherent complexity and variability of production and service delivery technology, people must be empowered with authority to make necessary decisions and must be enabled with knowledge to know when to exercise that authority. Aspects of TQM job designs have appeared throughout this discussion. We've discussed job enrichment, including provision of autonomy, creation of work modules, and development of trust and collaboration. We've seen these job attributes in the practices of organizations discussed throughout this chapter. But even as we close this chapter, we must raise a fundamental question: Can American workers adjust to the requirements for working together in teams and in collaboration with management?[95] Are the ideas of TQM totally applicable to the American worker? Is TQM the wave of the future? Do American managers have the ability and commitment to implement the necessary changes in jobs required by new technologies and new global realities?[96] Many contemporary observers warn us that the answers to all these questions must be yes because no other choice exists.[97]

Job design strategy focuses on jobs in the context of individuals' needs for economic well-being and personal growth. But let's put the strategy in a broader framework and include the issue of the sociotechnical system. Sociotechnical theory focuses on interactions between technical demands of jobs and social demands of people doing the jobs. The theory emphasizes that too great an emphasis on the technical system in the manner of scientific management or too great an emphasis on the social system in the manner of human relations will lead to poor job design. Rather, job design should take into account both the technology and the people who use the technology.

Sociotechnical theory and application of job design developed from studies undertaken in English coal mines from 1948 to 1958.[98] The studies became widely publicized for demonstrating the interrelationship between the social system and the technical system of organizations. The interrelationship was revealed when economic circumstances forced management to change how coal was mined (the technical system). Historically, the technical system consisted of small groups of miners (the social system) working together on "short faces" (seams of coal). But technological advancement improved roof control and safety and made longwall mining possible.

The new technical system required a change in the social system. The groups would be disbanded in favor of one-person, one-task jobs. Despite the efforts of management and even the union, miners eventually devised a social system that restored many characteristics of the group system. This experience has been completely described in organizational behavior literature and has stimulated a great deal of research and application.

There's no contradiction between sociotechnical theory and total quality management. In fact, the two approaches are quite compatible. The compatibility relates to the demands of modern technology for self-directed and self-motivated job behavior. Such job behavior is made possible in jobs designed to provide autonomy and variety. As worked out in practice, such jobs are parts of self-regulating work teams responsible for completing whole tasks. The work module concept pervades applications of sociotechnical theory.[99]

Numerous applications of sociotechnical design and total quality management are reported in the literature.[100] Some notable American examples include the Sherwin-Williams paint factory in Richmond, Kentucky, and the Quaker Oats pet food factory in Topeka, Kansas. Both factories were constructed from the ground up to include and allow for specific types of jobs embodying basic elements of autonomy and empowerment. Firms that don't have the luxury of building the plant from scratch must find ways to renovate both their technology and their job designs to utilize the best technology and people. Some of the most influential industrial and service organizations have confronted the necessity to design jobs to take advantage of the rapid pace of technological advance. In the contemporary global environment, sociotechnical system design has been incorporated in the total quality management approach to management.

Summary of Key Points

- Job design involves managerial decisions and actions that specify objective job depth, range, and relationships to satisfy organizational requirements as well as the social and personal requirements of jobholders.

- Contemporary managers must consider the issue of quality of work life when designing jobs. This issue reflects society's concern for work experiences that contribute to employees' personal growth and development.

- Strategies for increasing jobs' potential to satisfy the social and personal requirements of jobholders have gone through an evolutionary process. Initial efforts were directed toward job rotation and job enlargement. These strategies produced some gains in job satisfaction but didn't change primary motivators such as responsibility, achievement, and autonomy.

- During the 1960s, job enrichment became a widely recognized strategy for improving quality of work life factors. This strategy is based upon Herzberg's motivation theory and involves increasing jobs' depth through greater delegation of authority to jobholders. Despite some major successes, job enrichment isn't universally applicable because it doesn't consider individual differences.

- Individual differences are now recognized as crucial variables to consider when designing jobs. Experience, cognitive complexity, needs, values, valences, and perceptions of equity are some of the individual differences influencing jobholders' reactions to the scope and relationships of their jobs. When individual differences

YOU BE THE JUDGE COMMENT

JOB DESIGN AND ETHICS

No manager would dispute that jobs should be designed in a way that eliminates, or at least minimizes, the likelihood that employees may experience adverse physical or health consequences from performing their jobs. Inevitably, when this principle is applied at the workplace, the issue becomes much more complicated. Johnson Controls, Inc. created a fetal protection policy in 1982 at several of its 15 car battery plants. The policy banned women between the ages of 18 and 70 from jobs that include potential exposure to lead (which can cause birth defects in fetuses). Opponents of this policy (such as the United Auto Workers) claimed it was discriminatory and did nothing to protect male workers from unsafe working conditions.

The U.S. Supreme Court settled the case by striking down such policies. The Court argued that these policies create sex discrimination and that employers may not exclude women from jobs that are not more hazardous to women than to men, even though they may be hazardous to unborn children. Thus, the Court invalidated the fetal protection policy of an automobile battery manufacturer (see *United Auto Workers v. Johnson Controls, Inc.*, U.S. Supreme Court No. 89-1215, March 20, 1991).

So, what should companies do?

1. Eliminate or reduce workplace hazards where possible.
2. Educate employees (male and female) about job risk.
3. Talk with women about their pregnancies and give them every possible opportunity to comply with their doctors' advice.
4. Do not create separate policies to protect women only. Make sure the policy is inclusive so that all employees are provided with a safe and secure workplace.

Sources: Sue Shellenbarger, "Recent Suits Make Pregnancy Issues Workplace Priorities," *The Wall Street Journal,* January 14, 1998; Joann S. Lublin, "Decision Poses Dilemma for Employers," *The Wall Street Journal,* March 21, 1991, p. B1; and "Fetal Protection Policies," *HR Magazine,* January 1991, pp. 81–83.

---

are combined with environmental, situational, and managerial differences, job design decisions become increasingly complex.

- The most recently developed strategy of job design emphasizes the importance of core job characteristics as perceived by jobholders. Although measurements of individual differences remain a problem, managers should be encouraged to examine ways to increase positive perceptions of variety, identity, significance, autonomy, and feedback. By doing so, the potential for high-quality work performance and high job satisfaction is increased given that jobholders possess relatively high growth needs strength.

- Many organizations including Volvo, Citibank, General Motors, and General Foods have attempted job design with varying degrees of success. The current state of research knowledge is inadequate for making broad generalizations regarding exact causes of success and failure in applications of job design. Managers must diagnose their own situations to determine the applicability of job design in their organizations.

- Sociotechnical theory combines technological and social issues in job design practice. Sociotechnical theory is compatible with job design strategy and emphasizes the practical necessity to design jobs that provide autonomy, feedback, significance, identity, and variety.

- Total quality management (TQM) combines the ideas of job enrichment and sociotechnical theory. Managers who implement TQM design jobs that empower individuals to make important decisions about product/service quality. The empowerment process encourages participative management, team-oriented task modules, and autonomy.

Review and Discussion Questions

1. Why should organizations allow, even encourage, their employees to pursue non-work hobbies and volunteer opportunities? Would having such opportunities make you more likely to take a job with a particular company, or would it have no effect on your decision? Explain.

2. Explain the differences between job enlargement and job enrichment and analyze the relative advantages of these two approaches in organizations you have worked for.

3. What is the significance of the idea of quality of work life (QWL)? In particular, what would seem to be the trade-offs between meaningful jobs and productive jobs during periods of declining economic activity and unemployment?

4. There is a distinct move away from a "job" emphasis in some industries. Why is this occurring?

5. Assume that you are a restaurant supervisor in charge of 10 waiters. You notice that they appear bored with their jobs and that customer service is starting to decline. How can you redesign their jobs to make their work more interesting and more meaningful? Would you enrich or enlarge their jobs? Explain.

6. Describe the most meaningful job that you have ever had. Why was it meaningful? Do you agree with that part of job characteristics theory that posits that meaningful jobs tend to be more motivational?

7. Job enrichment is realized through changes to job depth. What changes can managers make to existing jobs that will provide employees with greater opportunities to exercise discretion?

8. Think about a current or previous job in which you were very motivated. What three factors motivated you the most about that job? Were they intrinsic or extrinsic outcomes?

9. Employees are increasingly interested in jobs with flexible work schedules. What factors are driving this interest?

10. As you understand the idea and practice of total quality management, do you believe that it's the wave of the future in American organizations? Explain.

Exercise

Exercise 6.1: *Job Design Preferences*

Objectives

1. To illustrate individual differences in preferences about various job design characteristics.

2. To illustrate how your preferences may differ from those of others.

3. To examine the most important and least important job design characteristics and how managers would cope with them.

Starting the Exercise

First you will respond to a questionnaire asking about your job design preferences and how you view the preferences of others. After working through the questionnaire individually, small groups will be formed. In the groups, discussion will focus on the individual differences in preferences expressed by group members.

Now how much do you know about job design?

6. True or false: The "position analysis questionnaire" is a method of job analysis that takes into account the human, task, and technological factors of jobs and job classes.
   a. True
   b. False

7. An example of a job that is high in depth and high in range is _____.
   a. receptionist
   b. accountant
   c. president/CEO
   d. firefighter

8. True or false: The O*NET is a comprehensive and flexible, Internet-accessible database created by the U.S. Department of Labor that describes occupations.
   a. True
   b. False

9. _____ refers to an employee's connections with other employees within the organization and his or her fit with the job, organization, and community.
   a. Job embeddedness
   b. Job connectivity
   c. Job attachment
   d. Job enlargement

10. For virtual teams to succeed, which of the following is true?
    a. Virtual team members must be carefully selected.
    b. Teams need to develop a sense of purpose and shared goals.
    c. Trust between team members should be cultivated early in the process.
    d. All (a–c) are correct.

REALITY CHECK ANSWERS

Before	After
1. c 2. c 3. c 4. b 5. a	6. a 7. c 8. a 9. a 10. d
Number Correct	Number Correct
_____	_____

Job design is concerned with a number of attributes of a job. Among these attributes are the job itself, the requirements of the job, the interpersonal interaction opportunities on the job, and performance outcomes. Individuals prefer certain attributes. Some prefer job autonomy, while others prefer to be challenged by different tasks. It is obvious that individual differences in preferences would be an important consideration for managers. An exciting job for one person may be a demeaning and boring job for another. Managers could use this type of information in attempting to create job design conditions that allow organizational goals and individual goals and preferences to be matched.

The Job Design Preference form is presented below. Please read it carefully and complete it after considering each characteristic listed. Due to space limitations, not all job design characteristics are included for your consideration. Use only those that are included on the form.

Phase I: 15 Minutes

Individually complete the A and B portions of the Job Design Preference form.

Phase II: 45 Minutes

1. The instructor will form groups of four to six students.
2. Discuss the differences in the rankings individuals made on the A and B parts of the form.
3. Present each of the A rank orders of group members on a flip chart or the blackboard. Analyze the areas of agreement and disagreement.
4. Discuss what implications the A and B rankings would have to a manager who would have to supervise a group such as the group you are in. That is, what could a manager do to cope with the individual differences displayed?

Job Design Preference Form

A. Your Job Design Preferences

Decide which of the following is most important to you. Place a 1 in front of the most important characteristic. Then decide which is the second most important characteristic to you and place a 2 in front of it. Continue numbering the items in order of importance until the least important is ranked 10. There are no right answers, since individuals differ in their job design preferences. Do not discuss your individual rankings until the instructor forms groups.

_____ Variety in tasks
_____ Feedback on performance from doing the job
_____ Autonomy
_____ Working as a team
_____ Responsibility
_____ Developing friendships on the job
_____ Task identity
_____ Task significance
_____ Having the resources to perform well
_____ Feedback on performance from others (e.g., the manager, co-workers)

B. Others' Job Design Preferences

In the A section you have provided your preferences. Now number the items as you think others would rank them. Consider others who are in your course, class, or program, that is, those who are also completing this exercise. Rank the factors from 1 (most important) to 10 (least important).

_____ Variety in tasks
_____ Feedback on performance from doing the job
_____ Autonomy
_____ Working as a team
_____ Responsibility
_____ Developing friendships on the job
_____ Task identity
_____ Task significance
_____ Having the resources to perform well
_____ Feedback on performance from others (e.g., the manager, co-workers)

Case

Case 6.1: *The Hovey and Beard Company Case*

Part 1

The Hovey and Beard Company manufactured a variety of wooden toys, including animals, pull toys, and the like. The toys were manufactured by a transformation process that began in the wood room. There, toys were cut, sanded, and partially assembled. Then the toys were dipped into shellac and sent to the painting room.

In years past, the painting had been done by hand, with each employee working with a given toy until its painting was completed. Most of the toys were only two colors, although a few required more than two. Now, in response to increased demand for the toys, the painting operation was changed so the painters sat in a line by an endless chain of hooks. These hooks moved continuously in front of the painters and passed into a long horizontal oven. Each painter sat in a booth designed to carry away fumes and to backstop excess paint. The painters would take a toy from a nearby tray, position it in a jig inside the painting cubicle, spray on the color according to a pattern, and then hang the toy on a passing hook. The rate at which the hooks moved was calculated by the engineers so that each painter, when fully trained, could hang a painted toy on each hook before it passed beyond reach.

The painters were paid on a group bonus plan. Since the operation was new to them, they received a learning bonus that decreased by regular amounts each month. The learning bonus was scheduled to vanish in six months, by which time it was expected that they would be on their own—that is, able to meet the production standard and earn a group bonus when they exceeded it.

Questions

1. Assume that the training period for the new job setup has just begun. What change do you predict in the level of output of the painters? Increase, decrease, or stay the same? Why?

2. What other predictions regarding the behavior of these painters do you make based upon the situation described so far?

Part 2

By the second month of the training period, trouble developed. The painters learned more slowly than had been anticipated, and it began to look as though their production would stabilize far below what was planned. Many of the hooks were going by empty. The painters complained that the hooks moved too fast and that the engineer had set the rates wrong. A few painters quit and had to be replaced with new ones. This further aggravated the learning problem. The team spirit that the management had expected to develop through the group bonus was not in evidence except as an expression of what the engineers called "resistance." One painter, whom the group regarded as its leader (and the management regarded as the ringleader), was outspoken in taking the complaints of the group to the supervisor. These complaints were that the job was messy, the hooks moved too fast, the incentive pay was not correctly calculated, and it was too hot working so close to the drying oven.

Part 3

A consultant was hired to work with the supervisor. She recommended that the painters be brought together for a general discussion of the working conditions. Although hesitant, the supervisor agreed to this plan.

The first meeting was held immediately after the shift was over at 4 p.m. It was attended by all eight painters. They voiced the same complaints again: The hooks went by too fast, the job was too dirty, and the room was hot and poorly ventilated. For some reason, it was this last item that seemed to bother them most. The supervisor promised to discuss the problems of ventilation and temperature with the engineers, and a second meeting was scheduled. In the next few days the supervisor had several talks with the engineers. They, along with the plant superintendent, felt that this was really a trumped-up complaint and that the expense of corrective measures would be prohibitively high.

The supervisor came to the second meeting with some apprehensions. The painters, however, did not seem to be much put out. Rather, they had a proposal of their own to make. They felt that if several large fans were set up to circulate the air around their feet, they would be much more comfortable. After some discussion, the supervisor agreed to pursue the idea. The supervisor and the consultant discussed the idea of fans with the superintendent. Three large fans were purchased and installed.

The painters were jubilant. For several days the fans were moved about in various positions until they were placed to the satisfaction of the group. The painters seemed completely satisfied with the results, and the relations between them and the supervisor improved visibly.

The supervisor, after this encouraging episode, decided that further meetings might also prove profitable. The painters were asked if they would like to meet and discuss other aspects of the work situation. They were eager to do this. Another meeting was held and the discussion quickly centered on the speed of the hooks. The painters maintained that the engineer had set them at an unreasonably fast speed and that they would never be able to fill enough of them to make a bonus.

The discussion reached a turning point when the group's leader explained that it wasn't that the painters couldn't work fast enough to keep up with the hooks but that they couldn't work at that pace all day. The supervisor explored the point. The painters were unanimous in their opinion that they could keep up with the belt for short periods if they wanted to. But they didn't want to because if they showed they could do this for short periods then they would be expected to do it all day. The meeting ended with an unprecedented request by the painters: "Let us adjust the speed of the belt faster or slower depending on how we feel." The supervisor agreed to discuss this with the superintendent and the engineers.

The engineers reacted negatively to the suggestion. However, after several meetings it was granted that there was some latitude within which variations in the speed of the hooks would not affect the finished product. After considerable argument with the engineers, it was agreed to try the painters' idea.

With misgivings, the supervisor had a control with a dial marked "low, medium, fast" installed at the booth of the group leader. The speed of the belt could now be adjusted anywhere between the lower and upper limits that the engineers had set.

Questions

1. What changes do you now expect in the level of output of the painters? Increase, decrease, or stay the same? Why?
2. What changes do you expect in the feelings of the painters toward their work situation? More positive, more negative, or no change? Why?
3. What other predictions do you make about the behavior of the painters?

Part 4

The painters were delighted and spent many lunch hours deciding how the speed of the belt should be varied from hour to hour throughout the day. Within a week the pattern had settled down to one in which the first half hour of the shift was run on a medium speed (a dial setting slightly above the point marked "medium"). The next two and a half hours were run at high speed, and the half hour before lunch and the half hour after lunch were run at low speed. The rest of the afternoon was run at high speed with the

exception of the last 45 minutes of the shift, which was run at medium.

The constant speed at which the engineers had originally set the belt was actually slightly below the "medium" mark on the control dial; the average speed at which the painters were running the belt was on the high side of the dial. Few, if any, empty hooks entered the oven, and inspection showed no increase of rejects from the paint room.

Production increased, and within three weeks (some two months before the scheduled ending of the learning bonus) the painters were operating at 30 to 50 percent above the level that had been expected under the original arrangement. Naturally, their earnings were correspondingly higher than anticipated. They were collecting their base pay, earning a considerable piece-rate bonus, and still benefiting from the learning bonus. They were earning more now than many skilled workers in other parts of the plant.

Questions

1. How do you feel about the situation at this point?
2. Suppose that you were the supervisor. What would you expect to happen next? Why?

Part 5

Management was besieged by demands that the inequity between the earnings of the painters and those of other workers in the plant be taken care of. With growing irritation between the superintendent and the supervisor, the engineers and supervisor, and the superintendent and engineers, the situation came to a head when the superintendent revoked the learning bonus and returned the painting operation to its original status: The hooks moved again at their constant, time-studied, designated speed.

Production dropped again and within a month all but two of the eight painters had quit. The supervisor stayed on for several months, but, feeling aggrieved, left for another job.

CHAPTER SEVEN

Evaluation, Feedback, and Rewards

Learning Objectives

After completing Chapter 7, you should be able to:

- **Describe** several purposes of performance evaluation.

- **Explain** why a 360-degree feedback program is considered more comprehensive.

- **Discuss** different types of reinforcement schedules.

- **Compare** intrinsic and extrinsic rewards.

- **Describe** the relationship between intrinsic rewards and organizational commitment.

- **Understand** the role rewards play in turnover, absenteeism, performance, and commitment.

- **Identify** several innovative reward systems.

Organizations use a variety of rewards to attract and retain people and to motivate them to achieve their personal and organizational goals. Managers must address almost daily the manner and timing of distributing rewards, such as pay, transfers, promotions, praise, and recognition. Rewards also can help create a climate that results in more challenging and satisfying jobs. Because these rewards are considered important by employees, they have significant effects on behavior and performance. In this chapter we are concerned with how rewards are distributed by managers. We discuss the reactions of people to rewards and examine the response of employees to rewards received in organizational settings. Additionally, we present the role of rewards in organizational absenteeism, turnover, commitment, and job performance.

Before individuals can be rewarded, there must be some basis for distributing rewards. Some rewards may accrue to all individuals simply by virtue of their employment with the organization. These are what are known as *universal* or *across-the-board rewards*. Other rewards may be a function of tenure or seniority. Many rewards, however, are related to job performance.[1] To distribute these rewards equitably, it is necessary to evaluate employee performance. Thus, we begin this chapter with a look at performance evaluation. Developing effective evaluation systems is just as critical to organizational success as developing effective reward systems. Both systems represent efforts to influence employee behavior. To achieve maximum effectiveness, it is necessary to carefully link employee evaluation systems with reward systems.

Evaluation of Performance

Virtually every organization of at least moderate size has a formal employee performance evaluation system. Assessing and providing feedback about performance is considered essential to an employee's ability to perform job duties effectively.[2] In

How much do you know about performance evaluation?

1. True or false: There are many different purposes for conducting performance appraisals, including the identification of high-potential employees and the evaluation of previous training programs.
   a. True
   b. False

2. Some performance appraisals have a _____ orientation; whereas other performance appraisals have more of a(n) _____ orientation.
   a. goal setting; empowerment
   b. judgmental; developmental
   c. perceptual; psychological
   d. None of the above (a–c) are correct.

3. Effort, self-motivation to adjust, and persistence are all elements of the _____ section of the "cognitive model of feedback."
   a. behavioral results
   b. mental processing
   c. cognitive evaluation
   d. individual characteristics

4. A _____ feedback program can include evaluations about an employee's performance from co-workers, supervisors, subordinates, and customers.
   a. global
   b. complete
   c. 360-degree
   d. certified

5. _____ are behaviors that can be influenced by altering the consequences (rewards and punishments) that follow these behaviors.
   a. Outcomes
   b. Reinforcers
   c. Operants
   d. Conditions

discussing this topic, we will identify the purposes performance evaluation may serve and examine what the focus of evaluations should be. We also will look at a number of performance evaluation methods, examining their strengths and weaknesses.

Purposes of Evaluation

The basic purpose of evaluation, of course, is to provide information about work performance.[3] More specifically, however, such information can serve a variety of purposes. Some of the major ones are:

1. Provide a basis for reward allocation, including raises, promotions, transfers, layoffs, and so on.
2. Identify high-potential employees.
3. Validate the effectiveness of employee selection procedures.
4. Evaluate previous training programs.
5. Stimulate performance improvement.
6. Develop ways of overcoming obstacles and performance barriers.

CULTURAL DIFFERENCES IN PERFORMANCE EVALUATIONS

Performance evaluations, like many other management procedures, are not universally the same across all cultures. The primary purpose served by evaluations, the procedures used to conduct evaluations, and the manner in which information is communicated are just a few of the components of performance evaluation that may differ as a function of the culture in which the evaluation is being conducted. Below are examples of some differences that exist between the United States, Saudi Arabia, and Japan. For each country, the descriptions of the various components reflect usual or typical practice. Clearly, within any single country there will be variations between organizations and, less frequently, within organizations.

Sources: Adapted from a report of the Association of Cross-Cultural Trainers in Industry, Southern California, 1984; and from P.R. Harris and R.T. Moran, *Managing Cultural Differences,* 6th ed. (Burlington, MA: Butterworth-Heinemann, 2004).

Component	United States	Saudi Arabia	Japan
Purpose	Fairness, employee development	Placement	Employee development
Who conducts evaluation?	Supervisor	Manager several layers higher	Mentor and supervisor
Frequency	Once a year or periodically	Once a year	Developmental appraisal once a month; evaluation appraisal after 12 years
Assumptions	Objective appraiser is fair	Subjective more important than objective	Objective and subjective equal importance
Manner of communication and feedback	Criticism direct and may be in writing	Criticism subtle and will not be in writing	Criticism subtle and given orally
Rebuttals	Employee will feel free to rebut	Employee will feel free to rebut	Employee will rarely rebut
Praise	Given individually	Given individually	Given to entire group

7. Identify training and development opportunities.
8. Establish supervisor–employee agreement on performance expectations.

These eight specific purposes can be grouped into two broad categories. The first four have a *judgmental orientation;* the last four have a *developmental orientation.* Evaluations with a judgmental orientation focus on past performance and provide a basis for making judgments regarding which employee should be rewarded and how effective organizational programs—such as selection and training—have been. Evaluations with a developmental orientation are more concerned with improving future performance by ensuring expectations are clear and by identifying ways to facilitate employee performance through training. These two broad categories are not mutually exclusive. Performance evaluation systems can, and do, serve both general purposes.

The general purpose for which performance evaluations are conducted will vary across different cultures, as will the frequency with which evaluations are conducted, who conducts them, and a variety of other components. The above Global OB illustrates some cultural differences in typical performance evaluations across three countries.

Focus of Evaluation

Effective performance evaluation is a continuous, ongoing process and, simply stated, involves asking two questions: "Is the work being done effectively?" and "Are employee skills and abilities being fully utilized?" The first question tends toward a judgmental orientation, while the second is more developmental in nature. Generally, evaluations should focus on translating the position responsibilities into each employee's day-to-day activities. Position responsibilities are determined on the basis of a thorough job analysis, a procedure discussed in detail in Chapter 6. Additionally, the evaluation should assist the employee in understanding these position responsibilities, the work goals associated with them, and the degree to which the goals have been accomplished.

Performance evaluations should focus on job performance, not individuals. If a software engineer's work comes to her by electronic communication and she forwards the completed work via e-mail to persons with whom she has no personal contact, should the fact that she cannot express herself well when talking to someone be an important factor in judging her performance? If we focus on her communication ability, we are concerned about her as an individual and are evaluating *her.* But if we look at this in relation to its effect on how well she does her job, we are evaluating her **performance**.

performance
A set of employee work-related behaviors designed to accomplish organizational goals.

When evaluating employee behavior, it is necessary to ensure not only that the focus of the appraisal remains on job performance, but that it also has proper weighting of relevant behaviors. Relevancy, in the context of performance evaluation, has three aspects: deficiency, contamination, and distortion. *Deficiency* occurs when the evaluation does not focus on all aspects of the job. If certain job responsibilities and activities are not considered, the evaluation is deficient. *Contamination* can be said to be the reverse of deficiency. It occurs when activities *not* part of the job are included in the evaluation. If we evaluate the software engineer mentioned in the previous paragraph on her verbal skills, this would be a form of contamination. Finally, *distortion* takes place in the evaluation process when an improper emphasis is given to various job elements. If, for example, placing the phones on automatic answering at the close of each business day is only a small element of a secretary's job, making that activity the major factor in evaluating his performance would be distorting that particular job element. Well-focused performance evaluations avoid deficiency, contamination, and distortion.

Improving Evaluations

It has been suggested that performance evaluation is the most important human resource function in an organization.[4] Developing an effective performance evaluation system constitutes a critical and challenging task for management. This means, among other things, maximizing the use and acceptance of the evaluations while minimizing dissatisfaction with any aspect of the system. Not all performance appraisal approaches are well received by managers and employees. For example, the forced rankings approach in which managers must place a certain percentage of employees into each performance category (e.g., above, at, and below average) has been met with resistance at many organizations. Some managers have difficulty labeling some of their employees as "below average" even if they perform at a slightly lower capacity than other employees in the department. A full treatment of performance evaluation problems and methods of overcoming them is beyond the scope of our discussion here. We offer, however, the following suggestions for improving the effectiveness of virtually any evaluation system.

1. Higher levels of *employee participation* in the evaluation process lead to more satisfaction with the system.

2. Setting *specific performance goals* to be met results in greater performance improvement than discussions of more general goals.

3. Evaluating subordinates' performance is an important part of a supervisor's job; managers should *receive training* in the process, and they should be evaluated on *how effectively* they discharge this part of their own job responsibilities.

4. Systematic evaluation of performance does little good if the results are not *communicated* to employees.

5. Performance evaluation feedback should not focus solely on problem areas; good performance should be *actively recognized and reinforced.*

6. Remember that while formal performance evaluation may take place on a set schedule (for example, annually), effective evaluation is a *continuous, ongoing process.*

To the extent that performance is linked with the organization's reward system, performance evaluation represents an attempt to influence the behavior of organizational members. That is, it is an attempt to *reinforce* the continuation or elimination of certain actions. The basic assumption is that behavior is influenced by its consequences and that it is possible to affect behavior by controlling such consequences. Consequently, we begin our discussion of rewarding individual behavior by examining the topic of reinforcement.

Performance Evaluation Feedback

Upon the completion of a performance evaluation, the manager (evaluator) usually is expected to provide feedback. The feedback session provides information concerning the rationale for the evaluation to the individual. If possible, objective information is used to guide the evaluated employee to improve or sustain performance. The need for feedback among people on and off the job is significant. People want to know how they are doing, how they are being perceived by others, and how they can make adjustments to perform better. Simply telling someone "you are doing OK," "keep up the good work," or "you're too emotional" is too vague and subjective to be useful to bring about improvement.

One of the most dreaded experiences of managers is delivering feedback to a poorly performing employee. Telling a person that you have evaluated his performance as inadequate, poor, or below expectations is difficult. Giving a person bad news is just not a comfortable, enjoyable experience.

An illustration of how dreaded providing feedback can be is an exercise used at PricewaterhouseCoopers. Staff members sitting opposite each other in a meeting are told they are to form an impression of the other person in the next few minutes. When the time has expired, the participants are informed that they will not be required to provide feedback of their impressions after all.[5] The exercise is designed to show how fearful people become when they are faced with informing someone about their impressions. Those dreaded feelings are a product of the top-down manner in which appraisal feedback has usually occurred. Managers typically tell subordinates what is wrong or right and how they should improve performance.

Purpose of Evaluation Feedback

Performance evaluation feedback can be instructional and/or motivational to the receiver (the evaluated person). Feedback instructs when it points out areas for improvement and teaches new behavior. For example, a sales associate may be informed that his reporting of expenses is not organized and is not detailed enough. A new program for preparing sales expense reports could improve his reports. Learning how to use the program permits the sales associate to use his laptop and the program to prepare reports that are considered accurate, informative, and timely.

Performance evaluation feedback is motivational when it provides a reward or promises a reward. A supervisor informing a technician that her report is superb and will serve as an example of an outstanding model is a form of reward via recognition. Receiving a compliment or sign of excellent work from a valued colleague (e.g., supervisor, peer, or subordinate) can be very motivational and energizing.

A meta-analysis of more than 20,000 feedback incidents revealed interesting results. First, while feedback did have an impact on increasing performance, the actual performance declined in over 38 percent of the reported feedback incidents.[6] This analysis of multiple studies suggests that managers need to understand how people process feedback. As Exhibit 7.1 illustrates, feedback is emitted from the person (self), others (supervisors, colleagues), and the job itself. This feedback impacts the person who processes the feedback before acting or behaving. Feedback does not simply lead directly to efforts to improve performance. The cognitive processing that occurs involves many characteristics and factors.

A Feedback Model

Exhibit 7.1 presents a sample of feedback sources, individual characteristics, and cognitive evaluation factors that have an impact on the eventual behavioral outcomes. People who possess high self-efficacy are candidates for wanting feedback. They want to verify and validate their competency or self-efficacy.

As Exhibit 7.1 points out, feedback can result in greater effort, a desire to make corrective adjustments, and persistence. These can be very positive behaviors that ultimately result in better or improved performance. Another possible consequence of feedback is disregarding it or simply not accepting it as valid.

Research and the practical implementation of feedback provide ways feedback can improve performance.[7] First, give feedback frequently, not once a year at a performance evaluation session. Second, permit the evaluated person to participate in the feedback sessions. This serves as a two-way exchange, problem-solving approach rather than an "evaluator telling" method. When employees participate they are

EXHIBIT 7.1

Cognitive Model of Feedback: Sample of Sources, Characteristics, Cognitive Evaluation, and Behavioral Results

Sources: Based on A.N. Kluger and A. DeNisi, "The Effects of Feedback Interventions on Performance: A Historical Review, a Meta-Analysis, and a Preliminary Feedback Intervention Theory," *Psychological Bulletin,* March 1996, pp. 254–84; and R. Kreitner and A. Kinicki, *Organizational Behavior* (New York: McGraw-Hill/Irwin, 2004), pp. 325–26.

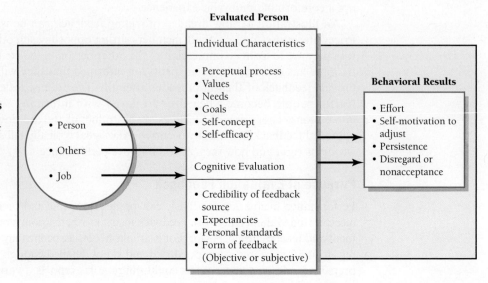

usually more satisfied with the feedback communication. Third, in providing feedback, do not solely focus on ineffective performance or problems. Praise, recognition, and encouragement serve as a form of positive reinforcement. Fourth, address results, goals, and goals accomplished, and not performer characteristics.[8] A golden rule of gaining and maintaining the respect of subordinates (evaluated employees) is to not attack or discuss their personality, attitudes, or values. These four guidelines are not perfect, nor do they always work effectively, but they are supported by research and they are not difficult to implement.

Multisource Feedback: A 360-Degree Approach

An increasing number of firms are using multisource feedback, instead of only a top-down feedback program. A recent survey suggests that 90 percent of Fortune 1000 firms use some form of multisource program. The increasing use of multisource programs is the result of calls for more fairness, clarity, and credibility in performance improvement programs.

In a 360-degree program, evaluators could include creditors, peers or team members, supervisors, subordinates, and the person. Anyone in the person's full domain (his or her circle or 360-degree range) could serve as an evaluator. For example, Google allows its managers and employees to request reviews from anyone across the organization, including peers, supervisors, customers, and suppliers.[9] It is assumed that this network has a truer picture of a person's performance than just a supervisor or any other category by itself.

As organizations attempt to improve the impact of their 360-degree feedback programs, several best practices are being used:[10]

1. *Use 360-degree feedback primarily for individual development.* This will help increase the acceptance of the program by employees.
2. *Integrate 360-degree feedback with other activities.* Assessment results can be followed by additional coaching and training, goal setting, and organizational development initiatives.
3. *Link the feedback process with the overall strategy and direction of the firm.* For example, build in customers if the firm's strategy is to become more customer-focused.
4. *Exert administrative control over every aspect of the 360-degree process.* This includes helping to choose raters and training everyone involved in the process.
5. *Make senior management role models.* When employees see senior managers receiving and acting on 360-degree feedback, they are more likely to take the initiative seriously.
6. *Use highly trained internal coaches to leverage the investment.* Coaches can help employees interpret results and create action plans for improvement.
7. *Evaluate the effectiveness or return on investment of the process.* Measure outcomes associated with the 360-degree feedback program and make modifications as necessary.

A comprehensive research study that analyzed the results of 24 research studies on multisource feedback reported modest (and positive) improvements in employee performance as a result of the feedback.[11] Another study reported that 360-degree feedback of 428 retail associate store managers was more valid in predicting assessment center performance than using managerial ratings alone.[12]

Arguments in Favor of 360-Degree Feedback

Research evidence is still insufficient to support the use of a multisource, 360-degree performance feedback program. The constant concern about fairness and credibility in evaluation is the major argument in favor of 360-degree programs. Multiple raters have different viewpoints of a person's performance. A supervisor has a single-person's perspective or overview. It is considered more thorough and credible to have multiple views being expressed.

There appears to be support among evaluated persons for a 360-degree program. Employee acceptance is important in using any management-initiated program.[13]

Arguments against 360-Degree Feedback

When information is being used to pinpoint performance, feedback providers may be reluctant to provide true ratings for fear that negative comments might be used against the person's career progress or salary progression. If feedback sources are concerned about the use of their ratings, they may inflate such ratings.[14]

Another argument against 360-degree programs involves the frequency of observation of performance. How often does a supplier or even a peer view, firsthand, the performance of a person? Differences in observation frequency across evaluators result in varying responses based not on actual or regular performance, but on what was observed on a limited number of occasions.[15]

In sum, the 360-degree feedback process, when developed, administered, and managed in a proper manner, offers promise to managers who are interested and brave enough to receive information on how they are doing. However, additional research is necessary to fine-tune 360-degree feedback programs and to determine whether they can make a major impact on employees' job performance.

There are available 360-degree feedback approaches for teams, as well. A software product called TeamWorks/360 focuses on the team as a group, rather than on individuals. Each team member rates the team's performance, then internal or external customers rate the team's performance. The software is used to provide ratings on 31 behaviors. All team members rate themselves on each of the behaviors. Team members can also evaluate other members of the team.[16]

A summary graph shows the team member how his or her self-rating compares with the views of other evaluators (e.g., other team members, customers). In addition, the report received by a team member indicates the five areas in which the member's performance was most effective and the five areas of least-effective performance.

Reinforcement Theory

Learning experts believe that reinforcement is the most important principle of learning. Desirable or reinforcing consequences (e.g., recognition in the feedback program of doing an excellent job) will increase the strength of a behavior (e.g., high-quality performance) and increase its probability of being repeated. Undesirable or punishment consequences will decrease the strength of a response and decrease its probability of being repeated.

operant
Behaviors amenable to control by altering the consequences (rewards and punishments) that follow them.

Attempts to influence behavior through the use of rewards and punishments that are consequences of the behavior are called *operant conditioning*. **Operants** are behaviors that can be controlled by altering the consequences that follow them. Most workplace behaviors such as performing job-related tasks, reading a budget report, or

EXHIBIT 7.2
**Rewards,
Reinforcement, and
Punishment**

	Desirable	Undesirable
Applied	I Positive reinforcement (behavior increases)	III Punishment (behavior decreases)
Withdrawn	II Punishment (behavior decreases)	IV Negative reinforcement (behavior increases)

coming to work on time are operants. A number of important principles of operant conditioning can aid the manager in attempting to influence behavior.

Reinforcement

Reinforcement is an extremely important principle of conditioning. Managers often use *positive reinforcers* to influence behavior. A positive reinforcer is a stimulus that, when added to the situation, strengthens the probability of a behavioral response. Thus, if the positive reinforcer has value (is desirable) to the person, it can be used to improve performance. This is shown in cell I of Exhibit 7.2. (However, a positive reinforcer that has value to one person may not have value to another person.) Sometimes *negative reinforcers* may be used. Negative reinforcement refers to an increase in the frequency of a response following removal of the negative reinforcer immediately after the response. As an example, exerting high degrees of effort to complete a job may be negatively reinforced by not having to listen to the "nagging" boss (undesirable). That is, completing the job through increased effort (behavior) minimizes the likelihood of having to listen to a nagging stream of unwanted advice (negative reinforcer) from a superior. This is illustrated by cell IV in Exhibit 7.2.

Reinforcement is different from a reward in that a reward is perceived to be desirable and is provided to a person after performance. All rewards are not reinforcers. Recall that reinforcers are defined as increasing the rate of behavior.

Punishment

punishment
Presenting an uncomfortable consequence for a particular behavior response or removing a desirable reinforcer because of a particular behavior response. Managers can punish by application or punish by removal.

Punishment is defined as presenting an uncomfortable or unwanted consequence for a particular behavioral response. It is an increasingly used managerial strategy.[17] Some work-related factors that can be considered punishments include a superior's criticism or being demoted. While punishment can suppress behavior if used effectively, it is a controversial method of behavior modification in organizations. It should be employed only after careful and objective consideration of all the relevant aspects of the situation. The dilemma of using punishment is displayed in cells II and III in Exhibit 7.2. Exhibit 7.2 compares positive and negative reinforcement and punishment when applied or withdrawn in a work setting.

Extinction

extinction
The decline in the response rate because of nonreinforcement.

Extinction means reducing unwanted behavior. When positive reinforcement for a learned response is withheld, individuals will continue to practice that behavior for some period of time. However, after a while, if the nonreinforcement continues, the behavior will decrease in frequency and intensity and will eventually disappear. The decline and eventual cessation of the response rate is known as **extinction.** For example, the continual telephone calls from a financial advisor that are not returned are eventually going to stop.

Reinforcement Schedules

continuous reinforcement
A schedule that is designed to reinforce behavior every time the behavior exhibited is correct.

It is extremely important to properly time the rewards or punishments used in an organization. The timing of these outcomes is called *reinforcement scheduling* (see Exhibit 7.3). In the simplest schedule, the response is reinforced each time it occurs. This is called **continuous reinforcement.** If reinforcement occurs only after some instances of a response and not after each response, an *intermittent reinforcement* schedule is being used. From a practical viewpoint, it is virtually impossible to reinforce continually every desirable behavior. Consequently, in organizational settings, almost all reinforcement is intermittent in nature.

An intermittent schedule means that reinforcement does not occur after every acceptable behavior. The assumption is that learning is more permanent when correct behavior is rewarded only part of the time. Ferster and Skinner have presented four types of intermittent reinforcement schedules.[18] Briefly, the four are:

1. *Fixed interval.* A reinforcer is applied only when the desired behavior occurs after the passage of a certain period of time since the last reinforcer was applied. An example would be to praise positive performance only once a week and not at other times. The fixed interval is one week.
2. *Variable interval.* A reinforcer is applied at some variable interval of time. A promotion is an example.

EXHIBIT 7.3 **Reinforcement Schedules and Their Effects on Behavior**

Source: Adapted from O. Behling, C. Schriesheim, and J. Tolliver, "Present Trends and New Directions in Theories of Work Effort," Journal Supplement Abstract Service, American Psychological Association, 1974, p. 57.

Schedule	Description	When Applied to Individual	When Removed by Manager	Organizational Example
Continuous	Reinforcer follows every response	Faster method for establishing new behavior	Faster method to cause extinction of new behavior	Praise after every new sale and order
Fixed interval	Response after specific time period is reinforced	Some inconsistency in response frequencies	Faster extinction of motivated behavior than variable schedules	Weekly, bimonthly, monthly paycheck
Variable interval	Response after varying period of time (an average) is reinforced	Produces high rate of steady responses	Slower extinction of motivated behavior than fixed schedules	Transfers, unexpected bonuses, promotions, recognition
Fixed ratio	A fixed number of responses must occur before reinforcement	Some inconsistency in response frequencies	Faster extinction of motivated behavior than variable schedules	Piece rate, commission on units sold
Variable ratio	A varying number (average) of responses must occur before reinforcement	Can produce high rate of response that is steady and resists extinction	Slower extinction of motivated behavior than fixed schedules	Random checks for quality yield praise for doing good work

3. *Fixed ratio.* A reinforcer is applied only if a fixed number of desired responses has occurred. An example would be paying a salesperson for an e-learning firm for each dollar of revenue above $6,000 for which she receives a 12 percent commission.

4. *Variable ratio.* A reinforcer is applied only after a number of desired responses, with the number of desired responses changing from situation to situation, around an average.

Research on reinforcement schedules has shown that higher rates of response usually are achieved with ratio rather than interval schedules. This finding is understandable since high response rates do not necessarily speed up the delivery of a reinforcer in an interval schedule as they do with ratio schedules. Occasionally, however, reinforcement schedule research has produced unexpected findings. For example, one study compared the effects of continuous and variable ratio piece-rate bonus pay plans. Contrary to predictions, the continuous schedule yielded the highest level of performance. One reason cited for the less-than-expected effectiveness of the variable ratio schedules was that some employees working on these schedules were opposed to the pay plan. They perceived the plan as a form of gambling, and this was not acceptable to them.[19]

Using a praise program can serve as reinforcement. The nearby Management Pointer provides some guidelines on how to use a praise program to reinforce desirable performance.

A Model of Individual Rewards

The main objectives of reward programs are: (1) to attract qualified people to *join* the organization, (2) to *keep* employees coming to work, and (3) to *motivate* employees to achieve high levels of performance. Exhibit 7.4 presents a model that attempts to integrate satisfaction, motivation, performance, and rewards. Reading the exhibit from left to right suggests that the motivation to exert effort is not enough to cause acceptable performance. Performance results from a combination of the effort of an individual and the individual's level of ability, skill, and experience. The performance results of the individual are evaluated either formally or informally by management, and two types of rewards can be distributed: intrinsic or extrinsic.[20] The rewards are evaluated by the individual, and to the extent the rewards are satisfactory and equitable, the individual achieves a level of satisfaction.

A significant amount of research has been done on what determines whether individuals will be satisfied with rewards. Lawler has summarized five conclusions based on the behavioral science research literature. They are:

1. *Satisfaction with a reward is a function both of how much is received and of how much the individual feels should be received.* This conclusion is based on the comparisons that people make. When individuals receive less than they feel they should, they are dissatisfied.

EXHIBIT 7.4
The Reward Process

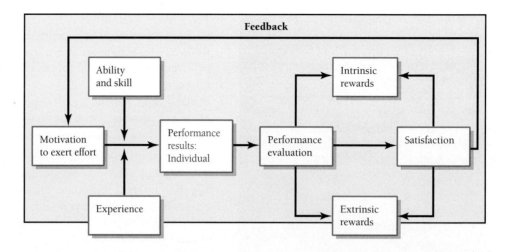

2. *An individual's feelings of satisfaction are influenced by comparisons with what happens to others.* People tend to compare their efforts, skills, seniority, and job performance with those of others. They then attempt to compare rewards. That is, they compare their own inputs with the inputs of others relative to the rewards received. This input–outcome comparison was discussed when the equity theory of motivation was introduced in Chapter 5.

3. *Satisfaction is influenced by how satisfied employees are with both intrinsic and extrinsic rewards.* Intrinsic rewards are valued in and of themselves; they are related to performing the job. Examples would be feelings of accomplishment and achievement. Extrinsic rewards are external to the work itself; they are administered externally. Examples would be salary and wages, fringe benefits, and promotions. The debate among researchers as to whether intrinsic or extrinsic rewards are more important in determining job satisfaction has not been settled because most studies suggest that both rewards are important. One clear message from the research is that extrinsic and intrinsic rewards satisfy different needs.

4. *People differ in the rewards they desire and in how important different rewards are to them.* Individuals differ on what rewards they prefer. In fact, preferred rewards vary at different points in a person's career, at different ages, and in various situations.

5. *Some extrinsic rewards are satisfying because they lead to other rewards.* For example, a large office or an office that has carpeting or drapes is often considered a reward because it indicates the individual's status and power. Money is a reward that leads to such things as prestige, autonomy and independence, security, and shelter.

The relationship between rewards and satisfaction is not perfectly understood, nor is it static. It changes because people and the environment change. However, any reward package should (1) be sufficient to satisfy basic needs (e.g., food, shelter, clothing), (2) be considered equitable, and (3) be individually oriented.[21]

One aspect of some reward programs that is not considered involves taxation. For example, announcing a $1,000 bonus could be great news by itself. However, if because of taxes the recipients get only $667, the news may be less positive. An important question to determine is, "Is it possible to reward an employee without inflicting the burden of tax liability?" Yes, firms can either "gross up" cash incentives or put them into employees' 401(k) retirement plans and health savings accounts.[22] Firms that gross up cash incentives provide employees with the full value of the bonus. For example, instead of issuing the $1,000 bonus, a company provides the employee with a check in the amount of $1,333. Thus, although the $1,333 is taxed, the employee still pockets $1,000.

Intrinsic and Extrinsic Rewards

The rewards shown in Exhibit 7.4 are classified into two broad categories: extrinsic and intrinsic. Whether rewards are extrinsic or intrinsic, it is important to first consider the rewards valued by the person since an individual will put forth little effort unless the reward has value. An *intrinsic reward* is defined as one that is self-administered by the person. It provides a sense of satisfaction or gratification and, often, a feeling of pride for a job well done. An *extrinsic reward* is initiated from outside the person. Receiving praise from a supervisor is extrinsic or initiated by someone other than the person. Both extrinsic and intrinsic rewards can have value. We will examine both types in the following sections.

Extrinsic Rewards

Financial Rewards: Salary and Wages   Money is a major extrinsic reward. It has been said, "Although it is generally agreed that money is the major mechanism for rewarding and modifying behavior in industry . . . very little is known about how it works."[23] To really understand how money modifies behavior, the perceptions and preferences of the person being rewarded must be understood, a challenging task for a manager. Unless employees can see a connection between performance and merit increases, money will not be a powerful motivator. Equally challenging is how motivation is affected after managers implement a pay cut during difficult economic times. The Organizational Encounter on page 192 discusses this issue in detail.

Many organizations utilize some type of incentive pay plan to motivate employees. Lawler presents the most comprehensive summary of the various pay plans and their effectiveness as motivators.[24] Each plan is evaluated on the basis of the following questions:

1. How effective is it in creating the perception that pay is related to performance?
2. How well does it minimize the perceived negative consequences of good performance?
3. How well does it contribute to the perception that important rewards other than pay (e.g., praise and interest shown in the employee by a respected superior) result in good performance?

A controversial issue regarding pay systems centers on whether they are public or private matters. Openness versus secrecy is not an either/or issue; it is a matter of degree. Some organizations will disclose the pay ranges, the pay decision criteria, and a schedule for receiving pay increases. Other organizations may present an entire array of employees and the pay increases each received in a particular performance review period.

Research indicates that a totally open pay system, in which there are no secrets about how much people are being paid, works best in organizations where employee performance can be measured in objective terms and there is low interdependence among employees. Organizations that specialize in selling to the public often employ individuals whose output can be measured and who do not have to work closely with other salespeople. A good example of this would be a personal selling organization such as Mary Kay Cosmetics, where the results of high-performing employees are

CUT PAY TO SAVE JOBS: FEW REWARDS DURING DIFFICULT TIMES

What do FedEx, Hewlett-Packard, Best Buy, *The New York Times*, CareerBuilder.com, and Capital One all have in common? In response to a recent worldwide recession, each one of these companies chose to cut employees' pay as a way to avoid layoffs. Why try to avoid layoffs? Even though employees are very sensitive about their pay and generally hate the idea of going back to lower pay levels, most see an across-the-board pay cut as a necessary evil during tough times. No one wants to see a co-worker, many with mortgages, car loans, children in college, and so on, get fired. By instituting a pay cut that includes the CEO and executives, an organization is seen as being socially responsible and compassionate. Also, by keeping the workforce intact, the organization won't find itself short-staffed when the economy picks up again. This will save the firm considerable time and money related to recruitment, selection, and training. A final benefit of the no-layoff approach is that customer service is preserved; in contrast, layoffs can lead to fewer and less-trained customer service personnel, ultimately reducing the quality of the firm's customer service capabilities.

In tough times, when employees are giving back 10 or 20 percent of their salaries and bonuses are being drastically reduced or eliminated, how can employees be "rewarded" so they don't leave the organization? One approach is to use "customized" or "tiered" pay cuts whereby some employees don't have to give back as much. This approach allows managers to protect top performers or lower earners who are more likely to live paycheck to paycheck. At FedEx, salaried workers who earn $150,000 or more received a 15 percent reduction in their pay; salaried employees making less gave back 10 percent; and hourly workers will go from a 40-hour to 32-hour workweek. Mark Herd, CEO

of Hewlett-Packard, took back as little as 2.5 percent from some employees but as much as 20 percent from others. Such a tiered approach allows managers to target pay cuts more precisely. A high-performing employee may be "rewarded" by receiving a small pay cut; it's hoped that this gesture will help keep the individual from leaving the firm.

A second approach to rewarding employees during tough times is to implement a reduced workweek or ask employees to volunteer for unpaid sabbaticals. According to a recent poll conducted by the Society for Human Resource Management (SHRM), approximately 20 percent of U.S. companies have shortened the workweek as a way to reduce pay. Matt Ferguson, CEO of CareerBuilder.com, right after implementing a pay cut for employees that he hoped would only last through the summer of 2009, "rewarded" the employees with only having to work a half day on Fridays. Ferguson gave employees time off as a way to compensate for the recent pay cuts.

Finally, employees can be "rewarded" by not being laid off, having to give back any portion of their salaries, or reducing their work hours. According to the aforementioned SHRM poll, several organizations took a variety of steps to save money and survive during the economic downturn, including implementing budget cuts across the whole organization (71 percent); not replacing employees who voluntarily leave the organization (63 percent); and implementing hiring freezes (52 percent). Many organizations and their employees hoped these steps would be sufficient to ward off any pay reductions and layoffs until the economy regained its health.

Sources: Michelle Conlin, "Pay Cuts Made Palatable," *BusinessWeek*, May 4, 2009, p. 67; Stephen Miller, "Employers Feel the Pain; More Staff and Pay Cuts Expected," *HR Magazine* 54, no. 5 (May 2009), p. 15; and Barbara Kiviat, "Do Pay Cuts Pay Off?" *Time*, April 27, 2009, p. GB.6.

made known to other employees and the public; for example, Mary Kay rewards its high achievers by buying them a new pink Cadillac. Since 1969, over 100,000 pink Cadillacs have been awarded to top performers worldwide.[25]

For the open pay system to be motivational for employees, measures need to be available for all important aspects of a job (e.g., number of new customers per quarter, increase in purchases by customer, etc.) and an employee's effort must be linked to short-term performance. In other words, a salesperson (and his or her peers) must see a same-month increase in pay (e.g., $300 for each new customer identified) as a result of finding two new customers that month.

If these conditions can be met, an open financial reward system can be well received. If, however, these conditions can't be met, the conflict, backlash, and hostility of an open system should be avoided with another system. Management in a less than fully open pay system should work at presenting information on how performance and financial rewards are linked. Illustrating that desirable job assignments, promotions, and results of performance appraisals are linked to improved financial rewards is an approach that takes on greater relevance when the pay system can't be totally open.[26]

Financial Rewards: Employee Benefits   According to the U.S. Bureau of Labor Statistics, organizations spend on average $18,325 a year on benefits for each employee.[27] This represents approximately 30 percent of a firm's compensation costs for each employee (the other 70 percent, or $42,370, is wages and salaries). Some benefits, however, such as the SAS Institute's subsidized child care center, workout center, and on-site medical care, are not entirely financial, but they do provide employees with valued rewards. The SAS Institute, the largest privately held software company in the world, believes in providing employees with many benefits in exchange for high-level performance and commitment.[28]

The major financial employee benefit in most organizations is the pension plan, and for most employees, the opportunity to participate in the pension plan is a valued reward. Employee benefits such as pension plans, hospitalization, and vacations usually are not contingent on the performance of employees, but are based on seniority or attendance.

Interpersonal Rewards   The manager has some power to distribute such interpersonal rewards as status and recognition. By assigning individuals to prestigious jobs, the manager can attempt to improve or remove the status a person possesses. However, if co-workers do not believe that a person merits a particular job, it is likely that status will not be enhanced. By reviewing performance, managers can, in some situations, grant what they consider to be job changes to improve status. The manager and co-workers both play a role in granting job status.

Lee Memorial Health System in Fort Myers, Florida, found out how powerful a simple recognition program can be. Lee Memorial received an award for being one of the top health care networks. Management wanted to thank its 5,000-plus employees for the reward the firm received. The firm decided that a customized key chain for each employee was the answer. The key chains had the words "Valued Employee Since _____," displayed on the top of the brass emblem with the employee's year-of-hire date.

The excitement stirred by the key chains was stunning. Everyone was excited, talking about the key chains, and pleased to be recognized. The employees appreciated the fact that each employee was recognized by their hire date. The time and minimal cost of $4.50 per employee for the "key chain recognition" was well worth the gesture.[29]

Promotions   For many employees, promotion does not happen often; some employees never experience it in their careers. The manager making a promotion reward decision attempts to match the right person with the job. Criteria often used to reach promotion decisions are performance and seniority. Performance, if it can be accurately assessed, is often given significant weight in promotion reward allocations.

Intrinsic Rewards

Completion   The ability to start and finish a project or job is important to some individuals. These people value what is called *task completion*. Some people have a need to complete tasks, and the effect that completing a task has on a person is a form of self-reward. Opportunities that allow such people to complete tasks can have a powerful motivating effect.

Achievement   Achievement is a self-administered reward that is derived when a person reaches a challenging goal. McClelland has found that there are individual differences in striving for achievement.[30] Some individuals seek challenging goals, while others tend to seek moderate or low goals. In goal-setting programs, it has

YOU BE THE JUDGE

YOUR REWARD PREFERENCES

Many theories attempt to explain what motivates employees. Numerous experts believe that rewards can be very motivational and help encourage high levels of performance. Think about which of the following rewards would be most motivational for you at work (rank-order your top five choices). Would the same rewards motivate your colleagues? Your supervisor?

1. Pay, bonuses, and other pay incentives.
2. Time off.
3. Flexible schedule.
4. Advancement and promotion opportunities.
5. Recognition from supervisor, peers, etc.
6. Ownership or profit-sharing.
7. Autonomy.
8. Personal challenge and growth.
9. Fun at work.
10. Social support and friends.
11. Job security.
12. Interesting work.

been proposed that difficult goals result in a higher level of individual performance than do moderate goals. However, even in such programs, individual differences must be considered before reaching conclusions about the importance of achievement rewards.

Autonomy   Some people want jobs that provide them with the right and privilege to make decisions and operate without being closely supervised. A feeling of autonomy could result from the freedom to do what the employee considers best in a particular situation. In jobs that are highly structured and controlled by management, it is difficult to create tasks that lead to a feeling of autonomy.

Personal Growth   The personal growth of any individual is a unique experience. An individual who is experiencing such growth senses his or her development and can see how his or her capabilities are being expanded. By expanding capabilities, a person can maximize or at least satisfy skill potential. Some people often become dissatisfied with their jobs and organizations if they are not allowed or encouraged to develop their skills. What is important to you in terms of rewards? This chapter's You Be the Judge feature asks for your ranking of 10 rewards.

Rewards Interact

The general assumption has been that intrinsic and extrinsic rewards have an independent and additive influence on motivation. That is, motivation is determined by the sum of the person's intrinsic and extrinsic sources of motivation. This straightforward assumption has been questioned by several researchers. Some have suggested that in situations in which individuals are experiencing a high level of intrinsic rewards, the addition of extrinsic rewards for good performance may cause a decrease in motivation.[31] Basically, the person receiving self-administered feelings of satisfaction is performing because of intrinsic rewards. Once extrinsic rewards are added, feelings of satisfaction change because performance is now thought to be due to the extrinsic rewards. The addition of the extrinsic rewards tends to reduce the extent to which the individual experiences self-administered intrinsic rewards.

The argument concerning the potential negative effects of extrinsic rewards has stimulated a number of research studies. Unfortunately, these studies report contradictory results.[32] Some researchers report a reduction in intrinsic rewards following the addition of extrinsic rewards for an activity.[33]

Other researchers have failed to observe such an effect.[34] A review of the literature found that 14 of 24 studies supported the theory that extrinsic rewards reduced intrinsic motivation.[35] However, 10 of the 24 studies found no support for the reducing effect theory. Of the 24 studies reviewed, only two used actual employees as subjects. All of the other studies used college students or grade school students. In studies of telephone operators and clerical employees, the reducing effect theory was not supported.[36] Managers need to be aware that no scientifically based and reported study substantiates that extrinsic rewards have a negative effect on intrinsic motivation.

Administering Rewards

Managers are faced with the decision of how to administer rewards. Three major theoretical approaches to reward administration are: (1) positive reinforcement, (2) modeling and social imitation, and (3) expectancy.

Positive Reinforcement

In administering a positive reinforcement program, the emphasis is on the desired behavior that leads to job performance rather than performance alone. The basic foundation of administering rewards through positive reinforcement is the relationship between behavior and its consequences. This relationship was discussed earlier in the chapter. While positive reinforcement can be a useful method of shaping desired behavior, other considerations concerning the type of reward schedule to use are also important. This relates to the discussion of continuous and intermittent schedules presented earlier. Management should explore the possible consequences of different types of reward schedules for individuals. It is important to know how employees respond to continuous, fixed-interval, and fixed-ratio schedules.

Modeling and Social Imitation

modeling
A method of administering rewards that relies on observational learning. An employee learns the behaviors that are desirable by observing how others are rewarded. It is assumed that behaviors will be imitated if the observer views a distinct link between performance and rewards.

Many human skills and behaviors are acquired by observational learning or, simply, imitation. Observational learning equips a person to duplicate a response, but whether the response actually is imitated depends on whether the model person was rewarded or punished for particular behaviors. If a person is to be motivated, he or she must observe models receiving reinforcements that are valued. To use **modeling** to administer rewards, managers must determine who responds to this approach. In addition, selecting appropriate models is a necessary step. Finally, the context in which modeling occurs needs to be considered. That is, if high performance is the goal and it is almost impossible to achieve that goal because of limited resources, the manager should conclude that modeling is not appropriate.[37]

Expectancy Theory

Some research suggests that expectancy theory constructs provide an important basis for classifying rewards.[38] From a rewards administration perspective, the expectancy approach, like the other two methods of administering rewards, requires managerial action. Managers must determine the kinds of rewards employees desire and do whatever is possible to distribute those rewards. Or they must create conditions so that what is available in the form of rewards can be applied. In some situations, it simply is not possible to provide the valued and preferred rewards. Therefore, managers often have to increase the desirability of other rewards.

ARE WOMEN RECEIVING EQUITABLE PAY TREATMENT?

On average, employed women receive less pay than employed men. According to the U.S. Bureau of Labor Statistics, women's earnings were approximately 80 percent of men's earnings in 2007. Although this finding represents some improvement since 1979, when women earned 62 percent as much as their male counterparts, there remains a gender-based pay gap. Does this mean women are being treated inequitably or unethically? Or could this pay gap merely reflect differences in the types of jobs held by women and men or the differences in seniority between the two groups? Or could it be that some women do not negotiate as effectively as men for higher salaries? The cause for the pay gap can be explained by all of these factors. However, significant pay differentials can still be found when women's pay is analyzed by age, education, and within occupation. This suggests that pay discrimination is occurring in many organizations.

In terms of age, the older a woman is, the less she makes relative to a man. Women in their peak earning years aged 45 to 54 and 55 to 64 make approximately 75 percent and 73 percent, respectively, as much as their male counterparts. This is an important issue when considering the increasing number of female-led single-parent households. When considering education, compared to men with a college degree, women with a college degree have seen their earnings grow at a faster rate. From 1979 to 2007, female college graduates' earnings increased by 33 percent (compared to an 18 percent increase for male college graduates' earnings), but this positive trend has not been sufficient to remove the male–female pay gap. Although more women than ever before are working in highly paid occupations (doctors, lawyers, business executives, etc.), there are substantial pay gaps within these and other occupations. While other gaps are somewhat smaller, they exist for virtually every job category. In addition, a larger percentage of women than men work in lower-paid occupations such as education and health care.

The 1963 amendment to the Fair Labor Standards Act known as the Equal Pay Act requires equal pay for equal work for men and women. Equal work is defined as work requiring equal skills, effort, and responsibility under similar working conditions. Since the passage of this legislation, the female–male pay gap has clearly narrowed. As the figures cited above indicate just as clearly, however, a great deal remains to be done.

A 1984 Supreme Court ruling permits women to bring suit on the grounds that they are paid less than men holding jobs of comparable worth based on job content evaluation. In this suit, Washington County, Oregon, prison matrons claimed sex discrimination because male prison guards, whose jobs were somewhat different, received substantially higher pay. The county had evaluated the males' jobs as having 5 percent more job content than the females' jobs, but paid the males 35 percent more. That same year, the state of Washington began wage adjustments for about 15,000 employees. This was the first of several adjustments aimed at eliminating state pay differentials between predominately female and male jobs by 1993.

While there are frequently legitimate reasons for pay differentials between women and men in comparable jobs (length of service in the position, for example), unfair differences still exist. To reward employees differently based solely on gender is not only unethical and illegal, it is poor business practice as well.

Sources: Adapted from U.S. Department of Labor, "Highlights of Women's Earnings in 2007," *U.S. Bureau of Labor Statistics Report 1008,* October 2008, pp. 1–91; Elizabeth Agnvall, "Women and Negotiation," *HR Magazine* 52, no. 12 (December 2007), pp. 69–74; Janet Stites, "Equal Pay for the Sexes," *HR Magazine* 50, no. 5 (May 2005), pp. 64–70; Stephanie Boraas and William M. Rodgers, III, "How Does Gender Play a Role in the Earnings Gap? An Update," *Monthly Labor Review* 126, no. 3 (March 2003) pp. 9–16; and U.S. Department of Labor, "Highlights of Women's Earnings in 2000," *Bureau of Labor Statistics Report 952,* August 2001, pp. 1–16.

A manager can, and often will, use principles from each of the three methods of administering rewards—positive reinforcement, modeling, and expectancy. Each of these methods indicates that employee job performance is a result of the application of effort. To generate the effort needed to achieve desirable results, managers can use positive reinforcers, modeling, and expectations.

What combination of methods to use is not the only issue in administering rewards. Organizational resources, competitive influences, labor market constraints, and government regulations are but a few of the many factors that must be considered in developing and maintaining reward programs. One particular issue that is receiving increasing attention is that of gender equity in reward administration. The above Organizational Encounter illustrates that women's salaries still trail those of men. To the extent that this reflects gender differences within the same jobs, this represents at least an ethical issue if not a legal one.

Rewards Affect Organizational Concerns

Rewards affect employee perceptions, attitudes, and behavior in a variety of ways. In turn, organizational efficiency and effectiveness are affected. Three important organizational concerns influenced by rewards are turnover and absenteeism, performance, and commitment. We will briefly examine each of these.

Turnover and Absenteeism

Some managers assume that high turnover is a mark of an effective organization. This view is somewhat controversial because a high quit rate means more expense for an organization. However, some organizations would benefit if disruptive and low performers quit.[39] Thus, the issue of turnover needs to focus on the *frequency* and on *who* is leaving.

Ideally, if managers could develop reward systems that retained the best performers and caused poor performers to leave, the overall effectiveness of an organization would improve. To approach this ideal state, an equitable and favorably compared reward system must exist. The feelings of *equity* and *favorable comparison* have an external orientation. That is, the equity of rewards and favorableness involve comparisons with external parties. This orientation is used because quitting most often means that a person leaves one organization for an alternative elsewhere.

There is no perfect means for retaining high performers. It appears that a reward system based on *merit* should encourage most of the better performers to remain with the organization. There also has to be some differential in the reward system that discriminates between high and low performers, the point being that the high performers must receive significantly more extrinsic and intrinsic rewards than the low performers.

Absenteeism is a costly and disruptive problem facing managers.[40] It is costly because it reduces output and disruptive because it requires that schedules and programs be modified. Absenteeism in the United States results in the estimated loss of more than 500 million workdays per year, about 5 days per employee or $600 per employee.[41] Other estimates suggest that the cost of lost productivity due to absenteeism is approximately $74 billion annually.[42] Employees go to work because they are motivated to do so. The level of motivation will remain high if an individual feels that attendance will lead to more valued rewards and fewer negative consequences than alternative behaviors.

Managers appear to have some influence over attendance behavior. They have the ability to punish, establish bonus systems, and allow employee participation in developing plans. Whether these or other approaches will reduce absenteeism is determined by the value of the rewards perceived by employees, the amount of the rewards, and whether employees perceive a relationship between attendance and rewards. These same characteristics appear every time we analyze the effects of rewards on organizational behavior.

Job Performance

Behaviorists and managers agree that extrinsic and intrinsic rewards can be used to motivate job performance. It is also clear that certain conditions must exist if rewards are to motivate good job performance: The rewards must be valued by the person, and they must be related to the level of job performance that is to be motivated.

Chapter 5 presented expectancy motivation theory, which stated that every behavior has associated with it (in a person's mind) certain outcomes or rewards or punishments. In other words, an assembly-line worker may believe that, by behaving in a certain way, he or she will get certain things. This is a description of the *performance-outcome expectancy*. The worker may expect that a steady performance of 10 units a day eventually will result in transfer to a more challenging job. On the other hand, the worker may expect that a steady performance of 10 units a day will result in being considered a rate-buster by co-workers.

valence
The strength of a person's preference for a particular outcome.

Each outcome has a **valence** or value to the person. Outcomes such as pay, promotion, a reprimand, or a better job have different values for different people because each person has different needs and perceptions. Thus, in considering which rewards to use, a manager has to be astute at considering individual differences. If valued rewards are used to motivate, they can result in the exertion of effort to achieve high levels of performance.

Organizational Commitment

commitment
A sense of identification, involvement, and loyalty expressed by an employee toward the company.

There is little research on the relationship between rewards and organizational commitment. **Commitment** to an organization involves three attitudes: (1) a sense of identification with the organization's goals, (2) a feeling of involvement in organizational duties, and (3) a feeling of loyalty to the organization.[43] Research evidence indicates that the absence of commitment can reduce organizational effectiveness.[44] People who are committed are less likely to quit and accept other jobs.[45] Thus, the costs of high turnover are not incurred. In addition, committed and highly skilled employees require less supervision. Close supervision and a rigid monitoring control process are time-consuming and costly. Furthermore, a committed employee perceives the value and importance of integrating individual and organizational goals. The employee thinks of his or her goals and the organization's goals in personal terms.

Intrinsic rewards are especially important for the development of organizational commitment. Organizations able to meet employee needs by providing achievement opportunities and by recognizing achievement when it occurs have a significant impact on commitment. Thus, managers need to develop intrinsic reward systems that focus on personal importance or self-esteem, integrate individual and organizational goals, and design challenging jobs.

Innovative Reward Systems

The typical list of rewards that managers can and do distribute in organizations has been discussed. We all know that pay, fringe benefits, and opportunities to achieve challenging goals are considered rewards by most people. It is also generally accepted that rewards are administered by managers through such processes as reinforcement, modeling, and expectancies. Managers are experimenting with newer and innovative, yet largely untested, reward programs. Seven different approaches to rewards that are not widely tested are skill-based pay, broadbanding, concierge services, team-based rewards, part-time benefits, gain-sharing, and employee stock ownership plans.

Skill-Based Pay

Skill-based pay is being used by a growing number of firms. In traditional compensation systems, workers are paid on the basis of their jobs. The hourly wage rate depends primarily on the job performed. In a skill-based plan, employees are paid at a rate based on their ability to develop and apply personal skills.[46] Typically, employees start at a basic initial rate of pay; they receive increases as their skills develop. Their pay rates are based on skill levels, no matter which jobs they are assigned.

In conventional pay systems, the job determines the pay rate and range. In the skill-based plan, however, the skills developed by employees are the key pay determinants. The skill-based pay plan approximates how professionals are compensated. In many organizations, professionals who do similar work are difficult to separate in terms of contributions made. Thus, surveys of what other firms pay professionals are used to establish pay grades and maturity curves. In skill-based plans, pay increases are not given at any specific time because of seniority. Instead, a raise is granted when employees demonstrate their skills to perform particular jobs.

Skill-based pay systems have at least four potential advantages:[47] (1) Since employees have more skills, the organization increases its flexibility by assigning workers to different jobs. (2) Because pay is not determined on the basis of the classification to which the job is assigned, the organization may need fewer distinct job classifications. (3) Fewer employees are needed because more workers are interchangeable. (4) The organization may experience reductions in turnover and absenteeism. Skill-based pay has worked well for a division of Rohm and Haas in La Porte, Texas. At this plant, employees learn all of the jobs to run a particular operation. The training takes about three years, and when it is successfully completed employees make approximately $12,000 a year more than when they started.[48]

A good place to begin the search and identification of key skills to perform well is with the already-exceptional performers. LEGO Systems, Inc., identified the skills of its top performers: technical skills, team achievement skills, and personal skills. Then, through focus groups and interviews with these top performers, the skills were clarified. LEGO used this information to build a competency model that served as the basis for linking pay to specific skills/competencies.[49]

Broadbanding

broadbanding
A pay system that reduces the actual number of pay grades to a relatively few broadly based pay grades. Places an emphasis on titles, grades, and job descriptions.

An element of financial reward that organizations are having problems with is the system of grading. Most systems have a large number of grades. The multiple grade approach is often out of alignment with the flatter, more team-oriented organizational designs institutions are moving toward. To counter this poor alignment, some firms are adopting what is called a banding or broadbanding approach. **Broadbanding** involves reducing numerous pay grades to a relatively few broadband grades.

An example of broadbanding would be placing all managers into one band; all technicians into a second band; all clerical personnel into a third band; and all part-time employees into a fourth band. Broadbanding emphasizes titles, grades, and job descriptions as presented in Exhibit 7.5.

Rather than concentrating on moving up a series of pay grades in a vertical system, employees could spend most, if not all, of their careers in a single band and move laterally as they acquire new skills or improve their performance. This type of pay system allows a person who needs to develop new skills to be placed in a lower band, but continue to be paid more.

How many pay bands are needed? There is no correct answer. Surveys suggest that organizations using broadbanding have from 1 to 18 bands.[50] The number of bands might depend on the levels in the firm's hierarchy, the key areas of accountability, or

EXHIBIT 7.5
Broadband Categories

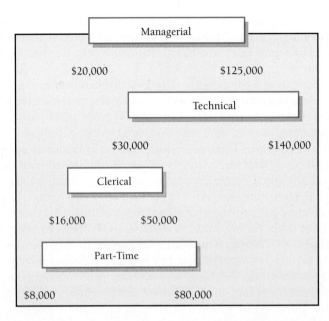

natural job clusters. General Electric has elected to use five bands for managerial personnel (professional, senior professional, leadership, executive, and senior executive). The results of GE's approach have not been subjected to careful analysis. Some critics of broadbanding at GE claim it is too gimmicky and is not as good as a well-designed, multiple-grade pay system.

At Scottish Bank, broadbanding was introduced with changes initiated by the chief executive officer. Fifteen pay grades covering all white-collar staff up to senior management were replaced by five broadbands.[51] Incremental pay progression and cost-of-living reviews were eliminated and totally flexible, merit-based increases were introduced. After about one year under the five broadband system, a number of modifications were made. Four distinct job family bands with levels in each were introduced. Also, pay progression to the band midpoint was guaranteed for effective performers within four years. The band also installed minimum pay increases for a growth in responsibilities and for the development of additional competencies. After these modifications, the broadband approach is now well received throughout the bank.

Broadbanding can make it easier to pay for skills and simplify the problem of placing employees and/or a job into a pay grade. It is easier because there are fewer pay grades. If a firm has 70 pay grades, the differences between each grade are small. What is the difference between a person being a 42 or a 43 grade? Broadbanding appears to have more flexibility for a person to make a lateral career move without punishing him or her by reducing pay. Traditional pay systems usually give no credit for the skills a person learned in the previous job. The person is simply paid on the basis of the new job. Why would someone be interested in moving laterally when everything is not included in the pay calculation?

Concierge Services

In Seattle, a vice president at the high-tech company Aventail has a tailor in his office to fit him for a new suit. Likewise, Baylor Health Care System in Dallas has unveiled its "Baylor Butler" concierge program to help its 15,000 employees balance their busy lives and schedules. To use the butler, employees visit the Web site or call a toll-free number to contact a concierge. The concierge helps with a variety of tasks, including making restaurant reservations, finding estimates for a home or automotive repair person, providing pet care vendors, doing personal shopping before the holidays, or picking up dry cleaning. The service is available 24 hours a day and 7 days a week.[52] This kind of employee benefit reward is not new, but it is attracting attention because of labor shortages, the clamor to balance work and life, the evaluation in benefit programs, and the Internet's ability to access services.[53]

The Society for Human Resource Management's 2008 Benefits Survey found that only 5 percent of employers report that they offer concierge services. Nevertheless, *Fortune* magazine's 100 Best Companies to Work For found 26 offering concierge services, including Zappos.com, Boston Consulting Group, AOL, and SC Johnson.

In many cases employees still have to pay for the most lavish services such as massages, but employers underwrite the location of the concierge. The availability of a concierge service for a wide range of "must do" activities is considered an attractive part of working for a particular firm. Freeing the employee to concentrate on performance can be considered an employer benefit worth the work and effort.

Team-Based Rewards

Individual pay-for-performance reward systems do not properly fit an organization that is designed around or uses teams. W. Edwards Deming (an originator of the total quality management approach) and other reward experts have clearly warned against putting individuals, who need to cooperate, under a reward system that fosters competition. Teams need to cooperate within the team structure and process. It is still difficult in a country that prides itself on individualism, such as the United States, to persuade employees to work together, to trust each other, and to be committed to group goals above individual work-related goals. People with strong individualism values become worried and skeptical about the so-called freeloader who doesn't perform well but gets the same rewards as everyone else.[54] It isn't fair. There are ways, however, to encourage poor performers to improve or leave. There are also methods to give special recognition and show respect to outstanding team leaders and performers.[55]

The design of a team-based reward system should follow the groupings in the overall organizational design. In situations where teams are relatively independent and measurable goals can be set and evaluated, rewards can be based on goal accomplishment.

In situations where teams are interdependent, a plant, division, or area reward plan may be the best system. Management must carefully analyze the independence–interdependence conditions.

Providing rewards to project teams is somewhat different. Since project team performance is usually short term and a onetime occurrence, it seems more appropriate to provide members with bonuses instead of permanent, base-pay merit rewards. Managers need to be consistent about how these teams are evaluated and should try to unite these short-term teams through recognition.[56]

The U.S. steel company, Nucor, which produces about 25 million tons of steel annually, has been rewarding its employee teams since 1966. Organized into groups of between 12 and 20 people (including supervisors and maintenance workers), Nucor pays team members based on the team's performance. HR managers at Nucor are careful to make sure the team-based pay supports the company's business strategy and doesn't undermine the individual employee's initiative. Nucor's team-based rewards program must be working; the company has been profitable each quarter since 1966 and has never laid off an employee.[57]

Although teams are here to stay, companies need to be careful in how they reward teams. Recent research suggests that team members feel strongly about being paid in a fair manner vis-à-vis other team members.[58] Companies need to apply team rewards consistently across team members and across time. Also, pay is not the only important motivator for team members; job security, challenging tasks, leadership style, and working with peers in a friendly working environment are important.[59] In sum, more research is needed to understand how to develop and manage effective team-based rewards.[60] Nucor's methods to reward teams appear to be working. However, additional long-term research into how other organizations are using team-based rewards is needed.[61] The Management Pointer on page 201 offers sound advice about team-based rewards systems.

Part-Time Benefits

The talent shortage has resulted in more employers relying more on people who work part-time. The U.S. Bureau of Labor Statistics defines "part-time" as working less than 35 hours per week. The number of part-timers (and their share of the workforce) has been growing in recent years. In April 2009, there were about 25.7 million part-timers in the U.S. workforce.[62] About 80 percent of employers provide vacation, holiday, and sick leave benefits, while about 70 percent offer some form of health care benefits.[63] Providing benefits to part-timers can be interpreted as a reward that is not mandatory. Companies such as UPS, Freddie Mac, and Starbucks are among those firms building a reputation for providing part-time employees with generous benefits packages, including health insurance, as a way to attract and retain top talent.

Most employers prorate benefits to their part-time workers. The most common way to calculate the rate for benefits is to divide the employee's average work hours in a full-time week. For example, if the average workweek in a firm is 40 hours, an employee who works 20 hours a week would receive benefits at 50 percent or one-half of the full-time rate.

One fear of smaller firms is that if a firm provides a full range of benefits to part-timers, some portion of full-timers will want to reduce their hours. In firms that are understaffed, having more full-timers opt for part-time status may result in a major operating crisis.

Gain-Sharing

Gain-sharing plans provide employees with a share of the financial benefits the organization accrues from improved operating efficiencies and effectiveness.[64] Probably the best-known example of gain-sharing is the Scanlon plan, named after its developer, Joseph Scanlon.[65] A typical Scanlon plan measures the labor costs required to produce goods or services during a base period. If future labor costs are less, a portion of the savings realized is shared with the employees responsible for the cost savings. In some companies, bonuses paid to workers under a Scanlon plan can equal or exceed the employee's usual salary. Scanlon plan companies typically rely on elaborate suggestion systems for receiving employee recommendations for operating efficiencies.

In a typical gain-sharing plan, an organization uses a formula to share financial gains with all employees in a single plant or location.[66] The organization establishes a historical base period of performance and uses this to determine whether or not gains in performance have occurred. Typically, only controllable costs are measured for the purpose of computing the gain. Unless a major change occurs in the organization's products or technology, the historical base figure stays the same over the duration of the plan.[67] The organization's performance is always compared to the time period before it implemented the gain-sharing plan. General Electric, Motorola, 3M, and TRW are among the thousands of firms using gain-sharing plans. GE has more than 10 gain-sharing plans in use.

Gain-sharing can take many forms. Simple cash awards for suggestions that are implemented is a form of gain-sharing. Virtually any program that shares cost reductions with employees may be considered gain-sharing. For example, Certified Transmissions, a chain of automotive transmission repair shops, faced escalating worker compensation costs because of high injury rates to its repairmen (not unusual in the automotive repair business). The company instituted a plan where all employees, including office staff, received a bonus each month there were no injuries. Bonus payments come from the money saved in reduced worker compensation costs, which have dropped to less than half of what the company had been paying before implementing the bonus plan.[68]

Successful gain-sharing programs require a strong commitment to operating efficiencies from both management and employees. In turn, such a commitment requires open communications, information sharing, and high levels of trust between all parties.

Goal-sharing is a follow-on to gain-sharing. Gain-sharing rewards employees based on financial performance. Goal-sharing has a broader approach. It refers to group incentive programs that reward employees for meeting specific goals. These goals often reflect job performance, quality, and service within a unit of a firm.[69]

At Weyerhaeuser in Federal Way, Washington, employees have no direct control over many of the financial aspects of the plant's success. The employees can make a difference in nonfinancial areas such as quality, safety, and efficiency. The employees set goals in these areas. By accomplishing the goals, the Weyerhaeuser employees earn a bonus. At Corning, Inc., the goal-sharing bonus is paid at the end of the year with a check that is separate from the regular paycheck. Corning has calculated that it receives $7.87 per each goal-sharing dollar it pays to employees.

Sears, Roebuck and Company has used goal-sharing at various stores. The goal-sharing unit is a specific store. Individual stores set their own goals. The goals relate to customer service and satisfaction.

Employee Stock Ownership Plans

ESOPs, as employee stock ownership plans are commonly called, are a relatively recent development in reward systems. They are somewhat like gain-sharing plans, a form of group incentive. Under ESOPs, companies make contributions of stock (or cash to purchase stock) to employees.[70] Typically, but not always, individual employee allocation is based upon seniority. ESOPs can provide a substantial nest egg for employees upon retiring or leaving the company. Organizations can benefit from improved performance from employees who now have a very direct financial stake in the company. An increasing number of organizations have instituted ESOPs, including Procter & Gamble, Polaroid, Lockheed, Brunswick Corporation, and Anheuser-Busch. Avis Corporation, one of the country's largest car rental firms, is wholly owned by its employees.

To create a more performance-oriented culture, Aquila, Inc. (formerly known as UtiliCorp.), a Kansas City–based utility, created a stock ownership plan. The goal of the plan is to provide 25 percent employee ownership. The company offers stock at a 15 percent discount and allows employees to buy shares in amounts of up to 20 percent of their base compensation. The 6 percent company match in the organization's 401(k) program also is awarded as stock. Even part of the annual incentive bonus for key employees is in the form of stock. Company officials report higher levels of satisfaction with the reward system since implementing the stock plan.[71]

Research on the effectiveness of employee stock ownership plans is mixed. Some companies, such as Brunswick, have attributed significant organizational performance improvements to the plans. Antioch Publishing Company has seen sales increase 13-fold since it instituted its ESOP. Company management reports that the ESOP has been important to that growth by making it easier to attract and retain good employees.[72] Other companies, however, see no apparent benefit from their plans. Like any other reward system, results will vary as a function of how well management introduces and implements the plan. Administering rewards is perhaps one of the most challenging and frustrating tasks that managers must perform.

Line of Sight: The Key Issue

Promotions, increased pay, recognition for a job well done, or the opportunity to own a part of an organization can be motivators if there is a clear line of sight between what the employee is doing and the reward. *Line of sight* means that the employee perceives that there is a "real" linkage between his or her performance and the rewards received. In the case of extrinsic rewards, organizations need to have systems that clearly tie rewards to desired performance.

Gain-sharing, stock options, and other extrinsic systems must be built around the line-of-sight concept. Unfortunately, accomplishing a clear line of sight is difficult. Merit-pay systems claim that they reward performance. Despite the notion of merit, employees do not always see or perceive the connection between rewards and performance. The practice of pay secrecy suggests that line of sight is difficult to achieve. Secret pay actions cloud any line-of-sight effort.

Intrinsic rewards are personal and come from the employee. However, organizations can influence intrinsic rewards and employees' perception of them by providing jobs that are challenging and by providing clear feedback on job performance. The design of a job should be carefully weighed when considering the line-of-sight issue. When jobs are designed with these issues in mind, the intrinsic rewards of working on the job become a top priority. Not all jobs can be enriched so that desired intrinsic rewards are provided to the employee. However, when jobs can be designed and enriched to provide a clear line of sight for matching intrinsic rewards and performance, the results have been positive. For example, the Mary Kay cosmetics company has designed jobs by making them autonomous and responsible. Sales representatives in most cases have found the jobs intrinsically rewarding and have linked their intrinsic rewards with exceptional performance. The line of sight of the job, rewards, and performance is validated constantly at Mary Kay.[73]

YOU BE THE JUDGE COMMENT

YOUR REWARD PREFERENCES

It's safe to say that not all employees are motivated by the same rewards. However, decades of employee surveys suggest that five factors play a consistently important role when it comes to motivating workers: good wages, appreciation for work done, job security, promotion and growth within the organization, and interesting work. The exact rank order of these factors has varied over the years. For example, a survey conducted in 1946 showed that "need to be appreciated for work done" was the top reward sought from respondents. The centralized decision making and hierarchical structures of many U.S. organizations in the post–World War II environment may have encouraged employees to seek recognition from superiors. In contrast, a 1992 survey reported that "good wages" was the most important motivational factor at work. Given the free market orientation of many employees in the 21st century and the frequent downsizing decisions of many organizations, this increased emphasis on extrinsic rewards (e.g., pay, bonuses, profit-sharing) continues.

Research suggests that the current workforce can be motivated in more ways than just good pay. The 5 Rs of motivation are

- Responsibility
- Respect
- Relationships
- Recognition
- Rewards

One more reward needs to be added to the 5 Rs, and that is jobs that afford work–life balance and flexibility. For example, Gen Y or Millennial workers and employees with child care or elder care needs tend to be more motivated (and retained longer) by jobs that allow them to work hard on their careers but also pursue their family and life interests. Companies should design jobs that allow employees to "own" them and feel accountable for their results. Respectful organizations not only say they value employees, but also show it by having "pro-people practices" such as continuous learning, extensive training, empowered teams, and equity in pay and promotion decisions. Relationships such as coaching, teaching, and supporting employees can produce favorable outcomes. Hard work and results should be recognized with promotions and public accolades. Rewards need to be awarded and allocated to those employees who most deserve them.

Sources: Laura Fitzpatrick, "We're Getting Off the Ladder," *Time,* May 25, 2009, p. 45; Ann Pomeroy, "The Future Is Now," *HR Magazine,* 52, no. 9 (September 2007), pp. 46–52; R. Brayton Bowen, "Today's Workforce Requires New Age Currency," *HR Magazine* 49, no. 3 (March 2004), pp. 101–7; and Carolyn Wiley, "What Motivates Employees According to Over 40 Years of Motivation Surveys," *International Journal of Manpower* 18, no. 3 (1997) pp. 263–80.

Summary of Key Points

- Performance evaluation serves several major purposes, including (1) providing a basis for reward allocation, (2) identifying high-potential employees, (3) validating the effectiveness of employee selection procedures, (4) evaluating previous training programs, and (5) facilitating future performance improvement.
- Feedback sessions should use objective information to help guide the evaluated employee to improve or sustain performance.
- A 360-degree feedback program involves the use of multiple sources of evaluation information collected from a full circle of evaluators (e.g., supervisors, subordinates, peers, and others).
- Reinforcement theory suggests that behavior is influenced by its consequences and that it is possible to affect behavior by controlling such consequences. Desired behaviors are reinforced through the use of rewards, while undesired behaviors can be extinguished through punishment. The timing of rewards and punishments is extremely critical and is controlled through the use of various *reinforcement schedules.*
- A useful model of individual rewards would include the suggestion that ability, skill, and experience, in addition to motivation, result in various levels of individual performance. The resulting performance is then evaluated by management, which

Now how much do you know about performance evaluation?

6. According to the terminology associated with reinforcement theory, _____ is the decline in a response rate because of nonreinforcement.
   a. eradication
   b. extinction
   c. destruction
   d. attrition

7. In the United States, the annual cost of lost productivity due to absenteeism is approximately $_____ billion.
   a. 15
   b. 58
   c. 74
   d. 91

8. True or false: Research suggests that giving extrinsic rewards to an employee who already has a high level of intrinsic motivation may result in the employee being *less* motivated.
   a. True
   b. False

9. True or false: Absenteeism in the United States results in more than 500 million lost workdays per year.
   a. True
   b. False

10. _____ plans provide employees with a share of the financial benefits the organization receives from improved operating efficiencies.
    a. Variable bonus
    b. Cafeteria benefit
    c. Continuous suggestion
    d. Gain-sharing

Reality Check Answers

Before	After
1. *a* 2. *b* 3. *a* 4. *c* 5. *c*	6. *b* 7. *c* 8. *a* 9. *a* 10. *d*
Number Correct	Number Correct
_____	_____

can distribute two types of rewards: intrinsic and extrinsic. These rewards are evaluated by the individual receiving them and, to the extent that they result in satisfaction, motivation to perform is enhanced.

- Organizational rewards can be classified as either extrinsic or intrinsic. Extrinsic rewards include salary and wages, fringe benefits, promotions, and certain types of interpersonal rewards. Intrinsic rewards can include such things as a sense of completion, achievement, autonomy, and personal growth.

- An effective reward system would encourage the best performers to remain with the organization, while causing the poorer performers to leave. To accomplish this, the system must be perceived as equitable. Additionally, the reward system should minimize the incidence of absenteeism. Generally, absenteeism will be less if an employee feels that attendance will lead to more valued rewards and fewer negative consequences.

- Both extrinsic and intrinsic rewards can be used to motivate job performance. For this to occur, certain conditions must exist: The rewards must be valued by the employee, and they must be related to the level of job performance that is to be motivated.

- In addition to standard organizational rewards such as pay, fringe benefits, advancement, and opportunities for growth, some organizations are experimenting with more innovative reward programs. Examples of such approaches include skill-based pay, broadbanding, concierge services, team-based rewards, part-time benefits, gain-sharing, and employee stock ownership plans.

Review and Discussion Questions

1. Why is providing feedback on poor performance a dreaded but necessary management experience?

2. Who should be included in a person's 360-degree domain when evaluating his or her performance?

3. What intrinsic rewards are important to you personally on a job and as a student?

4. From a managerial perspective, why is it impractical to provide continuous reinforcement in work environments? If it were practical, would it be a good idea? Explain.

5. The degree of employee satisfaction with the organization's reward system will significantly affect how successful the system is in influencing performance. Based on the research literature, what do we know about what influences whether individuals will be satisfied with the rewards they receive?

6. What are some problems that must be overcome to successfully administer a merit pay plan in an organization? What solutions can you offer for these problems?

7. The basic purpose of an evaluation is to provide information about work performance, but the information can also be used for other purposes. Name five other uses for an employee evaluation.

8. Why are team-based reward systems becoming more widely used?

9. This chapter discusses a number of innovative reward systems. Can you suggest other innovative approaches organizations might use? Identify potential problems with the approaches you suggest and try to find ways of overcoming them.

10. The gap between women's and men's pay is still considerable. What steps should employers and managers take to close this gap in a fair and consistent manner?

Exercise

Exercise 7.1: *Diagnosing a Work Performance Problem*

Background

Proper diagnosis is a critical aspect of effective motivation management. Often managers become frustrated because they don't understand the causes of observed performance problems. They might experiment with various "cures," but the inefficiency of this trial-and-error process often simply increases their frustration level. In addition, the accompanying misunderstanding adds extra strain to the manager–subordinate relationship. This generally makes the performance problem even more pronounced, which prompts the manager to resort

EXHIBIT 7.6 **Performance Diagnosis Model**

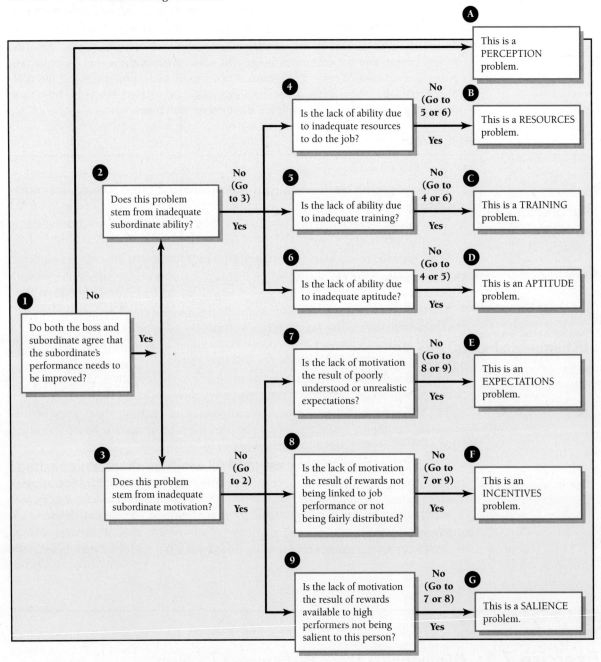

to more drastic responses, and a vicious, downward spiral ensues.

The performance diagnosis model in Exhibit 7.6 offers a systematic way for managers and subordinates to collaboratively pinpoint the cause(s) of dissatisfaction and performance problems. It assumes

that employees will work hard and be good performers if the work environment encourages these actions. Consequently, rather than jumping to conclusions about poor performance stemming from deficiencies in personality traits or a bad attitude, this diagnostic process helps managers focus their attention on improving the selection, job design, performance evaluation, and reward allocation systems. In this manner, the specific steps necessary to accomplish work goals and management's expectations are examined to pinpoint why the worker's performance is falling short.

The manager and low-performing subordinate should follow the logical discovery process in the model, step by step. They should begin by examining the current perceptions of performance, as well as the understanding of performance expectations, and then proceed through the model until the performance problems have been identified. The model focuses on seven of these problems.

A. *Perception problem.* "Do you agree your performance is below expectations?" A perception problem suggests that the manager and subordinate have different views of the subordinate's current performance level. Unless this disagreement is resolved, it is futile to continue the diagnostic process. The entire problem-solving process is based on the premise that both parties recognize the existence of a problem and are interested in solving it. If agreement does not exist, the manager should focus on resolving the discrepancy in perceptions, including clarifying current expectations (problem E).

B. *Resources problem.* "Do you have the resources necessary to do the job well?" (Ability has three components, and these should be explored in the order shown in the model. This order reduces a subordinate's defensive reactions.) Poor performance may stem from a lack of resource support. Resources include material and personnel support as well as cooperation from interdependent work groups.

C. *Training problem.* "Is a lack of training interfering with your job performance?" Individuals may be asked to perform tasks that exceed their current skill or knowledge level. Typically this problem can be overcome through additional training or education.

D. *Aptitude problem.* "Do you feel this is the right job-blend of work assignments for you?" This is the most difficult of the three ability problems to resolve because it is the most basic. If the *resupply* (providing additional resources) and *retraining* solutions have been explored without success, then more drastic measures may be

required. These include *refitting* the person's current job requirements, *reassigning* him to another position, or, finally, *releasing* him from the organization.

E. *Expectations problem.* "What are your performance expectations for this position? What do you think my expectations are?" This problem results from poor communications regarding job goals or job requirements. In some cases, the stated goals may be different from the desired goals. In other words, the employee is working toward one goal while the supervisor desires another. This often occurs when subordinates are not sufficiently involved in the goal- or standard-setting process. When this results in unrealistic, imposed expectations, motivation suffers.

F. *Incentives problem.* "Do you believe rewards are linked to your performance in this position?" Either the individual does not believe that "performance makes a difference" or insufficient performance feedback and reinforcement have been given. The manager should also ask, "Do you feel rewards are being distributed equitably?" This provides an opportunity to discuss subordinates' criteria for judging fairness. Often, unrealistic standards are being used.

G. *Salience problem.* "Are the performance incentives attractive to you?" Salience refers to the importance an individual attaches to available rewards. Often the incentives offered to encourage high performance simply aren't highly valued by a particular individual. The salience problem points out the need for managers to be creative in generating a broad range of rewards and flexible in allowing subordinates to choose among rewards.

Assignment

Option 1: Read the case below, "Joe's Performance Problems," and privately use the diagnostic model in Exhibit 7.6 to pinpoint plausible performance problems. Next, in small groups discuss your individual assessments, and list the specific questions you should ask Joe to accurately identify, from his point of view, the obstacles to his high performance. Finally, brainstorm ideas for plausible solutions. Be prepared to represent your group in role-playing a problem-solving interview with Joe.

Joe's Performance Problems

Joe joined your architectural firm two years ago as a draftsman. He is 35 years old and has been a draftsman since graduating from a two-year technical school right after high school. He is married and has four children. He has worked for four architectural firms in 12 years.

Joe came with mediocre recommendations from his previous employer, but you hired him anyway because you needed help desperately. Your firm's workload has been extremely high due to a local construction boom. The result is that a lot of the practices that contribute to a supportive, well-managed work environment have been overlooked. For instance, you can't remember the last time you conducted a formal performance review or did any career counseling. Furthermore, the tradition of closing the office early on Friday for a social hour was dropped long ago. Unfortunately, the tension in the office runs pretty high some days due to unbearable time pressures and the lack of adequate staff. Nighttime work and weekend work have become the norm rather than the exception.

Overall, you have been pleasantly surprised by Joe's performance. Until recently he worked hard and consistently produced quality work. Furthermore, he frequently volunteered for special projects, made lots of suggestions for improving the work environment, and demonstrated an in-depth practical knowledge of architecture and the construction business. However, during the past few months, he has definitely slacked off. He doesn't seem as excited about his work, and several times you have found him daydreaming at his desk. In addition, he has gotten into several heated arguments with architects about the specifications and proper design procedures for recent projects.

After one of these disagreements, you overheard Joe complaining to his officemate, "No one around here respects my opinion; I'm just a lowly draftsman. I know as much as these hotshot architects, but because I don't have the degree, they ignore my input, and I'm stuck doing the grunt work. Adding insult to injury, my wife has had to get a job to help support our family. I must be the lowest-paid person in this firm." In response to a question from a co-worker regarding why he didn't pursue a college degree in architecture, Joe responded, "Do you have any idea how hard it is to put bread on the table, pay a Seattle mortgage, work overtime, be a reasonably good father and husband, plus go to night school? Come on, be realistic!"

Exercise 7.2: *Making Choices about Rewards*

Objectives

1. To illustrate individual differences in reward preferences.
2. To emphasize how both extrinsic and intrinsic rewards are considered important.
3. To enable people to explore the reasons for the reward preferences of others.

Starting the Exercise

Initially individuals will work alone establishing their own lists of reward preferences after reviewing Exhibit 7.7. Then the instructor will set up groups of four to six students to examine individual preferences and complete the exercise.

The Facts

Presented in a random fashion in Exhibit 7.7 are some of the on-the-job rewards that could be available to employees.

Exercise Procedures

Phase I: 25 Minutes

1. Each individual should set up from Exhibit 7.7 a list of extrinsic and intrinsic rewards.
2. Each person should then rank-order from most important to least important the two lists.
3. From the two lists, rank the eight most important rewards. How many are extrinsic, and how many are intrinsic?

EXHIBIT 7.7
Some Possible Rewards for Employees

Company picnics	Smile from manager	Manager asking for advice
Watches	Feedback on performance	Informal leader asking for advice
Trophies	Feedback on career progress	Office with a window
Piped-in music	Larger office	The privilege of completing a job
Job challenge	Club privileges	from start to finish
Achievement opportunity	More prestigious job	
Time off for performance	More job involvement	
Vacation	Use of company recreation facilities	
Autonomy	Participation in decisions	
Pay increase	Stock options	
Recognition	Vacation trips for performance	

Phase II: 30 Minutes

1. The instructor will set up groups of four to six individuals.

2. The two lists in which the extrinsic and intrinsic categories were developed should be discussed.

3. The final rank orders of the eight most important rewards should be placed on a board or chart at the front of the room.

4. The rankings should be discussed within the groups. What major differences are displayed?

Case

Case 7.1: *The Politics of Performance Appraisal*

Every Friday, Max Steadman, Jim Coburn, Lynne Sims, and Tom Hamilton meet at Charley's after work for drinks. The four friends work as managers at Eckel Industries, a manufacturer of arc-welding equipment in Minneapolis. The one-plant company employs about 2,000 people. The four managers work in the manufacturing division. Max, 35, manages the company's 25 quality-control inspectors. Lynne, 33, works as a supervisor in inventory management. Jim, 34, is a first-line supervisor in the metal coating department. Tom, 28, supervises a team of assemblers. The four managers' tenure at Eckel Industries ranges from 1 year (Tom) to 12 years (Max).

The group is close-knit; Lynne, Jim, and Max's friendship stems from their years as undergraduate business students at the University of Minnesota. Tom, the newcomer, joined the group after meeting the three at an Eckel management seminar last year. Weekly get-togethers at Charley's have become a comfortable habit for the group and provide an opportunity to relax, exchange the latest gossip heard around the plant, and give and receive advice about problems encountered on the job.

This week's topic of discussion: performance appraisal, specifically the company's annual review process, which the plant's management conducted in the last week. Each of the four managers completed evaluation forms (graphic rating scales) on all of his or her subordinates and met with each subordinate to discuss the appraisal.

Tom: This was the first time I've appraised my people, and I dreaded it. For me, it's been the worst week of the year. Evaluating is difficult; it's highly subjective and inexact. Your emotions creep into the process. I got angry at one of my assembly workers last week, and I still felt the anger when I was filling out the evaluation forms. Don't tell me that my frustration with the guy didn't bias my appraisal. I think it did. And I think the technique is flawed. Tell me—what's the difference between a five and a six on "cooperation"?

Jim: The scales are a problem. So is memory. Remember our course in human resources in college? Dr. Philips said that, according to research, when we sit down to evaluate someone's performance in the past year, we will only be able to actively recall and use 15 percent of the performance we actually observed.

Lynne: I think political considerations are always a part of the process. I know I consider many other factors besides a person's actual performance when I appraise him.

Tom: Like what?

Lynne: Like the appraisal will become part of his permanent written record that affects his career. Like the person I evaluate today, I have to work with tomorrow. Given that, the difference between a five and a six on cooperation isn't that relevant, because frankly, if a five makes him mad and he's happy with a six . . .

Max: Then you give him the six. Accuracy is important, but I'll admit it—accuracy isn't my primary objective when I evaluate my workers. My objective is to motivate and reward them so they'll perform better. I use the review process to do what's best for my people and my department. If that means fine-tuning the evaluations to do that, I will.

Tom: What's an example of fine-tuning?

Max: Jim, do you remember three years ago when the company lowered the ceiling on merit raises? The top merit increase that any employee could get was 4 percent. I boosted the ratings of my folks to get the best merit increases for them. The year before that, the ceiling was 8 percent. The best they could get was less than what most of them received the year before. I felt they deserved the

4 percent, so I gave the marks that got them what I felt they deserved.

Lynne: I've inflated ratings to encourage someone who is having personal problems but is normally a good employee. A couple of years ago, one of my better people was going through a painful divorce, and it was showing in her work. I don't think it's fair to kick someone when they're down, even if their work is poor. I felt a good rating would speed her recovery.

Tom: Or make her complacent.

Lynne: No, I don't think so. I felt she realized her work was suffering. I wanted to give her encouragement; it was my way of telling her she had some support and that she wasn't in danger of losing her job.

Jim: There's another situation where I think fine-tuning is merited—when someone's work has been mediocre or even poor for most of the year, but it improves substantially in the last two, three months or so. If I think the guy is really trying and is doing much better, I'd give him a rating that's higher than his work over the whole year deserves. It encourages him to keep improving. If I give him a mediocre rating, what does that tell him?

Tom: What if he's really working hard, but not doing so great?

Jim: If I think he has what it takes, I'd boost the rating to motivate him to keep trying until he gets there.

Max: I know of one or two managers who've inflated ratings to get rid of a pain in the neck, some young guy who's transferred in and thinks he'll be there a short time. He's not good, but thinks he is and creates all sorts of problems. Or his performance is OK, but he just doesn't fit in with the rest of the department. A year or two of good ratings is a sure trick for getting rid of him.

Tom: Yes, but you're passing the problem on to someone else.

Max: True, but it's no longer my problem.

Tom: All the examples you've talked about involve inflating evaluations. What about deflating them, giving someone less than you really think he deserves? Is that justified?

Lynne: I'd hesitate to do that, because it can create problems. It can backfire.

Max: But it does happen. You can lower a guy's ratings to shock him, to jolt him into performing better. Sometimes, you can work with someone, coach him, try to help him improve, and it just doesn't work. A basement-level rating can tell him you mean business. You can say that isn't fair, and for the time being, it isn't. But what if you feel that if the guy doesn't shape up, he faces being fired in a year or two, and putting him in the cellar, ratings-wise, will solve his problem? It's fair in the long run if the effect is that he improves his work and keeps his job.

Jim: Sometimes, you get someone who's a real rebel, who always questions you, sometimes even oversteps his bounds. I think deflating his evaluation is merited just to remind him who's the boss.

Lynne: I'd consider lowering someone's true rating if they've had a long record of rather questionable performance, and I think the best alternative for the person is to consider another job with another company. A low appraisal sends him a message to consider quitting and start looking for another job.

Max: What if you believe the situation is hopeless, and you've made up your mind that you're going to fire the guy as soon as you've found a suitable replacement? The courts have chipped away at management's right to fire. Today, when you fire someone, you'd better have a strong case. I think once a manager decides to fire, appraisals become very negative. Anything good that you say about the subordinate can be used later against you. Deflating the ratings protects you from being sued and sometimes speeds up the termination process.

Tom: I understand your points, but I still believe that accuracy is the top priority in performance appraisal. Let me play devil's advocate for a minute. First, Jim, you complained about our memory limitations introducing a bias into appraisal. Doesn't introducing politics into the process further distort the truth by introducing yet another bias? Even more important, most would agree that one key to motivating people is providing true feedback—the facts about how they're doing so they know where they stand. Then you talk with them about how to improve their performance. When you distort an evaluation—however slightly—are you providing this kind of feedback?

Max: I think you're overstating the degree of fine-tuning.

Tom: Distortion, you mean.

Max: No, fine-tuning. I'm not talking about giving a guy a seven when he deserves a two, or vice versa. It's not that extreme. I'm talking about making slight changes in the ratings when you think that the change can make a big difference in terms of achieving what you think is best for the person and for your department.

Tom: But when you fine-tune, you're manipulating your people. Why not give them the most accurate evaluation and let the chips fall where they may? Give them the facts and let them decide.

Max: Because most of good managing is psychology. Understanding people, their strengths and shortcomings. Knowing how to motivate, reward, and act to do what's in their and your department's best interest. And sometimes, total accuracy is not the best path. Sometimes, it's not in anybody's best interest.

Jim: All this discussion raises a question. What's the difference between fine-tuning and significant distortion? Where do you draw the line?

Lynne: That's about as easy a question as what's the difference between a five and a six. On the form, I mean.

Questions

1. Based on your view of the objectives of performance evaluation, evaluate the perspectives about performance appraisal presented by the managers.

2. In your opinion, at what point does "fine-tuning" evaluations become unacceptable distortion?

3. Assume you are the vice president of human resources at Eckel Industries and that you are aware that fine-tuning evaluations is a prevalent practice among Eckel managers. If you disagree with this perspective, what steps would you take to reduce the practice?

CHAPTER EIGHT

Managing Misbehavior

Learning Objectives

After completing Chapter 8, you should be able to:

- **Explain** why the management of misbehavior is an important responsibility that managers must address.
- **Describe** some of the outcomes of misbehavior in terms of property, politics, interpersonal relations, and intrapersonal relations.
- **Explain** the different types of sexual harassment.

- **Discuss** why sexual harassment can be interpreted to be a form of violence.
- **Identify** why some consider the invasion of privacy rights to be a moral issue.
- **Discuss** how an organization's culture can impact what is referred to as the management of misbehavior norms.
- **Explain** why organizational researchers are now more willing to acknowledge that misbehavior is an important issue.

Managers often face problem behaviors in the work setting that must be solved to prevent additional negative consequences. An understanding of managing workers is incomplete without studying, discussing, anticipating, and addressing what we refer to in this chapter as managing employee misbehavior (MEM). This chapter recognizes that the majority of employee behavior is positive and directed toward the accomplishment of meaningful goals. However, occasionally managers need to deal with MEM in an organized, systematic manner.

The chapter will explore some of the available theory and increasing research concerning negative behavior in work settings. Obviously misbehavior is costly, reduces performance, and can impact the entire organization negatively.[1] Some organizational scientists have made recommendations regarding the management and analysis of misbehavior and its consequences. The chapter will explore a range of misbehavior from the minor to the most destructive; many forms will be omitted because of space limitations.

The Management of Misbehavior

Managing employee misbehavior requires an active posture in that managers are responsible for identifying, solving, and correcting problems. Some observers refer to workplace misbehavior as a serious form of antisocial behavior. Exhibit 8.1 lists misbehaviors in an organizational setting.

The list is only a partial presentation of misbehavior that needs management intervention. The popular press contains many stories and analyses of violent acts

Reality Check

How much do you know about managing misbehaving employees?

1. True or false: An employee's work environment has no influence on whether he or she will engage in substance abuse.
   a. True
   b. False

2. Sexual harassment is a specific type of misbehavior. Some refer to sexual harassment as a form of _____.
   a. white-collar crime
   b. business organization problem
   c. violence
   d. manufacturing policy issue

3. Employee theft losses to employers are at least _____ more than the total cost of street crime annually.
   a. 3 times
   b. 10 times
   c. 50 times
   d. 100 times

4. True or false: Employers can read e-mails sent over their computer systems even if employees are not informed of the policy.
   a. True
   b. False

5. A heuristic framework for helping managers cope with theft is called _____.
   a. crime stopper
   b. audit check
   c. steal
   d. honesty

(e.g., shootings) in the workplace, financial fraud and malfeasance (e.g., Bernie Madoff, Parmalat, Enron, and National Century Financial), and lawsuits filed and settled (e.g., Texaco, Mitsubishi, and Fox News) involving sexual harassment, identity theft, and discrimination.[2]

A number of major reviews of the organizational behavior literature suggest that organizational researchers tend to focus primarily on positive descriptions of what occurs at work.[3] The positive aspects, of which there are many, of leadership, motivation programs, and change projects are studied and discussed. Fewer scholars address employee misbehavior as an important concern.

EXHIBIT 8.1
Examples of Misbehavior at Work

Arson	Fraud	Sabotage
Blackmail	Incivility	Sexual harassment
Bribery	Intimidation	Spying on co-workers
Bullying	Kickbacks	Substance abuse
Cheating	Lying	Theft
Discrimination	Misinformation	Threats
Dishonesty	Privacy violations	Withholding information (concealment)
Espionage	Revenge	Withholding job effort

Although the majority of management researchers have largely ignored misbehavior in organizations,[4] other disciplines have studied it for years. Studies of the impact of an occupational structure on criminal workplace behavior, embezzlement, vandalism, sabotage, restriction of output, and goldbricking have been conducted by sociologists, occupational psychologists, criminologists, and anthropologists.[5] In a presidential address to the American Sociological Society, Sutherland introduced the notion of white-collar crime, defining it as "crime committed by a person of respectability and high social status in the course of his occupation."[6] Coleman proposed that white-collar crimes involve illegal acts, the identification of a beneficiary of the acts, and the social status of the actor (criminal). He further differentiated between *occupational* crime, or crimes to benefit the criminal conducted without organizational support, and *organizational* crime, which is conducted with the support of an organization.[7]

The Emergence in Management of the Study of Misbehavior

The concept of MEM has a cross-disciplinary theme. That is, a number of disciplines offer theories, research findings, and frameworks to examine MEM and its consequences. Vardi and Weitz discuss in detail a number of misbehavior categories including deviance, aggression, and political behavior. In their framework, employee deviance is concerned with the social conditions under which certain behaviors are considered deviate. Workplace aggression includes harmful and damaging behaviors. Political behavior is the misuse of power and influence. These three categories of misbehavior overlap and are interrelated in their framework.

The Vardi and Weitz framework has been adapted here to fit the goals of the chapter.[8] It is multidisciplinary, thorough, empirically supported, and can be examined through further testing, which will likely result inevitability in some modification. Exhibit 8.2 presents an adaptive, yet representative version of the Vardi and Weitz comprehensive model of organizational misbehavior.[9]

The discussion that follows will focus primarily on selected outcomes and selected interventions. Exhibit 8.2 suggests that misbehavior is a purposeful action on the part of individuals that is mediated by a person's beliefs and an organization's expectations. The intention to misbehave can result in a number of financially and socially costly outcomes.

Antecedents

Exhibit 8.2 displays four types of antecedents to misbehavior—individual, job, group, and organizational. The selection of characteristics displayed is based on available studies, frameworks, and discussions previously established on each of the factors. For example, when individuals perceive they are being mistreated by a manager, their preference for misbehaving may increase.[10] This attitude can then become internalized and impact co-workers. If, for example, co-workers agree that mistreatment has occurred, they can join in with their own misbehavior. Hackett found a relationship between employee dissatisfaction and increased absenteeism.[11] The intentional work misbehavior of the individual who perceives himself to be mistreated could have negative consequences for the person (dissatisfaction), the work group (dissatisfaction), and the organization (increased absenteeism). The model displayed in Exhibit 8.2 assumes that all misbehaviors (outcomes) are voluntarily committed.

EXHIBIT 8.2 **A Model of Organizational Misbehavior**

Source: Adapted from Yoav Vardi and Ely Weitz, *Misbehavior in Organizations: Theory, Research, and Management* (Mahwah, NJ: Lawrence Erlbaum, 2004), p. 251 with modifications.

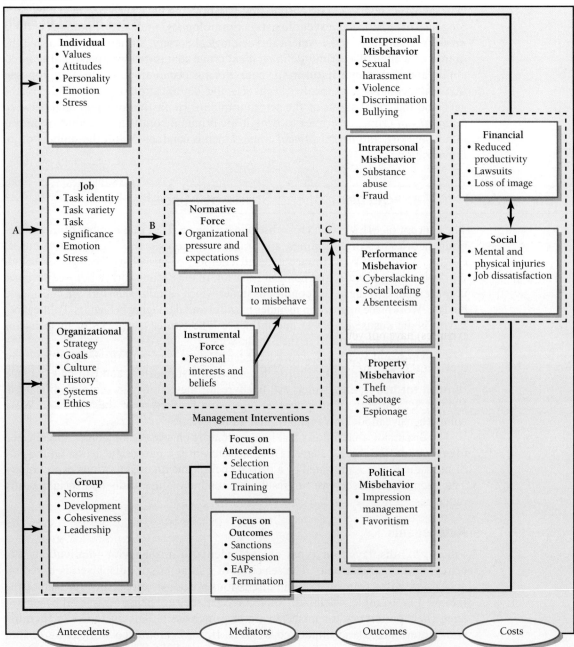

Mediators

A core concept in the model presented in Exhibit 8.2 is the "intention to misbehave." Accidental behaviors on the part of individuals are excluded. The intention to misbehave is defined as the behavior exhibited by an individual or group that is purposeful (intentional) and can be harmful to the person and others, as well as financially and socially costly.

The intention to misbehave is posited to mediate the relationship between antecedents and the outcomes that are expressions of the misbehavior.[12] Intentions are assumed to be the result of a normative force, or the person's expectations of how he or she is supposed to behave, and an instrumental force, which represents the individual's personal interests and beliefs. These two forces can influence a person's intention to misbehave as well as what type of misbehavior will be engaged in. For example, an angry employee may attempt to hurt the organization by hiding a crucial set of data to satisfy his need to retaliate (instrumental force), restrict his attendance (normative force), or misbehave in both ways.

Outcomes

The examples of misbehaviors (outcomes) presented in Exhibit 8.2 are some of the more researched, reported, and analyzed misbehaviors, but more examples exist. Five specific categories that are discussed in the literature are interpersonal, intrapersonal, performance, property, and political.[13] Some specific misbehaviors in these categories will be discussed later in the chapter.

Costs

The potential costs of employee misbehavior to individuals, groups, organizations, and other societal groups can be substantial. For example, the financial costs of the Enron debacle to employees (lost pensions), executives (imprisonment, lost careers), the community (Houston's economic and business infrastructure), and society (legal expenses) have not yet been calculated.[14] However, losses will reach billions of dollars. In addition to the financial costs of the Enron and other similar cases are substantial social costs (premature illness, depression, suicide, family instability). Are managers responsible for these costs? Some believe that managers have been given a "free ride" in the social cost responsibility area. The Organizational Encounter on page 220 illustrates examples of misbehavior in a number of organizations.

Management Interventions

Management interventions are the actions taken by managers (representing the organization) to prevent, control, or respond to harmful misbehavior. Exhibit 8.2 displays three specific points for management intervention—A, B, and C. At point A, management can carefully screen and refuse to hire "risky" individuals. Management can also intervene at other antecedent points: job, group, and organization. The problem with interventions at these points is that the person is already employed. The most efficient intervention point is during the preemployment phase.[15]

The intervention at B requires affecting the normative force, as well as the instrumental force. The goal of this intervention point is to reduce the possibility of a job, group, or organizational antecedent to trigger misbehavior. For example, some organizations use mentor programs to provide a role model of proper (normative) attitudes and behavior and communicate through mentor–mentee discussions the consequences of misbehaving (instrumental).

The intention of an intervention at C shifts from prevention to deterrence. The manager works to reduce the possibility of the intention to misbehave. A member of a team who values being part of the team may learn that misbehavior could mean being transferred (control) to another unit. She may decide that staying with the preferred unit is important and elect to behave properly. The threat of a transfer may be powerful enough to evoke a change in behavior.

MISBEHAVIOR: A FEW EXAMPLES

The reports of corporate crimes, fraud, and malfeasance continue to make headlines years after the Enron scandals hit newswires and television screens. Misbehavior is not gender, industry, country, or date specific. Managers and nonmanagers keep making headlines because they are alleged to have committed, have pleaded to committing, or have been convicted of a crime. A few samples of the carnage and misbehavior are:

- **Bernard L. Madoff Investment Securities:** The Securities and Exchange Commission (SEC) accused Madoff of deceiving investors to the tune of $65 billion. Engaging in a "Ponzi scheme," he traded and lost investor money but still paid these investors a certain return on investment with the money given by other investors. In 2009, the 70-year-old Madoff was found guilty of fraud and sentenced to 150 years in jail.

- **Rite Aid Corporation:** Federal prosecutors charged that the drugstore's former general counsel "tried to line his pocket with millions." Former CEO Martin Grass also pleaded guilty to conspiracy to defraud Rite Aid and its shareholders by inflating profits by $1.6 billion. He will serve up to eight years in federal prison and was fined $500,000.

- **Siemens Corporation:** Europe's largest engineering firm pleaded guilty in 2008 to charges of bribery and corruption and agreed to pay fines of $800 million in the United States and $540 million in Germany. Cash payments were made to foreign officials to help the company win lucrative contracts. It was alleged that three cash desks were set up at Siemens offices where managers could take out large sums of cash in suitcases to pay off officials.

- **Xerox Corporation:** The SEC alleged that Xerox, in an effort to hide deteriorating performance results, doctored its books using many fraudulent schemes, among them "cookie jar" reserves that could be dipped into when times were tough and manipulating office equipment leases to accelerate the booking of revenue and profit. Xerox paid the SEC a $10 million penalty to settle civil charges. Four top Xerox executives agreed to pay $22 million in fines and interest.

- **ImClone Systems Inc.:** This company claimed it had discovered a wonder drug for colorectal cancer called Erbitux. The Food and Drug Administration (FDA) refused to review the drug, citing missing evidence. Authorities proved Samuel Waksal, co-founder and CEO, tipped off family members and friends (e.g., Martha Stewart) that the FDA was refusing to conduct a review. This "tip" allowed individuals to sell the stock. Waksal was sentenced to 87 months in prison after pleading guilty to charges of securities fraud. He will also pay $4 million in fines and back taxes and is banned for life from leading a public company. Martha Stewart served five months in prison, two years probation, and for five months after her release she was confined to her home.

Sources: Adapted from Amir Efrati, Tom Lauricella, and Dionne Searcey, "Top Broker Accused of $50 Billion Fraud," *The Wall Street Journal*, December 12, 2008, p. A1; "Business: Bavarian Baksheesh: The Siemens Scandal," *The Economist* 389, no. 8611 (December 20, 2008), p. 112; "Martha Stewart," www.wikipedia.org/Martha_Stewart (accessed April 10, 2006); and Robert Franks et al., "Scandal Scorecard," *The Wall Street Journal*, October 3, 2003, pp. B1, B4.

These intervention points offer managers different opportunities to reduce the incidence or at least consequences or costs of misbehavior. Since every possible misbehavior can't be discussed, we select only a few. These have been selected because of the available literature and current discussion of them in the academic and popular press.

Selected Misbehaviors

The list of potential employee misbehaviors faced by managers is extensive. As stated earlier, Exhibit 8.1 represents only a partial list of misbehaviors. We now discuss a number of significant and widely publicized and researched misbehaviors.

Sexual Harassment

sexual harassment
Unwelcome advances, requests for sexual favors, and other types of verbal, psychological, or physical abuses.

Sexual harassment is an important topic and has been the subject of a considerable amount of research in recent years.[16] More than 70 percent of female employees report they have been the objects of sexually harassing behaviors while working. Sexual harassment is a form of aggression as well as unethical behavior.[17] Broadly defined, this misbehavior is characterized by unwelcome advances, requests for sexual favors, and other types of verbal, psychological, or physical abuses. From a legal perspective, there are several types of sexual harassment, including:[18]

1. *Quid pro quo.* This form of sexual harassment occurs when an employee's compliance with requests for sexual favors are linked to employment decisions (e.g., promotion or hiring).
2. *Hostile work environment.* This sexual harassment occurs when sex-related behavior interferes with an employee's work performance or creates an intimidating, hostile, or offensive working environment.
3. *Psychological.* This sexual harassment occurs when an employee "feels harassed" regardless of whether or not the sex-related behavior is illegal.

Sexual harassment occurs because of power differences, lust, and reasons that are not entirely understood. It occurs across gender lines and across sexual orientations.[19] It is not only misbehavior but is also illegal. Sexual harassment is a form of discrimination, but in addition, harassed employees can file claims for battery and defamation.

Flirting, joking, bantering, and other sexual interactions are daily occurrences in work settings. Not all of these interactions constitute sexual harassment. Consensual sexual interactions are those that reflect positive expressions of workers' sexual choices and desires. However, some workplace relationships can have a host of negative ramifications, including accusations of favoritism, decreased productivity, gossip, and in the case of a bad breakup, a strained work environment and even workplace violence.[20] Some companies ask employees to sign a "consensual relationship agreement" or "love contract." This agreement has to be signed by both dating employees and typically includes the following provisions:[21]

- The relationship is consensual.
- What the dating employees will do if the relationship stops being consensual.
- Both dating employees verify that they are aware of the company's policies on sexual harassment.
- The dating employees are told what happens if one or both of the dating employees break the contract.

O'Leary-Kelly and colleagues reviewed the research conducted on sexual harassment from 1995 to 2008.[22] They summarized sexual harassment research in terms of the various definitions of sexual harassment, predictors (personal, situational, and organizational) of sexual harassment, responses to sexual harassment (target, organizational, and observer), and the consequences of sexual harassment (turnover, work group productivity, job withdrawal). These researchers made the following conclusions about the evolution of sexual harassment research over the past 13 years: (1) There have been advances in theoretical models that guide research and empirical testing; (2) research is taking a broader focus to examine different types of harassers (e.g., clients) and a broader range of conduct (e.g., sexual assault); and (3) more has been learned about how sexual harassment is facilitated or inhibited by the organizational culture.[23]

Some individuals consider sexual harassment to be only of minimal concern or importance, not recognizing the damage done by sexually harassing misbehavior. Pryor and Stoller found that men who scored high on a characteristic designated "likelihood to sexually harass (LSH)" hold adversarial sexual beliefs, have difficulty understanding others' perspectives, and endorse traditional male sex stereotypes.[24] These high-LSH men view many harassing behaviors as only expressions or hints of attraction and sexual interest. Convincing men with LSH tendencies that sexual harassment hurts another person is difficult because of their hardened view about others' perspectives. For example, a recent study reported that males with high levels of LSH tend to give attractive females higher scores on performance appraisals.[25] These upwardly biased ratings can create fairness issues in relation to less attractive females who perform as well or better than their more attractive peers. Theory and research have proposed that men and women often view alleged sexual harassment behavior differently. Research shows that some behavior men consider friendly women interpret as sexual. Women tend to classify a wider range of behavior as sexually harassing than do men.[26] This stream of research suggests a basis for why men tend to be harassers more often than do women.

How can a manager recognize a behavior as sexual harassment?[27] There are a few tests for focusing on and categorizing particular behaviors:

The Family IQ Test. Would this occur if the sexual harasser's child were present? Would it be occurring if the spouse of the victim were present? Would you as an observer want the behavior or allow the actions to be done to your daughter?

The Public Forum Test. Is this a behavior you would like to see in the newspaper or hear about in a radio broadcast or on a television news program?

Dual Treatment. Is this done to other people, of both sexes, frequently?

These are general rules to help managers assess the behaviors of others, as well as their own behaviors. Considering the responses to these kinds of questions can help a manager govern his or her own behavior and decide how and when to intervene.

Aggression and Violence

The word *aggression* is used to describe many forms of behavior. Concisely put, **aggression** *at work* is the effort of an individual to bring harm to others with whom the person has worked or currently works at an organization (i.e., current or past). The attempt to bring harm is intentional and includes psychological as well as physical injury. There are over 2 million workplace physical assaults annually. Workplace violence accounts for about 18 percent of the violent crimes committed annually. According to the Occupational Safety and Health Administration (OSHA), workers who do the following activities are at an increased risk of being victims of workplace violence: exchange money, make deliveries, work alone, work late nights, or work in settings/homes with extensive contact with the public. High-risk occupations include: visiting nurses, psychiatric evaluators, phone and cable TV installers, retail workers, and taxi drivers.[28]

aggression
In the work setting this is behavior that brings harm to others with whom the aggressor works or has worked.

A review of the organization science literature suggests that aggression has only recently been considered worthy of study. Buss has categorized aggression along physical, verbal, active, passive, direct, and indirect dimensions.[29] Exhibit 8.3 shows his framework for classifying aggression. The Buss framework addresses interpersonal forms of aggression. Buss asserts that the aggressor consciously intends to bring harm to another person or the organization. Physical forms of aggression could involve an attack with fists, pushing, slapping, or use of a weapon. Verbal aggression is inflicted by words, gossip, or innuendo.

Active aggression brings harm through a specific behavior, while passive aggression is accomplished through withholding of something desired (e.g., deserved praise, information, resources). See Exhibit 8.3.

The direct form of aggression is found when the aggressor delivers harm personally. In indirect aggression another person produces the harm. Spreading a damaging rumor that harms an employee's chance to be promoted is an example of indirect aggression.

EXHIBIT 8.3 **Eight Types of Workplace Aggression Categorized by Buss**

Source: A.H. Buss, *The Psychology of Aggression* (New York: John Wiley & Sons, 1961).

Physical–Verbal Dimension	Active–Passive Dimension	Direct Dimension	Indirect Dimension
Physical	Active	*(Cell 1)* Homicide Assault Sexual assault Dirty looks Interrupting others Obscene gestures	*(Cell 2)* Theft Sabotage Defacing property Consuming needed resources
	Passive	*(Cell 3)* Intentional work slowdowns Refusing to provide needed resources Leaving area when target enters Preventing target from expressing self	*(Cell 4)* Showing up late for meetings Delaying work to make target look bad Failing to protect the target's welfare Causing others to delay action
Verbal	Active	*(Cell 5)* Threats Yelling Sexual harassment Insults and sarcasm Flaunting status Unfair performance evaluation	*(Cell 6)* Spreading rumors Whistle-blowing Talking behind target's back Belittling opinions Attacking protégé Transmitting damaging information
	Passive	*(Cell 7)* Failing to return phone calls Giving target the silent treatment Damning with faint praise Refusing target's request	*(Cell 8)* Failing to transmit information Failing to deny false rumors Failing to defend target Failing to warn of impending danger

O'Leary-Kelly, Griffin, and Glew suggest that individual differences play a role in aggression at work; however, they discourage investigating individual differences.[30] They contend that the best predictors of violence are demographic data, which are prohibited by law from being collected. Organizations rarely share information about worker aggression. The lack of individual-level research on aggression at work makes it difficult to determine with any confidence the role of individual differences in explaining workplace violence.

In the research attempting to find a link between individual differences and aggression, some of the individual differences studied include trait anger, negative affectivity, Type A behavior, attitude toward revenge, emotional reactivity, gender, and anxiety.[31] For example, studies report that males are more aggressive than females and score higher on attitude toward revenge than females.

Other studies on workplace violence, physical or emotional, report it can occur between colleagues, customers, and management. It includes, but is not limited to, threats, bomb scares, obscene phone calls or e-mail messages, sexual and verbal harassment, beatings, and shootings. Data from the Bureau of Labor Statistics' Census of Fatal Occupational Injuries reported that 11,613 workplace homicides occurred in the United States between 1992 and 2006 and averaged about 800 per year.[32] Unfortunately, in 2007, there was a substantial increase in homicides involving police officers and supervisors of retail sales workers.[33]

Nonfatal assaults result in millions of lost workdays and productivity and cost millions of dollars in compensation. Approximately 1 million people are assaulted annually while at work or on duty (including police officers and prison guards).

Although these data are alarming, they should not be exaggerated. The sensationalism of a disgruntled employee or ex-employee returning with a weapon and shooting people implies that there is an uncontrollable amount of rage and aggression in workplaces. There are surely too many misbehaving workers who resort to violence, but the majority of workplace homicides are the result of robberies and related crimes as opposed to co-workers settling differences.[34]

The increase in nonfatal violence and acts of aggression may be the result of downsizing, poor management observation and anticipation skills, increased insecurity, increased pressure for more productivity, and longer work hours. Employees now put in more time at work than they did 20 years ago. This extra push to work longer is assumed to be necessary to keep up with the competition. Management pressure to work harder and longer appears to be associated with increased levels of stress, burnout, frustration, anxiety, and fatigue. The possible implication is that employees resort to aggression and violence as the result of such pressures.

Bullying

bullying
Deliberate or unconscious repeated actions that are directed at another worker to cause humiliation or distress.

The notion of workplace bullying is being discussed and studied more frequently; however, still only a limited number of studies focus on bullying as misbehavior. **Bullying** is defined as repeated actions that are directed toward another worker, which are unwanted, which may be done deliberately or unconsciously, but clearly cause humiliation and distress, and create an unpleasant work setting. The behaviors of a bully are intended to be hostile actions or are considered by the victim to be hostile. Bullying differs from "normal" conflict with peers in that bullying is characterized by an imbalance of power, strong emotional reactions from the victim, a tendency to blame the victim, no effort to resolve the conflict, and an attempt to gain control through conflict.[35]

Organizational research on workplace bullying generally falls into two types: studies of the characteristics of victims and bullies; and studies that focus on the social context in which bullying occurs.[36] Researchers have found that many victims perceive envy as the reason for the hostility directed at them; they also have inadequate coping skills, are introverted, and have low self-esteem. Other researchers have found that overachievers are bullied more frequently than average performers.

Bullies have been known to possess high levels of aggression, but the research to develop a bully profile is sketchy, incomplete, and inconclusive.

Researchers have begun to consider the role of the social context and organizational structure of the workplace to see how they influence bullying behavior.[37] For example, lack of proper supervision, jobs done in isolation, social inequities in the workplace, and departments with low morale all provide a social context for bullying to occur.[38] Some believe that when high uncertainty exists, bullying is more likely to be present. The victim is the recipient of hostile acts more because of being a convenient target in a situation of uncertainty.

The role of an organization's culture or climate in nurturing a bully's behavior is captured by a number of examples of managers using intimidation, threats of firing, and promising disciplinary action "if performance is not improved." This form of bullying can become expected since it is a part of accepted behavior in the organization. Before its collapse, Enron's CEO Jeffrey Skilling was thought to use bullying tactics to obtain higher performance ratings (and higher pay/bonuses) for his key people.[39]

Einarsen suggests that bullying is an evolving process, with humiliating or punitive behaviors over time becoming an accepted pattern. In this view, bullying can thrive only when it is supported by an organization's culture.[40] Victims in a culture that supports bullying accept their fate through fear. Those victims who can't tolerate the continual bullying leave the organization through retirement, illness, or choice.

Some researchers believe that the proportion of bullied versus nonbullied employees acts as a measure of the mental health of an organization.[41] The unhealthier the organization, the higher the proportion of bullied versus nonbullied employees.

Incivility

incivility
In the workplace this is behavior that is designated as rude, discourteous, or demeaning toward others.

Workplace **incivility** involves acting rudely, discourteously, or in a demeaning manner toward others. It is on the low end of the continuum of abuse. Incivility isn't violence or harassment, but it is a lack of respect for others. Incivility appears to be proliferating outside and inside the workplace.[42] It is important for individuals who are interacting, working together, to conduct themselves in a civil way. It is also important for employees to treat customers or external individuals interacting with an organization with respect. Being civil or polite with regard to others in an organization constitutes what is called *organizational citizenship behavior* (OCB).[43]

Incivility includes condescending remarks, being disruptive in meetings, ignoring others, insulting another person, being abrupt, giving negative eye contact, not answering when asked a question, refusing to say "thank you" or "please," interrupting others when speaking, and sending "flaming" e-mails.

Co-workers are incivil at work for a number of reasons. Some have become so alienated that they feel no loyalty to their work, colleagues, or the organization.[44] In addition, there may be fears of what the future holds. Will I even have a job tomorrow? Or the workload may be overwhelming. Downsizing, managerial expectations, and pressure to work harder and longer create an increased workload.

As will be illustrated in Chapter 9, workplace stress is at a significant level. Individuals attempt to better manage stress but sometimes fail. The result is more rudeness, impoliteness, and improper etiquette. The concept of etiquette is ignored frequently (e.g., reading a fax addressed to someone else, interrupting a colleague when it is not necessary, ignoring someone in your space or area, and simply bad manners).

When incivility is prevalent or becomes a part of the work culture, the effects can be costly. Conflict emerges, which detracts from productivity. According to recent research, employees who are the recipients of uncivil behavior experience the following:[45]

- Increased job stress and dissatisfaction.
- Lower levels of creativity.
- Cognitive distraction and psychological distress.
- Disrupted relationships at work.
- Lower commitment to the organization.
- Higher turnover.

An Accountemps survey of executives from the largest 1,000 firms in the United States found that 13 percent of their time, or about six weeks a year, is spent resolving conflicts, many of which have a beginning in incivility.[46]

Some workers, after repeated incidents of incivility in the form of rudeness, become physically ill or suffer depression. These kinds of problems become costly in the form of increased sick days and high health insurance premiums.

To combat incivility problems, a growing number of firms are using training and education programs to involve participants in practicing civility and proper etiquette. Managers also practice better role, assignment, and scheduling etiquette with their employees. Some firms have gone to what they refer to as a "zero-tolerance" policy regarding incivility.[47] The policy is posted and communicated on the intranet explaining that poor behavior (e.g., incivility, rudeness) will not be tolerated. Infractions are linked to specific sanctions and these are part of the policy.[48]

A low-intensity form of incivility between colleagues can escalate to aggression or violence. For this and other reasons, incivility should not be permitted. The notion of "spiraling" from a slight, or something that was said, to violence has been studied by organizational researchers.[49] There has, however, been relatively little empirical attention to why some forms of incivility escalate (spiral) into something more serious and other forms do not. Even with limited research available it appears to be important for organizations to put a stop to incivility quickly and fairly. Some recommendations for stopping incivility include implementing a zero-tolerance policy (described above), managing proactively the climate of the organization, having leaders serve as role models, educating employees as to what is acceptable (and what's unacceptable) behavior, and punishing those individuals who engage in uncivil behaviors.[50] To ignore incivility because it is at the low end of the abuse scale is to allow it to become a part of the organization's norms and culture.[51] Neglecting incivility increases the chance that it will become more intense and perhaps more costly. Employees who indulge in incivility must be accountable regardless of their position and history in the organization.

Fraud

fraud
An intentional act of deceiving or misrepresenting to induce another individual or group to give up something of value.

Accounts of alleged and proven criminal fraud and unethical behavior involving organizations such as Enron, Tyco, and Arthur Andersen and individuals such as Bernard Madoff, Andrew Fastow, Martha Stewart, and Dennis Koslowski have flooded the media.[52] **Fraud** is defined as the intentional act of deceiving or misrepresenting to induce another individual or group to give up something of value. Managers and nonmanagers have been indicted and convicted of fraud. A study of over 12,000 employees found that 90 percent engaged at some time in workplace misbehaviors such as goldbricking, sick time abuses, and fraud. Surprisingly, about 33 percent of the employees actually stole money or merchandise on the job.[53] The researchers concluded the most common reason for committing fraud was *motivation*.

The concept of "wages in kind" suggests the more dissatisfied the employee is, the more motivated the individual will be to engage in fraud.[54] If an employee believes that fair treatment is not occurring at work or that compensation programs are unjust, he or she will take more risks to balance the scales.

Opportunity is another precondition of fraud. Research based on interviews of nearly 200 incarcerated embezzlers, including high-level business executives, revealed the majority committed fraud to meet their financial obligations.[55] The opportunity to *commit* and *conceal* the fraud was thought to be present (incorrectly as it turned out) by the incarcerated embezzlers. Such opportunity may partially explain the actions of Beazer Homes U.S.A., Inc. The Securities and Exchange Commission accused the former chief accounting officer of understating the company's income in filings between 2000 and 2005. Also, the company was accused of engaging in mortgage fraud activities. Beazer Homes will pay $53 million to settle these charges; $5 million is expected to be paid to the federal government and $48 million to victimized homeowners.[56] As described earlier in the chapter, Bernie Madoff thought he could conceal his $65 billion

YOU BE THE JUDGE

IS TONY A SAFE EMPLOYEE?

Tony works as an in-plant technician in a chemical plant in Gary, Indiana. He has worked exceptionally well after his release from a three-year prison sentence five years ago. As an ex-drug abuser and user who served his time, he thoroughly enjoys his job. In the past three months, for the first time in his work history, he has had a number of flashback seizures and interpersonal problems with a few colleagues. The flashbacks are a result of his use of the drug PCP years ago. The company's medical staff states that flashbacks are experienced by some ex-addicts.

As a technician Tony mixes and tests various chemicals according to procedures that must be carefully and correctly performed. A life-threatening mistake in mixing and testing could harm Tony or his co-workers. Tony's last seizure lasted a few minutes at the testing table. He had to be escorted from the test room.

The testing job is the only one available for which Tony is qualified. Should Tony be suspended? Fired? Are there other options that may be safe to take with regard to Tony?

Ponzi scheme from the SEC and his investors indefinitely. He was found guilty of fraud and will spend the rest of his life in jail.[57]

In a climate in which executive fraud appears daily in the media, experts believe that some degree of the big-stakes fraud engaged in by CEOs is caused by envy and jealousy, the thinking being, when a CEO considers a colleague is making $10 million annually there is inequity if he or she is making less.[58] The perceived inequity, the lack of discipline, and the ineffective application of laws encourage some CEOs to engage in fraudulent behaviors.

Thus, fraud is a combination of motive and opportunity. The opportunity to commit fraud is typically addressed through internal control systems. If the proper checks and balances exist, it is more difficult to defraud an organization. To deter opportunity, there should be a clear division of responsibility. If one person or group controls the financial and accounting books and the assets, the ability to behave fraudulently is limited only by the imagination.[59]

The use of internal controls is fine, but they can be overcome by strongly motivated people. Ensuring fairness, good working conditions, and sound leadership reduces the motivation to resort to fraud. The disgruntled, dissatisfied, and hopeless employee is a ready candidate for creating fraudulent schemes.

Substance Abuse at Work

Substance abuse among workers represents billions of dollars in organizational financial loss. Research in the U.S. workplace suggests that alcohol use directly impacts approximately 19 million people; and illicit drug use at work affects an estimated 4 million individuals.[60] Illicit drug use costs over $200 billion annually because of lost productivity, premature and preventable health problems, increased workers' compensation claims, and behavioral problems.[61]

A survey of full-time workers reported illicit drug users were more likely than nonusers to have worked for three or more employers in the past year, taken unexcused absences from work, and either voluntarily left an employer or been terminated in the past year.

Some substances not only are addictive, but also may be dangerous to associated nonusers. Assembly-line workers, transportation workers (e.g., drivers, pilots, ship captains), and various professionals (e.g., physicians, pharmacists) are singled out for

DRUG AND DRUG SWAB TESTING: IS IT GOOD PREVENTIVE MANAGEMENT OR SNEAKY?

One evening at Robert M. Sides, Inc., a music company in Williamsport, Pennsylvania, a team of testers swept through the firm's office after hours testing for the presence of drugs. They dragged and brushed a tool across telephone receivers, computer keyboards and mouses, doorknobs, armrests, and coffeepot handles. They also wiped or swabbed light switches. In the restrooms they dragged the tool across hot and cold fixtures on the sink.

These drug testers were hired by the firm to find out about on-the-job substance abuse and use. Organizations use drug-wipe testing because it is less invasive and costly than traditional drug testing. It costs about $10 per employee to test for five drugs including cannabis and cocaine. In comparison, a urine screen test performed by a laboratory costs about $35 per employee test.

According to the law, Robert M. Sides, Inc., has the right to perform such drug and swab tests. If drugs are being used at work, the employer has the right to examine its premises.

Not all firms want to engage in this type of after-hours tests because of their consideration for developing trust between employees and the firm. These firms consider the drug and swab approach to be sneaky. Also, the test can find that drugs were present but cannot identify who is the responsible party.

If the drug tests are used to acquire a general picture of the presence of drugs, it may be more acceptable to some firms. However, identifying a single or specific person is difficult. Buchanan Brodsky Enterprises, a firm that operates 19 car dealerships, uses drug and swab tests, but takes it one step further. It spot-tests employees. The employees are aware of the possibility that spot tests can be used. When employees are hired they receive a copy of the firm's spot-check policy and its rationale.

Source: Adapted from Kris Maher, "Armchair Drug Detection," *The Wall Street Journal,* January 20, 2004, pp. B1, B8.

study because of their impact on others. The majority of research on these subjects focuses on how organizations can detect and intervene to treat any substance abuse among these classes of employees.

Some researchers have investigated the work context in alleviating the substance abuse problem.[62] Is there a set of job-related stressors that contribute to substance abuse on and off the job? The results of investigating whether alcohol, marijuana, and cocaine use were related to working conditions or occupations were inconclusive. These researchers concluded that workers' substance use and abuse is a personal characteristic and has less to do with working conditions.

However, another study analyzed data collected from 2,790 U.S. workers to explore whether two work stressors—work overload and job insecurity—contribute to employee alcohol and illicit drug use before work.[63] The study found that these stressors do influence alcohol and illicit drug use before work, during the workday, and after work. This lends some support to the idea that the work environment can also contribute to employees' substance abuse.

Supporting the notion that the work environment can influence substance abuse, Bacharach and colleagues used survey data from employees to identify drinking problems.[64] It was found that a permissive workplace culture is the single most significant risk factor that drives employees to drink. When employees believe the organization will tolerate social drinking during work hours, there is a greater possibility that drinking will become a problem.

A study of experienced pharmacists provides an interesting view on the potential for substance abuse by knowledgeable professionals.[65] Despite being knowledgeable about addiction and abuse, pharmacists may become prescription-drug abusers. Interviews with 50 recovering drug-addicted pharmacists revealed a picture of how abuse occurred. The researchers propose that drug knowledge and familiarity may have contributed to the pharmacists' progressive prescription drug abuse. The pharmacists were deluded into believing they could overcome the addictive and harmful effects of the prescription drugs.

Organizations need to attempt to identify predictors of substance abuse before individuals become employed. However, no test can accurately predict future substance abuse. Drug testing for prospective employees and employees under suspicion of impairment and postaccident tests are used.[66] The Department of Defense requires noncommercial contractors to test some employees. The U.S. Department of Transportation requires drug testing for drivers in interstate commerce, airline personnel, and railroad employees.[67] These requirements cover preemployment, for-cause, postaccident, and random tests for sensitive positions. Improperly administered drug-testing programs can spell trouble for a company. The Federal Aviation Administration (FAA) plans to fine AMR Corp.'s American Airlines for allegedly violating employee drug- and alcohol-testing procedures. Between 2005 and 2007, the FAA claims that the airline "failed to properly oversee drug tests for flight attendants and a smaller number of mechanics. In some cases, the FAA said, employees knew beforehand that they would be tested."[68]

Some firms use drug swab testing to learn about their employees' substance abuse. One approach to drug swabbing is presented in the nearby Organizational Encounter.

Cyberslacking

The Internet has provided a technology feature that has enabled many employees to slack off their regular work. Employees have used the Internet for prohibited nonwork usage. Surfing the Internet for personal reasons is apparently widespread,[69] and some estimates put the cost to businesses of such Internet misuse at $85 billion per year.[70] Personal e-mails, online shopping, recreational surfing, listening to music, vacation planning, and house or apartment hunting are performed during working hours.

cyberslacking
The use of the Internet during office or work hours for personal reasons.

The use of the Internet for personal reasons is a form of "virtual goldbricking" or **cyberslacking.** This costs organizations in lost time and energy being devoted to nonorganization matters. Personal cyberslacking can also burden an organization's computer network. Employees who access pornography sites in offices may also contribute inordinately to sexual harassment behaviors.

Cyberslacking has increased, and so has workplace surveillance of employees. Many U.S. organizations now practice electronic monitoring of employees on the job.[71] E-mail, computer files, and interactions with customers are popular areas of monitoring. Electronic monitoring allows managers to review everything said, written, or read. Organizations have used electronic monitoring information to fire employees who mix personal and organizational business. A recent survey sponsored by the American Management Association and the ePolicy Institute reported that more than one-quarter of employers have fired employees for the misuse of e-mail, and about one-third have fired employees for misusing the Internet.[72] Misuse of the Internet was defined as:

- Viewing, uploading, or downloading offensive content.
- Violation of company policy.
- Excessive personal use.

Some organizations have barred the transmittal of pornography on their computers by using blocking software. Many organizations allow employees to send e-mail for some personal issues. These firms ease up on implementing a zero-tolerance policy because it appears to be too restrictive. Employees tend to respond coldly to zero-tolerance policies.

Lockheed Martin posts over 40 million e-mails per month. The firm's system crashed after an employee sent 60,000 co-workers an e-mail with an e-receipt requested about a national prayer day. Sending this kind of personal e-mail was prohibited.[73] Lockheed

EXHIBIT 8.4
Where Do Cyberslackers Surf?

Area of Surfing	Amount of Time (%)
General news	29.1%
Investment	22.5
Pornography	9.7
Travel	8.2
Entertainment	6.6
Sports	6.1
Shopping	3.5
Other	14.3

Martin spent hundreds of thousands of dollars to prevent any Lockheed Martin employee from sending an e-mail time bomb ever again. The cyberslacking employee was fired.[74] In addition to e-mail and Internet abuse, companies are increasingly monitoring employee blogs and online diaries that discuss organization or job-related information.[75] Some employees are under the mistaken belief that what they write in their blog is private and protected by the First Amendment right to free speech. In most states, employers can fire workers "at will" except for discriminatory reasons.[76]

Exhibit 8.4 shows how cyberslackers use their surfing time. Being able to eliminate all cyberslacking is not possible. However, having regulations, communicating them, and using them are needed to discourage this type of misbehavior.

Sabotage

sabotage
An extreme form of workplace violence instituted to disrupt, destroy, or damage equipment, data, or a work area.

A potentially costly form of misbehavior is **sabotage** that involves damaging or destroying an organization's or colleague's equipment, workspace, or data. Sabotage is a tangible expression of aggression or violence. Increasingly, co-workers are purposefully erasing databases and destroying other items. Employee sabotage can range from simple, pranklike behaviors to vandalism to computer bombs.[77] A former employee of an Eden Prarie, Minnesota–based company, Wand Corporation, used his company-issued password to introduce malicious software code that disrupted the company's IT infrastructure and destroyed data. The "logic bomb" attack destroyed 25 computers that ended up costing about $49,000 to replace. The saboteur pleaded guilty in federal court and may receive up to 10 years in prison.[78] Angry employees (and ex-employees) like this one covertly and overtly resort to sabotage to get even, to correct a perceived wrong, to take revenge, or to make a statement to others.[79]

Sabotage at its extreme is a form of violence. It has been described as misbehavior that includes a bit of revenge. The person resorting to sabotage is attempting to disrupt, destroy, or dismiss the organization.

Three types of sabotage targets exist: people, equipment, and operations.[80] In sabotaging people, the objective is to destroy the person's career, progress, reputation, or work area. The sabotage of equipment or operations involves physically destroying something.

The use of sabotage is usually the method of choice of people who are bored and not challenged, believe that something in their work history was very unfair to them, or want to gain an advantage over a colleague.

Management Pointer

SUGGESTIONS FOR BUILDING TRUST AND RESPECT

1. Listen attentively to what an individual is saying about work conditions, your style, fairness of rewards, and needs.

2. Work to help employees improve themselves and grow.

3. Lead by being an exceptional role model in terms of integrity, ethical behavior, and civility.

4. Display courtesy toward individuals at every level, status, and location.

5. Never lose your temper.

6. Never angrily reprimand, bully, or intimidate an employee privately or publicly.

7. Emphasize employee strengths, not weaknesses.

There are no available centralized data collected on incidents of sabotage. Reports suggest an increase in computer-related sabotage. The list of successful sabotage now includes lost information, replacing equipment, and increases in health care costs. It is estimated that employee fraud and abuse cost $400 billion annually.[81]

Theft

theft
Unauthorized taking, consuming, or transfer of money or goods owned by the organization.

Theft is defined as the unauthorized taking, consuming, or transfer of money or goods owned by the organization. This definition of theft should indicate that stealing is not limited to tangible property. Data, information, and intellectual property can and are stolen.

A few recent examples of theft in the workplace include:[82] A Maryland man recently stole 32 laptops from his nonprofit employer and tried to sell them on eBay. A chief financial officer changed the numbers on a spreadsheet to give himself a larger bonus. A regional vice president used his corporate credit card for $4,000 worth of Victoria's Secret lingerie. Theft by employees in any size organization is a serious issue that managers need to address. Theft costs money, is a specific act, and should be dealt with as soon as it is discovered. According to the National Retail Security Survey (NRSS), annual loss for the retail industry was a staggering $40.5 billion in 2008.[83] It is estimated that U.S. employee theft costs the equivalent of 7 percent of organizational revenue[84] and at least 10 times more than all of the nation's street crime annually.[85]

The Association of Certified Fraud Examiners and other experts have identified a number of trends and facts that managers should consider.[86] Exhibit 8.5 presents a few of these. The cost of theft points to the need for managers to intervene to attempt to control it through various programs. Electronic surveillance is increasingly used to stop or catch thieves. Organizations have also increased their use of honesty or integrity tests to point out theft-prone job candidates before hiring them.

The range of references to theft in both the law and research literature includes terms such as *misappropriation, stealing, petty larceny, grand theft,* and *embezzling*.[87] In many cases the employees in question do not use these terms for describing their behavior. Circumstances may be ambiguous. For example, an employee may make a long-distance telephone call on company time, equipment, and credit card. What is the motivation? Should this behavior be punished? Perhaps it was an emergency call and because of circumstances had to be made at the time. This may be hard to refute or establish.

Why do employees steal anything from their employers? This is a difficult question to answer. Some believe that people steal simply because they have an opportunity to do so. This perspective offers the employer the course of action to eliminate opportunities (e.g., implement inventory control systems, lock up merchandise, and install surveillance cameras). The elimination of all opportunities is problematic and likely impossible. The individuals who have the same opportunities as thieves and never steal are subjected to the same controls and surveillance.[88] Is this fair? Employees are different

EXHIBIT 8.5
Trends and Facts about Employee Theft

Facts	Percentage and Amount
The number of employees who steal are first-time offenders.	68.6%
Most employees that steal are men.	53.5%
As an employee's education increases, the incidence of theft declines.	
Thieves with a high school education.	56.9%
Tips received from colleagues that led to the discovery of thieves.	26 tips
U.S. retailers lose billions annually from theft.	Over $40 billion
Estimate of number of employees that steal something (e.g., pencil, paper) at least once.	75%

EXHIBIT 8.6
The Four STEAL Motives

Person's Intentions	Organization	Colleagues
Prosocial (Helpful)	**A**pprova**L** Follows manager's lead and norms condoning theft	**S**upport Follows work group norms condoning theft
Antisocial (Harmful)	**E**ven the score Wants to harm the organization	**T**hwart Opposes work group norms regarding theft

Source: Adapted from J. Greenberg, "The STEAL Motive: Managing the Social Determinants of Employee Theft," in *Antisocial Behavior in Organizations,* R.A. Giacalone and J. Greenberg, eds. (Thousand Oaks, CA: Sage Publications, 1997), pp. 85–108.

and should be treated fairly. Eliminating all opportunities for theft across the board may violate basic fairness.

Another perspective focuses on individual differences and developing, testing, and using profiling of individuals who are "prone" to steal. Employee theft is assumed to be better controlled at the entry point or when a person is selected for employment.[89] Although some promising research is being developed on integrity testing, the impact of trying to control the entry of individuals with a high propensity to steal is still debatable.[90] Additional suggestions for reducing negative behaviors such as theft are discussed in the Global OB on page 233.

The STEAL Model

Greenberg and associates believe that the motives underlying theft misbehavior are complex. These researchers categorize the motives behind theft as being prosocial or helpful and antisocial or harmful. The STEAL acronym refers to four motives behind theft behavior—S(upport), T(hwart), E(ven the score), and A(pprova)L.[91] Exhibit 8.6 presents these four motives and the intentions of the person.

Support motive: A work group with deviant norms about theft can have a powerful influence on theft behavior. Through its behaviors the group can display what, when, and where to steal. The group establishes the plan, shows how to execute it, and rewards participating members. The colleagues participating in the thefts are considered members in good standing.

The art of stealing and participating displays an allegiance to the group. The thief, by being recognized as a good group member, has his or her stealing behavior reinforced. Stealing is supported by the group and consequently more stealing occurs. The thief, under this type of support, considers the stealing behavior as accepted and good.

Thwart motive: The thwart motive opposes group norms that regulate theft. The rationale is to harm the employer by striking out at members of one's work group. It is an attempt to thwart the group's attempt to control theft.

By challenging group norms, a person who steals is likely to create strong pressure. The pressure can involve isolation, being chastised, having work flow disrupted, or being rudely treated. The responses from the challenged group members may be sullen or severe.

Even the score motive: An antisocial behavior is designed to inflict some form of harm on the organization. Evening the score is a way of attempting to harm an organization for something it has done (e.g., rejected a request, passed over for a promotion, reprimanded someone for not completing a job on time). Stealing is an attempt to bring about equity or balance in the mind of an aggrieved employee who acts to get even.

WHAT CAN ORGANIZATIONS DO TO PREVENT MISBEHAVIOR?

How can such misbehaviors as sexual harassment, violence, bullying, incivility, theft, fraud, substance abuse, and cyberslacking be prevented in organizations in the United States and around the globe? There's no "magic bullet" solution, but organizations can take steps to at least reduce the incidence of these counterproductive behaviors:

Step 1: *Lead by example.* Top leaders and managers should set the example by behaving in a fair, ethical, and courteous manner.

Step 2: *Create an ethical climate.* Ethical organizational climates can reduce certain workplace behaviors like bullying and increase positive outcomes such as organizational commitment.

Step 3: *Develop a companywide policy.* A zero-tolerance policy that prohibits violence, fraud, and so on needs to be communicated to all employees.

Step 4: *Train managers/employees.* Training should focus on how to identify and report inappropriate workplace behaviors.

Step 5: *Develop a crisis plan.* To be prepared to react to certain misbehaviors, the organization needs to develop a plan that will allow rapid response and damage control.

In addition to these five steps above, managers and leaders can also prevent many misbehaviors by being nice to employees. This commonsense advice is based on the extensive research on organizational justice (see Chapter 5). Positive behaviors can be enhanced in organizations when their leaders and managers do the following: distribute rewards (e.g., pay raises and promotions) in a fair manner; use procedures to make decisions that are unbiased and allow for corrections; are respectful and civil when interacting with and communicating decisions to employees; and reduce bureaucracy and increase the level of resources that employees need to do their jobs well.

Sources: Adapted from Fusun Bulutlar and Ela Unler Oz, "The Effects of Ethical Climates on Bullying Behavior in the Workplace," *Journal of Business Ethics* 86 (2009), pp. 273–95; Lynn Lieber, "Workplace Violence— What Can Employers Do to Prevent It?" *Employment Relations Today* 34, no. 3 (Fall 2007), pp. 91–100; and Wendi J. Everton, Jeffrey A. Jolton, and Paul M. Mastrangelo, "Be Nice and Fair or Else: Understanding Reasons for Employees' Deviant Behaviors," *Journal of Management Development* 26, no. 2 (2007), pp. 117–31.

In field studies researching the "evening the score" motive, Greenberg found that, consistent with Adam's equity motivation theory, theft rates were significantly higher in organizations in which employees' compensation was reduced than in comparison control groups. He also found that theft rates were low in organizations before compensation cuts and after regular rates of pay were reestablished.

ApprovaL motive: Most managers work to prevent theft. However, in some cases, an unwritten code of conduct permits (approves) some theft. For example, some managers permit the theft as a part of the worker's reward or may even participate in the stealing.

The impact of managerial approval can be significant. This efficient and convenient "looking the other way" is less troublesome than funding more traditional reward packages.

Greenberg offers suggestions that focus on managerial action to weaken the four STEAL motives.[92] He recommends rotating group membership, communicating the personal costs of theft, and treating employees equitably. The STEAL model provides a reasonable, but not complete, heuristic framework for helping managers cope with theft. There is no complete solution to employee theft. Recognizing the problem, attempting to understand the motives behind theft behavior, establishing a culture of trust and respect, and using fair, predictive selection tools to minimize the entry of those candidates with poor integrity and high dishonesty tendencies are some of the legal actions managers can take.

Privacy

Privacy in the workplace is an important issue facing managers and employees. The managerial perspective on privacy includes the right to do drug testing, electronic workplace searches, surveillance by tape recording or video, and monitoring off-duty conduct.[93] The emergence and growth of the Internet have created the issue of how technology at work can blur the lines between personal and professional behaviors. Surveys suggest that a majority of employers use some form of electronic monitoring and/or surveillance to track employee activity.

Privacy rights for public employees are found in the U.S. Constitution and are generally broader than the privacy rights of employees in the private sector. Privacy rights stem from different parts of the Bill of Rights. The First Amendment protects an employee's freedom of speech and association. The Fourth Amendment prohibits unreasonable searches and seizures. The Fifth Amendment ensures against self-incrimination, and the Fourteenth Amendment guarantees due process and equal protection. Various state constitutions also include a right to privacy.

Privacy violation through computer hacking is a worldwide problem.

E-Mail Privacy

Electronic mail is used widely in organizations. Groupware, instant messaging, and e-mail allow employees to share information in real time.[94] It has become a communication tool of choice. However, the proliferation of e-mail systems has brought about a number of issues that can create management–employee tensions. Pillsbury, UPS, and Intel have reserved the right to routinely inspect e-mail messages of employees.

The Fourth Amendment of the Constitution protects written communications from unreasonable searches and seizures. E-mail has the same immediacy as a telephone conversation, yet it has the permanence of a written document since these messages can be saved. These qualities have led the courts to regard e-mail as not being entitled to the same Fourth Amendment protection as telephone calls and written documents.

The courts have reaffirmed that employers can read e-mails sent over their computer systems even if employees are uninformed of the policies.[95] Preventing misbehavior and unprofessional messages takes precedence over an employee's privacy rights.

Despite its legality, some believe managerial review of e-mails is morally unacceptable. That is, management is misbehaving by snooping. Managers who indiscriminately inspect e-mails are violating the employee's moral right to privacy.

Privacy is not an easy concept. It can be defined broadly as the right to be left alone and to have some solitude. A more focused view of workplace **privacy** is that it is a condition that limits others' access to an individual's words, writings, opinions, and attitudes. Without privacy a person has no psychological solitude to plan, dream, or think.

privacy
A situation or condition that limits or forbids another person's access to an individual's records, data, or information.

The Organizational Threshold

A controversial question is whether employees give up all civil liberties once they cross into the organization. Are there any workplace rights, and shouldn't privacy be a top one? This question is more than a philosophical issue. There is a reciprocal aspect to privacy rights. The relationship between the employee and employer is reciprocal.[96] An employer expects employees not to share proprietary secrets, yet unless the employer respects employee privacy the reciprocal relationship is broken or damaged.

Routine examination of employee e-mails damages confidentiality. The e-mail is no longer confidential since a third party (e.g., management) reads the message and knows

YOU BE THE JUDGE COMMENT

IS TONY A SAFE EMPLOYEE?
Tony is doing exceptionally well, but there is a risk that one of his seizures may hurt someone. Tony should be reassigned until the seizures are brought under control. Endangering others is not an option for managers. Firing or suspending Tony is not a choice for a fair-minded, sensitive manager either. Find a job that he can accomplish until the seizure activity is corrected or stopped.

who is involved. Is it worth it to access e-mails if confidentiality and the reciprocal relationship is damaged or broken? Some firms say yes and others no. Those in favor believe that proprietary secrets will not be given up if employees know they may be monitored. Also, the use of e-mails for fraudulent purposes is reduced because of the fear of being caught.[97]

Those who oppose contend that a strict e-mail privacy policy provides employees with a sense of autonomy, self-confidence, and empowerment. Many employees value these factors, and they show it with higher morale and more loyalty to the organization.

Testing Policy

Organizations can utilize testing (e.g., medical, drug, psychological, or lie detector) if the test is designed to predict a person's ability to perform, is relatively noninvasive, and the results are private.[98] For example, the Americans with Disability Act (ADA) limits the use of medical testing. Employers can require a medical test only after a job offer is made. Also, the medical test results may not be passed on wholesale to the employer. Only the medical practitioner's conclusion about the person's ability to work without restrictions can be provided. Data on the medical test must be reviewed only by those with a "need to know."

Once a person becomes employed, the employer can conduct a medical examination only to determine "fitness-to-perform." Again only the examiner's general conclusion is provided.

Testing of any form should be carefully weighed in terms of costs and benefits. The key rule of thumb is that there be a strong work-related reason to require employees to be tested. If the reason is not apparent and significant, then testing should not be conducted.

Summary of Key Points

- Misbehavior in organizations is exhibited in many different forms. In general, the management of employee misbehavior (MEM) is the responsibility of managers in a formal sense. The groups to which misbehaving employees belong also have an informal role to play correcting or sanctioning misbehavior of colleagues.
- The MEM has a cross-disciplinary theme. A number of theories, studies, and models are available to trace antecedents, mediators, outcomes, and costs of organizational misbehavior.
- The intention to misbehave is proposed to mediate the relationship of antecedents and outcomes. These intentions are considered normative or instrumental.
- Management has a number of choices to intervene and correct or stop misbehavior. Included in the manager's choice set are interventions at the hiring point

(before entry), to impact normative or instrument behaviors, and to bring about deterrence.

- The possible misbehaviors confronted by managers and nonmanagers range from cyberslacking to sexual harassment to violence. If permitted to go unchecked, these misbehaviors result in lost productivity, higher costs, and lower morale.

- The consequences of misbehavior also include damaged, destroyed, or harmed equipment, information, and data. There can also be significant health costs.

- There is no "one best way" remedy for misbehavior. Individual differences, different goals, varied organizational cultures, and managerial knowledge and skill are all important factors to consider in coping with and attempting to correct misbehavior.

Review and Discussion Questions

1. A scholar commented, "Workplace aggression is wasteful in terms of human and financial resources." What is meant by this statement?

2. What roles do frustration, stress, and emotional disturbances play in the increase in incivility in organizations?

3. Some claim that white-collar crime is not as bad or harmful as nonmanagerial theft or sabotage of property. Do you agree? Why or why not?

4. What types of things might an employee do when seeking revenge against an organization? Against a co-worker?

5. There are three specific points or phases at which management has the opportunity to head off workplace violence. What are the points, and what actions can management take?

6. Can a person be required to take medical tests to be considered for a new role or job? What restrictions, if any, are placed on use of the test data?

7. As a manager, why would you be interested in learning how to deal with misbehavior?

8. Can Enron-type managerial misbehavior be stopped or eliminated? How?

9. What legal protections does an employee have against the employer's use of electronic surveillance?

10. In the near future, will organizations have at their disposal tests that can precisely identify job candidates with a high propensity to misbehave? Explain.

Case

Case 8.1: *Dealing with Violence at Work*

The U.S. Bureau of Labor Statistics' Census of Fatal Occupational Injuries reported that 11,613 workplace homicides occurred in the United States between 1992 and 2006 and averaged about 800 per year. The on-the-job homicide toll amounts to more than 10 percent of all fatal work injuries. There are many theories about why there is so much violence, but it is difficult to acquire an accurate and worthwhile prescription of how to stop the violence.

An example of the difficulty faced by managers involves the case of software tester Michael McDermott, who killed seven people at a Wakefield,

Reality Check

Now how much do you know about managing misbehaving employees?

6. Sabotage often targets equipment, operations, and _____.
   - a. people
   - b. files
   - c. systems
   - d. work products

7. Research suggests that employees who are the target of uncivil behavior may react in each of the following ways except for _____.
   - a. Lower levels of creativity
   - b. Increased violence against the harasser
   - c. Higher turnover
   - d. Increased job dissatisfaction

8. The opportunity to commit fraud in an organization is typically addressed through _____.
   - a. polygraph testing
   - b. internal controls
   - c. workshops
   - d. strict budgetary modeling

9. Workplace bullies have been known to possess high levels of _____.
   - a. self-confidence
   - b. aggression
   - c. sleep deprivation
   - d. social problems

10. Studies have found that managers spend about _____ percent of their time resolving workplace conflicts.
    - a. 2
    - b. 9
    - c. 13
    - d. 25

Reality Check Answers

Before	After
1. b 2. c 3. b 4. a 5. c	6. a 7. b 8. b 9. b 10. c
Number Correct	Number Correct
_____	_____

Massachusetts, Internet consulting company, Edgewater Technology, Inc. He is now serving a sentence of life without parole.

According to eyewitnesses, McDermott arrived at the Wakefield office of Edgewater Technology armed with a semiautomatic assault rifle, a 12-gauge shotgun, and a pistol. By the time the police captured him in the reception area, seven employees lay dead from gunfire.

What could have caused McDermott to "go crazy," as one witness described his behavior? What could have made him snap? Or did he snap?

The widespread belief that gunmen, like McDermott, erupt suddenly into an uncontrollable, murderous rage is deeply grounded in the popular vernacular often used to characterize these events: expressions like "going berserk," "going ballistic," or even "going postal" (a code word for workplace massacres coined after a string of post office shootings in the mid-1980s and early 1990s). The prevailing view is that mass killers are totally out of touch with reality (that is, psychotic) and select their victims randomly.

On the contrary, however, most workplace avengers do not just explode and start shooting spontaneously at anything that moves. Typically, these murderers act with calm deliberation, often planning their assault for days, if not weeks or months. Their preparations involve assembling the arsenal of weaponry as well as determining the most effective means of attack.

In his exit interview from Edgewater Technology, McDermott was assured that if he ever wanted to return, a position would be made for him. It was clear that he was held in high regard by management and staff alike. A huge party was thrown to send him off.

In addition, workplace mass murderers tend to be quite selective in targeting their victims. Rather than an act of sheer insanity, their homicide is an act of controlled revenge. Victims are chosen specifically because of the perceived harm that they have caused the perpetrator, who may himself feel like a victim of injustice.

It may be difficult to consider many of the slain employees of the Wakefield massacre to be in any way responsible for McDermott's adversities, no matter how paranoid his perceptions may have been. But if McDermott's motive was to strike back at Edgewater Technology, then executing anyone employed there would have fulfilled his mission.

In many instances, profoundly disgruntled workers imagine a wide-ranging network of unfairness on the job implicating nearly everyone. In effect, they seek to kill the company to harm the organization for not being fair, honest, and communicative. Innocent workers, although uninvolved with the killer's grievance, may be targeted as proxies for the corporate enterprise.

While still employed at the firm, McDermott was upset that Edgewater Technology was about to garnish his wages to pay back taxes he owed to the IRS. In his mind, conceivably, the company had gone from ally to enemy, joining hands with the federal government to ruin him financially. He apparently saw in mass murder his opportunity to make a preemptive strike against the firm.

Typically, the workplace avenger is a middle-aged white male who feels his job and financial well-being are in jeopardy. Facing yet another disappointment or failure at work, he senses that his career is slipping away. He also believes that he is not to blame for his employment troubles. Rather, it's the manager who gave him poor assignments or doesn't appreciate his hard work; it's his co-workers who get all the credit when profits go up; it's the human resources staff that is out to get him.

In support of his conspiratorial thinking, the workplace avenger before his deadly rampage typically suffers a catastrophic event, which, in his mind, represents the final straw.

For McDermott, the triggering episode may have involved the scheduled reduction in his take-home check for payment of back taxes as well as the news that his automobile was about to be repossessed. His financial woes had apparently grown too large for him to tolerate.

Reports from neighbors describe McDermott as a loner. Most mass killers are indeed isolated, socially and psychologically. Importantly, they lack the companionship of friends and family who might help ease them through the hard times and place employment troubles in perspective. Holidays like Christmas can sometimes intensify feelings of loneliness, especially for those individuals who lack support systems the rest of the year.

Unfortunately, the grieving families of the Edgewater Technology victims share a tragedy that too many others have suffered. For every incident of workplace homicide, thousands of workers are assaulted or threatened by an associate. When middle-aged workers face downsizing or major changes that disrupt their security, confidence, and routine, there is an increased probability that violence will be considered as a means to correct the wrong, the pain, and the perceived unfairness.

In response to rising levels of workplace violence, a wide range of books, seminars, and consultants have surfaced to help companies cope with the fearful threat of violence on the job. Some specialists focus on security concerns, others on promoting effective employee screening techniques or channels of communication to alert management to troublesome workers.

The term *profiling* has become a catchword for those who would search for telltale clues for identifying potential murderers before they strike. If there is indeed a profile of typical workplace avengers, can we spot them before they take matters and guns into their own hands? Regrettably, such prediction strategies are not very effective. There are likely tens of thousands of disgruntled employees in workplaces large and small who are frustrated, never smile, and live alone, yet very few will ever translate their inner feelings of anger into outward expressions of violence.

Yet in the aftermath of a mass killing, everyone becomes a psychologist when it comes to identifying murderous behavior. With the benefit of hindsight, neighbors and co-workers suddenly find all of the warning signs that they ignored beforehand—when they might have used such information possibly to prevent a massacre. As one of McDermott's co-workers suggested upon hearing about the shooting in Wakefield: "I knew right away it was McDermott." Of course, just like everybody else, the co-worker "knew" only after the tragic act had occurred.

Moreover, if management is too proactive and aggressive in trying to spot the so-called "ticking time bomb," they may do much more harm than good. If this employee perceives that he is being singled out in a negative way—even if it is to coerce him into counseling—his resentment and feelings of persecution can actually intensify. Although managers may not be able to predict the next Michael McDermott, they can strive to enhance the workplace climate for everyone.

If human assets are the major element in an organization's life, managers need to manage employee misbehavior promptly and in a calm, professional manner. Did McDermott display the "ticking time bomb" signs that co-workers identified? Retrospectively analyzing what occurred and what managers did or didn't do may have to become a top priority until worker rage, revenge, and violence are better understood and coped with as a part of management's responsibility.

Questions

1. Should managers be held accountable and liable for workplace violence such as what occurred at Edgewater Technology? Why or why not?

2. Why is it so difficult to develop a precise "profiling" strategy and approach to pinpoint violent employees like Michael McDermott before they commit such tragic, violent acts?

3. What should managers do if they suspect an employee has the potential to become violent?

Sources: James A. Fox, *The Will to Kill: Making Sense of Senseless Murder* (Boston, MA: Allyn and Bacon, 2001); Jeff R. Hearn and Wendy Parkin, *Gender, Sexuality, and Violence in Organizations: The Unspoken Forces of Organization Violations* (Thousand Oaks, CA: Sage Publications, 2002); and www.cdc.gov/niosh/topics/violence/ (accessed July 16, 2009).

CHAPTER NINE

Managing Individual Stress

Learning Objectives

After completing Chapter 9, you should be able to:

- **Define** what is meant by the term *stress*.
- **Describe** the components of the organizational stress model.
- **Explain** the differences in a problem-focused versus an emotion-focused strategy for coping with stress.

- **Discuss** how body systems are affected by stress.
- **Identify** some variables that moderate the stress process.
- **Describe** several different organizational and individual approaches to stress prevention and management.

The experience of work and life stress is certainly not new. Our cave-dwelling ancestors faced stress every time they left their caves and encountered their enemy, the saber-toothed tigers.[1] The tigers of yesteryear are gone, but they have been replaced by other predators—work overload, a nagging boss, computer problems, deadlines, downsizing, mergers, poorly designed jobs, marital disharmony, financial crises, accelerating rates of change. These work and nonwork predators create stress for individuals on and off the job.

Most economists and experts agree that in 2007 the world entered the worst economic recession since the Great Depression.[2] In the United States, the housing market collapsed and home foreclosures reached record levels, the banking system experienced tumultuous change and contraction, and companies laid off workers in the thousands.[3] For example, General Motors, Coca-Cola, Merck, and Chrysler all announced layoffs. The size of the layoffs worried many people. Xerox announced it would cut 5 percent or 3,000 employees from its workforce, Hewlett-Packard said it would release 7.5 percent or 24,600 of its employees, and Dell let go of 10 percent or 8,900 members of its worldwide workforce.[4] The federal government responded to the banking and financial crisis with a $787 billion stimulus package, a restructuring plan for the financial system, a housing recovery initiative, and an expansion of the role of the Federal Reserve.[5] Even with this attempt to stabilize the economy, there was still a great deal of uncertainty on the part of businesses, consumers, homeowners, and employees as to when things would turn around. Such economic uncertainty, combined with the real threat of losing one's job or home, left a lot of people feeling stressed and anxious. The saber-toothed tigers of yesterday have been replaced by new financial and job uncertainties, stress, and pressures.

This chapter focuses primarily on the individual at work in organizations and on the stress created in this setting. Much of the stress experienced by people in our industrialized society originates in organizations; the stress that originates elsewhere often interacts with and affects our behavior and performance in these same organizations. One of the complicating issues in understanding stress is that it has been defined in many ways. We begin this chapter with our definition of stress.

What Is Stress?

Stress means different things to different people. From a layperson's perspective, stress can be described as feeling tense, anxious, or worried. Scientifically, these feelings are all manifestations of the stress experience, a complex programmed response to perceived threat that can have both positive and negative results. The term *stress* itself has been defined in hundreds of ways in the literature. Virtually all of the definitions can be placed into one of two categories, however; stress can be defined as either a *stimulus* or a *response*.

A stimulus definition of stress is some event or characteristic of something that results in a disruptive consequence. It is, in that respect, an engineering definition of stress, borrowed from the physical sciences. In physics, stress refers to the external force applied to an object, for example, a bridge girder. The response is "strain," which is the impact the force has on the girder.

In a response definition, stress is seen partially as a response to some stimulus, called a stressor. A *stressor* is a potentially harmful or threatening external event or situation. Stress is more than simply a response to a stressor, however. In the

YOU BE THE JUDGE

IS THE ORGANIZATION RESPONSIBLE FOR AN EMPLOYEE'S STRESS?

The text refers to stress as an adaptive response to a situation that places special demands on a person. If those special demands are related to an employee's job, should the employer be responsible? One employee thought so. Here's what happened.

James Carter was an automobile assembly-line worker employed by General Motors Corporation. At work he was having a difficult time keeping up with the speed of the production line. The line moved past his workstation faster than he was sometimes able to perform the operations for which he

was responsible. Making the situation even more stressful for James was the fact that his manager frequently criticized him for his failure to keep up with line speed. Eventually the stress became more than he could cope with and he suffered a psychological breakdown. He wanted to be compensated for his "mental injury" and receive worker's disability payments. GM argued that it wasn't the job that caused the problem; thousands of workers perform essentially the same job in assembly plants without problems. It was Carter's reaction to the job, the company said, and thus GM was not responsible.

Was Carter's stress an injury? Was GM liable? You be the judge!

---

stress
An adaptive response, moderated by individual differences, that is a consequence of any action, situation, or event that places special demands on a person.

stressor
An external event or situation that is potentially harmful to a person.

response definition, stress is the consequence of the *interaction between* an environmental stimulus (a stressor) and the individual's response. That is, stress is the result of a unique interaction between stimulus conditions in the environment and the individual's predisposition to respond in a particular way. Using a response definition, we will define **stress** as an adaptive response, moderated by individual differences, that is a consequence of any action, situation, or event that places special demands on a person.

We thus think it is useful to view stress as the response of a person to certain stimulus conditions (actions, situations, events) or **stressors.** This allows us to focus attention on aspects of the organizational environment that are potential stress producers. Whether stress is actually felt or experienced by a particular individual will depend on that person's unique characteristics. Furthermore, note that this definition emphasizes that stress is an adaptive response.

Stress is the result of dealing with something (e.g., a person, an event, a problem) placing special demands on us. *Special* here means unusual, physically or psychologically threatening, or outside our usual set of experiences. Starting a new job assignment, changing bosses, having a flat tire, missing a plane, making a mistake at work, having a performance evaluation meeting with the boss—all of these actions, situations, or events may place special demands on us. In that sense, they are potential stressors. We say *potential* because not all stressors will always place the same demands on people. For example, having a performance appraisal meeting with the boss may be extremely stressful for Lynn and not the least stressful for her co-worker, Sabrina. Such a meeting makes special demands of Lynn; for Sabrina it does not. For Lynn the meeting is a stressor; for Sabrina it is not.[6]

For an action, situation, or event to result in stress, it must be perceived by the individual to be a source of threat, challenge, or harm. If there are no perceived consequences—good or bad—there is no potential for stress. Three key factors determine whether an experience is likely to result in stress: importance, uncertainty, and duration.

Importance relates to how significant the event is to the individual. For example, suppose you are facing a job layoff. The more significant that layoff is to you, the more likely you are to find it stressful. If you expect the layoff to be followed by a period of prolonged unemployment, you will probably view it as a more important event than if immediate reemployment is assured.

Uncertainty refers to a lack of clarity about what will happen. Rumors of an impending layoff may be more stressful to some people than knowing for certain they will be laid off. At least in the latter case, they can make plans for dealing with the situation. Frequently, *not* knowing places more demands on people than does knowing, even if the known result is perceived as negative.

Finally, *duration* is a significant factor. Generally, the longer special demands are placed on us, the more stressful they are. Being given a distasteful job assignment that lasts only a day or two may be mildly upsetting, while the same assignment lasting for six months could be excruciating. Most people can endure short periods of strenuous physical activity without tiring; prolong the duration, however, and even the fittest among us will become exhausted. The same holds true for stress and stressors. Stress of short duration is sometimes referred to as *acute stress.* It may last a few seconds, a few hours, even a few days. Long-duration stress, on the other hand, is sometimes referred to as *chronic stress.* Chronic stress may last for months and years. It is the ongoing tension experienced by the people of the Middle East or the turmoil that ethnic rivalries have brought to the people of Chechnya and Russia. It is the unrelenting pressure of a job one finds unsatisfying, the constant demands made by an unreasonable boss, or the never-ending struggle to advance in one's chosen career.

Stress Model

For most employed people, work and work-related activities and preparation time represent much more than a 40-hour-a-week commitment. Work is a major part of our lives, and work and nonwork activities are highly interdependent. The distinction between stress at work and stress at home has always been an artificial one. With the explosive increase of dual-career couples in the latter part of the 20th century, even this artificial distinction has become blurred. Our primary concern here, however, is with direct work-related stressors.

The model shown in Exhibit 9.1 is designed to help illustrate the link among organizational stressors, stress, and outcomes. Recall from our earlier definition that stress is a response to an action, situation, or event that places special demands on an individual. These occurrences are represented in Exhibit 9.1 as *stressors,* divided into four main categories: individual, group, organizational, and nonwork or extraorganizational. The first three stressor categories are work-related.

The experience of work-related and extraorganizational stress produces outcomes: behavioral, cognitive, and physiological. The model in Exhibit 9.1 suggests that the relationship between stress and outcomes (individual and organizational) is not necessarily direct; similarly neither is the relationship between the stressors and stress. These relationships may all be influenced by stress moderators. Individual differences such as age, social support mechanisms, and personality are potential moderators. A *moderator* is a valuable attribute that affects the nature of a relationship. While numerous moderators are extremely important, we focus our attention on three representative ones: personality, Type A behavior, and social support.

The stress model provides managers with a framework for thinking about stress in the workplace. Consequently, it suggests that interventions may be needed and can be effective in improving negative stress consequences. Stress prevention and management

EXHIBIT 9.1   A Model of Stressors, Stress, and Outcomes

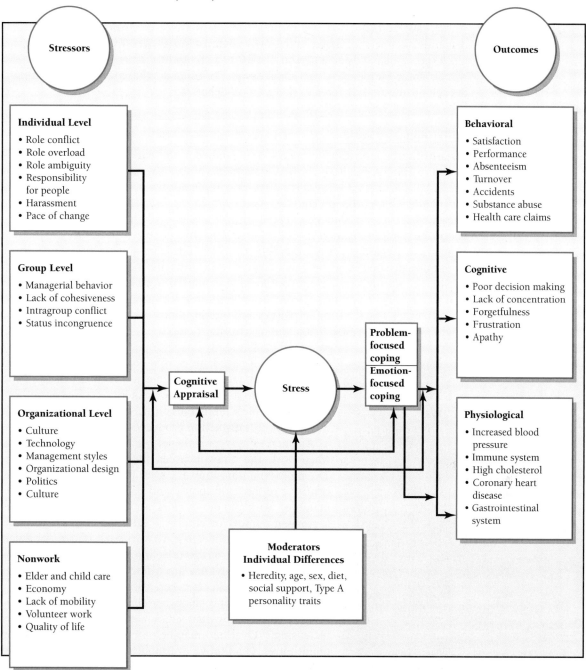

can be initiated by individuals or the organization. The intention of most preventive programs is to reduce the occurrence, intensity, and negative impact of stress. The management of stress attempts to eliminate or minimize negative consequences of stress. Prevention and the management of stress are challenging, however, as will be illustrated later in this chapter.

Work Stressors: Individual, Group, and Organizational

As we have said, stressors are those actions, situations, or events that place special demands on a person. Since, in the right circumstances, virtually any occurrence can place special demands on a person, the list of potential stressors is almost infinite. We will limit our examination to a small number of stressors that are relatively common in each of our model's three work-specific categories.

Individual Stressors

role conflict
Arises when a person receives incompatible messages regarding appropriate role behavior.

Stressors at the individual level have been studied more than any other category presented in Exhibit 9.1 Role conflict is perhaps the most widely examined individual stressor.[7] **Role conflict** is present whenever compliance by an individual to one set of expectations about the job conflicts with compliance to another set of expectations. Facets of role conflict include being torn by conflicting demands from a supervisor about the job and being pressured to get along with people with whom you are not compatible. Regardless of whether role conflict results from organizational policies or from other persons, it can be a significant stressor for some individuals. A recent analysis of 137 research studies that gathered information from 35,265 employees found that role conflict has a negative effect on employee performance.[8] Role conflict also leads to other problems for employees and organizations. A study at Goddard Space Flight Center determined that about 67 percent of employees reported some degree of role conflict. The study further found that Goddard employees who experienced more role conflict also experienced lower job satisfaction and higher job-related tension.[9] The researchers also found that the greater the power or authority of the people sending the conflicting messages, the greater was the job dissatisfaction produced by role conflict.

An increasingly prevalent type of role conflict occurs when work and nonwork roles interfere with one another. The most common nonwork roles involved in this form of conflict are those of spouse and parent. Balancing the demands of work and family roles is a significant daily task for a growing number of employed adults.[10] Pressure to work late, to take work home, to leave work early to care for a sick child, to spend more time traveling, and to frequently relocate in order to advance are a few examples of potential sources of role conflict between work and family.

Virtually everyone has experienced work overload, another common individual stressor, and the incidence rate is increasing.[11] Overload may be of two types: qualitative or quantitative. Qualitative overload occurs when people feel they lack the ability needed to complete their jobs or that performance standards have been set too high. Quantitative overload results from having too many things to do or insufficient time to complete a job. As organizations attempt to increase productivity, while decreasing workforce size, quantitative overload increases (and so does stress).[12] The New York law firm Cleary, Gottlieb, Steen, and Hamilton was sued by the father of an associate at the firm. The associate, unable to cope with workload, committed suicide by jumping off the roof of the firm's building.[13]

From a health standpoint, numerous studies have established that quantitative overload can cause biochemical changes, specifically, elevations in blood cholesterol levels. One study examined the relationship of overload, underload, and stress among 1,540 executives. Those executives on the low and high ends of the stress ranges reported more significant medical problems. This study suggests that the relationships among stressors, stress, and disease may be curvilinear. That is, those who are underloaded and those who are overloaded represent two ends of a continuum, each with a significantly elevated number of medical problems.[14] The underload–overload continuum is presented in Exhibit 9.2. The optimal stress level provides the best balance of challenge, responsibility, and reward. The potential negative effects of overload can be increased when overload is coupled with low ability to control the work demand.[15] Research suggests that when individuals experience high work demands with little or no control over these demands, the physiological changes that occur persist even after the individual has left work.[16]

Perhaps the most pervasive individual stressor of all is the unrelenting pace of change that is part of life today. At no other point in the history of industrialized society have we experienced such rapid change in the world around us. The last third of the 20th century included the advent of such wonders as communications satellites, moon landings, organ transplants, laser technology, nuclear power plants, intercontinental ballistic missiles, supersonic transportation, artificial hearts, and many other space-age developments. The pace of change within organizations has been no less remarkable at the start of the 21st century with two economic recessions, a global financial crisis, a major terrorist attack on U.S. soil, technological advances, and Internet-based phenomena like the explosion of social networking sites.

Many people who experience a great deal of change at work or in life show absolutely no negative effects or health problems. For some reason, these people can withstand the negative consequences of large doses of change that others cannot. Why this is so is an intriguing question. One organizational researcher, Suzanne Kobasa, has

EXHIBIT 9.2
The Underload–Overload Continuum

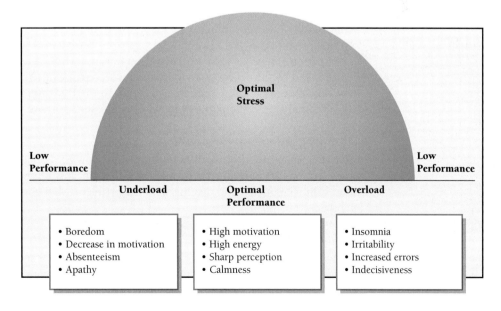

proposed that individuals who experience high rates of change without consequently suffering health problems might differ in terms of personality from those who are negatively affected. She refers to the personality characteristic in question as **hardiness.**[17] People with the hardiness personality trait seem to possess three important characteristics. First, they believe that they can control the events they encounter. Second, they are extremely committed to the activities in their lives. Third, they treat change in their lives as a challenge. In a longitudinal study to test the three-characteristic theory of hardiness, managers were studied over a two-year period. It was found that the more managers possessed hardiness characteristics, the smaller the impact of life changes on their personal health. Hardiness appeared to offset, or buffer, the negative impact of change.

It is proposed that hardiness is a factor that reduces stress by changing the way stressors are perceived. The hardy person is able to work through and around stressors, while the less hardy person becomes overwhelmed and unable to cope. The hardy respond by coping, attempting to control, and taking on the stressors as a challenge.[18] This type of response typically results in better behavioral, cognitive, and physiological consequences.[19]

Individual stressors abound. Not only can they cause stress but a number of other negative consequences as well. As we will see later in the chapter, stress consequences can affect not only health but a variety of job performance variables as well.

hardiness
A personality trait that appears to buffer an individual's response to stress. The hardy person assumes that he or she is in control, is highly committed to lively activities, and treats change as a challenge.

Group, Organizational, and Nonwork Stressors

The list of potential group and organizational stressors is a long one. In the next chapter, a number of group characteristics are discussed, including group norms, leadership, and the status hierarchy. Each of these can be a stressor for some group members, as can the different types of group conflict discussed in Chapter 10. One problem in discussing group and organizational stressors is identifying which are the most important. The paragraphs that follow briefly highlight the more significant stressors.

Participation

Participation refers to the extent that a person's knowledge, opinions, and ideas are included in the decision-making process. It is an important part of working in organizations for some people. Groups and organizations that do not encourage or allow participation will be a source of frustration to those who value it. Likewise, others will be frustrated by the delays often associated with participative decision making. Others may view shared decision making as a threat to the traditional right of a manager to have the final say. Participation will act as a stressor for these people.

Intra- and Intergroup Relationships

Poor relationships within and between groups can be a source of stress. Poor relationships may include low trust, lack of cohesion, low supportiveness, and lack of interest in listening to and dealing with the problems that confront a group or group member.

Organizational Politics

High levels of political behavior in organizations can be a source of stress for many employees. Office politics are consistently cited as a primary stressor in organizations.

Political activity, game playing, and power struggles can create friction, heighten dysfunctional competition between individuals and groups, and increase stress.

Organizational Culture

Like individuals, organizations have distinct personalities. The personality of an organization is shaped largely by its top executives. A tyrannical and autocratic executive team can create a culture filled with fear. Ernest Gallo is credited with being the stress producer at Gallo Winery because of the culture he has established with his hard-driving style, unrelenting insistence on superior performance, and low tolerance for failure.[20]

Lack of Performance Feedback

Most people want to know how they are doing and how management views their work. All too often, however, meaningful performance evaluation information is lacking, or the information is provided in a highly authoritarian or critical manner. Performance feedback information must be provided, and to minimize stress, it must occur in an open, two-way communication system.

Inadequate Career Development Opportunities

Career development opportunity stressors are those aspects of the organizational environment that influence a person's perception of the quality of his or her career progress. Career variables may serve as stressors when they become sources of concern, anxiety, or frustration. This can happen if an employee is concerned about real or imagined obsolescence, believes that promotion progress is inadequate, or is generally dissatisfied with the match between career aspirations and the current position.

Downsizing

Downsizing is the reduction of human resources by layoffs, attrition, redeployment, or early retirement.[21] As some organizations strive to cut costs, increasing numbers of employees are either downsized or fear being downsized. In either case, it is a potent stressor that can have negative effects for both individuals and organizations. Studies have shown, for example, that disability claims increase dramatically in companies that have recently downsized.[22] This increase comes both from employees who have been dismissed and from those who remain. That is probably why many companies have followed the lead of ReliaStar Bankers Security Life Insurance Co., which established a program to help employees cope with the stress of reorganization and layoffs.

Nonwork Stressors

Stress is also caused by factors outside the organization. Although the emphasis in this chapter is on work, nonwork stressors should not be ignored because they affect work. Raising children, caring for elders, volunteering in the community, taking college courses, and balancing family and work life are stressful for numerous people. The stress produced outside work is likely to impact a person's work behavior and performance. The distinction between work and nonwork is blurred, and overlapping stressors are significant in any discussion or analysis of stress.

The Global OB on page 250 illustrates nonwork stress referred to as work–life balance that management commuters face around the world.

A STRESS BALANCING ACT: HOPPING FROM THE HOME TO THE JOB AGAIN

The pressure of globalization and the changing nature of the work is forcing more and more managers from Europe, Asia, and North America to take a close look at their expectations about employee performance. As jobs around the world are becoming more stressful, complex, and challenging, a renewal or regeneration time becomes an issue for managers to consider. Even the travel part of global jobs has to be carefully evaluated in terms of stress.

Gone are the days when a manager assigned or transferred to work in another country (e.g., expatriate manager) has the family automatically packed up and shipped out. With many significant others and spouses now having their own careers and the importance of schooling for children, an overseas transfer introduces a form of stress trying to balance family life and work.

In Europe, the "eurocommuter" has emerged. That is, the transferred manager may be from Madrid, Spain, and is assigned for a period to Warsaw, Poland. To minimize stress, the eurocommuter travels on Monday morning to the job location, the family stays at the permanent residence, and the manager returns home for the weekend.

The stress of relocation is assumed by eurocommuters to be more significant than the stress of travel and being away from the family during the week. Not having to relocate means less disruption for the family. However, this does not eliminate the stress. Some experienced eurocommuters contend that about 12 months is the maximum time a manager should be expected to commute back and forth.

Whether this is a viable arrangement in other global locations such as Africa, Asia, Latin America, or North America is not known as yet.

The "eurocommuting" arrangement could be a positive approach for a short assignment. Individual managers have to decide for themselves whether it is best for them, their families, and their companies. Clearly, having managers who are willing to lead this type of lifestyle and travel back and forth can be beneficial to organizations. The stress of back and forth, being away from the family, and performing well on the job has to be compared to the stress of uprooting the family and relocating. There are no simple answers, but the "eurocommuter" approach is one choice that some managers and companies are considering.

Sources: Adapted from L. Dixon and M. Sim, "Short-Term Assignments Growing in Popularity," *Canadian HR Reporter* 21, no. 5 (March 2008), p. 17; "Have Job Will Travel—The Life of the Eurocommuter," *MWorld (Europe),* December 2002, pp. 1–3; "Balancing Act—All Work and No Play Makes Jack and Jill Look Elsewhere," *MWorld (Europe),* December 2003, pp. 8–10; see http://mworld.mce.be.

Cognitive Appraisal

As presented earlier in the model of stress in Exhibit 9.1, individuals using their own view of the situation conduct a perceptual evaluation. This is their interpretation of the situation or stressors. This perceptual process explains why one person's interpretation of stressors may be different from another person's.

The appraisal process occurs in two steps: primary and secondary.[23] A primary appraisal leads to categorizing a stressor as positive, negative, or meaningless. For example, a manager of a large retail store observes a 20 percent reduction in sales in November leading up to the holiday season. This is not good news given that many retailers earn the lion's share of their sales and profits during the holidays. The secondary appraisal involves a determination of whether something can be done to reduce the stress.[24] That is, is there some way I can fix the problem? The manager can't change consumer confidence but can certainly decrease hiring, control wasteful spending, increase advertising, and run storewide sales.

Coping with Stress

problem-focused coping
The actions taken by an individual to cope with a stressful person, situation, or event.

Through the primary and secondary appraisal, a coping approach is decided upon and applied. The two types of coping are: problem-focused and emotion-focused. **Problem-focused coping** is the actions taken to deal directly with the source of the stress. For example, workers facing a disrespectful manager may deal with his harassing style by being absent from work. This absenteeism enables the workers to be removed, some of the time, from the disrespectful manager.

emotion-focused coping
The actions taken by a person to alleviate stressful emotions. The actions center on avoidance or escape from a person, problem, or event.

Emotion-focused coping is the steps a person takes to address or alleviate stressful feelings and emotions. For example, employees who travel frequently as part of the job may alleviate their stressful feelings and emotions by exercising regularly or by reading light, nonwork-oriented fiction or poetry. If these coping activities are successful, the frequent travelers' feelings and emotions are kept in check.

Research illustrates that individuals use both kinds of coping approaches to deal with stressors. Some of the more popular problem-focused coping strategies include time management, working with a mentor, and training to improve competencies. A few of the more popular emotion-focused coping strategies include meditation, biofeedback, exercise, joining a work support group, and personal days off.

Stress Outcomes

The effects of stress are many and varied. Some effects are positive, such as self-motivation and stimulation to satisfy individual goals and objectives. Some stress consequences are disruptive, counterproductive, and even potentially dangerous. Additionally, as was suggested earlier (see again Exhibit 9.2), there are consequences associated with *too little* stress as well as too much. Not all individuals will experience the same outcomes. Research suggests, for example, that one of many factors influencing stress outcomes is type of employment. In one study, conducted at the Institute for Social Research at the University of Michigan, a sample of 2,010 employees was chosen from 23 occupations to examine the relationship between stress and stress consequences. The occupations were combined into four specific groups—blue-collar workers (skilled and unskilled) and white-collar workers (professional and nonprofessional).

Blue-collar workers reported the highest subjective effects, including job dissatisfaction; white-collar workers, the lowest. The unskilled workers reported the most boredom and apathy with their job conditions. They specifically identified a number of major stressors that created their psychological state: underutilization of skills and abilities, poor fit of the job with respect to desired amounts of responsibility, lack of participation, and ambiguity about the future. Skilled blue-collar workers shared some of these stressors and consequences with their unskilled counterparts, but not all; they reported above-average utilization of their skills and abilities but less responsibility and more ambiguity. White-collar professionals reported the fewest negative consequences. In all groups, however, there were indications that job performance was affected.[25]

In examining stress outcomes, the distinction in our model between organizational and individual outcomes is somewhat arbitrary. For example, a decrement in job performance due to stress is clearly an individual outcome; it is the individual's performance that is being affected. Just as clearly, however, the organization experiences important consequences from stress-related performance decrements.

Individual Outcomes

The emergence or evolution of stress outcomes takes time to identify or pinpoint. For example, a promoted employee develops an uncharacteristic pattern of Friday and Monday absences. A salesperson begins to lose repeat business; nonrenewing customers complain that he has become inattentive and curt in his dealings with them. A formerly conscientious nurse forgets to administer medications, with potentially serious patient consequences. An assembly worker experiences a significant increase in the percentage of her production rejected by the quality-control unit. A software designer

STRESS AND DEATH IN JAPAN

Have you ever felt or heard someone express the feeling, "This job is going to kill me!" Chances are you—or the person you heard—didn't literally believe that. If you were a Japanese worker, however, you might be very serious. Polls indicate that over 40 percent of Japanese workers aged 30 to 60 believe they will die from the stress of overwork, what the Japanese call *karoshi*. The victims of *karoshi* are known in their companies as *moretsu shain* (fanatical workers) and *yoi kigyo senshi* (good corporate soldiers).

In 1990, the average Japanese worker put in 2,124 hours a year—over 500 hours more than the Germans and French and about 250 hours more than Americans. Following the passage of two laws aimed at reducing the average number of hours worked by an employee, the Japanese figure had fallen to about 1,843 hours per year; however, this average is still above most other countries. At the same time, however, the nation's economic slump heightened the level of workplace anxiety. Many firms have been forced to downsize for the first time since 1945.

A Japanese Health Ministry report called *karoshi* the second-leading cause of death among workers (the first is cancer). Fierce competition among employees, as well as a strong sense of responsibility to their companies, leads many workers to stay at the office well into the night. When they do go home, they are tense and anxious because they feel that they should really be back at work. Some workers deal with the pressure by disappearing. As many as 10,000 men disappear each year, choosing to drop out rather than face the pressure of their jobs. Reports indicate over 140 cases of *karoshi* per year.

A *karoshi* hotline includes contact numbers, doctor and lawyer names, and a brief history of the concept of "death from overwork."

Sources: Adapted from A. Kanai, "Karoshi (Work to Death) in Japan," *Journal of Business Ethics* 84 (2009), pp. 209–16; Daniel Gross, "Why 'Steady' Lost," *Newsweek*, July 20, 2009; "Karoshi Hotline," http://karoshi.jp\english\index.html (accessed May 14, 2006); and Boye Lafayette de Mente, "Karoshi: Death from Overwork," *Japan's Cultural Code Words*, May 2002, pp. 1–6.

displays sudden, apparently unprovoked outbursts of anger. Each of these individuals is experiencing the effects and consequences of excessive stress.

Stress can produce *psychological consequences*—anxiety, frustration, apathy, lowered self-esteem, aggression, and depression. With respect to depression, a comprehensive survey of American workers concluded that a third of them experienced job stress–related depression.[26] Nor are such consequences restricted to American workers, as the Global OB demonstrates.

There is a stigma associated with depression.[27] Part of the stigma comes because most people lack an understanding of depression and its frequency. Unfortunately, most managers are not aware of these facts:

- According to the National Mental Health Association, the cost of depression is $44 billion a year in medical bills, lost productivity, and absenteeism.[28]
- Research suggests that depression is one of the most powerful conditions in the United States that leads to higher absenteeism and decreased worker productivity.[29]
- The World Health Organization predicts that by 2020, depression will be the second most common disability, after heart disease.[30]
- Depression is difficult to detect, especially within the present health care system.[31]

The *Diagnostic and Statistical Manual of Mental Disorders* (DSM-IV) is the diagnostic tool used to detect depression. The DSM-IV indicates that the diagnosis of depression requires the presence of either a depressed mood or diminished interest in all or most activities, marked psychomotor retardation, significant appetite or weight change, changes in sleep, fatigue or loss of energy, problems thinking or concentrating, feelings of worthlessness, excessive feelings of guilt, or thoughts of suicide or death. These signs must be persistent over the course of two weeks.

Managerial understanding of these symptoms can help the organization, especially when the manager asks professional counselors to intervene. It would be unwise for managers to ignore depression or to attempt to counsel workers suspected of being depressed. Being aware of depression symptoms and situations that precipitate it is the first line of intervention. Unfortunately, the stigma of depression results in a lack of understanding of its pervasiveness, costs, and treatment possibilities.[32]

Some stress outcomes may be *cognitive*. Cognitive outcomes would include poor concentration, inability to make sound decisions or any decisions, mental blocks, and decreased attention spans. Other effects may be *behavioral*. Such manifestations as accident proneness, impulsive behavior, alcohol and drug abuse, and explosive temper are examples.

Finally, *physiological outcomes* could include increased heart rate, elevated blood pressure, sweating, hot and cold flashes, increased blood glucose levels, and elevated stomach acid production. One way to envision the physiological impact of stress is to imagine oneself in a traumatic situation—your car is stalled on a railroad track and you hear the whistle of an oncoming train. This is the kind of sequence that occurs:[33]

- Steroid hormones and stress hormones are released by a signal to the brain area called the hypothalamic–pituitary adrenal (HPA) system. Cortisol is very important in marshalling systems through the body—heart, lungs, circulation, immune system—to deal with the stalled car and oncoming danger.
- The HPA releases neurotransmitters (chemical signals) called catecholamine. The catecholamine triggers an emotional response to the stressful situation—most likely fear of the danger.
- During the crisis, the catecholamine suppresses parts of the brain dealing with memory, concentration, and rational thought.
- Heart rate and blood pressure increase.
- The digestive system shuts down.

These are only a few of the physiological effects of the stress caused by the stalled car and the oncoming train. Once the threat has passed and the car is moved safely off the tracks, the stress hormones return to normal. Other body systems also normalize.

Stress-related work conditions that can possibly produce physiological effects similar to the stalled car episode include:

- Pressure in front of colleagues from a manager to work harder, faster, and longer.
- Poor, hostile relationships with colleagues.
- An accident or violence at work that injures friends or other employees.
- Being required to complete work for which you know you do not have the skills or competencies.
- Making an extremely important presentation to a group.

Some research shows that repeated release of stress hormones eventually produces hyperactivity in the HPA, and this can result in long-term sleep, anxiety, and depression problems.[34] The physiological stress response is like a rocket ready to be launched. Virtually all systems (e.g., heart, blood vessels, lungs, immune system, and brain) are altered to meet the perceived problem (e.g., danger, uncertainty, work-related problems).

Some stress outcomes combine effects from several of the categories of consequences described above. Consider, for example, the following two scenarios:

> Bob is a teacher in an inner-city high school. He barely remembers the time when he could not wait for the start of each school day; now he cannot wait until each day ends. As much as he could use the money, he quit teaching optional summer school three summers ago. He needs that break to recharge his batteries, which seem to run down

earlier with each passing school year. Many of his students are moody, turned off to society, and abusive to others.

Paula works as an air traffic controller in the second-busiest airport in the country. Every day, the lives of literally thousands of people depend on how well she does her job. Near misses are an everyday occurrence; avoiding disasters requires quick thinking and a cool head. At 31 years of age, Paula is the third oldest controller in the tower. She knows there are few controllers over the age of 40, and she is certain she will never be one. To make matters worse, she is in the final stages of a divorce. Paula was told after her last physical that she had developed a stomach ulcer. She is thinking of going into the nursery business with her sister; having responsibility for the well-being of shrubs and trees, rather than people, is very attractive to her.

burnout
A psychological process, brought about by unrelieved work stress, resulting in emotional exhaustion, depersonalization, and feelings of decreased accomplishment.

Bob and Paula are both experiencing job burnout. **Burnout** is a psychological process, brought about by unrelieved work stress, that results in emotional exhaustion, depersonalization, and feelings of decreased accomplishment.[35] Exhibit 9.3 displays some indicators of these three burnout outcomes. A recent research study found that burnout is linked to several aspects of ill health, including sleep disturbances, systematic inflammation, impaired immunity functions, and blood coagulation.[36] Burnout tends to be a particular problem among people whose jobs require extensive contact with and/or responsibility for other people. Indeed, much of the research that has been conducted on burnout has centered on the so-called helping professions: teachers, nurses, physicians, social workers, therapists, police, and parole officers.[37] The nearby Organizational Encounter presents some of the myths that surround the burnout concept.

A very important idea implicit in this conceptualization of burnout relates to job involvement. A high degree of involvement in, identification with, or commitment to one's job or profession is a necessary prerequisite for burnout. It is unlikely that one would become exhausted without putting forth a great deal of effort. Thus, the irony of burnout is that those most susceptible are those most committed to their work; all else being equal, lower job commitment equals lower likelihood of burnout. Various individual variables also affect the likelihood of developing burnout. For example, women are more likely to burn out than men, younger employees are more susceptible than older ones (particularly beyond age 50), and unmarried workers are more likely to burn out than married ones.

Organizations contribute to employee job burnout in a variety of ways. Research identifies four factors that are particularly important contributors to burnout: high levels of work overload, dead-end jobs, excessive red tape and paperwork, and poor communication and feedback, particularly regarding job performance. In addition, factors that have been identified in at least one research study as contributing to burnout include role conflict and ambiguity, difficult interpersonal relationships, and reward systems that are not contingent upon performance.[38]

EXHIBIT 9.3   Burnout Indicators

Source: John M. Ivancevich, Michael T. Matteson, Sara M. Freedman, and James S. Phillips, "Worksite Stress Management Interventions," *American Psychologist*, February 1990, p. 253.

Emotional Exhaustion	Depersonalization	Low Personal Accomplishment
Feel drained by work	Have become calloused by job	Cannot deal with problems effectively
Feel fatigued in the morning	Treat others like objects	Do not have a positive influence on others
Frustrated	Do not care what happens	Cannot understand others' problems
Do not want to work with	to other people	or identify with them
other people	Feel other people blame you	No longer feel exhilarated by your
		job

MYTHS AND BURNOUT

Christina Maslach is a leading expert on job burnout and author of the Maslach Burnout Inventory (MBI), the most widely used survey measure used in the field. *The Wall Street Journal* used its own survey to examine the concept Maslach clearly presented years ago. *The Wall Street Journal* interviewed managers in an attempt to understand managerial behavior that seems to push employees over the edge into job burnout. In the process, three myths were uncovered that organizations need to dispel if they are to reduce incidents of burnout among their staff.

Myth One: When a Client Says Jump, the Only Answer Is "How High?"

Lawyers, accountants, and management consultants are particularly vulnerable to believing in this myth even when it appears to result in high levels of burnout and turnover within their staffs. However, the study reported that a few professional firms are taking steps to integrate personal needs and concerns with the work lives of their employees. For example, Deloitte & Touche has implemented a policy that limits employees' travel time. It is no longer company policy for employees to spend all five working days of the week at clients' offices. At a maximum, employees are to spend only three nights (four working days) away from home and work the fifth day in their own offices each week, even when on lengthy assignments.

Myth Two: Reining in Employees' Workloads Will Turn Them into Slackers

Managers often behave as though a reduction in work overload will cause productivity to drop. Yet, studies often show the opposite result. Ernst & Young has a committee that monitors its staff accountants' workloads to head off burnout situations. The company says that its policies are raising retention rates and improving client service. A senior manager at Ernst observed that employees typically won't admit to burning out; thus having some compassionate, objective overview is useful.

Myth Three: If Employees Are Working Themselves into the Ground, It's Their Own Fault

Although this attribution may sometimes be true for some people, it is far from true for most. At the International Food Policy Research Institute, a nonprofit research organization in Washington, D.C., consultants discovered that a "crisis mentality" was driving scientists and support staff to work incredibly long hours. Management of the institute assumed that either (1) employees wanted to work these hours or (2) employees were managing their time poorly. Neither of these assumptions was valid. Rather, a shift in research focus coupled with an increased emphasis on using research teams allied with groups from other agencies and organizations had created an inefficient pattern of work for many people. Meetings, phone calls, and other forms of coordinated activity were eating up the workday, driving more productive research and writing into the evening hours.

Sources: Adapted from Christina Maslach, "How to Prevent Burnout," *New Zealand Management,* April 2005, pp. 43–48; and Sue Schellenbarger, "Three Myths That Make Managers Push Staff to the Edge of Burnout," *The Wall Street Journal,* March 17, 1999, p. B1.

Organizational Consequences

As illustrated in Exhibit 9.1, a number of the behavioral, cognitive, and physiological outcomes that are individually linked also have organizational consequences. While the organizational consequences of stress are many and varied, they share one common feature: stress costs organizations money. Although precise figures are lacking, based on a variety of estimates and projections from government, industry, and health groups, we place the costs of stress at about $250 billion annually. This estimate, which probably is conservative (some estimates are as high as $300 billion annually),[39] attempts to consider the dollar effects of reductions in operating effectiveness resulting from stress. The effects include poorer decision making and decreases in creativity. The huge figure also reflects the costs associated with mental and physical health problems arising from stress conditions, including hospital and medical costs, lost work time, turnover, sabotage, and a host of other variables that may contribute to stress costs. Because employers pay about 80 percent of all private health insurance premiums, and workers' compensation laws increasingly include provisions for awarding benefits for injuries stemming from stress in the workplace, it is clear that organizational consequences are significant.

Excessive stress increases job dissatisfaction. As we saw in Chapter 3, job dissatisfaction can be associated with a number of dysfunctional outcomes, including increased turnover, absenteeism, and reduced job performance. If productivity is reduced just 3 percent, for example, an organization employing 1,000 people would need to hire an additional 30 employees to compensate for that lost productivity. If annual employee costs are $40,000 per employee including wages and benefits, stress is costing the company $1.2 million just to replace lost productivity. This doesn't include costs associated with recruitment and training. Nor does it consider that decreases in quality of performance may be more costly for an organization than quantity decreases. Customer dissatisfaction with lower-quality goods or services can have significant effects on an organization's growth and profitability.

Further examples of organizational costs associated with stress include:

- The American Medical Association claims that stress was the cause of 80 to 85 percent of all human illness and disease or at the very least had a detrimental effect on individuals' health.[40]
- Stressed workers smoke more, eat less well, have more problems with alcohol and drugs, have more family problems, and have more problems with co-workers.[41]
- American businesses lose an estimated $200 billion to $300 billion per year to stress-related productivity decrease and other costs. This is higher than the total cost related to all strikes and the net profit from all Fortune 500 companies.[42]
- In Canada stress-related costs are estimated at $16 billion and in Great Britain costs are $7.3 billion annually.[43]
- Forty percent of employee turnover is due to excessive stress.[44]
- Over 500 million workdays are lost annually due to stress-related absenteeism.

Estimates and projections such as these (including our own estimate of annual stress-related costs) should be treated cautiously. There are simply too many variables to measure costs precisely. There is no doubt, however, that the consequences of excessive stress are significant in both individual and organizational terms.

Stress Moderators

Stressors evoke different responses from different people. Some people are better able to cope with a stressor than others. They can adapt their behavior in such a way as to meet the stressor head-on. On the other hand, some people are predisposed to stress; that is, they are not able to adapt to the stressor.

The model presented in Exhibit 9.1 suggests that various factors can moderate the relationships among stressor, stress, and consequences. A *moderator* is a condition, behavior, or characteristic that qualifies the relationship between two variables. The effect may be to intensify or weaken the relationship. The relationship between the number of gallons of gasoline used and total miles driven, for example, is moderated by driving speed. At very low and very high speeds, gas mileage declines; at intermediate speeds, mileage increases. Thus, driving speed affects the relationship between gasoline used and miles driven.

Many conditions, behaviors, and characteristics may act as stress moderators, including such variables as age, gender, and the hardiness construct discussed earlier in the chapter. In this section, we will briefly examine three representative types of moderators: (1) personality, (2) Type A behavior, and (3) social support.

Personality

As discussed in Chapter 3, the term *personality* refers to a relatively stable set of characteristics, temperaments, and tendencies that shape the similarities and differences in people's behavior. The number of aspects of personality that could serve as stress moderators is quite large. We will confine our attention to those aspects of personality previously identified in Chapter 3: the Big Five model, locus of control, and self-efficacy.

As you may recall from Chapter 3, the Big Five model of personality is made up of five dimensions: extroversion, emotional stability, agreeableness, conscientiousness, and openness to experience. Of these, *emotional stability* is most clearly related to stress. Those high on this dimension are most likely to experience positive moods and feel good about themselves and their jobs. While they certainly experience stress, they are less likely to be overwhelmed by it and are in a better position to recover from it. To a somewhat lesser degree, those high on *extroversion* are also more predisposed to experience positive emotional states. Because they are sociable and friendly, they are more likely to have a wider network of friends than their introverted counterparts; consequently, they have more resources to draw upon in times of distress.

If you are low on *agreeableness* you tend to be antagonistic, unsympathetic, and even rude, toward others. You are also probably somewhat mistrusting of others. These attributes increase the likelihood you will find other people to be a source of stress, and since others are more likely to find interacting with you stressful as well, an interpersonal relationship environment full of stressful situations is created.

Conscientiousness is the Big Five dimension most consistently related to job performance and success. To the extent that good performance leads to satisfaction and other rewards, those high on conscientiousness are less likely to experience stress with respect to these aspects of their jobs. Those low on this dimension, however, are more likely to be poorer performers, receive fewer rewards, and generally be less successful in their careers—not a recipe for low stress levels!

Finally, those high on *openness to experience* are better prepared to deal with stressors associated with change because they are more likely to view change as a challenge, rather than a threat.

Type A Behavior Pattern

Type A behavior pattern
Associated with research conducted on coronary heart disease. The Type A person is an aggressive driver who is ambitious, competitive, task-oriented, and always on the move.

In the 1950s, two medical cardiologists and researchers, Meyer Friedman and Ray Rosenman, discovered what they called the **Type A behavior pattern**.[45] They searched the medical literature and found that traditional coronary risk factors such as dietary cholesterol, blood pressure, and heredity could not totally explain or predict coronary heart disease (CHD). Coronary heart disease is the term given to cardiovascular diseases that are characterized by an inadequate supply of oxygen to the heart. Other factors seemed to the two researchers to be playing a major role in CHD. Through interviews with and observation of patients, they began to uncover a pattern of behavior or traits. They eventually called this the Type A behavior pattern (TABP).

The person with TABP has these characteristics:

- Chronically struggles to get as many things done as possible in the shortest time period.
- Is aggressive, ambitious, competitive, and forceful.
- Speaks explosively, rushes others to finish what they are saying.
- Is impatient, hates to wait, considers waiting a waste of precious time.

- Is preoccupied with deadlines and is work-oriented.
- Is always in a struggle with people, things, events.
- Displays or hides anger and hostility toward others.

Supporting the pioneering research of Rosenman and Friedman, who suggested that Type As have more heart attacks than do Type Bs, a recent analysis of data from 161 research studies conducted over the past 30 years found that Type A behavior (hostility and aggression) was associated with increased cardiovascular (heart rate or blood pressure) reactivity.[46]

Type B behavior pattern
The Type B person is relaxed, patient, steady, and even-tempered. The opposite of the Type A person.

In contrast, the **Type B behavior pattern** individual mainly is free of the TABP characteristics and generally feels no pressing conflict with either time or persons. The Type B may have considerable drive, wants to accomplish things, and works hard, but the Type B has a confident style that allows him or her to work at a steady pace and not to race against the clock. The Type A has been likened to a racehorse; the Type B, to a turtle.

Two major components of Type A behavior pattern are impatience and hostility. A study of 3,308 black and white men and women supported by the National Institutes of Health studied the effects of Type A, depression, and anxiety on long-term physical risk. Type A components were assessed at a baseline period and 15 years later. After 15 years, participants in the highest quartile of hostility had an 84 percent higher risk of hypertension.[47] No significant relationships were shown for the other factors. Results were similar for white and black participants.

A study of patients who underwent diagnostic coronary arteriography for suspected coronary heart disease illustrated involvement of hostility. Analysis showed that hostility was related to the presence of arteriosclerosis more than other Type A behavior pattern dimensions.[48]

Social Support

Both the quantity and quality of the social relationships individuals have with others appear to have a potentially important effect on the amount of stress they experience and on the likelihood that stress will have adverse effects on their mental and physical health. Social support can be defined as the comfort, assistance, or information one receives through formal or informal contacts with individuals or groups. A number of studies have linked social support with aspects of health, illness, burnout, and stress.[49]

Social support may take the form of emotional support (expressing concern, indicating trust, boosting esteem, listening); appraisal support (providing feedback and affirmation); or informational support (giving advice, making suggestions, providing direction). People who can serve as sources of social support at work include supervisors, co-workers, subordinates, and customers or other nonorganizational members with whom an employee might have contact. Nonwork support sources include family members (immediate and extended), friends, neighbors, caregivers (ministers, for example), health professionals (physicians, psychologists, counselors), and self-help groups (Alcoholics Anonymous, Weight Watchers).

A co-worker listening to a friend who failed to receive a desired promotion, a group of recently laid-off workers helping each other find new employment, or an experienced employee helping a trainee learn a job are all examples of providing support. Social support is effective as a stress moderator because it buffers the negative impact of stressors by providing a degree of predictability, purpose, and hope in upsetting and threatening situations.

A number of studies reinforce what we know to be true for our own experiences. Social support has been shown to reduce stress among employed individuals ranging from unskilled workers to highly trained professionals; it is consistently cited as an effective stress coping technique, and it has been associated with fewer health complaints experienced during periods of high stress.[50]

Stress Prevention and Management

An astute manager never ignores a turnover or absenteeism problem, workplace drug abuse, a decline in performance, hostile and belligerent employees, reduced quality of production, or any other sign that the organization's performance goals are not being met. The effective manager, in fact, views these occurrences as symptoms and looks beyond them to identify and correct the underlying causes. Yet most managers likely will search for traditional causes such as poor training, defective equipment, or inadequate instructions regarding what needs to be done. In all likelihood, stress will not be on the list of possible problems. Thus, the very first step in any attempt to deal with stress so that it remains within tolerable limits is recognition that it exists. Once that is accomplished, a variety of approaches and programs for preventing and managing organizational stress are available.

Exhibit 9.4 presents how organizational stress management programs can be targeted. Programs are targeted to (1) identify and modify work stressors, (2) educate employees in modifying and understanding stress and its impact, and (3) provide

EXHIBIT 9.4 Organizational Stress Management Program Targets

Source: John M. Ivancevich, Michael T. Matteson, Sara M. Freedman, and James S. Phillips, "Worksite Stress Management Interventions," *American Psychologist,* February 1990, p. 253.

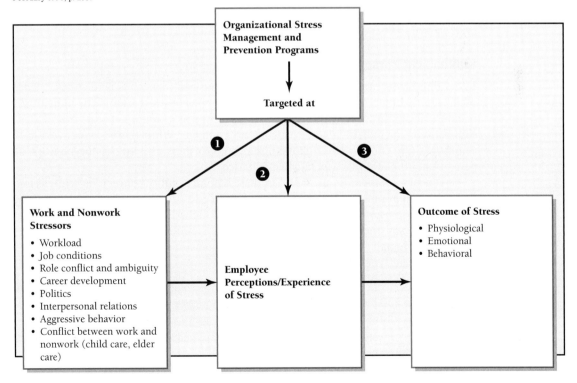

Management Pointer

SOCIAL SUPPORT

Developing Social Support

As a manager, you can take actions to help create a supportive work environment. These include:

1. Set an example by being a source of support for others, particularly subordinates.

2. Encourage open communication and maximum exchange of information.

3. Make certain you provide subordinates with timely performance feedback, presented in an encouraging, nonthreatening manner.

4. Provide for mentoring of the less experienced by more senior members of the work group.

5. Work to maintain and increase work group cohesion (see Chapter 10 for specifics regarding how to do this).

employees support to cope with the negative impact of stress. In a rapidly changing work environment, this type of targeting is difficult to accomplish. However, a trained, educated, and knowledgeable workforce can make modifications with the help of management in how work is performed. Some of the targeted, corrective programs include:

- Training programs for managing and coping with stress.
- Redesigning work to minimize stressors.
- Changes in management style to one of more support and coaching to help workers achieve their goals.
- More flexible work hours and attention paid to work–life balance and needs such as child and elder care.
- Better communication and team-building practices.
- Better feedback on worker performance and management expectations.

These and other efforts are targeted to prevent and/or manage stress. The potential for success of any prevention or management-of-stress program is good if there is a true commitment to understanding how stressors, stress, and outcomes are linked.

There is a very important distinction between preventing stress and managing it. Stress prevention focuses on controlling or eliminating stressors that might provoke the stress response. Stress management suggests procedures for helping people cope effectively with or reduce stress already being experienced. In this concluding section of the chapter, we will examine organizational programs and individual approaches to stress prevention and management, with the emphasis on management. First, however, we will look at a way of thinking about organizational stress prevention.

Maximizing Person–Environment Fit

In defining stress earlier in the chapter, we emphasized that stress is the consequence of the interaction between an environmental stimulus (a stressor) and the individual's response. From this perspective, stress may be viewed as a consequence of the relationship between the individual and the work environment. While there are many ways of thinking about individual–organizational relationships and stress, the concept of person–environment fit is the most widely used.[51]

Person–environment fit occurs when there is compatibility between individuals and their work environments. When an employee perceives that he or she fits well with the organization, the employee is more likely to have higher levels of organizational commitment, job satisfaction, and adjustment, while experiencing lower levels of stress.[52] Although originally thought of as a single dimension, researchers have identified several different types of P–E fit, including:[53]

1. *Person–organization fit*: Degree to which employees/applicants and organizations are compatible and meet each others' needs. An employee who doesn't fit with the organizational culture will experience stress and may end up leaving the organization.

2. *Person–job fit*: Extent to which an employee's/applicant's skills, abilities, and experience match the demands and requirements of the organization. To the extent that the individual's talents don't match the job requirements, stress results.

3. *Person–vocation fit*: Degree to which an individual has chosen a compatible career. People pursue careers for a variety of reasons—financial, interest, parental pressure, luck, etc. When an individual questions a career choice and regrets it, he or she is likely to experience stress.

4. *Person–group fit*: Extent to which there's interpersonal compatibility between individuals and their work groups. An employee can perceive a good fit with the organization, job, and career, but can't stand working with a certain group of co-workers, customers, or vendors. This misfit with the group will create stress for the employee.

By improving the quality of, or maximizing, the fit between the employee and the organizational environment, potential stressors are eliminated and stress is prevented. This P–E fit approach is somewhat similar to—and very consistent with—the concept of the psychological contract that was developed in Chapter 5. Violations of the psychological contract represent breakdowns in P–E fit.

There are numerous strategies for maximizing P–E fit. Ideally, the process begins before an individual even joins the organization. Employee recruitment programs that provide realistic job previews help potential employees determine whether the reality of the job matches their needs and expectations. Selection programs that are effective in ensuring that potential employees possess the requisite skills, knowledge, experience, and abilities for the job are key elements in maximizing fit.

Job skills and knowledge are not the only important factors to consider in employee selection, however. Fit can be maximized by closely linking personal predispositions to relevant aspects of the work environment as well. For example, as was suggested earlier, individuals with a low tolerance for ambiguity who find themselves in jobs or organizational environments in which there is little structure will very likely experience stress. Other examples include: An individual who is by nature authoritarian will experience stress in a participative organization; those who value intrinsic satisfaction will be frustrated by an environment that provides only extrinsic rewards; those wishing autonomy will be distressed by tight controls; and individuals with a high need for performance feedback will be stressed by supervisors who never communicate performance information.

Once a person is working in the organization, a critical variable in maximizing fit and preventing stress is effective socialization. Socialization is the process by which the individual learns and internalizes the values, expected behaviors, and social knowledge that are important for becoming an effective organizational member. The stages and characteristics of effective socialization were discussed in detail in Chapter 2, and you may wish to refer to that discussion in the present context of maximizing P–E fit.

Organizational Stress Prevention and Management Programs

In addition to the variety of activities that may be undertaken to improve person–environment fit, an increasing number of organizations have developed very specific stress prevention and/or management programs. Some of these programs focus on a specific issue or problem, such as alcohol or drug abuse, career counseling, job relocation, or burnout. Clark Nuber, a $25 million accounting and consulting firm near Seattle, has created a people-oriented culture that encourages its tax specialists to limit the amount they work each week to 55 hours (low for the accounting industry).[54] The company's stress-lowering approach to managing its people has led to it being named one of the Best Companies to Work For in America in 2008 and 2007. Circles, a Boston-based marketing firm, allows employees who have been with the firm for at least five years to take a 30-day paid sabbatical to avoid burnout and recharge their batteries.[55]

A variety of organizations such as Verizon Communications, Accenture, Ernst & Young, IBM, Dow Chemical, and Microsoft are also helping employees avoid burnout (and in so doing increase retention) by helping them to change careers without leaving the firm.[56] Verizon offers employees career-related courses and résumé-writing tips. IBM offers a skills-evaluation assessment to recommend career paths for which the employee might fit. Accenture assigns employees a career counselor and has a Web page for employees who are considering an internal career change. The Web page even has video clips of individuals who have made career changes within the firm. Such career-assistance programs are designed to reduce employee turnover and increase productivity.

Still other programs may target a specific group within the organization. An example is the Resident Assistance Program in place at Baylor College of Medicine. This program was designed to help medical residents cope successfully with the multitude of stressors they encounter.[57] Some programs may focus on a particular technique, such as developing relaxation skills. (For an example of a somewhat unusual focus, see the nearby Organizational Encounter on laughter.) Others are more general in nature, using a variety of approaches and geared to a cross-section of employees, such as the Employee Assistance Program at B. F. Goodrich, the Coors Brewing Company Wellness Program, and the Emotional Health Program at Equitable Life. Two specific types of organizational programs have become particularly popular during the last two decades: employee assistance programs and wellness programs.

Employee Assistance Programs (EAPs)

employee assistance program
An employee benefit program designed to deal with a wide range of stress-related problems, including behavioral and emotional difficulties, substance abuse, and family and marital discord.

Originally conceived as alcohol abuse programs, most **employee assistance programs** (EAPs) are designed to deal with a wide range of stress-related problems, both work and nonwork related, including behavioral and emotional difficulties, substance abuse, family and marital discord, and other personal problems. B. F. Goodrich, IBM, Xerox, and Caterpillar have such programs. EAPs have been based on the traditional medical approach to treatment. General program elements include:

- *Diagnosis.* Employee with a problem asks for help; EAP staff attempts to diagnose the problem.
- *Treatment.* Counseling or supportive therapy is provided. If in-house EAP staff is unable to help, employee may be referred to appropriate community-based professionals.
- *Screening.* Periodic examination of employees in highly stressful jobs is provided to detect early indications of problems.
- *Prevention.* Education and persuasion are used to convince employees at high risk that something must be done to assist them in effectively coping with stress.

An increasing number of employers believe that good health among employees is good for the organization. Blue Cross/Blue Shield determined that every dollar spent on the psychological care of employees with breast cancer saved $2.50 to $5.10 in overall medical expenses. The public school system of Orange County, Florida, found that the cost of medical claims dropped by 66 percent over five years for employees who used the EAP. At the end of five years, the same employees were taking 36 percent fewer sick leaves. At McDonnell Douglas (now Boeing), workers treated for alcohol and drug problems missed 44 percent fewer days of work after the EAP was set up.[58]

In addition to these health- and medical-oriented services offered through EAPs, the recent economic recession, where layoffs, salary reductions, home foreclosures, and other financial stresses have affected employees, has led some companies to offer a variety of support services aimed at helping them through these difficult times.[59] For

DEALING WITH STRESS CAN BE A LAUGHING MATTER

Stressed individuals have higher levels of the hormone cortisol. Laughter lowers cortisol levels. Children laugh about 400 times a day, while adults laugh about 15 times a day. Is it possible to get adults to laugh more at work and reduce those cortisol levels?

While passengers were preparing to board a Southwest Airlines flight, a Southwest customer service agent came over the public address system to announce, "Southwest Airlines would like to congratulate one of our first-time fliers who is celebrating his 89th birthday." This was a nice and fun announcement, typical of what the airline's employees try to do on a daily basis. Southwest Airlines also established a Belly Laugh Day; at 1:24 p.m. on January 24, people are supposed to laugh out loud to celebrate the joy of laughter.

The above typifies the Southwest Airlines culture, where it is believed that if employees are having fun they are going to do their jobs better and be less likely to experience dissatisfaction, stress, and burnout. Increasingly, companies are turning to humor as a way of improving employee morale and combating stress. A growing number of "humor consultants" are being hired by companies nationwide to lighten up an overworked, anxious workforce. Research supports the conclusion that humor boosts the human immune system, reduces stress, and helps keep people well. Other research shows decreases in production of stress hormones while people are laughing.

One group of humor consultants is developing a program called Subjective Multidimensional Interactive Laughter Evaluation (SMILE), which will survey humor preferences and coping styles and help tailor a personalized humor approach to stress reduction. What kind of organization would use such a program, or hire a humor consultant? The answer seems to be companies suffering from low morale, cutbacks, or buyouts. Corporations undergoing downsizing are major users.

The rationale for these programs is that humor is a set of skills that some people have developed better than others. For those in need of skill development, humor programs can help people increase the tools they have to combat stress.

Sources: Adapted from www.blogsouthwest.com/blog/belly-laugh-day (accessed July 20, 2009); D. Kulisek, "Laugh It Off," *Quality Progress* 41, no. 8 (2008), pp. 62–63; Charles S. Lauer, "Tracking Laughs," *Modern Healthcare* 37, no. 13 (March 2007), p. 22; and Francis X. Frei, "Rapid Rewards at Southwest Airlines," *Harvard Business School Cases*, September 2, 2003.

example, Telemundo Network (a division of NBC Universal) offers on-site financial planning and stress management workshops throughout the country via EAPs and employee groups. Blue Cross and Blue Shield of North Carolina believes that sharing information about the health of the company is important to reduce employee stress; the firm holds town hall meetings and an executive blog shares "top level" information and invites employee feedback. Alcoa also believes in keeping employees in the loop and uses e-mail, daily management notes, a biweekly employee publication, and an internal TV system to communicate with employees about the state of the company.[60]

Crucial to the success of any EAP is trust. Employees must trust that (1) the program can and will provide real help, (2) confidentiality will be maintained, and (3) use of the program carries no negative implications for job security or future advancement. If employees do not trust the program or company management, they will not participate. EAPs with no customers cannot have a positive effect on stress prevention and management.

Wellness Programs

wellness program
An employee program focusing on the individual's overall physical and mental health. Wellness programs may include a variety of activities designed to identify and assist in preventing or correcting specific health problems, health hazards, or negative health habits.

Wellness programs, sometimes called health promotion programs, focus on the employee's overall physical and mental health. Simply stated, any activity an organization engages in that is designed to identify and assist in preventing or correcting specific health problems, health hazards, or negative health habits can be thought of as wellness-related. This includes not only disease identification but lifestyle modification as well. Among the most prevalent examples of such programs are those emphasizing hypertension identification and control, smoking cessation, physical fitness and exercise, nutrition and diet control, and job and personal stress management.

We include wellness programs in a discussion of stress management for several reasons. First, stress prevention and management are a vital part of wellness, and, as we have already noted, it is frequently a component of wellness programs. Second, many of the concerns of wellness programs are at least partially stress-related. Stress has been cited as the greatest cause of poor health habits,[61] and poor health habits are what wellness programs attempt to change. Third, stress management contributes to healthier, more productive, and more effective employees, and consequently to healthier, more productive, and more effective organizations. Corporate wellness programs simply extend these payoffs. Fourth, it is impossible to divorce the topic of stress from health. In a sense, wellness programs represent a broad-based, contemporary extension of stress programs; their focus is concern for employee health and quality-of-life issues.

Examples of well-established wellness programs (all of which include a stress reduction component) include Aetna's Wellness Works program, Mass Mutual's Wellness Partnership, 3M's Lifestyle 2000 program, CIGNA'S Healthy Life program, Warner-Lambert's LifeWise program, and Control Data's StayWell program. StayWell has been so successful that it is now marketed to other companies. Wellness programs, however, are not restricted to large companies like those just cited. Approximately 50 percent of smaller firms provide some form of wellness program for their workers.[62]

Johnson & Johnson's wellness program, started more than 30 years ago, successfully promotes a global culture of health to its 120,000 employees worldwide. Known as the Health & Wellness Program, its overriding goals are to "optimize . . . the health and productivity of J&J employees worldwide . . . while helping to control health care costs."[63] During a four-year internal study of the effects of its wellness program, J&J reported a reduction of $224.66 per employee per year over the four-year period. This saved the company more than $38 million between 1995 and 1999.

Roche Pharmaceutical of Nutley, New Jersey, found that it spent only 3 percent of medical benefit dollars on preventive health measures. This small expenditure was despite the fact that 39 percent of the health claims submitted were the result of preventable conditions. Roche management concluded that focusing on prevention would mean healthier, more productive, less stressed, more creative, and less absent employees. Roche named its wellness program "Choosing Health."[64]

Choosing Health starts at the individual level by assessing employee health risks via a 76-item survey that takes 15 minutes to complete. A health profile is provided and sent directly to the employee's home. All employee responses and profiles are confidential and not released to a third party. The company also provides on-site screening for such ailments as high blood pressure, high cholesterol, and breast and skin cancers. Roche's Human Resource Management (HRM) group receives only aggregated data showing risks with the general population. HRM then patterns preventive health programs after the health risks and education needs of employees as a group. Almost 100 percent of Roche employees participate in Choosing Health.

The Roche program provides a $100 incentive for completing 100 sessions at a fitness facility or in a group exercise program. In the second year of the program, 23 percent of Choosing Health participants had reduced their health risks. A part of Choosing Health is an evaluation process to evaluate the impact of the program. In two years, the average lifestyle score increased from 63 to 68 (100 is the optimal score). Roche is constantly working to align prevention, intervention, employee health, and productivity.

Simply offering an EAP or wellness program does not guarantee positive results for either employers or the sponsoring organization. While many factors determine how successful any particular program will be, a number of recommendations, if followed, will increase the likelihood of achieving beneficial outcomes. Among the more important are:

1. Top-management support, including both philosophical support and support in terms of staff and facilities, is necessary.
2. Unions should support the program and participate in it where appropriate. This can be particularly difficult to accomplish. Many unions take the position that instead of helping employees deal with stress, management should focus on eliminating those conditions that contribute to the stress in the first place.
3. The greatest payoff from stress prevention and management comes not from one-shot activities, but from ongoing and sustained effort; thus, long-term commitment is essential.
4. Extensive and continuing employee involvement would include involvement not only in the initial planning but in implementation and maintenance as well. This is one of the most critical factors for ensuring representative employee participation.
5. Clearly stated objectives lay a solid foundation for the program. Programs with no or poorly defined objectives are not likely to be effective or to achieve sufficient participation to make them worthwhile.
6. Employees must be able to participate freely, without either pressure or stigma.
7. Confidentiality must be strictly adhered to. Employees must have no concerns that participation will in any way affect their standing in the organization.

Individual Approaches to Stress Prevention and Management

Organization members do not have to—nor should they—rely on formal organizational programs to assist in stress prevention and management. There are many individual approaches to dealing with stressors and stress. A few of the more popularly cited and frequently used approaches for individual stress prevention and management are discussed below. These approaches may be included in the range of options available within an organizational stress management or wellness program. The effectiveness of these techniques varies greatly. What one person finds useful, another may not. There is still a great deal we do not know regarding the effects of individual differences on stress management outcomes.[65]

Cognitive Techniques

The basic rationale for some individual approaches to stress management, known collectively as cognitive techniques, is that a person's response to stressors is mediated by cognitive processes or thoughts. The underlying assumption of these techniques is that people's thoughts, in the form of expectations, beliefs, and assumptions, are labels they apply to situations, and these labels elicit emotional responses to the situation. Thus, for example, if an individual labels the loss of a promotion a catastrophe, the stress response is to the label, not to the situation. Cognitive techniques of stress management focus on changing labels or cognitions so that people appraise situations differently. This reappraisal typically centers on removing cognitive distortions such as magnifying (not getting the promotion is the end of the world for me), overgeneralizing (not getting promoted means my career is over; I'll never be promoted in any job, anywhere), and personalization (since I didn't get the promotion it's clear I'm a terrible person). All cognitive techniques have a similar objective: to help people gain more control over their reactions to stressors by modifying their cognitions.[66]

Relaxation Training

The purpose of this approach is to reduce a person's arousal level and bring about a calmer state of affairs, both psychologically and physiologically. Psychologically, successful relaxation results in enhanced feelings of well-being, peacefulness and calm, a clear sense of being in control, and a reduction in tension and anxiety; physiologically, decreases in blood pressure, respiration, and heart rate should occur. Relaxation techniques include breathing exercises; muscle relaxation; autogenic training, which combines elements of muscle relaxation and meditation; and a variety of mental relaxation strategies, including imagery and visualization.[67]

Meditation

Many of the meditative forms that have achieved some degree of popularity in this country are derivatives of Eastern philosophies. Included in this category are Zen meditation and Nam Sumran, or Sikh meditation. Perhaps the most widely practiced in the United States is transcendental meditation, or TM. Its originator, Maharishi Mahesh Yogi, defined TM as turning the attention toward the subtler levels of thought until the mind transcends the experience of the subtlest state of thought and arrives at the source of thought.[68] The basic procedure used in TM is simple, but the effects claimed for it are extensive. One simply sits comfortably with closed eyes and engages in the repetition of a special sound (a mantra) for about 20 minutes twice a day. Studies indicate that TM practices are associated with reduced heart rate, lowered oxygen consumption, and decreased blood pressure.[69]

Biofeedback

Individuals can be taught to control a variety of internal body processes by using a technique called *biofeedback*. In biofeedback, small changes occurring in the body or brain are detected, amplified, and displayed to the person. Sophisticated recording and computer technology make it possible for a person to attend to subtle changes in heart rate, blood pressure, temperature, and brain-wave patterns that normally would be unobservable. Most of these processes are affected by stress.[70]

The potential role of biofeedback as an individual stress management technique can be seen from the bodily functions that can, to some degree, be brought under voluntary control. These include brain waves, heart rate, muscle tension, body temperature, stomach acidity, and blood pressure. Most if not all of these processes are affected by stress. The potential of biofeedback is its ability to help induce a state of relaxation and restore bodily functions to a nonstressed state. One advantage of biofeedback over nonfeedback techniques is that it gives precise data about bodily functions. By interpreting the feedback, individuals know how high their blood pressure is, for example, and discover, through practice, means of lowering it.

Biofeedback training has been useful in reducing anxiety, lowering stomach acidity (and thus reducing the likelihood of ulcer formation), controlling tension and migraine headaches, and, in general, reducing negative physiological manifestations of stress. Despite these positive results, people looking to biofeedback for stress control should understand that success requires training and the use of equipment that may be very expensive.

YOU BE THE JUDGE COMMENT

IS THE ORGANIZATION RESPONSIBLE FOR AN EMPLOYEE'S STRESS?

This case requires management to consider the consequences of Carter's claim. If Carter is compensated because of his claim, other employees will likely also make claims. Management should determine if Carter can be transferred to a slower-paced job. They should also determine Carter's history and record on this job. Is his not keeping pace something new or has it been a chronic problem?

GM will have to examine its selection program to determine if individuals have to be better screened. This would be a difficult case for Carter to win in court. However, in some states his claim of stress as an injury would be heard and contested under worker's compensation laws.

Summary of Key Points

- Stress is an adaptive response moderated by individual differences, that is, a consequence of any action, situation, or event that places special demands on a person.

- Stress can have psychological, behavioral, and physiological consequences. The relationship between stress and physiological consequences is complex and can potentially be serious to the health of individuals who can't or don't cope with the stressors linked to the stress.

- Major variables in the model of organizational stress presented in this chapter are: (1) work stressors (work environment, individual, group, and organizational); (2) stress itself; (3) stress consequences (organizational and individual); (4) stress moderators (personality, Type A behavior, and social support); and (5) stress prevention and management (maximizing person–environment fit, organizational programs, and individual approaches).

- Stressors are actions, situations, or events that place special demands on a person. Three important categories of stressors are: (1) work environment (e.g., chemicals, radiation, temperature); (2) individual stressors (e.g., role conflict, work overload, change); and (3) group and organizational stressors (e.g., politics, culture, interpersonal relationships, downsizing).

- While some consequences of stress are positive, many are dysfunctional. Negative individual consequences include accident proneness, poor concentration, drug and alcohol abuse, and burnout. Organizational consequences may include absenteeism, turnover, increased health and medical costs, and quantitative and qualitative decrements in productivity.

- Some factors affect the nature of the stress response. These are called stress moderators. Three important moderators are personality, Type A behavior, and social support.

- Individuals take problem-focused and/or emotion-focused steps to deal directly with stress. In most cases a combination of these two types of coping strategies is used.

- Stress prevention and management strategies include (1) maximizing person–environment fit, (2) organizational programs such as employee assistance and wellness, and (3) individual approaches such as cognitive techniques, relaxation training, meditation, and biofeedback.

Review and Discussion Questions

1. It has been suggested that "stress is in the eyes of the beholder." What does this mean? Do you agree?
2. Why should managers not even attempt to counsel or provide advice to any employee suspected of being depressed?
3. The issue of who should be responsible for dealing with work stress—the individual or the organization—is an important one. What do you think? What are your arguments for and against each position?
4. Do you think some types of jobs or organizations attract Type A individuals? Do some attract Type B individuals? Why?
5. What role can managers play in helping their employees use a problem-focused strategy to cope with excessive job stress?
6. Work underload may be every bit as dysfunctional as work overload. Can you think of other work variables where "too little" may be as counterproductive as "too much"?
7. What are the different kinds of person–environment fit? What can employees and managers do to maximize these different types of fit?
8. What is the relationship between stress and personality? What aspects of personality might tend to increase stress? Decrease it?
9. Why are people in certain occupations more susceptible to burnout? What kinds of things might organizations do to reduce the likelihood their members will experience burnout?
10. Increasingly, some global workers are being sent on overseas assignments. What stressors might be unique to such assignments? What might organizations do to minimize their impact?

Exercise

Exercise 9.1 *Behavior Activity Profile—Type A Measure*

Each of us displays certain kinds of behaviors, thought patterns, and personal characteristics. For each of the 21 sets of descriptions below, circle the number that you feel best describes where you are between each pair. The best answer for each set of descriptions is the response that most nearly describes the way you feel, behave, or think. Answer these in terms of your regular or typical behavior, thoughts, or characteristics.

1. I'm always on time for appointments.   7 6 5 4 3 2 1   I'm never quite on time.
2. When someone is talking to me, chances are I'll anticipate what they are going to say by nodding, interrupting, or finishing sentences for them.   7 6 5 4 3 2 1   I listen quietly without showing any impatience.
3. I frequently try to do several things at once.   7 6 5 4 3 2 1   I tend to take things one at a time.

Now how much do you know about managing stress?

6. True or false: The typical Type A behavior pattern (TABP) is considered a moderator of the stressor, stress, and consequences relationship.
   a. True
   b. False

7. Stress is considered to be an _____ response.
   a. environmental
   b. adaptive
   c. energy access
   d. obstacle

8. A person is in a state of _____ when compliance with one set of expectations is in conflict with compliance in another set of expectations.
   a. eustress
   b. delegation
   c. role conflict
   d. status compliance

9. The underload–overload optimal stress continuum graphically represents _____.
   a. a negative threshold
   b. an equation
   c. biochemical changes
   d. an inverted "U"

10. True or false: Over a four-year period, Johnson & Johnson's wellness program saved the company over $38 million.
    a. True
    b. False

REALITY CHECK ANSWERS

Before	After
1. c 2. c 3. a 4. b 5. a	6. a 7. b 8. c 9. d 10. a
Number Correct	Number Correct
_____	_____

4. When it comes to waiting in line (at banks, theaters, etc.), I really get impatient and frustrated.   It simply doesn't bother me.

5. I always feel rushed.   7 6 5 4 3 2 1   I never feel rushed.

6. When it comes to my temper, I find it hard to control at times.   7 6 5 4 3 2 1   I just don't seem to have one.

7. I tend to do most things like eating, walking, and talking rapidly.   7 6 5 4 3 2 1   Slowly.

TOTAL SCORE 1–7 _____ = S

8. Quite honestly, the things I enjoy most are job-related activities.   7 6 5 4 3 2 1   Leisure-time activities.

9. At the end of a typical workday, I usually feel like I needed to get more done than I did.   7 6 5 4 3 2 1   I accomplished everything I needed to.

10. Someone who knows me very well would say that I would rather work than play.   7 6 5 4 3 2 1   I would rather play than work.

11. When it comes to getting ahead at work, nothing is more important.   7 6 5 4 3 2 1   Many things are more important.

12. My primary source of satisfaction comes from my job.   7 6 5 4 3 2 1   I regularly find satisfaction in nonjob pursuits, such as hobbies, friends, and family.

13. Most of my friends and social acquaintances are people I know from work.   7 6 5 4 3 2 1   Not connected with my work.

14. I'd rather stay at work than take a vacation.   7 6 5 4 3 2 1   Nothing at work is important enough to interfere with my vacation.

TOTAL SCORE 8–14 _____ = J

15. People who know me well would describe me as hard driving and competitive.   7 6 5 4 3 2 1   Relaxed and easygoing.

16. In general, my behavior is governed by a desire for recognition and achievement.   7 6 5 4 3 2 1   What I want to do—not by trying to satisfy others.

17. In trying to complete a project or solve a problem, I tend to wear myself out before I'll give up on it.   7 6 5 4 3 2 1   I tend to take a break or quit if I'm feeling fatigued.

18. When I play a game (tennis, cards, etc.) my enjoyment comes from winning.   7 6 5 4 3 2 1   The social interaction.

19. I like to associate with people who are dedicated to getting ahead.   7 6 5 4 3 2 1   Easygoing and take life as it comes.

20. I'm not happy unless I'm always doing something.   7 6 5 4 3 2 1   Frequently, "doing nothing" can be quite enjoyable.

21. What I enjoy doing most are competitive activities.   7 6 5 4 3 2 1   Noncompetitive pursuits.

TOTAL SCORE 15–21 _____ = H

Source: Copyright © 1982 by Michael T. Matteson and John M. Ivancevich.

Impatience (S)	Job Involvement (J)	Hard Driving and Competitive (H)	Total Score (A) S+J+H

The Behavior Activity Profile attempts to assess the three Type A coronary-prone behavior patterns, as well as provide a total score. The three a priori types of Type A coronary-prone behavior patterns are shown:

Items	Behavior Pattern	Characteristics
1–7	Impatience (S)	Is anxious to interrupt Fails to listen attentively Gets frustrated by waiting (e.g., in line, for others to complete a job)
8–14	Job Involvement (J)	Focal point of attention is the job Lives for the job Relishes being on the job Gets immersed in job activities
15–21	Hard driving/Competitive (H)	Is hardworking, highly competitive Is competitive in most aspects of life, sports, work, etc. Races against the clock
1–21	Total score (A)	Total of S + J + H represents your global Type A behavior

Score ranges for total score are:

Score	*Behavior Type*
122 and above	Hard-core Type A
99–121	Moderate Type A
90–98	Low Type A
80–89	Type X
70–79	Low Type B
50–69	Moderate Type B
40 and below	Hard-core Type B

Percentile Scores

Now you can compare your score to a sample of over 1,200 respondents.

Percentile Score Percent of Individuals Scoring Lower	Raw Score	
	Males	**Females**
99%	140	132
95%	135	126
90%	130	120
85%	124	112
80%	118	106
75%	113	101
70%	108	95
65%	102	90
60%	97	85
55%	92	80
50%	87	74
45%	81	69
40%	75	63
35%	70	58
30%	63	53
25%	58	48
20%	51	42
15%	45	36
10%	38	31
5%	29	26
1%	21	21

Case

Case 9.1: *No Response from Monitor 23*

Loudspeaker: Ignition Minus 45 Minutes

Paul Keller tripped the sequence switches at control monitor 23 in accordance with the countdown instruction just to his left. All hydraulic systems were functioning normally in the second stage of the spacecraft booster checkpoint 1 minus 45. Keller automatically snapped master control switch to GREEN and knew that his electronic impulse along with hundreds of others from similar consoles within the Cape Canaveral complex signaled continuation of the countdown.

Free momentarily from data input, Keller leaned back in his chair, stretched his arms above his head, and then rubbed the back of his neck. The monitor lights on console 23 glowed routinely.

It used to be an incredible challenge, fantastically interesting work at the very fringe of man's knowledge about himself and his universe. Keller recalled his first day in Brevard County, Florida, with his wife and young daughter. How happy they were that day. Here was the future, the good life . . . forever. And Keller was going to be part of that fantastic, utopian future.

Loudspeaker: Ignition Minus 35 Minutes

Keller panicked! His mind had wandered momentarily, and he lost his place in the countdown instructions. Seconds later he found the correct place and tripped the proper sequence of switches for checkpoint 1 minus 35. No problem. Keller snapped master control to GREEN and wiped his brow. He knew he was late reporting and would hear about it later.

Damn! he thought, I used to know countdown cold for seven systems monitors without countdown instructions. But now . . . you're slipping Keller . . . you're slipping, he thought. Shaking his head, Keller reassured himself that he was overly tired today . . . just tired.

Loudspeaker: Ignition Minus 30 Minutes

Keller completed the reporting sequence for checkpoint 1 minus 30, took one long last drag on his cigarette, and squashed it out in the crowded ashtray. Utopia? Hell, it was one big rat race and getting bigger all the time. Keller recalled how he once naively felt that his problems with Naomi would disappear after they left Minneapolis and came to the Cape with the space program. Now, 10,000 arguments later, Keller knew there was no escape.

Only one can of beer left, Naomi? One stinking lousy can of beer, cold lunch meat, and potato salad? Is that all a man gets after 12 hours of mental exhaustion?

Oh, shut up, Paul! I'm so sick of you playing Mr. Important. You get leftovers because I never know when you're coming home . . . your daughter hardly knows you . . . and you treat us like nobodies . . . incidental to your great personal contribution to the Space Age.

Don't knock it, Naomi. That job is plenty important to me, to the Team, and it gets you everything you've ever wanted . . . more! Between this house and the boat, we're up to our ears in debt.

Now don't try to pin our money problems on me, Paul Keller. You're the one who has to have all the same goodies as the scientists earning twice your salary. Face it, Paul. You're just a button-pushing technician regardless of how fancy a title they give you. You can be replaced, Paul. You can be replaced by any S.O.B. who can read and punch buttons.

Loudspeaker: Ignition Minus 25 Minutes

A red light blinked ominously indicating a potential hydraulic fluid leak in subsystem seven of stage two. Keller felt his heartbeat and pulse rate increase. Rule 1 . . . report malfunction immediately and stop the count. Keller punched POTENTIAL ABORT on the master control.

Loudspeaker: The Count Is Stopped at Ignition Minus 24 Minutes 17 Seconds

Keller fumbled with the countdown instructions. Any POTENTIAL ABORT required a cross-check to separate an actual malfunction from sporadic signal error. Keller began to perspire nervously as he initiated standard cross-check procedures.

"Monitor 23, this is Control. Have you got an actual abort, Paul?" The voice in the headset was cool, but impatient, "Decision required in 30 seconds."

"I know, I know," Keller mumbled, "I'm cross-checking right now."

Keller felt the silence closing in around him. Cross-check one proved inconclusive. Keller automatically followed detailed instructions for cross-check two.

"Do you need help, Keller?" asked the voice in the headset.

"No, I'm O.K."

"Decision required," demanded the voice in the headset. "Dependent systems must be deactivated in 15 seconds." Keller read and reread the console data. It looked like a sporadic error signal . . . the system appeared to be in order.

"Decision required," demanded the voice in the headset. "Continue count," blurted Keller at last. "Subsystem seven fully operational." Keller slumped back in his chair.

Loudspeaker: The Count Is Resumed at Ignition Minus 24 Minutes 17 Seconds

Keller knew that within an hour after liftoff, Barksdale would call him in for a personal conference. "What's wrong lately, Paul?" he would say. "Is there anything I can help with? You seem so tense lately." But he wouldn't really want to listen. Barksdale was the kind of person who read weakness into any personal problems and demanded that they be purged from the mind the moment his men checked out their consoles.

More likely Barksdale would demand that Keller make endless practice runs on cross-check procedures while he stood nearby . . . watching and noting any errors . . . while the pressure grew and grew.

Today's performance was surely the kiss of death for any wage increase too. That was another of Barksdale's methods of obtaining flawless performance . . . which would surely lead to another scene with Naomi . . . and another sleepless night . . . and more of those nagging stomach pains . . . and yet another imperfect performance for Barksdale.

Loudspeaker: Ignition Minus 20 Minutes

The monitor lights at console 23 blinked routinely. "Keller," said the voice in the earphone. "Report, please."

"Control, this is Wallace at monitor 24. I don't believe Keller is feeling well. Better send someone to cover fast!"

Loudspeaker: The Count Is Stopped at 19 Minutes 33 Seconds

"This is Control, Wallace. Assistance has been dispatched and the count is on temporary hold. What seems to be wrong with Keller?"

"Control, this is Wallace, I don't know. His eyes are open and fixed on the monitor, but he won't respond to my questions. It could be a seizure or . . . a stroke."

Questions

1. Is there any way of avoiding the more serious manifestations (as with Paul Keller) of pressure on the job? Explain.
2. Are there any early warning signs given by employees under stress? If so, what are they?
3. What is the proper role of the supervisor here? Should he refer Keller to a professional counselor?

Source: Robert D. Joyce, *Encounters in Organizational Behavior* (New York: Pergamon Press, 1972), pp. 168–72.

Group Behavior and Interpersonal Influence

Coming together is a beginning; keeping together is progress; working together is success.

Henry Ford

CHAPTER TEN

Groups and Teams

Learning Objectives

After completing Chapter 10, you should be able to:

- **Understand** that the term *group* can be viewed from a number of perspectives.
- **Identify** the elements in the process of group formation and development.
- **Describe** the stages of group formation.
- **Identify** several ways to guard against groupthink.

- **Discuss** relevant criteria for group effectiveness.
- **Identify** the characteristics that distinguish a group from a team.
- **Describe** the differences between a self-managed work team and a virtual team.
- **Describe** the factors important to team success.

The existence of groups can alter a person's motivation or needs and can influence the behavior of people in an organizational setting. Organizational behavior is more than simply the logical composite of the behavior of separate individuals. It is not their sum or product but rather a much more complex phenomenon, a very important part of which is the group. This chapter provides a model for understanding the nature of groups in organizations. It explores various types of groups, the reasons for their formation, their characteristics, and some end results of group membership. It also focuses on a special form of groups—teams—that is playing an increasingly larger role in current organizational processes. The current understanding of teams builds on theories, research findings, and applications of groups and their formation, maturity, and effectiveness.

group
Two or more individuals interacting to accomplish a common goal.

team
Mature group with member interdependence and motivation to achieve a common goal.

Groups and teams are not the same. A **group** is two or more individuals interacting with each other to accomplish a common goal. **Teams** are mature groups with a degree of member interdependence and motivation to achieve a common goal. Teams start out as groups, but not all groups become mature and interdependent or teams.

Teams and groups share many common characteristics. First, as already noted, they can be formed when two or more individuals interact. Second, both teams and groups provide structure for the work and interaction of their members. Third, their members can perform specific technical, leadership, problem-solving, and emotional roles. Last, members of groups and teams share a common goal(s).

Exhibit 10.1 presents some of the differences between groups and teams. Depth of commitment distinguishes groups and teams. Groups are accountable to a manager and are often randomly formed (e.g., hiring different people over time), resulting in a varied mix of skills. Teams are internally accountable to one another, and each member's skills complement those of the other team members. Group members create and share norms of performance and behavior. On the other hand, teams share a culture, a set of rituals and processes, and a philosophy in working together.

Teams over time develop synergy or a special energy by leveraging the creativity, actions, and behaviors of members. A team's work and performance are said to be synergistic, or

How much do you know about groups and teams?

1. A(n) _____ is a group of individuals who are working as a unit to complete a project or job assignment.
    a. informal group
    b. command group
    c. task group
    d. formal group

2. Assigning group members to a secretive research and development project that operates outside of normal company operations in order to create innovative products is known as a _____.
    a. stealth operation
    b. skunkworks
    c. quiet development zone
    d. basement barrier

3. In a manufacturing setting, employees whose performance is similar to the standard performance of other employees (i.e., group norm) who perform similar tasks are said to be operating in the _____.
    a. zone of acceptance
    b. zone of accomplishment
    c. zone of goal achievement
    d. zone of agreement

4. Making a group more homogeneous and smaller are two steps that can _____ group members.
    a. increase conflict among
    b. decrease the amount of communication between
    c. have no effect on
    d. increase group cohesion among

5. In a work setting, an employee who produces more than anyone else in the group is known as a _____.
    a. zone hitter
    b. rate-buster
    c. norm expander
    d. None of the above (a–c) are correct.

greater than the work and performance of individuals working alone on the team. For example, the now famous animation studio Pixar was so cash-strapped during its early years that it almost went out of business.[1] What saved the company? A six-person team at Pixar created several high-quality short films (one was awarded an Oscar in 1988) and commercials that brought in $2.1 million in revenue and attracted the attention of executives at Disney, ultimately leading to a joint venture between the two companies in 1991.[2] Teams from both companies joined forces and released the blockbuster film *Toy Story*, which was the highest-grossing film in 1995 earning $362 million worldwide. Since that time, Disney purchased Pixar for $7.4 billion but has been careful to preserve the creative team environment that has helped the Disney and Pixar partnership create such popular animated films as *Finding Nemo, The Incredibles, Cars, Ratatouille, Wall-E,* and *Up*.[3]

Another example of synergistic teamwork and performance is the trauma team at Ben Taub General Hospital, Houston's busiest emergency room.[4] Physicians, nurses, aides, technicians, and specialists work on teams to treat life-and-death cases. Trauma teams are committed to saving lives under serious circumstances. Each member brings a

EXHIBIT 10.1
Comparison of Groups and Teams

Dimension	Formal Work Group	Team
Goals	Works on common goals	Total commitment to common goals
Accountability	To manager	To team members and team leader
Skill levels	Random	Complementary
Performance evaluation	By manager	By team members and team leader
Culture	Marked by change and conflict	Based on collaboration and goal attainment
Performance outcomes	Positive, neutral, or negative	Synergistic or greater than sum of members' contributions
Definition of success	By manager's aspirations	By members' and team leader's aspirations

special set of skills to the trauma patient. There is no time for conflict, since collaboration is essential for lives to be saved. Members of the trauma team depend on each other and are accountable to each other.

As a team, the Ben Taub unit has acquired a local and national reputation for accomplishing exceptional results in saving patients. The synergistic results could be accomplished only by a committed and dedicated team of professionals.[5] The trauma team is an actual example of the distinct characteristics and differences presented in Exhibit 10.1. Not all teams have such crucial life-and-death circumstances regularly facing them. Also, to effectively utilize teams in organizations, managers and leaders need to understand the distinctions illustrated in Exhibit 10.1.

The Nature of Groups

Groups are a pervasive part of modern life. All of us have been—and are—members of many different groups—school groups, work groups, family groups, social groups, religious groups. There are small groups and large groups, permanent groups and temporary groups, formal groups and informal groups. Some groups are successful, some are not. Some groups bring out the best in their members, while others may bring out the worst. These are just a few of the multitude of ways in which groups may be characterized.

As indicated earlier, the following definition of groups will be used throughout this chapter: two or more individuals interacting with each other to accomplish a common goal.

One way of viewing this definition is to think of it in terms of specifying three minimum requirements that must be met for a group to exist. The first requirement deals with size. There must be *two or more individuals* for there to be a group. One person does not constitute a group. Note that in this definition, while there is a minimum size requirement, there is no maximum.

The second requirement specifies that there must be some form of exchange or communication between these individuals. That is, they must *interact with each other* in some manner. We usually think of interaction between group members as occurring in a face-to-face verbal exchange, but that does not have to be the case. In nominal groups (discussed in Chapter 14), for example, the members might never speak with one another; their only interactions are typically in writing. At a noisy construction site, the communication between a supervisor and an ironworker may only come in the form of gestures, yet no one would suggest there was no important interaction occurring. You can have a collection of individuals who do not interact with one another; they are just that—a collection of individuals, not a group.

EXHIBIT 10.2   A Model of Group Formation and Development

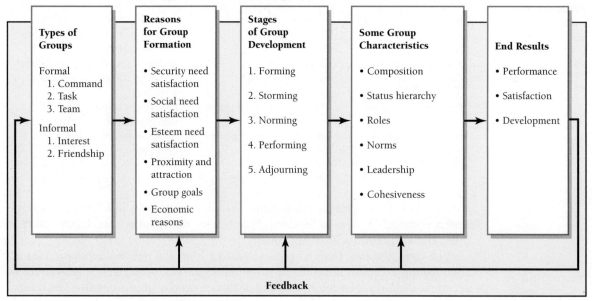

Types of Groups	Reasons for Group Formation	Stages of Group Development	Some Group Characteristics	End Results
Formal 1. Command 2. Task 3. Team Informal 1. Interest 2. Friendship	• Security need satisfaction • Social need satisfaction • Esteem need satisfaction • Proximity and attraction • Group goals • Economic reasons	1. Forming 2. Storming 3. Norming 4. Performing 5. Adjourning	• Composition • Status hierarchy • Roles • Norms • Leadership • Cohesiveness	• Performance • Satisfaction • Development

Feedback

The final requirement in our definition of groups is that of attempting to *accomplish a common goal.* If there is no common goal or purpose, there is no group by our definition. A common goal is a goal toward which individual members are willing to work. For example, a common goal of most sports teams is to achieve a high enough level of teamwork to win the game. Yes, a team "star" can make a substantial contribution to that victory, but it generally takes a team to win a game.

An Integrated Model of Group Formation and Development

Although every group is different, possessing its own unique attributes and dynamics, it is also true that in many important ways groups tend to display similar patterns of evolution. Exhibit 10.2 presents a model of group formation and development that we will follow in discussing this important organizational behavior and management topic. The model suggests that the end results of group activity are shaped by a number of antecedent variables, each category of which we will examine in this chapter. Each segment of the model can (and, in reality, does) influence each of the other segments.

Types of Groups

formal group
A group formed by management to accomplish the goals of the organization.

An organization has technical requirements that arise from its stated goals. The accomplishment of these goals requires that certain tasks be performed and that employees be assigned to perform these tasks. As a result, most employees will be members of a group based on their position in the organization. These are **formal groups.** Whenever individuals associate on a fairly continuous basis, there is a tendency for groups to form whose activities may be different from those required by the

informal group
A group formed by individuals and developed around common interests and friendships rather than around an organizational goal.

command group
A group of subordinates who report to one particular manager. The command group is specified by the formal organization chart.

task group
A group of individuals who are working as a unit to complete a project or job task.

organization. These are **informal groups.** Both formal groups and informal groups, it will be shown, exhibit the same general characteristics.

Formal Groups

The demands and processes of the organization lead to the formation of different types of groups. Specifically, at least two types of formal groups exist: command and task.

Command Group

The **command group** is specified by the organization chart and is made up of the subordinates who report directly to a given supervisor. The authority relationship between a department manager and the supervisors, or between a senior nurse and her subordinates, is an example of a command group.

Task Group

A **task group** comprises the employees who work together to complete a particular task or project. For example, when an emergency call comes in to put out a warehouse blaze, firefighters in a city fire department are trained to deal with the situation by performing a variety of tasks. These activities create a situation in which several firefighters must communicate and coordinate with one another to address the emergency situation. These required tasks and interactions facilitate the formation of a task group.[6] Another example would be the nurses assigned to duty in the emergency room of a hospital; they constitute a task group, since certain activities (e.g., taking a medical history, triage assessment, assisting the physician, comforting the patient's family, etc.) are required when a patient needs to be treated.

Informal Groups

Informal groups are natural groupings of people in work environments in response to social needs. In other words, informal groups are not deliberately created; they evolve naturally. Two specific types of informal groups are *interest* and *friendship.* The boundaries between these two types of groups often become blurred. For example, assume a group of employees from different departments of a company respond to a volunteer opportunity to serve the homeless at a nearby soup kitchen. This interest group evolves into a friendship group as a result of this bonding experience.

interest group
A group that forms because of some special topic of interest. Generally, when the interest declines or a goal has been achieved, the group disbands.

friendship group
An informal group that is established in the workplace because of some common characteristic of its members and that may extend the interaction of its members to include activities outside the workplace.

Interest Groups

Individuals who may not be members of the same command group, task group, or team may come together to achieve some mutual objective. Examples of **interest groups** include employees grouping together to present a unified front to management for more benefits and waitresses "pooling" their tips. Note that the objectives of such groups are not related to those of the organization, but are specific to each group.

Friendship Groups

Many groups form because the members have something in common such as age, political beliefs, or ethnic background. These **friendship groups** often extend their interaction and communication to off-the-job activities.

A distinction has been made between two broad classifications of groups—formal and informal. The major difference between them is that formal command and task groups and teams are designated by the formal organization as a means to an end.

Informal interest and friendship groups are important for their own sake. They satisfy a basic human need for association. If employees' affiliation patterns were documented, it would become rapidly apparent that they belong to numerous and often overlapping groups. Why so many groups exist is the question to which we turn next.

Why People Form Groups

Formal and informal groups form for various reasons.[7] Some of the reasons involve need satisfaction, proximity, attraction, goals, and economics.

One of the most compelling reasons people join groups is because they believe membership in a particular group will help them to satisfy one or more important needs. *Social needs,* for example, can be satisfied through groups that provide a vehicle for members to interact with one another. Indeed, it is difficult to imagine being able to fulfill general social needs without participating in at least some groups. *Security needs* may be partially met by membership in a group that acts as a buffer between employees and the organizational system. Without such a group, an individual may feel alone in facing organizational demands. This "aloneness" leads to a degree of insecurity that can be offset by group membership. *Esteem needs* may be partially met by belonging to a high-status or prestige group in which membership is difficult to obtain. An example would be the million-dollar roundtable in the life insurance business, or an honors organization in college.

Proximity and attraction are two related reasons people form groups. *Proximity* involves the physical distance between employees performing a job. Walking distance, rather than straight-line distance, is a better predictor of the amount of interaction that will occur. It is much easier to interact with a co-worker 10 yards away and separated by two desks than it is to interact with someone 1 yard away but separated by a wall. *Attraction* designates the attraction of people to each other because of perceptual, attitudinal, performance, or motivational similarity. Proximity makes it easier to determine areas of common attraction. Thus, both of these factors work together to facilitate group formation.

Group goals, if clearly understood, can be reasons people are drawn to a group. For example, an individual may join a group that meets after work to become familiar with a new personal computer system. Assume that this system is to be implemented in the work organization over the next year. The person who voluntarily joins the after-hours group believes that learning the new system is a necessary and important goal for employees.

Finally, in many cases groups form because individuals believe they can derive greater *economic benefits* from their jobs if they organize. For example, individuals working at different points on an assembly line may be paid on a group-incentive basis where the production of the group determines the wages of each member. By working and cooperating as a group, the workers may obtain higher economic benefits. Or executives in a corporation may form a group to review executive compensation in hopes of increasing their own economic payoffs. Whatever the circumstances, the group members have a common interest—increased economic benefits—that leads to group affiliation.

Stages of Group Development

Groups learn just as individuals do. The performance of a group depends both on individual learning and on how well the members learn to work with one another. For example, a new product committee formed for the purpose of developing a response to a competitor may evolve into a very effective team, with the interests of the company being most important. However, it may also be very ineffective if its members are more concerned about their individual departmental goals than about developing a response to a competitor. This section describes some general stages through which groups evolve and points out the sequential development process involved.[8]

One widely cited model of group development assumes that groups proceed through as many as five stages of development: (1) forming, (2) storming, (3) norming, (4) performing, and (5) adjourning.[9] Although identifying the stage a group is in at a specific time can be difficult, it is nonetheless important to understand the development process. At each stage, group behaviors differ and, consequently, each stage can influence the group's end results.

Forming

The first stage of group development is *forming,* and it is characterized by uncertainty (and, frequently, confusion) about the purpose, structure, and leadership of the group. Activities tend to focus on group members' efforts to understand and define their objectives, roles, and assignments within the group. Patterns of interaction among group members are tried out and either discarded or adopted, at least temporarily. The more diverse the group is, the more difficult it is to maneuver through this stage and the longer it takes. That is why this is a particularly sensitive stage in the formation of multicultural groups. Generally, this stage is complete when individuals begin to view themselves as part of a group.

> Student group example: After being assigned a semester-long group project by their professor, newly formed student groups meet to figure out how to get started on the project, who will do what task, etc.

Storming

The *storming* stage of group development tends to be marked with conflict and confrontation. This generally emotionally intense stage may involve competition among members for desired assignments and disagreements over appropriate task-related behaviors and responsibilities. A particularly important part of storming can involve redefinition of the groups' specific tasks and overall goals.

Individually, group members are likely to begin to decide the extent to which they like the group tasks and their degree of commitment to them. While members may accept the group at one level, at another level they may resist the control the group imposes on them. Some group members may begin to withdraw during storming, making this stage a particularly critical one for group survival and effectiveness. It is essential that the conflict that typifies storming be managed, as opposed to being suppressed. Suppression of conflict at this point is likely to create negative effects that can seriously hinder group functioning in later stages.

> Student group example: Group members argue over what to do about one of the five team members who missed two early (and important) meetings and deadlines.

Norming

While storming is marked by conflict and confrontation, *norming* is characterized by cooperation and collaboration. It is also the stage where group cohesion begins significant development. There tends to be an open exchange of information, acceptance of differences of opinion, and active attempts to achieve mutually agreed-upon goals and objectives. There is a strong degree of mutual attraction and commitment and feelings of group identity and camaraderie. Behavioral norms are established and accepted by the completion of this stage, as are leadership and other roles in the group. (The specific important impact of norms on group functioning is addressed in a subsequent section on group characteristics.)

> Student group example: Students have agreed upon key goals and objectives and have developed a true sense of "teamwork"; the leader is accepted and members have accepted their individual roles.

Performing

The fourth, and what may be the final stage, is performing. *Performing* is that stage where the group is fully functional. The group structure is set, and the roles of each member are understood and accepted. The group focuses its energies, efforts, and commitments on accomplishing the tasks it has accepted.

For some groups, this stage marks the attainment of a level of effectiveness that will remain more or less constant. For others, the process of learning and development will be ongoing so that group effectiveness and efficiency continue. In the former case, group performance will be maintained at a level sufficient to ensure survival; in the latter case, the group will record increasingly higher levels of achievement. Which way any particular group will go will depend on a number of variables; in particular, how successfully the group completed earlier development stages.

> Student group example: Group members and the group leader perform their tasks effectively and make a great deal of progress toward achieving their goals and objectives.

Adjourning

The *adjourning* stage involves the termination of group activities. Many groups, of course, are permanent and never reach the adjourning stage. For temporary groups, however, such as committees, project groups, task forces, and similar entities, this stage includes disbandment. Customary task activities are complete and the group focuses on achieving closure. This stage can be marked by very positive emotions centering on successful task accomplishment and achievement. It may also be a source of feelings of loss, disappointment, or even anger. The latter may be especially true in the case of permanent groups that fail to survive because of organizational downsizing, merging, or bankruptcy. Increasingly, adjournment is becoming an expected stage of group development, however. Many organizations are relying on temporary groups for problem-solving tasks and product development. Hewlett-Packard and 3M are two examples of companies using temporary groups. At these organizations, project teams may have a life cycle ranging from less than a month to several years.

Not all groups progress smoothly and predictably through these stages. Numerous factors can either hinder or facilitate the process. For example, if new members are constantly entering the group while others are leaving, the group may never complete the performing stage. Other factors that may influence the pattern of group development include the context or environment in which the group operates and group members' awareness of time and deadlines.

> Student group example: The group completes the assignment and submits it to the professor for a grade. After final exams are over, the group gets together for pizza to celebrate the successful completion of the project.

Characteristics of Groups

As groups evolve through their various stages of development, they begin to exhibit certain characteristics. To understand group behavior, you must be aware of these general characteristics. Some of the more important ones are composition, status hierarchy, roles, norms, leadership, and cohesiveness.

Composition

Group composition relates to the extent to which group members are alike. Members of a *homogeneous group* share a number of similar characteristics. Characteristics may be demographic (race, gender, socioeconomic background, education, age, or cultural origin), personality, skills and abilities, or work experience, to name just a few. A *heterogeneous group,* on the other hand, is composed of individuals who have few or no similar characteristics.

Group composition can be extremely important because it can influence a number of other characteristics and outcomes. All else being equal, for example, homogeneous groups are likely to be more cohesive than heterogeneous ones. On the other hand, heterogeneous groups may outperform homogeneous ones in certain situations because they have a richer variety of knowledge, information, and experience to draw upon.[10] As organizational diversity increases, at least with respect to demographic characteristics, groups will become more heterogeneous in composition. While this offers numerous opportunities for increasing group performance, it also makes the effective management of groups a more challenging task.[11] Sometimes explicit decisions to include individuals with certain characteristics in the composition of a group can have unintended consequences, as this chapter's You Be the Judge demonstrates.

Status Hierarchy

Status and *position* are so similar that the terms often are used interchangeably. The status assigned to a particular position is typically a consequence of certain characteristics that differentiate one position from other positions. In some cases, a person is given status because of such factors as job seniority, age, or assignment. For example, the oldest worker may be perceived as being more technically proficient and is attributed status by a group of technicians. Thus, assigned status may have nothing to do with the formal status hierarchy.

The status hierarchy, and particularly the deference paid to those at the top of the hierarchy, may sometimes have unintended—and undesirable—effects on performance. A vivid example occurred several years ago when a commercial jetliner ran out of fuel and landed short of the runway in Portland, Oregon, killing 10 of the 189 persons aboard. The plane ran out of fuel while flight members were preoccupied with a landing-gear problem that had forced them to circle Portland for some time. The Air Transportation Safety Board's report of the accident showed that both the copilot and the flight engineer knew the fuel situation was becoming critical, but they did not do enough to warn the captain. A study of the transcript of the cockpit conversation that took place before the crash confirms that warnings were made but were subtle, gentle, and extremely deferential to the senior captain in his position at the top of the status hierarchy.[12]

YOU BE THE JUDGE

USING GENDER TO INCREASE WORK GROUP DIVERSITY

Southwood Psychiatric Hospital is a treatment facility with an emphasis on the treatment of emotionally disturbed and sexually abused children. When hospital management reassigned a female child care specialist to the night team (the night team works from 11 p.m. to 7 a.m.), she was very upset. The specialist characterized the new assignment as being less desirable than assignment to the day-treatment team.

Hospital management assigned her to the night team because she was female and the night-treatment team was not very diverse; in fact, it was made up of all men. Recently, some female patients had indicated they were uncomfortable asking male specialists to assist them with certain needs during the night (e.g., going to the restroom, getting changed into pajamas, etc.). Hospital management, in an effort to make these female patients feel more comfortable, reassigned the female child care specialist to night duty.

Was this a reasonable way for Southwood Psychiatric Hospital to increase work group diversity? Do you think that this transfer will affect the reassigned female child care specialist's attitude toward her job, patients, or hospital management?

Roles

Each position in the group structure has an associated role that consists of the behaviors expected of the occupant of that position.[13] For example, the director of nursing services in a hospital is expected to lead, organize, and control the entire nursing department. The director is also expected to assist in preparing and administering the budget for the department. A nursing supervisor, on the other hand, is expected to supervise the activities of nursing personnel engaged in specific nursing services such as obstetrics, pediatrics, and surgery. These expected behaviors generally are agreed on not only by the occupants, the director of nursing, and the nursing supervisor, but also by other members of the nursing group and other hospital personnel.

In addition to an *expected role* there are also perceived and enacted roles. The *perceived role* is the set of behaviors that a person in a position believes he or she should enact. As discussed in Chapter 4, perception can be distorted or inaccurate. The *enacted role,* on the other hand, is the behavior that a person actually carries out. Thus, three possible role behaviors can result. Conflict and frustration may arise from differences in these three role types. In fairly stable or permanent groups, there typically is good agreement between expected and perceived roles. When the enacted role deviates too much from the expected role, the person either can become more like the expected role or leave the group.

Through membership in different groups, individuals perform multiple roles. For example, first-line supervisors are members of the management team but also are members of the group of workers they supervise. These multiple roles result in a number of expected role behaviors. In many instances, the behaviors specified by the different roles are compatible. When they are not, however, the individual may experience role conflict. In the case of first-line supervisors, for example, top management has a set of expectations that stresses the supervisor's role in the management group. However, the supervisor is part of the group she is supervising and may have close friendship ties with the other members of the group, who may be former working peers. Similarly, a physician placed in the role of hospital administrator also may experience this type of role conflict. Sometimes, the conflict is between the individual's role as a work group member on the one hand and a member of the larger organizational group on the other.

Norms

Norms are the standards shared by members of a group, and they have certain characteristics that are important to group members. First, norms are formed only with respect to things that have significance for the group. They may be written, but very often they can be verbally communicated to members. In many cases they may never be formally stated but somehow are known by all group members. If production is important, then a production norm will evolve. If helping other group members complete a task is important, then an assistance norm will develop. Conversely, if these are not important concerns to the group, no standards for appropriate behavior in these areas will evolve; group members will be free to behave in whatever manner seems reasonable to them.

Second, norms are accepted in various degrees by group members. Some norms are completely accepted by all members, while other norms are only partially accepted. For example, research suggests that employees' behavior can be influenced by an overly permissive group norm regarding absenteeism; basically, these employees will be absent more often than employees who are more concerned about the consequences of excessive absenteeism.[14]

Third, norms may apply to every group member, or they may apply to only some group members. For example, every member may be expected to comply with the production norm, while only group leaders may be permitted to disagree verbally with a management directive.

Groups develop norms for regulating many different aspects of their members' behavior.[15] For example, research suggests that positive feelings such as the joy and contentment of group members can create a group norm whereby the group is positive and upbeat.[16] Positive group affect has been shown to reduce group members' absenteeism and conflict while enhancing cooperation, performance, and member well-being.[17] In work groups, however, the most common norm relates to productivity, and group productivity norms specify "acceptable" production behavior. It is important to understand that the group's perception of what is an acceptable level of production may be significantly different from management's perception. The group's production norm may differ from management's for a number of reasons, including a fear of rate-cutting if production is too high or a fear of reprisal if production falls too low.

Exhibit 10.3 illustrates where a group's production norm might fall on a productivity continuum. The zone of acceptance depicted in the exhibit represents minor deviations above and below the norm that would be deemed acceptable to the group. Group members greatly exceeding the norm might be referred to as rate-busters, while those producing well below group expectations might be known as slackers.

Norm Conformity

An issue of concern to managers is why employees conform to group norms.[18] This issue is especially important when a person with skill and capability is performing significantly below his or her capacity so that group norms are not violated. A number of variables may influence conformity to group norms. The *personal characteristics* of the individual play a role. For example, research indicates that persons of high intelligence are less likely to conform than less intelligent individuals, and authoritarian personality types conform more than do nonauthoritarians.[19] *Situational factors,* such as group size and structure, may influence conformity. For example, conformity may become more difficult in larger groups or in those whose members are geographically separated. *Intergroup relationships,* which include such factors as the kind of pressure

EXHIBIT 10.3
Hypothetical Production Norm and Its Zone of Acceptance

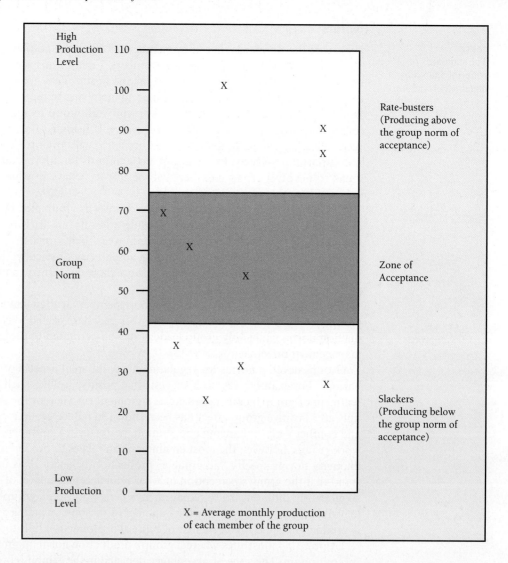

X = Average monthly production of each member of the group

the group exerts and the degree to which the member identifies with the group, are another potentially important variable.

The degree of conformity with group norms may also be influenced by cultural factors. Some cultures with a more collective tradition may place greater emphasis on the group and on conformity with norms than might cultures with a more individualistic orientation. Typical examples of these two orientations are Japan and the United States. Groups have traditionally played a far greater role in Japanese society than they have in the United States.

Leadership

The leadership role is an extremely crucial characteristic of groups as the leader exerts influence over the other members of the group.[20] In the formal group the leader can exercise legitimately sanctioned power. That is, the leader can reward or punish members who do not comply with the orders or rules. Sometimes, however, there is no single formal leader, even in a formal group. Such a condition may exist in the case of

NO BOSSES LEFT AT TEXAS INSTRUMENTS MALAYSIA

Because of the demographics of Malaysia and the shortage of highly skilled professional workers, Texas Instruments Malaysia (TIM) needed to find a new way to recruit, reward, and retain staff. The answer was to push job responsibility to the lowest level. The move to do so eliminated group leaders.

Since TIM was formed in 1972 to produce integrated circuits (it now produces more than 3 million a day), it has relied heavily on group and team structures. Early manifestations of this took the form of quality improvement teams as TIM adopted total quality management practices. By the late 1980s TIM managers began to put operator self-control into practice. They did this in two ways: first by teaching operators how to recognize problems and arrive at solutions; and second by giving them the responsibility, discretion, and authority to do something about a problem when they discovered one.

From there it became a logical progression to move toward eliminating group leaders. By 1992 nearly 90 percent of TIM workers were members of self-managed teams. Today that figure is virtually 100 percent. All day-to-day responsibility for business operating decisions such as stock control, quality, cost, delivery, and service is in the hands of the teams. Line managers have become a thing of the past. Indeed, the only formal leaders left at TIM are senior executives in control of strategy and finance. Such employee empowerment has been achieved by sharing information with workers and replacing a hierarchical management culture with one that is based on self-management.

Getting rid of the bosses has saved TIM $50 million in quality improvements over 10 years; productivity per employee has gone through the roof; production cycle time has been reduced by half; and absenteeism and tardiness records have dramatically improved. With increased productivity, increased profitability, and decreased organizational bureaucracy, TIM seems to be both a worker's and a management paradise.

Sources: W. Alan Randolph and Marshall Sashkin, "Can Organizational Empowerment Work in Multinational Settings?" *Academy of Management Executive* 16, no. 1 (2002), pp. 102–15; and "Bosses Not Instrumental at Texas Instruments," *Journal of Management Development,* September 1995, pp. 29–31.

autonomous work groups. Self-managed teams, for example, may collectively share leader duties among the group members. At Volvo's plant in Uddevalla, Sweden, for example, production of the Volvo 940 luxury sedan is carried out by teams that do not have a supervisor. Each team handles its own production scheduling and quality control operations. Even hiring decisions are made by the team as a whole. The Global OB describes a similar situation at Texas Instruments Malaysia.

The leadership role also is a significant factor in an informal group. The person who becomes an informal group leader generally is viewed as a respected and high-status member who embodies the values of the group, aids the group in accomplishing its goals, and enables members to satisfy needs. Additionally, the leader is the choice of group members to represent their viewpoint outside the group and usually is concerned with maintaining the group as a functioning unit.

Cohesiveness

Formal and informal groups seem to possess a closeness or commonness of attitude, behavior, and performance. This closeness has been referred to as *cohesiveness.* Cohesiveness typically is regarded as a force. It acts on the members to remain in a group and is greater than the forces pulling the members away from the group. A cohesive group, then, comprises individuals who are attracted to one another. A group that is low in cohesiveness does not possess interpersonal attractiveness for the members.

Since highly cohesive groups are composed of individuals who are motivated to be together, management tends to expect effective group performance. This logic is not supported conclusively by research evidence. In general, as the cohesiveness of a work group increases, the level of conformity to group norms also increases. But these norms may be inconsistent with those of the organization.

EXHIBIT 10.4 **The Relationship between Group Cohesiveness and Organizational Goals**

		Agreement with Organizational Goals	
		Low	**High**
Degree of Group Cohesiveness	**Low**	Performance probably oriented away from organizational goals	Performance probably oriented toward organizational goals
	High	Performance oriented away from organizational goals	Performance oriented toward organizational goals

There are, of course, numerous sources of attraction to a group. These might include:

1. The goals of the group and the members are compatible and clearly specified.
2. The group has a charismatic leader.
3. The reputation of the group indicates that the group successfully accomplishes its tasks.
4. The group is small enough to permit members to have their opinions heard and evaluated by others.
5. The members are attractive in that they support one another and help one another overcome obstacles and barriers to personal growth and development.[21]

Cohesiveness and Performance

The concept of cohesiveness is important for understanding groups in organizations.[22] The degree of cohesiveness in a group can have either positive or negative effects, depending on how group goals match those of the formal organization.[23] In fact, four distinct possibilities exist, as illustrated in Exhibit 10.4.

Exhibit 10.4 indicates that if cohesiveness is high and the group accepts and agrees with formal organizational goals, then group behavior probably will be positive from the formal organization's standpoint. However, if the group is highly cohesive but has goals that are not congruent with those of the formal organization, then group behavior probably will be negative from the formal organization's perspective.

Exhibit 10.4 also indicates that if a group is low in cohesiveness and the members have goals that are not in agreement with those of management, then the results probably will be negative from the standpoint of the organization. Behaviors will be more on an individual basis than on a group basis because of the low cohesiveness. On the other hand, it is possible to have a group low in cohesiveness, where the members' goals agree with those of the formal organization. Here, the results probably will be positive, although again more on an individual basis than on a group basis.

From a managerial perspective, it may sometimes be desirable to alter the cohesion of a work group. If the group has high productivity norms, for example, but is not particularly cohesive, increasing cohesiveness can be very beneficial.

Management Pointer

INCREASING GROUP COHESION

As a manager, you may find that members of your work group aren't getting along as well as they should. To improve cooperation within the group and its overall productivity, you may want to increase the cohesion level of the group. Some strategies for *increasing* group cohesion include:

1. Reaching joint agreement on group goals.
2. Making the group more homogeneous in its composition.
3. Increasing the frequency of interaction among group members.
4. Making the group smaller (decrease number of members).
5. Physically and/or socially isolating the group from other groups.
6. Allocating rewards to the group rather than to individuals.
7. Giving the group and group members more responsibility and resources to accomplish its goals.

To *decrease* group cohesion, do the opposite of the strategies above (e.g., induce disagreement on group goals, make the group more heterogeneous, etc.).

Increasing cohesion may bring about increased performance, as well as contribute to group members' satisfaction. The nearby Management Pointer suggests ways to increase group cohesion.

Sometimes *decreasing* cohesion may be in the best interest of the organization. A group whose goals are counter to those of the larger organization would be an example. This could occur during periods of labor unrest or while the organization is experiencing an external threat such as a hostile takeover. Or it may simply be a need to offset the negative effects of groupthink (discussed below).

Attempts to alter the cohesiveness of any group may not work; the opposite of what was intended may be the result. This is particularly true when reducing cohesion is being attempted. The group may see the effort as a threat, which may increase cohesiveness as the group unites to defend itself. Managers should exercise great care in deciding whether to influence the cohesion of work groups.

Groupthink

Why did so many financial experts miss the signs of the collapse of the housing bubble and financial crisis? With few exceptions, most of the key leaders and executive teams from large financial firms such as Bear Stearns, Lehman Brothers, and Merrill Lynch did not act on early information that suggested a major meltdown was imminent.[24] In hindsight, early warning signs were there. For example, Warren Buffett, the investment guru, came out in 2002 against the use of complicated derivatives. Also, Edward Gramlich, the governor of the Federal Reserve in 2001, complained about predatory lenders who were giving mortgages to buyers who could not afford them.[25] Unfortunately, financial service firm leaders and government regulators, as a group, decided to ignore these signals and to continue behaving as if the ride would never end.

Highly cohesive groups are important forces in influencing organizational behavior. One author has provided a provocative analysis of highly cohesive groups.[26] In his book, Irving Janis analyzed foreign policy decisions by a number of presidential administrations and concluded that those made by such groups often included a decision-making process he called *groupthink*. Janis defines **groupthink** as the "deterioration of mental efficiency, reality testing, and moral judgment" in the interest of group solidarity.[27] According to Janis, groups suffering from groupthink tend to display a number of common characteristics. Among these characteristics are the following:

> **groupthink**
> The deterioration of the mental efficiency, reality testing, and moral judgment of the individual members of a group in the interest of group solidarity.

Illusion of invulnerability. Group members collectively believe they are invincible.

Tendency to moralize. Opposition to the group's position is viewed as weak, evil, or unintelligent.

Feeling of unanimity. All group members support the leader's decisions. Members may have reservations about decisions but do not share these views. Rather than appearing weak, members keep dissenting views to themselves. This indicates how the pressure toward group solidarity can distort the judgment of individual members.

Pressure to conform. Formal and informal attempts are made to discourage discussion of divergent views. Groups exert significant pressure on individual members to conform.

Opposing ideas dismissed. Any individual or outside group that criticizes or opposes a decision receives little or no attention from the group. Group members tend to show strong favoritism toward their own ideas in the manner by which information is processed and evaluated, thereby ensuring that their own ideas will win out.

The ramifications of groupthink can be quite severe. Some researchers believe that the final "go/no go" decision at the time of the launch of the doomed space shuttle Challenger on January 28, 1986, was influenced by groupthink.[28] The findings of other research contradict this belief and report that the tragedy had nothing to do with groupthink, but rather was a result of two key symptoms related to the tragedy: (1) excessive faith in the established system, and (2) a short-range and self-interested preoccupation with meeting objectives and goals.[29]

Certainly, some level of group cohesiveness is necessary for a group to achieve often complex organizational goals and objectives. If seven individuals from seven different organizational units are responsible for a task, the task may never be completed effectively.[30] The point, however, is that more cohesiveness may not necessarily be better. While members of task groups may redefine solving a problem to mean reaching agreement rather than making the best decision, members of cohesive groups may redefine it to mean preserving relations among group members and preserving the image of the group. Some research suggests that, even among highly cohesive work groups, groupthink is not a factor if the group is composed of highly dominant individuals.[31]

Janis suggests that groups can guard against groupthink in several ways, including:

1. Encourage the group to state objections and doubts.
2. Leader should avoid taking sides or (prematurely) endorsing a particular course of action.
3. Break the group into subgroups to work on the same problem and then share the proposed solutions with the group.
4. Invite in outside experts to give feedback on group processes and proposed solutions.
5. Assign a group member to play devil's advocate so that important objections are raised.

End Results

Groups exist to accomplish objectives. In the case of work groups, those objectives are generally related to the performance of specific tasks, which in turn are designed to result in attainment of formal organizational outcomes. Measurable production (e.g., number of units assembled, percent of market captured, number of customers served) is perhaps the most obvious, but certainly not the only, end result of work group activities.

While some form of production output (goods, services, ideas, etc.) is typically an important measure of group performance and effectiveness, it is not the only consideration. Organizational researcher Richard Hackman identifies three important criteria of group effectiveness:[32]

1. *The extent to which the group's productive output meets the standards of quantity, quality, and timeliness of the users of the output.* For example, a group that produced a product that was unacceptable to a customer could not be considered effective no matter what the group or others thought about the product.
2. *The extent to which the group process of actually doing the work enhances the capability of group members to work together interdependently in the future.* This suggests that even though the group might produce a product meeting the standards

mentioned in the first criterion, if that end result was obtained in a manner destructive to future working relationships, the group is not effective. The fact that a group is a temporary one, such as a task force or project team, does not negate the importance of this criterion of effectiveness.

3. *The extent to which the group experience contributes to the growth and well-being of its members.* This criterion relates to the end results of development and satisfaction, which were specified in Exhibit 10.2. It is not necessary for a group to have member development and satisfaction as a stated objective for this to be a legitimate test of group effectiveness. When group participation does not contribute to personal or professional development and/or does not lead to any personal need satisfaction, this may have negative consequences. It suggests group productivity may not continue over an extended period, and it may have implications for the quality of group members' participation in subsequent groups.

These criteria are important ones for virtually any work group. However, they are particularly relevant for assessing the effectiveness of self-managed teams (SMTs). It is critical that SMTs enhance the capabilities of their members to work together interdependently in the future. Similarly, team member growth and well-being are equally necessary ingredients for SMT success.

Teams

As indicated at the start of this chapter, a team is viewed as a mature group comprising people with interdependence, motivation, and a shared commitment to accomplish agreed-upon goals. Admittedly, the distinction between a team and a group can be arbitrary and is sometimes vague. A total commitment to common goals and accountability to the team is what makes a team stand out and distinguish itself from immature, developing groups.

The use of teams has increased so significantly in U.S. organizations for a number of reasons. To a certain extent it has been triggered by the belief that teams have been an important contributor to Japan's economic accomplishments.[33] Additional reasons have to do with specific perceived benefits derived from using teams. These include potential quality improvements; enhanced productivity gains from bringing individuals with complementary skills together; and organizational restructuring efforts, particularly those with the objective of flattening the structure. Finally, many companies are moving to teams in response to other firms' success stories. The phenomenal success of Microsoft Corporation is attributed in part to its extensive use of software research and development teams, a point not lost on other firms in the industry that have implemented the same practice.

Types of Teams

There is no standard classification system for describing different types of teams. Distinctions among teams can be made on the basis of size, composition, organizational level, duration (temporary versus permanent), objectives, and potential contribution to organizational performance, to name only a few distinguishing characteristics. We will use a number of these to categorize important types of teams in organizations today—problem-solving teams, research and development teams, and the previously mentioned self-managed teams (SMT).

Problem-Solving Teams

As the name implies, problem-solving teams are formed to deal with problems. The problem may be very specific and known, or the team may be set up to deal with potential future problems that have not yet been identified. In the former case, the team is usually of temporary duration. It is put together to deal with a current problem and then dissolved. The life span of such teams may vary from a few days to many months, occasionally a year or longer.

quality circle
A small group of employees who meet on a regular basis, usually on company time, to recommend improvements and solve quality-related problems. Frequently a part of total quality management efforts.

Quality circles are examples of permanent problem-solving teams. A **quality circle** is a team of employees committed to recommending and implementing work and product improvements and solving quality-related problems. Circles typically comprise 6 to 12 employees who perform related jobs. Circle members are usually trained in group processes (for example, structured techniques for diagnosing problems and brainstorming).[34] A recent analysis of 36 research studies that focused on quality circles found that such participative techniques have a positive impact on employee performance.[35] Temporary or permanent problem-solving teams are increasingly being used by organizations that realize teams can significantly outperform individuals in many situations.[36] AT&T, for example, has effectively used problem-solving teams to address customer needs, resulting in quicker response time and increased customer satisfaction.

Cross-Functional Teams

A cross-functional team is one consisting of members from different functional departments (e.g., engineering, accounting, human resources, marketing). This type of team forms to address a specific problem. In most cases team members come from different departments and different levels (managers and nonmanagers). Organizations have used cross-functional, boundary-spanning teams for years. For example, at Caterpillar's tractor division, cross-functional teams working on product design and testing include a product designer, engineers, purchasing and marketing members, assembly workers, and even suppliers.[37]

At Boeing, a cross-functional team of specialists is stationed in one location to oversee the global production network of the company's twin-engine, long-haul 787 aircrafts. The supply chain originates in Japan and crosses North America, Europe, Russia, India, Australia, and ends in China.[38]

Using the skills, competencies, and experience of individuals from diverse areas within a firm can increase camaraderie, trust, and performance. However, cross-functional teams may take time to become effective. Building trust and commitment in cross-functional teams is challenging because of previous impressions, attitudes, and relationships that are formed before the team is assembled.

Virtual Teams

A popular response to increasing competition, the need for faster decisions, and technological advancements has been the creation of virtual teams. Working across distances via e-mail, desktop and real-time conferencing, videoconferencing, electronic bulletin boards, and other technologies is challenging for leaders. Virtual teams can be connected via computer and telecommunications technology. A **virtual team** is defined as a number of people geographically separated who are assembled by using various technologies to accomplish specific goals. A virtual team's membership rarely meets face to face.

virtual team
A geographically distributed, functionally and/or culturally diverse group of individuals who rely on interactive technology such as e-mail, text-based chat, Web casts, and videoconferencing to work together.

Virtual teams can meet without concern for space, time, or physical presence. Team members use communications links to perform their work, individual and team tasks, and roles. Companies such as Hewlett-Packard, IBM, Compaq, and Procter & Gamble have partially or fully eliminated traditional offices for providing customer services. Virtual teams work together to accomplish a wide range of tasks, including responding to customer requests, complaints, and suggestions.[39] A developer of tele-communication support systems, GlobeCOM is headquartered in New York but has satellite offices in more than 100 countries. The company has created over 50 virtual teams to design hardware and software applications, and to provide support for customers across five continents.[40]

The efficient and successful use of technology is one of a number of important factors contributing to the success of virtual teams. Possible technologies to use with virtual teams include desktop videoconferencing systems, collaborative software systems, smart phones, and Internet/intranet systems.[41] Each technology needs to be evaluated in terms of its effectiveness and cost benefits regarding the generation of ideas and plans, solving routine and complex problems, and negotiating interpersonal or other forms of conflict.

As virtual team members interact, it is important for leaders to coach, build trust, evaluate performance, and provide feedback.[42] Since the virtual team is geographically dispersed and uses technology links, leaders are challenged in performing their motivational team-building supportive roles. Virtual team members performing work anytime, anyplace are difficult to lead and manage in the traditional sense. Those charged with leading virtual teams must be technologically linked to members and must be willing to permit a great deal of autonomy and decision-making independence to members.[43] The hierarchical command and control process is minimized when using virtual teams. Virtual team members must be self-reliant but remain connected to and knowledgeable about the goals of the organization.

The dispersion of virtual team members creates a challenge for leaders in terms of creating a sense of team.[44] Something intangible is lost when team members do not have the opportunity to work and meet face to face. The use of Lotus Notes as a collaborative tool is an attempt to bring about a team feeling. Team members connect to electronic discussions to learn about policies, strategies, and expertise. Whether Lotus Notes can address the loss of personal contact is subject to debate and empirical study.[45]

An empirical study of the development of trust in 29 global virtual teams that were connected via e-mail provided interesting findings. The highest level of trust among virtual teams pointed to three traits. First, members began their interactions with nonwork social interactions, providing personal background information. Second, each member had a set of clear task roles. Third, all team members demonstrated positive attitudes. The study also illustrated that low-trust virtual teams were less productive than high-trust virtual teams.

The new competitive pressures and challenges for increased worker autonomy, empowerment, and work–life balance suggest that virtual teams and telecommuting (work carried out in a remote location away from a main office, factory, or plant) are a reality. By permitting employees to telecommute, companies such as Cisco Systems, Sun Microsystems, Deloitte, IBM, and Google have saved costs either through lower turnover, higher productivity, or reduced real estate costs.[46] The use of computers and telecommunication technology (e.g., BlackBerry) is likely to increase the dispersion and connectivity of employees. About 8 million American employees already telework, and a large percentage of individuals express a desire to have this option.[47] Virtual teams and virtual offices (usually at home) are very likely to become even more significant. New ways to effectively manage and lead organizations with virtual work arrangements need to be examined and studied. Ford Motor Company and Delta Airlines in February 2000 announced that any employee wanting one would be provided a personal computer for home use. These two firms believe that computer use, wherever it occurs, can benefit the performance of individuals working in the traditional setting or in a virtual arrangement.[48]

VIRTUAL WORK ARRANGEMENT ISSUES TO CONSIDER

Virtual employees? They're part of the mainstream now. But working from home hasn't been the panacea for work–life balance that many of us thought it was going to be. In fact, says Christena Nippert-Eng, an associate professor of sociology, the anxiety level has increased. "We feel less able than ever to place appropriate boundaries around the workday, while at the same time, we realize the need for those boundaries more than ever before."

Fascinated by the rituals of today's overconnected and underrested workers, Nippert-Eng has been exploring the boundaries—or the lack thereof—of the American workplace. She has come up with a couple of new species. Are you an *integrator*? They're the ones who have a single date book for their business and personal appointments and have desks littered with family snapshots. A *segmenter*? They'd rather be tortured than disclose the name of their cat to an office worker or have their work keys on the same ring as their home keys.

Overall, though, the new world of 24/7 work is becoming more integrationist, and that will have implications for people and companies. In an interview with *Fast Company,* Nippert-Eng talked about the future of the virtual workplace.

Why Don't More People Feel Better about Working at Home?

"Telecommuting is a move toward integration: the home broadband hookup to the office network and the wireless remote access to the e-mail server. But we are still a heavily segmenting culture. People are glad they are home when the kids get home, but few say that they are more comfortable with their work–life balance today than they were five or six years ago. The only people I've talked to who don't have these 'boundary' issues are the ones who don't own a home or who aren't married, or whose spouse works in the same kind of environment that they do."

What Are Some of the Specific Sources of Anxiety?

"When you're in the office, no one ever doubts whether you're working or not. You could be balancing your checkbook, but the fact that you're there is a reassurance. When you work at home, people don't really believe that you're working. So a common reaction is to say, 'I will respond to every e-mail within 30 seconds. I will be on my computer again at the end of the evening, so that

when people come in they will see stuff waiting for them.' It becomes another source of stress.

"Another source of anxiety is that there's no independent way for a manager to assess whether or not you're doing a good job. 'Being there when I need you' is pretty much still the standard. I know managers who actually up the productivity ante for people who work from home.

"At the same time, how do you establish an appropriate boundary between home and work? Most people have no idea when they should start and end the workday. Their day turns into this incredibly frantic, highly insecure, fast-paced mode where all time is work time and every day is a workday. There's no such thing as vacation anymore."

What Will It Take for These Arrangements to Work Better?

"From the point of view of the person working at home, do not ask your colleagues to do anything for you that they wouldn't normally do if you were there in the office. I'm hearing about colleagues who actually sabotage the work of teleworkers. These are people who choose not to do this boundary-blurring stuff and who resent office mates who do. Interview colleagues once a week early on, and keep asking them how it is working out for them.

"For an organization to be effective with people who work from home, supervisors must create arrangements that are as flexible as possible—but they must also make sure that the workday ends. Companies also need to look closely at the norms and at the expectations they have for their workers. Some supervisors are uncomfortable managing home–work integrators. Plenty of managers still want instantaneous hand-holding from their subordinates. They need to understand their own home–work boundaries and how they assess who's worthy of promotion.

"There's one last thing that both sides need to understand: Yes, you are going to lose time that could be spent working on other matters while you are duking out these issues. But if you don't, you'll run into bigger problems down the road."

Sources: Jennifer Reingold, "There's No Place (to Work) Like Home," *Fast Company* (online), December 19, 2007 (accessed June 4, 2009); Kelley M. Butler, "Phoning It In: Survey Results Report Productivity Lag among Teleworkers," *Employee Benefit News,* March 1, 2006, pp. 1–3; and Jennifer Reingold, "There's No Place (to Work) Like Home," *Fast Company,* November 2000, pp. 76–77.

The above Organizational Encounter indicates that teleworking is not always easy or successful.

Research and Development Teams

Research and development (R&D) teams are used to develop new products. Their use is most extensive in high-tech industries such as aviation, electronics, and computers. R&D teams are usually composed of representatives of many different departments or functions in the organization, making them cross-functional in nature. For example, a computer company may form a cross-functional R&D team made up of representatives from marketing, sales, engineering, purchasing, and finance to develop plans for a new product. Such a team, representing expertise from all the relevant areas of the company, can significantly reduce the amount of time required to bring a new product to the marketplace.

In some organizations, R&D teams have been set up to expedite innovation and creative new product design. Originally coined by a Lockheed engineer during World War II, such groups are referred to as **skunkworks**.[49] Such teams often have their own facilities, somewhat isolated from the rest of the organization. This may facilitate prolonged team interaction without interruption by day-to-day routines and problems. Skunkworks team members often become almost fanatical in the extent to which they identify with their products. At Hewlett-Packard, it is rumored that skunkworks teams are quietly trying to develop an operating system that can one day replace Microsoft Windows.[50] Hewlett-Packard, the No. 1 maker of PCs, wants to compete against the easier-to-use Apple brand of computers. When Ford Motor Company almost abandoned development of a new Mustang coupe because of cost considerations, it was a skunkworks team that over an eight-week period (with team members sleeping on the workplace floor in shifts) solved the engineering and related cost problems.[51]

skunkworks
A secretive research and development project that operates outside of normal company operations to create innovative products.

Self-Managed Teams

self-managed team (SMT)
Small group of individuals empowered to perform activities with minimal outside direction.

As discussed in Chapter 6, **self-managed teams (SMTs)** are small groups of individuals who are empowered to perform certain activities based on procedures established and decisions made within the team, with minimal or no outside direction. Organizations using SMTs include such industry leaders as AT&T, Campbell Soup, Chevron Chemical, Coca-Cola, Federal Express, General Electric, General Mills, Honeywell, Motorola, Procter & Gamble, Texas Instruments, and Xerox. As a result of global competition, multinational firms increasingly are using SMTs in their foreign affiliates as well.[52]

SMTs are not for everyone, nor have they been successful in every organization. When US West formed its teams, for example, the company sold the concept to employees promising teamwork, empowerment, and no loss of jobs. Many employees later felt that was just a cover for downsizing. As one ex-employee put it, "We showed them how to streamline the work, and now 9,000 people are gone. It makes you feel used."[53]

Before implementing SMTs, organizations should make certain such teams are consistent with the organization's: (1) business requirements, (2) values and goals, and (3) competencies. Once implemented, success depends on management commitment, receptivity to change, and employee trust in management. Without all of these, both individuals and organizations are likely to find the effort unsatisfactory.[54]

Team Effectiveness

Teams represent one form or type of group. As such, factors influencing the effectiveness of any group are important in determining team effectiveness. Previously discussed group characteristics such as composition, norms, leadership, and cohesion are examples. Some issues, however, are particularly important when it comes to developing effective teams. We will briefly examine four: training, communications, empowerment, and rewards. (The Management Pointer on page 298 suggests additional considerations.)

Training

Effective teams don't just happen. In addition to their individual task-related skills and abilities, team members must also know how to function effectively as team members. This almost always suggests training. Depending on the type and purpose of the team, training may be needed in problem-solving skills, creative thinking, or interpersonal skills. Certainly, at the very least, team members must be well-versed in the company's philosophy regarding teams, the team mission, and new roles and responsibilities individuals will have as a consequence of being part of the team. It has been suggested that without proper training the only thing management gets from creating teams is a guarantee that more time will be spent making worse decisions.

Whether a member of a student project group or a self-managed work team in an organization, what does it take to be an excellent team member? Research indicates that the following seven skills are highly desirable for team members to be effective:[55]

1. *Open-mindedness.* New projects often require team members to be thrust into a new situation with new team members. Individuals who can keep an open mind will tend to be more successful in dealing with these changes.

2. *Emotional stability.* The more stable an individual is, the faster she is expected to adjust to the different situations confronted by teams.

3. *Accountability.* When individual team members accept responsibility for their own performance and contributions, team effectiveness increases.

4. *Problem-solving abilities.* Team members should be able to analyze problems and develop alternative solutions to those problems.

5. *Communication skills.* Such skills will facilitate an open exchange of ideas and the creation of better solutions to problems.

6. *Conflict resolution skills.* Some disagreement within the group is healthy and will lead to better overall group performance. Too much conflict can lead to breakdowns in communication and a decrease in group cohesion.

7. *Trust.* Perhaps the most important characteristic of a good team member, trust must be present for the group to function at a high level of performance.

Communications

One of the more significant effects creating teams has on an organization's management is an increased need for information. Team members need information to accomplish their objectives. Much of this is information that has traditionally been management's exclusive domain. If teams are to be effective, however, full disclosure of formerly restricted information may be necessary. Management—particularly middle management—is often threatened by this, fearing a loss of decision-making power. The failure of many team efforts can be traced directly to management's unwillingness to share information with the teams it has created.

Empowerment

Along with information, teams must have the authority to make decisions and act autonomously. Whether a problem-solving team, an R&D team, or an SMT, teams that lack authority are generally less effective. In addition to hindering taking action, lack of authority suggests to team members that management doesn't really trust them in the first place, further reducing team effectiveness.

Being given insufficient authority is typically the root of team empowerment problems. It should be noted, however, that sometimes teams may be given *too much* authority. This is particularly a danger in the early stages of team involvement. Team members may be unaccustomed to making decisions and be overwhelmed by the degree of authority they suddenly possess. This is another reason training is such an important factor in team success.

Rewards

The reward system in most organizations is individually based. That is, organizational members are rewarded based on evaluation of their individual performance. While the individual's contribution to team success is a legitimate part of the reward system, team success must also be factored in. To the extent that teams perform well, the team should be rewarded. Distribution of that reward to individual team members is an important, but separate issue. Rewards can be allocated to teams in a number of ways. With problem-solving teams, for example, an incentive system is frequently used, wherein the team receives a percentage of the savings realized by the organization. Many organizations using SMTs have modified their reward structure to include some form of profit sharing. Regardless, it is important that teams be rewarded for their contribution to organizational objectives.

As we noted at the start of this chapter, the use of work groups in organizations is rapidly increasing. Groups hold the potential for simultaneously increasing both the productivity and satisfaction of group members. As organizations move through the first decade of the 21st century, it is difficult to overstate the importance of the role groups and teams are assuming in organizational life. Organizational structure, the design of work, performance feedback and reward systems, decision-making procedures, and organizational development strategies, to name a few, are all being profoundly affected by groups and teams. As we will see in the next chapter, group effects are not always positive.

Summary of Key Points

- Groups can be viewed from a number of perspectives, including perception, organization, and motivation. For our purposes, a group may be thought of as two or more individuals interacting with each other to accomplish a common goal.

- Formal groups are created to facilitate the accomplishment of an organization's goals. Command groups, specified by the organization chart; task groups, comprising employees working together to complete a specific project; and teams, comprised of people interacting closely together with a shared commitment, are three types of formal groups. Informal groups are associations of individuals in the work situation in response to social needs. Interest groups and friendship groups are two types of informal groups.

- Formal and informal groups exist for a number of reasons. Need satisfaction may be a compelling reason to join a group. Security, social, and esteem needs are typical examples. Proximity and attraction may be another reason. That is, people may form groups because their physical location encourages interaction they enjoy. People may also form groups to facilitate the accomplishment of common goals. Finally, some groups form because individuals believe they can derive economic benefits from group membership.

- As groups form and develop, they tend to go through several sequential stages. These are: (1) *forming,* characterized by uncertainty and confusion; (2) *storming,* marked by conflict and confrontation; (3) *norming,* where group cohesion begins significant development; (4) *performing,* where the group becomes fully functional; and (5) *adjourning,* which involves the termination of group activities.

- The model of the process of group formation and development presented in the chapter has a number of elements. These include the different types of groups, the reasons groups are formed, stages in group development, important characteristics of groups, and end results of group activity.

- To understand group behavior, it is essential to be aware that formal and informal groups exhibit certain characteristics. These include the composition of the group; the status hierarchy that exists and the basis used for determining member status; the norms or behaviors the group expects its members to adhere to; the type of leadership in the group; and the degree of cohesiveness that exists within the group.

- Relevant criteria for group effectiveness include (1) the extent to which group output meets expected standards of quantity, quality, and timeliness; (2) the extent to which the group process enhances the capability of group members to work together interdependently in the future; and (3) the extent to which the group experience contributes to the growth and well-being of the group.

- A team is a special kind of unit. Different types of teams include problem-solving teams, cross-functional teams, virtual teams, research and development teams, and self-managed teams.

Review and Discussion Questions

1. Think of a formal group to which you belong. Describe the group in terms of the characteristics of groups discussed in this chapter.

2. Have you ever been part of a virtual team? Describe it. What are the advantages and disadvantages of virtual work arrangements?

3. Why is it important for managers to be familiar with the concepts of group behavior?

4. Are groups more effective in problem solving than individuals?

5. Why is groupthink something to be avoided? How might a manager attempt to ensure that groupthink doesn't occur in his or her group?

6. What is the relationship between group norms and group cohesiveness? What roles do both cohesiveness and norms play in shaping group performance?

7. Describe a situation in which you were part of a formal work group (while working in a job or as a student) and one of the members of the group did not contribute much work to the group effort or project. How did the other group members deal with this person? How did this person's behavior affect the attitude of the other group members?

8. Thinking back to a recent student or work group project in which you participated, how effective were you as a team member? What behaviors did you engage in that contributed to your and the group's effectiveness? (Refer to the seven characteristics of effective team members presented in this chapter.)

9. Is leadership a more or less important consideration in self-managed teams than in other types of groups? Why or why not?

10. If you were creating a research and development team for an organization, what kinds of factors would you consider in deciding the composition of the team? Would these factors be different if you were putting together a problem-solving team?

Reality Check

Now how much do you know about groups and teams?

6. Playing devil's advocate and inviting outside experts to give feedback on group processes and proposed solutions are two ways to guard against _____.
   a. group collectivism
   b. group conflict
   c. groupthink
   d. group overlap

7. _____ is the deterioration of the mental efficiency, reality testing, and moral judgment of the individual members of a group in the interest of group solidarity.
   a. Group dissolution
   b. Group justification
   c. Groupthink
   d. Group cohesion

8. A _____ team is a geographically distributed, functionally and/or culturally diverse group of individuals who rely on interactive technology such as e-mail, Web casts, and videoconferencing to work together.
   a. virtual
   b. matrix
   c. cross-regional
   d. high-tech

9. True or false: Communication, conflict resolution, and problem-solving skills will help a person be a better team member.
   a. True
   b. False

10. The "performing stage" of group development is characterized by _____.
   a. terminating group activities
   b. conflict and confrontation
   c. accomplishing accepted tasks
   d. developing group cohesion

REALITY CHECK ANSWERS

Before	After
1. c 2. b 3. a 4. d 5. b	6. c 7. c 8. a 9. a 10. c
Number Correct	Number Correct
_____	_____

YOU BE THE JUDGE COMMENT

USING GENDER TO INCREASE WORK GROUP DIVERSITY

Having a more diverse work group for the night shift at Southwood Psychiatric Hospital would help some of the young female patients feel more comfortable. This goal seems very positive, and the hospital administration would be on the right track in improving patient care at the facility. Unfortunately, the reassignment of a female child care specialist from the day to the night shift (where she'd be the only female employee!) may have negative repercussions for her, the department, and the hospital. Because the specialist dislikes the "graveyard" shift and would miss her friends from the day shift, it is possible that the reassigned specialist will take out her frustration over the forced reassignment by reducing effort on the job, being less likely to engage in those "extra" helping behaviors such as filling in for absent co-workers, staying late when necessary, and so on. She may even begin looking for another job where she can get back to working the day shift.

What should the hospital do differently to increase work group diversity on the night shift without forcing a female specialist to transfer from day shift? The hospital should explain to the day shift specialists why female specialists are needed for the night shift. Next, the hospital should ask for female volunteers from the day shift to transfer to the night shift. If necessary, higher pay could be offered as an incentive. If that doesn't work, a rotation system could be implemented in which two or three female specialists are transferred to the night shift (as a team) for three to six months at a time, then return to the day shift after completing their tours of duty. At that point, a different team could be transferred temporarily to the night shift, and so on. In sum, Southwood Psychiatric Hospital needs to increase the gender diversity of its night shift, but needs to do it in a way that is perceived as fair to the child care specialists on the day shift.

Exercise

Exercise 10.1: *Participating In and Observations of Group Processes*

Objectives

1. To provide experience in participating in and observing groups undertaking a specific task.
2. To generate data that can be the focus of class discussion and analysis.

Starting the Exercise

The Situation

You are appointed to a personnel committee in charge of selecting a manager for the department that provides administrative services to other departments. Before you begin interviewing candidates, you are asked to develop a list of the personal and professional qualifications the manager needs. The list will be used as the selection criteria.

The Procedure

1. Select five to seven members to serve on the committee.
2. Ask the committee to rank the items in the following list in their order of importance in selecting the department head.

Source: Kae H. Chung and Leon C. Megginson, *Organizational Behavior* (New York: Harper & Row, 1981), pp. 241–44. Used by permission.

3. The students not on the committee should observe the group process. Some should observe the whole group, and others individual members. The observers can use observation guides A and B.
4. The observers should provide feedback to the participants.
5. The class should discuss how the committee might improve its performance.

Selection Criteria

_____ Strong institutional loyalty

_____ Ability to give clear instructions

_____ Ability to discipline subordinates

_____ Ability to make decisions under pressure

_____ Ability to communicate

_____ Stable personality

_____ High intelligence

_____ Ability to grasp the overall picture

_____ Ability to get along well with people

_____ Familiarity with office procedures

_____ Professional achievement

_____ Ability to develop subordinates

A. Group Process Observation Guide

Instructions: Observe the group behavior in the following dimensions. Prepare notes for feedback.

Group Behaviors	Description	Impact
Group Goal: Are group goals clearly defined?		
Decision Procedure: Is the decision procedure clearly defined?		
Communication Network: What kind of communication network is used? Is it appropriate?		
Decision Making: What kind of decision process is used? Is it appropriate?		
Group Norm: Observe the degrees of cohesiveness, compatibility, and conformity.		
Group Composition: What kind of group is it?		
Other Behavior: Is there any behavior that influences the group process?		

B. Individual Role Observation Guide

Instructions: Observe one committee member. Tabulate (or note) behaviors that he or she exhibits as the group works.

Initiating Ideas: Initiates or clarifies ideas and issues.	**Confusing Issues:** Confuses others by bringing up irrelevant issues or by jumping to other issues.
Managing Conflicts: Explores, clarifies, and resolves conflicts and differences.	**Mismanaging Conflicts:** Avoids or suppresses conflicts or creates "win-or-lose" situations.
Influencing Others: Appeases, reasons with, or persuades others.	**Forcing Others:** Gives orders or forces others to agree.
Supporting Others: Reinforces or helps others to express their opinions.	**Rejecting Others:** Deflates or antagonizes others.
Listening Attentively: Listens and responds to others' ideas and opinions.	**Showing Indifference:** Does not listen or brushes off others.
Showing Empathy: Shows the ability to see things from other people's viewpoint.	**Self-Serving Behavior:** Exhibits behavior that is self-serving.
Exhibiting Positive Nonverbal Behaviors: Pays attention to others, maintains eye contact, composure, and other signs.	**Exhibiting Negative Nonverbal Behaviors:** Tense facial expression, yawning, little eye contact, and other behaviors.

Exercise 10.2: *What to Do with Johnny Rocco*

Objectives

1. Participating in a group assignment playing a particular role.
2. Diagnosing the group decision process after the assignment has been completed.

Starting the Exercise

After reading the material relating to Johnny Rocco, a committee is formed to decide his fate. The chairperson of the meeting is Johnny's supervisor, who should begin by assigning roles to the group members. These roles (shop steward, head of production, Johnny's co-worker, director of personnel, and the social worker who helped Johnny in the past) represent points of view the chairperson feels should be included in this meeting. (Johnny is not to be included.) Two observers should be assigned.

After the roles have been assigned, each role-player should complete the personal preference part of the worksheet, ordering the alternatives according to their appropriateness from the vantage point of his or her role.

Once the individual preferences have been determined, the chairperson should call the meeting to order. The following rules govern the meeting: (1) the group must reach a consensus ordering of the alternatives; (2) the group cannot use a statistical aggregation, or majority vote, decision-making process; (3) members should stay "in character" throughout the discussion. Treat this as a committee meeting consisting of members with different backgrounds, orientations, and interests who share a problem.

Personal Preference	Group Decision	Worksheet
_____	_____	Give Johnny a warning that at the next sign of trouble he will be fired.
_____	_____	Do nothing, as it is unclear that Johnny did anything wrong.
_____	_____	Create strict controls (do's and don'ts) for Johnny with immediate strong punishment for any misbehavior.
_____	_____	Give Johnny a great deal of warmth and personal attention and affection (overlooking his present behavior) so he can learn to depend on others.
_____	_____	Fire him. It's not worth the time and effort spent for such a low-level position.
_____	_____	Talk over the problem with Johnny in an understanding way so he can learn to ask others for help in solving his problems.
_____	_____	Give Johnny a well-structured schedule of daily activities with immediate and unpleasant consequences for not adhering to the schedule.
_____	_____	Do nothing now, but watch him carefully and provide immediate punishment for any future misbehaviors.
_____	_____	Treat Johnny the same as everyone else, but provide an orderly routine so he can learn to stand on his own two feet.
_____	_____	Call Johnny in and logically discuss the problem with him and ask what you can do to help him.
_____	_____	Do nothing now, but watch him so you can reward him the next time he does something good.

After the group has completed the assignment, the two observers should discuss the group process using the Group Process Diagnostic Questions as a guide. Group members should not look at these questions until after the group task has been completed.

Johnny Rocco

Johnny has a grim personal background. He is the third child in a family of seven. He has not seen his father for several years, and his recollection is that his father used to come home drunk and beat up every member of the family; everyone ran when he came staggering home.

His mother, according to Johnny, wasn't much better. She was irritable and unhappy and she always predicted that Johnny would come to no good end. Yet she worked when her health allowed her to do so to keep the family in food and clothing. She always decried the fact that she was not able to be the kind of mother she would like to be.

Johnny quit school in the seventh grade. He had great difficulty conforming to the school routine—misbehaving often, being truant quite frequently, and engaging in numerous fights with schoolmates. On several occasions he was picked up by the police and, along with members of his group, questioned during several investigations into cases of both petty and grand larceny. The police regarded him as "probably a bad one."

The juvenile officer of the court saw in Johnny some good qualities that no one else seemed to sense. This man, Mr. O'Brien, took it upon himself to act as a "big brother" to Johnny. He had several long conversations with Johnny, during which he managed to penetrate to some degree Johnny's defensive shell. He represented to Johnny the first semblance of personal interest in his life. Through Mr. O'Brien's efforts, Johnny returned to school and obtained a high school diploma. Afterward, Mr. O'Brien helped him obtain a job.

Now, at age 20, Johnny is a stockroom clerk in one of the laboratories where you are employed. On the whole, Johnny's performance has been acceptable, but there have been glaring exceptions. One involved a clear act of insubordination on a fairly unimportant matter. In another Johnny was accused, on circumstantial grounds, of destroying some expensive equipment. Though the investigation is still open, it now appears that the destruction was accidental.

Johnny's supervisor wants to keep him on for at least a trial period, but he wants "outside" advice as to the best way of helping him grow into greater re-

sponsibility. Of course, much depends on how Johnny behaves in the next few months. Naturally, his supervisor must follow personnel policies that are accepted in the company as a whole. It is important to note that Johnny is not an attractive young man. He is rather weak and sickly and shows unmistakable signs of long years of social deprivation.

A committee is formed to decide the fate of Johnny Rocco. The chairperson of the meeting is Johnny's supervisor and should begin by assigning roles.

Group Process Diagnostic Questions

Communications

1. Who responded to whom?
2. Who interrupted? Was the same person interrupted consistently?
3. Were there identifiable "communication clusters"? Why or why not?
4. Did some members say very little? If so, why? Was level of participation ever discussed?
5. Were efforts made to involve everyone?

Decision Making

1. Did the group decide how to decide?
2. How were decisions made?
3. What criterion was used to establish agreement?
   a. Majority vote?
   b. Consensus?
   c. No opposition interpreted as agreement?
4. What was done if people disagreed?
5. How effective was your decision-making process?
6. Does every member feel his or her input into the decision-making process was valued by the group, or were the comments of some members frequently discounted? If so, was this issue ever discussed?

Leadership

1. What type of power structure did the group operate under?
   a. One definite leader?
   b. Leadership functions shared by all members?
   c. Power struggles within the group?
   d. No leadership supplied by anyone?
2. How does each member feel about the leadership structure used? Would an alternative have been more effective?
3. Did the chairperson provide an adequate structure for the discussion?

4. Was the discussion governed by the norms of equity?

5. Was the chairperson's contribution to the content of the discussion overbearing?

Awareness of Feelings

1. How did members in general react to the group meetings? Were they hostile (toward whom or what?), enthusiastic, apathetic?

2. Did members openly discuss their feelings toward each other and their role in the group?

3. How do group members feel now about their participation in this group?

Task Behavior

1. Who was most influential in keeping the group task-oriented? How?

2. Did some members carry the burden and do most of the work, or was the load distributed evenly?

3. If some members were not contributing their fair share, was this ever discussed? If so, what was the outcome? If not, why?

4. Did the group evaluate its method of accomplishing a task during or after the project? If so, what changes were made?

5. How effective was your group in performing assigned tasks? What improvements could have been made?

Source: Adapted from David A. Whetton and Kim S. Cameron, *Developing Management Skills* (Glenview, IL: Scott, Foresman and Company, 1984), pp. 450–53.

Case

Case 10.1: *Electrolux Cleans Up*

Boosting R&D and Getting All Units on the Same Page Delivers a Rebound

You will never meet Catherine, Anna, Maria, or Monica. But the future success of Sweden's Electrolux depends on what these four women think. Catherine, for instance, a Type A career woman who is a perfectionist at home, loves the idea of simply sliding her laundry basket into a washing machine, instead of having to lift the clothes from the basket and into the washer. That product idea has been moved onto the fast track for consideration.

So, just who are Catherine and the other women? Well, they don't actually exist. They are composites based on in-depth interviews with some 160,000 consumers from around the globe. To divine the needs of these mythical customers, 53 Electrolux employees, including designers, engineers, and marketers hailing from various divisions, gathered in Stockholm for a weeklong brainstorming session. The Catherine team began by ripping photographs out of a pile of magazines and sticking them onto poster boards. Next to a picture of a woman wearing a sharply tailored suit, they scribbled some of Catherine's attributes: driven, busy, and a bit overwhelmed.

With the help of these characters, Electrolux designers and engineers are searching for the insights they'll need to dream up the next batch of hot prod-

ucts. It's a new way of doing things for Electrolux, but then again, a lot is new at the company. When Chief Executive Hans Stråberg took the helm in 2002, the world's No. 2 maker of home appliances after Whirlpool Corp. faced spiraling costs while its middle-market products were gradually losing out to cheaper goods from Asia and Eastern Europe. Competition in the United States, where Electrolux gets 40 percent of its sales, was ferocious. The company's stock was treading water.

Stråberg had no choice but to do something radical. He began shuttering plants in Western Europe and the United States and shifting work to lower-cost locales in Asia and Eastern Europe. He also is spinning off the outdoor products division. But this is no ordinary corporate makeover. Stråberg is also breaking down barriers between departments and forcing his designers, engineers, and marketers to work together to come up with new products. To speed the transition, he recruited executives from companies with strong track records in innovation, including Procter & Gamble and PepsiCo.

At the Stockholm brainstorming session, for example, the group leader, Kim Scott, was a recent P&G defector. She urged everyone "to think of yourselves as Catherine." The room buzzed with discussion. Ideas were refined, sketches drawn up. The group settled on three concepts: Breeze, a clothes steamer that also removes stains; an Ironing Center, similar to a pants press but for shirts; and Ease, the washing machine that holds a laundry basket inside its drum.

Half the group raced off to the machine shop to turn out a prototype for Breeze, while the rest stayed upstairs to bang out a marketing plan. Over the next hour, designer Lennart Johansson carved and sandpapered a block of peach-colored polyurethane until a contraption that resembled a cross between an electric screwdriver and a handheld vacuum began to emerge. The designers in the group wanted the Breeze to be smaller, but engineer Giuseppe Frucco pointed out that would leave too little space for a charging station for the 1,500-watt unit.

For company veterans such as Frucco, who works at Electrolux's fabric care research and development center in Porcia, Italy, this dynamic groupthink is a refreshing change: "We never used to create new products together," he says. "The designers would come up with something and then tell us to build it." The new way saves time and money by avoiding the technical glitches that crop up as a new design moves from the drafting table to the factory floor.

To support the innovation drive, Stråberg has bumped up spending on R&D from 0.8 percent of sales to 1.2 percent and is aiming for 2 percent eventually. What he's gunning for are products that consumers will gladly pay a premium for: gadgets with drop-dead good looks and clever features that ordinary people can understand without having to pore through a thick users' manual. "Consumers are prepared to pay for good design and good performance," he says.

Electrolux isn't the only appliance maker on an innovation kick. In 1999, Whirlpool Corp. launched a program that allows all of its 68,000 employees to contribute design ideas, yielding a flood of new products.

Eye-Catching Design

But few have pulled off the range of hot new offerings that Electrolux has. One clear hit is a cordless stick-and-hand vacuum, called Pronto in the United States. Available in an array of metallic hues with a rounded, ergonomic design, this is the Cinderella of vacuums. Too attractive to be locked up in the broom closet, it calls out to be displayed in your kitchen. In Europe, it now commands 50 percent of the market for stick vacs, a coup for a product with fewer than two years on the market. The Pronto is cleaning up in the United

States, too. Stacy Silk, a buyer at retail chain Best Buy Co., says it is one of her hottest sellers, even though it retails for around $100, double the price of comparable models. "The biggest thing is the aesthetics," Silk says. "That gets people to walk over and look."

Stråberg, who spent decades running Electrolux operations in the United States, is crafting these new products even while moving away from many traditional tools of customer research. The company relies less heavily on focus groups and now prefers to interview people in their homes where they can be videotaped pushing a vacuum or shoving laundry into the washer. "Consumers think they know what they want, but they often have trouble articulating it," says Henrik Otto, senior vice president for global design, whom Stråberg lured away from carmaker Volvo. "But when we watch them, we can ask, 'why do you do that?' We can change the product and solve their problems."

The new approach yielded strong results. After dropping for two straight years, annual sales rose 8 percent, to $16.5 billion, in 2005. Operating income jumped 42 percent in the fourth quarter, compared with the year before, though it rose by less than 2 percent, to $881 million, for the year as a whole. Johan Hjertonsson, director of the consumer innovation program, says product launches have almost doubled in quantity. And the number of launches that result in outsized unit sales is now running at 50 percent of all introductions, from around 25 percent previously. Though the recent economic downturn has dampened sales for most companies in this and other retail product areas, Electrolux still maintains a 5 percent market share of the profitable household appliance market in North America in 2008. Catherine would be pleased.

Questions

1. How did Electrolux Chief Executive Stråberg break down barriers (and increase communication) between departments? Why did he do this? Explain.

2. What are the advantages for Electrolux of having individuals from different departments and functional areas work together on product design? Describe.

3. In an era with intense competition and several low-cost products on the market, how can Electrolux use teamwork and groups to succeed? Describe.

Source: Excerpted from Ariane Sains, Stanley Reed, and Michael Arndt, "Electrolux Cleans Up," *BusinessWeek*, February 27, 2006, pp. 42–43; also see http://ir.electrolux.com/html/annual2008-1-en/20090316/?page=1&mode=50&noConflict=1 (accessed June 9, 2009).

Managing Conflict and Negotiations

Learning Objectives

After completing Chapter 11, you should be able to:

- **Explain** the contemporary perspective on conflict.
- **Distinguish** between functional and dysfunctional conflict.
- **Understand** why intergroup conflict occurs.
- **Identify** several consequences of dysfunctional intergroup conflict.

- **Describe** five approaches for managing conflict through resolution.
- **Discuss** how increased globalization has changed negotiating tactics.
- **Distinguish** between win–win and win–lose negotiation.
- **Identify** the major types of third-party negotiations.

For any organization to perform effectively, interdependent individuals and groups must establish working relationships across organizational boundaries, between individuals, and among groups. Individuals or groups may depend on one another for information, assistance, or coordinated action. Such interdependence may foster either cooperation or conflict.

For example, the production and marketing executives of a firm may meet to discuss ways to deal with foreign competition. Such a meeting may be reasonably free of conflict. Decisions get made, strategies are developed, and the executives return to work. Thus, there is intergroup cooperation to achieve a goal. However, this may not be the case if sales decline because the firm is not offering enough variety in its product line. The marketing department desires broad product lines to offer more variety to customers, while the production department desires narrow product lines to keep production costs manageable and to increase productivity. Conflict is likely to occur at this point because each function has its own goals that, in this case, conflict. Thus, groups may cooperate on one point and conflict on another.

Conflict also can occur between similar groups and leaders within the same organization. For example, Microsoft had to manage some intergroup conflict between its traditional Microsoft Office team and a new innovative software engineering group when the latter was assembled to create NetDocs. The NetDocs initiative was formed to completely rethink the Office concept and to create a Web-based subscription service that would offer some of the same functions of Office, such as word processing and spreadsheets. There were major differences within Microsoft regarding the need to offer such a Web-based service and concern that it would substantially cannibalize sales of the traditional Office software program. Eventually, the NetDocs team was dissolved into the Office team and as a result, Microsoft lost its head start in the

How much do you know about managing conflict and negotiations?

1. _____ conflict is a confrontation or interaction between groups that hinders the achievement of organizational goals.
   a. Negligent
   b. Psychological
   c. Task-oriented
   d. Dysfunctional

2. True or false: The risk of intergroup conflict is low when two departments (e.g., manufacturing and shipping departments) in a company are sequentially interdependent.
   a. True
   b. False

3. In conflict situations where a group's members feel threatened, a group is likely to do each of the following except _____.
   a. become more loyal to the group
   b. desire strong, autocratic leadership
   c. become more consensus-oriented
   d. become more task-oriented

4. _____ is a type of planned intervention that is meant to build self-awareness and camaraderie among members of a team.
   a. Team building
   b. Conflict development
   c. Team formation
   d. Conflict avoidance

5. Distorted perceptions, negative stereotyping, and decrease in communication are changes _____ and occur due to dysfunctional conflict.
   a. between groups
   b. within groups
   c. Both *a* and *b* are correct.
   d Neither *a* nor *b* is correct.

"cloud computing" online software market. This forgone opportunity is important because Google has steadily built a suite of online software applications that resemble Microsoft Office products and could eventually pose a threat to Microsoft's dominance in office productivity software.[1]

This chapter will focus primarily on conflict that occurs between groups in organizations. Types and causes of intergroup conflict, results of intergroup conflict, and ways to manage intergroup conflict will be discussed in detail. Later in the chapter, we will cover negotiations from an individual manager perspective. We will include a discussion of negotiation tactics and interpersonal negotiation styles, as well as a comparison of cross-cultural differences in negotiation approaches. We end the chapter with a list of steps to improve negotiation effectiveness.

A Contemporary Perspective on Intergroup Conflict

In the past many organizational practitioners operated on the assumption that any and all conflict was bad and thus should be eliminated. Today we understand that is not the case. A more accurate and enlightened view is that conflict is neither inherently good nor bad, but it is inevitable. It is true that too much conflict can have negative consequences because it requires time and resources to deal with it and because it diverts energy that could more constructively be applied elsewhere. Too little conflict, on the other hand, can also be negative in that such a state can lead to apathy and lethargy and provide little or no impetus for change and innovation. If everything is going smoothly, people may become too comfortable to want to make changes that could improve organizational effectiveness.

Some conflict situations produce nothing positive. Other conflict situations, however, may be beneficial if they are used as instruments for change or innovation. For example, evidence suggests conflict can improve the quality of decision making and employee relations in organizations.[2] Thus, in dealing with conflict the critical issue is not so much the conflict itself but how it is managed. Using this perspective, we can define conflict in terms of the effect it has on the organization. In this respect, we shall discuss both *functional* and *dysfunctional conflict*.[3]

Functional Conflict

functional conflict
A confrontation between groups that enhances and benefits the organization's performance.

A **functional conflict** is a confrontation between groups that enhances and benefits the organization's performance. For example, two departments in a hospital may be in conflict over the most efficient and adaptive method of delivering health care to low-income rural families. The two departments agree on the goal but not on the means to achieve it. Whatever the outcome, low-income rural families probably will end up with better medical care once the conflict is settled. Without this type of conflict in organizations, there would be little commitment to change, and most groups likely would become stagnant. Functional conflict can lead to increased awareness of problems that need to be addressed, result in broader and more productive searches for solutions, and generally facilitate positive change, adaptation, and innovation.

Dysfunctional Conflict

dysfunctional conflict
A confrontation or interaction between groups that harms the organization or hinders the achievement of organizational goals.

A **dysfunctional conflict** is any confrontation or interaction between groups that harms the organization or hinders the achievement of organizational goals. Management must seek to eliminate dysfunctional conflict.

Beneficial conflicts can often turn into harmful ones. In most cases, the point at which functional conflict becomes dysfunctional is impossible to identify precisely. The same level of stress and conflict that creates a healthy and positive movement toward goals in one group may prove extremely disruptive and dysfunctional in another group (or at a different time for the same group). A group's tolerance for stress and conflict can also depend on the type of organization it serves. Auto manufacturers, professional sports teams, and crisis organizations such as police and fire departments would have different points where functional conflict becomes dysfunctional than would organizations such as universities, research and development firms, and motion-picture production firms.

A recent research study analyzed how an initial conflict between different groups at a community hospital in the Midwest escalated into a full-blown "war."[4] The conflict began when physicians perceived that the hospital administration (i.e., the CEO and her administrative team) was ignoring or blocking recommendations that could improve the quality of patient care at the hospital. The physicians wanted to maintain control over decisions that could affect their patients. The administration responded to this perceived attack from the physicians by withholding even more support for the physicians' recommendations. The physicians responded by launching a campaign to remove the CEO from her position. These retaliations and countermoves escalated, ultimately costing the administrative and medical groups countless hours of time, energy, and stress that could have been better spent on improving the quality of care for patients.[5]

Conflict and Organizational Performance

As previously indicated, conflict may have either positive or negative consequences for the organization, depending on how much exists and how it is managed. Every organization has an optimal level of conflict that can be considered highly functional—it helps generate positive performance. When the conflict level is too low, performance can also suffer. Innovation and change are less likely to occur, and the organization may have difficulty adapting to its changing environment. If a low conflict level continues, the very survival of the organization can be threatened. On the other hand, if the conflict level becomes too high, the resulting chaos also can threaten the organization's survival. An example is the popular press coverage of the results of "dissension" in labor unions and its impact on performance. If fighting between rival factions in the union becomes too great, it can render the union less effective in pursuing its mission of furthering members' interests. The relationship between the level of intergroup conflict and organizational performance that is consistent with a contemporary perspective is presented in Exhibit 11.1 for three hypothetical situations.

Stages of Conflict

perceived conflict
The first stage of the conflict process. Perceived conflict exists when there is a cognitive awareness on the part of at least one party that events have occurred or that conditions exist favorable to creating overt conflict.

Although some conflicts can become intense and full blown virtually instantaneously, usually intergroup conflicts develop over time. When this happens, the conflict typically passes through several stages of evolution. **Perceived conflict** exists when there is a cognitive awareness on the part of at least one group that events have occurred or that conditions exist favorable to creating overt conflict. Or perceived conflict may be part of a company's annual budget planning process, when each department attempts to maximize the resources it receives, potentially at the expense of every other department.

EXHIBIT 11.1   Relationship between Intergroup Conflict and Organizational Performance

	Level of Intergroup Conflict	Probable Impact on Organization	Organization Characterized By	Level of Organizational Performance
Situation I	Low or none	Dysfunctional	• Slow adaptation to environmental changes • Few changes • Little stimulation of ideas • Apathy • Stagnation	Low
Situation II	Optimal	Functional	• Positive movement toward goals • Innovation and change • Search for problem solutions • Creativity and quick adaptation to environmental changes	High
Situation III	High	Dysfunctional	• Disruption • Interference with activities • Coordination difficult • Chaos	Low

felt conflict
The second stage of conflict that includes emotional involvement. It is "felt" in the form of anxiety, tension, and/or hostility.

Perceived conflict may or may not lead to **felt conflict.** The felt stage of conflict represents an escalation that includes emotional involvement. It is "felt" in the form of anxiety, tension, and/or hostility. Because such feelings are generally a source of discomfort, the parties involved may be motivated to try to reduce the negative emotions. This, in turn, can lead to positive or negative attempts to deal with the conflict. Typically, all parties to a conflict need to experience both perceived and felt conflict to be sufficiently motivated to attempt resolution.

manifest conflict
The final stage in conflict. At the manifest conflict stage, the conflicting parties are actively engaging in conflict behavior. Manifest conflict is usually very apparent to noninvolved parties.

The final stage is that of **manifest conflict.** Manifest conflict is not only perceived and felt, it is acted upon. That is, at the manifest stage the conflicting groups are actively engaging in conflict behavior through verbal, written, or even physical attacks. In manifest conflict, it is usually very apparent to noninvolved parties that problems exist. Although it is possible to resolve manifest conflict, it is far better to deal with conflict at an earlier stage. Additionally, manifest conflict is more likely to have longer-lasting effects than either perceived or felt conflict.

Every conflict situation leaves a conflict aftermath that affects the way both groups perceive and act upon subsequent conflicts. Generally the earlier conflicts can be resolved, the more likely the aftermath will facilitate positive future interactions between the conflicting groups. While manifest conflicts can have functional aftermaths, the likelihood of dysfunctional outcomes increases as conflict moves from perceived to felt to manifest.

What Causes Intergroup Conflict?

Every group comes into at least partial conflict with every other group with which it interacts. This tendency is known as "the law of interorganizational conflict."[6] In this section we examine three of the more important factors that contribute to group conflict: work interdependence, goal differences, and perceptual differences.

Work Interdependence

Work interdependence occurs when two or more organizational groups must depend on one another to complete their tasks. The conflict potential in such situations ranges from relatively low to very high, depending on the nature of the interdependence. Three distinct types of interdependence among groups have been identified: pooled, sequential, and reciprocal. Exhibit 11.2 provides a visual representation of these three types.

pooled interdependence
Interdependence that requires no interaction between groups because each group, in effect, performs separately.

Pooled interdependence requires no interaction among groups because each group, in effect, performs separately. However, the pooled performances of all the groups determine how successful the organization is. For example, the staff of an IBM sales office in one region may have no interaction with its peers in another region. Similarly, two bank branches will have little or no interaction. In both cases, however, the groups are interdependent because the performance of each must be adequate if the total organization is to thrive. The conflict potential in pooled interdependence is relatively low, and management can rely on standard rules and procedures developed at the main office for coordination.

sequential interdependence
Interdependence that requires one group to complete its task before another group can complete its task.

Sequential interdependence requires one group to complete its task before another group can complete its task. Tasks are performed in a sequential fashion. In a manufacturing plant, for example, the product must be assembled before it can be painted. Thus, the assembling department must complete its task before the painting department can begin painting.

EXHIBIT 11.2
Types of Interdependence

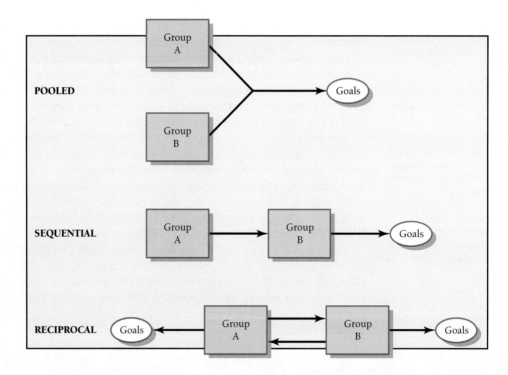

Under these circumstances, since the output of one group serves as the input for another, conflict between the groups is more likely to occur. Coordinating this type of interdependence involves effective use of the management function of planning.

Reciprocal interdependence requires the output of each group to serve as input to other groups in the organization. Consider the relationships that exist between the anesthesiology staff, nursing staff, technician staff, and surgeons in a hospital operating room. This relationship creates a high degree of reciprocal interdependence. The same interdependence exists among groups involved in space launchings. Another example is the interdependence among airport control towers, flight crews, ground operations, and maintenance crews. Clearly, the potential for conflict is great in any of these situations. Effective coordination involves management's skillful use of the organizational processes of communication and decision making.

All organizations have pooled interdependence among groups. Complex organizations also have sequential interdependence. The most complicated organizations experience pooled, sequential, and reciprocal interdependence among groups. The more complex the organization, the greater are the potentials for conflict and the more difficult is the task facing management.

reciprocal interdependence
Interdependence that requires the output of each group in an organization to serve as input to other groups in the organization.

Goal Differences

Ideally, interacting groups will always view their goals as mutually compatible and behave in such a way as to contribute to the attainment of both sets of goals. Realistically, however, this is frequently not the case. Several problems related to differences in goals can create conflicts.

Groups with *mutually exclusive goals* can find themselves in conflict. For example, marketing departments usually have a goal of maximizing sales, while credit departments seek to minimize credit losses. Depending on which department prevails, different customers might be selected. Some incompatible goals may be more apparent than real; in these situations, conflicting groups need to refocus on larger organizational objectives.

When *limited resources* must be allocated between groups, mutual dependencies increase and any differences in goals become more apparent. If money, space, labor, and materials were unlimited, every group could pursue its own goals. But in virtually all cases, resources must be allocated or shared. When groups conclude that resources have not been allocated in an equitable manner, pressures toward conflict increase.[7] When the limited resource is money, conflict potential is particularly strong.

Finally, the *different time horizons* needed by groups to achieve their goals can be a source of conflict. Research scientists working for a chemical manufacturer may have a time perspective of several years, while the same firm's manufacturing engineers may work within time frames of several months. A bank president might focus on 5- and 10-year time spans, while middle managers of the bank may concentrate on much shorter periods. With such differences in time horizons, problems and issues deemed critical by one group may be dismissed as unimportant by another, and conflicts may erupt.

Perceptual Differences

Goal differences can be accompanied by differing perceptions of reality, and disagreements over what constitutes reality can lead to conflict. For instance, a problem in a hospital may be viewed in one way by the medical staff and in another way by the nursing staff. Alumni and faculty may have different perceptions concerning the importance of a winning football program. Many factors cause organizational groups to form differing perceptions of reality.[8] Major factors include status incongruency, inaccurate perceptions, and different perspectives.

Status incongruency conflicts concerning the relative status of different groups are common. Usually, many different status standards are found in an organization, rather than an absolute one. The result is many status hierarchies. For example, status conflicts often are created by work patterns—which group initiates the work and which group responds. A production department, for instance, may perceive a change as an affront to its status because it must accept a sales group's initiation of work. This status conflict may be aggravated deliberately by the sales group. Academic snobbery is certainly a fact of campus life at many colleges and universities. Members of a particular academic discipline may perceive themselves, for one reason or another, as having a higher status than those of another discipline.

Inaccurate perceptions often cause one group to develop stereotypes about other groups. While the differences between groups may actually be quite small, each group will tend to exaggerate them. Thus, you will hear that "all women executives are aggressive," or "all bank trust officers behave alike," or "all professors think their course is the only important one." When the differences between the groups are emphasized, the stereotypes are reinforced, relations deteriorate, and conflict develops.

The example given earlier of alumni and faculty having different perceptions concerning the importance of a winning football program is an example of *different perspectives*. Alumni may wish for a winning football season because that shows a form of institutional success in a very visible public manner. Faculty, on the other hand, may see the football program as a distraction from the school's primary objective of creating and disseminating knowledge. The two groups simply may have a different view of what is most important. Group goals, experience, values, and culture all may contribute to different ways of seeing the world. The different perspectives growing out of different organizational cultures can explain why conflict frequently results when companies are merged.

The nearby Management Pointer provides suggestions for minimizing the role perceptual differences may play in causing conflict.

The Consequences of Dysfunctional Intergroup Conflict

Behavioral scientists have spent more than four decades researching and analyzing how dysfunctional intergroup conflict affects those who experience it.[9] They have found that groups placed in a conflict situation tend to react in fairly predictable ways. We shall examine a number of the changes that can occur *within groups* and *between groups* as a result of dysfunctional intergroup conflict.

> **Management Pointer**
>
> **MINIMIZING PERCEPTUAL BASES FOR CONFLICT**
>
> Perceptual differences can lead to conflict. To reduce the likelihood this will happen:
>
> 1. Communicate effectively! Reduce inaccurate perceptions by ensuring that groups have sufficient information to make accurate judgments.
> 2. Help develop a group's social sensitivity. Help the group understand the basis for another group's perspective (understanding does not necessarily mean agreeing with the other group's position).
> 3. Emphasize behavioral flexibility. Engage in actions (e.g., sharing information) based upon an understanding of the other group's perspective.

Changes within Groups

Many changes are likely to occur within groups involved in intergroup conflict. Unfortunately, these changes generally result in either a continuance or an escalation of the conflict.

Increased Group Cohesiveness

When groups are engaged in a conflict, their cohesion tends to increase. Competition, conflict, or perceived external threat usually result in group members putting aside individual differences and closing ranks. Members become more loyal to the group, and group membership becomes more attractive. This increase in cohesion is necessary to mobilize group resources in dealing with the "enemy" and tends to result in the suppression of internal disagreements. This tendency toward increased cohesion in the face of threat was seen in Kosovo. Ethnic groups in the former Yugoslavia have historically had difficulties getting along with each other.

Emphasis on Loyalty

The tendency of groups to increase in cohesiveness suggests that conformity to group norms becomes more important in conflict situations. In reality, it is not unusual for groups to overconform to group norms in conflict situations. This may take the form of blind acceptance of dysfunctional solutions to the conflict and result in groupthink, as discussed in the previous chapter. In such situations, group goals take precedence over individual satisfaction as members are expected to demonstrate their loyalty. In major conflict situations, interaction with members of "the other group" may be outlawed.

Rise in Autocratic Leadership

In extreme conflict situations where threats are perceived, democratic methods of leadership are likely to become less popular. Group members want strong leadership. This was true in the air traffic controllers' strike, discussed in the next chapter. Professional sports offer a number of examples, including the National Football League players' strike in 1987 and the Major League Baseball Players Association strike in 1994, which led to cancellation of the World Series for the first time in 90 years. In this strike, Union President Donald Fehr had tremendous authority from the players to do what he believed was best. Another sign of strong leadership is the fact that the Major League

Baseball players union was able to delay drug-testing programs until 2004 despite several years of suspicion that players were taking performance-enhancing drugs.[10]

Focus on Activity

When a group is in conflict, its members usually emphasize doing what the group does and doing it very well. The group becomes more task-oriented. Tolerance for members who goof off is low, and there is less concern for individual member satisfaction. The emphasis is on accomplishing the group's task and defeating the "enemy" (the other group in the conflict).

Changes between Groups

During conflicts, certain changes will probably occur between the groups involved.

Distorted Perceptions

During conflicts, the perceptions of each group's members become distorted. Group members develop stronger opinions of the importance of their units. Each group sees itself as superior in performance to the others and as more important to the survival of the organization than other groups. In a conflict situation, nurses may conclude that they are more important to a patient than physicians, while physicians may consider themselves more important than hospital administrators. The marketing group in a business organization may think, "Without us selling the product, there would be no money to pay anyone else's salary." The production group, meanwhile, will say, "If we don't make the product, there is nothing to sell." Ultimately, none of these groups is more important, but conflict can cause their members to develop gross misperceptions of reality.

Negative Stereotyping

As conflict increases and perceptions become more distorted, all the negative stereotypes are reinforced. A management representative may say, "I've always said these union guys are just plain greedy. Now they've proved it." The head of a local teachers union may say, "Now we know that what all politicians are interested in is getting re-elected, not the quality of education." When negative stereotyping is a factor in a conflict, the members of each group see fewer differences within their unit and greater differences between the groups than actually exist.

Decreased Communications

Communications between the groups in conflict usually break down. This can be extremely dysfunctional, especially where sequential interdependence or reciprocal interdependence relationships exist between groups. The decision-making process can be disrupted, and the customers or others whom the organization serves can be affected. Consider the possible consequences to patients, for instance, if a conflict between hospital technicians and nurses continues until it lowers the quality of health care.

While these are not the only dysfunctional consequences of intergroup conflict, they are the most common, and they have been well documented in the research literature. Other consequences, such as violence and aggression, are less common but also occur.

Also, tension occasionally results in creativity among individuals and groups. Michael Eisner, ex-chairman of Walt Disney, suggested that creative tension produced a steady stream of ideas.[11] He indicated that, at Disney, common sense and conflict yielded the needed creativity. Without conflict and common sense, Eisner believed, the creative sparks needed to keep coming up with new ideas would be lost. Many of his critics believed that Eisner was too confrontational to be effective in his position of CEO.[12] When intergroup conflicts occur, some form of managerial intervention is usually necessary. How managers can deal with these situations is the subject of the next section.

Managing Intergroup Conflict through Resolution

Since managers must live with intergroup conflict, they must confront the problem of managing it.[13] In this section we will examine several approaches to managing conflict. Exhibit 11.3 provides a framework, in the form of a conflict-resolution grid, for examining these various approaches.[14] As the exhibit suggests, one way of viewing conflict-resolution efforts between groups is to examine the extent to which a conflicting group has an internal and external focus with respect to resolution strategies. An *internal focus* represents the extent to which a group is intent upon addressing its own concerns in a conflict situation. An *external focus* reflects the extent to which a group is intent on addressing the concerns of the other group (or groups) involved in the conflict. From this perspective, internal and external foci are not opposite ends of the same dimension. Rather, they are two separate dimensions. Varying degrees of focus on these two dimensions lead to five approaches to resolving intergroup conflict. Depending upon the nature and conditions of the conflict, each of these five approaches can represent an effective approach for conflict-resolution management. We will examine each of these approaches separately.

Dominating

A dominating approach to conflict resolution represents a group's maximum focus on meeting its own concerns, coupled with a minimal focus on meeting the concerns of the other group. Dominating tends to be a power-oriented approach. That is, to be successful it requires that the using group have sufficient power to "force" its resolution on the other group. A group may hold the balance of power because it is higher up in the organizational hierarchy (that is, it has more authority); it controls critical resources (for example, budgets, personnel, or important knowledge); it has allied with powerful groups; or for a variety of other reasons.

EXHIBIT 11.3
Conflict-Resolution Grid

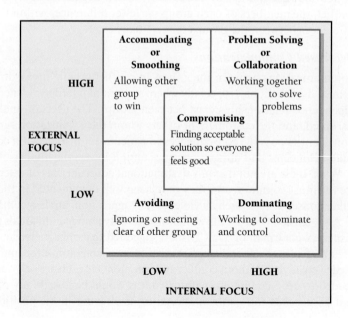

It is not unusual for both groups in a conflict to attempt a dominating approach to resolving their differences. Frequently in such cases, this means that one of the groups has overestimated its own power relative to that of the other group. In such cases, the outcome can have negative consequences for one or both groups. In labor disputes, for example, both management and the union may adopt a dominating approach to resolving their differences. The end result of this kind of power play may be a prolonged strike that is costly to both sides. The Organizational Encounter on page 320 describes five different approaches that people use to handle conflict in a negotiating context.

Despite the potential problems associated with the use of domination as a means of resolving conflict, it may be very appropriate and useful in some instances. There are times (for example, emergency situations) when differences must be settled quickly. When rapid and decisive action is important, dominating can represent the most time-effective means of resolution. Dominating may also be the best approach in resolving important issues when unpopular courses of action must be taken, such as layoffs, implementing new schedules, or enforcing unpopular policies and procedures.

Accommodating

In many respects, accommodating is just the opposite approach from dominating. An accommodating party places maximum emphasis on meeting the needs of the other group, while minimizing its own concerns. Although accommodation may appear to be "giving in," this may be an extremely beneficial approach for a conflicting group to use in some situations. For example, issues over which groups might conflict are not always of equal importance to each group. If the issue is critical to one group and of little importance to the other, obliging the first group through accommodating costs the second group little and may be seen as a goodwill gesture that helps maintain a cooperative relationship. Accommodating may also purchase "credits" that can be used in subsequent conflicts when the issues are more important to the obliging group. Finally, there may be instances when preserving the peace and avoiding disharmony are more important than reaching a resolution that maximizes a particular group's concerns.

Problem Solving

Problem solving represents what might appear to be the theoretically ideal or best approach to conflict resolution. However, it can be an extremely difficult approach to implement effectively. Problem solving, sometimes called collaborating or integrating, seeks to resolve conflict by placing maximum focus on both groups' concerns. Successful problem solving requires that conflicting groups display a willingness to work collaboratively toward an integrative solution that satisfies the needs of all concerned. The greatest obstacle that must be overcome is the win–lose mentality that so often characterizes conflicting groups. Unless the parties involved can rise above that kind of thinking, problem solving is not likely to be successful.

The potential benefits of using a problem-solving approach are significant. When conflicting parties truly collaborate, this can result in a merger of insight, experience, knowledge, and perspective that leads to higher-quality solutions than would be obtained by any other approach. Additionally, because both parties' concerns are incorporated into the resolution, commitment to the effective implementation of the solution is high. Sometimes the problem-solving process is aided by focusing on a superordinate goal. A **superordinate goal** is one that cannot be attained by one group singly and supersedes all other concerns of any of the individual groups involved in

superordinate goal
A goal that cannot be achieved without the cooperation of the conflicting groups.

HOW DO YOU HANDLE CONFLICT?

Are you the kind of person who thrives on arguing with other people, regardless of the topic being discussed? Or do you tend to shy away from disagreements to maintain harmony? Understanding your preferred conflict management style can help you to be a more effective co-worker and manager. As a student, such knowledge will help you work better with other students on group projects—especially at the end of the semester, when multiple deadlines can stress everyone's patience.

Complete the following self-assessment by circling one of the numbers from the following scale to describe your reaction to each of the statements below:

| 1 = Never . . . | 2 = Rarely . . . | 3 = Sometimes . . . | 4 = Often . . . | 5 = Very often |

Statement		Circle One			
1. I work to come out victorious, no matter what.	1	2	3	4	5
2. I try to put the needs of others above my own.	1	2	3	4	5
3. I look for mutually satisfactory solutions.	1	2	3	4	5
4. I try not to get involved in conflicts.	1	2	3	4	5
5. I strive to investigate issues thoroughly and jointly.	1	2	3	4	5
6. I never back away from a good argument.	1	2	3	4	5
7. I strive to foster harmony.	1	2	3	4	5
8. I negotiate to get a portion of what I propose.	1	2	3	4	5
9. I avoid open discussions of controversial subjects.	1	2	3	4	5
10. I openly share information with others in resolving disagreements.	1	2	3	4	5

Scoring and Interpretation

Competing	Q1 _____	+ Q6 _____	= Total
Collaborating	Q5 _____	+ Q10 _____	= Total
Avoiding	Q4 _____	+ Q9 _____	= Total
Accommodating	Q2 _____	+ Q7 _____	= Total
Compromising	Q3 _____	+ Q8 _____	= Total

Your preferred conflict-handling style is: _____ (category with highest score).
Your backup conflict-handling style is: _____ (category with 2nd highest score).

Competing: High scores on Q1 and Q6 indicate that your preferred style is to focus on winning in a negotiation setting. Conflict is seen as a part of the negotiation process, a means to receive what you desire. You enjoy the negotiation process. Trial attorneys fit this type of conflict management style.

Collaborating: People who have high scores on Q5 and Q10 tend to enjoy the negotiation process because it gives them an opportunity to probe deeply into difficult problems and help produce solutions that are acceptable to multiple parties. Real estate brokers tend to handle conflict in this manner.

Avoiding: Scoring high on Q4 and Q9 indicates that you prefer to avoid conflict and opportunities to negotiate. Although avoidance of conflict can help keep teams functioning when interpersonal difficulties arise, it can also lead to a variety of problems and dysfunctional behavior if issues are left unaddressed and unresolved. Professional politicians tend to be avoiders.

Accommodating: People with high scores on Q2 and Q7 use their relationship-building skills and empathy toward other people's emotions to help solve other people's problems. High accommodators place a good deal of emphasis on the needs of others. These types of negotiators are good in sales-based roles where relationships are critical. An example of this would be the account manager of a large natural gas company who is assigned to one large account for a three-year period.

Compromising: High scores on Q3 and Q8 indicate that your preferred conflict resolution style is to try to "close the gap" in two parties' desires by using some type of fair criteria that appear reasonable to both sides. Compromisers tend to want to preserve the relationship between parties. An example of a compromiser would be a team leader who is trying to work out a problem between two of her direct reports. She wants to resolve the problem quickly and have both parties feel that the outcome is fair.

Sources: Adapted from G. Richard Shell, "Bargaining Styles and Negotiation: The Thomas-Kilmann Conflict Mode Instrument in Negotiation Training," *Negotiation Journal* 17, no. 2 (April 2001), pp. 155–74; and K.W. Thomas, "Conflict and Conflict Management," in *Handbook of Industrial Psychology and OrganizationalPsychology, Vol. II,* ed. M. Dunnette (Chicago: Rand McNally, 1976), pp. 889–935.

the conflict. For example, members of the United Auto Workers union at the Ford Motor Company, in response to a major downturn in automobile sales and profitability, agreed to caps on overtime and unemployment pay and reductions in wage increases because the survival of the company was threatened.[15]

Avoiding

Frequently, some way can be found to avoid conflict. While avoiding may not bring any long-run benefits, it can be an effective and appropriate strategy in some conflict situations. Foremost among these is when avoiding is used as a temporary alternative. When the conflict is a particularly heated one, for example, temporary avoidance gives the involved parties an opportunity to cool down and regain perspective. Avoiding may also buy time needed by one or more of the groups to gather additional information necessary for a longer-range solution. Avoiding may also be appropriate when other parties are in a better position to resolve the conflict or when other matters that are more important need to be addressed. Unfortunately, people have a great temptation to overuse an avoiding approach; the number of situations where avoiding is the most effective strategy for dealing with a conflict is typically less than we would like it to be. Nonetheless, as a temporary expedient, avoiding can be a useful prelude to the implementation of a longer-range strategy.

Compromising

Compromising is a traditional method for resolving intergroup conflicts. With compromise, there is no distinct winner or loser, and the resolution reached probably is not ideal for either group. Compromising can be used very effectively when the goal sought (for example, money) can be divided equitably. If this is not possible, one group must give up something of value as a concession.

Compromising might be useful when two conflicting parties with relatively equal power are both strongly committed to mutually exclusive goals. It may also represent a way of gaining a temporary settlement to particularly complex and difficult issues. We saw earlier that problem solving was a desirable but difficult approach to conflict resolution. Compromise is a good "backup" strategy that conflicting parties can fall back on if their attempts at problem solving are unsuccessful. Sometimes, compromising may involve third-party interventions.[16] Such intervention may take the form of appealing to a managerial higher authority or a decision to submit the conflict to some form of mediation or arbitration.

Compromising is a middle-of-the-road approach. It typically involves giving up more than dominating, but less than accommodating. Additionally, it addresses issues more directly than avoiding, but with less depth than problem solving.

Each of these five approaches just discussed has assets and liabilities, and each is effective or ineffective in different situations. The Management Pointer highlights when each might be most appropriate.

Management Pointer

WHEN TO USE THE DIFFERENT CONFLICT-RESOLUTION APPROACHES

While there are many different situations in which each of the approaches is valid, keep these general points in mind:

- Use a *dominating* approach on important issues where you are certain you are right and where the benefit of a resolution outweighs the drawback of possible negative feelings by the dominated group.

- Use an *accommodating* approach in disputes that are of far greater importance to the other group than they are to your group.

- Use a *problem-solving* approach when both groups are willing to invest time and effort to reach a resolution that maximizes everyone's outcome.

- Use an *avoiding* approach primarily as a temporary expedient to buy more time.

- Use a *compromising* approach as a middle ground. It is a good backup approach when other approaches (mainly dominating and problem solving) fail to resolve the issue.

EXHIBIT 11.4   An Overview of Intergroup Conflict

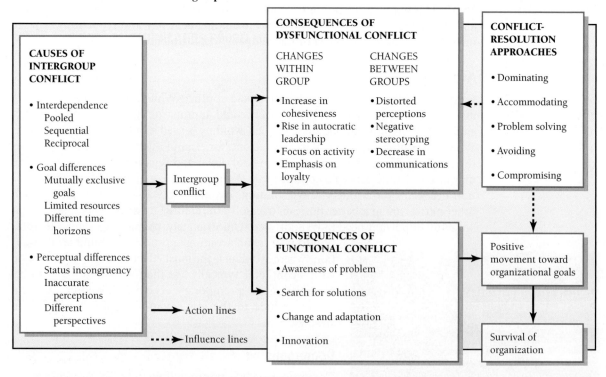

What this chapter has said thus far about intergroup conflict is summarized in Exhibit 11.4. The exhibit illustrates the relationship between causes and types of conflict, the consequences of conflict, and approaches to conflict resolution. Keep in mind that views of conflict and approaches to conflict resolution vary across cultures. Important aspects of conflict are viewed and experienced differently in different nations. The Global OB on page 323 illustrates this.

Stimulating Constructive Intergroup Conflict

Throughout this chapter we have stressed that some conflict is beneficial. This point was first made in the discussion on the contemporary perspective on conflict and is noted again in Exhibit 11.4, which details some of the functional consequences of intergroup conflict. We have already examined the situation where conflict is dysfunctional because it is too high; we have said little, however, regarding situations in which there is an insufficient amount of conflict. If groups become too complacent because everything always operates smoothly, management might benefit from stimulating conflict. Lack of any disagreement can lead to suboptimum performance, including inferior decision making.

A variety of research supports this conclusion. In one study, experimental and control groups were formed to solve a problem. The experimental groups had a member, a confederate of the researcher, whose job was to challenge the majority view of the groups he or she had been planted in as the group attempted to solve the problem. The control groups had no such member. In every case, the experimental groups outperformed the control groups.[17]

CONFLICT RESOLUTION: HOW JAPANESE AND AMERICANS DIFFER

Rensis Likert, the renowned social scientist and management expert, once observed that the strategies used by a society and its organizations for dealing with conflict reflect the basic values and philosophy of that society. In ideal circumstances, conflicts can be difficult to resolve; once the confounding variable of intercultural differences is added, conflict resolution becomes even more complex. Consider, for example, Japanese and American differences in the table below.

These broad generalizations may not apply in specific situations or with specific individuals or groups, but they point out that intercultural conflicts—and successful intercultural conflict resolution—are affected by differing cultural perspectives, values, and styles of interacting. All of these are significant factors that cannot be ignored in the conflict-resolution process.

Japanese	American	Japanese	American
Resolution involves long-term perspective	Short-term perspective	Takes time; process is important; win–win approach	Time is money; win–lose approach
Cooperation based on team spirit	Spirit of competition and rivalry	Emotional sensitivity highly valued	Emotional sensitivity not highly valued
Disagreement with superior often, but polite	Disagreement with superior seldom, but violent	Good of the group is ultimate aim	Profit motive or good of individual ultimate aim
Disputes settled through conferral and trust	Disputes settled through contracts and bringing arbitration	Face-saving crucial; decisions often made to save someone from embarrassment	Decision made on cost–benefit basis; face-saving not always important

Sources: Based on materials from Tae-Yeol Kim, Chongwei Wang, Mari Kondo, and Tae-Hyun Kim, "Conflict Management Styles: The Differences among the Chinese, Japanese, and Koreans," *International Journal of Conflict Management* 18, no. 1 (2007), pp. 23–41; Catherine Tinsley, "Models of Conflict Resolution in Japanese, German, and American Cultures," *Journal of Applied Psychology* 83 (1998), pp. 316–23; P. Casse, *Training for the Multicultural Manager: A Practical and Cross-Cultural Approach to the Management of People* (Washington, DC: Society of Intercultural Education, Training, and Research, 1982); and B.J. Punnett, *Experiencing International Management* (Boston: PWS-Kent, 1989).

While lack of conflict may prove beneficial in the short run, it can lead to situations where one group holds tremendous influence over another. For example, observers of the Japanese style of participatory management question whether the lack of conflict between managers and employees in Japanese firms is healthy.[18]

Raising conflict levels can yield a number of benefits. Some conflict is probably necessary to stimulate the critical evaluation of organizational policies and processes and to lay the groundwork for change. Lack of conflict leads to acceptance of the status quo and discourages innovation. Increasing conflict can be an effective antidote for groupthink (discussed in the previous chapter). As was suggested in Exhibit 11.1, organizational performance suffers not only when conflict levels are too high but also when they are too low.

What can management do to increase conflict to achieve functional consequences? Four possible strategies are discussed below.

Bringing Outside Individuals into the Group

A technique widely used to "bring back to life" a stagnant organization or subunit of an organization is to hire or transfer in individuals whose attitudes, values, and backgrounds differ from those of the group's present members. Many college faculties consciously seek new members with different backgrounds and often discourage the hiring of graduates of their own programs. This is to ensure a diversity of viewpoints among the faculty.

The technique of bringing in outsiders is also used widely in government and business. Recently, a bank president decided not to promote from within for a newly created position of marketing vice president. Instead, he hired a highly successful executive from the very competitive consumer products field. The bank president believed that, while the outsider knew little about marketing financial services, her approach to, and knowledge of, marketing was what the bank needed to become a strong competitor.

Altering the Organization's Structure

Changing the structure of the organization not only can help resolve intergroup conflict, but it is also excellent for *creating* conflict. For example, a school of business typically has several departments. One, named the Department of Business Administration, includes all of the faculty members who teach courses in management, marketing, finance, production management, and so forth. Accordingly, the department is rather large, with 32 members under one department chairperson, who reports to the dean. A new dean recently has been hired, and he is considering dividing the business administration unit into several separate departments (e.g., departments of marketing, finance, management), each with five or six members and a chairperson. The reasoning is that reorganizing in this manner will create competition among the groups for resources, students, faculty, and so forth, where none existed before because there was only one group. Whether this change will improve performance remains to be seen.

Stimulating Competition

Many managers utilize various techniques to stimulate competition among groups. The use of a variety of incentives, such as awards and bonuses for outstanding performance, often stimulates competition. If properly utilized, such incentives can help maintain a healthy atmosphere of competition that may result in a functional level of conflict. Incentives can be given for least defective parts, highest sales, best teacher, greatest number of new customers, or in any area where increased conflict is likely to lead to more effective performance.

Using Programmed Conflict

Increasingly, organizations are turning to programmed conflict to increase creativity and innovation and to improve decision making. Programmed conflict is conflict that is deliberately and systematically created even when no real differences appear to exist. It is "conflict that raises different opinions regardless of the personal feelings of the managers."[19] One popular form of programmed conflict is devil's advocacy. In **devil's advocacy,** someone or some group is assigned the role of critic with the job of uncovering all possible problems with a particular proposal. The role of the devil's advocate is to ensure that opposing views are presented and considered before any final decision is made.

Numerous organizations use some form of programmed conflict. Royal Dutch Shell regularly uses a devil's advocacy approach. Before Anheuser-Busch makes a major decision, such as entering a market or building a plant, it assigns groups the job of making the case for each side of the question. IBM has a system that encourages employees to disagree with their bosses. All of these companies have the same goal: to improve organizational performance by stimulating conflict.

devil's advocacy
A form of programmed conflict in which someone or some group is assigned the role of critic whose job it is to uncover all possible problems with a particular proposal.

Negotiations

Frequently, an important part of the process of conflict resolution involves negotiations. Negotiations may be viewed as a process in which two or more parties attempt to reach acceptable agreement in a situation characterized by some level of disagreement. In an

YOU BE THE JUDGE

LOWBALLING IN SALARY NEGOTIATIONS: HOW WOULD YOU HANDLE IT?

Assume you have been interviewing with a company that you have wanted to get a job with for a long time. The interviews went reasonably well and you like what you heard about the job itself, the organizational culture, and the people with whom you would be working on a day-to-day basis. To be prepared and get the best possible starting salary, you've done some research and found that the salary range for this position is $35,000 to $40,000. You would like to earn more but figure that it's worth paying your dues for a while to have this job and be with a good company with room to move up quickly.

When the HR manager presents you with the initial offer, you're surprised and a little shocked. The starting salary is closer to $30,000. You say you have to think about it. At home, you recall that the HR manager called this an "initial offer." Rather than reject the offer and move on to interviewing with other companies, you believe this low initial offer is the HR manager's way of lowballing, or providing you with an extremely low offer as a way to lower salary expectations.

If you are correct in assuming that this is merely a negotiation tactic, what should you do?

Should you submit a counteroffer in the amount of $45,000 and indicate that you believe this is more in line with your compensation requirements? Should you just forget the whole thing and move on to other employment opportunities? In either case, what's your opinion of the HR manager's offer?

---

organizational context, negotiation may occur (1) between two people (as when a manager and subordinate decide on the completion date for a new project the subordinate has just received); (2) within a group (most group decision-making situations); (3) between groups (such as the purchasing department and a supplier regarding price, quality, or delivery date), which has been the focus in this chapter; and (4) over the Internet. The Internet now serves as a place to negotiate jobs, consulting projects, training program prices, and supplier product prices. The one difference in negotiating on the Internet is that it is done with written communication only. Many of the skills discussed in this section apply to both face-to-face negotiations and Internet transactions.

Regardless of the setting or the parties involved, negotiations usually have at least four elements.[20] First, some disagreement or *conflict exists.* This may be perceived, felt, or manifest. Second, there is some degree of *interdependence between the parties.* Third, the situation must be conducive to *opportunistic interaction.* This means that each party has both the means and inclination to attempt to influence the other. Finally, there exists some *possibility of agreement.* In the absence of this latter element, of course, negotiations cannot bring about a positive resolution. Often, negotiation is required when it is least expected, as illustrated in this chapter's You Be the Judge.

When negotiations are successful, each party feels that it has significantly benefited from the resolution. When they fail, however, the conflict often escalates.

Win–Lose Negotiating

The classical view suggests negotiations are frequently a form of a zero-sum game. That is, to whatever extent one party wins something, the other party loses. A zero-sum situation assumes limited resources, and the negotiation process is to determine who will receive these resources. This is also known as *distributive negotiating.* The term refers to the process of dividing, or "distributing," scarce resources. Such a win–lose approach characterizes numerous negotiating situations. Buying an automobile is a classic example. As the buyer, the less you pay the less profit the seller makes; your "wins" (in the form of fewer dollars paid) are the seller's "losses" (in the form of fewer dollars of profit). Note that in win–lose negotiating, one party does not necessarily "lose" in an absolute sense. Presumably the party selling the car still made a profit, but to the extent the selling price was lowered to make the sale, the profit was lower.

In organizations, win–lose negotiating is quite common. It characterizes most bargaining involving material goods, such as the purchase of supplies or manufacturing raw materials. Win–lose negotiating can be seen in universities where each college attempts to negotiate the best budget for itself, invariably at the expense of some other college. Frequently, the most variable examples of distributive negotiations in organizations are those that take place between labor and management. Issues involving wages, benefits, working conditions, and related matters are seen as a conflict over limited resources.

Win–Win Negotiating

Win–win, or integrative, negotiating brings a different perspective to the process. Unlike the zero-sum orientation in win–lose, win–win negotiating is a positive-sum approach. Positive-sum situations are those where each party gains without a corresponding loss for the other party. This does not necessarily mean that everyone gets everything they wanted, for seldom does that occur. It simply means that an agreement has been achieved that leaves all parties better off than they were before the agreement.

It may seem as if a win–win approach is always preferable to a win–lose one. Why should there be a winner and a loser if instead there can be two winners? Realistically, however, not every negotiating situation has an integrative payoff. Some situations really are distributive; a gain for one side must mean an offsetting loss for the other. In the automobile purchase example cited earlier, it is true that both the purchaser and the seller can "win" in the sense that the purchaser obtains the car and the seller makes a profit. Nonetheless, this is essentially a distributive situation. The purchaser can obtain a better deal *only* at the loss of some profit by the seller. There is simply no way the purchaser can get the lowest price while the seller obtains the highest profit.

Even if the nature of what is being negotiated lends itself to a win–win approach, the organization of the negotiators may not. Win–win, or integrative, negotiating can work only when the issues are integrative in nature and all parties are committed to an integrative process. Typically, union and management bargaining includes issues that are both distributive and integrative in nature. However, because negotiators for both sides so frequently see the total process as distributive, even those issues that truly may be integrative become victims of a win–lose attitude, to the detriment of both parties.

Negotiation Tactics

To achieve a win–win or win–lose negotiation outcome, a variety of specific negotiation tactics can be employed by managers.[21] Some of the most frequently used tactics will be discussed next.

1. *Good-guy/bad-guy team.* Anyone who has read a detective story or seen a TV police show is familiar with this tactic. The bad-guy member of the negotiating group advocates such extreme positions that whatever the good guy says sounds reasonable.

2. *The nibble.* This tactic involves getting an additional concession or perk after an agreement has been reached. An example would be the request for an additional point on an exam grade by a student after an agreement was reached with the professor that the student would receive three extra points.

3. *Joint problem solving.* A manager should never assume that the more one side wins, the more the other loses. Feasible alternatives not yet considered may exist. For instance,

to decrease the hundreds of calls that the service department receives each day at a computer software firm, maybe the Web site designer could add a list of frequently asked questions to the company's Web site. This would decrease the number of calls and thus alleviate some conflict between the service and Web site design departments.

4. *Power of competition.* Tough negotiators use competition to make opponents think they don't need them. A line manager may use this tactic by threatening that his group will procure computer services outside the organization if the headquarters' computer staff doesn't comply with its service demands. The most effective defense against this tactic is for the opposing manager to remain objective. Don't commit quickly to unfavorable terms because of the fear of quick action on the other group's part.

5. *Splitting the difference.* This can be a useful technique when two groups come to an impasse. Managers should be careful, however, when the other group offers to split the difference too early. It may mean the other group has already received more than it thinks it deserves.

Increasing Negotiation Effectiveness

Just as there is no one best way to manage, neither is there one best way to negotiate. The selection of specific negotiation strategies and tactics depends on a number of variables. The nature of the issues being negotiated is a critical consideration. For example, how one approaches negotiating distributive issues may be quite different from the strategy employed for negotiating integrative ones. The context or environment in which the negotiations are occurring may also be an important consideration, as may be the nature of the outcomes that are desired from the negotiating process. In many negotiating situations this last consideration may be the most important.

One useful way to think about desired outcomes is to distinguish between *substantive* and *relationship* outcomes.[22] *Substantive* outcomes have to do with how the specific issue is settled. To strive to end up with a bigger piece of the pie than the other party is to focus on a substantive outcome. On the other hand, to negotiate in a manner designed primarily to maintain good relations between the parties—irrespective of the substantive result—is to focus on *relationship* outcomes. While the two concerns are not mutually exclusive, the relative importance assigned them will affect a manager's choice of negotiation strategies.

One model for increasing negotiating effectiveness is found in the work of the Dutch management practitioner Willem Mastenbroek. Although the model is extremely comprehensive, the key focus is on four activities.[23]

1. *Obtaining substantial results.* This refers to activities that focus on the content of what is being negotiated. Desirable outcomes cannot be achieved if the negotiations do not stay constructively focused on the real issues. A judicious exchange of information regarding goals and expectations of the negotiating process is an example of this type of activity.

2. *Influencing the balance of power.* The final outcome of negotiations is almost always directly related to the power and dependency relationships between the negotiators. Neither attempts to increase one's power through dominance nor responding with total deference to the other party's attempt to increase their power represents the most effective means of dealing with power issues. Achieving subtle shifts in the balance of power through the use of persuasion, facts, and expertise are almost always more effective.

3. *Promoting a constructive climate.* This relates to activities designed to facilitate progress by minimizing the likelihood that tension or animosity between the parties becomes disruptive. Specific activities might include attending to each party's opinions, acting in a predictable and serious manner, treating each party with respect, and showing a sense of humor. Being on different sides of an issue does not have to mean being at odds personally.

4. *Obtaining procedural flexibility.* These are activities that allow a negotiator to increase negotiating effectiveness through increasing the type and number of options available for conducting the negotiations. The longer a negotiator can keep the widest variety of options open, the greater the likelihood of reaching a desirable outcome. Examples include judicious choice of one's initial position, dealing with several issues simultaneously, and putting as many alternatives on the table as possible.

Using Third-Party Negotiations

Negotiations do not always take place only between the two parties directly involved in the disagreement. Sometimes third parties are called in when negotiations between the main parties have broken down or reached an impasse. At other times, third parties may be part of the negotiation from the beginning. In some instances, third-party involvement is imposed on the disputing parties; in others, the parties themselves voluntarily seek out third-party assistance. In any event, the instances of third-party negotiations appear to be increasing.

There are different kinds of third-party interventions, and third-party involvement has been characterized in many different ways. One such typology suggests four basic kinds of interventions.[24] *Mediation* is where a neutral third party acts as a facilitator through the application of reasoning, suggestion, and persuasion. Mediators facilitate resolution by affecting how the disputing parties interact. Mediators have no binding authority; the parties are free to ignore mediation efforts and recommendations. *Arbitration* is where the third party has the power (authority) to impose an agreement. In conventional arbitration, the arbitrator selects an outcome that is typically somewhere between the final positions of the disputing parties. In final-offer arbitration, the arbitrator is mandated to choose one or the other of the parties' final offers, and thus has no real control over designing the agreement.[25] *Conciliation* occurs where the third party is someone who is trusted by both sides and serves primarily as a communication link between the disagreeing parties. A conciliator has no more formal authority to influence the outcome than does a mediator. Finally, *consultation* is where a third party trained in conflict and conflict-resolution skills attempts to facilitate problem solving by focusing more on the relations between the parties than on the substantive issues. The chief role of the consultant is to improve the negotiating climate so that substantive negotiations can take place in the future.

It is not uncommon for managers to serve as third parties in negotiations. Situations in which this could occur would include two subordinates who are having a disagreement, an employee and a dissatisfied customer, or disputes between two departments, both of which report to the manager. As a third party, the manager could be called upon to assume any and all of these four types of roles.

Team Building

team building
A type of planned intervention that is meant to build self-awareness and camaraderie among members of a team.

Team building is a type of planned intervention that is meant to build self-awareness and camaraderie among members of a team.[26] With the help of a trained facilitator, team-building exercises can be performed within the organization or at some outside location. Examples of outside activities include high ropes course, river rafting, and overnight camping trips. Effective team-building activities can help develop stronger relationships among employees, which can help prevent (or at least decrease) interpersonal conflict at the office. Ineffective team-building approaches focus too much on a onetime event that is entertaining, feels good, and serves as a momentary distraction from the normal office routine, but doesn't have a long-term impact on team success.

Some ways to increase the effectiveness (and thus, return on investment) of team-building exercises include:[27]

1. Consider whether the employees want to function as a team. Or do they see themselves as "loners" who'd rather work as independently as possible? If it's the latter, supervisors should communicate how better teamwork could add value and increase individual rewards.

2. Link the team-building activity to business results. The activity should have a direct linkage to the overall strategies of the organization. If the organization wants to decrease the amount of dysfunctional conflict between departments, then the team-building exercises should be designed to help participants build their actionable knowledge in this area.

3. Follow up after the team-building event. The outcomes from the team-building activity should be revisited in three or six months to assess whether it has achieved the desired goals. Based on the example in number 2 above, managers should attempt to measure whether the team building helped boost rapport among employees and, consequently, decreased the number and intensity of dysfunctional conflicts between departments. (For more on team building, see Chapter 17).

Negotiating Globally

The number of global negotiations is increasing rapidly. The global deals, markets, and relationships that organizations are forming require careful attention to culture's impact on style.[28] Individuals steeped in specific cultures negotiate differently. Labeling any culture's negotiating style is too general and constraining. However, general characteristics and tendencies have been observed and noted. The former ambassador from Singapore to the United States noted that American negotiators generally (1) are prepared, (2) are plain speaking, (3) are pragmatic, (4) understand that concessions may be required, and (5) are very specific and candid. Others have described American negotiators as blunt, arrogant, and rushed.[29] The weaknesses of American negotiators appear to center on impatience, legalism, and poor listening skills. The strengths of American negotiators focus on friendliness, fairness, and flexibility.

Exhibit 11.5 describes more than 300 negotiators from 12 countries.[30] The Japanese emphasized a win–win or integrative approach more than any other countries' negotiators. The results also indicate the direct communication styles used by Argentinean, American, and German negotiators. A recent research study that looked at cultural influences on negotiations in Finland, Mexico, Turkey, and the United States found that negotiators should not automatically assume that the process will be win–win or win–lose.[31] Even though cultural differences in negotiations exist, each negotiator needs to "explore the attitudes of the specific parties with whom they are negotiating." For example, Finnish negotiators are as likely to pursue a win–win approach as a win–lose approach. The American negotiator needs to be ready to adjust to the other party's negotiation style.

The differences in negotiating style are extensive. Political systems, legal policies, ideology, traditions, and culture certainly play a role. The international experience of the negotiators also has an impact on the style utilized. Being familiar with the

EXHIBIT 11.5
Cultural Effects on Negotiating Style

Source: Adapted from J.W. Salacuse, "Ten Ways That Culture Affects Negotiating Style: Some Survey Results," *Negotiation Journal,* July 1998, pp. 221–40.

NEGOTIATING ATTITUDE: WIN–WIN OR WIN–LOSE?

	Japan	China	Argentina	France	India	USA	UK	Germany	Mexico	Nigeria	Brazil	Spain
Win–Win (%)	100	82	81	80	78	71	59	55	50	47	44	37

PERSONAL STYLE: FORMAL OR INFORMAL?

	Nigeria	Spain	China	Mexico	UK	Argentina	Germany	Japan	India	Brazil	France	USA
Formal (%)	53	47	46	42	35	35	27	27	22	22	20	17

COMMUNICATION STYLE: DIRECT OR INDIRECT?

	Japan	France	China	UK	Brazil	India	Germany	USA	Argentina	Spain	Mexico	Nigeria
Indirect (%)	27	20	18	12	11	11	9	5	4	0	0	0

AGREEMENT FORM: GENERAL OR SPECIFIC?

	Japan	Germany	India	France	China	Argentina	Brazil	USA	Nigeria	Mexico	Spain	UK
General (%)	46	45	44	30	27	27	20	22	20	17	16	11

communication style, time orientation, group versus individual orientation, religious orientation, and customs of the culture of the counterpart negotiator is an important step to take in preparing for global negotiations.[32] Knowing something about another person's culture is a sign of respect that is appreciated at the negotiating table.

Improving Negotiations

In one form or another, negotiation is becoming an increasingly important part of the manager's job. A review of the topic of negotiation by Wall and Blum concludes with a set of recommendations for managers on how to improve the negotiation process. They offer the following suggestions:[33]

1. Begin the bargaining with a positive overture—perhaps a small concession—and then reciprocate the opponent's concessions.
2. Concentrate on the negotiation issues and the situational factors, not on the opponent or his or her characteristics.
3. Look below the surface of your opponent's bargaining and try to determine his or her strategy.
4. Do not allow accountability to your constituents or surveillance by them to spawn competitive bargaining.

5. If you have power in a negotiation, use it—with specific demands, mild threats, and persuasion—to guide the opponent toward an agreement.

6. Be open to accepting third-party assistance.

7. In a negotiation, attend to the environment and be aware that the opponent's behavior and power are altered by it.

Summary of Key Points

- A contemporary perspective on conflict recognizes that conflict is neither inherently good nor bad but can be either depending on how it is dealt with. Rather than eliminating conflict, this view stresses that what is important is that conflict be effectively managed.

- A functional conflict is a confrontation between groups that enhances and benefits the organization's performance. Functional conflict can contribute to creativity, innovation, and improved decision making, among other benefits. Dysfunctional conflict, on the other hand, harms the organization or hinders the achievement of organizational goals.

- Levels of conflict can be related to overall organizational performance. Too much conflict can be disruptive, creating chaos and damaging interpersonal relations. Too little conflict can also detract from performance. If conflict levels are too low, innovation and change are less likely to occur. Each organization has an optimal level of conflict that can be extremely functional.

- Conflict is inevitable. Every group will sometimes come into conflict with one or more other groups. Numerous factors contribute to intergroup conflict. Three particularly important ones are (1) the interdependent nature of the relationship between work groups, (2) differences in goals, and (3) differences in perceptions.

- Groups involved in dysfunctional conflict tend to react in fairly predictable ways. Some changes occur *within* the groups involved in conflict; others take place *between* the groups. Within-group changes include increased cohesiveness, emphasis on group loyalty, a rise in autocratic leadership, and a focus on task-oriented activity. Between-group changes include an increase in perceptual distortion, negative stereotyping of the other group, and decreased communication.

- One way of viewing conflict resolution is from the perspective of a conflict-management grid. Such a grid points out five distinct approaches to group conflict resolution: dominating, accommodating, problem solving, avoiding, and compromising.

- Sometimes conflict levels are too low, and the objective becomes stimulating functional conflict between groups. Techniques available for stimulating conflict include bringing outsiders into the group, altering the organization's structure, creating competition between groups, and using programmed conflict.

- Win–lose negotiating is a form of zero-sum game. That is, to the extent one party wins something, the other party loses. Win–win negotiating is a positive-sum approach, wherein each party gains without a corresponding loss for the other party.

- There is an increasing use of third parties in negotiations. In some cases, third parties may be part of the entire process; in others, they may be called in only when an impasse is reached. Different types of third-party negotiations include mediation, arbitration, conciliation, and consultation.

- Negotiating with individuals from different countries and cultures poses a number of issues. Showing knowledge about a person's culture is one way to establish rapport and respect with another negotiator.

YOU BE THE JUDGE COMMENT

LOWBALLING IN SALARY NEGOTIATIONS: HOW WOULD YOU HANDLE IT?

Because you think you're going to like the job itself, the organizational culture, and co-workers, it's worth trying to negotiate for a better starting salary. It wouldn't make sense to walk away at this point and start the process all over again at another organization (where the same thing could happen!). What's your next step? If you're annoyed and frustrated by the low initial offer, you might respond with a win–lose negotiation strategy by countering with a salary request of $40,000 or higher. This might work, but chances are the HR manager will perceive you as unreasonable or out of his or her price range and will not meet your demand. The negotiation will likely be concluded and the offer withdrawn.

Another approach to the HR manager's initial lowball offer of $30,000 is to use a win–win negotiation approach where you first explain how your skill set and education are appropriate for the job and that with time and effort, you envision making a meaningful contribution to the organization. Then, you can indicate that you heard the going rate for this position was between $35,000 and $40,000, and thus you would be willing to start at $37,500 (the midpoint). You can explain that the midpoint is fair because you already have some of the skills and the required energy to hit the ground running in the job (i.e., perform reasonably well soon after starting the job and getting to know the organization, co-workers, etc.), but will become even more productive over time as you gain experience in the position. Thus, if you and the HR manager agree to the starting salary of $37,500, it's a win–win for the organization and you as a candidate.

Review and Discussion Questions

1. What is the difference between functional and dysfunctional conflict? Can conflict that starts off as functional become dysfunctional? Can dysfunctional conflict be changed to functional?

2. Can you think of situations with which you are familiar that would have benefited from more intergroup conflict? How could additional conflict have improved the situation?

3. When intergroup conflict occurs, changes take place within and between conflicting groups. What are these changes? Which changes generally are positive? Which are negative?

4. Is there a relationship between the level of intergroup conflict and organizational performance? How can an organization achieve optimal levels of conflict?

5. What are some of the major reasons intergroup conflict occurs? In your personal experience, what is the most frequent reason?

6. If you were about to begin negotiating with a person from Brazil, what would you want to know about his cultural background? Would it make a difference in the knowledge you seek if the Brazilian negotiator were a woman? Discuss.

7. What are the possible consequences of dysfunctional conflict? Are some of these consequences more or less likely to occur in organizational conflict situations?

8. People handle conflict in different ways. Assume you are a team leader and two of your team members (who report to you) are trying to negotiate who will take the major share of the work on a new project. Both feel they are overworked already and neither one wants the additional responsibility. Assume one of the team members has a competing style of conflict resolution, while the other individual prefers a collaborative style. What do you think the outcome of this negotiation will be? Explain your answer.

9. What are the four elements that are typically part of all negotiations? Are there likely to be differences in these elements depending on whether the negotiations are of a win–win or a win–lose nature?

10. Think about the last time you had to negotiate something (e.g., a higher grade, the purchase of a new or used car, etc.). Which of the following negotiation tactics were used by you and/or the other party: good guy/bad guy, the nibble, joint problem solving, power of competition, or splitting the difference? Identify which tactic was introduced and explain how it was used.

Now how much do you know about managing conflict and negotiations?

6. "The nibble" and "splitting the difference" are both examples of _____.
   a. intergroup conflict
   b. team-building exercises
   c. negotiation tactics
   d. dysfunctional conflict

7. _____ interdependence requires no interaction between groups because each group can perform its tasks separately.
   a. Pooled
   b. Joint
   c. Collective
   d. Unique

8. Thinking back to the different approaches to conflict resolution, the _____ approach is when one group places maximum focus on meeting its own concerns.
   a. avoiding
   b. collaborating
   c. compromising
   d. dominating

9. True or false: The dominating approach to conflict resolution is appropriate to use when your group is certain it is right and where the benefit of a resolution outweighs the drawback of possible negative feelings by the dominated group.
   a. True
   b. False

10. Bringing outside individuals into the group, stimulating competition among groups, and using a devil's advocate form of programmed conflict are all ways of _____.
    a. making groups fight with each other
    b. stimulating constructive intergroup conflict
    c. forcing one group to dominate another group
    d. None of the above (a–c) are correct.

REALITY CHECK ANSWERS

Before	After
1. *d* 2. *b* 3. *c* 4. *a* 5. *a*	6. *b* 7. *a* 8. *d* 9. *a* 10. *b*
Number Correct	Number Correct
_____	_____

Exercise

Exercise 11.1: *Third-Party Conflict Resolution*

Purpose

To understand the criteria that third parties use when they intervene and attempt to resolve others' conflicts.

Introduction

In addition to being involved in their own conflicts, managers are often called upon to intervene and to settle conflicts between other people. The two activities in this section are designed to explore how third parties may enter conflicts for the purpose of resolving them and to practice one very effective approach to intervention. In the exercise, you will read about a manager who has a problem deciding how to intervene in a dispute, and you will discuss this case in class.

Step 1: 5 Minutes

Read "The Seatcor Manufacturing Company" case.

The Seatcor Manufacturing Company

You are senior vice president of operations and chief operating officer of Seatcor, a major producer of office furniture. Joe Gibbons, your subordinate, is vice president and general manager of your largest desk assembly plant. Joe has been with Seatcor for 38 years and is two years away from retirement. He worked his way up through the ranks to his present position and has successfully operated his division for five years with a marginally competent staff. You are a long-standing personal friend of Joe's and respect him a great deal. However, you have always had an uneasy feeling that Joe has surrounded himself with minimally competent people by his own choice. In some ways, you think he is threatened by talented assistants.

Last week you were having lunch with Charles Stewart, assistant vice president and Joe's second-in-command. Upon your questioning, it became clear that he and Joe were engaged in a debilitating feud. Charles was hired last year, largely at your insistence. You had been concerned for some time about who was going to replace Joe when he retired, especially given the lack of really capable managerial talent on Joe's staff. Thus, you prodded Joe to hire your preferred candidate—Charles Stewart. Charles is rela-

tively young (39), extremely tenacious and bright, and a well-trained business school graduate. From all reports, he is doing a good job in his new position.

Your concern centers around a topic that arose at the end of your lunch. Charles indicated Joe Gibbons is in the process of completing a five-year plan for his plant. This plan is to serve as the basis for several major plant reinvestment and reorganization decisions that would be proposed to senior management. According to Charles, Joe Gibbons has not included Charles in the planning process. You had to leave lunch quickly and were unable to get much more information from Charles. However, he did admit that he was extremely disturbed by this exclusion and that his distress was influencing his work and probably his relationship with Joe.

You consider this a very serious problem. Charles will probably have to live with the results of any major decisions about the plant. More important, Joe's support is essential if Charles is to properly grow into his present and/or future job. Joe, on the other hand, runs a good ship and you do not want to upset him or undermine his authority. Moreover, you know Joe has good judgment; thus, he may have good reason for what he is doing. How would you proceed to handle this issue?

Step 2: 5 Minutes

Before discussing this case with anyone else, answer the following two questions:

1. Assume you were the senior vice president of operations. Exactly what would you do in this situation regarding the conflict between Joe and Charles?
2. Why would you take this action—i.e., what are your primary objectives by intervening in this way?

Step 3: 20–30 Minutes

The instructor will discuss this case with the entire class.

Step 4: 10–15 Minutes

The instructor will summarize the case discussion and present a framework for understanding how participants analyzed the case and decided to intervene.

Source: Developed by Roy J. Lewicki, The Ohio State University. Used with permission.

Exercise

Exercise 11.2 *World Bank: An Exercise in Intergroup Negotiation*

Step 1

The class is divided into two groups. The size of each group should be no more than 10. Those not in one of the two groups are designated as observers. However, groups should not have fewer than six members each. The instructor will play the role of the referee/banker for the World Bank.

Step 2

Read the World Bank Instruction Sheet.

Step 3

Each group or team will have 15 minutes to organize itself and plan strategy before beginning. Before the first round, each team must choose (*a*) two negotiators, (*b*) a representative, (*c*) a team recorder, and (*d*) a treasurer.

Step 4

The referee/banker will signal the beginning of round one and each following round and also end the exercise in about one hour.

Step 5

Discussion. In small groups or with the entire class, answer the following questions:

1. What occurred during the exercise?
2. Was there conflict? What type?
3. What contributed to the relationships among groups?
4. Evaluate the power, leadership, motivation, and communication among groups.
5. How could the relationships have been more effective?

World Bank General Instruction Sheet

This is an intergroup activity. You and your team are going to engage in a task in which money will be won or lost. *The objective is to win as much as you can.* Two teams are involved in this activity, and both teams receive identical instructions. After reading these instructions, your team has 15 minutes to organize itself and plan its strategy.

Each team represents a country. Each country has financial dealings with the World Bank. Initially, each country contributed $100 million to the World Bank. Countries may have to pay further monies or may receive money from the World Bank in accordance with regulations and procedures described below under sections headed Finances and Payoffs.

Each team is given 20 cards. These are your *weapons.* Each card has a marked side (X) and an unmarked side. The marked side of the card signifies that the weapon is armed. Conversely, the blank side shows the weapon to be unarmed.

At the beginning, each team will place 10 of its 20 weapons in their armed positions (marked side up) and the remaining 10 in their unarmed positions (marked side down). These weapons will remain in your possession and out of sight of the other team at all times.

There will be *rounds* and *moves.* Each round consists of seven moves by each team. There will be two or more rounds in this simulation. The number of rounds depends on the time available. Payoffs are determined and recorded after each round.

1. A move consists of turning two, one, or none of the team's weapons from armed to unarmed status, or vice versa.
2. Each team has two minutes to move. There are 30-second periods between moves. At the end of two minutes, the team must have turned two, one, or none of its weapons from armed to unarmed status, or from unarmed to armed status. If the team fails to move in the allotted time, no change can be made in weapons status until the next move.
3. The length of the $2\frac{1}{2}$-minute period between the beginning of one move and the beginning of the next is fixed and unalterable.

Each new round of the experiment begins with all weapons returned to their original positions, 10 armed and 10 unarmed.

Finances

The funds you have contributed to the World Bank are to be allocated in the following manner:

$60 million will be returned to each team to be used as your team's treasury during the course of the decision-making activities.

$40 million will be retained for the operation of the World Bank.

Payoffs

1. *If there is an attack:*
   a. Each team may announce an attack on the other team by notifying the referee/banker during the 30 seconds following any two-minute period used to decide upon the move (including the seventh, or final, decision period in any round). The choice of each team during the decision period just ended counts as a move. An attack may not be made during negotiations.
   b. If there is an attack (by one or both teams), two things happen: (1) the round ends, and (2) the World Bank levies a penalty of $5 million for each team.
   c. The team with the greater number of armed weapons wins $3 million for each armed weapon it has over and above the number of armed weapons of the other team. These funds are paid directly from the treasury of the losing team to the treasury of the winning team. The referee/bankers will manage this transfer of funds.
2. *If there is no attack:* At the end of each round (seven moves), each team's treasury receives from the World Bank $2 million for each of its weapons that is at that point unarmed, and each team's treasury pays to the World Bank $2 million for each of its weapons remaining armed.

Negotiations

Between moves, each team has the opportunity to communicate with the other team through its negotiators.

Either team may call for negotiations by notifying the referee/bankers during any of the 30-second periods between decisions. A team is free to accept or reject any invitation to negotiate.

Negotiators from both teams are *required* to meet after the third and sixth moves (after the 30-second period following that move, if there is no attack).

Negotiations can last no longer than three minutes. When the two negotiators return to their teams, the two-minute decision period for the next move begins once again.

Negotiators are bound only by: (*a*) the three-minute time limit for negotiations, and (*b*) their required appearance after the third and sixth moves. They are otherwise free to say whatever is necessary to benefit themselves or their teams. The teams similarly are not bound by agreements made by their negotiators, even when those agreements are made in good faith.

Special Roles

Each team has 15 minutes to organize itself to plan team strategy. During this period before the first round begins, each team must choose persons to fill the following roles. (Each team must have each of the following roles, which can be changed at any time by a decision of the team.)

- *Negotiators*—activities stated above.
- A *representative*—to communicate team decisions to the referee/bankers.
- A *recorder*—to record the moves of the team and to keep a running balance of the team's treasury.
- A *treasurer*—to execute all financial transactions with the referee/bankers.

Source: Adapted from John E. Jones and J. William Pfeiffer, eds., *The 1975 Annual Handbook for Group Facilitators* (San Diego, CA: University Associates, 1975).

Case

Case 11.1: *Conflict at Walt Disney Company: A Distant Memory?*

Even in the midst of a severe recession that has depressed tourism and a digital revolution in the media business, Disney is faring better than many of its rival companies. Although spending at its theme parks is down and fewer people are buying DVDs of recently released Disney movies (e.g., *Bolt* and *Beverly Hills Chihuahua*), Disney has positioned itself well to ride out the recession by having a broad mix of businesses in its portfolio. For example, Disney's sports cable network, ESPN, and ABC Family and Disney channels have reported an increase in operating profits in 2009. The creation and marketing of well-known franchises such as the Jonas Brothers is helping to fuel the company's success. The Jonases have already performed onstage to over a million people, sold over 750,000 copies of a book, starred in their own TV show on the Disney Channel, and will star in an upcoming full-length movie. Also, in an attempt to capture a larger share of the growing online viewer market, Disney recently bought an equity stake in Hulu, the online video platform. In addition, the Disney Pixar creative partnership (Disney bought Pixar) is continuing to produce popular and profitable animated movies such as *Wall-E* and *Up*.

To what degree have these business decisions been successful? Disney was ranked 67th in the Fortune 500 list of largest companies in 2008. Also, it surpassed other media companies, including Time Warner and News Corp., in terms of its stock performance and return on invested capital. Disney has become the largest media conglomerate in the world with a market value of about $40 billion.

Who has been the driving force behind many of these business decisions? Robert ("Bob") Iger took over as CEO in 2005. Known to many as "hardworking and likable," Iger has not only had to make a series of important business decisions regarding Disney's current businesses and future direction, but he has also had to repair several important relationships that the former CEO, Michael Eisner, strained during the later stage of his 22-year tenure.

Disney's controversial ex-CEO, Eisner, was credited with helping to turn around Disney in

the 1980s and once again making it into a formidable American company. In the mid-1990s, Eisner astutely guided the company to add Capital Cities/ABC and ESPN to its theme park and film businesses. Following these and other well-received decisions, Eisner's abrasive style and tendency toward micromanagement led to a series of public disputes and feuds with key players in the Disney world. Eisner fought with Miramax founders Harvey and Bob Weinstein over the financial details related to Disney's purchase of Miramax films. Eisner and Steve Jobs, then CEO of animated film producer Pixar, bumped heads several times. While testifying in front of Congress about movie piracy, Eisner made some negative comments about Apple Computer (of which Jobs is also CEO). Jobs took this jab personally and did not forgive Eisner for making these comments. This feud eventually culminated with Jobs threatening to not renew the Disney–Pixar partnership after the release of *Cars* in 2006 if Eisner was still CEO of Disney. Eisner had a long-running dispute with two (former) influential members of Disney's Board of Directors, Roy Disney and Stanley Gold, both of whom were outspoken critics of Eisner and his management team. For several years, these long-standing board members repeatedly called for Eisner's resignation.

Soon after Iger took over as CEO at Disney in 2005, he reached out and reconciled the company's differences with Roy Disney and Stanley Gold. They agreed to cease their "SaveDisney" campaign and work cooperatively with Iger. The dispute with the Weinstein bothers was resolved by making a settlement payment of $100 million (Disney kept the Miramax name and film library estimated at a worth of $2 billion). Iger repaired the relationship with Steve Jobs and Pixar, ultimately paving the way for Disney to pay $7.4 billion in stock to acquire Pixar Animation Studios in 2006 and adding Steve Jobs to the Disney Board of Directors.

In sum, the change in leadership at Disney from Michael Eisner to Bob Iger seems to have been a prudent one. Iger and his management team have made a series of good business decisions while systematically repairing key relationships that were strained during Eisner's reign as CEO.

Questions

1. How would you describe the conflict between Michael Eisner and the Weinstein brothers, the two board members (Disney and Gold), and Steve Jobs? Was it functional or dysfunctional?

2. Think back to the stages of conflict described in this chapter. Which stage best described the conflict between Eisner and Jobs? Was it perceived, felt, or manifest?

3. Which of the following best describes Michael Eisner's and Bob Iger's approaches to resolving conflict: dominating, problem solving, avoiding, or accommodating? Explain.

4. To what degree do you think Iger's calmer and less confrontational approach to running Disney has helped the company position itself to survive a major economic recession?

Sources: Written by Robert Konopaske of Texas State University and adapted from Matthew Garrahan, "Box Office Flops and Weak DVD Sales Hit Disney," *Financial Times,* May 6, 2009, p. 17; Matthew Garrahan, "Disney Succumbs to Recessionary Forces with Steep Falls in Profits," *Financial Times,* February 4, 2009, p. 13; Richard Siklos, "Bob Iger Rocks Disney," *Fortune,* January 19, 2009, p. 80; Meredith Downes, Gail S. Russ, and Patricia A. Ryan, "Michael Eisner and His Reign at Disney," *Journal of the International Academy of Case Studies* 13, no. 4 (2007), p. 79–87; Patricia Sellers, "Disney's Mr. Calm Unreels Miramax," *Fortune,* March 21, 2005, p. 30; and Christopher Parkes, "Eisner to Sever All Ties with Walt Disney," *Financial Times,* September 21, 2004, p. 33.

CHAPTER TWELVE

Power, Politics, and Empowerment

Learning Objectives

After completing Chapter 12, you should be able to:

- **Distinguish** between *influence* and *power*.
- **Identify** five interpersonal power bases.
- **Describe** three forms of structural power.
- **Discuss** the concepts of *powerlessness* and *empowerment*.
- **Identify** the contingencies that influence subunit power.

- **Explain** what is meant by the term *illusion of power*.
- **Describe** several frequently used influence tactics.
- **Discuss** the criteria for determining ethical behavior.
- **Identify** the considerations involved in using power effectively.

Power is a pervasive part of the fabric of organizational life.[1] Managers and nonmanagers use it. They manipulate power to accomplish goals and, in many cases, to strengthen their own positions. A person's success or failure in using or reacting to power is determined largely by understanding power, knowing how and when to use it, and being able to anticipate its probable effects.[2] The purpose of this chapter is to examine power and its uses in organizations. We will look at sources (bases) of power, how power is used, and the relationship between power and organizational politics.

The Concept of Power

The study of power and its effects is important to understanding how organizations operate. It is possible to interpret every interaction and every social relationship in an organization as involving power.[3] How organizational subunits and individuals are controlled is related to the issue of power and influence. The terms *power* and *influence* are frequently used interchangeably in the management literature; however, there is a subtle, yet important, difference between them. **Influence** is a transaction in which person B is induced by person A to behave in a certain way. For example, if an employee works overtime at the boss's request, that employee has been influenced by the boss.

Like influence, power involves a relationship between two people. Robert Dahl, a political scientist, captures this important relational focus when he defines power as saying "A has power over B to the extent that he can get B to do something B would not otherwise do."[4] What is the difference between this definition of power and our earlier definition of influence? **Power** represents the capability to get someone to do something; influence is the exercise of that capability. Another way of stating the distinction is to say that power is the potential to influence, while influence is power in action. Thus you

influence
Transaction in which person B is induced by person A to behave in a certain way.

power
The capability to get someone to do something.

How much do you know about power, politics, and empowerment?

1. Having influence over others (e.g., subordinates) based on the position within the organization that person holds is known as _____ power.
   a. expert
   b. intense
   c. coercive
   d. legitimate

2. True or false: Referent power is based on a subordinate's liking of a supervisor who provides the subordinate with important and meaningful work assignments.
   a. True
   b. False

3. True or false: Two of the reasons empowerment is not a universally accepted practice within all organizations is: (1) not everyone wants to be empowered and (2) some employees are not able to make responsible decisions.
   a. True
   b. False

4. An example of coping with uncertainty that can ultimately lead to your department acquiring more power within the company is _____.
   a. being located at the center of the organization
   b. preventing market share decline by developing new products
   c. possessing employees who have the only talent to complete the job
   d. None of the above (a–c) are correct.

5. Milgram's experiment on obedience revealed that 65 percent of participants in his study were willing to administer _____ shocks when asked to do so by the experimenter even though screams could be heard coming from the nearby booth where subjects were allegedly receiving the administered shocks.
   a. moderate
   b. very strong
   c. intense
   d. XXX (most severe)

may have power (the capacity to influence) but not use it; on the other hand, you cannot influence anyone (induce certain behavior in another person) without power.

We frequently speak of someone having power over someone else. While this is correct, it is important to stress that power is not an attribute of a particular person. Rather, it is an aspect of the relationship that exists between two (or more) people. No individual or group can have power in isolation; power must exist in relation to some other person or group. If A has power over B, it is, in part, because B is willing for that to be an aspect of the relationship between them. If and when B no longer desires that to be part of the relationship with A, A will no longer have power over B and no longer be able to influence B's behavior. Thus, *obtaining, maintaining,* and *using* power are all essential to influencing the behavior of people in organizational settings.

Some power relationships in organizations are *symmetrical.* This means that both parties are equal, or have the same amount of power. Other power relationships are *asymmetrical,* meaning one person in the relationship has more power than the other. Symmetry is a property that can change over time, as a person or group gains or loses power.[5] To understand how power can shift, it is important to know where power is obtained.

Where Does Power Come From?

Power is obtained in a variety of ways in an organization. Since power facilitates the organization's adaptation to its environment, the people and groups within the organization that are able to assist in that adaptation are the ones that will hold power. Two important categories of power in an organization are *interpersonal* and *structural*. Within each of these two categories are several specific sources of power. Let's look at these in some detail.

Interpersonal Power

In what is considered a classic essay in the management and organizational behavior literature, John French and Bertram Raven suggested five interpersonal sources, or bases, of power: legitimate, reward, coercive, expert, and referent.[6] As we shall see, these sources of power are not equally available to all organizational members.

Legitimate Power

legitimate power
Capacity to influence derived from the position of a manager in the organizational hierarchy. Subordinates believe that they "ought" to comply.

authority
The ability to influence others based on the perceived power of one's position and role within an organization.

Legitimate power refers to a person's ability to influence others because of the position within the organization that person holds. Legitimate or position power, as it is sometimes called, is derived from the position itself. That is, the organization has given to an individual occupying a particular position the right to influence—command— certain other individuals. This formal power is what we call **authority**. Orders from a manager in an authority position are followed because the manager has the legitimate power to command certain subordinates in lower positions. Not following orders subjects the offender to disciplinary action just as not following society's legal directives subjects one to disciplinary action in the form of arrest and penalty. Organizational authority has the following characteristics:

1. *It is invested in a person's position.* An individual has authority because of the position she holds, not because of any specific personal characteristics.
2. *It is accepted by subordinates.* The individual in a legal authority position exercises authority and can gain compliance because he or she has a legitimate right.
3. *Authority is used vertically.* Authority flows from the top down in the hierarchy of an organization.

Possessing legitimate power, or authority, does not mean that all orders will be followed by those who are subordinate to the individual in authority. For a subordinate to comply with an order from a superior requires that the order fall within the subordinate's zone of indifference. The term *zone of indifference* may be explained as follows: If all possible orders that might be directed to an individual from a superior were arranged in the order of their acceptability to the individual, some would be clearly acceptable while others might be clearly unacceptable. For example, a request by a manager that a subordinate complete her expense report might be an acceptable order. It would lie within her zone of indifference; that is, she is relatively indifferent to the request as far as the question of her boss's authority is concerned.

However, if the boss were to request that she record expenses she did not incur, or that she otherwise "pad" the expense report, such a request might well fall outside her zone of indifference. She may elect not to comply because she is no longer indifferent with respect to such an order. A person's zone of indifference may be wider or narrower depending on a number of factors such as the extent to which the boss has a source of power other than authority.

Reward Power

reward power
An influence over others based on hope of reward.

Reward power is based on a person's ability to reward a follower for compliance. It occurs when someone possesses a resource that another person wants and is willing to exchange that resource in return for certain behavior. Reward power is used to back up the use of legitimate power. If followers value the rewards or potential rewards the manager can provide (recognition, a good job assignment, a pay raise, opportunity to attend a training program, etc.), they may respond to orders, requests, and directions. Note, however, that if what a manager is offering as a reward has no value to an individual, it will not likely influence behavior.

Coercive Power

coercive power
Influence over others based on fear.

The opposite of reward power is **coercive power,** power to punish. Followers may comply out of fear. A manager may block a promotion or criticize a subordinate for poor performance. These practices and the fear they will be used are coercive power. Of course, one need not be in a position of authority to possess coercive power. For example, fear of rejection by co-workers for not complying with what they want represents coercive power even though one's co-workers have no formal authority.

Expert Power

expert power
Capacity of influence related to some expertise, special skill, or knowledge.

A person has **expert power** when he or she possesses special expertise that is highly valued. Experts have power even when their formal position in the organizational hierarchy is low. A person may possess expertise on technical, administrative, or personal matters. The salesperson who has a knack for landing new accounts, the software developer who always has an elegant solution for a program's bugs, the college dean who consistently raises the most money—all have enhanced ability to influence others because of their special expertise. The more difficult it is to replace the expert, the greater degree of expert power he or she possesses. Expert power is not unlimited, however; occasionally, individuals' expertise does not bestow upon them as much power as they believe it does. Expert power is a personal characteristic, while legitimate, reward, and coercive power are largely prescribed by the organization.

Referent Power

referent power
Power based on a subordinate's identification with a charismatic superior.

Many individuals identify with and are influenced by a person because of the latter's personality or behavioral style. The charisma of the person is the basis of **referent power.** A person with charisma is admired because of his or her characteristics. The strength of a person's charisma is an indication of his or her referent power. *Charisma* is a term that is often used to describe politicians, entertainers, or sports figures. Some managers are regarded as extremely charismatic by their subordinates. Jack Welch, former CEO at General Electric, and Steve Jobs, CEO of Apple, are examples of charismatic leaders. Certain aspects of charismatic leadership will be discussed in more detail in Chapter 15.

The five sources of interpersonal power can be divided into two major categories: organizational and personal. Legitimate, reward, and coercive power are primarily prescribed by the organization, the position, or specific interaction patterns. A person's legitimate power can be changed by transferring the person, rewriting the job description, or reducing the power by restructuring the organization. Expert and referent power are very personal. They are the result of an individual's personal expertise or style and, as such, are grounded in the person and not the organization.

These five types of interpersonal power are not independent of each other; a person can use these power sources effectively in various combinations. Some research has suggested, for example, that when subordinates believe a manager's coercive power is increasing, they also perceive a drop in reward, referent, and legitimate power. Finally, different power sources are not always equally well received. Some types of power are more likely to engender positive responses than are others. The nearby Management Pointer provides further information.

Structural Power

Power is frequently prescribed by structure within the organization. Structural sources of power result from the nature of the organizational social system rather than from attributes of an individual.[7] The structure of an organization is the control mechanism by which the organization is governed. In the organization's structural arrangements, decision-making discretion is allocated to various positions. Also, the structure greatly affects the patterns of communication and the flow of information within the system. Thus, organizational structure creates formal power and authority by specifying certain individuals to perform specific tasks and make certain decisions. Structure also significantly impacts informal power through its effect on information and communication flows within the system.

An example will help illustrate these concepts. At Bank of America, individuals in loan officer positions possess formal power and authority (e.g., the power to reject loan applications) by virtue of the role they play within the structure of the bank. Customer service managers perform different roles and, as such, they have different types of formal power and authority (e.g., the power to give a customer a refund for a bounced-check service fee). The power these employees possess is bestowed upon them by the organizational structure of the bank. In addition, both loan officers and customer service managers can develop their informal power by being plugged into the flow of information within the bank's system.

Every organization has its own unique structure and, as such, power will be distributed in different ways. Organizations with very few levels of management between the customer and the top leadership are likely to see a more balanced distribution of power among their employees than are traditional multilevel organizations with several layers of management.

We have already discussed how formal position is associated with power and authority. Certain rights, responsibilities, and privileges accrue from a person's position. Other forms of structural power exist, however, because of resources, decision making, and information.[8]

Management Pointer

SUBORDINATE RESPONSES TO DIFFERENT POWER SOURCES

All things being equal, subordinates respond differently to different types of power. When using power, keep the following generalizations about the five sources of interpersonal power in mind:

1. The use of *legitimate* or *reward* power will typically result in compliance. Compliance means that subordinates will obey your requests, but are unlikely to exert more than the minimal effort necessary.

2. The use of *coercive* power may result in resistance. Resistance means that subordinates may only pretend to comply with your requests, and they may openly resist.

3. The use of *expert* or *referent* power frequently results in commitment. Commitment means subordinates are likely to exert high levels of effort to accomplish what you ask, perhaps even exceeding what you requested.

Remember these are general findings, and each situation is different. Nonetheless, this suggests that even when you have the authority (legitimate power) to order something done, an expert- or referent-based influence attempt is likely to achieve better results.

Resources

Kanter argues quite convincingly that power stems from (1) access to resources, information, and support, and (2) the ability to get cooperation in doing necessary work.[9] Power occurs when a person has open channels to resources—money, human resources, technology, materials, customers, and so on. In organizations, vital resources

GOOGLE IN CHINA: 'DO NO EVIL'?

In an attempt to influence the powerful forces of economic and social change, leaders in the Chinese government are exerting control over companies that provide Internet services in China. In January 2006, Google launched a censored version of its search engine (www.google.cn) in mainland China. As part of the agreement to permit Google access to the potentially massive market of Internet users, the Chinese government required that Google restrict certain types of information from Chinese users when certain keyword searches are performed. For example, when the term *Chinese government corruption* is entered into the U.S. version of the Google search engine, 1,830,000 hits are recorded. In contrast, when the same search term is entered into the Chinese version of the Google search engine (www.google.cn), only 1,030,000 hits appear. As of the writing of this book, a Chinese user will receive only 56 percent of the search term hits compared to a user in the United States.

What does Google have to say about this controversial censorship practice? According to Andrew McLaughlin, Google's senior policy counsel: "While removing search results is inconsistent with Google's mission, providing no information . . . is more inconsistent with our mission." Also, Google believes that establishing a presence in the Chinese market is an important first step that could eventually lead to large profits for its shareholders while simultaneously getting more information to the average Chinese user.

Google is not alone. The Chinese government has also exerted considerable influence over other high-tech information providers. Microsoft removed some Chinese blogs and filtered such keywords as *democracy* on its China-based Web portal. Also, Yahoo! allegedly provided information to the Chinese government that resulted in the arrest and 10-year jail sentence of a man who e-mailed pro-democracy material.

Technology companies Google, Yahoo!, and Microsoft are trying to create a road map for doing business in countries like China that restrict free speech and freedom of expression. These companies have endorsed the Global Network Initiative, which encourages technology companies to protect users' personal information and privacy. The initiative also pushes companies to take a hard look at a country's track record in freedom of expression before investing there. However, some critics don't believe the Global Network Initiative goes far enough toward curbing rights abuses. For example, Google, Yahoo!, and Microsoft will still need to abide by China's strict local laws.

In sum, the power and influence of the Chinese government are evidenced by the manner in which companies such as Google, Microsoft, and Yahoo! are engaging in self-censorship in China. Whether this is fair or ethical is up to the leaders (and customers) of these companies to decide.

Sources: Adapted from Jessica E. Vascellaro, "Google, Yahoo, Microsoft Set Common Voice Abroad: Principles Aim to Define Conduct with Nations That Restrict Speech, Lack Privacy Protections and Censor Search Results," *The Wall Street Journal* (Eastern Edition), October 28, 2008, p. B7; "Special Report: The Party, the People and the Power of Cyber-Talk," *The Economist,* April 29, 2006, p. 28; Dan Nystedt, "Taiwan President Blasts Google, Yahoo on China," *Computerworld,* April 17, 2006, p. 14; Amy Schatz, "Tech Firms Defend China Web Policies," *The Wall Street Journal,* February 16, 2006, p. A3; and "Review and Outlook Editorial: G**gle in China," *The Wall Street Journal,* January 30, 2006.

are allocated downward along the lines of the hierarchy. The top-level manager has more power to allocate resources than do other managers further down the managerial hierarchy. The lower-level manager receives resources that are granted by top-level managers. To ensure compliance with goals, top-level managers (e.g., presidents, vice presidents, directors) allocate resources on the basis of performance and compliance. Thus, a top-level manager usually has power over a lower-level manager because the lower-level manager must receive resources from above to accomplish goals.

Decision-Making Power

The degree to which individuals or subunits (e.g., a department or a special project group) can affect decision making indicates the amount of power acquired. A person or subunit with power can influence how the decision-making process occurs, what alternatives are considered, and when a decision is made.[10] Individuals who influence a decision-making process and its outcomes may or may not have formal authority. For example, research has shown that Eleanor Roosevelt, spouse of President Franklin Delano Roosevelt, exerted informal political influence over Congress even though she was not an elected official.[11] She lacked formal authority but was adept at influencing certain decisions made by Congress. In other cases, individuals with formal authority have exerted decision-making power. When Richard J. Daley was mayor of Chicago, he was recognized as a power broker. He not only influenced the decision-making process, but he also had the power to decide which decisions would be given priority in the city council and when decisions would be made. He was a powerful politician because he was considered to be an expert at controlling each step in important decisions. Another example of the power of politicians is the Chinese government's censorship of U.S. information providers in China (see the Global OB).

Information Power

Knowledge is considered by some experts to be more powerful than any part or structure of an organization. *Knowledge* is defined as a conclusion or analysis derived from data and information.[12] Data are facts, statistics, and specifics. Information is the context in which data are placed.

Microsoft, Google, Walmart, Amazon, Nestlé, and Nokia did not become prominent, profitable companies because they were richer than Chrysler, General Foods, or Sears. They were able to utilize and leverage their intellectual capital more effectively. That is, these firms used the knowledge, information, experience, and creativity possessed by employees to gain a competitive advantage in their industries.

An excellent television commercial featuring Federal Express illustrates how knowledge and information have become valued assets in organizations. In the commercial a ranting, scowling boss rushes into a room to reprimand an employee about a package that he has been informed has not arrived on time. A complaining customer triggered the ranting. The boss continues blasting the employee as she taps on her computer's keyboard. The employee finally announces that her screen shows the package arrived and was signed for at a specific time. All of the employee's colleagues cheer her result. She had knowledge and information that disputed the boss's ranting. Employees and customers at Federal Express were able to track the package to the minute. The tracking (information) provides the knowledge about when the package was delivered.[13]

Having access to relevant and important knowledge information is power. Accountants generally do not have a particularly strong or apparent interpersonal power base in an organization. Rather, accountants have power because they control important information. Information is the basis for making effective decisions. Thus, those who possess information needed to make optimal decisions have power. The accountant's position in the organization structure may not accurately portray the amount of power that he or she wields. A true picture of a person's power is provided not only by the person's position but also by the person's access to relevant information.

A number of organizational situations can serve as the source of either power or powerlessness (not acquiring power). The powerful manager exists because he or she allocates required resources, makes crucial decisions, and has access to important information.[14] He or she is likely to make things happen. The powerless manager, however, lacks the resources, information, and decision-making prerogatives needed to be productive. Exhibit 12.1 presents some of the common symptoms and sources of powerlessness of first-line supervisors, staff professionals, and top-level managers. This exhibit indicates that a first-line manager, for example, may display a number of symptoms of powerlessness such as supervising very closely and not showing much concern about training or developing subordinates. If these symptoms persist, it is likely that the individual is powerless.

EXHIBIT 12.1   Symptoms and Sources of Powerlessness

Source: Reprinted by permission of the *Harvard Business Review*. Adapted from "Power Failures in Management Circuits," by Rosabeth Moss Kanter (July–August 1979), p. 73. Copyright © 1979 by the President and Fellows of Harvard College; all rights reserved.

Position	Symptoms	Sources
First-line supervisors (e.g., manager)	Supervise too closely; fail to train subordinates; not sufficiently oriented to the management team; inclined to do the job themselves	Routine, rule-minded jobs: limited lines of communication; limited advancement opportunities for themselves and their subordinates
Staff professionals (e.g., corporate lawyer, personnel/human resources specialist)	Create islands and set themselves up as experts; use professional standards as basis for judging work that distinguishes them from others; resist change and become conservative risk takers	Their routine tasks are only adjuncts to real line job; blocked career advancement replaced by outside consultants for nonroutine work
Top-level managers (e.g., chief executive officer, vice president)	Short-term horizon; top-down communication systems emphasized; reward followers to think like the manager, do not welcome bearers of bad news	Uncontrollable lines of supply; limited or blocked lines of information about lower managerial levels; diminished lines of support because of challenges to legitimacy

Empowerment

The chief of the Los Angeles Police Department directs approximately 10,000 sworn officers, 3,000 civilian employees, and an annual budget in excess of $1 billion. By any definition it is a powerful position. During his six years in the job, William Bratton vigorously fought crime in Los Angeles and instilled this passion in the officer ranks of the LAPD. Promoting only those commanders who shared his vision of crime reduction, Bratton's ideas, policies, and legacy led to a 41 percent drop in homicides and a 33 percent decrease in other major crimes in Los Angeles from 2002 to 2008.[15] His previous position as New York City police commissioner from 1993 to 1998 resulted in a similar remarkable reduction in violent crime.[16] He didn't accomplish that, however, because he had amassed a great deal of power; rather, he accomplished it because he gave a great deal of his power away by pushing decision-making authority far down the organizational hierarchy. He *empowered* officers at the precinct to take actions that previously could only be done at the commissioner's office level.[17] **Empowerment** has been defined by Conger and Kanungo as "a process of enhancing feelings of self-efficacy among organizational members through the identification of conditions that foster powerlessness and through their removal by both formal organizational practices and informal techniques of providing efficacy information."[18]

empowerment
Encouraging and/or assisting individuals and groups to make decisions that affect their work environments.

Despite the commonsense appeal of empowering employees, empowerment is not universally embraced for a number of reasons, such as:

1. Managers fear the loss of power, control, and authority.
2. Employees are not able to make responsible decisions.
3. Empowering employees was attempted before and it failed.
4. Sharing proprietary information means leaking ideas, plans, and knowledge to competitors.
5. Not everyone wants to be empowered. Those resisting empowerment become isolates, misfits, and not team players in the minds and perceptions of advocates of empowerment.[19]

Despite the skepticism and resistance inherent in the five reasons above, learning to leverage empowerment as a means to strengthen the capabilities and commitment of employees is one of the most important challenges facing managers today.[20] The empowerment process is presented in a staged sequence within organizations. The first stage involves identifying the conditions existing in the organization that lead to feelings of powerlessness on the part of organizational members. These conditions could find their origin in organizational factors (such as poor communications or highly centralized resources), management styles (such as authoritarianism), reward systems (nonmerit-based rewards, low incentive value rewards), or the nature of the jobs (low task variety, unrealistic performance goals).

The diagnoses completed in the first stage lead to the implementation of empowerment strategies and techniques in the second stage. Use of participative management, establishing goal-setting programs, implementing merit-based pay systems, and job enrichment through redesign are examples of possible empowerment activities. The use of these programs is designed to accomplish two objectives in the third stage. One is simply to remove the conditions identified in the first stage as contributing to powerlessness. The second, and more important, is to provide self-efficacy information to subordinates. Self-efficacy describes a belief in one's effectiveness. Individuals high in self-efficacy tend to be confident and self-assured and feel they are likely to be successful in whatever endeavors they undertake.

Receiving such information results in feelings of empowerment in the fourth stage. This is because increasing self-efficacy strengthens effort–performance expectancies. You will recall from the discussion of expectancy theory in Chapter 5 that this means increasing the perceived probability of successful performance, given effort. Finally, the enhanced empowerment feelings from stage four are translated into behaviors in the fifth and final stage. These behavioral consequences of empowerment include increased activity directed toward task accomplishment.

Thus, by helping organizational members feel more assured of their capability to perform well, and by increasing the linkages between effort and performance, empowerment can lead to what has been described as a "culture of contribution."[21] Such a culture can be found, for example, in Newfield Exploration, a New York Stock Exchange–listed oil and gas exploration company with a 2009 capital budget of $1.45 billion,[22] which has only two levels of management in the entire company. Because each employee has critical decision-making authority, everyone understands that the success of the company is in large measure dependent on the contribution they make. The company's success, in turn, directly affects the employees, since each employee is also an owner.

As we have already noted in previous chapters, organizations are increasingly relying on a variety of team structures to complete many work tasks. One benefit of team approaches is the increased empowerment of team members.[23] In the case of self-managed teams, for example, empowerment is fostered in at least two ways. First, additional formal decision-making control is delegated to the team. This

Management Pointer

INCREASING YOUR EFFECTIVENESS IN EMPOWERING OTHERS

1. Delegate authority, also. When you delegate responsibility, make certain you are also delegating authority to go along with it.

2. Be a "partner." Be prepared to give up your managerial "parent" role and assume a "partner" role.

3. Be supportive. Assure your subordinates through words and deeds that it is OK to make mistakes.

4. Share information. Empowered employees must have sufficient information to be able to see the "big picture."

5. Provide training opportunities. Encourage employees to develop skills to successfully perform new job responsibilities.

6. Provide constructive performance feedback. It is particularly important for newly empowered employees. Feedback enhances learning and can provide needed assurance that the job is being mastered.

empowers the team to make decisions and take actions that previously were reserved for—or at least required the approval of—a higher level. Second, because team members usually have broader responsibilities, they acquire additional skills, knowledge, and experiences. This increased expertise makes them more valuable to the organization, effectively increasing their influence. The Management Pointer on page 347 provides suggestions for successfully empowering subordinates.[24]

Interdepartmental Power

strategic contingency
An event or activity that is extremely important for accomplishing organizational goals.

The primary focus to this point has been on individual power and how it is obtained. However, it is also important to consider subunit or interdepartmental power. A subunit (business unit or strategic business unit) is a semiautonomous part of an overall organization that is a center for coordinated actions. Its organization is usually based on a product line or product lines and it competes against specific competitors. Subunit power is the focus of the strategic contingency theory developed by Hickson. A **strategic contingency** is an event that is extremely important for accomplishing organizational goals.[25] Crozier, a French sociologist, provided insight into the idea of strategic contingencies. He studied the relationships between workers in the production and maintenance departments of French tobacco-processing plants. Crozier found that the production workers enjoyed job security because of tenure, were protected against unfair disciplinary action, and were not replaced or transferred arbitrarily. The production workers were less skilled than the maintenance workers. The maintenance workers were highly skilled and were recruited and selected only after going through a rigorous screening process.

The production workers were dependent on the maintenance workers. This power differential was explained in terms of the control exercised by the maintenance workers over an important contingency. If machines were shut down, the entire plant came to a halt. Efficiently functioning machines were needed to accomplish output goals. Since the maintenance workers, at the request of the production workers, repaired machines that were down, they possessed significant power.

When machines were down, the job performance of the production workers suffered. Stoppages totally disrupted the workflow and the output of the production workers. Crozier proposed that the maintenance workers controlled a strategically contingent factor in the production process. Crozier's study provided clear evidence of subunit power differences. The study also stimulated other studies that eventually resulted in a strategic contingencies explanation of power differences.[26]

Using the work of Crozier and Hickson and their associates, it is possible to develop a concise explanation of strategic contingencies. The model presented in Exhibit 12.2 suggests that subunit power, the power differential between subunits, is influenced by (1) the degree of ability to cope with uncertainty, (2) the centrality of the subunit, and (3) the substitutability of the subunit.

Coping with Uncertainty

Unanticipated events can create problems for any organization or subunit. It is, therefore, the subunits most capable of coping with uncertainty that typically acquire power. There are three types of coping activities. First is *coping by prevention.* Here a subunit works at reducing the probability that some difficulty will arise. One example of a coping technique is designing a new product to prevent lost sales because of new competition in the marketplace.

EXHIBIT 12.2
**A Strategic
Contingency Model of
Subunit Power**

Sources: This figure is based
on the detailed research work
conducted by D.J. Hickson,
C.R. Hinnings, C.A. Lee, R.E.
Schneck, and J.M. Pennings,
"A Strategic Contingency
Theory of Intraorganizational
Power," *Administrative Science
Quarterly,* June 1971, pp.
216–29; and C.R. Hinnings,
D.J. Hickson, J.M. Pennings,
and R.E. Schneck, "Structural
Conditions of Intraorganiza-
tional Power," *Administrative
Science Quarterly,* March
1974, pp. 22–44.

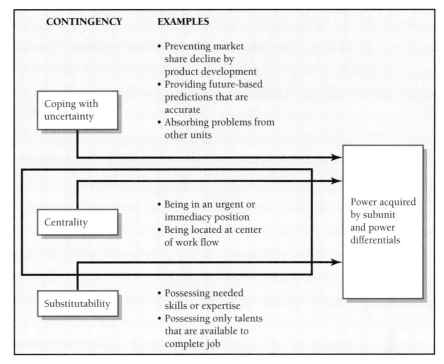

Second is *coping by information.* The use of forecasting is an example. Possessing timely forecasting information enables a subunit to deal with such events as competition, strikes, shortages of materials, and shifts in consumer demand. Planning departments conducting forecasting studies acquire power when their predictions prove accurate.

Third is *coping by absorption.* This coping approach involves dealing with uncertainty as it impacts the subunit. For example, one subunit might take a problem employee from another subunit and attempt to retrain and redirect that employee. This is done as a favor so that the other subunit will not have to go through the pain of terminating or continuing to put up with the employee. The subunit that takes in the problem employee gains the respect of other subunits, which results in an increase in power.

The relation of coping with uncertainty to power was expressed by Hickson as follows: "The more a subunit copes with uncertainty, the greater its power within the organization."[27]

Centrality

The findings of a number of research studies strongly suggest that centrality can be a significant source of subunit power.[28] The subunits that are most central to the flow of work in an organization typically acquire power. No subunit has zero centrality since all subunits are somehow interlinked with other subunits. A measure of centrality is the degree to which the work of the subunit contributes to the final output of the organization. Since a subunit is in a position to affect other subunits, it has some degree of centrality and therefore power.

Also, a subunit possesses power if its activities have a more immediate or urgent impact than those of other subunits. For example, Ben Taub General Hospital is a major public hospital in Houston. The emergency and trauma treatment subunit is extremely important and crucial, and it contains significant power within the hospital.

Failures in this subunit could result in the death of emergency victims. On the other hand, the psychiatric subunit does important work but not of the crucial and immediate type. Therefore, it has significantly less subunit power than the emergency and trauma treatment subunit.

Substitutability

substitutability
The ability of various work units to perform the activities of other work units.

Substitutability refers to the ability of other subunits to perform the activities of a particular subunit. If an organization has or can obtain alternative sources of skill, information, and resources to perform the job done by a subunit, the subunit's power will be diminished. Training subunits lose power if training work can be done by line managers or outside consultants. On the other hand, if a subunit has unique skills and competencies (e.g., the maintenance workers in Crozier's study discussed earlier) that would be hard to duplicate or replace, this tends to increase the subunit's power over other subunits.

Hickson et al. capture the importance of substitutability power when they propose that the lower the substitutability of the activities of a subunit, the greater is its power within the organization.[29]

The Illusion of Power

Admittedly, some individuals and subunits have vast amounts of power to get others to do things the way they want them done. However, there are also illusions of power. Imagine that one afternoon your supervisor asks you to step into his office. He starts the meeting: "You know we're really losing money using that Beal stamping machine. I'd like you to do a job for the company. I want you to destroy the machine and make it look like an accident." Would you comply with this request? After all, this is your supervisor, and he is in charge of everything—your pay, your promotion opportunities, your job assignments. You might ask yourself, "Does my supervisor have this much power over me?"

Where a person or subunit's power starts and stops is difficult to pinpoint. You might assume that the supervisor in the hypothetical example has the specific power to get someone to do this unethical and illegal "dirty work." However, even individuals who seemingly possess only a little power can influence others. A series of studies conducted by Milgram focused on the illusion of power. In these studies, subjects who had been voluntarily recruited thought they were administering electrical shocks of varying intensity to other subjects.[30] Ostensibly the experiment was designed to study the effects of punishment on learning. In reality, the studies focused on obedience to authority. Exhibit 12.3 displays the surprising results.

At the experimenter's direction, 26 of 40 subjects, or 65 percent, continued to increase the intensity of the shocks they thought they were administering to another person all the way to the maximum voltage even though the control panel indicated increasing voltage dosages as "intense," "extreme," "danger," and "severe shock." Additionally, screams could be heard coming from the booth, and the subject allegedly receiving the shock begged the experimenter to stop the project. Despite this, and even though the subjects were uncomfortable administering the shocks, they continued. Milgram stated:

> I observed a mature and initially poised businessman enter the laboratory, smiling and confident; within 20 minutes he was reduced to a twitching, stuttering wreck, who was rapidly approaching a point of nervous collapse . . . yet he continued to respond to every word of the experimenter and obeyed to the end.[31]

EXHIBIT 12.3
Results of Milgram's Classic Experiment on Obedience

Source: Based on descriptions and data presented in S. Milgram, "Behavioral Study of Obedience," *Journal of Abnormal and Social Psychology,* October 1963, pp. 371–78.

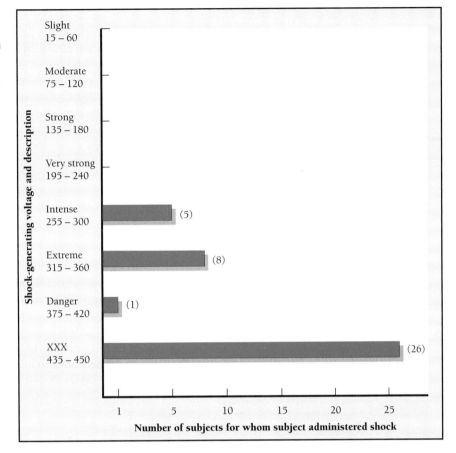

Why did the subjects obey the experimenter? Although the experimenter possessed no specific power over the subjects, he appeared to be a powerful person. He created an illusion of power. The experimenter, dressed in a white lab coat, was addressed by others as "doctor" and was very stern. The subjects perceived the experimenter as possessing legitimacy to conduct the study. The experimenter apparently did an excellent job of projecting the illusion of having power.

The Milgram experiments indicate that possessing power in a legitimate way is not the only way power can be exerted. Individuals who are perceived to have power may also be able to significantly influence others. Power is often exerted by individuals who have only minimal or no actual power. The "eye of the beholder" plays an important role in the exercise of power.

Jim Clark, an engineer, Stanford professor, and real estate developer, has created an almost cultlike illusion of power in Silicon Valley. His ideas and his involvement with Netscape, WebMD, and Silicon Graphics have helped reshape entire industries. He was the idea person behind each of these three companies. For example, at Silicon Graphics, Clark invented 3-D chips, which gave the firm a technological lead over other makers of high-priced workstations.[32] The chips allowed for the creation of the digital dinosaurs in the Oscar-winning hit movie *Jurassic Park.*

Clark grasped the commercial power of the Internet ahead of other geniuses. Few people had heard of a Web browser, which Clark's firm Netscape commercialized. Clark has taken his seemingly far-out ideas and has converted them into billions of dollars, making a lot of investors and employees very wealthy. His commercialization of ideas has created a halo about Clark. The illusion is that he has the Midas touch. A closer examination of his history and background illustrates a mystique and some myth surrounding Jim Clark.

Clark has experienced a variety of ups and downs as a result of being a player in the Internet revolution. For example, he has admitted to losing money in the formerly billion-dollar firm Healtheon. The company was created to bring the efficiencies of the Internet to the medical world. After a time, the company was folded into another one of Clark's ventures, WebMD. Clark also has experienced mixed results with his investments in other Internet firms, including an online photography Web site, Shutterfly, and a financial services company, myCFO.[33] Yet, Clark still has power to influence investors. The mention of his name in a deal creates a buzz and interest in being a part of the next Jim Clark idea and business.

Political Strategies and Tactics

Individuals and subunits continually engage in politically oriented behavior.[34] By politically oriented behavior we mean a number of things:

1. Behavior that usually is outside the legitimate, recognized power system.
2. Behavior that is designed to benefit an individual or subunit, often at the expense of the organization in general.
3. Behavior that is intentional and is designed to acquire and maintain power.

As a result of politically oriented behaviors, the formal power that exists in an organization often is sidetracked or blocked. In the language of organizational theory, political behavior results in the displacement of power.

Research on Politics

A number of studies have been conducted to explore political behavior and perceptions in organizations. A study that assessed the political skill of about 700 employees suggested that political skill can be accurately broken down into four distinct factors: social astuteness, interpersonal influence, networking ability, and apparent sincerity.[35] A related study found that of these four factors, social astuteness (i.e., being sensitive to others) is the strongest predictor of supervisor ratings and leadership effectiveness.[36] Being sensitive to the needs and feelings of others is an important survival skill in today's office environment.

Another study of 142 purchasing agents examined their political behavior. The job objective of the purchasing agents was to negotiate and fill orders in a timely manner. However, the purchasing agents also viewed their jobs as being a crucial link with the environment—competition, price changes, market shifts.[37] Thus, the purchasing agents considered themselves information processors. The vital link of the purchasing agents with the external environment placed them in conflict with the engineering department. As a result of the conflict, attempts to influence the engineering subunit were a regular occurrence.

This study discovered a variety of political tactics used by the purchasing agents. They included:

1. *Rule evasion.* Evading the formal purchase procedures in the organization.
2. *Personal-political.* Using friendships to facilitate or inhibit the processing of an order.
3. *Educational.* Attempting to persuade engineering to think in purchasing terms.

EXHIBIT 12.4 **Personal Characteristics of Effective Organizational Politicians**

Source: Adapted from R.W. Allen, D.L. Madison, L.W. Porter, P.A. Renwick, and B.T. Mayes, "Organizational Politics: Tactics and Characteristics of Its Actors," *California Management Review,* December 1979, p. 78.

Personal Characteristics	Combined Groups	Chief Executive Officers	Staff Managers	Supervisors
Articulate	30%	37%	39%	13%
Sensitive	30	50	21	17
Socially adept	20	10	32	17
Competent	17	10	21	21
Popular	17	17	11	24
Extroverted	16	17	14	17
Self-confident	16	10	21	17
Aggressive	16	10	14	24
Ambitious	16	20	25	4
Devious	16	13	14	21
Organization person	13	20	4	14
Highly intelligent	12	20	11	3
Logical	10	3	21	7

4. *Organizational.* Attempting to change the formal or informal interaction patterns between engineering and purchasing.

These political tactics, used by the purchasing agents to accomplish their goals, (1) were outside the legitimate power system, (2) occasionally benefited the purchasing agent at the expense of the rest of the organization, and (3) were intentionally developed so that more power was acquired by the purchasing agent.

Another study of political behavior was conducted in the electronics industry in Southern California. A total of 87 managers (30 chief executive officers, 28 higher-level staff managers, and 29 supervisors) were interviewed and asked about a number of aspects of organizational political behavior.[38] Among other questions, the managers were asked to describe the personal characteristics of organizational members who were effective "politicians." These characteristics are presented in Exhibit 12.4, along with the percentage of each group of managers who thought the characteristic was associated with effective political behavior.

A total of 13 characteristics were identified as being important, headed by articulateness, sensitivity, and social adeptness. As Exhibit 12.4 shows, there was a fairly high level of agreement between the three levels of managers on what characteristics were regarded as important. There were, however, some exceptions. For example, supervisors saw *ambitiousness* as being far less-often associated with effective political behavior (4 percent) than did CEOs (20 percent) and staff managers (25 percent). On the other hand, many more staff managers (21 percent) than CEOs (3 percent) or supervisors (7 percent) thought being *logical* was a characteristic of effective political players. It is probably reasonable to conclude that some of the differences between the groups were attributable to different perspectives. It is also probably the case that different political behaviors were used at different levels within the organization.

Playing Politics

The managers in the study described above were aware of political behavior because it was part of their organizational experiences. As the researchers noted, the study was not designed to either praise or criticize organizational political behavior. Instead, it was intended to show that politics is a fact of organizational life. Politics and political behavior exist in every organization. In this section, we will briefly examine a couple of different ways that the study of political behavior, or "playing politics," has been approached in organizations. We will close the section with a look at one specific political strategy that is receiving a great deal of attention currently, *impression management.*

Game Playing

Political behavior in organizations has been described by many researchers in terms of game playing. Henry Mintzberg has identified 13 types of political games played in organizations.[39] These games, played at all organizational levels by both managers and nonmanagers, are intended to accomplish a variety of purposes. Games are played to (1) resist authority (the insurgency game); (2) counter the resistance to authority (the counterinsurgency game); (3) build power bases (the sponsorship game and coalition-building game); (4) defeat rivals (the line-versus-staff game); and (5) bring about organizational change (the whistle-blowing game).

Let's look at one of Mintzberg's games. The insurgency game is played to resist authority, and there are many different ways to play. For example, suppose a plant foreman is instructed to reprimand a particular worker for violating company policies. The reprimand can be delivered according to the foreman's feelings and opinions about its worth and legitimacy. If the reprimand is delivered in a halfhearted manner, accompanied by a sly wink, it will probably have an effect very different from what was expected. Insurgency in the form of not delivering the reprimand as expected by a higher authority would be difficult for that authority to detect and correct. Technically, the foreman followed orders. Practically, however, he resisted those orders.

Insurgency, along with the rest of Mintzberg's games, is practiced in all organizations. Games are played within and between subunits, and they are played by individuals who are sometimes representing themselves and sometimes representing their units. It is unrealistic to assume that game playing can be eliminated. Even in the most efficient, profitable, productive, and responsible organizations, political games are being played.

Political Influence Tactics

Influence is what playing politics is all about. Individuals and groups engage in political behavior to influence the perceptions or behaviors of other individuals and groups. Accordingly, the means or tactics used to accomplish this have been the focus of much research. One particularly interesting approach has been refined over a period of many studies by several different researchers.[40] This research stream has identified nine specific tactics used by individuals to influence their superiors, co-workers, and subordinates to do what they wanted them to do. These tactics are:

1. *Consultation.* Used to gain your support for a course of action by letting you participate in the planning for the action.
2. *Rational persuasion.* Used to convince you that a particular course of action is "logically" the best course because it is in your best interest.
3. *Inspirational appeals.* Used to gain support by appealing to your values or ideals, or by increasing your confidence that the desired course of action will be successful.
4. *Ingratiating tactics.* Used to create a sense of obligation because someone is doing something nice for you. Designed to make it difficult for you not to support the course of action desired by the ingratiator.

5. *Coalition tactics.* Used to gain your support by seeking the help of others to persuade you, or by using the support of others as an argument for you to also give your support.

6. *Pressure tactics.* Used to gain your support for a particular course of action through demands, intimidation, or threats.

7. *Legitimating.* Used to gain your support by claiming the authority to ask for your support, or by claiming that such support is consistent with organizational policies or rules.

8. *Personal appeals.* Used to appeal to your feelings of loyalty and friendship to gain your support.

9. *Exchange tactics.* Used to gain your support by the promise that you will receive a reward or benefit if you comply, or by reminding you of prior favors you must now reciprocate.

Not all these tactics are equally effective in bringing about desired results. Exhibit 12.5 shows the results from one study that assessed the effectiveness of each tactic. Over 500 cases involving the use of influence tactics were analyzed in terms of leading to one of three outcomes:

1. *Commitment* results when you agree internally with the decision, action, or request, are enthusiastic about it, and are likely to exert unusual effort to carry out the request.

2. *Compliance* occurs when you carry out the request but are apathetic about it and make only a minimal effort to do it.

3. *Resistance* results when you are opposed to the request and try to avoid doing it.[41]

As can be seen from the exhibit, inspirational appeals and consultation were more effective than the rest of the tactics, with inspiration resulting in commitment 90 percent of the time it was used. On the other hand, legitimating, coalition, and pressure were less effective than the other tactics. Variables other than the type of influence tactic used can impact the success of the influence attempt. Even the use of a tactic such as pressure can sometimes result in commitment. Likewise, any tactic may result in resistance if it is used in an unskillful manner or if the request being made is clearly objectionable.[42]

In a meta-analysis of how influence tactics relate to work outcomes, researchers analyzed 31 studies that were conducted between 1973 and 2000.[43] These studies were

EXHIBIT 12.5
Frequency of Outcomes for the Use of Political Influence Tactics

Source: Adapted from Cecilia M. Falbe and Gary Yukl, "Consequences for Managers of Using Single Influence Tactics and Combinations of Tactics," *Academy of Management Journal,* August 1992, p. 647.

Influence Tactic	Outcomes		
	Resistance	Compliance	Commitment
1. Consultation	18%	27%	55%
2. Rational persuasion	47	30	23
3. Inspiration	0	10	90
4. Ingratiation	41	28	31
5. Coalition	53	44	3
6. Pressure	56	41	3
7. Legitimating	44	56	0
8. Personal appeals	25	33	42
9. Exchange	24	41	35

combined into one overall study to answer several questions related to employees' use of influence tactics:

1. Do influence tactics result in higher performance assessments from supervisors?
2. Do employees who use influence tactics receive more pay raises and promotions?
3. Which influence tactics are most effective?

The researchers reported that those individuals who use ingratiating behaviors and who use logic to convince others of a particular course of action have a greater chance of succeeding at their careers than do those who do not use those tactics. Ingratiating and rational persuasion tactics have a stronger impact in terms of higher performance assessments (as opposed to pay raises and promotions) because supervisors have control over the employee's performance assessment but often have little influence over pay raises and promotions. These latter outcomes are more related to the organization's financial situation and market conditions.

Interestingly, the researchers noted that an individual's use of pressure tactics resulted in both positive and negative outcomes. Their use had a negative effect on the individual's supervisory assessment but a positive effect on the employee's receipt of pay and promotions. It appears that individuals who aggressively seek out and ask for pay increases and promotions are more likely to receive them. However, those same behaviors are likely to lead the individual's supervisor to give lower performance assessments.

Impression Management

impression management
A political strategy that refers to actions individuals take to control the impressions that others form of them.

Impression management refers to the actions individuals take to control the impressions that others form of them.[44] Impression management is universal. Employers do it, as do employees; students do it with professors and professors do it with students; parents and children do it with each other. Research suggests that a significant part of behavior in organizations is motivated by the desire of organization members to be perceived by others in certain ways.[45] Virtually everyone makes a deliberate effort in some situations to create a desirable impression. Some of the political influence tactics discussed in the previous section represent attempts at impression management. Consultation, for example, is used to create the impression that you are participative and that you want, value, and respect input from the person you are trying to influence. Ingratiation is designed to project an impression of you as a nice, thoughtful, or friendly person.

Impression management has increasingly gained the attention of organizational researchers. The desire to present ourselves in the best possible light when the stakes are high is a widely held desire. Effective impression management can be quite useful. An obvious example is the use of impression management tactics during the employment interview.[46] It could be argued that at no time is successful impression management more important; if you fail to create a favorable impression, you're not likely to be offered the job!

self-promotion
An impression management tactic whereby individuals communicate their accomplishments to appear able and competent.

After reviewing 20 years of research on impression management behaviors, researchers found that effectively managing the way others see us is linked to a variety of favorable outcomes not just in job interviews, but also in performance appraisals and overall career success.[47] These researchers identified and organized 31 impression management tactics that can result in either good or bad effects to an individual's image.[48] For example, an employee might use **self-promotion** during an interview to receive a job offer. Alternatively, an employee who uses **intimidation** to convince his or her teammates to pursue a certain approach to a project is likely to hurt his or her image as a team player.

intimidation
An impression management tactic whereby individuals use threats and harassment to appear powerful.

Impression management does not necessarily imply that a *false* impression is being conveyed. Clearly, some impressions are designed to mislead. Creating blatantly false impressions, however, can damage your credibility and reputation.

Many impression management tactics are designed to emphasize the positive. Self-promotion, such as acclaiming your accomplishments, is an example. Flattering others is another example. Other impression management tactics may be aimed at reducing negatives. Providing an excuse for why you made a mistake, for example, may be designed to further the impression that the error was beyond your control. Or simply admitting responsibility for the mistake may be designed to demonstrate willingness to take responsibility. When ex–Attorney General Janet Reno accepted responsibility for the decision to launch the disastrous raid on the Branch Davidian complex in Waco, Texas, her stock soared because the public found it refreshing that someone in Washington was taking responsibility instead of blaming somebody else.

self-handicapping
Any action taken in advance of an outcome that is designed to provide either an excuse for failure or a credit for success.

One very effective impression management technique, self-handicapping, is designed to make the best of an as yet undetermined outcome. **Self-handicapping** refers to any action taken in advance of an outcome that is designed to provide either an excuse for failure or a credit for success. A self-handicap provides a persuasive causal explanation for potential failure, while setting the stage for the individual to receive more credit for success than would otherwise be the case.[49] For example, a quarterback who lets everyone know about his sore arm is not expected to have a good game. If he plays poorly, everyone attributes it to his sore arm rather than his ability or lack of effort; if he does well, he did so despite his handicap, suggesting truly extraordinary ability or effort. The employee who reports being up all night with a sick child the day of a scheduled presentation to management is another example. If the presentation goes poorly, there is a reason beyond the employee's control; if it goes well, the employee excelled under adverse conditions.

Ethics, Power, and Politics

Issues of power and politics often involve ethical issues as well. For example, if power is used within the formal boundaries of a manager's authority and within the framework of organizational policies, job description, procedures, and goals, it is really nonpolitical power and most likely does not involve ethical issues. When the use of power is outside the bounds of formal authority, policies, procedures, job descriptions, and organizational goals, it is political in nature. When this occurs, ethical issues are likely to be present. Some examples might include bribing government officials, lying to employees and customers, polluting the environment, and a general "ends justify the means" mentality. This chapter's You Be the Judge discusses whether business schools can teach ethics to their students.

Managers confront ethical dilemmas in their jobs because they frequently use power and politics to accomplish their goals. Each manager, therefore, has an ethical responsibility. Researchers have developed a framework that allows a manager to integrate ethics into political behavior. These researchers recommend that a manager's behavior must satisfy certain criteria to be considered ethical.[50]

1. *Utilitarian outcomes.* The manager's behavior results in optimization of satisfaction of people inside and outside the organization. In other words, it results in the greatest good for the greatest number of people.

2. *Individual rights.* The manager's behavior respects the rights of all affected parties. In other words, it respects basic human rights of free consent, free speech, freedom of conscience, privacy, and due process.

3. *Distributive justice.* The manager's behavior respects the rules of justice. It does not treat people arbitrarily but rather equitably and fairly.

What does a manager do when a potential behavior cannot pass the three criteria? The behavior may still be considered ethical in the particular situation if it passes the *criterion of overwhelming factors.* To justify the behavior, it must be based on tremendously overwhelming factors in the nature of the situation, such as conflicts among criteria (e.g., the manager's behavior yields both positive and negative results), conflicts within the criteria (e.g., a manager uses questionable means to achieve a positive result), or an inability to employ the first three criteria (e.g., the manager acts with incomplete or inaccurate information). The Organizational Encounter on page 360 presents a decision-tree approach to the application of these criteria.

With the increased emphasis on empowerment, ethical issues are even more prevalent. In an empowered organization where decisions are forced down to the lowest levels, employees need to understand the importance of being constantly aware of the ethical implications of what they do.[51] Many companies are instituting ethics training programs to assist newly empowered employees in making ethical decisions. For example, Best Buy provides annual ethics training to its 140,000 employees across the United States and Canada. After early experimentation, the company's chief ethics officer decided that newly hired administrative staff would receive ethics training via the traditional classroom approach during orientation, but retail store employees were given the option of learning the company's ethics policies via computer-based training.[52]

Using Power to Manage Effectively

Nothing gets done in any organization until someone makes it happen. Making the right things happen is what a manager's job is all about.[53] To be effective a manager must successfully influence the activities of other organizational members. As we pointed out at the start of this chapter, influence requires the exercise of power. To influence successfully, power must be used effectively. Organizational theorist and researcher Jeffrey Pfeffer has identified several important considerations in using power to manage effectively. We close this chapter with a look at Pfeffer's conclusions in this regard:[54]

Recognize that there are multiple interests in nearly every organization. Not everyone has the same interests, and not everyone's interests are necessarily compatible with yours. It is important to understand the organization's political landscape by knowing what interests exist and to whom they belong.

Know what position relevant individuals and groups hold with respect to issues important to you. When this perspective is different from yours it is also important to understand the basis for the difference. It is much easier to influence those who agree with us than it is to affect the behavior of those who do not. Knowing why someone's perspective is different from yours makes the task of exercising influence easier. Understanding why subordinates dislike a new incentive pay plan, for example, affords you a better opportunity to diagnose how they are likely to respond to different attempts you might make to sell them on its merits.

YOU BE THE JUDGE

CAN BUSINESS SCHOOLS TEACH ETHICS?

Easy credit, bankers' relaxed attitude toward risk, predatory lending practices, and the failure of regulators to intervene are all major causes of the latest financial crisis. However, according to John C. Bogle, founder and former CEO of the Vanguard Group of Mutual Funds, more rudimentary underlying causes of the worldwide financial crisis were that "self-interest got out of hand" and "unchecked market forces overwhelmed traditional standards of professional conduct, developed over centuries."[55] Bogle is placing part of the blame for our current crisis on unethical leadership, poor decision making, and/or outright greed. Should business schools in the United States share in the blame? The issue at hand is whether business schools have a responsibility—and the ability—to teach ethical behavior to business students.[56] This is not a new concept. Recent research suggests that a large majority of top MBA programs require students to study ethics or corporate social responsibility as part of their curricula. Harvard Business School offered its first business ethics course—"Social Factors in Business Enterprise"—nearly 100 years ago. Keeping pace with this tradition, starting in January 2004, Harvard Business School has required all students to take the ethics course "Leadership, Governance, and Accountability." Other schools, like Indiana University's Kelley School of Business, are also taking steps to ensure that their students abide by ethical standards. Students of the Kelley School of Business must follow a 20-page code of conduct that prohibits cheating, fabrication, and plagiarism, while promoting professional conduct with recruiters.

Experts and professors differ in their opinions regarding whether ethical behavior can be taught. Some believe that students' values are already formed and that no amount of classroom training will make an individual behave ethically. Others believe that by educating students on the severe consequences of unethical business decisions, such teaching will help deter unethical behavior in the future. For example, at the Tuck School of Business at Dartmouth College, students attend a panel that features an ex-convict who was involved in a $100 million fraud.

Should business schools require all students to take a specific ethics course? Or is it better to add an ethics component to all required courses, like accounting, management, and marketing? You be the judge!

Understand that to get things done you must have power, and in the case of those who oppose you, you must have more power than they do. This means it is essential that you know where power comes from and how these sources of power can be nurtured. It is important to recognize that there is nothing wrong with the acquisition and use of power if it is done in a professional and ethical manner. However effective you are as a manager, increasing your influence will further increase your effectiveness.

Finally, *recognize the strategies and tactics through which organizational power is developed and used.* This includes understanding the importance of timing, the use of the organization's structure, and the various forms of interpersonal power. As Pfeffer concludes, "We need to understand strategies and tactics of using power so that we can consider the range of approaches available to us, and use what is likely to be effective."[57]

An organizational member does not have to be in a formal leadership position to possess or use power. Having and using power, however, is an integral part of leadership. In this chapter we have examined the relevant aspects of power. In the chapters that follow, we turn our attention to the organizational processes of communication, decision making, and leadership.

USING AN ETHICAL DECISION TREE

Political behavior is pervasive. As the text indicates, such behavior is inherently neither good nor bad. In determining whether a particular choice of behaviors is ethical or unethical, based on the criteria discussed in the text, a manager might find the following decision tree useful.

Application of this decision-tree approach is certainly not a panacea. There may be situations in which one or more of these criteria cannot be employed or in which there is a conflict among criteria. Making the ethically correct political behavior choice is neither always easy nor always possible. However, models such as this one can be of assistance to managers in their decision making.

Source: Adapted from G.F. Cavanagh, D.J. Moberg, and M. Velasquez, "The Ethics of Organizational Politics," *Academy of Management Review,* July 1981, p. 368.

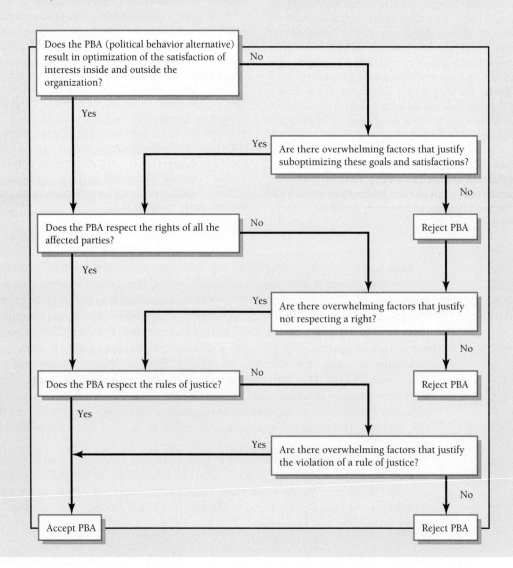

YOU BE THE JUDGE COMMENT

CAN BUSINESS SCHOOLS TEACH ETHICS?

There is considerable debate inside and outside business schools regarding whether (and how) ethics can be taught to college students who have long passed the "formative years." As the debate continues, many schools are offering ethics both as stand-alone courses and as supplements to other business courses (e.g., ethical decision making in accounting). Students at the Haas School of Business at the University of California at Berkeley, at the University of Maryland, and at Pepperdine University have the opportunity to interact with convicted white-collar criminals in the hope that the students will learn from these individuals' mistakes. A comprehensive ethics course at the University of California at Irvine evaluates the ethical, financial, and legal actions that contributed to Enron's demise.

Many ethics experts agree that if a course or supplement is offered to college students, it requires instructors who have received adequate training in cases, theories, and other pedagogical tools designed to convey a thorough grounding in ethical issues and decision making. Also, any instructor who plans on designing a course in ethics should address the following issues. (1) What are the objectives and learning outcomes of the course? (2) What kind of learning environment is necessary? (3) What learning processes need to be used to achieve the outcomes? (4) What are the roles of the students in the learning experience?

In sum, teaching ethics in business schools is a challenging, but meaningful, goal that should be considered by university administration and faculty. Whether done as a stand-alone course or an integrated module to functional courses, proper training and pedagogical tools for instructors can increase the overall effectiveness of these courses.

Sources: Carolyn Y. Nicholson and Michelle DeMoss, "Teaching Ethics and Social Responsibility: An Evaluation of Undergraduate Business Education at the Discipline Level," *Journal of Education for Business* 84, no. 4 (2009), pp. 213–18; Lisa Jones Christensen, Ellen Peirce, Laura P. Hartman, W. Michael Hoffman, Jamie Carrier, "Ethics, CSR, and Sustainability Education in the Financial Times Top 50 Global Business Schools: Baseline Data and Future Research Directions," *Journal of Business Ethics* 73, no. 4 (2007), pp. 347–68; Ronald R. Sims and Edward L. Felton, Jr., "Designing and Delivering Business Ethics Teaching and Learning," *Journal of Business Ethics* 63, no. 3 (February 2006), pp. 297–312; and Mark C. Baetz and David J. Sharp, "Integrating Ethics Content into the Core Business Curriculum: Do Core Teaching Materials Do the Job?" *Journal of Business Ethics* 51, no. 1 (April 2004), pp. 53–62.

Summary of Key Points

- Power is the capability one party has to affect the actions of another party. Influence is a transaction in which one party induces another party to behave in a certain way. Another way of making the distinction is to think of power as the potential to influence, and influence as power in action.

- French and Raven introduced the notion of five interpersonal power bases: legitimate (position based), reward, coercive (punishment based), expert, and referent (charismatic). These five bases can be divided into two major categories: organizational and personal. Legitimate, reward, and coercive power are primarily prescribed by an organization, while expert and referent power are based on personal qualities.

- Organizational structure creates power by specifying certain individuals to perform certain tasks. Three important forms of structural power include (1) access to resources, (2) ability to affect decision-making processes, and (3) having access to relevant and important information.

- Powerlessness occurs when an individual has little or no access to the bases of interpersonal or structural power. Empowerment refers to a process whereby conditions that contribute to powerlessness are identified and removed. Two important factors in empowerment are helping organizational members feel confident about their ability to perform well and increasing the linkages between effort and performance.

- The strategic contingency approach addresses subunit power. A strategic contingency is an event or activity that is extremely important for accomplishing organizational goals. The strategic contingency factors that have been disclosed by research include coping with uncertainty, centrality, and substitutability.

- Individuals with very little or no real power may still influence others because they *appear* to be powerful. This is the illusion of power that was clearly illustrated in the Milgram experiments on obedience.

- Frequently used influence tactics include consultation, rational persuasion, inspirational appeals, ingratiating tactics, coalition building, use of pressure, legitimating, personal appeals, and exchange tactics. A particularly important and frequently used tactic is that of impression management.

- A manager's behavior should satisfy certain criteria to be considered ethical. These include the (1) *criterion of utilitarian outcomes* (the greatest good for the greatest number); (2) *criterion of individual rights* (respecting rights of free consent, speech, privacy, and due process); and (3) *criterion of distributive justice* (respecting the rules of justice).

- Using power to manage effectively means (1) recognizing that there are multiple interests in every organization, (2) knowing what position others hold with respect to issues important to you, (3) understanding that getting things done requires having and using power, and (4) recognizing the strategies and tactics through which organizational power is developed and used.

Review and Discussion Questions

1. Think about a previous job you have held. Which, if any, were the sources of your power? Did you attempt to increase your power? If so, how?

2. What is meant by the term *empowerment?* Why is empowerment a concept that is resisted by some and rejected by others?.

3. If you wanted to gain compliance from subordinates, what type of power would you use? Explain what compliance means.

4. Assume that the printing process is a strategic contingency for a publishing company, and that only one group of employees knows how to operate the printing press. How could the environment be changed to more evenly balance power within the printing department?

5. How the illusion of power can be just as effective as actual power was clearly illustrated in the "obedience to authority" experiments conducted by Milgram. Can you think of other examples where people have responded to the illusion of power? Does this happen in organizations?

6. Political games are played at all organizational levels by both managers and non-managers. Identify the purposes for which these games are played.

7. A number of frequently used influence tactics were discussed in the text. How many have you witnessed being used in organizations of which you were a member? What other tactics have you seen used?

8. The use of power and politics often involves ethical issues. What are the criteria that may be used to determine the extent to which a manager's behavior is ethical? Are there ever legitimate exceptions to these criteria?

9. Which power would you prefer to develop for yourself: *expert power* or *legitimate power*? What are the advantages and disadvantages of each of these sources of power? Explain.

10. When was the last time you engaged in impression management? Was it effective? Why or why not? How might you use impression management to get a promotion? To receive a better grade in a course?

Now how much do you know about power, politics, and empowerment?

6. _____ refers to encouraging or assisting individuals and groups to make decisions that affect their work environments.
   a. Groupthink
   b. Empowerment
   c. Job enlargement
   d. Problem solving

7. Consultation, ingratiating tactics, and personal appeals are all known as _____ tactics.
   a. political influence
   b. developmental
   c. devil's advocate
   d. compliance

8. True or false: Self-promotion and intimidation are two types of impression management tactics.
   a. True
   b. False

9. True or false: Referent power is based on a subordinate's identification with a superior.
   a. True
   b. False

10. A lower-level employee can build his or her _____ power by developing special skills and knowledge that are highly valued within the department or organization.
    a. legitimate
    b. reward
    c. coercive
    d. expert

REALITY CHECK ANSWERS

Before	After
1. *d* 2. *b* 3. *a* 4. *b* 5. *d*	6. *b* 7. *a* 8. *a* 9. *a* 10. *d*
Number Correct	Number Correct
_____	_____

Exercise 12.1: *Empowerment Profile*

Step 1

Complete the following questionnaire. For each of the following items, select the alternative with which you feel more comfortable. While for some items you may feel that both (*a*) and (*b*) describe you or neither is ever applicable, you should select the alternative that better describes you most of the time.

1. When I have to give a talk or write a paper, I . . .
    _____ *a.* Base the content of my talk or paper on my own ideas.
    _____ *b.* Do a lot of research, and present the findings of others in my paper or talk.

2. When I read something I disagree with, I . . .
    _____ *a.* Assume my position is correct.
    _____ *b.* Assume what's presented in the written word is correct.

3. When someone makes me extremely angry, I . . .
    _____ *a.* Ask the other person to stop the behavior that is offensive to me.
    _____ *b.* Say little, not quite knowing how to state my position.

4. When I do a good job, it is important to me that . . .
    _____ *a.* The job represents the best I can do.
    _____ *b.* Others take notice of the job I've done.

5. When I buy new clothes, I . . .
    _____ *a.* Buy what looks best on me.
    _____ *b.* Try to dress in accordance with the latest fashion.

6. When something goes wrong, I . . .
    _____ *a.* Try to solve the problem.
    _____ *b.* Try to find out who's at fault.

7. As I anticipate my future, I . . .
    _____ *a.* Am confident I will be able to lead the kind of life I want to lead.
    _____ *b.* Worry about being able to live up to my obligations.

8. When examining my own resources and capacities, I . . .
    _____ *a.* Like what I find.
    _____ *b.* Find all kinds of things I wish were different.

9. When someone treats me unfairly, I . . .
    _____ *a.* Put my energies into getting what I want.
    _____ *b.* Tell others about the injustice.

10. When someone criticizes my efforts, I . . .
    _____ *a.* Ask questions to understand the basis for the criticism.
    _____ *b.* Defend my actions or decisions, trying to make my critic understand why I did what I did.

11. When I engage in an activity, it is very important to me that . . .
    _____ *a.* I live up to my own expectations.
    _____ *b.* I live up to the expectations of others.

12. When I let someone else down or disappoint them, I . . .
    _____ *a.* Resolve to do things differently next time.
    _____ *b.* Feel guilty, and wish I had done things differently.

13. I try to surround myself with people . . .
    _____ *a.* Whom I respect.
    _____ *b.* Who respect me.

14. I try to develop friendships with people who . . .
    _____ *a.* Are challenging and exciting.
    _____ *b.* Can make me feel a little safer and a little more secure.

15. I make my best efforts when . . .
    _____ *a.* I do something I want to do when I want to do it.
    _____ *b.* Someone else gives me an assignment, a deadline, and a reward for performing.

16. When I love a person, I . . .
    _____ *a.* Encourage him or her to be free and choose for himself or herself.

——————— *b.* Encourage him or her to do the same thing I do and to make choices similar to mine.

17. When I play a competitive game, it is important to me that I . . .
——————— *a.* Do the best I can.
——————— *b.* Win.

18. I really like being around people who . . .
——————— *a.* Can broaden my horizons and teach me something.
——————— *b.* Can and want to learn from me.

19. My best days are those that . . .
——————— *a.* Present unexpected opportunities.
——————— *b.* Go according to plan.

20. When I get behind in my work, I . . .
——————— *a.* Do the best I can and don't worry.
——————— *b.* Worry or push myself harder than I should.

Step 2

Score your responses as follows:

- Total your (*a*) responses: ———————
- Total your (*b*) responses: ———————

Step 3

Discussion. In small groups or with the entire class, answer the following questions:

1. What did you learn about yourself?
2. Would your closest friend agree with the scores or the scoring for (*a*) and (*b*)?
3. How could an organization use information gathered from this type of empowerment profile?

Source: "The Empowerment Profile," from *The Power Handbook* by Pamela Cuming. Copyright © 1980 by CBI Publishing. Reprinted by permission of Van Nostrand Reinhold Co., Inc.

Exercise

Exercise 12.2: *How Political Are You?*

Mark each of the following statements either mostly true or mostly false. In some instances, "mostly true" refers to "mostly agree," and "mostly false" refers to "mostly disagree." We are looking for general tendencies, so don't be concerned if you are uncertain as to the more accurate response to a given statement.

	Mostly True	Mostly False
1. I would stay late in the office just to impress my boss.	———	———
2. Why teach your subordinates everything you know about your job? One of them could then replace you.	———	———
3. I have no interest in using gossip to personal advantage.	———	———
4. Be extra careful about ever making a critical comment about your firm, even if it is justified.	———	———
5. I would go out of my way to cultivate friendships with powerful people.	———	———
6. I would never raise questions about the capabilities of my competition. Let his or her record speak for itself.	———	———
7. I am unwilling to take credit for someone else's work.	———	———
8. If I discovered that a co-worker was looking for a job, I would inform my boss.	———	———
9. Even if I made only a minor contribution to an important project, I would get my name listed as being associated with that project.	———	———
10. There is nothing wrong with tooting your own horn.	———	———
11. My office should be cluttered with personal mementos, such as pencil holders and decorations, made by my friends and family.	———	———
12. One should take action only when one is sure that it is ethically correct.	———	———

	Mostly True	Mostly False
13. Only a fool would publicly correct mistakes made by the boss.	_____	_____
14. I would purchase stock in my company even though it might not be a good financial investment.	_____	_____
15. Even if I thought it would help my career, I would refuse a hatchet-man assignment.	_____	_____
16. It is better to be feared than loved by your subordinates.	_____	_____
17. If others in the office were poking fun at the boss, I would decline to join in.	_____	_____
18. To get ahead, it is necessary to keep self-interest above the interests of the organization.	_____	_____
19. I would be careful not to hire a subordinate who might outshine me.	_____	_____
20. A wise strategy is to keep on good terms with everybody in your office even if you don't like everyone.	_____	_____

Source: A.J. DuBrin, *Winning Office Politics* (Englewood Cliffs, NJ: Prentice Hall, 1990), pp. 19–27. Used by permission of the publisher, Prentice Hall/A Simon & Schuster Company, Englewood Cliffs, NJ.

Case

Case 12.1: *The Power and Politics of Privacy on Social Networking Sites*

Facebook, with an estimated 300 million users, and MySpace, with 115 million monthly visitors worldwide, are the two largest and most popular social networking sites in the United States. Both companies state that they do not distribute users' information to third parties. However, advocacy groups concerned about online privacy rights and some users are increasingly wary about how these and other networking sites might be using and whether they are adequately protecting personal information. A common source of discomfort is whether users' personal information will be used to generate targeted ads directed at them. A recent manifestation of this wariness occurred February 4, 2009, after Mark Zuckerberg, CEO of Facebook, quietly changed the terms of use that govern how and for how long Facebook can use users' information posted to the popular Web site. About two weeks later, the consumer-advocacy blog Consumerist.com highlighted that the change in user policy would allow Facebook to continue to use information posted by users for marketing, promotional, or other purposes even after users had deleted the information from their Facebook accounts. Consumerist.com stated that the change in policy would allow Facebook to do anything it wanted with posted content, for as long as it wanted (even after a user closed his or her Facebook account). Following this realization, many users and consumer privacy advocacy groups railed against the change in terms of use at

Facebook. Presumably as a result of the public's reaction, Zuckerberg declared two weeks after the initial change that the company would return to its original terms of use while the feedback was analyzed. Zuckerberg announced that the company would work on a major revision of the terms and invited users to provide ideas on its Web site: "Facebook Bill of Rights and Responsibilities."

This wasn't the first time that Facebook experienced problems related to user privacy. In November 2007, Facebook lauched an advertising program, Beacon, that was developed to track the purchasing and other activities of Facebook users on 44 Web sites and then send notifications of these activities to the users' friends on Facebook. For example, if a user made an online purchase of a book on one of the 44 Web sites, this would act as an indirect referral to his or her friends on Facebook, which might spur additional purchases of the book. The problem started when a senior research engineer from a Palo Alto–based antispyware company, CA Inc., discovered that Beacon was also "tracking the activities of both members and nonmembers on Facebook and partner sites." Moreover, the program was set up in such a way that a message would be sent to a user's friends automatically unless the user figured out how to change his or her preferences on the Facebook Web site. Within two months of rolling out the Beacon software, CEO Zuckerberg apologized for how the rollout was handled and took steps to increase users' privacy related to their activities on the partner sites.

Zuckerberg is at the cutting edge of the intersection between technology and online privacy. In a recent blog post, he complained that his Facebook users can be inconsistent; on one hand, they want continually expanded services (e.g., more relevant ads and information about their friends), but on the other hand, they expect that their privacy will be protected and their information will not be shared with outside advertisers and third parties.

The battle over online privacy does not stop with social networking Web sites in the United States. Social network users in the 27-nation European Union are protected by strict privacy laws. The regulations "require Web sites to warn users of privacy risks and limit the sites' ability to target advertising based on members' race, religion or other sensitive categories." In the United Kingdom, privacy activists have recently reacted to Google's announcement that it would use "behavioral targeting" to generate display advertising when search results appear on users' screens. The British government is considering monitoring Facebook, MySpace, and Bebo for signs of terrorist communications and activity.

In sum, the debate over online privacy is not going away anytime soon. Several politically influential and powerful stakeholders with different priorities have a stake in the outcome: Users want their personal information protected; social networking companies want to use personal information to generate advertising revenue; advertising firms want to target their products/services to specific market segments; privacy advocacy groups want to limit the disclosure of users' personal information; technology companies want to facilitate greater information sharing; and governments want to monitor networking Web sites for signs of malevolent activities.

Questions

1. What is your opinion regarding these online privacy issues? To what extent are you concerned about how your personal information on Facebook, MySpace, and Google is used? Explain.

2. Looking back at the section on "political influence tactics" in this chapter, which tactics did Facebook's CEO Mark Zuckerberg use after he changed the original terms of use on February 4, 2009? Describe.

3. Of the stakeholders listed in the last paragraph of the case, which group do you think is most powerful in terms of shaping the future direction of online privacy issues? Explain.

Sources: Written by Robert Konopaske of Texas State University and adapted from Matthew Dalton, "EU Lays Out Web Privacy Rules," *The Wall Street Journal*, June 24, 2009, p. B8; Richard Waters, "Facebook Politics," *Financial Times,* April 28, 2009; Maija Palmer, "Online Privacy," *Financial Times,* March 27, 2009, p. 8; Frank Hayes, "About Face," *Computerworld* 43, no. 8 (February 23, 2009), p. 40; Jessica E. Vascellaro, "Facebook Performs About-Face on Data," *The Wall Street Journal,* February 19, 2009, p. B6; Ellen McGirt, J.L. August, and Anne C. Lee, "MySpace, the Sequel," *Fast Company,* September 2008, pp. 92–100; Randall Rothenberg, "Facebook's Flop," *The Wall Street Journal,* December 14, 2007, p. A21; Heather Havenstein and Jaikumar Vijayan, "Facebook Fiasco May Lead to Closer Look at Online Privacy Issues," *Computerworld,* December 10, 2007, p. 11; and Kevin Allison, "Facebook in Apology over Controversial Ad Technology," *Financial Times,* December 6, 2007, p. 26; http://www.facebook.com/press/info.php?factsheet.

Organizational Processes

The real leader has no need to lead—he is content to point the way.
Henry Miller, The Wisdom of the Heart *(1941)*

CHAPTER THIRTEEN

Communication

Learning Objectives

After completing Chapter 13, you should be able to:

- **Explain** the elements in the communication process.
- **Compare** the four major directions of communication.
- **Describe** the role played by interpersonal communication in organizations.

- **Discuss** multicultural communication.
- **Identify** significant barriers to effective communication.
- **Describe** ways in which communication in organizations can be improved.

Communicating, like the process of decision making discussed in the next chapter, pervades everything that all organizational members—particularly managers—do. The managerial functions of planning, organizing, leading, and controlling all involve communicative activity. In fact, communication is an absolutely essential element in all organizational processes.

The Importance of Communication

Communication is the glue that holds organizations together. Communication assists organizational members to accomplish both individual and organizational goals, implement and respond to organizational change, coordinate organizational activities, and engage in virtually all organizationally relevant behaviors. Yet, as important as this process is, breakdowns in communication are pervasive. This idea was captured in a now famous line from the Oscar-winning movie *Cool Hand Luke:* "What we have is a failure to communicate." We have all failed at communication from time to time; whether fumbling for the right words when asking your supervisor for a raise or having a negative exchange with a co-worker over something you wrote in a text message to him or her. Improving our ability to communicate effectively should be a top priority. Great communicators can achieve great things!

To the extent that organizational communications are less effective than they might be, organizations will be less effective than they might be. For example, in many companies, new-employee orientation programs represent the first important opportunity to begin the process of effective communication with employees. At Marriott International, the worldwide hotel and resort chain, 40 percent of new employees who leave the organization do so during the first three months on the job. At least that had been true historically. Recently, the rate of departures has been significantly reduced because Marriott has embarked on a concerted effort to improve the content and manner in which it communicates with new employees during orientation. In addition to formally providing more information, each new employee is assigned a "buddy" who

How much do you know about communication?

1. Communication that flows across functions in an organization is known as _____ communication.
   a. multipurpose
   b. cross-functional
   c. horizontal
   d. Both *a* and *b* are correct.

2. True or false: Nonverbal messages can be influenced by the gender and race of the sender of these messages.
   a. True
   b. False

3. _____ refers to the amount of information that can be transmitted or communicated in an effective manner.
   a. Information loading
   b. Data allocation
   c. Message enlargement
   d. Information richness

4. True or false: In 2008, it was estimated that spam e-mail messages cost U.S. organizations over $17 billion in lost employee productivity and the use of computer resources and personnel to filter and remove it.
   a. True
   b. False

5. Each of the following is an outcome of the use of competitive intelligence except for _____.
   a. loss of competitive advantage
   b. lost market share
   c. lost company reputation
   d. increased research and development costs

serves as a vital communication link to which the newcomer has unrestricted access. Marriott helps ensure that its frontline service personnel communicate effectively with their guests by first ensuring that Marriott communicates effectively with its employees, starting from their very first day on the job.

It would be extremely difficult to find an aspect of a manager's job that does not involve communication. Serious problems arise when directives are misunderstood, when casual kidding in a work group leads to anger, or when informal remarks by a top-level manager are distorted. Each of these situations is a result of a breakdown somewhere in the communication process.

Accordingly, the pertinent question is not whether managers engage in communication because communication is inherent to the functioning of an organization. Rather, the pertinent question is whether managers will communicate well or poorly. In other words, communication itself is unavoidable in an organization's functioning; *effective* communication is avoidable. *Every manager must be a communicator.* In fact, everything a manager does communicates something in some way to somebody or some group, but with what effect? While this may appear an overstatement at this point, it will become apparent as you proceed through the chapter. Despite the tremendous advances in communication and information technology, communication among people in organizations leaves much to be desired.[1] It is a process that occurs within people.

EXHIBIT 13.1
The Communication
Process

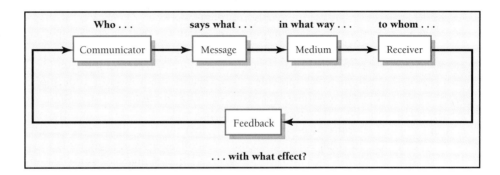

The general process of communication is presented in Exhibit 13.1. The process contains five elements—the communicator, the message, the medium, the receiver, and feedback. It can be simply summarized as: Who . . . says what . . . in what way . . . to whom . . . with what effect?[2] To appreciate each element in the process, we must examine how communication works.

The Communication Process

How Communication Works

Communication experts tell us that effective communication is the result of a common understanding between the communicator and the receiver. In fact, the word *communication* is derived from the Latin *communis,* meaning "common." The communicator seeks to establish a "commonness" with a receiver. Hence, we can define **communication** as the *transition of information and understanding through the use of common symbols from one person or group to another.* The common symbols may be verbal or nonverbal. You will see later that in the context of an organizational structure, information can flow up and down (vertical), across (horizontal), and down and across (diagonal).

The most widely used contemporary model of the process of communication has evolved mainly from the work of Shannon, Weaver, and Schramm.[3] These researchers were concerned with describing the general process of communication that could be useful in all situations. The model that evolved from their work is helpful for understanding communication. The basic elements include a communicator, an encoder, a message, a medium, a decoder, a receiver, feedback, and noise. The model is presented in Exhibit 13.2. Each element in the model can be examined in the context of an organization.

communication
The transmission of information and understanding through the use of common symbols.

EXHIBIT 13.2
A Communication
Model

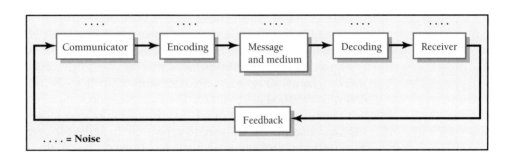

The communication process works extremely well at the world's largest food producer, Nestlé. The company, which has over 283,000 employees, sells much more than just chocolate, including coffee, ice cream, frozen foods, and pet care products.[4] The company has entered the e-revolution by using the Web for continuous communication. Nestlé provides store owners the option of ordering its chocolates and other products via a Web site: NestleEZOrder.com. The system will eliminate most of the 100,000 phoned or faxed orders a year from mom-and-pop shops.[5] Nestlé buyers have purchased cocoa beans and other raw ingredients on a country-by-country basis with little information about how colleagues were buying the same products. Now they share price information via the Internet and pick suppliers offering the best deals.

Nestlé has traditionally processed its own cocoa butter and powder and manufactured most of its own chocolate. The Web now lets Nestlé communicate regularly with suppliers, making outsourcing a viable option.

In the past, Nestlé guessed at how many Butterfinger bars it might be able to sell in a promotion. Today, electronic links with supermarkets and other partners provide real-time feedback and information.

The Nestlé approach involves each of the elements in the communication process. The difference with Nestlé today and Nestlé yesterday is that some of the firm's exchanges of messages and feedback are performed electronically. Nestlé believes that face-to-face and electronic communicators are needed to operate a profitable business around the world.

The Elements of Communication

Communicator

In an organizational framework, the communicator is an employee or manager with ideas, intentions, information, and a purpose for communicating.

Encoding

Given the communicator, an encoding process must take place that translates the communicator's ideas into a systematic set of symbols—into a language expressing the communicator's purpose. For example, a manager often takes accounting information, sales reports, and computer data and translates them into one message (i.e., an overall status report). The function of encoding, then, is to provide a form in which ideas and purposes can be expressed as a message.

Message

The result of the encoding process is the message. The purpose of the communicator is expressed in the form of the message—either *verbal* or *nonverbal*. Managers have numerous purposes for communicating, such as to have others understand their ideas, to understand the ideas of others, to gain acceptance of themselves or their ideas, or to produce action. The message, then, is what the individual hopes to communicate to the intended receiver, and the exact form it takes depends, to a great extent, on the medium used to carry the message. Decisions relating to the two are inseparable.

Not as obvious, however, are *unintended messages* that can be sent by silence or inaction on a particular issue as well as decisions of which goals and objectives not to pursue and which method not to utilize. For example, a decision to utilize one type of performance evaluation method rather than another may send a "message" to certain people. Messages may also be designed to appear on the surface to convey certain information, when other information is what is really being conveyed. Related to this are messages

CONFUSING THE PEOPLE AND CLOUDING THE ISSUE

Unfortunately, not all organizational communications are meant to clarify; sometimes they are designed to confuse. At other times, protecting the communicator may be the primary objective. Some words and phrases are so frequently used to convey a meaning other than the apparent one that their use has become institutionalized. Below are humorous examples of alternative interpretations to what otherwise appear as straightforward words or messages.

It is in process—It's so wrapped up in red tape that the situation is hopeless.

We will look into it—By the time the wheel makes a full turn, we assume you will have forgotten about it.

Under consideration—Never heard of it.

Under active consideration—We're looking in our files for it.

We're forming a committee/task force—We need more time to think of an answer.

Let's get together on this—I'm assuming you're as confused as I.

For appropriate action—Maybe you'll know what to do with this.

Note and initial—Let's spread the responsibility for this.

It is estimated—This is my guess.

We are aware of it—We had hoped that the person who started it would have forgotten about it by now.

We will advise you in due course—If we figure it out, we'll let you know.

Give us the benefit of your thinking—We'll listen to you as long as it doesn't interfere with what we have already decided to do.

She's in a conference—I don't have any idea where she is.

We are activating the file—We're e-mailing it to as many people as we can think of.

Let me bring you up to date—We didn't like what you were going to do, so we already did something else.

A reliable source—The person you just met.

An informed source—The person who told the person you just met.

An unimpeachable source—The person who started the rumor to begin with.

designed to protect the sender, rather than to facilitate understanding by the receiver. The above Organizational Encounter provides examples of these latter types of messages.

Medium

The *medium* is the carrier of the message. Organizations provide information to members in a variety of ways, including face-to-face communications, e-mails, intranets, telephone, group meetings, memos, policy statements, reward systems, production schedules, and sales forecasts. The increased use of electronic media based upon computer and telecommunication technologies has increased interest in the role of the medium in various aspects of organizational communications.[6]

Decoding-Receiver

For the communication process to be completed, the message must be decoded in terms of relevance to the receiver. *Decoding* is a technical term for the receiver's thought processes. Decoding, then, involves interpretation. *Receivers* interpret (decode) the message in light of their own previous experiences and frames of reference. Thus, a salesperson is likely to decode a memo from the company president differently than a production manager will. A nursing supervisor is likely to decode a memo from the hospital administrator differently than the chief of surgery will. The closer the decoded message is to the intent desired by the communicator, the more effective is the communication. This underscores the importance of the communicator being "receiver-oriented."

Feedback

Provision for feedback in the communication process is desirable. *One-way* communication processes are those that do not allow receiver-to-communicator feedback. This may increase the potential for distortion between the intended message and the received message. A feedback loop provides a channel for receiver response that enables the communicator to determine whether the message has been received and has produced the intended response. *Two-way* communication processes provide for this important receiver-to-communicator feedback.[7]

For the manager, communication feedback may come in many ways. In face-to-face situations, *direct* feedback through verbal exchanges is possible, as are such subtle means of communication as facial expressions of discontent or misunderstanding. In addition, *indirect* means of feedback (such as declines in productivity, poor quality of production, increased absenteeism or turnover, and lack of coordination and/or conflict between units) may indicate communication breakdowns. Some companies take employee feedback very seriously. DHL Express has created a "power line" for its 33,000 full-time employees and independent contractors to report complaints.[8] Also, Cabela's, a 14,000-employee outdoor outfitter, has set up hotlines so that workers can report complaints anonymously without fear of reprisal from their managers or supervisors. A similar hotline has been established to elicit complaints from its vendors. Such feedback from employees and vendors helps keep Cabela's decision makers plugged into business in the field.[9]

Noise

In the framework of human communication, noise can be thought of as those factors that distort the intended message. Noise may occur in each of the elements of communication. For example, a manager who is under a severe time constraint may send out a hastily written e-mail to his or her subordinates, only to discover that the wording in the e-mail angers several employees. They may think the manager's e-mail is rude and pushy. In this case the subordinates have attached a different meaning to the message contained in the e-mail and have practically ignored the actual information sent by the manager.

The elements discussed in this section are essential for communication to occur. They should not, however, be viewed as separate. They are, rather, descriptive of the acts that have to be performed for any type of communication to occur. The communication may be vertical (superior–subordinate, subordinate–superior) or horizontal (peer–peer). Or it may involve one individual and a group. But the elements discussed here must be present.

Nonverbal Messages

nonverbal communication
Messages sent with body posture, facial expressions, and head and eye movements.

The information sent by a communicator that is unrelated to the verbal information— that is, nonverbal messages or **nonverbal communication**—is a relatively recent area of research among behavioral scientists. The major interest has been in the *physical cues* that characterize the communicator's presentation. These cues include such modes of transmitting nonverbal messages as head, face, and eye movements, posture, physical distance, gestures, tone of voice, handshakes, and clothing and dress choices.[10] Nonverbal messages themselves are influenced by factors such as the gender and race of the communicator.[11]

Unique Qualities of Nonverbal Communication

Some nonverbal messages are spontaneous and unregulated expressions of emotion, while others are conscious and deliberately presented.[12] Through nonverbal behavior, particularly body movements, we say, "Help me, I'm lonely. Take me, I'm available. Leave me alone, I'm depressed." We act out our state of being with nonverbal body language. We lift one eyebrow for disbelief. We rub our noses for puzzlement. We clasp our arms to isolate ourselves or to protect ourselves. We shrug our shoulders for indifference, wink one eye for intimacy, tap our fingers for impatience, slap our forehead for forgetfulness.[13]

Nonverbal messages may differ from other forms of communication behavior in several ways. For example, nonverbal behavior can be difficult to suppress (e.g., an involuntary frown indicating displeasure). Such unconscious behavior can contradict the message the communicator is sending verbally. Another way in which nonverbal messages differ from other forms is that they are more apparent to the people who observe them than they are to the people who produce them. This can make it very difficult for the sender to know how successfully she or he produced the nonverbal message that was intended. Finally, many nonverbal messages are susceptible to multiple interpretations. Even something as common as a smile may have many different meanings. Smiles may indicate genuine happiness, contempt, deceit, fear, compliance, resignation—even, on occasion, anger.

Research Findings

Research indicates that facial expressions and eye contact and movements generally provide information about the *type* of emotion, while such physical cues as distance, posture, and gestures indicate the *intensity* of the emotion. These conclusions are important to managers. They indicate that communicators often send a great deal more information than is obtained in verbal messages. To increase the effectiveness of communication, a person must be aware of the nonverbal as well as the verbal content of the messages.

When verbal and nonverbal messages conflict, receivers tend to place more faith in nonverbal cues. When this type of conflict occurs, a judgment on what message to decipher is going to be made (e.g., "the customer said that price wasn't important, but she looked away from me when she said it; I think it's very important to her"). Thus, our co-workers, supervisors, and customers are constantly examining our nonverbal and verbal cues. Some of the most common nonverbal cues people study include eye contact, facial expressions (the human face displays over 250,000), posture, and gestures. Being aware of these main cue initiators is important. For example, sustained eye contact in some cultures is considered impolite. While the thumbs-up for a successful effort is a cue in the United States for a "job well done," it is an obscene gesture in Spain and parts of Latin America.

Being aware of nonverbal messages requires an awareness of their existence and importance. A good way to examine your own nonverbal impression and presence is to videotape yourself making a formal presentation. A review of the videotape will help determine the alignment of verbal and nonverbal messages.

Communicating within Organizations

The design of an organization should provide for communication in four distinct directions: downward, upward, horizontal, and diagonal. Since these directions of communication establish the framework within which communication in an organization occurs, let us briefly examine each one. This examination will enable you to better appreciate the barriers to effective organizational communication and the means to overcome them.

Downward Communication

downward communication
Communication that flows from individuals in higher levels of the organization's hierarchy to those in lower levels.

This type of communication flows downward from individuals in higher levels of the hierarchy to those in lower levels. The most common forms of **downward communication** are job descriptions, memos and e-mails from the CEO, policy statements, hiring and operating procedures, manuals, and company publications. In many organizations, downward communication is often incomplete, inadequate, and inaccurate, as evidenced in the often-heard statement among organization members that "we have absolutely no idea what's happening." Such complaints indicate inadequate downward communication and the need of individuals for information relevant to their jobs. The absence of relevant company- and job-related information can create unnecessary stress among organization members.[14] Employees go through four stages when high-level decisions are developed and implemented: first, employees *speculate* about what's going to happen (e.g., I think there's going to be a layoff); second, when the official announcement is made, employees *digest* the news and why the decision is being made (e.g., sales are down 30 percent so a layoff was inevitable); third, they *deliberate* by discussing the announcement with their peers; and, fourth, employees make a *conclusion* about the decision. This last step will lead the employees to "embrace, accept, endure, reject, or passively resist" the decision.[15] Decision makers who communicate and respond to these stages will increase the likelihood that employees will accept and embrace the announced changes.

Upward Communication

upward communication
Upward communication flows from individuals at lower levels of the organizational structure to those at higher levels. Among the most common upward communication flows are suggestion boxes, group meetings, and appeal or grievance procedures.

An effective organization needs **upward communication** as much as it needs downward communication. In such situations, the communicator is at a lower level in the organization than the receiver. Some of the most common upward communication flows are suggestion boxes, group meetings, and appeal or grievance procedures. In their absence, people somehow find ways to adopt nonexistent or inadequate upward communication channels. This has been evidenced by the emergence of "underground" employee publications in many large organizations.

Upward communication serves a number of important functions. Organizational communication researcher Gary Kreps identifies several:[16]

1. It provides managers with feedback about current organizational issues and problems, and information about day-to-day operations that they need for making decisions about directing the organization.
2. It is management's primary source of feedback for determining the effectiveness of its downward communication.
3. It relieves employees' tensions by allowing lower-level organization members to share relevant information with their superiors.
4. It encourages employees' participation and involvement, thereby enhancing organizational cohesiveness.

Horizontal Communication

horizontal communication
Communication that flows across functions in an organization.

Often overlooked in the design of most organizations is the provision for **horizontal communication.** When the chairperson of the accounting department communicates with the chairperson of the marketing department concerning the course offerings in a college of business administration, the flow of communication is horizontal. Although vertical (upward and downward) communication flows are the primary considerations in organizational design, effective organizations also need horizontal communication. Horizontal communication—for example, communication between production and sales in a business organization and among the different departments or colleges within a university—is necessary for the coordination and integration of diverse organizational functions.

Since mechanisms for ensuring horizontal communication ordinarily do not exist in an organization's design, its facilitation is left to individual managers. Peer-to-peer communication often is necessary for coordination and also can provide social need satisfaction.

Diagonal Communication

diagonal communication
Communication that cuts across functions and levels in an organization.

While it is probably the least-used channel of communication in organizations, **diagonal communication** is important in situations where members cannot communicate effectively through other channels. For example, the comptroller of a large organization may wish to conduct a distribution cost analysis. One part of that task may involve having the sales force send a special report directly to the comptroller rather than going through the traditional channels in the marketing department. Thus, the flow of communication would be diagonal as opposed to vertical (upward) and horizontal. In this case, a diagonal channel would be the most efficient in terms of time and effort for the organization.

Communicating Externally

Organizations are involved in communicating externally to introduce products and services, to increase awareness of key brands, to project a positive image and reputation, to attract employees, and to gain attention.[17] The typical external communication program includes four distinct programs:

- *Public relations* involves the communication of a positive image, exemplary corporate/organization citizenship, and promotion of an identity as a contributor to society and the immediate community. If a full-time public relations staff is not used, some type of arrangement with a professional firm may be used.
- *Advertising* involves illustrating products or services in a positive manner and building brand loyalty. This form of communication is designed to attract customers, clients, or patients.
- *Promoting* the culture and opportunities available to prospective employees. This communication is designed to attract employee talent to sustain and grow the organization.
- *Customer/client/patient surveys* are used to gather feedback about the experience of external constituents with the organization. This information is used to make modifications or changes in service, products, or relationships.

Each of these four communication programs is used to collect or disseminate information. The internal and external communication programs provide ideas, information, connections, and insight into what individuals and groups are saying, what is important, and what needs modification.

Information Richness

information richness
Refers to the amount of information that can be transmitted or communicated in an effective manner.

There are many different ways to communicate both within the organization, to supervisors and co-workers, and outside the organization, to customers and vendors. Communication media differ in their **information richness**. The richness of communication refers to the amount of information that can be transmitted in an effective manner.[18] A medium that enables high richness, such as a face-to-face interaction, is more likely to result in common understanding between individuals or a group when compared to a

EXHIBIT 13.3 **Common Communication Media in 21st Century Organizations**

Source: Adapted from Robert H. Lengel and Richard L. Daft, "The Selection of Communication Media as an Executive Skill," *Academy of Management Executive* 2, no. 3 (1988), pp. 225–32.

Media	Richness	Example	Benefit
Face-to-face	Very high	Ask supervisor for a raise.	Ability to adjust message according to real-time feedback.
Telephone conversation, video conference	High	Meeting with virtual group members.	Efficient, less costly, and less time-consuming than traveling to central location.
Memos, letters, faxes, personalized e-mail, voice mail	Low	Communicate a customer service policy to customer.	Efficient and cost-effective way to communicate routine information.
General e-mail, financial reports, flyers, bulletin boards, computer reports	Very low	Annual report to shareholders.	Standardized information for large audience.

low-in-richness medium, such as a generalized e-mail sent to all employees. Exhibit 13.3 provides examples of communication media typically used by employees and the level of richness contained within each medium.

Face-to-face communication is high in richness because verbal and nonverbal cues can be exchanged and observed. This form of communication is also in "real time" and consequently permits on-the-spot feedback. If a person fails to understand a communication, a request for clarification can immediately be presented.

Information richness is low in the case of an e-mail to a general population (e.g., a department, the entire project team, a subsidiary company). The impersonal nature of this type of communication is obvious. A specific individual is not being addressed, so feedback is not likely to occur in this type of communication.

How Technology Affects Communication

Internet/Intranet/Extranet

Internet
A global network of integrated computers that provides users with information, video, documents, and a vast array of communication capabilities.

The Internet has become a very popular resource for millions of people throughout many parts of the world. Developed in the 1960s by the U.S. Department of Defense as a way to ensure that communications could survive a military attack, the **Internet** is an organization of computer networks connecting everything from large supercomputers at government agencies to mainframes at businesses to PCs at individuals' homes.[19] Whether downloading music for iTunes, updating your status on social networking Web sites such as MySpace.com or Facebook.com, or conducting research for a paper, Internet users in the United States number over 203 million.[20] Some estimates suggest that worldwide Internet usage has grown from 361 million in 2000 to approximately 1.6 billion as of March 2009.[21]

The term *Internet* is used to cover many services and information technologies. The World Wide Web is the service that currently has the most applicable communication protocols and technology for business on the Internet. Internet services include electronic mail (e-mail), newsgroups, and chat rooms. The Web brings graphics, interaction, and hyperlinking capabilities to the Internet and allows for multimedia content such as voice and video. A common mistake is to think that the Internet and the Web are the same.

intranet
A private, protected electronic communication system within an organization; intranets allow certain stakeholders to gain access to internal organizational information.

An **intranet** is a private, protected electronic communication system within an organization. If it is connected to the Internet, it has its privacy protected by what are called *firewalls*. A firewall is a network mode set up internally to prevent traffic to cross into the private domain. Intranets are used to communicate such things as proprietary organizational information, company plans, confidential medical records, training programs, compensation data, and company records.

For example, American Airlines uses the employee portal "Jetnet" to automate employee travel reservations (employees travel for free) and enrollment in benefits. The use of this intranet has saved the company approximately $3 million per year.[22]

extranet
A private, protected electronic communication system that is designed to connect employees with individuals external to the organization such as vendors, customers, or other strategic partners.

An **extranet** is designed to connect employees with individuals external to the organization, such as vendors, customers, and other strategic partners. At Campbell Soup Company, extranet portals are being developed to get retailers and consumers more involved in new product development.[23] At chocolate manufacturer Hershey, IT employees recently completed an extranet that will allow customers and retailers to check the status of their orders online.[24]

Electronic Mail, Messaging, and Social Networking

The use of e-mail will continue to expand rapidly in the coming years. For example, some estimates indicate the number of e-mail users globally will increase from 1.2 billion in 2007 to 1.6 billion in 2011.[25] In the past, some e-mail users sent out unedited, poorly written messages on the fly. This type of sloppiness has been criticized and is discouraged in organizations. The privacy of e-mail is another serious issue. Supervisors, colleagues, and others can access e-mail messages. Consequently, care must be exercised in properly using e-mails as a communication approach.

The permanency of e-mail messages is another issue that astute users of e-mail communications have learned to consider. Erased messages can remain on disk drives, servers, and social networking sites indefinitely. In the wake of the Enron case, e-mail storage and record keeping have become important issues for many companies. For example, federal regulators fined five Wall Street firms a total of $8.25 million for failing to adequately maintain e-mail files that adhere to record-keeping standards.[26]

Websense Inc. is a maker of employee-monitoring software that identifies improper use of the Internet and personal (not work-related) e-mails. Nearly one-third of those companies polled by Websense had fired workers for improper use of the Internet. Nearly three-quarters of major U.S. companies are now recording and reviewing employees' communications, including e-mail, telephone calls, and Internet connections. For example, Chevron and Microsoft both settled sexual harassment lawsuits for $2.2 million apiece as a result of internally circulated e-mails that could have created hostile work environments.[27]

E-mail is an effective way of communicating simple messages. Complex data and information should probably be sent in hard copy documents. Think simple. Secure your e-mails. Always use correct and professional language in preparing and sending e-mails.

In addition to e-mail, the growth of instant messaging (IM) has also been explosive within recent years. This has been fueled by free consumer services such as AOL Instant Messenger, Microsoft's MSN Messenger, Google's Talk, and Yahoo! Messenger. Now, more and more organizations are installing internal IM systems such as IBM's Lotus SameTime software.[28] Corporate use of IM is expected to grow rapidly because IM offers real-time communication among geographically dispersed employees; is an inexpensive alternative to multiple telephone calls and travel; creates a document trail for future reference; offers integration with voice and video; and demands the immediate attention of its users.[29]

Driven by the increased need to conduct business from anywhere at any time, text messaging from cell phones is also gaining in popularity.[30] Given that most employees, customers, and vendors have cell phones in the United States, many companies are exploring ways to use text messaging to connect with potential customers, increase sales, and enhance customer satisfaction.[31] For example, *American Idol,* ESPN, and Disney encourage viewers to get involved with their televised programs by texting votes and messages to the show. CNN asks viewers to text in questions and opinions about current events.

Texting to reach customers has many advantages compared with the more traditional methods such as TV, radio, e-mail, newspapers, magazines, or direct mail, including:[32]

- Texting is less expensive than many other forms of advertising and marketing.
- There's less spam because cell phone companies block most of it.
- Texting is the favorite form of communication among young consumers, making them an attractive target market.
- People read 95 percent of text messages because they are generally from known sources and friends.

Another way in which technology is transforming communication is with the explosion in popularity of social networking sites such as Facebook, MySpace, and LinkedIn. Serving a variety of human and business needs, social networking sites are rapidly becoming part of the communication fabric of organizations. Although conventional wisdom suggests these sites are the exclusive domain of teenagers and twenty-somethings, this new era of social networking is reaching far and wide. The social networking and microblogging Web site Twitter has been creating a buzz in many circles. For example, the U.S. Department of State, realizing that social networking sites such as Twitter were helping broadcast images of the protests against Iran's election results in 2009, asked the company to delay maintenance to keep the tweets flowing.[33] This was significant given the Iranian government's attempt to censor more traditional news outlets and reporters. A recent article in *BusinessWeek* featured the former CEO of General Electric, Jack Welch, and his spouse discussing how the pair "tweets" (i.e., sends short messages of 140 characters or less) on a daily basis and see Twitter as "a high-value way for companies to help brand themselves and microtarget consumer groups, as well as another tool for managers to interact with their people, and vice versa."[34]

Individuals, groups, and organizations use social networking sites and blogs for a variety of purposes. Current or former employees use these Web sites to discuss a company's policy or an unpopular supervisor. A group of customers excited about a new product (e.g., the release of the iPhone) could create such a buzz around the launch of that product that its sales get a boost. Accenture has developed its own social networking program called "Performance Multiplier" to enable employees to post updates, photos, and weekly goals related to their performance. The program aims for employees to receive and use informal feedback from managers and employees so that they can improve their performance.[35]

Risks are associated with the often informal and boundaryless world of social networking sites. For example, Virgin Atlantic fired a cabin crew for complaining on the Internet about passengers and making jokes about faulty jet engines.[36] Employers are establishing guidelines to prevent public disclosures that could hurt an organization's reputation or create a social networking scandal.[37] General Electric has set up an internal "Tweet Squad" consisting of young hipster employees who help older employees and managers refine their social networking skills. Also, IBM has established the following guidelines to help its employees understand what they can and cannot say on blogs and social networking sites:[38]

- Employees are personally responsible for all content that is published online.
- What is published might become public for a long time. Keep this in mind.
- Employees should be transparent about their role at IBM in all posts.
- Employees should get permission before reporting on internal/private conversations.
- When necessary, employees should promptly correct mistakes and edit previous posts.

Social networking sites have given individuals a powerful communication tool; once information is posted, it can be accessed within seconds from any Internet-enabled cell phone or PC around the globe. E-mail and instant/text messaging are also powerful Internet-based communication tools. Some observers are concerned that employees are becoming overly distracted by frequently stopping their work to check their voice mail, respond to e-mail/instant messages/tweets, check out the latest videos on YouTube, and/or update their Facebook or MySpace page. Basex, a New York City–based business research company, estimated, "These distractions consume as much as 28 percent of the average U.S. worker's day . . . and sap productivity to the tune of $650 billion a year."[39] Given the high stakes associated with these technology-based forms of communication, managers and employees will continue to explore and exploit them for the foreseeable future.

Smart Phones

This type of wireless device will continue to gain in popularity as businesspeople attempt to stay connected at virtually all times. According to market research firm SNL Kagan, approximately 84 percent of Americans had cell phones in 2007.[40] The success of the mobile phone is being challenged by the "smart phone," such as Apple's iPhone and Research in Motion's BlackBerry, which enables businesspeople to access e-mail, text, download software applications ("apps"), and browse the Internet while they go from city to city, and allows them to store addresses, phone numbers, customer prices, and other data critical to day-to-day functioning.[41] Such growth reflects the need for managers to stay organized and connected with colleagues, customers, and other important stakeholders from virtually anywhere, anytime. Research firm Gartner estimates that 139 million people used smart phones worldwide in 2008, but this number was expected to increase to 295 million by 2010.[42] Given such a growing market, companies such as Apple, Motorola, Samsung, Nokia, Verizon, Palm, and Microsoft are all competing to take as much market share as possible.

Voice Mail

The primary method by which employees communicate internally, leaving a recorded message accounts for approximately 90 percent of telephone communication within organizations today. Voice mail, more popular than e-mail, serves many functions, but one of the most important is message storage. Incoming messages are delivered without interrupting receivers and allow communicators to focus on the reason for their call. Voice mail minimizes inaccurate message-taking and differences in time zones.

Employees today are encouraged to develop the ability to leave concise, professional, and courteous voice-mail messages. Best practices include the following:[43]

- Organize your thoughts before picking up the telephone.
- Identify a specific, brief request that can be delivered via voice mail.

- State your name, the time and date, your company name, and the purpose of your call.
- Be precise and keep the message simple.
- Say what you would like the receiver to do.
- Give a reason for the request.
- Say "thank you."
- Finish with, "Feel free to call me at the following number . . . ."

Videoconferencing, Teleconferencing, and e-Meetings/Collaboration

Videoconferencing refers to technologies associated with viewing, and *teleconferencing* refers to technologies primarily associated with speaking. Often the terms are used interchangeably. Both technologies enable individuals to conduct meetings without getting together face-to-face.

These technologies enable participants to interact at the same time even when they are dispersed around the globe. Videoconferencing, in particular, is being used by an increasing number of companies as they attempt to increase productivity and lower travel costs. For example, W. R. Grace & Company, a $2 billion specialty chemical manufacturer, holds between 40 and 60 videoconferences per month. The firm's $200,000 investment in videoconferencing equipment paid for itself within two months in travel savings.[44]

Another form of conferencing is Web conferencing (or "webinars") in which the Internet is used to conduct real-time e-meetings or presentations of geographically dispersed participants. Participants connect to the Web conference via a personal computer or other Internet-enabled device. In addition to presentations, Web conferencing and online collaboration software allow voice, video, instant messaging, document sharing, and presentations among participants.[45] These capabilities help facilitate online collaboration on projects and other work assignments. Online collaboration services are offered by several companies including Citrix Sytems' "GoToMeeting" and Microsoft's "Office Live Meeting Service."[46]

Electronic meeting software (EMS), or meetingware, uses networked computers to automate meetings. A large screen at the front of the room is the focal point. The screen serves as an electronic flip chart displaying comments, ideas, and responses of participants. Meetingware allows facilitators to poll meeting participants, analyze voting results, and create detailed reports.

Meetingware is helpful when large groups must reach decisions quickly. Instead of one by one, meeting participants can simultaneously provide a vote, an opinion, or an idea. At Hewlett-Packard, meetingware has accelerated new product development by 30 percent.[47] Structured electronic meetings are 20 to 30 percent shorter than face-to-face meetings.

Advancements in information technologies are continuing and are providing organizational members with additional ways to communicate. Technologies, however, will not solve all communication problems. Overloading employees with new "toys," additional information, and technologies to learn can result in less efficiency. Also, the social interaction and personal touch can be lost by relying solely on electronic technologies for communication. Electronic communication omits many verbal and most nonverbal cues that people use to acquire feedback. Guarding against anonymity and depersonalization are concerns when using many of the information technologies such as e-mail, videoconferencing, and electronic meetings.

Interpersonal Communication

interpersonal communication
Communication that flows from individual to individual in face-to-face and group settings.

Within an organization, communication flows from individual to individual in a variety of ways, from face-to-face and group settings to instant messaging and videoconferencing. Such flows are termed **interpersonal communication** and can vary from direct orders to casual expressions. Interpersonal behavior could not exist without interpersonal communication. In addition to providing needed information, interpersonal communication also influences how people feel about the organization. For example, research indicates that satisfaction with communication relationships affects organizational commitment.[48]

The problems that arise when managers attempt to communicate with other people can be traced to *perceptual differences* and *interpersonal style differences.* We know from Chapter 4 that each manager perceives the world in terms of his or her background, experiences, personality, frame of reference, and attitude. The primary way in which managers relate to and learn from the environment (including the people in that environment) is through information received and transmitted. And the way in which managers receive and transmit information depends, in part, on how they relate to two very important *senders* of information—*themselves* and *others.*

In research involving interpersonal communication, it has been found that only 7 percent of the "attitudinal" meaning of a message comes from words spoken. Over 90 percent of meaning results from nonverbal cues.[49] These silent signals exert a strong influence on the receiver. However, interpreting them is by no means scientifically based. For example, does a downward glance during a brief encounter in an office mean modesty, embarrassment, a lack of respect, or fatigue?

Multicultural Communication

multicultural communication
This occurs when two or more individuals from different cultures communicate with one another.

Multicultural communication occurs when two or more individuals from different cultures communicate with one another, whether it is through a face-to-face meeting, an instant messaging exchange, or a videoconference. Cultural anthropologists Edward T. and Mildred R. Hall theorize that culture is communication and that communication can be divided into several culturally determined parts: words, space, time, and behavior.[50] Within each of these categories, examples of the challenges of communicating across cultures are common.

Words

An often-repeated and much-enjoyed joke in Latin America and Europe poses this question: "If someone who speaks three languages is called *trilingual,* and someone who speaks two languages is called *bilingual,* what do you call someone who speaks only one language?" The answer is "an American." Although certainly not universally true, this story makes a telling point. While the average European speaks several languages, the typical American is fluent only in English. One research report indicates 23,000 American college students study Japanese; in the same year, 20 million Japanese were studying English.[51] The Global OB illustrates how important it is to understand language in a cross-cultural context.

In the global business environment of today, foreign language training and fluency are a business necessity. It is true that English is an important business language and that many nonnative speakers have learned to conduct business in English. However, the vast majority of the world's population neither speaks nor understands English.

CROSS-CULTURAL COMMUNICATION PROBLEMS

Communicating exactly what you want to communicate, rather than more, less, or something altogether different, can be a challenge when the communication occurs within a single culture. Achieving the desired results cross-culturally can present special problems.

Many of the difficulties encountered with cross-cultural communications stem from the fact that different languages are involved and direct translation is not always feasible. American automobile manufacturers have learned this lesson. When Ford Motor Company introduced its Fiera truck line in some developing countries, it discovered that Fiera is a Spanish slang word meaning "ugly woman." Chevrolet discovered that in Italian Chevrolet Nova translates as "Chevrolet no go." Similarly, GM's "Body by Fisher" logo translates in at least one language into "Corpse by Fisher." Such problems are not restricted to carmakers. Coca-Cola, for example, has had its share of translation problems. In Chinese, Coca-Cola becomes "Bite the head of a dead tadpole." In some parts of Asia the familiar Coke advertis-

ing slogan "Coke adds life" is translated as "Coke brings you back from the dead."

Language translation is not the only source of problems. Head, hand, and arm gestures may mean different things in different cultures. In some countries, for example, moving one's head from side to side means "yes," while bobbing it up and down means "no"—just the reverse of U.S. meaning. Or take the familiar A-OK hand gesture. In the United States it means things are fine, or everything is working. In France it simply means "zero." In Japan, on the other hand, it is a symbol representing money. There it may be used to indicate that something is too expensive. And in Brazil, the gesture is interpreted as obscene.

Many other aspects of the communication process can cause difficulties. Different cultural interpretations of the significance of eye contact and the physical distance maintained between two people talking with one another and differences in accepted forms of address are but a few examples. Effective cross-cultural communications require that we become less ethnocentric and more culturally sensitive.

Nor is language per se the only barrier to effective cross-cultural communications; in fact, it may be one of the easiest barriers to overcome. In addition to verbal language issues, numerous other culturally related variables can hinder the communication process, not the least of which are space and time.

Space

Every person has an invisible boundary of space that surrounds his or her person. In some cultures (e.g., Northern Europe), the boundaries are large; whereas in other cultures (e.g., Middle Eastern countries), this space can be quite small.[52] The amount of personal space maintained by an individual can shift temporarily depending on his physical surroundings (e.g., a crowded elevator) or the degree of intimacy with the person he is interacting with (e.g., spouse). Misunderstandings can occur when a businessman from a culture where men touch and embrace one another as part of normal everyday life initiates physical contact with his counterpart from a culture where touching between men is rare and occurs only with family members. The latter individual will feel uncomfortable and may misunderstand the intent of the physical contact.

Time

Individuals in Asia, the Middle East, and Latin America tend to view time as polychronic. Managers from *polychronic* time cultures do many things at once, are subject to interruptions, are committed to human relationships, change plans often, and base promptness on the relationship. However, managers from *monochronic* cultures do one thing at a time, take time commitments seriously, adhere to plans, follow rules of privacy, show respect for private property, and emphasize promptness.[53] The most common example of misunderstandings occurs with regard to appointment times. An American executive arrives at her Mexican counterpart's office about 10 minutes before their scheduled meeting and discovers that the individual won't be arriving for another hour or so. Infuriated by the lack of respect and casual attitude of the Mexican, she sits and fumes until the meeting takes place.

Despite innumerable differences, multicultural communication can be successful. Businesspeople from different cultures effectively and efficiently communicate with each other hundreds, perhaps thousands, of times every business day. By and large, the senders and receivers of those successful communications exhibit some, or all, of the following attributes:

1. *Preparation*. They have made it a point to familiarize themselves with significant cultural differences that might affect the communication process. They do this through study, observation, and consultation with those who have direct or greater experience with the culture than do they.

2. *Outside thinking*. They make a conscious, concerted effort to lay aside ethnocentric tendencies. This does not mean they must agree with values, customs, interpretations, or perspectives different from their own; awareness, not acceptance, is what is required to facilitate communications.

3. *Humility*. Perhaps most importantly, despite their efforts at doing what is described in the above two points, they maintain a posture of "knowing they do not know." This simply means that in the absence of direct, usually extensive, ongoing exposure to another culture, they may be unaware of nuances in the communication process. Rather than assuming understanding is complete unless demonstrated otherwise, they assume it is *in*complete until shown otherwise.

In the two chapter sections that follow, you will be able to identify barriers to effective communications, which may be especially relevant in multicultural contexts, as well as find techniques for improving communications, which are particularly important in the same contexts.

Four Seasons, the luxury hotel chain, understands multicultural communication very well. In recruiting and selecting overseas managers, the Four Seasons profile includes strong listening skills, alertness to body language, and open minds.[54] Four Seasons believes that culture is learned and that open-mindedness allows managers to learn new attitudes to deal with the diversity of customers.

Barriers to Effective Communication

A good question at this point is: "Why does communication break down?" On the surface, the answer is relatively easy. We have identified the elements of communication as the communicator, encoding, the message, the medium, decoding, the receiver, and feedback. If noise exists in these elements in any way, complete clarity of meaning and understanding will not occur. A manager has no greater responsibility than to develop effective communications. In this section, we discuss several barriers to effective communication that can exist both in organizational and interpersonal communications.

Frame of Reference

Different individuals can interpret the same communication differently depending on their previous experiences. This results in variations in the encoding and decoding process. Communication specialists agree that this is the most important factor that breaks down the "commonness" in communications. When the encoding and decoding processes are not alike, communication tends to break down. Thus, while the communicator actually is speaking the "same language" as the receiver, the message conflicts with the way the receiver "catalogs" the world. If a large area is shared in common, effective communication is facilitated. If a large area is not shared in common—if there has been no common experience—then communication becomes impossible or, at best, highly distorted. The important point is that communicators can encode and receivers can decode only in terms of their experiences. As a result, distortion often occurs because of differing frames of reference.

Frames of reference and one's interpretation of events can vary based on one's organizational experience and standing: manager versus employee; entry level versus senior employee; staff versus line employee; accounting versus marketing department employee; headquarters versus affiliate employee; and so on. As a result, the needs, values, attitudes, and expectations of different individuals in the organization will differ, and this difference will often result in unintentional distortion of communication. This is not to say that one group is wrong or right. All it means is that, in any situation, individuals will choose the part of their own past experiences that relates to the current experience and is helpful in forming conclusions and judgments.

Selective Listening

A vital part of the communication process involves listening. About 75 percent of communication is listening. Most people spend only between 30 and 40 percent of their time listening.[55] This means that there are a lot of listening errors and deficiencies. Most speakers talk at a rate of about 150 words per minute. A good listener can process and understand oral communication at a rate of about 400 words per minute.

Listening takes place in four phases—perception, interpretation, evaluation, and action. Barriers can obstruct and block the listening process. The meaning attached to a manager's request is colored by a person's cultural, educational, and social frames of reference. Thus, *interpretation* of the manager's meaning may be different because of frame-of-reference differences.

The method of *evaluation* used is influenced by attitudes, preferences, and experience. The type of *action* taken involves memory and recall. Sometimes memory failures do not permit the best actions.

Selective listening is a form of selective perception in which we tend to block out new information, especially if it conflicts with what we believe. When we receive a directive from management, we notice only those things that reaffirm our beliefs. Those things that conflict with our preconceived notions we either do not note at all or we distort to confirm our preconceptions.

For example, a notice may be sent to all operating departments that costs must be reduced if the organization is to earn a profit. The communication may not achieve its desired effect because it conflicts with the "reality" of the receivers. Thus, operating employees may ignore or be amused by such information in light of the large salaries, travel allowances, and expense accounts of some executives. Whether they are justified is irrelevant; what is important is that such preconceptions result in breakdowns in communication.

A few worthwhile listening pointers are apparent in observing Oprah Winfrey, the celebrated talk show host. Oprah blocks out distractions and focuses on the talker (guest, audience member); she is always actively involved with great eye contact, listens empathically without interrupting, and paraphrases her guest's comments and ideas. She is a master at making sure the speaker is understood. Managers could learn a lot about listening in general, selective listening, and empathic listening from Oprah. Her style and approach make guests feel important, welcomed, and understood.

Value Judgments

In every communication situation, *value judgments* are made by the receiver. This basically involves assigning an overall worth to a message before receiving the entire communication. Value judgments may be based on the receiver's evaluation of the communicator or previous experiences with the communicator, or on the message's anticipated meaning. For example, a restaurant manager may not pay attention to the complaints of one of her waitstaff if this employee is known as a "whiner" and a constant complainer. In essence, the manager has categorized this employee's communication style and will react to the complaints only if she hears the same complaints from other employees.

Source Credibility

Source credibility refers to the trust, confidence, and faith that the receiver has in the words and actions of the communicator. The level of credibility the receiver assigns to the communicator in turn directly affects how the receiver views and reacts to the words, ideas, and actions of the communicator.

Thus, how subordinates view a communication from their manager is affected by their evaluation of the manager. This, of course, is heavily influenced by previous experiences with the manager. Again we see that everything done by a manager communicates. A group of hospital medical staff that views the hospital administrator as less than honest, as manipulative, and as not to be trusted is apt to assign nonexistent motives to any communication from the administrator. Union leaders who view management as exploiters and managers who view union leaders as political animals are likely to engage in little real communication.

Filtering

Filtering, a common occurrence in upward communication in organizations, refers to the manipulation of information so that the receiver perceives it as positive. Subordinates cover up unfavorable information in messages to their superiors. The reason for filtering should be clear; this is the direction (upward) that carries control information to management. Management makes merit evaluations, grants salary increases, and promotes individuals based on what it receives by way of the upward channel. The temptation to filter is likely to be strong at every level in the organization.

At General Electric, under the strong leadership of ex-CEO Jack Welch, filtering was sometimes a problem. CEO Welch had a reputation for being tough, aggressive, quick to fire employees, impatient, and intimidating, which led to his being both highly admired and feared.[56] When employees (such as the GE senior executives under Jack Welch) are apprehensive about communicating information to a superior, filtering can and does occur.

In-Group Language

In-group language or technical jargon is not always easy to understand, especially for an outsider. For example, a judge in the federal antitrust trial against Microsoft Corporation actually had to ask another computer company to define two words: *bundling* and *integration.* U.S. District Judge Thomas Penfield Jackson questioned a witness from Apple Computer Inc. about the meaning of the two words.[57] Sometimes a company creates its own internal language as a way to differentiate its products, processes, or services from those of other companies. Starbucks, named to Fortune's 100 Best Companies to Work For in 2009, is a prime example of how a company can create its own lingo or jargon; with its now ubiquitous "short," "tall," "grande," and "venti" sizes of coffee that replaced the more pedestrian "small," "medium," "large," and "extra large" sizes.[58] In addition, customers can order any of the following drinks: an Iced Quad Venti with Whip Skinny Caramel Macchiato, a Tall Green Tea Frappuccino Blended Crème, or just a Tall Americano.[59] To help customers learn the language of ordering, Starbucks published a 22-page booklet titled "Make It Your Drink."[60]

In addition to individual businesses, occupational, professional, and social groups also develop words or phrases that have meaning only to members. Such special language can serve many useful purposes. It can provide members with feelings of belonging, cohesiveness, and, in many cases, self-esteem. It also can facilitate effective communication *within* the group. The use of *in-group language* can, however, result in severe communication breakdowns when outsiders or other groups are involved. This is especially the case when groups use such language in an organization, not for the purpose of transmitting information and understanding, but rather to communicate a mystique about the group or its function.

Status Differences

Organizations often express hierarchical rank through a variety of symbols—titles, offices, carpets, and so on. Such *status differences* can be perceived as threats by persons lower in the hierarchy, and this can prevent or distort communication. Rather than look incompetent, a nurse may prefer to remain quiet instead of expressing an opinion or asking a question of the nursing supervisor.

Many times superiors, in an effort to utilize their time efficiently, make this barrier more difficult to surmount. The governmental administrator or bank vice president may be accessible only by making an appointment or by passing the careful quizzing of an administrative assistant. This widens the communication gap between superior and subordinates.

Time Pressures

The pressure of time is an important barrier to communication. An obvious problem is that managers do not have the time to communicate frequently with every subordinate. However, time pressures often can lead to far more serious problems than this. *Short-circuiting* is a failure of the formally prescribed communication system that often results from time pressures. What it means simply is that someone has been left out of the formal channel of communication who normally would be included.

For example, suppose a salesperson needs a rush order for a very important customer and goes directly to the production manager with the request since the production manager owes the salesperson a favor. Other members of the sales force get word of this and become upset over this preferential treatment and report it to the sales manager. Obviously, the sales manager would know nothing of the deal, since he or she has been short-circuited. In some cases, however, going through formal channels is extremely costly or is impossible from a practical standpoint. Consider the impact on a hospital patient if a nurse had to report a critical malfunction in life-support equipment to the nursing team leader, who in turn had to report it to the hospital engineer, who would instruct a staff engineer to make the repair.

Communication Overload

One of the vital tasks performed by a manager in decision making, and one of the necessary conditions for effective decisions, is acquiring *information*.[61] Because of the advances in communication technology, the difficulty is not in generating information. In fact, the last decade often has been described as the "Information Era" or the "Age of Information." Managers often feel buried by the deluge of information and data to which they are exposed, and they cannot absorb or adequately respond to all of the messages directed to them. They "screen out" the majority of messages, which in effect means that these messages are never decoded. Thus, the area of organizational communication is one in which more is not always better.

spam
A barrier to effective e-mail communication, this is unsolicited commercial solicitations that enter and clutter an employee's e-mail in-box.

A frequently cited barrier to effective e-mail communication is **spam,** unsolicited commercial solicitations that enter a person's e-mail in-box. Although estimates vary, approximately 2.3 billion spam messages are sent in the United States on a daily basis. According to the e-mail messaging research firm Ferris Research, approximately 40 trillion spam messages were sent worldwide in 2008, costing businesses around the globe approximately $140 billion in time and resources to deal with these unwanted messages.[62] One of the largest known spammers (Scott Richter, the "spam king") is equipped to send out an astonishing 1 billion e-mails per hour.[63] How does this affect organizations? It's estimated that about 20 percent of all inbound corporate e-mail messages are unsolicited junk e-mail. Employees have to identify and delete these unwanted messages or rely on spam filtering software to take care of them. The spam problem is getting so large that spam cost U.S. organizations in 2008 an estimated $17 billion in lost employee productivity and the use of computer resources and personnel to filter and remove it.[64]

Employees and organizations alike need to manage the amount of spam that clogs their e-mail systems. There is some relief due to the passage of a federal anti-spam law, "Controlling the Assault of Non-Solicited Pornography and Marketing Act of 2003" (a.k.a., "CAN-SPAM" Act). But the law still allows a large number of unsolicited e-mails to get through.[65] Filters, anti-spam services, and software can be used to decrease spam.[66] Also, a recent court ruling that ordered Scott Richter, the "spam king," to pay Microsoft $7 million to settle a lawsuit and to agree to stop sending unsolicited e-mails is a victory against current and would-be spammers.[67] Until spam is prohibited, employees need to develop fast and effective ways to block and delete spam without accidentally missing e-mail from real customers and co-workers.

The barriers to communication that have been discussed here, while common, are by no means the only ones. Examining each barrier indicates that they are either *within individuals* (e.g., frame of reference, value judgments) or *within organizations* (e.g., in-group language, filtering). This point is important because attempts to improve communication must focus on changing people and/or changing the organizational structure.

Improving Communication in Organizations

Managers striving to become better communicators have two separate tasks they must accomplish. First, they must improve their *messages*—the information they wish to transmit. Second, they must seek to improve their own *understanding* of what other people are trying to communicate to them. As organizations become increasingly diverse, the opportunities for communication breakdowns will most likely increase. Before examining the general means that managers can use to improve communication, consult the Management Pointer on page 392, which presents very specific ways to improve communication in diverse organizations. The bottom line of this final section of the chapter is that managers must become better encoders and decoders. They must strive not only to be understood but also to understand. The techniques discussed here can contribute to accomplishing these two important tasks.

Following Up

Following up involves assuming that you are misunderstood and, whenever possible, attempting to determine whether your intended meaning actually was received. As we have seen, meaning often is in the mind of the receiver. An accounting unit leader in a government office passes on to staff members notices of openings in other agencies. While longtime employees may understand this as a friendly gesture, a new employee might interpret it as an evaluation of poor performance and a suggestion to leave.

Regulating Information Flow

The regulation of communication can ensure an optimum flow of information to managers, thereby eliminating the barrier of "communication overload." Communication is regulated in terms of both quality and quantity. The idea is based on the *exception principle* of management, which states that only significant deviations from policies and procedures should be brought to the attention of superiors. In terms of formal communication, then, superiors should be communicated with only on matters of exception and not for the sake of communication.

Utilizing Feedback

Earlier in the chapter, feedback was identified as an important element in effective two-way communication. It provides a channel for receiver response that enables the communicator to determine whether the message has been received and has produced the intended response.[68]

In face-to-face communication, direct feedback is possible.[69] In downward e-mail communication, however, inaccuracies often occur because of insufficient opportunity for feedback from receivers. An e-mail from the vice president of human resources addressing an important policy change in benefits may be sent to all employees, but this does not guarantee that communication has occurred. Due to an excessive amount of e-mails in employees' in-boxes, the new message may not be read by every employee. Personal follow-up on the part of departmental supervisors will help ensure that everyone is aware of the new benefits policy.

Empathy

Empathy involves being receiver-oriented rather than communicator-oriented. The form of the communication should depend largely on what is known about the receiver. Empathy requires communicators to place themselves in the shoes of the receiver to anticipate how the message is likely to be decoded. Empathy is the ability to put oneself in the other person's role and to assume that individual's viewpoints and emotions. Remember that the greater the gap between the experiences and background of the communicator and the receiver, the greater is the effort that must be made to find a common ground of understanding—where there are overlapping fields of experience.

YOU BE THE JUDGE

WHAT TO DO ABOUT THE GRAPEVINE!

There are those who believe that the grapevine—the gossip chain—is the speediest, most efficient channel of communication in an organization. Research also points out that it is accurate. At least 75 percent of the gossip that travels through the grapevine is said to be true. Thus, many believe that the grapevine is a very useful channel of communication and should, therefore, be utilized by managers. It can serve as an early warning system for employees, serving up bad news long before any formal announcements are made. It can promote closeness among employees, allowing them to let off steam and alleviate stress. It provides managers the opportunity to float trial balloons (e.g., concerning a plan they're considering putting into action) and thus receive early indications of people's reactions. Finally, it can serve as a medium for building and maintaining a firm's culture. Via gossip, the company war stories and those stories that communicate the firm's values can be told.

On the other hand, there are those who believe that the grapevine carries a very costly downside—a negative impact on productivity. The argument is that gossip takes time and saps employee morale. While 75 percent of the grapevine gossip may be true, it is the remaining 25 percent that carries false and destructive rumors that employees spend costly time worrying about. As a result, managers spend a disproportionate amount of time dealing with situations caused by rumor and gossip, not reality. Managers may also be held personally liable for defamation as a result of workplace conversations that may disclose confidential information or start rumors. Finally, while managers have used the grapevine for years as an early warning system or break-it-to-them gently tool, it can no longer even serve in this capacity in many organizations because younger employees disbelieve all company communication, whether by official memo or gossip.

Because the grapevine is not likely to go away, it is important for management not to ignore it. What things can management do to curb gossip?

Sources: Adapted from A. Van Iterson and S. Clegg, "The Politics of Gossip and Denial in Interorganizational Relations," *Human Relations* 61, no. 8 (2008), pp. 1117–37; Poul Houman Andersen, "Listening to the Global Grapevine: SME Export Managers' Personal Contacts as a Vehicle for Export Information Generation," *Journal of World Business* 41, no. 1 (February 2006), pp. 81–96; Lisa A. Burke and Jessica Morris Wise, "The Effective Care, Handling, and Pruning of the Office Grapevine," *Business Horizons* 46, no. 3 (May/June 2003) pp. 71–76; and M. Kennedy, "Who Pruned the Grapevine?" *Across the Board*, March 1997, pp. 55–56.

Repetition

Repetition is an accepted principle of learning. Introducing repetition or redundancy into communication (especially that of a technical nature) ensures that if one part of the message is not understood, other parts will carry the same message. New employees often are provided with the same basic information in several different forms when first joining an organization. Likewise, students receive much redundant information when first entering a university. This is to ensure that registration procedures, course requirements, and other key issues are communicated.

Encouraging Mutual Trust

We know that time pressures often negate the possibility that managers will be able to follow up communication and encourage feedback or upward communication every time they communicate. Under such circumstances, an atmosphere of mutual confidence and trust between managers and their subordinates can facilitate communication. Managers who develop a climate of trust will find that following up on each communication is less critical and that no loss in understanding will result among subordinates from a failure to follow up on each communication. This is because they have fostered high "source credibility" among subordinates.

Effective Timing

Individuals are exposed to thousands of messages daily. Many of these messages are never decoded and received because of the impossibility of taking them all in. While managers are attempting to communicate with a receiver, other messages are being received simultaneously. Thus, the message that managers send may not be "heard." Messages are more likely to be understood when they are not competing with other messages.[70] On an everyday basis, effective communication can be facilitated by properly timing major announcements. The barriers discussed earlier often are the result of poor timing that results in distortions and value judgments.

Simplifying Language

Complex language has been identified as a major barrier to effective communication. Students often suffer when their teachers use technical jargon that transforms simple concepts into complex puzzles. Universities are not the only place where this occurs, however. Government agencies are also known for their often-incomprehensible communications. We already have noted instances where professional people use in-group language in attempting to communicate with individuals outside their group. Managers must remember that effective communication involves transmitting *understanding* as well as information. If the receiver does not understand, then there has been no communication. Managers must encode messages in words, appeals, and symbols that are meaningful to the receiver.

Using the Grapevine

The grapevine is an important information communication channel that exists in all organizations. It basically serves as a bypassing mechanism, and in many cases it is faster than the formal system it bypasses. The grapevine has been aptly described in the following manner: "With the rapidity of a burning train, it filters out of the woodwork, past the manager's office, through the locker room, and along the corridors." Because it is flexible and usually involves face-to-face communication, the grapevine transmits information rapidly. The resignation of an executive may be common knowledge long before it is officially announced.

On the other hand, the grapevine is not a formal channel of communication. Thus, there are those who believe that managers should avoid using the grapevine because to not do so borders on being unethical as well as potentially dangerous. This chapter's You Be the Judge examines the very real issue of what to do about the grapevine.

Promoting Ethical Communications

It is incumbent upon organizational members to deal ethically with one another in their communication transactions. Kreps postulates three broad principles applicable to internal organizational communications.[71] The first is that organizational members should not intentionally deceive one another. This may not be as simple a principle to conform to as it may seem. While lying clearly violates it, is communicating less than you know to be true a breach of ethics? There is no hard and fast answer. The second principle is that organization members' communication should not purposely harm any other organization member. This is known as nonmalfeasance, or refraining from doing harm. Finally, organization members should be treated justly. This too can be difficult, for justice is a relative principle that must be evaluated in a specific context.

Competitive Intelligence

Gathering information, data, and ideas from competitors has become a big business. Is it ethical? Spying on someone or another business is distasteful to some, but the price of surviving is necessary to others. Some managers propose that if the law is not broken, gathering intelligence through reviewing memos, posing as a customer, surfing a competitor's Web site, listening carefully to comments, attending trade shows, and talking to loose-lipped employees is all about business. Some companies go so far as to hire a "spy" to gain access to a competitor's organization by blending in with authorized employees to get past security guards, posing as an IT repair technician or posing as an actual employee.[72] Regardless of how one looks at it, the increased use of competitive intelligence over the past 15 years has proven costly to many U.S. companies. The FBI estimates that U.S. firms lose approximately $250 billion annually as a result of competitive intelligence leakages.[73] One survey found that the four most significant outcomes of competitive intelligence leakages are: (1) loss of competitive advantage; (2) lost market share; (3) increased research and development costs; and (4) higher insurance premiums.[74]

Competitive intelligence—a system for gathering information (all forms of communication) that affects a firm, analyzing the data, and taking action—is becoming an accepted practice. Used properly and with concern for ethical behavior, competitive intelligence can speed a firm's reaction to changes, help outmaneuver competitors, and protect a firm's own secrets. There is no one method of gathering intelligence, but a number of tools are available. Web monitoring services (such as www.knowx.com), Internet links, and books provide communication that might be useful.[75]

An example of an unethical practice of competitive intelligence was discovered by the Granite Island Group in Gloucester, Massachusetts. The firm sweeps offices for technical surveillance devices. The firm found a videoconferencing camera that turned itself on and recorded a client's board meeting. A rival of the Granite Island client had set up a system to activate the camera remotely and look and listen in on the discussion.[76]

Another example occurred when an employee was recruited to spy on her own company. A salesclerk in a retail outlet of a telecommunications organization was told that she was needed to be part of a top secret "anti-fraud team." She was sworn to secrecy and told that only the CEO, a vice president, and "Richard" (a con artist) knew of the team. After the employee sent several files to a secret e-mail account, she was given a bonus of $15,000 and months later, another bonus of $30,000. At that point, "Richard" let her in on the actual scheme and she felt she was in too deep to get out of the situation.[77]

Competitive intelligence does not have to involve turning on cameras from a remote area. Listening to a rival's public statements, which is perfectly ethical, could reveal protected information. A West Coast provider of insurance in an interview gave information about a new wellness product. A Web-based monitoring service picked this information up. Competitors seized on the information and got to the market first with their own wellness protection policies.

In conclusion, it would be hard to find an aspect of a manager's job that does not involve communication. If everyone in the organization had common points of view, communicating would be easy. Unfortunately, this is not the case. Each member comes to the organization with a distinct personality, background, experience, and frame of reference. The structure of the organization itself influences status relationships and the distance levels between individuals, which in turn influence the ability of individuals to communicate.

YOU BE THE JUDGE COMMENT

WHAT TO DO ABOUT THE GRAPEVINE!

As a supervisor or manager, your essential first step in dealing with gossip is to make sure you are plugged into the grapevine. You have to know what the latest gossip is before you can effectively deal with it. Try not to be so task-oriented that you miss hearing the rumors that have been making the rounds. For example, a subordinate might make a joke during a meeting or a hallway chat about a large customer that is thinking about pulling its account and going with a competitor. This is an obvious attempt by the subordinate to get more information about the rumor from you; in fact, she may be waiting to see if you confirm or deny it. When you start to hear similar comments or questions from other employees, it's time to start dealing with the gossip.

Dealing with gossip can be done formally (e.g., official e-mail or announcement during a meeting) or informally (e.g., hallway or lunch conversations with key employees). Either way, supervisors or managers who want to try to influence the impact of these informal messages need to be proactive and address employees' concerns. By not doing anything, managers are contributing to the unproductive time and energy that many employees will spend on trying to gather and interpret information about the rumor. This is especially so if the rumors have job-related consequences such as a potential merger or layoff situation. In sum, it's better to be a proactive communicator rather than a manager who allows rumors and gossip to undermine employees' time, energy, and ultimately, productivity.

In this chapter we have tried to convey the basic elements in the process of communication and what it takes to communicate effectively. These elements are necessary whether the communication is face-to-face or written and communicated vertically, horizontally, or diagonally within an organizational structure.

We have discussed several common communication barriers and several means to improve communication. Exhibit 13.4 illustrates the means that can be used to facilitate more effective communication. Often there is not enough time to utilize many of the techniques for improving communication, and skills such as empathy and effective listening are not easy to develop. Exhibit 13.4 shows that communicating is a matter of transmitting and receiving. Managers must be effective at both. They must understand as well as be understood.

EXHIBIT 13.4
Improving Communications in Organizations (Narrowing the Communication Gap)

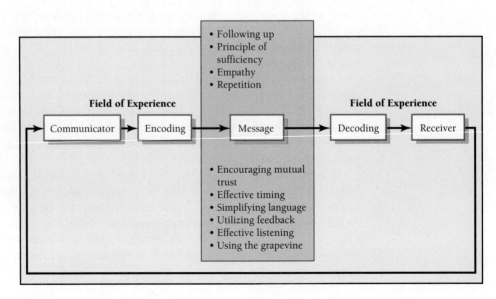

Summary of Key Points

- Communication is one of the vital processes that breathes life into an organizational structure. The process contains five elements: the *communicator,* who initiates the communication; the *message,* which is the result of encoding and which expresses the purpose of the communicator; the *medium,* which is the channel or carrier used for transmitting the message; the *receiver* for whom the message is intended; and *feedback,* a mechanism that allows the communicator to determine whether the message has been received and understood.

- Communication flow moves in one of four directions. Downward communications are the most common and include job instructions, procedures, and policies. An upward flow can be just as important and may involve the use of suggestion boxes, group meetings, or grievance procedures. Horizontal and diagonal communications serve an important coordinative function.

- Information technologies such as e-mails, voice mails, videoconferencing, and electronic meetings are becoming common in organizations of all sizes. Caution must be taken in how, when, and where these technologies are used.

- Interpersonal communication flows from individual to individual in face-to-face and group settings. In addition to providing needed information, interpersonal communication can also influence how people feel about the organization and its members. *Interpersonal style* is a term used to describe the way an individual prefers to relate to others in interpersonal communication situations.

- In the international business environment, needing to communicate with members of other cultures is becoming common. In addition to obvious language problems, different cultural customs, values, and perspectives can serve to complicate effective communications. A significant barrier is *ethnocentrism,* which is the tendency to consider the values of one's own country superior to those of other countries.

- There are numerous barriers to effective communication. Among the more significant are frame of reference, selective listening, value judgments, source credibility, filtering, in-group language, status differences, time pressures, and communication overload.

- Improving organizational communications is an ongoing process. Specific techniques for doing this include following up, regulating information flow, utilizing feedback, empathy, repetition, encouraging mutual trust, effective timing, simplifying language, effective listening, using the grapevine, and promoting ethical communications.

Reality Check

Now how much do you know about communication?

6. According to Shannon and Weaver's and Schramm's communication model, the communicator (or sender) _____ a message that is later interpreted by a receiver.
   a. encodes
   b. elaborates
   c. modifies
   d. None of the above (a–c) are correct.

7. When a subordinate communicates with his or her supervisor, this is known as _____ communication.
   a. elite
   b. upward
   c. vertical
   d. developmental

8. Which of the following communication media is highest in richness?
   a. Voice-mail message
   b. Videoconference
   c. Business letter
   d. Computer report

9. True or false: Companies use texting to reach customers because it is less expensive than other forms of advertising and it's a popular form of communication among young consumers.
   a. True
   b. False

10. A private, protected electronic communication system within an organization is known as an _____.
    a. extranet
    b. Internet
    c. intranet
    d. information-net

REALITY CHECK ANSWERS

Before	After
1. c 2. a 3. d 4. a 5. c	6. a 7. b 8. b 9. a 10. c
Number Correct	Number Correct
_____	_____

Review and Discussion Questions

1. Can you think of a communication transaction you have been part of when an encoding or decoding error was made? Why did it happen, and what could have been done to avoid it?

2. Why do you think that downward communication is much more prevalent in organizations than upward communication? How easy would it be to change this?

3. Due to the increase in spam and other nonessential e-mail messages (e.g., jokes and chain letters) that employees receive, some claim that reading, processing, and responding to e-mail messages can drain employee productivity. What can be done to help employees better manage their e-mail communication?

4. In your experience, which of the barriers to effective communication discussed in the chapter is responsible for the most communication problems? Which barrier is the hardest to correct?

5. Discuss some of the advantages of using texting to reach customers as compared with the more traditional methods such as TV, radio, newspapers, magazines, or direct mail?

6. Can you think of reasons some individuals might prefer one-way communications when they are the sender and two-way when they are the receiver? Explain.

7. A study once revealed that 55 percent of our communication time is spent transmitting and 45 percent is spent receiving. If true, what are the implications of this finding?

8. "Organizations should be less concerned with improving communication than with reducing the volume of information they disseminate to employees." Do you agree or disagree with this statement? Explain.

9. How does communication affect the interpersonal influence topics discussed in Chapters 9–11?

10. Think of a time when you were trying to communicate with someone from another culture who did not speak your native language well. What steps did you take to understand this person? What was the most difficult or challenging aspect of the situation?

Exercise

Exercise 13.1: *Your Communication Style*

To determine your preferred communication style, select the one alternative that most closely describes what you would do in each of the 12 situations below. Do not be concerned with trying to pick the correct answer; select the alternative that best describes what you would actually do. Circle the letter *a, b, c,* or *d.*

1. Wendy, a knowledgeable person from another department, comes to you, the engineering supervisor, and requests that you design a special product to her specifications. You would:

a. Control the conversation and tell Wendy what you will do for her.

b. Ask Wendy to describe the product. Once you understand it, you would present your ideas. Let her realize that you are concerned and want to help with your ideas.

c. Respond to Wendy's request by conveying understanding and support. Help clarify what is to be done by you. Offer ideas, but do it her way.

    d. Find out what you need to know. Let Wendy know you will do it her way.

2. Your department has designed a product that is to be fabricated by Saul's department. Saul has been with the company longer than you have; he knows his department. Saul comes to you to change the product design. You decide to:
   a. Listen to the change and why it would be beneficial. If you believe Saul's way is better, change it; if not, explain why the original idea is superior. If necessary, insist that it be done your way.
   b. Tell Saul to fabricate it any way he wants to.
   c. You are busy; tell Saul to do it your way. You don't have the time to listen and agree with him.
   d. Be supportive; make changes together as a team.

3. Upper management has a decision to make. They call you to a meeting and tell you they need some information to solve a problem they describe to you. You:
   a. Respond in a manner that conveys personal support and offer alternative ways to solve the problem.
   b. Respond to their questions.
   c. Explain how to solve the problem.
   d. Show your concern by explaining how to solve the problem and why it is an effective solution.

4. You have a routine work order. The work order is to be placed verbally and completed in three days. Sue, the receiver, is very experienced and willing to be of service to you. You decide to:
   a. Explain your needs, but let Sue make the other decisions.
   b. Tell Sue what you want and why you need it.
   c. Decide together what to order.
   d. Simply give Sue the order.

5. Work orders from the staff department normally take three days; however, you have an emergency and need the job today. Your colleague Jim, the department supervisor, is knowledgeable and somewhat cooperative. You decide to:
   a. Tell Jim that you need it by 3 p.m. and return at that time to pick it up.
   b. Explain the situation and how the organization will benefit by expediting the order. Volunteer to help any way you can.

    c. Explain the situation and ask Jim when the order will be ready.
    d. Explain the situation and together come to a solution to your problem.

6. Danielle, a peer with a record of high performance, has recently had a drop in productivity. Her problem is affecting her performance. You know Danielle has a family problem. You:
   a. Discuss the problem; help Danielle realize the problem is affecting her work and yours. Supportively discuss ways to improve the situation.
   b. Tell the boss about it and let him decide what to do about it.
   c. Tell Danielle to get back on the job.
   d. Discuss the problem and tell Danielle how to solve the work situation; be supportive.

7. You are a knowledgeable supervisor. You buy supplies from Peter regularly. He is an excellent salesperson and very knowledgeable about your situation. You are placing your weekly order. You decide to:
   a. Explain what you want and why; develop a supportive relationship.
   b. Explain what you want and ask Peter to recommend products.
   c. Give Peter the order.
   d. Explain your situation and allow Peter to make the order.

8. Jean, a knowledgeable person from another department, has asked you to perform a routine staff function to her specifications. You decide to:
   a. Perform the task to her specification without questioning her.
   b. Tell her that you will do it the usual way.
   c. Explain what you will do and why.
   d. Show your willingness to help; offer alternative ways to do it.

9. Tom, a salesperson, has requested an order for your department's services with a short delivery date. As usual, Tom claims it is a take-it-or-leave-it offer. He wants your decision now, or within a few minutes, because he is in the customer's office. Your action is to:
   a. Convince Tom to work together to come up with a later date.
   b. Give Tom a yes or no answer.
   c. Explain your situation and let Tom decide if you should take the order.

10. As a time-and-motion expert, you have been called in regards to a complaint about the standard time it takes to perform a job. As you analyze the entire job, you realize one element should take longer, but other elements should take less time. The end result is a shorter total standard time for the job. You decide to:
    a. Tell the operator and foreman that the total time must be decreased and why.
    b. Agree with the operator and increase the standard time.
    c. Explain your findings. Deal with the operator and/or foreman's concerns, but ensure compliance with your new standard.
    d. Together with the operator, develop a standard time.

11. You approve budget allocations for projects. Marie, who is very competent in developing budgets, has come to you. You:
    a. Review the budget, make revisions, and explain them in a supportive way. Deal with concerns, but insist on your changes.
    b. Review the proposal and suggest areas where changes may be needed. Make changes together, if needed.
    c. Review the proposed budget, make revisions, and explain them.
    d. Answer any questions or concerns Marie has and approve the budget as is.

12. You are a sales manager. A customer has offered you a contract for your product with a short delivery date. The offer is open for days. The contract would be profitable for you and the organization. The cooperation of the production department is essential to meet the deadline.

Tim, the production manager, and you do not get along very well because of your repeated requests for quick delivery. Your action is to:
    a. Contact Tim and try to work together to complete the contract.
    b. Accept the contract and convince Tim in a supportive way to meet the obligation.
    c. Contact Tim and explain the situation. Ask him if you and he should accept the contract, but let him decide.
    d. Accept the contract. Contact Tim and tell him to meet the obligation. If he resists, tell him you will go to the boss.

To determine your preferred communication style, in the chart below, circle the letter you selected as the alternative you chose in situations 1–12. The column headings indicate the style you selected.

	Autocratic	Consultative	Participative	Laissez Faire
1.	a	b	c	d
2.	c	a	d	b
3.	c	d	a	b
4.	d	b	c	a
5.	a	b	d	c
6.	c	b	a	b
7.	c	a	b	d
8.	b	c	d	a
9.	b	d	a	c
10.	a	c	d	b
11.	c	a	b	d
12.	d	b	a	c
Total				

Source: Robert N. Lussier, *Human Relations in Organizations: A Skill-Building Approach* (Homewood, IL: Irwin, 1993), pp. 153–56.

Case

Case 13.1: *The Road to Hell*

John Baker, chief engineer of the Caribbean Bauxite Company Limited of Barracania in the West Indies, was making his final preparations to leave the island. His promotion to production manager of Keso Mining Corporation near Winnipeg—one of Continental Ore's fast-expanding Canadian enterprises—had been announced a month before, and now everything had been tidied up except the last vital interview with his successor, the able young Barracanian

Matthew Rennalls. It was vital that this interview be a success and that Rennalls leave Baker's office uplifted and encouraged to face the challenge of his new job. A touch on the bell would have brought Rennalls walking into the room, but Baker delayed the moment and gazed thoughtfully through the window, considering just exactly what he was going to say and, more particularly, how he was going to say it.

Baker, an English expatriate, was 45 years old and had served his 23 years with Continental Ore in many different places: the Far East; several countries of Africa; Europe; and, for the last two years, the West Indies. He had not cared much for his previous assignment in Hamburg and was delighted when the West Indian appointment came through. Climate was not the only attraction. Baker had always preferred working overseas in what were called the developing countries because he felt he had an innate knack—more than most other expatriates working for Continental Ore—of knowing just how to get on with regional staff. Twenty-four hours in Barracania, however, soon made him realize that he would need all of his innate knack if he were to deal effectively with the problems in this field that awaited him.

At his first interview with Glenda Hutchins, the production manager, the whole problem of Rennalls and his future was discussed. There and then it was made quite clear to Baker that one of his most important tasks would be the grooming of Rennalls as his successor. Hutchins had pointed out that not only was Rennalls one of the brightest Barracanian prospects on the staff of Caribbean Bauxite—at London University he had taken first-class honors in the B.Sc. engineering degree—but, being the son of the minister of finance and economic planning, he also had political pull.

Caribbean Bauxite had been particularly pleased when Rennalls decided to work for it rather than for the government in which his father had such a prominent post. The company ascribed his action to the effects of its vigorous and liberal regionalization program that, since World War II, had produced 18 Barracanians at the middle-management level and given Caribbean Bauxite a good lead in this respect over all other international concerns operating in Barracania. The success of this timely regionalization policy had led to excellent relations with the government—a relationship that gained added importance when Barracania, three years later, became independent, an occasion that encouraged a critical and challenging attitude toward the role foreign interest would have to play in the new Barracania. Hutchins, therefore, had little difficulty convincing Baker that the successful career development of Rennalls was of the first importance.

The interview with Hutchins was now two years in the past, and Baker, leaning back in his office chair, reviewed just how successful he had been in the grooming of Rennalls. What aspects of the latter's character had helped, and what had hindered? What about his own personality? How had that helped or hindered? The first item to go on the credit side, without question, would be the ability of Rennalls to master the technical aspects of his job. From the start he had shown keenness and enthusiasm, and he had often impressed Baker with his ability in tackling new assignments and the constructive comments he invariably made in departmental discussions. He was popular with all ranks of Barracanian staff and had an ease of manner that stood him in good stead when dealing with his expatriate seniors.

These were all assets, but what about the debit side? First and foremost was his racial consciousness. His four years at London University had accentuated this feeling and made him sensitive to any sign of condescension on the part of expatriates. Perhaps to give expression to this sentiment, as soon as he returned home from London, he threw himself into politics on behalf of the United Action Party, which later won the preindependence elections and provided the country with its first prime minister.

The ambitions of Rennalls—and he certainly was ambitious—did not, however, lie in politics. Staunch nationalist he was, but he saw that he could serve himself and his country best—for was not bauxite responsible for nearly half the value of Barracania's export trade?—by putting his engineering talent to the best use possible. On this account, Hutchins found that he had an unexpectedly easy task in persuading Rennalls to give up his political work before entering the production department as an assistant engineer.

It was, Baker knew, Rennalls' well-repressed sense of racial consciousness that had prevented their relationship from being as close as it should have been. On the surface, nothing could have seemed more agreeable. Formality between the two was minimal. Baker was delighted to find that his assistant shared his own peculiar "shaggy dog" sense of humor, so jokes were continually being exchanged. They entertained one another at their houses and often played tennis together—and yet the barrier remained invisible, indefinable, but ever present. The existence of this screen between them was a constant source of frustration to Baker, since it indicated a weakness he was loathe to accept. If successful with people of all other nationalities, why not with Rennalls?

At least he had managed to break through to Rennalls more successfully than had any other expatriate. In fact, it was the young Barracanian's attitude—sometimes overbearing, sometimes cynical—toward other company expatriates that had been one of the subjects Baker raised last year when he discussed Rennalls' staff report with him. Baker knew, too, that he would have to raise the same subject again in the forthcoming interview, because Martha Jackson, the senior drafter, had complained only yesterday about the rudeness of Rennalls. With this thought in mind, Baker leaned forward and spoke into the intercom: "Would you come in, Matt, please? I'd like a word with you." Rennalls came in, and Baker held out a box and said, "Do sit down. Have a cigarette."

He paused while he held out his lighter, and then went on. "As you know, Matt, I'll be off to Canada in a few days' time, and before I go, I thought it would be useful if we could have a final chat together. It is indeed with some deference that I suggest I can be of help. You will shortly be sitting in this chair and doing the job I am now doing, but I, on the other hand, am 10 years older, so perhaps you can accept the idea that I may be able to give you the benefit of my long experience."

Baker saw Rennalls stiffen slightly in his chair as he made this point, so he added in explanation, "You and I have attended enough company courses to remember those repeated requests by the personnel manager to tell people how they are getting on as often as the convenient moment arises, and not just the automatic once a year when, by regulation, staff reports have to be discussed."

Rennalls nodded his agreement, so Baker went on, "I shall always remember the last job performance discussion I had with my previous boss back in Germany. She used what she called the 'plus and minus technique.' She firmly believed that when seniors seek to improve the work performance of their staff by discussion, their prime objective should be to make sure the latter leave the interview encouraged and inspired to improve. Any criticism, therefore, must be constructive and helpful. She said that one very good way to encourage a person—and I fully agree with her—is to discuss good points, the plus factors, as well as weak ones, the minus factors. So I thought, Matt, it would be a good idea to run our discussion along these lines."

Rennalls offered no comment, so Baker continued. "Let me say, therefore, right away, that as far as your own work performance is concerned, the pluses far outweigh the minuses. I have, for instance, been most impressed with the way you have adapted your considerable theoretical knowledge to master the practical techniques of your job—that ingenious method you used to get air down to the fifth shaft level is a sufficient case in point. At departmental meetings I have invariably found your comments well taken and helpful. In fact, you will be interested to know that only last week I reported to Ms. Hutchins that, from the technical point of view, she could not wish for a more able person to succeed to the position of chief engineer."

"That's very good indeed of you, John," cut in Rennalls with a smile of thanks. "My only worry now is how to live up to such a high recommendation."

"Of that I am quite sure," returned Baker, "especially if you can overcome the minus factor which I would like now to discuss with you. It is one that I have talked about before, so I'll come straight to the point. I have noticed that you are more friendly and get on better with your fellow Barracanians than you do with Europeans. In point of fact, I had a complaint only yesterday from Ms. Jackson, who said you had been rude to her—and not for the first time, either.

"There is, Matt, I am sure, no need for me to tell you how necessary it will be for you to get on well with expatriates, because until the company has trained up sufficient men of your caliber, Europeans are bound to occupy senior positions here in Barracania. All this is vital to your future interests, so can I help you in any way?"

While Baker was speaking on this theme, Rennalls sat tensed in his chair, and it was some seconds before he replied. "It is quite extraordinary, isn't it, how one can convey an impression to others so at variance with what one intends? I can only assure you once again that my disputes with Jackson—and you may remember also Godson—have had nothing at all to do with the color of their skins. I promise you that if a Barracanian had behaved in an equally peremptory manner, I would have reacted the same way. And again, if I may say it within these four walls, I am sure I am not the only one who has found Jackson and Godson difficult. I could mention the names of several expatriates who have felt the same. However, I am really sorry to have created this impression of not being able to get on with Europeans—it is an entirely false one—and I quite realize that I must do all I can to correct it as quickly as possible. On your last point, regarding Europeans holding senior positions in the company for some time to come, I quite accept the situation. I know that Caribbean Bauxite—as it has been for many years now—will promote Barracanians as soon as their experience warrants it. And, finally, I would like to assure you, John—and my father thinks the same, too—that I am very happy in my work here and hope to stay with the company for many years to come."

Rennalls had spoken earnestly, and Baker, although not convinced by what he had heard, did not think he could pursue the matter further except to say, "All right, Matt, my impression may be wrong, but I would like to remind you about the truth of that old saying, 'What is important is not what is true, but what is believed.' Let it rest at that."

But suddenly Baker knew that he did not want to "let it rest at that." He was disappointed once again at not being able to break through to Rennalls and at having again had to listen to his bland denial that there was any racial prejudice in his makeup.

Baker, who had intended to end the interview at this point, decided to try another tack. "To return for a moment to the plus and minus technique I was telling you just now, there is another plus factor I forgot to mention. I would like to congratulate you not only on the caliber of your work, but also on the ability you have shown in overcoming a challenge that I, as a European, have never had to meet.

"Continental Ore is, as you know, a typical commercial enterprise—admittedly a big one—that is a product of the economic and social environment of the United States and Western Europe. My ancestors have all been brought up in this environment of the past 200 or 300 years, and I have, therefore, been able to live in a world in which commerce (as we know it today) has been part and parcel of my being. It has not been something revolutionary and new that has suddenly entered my life. In your case," went on Baker, "the situation is different, because you and your forebears have only had some 50 and not 200 or 300 years. Again, Matt, let me congratulate you—and people like you—on having so successfully overcome this particular hurdle. It is for this very reason that I think the outlook for Barracania—and particularly Caribbean Bauxite—is so bright."

Rennalls had listened intently, and when Baker finished, he replied, "Well, once again, John, I have

to thank you for what you have said, and, for my part, I can only say that it is gratifying to know that my own personal effort has been so much appreciated. I hope that more people will soon come to think as you do."

There was a pause, and, for a moment, Baker thought hopefully that he was about to achieve his long-awaited breakthrough. But Rennalls merely smiled back. The barrier remained unbreached. There were some five minutes' cheerful conversation about the contrast between the Caribbean and Canadian climates and whether the West Indies had any hope of beating England in the Fifth Test before Baker drew the interview to a close. Although he was as far from ever knowing the real Rennalls, he was nevertheless glad that the interview had run along in this friendly manner and, particularly, that it had ended on such a cheerful note.

This feeling, however, lasted only until the following morning. Baker had some farewells to make, so he arrived at the office considerably later than usual. He had no sooner sat down at his desk than his secretary walked into the room with a worried frown on her face. Her words came fast. "When I arrived this morning, I found Mr. Rennalls already waiting at my door. He seemed very angry and told me in quite a peremptory manner that he had a vital letter to dictate that must be sent off without any delay. He was so worked up that he couldn't keep still and kept pacing about the room, which is most unlike him. He wouldn't even wait to read what he had dictated. Just signed the page where he thought the letter would end. It has been distributed, and your copy is in your tray."

Puzzled and feeling vaguely uneasy, Baker opened the envelope marked "Confidential" and read the following letter:

FROM: Assistant Engineer

TO: The Chief Engineer Caribbean Bauxite Limited

SUBJECT: Assessment of Interview Between Messrs. Baker and Rennalls

DATE: 14th August 1982

It has always been my practice to respect the advice given me by seniors, so after our interview, I decided to give careful thought once again to its main points and so make sure that I had understood all that had been said. As I promised you at the time, I had every intention of putting your advice to the best effect.

It was not, therefore, until I had sat down quietly in my home yesterday evening to consider the interview objectively that its main purport became clear. Only then did the full enormity of what you said dawn on me. The more I thought about it, the more convinced I was that I had hit upon the real truth—and the more furious I became. With a facility in the English language which I—a poor Barracanian—cannot hope to match, you had the audacity to insult me (and through me every Barracanian worth his salt) by claiming that our knowledge of modern living is only a paltry 50 years old, while yours goes back 200 to 300 years. As if your materialistic commercial environment could possibly be compared with the spiritual values of our culture! I'll have you know that if much of what I saw in London is representative of your boasted culture, I hope fervently that it will never come to Barracania. By what right do you have the effrontery to condescend to us? At heart, all you Europeans think us barbarians, or, as you say amongst yourselves, we are "just down from the trees."

Far into the night I discussed this matter with my father, and he is as disgusted as I. He agrees with me that any company whose senior staff think as you do is no place for any Barracanian proud of his culture and race. So much for all the company claptrap and specious propaganda about regionalization and Barracania for the Barracanians.

I feel ashamed and betrayed. Please accept this letter as my resignation, which I wish to become effective immediately.

cc: Production Manager
Managing Director

Questions

1. What, in your opinion, did Baker hope to accomplish as a result of his conversation with Rennalls? Did he succeed? Why or why not?

2. Did nonverbal communications play a part in this case? Be specific and give examples.

3. What could Baker and Rennalls have done to improve the situation described in this case?

Source: Reprinted by permission of the Industrial Relations Center, The University of Chicago.

CHAPTER FOURTEEN

Decision Making

Learning Objectives

After completing Chapter 14, you should be able to:

- **Contrast** programmed with nonprogrammed decisions.
- **Identify** the steps in the decision-making process.
- **Discuss** priority setting.

- **Describe** the conditions governing alternative-outcome relationships.
- **Explain** the role of behavioral influences on decision making.
- **Compare** individual and group decision making.
- **Identify** specific techniques for stimulating creativity.

Decision making is defined as the process of choosing a particular action that deals with a problem or opportunity. The quality of the decisions that managers make is the yardstick of their effectiveness.[1] Sometimes just one or two exceptionally good or exceptionally poor decisions can have significant effects on a manager's career or an organization's success. Union Carbide management made several poor decisions in the aftermath of the cataclysmic accident involving the release of methyl isocyanate in Bhopal, India, in 1984. This tragic event took the lives of more than 2,000 people. The accident itself, as well as subsequent decisions made regarding the handling of the accident, had profound effects on Union Carbide. Worldwide indignation and censure contributed to a collapse in the value of the company's stock, a downgrading of its credit rating, a hostile takeover attempt (by GAF Corp.), and damage claims totaling *billions* of dollars.

Another example of poor decision making can be traced to the executives at Ford Motor Company regarding the design of the Pinto. Faced with growing competition, Ford needed a small car in its lineup and rushed the Pinto through design and into production. In this rush to market, engineers made a fatal error; the placement of the Pinto fuel tank made it likely to rupture in the event of a rear-end collision. Testing revealed this flaw to engineers, but assembly equipment had already been purchased and replacing the fuel system with a safer alternative was considered to be cost-prohibitive. However, in an effort to fix the problem, the engineers worked within the existing design and developed a modification. The cost of this fix, estimated by Ford to be approximately $11 per vehicle, was determined to be more than the payout for potential lawsuits related to the projected number of deaths per year (180) and the estimated settlement per death.[2]

Because decision making is so very important and can have such significant effects on employees, customers, shareholders, and a company's reputation, as illustrated in the examples above, it has been suggested that management *is* decision making. It would be a mistake, however, to conclude that only managers make decisions. Increasingly, nonmanagers are making important decisions in organizations. Thus, while decision making is an important managerial process, it is fundamentally a *people* process.

How much do you know about decision making?

1. _____ decisions are required for unique and complex management problems.
   a. Nonprogrammed
   b. Developmental
   c. Exceptional
   d. Both *b* and *c* are correct answers.

2. The guidelines or beliefs that a person uses when confronted with a situation in which a choice must be made are known as _____.
   a. mission statements
   b. vision
   c. values
   d. ethical evaluation

3. _____ is a concept that assumes that decision making is fraught with constraints and limitations.
   a. Information conception
   b. Groupthink
   c. Bounded rationality
   d. Psychological overload

4. A mental state of anxiety that occurs when there is a conflict within an individual after a decision is made is known as _____.
   a. thought disturbance
   b. cognitive dissonance
   c. mental misalignment
   d. None of the above (*a–c*) are correct.

5. While managers at all levels make various types of decisions, supervisors are typically confronted with _____ decisions while executives focus their time on _____ decisions.
   a. ethical, unethical
   b. nonprogrammed, programmed
   c. personnel, strategic
   d. programmed, nonprogrammed

This chapter, therefore, describes and analyzes decision making in terms that reflect the ways in which people make decisions based on their understanding of individual, group, and organizational goals and objectives.

Types of Decisions

Managers in organizations may be separated by background, lifestyle, and distance, but sooner or later they must all make decisions. Even when the decision process is highly participative, with full involvement by subordinates, the manager ultimately is responsible for the outcomes of a decision. In this section, we present a classification system into which various kinds of decisions can be placed, regardless of whether the manager makes the decision unilaterally or in consultation with, or by delegation to, subordinates.

Researchers and experts in the field of decision making have developed several ways of classifying different types of decisions. For the most part, these classification systems are similar, differing mainly in terminology. We use the widely adopted distinction suggested by Herbert Simon.[3] Simon distinguishes between two types of decisions:

programmed decisions
Situations in which specific procedures have been developed for repetitive and routine problems.

nonprogrammed decisions
Decisions required for unique and complex management problems.

1. *Programmed decisions.* If a particular situation occurs often, a routine procedure usually will be worked out for solving it. Decisions are **programmed** to the extent that they are repetitive and routine and a definite procedure has been developed for handling them. For example, Amazon.com has established a precise procedure to guide the return process. These steps are so systemized that they are literally "programmed" and carried out in an automatic manner with minimal human intervention.[4]

2. *Nonprogrammed decisions.* Decisions are **nonprogrammed** when they are novel and unstructured. There is no established procedure for handling the problem, either because it has not arisen in exactly the same manner before or because it is complex or extremely important. Such decisions deserve special treatment. A vivid illustration of nonprogrammed decision making can be seen in the actions taken by the I.H. Caffey Distributing Company in the aftermath of a natural disaster. In the predawn hours of a May morning, a tornado ripped the company's distribution center in half. While Caffey had a disaster plan in place, this level of destruction was something the team had never dreamed of, and it happened as the company was entering its busiest time of the year. With over $100 million in damages, it was at risk of losing millions of dollars more in revenue. Quick and decisive decision making by company leaders allowed the company to make 25 percent of its deliveries within three days and deliver 75 percent of its orders within the week.[5] The decisions that helped this company recover quickly were nonprogrammed ones that the Caffey executives had never been faced with before.

While the two classifications are broad, they point out the importance of differentiating between programmed and nonprogrammed decisions. The management of most organizations faces great numbers of programmed decisions in their daily operations. Such decisions should be treated without expending unnecessary organizational resources on them. On the other hand, the nonprogrammed decision must be properly identified as such, since it is this type of decision that forms the basis for allocating billions of dollars worth of resources in our economy every year. Unfortunately, it is the human part of this type of decision-making process that we know the least about.[6] Exhibit 14.1 presents a breakdown of the different types of decisions, with examples

EXHIBIT 14.1   Types of Decisions

	Programmed Decisions	**Nonprogrammed Decisions**
Type of problem	Frequent, repetitive, routine, much certainty regarding cause-and-effect relationships	Novel, unstructured, much uncertainty regarding cause-and-effect relationships
Procedure	Dependence on policies, rules, and definite procedures	Necessity for creativity, intuition, tolerance for ambiguity, creative problem solving
Examples	*Business firm:* Periodic reorders of inventory	*Business firm:* Diversification into new products and markets
	University: Necessary grade point average for good academic standing	*University:* Construction of new classroom facilities
	Health care: Procedure for admitting patients	*Health care:* Purchase of experimental equipment
	Government: Merit system for promotion of state employees	*Government:* Reorganization of state government agencies

of each type, in different kinds of organizations. The exhibit illustrates that programmed and nonprogrammed decisions require different kinds of procedures and apply to distinctly different types of problems.

Traditionally, programmed decisions have been handled through rules, standard operating procedures, and the structure of the organization that develops specific procedures for handling them. Operations researchers—through the development of mathematical models—have facilitated the handling of these types of decisions.

On the other hand, nonprogrammed decisions usually have been handled by general problem-solving processes, judgment, intuition, and creativity. Unfortunately, the advances that modern management techniques have made in improving nonprogrammed decision making have not been nearly as great as the advances they have made in improving programmed decision making.[7]

Ideally, the main concern of top management should be nonprogrammed decisions, while first-level managers are typically concerned with programmed decisions. Middle managers in most organizations also concentrate on programmed decisions, but will increasingly participate in nonprogrammed decisions. In other words, the nature, frequency, and degree of certainty surrounding a problem should dictate at what level of management the decision should be made.

Obviously, problems arise in those organizations where top management expends much time and effort on programmed decisions.[8] One unfortunate result of this practice is a neglect of long-range planning, which is subordinated to other activities, whether the organization is successful or is having problems. If the organization is successful, this justifies continuing the policies and practices that have achieved success. If the organization experiences difficulty, its current problems have first priority and occupy the time of top management. In either case, long-range planning is neglected.

Finally, the neglect of long-range planning usually results in an overemphasis on short-run control. This results in a lack of delegation of authority to lower levels of management, which often has adverse effects on motivation and satisfaction.

A Rational Decision-Making Process

decision
A means to achieve some result or to solve some problem. The outcome of a process that is influenced by many forces.

Decisions should be thought of as means rather than ends. They are the *organizational mechanisms* through which an attempt is made to achieve a desired state. They are, in effect, an *organizational response* to a problem. Every decision is the outcome of a dynamic process that is influenced by a multitude of forces. Exhibit 14.2 diagrams a rational decision-making process. The reader should not, however, interpret this outline to mean that decision making is a fixed procedure. It is a sequential process rather than a series of steps. This sequence diagram enables us to examine each element in the normal progression that leads to a decision.

Examination of Exhibit 14.2 reveals that it is more applicable to nonprogrammed decisions than to programmed decisions. Problems that occur infrequently, with a great deal of uncertainty surrounding the outcome, require that the manager utilize the entire process. For problems that occur frequently, however, this is not necessary. If a policy is established to handle such problems, it will not be necessary to develop and evaluate alternatives each time a similar problem arises.

Establishing Specific Goals and Objectives and Measuring Results

Goals and objectives are needed in each area where performance influences the effectiveness of the organization. If goals and objectives are adequately established, they will dictate what results must be achieved and the measures that indicate whether or not they have been achieved. Goal setting is appropriate for individuals, teams, and both large and small

EXHIBIT 14.2
**The Rational
Decision-Making
Process**

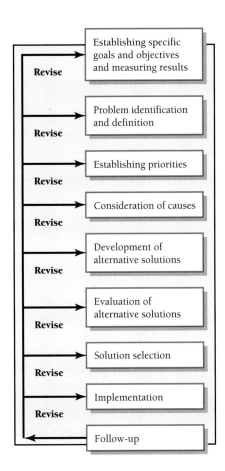

Revise → Establishing specific goals and objectives and measuring results

Revise → Problem identification and definition

Revise → Establishing priorities

Revise → Consideration of causes

Revise → Development of alternative solutions

Revise → Evaluation of alternative solutions

Revise → Solution selection

Revise → Implementation

Follow-up

organizations. University of Houston alumnus and entrepreneur Danny Klam knows the power of goal setting all too well. He owns three Simply Splendid Donuts and Ice Cream shops. His business, open for just five years, grossed over $750,000 in 2008 and is projecting an annual growth rate of 60 percent. Klam's "secret" of success may be found in a simple quote, "You have to keep your priorities straight."[9] To keep priorities, you must set and prioritize goals and monitor your progress toward the achievement of those goals.

Problem Identification and Definition

A necessary condition for a decision is a problem—if problems did not exist, there would be no need for decisions. Problems typically result from a determination that a discrepancy exists between a desired state and current reality.[10] This underscores the importance of establishing goals and objectives. How critical a problem is for the organization is measured by the gap between the levels of performance specified in the organization's goals and objectives and the levels of performance attained. Thus, a gap of 20 percent between a sales volume objective and the volume of sales actually achieved signifies that some problem exists.

It is easy to understand that a problem exists when a gap occurs between desired results and actual results. However, certain factors often lead to difficulties in identifying exactly what the problem is.[11] These factors are:

1. *Perceptual problems.* As noted in Chapter 4, individual feelings may act in such a way as to protect or defend us from unpleasant perceptions. Negative information

may be selectively perceived in such a way as to distort its true meaning or it may be ignored. For example, a college dean may fail to identify increasing class sizes as a problem while at the same time being sensitive to problems faced by the president of the university in raising funds for the school.

2. *Defining problems in terms of solutions.* This is really a form of jumping to conclusions. For example, a sales manager may say, "The decrease in profits is due to our poor product quality." The sales manager's definition of the problem suggests a particular solution—the improvement of product quality in the production department. Certainly, other solutions may be possible. Perhaps the sales force has been inadequately selected or trained. Perhaps competitors have a superior product.

3. *Identifying symptoms as problems.* "Our problem is a 32 percent decline in orders." While it is certainly true that orders have declined, the decline in orders is really a symptom of the real problem. When the manager identifies the real problem, the cause of the decline in orders will be found.

Problems usually are of three types: opportunity, crisis, or routine.[12] Crisis and routine problems present themselves and must be attended to by the managers. Opportunities, on the other hand, usually must be found. They await discovery, and they often go unnoticed and eventually are lost by an inattentive manager. This is because, by their very nature, most crises and routine problems demand immediate attention. Thus, a manager may spend more time in handling problems than in pursuing important new opportunities. Many well-managed organizations try to draw attention away from crises and routine problems and toward longer-range issues through planning activities and goal-setting programs. An organization that has benefited from effective decision making is Facebook, the social networking company. Facebook recently announced it has doubled its registered users in less than a year and is projecting annual revenue growth of over 70 percent in an otherwise weak economy. Its secret isn't really all that secret. Facebook sees itself as an advertising company. In founding the firm, CEO Mark Zuckerberg noted an imbalance between where people spent their time and where advertisers were spending their money; so, he devised a novel way to advertise online. The company is following Zuckerberg's original vision and in so doing is achieving great results. Facebook, however, has not been without its problems. In 2009, Facebook decided to change its "terms of service," effectively transferring ownership of all user-posted materials to the company. Facebook claimed that the change was simply a clarification of an existing company policy, but the public saw it differently. Internet users, already spooked over privacy concerns, blogged against the change implemented by Facebook. Internet advocates threatened to lodge a complaint with the U.S. Federal Trade Commission. Rather than ignore this self-created crisis, Facebook took decisive action and reversed the decision. The CEO promised that in the future, members would have a voice in changes to ownership of user content. This quick and clear action ended the panic and reassured users it was safe to stay with Facebook.[13]

Establishing Priorities

All problems are not created equal. Deciding whether to launch a new product in response to a competitor's move is probably a more significant decision than whether the employee lounge should be repainted. The process of decision making and solution implementation requires resources. Unless the resources the organization has at its disposal are unlimited, it is necessary to establish priorities for dealing with problems. This, in turn, means being able to determine the significance level of the problem.

Determining problem significance involves consideration of three issues: urgency, impact, and growth tendency.

Urgency relates to time. How critical is the time pressure? Putting out a fire in the office is more urgent than fixing a stalled elevator. The potential for stopgap measures also impacts urgency. For example, if people in the stalled elevator can be released before the elevator is repaired, that reduces the urgency of making repairs. *Impact* describes the seriousness of the problem's effects. Effects may be on people, sales, equipment, profitability, public image, or any number of other organizational resources. *Growth tendency* addresses future considerations. Even though a problem may currently be of low urgency and have little impact, if allowed to go unattended it may grow. The decision to cut back on routine preventive maintenance of plant equipment as a cost-cutting measure may not create a significant problem immediately. Over time, however, major difficulties may arise.

The more significant the problem, as determined by its urgency, impact, and growth tendency, the more important it is that it be addressed. A critical part of effective decision making is determining problem significance.

Consideration of Causes

While not impossible, it is ordinarily difficult and ill-advised to determine a solution to a problem when the problem cause is unknown. If an organization wishes to address the problem of declining sales, how can it decide on an appropriate solution if it does not know the reason for the decline? If sales are falling because the product is no longer price competitive, possible solutions will be quite different than if declining sales are due to poor service after the sale. Proper identification of causes helps the decision maker avoid solving the wrong problem.[14]

Frequently, the search for problem causes leads to a better definition of the real problem. Causes can be turned into new—and better—problem statements. One method that has been successfully used to find the underlying cause of a problem is the "Five Whys." This approach simply directs the problem solver to repeatedly ask "why." The "Five" in the method's name reflects a general rule that after an individual asks why five times, he or she will have worked through the various outer layers of a problem and found the true issue.[15] For example, if a bank experiences a large increase in customer account closures, management may assume that the closures are due to poor customer service. Asking a few ex-customers why the service is poor uncovers a perception that the tellers have become less pleasant than in the past. Asking some tellers why their mood has changed finds the unpleasantness is related to a recent change in the dress code. Asking why the dress code modification is causing an issue leads to the discovery that it was improperly rolled out and tellers feel it was forced on them "overnight." Finally, bank managers can ask why the rollout of the dress code was ineffective, correct those issues, and attempt to improve employee morale, ultimately restoring a high level of customer service.

Development of Alternative Solutions

Before a decision is made, feasible alternatives should be developed (actually these are potential solutions to the problem) and the potential consequences of each alternative should be considered. This is really a search process in which the relevant internal and external environments of the organization are investigated to provide information that can be developed into possible alternatives.[16] Obviously, this search is conducted within certain time and cost constraints, since only so much effort can be devoted to developing alternatives.

For example, a sales manager may identify an inadequately trained sales force as the cause of declining sales. The sales manager then would identify possible alternatives for solving the problem, such as (1) a sales training program conducted at the home office by management, (2) a sales training program conducted by a professional training organization at a site away from the home office, or (3) more intense on-the-job training.

Evaluation of Alternative Solutions

Once alternatives have been developed, they must be evaluated and compared. In every decision situation, the objective is to select the alternative that will produce the most favorable outcomes and the least unfavorable outcomes. This again points to the necessity of objectives and goals since, in selecting from among alternatives, the decision maker should be guided by the previously established goals and objectives. The alternative-outcome relationship is based on three possible conditions:

- *Certainty.* The decision maker has complete knowledge of the probability of the outcome of each alternative.
- *Uncertainty.* The decision maker has absolutely no knowledge of the probability of the outcome of each alternative.
- *Risk.* The decision maker has some probable estimate of the outcomes of each alternative.

Wouldn't it be wonderful if on a particular day early in the morning you knew for certain what the New York Stock Exchange was going to do that day? Knowing exactly what the future will be would lead to decisions about stock investments that would always optimize the results. Of course, certainty in most decision making at work, home, and in the stock market is not possible. There are greater or lesser degrees of certainty.

The degree of certainty in decision making is expressed as a risk. When a decision maker lacks certainty about an outcome from a specific action (e.g., investment in a stock, receiving a promotion based on annual performance), there is a degree of risk. A probability expresses the degree of risk. One famous company that kept many investors and e-business experts in uncertainty was Amazon.com. For many years since it was founded in 1994, CEO Jeff Bezos worked hard to convince investors, critics, and his own managers that the company would eventually show a profit. Despite his optimism, many experts gave a low probability that Amazon.com would ever report a profit. Much to the delight of those investors and managers who rode out this risk, Amazon.com reported its first profit in the fourth quarter of 2001.[17] Since then, the company has continued to show a profit and has reached $19.7 billion in sales.[18] Uncertain situations exist when managers have no or such little information that they are not able to even assign a probability to various decisions and their possible outcomes. By gathering information or studying a situation, the degree of uncertainty facing a decision maker can sometimes be reduced.

In evaluating alternative solutions, two cautions should be kept in mind. First, this phase of the decision-making process must be kept separate and distinct from the previous step, identifying solutions. This is particularly true in a group decision-making context. When alternatives are evaluated as they are proposed, this may restrict the number of alternative solutions identified. If evaluations are positive, the process may end prematurely by settling on the first positive solution. On the other hand, negative evaluations make it less likely for someone to risk venturing what may be an excellent solution for fear of being criticized or thought less of.

The second caution is to be wary of solutions that are evaluated as being "perfect." This is particularly true when the decision is being made under conditions of uncertainty. If a solution appears to have no drawbacks or if, in a group setting, there is unanimous agreement on a course of action, it may be useful to assign someone to take a devil's advocate position. The job of a **devil's advocate** is to be a thorough critic of the proposed solution. Research supports the benefits of devil's advocacy and the conflict a devil's advocate may cause, thus forcing a decision maker to reexamine assumptions and information.[19]

devil's advocate
An appointed critic of proposed group actions whose intent is to uncover underlying issues with the prevailing direction of the group.

Solution Selection

The purpose of selecting a particular solution is to solve a problem to achieve a predetermined objective. This point is an extremely important one. A decision is not an end in itself but only a means to an end. The selection of an alternative should not be viewed as an isolated act. If it is, the factors that led to and lead from the decision are likely to be excluded. Specifically, the steps following the decision should include implementation and follow-up. The critical point is that decision making is more than an act of choosing; it is a dynamic process.

Unfortunately for most managers, situations rarely exist in which one alternative achieves the desired objective without having some positive or negative impact on another objective. Situations often exist where two objectives cannot be optimized simultaneously. If one objective is *optimized,* the other is *suboptimized.* For example, when JPMorgan Chase & Co. was planning on outsourcing millions of dollars of additional work to India, it was called to task by more than three dozen members of Congress. The bank had just received $25 billion in taxpayer money as part of the government's Troubled Asset Relief Program, an initiative intended to stabilize a troubled U.S. financial industry.[20] Outsourcing to India was a means for the bank to reduce expenses and would help expedite its return to financial health. Congress wanted not only to ensure the continued solvency of the bank but also to stabilize U.S. employment. These simultaneous goals of Congress conflicted with the bank's directive to regain its financial health by reducing expenses through outsourcing.

A situation could also exist where attainment of an organizational objective would be at the expense of a societal objective. The reality of such situations is seen clearly in the rise of ecology groups, environmentalists, and the consumerist movement. Apparently, these groups question the priorities (organizational as against societal) of certain organizational decision makers. Whether an organizational objective conflicts with another organizational objective or with a societal objective, the values of the decision maker will strongly influence the alternative chosen.

In managerial decision making, optimal solutions often are impossible. This is because the decision maker cannot possibly know all of the available alternatives, the consequences of each alternative, and the probability of occurrence of these consequences.[21] Thus, rather than being an *optimizer,* the decision maker is a *satisfier,* selecting the alternative that meets an acceptable (satisfactory) standard.

Implementation

Any decision is little more than an abstraction if it is not implemented, and it must be effectively implemented to achieve the objective for which it was made. It is entirely possible for a "good" decision to be hurt by poor implementation. In this sense, implementation may be more important than the actual choice of the alternative.

Since, in most situations, implementing decisions involves people, the test of the soundness of a decision is the behavior of the people involved relative to the decision. While a decision may be technically sound, it can be undermined easily by dissatisfied subordinates. Subordinates cannot be manipulated in the same manner as other resources. Thus, a manager's job is not only to choose good solutions but also to transform such solutions into behavior in the organization. This is done by effectively communicating with the appropriate individuals and groups.[22]

Follow-Up

Effective management involves the periodic measurement of results. Actual results are compared with planned results (the objective), and if deviations exist, changes must be made. Here again, we see the importance of measurable objectives. If such objectives do not exist, then there is no way to judge performance. If actual results do not match planned results, changes must be made in the solution chosen, in its implementation, or in the original objective if it is deemed unattainable. If the original objective must be revised, then the entire decision-making process will be reactivated. The important point is that once a decision is implemented, a manager cannot assume that the outcome will meet the original objective. Some system of control and evaluation is necessary to make sure the actual results are consistent with the desired results.

Sometimes the result or outcome of a decision is unexpected or is perceived differently by different people, and dealing with this possibility is an important part of the follow-up phase in the decision process.

Alternatives to Rational Decision Making

Decision makers do not follow to the letter the decision-making process presented in Exhibit 14.2. Time pressures, incomplete information, limited human resources, and many other factors may impact the decision-making process.

Administrative Decision Making

March and Simon offer a descriptive approach that is described as the administrative decision-making model.[23] In this model decision makers are depicted as operating with incomplete information and being impacted by their cognitive abilities and by psychological and sociological factors. Managers who are faced with limitations and restrictions often use what is referred to as the **bounded rationality approach.** In this approach the decision makers are assumed to have a limited or incomplete view of the problems or opportunities facing them. The number of solutions that can be implemented is limited by the capabilities of the decision maker and the resources that are available. Since the information, data, and knowledge are not perfect, which decision is best is unknown.

In the bounded rationality approach, the following assumptions are made:

bounded rationality approach
This approach assumes that decision making is not a perfectly rational process, but rather one that is fraught with constraints and limitations. Though not optimal, decisions are thought to be satisfactory and acceptable.

- Managers (decision makers) rarely have all the information they need or want.
- Decision makers are not aware of all possible alternatives and are not able to predict consequences.
- Early alternatives and solutions are quickly adopted because of constraints and limitations.
- The organization's goals constrain decision making.
- Conflicting goals of different constituents (e.g., employees, suppliers, customers, and boards) can restrict decisions, forcing a compromise solution.

These bounded rationality–type assumptions point to making decisions that are constrained, limited, but good enough. This type of decision is referred to as a "satisfying decision," that is, making a decision that is acceptable and good enough, but if everything were perfect it might not be the optimal decision. Decision makers are satisfiers because of the circumstances and the need to move forward. For example, few people find their ideal, perfect, or optimal job. People need to earn a living, and, after what each considers to be a thorough search, a person takes an acceptable or good-enough offer. There is some degree of satisfying in almost all decisions that people make.

Southwest Airlines offers no-frills, typically on-time, and competitively priced air travel. If a traveler wants an optimal experience with a good meal, refreshments, comfortable seating, and quietness, then Southwest is not the way to fly. A traveler (decision maker) would be satisfied by electing to travel Southwest, but he or she may not be optimizing the travel experience.

Intuitive Decision Making

Managers sometimes simply make decisions based on a "gut" feeling or intuition.[24] An intuitive decision maker uses experience, self-confidence, and self-motivation to process information, data, and the environment to address a problem or opportunity. Intuitive decision making involves an unconscious process that incorporates the decision maker's personality and experience in reaching a decision. Intuitive decision making occurs frequently because:

- High levels of uncertainty about a problem, the goals, and the decision criteria can exist.
- In some situations there is no history or past experience to draw upon.
- Time pressures are intense.
- An excessive number of alternatives can be difficult to thoroughly analyze.

These factors suggest that when uncertainty is high, time pressures are bearing down, and complexity exists, intuitive decision making is likely to be involved. The rational and administrative explanations of decision making are appealing because some logic and system is associated with each of these processes.[25] However, in chaotic, rapidly changing, and pressure-packed situations, a lot of intuitive decision making is likely to occur. Perhaps it is best to combine the more systematic and intuitive approaches when attempting to reach decisions.[26]

Even when managers combine systematic and intuitive approaches, decisions can still turn out to be flawed and costly to the organization. The Organizational Encounter on page 418 reviews some of these failed decisions and several causes that may have contributed to them.

Behavioral Influences on Decision Making

A number of behavioral factors influence any decision-making process (e.g., rational, administrative, intuitive). Some of these factors influence only certain aspects of the process, while others influence the entire process. However, each may have an impact and, therefore, must be understood to fully appreciate decision making as a process in organizations. Four behavioral factors—values, propensity for risk, potential for dissonance, and escalation of commitment—are discussed in this section. Each of these factors has been shown to have a significant impact on the decision-making process.

DO GOOD COMPANIES MAKE POOR DECISIONS?

In December 2008, facing an unprecedented downturn in business, the CEOs of GM, Ford, and Chrysler traveled to Washington asking for $25 billion in government loans, lest they face bankruptcy. These highly experienced executives each took their own corporate jets to jointly testify in front of Congress. While the use of corporate jets may have been the most time-efficient means to reach Washington, the executives failed to consider the political impact of taking a private plane to plead poverty and to ask for taxpayer relief. Although the need for funding may have been legitimate, their decision to take corporate jets so enraged Congress that the executives were sent away with a scolding. *Fortune* magazine identified the trip as the "dumbest" moment in business in 2008. When they returned to Congress for a second time to again request public funding for their firms, the CEOs drove their companies' fuel-efficient vehicles from Detroit to Washington. While they intended to make a positive statement through their choice of transportation, many in the public questioned if this was the best use of an executive's time. The long drive from Detroit to Washington by the automobile industry's executives was identified by *Fortune* as the second "dumbest" business moment of the year. How could these experienced executives leading billion-dollar companies make such bad decisions over something as simple as how to get to Washington? They could have reasonably taken a commercial flight as do thousands of other executives and businesspeople. Researcher Paul C. Nutt has studied hundreds of actual managerial decisions

and found that approximately 50 percent of these decisions failed. He has analyzed such decisions as the Firestone Tire recall, the building of the Denver International Airport, and Quaker's acquisition of Snapple. He concludes that managers who fall victim to any of the following decision-making traps are more likely to make poor or failed decisions:

1. Failing to understand people's concerns and competing claims.
2. Overlooking people's interests and commitments.
3. Defining expectations in an unclear manner.
4. Limiting the search for alternatives and remedies.
5. Misusing evaluations of possible alternatives.
6. Ignoring or downplaying ethical questions.
7. Neglecting to analyze the results of the decision to understand what worked and didn't work.

Although decisions are usually made without the benefit of perfect information and unlimited time to search for and evaluate alternative solutions, managers should try to avoid the common decision-making traps that can lead to expensive and time-consuming failed decisions.

Sources: Adapted from Paul C. Nutt, *Why Decisions Fail: Avoiding the Blunders and Traps That Lead to Debacles* (San Francisco: Berrett-Koehler, 2002); Peter Valdes-Dapena, "21 Dumbest Moments in Business 2008," *Cnnmoney.com;* http://money.cnn.com/galleries/2008/fortune/0812/gallery.dumbest_moments_2009.fortune/index.html (accessed April 21, 2009).

Values

values
The guidelines and beliefs that a person uses when confronted with a situation in which a choice must be made.

In the context of decision making, **values** can be thought of as the guidelines a person uses when confronted with a situation in which a choice must be made. Values are acquired early in life and are a basic (often taken-for-granted) part of an individual's thoughts. The influence of values on the decision-making process is profound:

In *establishing objectives,* it is necessary to make value judgments regarding the selection of opportunities and the assignment of priorities.

In *developing alternatives,* it is necessary to make value judgments about the various possibilities.

In *choosing an alternative,* the values of the decision maker influence which alternative is chosen.

In *implementing a decision,* value judgments are necessary in choosing the means for implementation.

In the *evaluation and control* phase, value judgments cannot be avoided when corrective action is taken.

It is clear that values pervade the decision-making process. As one example, consider the issue of ethics in decision making. An ethical decision can be viewed as one

YOU BE THE JUDGE

ETHICS AND THE *CHALLENGER* DECISION

Millions of Americans of all ages watched the live TV presentation of the launch of the space shuttle *Challenger* on January 28, 1986. Less than two minutes after liftoff, the *Challenger* exploded. All seven crew members perished. In hindsight, it became clear that the launch should have been canceled. The issue we are examining here is, was it as clear before the launch? Consider the following:

During the evening before the launch, a teleconference took place between representatives of Morton Thiokol (manufacturer of the booster rocket), the Marshall Space Flight Center (MSFC), and the Kennedy Space Center. Morton Thiokol engineers expressed concern about the integrity of the O-ring seals at temperatures below 53 degrees (temperatures at the launch site were below freezing). The Thiokol senior engineer concluded the data supported a no-launch decision. The director of space engineering at the MSFC indicated he was "appalled" by the Thiokol recommendation but would not launch over the contractor's objections. At that point, the MSFC chief of solid rockets gave his view, concluding the data presented were inconclusive.

Based on NASA's rule that contractors had to prove it was safe to fly, the statement that the data were inconclusive should have stopped the launch. However, a Thiokol vice president who was also on the line requested an off-line caucus to reevaluate the data. During the caucus, two engineers attempted to make themselves heard as management representatives began a discussion. Their attempts were met with cold stares as management representatives struggled to compile data that would support a launch decision. Returning to the teleconference, the Thiokol VP read a launch support rationale and recommended that it proceed.

NASA, for its part, accepted the recommendation without any discussion. It was consistent with its desires. Several delays had already occurred and it feared a loss of public and political interest. Besides, the president was giving his State of the Union address that evening and surely the launch would get a favorable mention.

What is your opinion on the ethics of the decision? Recall that the text defines an ethical decision as one that is both legal and morally acceptable to society.

Sources: "Washington Outlook," *Aviation Week & Space Technology* 168, no. 19 (2008), pp. 23–26; Scott Richardson, "Our Destiny Is Out There," *Knight Ridder Tribune Business News,* January 29, 2006, p. 1; Robert D. Dimitroff, Lu Ann Schmidt, and Timothy D. Bond, "Organizational Behavior and Disaster: A Study of Conflict at NASA," *Project Management Journal* 36, no. 2 (2005), pp. 28–38; Mark Maier, "Ten Years after a Major Malfunction: Reflections on 'The Challenger Syndrome,'" *Journal of Management Inquiry* 11, no. 3, (September 2002), pp. 282–94; M.P. Miceli and J.P. Near, "Whistleblowing: Reaping the Benefits," *Academy of Management Executive,* August 1994, pp. 65–72; R. March, C. Stubbart, V. Traub, and M. Cavanaugh, "The NASA Space Shuttle Disaster: A Case Study," *Journal of Management Case Studies,* Winter 1987, pp. 300–318; and G. Whyte, "Decision Failures: Why They Occur and How to Prevent Them," *Academy of Management Executive,* August 1991, pp. 23–31.

that is legal and morally acceptable to society; an unethical decision is either illegal or morally unacceptable.[27] To a large extent, a decision maker's willingness to make ethical or unethical decisions will be influenced by his or her values. Well-publicized recent scandals involving numerous organizations such as Enron, Arthur Andersen, WorldCom, Tyco, HealthSouth, Freddie Mac, the New York Stock Exchange, and the $7 trillion mutual fund industry have heightened awareness of the critical role that values play in decision making.[28] This chapter's You Be the Judge presents another powerful example.

Ethical scandals continue to gain the public's attention. Ethical problems are not just limited to business organizations; they also impact health care, the legal profession, and government organizations. The scandals are global.[29] Why do some individual decision makers in every profession, occupation, and country resort to unethical choices? Philosophers and social scientists have studied this problem and found that no one set of explanations applies to all cases.

Some of the most cited explanations of why decision makers still make unethical choices include:

• They feel pressure to perform exceptionally well. This pressure to produce top-level results (financially) is continuous.

- They think since everyone else is doing it, so must they to remain competitive. This is the keeping-up-with-the-Joneses explanation.
- The practice of being secretive and nonrevealing is considered important in some organizations. This results in the practice of stonewalling or willingly hiding or holding onto relevant data and information. Examples of hiding research and survey information include Dow Corning's silicone gel used in breast implant studies, Ford Pinto's rear gas tank defect problems (resulting in explosions and deaths), and B. F. Goodrich rewarding employees who falsified and withheld data on the quality of aircraft brakes.
- They fail to take responsibility for problems.
- They focus on cost before safety when there is a choice.

Improving the record of making ethical decisions is difficult.[30] Values are difficult to change. Efforts to promote ethical decision making focus on training, preparation of a code of ethics, having top executives serve as proactive role models, and personally examining the situation or decision to be made. When examining the situation, the decision maker should consider doing what is legal, doing what is right, being fair, and answering the question, "Could the decision meet the 'sunshine' test," or "if it is published in the newspaper, would the reader consider the decision ethical?"

Ethical decision making starts with the values that guide an individual's decision making. There are no simple prescriptions, but there are right, fair, honest, and open ways of making decisions. Many decisions have an ethical dimension that requires thought, reflection, caution, and attention.[31] Considering the rights of others, adhering to strong values, and living up to high standards of behavior are the starting points for facing inevitable ethical dilemmas when making decisions.

Propensity for Risk

From personal experience, you undoubtedly are aware that decision makers vary greatly in their propensity for taking risks. This one specific aspect of personality strongly influences the decision-making process. A decision maker who has a low aversion to risk will establish different objectives, evaluate alternatives differently, and select different alternatives than will another decision maker in the same situation who has a high aversion to risk. The latter will attempt to make choices where the risk or uncertainty is low or where the certainty of the outcome is high. You will see later in the chapter that many people are bolder and more innovative and advocate greater risk taking in groups than as individuals. Apparently, such people are more willing to accept risk as members of a group.

Risk propensity is also affected by whether potential outcomes are characterized in terms of losses or gains. This, in turn, depends on how the decision maker "frames" the decision. *Framing* refers to the decision maker's perception, in terms of gains or losses, of the decision's possible outcomes.[32] When the choice is perceived as being between losses, there is a greater propensity to take risks than when it is perceived as being between gains. For example, when a large number of individuals are confronted with the choice of losing $100 for certain or taking a gamble on a coin flip with an equal expected value (i.e., if it comes up heads you lose $200; if it comes up tails you lose nothing), most people will choose the gamble. On the other hand, when confronted with the choice between a certain gain of $100 or a coin flip with an equal expected value (heads you receive $200; tails you receive nothing), most people opt for the certain $100.

Potential for Dissonance

Much attention has been focused on the forces and influences affecting the decision maker before a decision is made and on the decision itself. But only recently has attention been given to what happens *after* a decision has been made. Specifically, behavioral scientists have focused attention on the occurrence of post-decision anxiety.

cognitive dissonance
A mental state of anxiety that occurs when there is a conflict among an individual's various cognitions (for example, attitudes and beliefs) after a decision has been made.

Such anxiety is related to what Festinger calls cognitive dissonance.[33] Festinger's **cognitive dissonance** theory states that there is often a lack of consistency or harmony among an individual's various cognitions (attitudes, beliefs, and so on) after a decision has been made. That is, there will be a conflict between what the decision maker knows and believes and what was done, and as a result the decision maker will have doubts and second thoughts about the choice that was made. In addition, there is a likelihood that the intensity of the anxiety will be greater when any of the following conditions exist:

1. The decision is an important one psychologically or financially.
2. There are a number of forgone alternatives.
3. The forgone alternatives have many favorable features.

Each of these conditions is present in many decisions in all types of organizations. You can expect, therefore, that post-decision dissonance will be present among many decision makers, especially those at higher levels in the organization.

Dissonance can be reduced by admitting that a mistake has been made. Unfortunately, many individuals are reluctant to admit they have made a wrong decision and will be more likely to use one or more of the following methods to reduce their dissonance:

1. Seek information that supports the wisdom of their decision.
2. Selectively perceive (distort) information in a way that supports their decision.
3. Adopt a less favorable view of the forgone alternatives.
4. Minimize the importance of the negative aspects of the decision and exaggerate the importance of the positive aspects.

While each of us may resort to some of this behavior in our personal decision making, it is easy to see how a great deal of it could be extremely harmful in terms of organizational effectiveness. The potential for dissonance is influenced heavily by one's personality, specifically one's self-confidence and ability to be persuaded. In fact, all of the behavioral influences are closely interrelated and are isolated here only for discussion purposes.[34] For example, what kind of a risk taker you are and your potential for anxiety following a decision are very closely related, and both are strongly influenced by your personality, your perceptions, and your value system. Before managers can fully understand the dynamics of the decision-making process, they must appreciate the behavioral influences on themselves and other decision makers in the organization when they make decisions.

While all leaders may face decisions that leave them second-guessing, the consequences of decisions that literally deal with life and death can leave them particularly susceptible to cognitive dissonance. Perhaps no individual has made a single decision of greater impact on human life than President Harry Truman. Thrust into the Oval Office after the unexpected death of his predecessor, Truman was the president of a country at war. Rather than pursue a prolonged and bloody invasion of Japan to end World War II, Truman made the controversial decision to authorize the use of atomic weapons. This decision potentially saved the lives of hundreds of thousands of U.S. servicemen, but in doing so he also ordered an estimated 150,000 civilians to their deaths. This was not the last decision of grave consequence that Truman had to face. For example, he also involved the country in the Korean War, desegregated the military, and formed the North Atlantic Treaty Organization (NATO). It is interesting to consider how Truman weighed the costs associated with such decisions and managed the dissonance he must have experienced while and after making such impactful decisions. Even though he surely felt he was making the right decisions, how did Truman balance the costs associated with these decisions? Truman is credited with saying the following, which may provide insight into how he viewed the president's role in decision making: "Being a president is like riding a tiger. You have to keep on riding or be swallowed."[35] Perhaps Truman was saying that his focus on the present saved him from being consumed by the decisions of his past.

Escalation of Commitment

Gamblers who place larger and larger wagers in an effort to recoup earlier losses are displaying a decision-making behavior called *escalation of commitment.* Decision makers who are unclear about their goals, have a fear of failure, are feeling pressure, and work in a culture with low trust are likely to be candidates for escalation of decision making. **Escalation of commitment** refers to an increasing commitment to a previous decision when a "rational" decision maker would withdraw.[36] It typically results from a need to turn a losing or poor decision into a winning or good decision. Examples of escalation of commitment abound in daily life. President Lyndon Johnson's decision to continue increasing U.S. troop involvement in the Vietnam War is a frequently cited example. The savings and loan crisis of the 1980s grew out of decisions made by loan officers to make increasingly riskier loans in an escalating effort to recoup losses resulting from previous poor loan decisions. The decision made by Bureau of Alcohol, Tobacco, and Firearms agents to move forward with the raid on the heavily armed Branch Davidian compound outside Waco, Texas, also appears to have been an example of escalation of commitment.

Escalation of commitment can result from becoming too ego-involved in a decision process. Because failure is threatening to an individual's self-esteem, people tend to ignore negative information. It can also be the result of peer pressure, which makes it difficult for a decision maker to reverse a course of action he or she has publicly supported in the past. In either case, it involves loss of objectivity in the decision-making process.

A classic case of escalation of commitment may be seen as leading to the demise of the Joseph Schlitz Brewing Company. The brewer's marketing slogan, "When you're out of Schlitz, you're out of beer," correctly communicated the company's level of market dominance. For several years, Schlitz had been the market leader in the United States but in 1957 fell to second place behind Anheuser-Busch. In 1970, Schlitz executives made a bold decision. Attempting to recapture their top market position, they altered the recipe and the brewing process so that they could make their beer more quickly and cheaply. They substituted corn syrup for malt, changed the stabilizers in the beer, and decreased the brewing time from 40 to 15 days.

While these innovations immediately decreased costs and increased output, not surprisingly, the taste of the beer was found to be inferior. Worse, the formulation tended to break down and the ingredients would coagulate and sink, looking disturbingly like mucus at the bottom of the can. Even after the brewery realized it was shipping what was perceived as "snot beer," it decided to do nothing. Rationalizing that most of the beer would not be subject to the conditions that promoted the coagulation, what executives benignly termed "hazing," action was withheld for months before a massive

escalation of commitment
An increasing adherence to a previous decision when a rational decision maker would withdraw.

MAKING DECISIONS IN DIVERSE CULTURES

Organizational decision making in the United States is presumed to be based on thorough and objective analysis of relevant information. Whether this is true in actual practice is arguable, but it does represent what is supposed to happen ideally. This is not the ideal in every society, however. In some countries, it is inappropriate for senior executives to consult subordinates before making a decision; in other countries it is equally inappropriate for them not to consult subordinates. In almost every aspect of decision making, different cultural norms dictate different ways of proceeding. A few examples follow:

1. In some cultures (the United States, for example), problems are more likely to be seen as requiring solutions, whereas in others (Thailand, for example), problems are more likely to be seen as situations requiring acceptance.

2. Americans value following the chain of command during the decision-making process. Swedes, on the other hand, will not hesitate to go around or over someone in the chain if doing so is helpful to the decision process. Such behavior would be viewed as inappropriate in American organizations and perfectly acceptable in Swedish ones.

3. Mexicans, who value tradition and history, will tend to adopt tried and proven solutions to current problems. Australians are more present-oriented—and more aggressive—and are more likely to try unique and innovative alternative solutions.

4. Germans tend to process their decisions through committees, frequently composed primarily of technical experts. The French, who tend to be highly centralized, would not likely use committees.

5. In high power-distance cultures such as India, decisions are made at the highest level of the organization. In a low power-distance culture such as Sweden, on the other hand, the lowest-level employees expect to make their own decisions.

The differences between Japanese and American management practices are often subjects of debate and discussion. Decision making is a part of management practice, and many differences in the decision-making process exist between these two countries. For example, the Japanese are much more consensus-oriented than are Americans. Japanese decision making is often described by the word *nemawashi,* which means "root-binding." Each employee has a sense of running the organization because nothing gets done until everyone agrees. Many—if not most—American managers would find this approach frustrating and agonizingly slow. Japanese are also likely to spend much more time on deciding if a decision is even needed and on what the decision is about than their American counterparts. Because of this, they tend to direct their attention to major decisions, in contrast to American managers who often focus (by Japanese thinking) on minutiae.

These are only a few examples of the many cultural variations in decision making. They explain why cross-cultural decision making can be very difficult.

---

recall of over 10 million cans was ordered. Schlitz never recovered and was eventually bought out by a smaller brewer. Schlitz's commitment to its formula change caused its downfall. Interestingly, the current owner of the Schlitz brand name has just reintroduced the original recipe and it is being well received.[37]

Each of the behavioral influences just discussed—values, propensity for risk, potential for dissonance, and escalation of commitment—are influenced by the culture to which the decision maker has been exposed as well as the cultural context in which the decision is being made. As organizational decision making transcends national boundaries, cultural influences—and differences—become increasingly significant. Many cultural differences affect decision making. The above Global OB provides examples.

Group Decision Making

In most organizations, a great deal of decision making is achieved through committees, teams, task forces, and other kinds of groups.[38] Managers frequently face situations in which they must seek and combine judgments in group meetings. This is especially true for nonprogrammed problems, which are novel and have much uncertainty regarding the outcome. In most organizations, it is unusual to find decisions being made on such problems by one individual on a regular basis.

The increased complexity of many nonprogrammed decisions requires specialized knowledge in numerous fields, usually not possessed by one person. This requirement, coupled with the reality that the decisions made eventually must be accepted and implemented by many units throughout the organization, has increased the use of the collective approach to the decision-making process. Perhaps no organization models team effectiveness better than the U.S. Army Special Forces or Green Berets. These soldiers are expected to operate on missions that are "special" or outside of typical parameters. They are trained to ignore the "inept conventional mentality to find intelligent solutions to unconventional situations." Green Berets are experts in multiple specialty areas. When teams are deployed, each soldier has a specific role; however, each person is also cross-trained in at least one other team member's area. Teams are expected to operate in remote locations for extended periods with limited (if any) support or guidance from their command. Their success is determined by their ability to collectively and creatively implement solutions to novel situations.[39]

Individual versus Group Decision Making

Considerable debate has occurred over the relative effectiveness of individual versus group decision making. Groups usually take more time to reach a decision than individuals do. But bringing together individual specialists and experts has its benefits since the mutually reinforcing impact of their interaction results in better decisions. In fact, a great deal of research has shown that consensus decisions with five or more participants are superior to individual decision making, majority vote, and leader decisions. Unfortunately, open discussion has been found to be negatively influenced by such behavioral factors as the pressure to conform; the influence of a dominant personality type in the group; "status incongruity," as a result of which lower-status participants are inhibited by higher-status participants and "go along," even though they believe that their own ideas are superior; and the attempt of certain participants to influence others because these participants are perceived to be experts in the problem area.[40] Additionally, framing effects occur more frequently in groups.[41]

Certain decisions appear to be better made by groups, while others appear better suited to individual decision making. Nonprogrammed decisions appear to be better suited to group decision making. Usually calling for pooled talent, the decisions are so important that they are frequently made by top management and, to a somewhat lesser extent, by middle managers.

In terms of the decision-making process itself, the following points concerning group processes for nonprogrammed decisions can be made:

1. In *establishing goals and objectives,* groups probably are superior to individuals because of the greater amount of knowledge available to groups.

2. In *identifying causes and developing alternative solutions,* the individual efforts of group members are necessary to ensure a broad search in the various functional areas of the organization.

3. In *evaluating alternative solutions,* the collective judgment of the group, with its wider range of viewpoints, seems superior to that of the individual decision maker.

EXHIBIT 14.3
Probable Relationship between Quality of Group Decision and Method Utilized

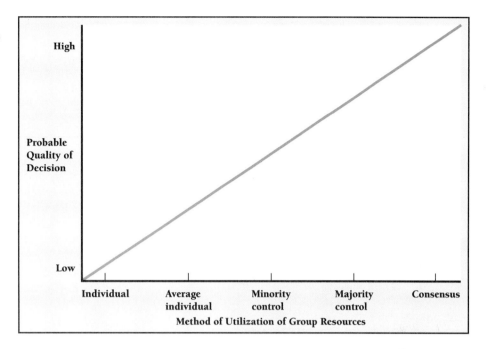

4. In *solution selection,* it has been shown that group interaction and the achievement of consensus usually results in the acceptance of more risk than would be accepted by an individual decision maker. In any event, the group decision is more likely to be accepted as a result of the participation of those affected by its consequences.

5. *Implementation and follow-up* of a decision, whether or not made by a group, usually are accomplished by individual managers. Thus, since a group ordinarily is not responsible, the responsibility for implementation and follow-up necessarily rests with the individual manager.

Exhibit 14.3 summarizes the research on group decision making. It presents the relationship between the probable quality of a decision and the method utilized to reach the decision. It indicates that, as we move from "individual" to "consensus," the quality of the decision improves. Note also that each successive method involves a higher level of mutual influence by group members. Thus, for a complex problem requiring pooled knowledge, the quality of the decision is likely to be higher as the group moves toward achieving consensus.[42] The final section of the chapter examines ways to increase creativity in group decision making. Before progressing, however, examine the Management Pointer on page 426, which presents techniques to increase your individual creativity.

Creativity in Group Decision Making

creativity
Process by which an individual, group, or team produces novel and useful ideas to solve a problem or capture an opportunity.

Since most decisions involve some degree of risk, there is a need for creativity to solve problems and seize opportunities. **Creativity** is a process by which an individual, group, or team produces novel and useful ideas to solve a problem or capture an opportunity. In organizations, moving away from logical, linear, or "in the box" thinking describes creativity. This is called *lateral thinking* or a process of generating novel ways to solve problems faced by an individual or group.

Creative decision makers share some common characteristics such as:

- *Perseverance.* They stay longer attacking problems.
- *Risk-taking propensity.* They take moderate to high risks and stay away from extreme risks.
- *Openness.* They are open to new experiences and are willing to try new approaches.
- *Tolerance of ambiguity.* They can tolerate a lack of structure, some lack of clarity, and not having complete information, data, and answers.

These characteristics of creative individuals fit many of the popular stars of the general press, including Michael Dell (Dell computers), Bill Gates (Microsoft), and Hiroyuki Yoshino (Honda Motor Company). Their backgrounds and creativity characteristics are cited quite often. One less publicized, yet creative decision maker who personifies perseverance, risk taking, openness, and an ability to deal with ambiguity is Meg Whitman. She has worked at Procter & Gamble, Bain & Co., and Disney searching for her ideal job.[43]

Meg Whitman joined FTD (flowers) as CEO and kept learning and making what colleagues call fast and nononsense decisions. She took an opportunity at eBay when it was a maze of conflict, uncertainty, and risk. Whitman was open to new ideas, withstood unrelenting criticism for her decisions, and stuck to her plan. When the eBay system crashed and service was turned off, Whitman jumped in and corrected the problems. She persevered and creatively helped eBay achieve unheard-of success. She took risks, became wealthy, and is an example of an unrecognized (by most people) leader, serving as a role model of a creative decision maker.[44]

Groups and teams can have even more creative potential than individuals such as Meg Whitman. This is especially true when the task is complex and novel and there is uncertainty. Groups have creative potential because of combined expertise, resources, and experience.

But if groups are potentially better suited to nonprogrammed decisions than individuals are, an atmosphere fostering group creativity must be created. In this respect, group decision making may be similar to and may utilize brainstorming in that discussion must be free-flowing and spontaneous. All group members must participate, and the evaluation of individual ideas must be suspended in the beginning to encourage participation, even though ultimately a decision must be reached.

Management Pointer

INCREASING YOUR CREATIVITY

As knowledge-based organizations become the norm, creativity is a competence that these organizations need. The real value in such organizations is not in their physical assets but in their intellectual assets—the ideas and insights in the minds of their employees. Such organizations cannot survive without creativity and are discovering that it is a skill that can be developed. Here are some tips for becoming more creative.

1. Get out of the office. A walk in the park or a trip to a toy store may be more productive than sitting at your desk with a pencil and pad.
2. Be childlike. Some believe this is the most important tip because creativity seems to be connected with age.
3. Be a maverick. The best ideas and decisions often come from those who don't care what others are thinking or how they are doing things.
4. Sit on the other side of the room. Break your routine, drive to work a different way.
5. Ask "What if . . . ?" This question can stimulate thought for you and plenty of discussion in a group.
6. Listen. No one has a monopoly on good ideas. Ask others, and listen.

Techniques for Stimulating Creativity

In many instances, group decision making is preferable to individual decision making, but consider the statement, "A camel is a racehorse designed by a committee." While the necessity and the benefits of group decision making are recognized, numerous problems also are associated with it, some of which already have been noted. Practicing managers need specific techniques that will enable them to increase the benefits from group decision making while reducing the associated problems. If problems are not addressed, then a group's creativity can be substantially diminished.[45]

We shall examine three techniques that, when properly utilized, have been found to be extremely useful in increasing the creative capability of a group in generating ideas, understanding problems, and reaching better decisions. Increasing the creative capability of a group is especially necessary when individuals from diverse sectors of the organization must pool their judgments and create a satisfactory course of action for the organization. The three techniques are brainstorming, the Delphi technique, and the nominal group technique.

Brainstorming

brainstorming
The generation of ideas in a group through noncritical discussion.

In many situations, groups are expected to produce creative or imaginative solutions to organizational problems. In such instances, **brainstorming** often has been found to enhance the creative output of the group. The technique of brainstorming includes a strict series of rules. The purpose of the rules is to promote the generation of ideas while, at the same time, avoiding the inhibitions of members that usually are caused by face-to-face groups. The basic rules are:

No idea is too ridiculous. Group members are encouraged to state any extreme or outlandish idea.

Each idea presented belongs to the group, not to the person stating it. In this way, it is hoped that group members will utilize and build on the ideas of others.

No idea can be criticized. The purpose of the session is to generate, not evaluate, ideas.

Brainstorming is widely used in advertising agencies where it apparently is effective. It has been less successful in other situations because there is no evaluation or ranking of the ideas generated. Thus, the group never really concludes the problem-solving process. Other issues that can decrease the effectiveness of brainstorming in teams include:[46]

1. *Social loafing.* Team members tend to not work as hard mentally or physically as they would alone, so social loafing can decrease the quality and quantity of ideas generated from the brainstorming session.
2. *Conformity.* If members of the team are overly concerned that their ideas and suggestions will be viewed critically by others, then they will be less likely to provide innovative and creative suggestions.
3. *Idea production blocking.* This occurs when a team member has to wait his or her turn to provide an idea that contributes to the brainstorming session. The delay may cause the individual to forget what he or she was going to say, or to not listen to what is being said by other contributors.
4. *Downward norm setting.* When a brainstorming session is not well managed, the lowest-performing members tend to pull down the overall performance of the team to their level.

These problems can be minimized, and the performance of team members who engage in brainstorming activities can be enhanced, by: (1) setting specific goals for the teams to achieve; (2) providing meaningful incentives for teams that perform well; and (3) having a skilled facilitator manage the process.

The Delphi Technique

This technique involves the solicitation and comparison of anonymous judgments on the topic of interest through a set of sequential questionnaires that are interspersed with summarized information and feedback of opinions from earlier responses.[47]

Delphi technique
Method of decision making that compares anonymous judgments on a topic of interest through a set of sequential questionnaires.

The **Delphi technique** retains the advantage of having several judges while removing the biasing effects that might occur during face-to-face interaction. The basic approach has been to collect anonymous judgments by mail questionnaires. For example, the members independently generate ideas to answer the first questionnaire and return it. The staff members summarize the responses as the group consensus and feed this summary back along with a second questionnaire for reassessment. Based on this feedback, the respondents independently evaluate their earlier responses. The underlying belief is that the consensus estimate will result in a better decision after several rounds of anonymous group judgment. While it is possible to continue the procedure for several rounds, studies have shown essentially no significant change after the second round of estimation.

The Nominal Group Technique (NGT)

NGT has gained increasing recognition in health, social service, education, industry, and government organizations.[48] The term **nominal group technique (NGT)** was adopted by earlier researchers to refer to processes that bring people together but do not allow them to communicate verbally. Thus, the collection of people is a group "nominally," or in name only. You will see, however, that NGT in its present form combines both verbal and nonverbal stages.

nominal group technique (NGT)
Method of decision making that occurs in a highly structured meeting; group decision is based on mathematical assessment of votes.

Basically, NGT is a structured group meeting that proceeds as follows: A group of individuals (7 to 10) sit around a table but do not speak to one another. Rather, each person writes ideas on a pad of paper. After five minutes, a structured sharing of ideas occurs. Each person around the table presents one idea. A person designated as recorder writes the ideas on a flip chart in full view of the entire group. This continues until all of the participants indicate that they have no further ideas to share. There is still no discussion.

The output of this phase is a list of ideas (usually between 18 and 25). The next phase involves structured discussion in which each idea receives attention before a vote is taken. This is achieved by asking for clarification or stating the degree of support for each idea listed on the flip chart. The next stage involves independent voting in which each participant, in private, selects priorities by ranking or voting. The group decision is the mathematically pooled outcome of the individual votes. Exhibit 14.4 illustrates the nominal group technique.

Both the Delphi technique and NGT have had excellent success records. Basic differences between them are:

1. Delphi participants typically are anonymous to one another, while NGT participants become acquainted.
2. NGT participants meet face-to-face around the table, while Delphi participants are physically distant and never meet face-to-face.
3. In the Delphi process, all communication between participants is by way of written questionnaires and feedback from the monitoring staff. In NGT, communication is direct between participants.[49]

EXHIBIT 14.4
Four-Step Nominal
Group Technique

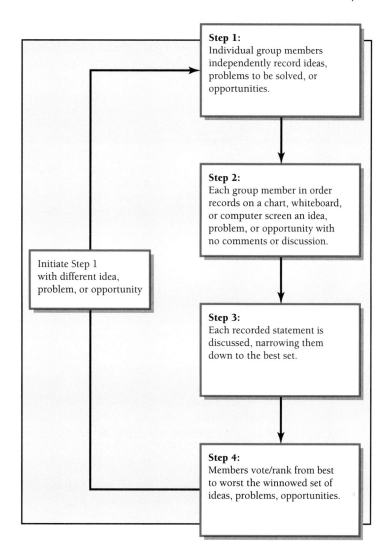

Initiate Step 1
with different idea,
problem, or opportunity

Step 1:
Individual group members
independently record ideas,
problems to be solved, or
opportunities.

Step 2:
Each group member in order
records on a chart, whiteboard,
or computer screen an idea,
problem, or opportunity with
no comments or discussion.

Step 3:
Each recorded statement is
discussed, narrowing them
down to the best set.

Step 4:
Members vote/rank from best
to worst the winnowed set of
ideas, problems, opportunities.

Practical considerations often influence which technique is used. For example, such factors as the number of working hours available, costs, and the physical proximity of participants will influence which technique is selected.

Our discussion here has not been designed to make the reader an expert in the Delphi process or NGT. Our purpose throughout this section has been to indicate the frequency and importance of group decision making in every type of organization. The three techniques discussed are practical devices to improve the effectiveness of group decisions.

Decision making is a common responsibility shared by all executives, regardless of functional area or management level. Every day, managers are required to make decisions that shape the future of their organization as well as their own futures. The quality of a manager's decisions is the yardstick of his or her effectiveness. Some of these decisions may have a strong impact on the organization's success, while others will be important but less crucial. However, all of the decisions will have some effect (positive or negative, large or small) on the organization.

YOU BE THE JUDGE COMMENT

ETHICS AND THE *CHALLENGER* DECISION

The explosion of the space shuttle *Challenger* and loss of seven crew members was a tragic event that stands in contrast to the many successful missions by the U.S. space program over the past 50 years. Unfortunately, the evidence suggests that the *Challenger* should not have been launched given that the data on the potential performance of the O-rings in temperatures under 53 degrees Fahrenheit were inconclusive. It appears that the political pressure was greater than the ability of key decision makers at Morton Thiokol, the Marshall Space Flight Center, and the Kennedy Space Center to recommend that the *Challenger* launch be delayed again. It is likely that fear, pride, career considerations, organizational pressures to succeed, and/or the ever-present urgency for public and political support for the space program took precedence over the safety of the crew. With the advantage of 20–20 hindsight, the decision to "go" may have been a legal decision, but certainly not an ethical one.

Summary of Key Points

- Decisions may be classified as programmed or nonprogrammed, depending on the type of problem. Decisions are *programmed* to the extent that they are repetitive and routine and a definite procedure has been developed for handling the problem. Decisions are *nonprogrammed* when they are novel and unstructured and there is no established procedure for handling the problem.

- Because not all problems are of the same importance, it is necessary to prioritize them. How significant a problem is depends on at least three attributes: urgency, impact, and growth tendency. *Urgency* relates to time and how critical time pressures are in dealing with a problem. *Impact* describes the seriousness of the problem's effects. *Growth tendency* addresses the likelihood of future changes in problem urgency or impact.

- The relationship between alternatives and outcomes is based on three possible conditions. *Certainty* exists when the decision maker has complete knowledge of the probability of the outcome of each alternative. *Uncertainty* exists when absolutely no such knowledge is available. *Risk* is an intermediate condition, wherein some probable estimate of outcomes can be made.

- The decision-making process entails following a number of steps. Sequentially, these are: (1) establishing specific goals and objectives and measuring results, (2) problem identification and definition, (3) establishing priorities, (4) consideration of causes, (5) development of alternative solutions, (6) evaluation of alternative solutions, (7) solution selection, (8) implementation, and (9) follow-up.

- The decision-making process is influenced by behavioral factors. Different decision makers may behave differently at any step in the decision-making process. Behavioral factors include values, propensity for risk, potential for dissonance, and escalation of commitment.

- Research suggests that decisions made by groups are superior to those made by individuals. However, some aspects of group decision making tend to have negative effects. These include pressure to conform and the disproportionate influence exerted by a dominant group member.

- One of the advantages of group decision making is that it can facilitate the identification of creative and innovative solutions to problems. Three specific techniques for stimulating creativity in groups are brainstorming, the nominal group technique, and the Delphi technique.

Review and Discussion Questions

1. Risk is an inevitable part of decision making. Thinking back to an important career-related decision you made recently, how much risk was involved in the decision? How did you go about weighing the risks associated with the possible outcomes? How much risk are you willing to tolerate to be successful in your career?

2. Why is it important to establish priorities among different problems? Under what conditions might it be necessary to reevaluate priorities?

3. Increasingly today, decisions are made in a global context. Can you think of some techniques that might be employed to reduce the likelihood of difficulties when decision makers from different cultures are working together to solve a problem?

4. How do you cope with cognitive dissonance after making a decision? Are you successful? By what criteria?

5. Think of a reasonably important nonprogrammed decision you made recently. Did you employ an approach similar to the decision-making process outlined in Exhibit 14.2? How good was your decision? Could it have been improved by using the decision-making process? Explain.

6. Given all of the corporate scandals (e.g., Enron, Tyco) that have been in the news, how important a role should ethics play in decision making? Should leaders and managers—and organizations—be evaluated on the extent to which they make ethical decisions?

7. What role does personality play in decision making? Can you think of an example from your experience where the personality of a decision maker clearly influenced his or her decision?

8. Creativity requires nonconformity of thinking. Does that explain why so many organizational decisions are noncreative? Aside from the specific techniques discussed in the chapter, what can be done to stimulate creative decision making in an organization?

9. Bounded rationality appears to be a better explanation of how decision making actually occurs. What makes this better than a rational explanation of decision making?

10. "Decisions should be thought of as means rather than ends." Explain what this statement means and what effect it should have on decision making.

Reality Check

Now how much do you know about decision making?

6. Defining problems in terms of solutions (i.e., jumping to conclusions) is a mistake that can undermine good decision making in the _____ stage of rational decision making.
   a. establishing specific goals
   b. problem identification and definition
   c. establishing priorities
   d. implementation

7. Which of the following is a technique that promotes the generation of ideas in a group through noncritical discussion?
   a. Ethical decision making
   b. Brainstorming
   c. The normal group technique
   d. Utilization development

8. True or false: Managers rarely rely on "gut" feeling or intuition when making decisions.
   a. True
   b. False

9. True or false: When a group uses a consensus approach to decision making, the quality of the decisions it makes tends to be low.
   a. True
   b. False

10. Assume you have to choose between two good job offers. One provides a higher salary, but the other is located in a city that you really like. You're anxious about the decision and not sure which job to accept. You are likely experiencing _____.
    a. decision shock
    b. cognitive dissonance
    c. repetitive information overload
    d. None of the above (a–c) are correct.

REALITY CHECK ANSWERS

Before	After
1. *a* 2. *c* 3. *c* 4. *b* 5. *d*	6. *b* 7. *b* 8. *b* 9. *b* 10. *b*
Number Correct	Number Correct
_____	_____

Exercise 14.1: *How Biased Is Your Decision Making?*

Step 1

Answer each of the problems below.

1. A certain town is served by two hospitals. In the larger hospital, about 45 babies are born each day, and in the smaller hospital, about 15 babies are born each day. Although the overall proportion of boys is about 50 percent, the actual proportion at either hospital may be greater or less than 50 percent on any day. At the end of a year, which hospital will have the greater number of days on which more than 60 percent of the babies born were boys?
   a. The large hospital.
   b. The small hospital.

c. Neither—the number of days will be about the same (within 5 percent of each other).

2. Linda is 31, single, outspoken, and very bright. She majored in philosophy in college. As a student, she was deeply concerned with discrimination and other social issues and participated in antinuclear demonstrations. Which statement is more likely:

   a. Linda is a bank teller.

   b. Linda is a bank teller and active in the feminist movement.

3. A cab was involved in a hit-and-run accident. Two cab companies serve the city: the Green, which operates 85 percent of the cabs, and the Blue, which operates the remaining 15 percent. A witness identifies the hit-and-run cab as Blue. When the court tests the reliability of the witness under circumstances similar to those on the night of the accident, he correctly identifies the color of a cab 80 percent of the time and misidentifies it the other 20 percent. What's the probability that the cab involved in the accident was Blue, as the witness stated?

4. Imagine that you face this pair of concurrent decisions. Examine these decisions, then indicate which choices you prefer:

   Decision I: Choose between:

   a. A sure gain of $240.

   b. A 25 percent chance of winning $1,000 and a 75 percent chance of winning nothing.

   Decision II: Choose between:

   c. A sure loss of $750.

   d. A 75 percent chance of losing $1,000 and a 25 percent chance of losing nothing.

   Decision III: Choose between:

   e. A sure loss of $3,000.

   f. An 80 percent chance of losing $4,000 and a 20 percent chance of losing nothing.

5. *a.* You've decided to see a Broadway play and have bought a $40 ticket. As you enter the theater, you realize you've lost your ticket. You can't remember the seat number, so you can't prove to the management that you bought a ticket. Would you spend $40 for a new ticket?

   b. You've reserved a seat for a Broadway play for which the ticket price is $40. As you enter the theater to buy your ticket, you discover you've lost $40 from your pocket. Would you still buy the ticket? (Assume you have enough cash left to do so.)

6. Imagine you have operable lung cancer and must choose between two treatments—surgery and radiation therapy. Of 100 people having surgery, 10 die during the operation, 32 (including those original 10) are dead after one year, and 66 after five years. Of 100 people having radiation therapy, none dies during treatment, 23 are dead after one year, and 78 after five years. Which treatment would you prefer?

Step 2

Your instructor will give you the correct answer to each problem.

Step 3

Discussion. In small groups, with the entire class, or in written form, as directed by your instructor, answer the following questions:

1. *Description:*

   How accurate were the decisions you reached?

2. *Diagnosis:*

   What biases were evident in the decisions you reached?

3. *Prescription:*

   How could you improve your decision making to make it more accurate?

Sources: Adapted from D. Kahneman and A. Tversky, "Rational Choice and the Framing of Decisions," *Journal of Business* 59, no. 4 (1986), pp. S251–78; A. Tversky and D. Kahneman, "The Framing of Decisions and the Psychology of Choice," *Science* 211 (1981), pp. 453–58; D. Kahneman and A. Tversky, "Extensional vs. Intuitive Reasoning," *Psychological Review* 90 (1983), pp. 293–315; and K. McKean, "Decisions, Decisions," *Discover Magazine*, June 1985.

Exercise 14.2: *Group Decision Making*

Purpose

1. Identify the pros and cons of group versus individual decision making.
2. Experience a group decision-making situation.
3. Practice diagnosing work-group effectiveness.

Introduction

Much of the work that occurs in organizations is done in groups. In fact, the more important a task, the more likely it is to be assigned to a group. The belief is that groups make better decisions and are better at solving problems than individuals. However, the evidence on this subject is contradictory and seems to suggest that "it depends." Groups are more effective under some circumstances and individuals under others. Assets and liabilities are associated with both. Because so much important work is done in groups, it is necessary for group members to learn to minimize the liabilities and capitalize on the assets of the group problem solving.

Sources: Wilderness Survival is reprinted from: J. William Pfeiffer and John E. Jones, eds., *1976 Annual Handbook for Group Facilitators* (San Diego, CA: University Associates, Inc., 1976). Used with permission. The Group Effectiveness Checklist is based on the ideas presented in I.L. Janis, "Groupthink," *Psychology Today,* November 1971. N.R.F. Maier, "Assets and Liabilities in Group Problem Solving: The Need for an Integrative Function," *Psychological Review* 74 (1967), pp. 239–49.

Instructions

1. Read the directions below and complete the Wilderness Survival Worksheet.
2. Form groups of five to seven people.
3. In groups, read the directions for and complete the Wilderness Survival Group Consensus Task.
4. Calculate your scores using the directions.
5. Interpret your score.
6. Participate in a class discussion.

Wilderness Survival Worksheet

Directions: Here are 12 questions concerning personal survival in a wilderness situation. Your first task is to *individually* select the best of the three alternatives given under each item. Try to imagine yourself in the situation depicted. Assume that you are alone and have a minimum of equipment, except where specified. The season is fall. The days are warm and dry, but the nights are cold.

After you have completed the task individually, you will again consider each question as a member of a small group. Both the individual and group solutions will later be compared with the "correct" answers provided by a group of naturalists who conduct classes in woodland survival.

	Your Answer (a, b, or c)	Your Group's Answer (a, b, or c)
1. You have strayed from your party in trackless timber. You have no special signaling equipment. The best way to attempt to contact your friends is to: a. Call for "help" loudly but in a low register. b. Yell or scream as loud as you can. c. Whistle loudly and shrilly.	_____	_____
2. You are in "snake country." Your best action to avoid snakes is to: a. Make a lot of noise with your feet. b. Walk softly and quietly. c. Travel at night.	_____	_____
3. You are hungry and lost in wild country. The best rule for determining which plants are safe to eat (those you do not recognize) is to: a. Try anything you see the birds eat. b. Eat anything except plants with bright red berries. c. Put a bit of the plant on your lower lip for five minutes; if it seems all right, try a little more.	_____	_____

4. The day becomes dry and hot. You have a full canteen of water (about one liter) with you. You should:
   a. Ration it—about a capful a day.
   b. Not drink until you stop for the night, then drink what you think you need.
   c. Drink as much as you think you need when you need it.

5. Your water is gone; you become very thirsty. You finally come to a dried-up watercourse. Your best chance of finding water is to:
   a. Dig anywhere in the streambed.
   b. Dig up plant and tree roots near the bank.
   c. Dig in the streambed at the outside of a bend.

6. You decide to walk out of the wild country by following a series of ravines where a water supply is available. Night is coming on. The best place to make camp is:
   a. Next to the water supply in the ravine.
   b. High on a ridge.
   c. Midway up the slope.

7. Your flashlight glows dimly as you are about to make your way back to your campsite after a brief foraging trip. Darkness comes quickly in the woods and the surroundings seem unfamiliar. You should:
   a. Head back at once, keeping the light on, hoping the light will glow enough for you to make out landmarks.
   b. Put the batteries under your armpits to warm them, and then replace them in the flashlight.
   c. Shine your light for a few seconds, try to get the scene in your mind, move out in the darkness, and repeat the process.

8. An early snow confines you to your small tent. You doze with your small stove going. There is danger if the flame is:
   a. Yellow.
   b. Blue.
   c. Red.

9. You must ford a river that has a strong current, large rocks, and some white water. After carefully selecting your crossing spot, you should:
   a. Leave your boots and pack on.
   b. Take your boots and pack off.
   c. Take off your pack, but leave your boots on.

10. In waist-deep water with a strong current, when crossing the stream, you should face:
    a. Upstream.
    b. Across the stream.
    c. Downstream.

11. You find yourself rimrocked; your only route is up. The way is mossy, slippery rock. You should try it:
    a. Barefoot.
    b. With boots on.
    c. In stocking feet.

12. Unarmed and unsuspecting, you surprise a large bear prowling around your campsite. As the bear rears up about 10 meters from you, you should:
    a. Run.
    b. Climb the nearest tree.
    c. Freeze, but be ready to back away slowly.

Compare your answers to the "expert answers."

Number Correct (individual)   Number Correct (group)

Wilderness Survival Group Consensus Task

Directions: You have just completed an individual solution to Wilderness Survival. Now your small group will decide on a group solution to the same dilemmas.

A decision by consensus is difficult to attain, and not every decision may meet with everyone's unqualified approval. However, there should be a general feeling of support from all members before a group decision is made. Do not change your individual answers, even if you change your mind in the group discussion.

Outcome	Group 1	Group 2	Group 3
Range of individual scores (low–high)			
Average of individual scores			
Group score			

Expert Answers

Below are the recommended courses of action for the scenarios on the Wilderness Survival Worksheet. These responses are considered to be the best rules of thumb for most situations; specific situations, however, might require other courses of action.

1. (a) *Call "Help" loudly but in a low tone.* Low tones carry farther, especially in dense woodland.

2. (a) *Make a lot of noise with your feet.* Snakes do not like people and will usually do everything they can to get out of the way.

3. (c) *Put a bit of the plant on your lower lip for five minutes; if it seems all right, try a little.* The best approach, of course, is to eat only those plants that you recognize as safe. But when you are in doubt and very hungry, you may use the lip test. If the plant is poisonous, you will get a very unpleasant sensation on your lip.

4. (c) *Drink as much as you think you need when you need it.* The danger here is dehydration, and once the process starts, your liter of water will not do much to reverse it.

5. (c) *Dig in the streambed at the outside of a bend.* This is the part of the river or stream that flows the fastest, is less silted, deepest, and the last part to go dry.

6. (c) *Midway up the slope.* A sudden rainstorm might turn the ravine into a raging torrent. The ridgeline increases your exposure to rain, wind, and lightning should a storm break. The best location is on the slope.

7. (b) *Put the batteries under your armpits to warm them, and then replace them in the flashlight.* Flashlight batteries lose much of their power, and weak batteries run down faster, in the cold. Warming the batteries, especially if they are already weak, will restore them for a while.

8. (a) *Yellow.* A yellow flame indicates incomplete combustion and a strong possibility of carbon monoxide buildup. This can be deadly.

9. (a) *Leave your boots and pack on.* Sharp rocks or uneven footing demand that you keep your boots on. If your pack is fairly well balanced, wearing it will provide you the most stability in the swift current.

10. (b) *Across the stream.* Facing upstream is the worst alternative; the current could push you back, and your pack would provide the unbalance to pull you over. You have the best stability facing across the stream, keeping your eye on the exit point on the opposite bank.

11. (c) *In stocking feet.* Here you can pick your route to some degree, and you can feel where you are stepping. Normal hiking boots become slippery, and going barefooted offers your feet no protection at all.

12. (c) *Freeze, but be ready to back away slowly.* Sudden movement will probably startle the bear a lot more than your presence. If the bear is seeking some of your food, do not argue; let the bear forage and be gone. Otherwise, back very slowly toward some refuge (trees, rock outcrop, etc.).

Source: Adapted from Jack Gordon, ed. *Pfeiffer's Classic Activities for Building Better Teams* (New York: John Wiley & Sons, 2003).

Case

Case 14.1: *Bank of America CEO under Pressure*

The mood at the April 29, 2009, Bank of America (B of A) shareholder meeting was tense. Stock prices had plummeted from a high of over $52 in 2006 to a close the previous day of $8.15. Although there was some consolation in that the stock was recovering from its recent low of $2.53, the realization that even with this bounce, the bank's stock had lost 85 percent of its value left little room for celebration. While some of the poor performance could be blamed on the economy as a whole, the Dow Jones Average was down much less at 33 percent; as a result, shareholders were increasingly looking at the actions of management and questioning their wisdom.

By the time of the meeting, B of A had received approximately $45 billion in funding from the U.S. government's Troubled Asset Relief Program (TARP). This huge cash influx was initially justified by the government as needed to stabilize this bank that was deemed too big to be allowed to fail. The most recent installment of $20 billion was seen as protecting the earlier investments of $25 billion. In exchange for the TARP funding, B of A issued shares of preferred stock to the government and dramatically cut its dividend to the owners of common stock from what had been 64 cents a share in 2008 to one cent a share. While the decisions that led to the near collapse of the bank had shareholders upset, recent revelations concerning the bank's merger with Merrill Lynch (ML) had focused their anger.

The previous September, the same month that brokerage house Lehman Brothers filed for bankruptcy and mortgage giants Fannie Mae and Freddie Mac were taken over by the government, the Treasury Department intensely negotiated a weekend deal for B of A to purchase troubled ML. The government justified this aggressive and rapid move as needed to stop a potential for multiple failures in the banking sector; and B of A, with Treasury assurances of support, complied with the government's strategy. After the negotiation, B of A CEO Kenneth Lewis, seeing a continuing decline of ML's value, attempted to exercise a negotiated right to opt out of the deal. Lewis claims when he did so Treasury Secretary Henry Paulson told him pursuing that option would

cause the Treasury to move to remove the board and the management of the company. Lewis also claimed that Fed Chairman Ben Bernanke and Paulson insisted that ML's losses (which grew to $15 billion) be kept from the public.

Not surprisingly, the Treasury and Federal Reserve recount a different version of these conversations. These agencies admit to seeing an urgent need to save ML from collapse but claim not to have threatened Lewis with his job or insisted on secrecy. The government's position was that they advised Lewis that the escape clause was not applicable and that an attempt to exercise it or pronouncements regarding ML would simply hurt the value of B of A.

Regardless of what was actually said in these high-level conversations, Lewis agreed to a deal that he knew was damaging to shareholders in order to help the government save the financial system. It appears that Lewis was confronted with at least three competing outcomes: protect shareholder wealth; protect the financial system in general, which no doubt would have a negative impact on B of A if it failed; and appease powerful government officials.

Adding to the issue were concerns over ML's questionable expenditures before the acquisition. Even though ML was losing billions of dollars, it was only after pressure from the New York Attorney General that the company dropped $200 million in bonuses to three top executives. Perhaps showing the ultimate disconnect from the reality of the firm's situation, the former ML CEO spent $1.22 million redecorating his office. Included in the CEO's new office were a rug valued at $87,784 and a $35,115 commode. These acts suggest significant flaws in the decision-making processes of the ML leadership. While the public was upset with ML for its excesses, B of A shareholders were dumbfounded as to why their company saved them.

Angered by Lewis's actions, a large and organized group of shareholders promised to make the annual meeting exciting and vote out the entire board. The bank also prepared for the meeting by hiring two "proxy solicitors" to help canvass the votes in their favor and by making statements that the ML deal would be good for shareholders in the long run.

More than 2,000 people attended the meeting. Numerous shareholders stood up and demanded the dismissal of Lewis, accusing him of using poor judgment and only trying to save his job, essentially placing his own interests before those of the shareholders. Lewis also had his supporters at the meeting expounding on how his leadership had saved the bank and perhaps the country. Rarely is such confrontation seen at shareholder meetings; the election for the board was so close that the votes required multiple counts. At the end of the day, Lewis had won reelection to the position of CEO but was forced to step down as chairman of the board. As financial pundits analyzed the election results, multiple interpretations emerged. One view of the election was that Lewis was still firmly in charge of the bank as his replacement as chairman was a board insider. Others saw this split in responsibility as a precursor to Lewis's departure.

Questions

1. B of A CEO Kenneth Lewis, in approving the ML acquisition, made a decision that many believed was not in the best interest of the bank. Critique the decision to go ahead with the ML acquisition. What would you have done?

2. Hired to help turn around a failing company, ML's CEO spent over $1 million redecorating his office. What decision-making errors do you suspect occurred in that situation and what may have prevented them?

3. What ethical concerns do you have regarding the events of the case? How might the decision-making processes have been modified to avoid these issues?

Sources: Written by Dr. Michael Dutch, Greensboro College, Greensboro, North Carolina (2009). Adapted from "Blundering Herd: Dark Days at Merrill Lynch," Guardian.co.uk, http://www.guardian.co.uk/business/2009/apr/28/merrill-lynch-banking (accessed April 20, 2009); Pallavi Gogoi and Barbara Hagenbaugh, "Bank of America Gets $20B from Government," *USA Today*, January 16, 2009; Pallavi Gogoi, "Lewis: B of A Pushed to Merrill Deal," *USA Today*, April 24, 2009; Christina Rexrode, "Key Vote at BofA Stirs Up Hostility," *The Charlotte Observer*, April 26, 2009; Jonathan Stempel, "UPDATE 9-B of A's Lewis Ousted as Board Chairman, Stays as CEO," *Forbes.com*, www.forbes.com/feeds/afx/2009/04/29/afx6358265.html (accessed April 30, 2009).

CHAPTER FIFTEEN

Leadership

Learning Objectives

After completing Chapter 15, you should be able to:

- **Define** the term *leadership*.
- **Discuss** the trait approach to leadership.
- **Describe** two major behavior approaches to leadership.
- **Explain** what situational approaches are and describe several significant ones.
- **Identify** a number of substitutes for leadership.

Leadership has been a topic of interest, speculation, and debate since the time of Plato. In organizations around the world, from massive conglomerates to small custom fabrication shops, the same lament emerges: Where are the leaders? Who are the best leaders? What are the attributes of the best leaders? The measure of effectiveness of leading that no one is tired of reading and reflecting about is *results achieved.*[1]

During the study of history we have learned a great deal about what leadership is—and about what it isn't. Despite all the thousands of studies that have been conducted, however, there is still a great deal we do not know. In this chapter we will examine some of what we do know about leadership. We will provide a concise historical and contemporary overview of leadership, and we will focus on some very current and emerging leadership concepts and consider applications that provide value.

While a great many aspects of leadership have been studied, most organizational researchers and behavioral scientists have focused on two important leadership issues: (1) why some organizational members become leaders while others do not, and (2) why some leaders are successful while others are not. Both these issues are thought to be important because leadership is so vital and energizing. It has been suggested that when groups, teams, or organizations are successful, their leadership receives too much credit, and when they fail their leadership gets too much of the blame. Nonetheless, leaders do make a difference, and leadership is a critical variable in shaping organizational effectiveness.

What Is Leadership?

With so much interest in leadership, it might be assumed that everyone is in general agreement about what constitutes leadership. Such is not the case, as can clearly be seen in the diversity of whom we consider to be leaders. A 2009 *Time* magazine poll of the "100 most influential people" in the world included: Barack Obama, Chesley ("Sully") Sullenberger, Hillary Clinton, Rush Limbaugh, Oprah Winfrey, Ted Turner, and Ted Kennedy.[2] These individuals operate in distinct environments and toward divergent objectives. While most would agree that they are leaders, what leads to their success may not be as clear. Can one precisely define what allowed Ted Kennedy to be elected eight times to the U.S. Senate? If he had switched places with Ted Turner, would those same characteristics and traits have led him to comparable successes in the global media industry?

leadership
Using influence in an organizational setting or situation, producing effects that are meaningful and have a direct impact on accomplishing challenging goals.

Leadership qualities important in one situation may be different from those required in another.[3] It is unlikely that any of the individuals on the 100 most influential list would be equally successful in another's context or industry. Leadership does not take place in a vacuum. Every leader must deal with three important variables: the people who are being led, the task that the people are performing, and the environment in which the people and the task exist. Because these three variables are different in every situation, what is expected and needed from a leader will be different in every situation.

The fact that leaders and leadership situations differ has led to numerous leadership definitions. Some definitions of leadership are based on leader characteristics, some on leader behaviors, still others on outcomes or end results. A definition of leadership needs to be sufficiently broad to accommodate different theories, research findings, and applications. We define **leadership** as the process of influencing others to facilitate the attainment of organizationally relevant goals.[4] Note that as specified by this definition you do not have to be in a formal leadership position to exert leadership behavior. The role of informal leader can be every bit as important to a group's success as is that of the formal leader.

Differences in definitions, leadership expectations, and the three significant variables that are a part of all leadership situations (people, task, environment) notwithstanding, there are some leadership commonalities. For example, Warren Bennis, who has devoted decades to researching leadership issues,[5] concludes that virtually all leaders of effective groups share four characteristics:

1. They provide direction and meaning to the people they are leading. This means they remind people what is important and why what they are doing makes an important difference.
2. They generate trust.
3. They favor action and risk taking. That is, they are proactive and willing to risk failing in order to succeed.
4. They are purveyors of hope. In both tangible and symbolic ways they reinforce the notion that success will be attained.[6]

The Organizational Encounter on page 442 illustrates that the most unlikely person can display leadership. As the Encounter illustrates, some individuals obviously possess characteristics that are so attractive to others that they are considered leaders.

Is Leadership Important?

Leaders such as SAS's Jim Goodnight can make a difference in end results in categories such as performance, goal attainment, and individual growth and development. However, the specific behavior and the processes used by leaders to make such a difference are somewhat ambiguous.

Empirical evidence of the magnitude of the effects of leadership on performance is modest. Several reasons have been cited to explain these modest effects.[7] First, those selected as leaders are similar in background, experience, and qualifications. The similarity across selected individuals reduces the range of characteristics exhibited by leaders. Second, leaders at even the highest levels do not have unilateral control over resources. Major decisions require approval, review, and the use of modifications suggested by others. Third, many factors cannot be controlled by a leader. Labor markets, environmental factors, and policies are often outside a leader's direct control. External factors may be overwhelming and uncontrollable, no matter how astute, insightful, and influential a leader may be.

Over the years researchers have continued to find only a modest effect of leadership on performance. One study of 167 firms in 13 industries over a 20-year period found that the administration factor (i.e., a combination of leadership and managership) had a limited effect on sales, profits, and profit margins.[8] Reanalysis of the same data found that leadership accounted for more variance in performance than did many of the other variables studied, but most of the variance is unexplained.[9]

Manz and Sims have clearly pointed out another wave of thinking that emphasizes the replacement of "bosses" with teams of employees who serve as their own bosses.[10] The concept has been labeled variously as *self-managing teams, empowerment teams,* and *autonomous work groups.* The teams described by Sims and Manz may not have bosses, but they do have leaders. As these organizational researchers state, "No successful team is without leadership." Manz and Sims have described "superleaders," individuals who lead others to lead themselves to higher levels of performance. Team leaders sometimes emerge or are sometimes appointed. They can be called coordinators, facilitators, or coaches. They exert influence from a position of respect or expertise that is accepted by the other team members. The Organizational

LEADERSHIP HAS NO AGE LIMITS

While many high school seniors spend their spare time wondering who will be their prom date or who will win the next school sporting event, Michael Sessions had bigger things on his mind. Turning 18 years old in his senior year in high school, Michael decided he wanted to be mayor of his hometown, Hillsdale, Michigan, a community of 8,200 residents 85 miles outside of Detroit. Not able to be listed on the ballot because he was too young at the time of the filing deadline, he launched a write-in campaign against the unopposed incumbent. He used $700 of his savings as campaign funds and went door-to-door trying to meet as many people as possible. Although he had recently lost the election to become his class vice president, Michael beat the 51-year-old incumbent for the position of mayor by a margin of two votes. While the position is largely ceremonial, Michael is responsible for running city council meetings and making city commission appointments. Hillsdale High School government and economics teacher Steven Brower described Michael as a go-getter who approached the race for mayor as if he were running for president of the United States. Asked why he ran, Michael told ABC News that he wanted to make a difference.

Michael has kept his campaign promises and added an additional full-time firefighter and made City Hall a friendlier and more service-oriented organization. However, Michael's tenure as mayor has not been without controversy. He has been involved with the dismissal of the longtime city manager and survived a recall election due to a misdemeanor conviction related to the sending of disparaging e-mails about his former friend and campaign manager. Michael has decided not to seek reelection as he is unsure where his post-college career will take him.

Sources: "College-Student Mayor Not Seeking Re-Election," *Newsmax.com*, www.newsmax.com/us/teen_mayor/2009/04/14/202964.html (accessed April 14, 2009); Korie Wilkins, "Young Mayor Emerges Wiser: Hillsdale's Michael Sessions, 20, Beats Cancer, Recall Effort," *WZZM13.com*, October 15, 2007, www.wzzm13.com/news/news_article.aspx?storyid = 82273; Wendy Koch, "'Go-Getter,' 18, Ousts Mayor in Michigan," USAToday.com, November 9, 2005, www.usatoday.com/news/nation/2005-11-09-kid-mayor_x.htm; and Brian Wise and Jen Brown, "High School Senior Elected Mayor of Mich. Town," ABC News, November 9, 2005, http://abcnews.go.com/GMA/story?id = 1296769.

Encounter "Growing Leaders" shows that some companies work hard at grooming leaders for the future.

Trait Approaches

Thinking and discussion about leadership have evolved over the years from a trait-based approach to the concept of teams without bosses. To understand this evolution in views of leadership, it is helpful to trace the historical foundations, some considered today to be rather simplistic and some so complex that practitioners now find little value in them.

Much of the early discussion and research on leadership focused on identifying intellectual, emotional, physical, and other personal traits of effective leaders. This approach assumed that a finite number of individual traits of effective leaders could be found. To a significant extent, the personnel testing component of scientific management supported the **trait theory of leadership**.[11] In addition to being studied by testing, the traits of leaders have been examined by observation of behavior in group situations, by choice of associates (voting), by nomination or rating by observers, and by analysis of biographical data.

trait theory of leadership
An attempt to identify specific characteristics (physical, mental, personality) associated with leadership success. The theory relies on research that relates various traits to certain success criteria.

Intelligence

In a review of 33 studies, Ralph Stogdill found that leaders were more intelligent than followers.[12] One significant finding, however, was that extreme intelligence differences between leaders and followers might be dysfunctional. For example, a leader with a relatively high IQ attempting to influence a group whose members have average IQs may be unable to understand why the members don't comprehend the problem. In addition, such a leader may have difficulty communicating ideas and policies. A 2007 study examined the relationship between leader ability and IQ in a population of

GROWING LEADERS

George Buckley, CEO of 3M, was recently quoted as saying, "I'd sooner own a fish farm than be reliant on catching a few." Of course, Buckley wasn't talking about fish but rather how 3M prefers internal development of leaders over external recruitment to fill its ranks. Developing leaders is seen as an investment at 3M. Buckley realizes that some of the leaders he "raises" will likely end up with other organizations, but the increased availability of internal talent for those who stay makes the effort well worth it.

Buckley's approach to leader development is simple. He states, "There is a difference between a leader and a manager. A leader is as much about inspiration as anything else. A manager is more about process. We try to mix both into our development. In the end, maybe you can't plant leadership in a person, but you certainly can enhance it in a person." The company's methods

must be working, as it was named by the Hay Group and *Chief Executive* magazine as the "Best Company for Leaders."

More than 1,000 firms headquartered in 89 countries were considered in the Hay Group/*Chief Executive* study. Obtaining the No. 1 spot on this list was no easy task; 3M narrowly edged out Procter & Gamble and General Electric for first place on the list of the best companies for leaders. Other notable companies on the list included Coca-Cola, Southwest Airlines, and PepsiCo.

Does growing your own leadership talent have any real benefit? Perhaps it's not a coincidence that 3M was also listed by *Fortune* magazine as one of the top 20 most admired companies in the world.

Sources: Adapted from Del Jones, "3M CEO Emphasizes Importance of Leaders," *USA Today*, May 18, 2009; J.P. Donlon, "Best Companies for Leaders," *Chief Executive*, February 2009; and Geoff Colvin, "The World's Most Admired Companies 2009," *Fortune*, March 16, 2009.

police officers and suggested that although IQ is important for leaders, emotional intelligence (covered in Chapter 4) is a better predictor of leadership ability in certain contexts.[13]

Personality

Edwin Ghiselli reported several personality traits associated with leader effectiveness.[14] He found that the ability to initiate action independently was related to the respondent's level in the organization. The higher the person went in the organization, the more important this trait became. Ghiselli also found that self-assurance was related to hierarchical position in the organization. Finally, he found that persons who exhibited individuality were the most effective leaders. Studies continue to find a relation between personality characteristics and leader effectiveness. A recent study looked at the "Big Five" personality traits along with leader self-efficacy (the belief in one's potential for success) and several perceived job characteristics. The study confirmed a relation between personality characteristics and leadership assessments; most notable was a strong relationship between leader self-efficacy and leader performance.[15]

Physical Characteristics

Studies of the relationship between effective leadership and physical characteristics such as age, height, weight, and appearance provide contradictory results. Being taller and heavier than the group average is certainly not advantageous for achieving a leader position. However, some organizations believe a physically large person is needed to secure compliance from followers. This notion relies heavily on coercive power. Nonetheless, Truman, Gandhi, Napoleon, and Stalin are examples of individuals of small stature who rose to powerful leadership positions. Even when the use of physical attributes was being promoted as a principal technique to select leaders, the method was questioned. A 1944 book on selection stated, "Do not fall into the error of judging character from facial or other physical characteristics," advocating instead other, more "scientific" approaches.[16] While this 65-year-old advice is generally taken today as

EXHIBIT 15.1

Traits Associated with Leadership Effectiveness

Source: Adapted from Bernard M. Bass, *Stogdill's Handbook of Leadership* (New York: Free Press, 1982), pp. 75–76.

Intelligence	Personality	Abilities
Judgment	Adaptability	Ability to enlist cooperation
Decisiveness	Alertness	Cooperativeness
Knowledge	Creativity	Popularity and prestige
Fluency of speech	Personal integrity	Sociability (interpersonal skills)
	Self-confidence	Social participation
	Emotional balance and control	Tact, diplomacy
	Independence (nonconformity)	

true, our understanding of scientific approaches has evolved to the extent that it may be questioned. In a study using pictures of company CEOs, subjects' facial evaluations of CEOs were found to be related to company performance.[17] This study suggests the need for further research on the relationship between physical appearance and leadership outcomes.

Supervisory Ability

Using the leaders' performance ratings, Ghiselli found a positive relationship between supervisory ability and level in the organizational hierarchy.[18] The supervisor's ability is defined as the "effective utilization of whatever supervisory practices are indicated by the particular requirements of the situation."[19] Once again, a valid measurement of the concept is needed—and finding such precision is still a difficult problem to resolve.

Exhibit 15.1 summarizes a number of the most researched traits of leaders (traits found most likely to characterize successful leaders). Some studies have reported that these traits contribute to leadership success. However, leadership success is neither primarily nor completely a function of these or other traits.

Although in some studies traits such as those in Exhibit 15.1 have differentiated effective from ineffective leaders, research findings are still contradictory for a number of possible reasons. First, the list of potentially important traits is endless. Every year, new traits—such as the sign under which a person is born, handwriting style, and order of birth—are added to personality, physical characteristics, and intelligence. This continual "adding on" results in more confusion among those interested in identifying leadership traits. Second, trait test scores aren't consistently predictive of leader effectiveness. Leadership traits don't operate singly to influence followers, but act in combination. This interaction influences the leader–follower relationship. Third, patterns of effective behavior depend largely on the situation: Leadership behavior that's effective in a bank may be ineffective in a laboratory. Finally, the trait approach fails to provide insight into what the effective leader does on the job. Observations are needed that describe the behavior of effective and ineffective leaders.

Despite its shortcomings, the trait approach is not completely invalid. Kirkpatrick and Locke found evidence that effective leaders are different from other people.[20] Their review of the literature suggests that drive, motivation, ambition, honesty, integrity, and self-confidence are key leadership traits. Kirkpatrick and Locke believe that leaders don't have to be great intellects to succeed. However, leaders do need to have the "right stuff" or right traits to have a good chance to be effective.

Behavioral Approaches

In the 1940s, researchers began to explore the notion that how a person acts determines that person's leadership effectiveness. Instead of searching for traits, these researchers examined leader *behaviors* and their impact on the performance and satisfaction of followers.

Job-Centered and Employee-Centered Leadership

In 1947, Rensis Likert began studying how best to manage the efforts of individuals to achieve desired performance and satisfaction objectives. The purpose of most leadership research by the Likert-inspired team at the University of Michigan was to discover the principles and methods of effective leadership. The effectiveness criteria used in many of the studies included:

Productivity per work hour, or other similar measures of the organization's success in achieving its production goals.

Job satisfaction of members of the organization.

Turnover, absenteeism, and grievance rates.

Costs.

Scrap loss.

Employee and managerial motivation.

Studies were conducted in a wide variety of organizations: chemical, electronics, food, heavy machinery, insurance, petroleum, public utilities, hospitals, banks, and government agencies. Data were obtained from thousands of employees doing different job tasks, ranging from unskilled work to highly skilled research and development work.

job-centered leader
Focuses on encouraging employees to complete the task and uses close supervision so that individuals perform their tasks using acceptable and timely procedures.

Through interviewing leaders and followers, researchers identified two distinct styles of leadership, referred to as *job-centered* and *employee-centered*. The **job-centered leader** focuses on completing the task and uses close supervision so that subordinates perform their tasks using specified procedures.

employee-centered leader
Focuses on having people complete the work and believes in delegating decision making and aiding employees in satisfying their needs by creating a supportive work environment.

The **employee-centered leader** focuses on the people doing the work and believes in delegating decision making and aiding employees in satisfying their needs by creating a supportive work environment. The employee-centered leader is concerned with followers' personal advancement, growth, and achievement. Such leaders emphasize individual and group development with the expectation that effective work performance will naturally follow.

Initiating Structure and Consideration

One of the more significant leadership research programs that developed after World War II was led by Edwin Fleishman and his associates at The Ohio State University. This important research program yielded a two-factor theory of leadership.[21] A series of studies isolated two leadership factors, referred to as *initiating structure* and *consideration*.

initiating structure
Designates behavior in which the leader organizes and defines the relationships in the group, tends to establish well-defined patterns and channels of communication, and spells out ways of getting the job done.

consideration
Involves behavior indicating friendship, mutual trust, respect, warmth, and rapport between the leader and the followers.

Initiating structure designates behavior in which the leader organizes and defines the relationships in the group, tends to establish well-defined patterns and channels of communication, and spells out ways of getting the job done. The leader with a high initiating structure tendency focuses on goals and results. **Consideration** involves behavior indicating friendship, mutual trust, respect, warmth, and rapport between the leader and the followers. The leader with a high consideration overview supports open communication and participation.

These dimensions are measured by two separate questionnaires. The Leadership Opinion Questionnaire (LOQ) assesses how leaders think they behave in leadership roles. The Leader Behavior Description Questionnaire (LBDQ) measures perceptions of subordinates, peers, or superiors.

The original premise suggested by the Ohio State researchers was that a high degree of consideration and a high degree of initiating structure (high–high) was most desirable. Since the original research was undertaken to develop the questionnaire, there have been numerous studies of the relationship between these two leadership dimensions and various effectiveness criteria. In a study at International Harvester, researchers began to find some more complicated interactions of the two dimensions. Supervisors who scored high on initiating structure not only had high proficiency ratings from superiors but also had more employee grievances. A high consideration score was related to lower proficiency ratings and lower absences.[22] A recent review of the literature found that initiating structure was consistently associated with leader and group performance, and consideration was associated with follower satisfaction, motivation, and leader effectiveness.[23]

The OSU personal–behavioral theory has been criticized for simplicity (e.g., only two dimensions of leadership), lack of generalizability, and reliance on questionnaire responses to measure leadership effectiveness. Organizational researchers have cautioned against reliance on questionnaire measures of leadership-initiating factors. One convincing argument is that when raters know about a leader's performance, their ratings of her behavior may be substantially distorted. Hence, correlations between past performance and rated behavior may reflect performance-induced distortions in behavioral ratings as well as real causal effects of past behavior on performance.[24]

Why Trait and Behavioral Approaches Fall Short

Both trait and behavioral approaches to leadership have helped us better understand the dynamics of leadership situations. Trait approaches consider personal characteristics of the leader that may be important in achieving success in a leadership role. There is no doubt that certain characteristics may be helpful—even essential—in some situations. These same characteristics, however, may be unimportant—even detrimental—in other situations. Similarly, the behavioral approaches attempt to specify which kinds of leader behaviors are necessary for effective leadership. And here again there is no doubt that certain behaviors may be important in some situations, but may be irrelevant or damaging in others. Initiating-structure behaviors on the part of the leader, for example, may be critical to successful task completion in some situations; in others, where workers know exactly what needs to be done, such behaviors may detract from employee performance and satisfaction.

At the start of the chapter we suggested that leaders needed to deal with three important variables: the people being led, the task being performed, and the environment in which the work was occurring. Trait and behavior approaches fail to consider this interaction among people, tasks, and environments. All three variables are an important part of the leadership situation, yet trait and behavior approaches ignore task and environment considerations.

Situational Approaches

When the search for the "best" set of traits or behaviors failed to discover an effective leadership mix and style for all situations, situational theories of leadership evolved that suggest leadership effectiveness is a function of various aspects of the leadership *situation*. A number of situational approaches have been proposed and studied. We will examine several of the more significant ones.

Only after inconclusive and contradictory results evolved from much of the early trait and behavior research was the importance of the situation studied more closely by those interested in leadership. As the importance of situational factors became more recognized, leadership research became more systematic, and situational models of leadership began to appear in the literature. Each model has its advocates, and each attempts to identify the leader behaviors most appropriate for a series of leadership situations. Also, each model attempts to identify the leader-situation patterns or interactions for effective leadership.

Fiedler's Contingency Leadership Model

The contingency model of leadership effectiveness was developed by Fiedler[25] and postulates that the performance of groups is dependent on the interaction between leadership style and situational favorableness. Leadership style is measured by the *Least-Preferred Coworker Scale* (LPC), an instrument developed by Fiedler that assesses the degree of positive or negative feelings held by a person toward someone with whom he or she least prefers to work. Low scores on the LPC are thought to reflect a *task-oriented*, or controlling, structuring leadership style. High scores are associated with a *relationship-oriented*, or passive, considerate leadership.

leader–member relations
A factor in the Fiedler contingency model that refers to the degree of confidence, trust, and respect that the leader obtains from the followers.

Fiedler proposes three factors that determine how favorable a leader's environment is, or what is designated the degree of situational favorableness. **Leader–member relations** refers to the degree of confidence, trust, and respect the followers have in their leader. This is the most important factor. **Task structure** is the second most important factor and refers to the extent to which the tasks the followers are engaged in are structured. That is, is it clearly specified and known what followers are supposed to do, how they are to do it, when and in what sequence it is to be done, and what decision options they have (high structure)? Or are these factors unclear, ambiguous, unspecifiable (low structure)? **Position power** is the final factor and refers to the power inherent in the leadership position. Generally, greater authority equals greater position power.

task structure
A factor in the Fiedler contingency model that refers to how structured a job is with regard to requirements, problem-solving alternatives, and feedback on how correctly the job has been accomplished.

Together, these three factors determine how favorable the situation is for the leader. Good leader–member relations, high task structure, and strong position power constitute the most favorable situation. Poor relations, low degree of structure, and weak position power represent the least favorable situation. The varying degrees of favorableness and the corresponding appropriate leadership style are shown in Exhibit 15.2.

position power
A factor in the Fiedler contingency model that refers to the power inherent in the leadership position.

Fiedler contends that a permissive, more lenient (relationship-oriented) style is best when the situation is moderately favorable or moderately unfavorable. Thus, if a leader is moderately liked and possesses some power, and the job tasks for subordinates are somewhat vague, the leadership style needed to achieve the best results is relationship-oriented. In contrast, when the situation is highly favorable or highly unfavorable, a task-oriented approach generally produces the desired performance. Fiedler bases his conclusions regarding the relationship between

EXHIBIT 15.2
Summary of Fiedler's Situation Variables and Their Preferred Leadership Styles

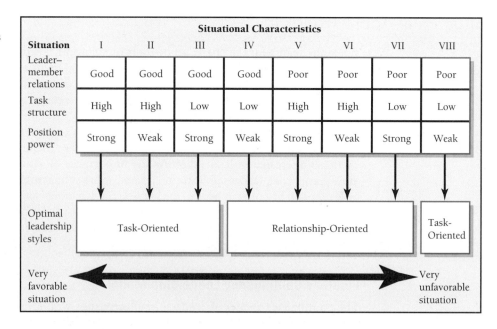

leadership style and situational favorableness on more than two decades of research in business, educational, and military settings.[26] The Management Pointer suggests several steps leaders can take to modify various situations.

Fiedler is not particularly optimistic that leaders can be trained successfully to change their preferred leadership style. Consequently, he sees changing the favorableness of the situation as a better alternative. In doing this, the first step Fiedler recommends is to determine whether leaders are task- or relationship-oriented. Next, the organization needs to diagnose and classify the situational favorableness of its leadership positions. Finally, the organization must select the best strategy to bring about improved effectiveness. If leadership training is selected as an option, then it should devote special attention to teaching participants how to modify the environments and their jobs to fit their styles of leadership. That is, leaders should be trained to change their leadership situations. Fiedler believes that a leader's style, whether relationship-oriented or task-oriented, is fixed or enduring. Altering the situation to fit the leader's style is what he recommends. Fiedler suggests that when leaders can recognize the situations in which they are most successful, they can then begin to modify their own situations.

Critique of Fiedler's Contingency Model

Fiedler's model and research have elicited both support and criticisms.[27] Some researchers have called attention to the questionable measurement of the LPC, finding its reliability and validity to be low. Others have criticized the fact that Fiedler's variables are not precisely defined. For example, at what point does a "structured" task become an "unstructured" task? Still others feel that the model is flawed because it too readily accommodates nonsupportive results.

Despite supporters and detractors, Fiedler's contingency model has made significant contributions to the study and application of leadership principles. Fiedler called direct attention to the situational nature of leadership. His view of leadership stimulated numerous research studies and much-needed debate about the dynamics of leader behavior. Certainly, Fiedler has played one of the most prominent roles in encouraging the scientific study of leadership in work settings. He pointed the way and made others uncomfortably aware of the complexities of the leadership process.

Vroom-Jago Leadership Model

Victor Vroom and Philip Yetton initially developed a leadership decision-making model that indicated the situations in which various degrees of participative decision making would be appropriate.[28] In contrast to Fiedler's work on leadership, Vroom and Yetton attempted to provide a normative model that a leader can use in making decisions. The term *normative* refers to the fact that the model provides norms or guidelines leaders can use for dealing with decision-making situations. Their approach assumed that no one single leadership style was appropriate; rather, the leader must be flexible enough to change leadership styles to fit specific situations. In developing the model, Vroom and Yetton made these assumptions:

1. The model should be of value to managers in determining which leadership styles they should use in various situations.
2. No single style is applicable to all situations.
3. The main focus should be the problem to be solved and the situation in which the problem occurs.
4. The leadership style used in one situation should not constrain the styles used in other situations.
5. Several social processes influence the amount of participation by subordinates in problem solving.

> **Vroom-Jago leadership model**
> A leadership model that specifies which leadership decision-making procedures will be most effective in each of several different situations. Two of the proposed leadership styles are autocratic (AI and AII); two are consultative (CI and CII); and one is oriented toward joint decisions (decisions made by the leader and the group, GII).

After a number of years of research and application, the original model has been revised by Vroom and Jago to further improve its accuracy.[29] To understand the **Vroom-Jago leadership model,** it is important to consider three critical components: (1) specification of the criteria by which decision effectiveness are judged, (2) a framework for describing specific leader behaviors or styles, and (3) key diagnostic variables that describe important aspects of the leadership situation.

Decision Effectiveness

> **decision quality**
> An important criterion in the Vroom-Jago model that refers to the objective aspects of a decision that influence subordinates' performance aside from any direct impact on motivation.

Selection of the appropriate decision-making process involves considering two criteria of decision effectiveness: decision quality and subordinate commitment. **Decision quality** refers to the extent to which the decision impacts job performance. For example, deciding whether to paint the stripes in the employee parking lot yellow or white requires low decision quality because it has little or no impact on job performance. On the other hand, a decision regarding at what level to set production goals requires high decision quality. *Subordinate commitment* refers to how important it is that the subordinates be committed to or accept the decision in order that it may be successfully implemented. Deciding which color paint to use in the parking lot does not really require employee commitment to be successfully implemented; just as clearly, setting production goals at a particular level does require employee commitment if those goals are to be achieved.

In addition to quality and commitment considerations, decision effectiveness may be influenced by time considerations. A decision is not an effective one, regardless of quality and commitment, if it takes too long to make. Even a decision made relatively quickly, if it is a participative one involving a number of people, may be costly in terms of total time spent. Thus, a decision made at a meeting of 15 department members and the department manager that takes two hours has used 32 work hours. In terms of overall organizational effectiveness, this may represent a larger opportunity cost than can be justified.

Decision Styles

The Vroom-Jago model makes a distinction between two types of decision situations facing leaders: individual and group. Individual decision situations are those whose solutions affect only one of the leader's followers. Decision situations that affect several followers are classified as group decisions. Five different leadership styles that fit individual and group situations are available. Described in Exhibit 15.3, these styles are categorized as follows:

1. Autocratic (A): You (the leader) make the decision without input from your subordinates or you (the leader) secure input from subordinates and then make the decision.
2. Consultative (C): Subordinates have some input, but you make the decision.
3. Group (G): The group makes the decision; you (as leader) are just another group member.
4. Delegated (D): You give exclusive responsibility to subordinates.

For group decisions, leaders can choose from styles AI, AII, CI, CII, and GII. For individual decisions, leaders can choose from styles AI, AII, CI, GI, and DI.

EXHIBIT 15.3   **Vroom-Jago Decision Styles**

Individual Level	Group Level
AI. You solve the problem or make the decision yourself, using information available to you at that time.	**AI.** You solve the problem or make the decision yourself, using information available to you at that time.
AII. You obtain any necessary information from the subordinates, then decide on the solution to the problem yourself. The role played by your subordinates in the decision is clearly one of providing specific information that you request.	**AII.** You obtain any necessary information from subordinates, then decide on the solution to the problem yourself. The role played by your subordinates in making the decision is clearly one of providing specific information that you request.
CI. You share the problem with the relevant subordinate, getting ideas and suggestions. Then *you* make the decision. This decision may or may not reflect your preferred decision.	**CI.** You share the problem with the relevant subordinates individually, getting their ideas and suggestions without bringing them together as a group. Then *you* make the decision. This decision may or may not reflect your subordinates' influence.
GI. You share the problem with one of your subordinates, and together you analyze the problem and arrive at a mutually satisfactory solution in an atmosphere of free and open exchange of information and ideas.	**CII.** You share the problem with your subordinates in a group meeting. In this meeting, you obtain their ideas and suggestions. Then you make the decision, which may or may not reflect your subordinates' influence.
DI. You delegate the problem to one of your subordinates, providing him or her with any relevant information that you possess, but giving him or her responsibility for solving the problem alone. Any solution the person reaches receives your support.	**GII.** You share the problem with your subordinates as a group. Together, you generate and evaluate alternatives and attempt to reach a consensus on a solution. You do not try to influence the group to adopt "your" solution, and you are willing to accept and implement any solution that has the support of the entire group.

Diagnostic Procedure

To determine the most appropriate decision-making style for a given situation, Vroom suggests leaders perform a situational diagnosis by asking a series of questions, as follows:[30]

1. How important is the technical quality of the decision?
2. How important is subordinate commitment to the decision?
3. Do you have sufficient information to make a high-quality decision?
4. Is the problem well structured?
5. If you were to make the decision by yourself, is it reasonably certain that your subordinates would be committed to the decision?
6. Do subordinates share the organizational goals to be attained in solving this problem?
7. Is conflict among subordinates over preferred solutions likely?
8. Do subordinates have sufficient information to make a high-quality decision?

Each of these questions may be thought of as representing a dichotomy. That is, they may be answered yes or no, or high or low. Within the framework of the model, however, it is possible for responses to fall between dichotomized extremes. Answers of "probably" and "maybe" may reflect subtle differences among situations, particularly those that in some way may be ambiguous or unclear. The capacity of the model to treat these questions as continuous scales is one of the significant additions to the revised Vroom-Jago model.

Application of the Model

Actual application of the Vroom-Jago model can vary significantly in its degree of complexity, sophistication, and specificity, depending on the particular purpose for which it is used and the needs of the decision maker. In its simplest form, application of the model can be expressed as a set of decision-making rules of thumb. Exhibit 15.4 lists, as an example, four of the rules that apply to the model as discussed here.

Validity of the Model

The Vroom-Jago model lacks complete empirical evidence establishing its validity. Certainly the model is thought to be consistent with what we now know about the benefits and costs of subordinate participation in decision making. Moreover, it represents a direct extension of the original Vroom-Yetton model, for which ample validation

EXHIBIT 15.4

Example of Vroom-Jago Rules of Thumb

Source: Abridged from V. Vroom and A. Jago, *The New Leadership* (Englewood Cliffs, NJ: Prentice Hall, 1988). Copyright 1987 by V. Vroom and A. Jago. Used with permission of the authors.

Rules to improve decision quality:
1. Avoid the use of AI when
   a. The leader lacks the necessary information.
2. Avoid the use of GII when
   a. Subordinates do not share the organizational goals.
   b. Subordinates do not have the necessary information.
3. Avoid the use of AII and CI when
   a. The leader lacks the necessary information.
   b. The problem is unstructured.
4. Move toward GII when
   a. The leader lacks the necessary information.
   b. Subordinates share the organizational goals.
   c. There is conflict among subordinates over preferred solutions.

evidence does exist.[31] Nonetheless, without additional evidence that the use of the model can improve decision effectiveness and, by extension, leadership success, its value as a theoretical contribution and as a practical tool has not been fully determined.

Path–Goal Leadership Model

path–goal leadership model
A theory that suggests it is necessary for a leader to influence the followers' perception of work goals, self-development goals, and paths to goal attainment. The foundation for the model is the expectancy motivation theory.

Like the other situational or contingency leadership approaches, the **path–goal leadership model** attempts to predict leadership effectiveness in different situations. According to this model, leaders are effective because of their positive impact on followers' motivation, ability to perform, and satisfaction. The theory is designated *path–goal* because it focuses on how the leader influences the followers' perceptions of work goals, self-development goals, and paths to goal attainment.[32]

The foundation of path–goal theory is the expectancy motivation theory discussed in Chapter 5. The early theoretical work on the path–goal theory proposed that leaders will be effective by making rewards available to subordinates and by making those rewards contingent on the subordinates' accomplishment of specific goals. It is argued by some that an important part of the leader's job is to clarify for subordinates the kind of behavior most likely to result in goal accomplishment. This activity is referred to as **path clarification**.

path clarification
The leader's efforts to clarify for employees the kind of behavior most likely to result in goal accomplishment.

The early path–goal work led to the development of a theory involving four specific styles of leader behavior (directive, supportive, participative, and achievement) and three types of subordinate attitudes (job satisfaction, acceptance of the leader, and expectations about effort-performance-reward relationships).[33] The *directive leader* tends to let subordinates know what is expected of them. The *supportive leader* treats subordinates as equals. The *participative leader* consults with subordinates and uses their suggestions and ideas before reaching a decision. The *achievement-oriented leader* sets challenging goals, expects subordinates to perform at the highest level, and continually seeks improvement in performance.

Two types of situational or contingency variables are considered in the path–goal theory. These variables are the *personal characteristics of subordinates* and the *environmental pressures and demands* with which subordinates must cope to accomplish work goals and derive satisfaction.

An important personal characteristic is subordinates' perception of their own ability. The higher the degree of perceived ability relative to the task demands, the less likely the subordinate is to accept a directive leader style. This directive style of leadership would be viewed as unnecessarily close. In addition, it has been discovered that a person's *locus of control* also affects responses. Individuals who have an internal locus of control (they believe that rewards are contingent on their efforts) are generally more satisfied with a participative style, while individuals who have an external locus of control (they believe that rewards are beyond their personal control) are generally more satisfied with a directive style.[34]

The environmental variables include factors that are not within the control of the subordinate but are important to satisfaction or to the ability to perform effectively.[35] These include the tasks, the formal authority system of the organization, and the work group. Any of these environmental factors can motivate or constrain the subordinate. The environmental forces may also serve as a reward for acceptable levels of performance. For example, the subordinate could be motivated by the work group and receive satisfaction from co-workers' acceptance for doing a job according to group norms.

Based on mixed research results, a revised theoretical formation of the path–goal model has been presented. House, in his revised framework, proposes that research

EXHIBIT 15.5   Framework of Revised Path–Goal Leadership Perspective

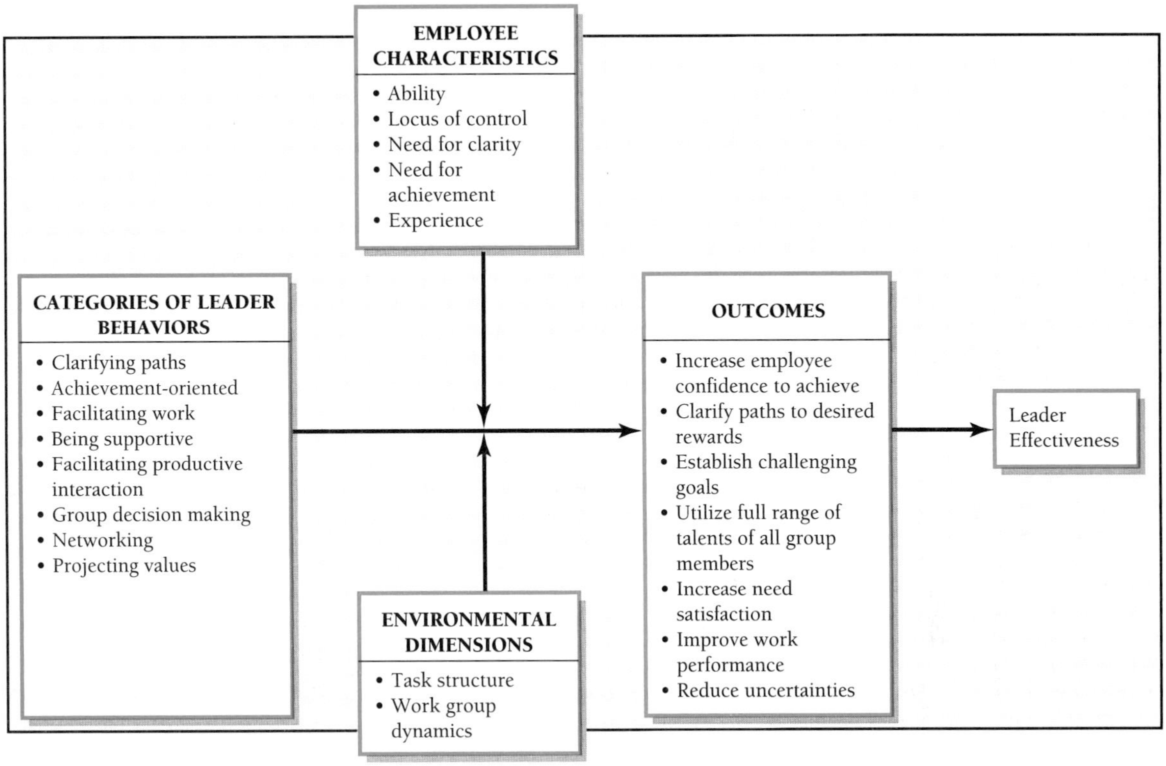

points out the complexity of leadership and a need for more categories of leadership behavior.[36] House emphasizes the significance of intrinsic motivation and empowerment initiated by leaders. Exhibit 15.5 illustrates the characteristics of House's revised path–goal framework.

Critique of the Path–Goal Model

The revised path–goal model has not been sufficiently tested to conclude that it provides an accurate portrayal of leadership in organizational settings. Some interesting questions remain about its predictive power. Much of the research to date has involved only partial tests of the original and the revised path–goal model.[37]

On the positive side, however, the path–goal model is an improvement over the trait and personal–behavioral theories. It attempts to indicate which factors affect the motivation to perform. In addition, the path–goal approach introduces both situational factors and individual differences when examining leader behavior and outcomes such as satisfaction and performance. The path–goal approach makes an effort to explain why a particular style of leadership works best in a given situation. As more research accumulates, this type of explanation will have practical utility for those interested in the leadership process in work settings.

Hersey-Blanchard Situational Leadership Theory

Managers often complain that esoteric theories don't help them do a better job on the production line, in the office, or in a research and development lab. They want something they can apply and use. Hersey and Blanchard developed a situational leadership

situational leadership theory (SLT)
An approach to leadership advocating that leaders understand their own behavior and the readiness of their followers. This approach requires diagnostic skills in human behavior on the part of the leader.

theory that has definitely appealed to many managers.[38] Managers in large firms and small businesses have used the **situational leadership theory (SLT)** and enthusiastically endorse its value. The appeal of SLT may be that its approach is intuitive and can be effectively summarized in a page.[39]

SLT's emphasis is on followers and their level of maturity or "readiness." The leader must properly judge or intuitively know followers' readiness level and then use a leadership style that fits the level. Readiness is defined as the ability and willingness of people (followers) to take responsibility for directing their own behavior. It's important to consider two types of readiness: job and psychological. A person high in job readiness has the knowledge and abilities to perform the job without a manager structuring or directing the work. A person high in psychological readiness has the self-motivation and desire to do quality work. Again, this person has little need for direct supervision.

Hersey and Blanchard used the Ohio State studies to further develop four leadership styles available to managers:

- *Telling*—the leader defines the roles needed to do the job and tells followers what, where, how, and when to do the tasks.
- *Selling*—the leader provides followers with structured instructions, but is also supportive.
- *Participating*—the leader and followers share in decisions about how best to complete a high-quality job.
- *Delegating*—the leader provides little specific, close direction or personal support to followers.

By determining followers' readiness levels through discussions, observation, field surveys, and interviews, a manager can choose from among the four leadership styles. Exhibit 15.6 presents characteristics of the SLT.

Application of the model works as follows. Suppose a manager determines that his recently hired followers are unsure of themselves and insecure about how to perform the job. The followers are placed at the RI readiness state. By moving from RI to the leadership style development curve, the intersection of the vertical line would be at the telling style point. That is, an RI follower requires a leader who is high on task orientation, gives direct instructions, and is low in support behavior. Task behavior is needed more for this person than supportive behavior. In fact, research is available to support the SI style over any of the others.[40] Some may assume that a participative (S3) style is best. However, asking an insecure follower to participate may result in more insecurity about making a mistake or saying something that's considered dumb.

A follower will be more ready to take on more responsibility as other leadership styles become more effective. For example, an R&D lab with expert, experienced scientists who are totally able and willing to do the job would flourish under a delegative (S4) style of leadership. Using the readiness indicator with the four-style model helps the manager conceptualize what's best for followers.

Blanchard responded to some critics of the SLT by revising the original model.[41] He retitled various terms, calling task behavior *directive behavior*, and relationship behavior *supportive behavior*. The four leadership styles are now called S1—directing, S2—coaching, S3—supporting, and S4—delegating. Readiness is now called the *development level of followers*. The development level is defined in terms of followers' current competence and commitment to do the job.

EXHIBIT 15.6
The Hersey-Blanchard Situational Leadership Model

Source: P. Hersey and K.H. Blanchard, *Management of Organizational Behavior: Utilizing Human Resources,* 5th ed. (Englewood Cliffs, NJ: Prentice Hall, 1988), p. 171. The original model published in the first edition in 1969 used the label *maturity* instead of *readiness.*

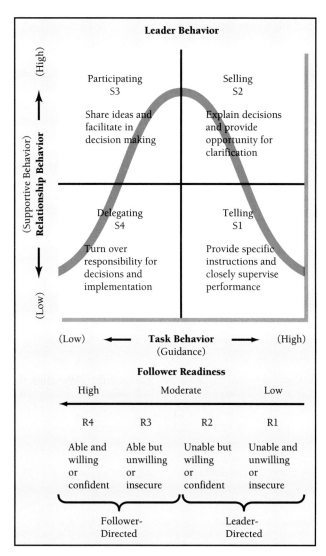

Critique of SLT

Although a number of managers find this model attractive, there are some serious unanswered questions. The most important may be, does it really work? Testing of the model has been very limited. Even the developers, Hersey and Blanchard, have failed to provide significant evidence (1) that predictions can be made from the model, and (2) of which style is best. Another issue revolves around the notion that a leader can change or adapt her style to fit a follower or group. Are people in leadership positions that adaptable? Again, research is needed to validate leader flexibility.[42]

Despite the words of caution about limited research and flexibility, many managers like the SLT. It is considered practical, meaningful, and useful in training managers to think and behave like leaders. As leadership continues to command attention in organizations, the SLT remains a popular way to express what leaders should be doing at work.

Comparing the Situational Approaches

The four situational leadership models have some similarities and some differences. They are similar in that they (1) focus on the dynamics of leadership, (2) have stimulated research on leadership, and (3) remain controversial because of measurement problems, limited research testing, or contradictory research results.

Exhibit 15.7 summarizes the themes of each model. Fiedler's model, the most tested, is perhaps the most controversial. His view of leader behavior centers on task- and relationship-oriented tendencies and how these interact with task and position power. The path–goal approach emphasizes the instrumental actions of leaders and four styles for conducting these actions (directive, supportive, participative, and achievement-oriented).

The situational variables discussed in each approach differ somewhat. There is also a different view of outcome criteria for assessing how successful the leader behavior has been: Fiedler discusses leader effectiveness, and the path–goal approach focuses on satisfaction and performance.

EXHIBIT 15.7   Summary Comparison of Four Important Situational Models of Leadership

	Fiedler's Contingency Model	Vroom, Yetton, and Jago	House's Path–Goal Model	Hersey-Blanchard Situational Leadership Theory
Leadership qualities	Leaders are task- or relationship-oriented. The job should be engineered to fit the leader's style.	Leaders make either individual or group decisions and can choose from five different styles.	Leaders can increase followers' effectiveness by applying proper motivational techniques.	Leader must adapt style in terms of task behavior and relationship behavior on the basis of followers.
Assumptions about followers	Followers prefer different leadership styles, depending on task structure, leader–member relations, and position power.	Followers participate in varying degrees in decisions involving problems.	Followers have different needs that must be fulfilled with the help of a leader.	Followers' maturity level (readiness) to take responsibility influences the leadership style that is adopted.
Leader effectiveness	Effectiveness of the leader is determined by the interaction of environment and personality factors.	Effective leaders select the appropriate decision set and permit the optimal participation for followers.	Effective leaders are those who clarify for followers the paths or behaviors that are best suited.	Effective leaders are able to adapt directing, coaching, supporting, and delegating style to fit the followers' levels of maturity.
History of research: problems	If investigations not affiliated with Fiedler are used, the evidence is contradictory on the accuracy of the model.	Research support for the model is mixed and limited. The model is considered by some to be complex even though a computer program is available to trace decision ties used.	Model has generated modest research interest in past two decades.	Not enough research is available to reach a definitive conclusion about the predictive power of the theory.

Other Perspectives, Concepts, and Issues of Leadership

A number of leadership concepts are attracting the interest of practitioners and organizational researchers. Each of the concepts in this section has provided interesting, controversial, and insightful analysis or debates about their value in improving the general understanding of how leadership can effectively impact employees.

Charismatic Leadership

charismatic leader
The charismatic leader is one who creates an atmosphere of motivation based on an emotional commitment to and identity with his or her vision, philosophy, and style on the part of followers.

John F. Kennedy, Winston Churchill, Ray Kroc, and Walt Disney possessed an attractiveness that enabled them to make a difference with citizens, employees, and followers. The leadership approach of such people is referred to as charismatic leadership. Max Weber suggested that some leaders have a gift of exceptional qualities—a *charisma*—that enables them to motivate followers to achieve outstanding performance.[43] Such a charismatic leader is depicted as being able to play a vital role in creating change. People view the charismatic leader as a hero. Individuals who are able to take on hero qualities gain charisma. The **charismatic leader** is one who creates an atmosphere of motivation based on an emotional commitment to and identity with his or her vision, philosophy, and style on the part of followers. In the national political arena, if President John F. Kennedy was considered charismatic, President Jimmy Carter was not considered to be charismatic by most citizens.

Sam Walton was considered by many to possess charismatic qualities. He worked hard to explain his vision of retailing and serving the customer. As people responded to his vision and goals, Walton used his charm to press his viewpoint. He paid attention to his employees and his customers—the human assets of business. Walton had a "gift" for making other people feel good about working for him and buying his products and services.

Steven Jobs, co-founder of Apple, provides another example of a charismatic leader who works to inspire others. Jobs' impact, attractiveness, and inspiration were described as follows:

> When I walked through the Macintosh building with Steve, it became clear that he wasn't just another general manager bringing a visitor along to meet another group of employees. He and many of Apple's leaders weren't managers at all; they were impresarios. . . . Not unlike the director of an opera company, the impresario must cleverly deal with the creative temperaments of artists. . . . His gift is to merge powerful ideas with the performance of his artists.[44]

Defining Charismatic Leadership

Charisma is a Greek word meaning "gift." Powers that could not be clearly explained by logical means were called by the Greeks *charismatic*. It has been suggested that it is a combination of charm and personal magnetism that contributes to the remarkable ability to get other people to endorse your vision and promote it passionately.[45]

What Constitutes Charismatic Leadership Behavior?

What behavioral dimensions distinguish charismatic leaders from noncharismatic leaders? In the early work on charismatic leadership, explanations lacked specificity. Later empirical studies have examined the specific behavior and attributes of charismatic leaders, such as ability to inspire, a dominating personality, vision, and communication ability.[46] However, no specific set of behaviors and attributes is

EXHIBIT 15.8 **Behavioral Components of Charismatic and Noncharismatic Leaders**

Source: Adapted from Jay A. Conger and Rabindra N. Kanungo, "Toward a Behavioral Theory of Charismatic Leadership in Organizational Settings," *Academy of Management Review*, October 1987, pp. 637–47.

Component	Charismatic Leader	Noncharismatic Leader
Relation to status quo	Essentially opposed to status quo and strives to change it (Steve Jobs at Apple)	Essentially agrees with status quo and strives to maintain it
Future goal	Idealized vision highly different than status quo (Tom Monaghan with the Domino's Pizza concept)	Goal not too discrepant from status quo
Likableness	Shared perspective and idealized vision make him or her a likable and honorable hero worthy of identification and imitation (Lee Iacocca in first three years at Chrysler)	Shared perspective makes him or her likable
Expertise	Expert in using unconventional means to transcend the existing order (Al Davis, owner of the Oakland Raiders)	Expert in using available means to achieve goals within the framework of the existing order
Environmental sensitivity	Expert in using unconventional means to transcend the existing order (Warren Buffett, CEO of Berkshire Hathaway)	Low need for environmental sensitivity to maintain status quo
Articulation	Strong articulation of future vision and motivation to lead (Jim Clark, CEO of Netscape)	Weak articulation of goals and motivation to lead
Power base	Personal power based on expertise, respect, and admiration for a unique hero (Colin Powell, former secretary of state)	Position power and personal power (based on reward, expertise, and liking for a friend who is a similar other)
Leader–follower relationship	Elitist, entrepreneur, an exemplary (Mary Kay Ash of Mary Kay Cosmetics) Transforms people to share the radical changes advocated (Edward Land, inventor of Polaroid camera)	Egalitarian, consensus seeking or directive Nudges or orders people to share his or her views

universally accepted by researchers and practitioners. A descriptive behavioral framework that builds upon empirical work has been offered. The framework presented in Exhibit 15.8 assumes that charisma must be viewed as an attribution made by followers within the work context.

Many leaders, of course, are not charismatic. These leaders exhibit behaviors similar to those described in Exhibit 15.8 as "noncharismatic." This does not necessarily mean, however, that they are ineffective. On the contrary, outstanding administrative skills or keen analytical abilities, for example, can contribute to effectiveness in noncharismatic leaders. Bill Gates of Microsoft is not often viewed as a charismatic leader. However, he has been very analytical, innovative, efficient—and successful. Despite his somewhat noncharismatic style, Gates helped build Microsoft into one of the world's most powerful organizations. Such observations about the successful performance of noncharismatic leaders such as Gates suggests that research has not been definitive regarding the impact of charisma on organizational performance. For example, one study examining CEO charisma and stock performance found that success leads to perceptions of charismatic leadership; however, charisma did not lead to subsequent organizational success.[47]

Two Types of Charismatic Leaders

Charismatic leaders may be characterized in different ways. Two such ways, or types, are *visionary* and *crisis-based*. Most discussions of charismatic leadership emphasize *visionary* leadership. It's argued that the first requirement for exercising charismatic leadership is expressing a shared vision of what the future could be. Through communication ability, the visionary charismatic leader links followers' needs and goals to job or organizational goals. Linking followers with the organization's direction, mission, and goals is easier if they're dissatisfied or unchallenged by the current situation. Visionary charismatic leaders have the ability to see both the big picture and the opportunities the big picture presents.[48]

An example of a visionary charismatic leader is Felipe Alfonso, who headed the Asian Institute of Management (AIM) while also serving as the CEO of Manila Electric Company (MERALCO). He is considered a tireless and charismatic leader who formulates a vision of the future, while bringing people together to seize opportunities.

AIM has trained and developed many of the top professional, entrepreneurial, and socially responsible leaders of Asia and the rest of the world. It has graduated over 20,000 students from 68 countries.[49]

The Manila Electric Company provides more than half of the Philippines' total electric consumption, and its franchise area produces 50 percent of the country's gross domestic product. Under Alfonso's leadership, both AIM and the Manila Electric Company have clarified their visions, attracted the best talent, and utilized the most advanced information technology. Earning the trust of people through serving them with integrity is one of Alfonso's major axioms. He prides himself on having visions of the future that are inspirational, ethical, and innovative.

Crisis-based charismatic leaders have an impact when the system must handle a situation for which existing knowledge, resources, or procedures are not adequate.[50] The crisis-produced charismatic leader communicates clearly what actions need to be taken and what their consequences will be.

One of the most publicized, respected, and now classic examples of crisis management leadership was James Burke, CEO of Johnson & Johnson in 1982. He received word of deaths in Chicago associated with a company product, Extra-Strength Tylenol capsules.[51] Five Chicago-area residents had purchased Tylenol and passed away within a few days. Medical examiners retrieved bottles from the victims' homes and found capsules laced with cyanide. Johnson & Johnson, under Burke's direction and leadership, recalled the product and advised consumers not to take any of the capsules. The Food and Drug Administration (FDA) suspected someone not connected with Johnson & Johnson had inserted cyanide in some capsules and returned the bottles to stores.

Burke led the company effort in a three-phase approach: (1) determine what happened, (2) assess and curtail the damage, and (3) restore Tylenol back into the market. Despite an FBI and Illinois investigation, the perpetrator was never found. Burke showed decisiveness in immediately recalling the product and informing the public. He didn't know the full extent of the

---

Management Pointer

ATTRIBUTES OF CHARISMATIC LEADERS

Want to become more charismatic? Focus on developing as many of these attributes as you can.

1. *Develop visionary thinking.* Establish idealized goals that represent significant improvement over the status quo.

2. *Communicate the vision.* Visions must be articulated in a manner that is consistent with followers' needs.

3. *Have conviction.* Charismatic leaders are perceived as being strongly committed to their visions and willing to sacrifice and take significant personal risk to achieve them.

4. *Exhibit extraordinary behaviors.* Engage in behaviors that are unconventional and counter to established norms. Such behaviors should be related to obtaining objectives, not just for show.

5. *Develop self-confidence.* Successful charismatic leaders have total confidence in their abilities to overcome obstacles and get things accomplished.

problem, but he communicated quickly and clearly. Under Burke's leadership, a more widespread tragedy was averted. He also helped rebuild the Tylenol brand, and he regained regular user confidence. The firm ran television commercials informing the public that it was doing everything possible to regain their trust. Subsequently, Johnson & Johnson designed a tamper-resistant package to prevent a future tragedy. Tylenol was sold only in a new triple-sealed package. Customers were asked to throw away their old Tylenol, call a toll-free number, and receive a coupon for a free triple-sealed package.

The knowledge available on charismatic leadership is still relatively abstract and ambiguous. Despite Weber's concept of charismatic authority, various frameworks of how charismatic leadership evolves, and some limited research results, much more theoretical and research work needs to be done. There is a void in our understanding of charismatic leaders who can be harmful and dangerous, such as Adolf Hitler and Joseph Stalin. The attributes of charismatic leaders are presented as developmental suggestions for managers in the Management Pointer on page 459.

Transactional and Transformational Leadership

Each of the leadership approaches discussed so far emphasizes the point that leadership is an exchange process. Followers are rewarded by the leader when they accomplish agreed-upon objectives. The leader serves to help followers accomplish the objectives.

Transactional Leadership

transactional leader
Helps the follower identify what must be done to accomplish the desired results (e.g., better-quality output, more sales or services, reduced cost of production) and ensures that employees have the resources needed to complete the job.

The exchange role of the leader has been referred to as *transactional*. Exhibit 15.9 presents the *transactional leadership* roles. The leader helps the followers identify what must be done to accomplish the desired results: for example, better-quality output, more sales or services, reduced cost of production. In helping the followers identify what must be done, the **transactional leader** considers followers' self-concept and esteem needs. The transactional approach uses path–goal concepts as part of its framework and explanation.

In using the transactional style, the leader relies on contingent rewards and on management by exception. Research shows that when contingent reinforcement is used, followers exhibit an increase in performance and satisfaction;[52] followers believe that accomplishing objectives will result in their receiving desired rewards. Using management by exception, the leader won't be involved unless objectives aren't being accomplished.

Transactional leadership is not often found in organizational settings. One national sample of U.S. workers showed that only 22 percent of the participants perceived a direct relationship between how hard they worked and how much pay they received.[53] That is, the majority of workers believed that good pay was not contingent on good performance. Although workers prefer a closer link between pay and performance, it was not present in their jobs. Why? There are probably a number of reasons, such as unreliable performance appraisal systems, subjectively administered rewards, poor managerial skills in showing employees the pay–performance link, and conditions outside the manager's control. Also, managers often provide rewards that aren't perceived by followers to be meaningful or important.

A small pay increase, a personal letter from the boss, or a job transfer may not be what employees want in the form of contingent rewards. Until managers understand what employees want, administer rewards in a timely manner, and emphasize the pay–performance link, there's likely to be confusion, uncertainty, and minimal transactional impact in leader–follower relationships.

EXHIBIT 15.9
Transactional
Leadership

Source: Bernard M. Bass,
Leadership and Performance
beyond Expectations (New
York: Free Press, 1985), p. 12.

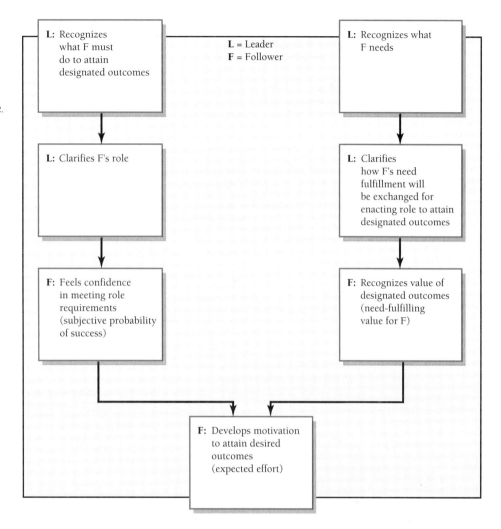

The Transformational Leader

transformational
leader
Motivates followers to
work for goals instead
of short-term self-
interest and for
achievement and
self-actualization
instead of security; is
able to express a clear
vision and inspire
others to strive to
accomplish the vision.

Another type of leader, referred to as the **transformational leader,** motivates followers
to work for goals instead of short-term self-interest and for achievement and self-
actualization instead of security.[54] In *transformational leadership,* viewed as a special
case of transactional leadership, the employee's reward is internal. By expressing a
vision, the transformational leader persuades followers to work hard to achieve the
goals envisioned. The leader's vision provides the follower with the motivation for
hard work that is self-rewarding (internal).

Transactional leaders will adjust goals, direction, and mission for practical reasons. Transformational leaders, on the other hand, make major changes in the
firm's or unit's mission, way of doing business, and human resources management
to achieve their vision. The transformational leader will overhaul the entire
philosophy, system, and culture of an organization. The transformational
leader uses and expounds upon attitudinal, charismatic, and transitive methods of
leadership.

The development of transformational leadership factors has evolved from research by Bass.[55] He identified five factors (the first three apply to transformational and the last two apply to transactional leadership) that describe transformational leaders. They are:

Charisma. The leader is able to instill a sense of value, respect, and pride and to articulate a vision.

Individual attention. The leader pays attention to followers' needs and assigns meaningful projects so that followers grow personally.

Intellectual stimulation. The leader helps followers rethink rational ways to examine a situation. He encourages followers to be creative.

Contingent reward. The leader informs followers about what must be done to receive the rewards they prefer.

Management by exception. The leader permits followers to work on the task and doesn't intervene unless goals aren't being accomplished in a reasonable time and at a reasonable cost.

One of the most important characteristics of the transformational leader is charisma. However, charisma by itself isn't enough for successful transformational leadership, as Bass clearly states:

> The deep emotional attachment which characterizes the relationship of the charismatic leader to followers may be present when transformational leadership occurs, but we can distinguish a class of charismatics who are not at all transformational in their influence. Celebrities may be identified as charismatic by a large segment of the public. Celebrities are held in awe and reverence by the masses that are developed by them. People will be emotionally aroused in the presence of celebrities and identify with them in their fantasy, but the celebrities may not be involved at all in any transformation of their public. On the other hand, with charisma, transformational leaders can play the role of teacher, mentor, coach, reformer, or revolutionary. Charisma is a necessary ingredient of transformational leadership, but by itself it is not sufficient to account for the transformational process.[56]

This relationship may be seen in a recent study where transformational leadership was shown to lead to higher levels of innovation when a climate for excellence (perhaps through charisma) has been created.[57]

Transformational leadership has been found to be related to an organization's socially oriented initiatives. The concept that a corporation needs to do more than the minimal requirements of the law in its treatment of its stakeholders has been termed **corporate social responsibility** (CSR). The stakeholders considered in CSR include employees, suppliers, customers, the community, and within the broader conceptualization of sustainability, the planet itself. Organizations recognized for their CSR activities include: Ben & Jerry's Homemade Ice Cream and Newman's Own.[58] The latter has donated over $280 million to charitable causes over the last 26 years,[59] and Ben & Jerry's routinely contributes over $1 million annually to its foundation to support community initiatives.[60]

In sum, CSR activities are believed to have positive effects for society and the organization undertaking them. Some organizational leaders see CSR expenditures as investments and look at them as strategic rather than social initiatives. This approach is confirmed by a recent study that found an association between transformational leadership and strategically oriented CSR activities.[61]

In addition to charisma, transformational leaders need assessment skills, communication abilities, and sensitivity to others. They must be able to articulate their vision, and they must be sensitive to the skill deficiencies of followers.

corporate social responsibility
Actions that corporations undertake to promote the public good beyond those required by law or the immediate interest of financial stakeholders.

YOU BE THE JUDGE

IF YOUR BOSS MAKES YOU SICK, CAN YOU GET A NEW ONE?

It is clearly illegal for anyone in a managerial or leadership role to discriminate against employees on the basis of such factors as gender, race, religion, age, disabilities, or national origin. Nor can leaders harass their employees in ways that contribute to a hostile work environment. But what if simply working for a particular boss makes an employee sick? Does the company have a legal obligation to get you a new boss? One employee of the New York Federal Reserve Bank (the Fed) thought so.

A manager at the Fed suffered a back injury, unrelated to work, and was given two medical leaves at full pay, each about six months long. In between, she worked about six months on a part-time schedule, also at full pay. At various times during this period she expressed dissatisfaction with her boss. While on her second leave, her physician and her psychologist both wrote the Fed recommending that she return to work but that certain accommodations be made for her because of her back injury. One of these accommodations was that she be given a new boss because she found working for her current one aggravated her back problem.

The Fed gave her two choices: (1) return to work under her current manager, receive ergonomic furniture, have flexibility to get up and move around periodically, and receive assistance from the personnel office in seeking a new position elsewhere in the Fed, or (2) resign, receive assistance in finding work elsewhere, and receive 26 weeks of severance pay and six months of medical benefits. When she failed to show up for work and did not accept the severance package, she was fired. She sued, claiming the Fed discriminated against her because of her disability and failed to make a reasonable accommodation for her as required by the Americans with Disabilities Act. Did the Fed discriminate? Was the employee being reasonable? You be the judge!

Coaching

Coaching is the everyday interaction of helping another employee increase his or her understanding of the work and improve performance. In Chapter 2, mentoring and socialization were discussed. Mentors are usually senior employees and are often similar in background, religion, ethnicity, and gender to protégés. Coaches come in all varieties and aren't always linked to seniority. Coaches possess skills, experience, and ability that leaders display. Included in the arsenal of exceptional coaches are a talent for observing, decisive decision making, exceptional communication ability, a good understanding of the reward–performance feedback that makes sense, and the ability to be nonjudgmental.[62]

From 1997 to 2002, Doug Blevins served as a kicking coach and a leader for the Miami Dolphins football team. This is remarkable because he has never attempted to kick a football in his life. Doug was born with cerebral palsy and has never walked.

Doug has exceptional observational and coaching skills. He breaks each kicking motion down to its component parts. He then studies the behavior, motions, and mechanics of the kickers and develops a practice plan for each kicker (punts, field goals, kick-offs) and drills them.

Doug Blevins offers a few hints on how to coach and lead that can be used in organizations:

1. Observe the detail.
2. Develop the person's strengths.
3. Work to improve people, not change them.
4. Require continual improvement.

5. Pace the person. Don't wear them out by working so hard all the time.

6. Believe that you can be the best.[63]

Kickers coached by Blevins are still scattered throughout the NFL. Many of these players marvel at Blevins' knowledge, communication, and motivational skills, and his work ethic. He has taken a different journey, but Doug Blevins is considered a consummate coach and leader. While no longer with the NFL, Blevins continues to coach at kicking camps and through individual instruction. He also travels throughout the United States as a motivational speaker.[64]

Coaches, like Doug Blevins, adopt the approach of teacher, not competitor, and of being helpful without being judgmental. The coach observes to understand fully what the pupil is doing. In organizations the objective of coaching is to improve performance. However, the focus is more long term than on the immediate work, role, or task. Coaching requires confronting the fact that a person is not skilled or talented enough at present to perform well. The buildup of skills to perform well often takes a lot of time and patience. Coaches need to be committed for the long term to be able to see results.

Practicing a number of coaching techniques is recommended for long-term success.[65] Included in the recommended set are:

- Practice active listening. Play back to the person what was heard.
- Support learning through action and reflection.
- Move from easy to hard skills.
- Set goals.
- Provide tactful feedback, positive and negative. Focus more on successes, but point out failures.

The essence of coaching and leading is to be creative and to look for positives. It may take a long time to observe successes, but a steady course can be very rewarding to both the coach and the pupil.

Servant Leadership

servant leader
A leader who emphasizes employee growth and service to others as worthwhile ends in and of themselves, placing others' needs in front of their own.

Should a leader be served by his or her followers? In 1977, Robert Greenleaf proposed the opposite. He wrote that a leader should be driven by a desire to serve, helping those who have a legitimate need regardless of their status and without an expectation of a reciprocal obligation. Greenleaf proposed that the leader should be a servant. While this desire to serve is the central characteristic of **servant leadership,** the approach is typically thought to also include leader humility, treating others as equals in relationships, and the application of high moral values. This form of leadership is associated with helping workers see themselves as whole and living purposeful lives.[66] Does servant leadership work? Dan Warmenhoven, chairman and chief executive officer of NetApp, would likely say "yes." His company has been named one of *Fortune* magazine's "World's Most Admired Companies" and one of *Forbes* magazine's "400 Best Big Companies in America."[67] In the contracting economic environment of 2009, NetApp continued to grow and had a $2 billion cash reserve on hand as a rainy day fund. His company, while "frugal," values and serves its employees. Company benefits include five paid days for volunteer work, and adoption and autism coverage that has cost $242,452 over the past three years. While the linkage between service leadership and organizational success has yet to be statistically supported, NetApp's performance implies that service leadership works.

THE VALUE OF GLOBAL EXPERIENCE

How does one become a leader of an organization such as 3M? One way is to go international! All but one of 3M's eight executive vice presidents has had significant international assignments, and the one who doesn't was born outside the United States. The current CEO of 3M, George Buckley, is also foreign born and has had significant management experience outside the United States. Is this pattern of acquiring international experience to prepare for senior leadership positions unique to 3M? A look at the leadership at the No. 2 organization on the list of best companies for leaders, Procter & Gamble, reinforces the idea that international experience is a must-have skill for today's business leaders. P&G's chairman and CEO, the vice chairman, the CFO, and the COO have all held positions in P&G's international operations. Such international experience builds knowledge of working with global stakeholders and competing successfully in diverse cultures and markets. Judging from the executives at 3M and P&G, it appears that global experience is increasingly becoming a requirement for moving to the pinnacle of the management ranks.

Taking one or more international management assignments within an organization can have a negative side. Some managers perceive such assignments as a gamble. Being out of sight in an overseas position can mean being out of mind of the top decision makers at headquarters. Managers in foreign operations may become isolated and lose touch with the political changes that constantly occur at the home office. These are very real risks associated with taking international assignments. However, many leaders and fast-track managers feel the benefits of going international outweigh the risks.

The globally experienced manager must make contact with the culture, cope with and learn firsthand about culture shock, and receive another culture's view of the organization, its products or services, and what employees think about various practices and programs. This broader global business perspective is considered to be crucial for advancement in some companies.

Not all global assignments are equal. Some managers prefer very brief stints. An assignment that lasts at least one year allows managers to experience the host country culture and learn the language.

Opportunities to acquire global experience tend to attract younger managers who already work on virtual and multifunctional projects. Global managers will experience expanded job responsibilities and will have to learn to cope with change, repatriation, communication problems, and a diverse workforce. The value added is hard to quantify. It is, however, according to expatriated managers an invaluable addition to their career path and progress.

Sources: J.P. Donlon, "Best Companies for Leaders," *Chief Executive*, February 2009 (accessed May 15, 2009); "Chairman of the Board and Chief Executive Officer," http://solutions.3m.com/wps/portal/3M/en_US/our/company/information/leadership/ceo-officers/chairman-ceo (accessed May 15, 2009); "PG.com, News, P&G Management Bios & Photos," http://phx.corporate-ir.net/phoenix.zhtml?c = 195341&p = irol-govmanage; and Justin Martin, "The Global CEO," *Chief Executive,* February 2004, pp. 41–46.

Multicultural Leadership

As each theory or approach to leadership is presented, perhaps it is necessary to ask: To what extent do particular leadership (influence) styles vary around the world? Effective leaders in a Nigerian manufacturing facility may be totally ineffective if transferred to the same type of manufacturing plant in South Africa. The leader's role is performed in a context (e.g., political, cultural). A leader's personality, efforts, or style may emerge from or be in conflict with the context. A leader in a specific national culture may need to apply various attitudes and behaviors to exercise the right blend of influence to accomplish relevant goal achievement.[68] The leadership needed to be effective cannot be generalized in a global context. The Global OB explains in a concise manner the value of acquiring global experience.

Cross-Cultural Research

A study by Bass et al. found that leadership attributes associated with effective leadership results vary across cultures. A considerable amount of research directly or indirectly supports the notion of cultural contingency in leadership. For example,

Hofstede's five cultural dimensions (discussed in Chapter 2) provide a good starting point to study cross-cultural leadership effectiveness characteristics. Employees who rank high on power distance (e.g., India, East Africa, and Indonesia) are more likely to prefer an autocratic style of leadership because they are more comfortable with a clear distinction between managers and subordinates. On the other hand, employees in countries that rank low on power distance (e.g., Austria) prefer a more participative style of leadership.[69] Hofstede concludes that participative management approaches that are highly recommended by many American researchers can be counterproductive in other cultures. He further suggests that American researchers tend to concentrate much of their analysis on leaders and not enough on subordinates and their attitudes toward leaders.

Other research points to additional differences in various aspects of leaders and leadership across cultures. Research has shown, for example, that in Nigeria and Taiwan (1) economic success is more likely to result from severe autocratic leadership styles, and (2) success decreases with increasing consideration for employees and their families.[70] As a further example, a recent study reported important differences in how U.S. and People's Republic of China managers deal with uncertainty and make decisions in ambiguous situations.[71] Studies such as these have important implications, particularly as the number of joint ventures among these countries increases.[72]

The effective multicultural leader in different global settings apparently needs various leadership skills that are not always so obvious. In cross-cultural studies of managers, Bass identified seven factors linked to leadership effectiveness:[73]

1. Preferred awareness (willingness to be aware of others' feelings).
2. Actual awareness (actual understanding of oneself and others).
3. Submissiveness (to rules and authority).
4. Reliance on others (in problem solving).
5. Favoring of group decision making.
6. Concern for human relations.
7. Cooperative peer relations.

The skills and other competencies of the leader, however, comprise only one variable in the leadership context. Other factors to consider include the subordinates, the peers, the superiors, the task, and the task environment. Leadership in a multicultural situation, whether the management of a joint venture, a diverse work group in the United States, or a subsidiary abroad, poses many challenging tasks. Researchers have considerable doubts about the generalizability of what is good leadership across national and cultural boundaries. The transferability of leadership practices must be carefully analyzed. Beyond broad generalizations, managers should conduct their own research, review available research, and consult with others to develop the appropriate leadership style for each unique context.

The complexity of global joint ventures or of leading a foreign subsidiary requires the careful study of the culture, history, expectations, and working environments that face the leader. There is no right or "universal" way to lead. However, differences in style and preferences, if known, can make the job of leading less frustrating. Influential leaders in any country carefully examine the entire leadership context and their own competencies and then act to achieve relevant organizational goals.

Substitutes for Leadership

Most approaches and explanations of leadership assume that leaders are necessary in all settings and situations. However, some researchers propose that there are substitutes for leadership. That is, there are situational variables that can be considered substitutes for leadership. These substitutes can increase or diminish a leader's ability to influence others.

Leadership substitutes include task, organizational, or subordinate characteristics that render relationship- and/or task-oriented leadership not only impossible but also unnecessary. A related concept is a *leadership neutralizer*—something that makes it impossible for leadership to make a difference.[74]

Researchers have identified a wide variety of individual, task, environmental, and organizational characteristics as leadership substitute factors that influence relationships between leader behavior and follower satisfaction and performance. Some of these variables (e.g., follower expectations of the leader behavior) appear to influence which leadership style will enable the leader to motivate the direct followers. Others, however, function as *substitutes for leadership*. Substitute variables tend to negate the leader's ability to either increase or decrease followers' satisfaction or performance.

Substitutes for leadership are claimed to be prominent in many organizational settings. However, the leadership approaches we have presented fail to include any substitutes for leadership in discussing the leader behavior–follower satisfaction and performance relationship.

Exhibit 15.10, based on previously conducted research, provides substitutes for only two of the more popular leader behavior styles: relationship-oriented and

EXHIBIT 15.10   Items That Assess Leader–Member Exchange

Source: Adapted from Steven Kerr and John M. Jermier, "Substitutes for Leadership: Their Meaning and Measurement," *Organizational Behavior and Human Performance,* December 1978, p. 378.

	Neutralizes	
Characteristic	**Relationship-Oriented Leadership**	**Task-Oriented Leadership**
Of the subordinate:		
1. Ability, experience, training, knowledge		X
2. Need for independence	X	X
3. "Professional" orientation	X	X
4. Indifference toward organizational rewards	X	X
Of the task:		
5. Unambiguous and routine		X
6. Methodologically invariant		X
7. Provides its own feedback concerning accomplishment		X
8. Intrinsically satisfying	X	
Of the organization:		
9. Formalization (explicit plans, goals, and areas of responsibility)		X
10. Inflexibility (rigid, unbending rules and procedures)		X
11. Highly specified and active advisory and staff functions		X
12. Close-knit, cohesive work groups	X	X
13. Organizational rewards not within the leader's control	X	X
14. Spatial distance between superior and subordinates	X	X

task-oriented. For each of these styles, Kerr and Jermier present substitutes (characteristics of the subordinate, the task, or the organization) that neutralize the style.[75] For example, an experienced, well-trained, knowledgeable employee doesn't need a leader to structure the task (e.g., a task-oriented leader). Likewise, a job (task) that provides its own feedback doesn't require a task-oriented leader to inform the employee how he's doing. Also, an employee in a close-knit, cohesive group doesn't need a supportive, relationship-oriented leader. The group substitutes for this leader. The impact of these effects can be seen in a recent study on R&D project teams where intrinsically satisfying tasks and worker ability were shown to be empirically related to improved organizational outcomes.[76]

Admittedly, we don't fully understand the leader–follower relationship in organizational settings.[77] We need to continue searching for guidelines and principles. Such searching now seems to be centered on more careful analysis of a situational perspective on leadership and on issues such as the cause–effect question, the constraints on leader behavior, and substitutes for leadership. We feel that it's better to study leaders and substitutes for leaders than to use catchy descriptions to identify leaders. Such study and analysis can result in developing programs to train, prepare, and develop employees for leadership roles.

Summary of Key Points

- Leadership is the process of influencing others to facilitate the attainment of organizationally relevant goals. Exercising leadership does not require that one be in a formal leadership position. Three important variables present in all leadership situations are people, task, and environment.

- A trait approach to leadership focuses on identifying the intellectual, emotional, physical, or other personal traits of effective leaders. Traits that have been identified include intelligence, personality, height, and supervisory ability. Trait approaches have failed to identify any universally accepted characteristics.

- Behavior approaches to leadership focus on the behavior of the leader. Job-centered and employee-centered leadership and initiating structure and consideration are examples of what has been identified as important leader behavior. Behavior approaches and trait approaches both fail to include the nature of the leadership situation in attempting to prescribe effective leadership approaches.

- Situational approaches emphasize the importance of considering the nature of the environment, or situation, in which leadership is exercised. Important situational approaches include Fiedler's contingency model; Vroom, Yetton, and Jago's normative decision-making model of leadership; the path–goal model; and Hersey and Blanchard's situational leadership theory.

- Charisma, transaction, and transformation are interesting and insightful ways of analyzing leadership. Charismatic leaders are able to attract and influence followers.

- Transformational leaders are able to influence others by using charisma, paying attention to followers, and stimulating others.

- The leader–member exchange explanation of leaders proposes that a leader can be effective by being flexible in using the appropriate style with various individuals.

YOU BE THE JUDGE COMMENT

IF YOUR BOSS MAKES YOU SICK, CAN YOU GET A NEW ONE?

No. The Fed attempted to reasonably accommodate this employee's back problem. The employee offered no solid proof of her claim that her current boss aggravated her back problem. Reasonable accommodation was offered in the form of furniture and ability to move around. Plus, the Fed offered to help her find a comparable position.

- Coaching is the use of skills in one-on-one interactions with individuals who learn from the coach.
- Leadership substitutes are factors that render leadership unnecessary or even impossible. Leadership substitutes negate the leader's ability to either increase or decrease follower satisfaction or performance. Substitutes can include cohesive work groups, intrinsically satisfying tasks, and high levels of subordinate ability, experience, and knowledge.

Review and Discussion Questions

1. Is coaching a specific leadership approach or is it another form of mentoring? Explain.
2. Over time, the many different approaches used to explain leadership have become increasingly involved and complex. Why do you think this has happened?
3. Organizations annually spend a great deal of money on leadership training. Is this a wise investment? Are there other, less costly ways of improving leadership effectiveness?
4. How can "evil" individuals such as Adolf Hitler influence followers? Explain this in terms of charisma.
5. Why would communication skill be considered important in every explanation of leadership covered in this chapter?
6. Realistically, how much control does a leader have over situational favorableness? How might a leader go about trying to improve favorableness? Does it really make sense for a leader to try to *decrease* favorableness?
7. It has been suggested that good leadership is knowing when to take charge and when to delegate. How consistent is this with the various situational approaches discussed in this chapter?
8. Is leadership more important in a large unit or a small unit? Explain.
9. Is there a cause-and-effect relationship between leader behavior and follower performance? What is the nature or direction of the relationship? How strong is the relationship?
10. What substitutes for leadership exist for a student preparing to take a final examination in a course offered as part of a firm's educational fringe-benefit program?

Now how much do you know about leadership?

6. Approaches to leadership that suggest leadership effectiveness is a function of various aspects of the leadership situation are called _____ theories of leadership.
   a. behavioral
   b. situational
   c. trait
   d. functional

7. _____ describes behavior in which the leader organizes and structures the way a job is to be accomplished.
   a. Pressure-centeredness
   b. Initiating structure
   c. Coping angle
   d. Managing scope

8. The most damaging critique of Fiedler's work on leadership centers on his measurement of the _____.
   a. job's goal
   b. least preferred co-workers
   c. leader's emotions
   d. attitude of subordinates

9. The emphasis of Hersey and Blanchard's situational leadership model is on followers and their level of _____.
   a. performance
   b. training
   c. readiness
   d. education

10. Most behavioral-style leadership theories discuss only _____ dimension(s).
    a. 1
    b. 2
    c. 3
    d. 4

REALITY CHECK ANSWERS

Before	After
1. *b* 2. *c* 3. *c* 4. *d* 5. *b*	6. *b* 7. *b* 8. *b* 9. *c* 10. *b*
Number Correct	Number Correct
_____	_____

Exercise

Exercise 15.1: *Task and People Orientations*

Are you task- or people-oriented? Or do you have a balanced style of leading? The following items describe the people- or task-oriented aspects of leadership. Use any past or present experience in leading a group of people as you complete the 34-item scale. Circle whether you would most likely behave in the described way, always (A), frequently (F), occasionally (O), seldom (S), or never (N).

A	F	O	S	N	1. I would most likely act as the spokesperson of the group.
A	F	O	S	N	2. I would encourage overtime work.
A	F	O	S	N	3. I would allow employees complete freedom in their work.
A	F	O	S	N	4. I would encourage the use of uniform procedures.
A	F	O	S	N	5. I would permit employees to use their own judgment in solving problems.
A	F	O	S	N	6. I would stress being ahead of competing groups.
A	F	O	S	N	7. I would speak as a representative of the group.
A	F	O	S	N	8. I would encourage members for a greater effort.
A	F	O	S	N	9. I would try out my ideas in the group.
A	F	O	S	N	10. I would let members do their work the way they think best.
A	F	O	S	N	11. I would be working hard for a promotion.
A	F	O	S	N	12. I would tolerate postponement and uncertainty.
A	F	O	S	N	13. I would speak for the group if there were visitors present.
A	F	O	S	N	14. I would keep the work moving at a rapid pace.
A	F	O	S	N	15. I would turn the members loose on a job and let them go to it.
A	F	O	S	N	16. I would settle conflicts when they occur in the group.
A	F	O	S	N	17. I would get swamped by details.
A	F	O	S	N	18. I would represent the group at outside meetings.
A	F	O	S	N	19. I would be reluctant to allow the members any freedom of action.
A	F	O	S	N	20. I would decide what should be done and how it should be done.
A	F	O	S	N	21. I would give some members some of my authority.
A	F	O	S	N	22. Things would usually turn out as I had predicted.
A	F	O	S	N	23. I would allow the group a high degree of initiative.
A	F	O	S	N	24. I would assign group members to particular tasks.
A	F	O	S	N	25. I would be willing to make changes.
A	F	O	S	N	26. I would ask the members to work harder.
A	F	O	S	N	27. I would trust the group members to exercise good judgment.
A	F	O	S	N	28. I would schedule the work to be done.
A	F	O	S	N	29. I would refuse to explain my actions.
A	F	O	S	N	30. I would persuade others that my ideas are to their advantage.
A	F	O	S	N	31. I would permit the group to set its own pace.
A	F	O	S	N	32. I would urge the group to beat its previous record.
A	F	O	S	N	33. I would act without consulting the group.
A	F	O	S	N	34. I would ask that group members follow standard rules and regulations.

T_____P_____

The T/P Leadership Questionnaire is scored as follows:

a. Circle the item numbers for statements 8, 12, 17, 18, 19, 29, 33, and 34.

b. Write the number 1 in front of a *circled item number* if you responded S (seldom) or N (never) to that statement.

c. Also write a number 1 in front of *item numbers not circled* if you responded A (always) or F (frequently).

d. Circle the numbers that you have written in front of the following statements: 3, 5, 8, 10, 15, 18, 19, 21, 23, 25, 27, 29, 31, 33, and 34.

e. Count the *circled number 1s*. This is your score for concern for people. Record the score in the blank following the letter P.

f. Count the *uncircled number 1s*. This is your score for concern for task. Record this number in the blank following the letter T.

Source: The T/P Leadership Questionnaire was adapted by J.B. Ritchie and P. Thompson. *Organization and People* (New York: West, 1984). Copyright 1969 by the American Research Association.

Exercise

Exercise 15.2: *Leadership Style Analysis*

Objectives

1. To learn how to diagnose different leadership situations using the Vroom-Jago model.
2. To learn how to apply a systematic procedure for analyzing situations.
3. To improve understanding of how to reach a decision.

Starting the Exercise

The instructor will form groups of four to five people to analyze each of the following three cases. Try to reach a group consensus on which decision style is best for the particular case. Each case should take a group between 30 and 45 minutes to analyze.

Exercise Procedures

Phase I (10–15 minutes): Individually read a case and select what you consider to be the best decision style.

Phase II (30–45 minutes): Join a group appointed by the instructor and reach a group consensus.

Phase III (20 minutes): Each group spokesperson presents the group's response and rationale to other groups.

These phases should be used for each of the cases.

Case I

Setting: Corporate headquarters
Your position: Vice president

As marketing vice president, you frequently receive nonroutine requests from customers. One such request, from a relatively new customer, is for extended terms on a large purchase ($2.5 million) involving several of your product lines. The request is for extremely favorable terms that you would not consider except for the high inventory level of most product lines at the present time due to the unanticipated slack period that the company has experienced over the last six months.

You realize that the request is probably a starting point for negotiations, and you have proved your abilities to negotiate the most favorable arrangements in the past. As preparation for these negotiations, you have familiarized yourself with the financial situation of the customer, using various investment reports that you receive regularly.

Reporting to you are four sales managers, each of whom has responsibility for a single product line. They know of the order, and, like you, they believe that it is important to negotiate terms with minimum risk and maximum returns to the company. They are likely to differ on what constitutes an acceptable level of risk. The two younger managers have developed a reputation of being "risk takers," whereas the two more senior managers are substantially more conservative.

Case II

Setting: Toy manufacturer

Your position: Vice president, engineering and design

You are a vice president in a large toy manufacturing company, and your responsibilities include the design of new products that will meet the changing demand in this uncertain and very competitive industry. Your design teams, each under the supervision of a department head, are therefore under constant pressure to produce novel, marketable ideas.

At the opposite end of the manufacturing process is the quality control department, which is under the authority of the vice president, production. When quality control has encountered a serious problem that may be due to design features, its staff has consulted with one or more of your department heads to obtain their recommendations for any changes in the production process. In the wake of consumer concern over the safety of children's toys, however, the responsibilities of quality control have recently been expanded to ensure not only the quality but also the safety of your products. The first major problem in this area has arisen. A preliminary consumer report has blacklisted one of your new products without giving any specific reason or justification. This has upset you and others in the organization since it was believed that this product would be one of the most profitable items in the coming Christmas season.

The consumer group has provided your company with an opportunity to respond to the report before it is made public. The head of quality control has therefore consulted with your design people, but you have been told that they became somewhat defensive and dismissed the report as "overreactive fanatic nonsense." Your people told quality control that, while freak accidents were always possible, the product was certainly safe as designed. They argued that the report should simply be ignored.

Since the issue is far from routine you have decided to give it your personal attention. Because your design teams have been intimately involved in all aspects of the development of the item, you suspect that their response was extreme and was perhaps governed more by their emotional reaction to the report than by the facts. You are not convinced that the consumer group is totally irresponsible, and you are anxious to explore the problem in detail and to recommend to quality control any changes that

may be required from a design standpoint. The firm's image as a producer of high-quality toys could suffer a serious blow if the report were made public and public confidence were lost as a result.

You will have to depend heavily on the background and experience of your design teams to help you in analyzing the problem. Even though quality control will be responsible for the decision to implement any changes that you may ultimately recommend, your own subordinates have the background of design experience that could enable you to set standards for what is "safe" and to suggest any design modifications that would meet these standards.

Case III

Setting: Corporate headquarters

Your position: Vice president, marketing

The sales executives in your home office spend a great deal of time visiting regional sales offices. As marketing vice president, you are concerned that the expenses incurred on these trips are excessive—especially now, when the economic outlook seems bleak and general belt-tightening measures are being carried out in every department.

Having recently been promoted from the ranks of your subordinates, you are keenly aware of some cost-saving measures that could be introduced. You have, in fact, asked the accounting department to review a sample of past expense reports, and it has agreed with your conclusion that several highly favored travel "luxuries" could be curtailed. For example, your sales executives could restrict first-class air travel to only those occasions when economy class is unavailable, and airport limousine service to hotels could be used instead of taxis where possible. Even more savings could be made if your personnel carefully planned trips such that multiple purposes could be achieved where possible.

The success of any cost-saving measures, however, depends on the commitment of your subordinates. You do not have the time (or the desire) to closely review the expense reports of these sales executives. You suspect, though, that they do not share your concerns over the matter. Having once been in their position, you know that they feel themselves to be deserving of travel amenities.

The problem is to determine which changes, if any, are to be made in current travel and expense account practices in light of the new economic conditions.

Case 15.1: *Rotating Leaders: Orpheus Orchestra*

The second week of January at Baruch High School in Manhattan, teenagers are noisily making their way to and from class. On the street below, a siren blares through Union Square. And in a classroom on one of the floors of the high school, musicians are sight-reading a piece of music. After several frustrating attempts, cellist Melissa Meell finally stops and shrugs her shoulders. "We're a long way from Carnegie Hall," she quips.

That kind of wisecrack would be typical of a clever 12th-grader who's struggling through her first Mozart symphony, hoping to ace her audition for all-city orchestra and get a crack at playing on the stage of that revered concert hall. But, in fact, Meell is 44, a professional musician, and a member of Orpheus—a Grammy-nominated chamber orchestra that's widely considered one of the best of its kind on the planet. Although she and her fellow musicians are just 19 days away from their next Carnegie Hall performance, they still sound as if they're playing rubber bands.

With such an imposing deadline at hand, why is this prestigious group of musicians rehearsing in such noisy surroundings? The school, it turns out, is its home. Orpheus has been the orchestra in residence at Baruch High School for more than three years and at Zicklin School of Business, which is affiliated with New York City's university system, since September 1999. Orpheus is a conductorless orchestra, and it was for that very reason that Baruch wanted the orchestra to take up residence there—so that students could watch Orpheus rehearse and observe firsthand how it uses collaboration and consensus-building to settle its creative differences. High school students would get a living lesson in conflict resolution. And business students, who would soon be working in a world where few people believe that a CEO has—or should have—all of the answers, would learn that self-governance makes a worthwhile model and that leadership is most effective when all levels of an organization have input.

Its self-governing and leadership abilities have made Orpheus more than just a group of gifted musicians. Orpheus has actually become a metaphor

for structural change—the kind of change that has bedeviled so many big companies and exasperated so many big-company CEOs. Orpheus's founder, Julian Fifer, 49, first became aware of the group's metamorphosis when a chairman of a large Japanese publishing company approached him several years ago. "He told me how much he had enjoyed our concert," Fifer recalls. "But then he confided that he didn't want his employees to discover us." Fifer was amused—and intrigued: If old-line business leaders resisted their self-governing process, presumably there were corporate mavericks who would find it compelling. That assumption proved to be correct. Several large companies, including Kraft Foods and Novartis AG, have hired Orpheus to demonstrate its process to their executives.

What do these executives find so compelling about Orpheus's sound and system? To them, the group is a radical, ongoing experiment to find out whether grassroots democracy and commitment to consensus can lead to transcendental performance—or whether it will all end in organizational chaos and muddled results. So what is the key to the orchestra's continued success? A set of insights about motivation, decision making, performance, and work that are as relevant in conference rooms as they are in concert halls.

Motivation: The Sweet Sound of Satisfaction

Those who aspire to a career as a classical musician and who are studying at a top conservatory have a few obvious career paths: Clearly, the more talented you are, the more options you have. Those who win or place well in big competitions can go on to sign recording contracts and to enjoy solo careers. They can also choose to join chamber music groups, as do many of their other colleagues. Virtually all—no matter how successful or well-known—teach. Some, however, are forced to do so to support themselves financially. Most orchestra musicians who want to perform full-time join symphony orchestras.

Those jobs offer relative stability and a decent income, but they are hard to come by. Even so, back in the early 1970s, when Orpheus's founding members were trickling out of music schools and into the New York freelance scene, taking such a job was not high on their list of career goals. "Many of us believed that joining a traditional orchestra would lead to a creative dead end," says Ronnie Bauch, 47, a violinist with Orpheus since 1974, "because you'd be under the thumb of its conductor for the next 30 or 40 years."

"Ironically, your conservatory training leaves you ill-equipped to play in large orchestras," adds Frank Morelli, 40, a bassoonist who joined Orpheus in the late 1970s but sometimes also plays in conductor-led groups. "Presumably, you've devoted so much time to studying music because you have a need for self-expression. If you've studied at a top school for the past four or so years, you've also got a certain amount of pride and ego invested in your career. And you're self-motivated because the competition is so steep. But all of those things can get in the way when you're sitting in an orchestra with a conductor telling you what to do."

Some observers of the orchestra scene today believe that the moral righteousness of Orpheus's early members was prophetic. "The climate in most conductor-led orchestras is appalling," says Harvey Seifter, 46, Orpheus's executive director, who left the theater world about two years ago to take on the delicate task of administering to the needs of this self-governing enterprise. "Orchestras take a lot of very smart people, many of whom learned to read music before they learned to read words, and, if they're violinists, sit them in the last row of the second-violin section, where they must unquestioningly follow someone who's waving a stick at them. Success is defined as how good you are at getting your bow to leap off your violin at the exact same nanosecond as all of the other violinists' bows."

That interpretation is in keeping with the results of a study conducted by Harvard psychology professor Richard Hackman. In the early 1990s, Hackman looked at job satisfaction among symphony musicians in 78 orchestras in four countries and found widespread discontent. Indeed, in this now well-known study, symphony members experienced the same levels of job satisfaction as the federal prison guards whom Hackman had studied earlier. Symphony musicians were, however, happier than professional hockey players.

"Most of them adapt," explains Hackman. "But they often do that by finding other ways to develop musically. One person said that he had to be very careful not to let his symphony job get in the way of making music."

For Fifer, the inspiration for Orpheus came from his chamber music experiences back at Juilliard. He found the sense of intimacy and connectedness that he felt with other musicians in those groups exciting and inspiring, and he longed to find a way to re-create that experience on a larger scale. "I loved chamber music's clarity of sound and flexibility of temperament," he says. "I wanted to bring that camaraderie and spirit into a larger setting. And in order for everyone to be able to communicate more effectively, it seemed necessary to do without a conductor."

So Fifer invited a select group of musicians to that first rehearsal, carefully choosing among those who he knew could take—as well as give—criticism. He named the group Orpheus, for the Greek god who created music so powerful that stones rose up and followed him. "We had no particular method for presenting interpretations and ideas on a piece, but our spirits were high, and we had a great deal of enthusiasm," he recalls. "It was as if we were calling out to anyone who would listen. 'Look Ma, no hands!'"

Decision Making: Everyone's a Leader (Just Not All at Once)

But could they do it? When Fifer's idea first took shape, he knew of no preexisting model for a conductorless group of Orpheus's size—anywhere. So his idea was an ambitious one: assembling a number of renegade musicians and building a sustainable enterprise fueled only (at least at first) by idealism and satisfaction. Still, the group pressed on, meeting at Chinese restaurants, rehearsing in churches, and performing at public libraries and housing projects, because city-owned property cost nothing to rent. Eventually, the group got a few annual grants from New York's arts commission, created a demo tape, and, in 1974, booked a small hall at Lincoln Center for its debut performance. In 1979, Orpheus made its first concert tour of Europe, and five years later, it signed a recording contract with the prestigious Deutsche Grammaphon label.

Even as performances gained recognition and attracted larger audiences, rehearsals remained a work in progress. At first, all 27 members of the group participated in every decision that had to be made for each piece—hundreds of tiny details involving dynamics, phrasing, and tempo. So that Orpheus wouldn't sound like dueling stereos, each decision had to be unanimous. And that could take a while, especially when 27 strong-willed musicians were involved, and the buck stopped with all of them. "Rehearsals were becoming free-for-alls," says Martha Caplin, 48, a violinist with the group since 1982. "We needed twice as many rehearsals just to try all of the ideas."

Any organization that operates on consensus risks the possibility of arriving at utterly wishy-washy decisions. If the agreement process is itself chaotic, that risk is even greater. To combat that problem, Orpheus decided to experiment with a new rehearsal method. Instead of just giving the floor to anyone who had an interpretation to offer, Orpheus formed smaller core groups, whose members would change regularly, that would rehearse each piece before the entire group began working on it.

"These core groups formulate one interpretation of a piece," Bauch emphasizes. "It's not necessarily *the* interpretation. Sometimes it's just a starting point." A core group does the same sort of preparation that a good conductor would do—researching the composer's other works, learning the history of the particular work that will be performed, and listening to recordings of that piece of music. Then the core group presents its ideas to the entire ensemble during the first read-through.

Another unusual aspect of Orpheus is the role that its concertmaster plays. In conductor-led orchestras, the concertmaster is usually more of a team captain. But in Orpheus, that function (which rotates regularly) is similar to that of a player-coach on a soccer team. Orpheus's concertmasters are responsible for actually running rehearsals, moderating debates among members, suggesting resolutions to those debates, and making sure that such discussions don't get too bogged down. Although the core group exerts its influence mostly in the early stages of rehearsing a piece, the concertmaster has more influence as performance dates near.

According to Fifer, having different people be concertmaster seemed the only logical way to run a group fueled by 1960s idealism. The decision to rotate core-group members was, however, more pragmatic: "That rotation method actually alleviates some of the pressure to try to get your way all of the time," admits Bauch. "Having to modulate our personalities and to take on different roles gives us an opportunity to develop leadership skills as well as a chance to be supportive." At first, the entire group voted on who would be the concertmaster for each piece. Eventually, Orpheus elected an executive committee that appoints a concertmaster according to an individual's particular musical expertise.

Not only do core groups and concertmasters change from concert to concert, but they also change from piece to piece. Such frequent changes in leadership require some preperformance planning. At the conclusion of every piece, Orpheus musicians bow and walk off stage. When they return for the next selection on the program, they take different seats, according to their part in that piece. This maneuvering is similar to that of the small chamber groups that Fifer envisioned when he formed Orpheus.

And also like those small chamber-music groups, different members of Orpheus give one another musical cues. Alert audience members will notice a musician use a nod of a head or a gesture of a bow, in a way inviting a fellow musician to join the "conversation" by offering that person a chance to pick up a musical thought. "At any time, you can be leading or following. 'Supporting' is the word that we like to use," says Bauch. "When I'm about to get a cue. I often find myself moving with the musician who's playing." That physical style of playing is usually not experienced in a standard symphony orchestra. It's as if members of Orpheus are all breathing with the same set of lungs.

For performances, Orpheus sits in a semicircle, with the center space (which is normally reserved for a conductor) empty. As a result, casual observers and some critics have erroneously referred to the ensemble as being "leaderless." In fact, "Orpheus exerts more leadership than any other orchestra I've examined," says Harvard's Hackman.

Performance: Practice Random Acts of Leadership

Soloists often adjust how loud they play a piece and how long they hold a note to the acoustics of a particular recital hall. Orpheus does the same. Those who have never worked with the group may find its methods fascinating. "One of the neatest things about Orpheus is that one of its musicians will go down and sit in the audience to hear how each piece sounds to a concertgoer's ears," says Susan Botti, a singer and composer who wrote a piece that Orpheus premiered. "I come from the theater, so I'm used to having people out where the audience sits taking notes and giving feedback during a run-through, but I've never seen that happen in an orchestra before."

Whether or not the concertmaster for a piece is particularly vocal, or the core group unusually opinionated, Orpheus's members all demonstrate great faith in the feedback from the colleague who's doing a sound check. "It's a crucial part of what we do," says Bauch. "On stage, you can't hear how a piece of music sounds to an audience, so you have to trust your colleague's ear. We used to vote on that kind of stuff at the last minute. Now that our listening skills are more refined, I think we trust one another more." (Bauch also has had an opportunity to hone another of his senses—just in case he'll need it on the concert stage: He helped taste-test New York Super Fudge Chunk ice cream for his childhood friends, Ben and Jerry.)

Bauch notes that changing core-group participants and the concertmaster position has given each orchestra member an intensive course in leadership training. "I've always been a quiet person, but in this group, speaking up is a matter of survival," says Susan Palma-Nidel, a flutist with Orpheus since 1980. "This experience has allowed me to discover strengths that I didn't know I had. Not only have I helped lead the group, but I've also been interviewed by the media—something I never thought I'd do. If I hadn't been forced to do those things, I'm not sure that I ever would have."

Questions

1. What would business organizations such as Kraft Foods gain from observing Orpheus in action?
2. Orpheus rotates the concertmaster position among core-group members. What is the logic of rotating the leader?
3. What are some of the substitutes for permanent leadership that exist within Orpheus?

Source: Adapted from Ron Lieber, "Leadership Ensemble," *Fast Company,* May 2000, p. 286, used by permission.

Organizational Design, Change, and Innovation

Where there is an open mind, there will always be a frontier.

Charles F. Kettering, quoted in Profile in America

CHAPTER SIXTEEN

Organizational Structure and Design

Learning Objectives

After completing Chapter 16, you should be able to:

- **Identify** the choices that must be made in designing an organizational structure.
- **Define** what is meant by the term *division of labor.*
- **Discuss** the role of delegation of authority in design decisions.
- **Describe** several forms of departmentalization.
- **Identify** the major advantages of matrix organizational design.

- **Explain** the importance of span of control.
- **Define** three important dimensions of structure.
- **Compare** mechanistic and organic organizational design.
- **Discuss** multinational organizational structure and design issues.
- **Explain** the meaning of the term *virtual organization.*

Organizational structure and design have always been important factors influencing the behavior of individuals and groups that comprise the organization; the new rules of operating in today's global business environment make structure and design considerations even more critical.[1] Today's managers are faced with an array of structural possibilities.[2] Ultimately, it is through the design of the structure that management establishes expectations for what individuals and groups will do to achieve the organization's purposes. But before these purposes can be accomplished, somebody must do some work. Not only must people do some work, but they must also do the right work. And that brings us to organizational structure, because it is through structure that managers decide how the organization's purposes will be accomplished.[3]

Managers achieve coordinated effort through the design of a structure of task and authority relationships. Design, in this context, implies that managers make a conscious effort to predetermine the way employees do their work. Structure refers to relatively stable relationships and processes of the organization. Organizational structure is considered by many to be "the anatomy of the organization, providing a foundation within which the organization functions."[4] Thus, the structure of an organization, similar to the anatomy of a living organism, can be viewed as a framework. The idea of structure as a framework "focuses on the differentiation of positions, formulation of rules and procedures, and prescriptions of authority."[5] Therefore, the purpose of structure is to regulate, or at least reduce, uncertainty in the behavior of individual employees.

Organizations are purposive and goal-oriented, so it follows that the structure of organizations also is purposive and goal-oriented. Our concept of organizational structure takes into account the existence of purposes and goals, and our attitude is that management should think of structure in terms of its contribution to organizational effectiveness, even though the exact nature of the relationship between structure and effectiveness is inherently difficult to know. Structural decisions should also reflect company values and incorporate ethical and environmental considerations. Indeed, as illustrated in this chapter's You Be the Judge, many issues relating to corporate social responsibility are at the core of some contemporary approaches to organizational design and structure.

Designing an Organizational Structure

organizational design
A specific organizational structure that results from managers' decisions and actions.

Managers who set out to design an organizational structure face difficult decisions. They must choose among a myriad of alternative frameworks of jobs, work projects, and departments. The process by which they make these choices is termed **organizational design,** and it means quite simply the decisions and actions that result in an organizational structure.[6] This process may be explicit or implicit, it may be "one-shot" or developmental, it may be done by a single manager or by a team of managers.[7] However the actual decisions come about, the content of the decisions is always the same.

The first decision focuses on individual jobs, the next two decisions focus on departments or groups of jobs, and the fourth decision considers the issue of delegation of authority throughout the structure.

1. Managers decide how to divide the overall task into successively smaller jobs. Managers divide the total activities of the task into smaller sets of related activities. The effect of this decision is to define jobs in terms of specialized activities and responsibilities. Although jobs have many characteristics, the most important one is their degree of specialization.

2. Managers decide the bases by which to group the individual jobs. This decision is much like any other classification decision, and it can result in groups containing jobs that are relatively homogeneous (alike) or heterogeneous (different).

3. Managers decide the appropriate size of the group reporting to each superior. As we have already noted, this decision involves determining whether spans of control are relatively narrow or wide.

4. Managers distribute authority among the jobs. Authority is the right to make decisions without approval by a higher manager and to exact obedience from designated other people. All jobs contain some degree of the right to make decisions within prescribed limits. But not all jobs contain the right to exact obedience from others. The latter aspect of authority distinguishes managerial jobs from nonmanagerial jobs. Managers can exact obedience; nonmanagers can't.

Thus, organizational structures vary depending upon the choices that managers make. If we consider each of the four design decisions to be a continuum of possible choices, the alternative structures can be depicted as follows:

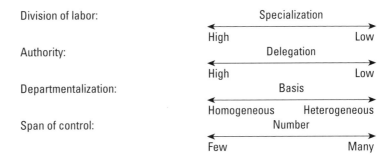

Organizational structures tend toward one extreme or the other along each continuum. Structures tending to the left are characterized by a number of terms including *classical, formalistic, structured, bureaucratic, System 1,* and *mechanistic.* Structures tending to the right are termed *neoclassical, informalistic, unstructured, nonbureaucratic, System 4,* and *organic.*[8] Exactly where along the continuum an organization finds itself has implications for its performance as well as for individual and group behavior.[9]

Division of Labor

division of labor
The process of dividing work into relatively specialized jobs to achieve advantages of specialization.

Division of labor concerns the extent to which jobs are specialized. Managers divide the total task of the organization into specific jobs having specified activities. The activities define what the person performing the job is to do. For example, activities of the job "accounting clerk" can be defined in terms of the methods and procedures required to process a certain quantity of transactions during a period of time.

YOU BE THE JUDGE

CAN ORGANIZATIONAL DESIGN IMPACT CORPORATE SOCIAL RESPONSIBILITY?

Fuji Heavy Industries (FHI), a Japanese company, has organized itself into four divisions: automobile, aerospace, industrial products, and "other." While most people may not be familiar with FHI, almost everyone has heard of its car brand, Subaru. FHI's other divisions produce a diverse range of products from military helicopters and airliner wings to sanitation vehicles. Although FHI is entrenched in classic "heavy industries," it is not your typical smokestack company.

FHI's corporate philosophy specifically includes its "aim to continuously promote harmony between people, society, and the environment." The company has also issued a specific environmental policy that states:

FHI recognizes the integral relationship between the environment and its business activities and strives to provide products that are friendly to the earth, society, and people. FHI is protecting the environment to ensure our future.

FHI doesn't stop there. Its "operating criteria for environmental conservation" expands on the environmental policy and includes the following points.

1. FHI is committed to environmental conservation and gives consideration to environmental impact at every step of product development, design, manufacture, sales, service, and disposal.

2. FHI observes the relevant laws, regulations, and agreements with communities and industries, while also promoting voluntary activities in accordance with its own environmental objectives and targets as determined by the company.

3. FHI recognizes the importance of continual improvement and efforts to prevent pollution and encourages every employee to act with self-awareness and responsibility.

4. FHI endeavors to raise environmental consciousness by providing educational opportunities for its employees according to their job status and job description.

5. FHI regularly performs audits and inspections to improve its environmental conservation activities.

6. FHI is committed to interacting within the community and engaging in joint activities to further environmental preservations.

FHI has done more than just issue statements. For example, many Subarus are engineered as super-ultra-low-emission and zero-emission vehicles. According to Environmental Protection Agency (EPA) fuel economy statistics, Subaru sells the most fuel-efficient fleet of all-wheel-drive vehicles in the market, but its commitment doesn't end there. Subaru's Indiana manufacturing plant (SIA) was the first auto assembly plant in the world that sends nothing from its manufacturing operation to a landfill. Subaru proudly proclaims that the average U.S. consumer sends more trash to a landfill each week than its SIA facility. As if that's not enough, SIA's 800 acres have been designated a "Backyard Wildlife Habitat" and are an animal sanctuary. The manufacturing campus is home to numerous forms of wildlife including the bald eagle. Subaru sponsors various community organizations including: the ASPCA, Leave No Trace Center for Outdoor Ethics, and the Geological Society of America.

FHI's environmental efforts aren't just limited to Subaru. It has developed ultra-light materials for use in aircraft and is involved in wind and other alternative energy initiatives. Even its sanitation vehicles are designed to be eco-friendly. FHI's commitment to the environment is embedded in its organization from the chairman to the line employee.

In your opinion, to what extent (if at all) should an organization be committed to the environment? While FHI may view its environmental initiatives as investments, whose funds are being invested? Is FHI doing too much or too little? You be the judge.

Sources: "Business Segments and Geographic Segments," Fuju Heavy Industries, www.fhi.co.jp/english/ir/finance/achievement.html (accessed April 3, 2009); "About Subaru of America, Inc.," Subaru of North America, www.subaru.com.company/news.index.html (accessed April 3, 2009); and "Fuji Heavy Industries," Subaru of North America, www.drive.subaru.com/OnlineX_Fuji.htm (accessed April 3, 2009).

The economic advantages of dividing work into specialized jobs are the principal historical reasons for the creation of organizations.[10] As societies became more and more industrialized and urbanized, craft production gave way to mass production. Mass production depends upon the ability to obtain the economic benefits of specialized labor, and the most effective means for obtaining specialized labor is through organizations. Although managers are concerned with more than the economic implications of jobs, they seldom lose sight of specialization as the rationale for dividing work among jobs.[11]

Division of labor in organizations can occur in three different ways:[12]

1. *Personal specialties.* Most people think of specialization in the sense of occupational and professional specialties. Thus, we think of accountants, software engineers, graphic designers, scientists, physicians, and the myriad of other specialties that exist in organizations and everyday life.

2. *Natural sequence of work.* For example, manufacturing plants often divide work into fabricating and assembly, and individuals will be assigned to do the work of one of these two activities. This particular manifestation of division of work is termed *horizontal specialization.*

3. *Vertical plane.* All organizations have a hierarchy of authority from the lowest-level manager to the highest-level manager. The CEO's work is different from the shift supervisor's.

Determining what each job in the organization should do is a key managerial decision. Jobs vary along a general dimension of specialization, with some jobs being more highly specialized than others. Managers can change an organization's structure by changing the degree of specialization of jobs. For example, Procter & Gamble (P&G) ex-CEO Edwin Artzt changed the degree of specialization of the company's sales reps. Artzt believed that sales reps interested in developing strong ties with customers lost their competitive instinct. He believed that team members devoted too much energy to building relationships within the team and with the customers and too little attention to building volume and profit. He reversed P&G's team approach in favor of sales representatives who represented narrow sectors such as soap and food products. One organizational effect of Artzt's decision had been a move to create separate sales groups within each sector. In terms of specialization of labor, sales representatives were given more specialized jobs (they sold fewer different products) and the organization had more specialized units (the sales units in each of the sectors).[13] Current CEO A.G. Lafley continues to refocus P&G's energies and has achieved significant financial success (e.g., company sales increased 19 percent to a total of $51.4 billion in 2004).[14]

The process of defining the activities and authority of jobs is analytical; that is, the total task of the organization is broken down into successively smaller ones. But then management must use some basis to combine the divided tasks into groups or departments containing some specified number of individuals or jobs. We will discuss these two decisions relating to departments in that order.

Delegation of Authority

delegation of authority
The process by which authority is distributed downward in an organization.

Managers decide how much authority should be delegated to each job and each jobholder. As we have noted, authority refers to individuals' right to make decisions without approval by higher management and to exact obedience from others. **Delegation of authority** refers specifically to making decisions, not to doing work. A sales manager can be delegated the right to hire salespeople (a decision) and the right to assign them to specific territories (obedience). Another sales manager may not have the right to hire but may have the right to assign territories. Thus, the degree of delegated authority can be relatively high or relatively low with respect to both aspects of authority. Any particular job involves a range of alternative configurations of authority delegation.[15] Managers must balance the relative gains and losses of alternatives.

Reasons to Decentralize Authority

Relatively high delegation of authority encourages the development of professional managers. This is one reason Microsoft's top two leaders, Bill Gates and Steve Ballmer, built a professional management structure that will help the organization ensure succession planning and live much longer than its founders.[16] Organizations that decentralize (delegate) authority enable managers to make significant decisions, to gain skills, and to advance in the company. By virtue of their right to make decisions on a broad range of issues, managers develop expertise that enables them to cope with problems of higher management. Managers with broad decision-making power often make difficult decisions. Consequentially, they are trained for promotion into positions of even greater authority and responsibility. Upper management can readily compare managers on the basis of actual decision-making performance. Advancement of managers on the basis of demonstrated performance can eliminate favoritism and minimize personality in the promotion process.

Second, high delegation of authority can lead to a competitive climate within the organization. Managers are motivated to contribute in this competitive atmosphere, since they're compared with their peers on various performance measures. A competitive environment in which managers compete on sales, cost reduction, and employee development targets can be a positive factor in overall organizational performance. Competitive environments can also produce destructive behavior if one manager's success occurs at the expense of another's. But regardless of whether it's positive or destructive, significant competition exists only when individuals have authority to do those things that enable them to win.

Finally, managers who have relatively high authority can exercise more autonomy and thus satisfy their desires to participate in problem solving. This autonomy can lead to managerial creativity and ingenuity, which contribute to the adaptiveness and development of the organization and managers. As we've seen in earlier chapters, opportunities to participate in setting goals can be positive motivators. But a necessary condition for goal setting is authority to make decisions. Many organizations, large and small, choose to follow the policy of decentralization of authority.

Decentralization of authority has its benefits, but these benefits aren't without costs. Organizations that are unable or unwilling to bear these costs will find reasons to centralize authority.

Reasons to Centralize Authority

Several reasons support centralizing authority. First, managers must be trained to make the decisions that go with delegated authority. Formal training programs can be quite expensive, which can more than offset the benefits.

Second, many managers are accustomed to making decisions and resist delegating authority to their subordinates. Consequently, they may perform at lower levels of effectiveness because they believe that delegation of authority involves losing control.

Third, administrative costs are incurred because new or altered accounting and performance systems must be developed to provide top management with information about the effects of their subordinates' decisions. When lower levels of management have authority, top management must have some means of reviewing the use of that authority. Consequently, they typically create reporting systems that inform them of the outcomes of decisions made at lower levels in the organization.

The fourth and perhaps most pragmatic reason to centralize is that decentralization means duplication of functions. Each autonomous unit must be truly self-supporting to be independent. But that involves a potentially high cost of duplication. Some organizations find that the cost of decentralization outweighs the benefits.[17]

Decision Guidelines

Like most managerial issues, whether authority should be delegated in a high or low degree cannot be resolved simply.[18] As usual, in managerial decision making, whether to centralize or decentralize authority can only be guided by general questions.

Departmental Bases

The rationale for grouping jobs rests on the necessity for coordinating them. The specialized jobs are separate, interrelated parts of the total task, whose accomplishment requires the accomplishment of each of the jobs. But the jobs must be performed in the specific manner and sequence intended by management when they were defined. As the number of specialized jobs in an organization increases, there comes a point when they can no longer be effectively coordinated by a single manager. Thus, to create manageable numbers of jobs, they are combined into smaller groups and a new job is defined—manager of the group.

The crucial managerial consideration when creating departments is determining the basis for grouping jobs. Of particular importance is the determination for the bases for departments that report to the top management position. In fact, numerous bases are used throughout the organization, but the basis used at the highest level determines critical dimensions of the organization. Some of the more widely used **departmentalization** bases[19] are described in the following sections.

departmentalization
The manner in which an organization is structurally divided. Some of the more publicized divisions are by function, territory, product, customer, and project.

Functional Departmentalization

Managers can combine jobs according to the functions of the organization. Every organization must undertake certain activities to do its work. These necessary activities are the organization's functions. The necessary functions of a manufacturing firm include production, marketing, finance, accounting, and human resources. These activities are necessary to create, produce, and sell a product. Necessary functions of a commercial bank include taking deposits, making loans, and investing the bank's funds. The functions of a hospital include surgery, psychiatry, housekeeping, pharmacy, nursing, and human resources.[20] Each of these functions can be a specific department, and jobs can be combined according to them. The functional basis is often found in relatively small organizations that provide a narrow range of products and services. It is also widely used as the basis in divisions of large multiproduct organizations.

Manufacturing organizations are typically structured on a functional basis (see Exhibit 16.1). The functions are engineering, manufacturing, reliability, distribution, finance, human resources, public relations, and purchasing. The functional basis has wide application in both service and manufacturing organizations. The specific configuration of functions that appear as separate departments varies from organization to organization.

The principal advantage of the functional basis is its efficiency. That is, it seems logical to have a department that consists of experts in a particular field such as production or accounting. By having departments of specialists, management creates efficient units. An accountant is generally more efficient when working with other accountants and other individuals who have similar backgrounds and interests. They can share expertise to get the work done.

EXHIBIT 16.1
Functional
Departmentalization
Structure

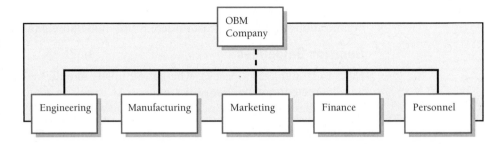

This classic form of organization is used to produce a classic snack, Lay's potato chips. A quick review of Frito-Lay North America's leadership structure indicates a functional organization. Reporting to president and CEO Al Carey are separate vice presidents responsible for the organization's public affairs, innovation, legal issues, marketing, operations, human resources, and sales. Although the division produces over 40 top brands and uses various distribution channels to reach different customer segments, this $12 billion business uses the functional form of organization to dominate the very competitive business of snack foods.[21]

A major disadvantage of this departmental basis is that, because specialists are working with and encouraging each other in their areas of expertise and interest, organizational goals may be sacrificed in favor of departmental goals. Accountants may see only their problems and not those of production or marketing or the total organization. In other words, the culture of and identification with the department are often stronger than identification with the organization and its culture.

Geographic Departmentalization

Another basis for departmentalizing is to establish groups according to geographic area. The logic is that all activities in a given region should be assigned to a manager. This individual is in charge of all operations in that particular geographic area.

In large organizations, geographic arrangements are advantageous because physical separation of activities makes centralized coordination difficult. For example, it is extremely difficult for someone in New York to manage salespeople in Kansas City. It makes sense to assign the managerial job to someone in Kansas City.

Large, multiunit retail stores are often organized along geographic lines. Specific retail outlets in a geographic area will comprise units, often termed *divisions,* which report to a regional manager who in turn may report to a corporate manager. For example, the manager of the Lexington, Kentucky, retail store of a national chain reports to the president, Midwest Division. The Midwest Division reports to the headquarters unit.

Territorial departmentalization provides a training ground for managerial personnel. The company is able to place managers in territories and then assess their progress in that geographic region. The experience that managers acquire in a territory away from headquarters provides valuable insights about how products and/or services are accepted in the field. Exhibit 16.2 depicts a territorial organization structure.

Product Departmentalization

Managers of many large, diversified companies group jobs on the basis of product. All jobs associated with producing and selling a product or product line will be placed under the direction of one manager. Product becomes the preferred basis as a firm grows by increasing the number of products it markets. As a firm grows, it's difficult

EXHIBIT 16.2
Territorial Departmentalization Structure

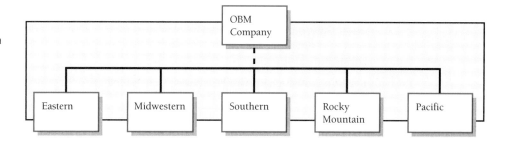

to coordinate the various functional departments and it becomes advantageous to establish product units. This form of organization allows personnel to develop total expertise in researching, manufacturing, and distributing a product line. Concentrating authority, responsibility, and accountability in a specific product department allows top management to coordinate actions.

The organizational structure using products as the basis for departments has been a key development in modern capitalism. The term *divisional organization* refers to this form of organizational structure. Most of the major and large firms of developed countries use it to some degree. The product-based divisions are often freestanding units that can design, produce, and market their own products, even in competition with other divisions of the same firm.[22]

A product department organization is shown in Exhibit 16.3 with three product divisions (small household appliances, large household appliances, and commercial appliances) reporting to the OBM corporate headquarters. Within each of these units we find production and marketing personnel. Since managers of product divisions coordinate sales, manufacturing, and distribution of a product, they become the overseers of a profit center. In this manner, profit responsibility is implemented in product-based organizations. Managers are often asked to establish profit goals at the beginning of a time period and then to compare actual profit with planned profit.

Wind River Systems, a global leader in device software optimization, has recently moved to this structure. It has organized itself into four product divisions: VxWorks, Linux, Tools, and Device Test. The company believes that doing so has allowed it to better respond to clients and permits the company to better measure the returns on investments.[23]

Product-based organizations foster initiative and autonomy by providing division managers with the resources necessary to carry out their profit plans. But such organizations face the difficult issue of deciding how much redundancy is necessary. Divisional structures contain some degree of redundancy because each division wants its own research, engineering, marketing, production, and all other functions necessary

EXHIBIT 16.3
Product Departmentalization Structure

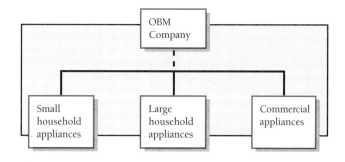

to do business. Thus, technical and professional personnel are found throughout the organization at the division levels. The cost of this arrangement can be exorbitant.

Customer Departmentalization

Customers and clients can be a basis for grouping jobs.[24] Examples of customer-oriented departments are the organizational structures of educational institutions. Some institutions have regular (day and night) courses and extension divisions. In some instances, a professor will be affiliated solely with the regular division or extension division. In fact, titles of some faculty positions specifically mention the extension division.

Another form of customer departmentalization is the loan department in a commercial bank. Loan officers are often associated with industrial, commercial, or agricultural loans. The customer will be served by one of these three loan officers.

The importance of customer satisfaction has stimulated firms to search for creative ways to serve people better. Since the Bell System broke up, competition for customers has forced AT&T to organize into customer-based units that identify with the needs of specific customers. Before the breakup, the firm was organized around functions. The move toward customer-based departments at Bell Labs was accompanied by efforts to implement total quality management (TQM), a customer-focused management practice that is reinforced in the customer-based structure.[25]

Some department stores are departmentalized to some degree on a customer basis, as shown in Exhibit 16.4. They have groupings such as retail store customers, mail-order customers, institutional customers, and government customers. Organizations with customer-based departments are better able to satisfy customer-identified needs than organizations that base departments on noncustomer factors.[26]

The Matrix Model

matrix model of organizational design
An organizational design that superimposes a product- or project-based design on an existing function-based design.

The **matrix model of organizational design** attempts to maximize the strengths and minimize the weaknesses of both the functional and product bases. In practical terms, the matrix design combines functional and product departmental bases.[27] Companies such as American Cyanamid, Avco, Carborundum, Caterpillar Tractor, Hughes Aircraft, ITT, Monsanto Chemical, National Cash Register, Prudential Insurance, TRW, and Texas Instruments are only a few users of matrix organization. Public sector users include public health and social service agencies.[28] Although the exact meaning of matrix organization varies in practice, it's typically seen as a balanced compromise between functional and product organization, between departmentalization by function and by product.[29]

Matrix organizations achieve the desired balance by superimposing, or overlaying, a horizontal structure of authority, influence, and communication on the vertical structure. In the arrangement shown in Exhibit 16.5, personnel assigned in each cell belong not only to the functional department, but also to a particular product or project.

EXHIBIT 16.4
Customer Departmentalization Structure

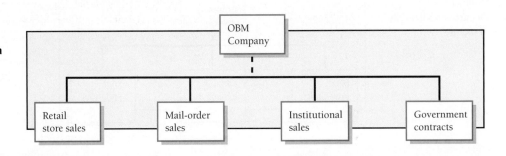

EXHIBIT 16.5 **Matrix Organizations**

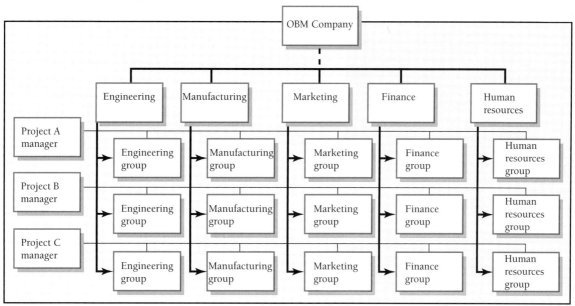

For example, manufacturing, marketing, engineering, and finance specialists are as-signed to work on one or more projects or products A, B, C, D, and E. As a conse-quence, personnel report to two managers: one in their functional department and one in the project or product unit. The existence of a *dual authority system* is a distinguish-ing characteristic of matrix organization. The potential conflict between allegiance to one's functional manager and one's project manager must be recognized and dealt with in matrix organizations.[30] In addition to the dual authority system, there are other unique characteristics of matrix organizations that need to be understood and managed carefully. The Management Pointer on page 492 offers tips for managers and employees who want to succeed within matrix organizations.

Matrix structures are found in organizations that (1) require responses to rapid change in two or more environments, such as technology and markets; (2) face uncertainties that generate high information-processing requirements; and (3) must deal with financial and human resources constraints.[31] Managers confronting these circumstances must obtain certain advantages that are most likely to be realized with matrix organization.[32]

Matrix organization facilitates the utilization of highly specialized staff and equipment. Each project or product unit can share the specialized resource with other units, rather than duplicating it to provide independent coverage for each. This is a particular advan-tage when projects don't require the specialist's full-time efforts. For example, a project may require only half a computer scientist's time. Rather than having several underutilized computer scientists assigned to each project, the organization can keep fewer of them fully utilized by shifting them from project to project. Such flexibility speeds response to com-petitive conditions, technological breakthroughs, and other environmental changes.

Advantages of Matrix Organization

A number of advantages can be associated with the matrix design. Some of the more important ones are as follows:

Efficient use of resources: Matrix organization facilitates the utilization of highly specialized staff and equipment. Each project or product unit can share the specialized resource with other units rather than duplicating it to provide independent coverage for each. This advantage is particularly so when projects require less than the full-time efforts of the specialist.

Flexibility in conditions of change and uncertainty: Timely response to change requires information and communication channels that efficiently get the information to the right people at the right time.[33] Matrix structures encourage constant interaction among project unit and functional department members. Information is channeled vertically and horizontally as people exchange technical knowledge, resulting in quicker response to competitive conditions, technological breakthroughs, and other environmental conditions.

Technical excellence: Technical specialists interact with other specialists while assigned to a project. These interactions encourage cross-fertilization of ideas, such as when a computer scientist must discuss the pros and cons of electronic data processing with a financial accounting expert.

Freeing top management for long-range planning: One stimulus for the development of matrix organizations is that top management is able to be less involved with day-to-day operations. This makes it possible for top management to delegate ongoing decision making, thus providing more time for long-range planning.

Improving motivation and commitment: Project and product groups are composed of individuals with specialized knowledge to whom management assigns, on the basis of their expertise, responsibility for specific aspects of the work. Consequently, decision making within the group tends to be more participative and democratic than in more hierarchical settings, ultimately fostering high levels of motivation and commitment.

Providing opportunities for personal development: Placed in groups consisting of individuals representing diverse parts of the organization, employees come to appreciate the different points of view expressed and become more aware of the total organization. Moreover, the experience broadens each specialist's knowledge not only of the organization but of other scientific and technical disciplines—engineers develop knowledge of financial issues; accountants learn about marketing.

Different Forms of Matrix Organization

Matrix organization forms can be depicted as existing in the middle of a continuum with formal and centralized organizations at one extreme and with fluid and decentralized organizations at the other. Ordinarily, the process of moving to matrix organization is evolutionary. That is, as the present structure proves incapable of dealing with rapid technological and market changes, management attempts to cope by establishing procedures and positions that are outside the normal routine.

This evolutionary process consists of the following steps:

Task force: When a competitor develops a new product that quickly captures the market, a rapid response is necessary. A convenient approach is to create a task force of individuals from each functional department and charge it with the responsibility to expedite the process. The task force achieves its objective, then dissolves, and members return to their primary assignment.

Teams: If the product or technological breakthrough generates a family of products that move through successive stages of new and improved products, the temporary task force concept is ineffective. A typical next step is to create permanent teams consisting of representatives from each functional department. The teams meet regularly to resolve interdepartmental issues and to achieve coordination.

Product managers: If the technological breakthrough persists so that new product development becomes a way of life, top management will create the roles of product managers. In a sense, product managers chair the teams, but they now are permanent positions. They have no formal authority over the team members but must rely on their expertise and interpersonal skill to influence them. Companies such as General Foods, Du Pont, and IBM make considerable use of the product management concept.

Product management departments: The final step in the evolution to matrix organization is the creation of product management departments with subproduct managers for each product line. In some instances, the subproduct managers are selected from specific functional departments and continue to report directly to their functional managers. Considerable diversity in the application of matrix organization exists, yet the essential feature is the creation of overlapping authority and the existence of dual authority.

Exactly where along the continuum an organization stops in the evolution depends on factors in the situation. Specifically and primarily important are the rates of change in technological and product developments. The resultant uncertainty and information required vary.

A fully developed matrix organization has product management departments along with the usual functional departments. Such organizations have product managers reporting to top management, with subproduct managers for each product line.

Span of Control

span of control
The number of subordinates reporting to a superior. The span is a factor that affects the shape and height of an organizational structure.

The determination of appropriate bases for departmentalization establishes the kinds of jobs that will be grouped together. But that determination doesn't establish the number of jobs to be included in a specific group, the issue of **span of control**. Generally, the issue comes down to the decision of how many people a manager can oversee; that is, will the organization be more effective if the span of control is relatively wide or narrow? The question is basically concerned with determining the volume of interpersonal relationships that the department's manager is able to handle. Moreover, the span of control must be defined to include not only formally assigned subordinates, but also those who have access to the manager. Not only may a manager be placed in a position of being responsible for immediate subordinates, but she may also be chairperson of several committees and task groups.[34]

The critical consideration in determining the manager's span of control is not the number of potential relationships. Rather it's the frequency and intensity of the actual relationships that are important. Not all relationships will occur, and those that do will vary in importance. If we shift our attention from potential to actual relationships as the bases for determining optimum span of control, at least three factors appear to be important.

Required Contact

In research and development as well as medical and production work, frequent contact and a high degree of coordination are needed between a superior and subordinates. Conferences and other forms of consultation often aid in attaining goals within a constrained time period. For example, the research and development team leader may have to consult frequently with team members so that a project is completed within a time period that will allow the organization to place a product on the market. Thus, instead of relying upon memos and reports, it is in the best interest of the organization to have as many in-depth contacts with the team as possible. A large span of control would preclude contacting subordinates so frequently, which could impede the project. In general, the greater the inherent ambiguity in an individual's job, the greater the need for supervision to avoid conflict and stress.[35]

Degree of Specialization

The degree of specialized employees is a critical consideration in establishing the span of control at all levels of management. It is generally accepted that a manager at the lower organizational level can oversee more subordinates because work at the lower level is more specialized and less complicated than at higher levels of management. Management can combine highly specialized and similar jobs into relatively large departments because the employees may not need close supervision.

Ability to Communicate

Instructions, guidelines, and policies must be communicated verbally to subordinates in most work situations. The need to discuss job-related factors influences the span of control. The individual who can clearly and concisely communicate with subordinates is able to manage more people than one who can't.

The widespread practice of downsizing and "flattening" organizations of all kinds has direct implications for the span-of-control decision. Downsizing reduces the number of all employees, but relatively more managers (usually middle managers) than nonmanagers.[36] Sam's Club stores eliminated 1,200 of the 3,000 management positions in its stores. While this 40 percent reduction in management was intended to create a more efficient operation and improve customer service, it also significantly impacted reporting relationships.[37] Downsizing increases the number of nonmanagers per manager; consequently, the average span of control of each manager increases. Whether the factors of required contact, degree of specialization, and ability to communicate have any bearing on the resultant spans of control can be debated. In fact, many middle managers whose spans of control have been widened believe that top management made the decision without regard to these factors.

Dimensions of Structure

The four design decisions (division of labor, delegation of authority, departmentalization, and span of control) result in a structure of organizations. Researchers and practitioners of management have attempted to develop their understanding of relationships between structures and performance, attitudes, effectiveness, and other variables thought to be important. This development of understanding has been hampered not only by the complexity of the relationships themselves, but also by the difficulty of defining and measuring the concept of organizational structure.

Although universal agreement on a common set of dimensions that measure differences in structure is neither possible nor desirable, some suggestions can be made. At present, three dimensions are often used in research and practice to describe structure: formalization, centralization, and complexity.[38]

Formalization

formalization
A dimension of organizational structure that refers to the extent to which rules, procedures, and other guides to action are written and enforced.

The dimension of **formalization** refers to the extent to which expectations regarding the means and ends of work are specified, written, and enforced. An organizational structure described as highly formalized would be one with rules and procedures to prescribe what each individual should be doing.[39] Such organizations have written standard operating procedures, specified directives, and explicit policies. In terms of the four design decisions, formalization is the result of high specialization of labor, high delegation of authority, the use of functional departments, and wide spans of control.[40]

1. High specialization of labor (as in the auto industry) is amenable to the development of written work rules and procedures. Jobs are so specialized as to leave little to the discretion of the jobholder.

2. High delegation of authority creates the need for checks on its use. Consequently, the organization writes guidelines for decision making and insists upon reports describing the use of authority.

3. Functional departments are made up of jobs with great similarities. This basis brings together jobs that make up an occupation such as accountants, engineers, and machinists. Because of the similarity of the jobs and the rather straightforward nature of the department's activities, management can develop written documents to govern those activities.

4. Wide spans of control discourage one-on-one supervision. There are simply too many subordinates for managers to keep up with on a one-to-one basis. Consequently, managers require written reports to inform them. Although formalization is defined in terms of written rules and procedures, we must understand how they're viewed by the employees. Some organizations have all the appearances of formalization, complete with thick manuals of rules, procedures, and policies, yet employees don't perceive them as affecting their behavior. Thus, where rules and procedures exist, they must be enforced if they're to affect behavior.[41]

Centralization

centralization
A dimension of organizational structure that refers to the extent to which authority to make decisions is retained in top management.

Centralization refers to the location of decision-making authority in the hierarchy of the organization. More specifically, the concept refers to delegation of authority among the jobs in the organization. Typically, researchers and practitioners think of centralization in terms of (1) decision making and (2) control. But despite the apparent simplicity of the concept, it can be difficult to apply.

The difficulty derives from three sources. First, people at the same level can have different decision-making authority. Second, not all decisions are of equal importance in organizations. For example, a typical management practice is to delegate authority to make routine operating decisions (i.e., decentralization), but to retain authority to make strategic decisions (i.e., centralization). Third, individuals may not perceive that they really have authority even though their job descriptions include it. Thus, objectively they have authority, but subjectively they don't.[42]

The relationships between centralization and the four design decisions are generally as follows:

1. The higher the specialization of labor, the greater the centralization. This relationship holds because highly specialized jobs do not require the discretion that authority provides.

2. The less authority that is delegated, the greater the centralization. By definition of the terms, *centralization* involves retaining authority in the top management jobs, rather than delegating it to lower levels in the organization.

3. The greater the use of functional departments, the greater the centralization. The use of functional departments requires that activities of the several interrelated departments be coordinated. Consequently, authority to coordinate them will be retained in top management.

4. The wider the spans of control, the greater the centralization. Wide spans of control are associated with relatively specialized jobs, which, as we've seen, have little need for authority.

Complexity

complexity
A dimension of organizational structure that refers to the number of different jobs and/or units within an organization.

Complexity is the direct outgrowth of dividing work and creating departments. Specifically, the concept refers to the number of distinctly different job titles, or occupational groupings, and the number of distinctly different units, or departments. The fundamental idea is that organizations with many different kinds of jobs and units create more complicated managerial and organizational problems than those with fewer jobs and departments.

Complexity, then, relates to differences among jobs and units. Therefore, it's not surprising that differentiation is often used synonymously with complexity. Moreover, it has become standard practice to use the term **horizontal differentiation** to refer to the number of different units at the same level;[43] **vertical differentiation** refers to the number of levels in the organization.[44] The relationships between complexity (horizontal and vertical differentiation) and the four design decisions are generally as follows:

horizontal differentiation
The number of different units existing at the same level in an organization. The greater the horizontal differentiation, the more complex is the organization.

vertical differentiation
The number of authority levels in an organization. The more authority levels an organization has, the more complex is the organization.

1. The greater the specialization of labor, the greater the complexity. Specialization is the process of creating different jobs and thus more complexity. Specialization of labor contributes primarily to horizontal differentiation.

2. The greater the delegation of authority, the greater the complexity of the organization. Delegation of authority is typically associated with a lengthy chain of command (that is, with a relatively large number of managerial levels). Thus, delegation of authority contributes to vertical differentiation.

3. The greater the use of geographic, customer, and product bases, the greater the complexity. These bases involve creating self-sustaining units that operate much like freestanding organizations. Consequently, there must be considerable delegation of authority and, thus, considerable complexity.[45]

4. Narrow spans of control are associated with high complexity. This relationship holds because narrow spans are necessary when the jobs to be supervised are quite different one from another. A supervisor can manage more people in a simple organization than in a complex organization. The apparently simple matter of span of

EXHIBIT 16.6
**Organizational
Dimensions and
Organizational
Decisions**

Dimensions	Decisions
High formalization	1. High specialization 2. Delegated authority 3. Functional departments 4. Wide spans of control
High centralization	1. High specialization 2. Centralized authority 3. Functional departments 4. Wide spans of control
High complexity	1. High specialization 2. Delegated authority 3. Territorial, customer, and product departments 4. Narrow spans of control

control can have profound effects on organizational and individual behavior. Hence, we should expect the controversy that surrounds it.

Relationships between dimensions of organizational structure and the four design decisions are summarized in Exhibit 16.6. It notes the causes of only high formalization, centralization, and complexity. However, the relationships are symmetrical—the causes of low formalization, centralization, and complexity are the opposite of those in the exhibit.

Organizational Design Models

The two models of organizational design described in this section are important ideas in management theory and practice. Because of their importance, they receive considerable theoretical and practical attention. Although many variations on these models can be found in practice, we will focus on the basic elements of *mechanistic* and *organic* organizational designs.

The Mechanistic Model

A body of literature that emerged during the early 20th century considered the problem of designing the structure of an organization as but one of a number of managerial tasks, including planning and controlling. These writers' objective was to define *principles* that could guide managers in performing their tasks. An early writer, Henri Fayol, proposed a number of principles that he had found useful in managing a large coal mining company in France.[46] Some of Fayol's principles dealt with the management function of organizing; four of these are relevant for understanding the **mechanistic model of organizational design.**

**mechanistic model of
organizational design**
The type of organizational design that emphasizes the importance of production and efficiency. It is highly formalized, centralized, and complex.

The Principle of Specialization

Fayol stated that specialization is the best means for making use of individuals and groups of individuals. At the time of Fayol's writings, the limit of specialization (that is, the optimal point) had not been definitively determined. Scientific management popularized a number of methods for implementing specialization of labor. These methods, such as work standards and motion-and-time study, emphasized technical (not behavioral) dimensions of work.

The Principle of Unity of Direction

According to this principle, jobs should be grouped according to specialty. Engineers should be grouped with engineers, salespeople with salespeople, accountants with accountants. The departmentalization basis that most nearly implements this principle is the functional basis.

The Principle of Authority and Responsibility

Fayol believed that a manager should be delegated sufficient authority to carry out her assigned responsibilities. Because the assigned responsibilities of top managers are considerably more important to the future of the organization than those of lower management, applying the principle inevitably leads to centralized authority. Centralized authority is a logical outcome not only because of top management's larger responsibilities but also because work at this level is more complex, the number of workers involved is greater, and the relationship between actions and results is remote.

The Scalar Chain Principle

scalar chain
The graded chain of authority created through the delegation process.

The natural result of implementing the preceding three principles is a graded chain of managers from the ultimate authority to the lowest ranks. The **scalar chain** is the route for all vertical communications in an organization. Accordingly, all communications from the lowest level must pass through each superior in the chain of command. Correspondingly, communication from the top must pass through each subordinate until it reaches the appropriate level.

Fayol's writings became part of a literature that, although each contributor made unique contributions, had a common thrust. Writers such as Mooney and Reilly,[47] Follett,[48] and Urwick[49] all shared the common objective of defining the principles that should guide the design and management of organizations. A complete review of their individual contributions won't be attempted here. However, we'll review the ideas of one individual, Max Weber, who made important contributions to the mechanistic model. He described applications of the mechanistic model and coined the term *bureaucracy.*

Bureaucracy

Bureaucracy has various meanings. The traditional usage is the political science concept of government by bureaus but without participation by the governed. In layman's terms, *bureaucracy* refers to the negative consequences of large organizations, such as excessive red tape, procedural delays, and general frustration.[50] But in Max Weber's writings, *bureaucracy* refers to a particular way to organize collective activities.[51] Weber's interest in bureaucracy reflected his concern for the ways society develops hierarchies of control so that one group can, in effect, dominate other groups.[52] Organizational design involves domination in the sense that authority involves the legitimate right to exact obedience from others. His search for the forms of domination that evolve in society led him to the study of bureaucratic structure.

According to Weber, the bureaucratic structure is "superior to any other form in precision, in stability, in the stringency of its discipline and its reliability. It thus makes possible a high degree of calculability of results for the heads of the organization and for those acting in relation to it."[53] The bureaucracy compares to other organizations "as does the machine with nonmechanical modes of production."[54] These words capture the essence of the mechanistic model of organizational design.

To achieve the maximum benefits of the bureaucratic design, Weber believed that an organization must have the following characteristics:

1. All tasks will be divided into highly specialized jobs.
2. Each task is performed according to a system of abstract rules to ensure uniformity and coordination of different tasks.
3. Each member or office of the organization is accountable for job performance to one, and only one, manager.
4. Each employee of the organization relates to other employees and clients in an impersonal, formal manner, maintaining a social distance with subordinates and clients.
5. Employment in the bureaucratic organization is based on technical qualifications and is protected against arbitrary dismissal.

These five characteristics of bureaucracy describe the kind of organizations Fayol believed to be most effective. Both Fayol and Weber described the same type of organization, one that functions in a machine-like manner to accomplish the organization's goals in a highly efficient manner. Thus, the term *mechanistic* aptly describes such organizations.

The mechanistic model achieves high levels of production and efficiency due to its structural characteristics:

1. It's highly complex because of its emphasis on specialization of labor.
2. It's highly centralized because of its emphasis on authority and accountability.
3. It's highly formalized because of its emphasis on function as the basis for departments.

These organizational characteristics and practices underlie a widely used organizational model. One of the more successful practitioners of the mechanistic model has been United Parcel Service (UPS).[55] This profitable delivery firm competes directly with the U.S. Postal Service (USPS) in the delivery of small packages. Even though the USPS is subsidized and pays no taxes, UPS has been able to better apply the mechanistic form and compete successfully by stressing efficiency of operations. It apparently achieves great efficiencies through a combination of automation and organizational design. Specialization and formalization are highly visible characteristics of UPS structure. UPS uses clearly defined jobs and an explicit chain of command. The tasks range from truck washers and maintenance personnel to top management and are arranged in a hierarchy of authority consisting of eight managerial levels. The high degree of specialization enables management to use many forms of written reports such as daily worksheets that record each employee's work quotas and performance. Company policies and practices are in written form and are routinely consulted in hiring and promotion decisions. Apparently, UPS has found the mechanistic form of organization to be well suited for its purposes.

UPS has more than 1,000 industrial engineers on its payroll. Their job is to design jobs and to set the standards that specify the way UPS employees do their jobs. For example, engineers instruct drivers to walk to the customer's door at the rate of three feet per second and to knock on the door. Company management believes that the standards aren't just a way to obtain efficiency and production, but also to provide the employee with important feedback on how he's doing the job. All in all, the company's efficiency bears testimony to its use of the mechanistic model.

The Organic Model

organic model of organizational design
The organizational design that emphasizes the importance of adaptability and development. It is relatively informal, decentralized, and simple.

The **organic model of organizational design** stands in sharp contrast to the mechanistic model due to their different organizational characteristics and practices. The most distinct differences between the two models are a consequence of the different effectiveness criteria each seeks to maximize. While the mechanistic model seeks to maximize efficiency and production, the organic model seeks to maximize satisfaction, flexibility, and development.

The organic organization is flexible to changing environmental demands because its design encourages greater utilization of human potential. Managers are encouraged to adopt practices that tap the full range of human motivations through job design that stresses personal growth and responsibility. Decision making, control, and goal setting are decentralized and shared at all levels of the organization. Communications flow throughout the organization, not simply down the chain of command. These practices are intended to implement a basic assumption of the organic model, which states that an organization will be effective to the extent that its structure is "such as to ensure a maximum probability that in all interactions and in all relationships with the organization, each member, in the light of his background, values, desires, and expectations, will view the experience as supportive and one which builds and maintains a sense of personal worth and importance."[56]

An organizational design that provides individuals with this sense of personal worth and motivation and that facilitates satisfaction, flexibility, and development would have the following characteristics:

1. It's relatively simple because of its deemphasis on specialization and its emphasis on increasing job range.
2. It's relatively decentralized because of its emphasis on delegation of authority and increasing job depth.
3. It's relatively informal because of its emphasis on product and customer as bases for departments.

A leading spokesperson and developer of ideas supporting applications of the organic model is Rensis Likert. His studies at the University of Michigan have led him to argue that organic organizations (Likert uses the term *System-4*) differ markedly from mechanistic organizations (Likert uses the term *System-1*) along a number of structural dimensions.[57]

The literature is filled with reports of efforts to implement organic designs in actual organizations.[58] Likert himself reports many of these studies.[59] One organization has received considerable attention for its efforts to implement organic principles. Thrivent Financial for Lutherans (the product of the merger between Aid Association for Lutherans and Lutheran Brotherhood) is a financial services business managing more than $65 billion in assets and serving nearly 3 million clients.[60] It has transformed its organization from a mechanistic to an organic structure in an effort to take advantage of benefits of the **self-managed team** concept. Before reorganization, Thrivent was organized mechanistically according to the traditional functions of the insurance industry, and employees were highly trained to deal with processing, underwriting, valuations, and premium services functions. Specialization resulted in considerable efficiency dealing with customers requiring the attention of one of the functions. But when multiple functions were involved, the organization became bogged down.

self-managed team
Groups of employees that complete an entire piece of work while having considerable autonomy over the way in which they accomplish their work.

Thrivent's management explored the potential benefits of establishing teams of employees that could handle all details of any customer transaction, whether health, life, or casualty insurance. The teams consist of individuals who once were responsible for functions; now they're responsible for customers and take initiative that once required management prodding. As a result of teams' assumption of responsibility for their own management, three levels of management have been eliminated from the organization. The organization is now simpler and more decentralized than before, and therefore more organic and less mechanistic.

Thrivent also implemented a form of employee compensation termed "pay for knowledge" to encourage employees to adopt the new work system. It provides individuals with pay increases for obtaining additional knowledge that enables them to improve their job performance. In the context of Thrivent's organic organization, employees needed to learn not only new technical knowledge, but also new interpersonal knowledge because working with other individuals in teams is critical to the success of the new organizational design.[61]

Multinational Structure and Design

As we have seen previously, four design decisions regarding division of labor, delegation of authority, departmentalization, and span of control shape the design of organizational structures. These decisions, in turn, are affected by a variety of factors. Foremost among them are the social, political, cultural, legal, and economic environments in which the organization is operating. Because of their very nature, multinational corporations frequently exist in very divergent environments. A multinational corporation may be categorized as consisting of a group of geographically dispersed organizations with different national subsidiaries.[62]

One approach to setting up a foreign subsidiary is that of replication. That is, the same organizational structure and operating policies and procedures that exist in the existing domestic organization are used. For example, when establishing its foreign subsidiaries, Procter & Gamble created an "exact replica of the United States Procter & Gamble organization" because it believed that using "exactly the same policies and procedures which have given our company success in the United States will be equally successful overseas."[63] The potential difficulty with such a practice is that it may result in the reliance upon organizational designs and management practices that are simply unsuitable for the environment of the host country. This may explain why foreign subsidiary organizational structures tend to evolve over time as the company becomes more internationalized.[64] The Global OB on page 502 discusses this concept in greater detail.

Of course, while important cross-country differences may dictate making adaptations in structure, policy, and management practices, even widely divergent countries can have similarities. One of the challenges to organizational researchers is to provide data to help better understand the degree of similarity and difference across national boundaries that has implications for organizational operations.

Corporations that cross national boundaries must decide how to include foreign activity in the organization. How should international activities be coordinated? In fact, foreign activities are but extensions of the domestic businesses, and how they're coordinated to achieve strategic outcomes involves issues not much different from those of local activities.[65] Japanese corporations' outstanding success in international markets has initiated great interest in the ways firms can and should organize if they're to compete with the Japanese. At the heart of the discussion is which departmental basis is appropriate under which circumstances.[66]

FEDEX AND THE ROMANS: IMPLICATIONS FOR ORGANIZATIONAL DESIGN

In the Oscar-nominated movie *Cast Away,* Tom Hanks portrays a time-obsessed FedEx employee sent to Russia to improve the efficiency of an underperforming operation. While the complexity of the international package delivery business is not the focus of the film, we do get a glimpse into some of the intricacies of the FedEx organization.

Founded in 1971, FedEx has grown into a $38 billion company, with over 290,000 "team members" deployed in 220 countries. The company operates 1,052 air express stations, 10 air hubs, and 34 ground hubs while using over 900 aircraft and 80,000 ground vehicles to make deliveries. The corporation commonly known as FedEx actually consists of several operating companies: FedEx Express, FedEx Ground, FedEx Freight, FedEx Office, FedEx Custom Critical, FedEx Trade Networks, and FedEx Services.

When asked about the organizational structure of FedEx, Fredrick W. Smith, chairman, president, and CEO, has said the following:

> If Julius Caesar were sitting in this room he would recognize FedEx's organizational structure. He invented it. He had a proconsul in Palestine, one in Gaul, and one in Britain. Each . . . had infantrymen, an archer, and so forth. Same with us. We have our person in Hong Kong, one in Brussels. Each has an IT person, each has a business unit head, each has a personnel person. The organizational structure of modern business was developed by the Romans.

Following this Roman model, the "proconsuls" in FedEx are their regional presidents, and their "armies" are impressive; for example, FedEx's Europe, Middle East, and Africa (EMEA) Region has 14,000 employees and three major air hubs that serve 89 countries. As trade barriers are lifted as a result of Eastern European countries' future membership in the European Union, EMEA will be well positioned for further geographic/regional expansion.

FedEx's largest "foreign legion" is its Asia Pacific (APAC) Region with an "army" of over 14,000 employees, two major air hubs, and direct service to over 30 countries. APAC's defining moment may have been its ability to become the sole U.S.-based express company to have aviation rights in China. APAC, based in Hong Kong, has recently extended its dominance in the region through the opening of a $150 million air hub at Baiyun International Airport in Guangzhou, China. This new facility is FedEx's largest air hub outside of the United States and is planned to be the center of the regional operation for the next 30 years.

While researchers and management experts develop innovative means to approach organizational design, FedEx's Smith expounds a system made popular by the Romans, and it appears to be working. His international regions are equipped with the tools needed to move quickly and decisively, which has allowed FedEx to become the world's dominant express delivery service.

Sources: Adapted from "FedEx Opens New Asian Pacific Hub in Guangzhou, China," FedEx, February 9, 2009, http://news.van.fedex.com/intl/cn?node= 12727 (accessed April 13, 2009); "FedEx Corporation," http://about.fedex. designcdt.com/our_company/company_information/fedex_corporation (accessed April 13, 2009); "Regional Facts," FedEx, http://about.fedex. designcdt.com/our_company/company_information/regional_facts (accessed April 13, 2009); and "FedEx Chief Takes Cue from Leaders in History," *USA Today,* June 29, 2005, www.usatoday.com/money/companies/ management/2005-06-19-fedex-advice_x.htm (accessed April 13, 2009).

The most prevalent departmental basis is *geographical.* This arrangement has national and regional managers reporting to a headquarters in the same national or regional area. Geographic-based organizations for multinational corporations (MNCs) have the same characteristics as those for domestic organizations. Each national or regional office has all the resources necessary to produce and market the product or service. This organizational form is suitable for organizations with limited product lines such as ITT and Charles Pfizer Corporation.

MNCs having a diversified product line may find certain advantages in the *product-based* organizational structure. This structure assigns worldwide responsibility for a product or product line to a single corporate office, and all foreign and domestic units associated with that product report to the corporate product office. Eastman Kodak uses the product-based structure to assign responsibility for worldwide research and development, manufacturing, marketing, and distribution of its products. The basic product unit, termed a *line of business* (LOB), makes its own decisions and succeeds or fails accordingly. Eastman Kodak believes this structure enables managers to respond more quickly to market conditions.[67] For example, Kodak is refocusing its business strategy away from the traditional film business to the growing digital technology arena and related products such as ink-jet printers and high-end digital printing.[68]

MNCs with very restrictive product lines such as firms in the mining industry may optimize results using the *function* approach. According to this structure, a corporate office for each business function such as production, marketing, and finance has authority over those functions wherever they take place throughout the world. Thus, production personnel in Europe and South America as well as North America will report to corporate officials in charge of production.[69] Although MNCs share certain common managerial and organizational problems, how they deal with them will reflect their own national culture as well as the local, host-country culture.

We can summarize our discussion of how MNCs organize by describing how many Japanese firms go about it. Typically they concentrate on a relatively narrow set of business activities, unlike their typical Western counterparts that enter several lines of business. One effect of this difference is that Japanese employees perform relatively fewer specialized jobs with relatively more homogeneous skills and experiences due to the fewer business specialties to be performed. The typical Japanese manufacturing job has less range than the typical Western manufacturing job. The authority associated with each job is relatively less in Japanese firms, although the Japanese practice of participative management enables individual workers to have a say in matters that immediately affect their own jobs. Middle managers in Japanese firms are expected to initiate opportunities for workers to be involved, and they are evaluated on this criterion as well as on economic and performance criteria.

Departments in Japanese firms are more often based on function and process than on product, customer, or location. The preference for the internal-oriented bases reflects again Japanese firms' preference to do business in fewer industries such that more complex divisional firms aren't as likely to develop. The Japanese have developed the practice of creating close ties with supplier organizations and thus have avoided the necessity of vertical integration as is the case of many Western business organizations.

The differences between organizational structures in Japan and in the West can be accounted for by differences in business practices. These business practices are no doubt due to national and cultural developments in how business is done, not in how organizations are structured.[70]

Virtual Organizations

One of the fastest-developing practices in business throughout the world involves firms in cooperative relationships with their suppliers, distributors, and even competitors. These networks of relationships enable organizations to achieve both efficiency and flexibility to exploit advantages of the mechanistic and organic organizational designs. These "virtual organizations" have become so pervasive that some experts refer to them as the models for 21st century organizations.[71] Cooperative relationships enable the principal organization to rely upon the smaller, closer-to-the-market partner to sense impending changes in the environment and to respond at the local level, thus relieving the parent organization of that necessity.

A **virtual organization** (e.g., meetings, teams, offices, firms, and alliances) is a collection of geographically distributed, functionally and/or culturally diverse aggregations of individuals that is linked by electronic forms of communication.[72] The virtual organization by necessity has to rely on somewhat blurred boundaries to forge relationships that are often governed by contract. The virtual unit is assembled and disassembled according to needs.

virtual organization
A collection of geographically distributed, functionally and/or culturally diverse aggregations of individuals that are linked by electronic forms of communication.

EXHIBIT 16.7
Characteristics of Virtual Organization and Some Consequences

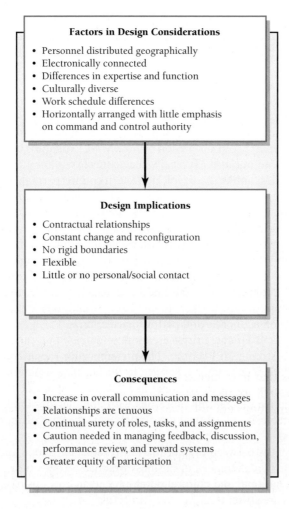

Factors in Design Considerations

- Personnel distributed geographically
- Electronically connected
- Differences in expertise and function
- Culturally diverse
- Work schedule differences
- Horizontally arranged with little emphasis on command and control authority

Design Implications

- Contractual relationships
- Constant change and reconfiguration
- No rigid boundaries
- Flexible
- Little or no personal/social contact

Consequences

- Increase in overall communication and messages
- Relationships are tenuous
- Continual surety of roles, tasks, and assignments
- Caution needed in managing feedback, discussion, performance review, and reward systems
- Greater equity of participation

An example of a virtual organization is Barclays' global bank. The organization is a global network created by electronically linking extant networks of small, regional banks. Customers of the regional banks feel like they are a part of a large entity, Barclays, because they are provided with worldwide services. The feeling of being part of a worldwide entity exists, as customers remain members of their local community banks as well.[73]

Exhibit 16.7 captures the main characteristics of virtual organizations. The characteristics are applicable to a movie production firm in which personnel are aggregated to complete a film; to an e-learning company preparing training courseware (that subject matter experts prepare) for delivery online to clients; to a manufacturing firm in which subcontractors—both domestically and globally based—provide raw materials, manufacturing processes, distribution and storage facilities, and research; and to development consortia, in which intellectual properties flow through the companies in a specific geographic region.

Exhibit 16.7 summarizes some of the factors, implications, and possible consequences of virtual organizations. These attributes can be applied to any type of virtual team, unit, organization, or consortia. Proponents of the virtual-style organization propose that the benefits of this type of arrangement are faster response time, autonomy, greater flexibility, and more efficient use of technical, behavioral, and professional expertise. The critics argue that virtual organizations mean increased conflict, decreased loyalty, a lack of any coherence in plans and strategies, information overload, and no social interaction fulfillment.

The Realities of Virtual Organizations

An organization is typically virtual to some degree.[74] At one extreme, a firm is virtual to the extent that each step in the process of providing a product or service is outside the firm's boundaries. Some publishing firms typically perform manuscript selection and marketing in-house, while writing, editing, printing, and distribution are done outside the firm and in many instances through virtual connectivity.

The other extreme finds the fully integrated, mechanistic-type organization performing all aspects of management, production, sales, finance, and distribution. But even most of these types of traditional firms are making contractual and logistical arrangements to have some activities performed externally.

Transaction-cost theorists have studied why certain activities are kept within the firm while others are contracted or performed outside. The decisions are based on minimizing the combined cost of production and governance. If only production costs are considered, it is argued that these costs can be reduced as more production activities are performed externally. However, the costs of governance are often higher when firms purchase goods and services in the open market rather than in-house.

The virtual organization is distinctively different from the mechanistic, organic, or matrix forms that have hierarchy, layers of management, and face-to-face control. The line and staff arrangement in these organizational design approaches is in-house. Virtual organizations are not always the best or most appropriate arrangement. The work, expertise, and goals of the firm must be reviewed carefully. The requirements of personal contact, regular hours, in-person negotiations, and employee needs must be determined. When there is a reasonable fit among the work, expertise, goals, and requirements, then a virtual organization should be considered as an option.

Work in e-commerce, consulting, marketing, and job searching seems best suited for virtual organizations. These jobs are service-oriented, require extensive communication, are dynamic, and are knowledge-based. There is also the issue of whether an organization has the managerial competence suited to lead, coordinate, facilitate, and provide constructive feedback to virtual organization workers. These and similar issues should be carefully evaluated before taking a plunge into virtual organization discussions, plans, or implementation.

The viability of a virtual organization as the proper design approach is centered on two major issues.[75] First is the conclusion that the virtual arrangement results in economic gains of acquiring goals and services from specialized firms, which are able to provide these factors efficiently. Second is the assumption that computers and telecommunications networks reduce the costs of coordination, allowing organizations to achieve these economic benefits without incurring the higher transaction costs associated with buying from an external supplier.

The exact form of the appropriate virtual organization varies. Some organizations develop relationships only with key suppliers. Other organizations develop relationships with marketers and distributors. In the extreme case, the parent organization functions much like a broker and deals independently with product designers, producers, suppliers, and markets. The critical managerial and organizational decisions involve which of the functions to buy, which to produce, and how to manage and coordinate the relationships with their partners. Managers in these organizations have less environmental uncertainty to deal with because they have, in a sense, subcontracted that responsibility to their counterparts in the network. Such organizational structures are, in a sense, boundaryless organizations.[76]

Virtual organizations have come a long way since they originated in Japan, where firms create alliances with other firms. These alliances take the form of cooperative agreements, consortia, and equity ownerships to establish networks of businesses. In Japan, this form of doing business is termed *keiretsu* and involves a very large financial institution, a very large industrial conglomerate, and smaller firms in a network of relationships that enable the large firm to produce the product and the smaller firms to supply components, do research and design, and perhaps distribute and market. The participating bank provides the financial requirements to support the network of cooperative relationships. This form of interorganizational network has enabled Japanese industry to grow without supply bottlenecks and damage to competition from domestic firms.

Boundaryless Organizations

The command and control, top-down, mechanistic organizational design is orderly, specific, and relies on defined roles for employees, managers, and nonmanagers. Companies such as Motorola, Oticon A/S, and Coca-Cola are continuously attempting to minimize and, in some cases, eliminate vertical and horizontal structures, tightly defined work roles, and top-down control. They are working to achieve what is referred to as a **boundaryless organization**. The assumption these and other firms are making is that rigid structure and too much specificity create barriers within a firm and between a firm and its external suppliers and customers.

boundaryless organization
A firm in which chains of command are eliminated, spans of control are unlimited, and rigid departments are replaced with empowered teams.

The minimization of layers results in a flatter hierarchy. There is still a hierarchy but there is less distance, less separation between top-level managers and other employees. The boundaryless organization also emphasizes participative decision making, multiple-hierarchy teams (executives, managers, operating employees), team building, and coordination. At Oticon A/S, a Danish hearing-aid manufacturer, hierarchy has been purposefully minimized. A project-team emphasis is used to oversee, coordinate, and plan all work. The functional departmental unit has been eliminated. Oticon A/S has concluded that functional departments create too many barriers to interaction, team building, and morale. Oticon A/S has decided to use project teams to tear down the barriers. Other firms, such as Xerox, use multidisciplinary teams that work on a single project from start to finish instead of using departmental units.

To be effective with a more pronounced boundaryless design, Oticon A/S and Xerox must have a high level of trust between employees. Trust in these arrangements exists when individuals make a good faith effort to behave in accordance with expectations, are honest in all interactions, and do not take advantage of others even when the opportunity is available.[77] Individuals also need to possess good skills and competencies so work can be performed without constant managerial monitoring and feedback.

The effective boundaryless organization breaks down barriers with external constituents and distance. Strategic alliances and telecommunicating are examples of how to break down barriers. The Japanese *keiretsu* relationship is an example of a vertical alliance between large corporations and their suppliers. Typically, the large business takes a minority ownership (e.g., 10 percent) in a supplier. The two organizations become bonded in a strategic partnership for their mutual gain. There is little room for communication, decision making, and strategic choice barriers in alliances. The leveraging of resources, achievement of goals, and reduction of risks are some of the reasons Coca-Cola and Apple Computer have adopted alliances to reduce unnecessary structural barriers with external constituents.

Telecommunicating (also called *teleworking*) is reducing barriers. The software engineer in Austin, Texas, and the engineering salesperson in Tacoma, Washington, are examples of millions of individuals who are doing their work outside of brick and mortar buildings. They represent a part of the virtual workforce. They are workers in boundaryless organizations that are connected via technology.

Conceptually, the boundaryless organization involves the breaking down of structure, hierarchy, specific roles, and distance. The virtual organization already discussed is one variation or type of boundaryless organization.

Summary of Key Points

- Four key managerial decisions determine organizational structures. These decisions are concerned with dividing the work, delegating authority, departmentalizing jobs into groups, and determining spans of control.

- The term *division of labor* concerns the extent to which jobs are specialized. Dividing the overall task of the organization into smaller related tasks provides the technical and economic advantages found in specialization of labor.

- Delegating authority enables an individual to make decisions and extract obedience without approval by higher management. Like other organizational issues, delegated authority is a relative, not absolute, concept. All individuals in an organization have some authority. The question is whether they have enough to do their jobs.

- There are several forms, or bases, of departmentalization. *Functional* departmentalization groups jobs by the function performed (i.e., marketing, production, accounting). *Territorial* departmentalization groups jobs on the basis of geographical location. *Product* departmentalization groups jobs on the basis of the department's output. *Customer* departmentalization groups jobs on the basis of the users of the good or service provided.

- An organizational design that attempts to maximize the benefits and minimize the weakness of both the functional and product forms is known as a matrix design. The benefits from this structure include the efficient use of resources, flexibility in conditions of change and uncertainty, technical excellence, freeing top management for long-range planning, improving motivation and commitment, and providing good opportunities for personal development.

- Span of control relates to the decision regarding how many people a manager can oversee. It is an important variable because managerial effectiveness can be compromised if spans of control are too large. Additionally, span of control affects the number of levels in an organization; the wider the span, the fewer the levels.

- Three important dimensions of structure are formalization, centralization, and complexity. *Formalization* refers to the extent to which policies, rules, and procedures exist in written form; *centralization* refers to the extent to which authority is retained in the jobs of top management; and *complexity* refers to the extent to which the jobs in the organization are relatively specialized.

- Two important organizational design models are termed *mechanistic* and *organic*. Mechanistic design is characterized by highly specialized jobs, homogeneous departments, narrow spans of control, and relatively centralized authority. Organic designs, on the other hand, include relatively despecialized jobs, heterogeneous departments, wide spans of control, and decentralized authority.

YOU BE THE JUDGE COMMENT

CAN ORGANIZATIONAL DESIGN IMPACT CORPORATE SOCIAL RESPONSIBILITY?

Do organizations have an obligation to support environmentally friendly or sustainable activities? Many students would say it is a moral imperative or that it's just good business; while other students might argue such behaviors do not contribute to many organizations' bottom lines. With an expanding population and limited resources, it is reasonable to project that without proper care, many of the resources that we depend upon both as businesspeople and as occupants of the planet will cease to be viable.

While individual governments may attempt to enforce "appropriate" behaviors, one of the challenges of supporting sustainability is that a unified global approach is needed. Absent this, a corporation that does not support the environmental initiatives of one government can simply move their operation to a less regulated country. While multinationals are routinely criticized for their behaviors, they may hold the key to initiating global sustainability activities.

Fuji Heavy Industries (FHI) has made the environment a feature in its corporate philosophy. The company's operating procedures call for regularly performed audits to not only ensure but also improve upon its environmental conservation activities. FHI's car brand, Subaru, established the first zero landfill auto manufacturing plant in the world and created a wildlife refuge on its manufacturing campus in Indiana. FHI was not obligated by law to undertake these activities but holds itself to these higher standards.

In a message from the president, Ikuo Mori, FHI's president and CEO, refers to a "social responsibility as a company that develops a variety of products centered on automotive businesses . . . (to) be a company that is trusted by the people of the world." FHI helps to build this trust through its environmental initiatives. FHI is a global organization whose commitment to sustainable operations is evident throughout.

Sources: "Message from the President," Fuji Heavy Industries, www.fhi.co.jp/english/outline/index.html (accessed April 4, 2009); and "Fuji Heavy Industries," Subaru of North America, www.drive.subaru.com/OnlineX_Fuji.htm (accessed April 3, 2009).

- It is important to be particularly attentive to structure and design considerations in multinational organizations. Differences in the social, political, cultural, legal, and economic environments of countries hosting subsidiaries of domestic organizations can dictate the need for different answers to design questions.
- Virtual organizations have become important ways of getting work done. Often termed "empty organizations," they serve as focal points for getting all the functions accomplished but without having to directly manage them.
- Boundaryless organizations, in which the hierarchy and chain of command are minimized and rigidly structured departments are eliminated, are being implemented to reduce barriers between people and constituencies.

Review and Discussion Questions

1. Why would a virtual organization design be popular in the movie industry?
2. "The more authority that is delegated to nonmanagers, the less authority managers have." Is this necessarily a true statement? Explain.
3. What barriers are reduced or eliminated by adopting a boundaryless organization?
4. What are some factors that may have important implications for structure and design decisions in multinational corporations?
5. Characterize the following organizations on the basis of their degree of formalization, centralization, and complexity: the university you are attending, the federal government, and a local branch of a national fast-food franchise.

6. Can you think of a particular company or type of industry that tends toward a mechanistic design? What advantages and disadvantages could you see if that organization or industry were to adopt a more organic design form?

7. What is the difference between organizational *structure* and *design*?

8. What cues might a manager have that suggest there is a problem with the design of an organization? Is changing an existing organization different from designing a new structure? Explain.

9. Changes in organizational size affect structure. In what ways might growth (increasing size) affect an organization's structure? In what ways might consolidation (decreasing size) affect structure?

10. What are some potential advantages of a matrix design?

Exercise

Exercise 16.1: *Paper Plane Corporation*

Objectives

1. To illustrate how division of labor can be efficiently structured.

2. To illustrate how a competitive atmosphere can be created among groups.

Starting the Exercise

Unlimited groups of six participants each are used in this exercise. These groups may be directed simultaneously in the same room. Approximately a full class period is needed to complete the exercise. Each person should have assembly instructions and a summary sheet, which are shown on the following pages, and ample stacks of paper (8½ by 11 inches). The physical setting should be a room large enough so that the individual groups of six can work without interference from the other groups. A working space should be provided for each group.

- The participants are doing an exercise in production methodology.

- Each group must work independently of the other groups.

- Each group will choose a manager and an inspector, and the remaining participants will be employees.

- The objective is to make paper airplanes in the most profitable manner possible.

- The facilitator will give the signal to start. This is a 10-minute, timed event utilizing competition among the groups.

- After the first round, everyone should report their production and profits to the entire group. They also should note the effect, if any, of the manager in terms of the performance of the group.

- This same procedure is followed for as many rounds as there is time.

Paper Plane Corporation: Data Sheet

Your group is the complete workforce for Paper Plane Corporation. Established in 1943, Paper Plane has led the market in paper plane production. Presently under new management, the company is contracting to make aircraft for the U.S. Air Force. You must establish an efficient production plant to produce these aircraft. You must make your contract with the Air Force under the following conditions:

1. The Air Force will pay $20,000 per airplane.

2. The aircraft must pass a strict inspection made by the facilitator.

3. A penalty of $25,000 per airplane will be subtracted for failure to meet the production requirements.

4. Labor and other overhead will be computed at $300,000.

5. Cost of materials will be $3,000 per bid plane. If you bid for 10 but only make 8, you must pay the cost of materials for those you failed to make or that did not pass inspection.

Source: Louis Potheni in Fred Luthans, *Organizational Behavior* (New York: McGraw-Hill, 1985). p. 555.

Now how much do you know about organizational structure and design?

6. The type of organizational design that emphasizes production and efficiency while being highly formalized, centralized, and complex is known as the _____ model.
   a. mechanistic
   b. automated
   c. organic
   d. artificial

7. True or false: Managers can shape an organization's structure by making decisions about division of labor, authority, departmentalization, and span of control.
   a. True
   b. False

8. _____ is the process by which authority is distributed downward in an organization.
   a. Job enlargement
   b. Vertical integration
   c. Delegation
   d. Horizontal utilization

9. Matrix organizations are best described by which of the following statements:
   a. They exist in the middle of a continuum with mechanistic organizations at one extreme and organic organizations at the other.
   b. They are generally more mechanistic than organic in nature.
   c. They provide an example of the application of Fayol's principles.
   d. They consist of a network of independent organizations that form a venture.

10. A collection of geographically distributed, functionally and/or culturally diverse aggregations of individuals that are linked by electronic forms of communication is known as a _____.
    a. distributed joint venture
    b. virtual organization
    c. strategic alliance
    d. None of the above (a–c) are correct.

REALITY CHECK ANSWERS

Before	After
1. *c* 2. *b* 3. *a* 4. *c* 5. *b*	6. *a* 7. *a* 8. *c* 9. *a* 10. *b*
Number Correct	Number Correct
_____	_____

Summary Sheet

Round 1:

Bid: _____ Aircraft @ $20,000 per aircraft = _____

Results: _____ Aircraft @ $20,000 per aircraft = _____

Less: $300,000 overhead; _____ × $3,000 cost of raw materials; _____ × $25,000 penalty

Profit: _____

Round 2:

Bid: _____ Aircraft @ $20,000 per aircraft = _____

Results: _____ Aircraft @ $20,000 per aircraft = _____

Less: $300,000 overhead; _____ × $3,000 cost of raw materials; _____ × $25,000 penalty
Profit: _____

Round 3:

Bid: _____ Aircraft @ $20,000 per aircraft = _____
Results: _____ Aircraft @ $20,000 per aircraft = _____
Less: $300,000 overhead; _____ × $3,000 cost of raw materials; _____ × $25,000 penalty
Profit: _____

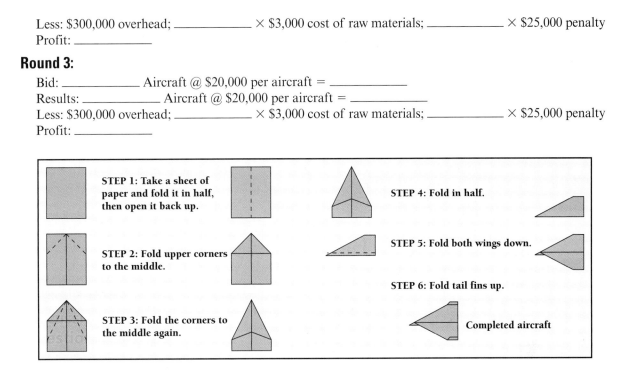

STEP 1: Take a sheet of paper and fold it in half, then open it back up.

STEP 2: Fold upper corners to the middle.

STEP 3: Fold the corners to the middle again.

STEP 4: Fold in half.

STEP 5: Fold both wings down.

STEP 6: Fold tail fins up.

Completed aircraft

Case

Case 16.1: *The Race for a Top-Selling Electric Car: Will Upstart Company Detroit Electric Beat Ford?*

In a recent article, *Forbes* automotive columnist Jerry Flint recounts Ford Motor's ambitious goal in 1966 that they would produce an electric car in five to 10 years. Flint recalls after numerous inquiries during the subsequent months and years, he was eventually told that five to 10 years, was a running target and that Ford was always five to 10 years from a viable electric car. Finally, in 2009, Ford announced that an electric version of the Ford Focus will be in the showrooms in 2011.

Unfortunately, this 43-year delay may end up dampening Ford's success in the electric car market. Within a few months of Ford's announcement, Detroit Electric Holdings Ltd., an automotive start-up based in Amsterdam, publicly stated it would start selling electric vehicles in the first quarter of 2010; initially in China, Europe, and the United Kingdom with sales opening up in the United States shortly afterward. The base vehicle will have a single-charge range of over 100 miles with models costing between

$23,000 and $26,000. By 2012, sales are expected to exceed 270,000 vehicles. Could a different business model and organizational structure explain the much faster launch of Detroit Electric's car in comparison to the much slower pace displayed by Ford?

Detroit Electric

While electric cars were produced under the Detroit Electric brand between 1907 and 1939, the current iteration of Detroit Electric was established in 2007. The firm's Netherlands-based engineering team has already patented an electric drive system and "Flux Motor" technology. Detroit Electric also developed an expertise in lithium polymer batteries. The company claims its technology is a significant improvement over its competitors, and allows for its vehicles to operate more efficiently and have increased ranges. In a period where the major auto manufacturers are losing billions of dollars, Detroit Electric has developed this technology and is projecting to sell hundreds of thousands of electric cars within the next five years. How much investment did Detroit Electric need to bring its car to its current stage? A relatively modest investment of $20 million. The company anticipates an additional $100 million investment will be necessary to bring the cars to market. To put this investment in context, Ford lost an average of $67 million a day in the fourth quarter of 2008. When asked how the company can do what has eluded the traditional automakers, Detroit Electric points out that it follows a different business model and organizational structure.

> We concentrate our funding on research and development of the motor, vehicle design, marketing and distribution, while utilizing original equipment manufacturer's (OEM) proven vehicle platforms.

Detroit Electric is a car company that doesn't design or build cars. While its Advanced Propulsion Lab subsidiary will produce motors and controllers and its Electric Energy subsidiary will produce batteries, the actual manufacturing of the car is outsourced. The company says this arrangement allows it to avoid a capital expense that could be fatal to its start-up.

Proton Holdings

Detroit Electric has licensed two of Proton Holdings' vehicles and contracted them to build cars under the Detroit Electric brand. Proton is Malaysia's largest auto manufacturer, and its largest investor in research and development. Detroit Electric CEO Albert Lam said of the arrangement, "We chose Proton due to its state-of-the-art production facility, commitment to research and development, cost efficiency, and stable, high-quality workforce."

Perusahaan Otomobil Nasional Berhad (Proton) was founded in 1983 and produced its first commercial vehicle in 1985. In addition to selling in its home country of Malaysia, it distributes cars in four international regions: UK/Western Europe, the Middle East, South East Asia, and Australasia. The company produces 270,000 cars annually in a wide variety of models including the world-renowned Lotus sports car line. Proton has almost 11,000 employees working in seven groups: engineering services, manufacturing, sales and distribution, property, financial services, investee and associate companies, and "others."

Questions

1. What organizational structure do you believe is being used to produce Detroit Electric vehicles?
2. Detroit Electric is on pace to introduce its electric vehicles to market just three years after its inception. Ford will have taken over 40 years to produce a viable electric car by 2011. How has differing organizational structure influenced the pace of development within these two companies?
3. The creation and manufacture of Detroit Electric's car involves organizations from countries around the world. What issues may arise from this cooperative arrangement of international companies?
4. How would you promote ethical behavior in the organization producing the Detroit Electric car?

Sources: Written by Dr. Michael Dutch, Greensboro College, Greensboro, North Carolina. Adapted from "Detroit Electric and Proton Announce Strategic Partnership to Produce Affordable and Practical Pure Electric Vehicles," Detroit Electric, March 30, 2009, http://Detroit-electric.co.uk/display_article.php?id=33 (accessed April 2, 2009); Jerry Flint, "The Myth of the Electric Car," Forbes.com, March 2, 2009, www.forbes.com/2009/03/18/ford-electric-cars-business-autos-jerry-flint.html (accessed April 2, 2009); "Corporate Information," Proton, www.proton.com/about_proton/corp_governance/index.php (accessed April 2, 2009); and Bill Vlasic, "Ford Reports a Record $14.6 Billion Loss for 2008," *The New York Times*, January 30, 2009, p. B3.

CHAPTER SEVENTEEN

Managing Organizational Change and Innovation

Learning Objectives

After completing Chapter 17, you should be able to:

- **Define** what is meant by *organizational change management*.
- **Identify** the major steps in undertaking organizational change effort.
- **Describe** how appreciative inquiry is conducted.
- **Discuss** the role of problem diagnosis in organizational change management.
- **Identify** a number of change methods and the relative depth of intervention each represents.

- **Recognize** the impediments and conditions that may limit change management effectiveness.
- **Discuss** the ethical implications of change management.
- **Understand** how adopting innovation is a natural outcome in organizations that effectively manage change.

As managers contemplate the futures of their organizations in the 21st century, they can't escape the inevitability of change. *Change* is certainly among the most frequently used words on the business pages of every newspaper in the world. Not only have entire countries and empires gone through dramatic and wrenching changes, but so also have companies such as IBM, Amazon.com, Intel, and Oracle. The USSR no longer exists, but neither do Linens 'n Things, Filene's Basement, KB Toys, and Circuit City. So it makes sense for this text devoted to the preparation of future managers to address the issues associated with managing change.

Well-known business writers state that contemporary business organizations confront changing circumstances that put bygone eras of change to shame by comparison. The combination of global competition, computer-assisted manufacturing methods, and instant communications has implications more far-reaching than anything since the beginning of the Industrial Revolution.[1] Popular literature and best sellers warn managers that their organizations' futures depend upon their ability to master change.[2] Many authors state that change is a pervasive, persistent, and permanent condition for all organizations. Not only are managers faced with continual change, but also the rate of change has been accelerating. Some have described the growth in the rate of change faced by organizations as exponential.[3]

Effective managers must view managing change as an integral responsibility rather than as a peripheral one.[4] In addition to managing change, contemporary and future

How much do you know about organizational change and innovation?

1. The use of power or authority to bring about a change in behavior, structure, or technology implies a reliance on _____.
   a. incentives
   b. history
   c. coercion
   d. evaluation

2. Individuals in general resist change because they _____ what may possibly happen to them.
   a. trust
   b. reinforce
   c. resent
   d. fear

3. The forces for change are usually classified as being _____ forces.
   a. environmental and regulatory
   b. internal and external
   c. management and leadership
   d. contingency and systems

4. A method of focusing on positive or potential opportunities associated with change is referred to as _____.
   a. network mining
   b. appreciative inquiry
   c. flex-site
   d. total quality systems

5. The implementation of the change method has two dimensions: _____ and _____.
   a. cost and commitment
   b. timing and scope
   c. cost and timing
   d. timing and commitment

managers will have to develop approaches for adopting and implementing innovation. Innovative products, processes, and practices have become the rule rather than the exception, and managing change and innovation has become a major management responsibility of the 21st century.

But we must accept the reality that not all organizations will successfully make the appropriate changes or adopt the effective innovations. Some researchers believe that organizations with the best chance for success are relatively small and compete in industries in which research and development expenditures have traditionally been relatively high and barriers to entry are relatively low. Such firms in these industries have had to change to survive, and they are likely to be the survivors in the first quarter of the 21st century.[5]

In the wake of globalization, new technologies, demographic shifts, emerging new markets, and new alliances, organizations must adapt at fast rates to survive. People in organizations now must change and adapt to advance their careers, to improve their productivity, and to carry out a variety of roles in organizations, with no time to spare. Likewise, organizations must be flexible, creative, and responsive to remain distinct,

LESSONS ABOUT SPEED FROM THE 17TH CENTURY

An interesting report in the *Academy of Management Executive* relates the story of the Swedish ship *Vasa*. The *Vasa* was a tremendous warship built in 1628 that cost over 5 percent of Sweden's gross domestic product to build. After going less than one mile, the vessel keeled over and sank 110 feet to the bottom of the Stockholm harbor. Fifty crewmembers perished with the ship.

The *Vasa's* story emphasizes the need for managerial realism in the development and launching of new products. A few of these lessons are:

- *Obsession with speed.* The *Vasa* was a radical new design, which contributed to uncertainty. Steps were skipped to make sure the ship was on schedule, and quality suffered.

- *Feedback failures.* Throughout changes in a process, continuous testing and feedback are needed. A more modern example than the *Vasa* is Lever Brothers' European launch of Persil Power (a detergent). After years of testing, Persil Power was launched containing manganese, which was believed to have superior cleaning properties. However, Procter & Gamble (P&G) launched a negative advertising campaign, claiming Persil Power damaged clothes and fabrics. Independent researchers confirmed P&G's claims and Persil's market share dwindled and the product was dropped.

- *Top-management meddling.* Sweden's King Gustav II Adolph was a one-person management team involved in all phases of the *Vasa* project. He had suffered military losses and wanted a hand in all decisions.

- *Appropriate top-management involvement.* A more hopeful modern example is Chairman Eiji Toyoda of Toyota Motors. The company was known for inexpensive cars when Toyoda challenged his engineers to "develop the best car in the world." He provided only general specifications, over $500 million, and then released the project to a team of engineers.

The *Vasa* tragedy, centuries ago, provides guidelines for today's managers. Value speed but do not violate common sense, and don't take shortcuts on quality, integrity, and providing feedback.

Sources: Adapted from Dottie E. Mayol, "The Swedish Ship *Vasa's* Reward," www.abc.se/~pa/publ/vasa.htm (accessed June 5, 2006); and Eric Kessler, Paul E. Bierly, III, and Shanthi Gopalakrishnan, "*Vasa* Syndrome: Insights from a 17th Century New-Product Disaster," *Academy of Management Executive* 15 (August 2001), pp. 80–91.

retain market share, and grow new businesses, strategies, and opportunities.[6] Just as the adage states, "Failing to plan is planning to fail." Organizations that fail to plan for, anticipate, and accurately adapt to change are likely not to survive. *Speed* is the catchword of the day. However, as the Global OB suggests, speed must be treated carefully if it is to become an advantage.

The forces for change are worldwide. A study of more than 12,000 managers in 25 companies shows them dealing with major restructuring, mergers, divestitures, acquisitions, downsizing, and international expansion.[7] Exhibit 17.1 shows the percentage of managers reporting such changes in six countries.

This chapter explores issues associated with managing change and innovation through reeducation and learning among individuals, groups, and organizations. Reeducation and learning, along with taking appropriate actions, maximize the probability that successful change will occur.

Alternative Change Management Approaches

Managers can undertake organizational change in various ways. In many instances the change process occurs at the expense of short-term losses in exchange for long-term benefits.[8] One extensive review of the literature identified several approaches that managers can use to manage planned change.[9] Although the terms vary from author to author and from proponent to proponent, the underlying theme is the same. The approaches to bringing about change range from the application of power, in any of its forms, to the application of reason. Midway between these two extremes is the approach that relies upon reeducation.

EXHIBIT 17.1
Managers Facing Organizational Change: A Cross-National Picture

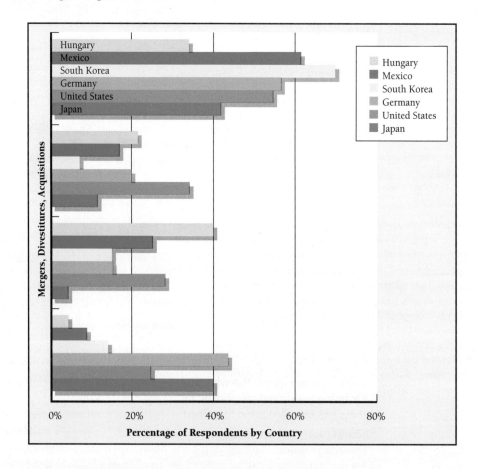

Managing Change through Power

The *application of power* to bring about change implies the use of coercion. Managers have access to power and can use their power to coerce nonmanagers to change in the direction they desire. Managers can implement power through their control over rewards and sanctions. They can determine the conditions of employment including promotion and advancement. Consequently, through their access to these bases of power, managers can bring to bear considerable influence in an organization.

The application of power often manifests in autocratic leadership, and contemporary organizations do not generally encourage managers to engage in such leadership behavior. In times past, autocratic management was a factor in the rise of labor unions as counterweights to the arbitrary use of managerial power. Except in crisis situations when the very existence of the organization is at stake, coercive power is typically not a good approach for bringing about change. This is particularly true for organizations that have traditionally allowed a great deal of employee participation. A recent study has found these organizations are likely to resist autocratic approaches to change.[10]

Managing Change through Reason

The *application of reason* to bring about change is based on the dissemination of information before the intended change. The underlying assumption is that reason alone will prevail and that the participants and parties to the change will all make the rational choice. The reason-based approach appeals to the sensibilities of those who take a utopian view of organizational worlds. But the reality of organizations requires that we recognize the existence of individual motives and needs, group norms and sanctions, and the fact that organizations exist as social as well as work units, all of which means that reason alone won't be sufficient to bring about change.

Managing Change through Reeducation

The middle-ground approach relies upon *reeducation* to improve the functioning of the organization. Reeducation implies a particular set of activities that recognizes that neither power nor reason can bring about desirable change. This set of activities has been the subject of much research and application and is generally understood to be the essence of organizational development.[11]

organizational development
The process of preparing for and managing change in organizational settings.

The term **organizational development** implies a normative reeducation strategy intended to affect systems of beliefs, values, and attitudes within the organization so that it can adapt better to the accelerated rate of change in technology, in our industrial environment, and in society in general. It also includes formal organizational restructuring, which is frequently initiated, facilitated, and reinforced by the normative and behavioral changes.[12]

The fact that organizational development is a process that brings about change in a social system raises the issue of the *change agent* (the individual or group who becomes the catalyst for change). Are change agents necessary for organizational improvement to occur? Once we recognize that organizational change involves substantial changes in how individuals think, believe, and act, we can appreciate the necessity of someone to play the role of change agent. But who should play the role? Existing managers? New managers? Or individuals hired specifically for that purpose? Depending upon the situation, any of these can be called upon to orchestrate the organizational change process.[13]

Managers who implement change programs are committed to making fundamental changes in organizational behavior. At the heart of the process are learning principles that enable individuals to unlearn old behaviors and learn new ones. The classic relearning sequence of unfreezing, moving, and refreezing is implemented in the systematic approach to change.[14]

Learning Principles in Change Management

To better understand how changes are brought about in individuals, we must apply appropriate principles of learning. Managers can design a theoretically sound change approach and not achieve any of the anticipated results because they overlooked the importance of providing motivation, reinforcement, and feedback to employees. These principles of learning originally stated by Kurt Lewin serve to unfreeze old learning, instill new learning, and refreeze that new learning.

Unfreezing old learning requires people to want to learn new ways to think and act. Unfreezing deals directly with resistance to change.[15] Individuals may not accept that they need more skill in a particular job or more understanding of the problems of other units of the firm. Some people recognize this need and are receptive to experiences that will aid them in developing new skills or new empathies. Others reject the need or play it down, because learning is to them an admission that they aren't completely competent in their jobs. These kinds of people face the prospect of change with different expectations and motivations. Determining the expectations and motivations of people isn't easy. It is, however, a task that managers must undertake to manage change: It is management's responsibility to show employees why they should want to change.

Movement to new learning requires training, demonstration, and empowerment. Training nonmanagerial employees hasn't been a high priority among American corporations, but lost market shares to foreign competitors that invest greater resources in training have encouraged American firms to make training a regular part of their employees' assignments. Through training and demonstration of the appropriateness of that training, employees can be empowered to take on behaviors they previously had only vaguely imagined possible. The new behaviors must be carefully and sensitively taught.

Refreezing the learned behavior occurs through the application of reinforcement and feedback. These two principles suggest that when people receive positive rewards, information, or feelings for doing something, they'll more likely do the same thing in a similar situation. The other side of the coin involves the impact of punishment for a particular response. Punishment will decrease the probability of doing the same thing another time. The principle, then, implies that it would be easier to achieve successful change through the use of positive rewards. Reinforcement can also occur when the knowledge or skill acquired in a training program is imparted through a refresher course. The ultimate goal of refreezing is to have the learned behavior become a habit. A habit goes beyond mere repetition of a behavior as the desired behavior becomes an automatic or default response to the situation.[16]

Management must guard against the possibility that what a person has learned at a training site is lost when that person is transferred to the actual work site. If things have gone well, only a minimum amount will be lost in this necessary transfer. A possible strategy for keeping the loss to a minimum is to make the training situation similar to the actual workplace environment. Another strategy is to reward the newly learned behavior. If the colleagues and superiors of newly trained people approve new ideas or new skills, these people will be encouraged to continue to behave in the new way.

If colleagues and superiors behave ambiguously or negatively in any way, the newly trained people will be discouraged from persisting with attempts to use what they've learned. This is one reason it has been suggested that superiors be trained before subordinates. The superior, if trained and motivated, can serve as a reinforcer and feedback source for the subordinate who has left the training confines and is now back on the job.

Change Agents: Forms of Intervention

change agent
A person who acts as the initiator for change activities. Can be internal members of the firm or external consultants.

Because managers tend to seek answers in traditional solutions, the intervention of an outsider is often necessary. The intervener, or **change agent,** brings a different perspective to the situation and challenges the status quo. The success of any change program rests heavily on the quality and workability of the relationship between the change agent and the key decision makers within the organization. Thus, the form of intervention used is a crucial consideration.[17]

To intervene is to enter into an ongoing organization or relationship among persons or departments, for the purpose of helping improve effectiveness. A number of forms of intervention are used in organizations.

External Change Agents

external change agents
A person from outside an organization who initiates change.

External change agents are temporary employees (e.g., change consultants) of the organization, since they're engaged only for the duration of the change process. They originate in a variety of organizations including universities, consulting firms, and training agencies. Many large organizations have individuals located at central offices who take temporary assignments with line units that are contemplating organizational change. At the conclusion of the change program, the change agent returns to headquarters.

The usual external change agent is a university professor or private consultant who has training and experience in the behavioral sciences. Such an individual will be contacted by the organization and be engaged after agreement is reached on the conditions of the relationship. Ordinarily, the change agent will have graduate degrees and experience in specialties that focus on individual and group behavior in organizational settings. With this kind of training, the external change agent has the perspective to facilitate the change process.

Internal Change Agents

internal change agent
A person, manager or nonmanager, working for an organization, who initiates change.

The **internal change agent** is an individual working for the organization who knows something about its problems.[18] The usual internal change agent is a recently appointed manager of an organization that has a record of poor performance; often, the individual takes the job with the expectation that major change is necessary. How successfully internal change agents undertake their roles has been extensively studied in recent years.

Raymond Smith's experience as an internal change agent clearly illustrates what such individual efforts can bring about.[19] When Smith became CEO of Bell Atlantic, he confronted the imperative of changing a slow-to-act bureaucracy into a fast-response entrepreneurial entity. The driving force behind the change was the deregulation of the communications industry. Rather than rely on outside consultants to transform the organization, Smith took on the role of champion of change with full understanding of all the demands that the role would place on him. He immediately began fact gathering and consensus building via discussions with managers and nonmanagers throughout the organization. His intent was to demonstrate by word and deed that Bell Atlantic had to change in fundamental ways if it was to survive in the competitive, deregulated environment.

Signs of progress include breaking down barriers between departments, sharing resources, and developing attitudes that encourage teamwork and idea sharing. Smith attributes much of his success to creating a sense of empowerment among Bell employees. Thus, they believe if they act for the good of the company and succeed, they and the company prosper. But if failure is the outcome, failure is shared by all. Smith reoriented the company to be consistent with the new environmental demands—competition.

Internal change agents are a rare breed. In a recent article, Jack Welch, former CEO of General Electric, estimated that no more than 10 percent of employees fit the category. Welch states that while all change agents must be leaders, not all leaders are change agents.[20]

External–Internal Change Agents

Some organizations use a combination external–internal change team to intervene and develop programs. This approach attempts to use the resources and knowledge base of both external and internal change agents. It involves designating an individual or small group within the organization to serve with the external change agent to spearhead the change effort. The internal group often comes from the human resource management unit, but it can also be a group of top managers. As a general rule, an external change agent will actively solicit the visible support of top management as a way to emphasize the importance of the change effort.[21]

Each of the three forms of intervention has advantages and disadvantages. The external change agent is often viewed as an outsider. When employees hold this belief, rapport needs to be established between the change agent and decision makers. The change agent's views on the organization's problems are often different from the decision maker's views, which leads to problems in establishing rapport. Differences in viewpoints often result in mistrust of the external change agent by the policymakers or a segment of the policymakers. Offsetting these disadvantages is the external change agent's ability to refocus the organization's relationship with the changing environmental demands. The external agent has a comparative advantage over the internal change agent when significant strategic changes must be evaluated.[22]

The internal change agent is often viewed as being more closely associated with one unit or group of individuals than with any other. This perceived favoritism leads to resistance to change by those who aren't included in the internal change agent's circle of close friends and personnel, but knowledge of this can be valuable in preparing for and implementing change. The internal change agent can often serve as the champion for change because of enlightened understanding of the organization's capability and because of personal persistence.[23]

The third type of intervention, the combination external–internal team, is the rarest, but it seems to have a reasonable chance for success. In this type of intervention, the outsider's objectivity and professional knowledge are blended with the insider's knowledge of the organization and its human resources. This blending of knowledge often results in increased trust and confidence among the parties involved. The combination external–internal team's ability to communicate and develop a more positive rapport can reduce resistance to any forthcoming change.

While change agents are expected to help organizations implement positive improvements, change agents themselves may create problems or issues. The actions of the change agents may create resistance, which if not properly addressed may lead to the failure of the initiative. Proper understanding of the sources of resistance and the means to address them is critical for successful change activities.[24]

Resistance to Change

Even in situations in which change is clearly the best choice, there may be fear, anxiety, and resistance. The more significant the change in structure, task, technology, and human assets, the more intense the fear, anxiety, and resistance. A large portion of whatever fear, anxiety, or resistance occurs is triggered by changes in routine, patterns, and habits. Researchers, however, have been more specific in categorizing resistance to change that results from individuals and organizational factors.[25]

Exhibit 17.2 presents a graphical portrayal of a variety of individual responses to a change in structure, technology, or people.

Individual Resistance

Individuals resist change because they fear what will happen to them. A number of individual impediments to change have been uncovered through research conducted in organizational settings. Reasons for resistance are the following:

- The threat of loss of position, power, status, quality of life, and authority.
- Economic insecurity regarding retention of the job or level of compensation.

EXHIBIT 17.2   Range of Individual Resistance Behaviors

Source: Concept for continuum and some behaviors stimulated by A.P. Goldstein, *Reducing Resistance: Methods for Enhancing Openness to Change* (Champaign, IL: Research Press, 2001).

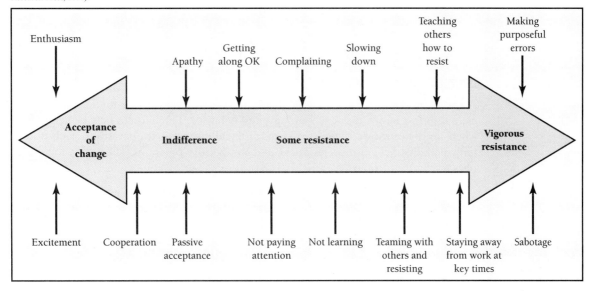

- The possible alteration of social friendships and interactivity. Redesign, shifts in work processes, and movement of people are considered to be threats to friendships, patterns of social on-the-job interactions, and routines.
- The natural human fear of the unknown brought about by change. The inability to predict with certainty how the new organizational design, manager, or compensation system is going to work creates a natural resistance.
- Failure to recognize or be informed about the need for change.
- Cognitive dissonance created because one is confronted with new people, processes, systems, technology, or expectations. The dissonance or discomfort created by what is new or different is another typical social psychological human process.[26]
- Feelings of inadequacy. People will seldom admit that they lack the skills to be good performers if a change occurs.
- Belief that what is going to be changed is wrong or a bad idea.

Each of these and other individually oriented points of resistance can be addressed through increased communication, information, and data. Face-to-face meetings, newsletters, e-mails, reports, speeches, conferences, and other methods of communication can lead to a better understanding and trust about changes. Other methods for dealing with individual resistance include having people participate in the entire change process, using change champions from within the group to serve as facilitators, and engaging in negotiations about the type and pace of changes. These approaches require management skill in leading the change approach.

Unfortunately, some managers use coercion, threats, and manipulation to implement changes. The drawbacks to these hands-on, top-down approaches include resentment, withdrawal, slowing down, anger, covert sabotage, and unethical behaviors.[27] These methods provide few long-term benefits that justify their implementation.

Trust, faith, and confidence in any change program are extremely important. Robert Shapiro, when serving as CEO of Monsanto, captured the essence of trust as follows:

> You can't get to good morale by lying. . . . You can't get innovation that way. You find an enormous amount of time and effort is dealing with the trust of others. Look at all the inefficiencies of lack of trust. It tells you that an honest organization is going to be much more efficient. It just makes good business sense.[28]

Organizational Resistance

A range of forces within an organization poses barriers to the implementation of changes in structure, tasks, technology, and behavior. These forces may be heightened when an organization consists of geographically separated operations, each potentially with distinct cultures, products, and competitive pressures.[29] Organizational barriers to change include:

- The professional and functional orientation of a department, unit, or team. Engineers perceive changes from an engineering background and experience. Likewise, education, training, and learning shape sales and marketing teams' perceptions. The organizational unit also creates its own norms and standards of behavior. Changes may alter relationships that impact these norms and standards.

- Structural inertia. Organizations are structured to promote stability. The structural arrangement is created in a way that it resists changes or forces that generate instability. This same type of structure at the organization level also exists at the group and team levels. Strong norms are resistant to change because of group members' comfort with a certain flow and pattern.

- Perceived threats to the power balance in an organization. The fear of losing position, status, and resource power or leverage creates a strong backlash. Change in how products are sold in mall stores, online, and through catalogs created resistance in Sears stores, units, and subunits based on the perception of power and its distribution in the firm. The online unit wanted more resources allocated to it while the store managers resisted the untested venture into online e-tailing.

- An aura and folklore, spurred by a previous failure, about the dangers associated with change. Because of Coca-Cola's failed experiment with changing the taste and flavor of Coke, future attempts to alter anything associated with Coke's formula will likely be met with skepticism, doubt, and caution. The same type of failure-driven resistance existed at Ford Motor Company for a least a full decade after the monumental financial losses associated with the introduction of the Edsel automobile. Ford was reluctant to introduce major style changes and new products for at least 10 years after the 1957 Edsel failure.

Strategies for Overcoming Resistance to Change

The range of individual and organizational resistance factors involves fear, anxiety, team behavior, politics, and uncertainty. Analyzing change and resistance involves a number of key considerations.[30] First, individuals and organizations must have a reason to change.

Second, the more involved people at all levels of the hierarchy are in the change planning, implementation, and monitoring, the higher the likelihood of success. Changes that are imposed on employees with little warning are likely to be resisted. As the Organizational Encounter on page 523 suggests, allowing people to participate in change has significant benefits.

ALLOW PEOPLE TO PARTICIPATE IN CHANGE

Leading a change requires the work, ideas, and creativity of more than a single change agent. Research shows that participation increases the likelihood of change success. Willie Pietersen described a change program he was involved with as the president of Sterling Winthrop's Health Business. The firm's main global product was Panadol, a headache remedy selling 6 billion tablets a year in 85 countries, but at that time doing so in many different kinds of packages. Pietersen wanted to convert the hodgepodge packaging into a single known brand. He faced stiff resistance from around the world. He described his challenge this way.

At a meeting I gave a talk about the power of global branding. I projected a slide of the Coca-Cola logo—but instead of using familiar colors and script, I used a random selection of different colors and fonts. There was a patchwork of labels and colors.

I did the same for Kodak. Instead of yellow and black, the Kodak logo was done in many different shades and sizes.

Then I put up a slide of Panadol's actual packaging from around the world. It looked like a collage of 20 different designs done by 20 different advertising agencies. There was silence in the audience. "This isn't a brand," I said. "This looks like a collection of different products having the same name. To remain competitive in an increasingly connected world, Panadol needs to be a global brand."

We broke up the large audience into smaller groups. The charge to each was to come up with an approach to harmonize Panadol's many images into a single brand.

After about an hour, I was told that many people were upset, frustrated, and angry. For years the authority and power was in the hands of the company's regional managers. I was accused of stripping away this power in favor of centralized control.

I looked at the podium and said, "I understand your fear of losing power. But you are incorrect. I'm asking you to help us come up with a globalization brand and strategy. I will appoint a team of regional managers to coordinate the effort. We'll need to select a single global advertising agency and package-design firm, but you will guide their work."

The regional manager audience was relieved and willingly and enthusiastically took up the task. Within four months, the regional manager team came up with a plan for creating and implementing a global Panadol brand image.

The lesson seems clear: Don't hand over a change approach and say, "Here, implement this." It's not going to work. We learned that participation works because more people are involved. Involving people requires people skills, patience, and managing emotions. It also requires a willingness to allow others to participate in the change process, planning, and implementation.

Sources: Adapted from Phred Dvorak, "Construction Firm Rebuilds Managers to Make Them Softer," *The Wall Street Journal,* May 16, 2006, www.online.wsj.com; "GSK at a glance; About GSK; GlaxoSmithKline," www.gsk.com/about/ataglance.htm (accessed March 11, 2009); and Willie Pietersen, "The Mark Twain Dilemma: The Theory and Practice of Change Leadership," *Journal of Business Strategy* 23 (September–October 2002), pp. 32–37.

Third, communication is an ongoing and not a onetime factor in successful change programs. Ever more communication is always needed in major change programs. Communication can educate and prepare the employees in a way that reduces fear, anxiety, and resistance.

Fourth, an organization contemplating change needs to identify and help guide champions or supporters of change. It is important to have the backing of powerful and influential people. They can serve as spokespersons and role models to help facilitate the change.

Finally, the creation of a learning organization or one that has the capacity, resilience, and flexibility to change is ideal.[31] In learning organizations such as Cisco Systems, Kimberly-Clark, Baxter Laboratories, and Wells Fargo, employees share ideas, make recommendations, and participate voluntarily in change from the outset.

Learning organizations have the following characteristics:[32]

- Open discussions and accessibility to information and data.
- Clear vision expressed at all levels.
- Strong emphasis on interdependence, worth, and importance of each person and unit.
- Clear goals and concepts of performance expectations.
- Commitment to learning, improving, and personal growth.

- Concern for measurable results whenever possible.
- A curiosity to try new methods and experiment, and acceptance of failure.

Any organization in any industry can become a learning system that can thrive on change. Setting aside old ways of thinking and minimizing the resistance to change can become a habit, especially in organizations that try to fit the learning model.

While the concept of learning organizations is appealing, empirical evidence to support its effectiveness, perhaps due to difficulties in measurement, has been limited.[33] Researchers continue to examine the topic, and a recent study has found learning organization behaviors were associated with net income per employee, self-reported financial measures, and the percentage of overall sales from new products.[34] In this time of shortened product life cycles, the ability to continually create new products may be the key for continued organizational success.

A Model for Managing Organizational Change

The process of managing change through reeducation can be approached logically. The several steps of this logical process are suggested in Exhibit 17.3. The model consists of specific steps generally acknowledged as being essential to successful change management.[35] A manager considers each of them, either explicitly or implicitly, when undertaking a change program. Prospects of initiating successful change can be enhanced when managers actively support the effort and demonstrate that support by implementing systematic procedures that give substance to the process.[36]

EXHIBIT 17.3   A Model for the Management of Organizational Development

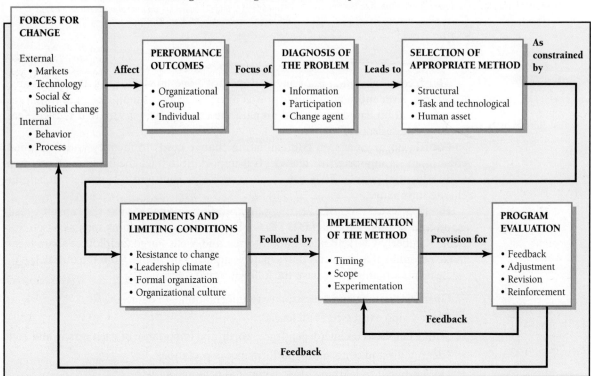

The model indicates that forces for change continually act on the organization; this assumption reflects the dynamic character of the modern world. At the same time, it's the manager's responsibility to sort out the information that reflects the magnitude of change forces.[37] The information is the basis for recognizing when change is needed; it's equally desirable to recognize when change isn't needed. But once managers recognize that something is malfunctioning, they must diagnose the problem and identify relevant alternative techniques.

Finally, the manager must implement the change and monitor the change process and change results. The model includes feedback to the implementation step and to the forces-for-change step. These feedback loops suggest that the change process itself must be monitored and evaluated. The mode of implementation may be faulty and may lead to poor results, but responsive action could correct the situation. Moreover, the feedback loop to the initial step recognizes that no change is final. A new situation is created within which problems and issues will emerge; a new setting is created that will itself become subject to change. The model suggests no final solution; rather, it emphasizes that the modern manager operates in a dynamic setting wherein the only certainty is change itself.

Forces for Change

The forces for change can be classified conveniently into two groups: *external forces* and *internal forces*. External forces are beyond management's control. Internal forces operate inside the firm and are generally within the control of management. Understanding and effectively exploiting these forces may allow an organization to improve upon its competitive position. Allowing these forces to occur without reaction will allow competing organizations to seize an advantage.[38]

External Forces

Organizations seldom undertake significant change without a strong shock from their environment. The external environment includes many economic, technological, and social/political forces that can trigger the change process. Those who study and practice organizational change agree that these environmental triggers are necessary but not sufficient to initiate change. Change also involves managers who are aware of the need for change and who take action.

economic forces
Forces in the environment that can influence what occurs within a firm, such as security markets, interest rates, foreign currency fluctuations, and competitors' pricing strategies.

The manager of a business has historically been concerned with reacting to **economic forces**. Competitors introduce new products, increase their advertising, reduce their prices, or increase their customer service. In each case, a response is required unless the manager is content to permit the erosion of profit and market share. At the same time, changes occur in customer tastes and incomes. The firm's products may no longer have customer appeal; customers may be able to purchase less expensive, higher-quality forms of the same products.

technology
An important concept that can have many definitions in specific instances but that generally refers to actions, physical and mental, that an individual performs upon some object, person, or problem in order to change it in some way.

The second source of environmental change forces is **technology**. The knowledge explosion has introduced new technology for nearly every business function. Computers have made possible high-speed data processing and the solutions to complex production problems. New machines and new processes have revolutionized how many products are manufactured and distributed. Computer technology and automation have affected not only the technical conditions of work, but the social conditions as well.[39] New occupations have been created, and others have been eliminated. Slowness to adopt new technology that reduces cost and improves quality will show up in the financial statements sooner or later.[40] Technological advance is a permanent fixture in the business world. As a force for change, it will continue to demand attention.

The third source of environmental change forces is *social and political change*. Business managers must be tuned in to the great social movements over which they have no control but that, in time, influence their firm's fate. Sophisticated mass communications and international markets create great potential for business, but they're also great threats to managers who can't understand what's going on.[41] Finally, the relationship between government and business becomes much closer as regulations are imposed and relaxed.

Comprehending implications of external forces requires organizational learning processes.[42] These processes, now being studied in many organizations, involve the capacity to absorb new information, process that information in the light of previous experience, and act on the information in new and potentially risky ways. But only through such learning experiences will organizations be prepared for the 21st century.

Internal Forces

Internal forces for change within the organization can usually be traced to process and behavioral problems. The process problems include breakdowns in decision making and communications. Decisions aren't being made, are made too late, or are of poor quality. Communications are short-circuited, redundant, or simply inadequate. Tasks aren't undertaken or aren't completed because the person responsible did not get the word. Because of inadequate or nonexistent communications, a customer order isn't filled, a grievance isn't processed, or an invoice isn't filed and the supplier isn't paid. Interpersonal and interdepartmental conflicts reflect breakdowns in organizational processes.

Low levels of morale and high levels of absenteeism and turnover are symptoms of behavioral problems that must be diagnosed. A wildcat strike or a walkout may be the most tangible sign of a problem, yet such tactics are usually employed because they arouse management to action. A certain level of employee discontent exists in most organizations—it's dangerous to ignore employee complaints and suggestions. The process of change includes the recognition phase—the point where management must decide to act or not to act.

In many organizations, the need for change goes unrecognized until some major catastrophe occurs. The employees strike or seek the recognition of a union before management finally recognizes the need for action. Whether it takes a whisper or a shout, the need for change must be recognized by some means; and once that need has been recognized, the exact nature of the problem must be diagnosed. If the problem isn't properly understood, the impact of change on people can be extremely negative.

Diagnosis of a Problem

Change agents facilitate the diagnostic phase by gathering, interpreting, and presenting data. Although the accuracy of data is extremely important, how the data are interpreted and presented is equally important. Interpretation and presentation are generally accomplished in one of two ways. First, the data are discussed with a group of top managers, who are asked to make their own diagnosis of the information; or, second, change agents may present their own diagnoses without making explicit their frameworks for analyzing the data. A difficulty with the first approach is that top management tends to see each problem separately. Each manager views his problem as being the most important and fails to recognize other problem areas. The second approach has inherent problems of communication. External change agents often have difficulty with the second approach because they become immersed in theory and various conceptual frameworks that are less realistic than the managers would like.

Appropriate action is necessarily preceded by diagnosis of the problem's symptoms. Experience and judgment are critical to this phase unless the problem is readily apparent to all observers. Ordinarily, however, managers can disagree on the nature of the problem. There's no formula for accurate diagnosis, but the following questions point the manager in the right direction:

1. What is the problem as distinct from the symptoms of the problem?
2. What must be changed to resolve the problem?
3. What outcomes (objectives) are expected from the change, and how will those outcomes be measured?

The answers to these questions can come from information ordinarily found in the organization's information system. Or it may be necessary to generate ad hoc information through the creation of committees or task forces. Meetings between managers and employees provide a variety of viewpoints that can be sifted through by a smaller group. Interviewing key personnel is an important problem-finding method. Another diagnostic approach that obtains broader-based information is the attitude survey.

The survey is a useful diagnostic approach if the potential focus of change is the total organization. If smaller units or entities are the focus of change, the survey technique may not be a reliable source of information. For example, if the focus of change is a relatively small work group, diagnosis of the problem is better accomplished through individual interviews followed by group discussion of the interview data. In this approach, the group becomes actively involved in sharing and interpreting perception of problems. However, the attitude survey can pose difficulties for organizations with relatively low levels of trust in management's sincerity to use the information in constructive ways.

Identification of individual employees' problems comes about through interviews and personnel department information. Consistently low performance evaluations indicate such problems, but it's often necessary to go into greater detail. Identifying individuals' problems is far more difficult than identifying organizational problems. Thus, the diagnostic process must stress the use of precise and reliable information.

To summarize, the data collection process can tap information in several ways. Five different approaches are useful for assorted purposes:[43]

1. Questionnaire data can be collected from large numbers of people.
2. Direct observations can be taken of actual workplace behavior.
3. Selected individuals in key positions can be interviewed.
4. Workshops can be arranged with groups to explore different perceptions of problems.
5. Documents and records of the organization can be examined for archival and current information.

Regardless of the data collection method, it is important to clearly understand a problem before initiating an organizational development activity. An effective and targeted needs assessment increases the likelihood that it will lead to improved organizational performance.[44]

Selection of Appropriate Methods

Managers have a variety of change and development methods to select from, depending on the objectives they hope to accomplish. One way of viewing objectives is from the perspective of the depth of the intended change.

Depth of intended change refers to the scope and intensity of the change efforts. A useful distinction here is between the formal and informal aspects of organizations. Formal organizational components are observable, rational, and oriented toward structural factors. The informal components are not observable to all people; they are affective and oriented to process and behavioral factors. Generally speaking, as one moves from formal aspects of the organization to informal aspects, the scope and intensity increase. As scope and intensity increase, so does the depth of the change.

The choice of a particular development method depends on the nature of the problem that management has diagnosed and the depth of the intended change. Examining several specific development methods is the focus of the rest of this section. For purposes of our discussion, we have grouped these methods into three categories: structural, task and technological, and human asset or people. The classification of methods that we use in no way implies a distinct division among the approaches. On the contrary, the interrelationships among them must be acknowledged and anticipated. As an illustration of this, we close this section with a look at approaches that are multifaceted and cut across our three categories.

Structural Approaches

Structural approaches to organizational change refer to managerial actions that attempt to improve effectiveness by introducing change through formal policies and procedures. Actual structural reorganization is the most direct example of this approach. Mergers and acquisitions, as well as the recent interest in downsizing, may set the stage for a variety of structural reorganizations. Generally, restructuring tends to focus on creating flatter, more organic organizations.

Not all structural approaches necessarily involve making actual changes in the organizational structure, however. Introduction of a zero-based budgeting system, for example, may represent a significant change in both policy and procedure, without altering the existing structure. Many organizations are revising their reward systems, emphasizing pay for performance. In such systems, pay is determined by achieved levels of either individual or team performance. Reward systems such as these also represent a structural approach to organizational change.

One method representing a structural approach to organizational change that has demonstrated effectiveness is *management by objectives (MBO)*. Another structural approach is referred to as *reengineering*.

Management by Objectives

management by objectives (MBO)
A process under which superiors and subordinates jointly set goals for a specified time period and then meet again to evaluate the subordinates' performance in terms of those previously established goals.

Management by objectives (MBO) is a process consisting of a series of interdependent and interrelated steps designed to facilitate planning and control, decision making, and other important management functions. It is also a management philosophy that reflects a proactive rather than reactive approach to managing.[45] Successful use of MBO depends on the ability of participants to define their objectives in terms of their contributions to the total organization and to be able to accomplish them.

The original work of Drucker[46] and subsequent writings by others provide the basis for three guidelines for implementing MBO:

1. Superiors and subordinates meet and discuss objectives that contribute to overall goals.
2. Superiors and subordinates jointly establish attainable objectives for the subordinates.

3. Superiors and subordinates meet at a predetermined later date to evaluate the subordinates' progress toward the objectives.

The exact procedures employed in implementing MBO vary from organization to organization and from unit to unit.[47] However, the basic elements of objective setting, participation of subordinates in objective setting, and feedback and evaluation usually are parts of any MBO program. The intended consequences of MBO include improved contribution to the organization, improved attitudes and satisfaction of participants, and greater role clarity. MBO is highly developed and widely used in business, health care, and governmental organizations.

While it is generally accepted that specific objectives or goals lead to improved performance, there are potential issues if too much emphasis is placed on goals. If goals are too narrowly focused, employees may be overly attentive to the goal area at the expense of other important areas. An excessive number of simultaneous goals may lead to an employee focusing only on one as a means of coping with what may be perceived as extreme job demands. Goals with overly aggressive timelines may encourage employees to take short-term actions that are not in the long-term best interest of the organization. Overly aggressive goals associated with personal rewards may also promote excessive risk taking by employees.[48] These potential pitfalls should not dissuade from the use of MBO or similar interventions; rather, MBO programs require care and thought in their design if they are expected to direct employee energies and productivity in the organization.

Reengineering

reengineering
Creating radical changes in processes, systems, and/or structures that meet customer needs efficiently and are economically sound.

Companies such as Mutual Benefit Life, Hewlett-Packard, and Ford, through initiative to change work flow, processes, and design, helped create what eventually became known as **reengineering.** The objective of reengineering is to create processes, systems, and structures that meet customer needs efficiently and in an economically sound manner. Instead of this objective catching the attention of managers, however, the notion of downsizing, introducing computerized systems to replace employees, and eliminating layers of management has dominated discussions, analysis, and critiques of reengineering.

James Champy and Michael Hammer popularized reengineering in their book *Reengineering the Organization.*[49] They advocate an approach to structure and process that begins with a clear, blank sheet of paper. This fresh start enables managers to design an entirely new (reengineered) organization to meet the needs of customers. The new approach must be implemented with careful training, education, and documentation to prevent the old structures and processes from reappearing out of habit and inertia. Reengineering consists of a process that evolves from unfreezing structures and processes, reinventing new structures and processes, and freezing them.

Reengineering consists of three strategies: streamlining, integrating, and transforming. Streamlining breaks the core process into segments to eliminate waste, delays, and slow response time. An example of streamlining is to discover the most efficient way to redesign on-site, instructor-led training so that it can be delivered on the Internet through online, asynchronous courseware.

Integrating is the unification of systems, processes, or work-related activities across functional lines, such as combining the course preparation, instruction, and graphical design and hosting activities in producing online courses to fit the diverse needs of online trainees.

Transforming involves benchmarking to locate "best in class" organizations. An example of transforming is to forget how the firm currently prepares and delivers online training courses. What do trainees want, when, and where? Is it possible to learn and pace the training skill, competency, or knowledge in such a way that each person literally controls and structures his or her own course?

Taco Bell used reengineering to change the firm. The firm started its reengineering work by asking customers what they wanted when visiting a Mexican-style fast-food restaurant. Instead of finding that customers wanted what other successful fast-food restaurants provided, Taco Bell found simplicity was the resounding response. Customers wanted from Taco Bell fast service, hot food, good-tasting food, and cleanliness. Fancy surroundings, expensive internal designs and furniture, and soothing music were not mentioned.

Taco Bell reinvented itself, the restaurant design, the price structure, and the treatment of customers. Small lot cooking was replaced with a central kitchen that controlled food quality very carefully. The central kitchen dispensed the food to restaurants, which were 30 percent kitchen and 70 percent customer service area instead of the reverse design.

Taco Bell streamlined, integrated, and transformed its typical restaurant design, pricing, food preparation, and customer service. The results have been the preparation of good food, served hot, and sold at a reasonable price in a clean environment.

Critics of reengineering point to the fear and anxiety raised by this structural change approach.[50] Reengineering has not lived up to the excessive hype and expectations established by a legion of management consultants and academic gurus. Despite these criticisms, some organizations continue today to use reengineering concepts such as streamlining, integration, and transformation. When these activities are used with caution, with concern for people, and for gaining and sustaining a fair competitive advantage, reengineering practices can be effective, well received, and cost efficient. On the other hand, when reengineering is the code word for downsizing, eliminating management layers, and having computers replace people, resistance, anxiety, and fear are likely to permeate an organization.

The continued growth of technology, particularly computing technology, may be changing the face of reengineering. The concept of plug-and-play computer components is being applied to organizations. Rather than overhauling an entire process, this new approach looks at the organization much like a computer—a collection of parts fitted together to achieve an end. These parts or operations can be analyzed and swapped out to improve efficiency much the same way one would upgrade a computer. This perspective, possible only through the advancement in control and communication technologies, allows projects to be implemented and potentially provide returns much faster than traditional reengineering projects.[51]

Task and Technological Approaches

Task and technological approaches to organizational change focus directly on the work itself that is performed in the organization. A task focus emphasizes job design changes, a topic discussed in detail in Chapter 6. Job enlargement, which increases range (the number of tasks performed), and job enrichment, which increases depth (the amount of discretion and responsibility the jobholder has), are primary examples of task approaches. Some of the newer systems of work scheduling may also be classified as task approaches. Recall, for example, our discussion of flexible work schedules in Chapter 6. By allowing individuals to choose when they perform their assigned tasks, management is hoping to increase satisfaction, productivity, and performance while decreasing absenteeism and turnover.

Technological approaches emphasize changes in the flow of work. This could include, for example, new physical plant layouts, changes in office design, and improved work methods and techniques. Many technological changes are related to advances in equipment design and capability. For example, computer-aided design (CAD) technology has transformed the job (and productivity) of draftspersons; computer-aided manufacturing (CAM) has removed many of the manual steps in taking a design to manufacture; laser-guided production equipment has dramatically increased the accuracy of many manufacturing processes; the desktop computer has altered millions of jobs; and, on a growing number of factory floors, robots are outnumbering people. Organizational researchers are just now beginning to examine some of the longer-term effects of technological change on individuals.[52]

An important aspect of task and technological approaches to organizational change is training. When jobs are redesigned, when work flow is changed, or when the use of new equipment must be mastered, training programs are an integral tool in providing the necessary new skills and knowledge. In fact, the most widely used methods for developing employee productivity are training programs.[53] A distinction can be made between on-the-job training and off-the-job training. On-the-job training generally focuses on teaching specific skills and techniques needed to master a job. An advantage is that the employees are actually producing while undergoing training. Corning Inc., the well-known glass manufacturing company, is an example of an organization that is extensively involved in on-the-job training. As employees master each job requirement, they receive credits that become part of their performance evaluations. Training at Corning, however, is not restricted to specific job skills. The company has developed an interactive set of workbooks to train employees in company culture, values, and organization.[54]

Frequently, organizations have provided training that supplements on-the-job efforts. Some of the advantages of off-the-job training are:

1. It lets executives get away from the pressures of the job and work in a climate in which "party-line" thinking is discouraged and self-analysis is stimulated.
2. It presents a challenge to executives that, in general, enhances their motivation to develop themselves.
3. It provides resource people and resource material—faculty members, fellow executives, and literature—that contribute suggestions and ideas for the executives to "try on for size" as they attempt to change, develop, and grow.

The theme of the advantages cited above is that trainees are more stimulated to learn by being away from job pressures. This is certainly debatable since it is questionable whether much of what is learned can be transferred back to the job. Attending a case-problem-solving program in San Diego is quite different from facing irate customers in Cleveland. Nonetheless, despite the difficulty of transferring knowledge from the classroom-type environment to the office, plant, or hospital, off-the-job training programs are still very popular and widely utilized.

People Approaches

Directly or indirectly, all organizational change efforts involve the human assets of the organization. MBO programs, for example, are designed to help individuals set realistic performance goals and objectives, and a variety of job training programs are aimed at increasing skills and knowledge needed to perform tasks. Thus, both the structural approaches and the task and technological approaches typically involve changes related to achieving fairly specific and narrow outcomes. What we are calling human asset or people approaches, however, are a category of change methods designed to result in a far less specific and much broader outcome of helping individuals learn and grow professionally, and perhaps personally.

YOU BE THE JUDGE

RESISTANCE TO CHANGE?

Jason and Hannah work for Pierpont Global Software. The company has just undergone a large change in its reward and evaluation systems. The 15-month change program is still being implemented in Jason and Hannah's unit. Hannah pays you a visit to complain about Jason's negative comments about the new reward and evaluation system.

She contends that Jason is talking to a group of young software engineers attempting to persuade them to resist, question, and drag their feet on using the evaluation portion of the system. Hannah wants you to intervene and immediately stop Jason from influencing others. She also complains that Jason is so noisy in the work area that she and others are distracted from doing their work.

Should you immediately call in Jason and ask him what's going on? You be the judge.

A necessary prerequisite to effective, lasting organizational change is individual change. Structural, task, and technological transformations will ultimately fail if the individuals involved are not receptive to change. Human asset approaches help prepare people for ongoing change and learning.

In the "You Be the Judge," Hannah was one of Jason's biggest advocates when he was recruited three years ago. They have worked together on three major projects that have all been successes for Pierpont. However, in the last few months you have heard about bickering between Jason and Hannah regarding a number of cost control issues in the unit. They are both respected informal leaders of the unit. The situation raises an issue involving change, management, and leadership. It asks you to examine conflict, colleagues, and managerial response centered on a change program and its aftermath. There is no simple solution, and the situation requires some caution.

The "learning organization" philosophy stresses the importance of change, learning, and human assets. According to Peter Senge, a leading advocate, learning organizations value continuing individual and collective learning.[55] To increase effectiveness, Senge argues, organizational members must put aside their old ways of thinking, learn to be open with others, understand how their company really works, develop plans everyone can agree on, and then work together to achieve those plans.[56] Human asset approaches assist in achieving one or more of those objectives. The Organizational Encounter on page 533 discusses some of the programs IBM utilizes to focus on diversity and the development of global markets.

Team Building

In recent years, organizations have shown renewed interest in effectively using work groups, or teams.[57] Anyone who has ever operated a business or organized any kind of project requiring the efforts of several people knows the difficulties involved in getting everyone to pull in the right direction, in the right way, and at the right time. One approach to minimizing these difficulties is that of team building.

The purpose of team building is to enable work groups to get their work done more effectively, to improve their performance. The work groups may be existing or relatively new command and task groups. The specific aims of the intervention include setting goals and priorities, analyzing the ways the group does its work, examining the group's norms and processes for communicating and decision making, and examining the interpersonal relationships within the group. As each of these aims is undertaken, the group is placed in the position of having to recognize explicitly the contributions, positive and negative, of each group member.

IBM PRACTICES WHAT IT PREACHES

Today more than ever, workforce diversity is a global workplace and marketplace topic. More companies are asking, "Do we look like our customers? Is our culture one that fosters inclusiveness and tolerance in each country where we do business?"

Tom Watson, Jr., president of IBM from 1952 to 1971, identified three cornerstones of his firm's approach to business: (1) respect each individual, (2) provide the best service possible to each customer, and (3) excellence must be a way of life. Watson led IBM to appreciate diversity long before the concept became popular, committing IBM to a global marketplace. This commitment remains today. IBM in its interpretation of diversity includes race, gender, physical disabilities, lifestyle, age, religion, economic status, geography, and sexual orientation.

A few examples of how IBM addresses global diversity include:

- A $50 million Global/Life Fund for 74 child care center relationships around the world.
- Eight executive task forces (Asian, black, Hispanic, Native American, gay/lesbian/bisexual/transgender, disabilities, men, and women.

- $1.3 billion to support IBM supplier diversity programs.
- Programs to address the digital divide around the world.
- Showcasing technology at six Global Accessibility Centers.
- Implementation of a global workforce strategy.

In the continuing struggle for talented, diverse employees, IBM takes initiative. The company illustrates by example, financial support, and results that it values diversity around the world, and its efforts are being recognized. IBM has been named as one of the DiversityInc Top 50 Companies for Diversity based upon its CEO commitment, human capital, supplier diversity, and corporate and organizational communications.

Sources: Adapted from "Training Best Practices 2006," *Training*, March 2006, pp. 60–62; J.T. Childs, Jr., "Managing Workforce Diversity at IBM: A Global HR Topic That Has Arrived," *Human Resource Management*, Spring 2005, pp. 73–77; and "Announcing the 9th Annual DiversityInc Top 50 Companies for Diversity," *DiversityInc*, March 20, 2009, www.diversityinc.com/public/5530.cfm.

The process by which these aims are achieved begins with diagnostic meetings. Often lasting an entire day, the meetings enable each group member to share with other members his or her perceptions of problems. Subsequently, a plan of action must be agreed on. The action plan should call on each of the group members, individually or as part of a subgroup, to undertake a specific action to alleviate one or more of the problems.

Team building is also effective when new groups are being formed because problems often exist when new organizational units, project teams, or task forces are created. Typically, such groups have certain characteristics that must be overcome if the groups are to perform effectively. For example:

1. Confusion exists as to roles and relationships.
2. Members have a fairly clear understanding of short-term goals but not long-term ones.
3. Group members have technical competence that puts them on the team and think that is sufficient.
4. Members often pay more attention to the tasks of the team than to the relationships among the team members.

To combat these tendencies, the new group could schedule team-building meetings during the first few weeks of its life.

Although the reports of team building indicate mixed results, the evidence suggests that group processes improve through team-building efforts.[58] This record of success accounts for the increasing use of team building as an organizational development (OD) method. The Organizational Encounter on Seagate (page 534) illustrates how one organization utilized a unique approach to team building. Team building is covered in greater depth in Chapter 10.

SEAGATE'S MORALE-ATHON

Team building is an important step in achieving goals, building morale, and getting to know your colleagues. There are various team-building exercises, techniques, and programs. One of the more interesting attempts to build better, stronger, and more productive teams is utilized by Seagate Technology, a manufacturer of computer hard drives.

Going inside Seagate's $9,000-a-head team-building blowout in New Zealand reveals some of the firm's philosophy and approaches to team building. Plenty of companies try to motivate the troops, but few go as far as Seagate Technology. As part of its Eco Seagate initiative, the $12.7 billion maker of computer storage hardware flies 200 select staffers annually to New Zealand for its Eco Seagate—an intense week of team building topped off by an all-day race in which Seagaters have to kayak, hike, bike, swim, and rappel down a cliff.

It's cocktail hour, and nervous getting-to-know-you chatter floats around the Queenstown chalet, where guests arrive by gondola. Staffers from a dozen countries are talking and gazing out at a stupendous mountain view of The Remarkables. The employees have been chosen from 1,200 who tried to get into Eco Seagate. (The company employs 45,000.) There are no age limits: The oldest racer in the sixth year of the event was 62.

This event, or social experiment, was former CEO Bill Watkins' pet project. He dreamed up Eco Seagate as a way to break down barriers, boost confidence, and make staffers better team players. "Some of you will learn about teamwork because you have a great team," he says.

Watkins knows about disastrous teams. When Seagate acquired his employer, Conner Peripherals, in 1996, hostility reigned as staffers jockeyed to guard their turf. "Corporate culture is the story of the company," says Watkins. "Back then, Seagate had lots of great stories—about people getting fired. We needed to create a different culture—one that was open, honest, and encouraged people to work together."

Five days into the Seagate team-building program, 40 teams are dropped on an island in the middle of Lake Wakatipu between 6 and 7 a.m. A conch sounds, and the teams race to their kayaks and paddle 1.5 miles to shore. Then, navigating with a compass, they trek over 4.3 miles of hilly terrain, mountain-bike 10.5 miles of rocks and ruts, then rappel 160 feet into a canyon for a hypothermic swim and hike.

Here's the reality: a ragged day of pain and suffering. After a slow start on the kayak, Five Elements runs past 20 teams on the hike, jumps on bikes, and pedals like mad to second place. "This pace is feeling a little leisurely," jokes Stuart Brown, 44, a program manager from Shakopee, Minnesota. Everyone laughs and speeds up. But an hour later they start to climb the big hill.

"Help me!" Engineer Kebiao Yuan, 41, is straddling his bike, so cramped he can't move. His teammates lift his leg over the bike, rub his knotted muscles, and squeeze a pack of sickeningly sweet energy gel into his mouth. Soon he's back on his machine, and Five Elements enters the final stretch of the bike leg. At the next transition point they ditch the bikes, run to the rim of a canyon, and rappel down. Then it's a 1.6-mile trek out, partly wading, partly swimming in 50-degree water. Too cold to feel anything at all, Five Elements crosses the finish line five hours and 51 minutes after the start—27 minutes after the first-place team, Fuel, and four hours before the stragglers.

At the finish line they find portable showers, dry clothes, and tables laden with grilled meats and salads. Miraculously, all 40 teams make it, carrying their silly kiwi birds.

Seagate Technology believes that the costs of its New Zealand extravaganza team-building program is worth the benefits. The thinking is that the team building leads to a more committed workforce, knowing and trusting colleagues more, and being motivated to help the company achieve its goal.

Sources: Adapted from Sarah Max, "Seagate's Morale-athon," *BusinessWeek*, April 3, 2006, pp. 110–111; www.seagate.com (accessed June 6, 2006); and "Company Snapshot," *Seagate.com*, www.seagate.com/www/en-us/about/investor_relations/company_information/company_snapshot (accessed June 16, 2009).

Ethics Training

While many organizations have codes of ethics, with few exceptions ethics training, particularly organizationwide effort, is a relatively recent development. While the content and methodology of ethics programs vary widely, most may be categorized as focusing on one or both of two general objectives: (1) developing employee awareness of business ethics and (2) focusing on specific ethical issues with which the employee may come in contact. By helping to develop employee awareness of ethical issues in decision making, organizations hope to:[59]

- Enable recognition of ethical components of a decision.
- Legitimize ethics as part of the decision-making process.

- Avoid variability in decision making caused by lack of norms or awareness of rules.
- Avoid confusion as to who is responsible for misdeeds.
- Provide decision-making frameworks for analyzing ethical choices.

The second objective, that of focusing on relevant ethical issues with which employees may be faced, may include dealing with conflict-of-interest situations, white-collar crime, or discharging one's job responsibilities within the context of local, state, and federal requirements. This latter category could encompass such diverse activities as employee safety, equal employment opportunity issues, product marketing claims, environmental protection, and sexual harassment.

Formal ethics training, particularly programs involving most or all levels within the organization, is too recent a phenomenon to draw conclusions about its effectiveness. It is clear, however, that however effective it may be, ethics training is not a cure-all.

Mentorship Programs

Formal mentorship programs represent an even more recent and less frequently used organizational change technique than ethics training. A mentor is a knowledgeable individual who is committed to providing support to other, usually junior, organizational members.[60] Mentoring programs help individuals develop by providing specific job instruction, disseminating organizational cultural norms and values, dispelling organizational myths, and generally transferring knowledge gained through years of being part of the organization. Mentoring relationships, of course, are not new; mentors and "mentees" have existed as long as have formal organizations. Formalizing such relationships, however, is a very new and largely unexplored concept.

A number of positive benefits to the organization have been identified as outcomes of mentoring programs.[61] These include (1) early identification of talent that might otherwise go unnoticed, (2) sensing by mentors of employee attitudes and morale, and (3) transmission of informal organizational expectations (corporate culture). Organizational benefits of mentoring can accrue at all levels of the company, up to and including the individual(s) being groomed for the presidency.

There are some caveats to keep in mind, however. Formalized mentor–mentee relationships should always be voluntary for both parties. And companies should not assume that every long-term employee who has the interest would make a good mentor. In this regard, some individuals should be discouraged from assuming this role, and it is a good idea for all prospective mentors to receive training or coaching on effective mentoring relationships. Finally, organizations must understand that not everything passed from mentors to mentees will be factually correct or organizationally desirable. The potential payoffs, however, both in terms of individual and organizational change, make such programs worth considering.

Introspection Development

Dealing with constant change, both planned and unplanned, is a significant facet in a growing number of work situations. Companies are learning that taking time for reflection can be an invaluable activity for many organizational members. Major companies, such as Aetna, PepsiCo, and AT&T, are incorporating various forms of introspection training into their management change programs. AT&T, for example, devotes approximately 20 percent of its annual executive training budget to courses that encourage development of introspection. Introspection involves a close examination of one's own thoughts and feelings. Some companies, such as AT&T, support specific training courses. Others, like Patagonia, the outdoor sportswear company, allow employees to take periodic sabbaticals to renew and recharge themselves. Regardless of the approach, successful introspection has a number of goals:[62]

1. *Developing objectivity*. Successful reflection requires objectively seeking and processing information about oneself.
2. *Learning*. Learning must result from introspection, not just once, but continually. The objective is to create a process that filters experiences through reflection to produce better decisions.
3. *Improving self-confidence*. Reflection is designed to help individuals become comfortable with their weaknesses as well as their strengths.
4. *Increased sense of personal responsibility* and willingness to look internally rather than projecting blame for negative outcomes externally.
5. Successful introspection should create an *increased tolerance for ambiguity and paradox,* attributes that are becoming virtual requirements for mastering today's organizational environments.
6. *Action taking*. Introspection does not mean we have to change, but it should enable us to more easily change when it is appropriate to do so.
7. *Achieving a balance in life*. Helping to sort out priorities in the conflict between work demands and one's nonwork life is an important payoff of successful introspection.
8. Introspection should open an individual's access to *creativity and intuition,* thus fostering innovation and higher-quality nonprogrammed decision making.
9. The ultimate goal is *egolessness,* or the ability to transcend selfish concerns. This translates into decision making centered on what is best for the unit, not what is most ego enhancing.

Introspection programs that allow time for examining oneself need to be scientifically studied. Instead of relying on common sense that self-examination sounds good, rigorous study of these types of programs is long overdue. While their adherents are strong believers, well-designed evaluation studies are lacking, and until more results are available, this type of change will be attempted only occasionally.

Multifaceted Approaches

Not all organizational change interventions fit neatly into one category or approach. Sometimes techniques from different categories may be used together in a multifaceted approach to development. As an example, a silver-mining company combined team building (a human asset approach) and MBO (a structural approach).[63] The program was aimed at improving productivity and safety in the mine.

Other OD interventions may be considered multifaceted because the technique used is itself so broad-based that it cuts across two or even all three categories. Currently, one such program is total quality management, or TQM. TQM is both a philosophy and system of management that, using statistical process control and group problem-solving processes, places the greatest priority on attaining high standards for quality and continuous improvement. Organizations such as IBM, Xerox, Ford, Johnson & Johnson, and Motorola have adopted some form of total quality management. Motorola's program, for example, focuses on achieving "Six Sigma quality." **Six Sigma** is a statistical measure that expresses how close a product comes to its quality goal. One sigma means approximately 68 percent of products reached the quality objective; three sigma means 99.7 percent have reached the goal; six sigma is 99.999997 percent perfect, or only 3.4 defects per 1 million parts.

Six Sigma
Powerful statistical tools and techniques to improve quality in manufacturing, human resource processes, and other operations within organizations.

There are many different versions of TQM. In actual operation, one company's TQM program may appear quite different from another company's. Despite large operational differences, the major components of most TQM programs are similar. One researcher describes key TQM components in the following manner:[64]

Goal: The goal of TQM is to establish quality as a dominant organizational priority, vital for long-term effectiveness.

Definition of quality: Quality is satisfying the customer. All quality improvements must begin with an understanding of customer needs and perceptions.

Nature of the environment: TQM changes the boundaries between the organization and its environment. Entities formerly considered part of the environment (suppliers, customers) are now considered part of organizational processes.

Role of management: Management's role is to create a system that can produce quality results; managers and the system are responsible for poor quality.

Role of employees: Employees are empowered to make decisions and take necessary steps to improve quality within the system designed by management. Additional training provides needed skills for this broader role.

Structural rationality: The organization is restructured as a set of horizontal processes that start with suppliers and end with customers. Teams are organized around processes to facilitate task accomplishment.

Philosophy toward change: Change, continuous improvement, and learning are necessary. Ideally, all organizational members are motivated toward constant improvement.

TQM represents one of the most comprehensive and far-reaching approaches to improving effectiveness. There are very few current or near-future organizational members who have not been or will not be affected in some way by TQM.

Appreciative Inquiry

The bulk of organizational change and development programs start any diagnosis with an emphasis on identifying problems, shortfalls, or deficiencies, such as sexual harassment problems, excessive costs or resource limits, and not meeting a previously established performance goal. This "deficit thinking" may cause organizations to overlook opportunities.[65] **Appreciative inquiry** (AI) is a method of focusing on *positive* aspects or potential opportunities.[66] AI proposes that organizations and individuals are creative enough to develop programs, relationships, and behaviors that address success, personal growth, and fulfillment. It searches for and attempts to bring out the best in people, the organization, and the external environment. AI involves the art and practice of asking probing questions that can strengthen an individual's or an organization's ability to anticipate, seize, and initiate positive potential.[67]

appreciative inquiry
A method of focusing on positive or potential opportunities. An approach that asks questions and requires answers in an attempt to seize and improve upon an organization's potential.

AI is described in a variety of ways:

- A methodology that takes the idea of the social construction of reality by using metaphors and narratives.
- A radically affirmative approach to change that lets go of problem-based management.
- A model of much-needed participatory science.

Exhibit 17.4 outlines what is referred to as the 4-D framework of appreciative inquiry. Pioneering work on refining this framework was conducted by consulting firm Marge Schiller and Associates in Avon Corporation in Mexico.[68]

The 4-D process begins with discovering or appreciating what is the "best" in the present situation being examined. This could involve determining what employees like about their work, unit, or colleagues. As this discussion evolves, the next "D" emerges,

EXHIBIT 17.4
4-D Framework for Appreciative Inquiry

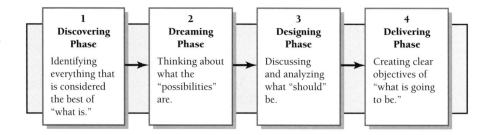

1 Discovering Phase	**2 Dreaming Phase**	**3 Designing Phase**	**4 Delivering Phase**
Identifying everything that is considered the best of "what is."	Thinking about what the "possibilities" are.	Discussing and analyzing what "should" be.	Creating clear objectives of "what is going to be."

dreaming. What would make the work, unit, or colleagues ideal? Talking about ideals and the value of being in an ideal situation, the process shifts to designing or exchanging thoughts and eventually formulating and constructing with others a collective model of what an ideal group, team, or work setting would be in terms of schedules, expectations, roles, responsibilities, rewards, and goals.

Once the ideal model is conceptualized, discussed, and modified, the focus shifts to the fourth "D," delivering. The idea now is to establish a plan, execution strategy, and set of goals for the situation. Instead of the "ideal," the theme is now the real situation or setting.[69]

A key issue regarding AI and change is: If one wants to inspire, mobilize, and sustain motivation, what is the best way—by focusing on problems, shortfalls, or deficits or by addressing opportunities to build on strengths? AI is positioned to probe and ask about peak, positive events, experiences, and models.

Avon Mexico used AI to develop opportunities for increasing the number of women in top management positions. A team of employees and consultants collected stories that described, analyzed, and portrayed gender equality and fairness at Avon Mexico. These stories were used as the basis of two-day training programs for Avon Mexico employees to devise additional programs and approaches for accomplishing gender equality. The AI process of discovery, dreaming, designing, and delivering served as the change approach used at Avon Mexico. Since the AI training approach was used, the company won the Catalyst Award for gender equality and more women are now in senior positions at Avon Mexico.[70]

Impediments and Limiting Conditions

The selection of any change method should be based on diagnosis of the problem, but the choice is tempered by certain conditions that exist at the time. Scholars identify three sources of influence on the outcome of management change programs that can be generalized to cover the entire range of interventions: leadership climate, formal organization, and organizational culture.

Leadership Climate

leadership climate
The nature of the work environment in an organization that results from the leadership style and administrative practices of managers.

The nature of the work environment that results from the leadership style and administrative practices of managers is termed the **leadership climate**. It can greatly affect a program. Any program that lacks management's support and commitment has only a slim chance of success.[71] The style of leadership may itself be the subject of change. For example, total quality management (TQM) attempts to move managers toward a certain style—open, supportive, and group centered. But participants may be unable to adopt such styles if the styles aren't compatible with their own manager's style.[72] One approach to leadership—transformational leadership—has as its basis a vision of transformation or change. Leadership approaches are presented in Chapter 15.

Formal Organization

formal organization
The recognized and sanctioned structure, policies, and rules of a unit or institution.

The **formal organization** includes the philosophy and policies of top management, as well as legal precedent, organizational structure, and the systems of control. Of course, each of these sources of impact may itself be the focus of a change effort. The important point is that a change in one must be compatible with all of the others.[73] It may be possible to design organizations that not only facilitate change, but actually welcome change.[74]

Organizational Culture

organizational culture
The pervasive system of values, beliefs, and norms that exists in any organization. The organizational culture can encourage or discourage effectiveness, depending on the nature of the values, beliefs, and norms.

Organizational culture refers to the pattern of beliefs resulting from group norms, values, and informal activities.[75] The impact of traditional behavior that's sanctioned by group norms, but not formally acknowledged, was first documented in the Hawthorne studies. A proposed change in work methods or the installation of an automated device can run counter to the expectations and attitudes of the work group, and, if such is the case, the selected method must be one that anticipates and manages the resulting resistance.[76]

Implementing a method that doesn't consider the constraints imposed by prevailing conditions within the present organization may, of course, amplify the problem that triggered the process. If management undertakes change in this way, the potential for subsequent problems is greater than would ordinarily be expected. Taken together, the prevailing conditions constitute the climate for change, and they can be positive or negative. You may recall from Case 16.1 Ford's 1966 announcement of a commercially viable electric car within 10 years.[77] Over 40 years later, the company has yet to market such a vehicle. In contrast, NASA moved from its first manned space mission to a successful lunar landing in just over eight years.[78] While technological issues and resource availability may partially explain these contrasting outcomes, differing organizational cultures may be the leading reason for NASA's success and Ford's delay.

Implementing the Method

The implementation of the change method has two dimensions: timing and scope. *Timing* refers to the selection of the appropriate time at which to initiate the intervention. *Scope* refers to the selection of the appropriate scale. Timing depends on a number of factors, particularly the organization's operating cycle and the groundwork preceding the program. Certainly, if a program is of considerable magnitude, it's desirable that it not compete with day-to-day operations; thus, the change might well be implemented during a slack period. On the other hand, if the program is critical to the organization's survival, then immediate implementation is in order. The scope of the program depends on the strategy. The program may be implemented throughout the organization. Or it may be phased into the organization level by level or department by department. The optimum strategy uses a phased approach, which limits the scope but provides feedback for each subsequent implementation.

The intervention that's finally selected is usually not implemented on a grand scale. Rather, it's implemented on a small scale in various units throughout the organization. For example, an MBO program can be implemented in one unit or at one level at a time. The objective is to experiment with the intervention (that is, to test the validity of the diagnosed solution). As management learns from each successive implementation, the total program is strengthened. Not even the most detailed planning can anticipate all the consequences of implementing a particular intervention. Thus, it's necessary to experiment and search for new information that can bear on the program.

As the experimental attempts provide positive signals that the program is proceeding as planned, there's reinforcement effect. Personnel will be encouraged to accept the change required of them and to enlarge their own efforts' scope. Acceptance of the change is facilitated by its positive results.

Evaluating Program Effectiveness

Bringing about effective change represents an expenditure of organizational resources in exchange for some desired result. The resources take the form of money and time that have alternative uses. The result is in the form of increased organizational effectiveness: production, efficiency, and satisfaction in the short run; adaptiveness and flexibility in the intermediate run; survival in the long run. Accordingly, some provision must be made to evaluate the program in terms of expenditures and results. In addition to providing information to evaluate a specific organizational change effort, evaluation provides a literature that can be accessed by others who are deciding whether to undertake OD. Reviews of the relative efficacy of interventions appear regularly.[79] The evaluation phase has two problems to overcome: obtaining data that measure the desired results and determining the expected trend of improvement over time.

The acquisition of information that measures the sought-after result is the easier problem to solve, although it certainly doesn't lend itself to naive solutions. The stimulus for change is the deterioration of effectiveness criteria that management has traced to structural and behavioral causes. The criteria may be any number of effectiveness indicators, including profit, sales volume, absenteeism, turnover, scrappage, or costs. The major source of feedback for those variables is the organization's information system. But if the change includes the expectation that employee satisfaction must be improved, the usual sources of information are limited, if not invalid. It's quite possible for a change to induce increased production at the expense of declining employee satisfaction. Thus, if the manager relies on the naive assumption that production and satisfaction are directly related, the change may be incorrectly judged successful when cost and profit improve.[80]

To avoid the danger of overreliance on production data, the manager can generate ad hoc information that measures employee satisfaction. The benchmark for evaluation would be available if an attitude survey was used in the diagnosis phase. The definition of *acceptable improvement* is difficult when evaluating attitudinal data, since the matter of how much more positive employees' attitudes should be is quite different from the matter of how much more productive they should be. Nevertheless, for a complete analysis of results, attitudinal measurements must be combined with production and other effectiveness measurements.

In a practical sense, a program's effectiveness can't be evaluated if objectives haven't been established before it's implemented. A program undertaken to make the organization "a better place to work" or to develop the "full potential of the employees" can't be evaluated. If, on the other hand, measurable criteria that are valid indicators of "better places to work" and "full employee potential" are collected during the diagnostic phase and subsequently tracked as the program is undertaken, bases for evaluation exist. A considerable body of literature describes methods of evaluation, and managers of change programs should consult it for guidance in program evaluation.

Generally, an evaluation model would follow the six steps of evaluative research:

1. Determining the objectives of the program.
2. Describing the activities undertaken to achieve the objectives.

3. Measuring the effects of the program.

4. Establishing baseline points against which changes can be compared.

5. Controlling extraneous factors, preferably through use of a control group.

6. Detecting unanticipated consequences.

Application of these six steps isn't always possible. For example, managers don't always specify objectives in precise terms, and control groups may be difficult to establish. Nevertheless, the difficulties of evaluation shouldn't discourage attempts to evaluate.

How Effective Are Change Interventions?

The critical test of alternative change interventions is whether they help to improve organizational effectiveness. This can be determined only through research. There's a rather long history of such research. The current practice appears to have shifted the focus from interventions directed at informal components to those directed at formal components. In particular, structural interventions have been the most widely used method as reported in the literature.[81] The increasing use of structure and job targets reflects the increasing importance of production and efficiency criteria of organizational effectiveness, the specific targets of such interventions. The priority of these criteria reflects the importance of external competitive pressures that emphasize quantity, quality, and cost improvements. Structural interventions target these variables for change, whereas human asset interventions target somewhat more nebulous but nonetheless important variables such as attitudes, problem-solving skills, motivation, openness, and trust. It's also possible that interventions that attempt to change individual and group behavior have waned in popularity because it's difficult to evaluate them through rigorous evaluative research designs.[82]

Research reviews of the record-of-change efforts conclude that multimethod approaches have better success than single-method ones. Nicholas, for example, compared effects of sensitivity training, team building, job enrichment, and job redesign and concluded that no one method is successful in all instances (an expected conclusion).[83] But he also found that significant changes occur when several methods combine. One such combination includes three discrete steps involving all levels of the organization. The three steps are (1) all employees participate in goal setting, decision making, and job redesign, (2) employee collaboration is developed through team building, and (3) the organizational structure is reorganized to accommodate the new levels of participation and collaboration. Application of these three steps can go a long way toward meeting some arguments against specific methods. The overriding managerial concern is transfer of learning to the work environment.[84] Only under these circumstances can methods be considered effective.

Management Pointer

STEPS TO TAKE WHEN MANAGING CHANGE

A manager confronted with the need to plan and implement change would be well advised to consider the following points:

1. Management and all those involved must have high and visible commitment to the effort.

2. People who are involved need to have advance information that enables them to know what is to happen and why they are to do what they are to do.

3. The effort (especially the evaluation and reward systems) must be connected to other parts of the organization.

4. The effort needs to be directed by line managers and assisted by a change agent if necessary.

5. The effort must be based on good diagnosis and must be consistent with the conditions in the organization.

6. Management must remain committed to the effort throughout all its steps, from diagnosis through implementation and evaluation.

7. Evaluation is essential and must consist of more than asking people how they felt about the effort.

8. People must see clearly the relationship between the effort and the organization's mission and goals.

9. The change agent, if used, must be clearly competent.

Guidelines for Managing Change

What then can managers do when they recognize the need to change their organization? Although no absolute guarantees can ensure success in every case, the accumulated experience of people involved with organizational change offers some guidelines. The Management Pointer, "Steps to Take When Managing Change," identifies the important points a manager should consider when contemplating a major organizational change.

Organizational change is a significant undertaking that managers should go about in a systematic way. The model for managing change offers a systematic process for bringing about organizational effectiveness.

Summary of Key Points

- The need to consider organizational change arises from changes in the internal and external environment. Changes in input, output, technological, and scientific subenvironments may indicate the need to consider the feasibility of a long-term, systematically managed program for changing the structure, process, and behavior of the organization. Even in the absence of environmental changes, organizational processes and behavior may become dysfunctional for achieving organizational effectiveness.

- The diagnosis of present and potential problems involves the collection of information that reflects the level of organizational effectiveness. Data that measure the current state of production, efficiency, satisfaction, adaptiveness, and flexibility must be gathered and analyzed. The purpose of diagnosis is to trace the causes of the problem. In addition to serving as the base for problem identification, the diagnostic data also establish the basis for subsequent evaluation.

- To diagnose the problem, managers can consider these analytical questions:

  1. What is the problem as distinct from its symptoms?
  2. What must be changed to resolve the problem?
  3. What outcomes are expected, and how will these outcomes be measured?

  The managerial response to these questions should be stated in terms of criteria that reflect organizational effectiveness. Measurable outcomes such as production, efficiency, satisfaction, adaptiveness, and flexibility must be linked to skill, structural, task and technological, and human resource changes necessitated by problem identification.

- Through diagnosis, management associates the problem with structural, task and technological, and human asset causes and selects the appropriate intervention. If employee participation is inappropriate because the necessary preconditions don't exist, management must unilaterally define the problem and select the appropriate method. Whatever the sources of the problem, the intervention must include provision for learning principles.

- The last step of the process is the evaluation procedure. The ideal situation would be to structure the procedure in the manner of an experimental design. That is, the end results should be operationally defined, and measurements should be taken, before and after, both in the organization undergoing change and in a second organization (the control group). If the scope of the program is limited to a subunit, a second subunit could serve as a control group. An evaluation not only enables management to account for its use of resources but also provides feedback. Based on this feedback, corrections can be made in the implementation phase.

YOU BE THE JUDGE COMMENT

RESISTANCE TO CHANGE?

Should you immediately call Jason in to determine what is going on? No, a better approach is to check with others in the unit to determine if Hannah is accurate in her analysis, while also listening to determine the opinions about the reward and evaluation system changes. By immediately stepping in and facing Jason with accusations made by his colleague, you're moving too quickly.

The problem between Jason and Hannah may have nothing to do with the accusations being made. Is this typical behavior for Jason? Is Hannah a meddler or a gossip? Is Hannah looking out for the best interest of the company? What do other team members say or indicate about the change? Your first steps should be diagnostic before deciding how to proceed next. Diagnose, listen, and then respond if it is necessary to take action.

Review and Discussion Questions

1. Discuss the 4-D framework used in conducting appreciative inquiry. How is it different from a traditional diagnosis approach used in organizational change?

2. Newly formed organizational units, project teams, or task forces often have problems or characteristics that must be overcome if the groups are to perform effectively. What are they?

3. Why is diagnosing a situation sometimes bypassed or avoided by managers?

4. Explain why programs to bring about significant change often must use more than one form of intervention.

5. As a manager, what ethical dilemmas might you face when instructed to downsize your department by one-third in order to increase the organization's long-run chance of survival?

6. Describe the relationship among the steps of the change model depicted in this chapter and the process of unfreezing–movement–refreezing. Which steps of the model are related to which elements of the relearning process?

7. How would you go about designing a training program that would cause managers in a small firm to recognize the need to change the way they manage if their industry has become more competitive in recent years?

8. How do employees resist change and what can managers do about overt and covert resistance?

9. When was the last time you changed a specific behavior (e.g., began to exercise, went on a diet, studied a new subject)? How successful were you in achieving and sustaining the change? Why?

10. Explain why organizational and individual change programs should be evaluated and why such an evaluation is so difficult to do.

Now how much do you know about organizational change and innovation?

6. Managerial actions that attempt to improve effectiveness by introducing change through formal policies and procedures are referred to as _____ approaches to change.
   a. structural
   b. policy
   c. people
   d. formal

7. Reengineering as a change strategy consists of streamlining, integrating, and _____.
   a. finalizing
   b. evaluating
   c. transforming
   d. producing

8. The concept of intervention in a change program refers to entering an organization unit, or project, for the purpose of helping to improve its _____.
   a. management
   b. leadership
   c. philosophy
   d. effectiveness

9. The concept of unfreezing old learning, instilling new learning, and refreezing the new learning was introduced by _____.
   a. Maslow
   b. Herzberg
   c. Fiedler
   d. Lewin

10. Peter Drucker introduced a concept that focuses on proactive management that is called _____.
    a. statistical process control
    b. management by objectives
    c. engineering reversal
    d. PERT

REALITY CHECK ANSWERS

Before		After	
1. *c* 2. *d* 3. *b* 4. *b* 5. *b*		6. *a* 7. *c* 8. *d* 9. *d* 10. *b*	
Number Correct		Number Correct	

Exercise 17.1: *Organization Development at J. P. Hunt*

Objective

To experience an OD technique—in this case the use of survey feedback—to diagnose strengths and weaknesses and develop an action plan.

Starting the Exercise

Set up four to eight members for the one-hour exercise. The groups should be separated from each other and asked to converse only with members of their own group. Each person should read the following:

J. P. Hunt department stores is a large retail merchandising outlet located in Boston. The company sells an entire range of retail goods (e.g., appliances, fashions, furniture, and so on) and has a large downtown store plus six branch stores in various suburban areas.

Similar to most retail stores in the area, employee turnover is high (i.e., 40 to 45 percent annually). In the credit and accounts receivable department, located in the downtown store, turnover is particularly high at both the supervisor and subordinate levels, approaching 75 percent annually. The department employs approximately 150 people, 70 percent of whom are female.

Due to rising hiring and training costs brought on by the high turnover, top department management began a turnover analysis and reduction program.

As a first step, a local management consulting firm was contracted to conduct a survey of department employees. Using primarily questionnaires, the consulting firm collected survey data from over 95 percent of the department's employees. The results are shown in Exhibit 17.5, by organizational level, along with industry norms developed by the consulting firm in comparative retail organizations.

The Procedure

1. Individually, each group member should analyze the data in the exhibit and attempt to identify and diagnose department strengths and problem areas.

2. As a group, the members should repeat step 1 above. In addition, suggestions for resolving the problems and an action plan for feedback to the department should be developed.

EXHIBIT 17.5 Survey Results for J. P. Hunt Department Store: Credit and Accounts Receivable Department

Variable	Survey Results*			Industry Norms*		
	Managers	Supervisors	Nonsupervisors	Managers	Supervisors	Nonsupervisors
Satisfaction and rewards						
Pay	3.30	1.73	2.48	3.31	2.97	2.89
Supervision	3.70	2.42	3.05	3.64	3.58	3.21
Promotion	3.40	2.28	2.76	3.38	3.25	3.23
Co-workers	3.92	3.90	3.72	3.95	3.76	3.43
Work	3.98	2.81	3.15	3.93	3.68	3.52
Performance–to–intrinsic rewards	4.07	3.15	3.20	4.15	3.85	3.81
Performance–to–extrinsic rewards	3.67	2.71	2.70	3.87	3.81	3.76
Supervisory behavior						
Initiating structure	3.42	3.97	3.90	3.40	3.51	3.48
Consideration	3.63	3.09	3.18	3.77	3.72	3.68
Positive rewards	3.99	2.93	3.02	4.24	3.95	3.91
Punitive rewards	3.01	3.61	3.50	2.81	2.91	3.08
Job characteristics						
Autonomy	4.13	4.22	3.80	4.20	4.00	3.87
Feedback	3.88	3.81	3.68	3.87	3.70	3.70
Variety	3.67	3.35	3.22	3.62	3.21	2.62
Challenge	4.13	4.03	3.03	4.10	3.64	3.58
Organizational practices						
Role ambiguity	2.70	2.91	3.34	2.60	2.40	2.20
Role conflict	2.87	3.69	2.94	2.83	3.12	3.02
Job pressure	3.14	4.04	3.23	2.66	2.68	2.72
Performance evaluation process	3.77	3.35	3.19	3.92	3.70	3.62
Worker cooperation	3.67	3.94	3.87	3.65	3.62	3.35
Work flow planning	3.88	2.62	2.95	4.20	3.80	3.76

*The values are scored from 1, very low, to 5, very high.

Case 17.1: *Nucor Corporation: Innovation, Change, and Motivation*

It was about 2 p.m. when three Nucor Corp. electricians got the call from their colleagues at the Hickman, Arkansas, plant. It was bad news: Hickman's electrical grid had failed. For a minimill steelmaker like Nucor, which melts scrap steel from autos, dishwashers, mobile homes, and the like in an electric arc furnace to make new steel, there's little that could be worse. The trio immediately dropped what they were doing and headed to the plant. Malcolm McDonald, an electrician from the Decatur, Alabama, mill, was in Indiana visiting another facility. He drove down, arriving at 9 o'clock that night. Les Hart and Bryson Trumble, from Nucor's facility in Hertford County, North Carolina, boarded a plane that landed in Memphis at 11 p.m. Then they drove two hours to the troubled plant.

No supervisor had asked them to make the trip, and no one had to. They went on their own. Camping out in the electrical substation with the Hickman staff, the team worked 20-hour shifts to get the plant up and running again in three days instead of the anticipated full week. There wasn't any direct financial incentive for them to blow their weekends, no extra money in their next paycheck, but for the company their contribution was huge. Hickman went on to post a first-quarter record for tons of steel shipped.

What's most amazing about this story is that at Nucor it's not considered particularly remarkable. "It could have easily been a Hickman operator going to help the Crawfordsville [Ind.] mill," says Executive Vice President John J. Ferriola, who oversees the Hickman plant and seven others. "It happens daily."

In an industry as Rust Belt as they come, Nucor has nurtured one of the most dynamic and engaged workforces around. The 21,700 nonunion employees at the company, based in Charlotte, North Carolina, don't see themselves as worker bees waiting for instructions from above. Nucor's flattened hierarchy and emphasis on pushing power to the front line lead its employees to adopt the mindset of owner-operators. It's a profitable formula: Nucor's 387 percent return to shareholders over five years handily beat almost all other companies in the Standard & Poor's 500 stock index, including new economy icons Amazon.com, Starbucks, and eBay. And the company has become more profitable as it has grown: Margins, which were 7 percent in 2000, reached 17 percent in 2008.

Nucor gained renown in the late 1980s for its radical pay practices, which base the vast majority of most workers' income on their performance. This was a major, dramatic change in pay systems at the time. An upstart nipping at the heels of the integrated steel giants, Nucor had a close-knit culture that was the natural outgrowth of its underdog identity. Legendary leader F. Kenneth Iverson's radical insight was: Employees, even hourly clock-punchers, will make an extraordinary effort if you reward them richly, treat them with respect, and give them real power.

Nucor is an upstart no more, and the untold story of how it has clung to that core philosophy even as it has grown into the largest steel company in the United States is in many ways as compelling as the celebrated tale of its brash youth. Iverson retired in 1999. Under CEO Daniel R. DiMicco, a 23-year veteran, Nucor has expanded to 22 plants while managing to instill its unique culture in all of the facilities it has bought, an achievement that makes him a more than worthy successor to Iverson.

Nucor's performance, even in a depressed economy, has been nothing less than sensational. It has grown into a company with 2008 sales of $23.6 billion, up from $4.6 billion when DiMicco took over in 2000. In 2008 net income was $1.8 billion, up from $311 million in 2000. "In terms of a business model," says Louis L. Schorsch, president and CEO of Nucor rival Mittal Steel USA, "They've won in this part of the world."

At Nucor, managing and leading is about an unblinking focus on the people on the front line of the business. It's about talking to them, listening to them, taking a risk on their ideas, and accepting the occasional failure. It's a culture built in part with symbolic gestures. Every year, for example, every employee's name goes on the cover of the annual report. And, like Iverson before him, DiMicco flies commercial, manages without an executive parking space, and really does make the coffee in the office when he takes the last cup. Although he has an Ivy League pedigree, including degrees from Brown

University and the University of Pennsylvania, DiMicco retains the plain-talking style of a guy raised in a middle-class family in Mt. Kisco, New York. Only 65 people—yes, 65—work alongside him at headquarters.

At times, workers and managers exhibit a level of passion for the company that can border on the bizarre. Executive Vice President Joseph A. Rutkowski, an engineer who came up through the mills, speaks of Nucor as a "magic" place, representing the best of American rebelliousness. He says, "We epitomize how people should think, should be."

Compared with other U.S. companies, pay disparities are modest at Nucor. Today, the typical CEO makes more than 400 times what a factory worker takes home. Last year, Nucor's chief executive collected a salary and bonus close to one quarter of that average. DiMicco did well by any reasonable standard, with a total 2008 compensation of $5.24 million, but that's because Nucor is doing well. Company returns are 13 percent higher than the industry average. When things are bad, DiMicco suffers, too. In 2003, as the company was dealing with an industry downturn and barely squeaked out a profit, DiMicco made $1.4 million. He gets few stock options, and most of his restricted stock and other longer-term bonuses don't materialize if the company doesn't beat the competition and outpace a sample group of other high-performing companies for good measure. Paul Hodgson, senior research associate at the Corporate Library, an organization that researches corporate governance issues, and an expert in the field who rarely has anything good to say about CEO compensation, calls Nucor's system a "best practice." Adds Hodgson: "Not too many companies get my vote of approval."

Executive pay is geared toward team building. The bonus of a plant manager, a department manager's boss, depends on the entire corporation's return on equity. So there's no glory in winning at your own plant if the others are failing. When Ferriola became general manager of Nucor's Vulcraft plant in Grapeland, Texas, in 1995, he remembers he wasn't in the job two days before he received calls from every other general manager in the Vulcraft division offering to help however they could. (Vulcraft manufactures the steel joists and decks that hold up the ceilings of shopping centers and other buildings.)

"It wasn't idle politeness. I took them up on it," says Ferriola. And they wanted him to, he notes. "My performance impacted their paycheck."

This high-stakes teamwork can be the hardest thing for a newly acquired plant to get used to. David Hutchins, a frontline supervisor or "lead man" in the rolling mill at Nucor's first big acquisition, its Auburn, New York, plant, describes the old way of thinking. The job of a rolling mill is to thin out the steel made in the hot mill furnace, preparing it to be cut into sheets. In the days before the Nucor acquisition, if the cutting backed up, Hutchins would just take a break. "We'd sit back, have a cup of coffee, and complain: "Those guys stink," he says. "At Nucor, we're not 'you guys' and 'us guys.' It's all of us guys. Wherever the bottleneck is, we go there, and everyone works on it."

As Nucor grows, existing facilities making products that overlap with those of acquired plants may need to find new businesses to branch into. So Nucor employees have to innovate themselves out of tough spots and into more profitable ones. Changes have to be made often to adapt to the environment. The Crawfordsville plant is among those that have felt some squeeze. It's famous as the place that pioneered the commercialization of the thin-strip casting of steel that made it possible for minimills such as Nucor to compete with the industry's old guard. But Crawfordsville is not on a large waterway, a disadvantage at a time of high fuel costs. As Nucor's oldest sheet mill, it can't make sheets as wide as many of Nucor's other mills, including a giant plant in Decatur acquired in 2002.

Questions

1. How would you describe the culture of Nucor?

2. Why is the type of executive pay practice at Nucor not found in many other companies?

3. If innovative solutions to problems are needed at Nucor, how do you think they will emerge? That is, will internal or external forces bring about the needed innovations? Explain.

Sources: Adapted from Nanette Byrnes and Michael Arndt, "The Art of Motivation," *BusinessWeek,* May 1, 2006, pp. 56–58; "CEO Compensation #258 Daniel R DiMicco," *Forbes.com,* April 22, 2009, www.forbes.com/lists/2009/12/best-boss-09_Daniel-R-DiMicco_2NN7.html; "Nucor 2008 Annual Report," February 26, 2009, http://media.corporate-ir.net/media_files/irol/10/107115/2008AnnualReport.pdf.

Quantitative and Qualitative Research Techniques for Studying Organizational Behavior and Management Practice

Sources of Knowledge about Organizations

The vast majority of the research reports and writing on organizations are contained in technical papers known as journals. Some of these journals, such as the *Academy of Management Review,* are devoted to topics of management and organization, while journals such as *Organizational Behavior and Human Decision Processes* focus largely on the results of empirical studies about organizational behavior, organizational psychology, and decision making. Such journals as the *Harvard Business Review* are general business journals, while the *American Sociological Review* and the *Journal of Applied Psychology* are general behavioral science journals. These business and behavioral science journals often contain articles of interest to students of management. Exhibit A.1 presents a selective list of journals.

The sources in Exhibit A.1 provide information, data, and discussion about what is occurring within and among organizations. This knowledge base provides managers with available research information that could prove useful in their own organizations or situations.

History as a Way of Knowing about Organizations

The oldest approach to the study of organizations is through the history of organizations, societies, and institutions. Throughout human history, people have joined with others to accomplish their goals, first in families, later in tribes and other more sophisticated political units. Ancient peoples constructed pyramids, temples, and ships; they

EXHIBIT A.1   **Selected Sources of Writing and Research on Organization**

1. *Academy of Management Journal*	14. *HR Focus*	27. *Management International Review*
2. *Academy of Management Review*	15. *HR Magazine*	28. *Management Review*
3. *Academy of Management Perspectives*	16. *Human Organization*	29. *Management Science*
4. *Academy of Management Learning and Education*	17. *Human Resource Management*	30. *Online Learning*
5. *Administrative Science Quarterly*	18. *Industrial and Labor Relations Review*	31. *Organizational Behavior and Human Decision Processes*
6. *Advanced Management Journal*	19. *Industrial Engineering*	32. *Organizational Dynamics*
7. *American Sociological Review*	20. *Industrial Management Review*	33. *Organizational Research Methods*
8. *Business Horizons*	21. *Journal of Applied Behavioral Science*	34. *Personnel Psychology*
9. *Business Management*	22. *Journal of Applied Psychology*	35. *Public Administration Review*
10. *California Management Review*	23. *Journal of Business*	36. *Sloan Management Review*
11. *Decision Sciences*	24. *Journal of International Business Studies*	37. *Strategic Management Journal*
12. *Fortune*	25. *Journal of Management*	38. *Training*
13. *Hospital and Health Services Administration*	26. *Journal of Management Studies*	39. *Training and Development*

created systems of government, farming, commerce, and warfare. For example, Greek historians tell us that it took 100,000 men and more than 20 years to build the Pyramid of Khufu in Egypt. It was almost as high as the Washington Monument and had a base that would cover eight football fields. Remember, these people had no construction equipment or computers. One thing they did have, though, was organization. While these "joint efforts" did not have formal names such as "XYZ Corporation," the idea of getting organized was quite widespread throughout early civilizations. The literature of the times refers to such managerial concepts as planning, staff assistance, division of labor, control, and leadership.[1]

The administration of the vast Roman Empire required the application of organization and management concepts. In fact, it has been said, "the real secret of the greatness of the Romans was their genius for organization."[2] The Romans used certain principles of organization to coordinate the diverse activities of the empire.

If judged by age alone, the Roman Catholic Church would have to be considered the most effective organization of all time. While its success is the result of many factors, one of these factors is certainly the effectiveness of its organization and management. For example, a hierarchy of authority, a territorial organization, specialization of activities by function, and use of the staff principle were integral parts of early church organization.

Finally, it is not surprising that some important concepts and practices in modern organizations can be traced to military organizations. This is because, like the church, military organizations were faced with problems of managing large, geographically dispersed groups. As did the church, military organizations adopted early the concept of staff as an advisory function for line personnel.

Knowledge of the history of organizations in earlier societies can be useful for the future manager. In fact, many of the early concepts and practices are being utilized successfully today. However, you may ask whether heavy reliance on the past is a good guide to the present and future. We shall see that time and organizational setting have much to do with what works in management.

Experience as a Way of Knowing about Organizations

Some of the earliest books on management and organizations were written by successful practitioners. Most of these individuals were business executives, and their writings focused on how it was for them during their time with one or more companies. They usually put forward certain general principles or practices that had worked well for them. Although using the writings and experiences of practitioners sounds practical, it has its drawbacks. Successful managers are susceptible to the same perceptual phenomena as each of us. Their accounts, therefore, are based on their own preconceptions and biases. No matter how objective their approaches, the accounts may not be entirely complete or accurate. In addition, the accounts also may be superficial since they often are after-the-fact reflections of situations in which, when the situations were occurring, the managers had little time to think about how or why they were doing something. As a result, the suggestions in such accounts often are oversimplified. Finally, as with history, what worked yesterday may not work today or tomorrow.[3]

Science as a Way of Knowing about Organizations

We have noted that a major interest in this book is the behavioral sciences, which have produced theory, research, and generalizations concerning the behavior and management of organizations. The interest of behavioral scientists in the problems of organizations is relatively new, becoming popular in the early 1950s, when an organization known as the Foundation for Research on Human Behavior was established. The objectives of this organization were to promote and support behavioral science research in business, government, and other types of organizations.

Many advocates of the scientific approach believe that practicing managers and teachers have accepted prevalent practices and principles without the benefit of scientific validation. They believe that scientific procedures should be used whenever possible to validate practice. Because of their work, many of the earlier practices and principles have been discounted or modified, and others have been validated.

Research in the Behavioral Sciences

Present research in the behavioral sciences is extremely varied with respect to the scope and methods used. One common thread among the various disciplines is the study of human behavior through the use of scientific procedures. Thus, it is necessary to examine the nature of science as it is applied to human behavior. Some critics believe that a science of human behavior is unattainable and that the scientific procedures used to gain knowledge in the physical sciences cannot be adapted to the study of humans, especially humans in organizations.

The authors do not intend to become involved in these arguments. However, we believe that the scientific approach is applicable to management and organizational studies.[4] Furthermore, as we have already pointed out, means other than scientific procedures have provided important knowledge concerning people in organizations.

The manager of the future will draw from the behavioral sciences just as the physician draws from the biological sciences. The manager must know what to expect from the behavioral sciences, their strengths and weaknesses, just as the physician must know what to expect from bacteriology and how it can serve as a diagnostic tool.

However, the manager, like the physician, is a practitioner. He or she must make decisions in the present, whether or not science has all the answers, and certainly cannot wait until it finds them before acting.

The Scientific Approach

Most current philosophers of science define *science* in terms of what they consider to be its one universal and unique feature: *method*. The greatest advantage of the scientific approach is that it has one characteristic not found in any other method of attaining knowledge: *self-correction*.[5] The scientific approach is an objective, systematic, and controlled process with built-in checks all along the way to knowledge. These checks control and verify the scientist's activities and conclusions to enable the attainment of knowledge independent of the scientist's own biases and preconceptions.

Most scientists agree that there is no single scientific method. Instead, scientists can and do use several methods. Thus, it probably makes more sense to say that there is a scientific approach. Exhibit A.2 summarizes the major characteristics of this approach. While only an "ideal" science would exhibit all of them, they are nevertheless the hallmarks of the scientific approach. They exhibit the basic nature—objective, systematic, controlled—of the scientific approach, which enables others to have confidence in research results. What is important is the overall fundamental idea that the scientific approach is a controlled rational process.

Methods of Inquiry Used by Behavioral Scientists

How do behavioral scientists gain knowledge about the functioning of organizations?[6] Just as physical scientists have certain tools and methods for obtaining information, so do behavioral scientists. These usually are referred to as research designs. In broad terms, three basic designs are used by behavioral scientists: the case study, the field study, and the experiment.

EXHIBIT A.2   **Characteristics of the Scientific Approach**

1. *The procedures are public.* A scientific report contains a complete description of what was done to enable other researchers in the field to follow each step of the investigation as if they were actually present.

2. *The definitions are precise.* The procedures used, the variables measured, and how they were measured must be clearly stated. For example, if examining motivation among employees in a given plant, it would be necessary to define what is meant by motivation and how it was measured (for example, number of units produced, number of absences).

3. *The data collection is objective.* Objectivity is a key feature of the scientific approach. Bias in collecting and interpreting data has no place in science.

4. *The finding must be replicable.* This enables another interested researcher to test the results of a study by attempting to reproduce them.

5. *The approach is systematic and cumulative.* This relates to one of the underlying purposes of science, to develop a unified body of knowledge.

6. *The purposes are explanation, understanding, and prediction.* All scientists want to know "why" and "how." If they determine "why" and "how" and are able to provide proof, they can then predict the particular conditions under which specific events (human behavior in the case of behavioral sciences) will occur. Prediction is the ultimate objective of behavioral science as it is of all science.

Case Study

A case study attempts to examine numerous characteristics of one or more people, usually over an extended time period. For years, anthropologists have studied the customs and behavior of various groups by actually living among them. Some organizational researchers have done the same thing. They have worked and socialized with the groups of employees they were studying.[7] The reports on such investigations usually are in the form of a case study. For example, a sociologist might report the key factors and incidents that led to a strike by a group of blue-collar workers.

The chief limitations of the case-study approach for gaining knowledge about the functioning of organizations are:

1. Rarely can you find two cases that can be meaningfully compared in terms of essential characteristics. In other words, in another firm of another size, the same factors might not have resulted in a strike.
2. Rarely can case studies be repeated or their findings verified.
3. The significance of the findings is left to the subjective interpretation of the researcher. Like the practitioner, the researcher attempts to describe reality, but it is reality as perceived by one person (or a very small group). The researcher has training, biases, and preconceptions that inadvertently can distort the report. A psychologist might give an entirely different view of a group of blue-collar workers than would be given by a sociologist.
4. Since the results of a case study are based on a sample of one, the ability to generalize from them may be limited.[8]

Despite these limitations, the case study is widely used as a method of studying organizations. It is extremely valuable in answering exploratory questions.

Field Study

In an attempt to add more reality and rigor to the study of organizations, behavioral scientists have developed several systematic field research techniques such as personal interviews, observation, archival data, and questionnaire surveys. These methods are used individually or in combination. They are used to investigate current practices or events, and with these methods, unlike with some other methods, the researcher does not rely entirely on what the subjects say. The researcher may personally interview other people in the organization—fellow workers, subordinates, and superiors—to gain a more balanced view before drawing conclusions.[9] In addition, archival data, records, charts, and statistics on file may be used to analyze a problem or hypothesis.

A very popular field study technique involves the use of expertly prepared questionnaires. Not only are such questionnaires less subject to unintentional distortion than personal interviews, but they also enable the researchers to greatly increase the number of individuals who participate. The questionnaire enables the collection of data on particular characteristics that are of interest to the researchers (for example, creativity, organizational justice, and role conflict).

In most cases, surveys are limited to a description of the current state of the situation. However, if researchers are aware of factors that may account for survey findings, they can make conjectural statements (known as hypotheses) about the relationship between two or more factors and relate the survey data to those factors. Thus, instead of just describing perceptions of performance evaluation, the researchers could make finer distinctions (for example, distinctions regarding job tenure, salary level, or education) among groups of ratees. Comparisons and statistical tests could then be applied to determine differences, similarities, or relationships. Finally, longitudinal studies involving observations made over time are used to describe changes that have taken place. Thus, in the situation described here, we can become aware of changes in overall ratee perceptions of appraisal interviews over time, as well as ratee perceptions relating to individual managers.[10]

Despite their advantages over many of the other methods of gaining knowledge about organizations, field studies are not without problems. Here again, researchers have training, interests, and expectations that they bring with them.[11] Thus, a researcher inadvertently may ignore a vital technological factor when conducting a study of employee morale while concentrating only on behavioral factors. Also, the fact that a researcher is present may influence how the individual responds. This weakness of field studies has long been recognized and is noted in some of the earliest field research in organizations.

Experiment

The experiment is potentially the most rigorous of scientific techniques. For an investigation to be considered an experiment, it must contain two elements—manipulation of some independent variable and observation or measurement of the results (dependent variable) while maintaining all other factors unchanged. Thus, in an organization, a behavioral scientist could change one organizational factor and observe the results while attempting to keep everything else unchanged.[12] There are two general types of experiments.

laboratory experiment
Experiment in which the researcher creates an environment in which the subject works. This setting permits the researcher to control closely the experimental conditions.

In a **laboratory experiment,** the environment is created by the researcher. For example, a management researcher may work with a small, voluntary group in a classroom. The group may be students or managers. They may be asked to communicate, perform tasks, or make decisions under different sets of conditions designated by the researcher. The laboratory setting permits the researcher to control closely the conditions under which observations are made. The intention is to isolate the relevant variables and to measure the response of dependent variables when the independent variable is manipulated. Laboratory experiments are useful when the conditions required to test a hypothesis are not practically or readily obtainable in natural situations and when the situation to be studied can be replicated under laboratory conditions. For such situations, many schools of business have behavioral science laboratories where such experimentation is done.

field experiment
Experiment in which the investigator attempts to manipulate and control variables in the natural setting rather than in a laboratory.

In a **field experiment,** the investigator attempts to manipulate and control variables in the natural setting rather than in a laboratory. Early experiments in organizations included manipulating physical working conditions such as rest periods, refreshments, and lighting. Today, behavioral scientists attempt to manipulate a host of additional factors.[13] For example, a training program might be introduced for one group of managers but not for another. Comparisons of performance, attitudes, and so on could be obtained later at one point or at several different points (a longitudinal study) to determine what effect, if any, the training program had on the managers' performances and attitudes.

The experiment is especially appealing to many researchers because it is the prototype of the scientific approach. It is the ideal toward which every science strives. However, while its potential is still great, the experiment has not produced a great breadth of knowledge about the functioning of organizations. Laboratory experiments suffer the risk of artificiality. The results of such experiments often do not extend to real organizations. Teams of business administration or psychology students working on decision problems may provide a great deal of information for researchers. Unfortunately, it is questionable whether this knowledge can be extended to a group of managers or nonmanagers making decisions under severe time constraints.[14]

Field experiments also have drawbacks. First, researchers cannot control every possible influencing factor (even if they knew them all) as they can in a laboratory. Here again, the fact that a researcher is present may make people behave differently, especially if they are aware that they are participating in an experiment. Experimentation in the behavioral sciences and, more specifically, experimentation in organizations are complex matters.

In a *true experiment,* the researcher has complete control over the experiment: the who, what, when, where, and how. A *quasi-experiment,* on the other hand, is an experiment in which the researcher lacks the degree of control over conditions that is possible in a true experiment. In the vast majority of organizational studies, it is impossible to completely control everything. Thus, quasi-experiments typically are the rule when organizational behavior is studied via an experiment.

Finally, with each of the methods of inquiry utilized by behavioral scientists, some type of measurement usually is necessary. For knowledge to be meaningful, it often must be compared with or related to something else. As a result, research questions (hypotheses) usually are stated in terms of how differences in the magnitude of some variable are related to differences in the magnitude of some other variable.

The variables studied are measured by research instruments. Those instruments may be psychological tests, such as personality or intelligence tests; questionnaires designed to obtain attitudes or other information; or in some cases, electronic devices to measure eye movement or blood pressure.

It is very important that a research instrument be both reliable and valid. Reliability is the consistency of the measure. In other words, repeated measures with the same instrument should produce the same results or scores. Validity is concerned with whether the research instrument actually measures what it is supposed to be measuring. Thus, it is possible for a research instrument to be reliable but not valid. For example, a test designed to measure intelligence could yield consistent scores over a large number of people but not be measuring intelligence.

Meta-Analysis

meta-analysis
A statistical procedure that pools the results of multiple research studies to derive an aggregated based result and interpretation of the findings.

A method of statistical analysis called **meta-analysis** that summarizes findings across independent studies is being used with some frequency.[15] The logic of meta-analysis is that researchers can arrive at a clearer, more accurate conclusion regarding a research area such as selection screening, team-building effectiveness, or conflict resolution methods by combining or aggregating the results of many studies of the area. It is assumed that aggregation of results presents a "truer or more accurate picture than would be found in any single study." A typical meta-analysis might combine 30 or 40 individual empirical studies. For example, Ones, Viswesvaran, and Schmidt studied the relationship between scores on a type of employment screening test called an *integrity (honesty) test* and certain aspects of behavior.[16] By using meta-analysis, Ones and her co-researchers combined the results of many different studies statistically and they estimated the correlation coefficient (.41) between the test score and supervising ratings of job performance.

There are some potential issues to be concerned about in using meta-analysis. What studies should be included in the aggregate pool? What level of research design rigor should be used to include studies in the pool? There is also the issue of including only published studies. How about studies with nonsupportive results that are generally not published? These are issues that need to be considered so that the "truest" picture can be provided.[17]

Qualitative Research

Instead of using experimental designs and concentrating on measurement issues, some researchers use qualitative research procedures. The notion of applying qualitative research methods to studying behavior within organizations recently has been addressed in leading research outlets.[18] The term *qualitative methods* is used to describe an array of interpretative techniques that attempt to describe and clarify the meaning of naturally occurring phenomena. It is by design rather open-ended and interpretative. The researcher's interpretation and description are the significant data collection acts in a qualitative study. In essence, qualitative data are defined as those (1) whose meanings are subjective, (2) that are rarely quantifiable, and (3) that are difficult to use in making quantitative comparisons.

Using both quantitative and qualitative methods in the same study can, in some cases, achieve a comprehensiveness that neither approach, if used alone, could achieve.[19] Another possible advantage of the combined use of the quantitative and qualitative methods is that the use of multiple methods could help check for congruence in findings. This is extremely important, especially when prescribing management interventions on the basis of research.[20]

The quantitative approach to organizational behavior research is exemplified by precise definitions, control groups, objective data collection, use of the scientific method, and replicable findings. The importance of reliability, validity, and accurate measurement is always stressed. On the other hand, qualitative research is more concerned with the meaning of what is observed. Since organizations are so complex, a range of quantitative and qualitative techniques can be used side by side to learn about individual, group, and organizational behavior.[21]

Qualitative methodology uses the experience and intuition of the researcher to describe the organizational processes and structures being studied. The data collected by a qualitative researcher requires him or her to become very close to the situation or problem being studied. For example, one qualitative method used is called the *ethnographic method* by anthropologists.[22] Here the researcher typically studies a phenomenon for long periods of time as a participant-observer. The researcher becomes part of the situation being studied to feel what it is like for the people in that situation. The researcher becomes immersed in other people's realities.

Participant observation usually is supplemented by a variety of quantitative data collection tools such as structured interviews and self-report questionnaires. A variety of techniques are used so that the researcher can check the results obtained from observation and recorded in field notes.

In training researchers in the ethnographic method, it is common to place them in unfamiliar settings. A researcher may sit with and listen to workers on a production line, drive around in a police car to observe police officers, or do cleanup work in a surgical operating room. The training is designed to improve the researcher's ability to record, categorize, and code what is being observed.

An example of qualitative research involvement is present in Van Maanen's participant-observer study of a big-city police department. He went through police academy training and then accompanied police officers on their daily rounds. He functioned with police officers in daily encounters. Thus, he was able to provide vivid descriptions of what police work was like.[23]

Other qualitative techniques include content analysis (e.g., the researcher's interpretation of field notes), informal interviewing, archival data surveys and historical analysis, and the use of unobtrusive measures (e.g., data whose collection is not influenced by a researcher's presence). An example of the last would be the wear and tear on a couch in a cardiologist's office. As reported in the discussion of Type A behavior pattern in Chapter 9, the wear and tear was on the edges of the couch, which suggested anxiety and hyperactive behavior. Qualitative research appears to rely more on multiple sources of data than on any one source. The available research literature suggests a number of characteristics associated with qualitative research.[24]

1. *Analytical induction.* Qualitative research begins with the up-close, firsthand inspection of organizational life.
2. *Proximity.* Researchers' desire to witness firsthand what is being studied. If the application of rewards is what is being studied, the researcher would want to observe episodes of reward distribution.
3. *Ordinary behavior.* The topics of research interest should be ordinary, normal, routine behaviors.
4. *Descriptive emphasis.* Qualitative research seeks descriptions for what is occurring in any given place and time. The aim is to disclose and reveal, not merely to order data and to predict.
5. *Shrinking variance.* Qualitative research is geared toward the explanation of similarity and coherence. Greater emphasis is placed on commonality and on things shared in organizational settings than on things not shared.
6. *Enlightening the consumer.* The consumer of qualitative research could be a manager. A major objective is to enlighten without confusing him or her. This is accomplished by providing commentary that is coherent and logically persuasive.

Researchers and managers do not have to choose either quantitative or qualitative research data and interpretation. There are convincing and relevant arguments that more than one method of research should be used when studying organizational behavior. Quantitative and qualitative research methods and procedures have much to offer practicing managers. Blending and integrating quantitative and qualitative research are what researchers and managers must do in the years ahead to better understand, cope with, and modify organizational behavior.

A

ability   A person's talent to perform a mental or physical task.

adaptiveness   A criterion of effectiveness that refers to the ability of the organization to respond to change that is induced by either internal or external stimuli. An equivalent term is *flexibility,* although adaptiveness connotes an intermediate time frame, whereas flexibility ordinariiy is used in a short-run sense.

affect   The emotional component of an attitude; often learned from parents, teachers, and peer group members.

affirmative action   The task of developing and implementing a program and process to achieve equality of opportunity in an organization.

aggression   In the work setting, this is behavior that brings harm to others with whom the aggressor works or has worked.

agreeableness   One of the Big Five personality dimensions; it is the tendency to be courteous, forgiving, tolerant, trusting, and softhearted.

alternative dispute resolution   The process of resolving conflicts, disputes, and problems through third-party interventions. Usually this process excludes lawyers.

appreciative inquiry   A method of focusing on positive or potential opportunities. An approach that asks questions and requires answers in an attempt to seize and improve upon an organization's potential.

attitudes   Mental states of readiness for need arousal.

attraction-selection-attrition (ASA) framework   The concept that attraction to an organization, selection by it, and attrition from it result in particular kinds of people being in the organization. These people, in turn, determine organizational behavior.

attribution theory   A process by which individuals attempt to explain the reasons for events.

authority   The ability to influence others based on the perceived power of one's position and role within an organization.

B

banking time off   A reward practice of allowing employees to build up time-off credits for such things as good performance or attendance. The employees then receive the time off in addition to the regular vacation time granted by the organization because of seniority.

baseline   The period of time before a change is introduced.

behavior   Anything a person does, such as talking, walking, thinking, or daydreaming.

behavior modification   An approach to motivation that uses the principles of operant conditioning.

Big Five personality model   A model of personality that suggests human personality is comprised of five central dimensions: extroversion, emotional stability, agreeableness, conscientiousness, and openness to experience.

boundaryless organization   A firm in which chains of command are eliminated, spans of control are unlimited, and rigid departments are replaced with empowered teams.

boundary-spanning role   The role of an individual who must relate to two different systems, usually an organization and some part of its environment.

bounded rationality approach   This approach assumes that decision making is not a perfectly rational process, but rather one that is fraught with constraints and limitations. Though not optimal, decisions are thought to be satisfactory and acceptable.

brainstorming   The generation of ideas in a group through noncritical discussion.

broadbanding   A pay system that reduces the actual number of pay grades to a relatively few broadly based pay grades. Places an emphasis on titles, grades, and job descriptions.

bullying   Deliberate or unconscious repeated actions that are directed at another worker to cause humiliation or distress.

burnout   A psychological process brought about by unrelieved work stress, resulting in emotional exhaustion, depersonalization, and feelings of decreased accomplishment.

C

cafeteria-style benefits plans   Plans that allow employees to choose benefits that suit them and to make adjustments to meet their changing needs.

case study   A detailed analysis and examination of a problem(s) that requires attention and resolution.

centralization   A dimension of organizational structure that refers to the extent to which authority to make decisions is retained in top management.

chameleon effect   The practice of mimicking another person's mannerisms, facial expressions, and body movements.

change agent   A person who acts as the initiator for change activities. Can be internal members of the firm or external consultants.

charismatic leader   The charismatic leader is one who creates an atmosphere of motivation based on an emotional commitment to and identity with his or her vision, philosophy, and style on the part of followers.

classical design theory   A body of literature that evolved from scientific management, classical organization, and bureaucratic theory. The theory emphasizes the design of a preplanned structure for doing work. It minimizes the importance of the social system.

classical organization theory   The body of literature that developed from the writings of managers who proposed principles of organization. These principles were intended to serve as guidelines for other managers.

coaching   The everyday interaction of helping, guiding, and encouraging another employee to improve his or her understanding of the work and improve performance.

coercive power   Influence over others based on fear. A subordinate perceives that failure to comply with the wishes of a superior would lead to punishment or some other negative outcome.

cognition   This is basically what individuals know about themselves and their environment. Cognition implies a conscious process of acquiring knowledge.

cognitive dissonance   A mental state of anxiety that occurs when there is a conflict among an individual's various cognitions (for example, attitudes and beliefs) after a decision has been made.

cohesiveness   The attractiveness strength existing between a group or team of individuals.

command group   A group of subordinates who report to one particular manager. The command group is specified by the formal organization chart.

commitment   A sense of identification, involvement, and loyalty expressed by an employee toward the company.

communication   The transmission of information and understanding through the use of common symbols.

competitive intelligence   A system of gathering, analyzing, and acting on information about another firm.

complexity   A dimension of organizational structure that refers to the number of different jobs and/or units within an organization.

compliance   Being in agreement with specific legal, organizational, or official requirements.

compressed workweek   An alternative work arrangement in which the standard five-day, 40-hour workweek is compressed. The most popular is four 10-hour days.

concierge services   An employee benefit that allows employees to pay for a provider to do everyday services on their behalf. Helping balance employees' busy lives, concierge services may include any/all of the following: doing personal shopping during the holidays, finding estimates for an automotive repair, and making restaurant reservations.

conflict   A situation where a person or group believes they are losing power, resources, or status because of another person or group.

conscientiousness   One of the Big Five personality dimensions; it is the tendency to be dependable, organized, thorough, and responsible.

conscious goals   The main goals a person is striving toward and is aware of when directing behavior.

consensus   In attribution theory, the degree to which other people are engaging in the same behavior.

consideration   Involves behavior indicating friendship, mutual trust, respect, warmth, and rapport between the leader and the followers.

consistency   In attribution theory, the degree to which a person engages in the same behaviors at different times.

content approaches to motivation   Theories that focus on the factors within a person that energize, direct, sustain, and stop behavior.

contingency approach to management   This approach to management is based on the belief that there is no one best way to manage in every situation but that managers must find different ways that fit different situations.

contingency design theory   An approach to designing organizations where the effective structure depends on factors in the situation.

continuous reinforcement   A schedule that is designed to reinforce behavior every time the behavior exhibited is correct.

corporate social responsibility   Actions that corporations undertake to promote the public good beyond those required by law or the immediate interest of financial stakeholders.

creativity   Process by which an individual, group, or team produces novel and useful ideas to solve a problem or capture an opportunity.

cultural diversity   The vast array of differences created by cultural phenomena such as history, economic conditions, personality characteristics, language norms, and mores.

cyberslacking   The use of the Internet during office or work hours for personal reasons.

D

decentralization   Basically, this entails pushing the decision-making point to the lowest managerial level possible. It involves the delegation of decision-making authority.

decision   A means to achieve some result or to solve some problem. The outcome of a process that is influenced by many forces.

decision acceptance   An important criterion in the Vroom-Jago model that refers to the degree of subordinate commitment to the decision.

decision quality   An important criterion in the Vroom-Jago model that refers to the objective aspects of a decision that influence subordinates' performance aside from any direct impact on motivation.

decoding   The mental procedure that the receiver of a message goes through to decipher the message.

delegated strategies   Strategies for introducing organizational change that allow active participation by subordinates.

delegation of authority   The process by which authority is distributed downward in an organization.

Delphi technique   A technique used to improve group decision making that involves the solicitation and comparison of anonymous judgments on the topic of interest through a set of sequential questionnaires interspersed with summarized information and feedback of opinions from earlier responses.

departmentalization   The manner in which an organization is structurally divided. Some of the more publicized divisions are by function, territory, product, customer, and project.

development   A criterion of effectiveness that refers to the organization's ability to increase its responsiveness to current and future environmental demands. Equivalent or similar terms include *institutionalization, stability,* and *integration.*

devil's advocacy   A form of programmed conflict in which someone or some group is assigned the role of critic whose job it is to uncover all possible problems with a particular proposal.

devil's advocate   An appointed critic of proposed group actions whose intent is to uncover underlying issues with the prevailing direction of the group.

diagonal communication   Communication that cuts across functions and levels in an organization.

distinctiveness   In attribution theory, the degree to which a person behaves similarly in different situations.

distributive justice   The perceived fairness of how resources and rewards are distributed throughout an organization. For example, employees make judgments about the fairness of the amount of their pay raises.

diversity   Refers to those attributes that make people different from one another. Primary dimensions of diversity include age, ethnicity, gender, physical attributes, race, and sexual/affectional orientation.

division of labor   The process of dividing work into relatively specialized jobs to achieve advantages of specialization.

downward communication   Communication that flows from individuals in higher levels of the organization's hierarchy to those in lower levels.

dysfunctional conflict   A confrontation or interaction between groups that harms the organization or hinders the achievement of organizational goals.

E

economic forces   Forces in the environment that can influence what occurs within a firm, such as security markets, interest rates, foreign currency fluctuations, and competitors' pricing strategies.

effectiveness   In the context of organizational behavior, *effectiveness* refers to the optimal relationship among five components: production, efficiency, satisfaction, adaptiveness, and development.

efficiency   A short-run criterion of effectiveness that refers to the organization's ability to produce outputs with minimum use of inputs. The measures of efficiency are always in ratio terms, such as benefit/cost, cost/output, and cost/time.

emotional intelligence (EI)   The handling of relationships and interactions with others.

emotional labor   The effort and work to manage your emotions to keep them under control.

emotional stability   One of the Big Five personality dimensions; it is the tendency to be calm, serene, relaxed, and secure.

emotion-focused coping   The actions taken by a person to alleviate stressful emotions. The actions center on avoidance or escape from a person, problem, or event.

emotions   A state of physiological arousal and changes in facial expressions, gestures, posture, and subjective feelings.

employee assistance program   An employee benefit program designed to deal with a wide range of stress-related problems, including behavioral and emotional difficulties, substance abuse, and family and marital discord.

employee-centered leader   Focuses on having people complete the work and believes in delegating decision making and aiding employees in satisfying their needs by creating a work supportive environment.

employee stock ownership plans (ESOPs)   An employee reward program in which organizations make contributions of stock (or cash to purchase stock) to employees. Stock allocation is typically, but not always, based on seniority.

empowerment   Encouraging and/or assisting individuals and groups to make decisions that affect their work environments.

encoding   The conversion of an idea into an understandable message by a communicator.

environmental forces   Forces for change beyond the control of the manager. These forces include marketplace actions, technological changes, and social and political changes.

equity theory   A theory of motivation that examines how a person might respond to perceived discrepancies between her input/outcome ratio and that of a reference person.

ERG theory   A need hierarchy theory of motivation comprised of three sets of needs: existence (E), relatedness (R), and growth (G).

escalation of commitment   An impediment to effective decision making, it refers to an increasing adherence to a previous decision when a rational decision maker would withdraw. It typically results from a need to turn a losing or poor decision into a winning or good decision.

expectancy   The perceived likelihood that a particular act will be followed by a particular outcome.

expectancy theory   A theory of motivation that suggests employees are more likely to be motivated when they perceive their efforts will result in successful performance and, ultimately, desired rewards and outcomes.

experiment   To be considered an experiment, an investigation must contain two elements—manipulation of some variable (independent variable) and observation of the results (dependent variable).

expert power   Capacity to influence related to some expertise, special skill, or knowledge. Expert power is a function of the judgment of the less-powerful person that the other person has ability or knowledge that exceeds his own.

external change agent   A person from outside an organization who initiates change.

extinction   The decline in the response rate because of nonreinforcement.

extranet   A private, protected electronic communication system that is designed to connect employees with individuals external to the organization, such as vendors, customers, or other strategic partners.

extrinsic rewards   Rewards external to the job, such as pay, promotion, or fringe benefits.

extroversion   One of the Big Five personality dimensions; it is a trait that indicates a person's outgoing, sociable behavior.

F

felt conflict   The second stage of conflict that includes emotional involvement. It is felt in the form of anxiety, tension, and/or hostility. See also *perceived conflict* and *manifest conflict*.

field experiment   Experiment in which the investigator attempts to manipulate and control variables in the natural setting rather than in a laboratory.

fixed-interval reinforcement   A situation in which a reinforcer is applied only after a certain period of time has elapsed since the last reinforcer was applied.

flextime   An arrangement that provides employees greater individual control over work scheduling. In a flextime schedule, employees can determine, within some limits, when they will go to work. In most flextime plans, employees may vary their schedule day to day, provided they work a specific number of hours a week.

formal group   A group formed by management to accomplish the goals of the organization.

formalization   A dimension of organizational structure that refers to the extent to which rules, procedures, and other guides to action are written and enforced.

formal organization   The recognized and sanctioned structure, policies, and rules of a unit or institution.

fraud   An intentional act of deceiving or misrepresenting to induce another individual or group to give up something of value.

friendship group   An informal group that is established in the workplace because of some common characteristic of its members and that may extend the interaction of its members to include activities outside the workplace.

functional conflict   A confrontation between groups that enhances and benefits the organization's performance.

functional job analysis (FJA)   A method of job analysis that focuses attention on the worker's specific job activities, methods, machines, and output. The method is used widely to analyze and classify jobs.

fundamental attribution error   A tendency to underestimate the importance of external factors and overestimate the importance of internal factors when making attributions about the behavior of others.

G

gain-sharing   A reward system in which employees share in the financial benefits the organization accrues from improved operating efficiencies and effectiveness. Gain-sharing can take many different forms including cash awards for suggestions and bonus plans.

glass ceiling An invisible barrier that blocks qualified individuals from making career progress or receiving a fair share of the rewards.

globalism The interdependency of transportation, distribution, communication, and economic networks across international borders.

Global Leadership and Organizational Behavior Effectiveness (GLOBE) project A large international research project that analyzed data on 62 cultures to identify and understand managers' perceptions of cultural practices and values from their home countries.

goal A specific target that an individual is trying to achieve; a goal is the target (object) of an action.

goal approach to effectiveness A perspective on effectiveness that emphasizes the central role of goal achievement as the criterion for assessing effectiveness.

goal commitment The amount of effort that is actually used to achieve a goal.

goal difficulty The degree of proficiency or the level of goal performance that is being sought.

goal intensity The process of setting a goal or of determining how to reach it.

goal orientation A concept that refers to the focus of attention and decision making among the members of a subunit.

goal participation The amount of a person's involvement in setting task and personal development goals.

goal setting The process of establishing goals. In many cases, goal setting involves a superior and subordinate working together to set the subordinate's goals for a specified period of time.

goal specificity The degree of quantitative precision of the goal.

Golem effect A self-fulfilling prophecy that causes a person to behave in a negative manner to meet low expectations.

grapevine An informal communication network that exists in organizations and short-circuits the formal channels.

group Two or more individuals interacting with each other to accomplish a common goal.

group cohesiveness The strength of the members' desires to remain in the group and the strength of their commitment to the group.

group norms Standards shared by the members of a group.

groupthink The deterioration of the mental efficiency, reality testing, and moral judgment of the individual members of a group in the interest of group solidarity.

H

halo effect In perception, it occurs when a person allows one important factor or characteristic to bias his or her view, impression, or evaluation.

hardiness A personality trait that appears to buffer an individual's response to stress. The hardy person assumes that he or she is in control, is highly committed to lively activities, and treats change as a challenge.

Hawthorne studies A series of studies undertaken at the Chicago Hawthorne Plant of Western Electric from 1924 to 1933. The studies made major contributions to the knowledge of the importance of the social system of an organization. They provided the impetus for the human relations approach to organizations.

health promotion program See *wellness program*.

horizontal communication Communication that flows across functions in an organization.

horizontal differentiation The number of different units existing at the same level in an organization. The greater the horizontal differentiation, the more complex is the organization.

I

impression management The attempt to influence others' perceptions of you; a political strategy that refers to actions individuals take to control the impressions that others form of them.

incentive plan criteria To be effective in motivating employees, incentives should (1) be related to specific behavioral patterns (for example, better performance), (2) be received immediately after the behavior is displayed, and (3) reward the employee for consistently displaying the desired behavior.

incivility In the workplace, this is behavior that is designated as rude, discourteous, or demeaning toward others.

influence A transaction in which a person or a group acts in such a way as to change the behavior of another person or group. Influence is the demonstrated use of power.

informal group A group formed by individuals and developed around common interests and friendships rather than around an organizational goal.

information flow requirements The amount of information that must be processed by an organization, group, or individual to perform effectively.

information richness Refers to the amount of information that can be transmitted or communicated in an effective manner. Face-to-face interactions are high in information richness; a general e-mail to all employees is low in information richness.

informational justice   An area of organizational science research that focuses on the perceived fairness of the communication provided to employees from authorities.

initiating structure   Designates behavior in which the leader organizes and defines the relationships in the group, tends to establish well-defined patterns and channels of communication, and spells out ways of getting the job done.

instrumentality   The relationship between first- and second-level outcomes.

interaction   Any interpersonal contact in which one individual acts and one or more other individuals respond to the action.

interest group   A group that forms because of some special topic of interest. Generally, when the interest declines or a goal has been achieved, the group disbands.

intergroup conflict   Conflict between groups; can be functional or dysfunctional.

internal change agent   A person, manager or nonmanager, working for an organization, who initiates change.

internal forces   Forces for change that occur within the organization and that usually can be traced to *process* and to *behavioral causes*.

Internet   A global network of integrated computers that provides users with information, video, documents, and a vast array of communication capabilities.

interpersonal communication   Communication that flows from individual to individual in face-to-face and group settings.

interpersonal justice   Judgments made by employees about the perceived fairness of the treatment received by employees from authorities.

interpersonal orientation   A concept that refers to whether a person is more concerned with achieving good social relations as opposed to achieving a task.

interpersonal rewards   Extrinsic rewards such as receiving recognition or being able to interact socially in the job.

interpersonal style   The way in which an individual prefers to relate to others.

interrole conflict   A type of conflict that results from facing multiple roles. It occurs because individuals simultaneously perform many roles, some of which have conflicting expectations.

intervention   The process by which either outsiders or insiders assume the role of a change agent in the OD program.

intimidation   An impression management tactic whereby individuals use threats and harassment to appear powerful.

intranet   A private, protected electronic communication system within an organization; intranets allow certain stakeholders to gain access to internal organizational information.

intrinsic rewards   Rewards that are part of the job itself. The responsibility, challenge, and feedback characteristics of the job are intrinsic rewards.

J

job analysis   The description of how one job differs from another in terms of the demands, activities, and skills required.

job-centered leader   Focuses on encouraging employees to complete the task and uses close supervision so that individuals perform their tasks using acceptable and timely procedures.

job content   The factors that define the general nature of a job.

job context   The physical environment and other working conditions, along with other factors considered to be intrinsic to a job.

job definition   The first subproblem of the organizing decision. It involves the determination of task requirements of each job in the organization.

job depth   The amount of control that an individual has to alter or influence the job and the surrounding environment.

job description   A summary statement of what an employee actually does on the job.

job design   The process by which managers decide individual job tasks and authority.

job embeddedness   Refers to an employee's connection with other employees within the organization, fit with the job/organization/community, and sacrifices that would be made if he or she were to leave the organization.

job enlargement   An administrative action that involves increasing the range of a job. Supposedly, this action results in better performance and a more satisfied workforce.

job enrichment   An approach developed by Herzberg that seeks to improve task efficiency and human satisfaction by means of building into people's jobs greater scope for personal achievement and recognition, more challenging and responsible work, and more opportunity for individual advancement and growth.

job evaluation   The assignment of dollar value to a job.

job range   The number of operations that a job occupant performs to complete a task.

job relationships   The interpersonal relationships that are required of or made possible by a job.

job requirements   Factors such as education, experience, degrees, licenses, and other personal characteristics required to perform a job.

job rotation   A form of training that involves moving an employee from one workstation to another. In addition to achieving the training objective, this procedure also is designed to reduce boredom.

job satisfaction   An attitude that workers have about their jobs. It results from their perception of the jobs.

job sharing   A form of alternative work arrangement in which two or more individuals share the same job. One jobholder might work in the mornings, while a second jobholder works in the afternoon. Job sharing increases employee discretion.

job specification   A product of a job analysis. A job specification identifies the minimum acceptable qualifications that a jobholder must have to perform the job at an acceptable level. It may include specifications for educational level, knowledge, skills, aptitudes, and previous experience.

K

kinesics   The study of communication through body movement, postures, gestures, and facial expressions.

L

laboratory experiment   Experiment in which the researcher creates an environment in which the subject works. This setting permits the researcher to control closely the experimental conditions.

leader–member relations   A factor in the Fiedler contingency model that refers to the degree of confidence, trust, and respect that the leader obtains from the followers.

leadership   Using influence in an organizational setting or situation, producing effects that are meaningful and have a direct impact on accomplishing challenging goals.

leadership climate   The nature of the work environment in an organization that results from the leadership style and administrative practices of managers.

learning   The process by which a relatively enduring change in behavior occurs as a result of practice.

learning transfer   An important learning principle that emphasizes the carryover of learning into the workplace.

legitimate power   Capacity to influence derived from the position of a manager in the organizational hierarchy. Subordinates believe that they "ought" to comply.

locus of control   Specifies a person's beliefs that he or she does not master his or her fate.

M

management by objectives (MBO)   A process under which superiors and subordinates jointly set goals for a specified time period and then meet again to evaluate the subordinates' performance in terms of those previously established goals.

manifest conflict   The final stage in conflict. At the manifest conflict stage, the conflicting parties are actively engaging in conflict behavior. Manifest conflict is usually very apparent to noninvolved parties. See also *perceived conflict* and *felt conflict*.

matrix model of organizational design   An organizational design that superimposes a product- or project-based design on an existing function-based design.

mechanistic model of organizational design   The type of organizational design that emphasizes the importance of production and efficiency. It is highly formalized, centralized, and complex.

mental ability   Refers to one's level of intelligence and can be divided into subcategories, including verbal fluency and comprehension, inductive and deductive reasoning, associative memory, and spatial orientation.

mentor   A person who provides one-on-one coaching, friendship, sponsorship, and role modeling examples to a less experienced protégé—a mentee.

meta-analysis   A statistical procedure that pools the results of multiple research studies to derive an aggregated based result and interpretation of the findings.

mission   The ultimate, primary purpose of an organization. An organization's mission is what society expects from the organization in exchange for its continuing survival.

modeling   A method of administering rewards that relies on observational learning. An employee learns the behaviors that are desirable by observing how others are rewarded. It is assumed that behaviors will be imitated if the observer views a distinct link between performance and rewards.

modified or compressed workweek   A shortened workweek. The form of the modified workweek that involves working four days a week, 10 hours each day, is called a 4/40. The 3/36 and 4/32 schedules also are being used.

mood   A long-lasting state of emotion.

motion study   The process of analyzing a task to determine the preferred motions to be used in its completion.

motivator-hygiene theory   The Herzberg approach that identifies conditions of the job that operate primarily to dissatisfy employees when they are not present (hygiene factors—salary, job security, work conditions, and so on). There also are job conditions that lead to high levels of motivation and job satisfaction. However, the absence of these conditions does not prove highly dissatisfying. The conditions include achievements, growth, and advancement opportunities.

multicultural communication   This occurs when two or more individuals from different cultures communicate with one another.

multiple roles   The notion that most individuals play many roles simultaneously because they occupy many different positions in a variety of institutions and organizations.

N

national culture   The sum total of the beliefs, rituals, rules, customs, artifacts, and institutions that characterize the population of a nation.

need for power   A person's desire to have an impact on others. The impact can occur by such behaviors as action, the giving of help or advice, or concern for reputation.

need hierarchy model   Maslow assumed that the needs of a person depend on what he or she already has. This in a sense means that a satisfied need is not a motivator. Human needs are organized in a hierarchy of importance. The five need classifications are: physiological, safety, belongingness, esteem, and self-actualization.

needs   The deficiencies that an individual experiences at a particular point in time.

noise   Interference in the flow of a message from a sender to a receiver.

nominal group technique (NGT)   A technique to improve group decision making that brings people together in a very structured meeting that does not allow for much verbal communication. The group decision is the mathematically pooled outcome of individual votes.

nonprogrammed decisions   Decisions required for unique and complex management problems.

nonverbal communication   Messages sent with body posture, facial expressions, and head and eye movements.

norms   The standards of behavior shared by members of a group.

O

openness to experience   One of the Big Five personality dimensions; it reflects the extent to which an individual is broad-minded, creative, curious, and intelligent.

operant   Behaviors amenable to control by altering the consequences (rewards and punishments) that follow them.

optimal balance   The most desirable relationship among the criteria of effectiveness. Optimal, rather than maximum, balance must be achieved in any case of more than one criterion.

organic model of organizational design   The organizational design that emphasizes the importance of adaptability and development. It is relatively informal, decentralized, and simple.

organizational behavior   The study of human behavior, attitudes, and performance within an organizational setting; drawing on theory, methods, and principles from such disciplines as psychology, sociology, and cultural anthropology to learn about *individual* perceptions, values, learning capacities, and actions while working in *groups* and within the total *organization;* analyzing the external environment's effect on the organization and its human resources, missions, objectives, and strategies.

organizational behavior modification   An operant approach to organizational behavior. This term is used interchangeably with the term *behavior modification.*

organizational climate   A set of properties of the work environment, perceived directly or indirectly by the employees, that is assumed to be a major force in influencing employee behavior.

organizational commitment   When an individual aligns very closely with the programs, goals, and systems of the organization.

organizational culture   The pervasive system of values, beliefs, and norms that exists in any organization. The organizational culture can encourage or discourage effectiveness, depending on the nature of the values, beliefs, and norms.

organizational design   A specific organizational structure that results from managers' decisions and actions. Also, the process by which managers choose among alternative frameworks of jobs and departments.

organizational development   The process of preparing for and managing change in organizational settings.

organizational justice   An area of organizational science research that focuses on perceptions and judgments by employees regarding the fairness of their organizations' procedures and decisions.

organizational politics   The activities used to acquire, develop, and use power and other resources to obtain one's preferred outcome when there is uncertainty or disagreement about choices.

organizational processes   The activities that breathe life into the organizational structure. Among the common organizational processes are communication, decision making, socialization, and career development.

organizational structure   The formal pattern of how people and jobs are grouped in an organization. The organizational structure is often illustrated by an organization chart.

organizations   Institutions that enable society to pursue goals that could not be achieved by individuals acting alone.

P

participative management   A concept of managing that encourages employees' participation in decision making and in matters that affect their jobs.

path clarification   The leader's efforts to clarify for employees the kind of behavior most likely to result in goal accomplishment.

path–goal leadership model   A theory that suggests it is necessary for a leader to influence the followers' perception of work goals, self-development goals, and paths to goal attainment. The foundation for the model is expectancy motivation theory.

perceived conflict   The first stage of the conflict process. Perceived conflict exists when there is a cognitive awareness on the part of at least one party that events have occurred or that conditions exist favorable to creating overt conflict. See also *felt conflict* and *manifest conflict*.

perception   The process by which an individual gives meaning to the environment. It involves organizing and interpreting various stimuli into a psychological experience.

performance   A set of employee work-related behaviors designed to accomplish organizational goals.

personal–behavioral leadership theories   A group of leadership theories that are based primarily on the personal and behavioral characteristics of leaders. The theories focus on *what* leaders do and/or *how* they behave in carrying out the leadership function.

person–organization fit   The extent to which a person's values and personality are perceived to fit the culture of the organization.

personality   A stable set of characteristics and tendencies that determine commonalities and differences in the behavior of people.

personality test   A test used to measure the emotional, motivational, interpersonal, and attitude characteristics that make up a person's personality.

person–role conflict   A type of conflict that occurs when the requirements of a position violate the basic values, attitudes, and needs of the individual occupying the position.

pooled interdependence   Interdependence that requires no interaction between groups because each group, in effect, performs separately.

position analysis questionnaire (PAQ)   A method of job analysis that takes into account the human, task, and technological factors of jobs and job classes.

position power   A factor in the Fiedler contingency model that refers to the power inherent in the leadership position.

power of human resources   The ability to get things done in the way one wants them to be done.

power illusion   The notion that a person with little power actually has significant power. The Milgram experiments indicate that the participants were obedient to commands given by an individual who seemed to have power, wore a white coat, was addressed as "doctor," and acted quite stern.

prejudice   A stereotype that doesn't change even when information disputing it is presented.

privacy   A condition that limits or forbids another person's access to an individual's records, data, or information.

problem-focused coping   The actions taken by an individual to cope with a stressful person, situation, or event.

procedural justice   The perceived fairness of the processes used by the organization to arrive at decisions such as who receives promotions, how pay raise are established, and how bonus payouts are allocated.

process   In systems theory, the process element consists of technical and administrative activities that are brought to bear on inputs to transform them into outputs.

process approaches to motivation   Theories that provide a description and analysis of the process by which behavior is energized, directed, sustained, and stopped.

production   A criterion of effectiveness that refers to the organization's ability to provide the outputs the environment demands of it.

programmed decisions   Situations in which specific procedures have been developed for repetitive and routine problems.

psychological contract   An unwritten agreement between an employee and the organization that specifies what each expects to give to and receive from the other.

psychological contract breach   Employee perception that the organization has failed to fulfill an unwritten exchange agreement.

punishment   Presenting an uncomfortable consequence for a particular behavior response or removing a desirable reinforcer because of a particular behavior response. Managers can punish by application or punish by removal.

Pygmalion effect   A self-fulfilling prophecy that causes a person to behave in a positive manner to meet expectations.

Q

qualitative overload   A situation in which a person feels that he or she lacks the ability or skill to do a job or that the performance standards have been set too high.

quality circle   A small group of employees who meet on a regular basis, usually on company time, to recommend improvements and solve quality-related problems. Frequently a part of *total quality management efforts*.

quality of work life (QWL)   Management philosophy and practice that enhance employee dignity, introduce cultural changes, and provide opportunities for growth and development.

quantitative overload   A situation in which a person feels that he or she has too many things to do or insufficient time to complete a job.

R

rapidity of change   The speed at which change occurs. Rapid change is found in many areas such as technology, demographics, globalism, and new products and services.

reciprocal causation of leadership   The argument that follower behavior has an impact on leader behavior and that leader behavior influences follower behavior.

reciprocal interdependence   Interdependence that requires the output of each group in an organization to serve as input to other groups in the organization.

reengineering   Creating radical changes in processes, systems, and/or structures that meet customer needs efficiently and are economically sound.

referent power   Power based on a subordinates' identification with a charismatic superior. The more powerful individual is admired because of certain traits, and the subordinate is influenced because of this admiration.

reward power   An influence over others based on hope of reward; the opposite of coercive power. A subordinate perceives that compliance with the wishes of a superior will lead to positive rewards, either monetary of psychological.

resistance to change   Behavioral, cognitive, or emotional upset and resistance to real or perceived work-related changes.

role   An organized set of behaviors.

S

sabotage   An extreme form of workplace violence instituted to disrupt, destroy, or damage equipment, data, or a work area.

satisfaction   A criterion of effectiveness that refers to the organization's ability to gratify the needs of its participants. Similar terms include *morale* and *voluntarism*.

scalar chain   The graded chain of authority created through the delegation process.

scientific management   A body of literature that emerged during the period 1890–1930 and that reports the ideas and theories of engineers concerned with such problems as job definition, incentive systems, and selection and training.

scope   The scale on which an organizational change is implemented (for example, throughout the entire organization, level by level, or department by department).

self-efficacy   Related to an individual's belief that he or she can successfully complete a task. People with high levels of self-efficacy firmly believe in their performance capabilities. The concept of self-efficacy includes three dimensions: magnitude, strength, and generality.

self-handicapping   Any action taken in advance of an outcome that is designed to provide either an excuse for failure or a credit for success.

self-managed team (SMT)   Groups of employees that complete an entire piece of work while having considerable autonomy over the way in which they accomplish their work.

self-serving bias   A frequent attribution error that is reflected in the tendency people have to take credit for successful work and deny responsibility for poor work.

self-promotion   An impression management tactic whereby individuals communicate their accomplishments to appear able and competent.

sequential interdependence   Interdependence that requires one group to complete its task before another group can complete its task.

servant leader   A leader who emphasizes employee growth and service to others as worthwhile ends in and of themselves, placing others' needs in front of his or her own.

sexual harassment   Unwelcome advances, requests for sexual favors, and other types of verbal, psychological, or physical abuses.

similar-to-me errors   Using yourself as a benchmark against which others are judged.

situational leadership theory (SLT)   An approach to leadership advocating that leaders understand their own behavior and the readiness of their followers. This approach requires diagnostic skills in human behavior on the part of the leader.

Six Sigma   Powerful statistical tools and techniques to improve quality in manufacturing, human resource processes, and other operations within organizations.

skunkworks   A secretive research and development project that operates outside of normal company operations to create innovative products.

socialization   The process by which an individual comes to appreciate the values, abilities, expected behaviors, and social knowledge essential for assuming an organizational role and for participating as an organization member.

social support   The comfort, assistance, or information an individual receives through formal or informal contacts with individuals or groups.

spam   A barrier to effective e-mail communication, this is unsolicited commercial solicitations that enter and clutter an employee's e-mail in-box.

span of control   The number of subordinates reporting to a superior. The span is a factor that affects the shape and height of an organizational structure.

status In an organizational setting, status relates to positions in the formal or informal structure. Status is designated in the formal organizations, whereas in informal groups it is determined by the group.

status consensus The agreement of group members about the relative status of members of the group.

stereotyping A translation step in the perceptual process that people use to classify or categorize events, people, or situations.

strategic contingency An event or activity that is extremely important for accomplishing organizational goals. Among the strategic contingencies of subunits are dependency, scarcity of resources, coping with uncertainty, centrality, and substitutability.

stress An adaptive response, moderated by individual differences, that is a consequence of any action, situation, or event that places special demands on a person.

stressor An external event or situation that is potentially harmful to a person.

structure The established patterns of interacting in an organization and of coordinating the technology and human assets of the organization.

structure (in group context) Used in the context of groups, the term *structure* refers to the standards of conduct that are applied by the group, the communication system, and the reward and sanction mechanism of the group.

substitutability The ability of various work units to perform the activities of other work units.

subunit (business unit or strategic business unit) A semiautonomous part of an overall organization that is a center for coordinated actions; usually it is organized around a product line and competes against other organizations.

superordinate goal A goal that cannot be achieved without the cooperation of the conflicting groups.

supportive organizational climate The amount of perceived support employees receive from their co-workers, supervisor, and other departments that helps them successfully perform their job duties.

survey A survey usually attempts to measure one or more characteristics in many people, usually at one point in time. Basically, surveys are used to investigate current problems and events.

System-4 organization The universalistic theory of organization design proposed by Likert. The theory is defined in terms of overlapping groups, linking-pin management, and the principle of supportiveness.

systems theory An approach to the analysis of organizational behavior that emphasizes the necessity for maintaining the basic elements of input-process-output and for adapting to the larger environment that sustains the organization.

T

tacit knowledge The work-related practical know-how that employees acquire through observation and direct experience on the job.

task group A group of individuals who are working as a unit to complete a project or job task.

task structure A factor in the Fiedler contingency model that refers to how structured a job is with regard to requirements, problem-solving alternatives, and feedback on how correctly the job has been accomplished.

team A formal group of people interacting very closely together with a shared commitment to accomplish agreed-upon objectives.

team building A type of planned intervention that is meant to build self-awareness and camaraderie among members of a team.

technology An important concept that can have many definitions in specific instances but that generally refers to actions, physical and mental, that an individual performs upon some object, person, or problem in order to change it in some way.

telecommuting An alternative work arrangement in which an employee works at home while being linked to the office via a computer and/or fax machine.

testing A source of error in experimental studies. The error occurs when changes in the performance of the subject arise because previous measurement of his performance made him aware that he was part of an experiment.

theft Unauthorized taking, consuming, or transfer of money or goods owned by the organization.

time orientation A concept that refers to the time horizon of decisions. Employees may have relatively short- or long-term orientations, depending on the nature of their jobs.

time study The process of determining the appropriate elapsed time for the completion of a task.

timing The point in time that has been selected to initiate an organizational change method.

tolerance for ambiguity The tendency to perceive ambiguous situations or events as desirable. On the other hand, intolerance for ambiguity is the tendency to perceive ambiguous situations or events as sources of threat.

total quality management (TQM) A philosophy and system of management that, using statistical process control and group problem-solving processes, places the greatest priority on attaining high standards for quality and continuous improvement.

trait theory of leadership An attempt to identify specific characteristics (physical, mental, personality) associated with leadership success. The theory relies on research that relates various traits to certain success criteria.

transactional leader   Helps the follower identify what must be done to accomplish the desired results (e.g., better-quality output, more sales or services, reduced cost of production) and ensures that employees have the resources needed to complete the job.

transformational leader   Motivates followers to work for goals instead of short-term self-interest and for achievement and self-actualization instead of security; is able to express a clear vision and inspire others to strive to accomplish the vision.

Type A behavior pattern   Associated with research conducted on coronary heart disease. The Type A person is an aggressive driver who is ambitious, competitive, task-oriented, and always on the move. Rosenman and Friedman, two medical researchers, suggest that Type As have more heart attacks than do Type Bs.

U

unilateral strategies   Strategies for introducing organizational changes that do not allow for participation by subordinates.

universal design theory   A point of view that states there is "one best way" to design an organization.

upward communication   Upward communication flows from individuals at lower levels of the organizational structure to those at higher levels. Among the most common upward communication flows are suggestion boxes, group meetings, and appeal or grievance procedures.

V

valence   The strength of a person's preference for a particular outcome.

values   The guidelines and beliefs that a person uses when confronted with a situation in which a choice must be made.

vertical differentiation   The number of authority levels in an organization. The more authority levels an organization has, the more complex is the organization.

virtual organizations   A collection of geographically distributed, functionally and/or culturally diverse aggregations of individuals that are linked by electronic forms of communications.

virtual teams   A geographically distributed, functionally and/or culturally diverse group of individuals who rely on interactive technology such as e-mail, Webcasts, and videoconferencing to work together.

Vroom-Jago leadership model   A leadership model that specifies which leadership decision-making procedures will be most effective in each of several different situations. Two of the proposed leadership styles are autocratic (AI and AII); two are consultative (CI and CII); and one is oriented toward joint decisions (decisions made by the leader and the group, GII).

W

wellness program   An employee program focusing on the individual's overall physical and mental health. Wellness programs may include a variety of activities designed to identify and assist in preventing or correcting specific health problems, health hazards, or negative health habits.

ENDNOTES

Chapter 1

[1]Sumantra Ghoshal and Christopher A. Bartlett, *The Individualized Corporation* (New York: Harper Business, 1997), pp. 7–8.

[2]Jeffrey Pfeffer and John F. Verga, "Putting People First for Organizational Success," *Academy of Management Executive* 13 (May 1999), p. 35.

[3]S. Nelson Gray, "Tipping Points: Building Momentum for Lasting Change," *Organizational Development Journal,* Summer 2005, pp. 71–77.

[4]Scott DeCarlo, "Forbes Global 2000: The World's Biggest Public Companies," *Forbes,* April 17, 2006, pp. 103–93.

[5]www.forbes.com/lists/2009/18/global-09_The-Global-2000_MktVal.html (accessed July 4, 2009).

[6]"Employment Status of the Population," *Monthly Labor Review,* May 2009, pp. 82–83.

[7]"Employment Status of the Population," *Monthly Labor Review,* January 2006, pp. 69–70.

[8]Michael T. Hannan, Laszlo Polos, and Glenn R. Carroll, "Cascading Organizational Change," *Management Sciences* 14 (September/October 2003), pp. 463–82.

[9]D. Denton, "Strategic (Big Picture) Technology," *Journal of American Academy of Business* 12, no. 2 (2008), pp. 60–68; E.F. Cranor and S. Greenstein, eds., *Communications Policy and Information Technology: Promises, Problems, and Prospects* (Cambridge, MA: MIT Press, 2002).

[10]W. Edwards Deming, *Out of the Crisis* (Cambridge, MA: MIT Press, 2000).

[11]M. Alavi and B.R. Gallupe, "Using Information Technology in Learning: Case Studies in Business and Management Education Programs," *Academy of Management Learning and Education* 2 (June 2003), pp. 139–53.

[12]Ibid.

[13]James C. Cooper, "The Mixed Blessing of Soaring Productivity," *BusinessWeek,* February 2009, p. 10.

[14]Ibid.

[15]David Ulrich, Steve Kerr, and Ron Ashkinas, *The GE Work-Out* (New York: McGraw-Hill, 2002).

[16]John M. Ivancevich, Peter Lorenzi, Steven J. Skinner, and Philip B. Crosby, *Management: Quality and Competitiveness* (Burr Ridge, IL: Irwin, 1997), pp. 30–52.

[17]Ibid., pp. 3–14.

[18]Claude S. George, Jr., *The History of Management Thought* (Englewood Cliffs, NJ: Prentice Hall, 1968), p. 47.

[19]Andrea Gabor, *The Capitalist Philosophers* (New York: Times Books, 2000), pp. 3–44.

[20]Henri Fayol, *General and Industrial Management,* trans. J.A. Conbrough (Geneva: International Management Institute, 1929).

[21]John M. Bartunek, Sara L. Rynes, and Duane Ireland, "What Makes Management Research Interesting, and Why Does It Matter?" *Academy of Management Journal,* February 2006, pp. 9–15.

[22]Ibid.

[23]Jonathan Birchall and Jenny Wiggins, "Retail Suppliers Chase the Value in a Shift to Thrift," *Financial Times,* May 7, 2009, p. 15; and Mark Sherrington, *Added Value* (New York: Palgrave Macmillan, 2003).

[24]E. Mayo, *The Social Problems of Industrial Civilization* (Cambridge, MA: Harvard University Press, 1945).

[25]F.J. Roethlisberger and W.J. Dickson, *Management and the Worker* (Cambridge, MA: Harvard University Press, 1939).

[26]H. McIlvaine Parsons, "Hawthorne: An Early OBM Experiment," *Journal of Organizational Behavior Management,* February 1992, pp. 27–44; and R.G. Greenwood, A.A. Bolton, and B.A. Greenwood, "Hawthorne a Half Century Later: Relay Assembly Participants Remember," *Journal of Management,* Fall–Winter 1983, pp. 217–31.

[27]J. Urbany, T. Reynolds, and J. Phillips, "How to Make Values Count in Everyday Decisions," *MIT Sloan Management Review,* 49, no. 4 (2008), pp. 75–80; Chris Turner, *All Hat and No Cattle* (New York: Perseus, 1999).

[28]Cindy Waxer, "501 Blues," *Business 2.0,* January 2000, pp. 53–54.

[29]See http://www.levistrauss.com/Downloads/AR_2008.pdf (accessed July 6, 2009).

[30]Cindy Waxer, "501 Blues."

[31]Levi Strauss & Co., Annual Report 2005; http://www.levistrauss.com/Company/ValuesAndVision.aspx (accessed July 6, 2009).

[32]"Can Levi's Be Cool Again?" *BusinessWeek,* March 13, 2000, pp. 144–48.

[33]"Organizational Effectiveness/HR Consulting," *Canadian HR Reporter,* 2006, pp. 1–10.

[34]Kim S. Cameron and David A. Whetten, "Perceptions of Organizational Effectiveness over Organizational Life Cycles," *Administrative Science Quarterly,* December 1981, pp. 525–44; and R. E. Quinn and Kim Cameron, "Organizational Life Cycles and Shifting Criteria of Effectiveness: Some Preliminary Evidence," *Management Science,* January 1983, pp. 33–51.

[35]Chris Argyris, *Flawed Advice and the Management Trap* (New York: Oxford University Press, 2000).

[36]Darryl D. Enos, *Performance Improvement: Making It Happen* (New York: St. Lucie Press, 2000).

[37]Ibid.

[38]Shaker A. Zahra, "The Changing Rules of Global Competitiveness in the 21st Century," *Academy of Management Executive,* February 1999, pp. 36–42.

[39]http://www.jdpower.com/autos/articles/2008-Initial-Quality:-Premium-Cars (accessed on July 6, 2009).

Chapter 2

[1]Robert Konopaske and John M. Ivancevich, *Global Organizational Behavior and Management* (Burr Ridge, IL: McGraw-Hill, 2004).

[2]See www.cia.gov/library/publications/the-world-factbook/geos/IN.html (accessed July 7, 2009).

[3]C.L. Cooper, S. Cartwright, and P.C. Earley, eds., *The International Handbook of Organizational Culture and Climate* (New York: John Wiley & Sons, 2001).

[4]Harrison M. Trice and Janice M. Beyer, *The Cultures of Work Organizations* (Englewood Cliffs, NJ: Prentice Hall, 1993).

[5]Geert Hofstede, *Cultures and Organizations* (New York: McGraw-Hill, 1991), pp. 8–10.

[6]Geert Hofstede, "National Cultures in Four Dimensions," *International Studies of Management and Organization,* Spring–Summer 1983, pp. 31–42.

[7]Geert Hofstede and Michael Harris Bond, "The Confucius Connection: From Cultural Roots to Economic Growth," *Organizational Dynamics* 16, no. 4 (1988), pp. 4–21.

[8]Ibid.

[9]See http://stuwww.uvt.nl/~csmeets/PAGE3.HTM (accessed July 8, 2009).

[10]Simcha Ronen and Oded Shenkar, "Clustering Countries on Attitudinal Dimensions: A Review and Synthesis," *Academy of Management Review,* August 1985, pp. 435–54.

[11]Mary Jo Hatch, "Dynamics of Organizational Culture," *Academy of Management Review,* October 1993, pp. 657–93.

[12]J. Colvin, "The 50 Best Companies for Asians, Blacks, and Hispanics," *Fortune,* September 2000, pp. 53–57.

[13]Robert House, Mansour Javidan, Paul Hanges, and Peter Dorfman, "Understanding Cultures and Implicit Leadership Theories across the Globe: An Introduction to Project GLOBE," *Journal of World Business* 37 (2002), pp. 3–10.

[14]Mansour Javidan, Gunter K. Stahl, Felix Brodbeck, and Celeste P.M. Wilderom, "Cross-Border Transfer of Knowledge: Cultural Lessons from Project GLOBE," *Academy of Management Executive* 19, no. 2 (2005), pp. 59–76.

[15]House et al., "Understanding Cultures and Implicit Leadership Theories."

[16]M. Javidan and A. Dastmalchian, "Managerial Implications of the GLOBE Project: A Study of 62 Societies," *Asia Pacific Journal of Human Resources* 47, no. 1 (2009), pp. 41–58.

[17]R.S. Gallagher, *The Soul of an Organization* (Chicago: Dearborn, 2003).

[18]Sarita Chawla and John Renesch, eds., *Learning Organizations: Developing Culture for Tomorrow's Workplace* (University Park, IL: Productivity Press, 2006), pp. 152–64.

[19]Ibid.

[20]Edgar H. Schein, *Organizational Culture and Leadership* (San Francisco: Jossey-Bass, 1985), p. 9.

[21]"Where Even Grumpy Is Happy—Disney World," *Economist.com/Global Agenda*, March 28, 2007 (accessed July 8, 2009).

[22]Michael Zwell, *Creating a Culture of Competence* (New York: John Wiley & Sons, 2000).

[23]Ibid.

[24]J. Freiburg and K. Freiburg, *NUTS! Southwest Airlines' Crazy Recipe for Business and Personal Success* (Austin, TX: Bard Books, 1996).

[25]Alan Farnham, "The Trust Gap," *Fortune,* December 4, 1989, pp. 56–74, 78.

[26]E. Bryant, "Leadership Southwest Style." *Training & Development* 61, no. 12 (December 2007), pp. 36–39.

[27]Ibid.

[28]Keom L. Freiberg, "The Heart and Spirit of Transformation Leadership: A Qualitative Case Study of Herb

Kelleher's Passion for Southwest Airlines," Doctoral Dissertation, University of San Diego, 1997, p. 234.

[29]"Airline," A&E Series on Southwest Airlines, www.southwest.com/programsservices/swa_story.html#stories (accessed April 15, 2006).

[30]Joshua Macht, "Letting the Air Out of Celebrity Leaders," *Business 2.0,* March 2002, pp. 94–95.

[31]Peter C. Reynolds, "Imposing a Corporate Culture," *Psychology Today*, March 1987, pp. 33–38.

[32]See http://about.nordstrom.com/aboutus/companyhist/companyhist.asp (accessed July 8, 2008).

[33]Michael H. Seid, "Understanding Why Companies Operate at the Head of the Pack," www.msaworldwide.com/upload (accessed April 15, 2006).

[34]S. Vitell and A. Singhapakdi, "The Role of Ethics Institutionalization in Influencing Organizational Commitment, Job Satisfaction, and Esprit de Corps," *Journal of Business Ethics* 81 no. 2 (2008), pp. 343–53.

[35]http://pepsico.com/Company/Leadership.aspx.

[36]Ibid.

[37]Schein, *Organizational Culture and Leadership,* pp. 83–89.

[38]Golnaz Sadri and Brian Lees, "Developing Corporate Culture as a Competitive Advantage," *Journal of Management Development* 20, no. 9/10 (2001), pp. 853–59.

[39]J. Cole, "De-Stressing the Workplace," *HR Focus* 76, no. 10, p. 1.

[40]F. Luthans, S. Norman, B. Avolio, and J. Avey, "The Mediating Role of Psychological Capital in the Supportive Organizational Climate – Employee Performance Relationship," *Journal of Organizational Behavior* 29, no. 2 (2008), pp. 219–38.

[41]Ibid.

[42]J. Sarros, B. Cooper, and J. Santora, "Building a Climate for Innovation through Transformational Leadership and Organizational Culture," *Journal of Leadership & Organizational Studies* 15, no. 2 (2008), pp. 145–58; and Jon R. Katzenbach, *The Path to Peak Performance* (Cambridge, MA: Harvard Business School Press, 2000).

[43]Leon de Caluwe and Hans Vermack, *Learning to Change: A Guide for Organization Change Agents* (Thousand Oaks, CA: Sage, 2003).

[44]G. Farias and H. Johnson, "Organizational Development and Change Management," *Journal of Applied Behavioral Science*, September 2000, pp. 376–79.

[45]Amy L. Kristof-Brown, Ryan D. Zimmerman, and Erin C. Johnson, "Consequences of Individuals' Fit at Work: A Meta-Analysis of Person-Job, Person-Organization, Person-Group, and Person-Supervisor Fit," *Personnel Psychology* 58, no. 2 (2005), pp. 281–342.

[46]J. Van Maanen and E.H. Schein, "Toward a Theory of Organizational Socialization," *Research in Organizational Behavior* 1 (1979), pp. 209–64.

[47]Edgar Schein, *The Corporate Cultural Survival Guide: Sense and Nonsense about Culture Change* (San Francisco: Jossey-Bass, 1999).

[48]Ibid.

[49]Samuel B. Bacharach, Pete Bamberger, Valerie McKinney, "Boundary Management Tactics and Logics of Action: The Case of Peer-Support Providers," *Administrative Science Quarterly,* December 2000, pp. 704–36.

[50]These stages are identified by Daniel C. Feldman, "A Contingency Theory of Socialization," *Administrative Science Quarterly,* September 1967, pp. 434–35. The following discussion is based heavily on this work as well as on Daniel C. Feldman, "A Practical Program for Employee Socialization," *Organizational Dynamics,* Autumn 1976, pp. 64–80; and Daniel C. Feldman, "The Multiple Socialization of Organization Members," *Academy of Management Review,* June 1981, pp. 309–18.

[51]J. Van Maanen, "People Processing: Strategies for Organizational Socialization," *Organizational Dynamics,* Summer 1978, pp. 18–36.

[52]Tammy Allen and Lillian Eby, eds., *The Blackwell Handbook of Mentoring: A Multiple Perspective Approach* (Malden, MA: Blackwell Publishing, 2007).

[53]Herminia Ibarra, "Making Partner: A Mentor's Guide for a Psychological Journey," *Harvard Business Review,* March–April 2000, pp. 146–55.

[54]Susan J. Wells, "Tending Talent," *HR Magazine* 54, no. 5 (May 2009), pp. 53–58.

[55]Allen and Eby, *The Blackwell Handbook of Mentoring: A Multiple Perspective Approach.*

[56]Kathy E. Kram, "Phases of the Mentor Relationship," *Academy of Management Journal,* December 1983, pp. 608–25.

[57]Wells, "Tending Talent."

[58]Ibid.

[59]Ibarra, "Making Partner."

[60]Kathryn Tyler, "Cross-Cultural Connections," *HR Magazine* 52, no. 10 (October 2007), pp. 77–81, 83.

[61]Ibarra, "Making Partner."

[62]Ronald D. Brown, "The Role of Identification in Mentoring Female Protégés," *Group and Organization Studies,* March–June 1986, p. 72.

[63]www.census.gov/Press-Release/www/releases/archives/population/012496.html (accessed July 11, 2009).

[64]Ibid.

[65]Robert J. Grossman, "Race in the Workplace," *HR Magazine,* March 2000, pp. 40–45; and David A. Thomas and Suzy Wetlauffer, "A Question of Color: A Debate on Race in the U.S. Workplace," *Harvard Business Review,* September–October 1997, pp. 118–32.

[66]Stanley F. Slater, Robert A. Weigand, and Thomas J. Zwirlein, "The Business Case for Commitment to Diversity," *Business Horizons* 51 (2008), pp. 201–9.

[67]Nancy R. Lockwood, "Workplace Diversity: Leveraging the Power of Difference for Competitive Advantage," *HR Magazine* 50, no. 6 (June 2005), pp. 1–11.

[68]Ibid.

[69]Robert Rodriguez, "Diversity Finds Its Place," *HR Magazine* 51, no. 8 (August 2006), pp. 56–62.

[70]Slater, et al., "The Business Case for Commitment to Diversity."

[71]Ibid.

[72]Rama D. Jager and Rafael Ortiz, *In the Company of Giants* (New York: McGraw-Hill, 1997).

[73]Ibid.

[74]Norma Carr-Ruffino, *Managing Diversity* (Cincinnati, OH: Thomas International Publishing, 1996), pp. 6–8.

[75]G.R. Carroll and M.T. Hannan, *The Demography of Corporations and Industries* (Princeton, NJ: Princeton University Press, 2000).

[76]David Jamieson and Julie O'Mara, *Managing Workforce 2000* (San Francisco: Jossey-Bass, 1991), pp. 84–89.

[77]Jacqueline A. Gilbert and John M. Ivancevich, "Value Diversity: A Tale of Two Organizations," *Academy of Management Review,* February 2000, pp. 93–110.

[78]M. Benefiel, "Irreconcilable Foes? The Discourse of Spirituality and the Discourse of Organizational Science," *Organization: The Interdisciplinary Journal of Organization Theory and Science* 10 (2003), pp. 385–93.

[79]Dennis Duchon and Donde Ashmos Plowman, "Nurturing the Spirit at Work: Impact on Work Unit Performance," *The Leadership Quarterly* 16 (2005), pp. 807–33.

[80]K.L. Dean, C.J. Fornaciari, and J.J. McGee, "Research in Spirituality, Religion, and Work," *Journal of Organizational Change Management* 168 (2003), pp. 378–95.

[81]G. Gotsis and Z. Kortezi, "Philosophical Foundations of Workplace Spirituality: A Critical Approach," *Journal of Business Ethics* 78, no. 4 (2008), pp. 575–600.

[82]I. Mitroff, "Spirituality in Organizations: Empirical Research," Discussant at the 2001 Academy of Management Meetings, 2001, Washington, DC.

[83]See http://group.aomonline.org/msr/ (accessed July 12, 2009).

[84]Duchon and Plowman, "Nurturing the Spirit at Work: Impact on Work Unit Performance."

[85]R. Kolodinsky, R. Giacalone, and C. Jurkiewicz, "Workplace Values and Outcomes: Exploring Personal, Organizational, and Interactive Workplace Spirituality," *Journal of Business Ethics* 81, no. 2 (2008), pp. 465–80.

[86]I. Mitroff and E. Denton, *A Spiritual Audit of Corporate America: A Hard Look at Spirituality, Religion, and Values in the Workplace* (San Francisco: Jossey-Bass, 1999).

[87]Ibid.

[88]P. Gibbons, "Spirituality at Work: Definitions, Measures, Assumptions, and Validity Claims," in *Work and Spirit: A Reader of New Spiritual Paradigms for Organizations,* ed. J. Biberman and M. Whitty (Scranton, PA: University of Scranton Press, 2000), pp. 111–31.

[89]J. Milliman, A.J. Czaplewski, and J. Ferguson, "Workplace Spirituality and Employee Work Attitudes," *Journal of Organizational Change Management* 16 (2003), pp. 426–47.

[90]R.A. Giacalone and C.L. Jurkiewicz, "Toward a Science of Workplace Spirituality," in *Handbook of Workplace Spirituality and Organizational Performance,* ed. R.A. Giacalone and C.L. Jurkiewicz (New York: Paulist Press, 2003).

[91]Pamela Chandler Lee, *Cognition and Affect in Leader Behavior: The Effects of Spirituality, Psychological Empowerment, and Emotional Intelligence on the Motivation to Lead* (New York: Proquest Information and Leading, 2006); and K. Krahnke, R.A. Giacalone, and C.L. Jurkiewicz, "Point–Counterpoint: Measuring Workplace Spirituality," *Journal of Organizational Change Management* 16 (2003), pp. 396–405.

Chapter 3

[1]B. Schneider, H.W. Goldstein, and D.B. Smith, "The ASA Framework: An Update," *Personnel Psychology,* Autumn 1996, pp. 757–74.

[2]David R. Hannah and Christopher D. Zatzick, "An Examination of Leader Portrayals in the U.S. Business Press following the Landmark Scandals of the Early 21st Century," *Journal of Business Ethics* 79 (2008), pp. 361–77; Ronald R. Sims and Johannes Brinkman, "Enron Ethics (Or: Culture Matters More than Codes)," *Journal of Business Ethics* 45, no. 3 (July 2003), pp. 243–55; Charlene Fishman, "Bad Business: What If You'd Worked for Enron?" *FastCompany* 58 (May 2002), pp. 102–11.

[3]Kenneth S. Kendler, Laura M. Thornton, and Nancy I. Pedersen, "Tobacco Consumption in Swedish Twins Reared Apart and Reared Together," *Archive of General Psychiatry* 57, no. 9 (September 2000), pp. 886–92; Thomas J. Bouchard, Sr., "Genetic and Environmental Influences on Intelligence and Special Mental Abilities," *American Journal of Human Biology,* April 1998, pp. 253–75; and Lawrence Wright, *Twins: And What They Tell Us about What We Are* (New York: John Wiley & Sons, 1999).

[4]Eden B. King, "The Effect of Bias on the Advancement of Working Mothers," *Human Relations* 61, no. 12 (December 2008), pp. 1677–1711; Denise Breeby, "Women's Work: Gender Equality vs. Hierarchy in the Life Sciences," *Contemporary Sociology,* March 2006, pp. 138–39.

[5]James L. Gibson, James H. Donnelly, Jr., John M. Ivancevich, and Robert Konopaske, *Organizations: Behavior, Structure, Processes,* 13th ed. (New York: McGraw-Hill, 2009).

[6]Susan J. Wells, "Counting on Workers with Disabilities," *HR Magazine,* 53, no. 4 (April 2008), pp. 45–50; Mitra Toossi, "Labor Force Projections to 2016—More Workers in Their Golden Years" *Monthly Labor Review,* November 2007, U.S. Bureau of Labor Statistics (http://www.bls.gov/opub/mlr/2007/11/art3full.pdf).

[7]"Conectiv and Subcontractors to Pay $1.65 Million to Black Workers Who Were Racially Harassed," U.S. Equal Employment Opportunity Commission, www.eeoc.gov/press/5-5-08.html (accessed May 7, 2009).

[8]V. Weaver, "Winning with Diversity," *BusinessWeek,* September 10, 2001, Special Section; and Luis R. Gomez-Mejia, David B. Balkin, and Robert L. Cardy, *Managing Human Resources,* 4th ed. (Upper Saddle River, NJ: Pearson/Prentice Hall, 2003), p. 125.

[9]Sadri Golnaz and Tran Hoa, "Managing Your Diverse Workforce through Improved Communication," *Journal of Management Development* 21, no. 3–4 (2002), pp. 227–38.

[10]Robert Konopaske and John M. Ivancevich, *Global Management and Organizational Behavior* (New York: McGraw-Hill, 2004), p. 217.

[11]Francesco Guerrera, "Women Crack Glass Ceiling from Above," *Financial Times,* July 23, 2008, p. 3; and Siri Terjesen and Val Singh, "Female Presence on Corporate Boards: A Multi-Country Study of Environmental Context," *Journal of Business Ethics* 83 (2008), pp. 55–63.

[12]Karen Auby, "A Boomer's Guide to Communicating with Gen X and Gen Y," *BusinessWeek*, August 25, 2008, pp. 63–64.

[13]John M. Ivancevich, *Human Resource Management,* 11th ed. (New York: McGraw-Hill, 2009).

[14]T.G. Reio and J. Sanders-Reio, "Sensation Seeking as an Inhibitor of Job Performance," *Personality and Individual Differences,* March 2006, pp. 631–42.

[15]S. Escorial, L.F. Garcia, L. Cuevas, and M. Juan-Espinosa, "Personality Level on the Big Five and the Structure of Intelligence," *Personality and Individual Differences,* April 2006, pp. 909–17.

[16]www.wonderlic.com.

[17]Sarah F. Gale, "Putting Job Candidates to the Test," *Workforce* 82, no. 4 (April 2003), pp. 64–68; and Jeff Barvian, "Just Call Me Leonard Zelig," *Training* 38, no. 6 (June 2001), p. 78.

[18]Daniel Goleman, *Working with Emotional Intelligence* (New York: Bantam, 1998).

[19]Margaret M. Hopkins and Diana Bilimoria, "Social and Emotional Competencies Predicting Success for Male and Female Executives," *The Journal of Management Development* 27, no. 1 (2008), pp. 13–35.

[20]Peter J. Jordan, Neal M. Ashkanasv, and Charlene E. J. Hartel, "Emotional Intelligence as a Moderator of Emotional and Behavioral Reactions to Job Insecurity," *Academy of Management Review* 27, no. 3 (2002), pp. 361–77.

[21]Steve J. Armstrong, "Experiential Learning and the Acquisition of Managerial Tacit Knowledge," *Academy of Management Learning & Education* 7, no. 2 (June 2008), pp. 189–208; Erich N. Brockmann and William P. Anthony, "Tacit Knowledge and Strategic Decision Making," *Group and Organization Management* 27, no. 4 (December 2002), pp. 436–56.

[22]Robert J. Sternberg, "Successful Intelligence," *Executive Excellence* 14, no. 8 (August 1997), p. 5.

[23]Jennifer Hedlund, George B. Forsythe, Joseph A. Horvath, and Wendy M. Williams, "Identifying and Assessing Tacit Knowledge: Understanding the Practical Intelligence of Military Leaders," *Leadership Quarterly* 14, no. 2 (April 2003), pp. 117–32.

[24]Ya Hui Michelle See, Richard E. Petty, and Leandre R. Fabrigar, "Affective and Cognitive Meta-Bases of Attitudes: Unique Effects on Information Interest and Persuasion," *Journal of Personality and Social Psychology* 94, no. 6 (June 2008), pp. 938–55; and Richard E. Petty, Pablo Brinol, and Zakary L. Tormala, "Thought Confidence as a Determinant of Persuasion: The Self-Validation Hypothesis," *Journal of Personality and Social Psychology* 82, no. 5 (May 2002), pp. 722–34.

[25]Robert Roe and Peter Ester, "Values and Work: Empirical Findings and Theoretical Perspectives," *Applied Psychology: An International Review,* January 1999, pp. 1–21.

[26]K. Krone, "Trends in Organizational Communication Research: Sustaining the Discipline, Sustaining Ourselves," *Communication Studies,* March 2005, pp. 95–105.

[27]G. R. Carter, "Assessing Organizational Communication: Strategic Communication Audits," *Journalism and Mass Communication,* Summer 2005, pp. 449–50.

[28]Maureen L. Ambrose, Anke Arnaud, and Marshall Schminke, "Individual Moral Development and Ethical Climate: The Influence of Person-Organization Fit on Job Attitudes," *Journal of Business Ethics* 77, no. 3 (February 2008), pp. 323–34; and Virginia Postrel, *The Future and Its Enemies* (New York: Free Press, 1999).

[29]Ben & Jerry's Homemade, Inc., *Annual Report 2005.*

[30]"100 Best Places to Work in IT 2008," *Computerworld,* June 30–July 7, 2008; and Gary Anthes, "A Way to Unwind," *Computerworld,* June 18, 2007, p. 74.

[31]Bryan D. Edwards, Suzanne T. Bell, Winfred Arthur, Jr., and Arlette D. Decuir, "Relationship between Facets of Job Satisfaction and Task and Contextual Performance," *Applied Psychology* 57, no. 3 (July 2008), pp. 441–65; Cynthia D. Fisher, "Why Do Lay People Believe That Satisfaction and Performance Are Correlated? Possible Sources of a Commonsense Theory," *Journal of Organizational Behavior* 24, no. 6 (September 2003), pp. 753–67; and Ann Marie Ryan, Mark Schmit, and Raymond Johnson, "Attitudes and Effectiveness: Examining Relations at an Organizational Level," *Personnel Psychology,* Winter 1996, pp. 853–82.

[32]J. A. Wagner III, "Participation's Effects on Performance and Satisfaction: A Reconsideration of Research Evidence," *Academy of Management Review,* April 1994, pp. 312–30.

[33]Rodger W. Griffeth, Peter W. Hom, and Stefan Gaertner, "A Meta-Analysis of Antecedents and Correlates of Employee Turnover: Update, Moderator Tests, and Research Implications for the Next Millennium," *Journal of Management* 26, no. 3 (2000), pp. 463–88; and Chi-sum Wong, Chun Hui, and Kenneth S. Law, "Causal Relationships between Attitudinal Antecedents to Turnover," *Academy*

of Management Best Paper Proceedings, August 1995, pp. 342–46. For a somewhat different view, see Thomas W. Lee, Terence R. Mitchell, Lowell Wise, and Steven Fireman, "An Unfolding Model of Voluntary Employee Turnover," *Academy of Management Journal,* February 1996, pp. 5–36.

[34]Bouchard, "Genetic and Environmental Influences."

[35]R.M. Guion and R.F. Gottier, "Validity of Personality Measures in Personnel Selection," *Personnel Psychology* 18 (1965), pp. 135–64.

[36]Margery Weinstein, "Personality Assessment Soars at Southwest," *Training* 45, no. 1 (January 2008), p. 14.

[37]L. Offermann and R. Spiros, "The Science and Practice of Team Development: Improving the Link," *Academy of Management Journal* 44 (2001), pp. 376–92; and W.L. Gardner and M.J. Martinko, "Using the Myers-Briggs Type Indicator to Study Managers: A Literature Review and Research Agenda," *Journal of Management* 22 (1996), pp. 45–82.

[38]James Michael, "Using the Myers-Briggs Type Indicator as a Tool for Leadership Development: Apply with Caution," *Journal of Leadership and Organizational Studies* 10, no. 1, pp. 68–84.

[39]J. Allick, "Personality Dimensions across Cultures," *Journal of Personality Disorders,* June 2005, pp. 212–32.

[40]Ibid.

[41]Timothy A. Judge, Daniel Heller, and Michael K. Mount, "Five-Factor Model of Personality and Job Satisfaction: A Meta-Analysis," *Journal of Applied Psychology* 87, no. 3 (June 2002), pp. 530–41.

[42]Timothy A. Judge and Remus Ilies, "Relationship of Personality to Performance Motivation: A Meta-Analytic Review," *Journal of Applied Psychology* 87, no. 4 (August 2002), pp. 797–807.

[43]Dishan Kamdar and Linn Van Dyne, "The Joint Effects of Personality and Workplace Social Exchange Relationships in Predicting Task Performance and Citizenship Performance," *Journal of Applied Psychology* 92, no. 5, pp. 1286–98; George A. Neuman and Julie Wright, "Team Effectiveness: Beyond Skills and Cognitive Ability," *Journal of Applied Psychology* 84, no. 3 (June 1999), pp. 379–89.

[44]Ryan Zimmerman, "Understanding the Impact of Personality Traits on Individuals' Turnover Decisions: A Meta-Analytic Path Model," *Personnel Psychology* 61, no. 2 (Summer 2008), pp. 309–48; Judge and Ilies, "Relationships of Personality to Performance Motivation"; and Judge et al., "Five-Factor Model."

[45]Michael K. Mount and Murray R. Barrick, "Five Reasons Why the 'Big Five' Article Has Been Frequently Cited," *Personnel Psychology* 51, no. 4 (1998), pp. 849–57.

[46]R.R. McCrae and P.T. Costa, "A Five-Factor Theory of Personality," in *Handbook of Personality,* 2nd ed., eds. L.A. Pervin and O.P. John (New York: Guilford, 1999), pp. 139–53.

[47]J.R. Rotter, "Generalized Expectancies for Internal versus External Control of Reinforcement," *Psychological Monographs* 1, no. 609, (1996), pp. 1–28.

[48]Jesus F. Salgado, "The Five Factor Model of Personality and Job Performance in the European Community," *Journal of Applied Psychology,* February 1997, pp. 30–43.

[49]James R. Detert, Linda Klebe Trevino, and Vicki L. Sweitzer, "Moral Disengagement in Ethical Decision Making: A Study of Antecedents and Outcomes," *Journal of Applied Psychology* 93, no. 2 (March 2008), pp. 374–91; L.K. Trevino and S.A. Youngblood, "Bad Apples in Bad Barrels: A Causal Analysis of Ethical Decision-Making Behavior and Human Resource Management," *Academy of Management Review,* July 1987, pp. 472–85.

[50]Marilyn E. Gist and Terence R. Mitchell, "Self-Efficacy: A Theoretical Analysis of Its Determinants and Malleability," *Academy of Management Review* 17, no. 2 (1992), pp. 183–201.

[51]Alexander D. Stajkovic and Fred Luthans, "Self-Efficacy and Work-Related Performance: A Meta-Analysis," *Psychological Bulletin* 124, no. 2 (1988), pp. 240–62.

[52]Albert Bandura and Edwin Locke, "Negative Self-Efficacy and Goal Effects Revisited," *Journal of Applied Psychology* 88, no. 1 (February 2003), pp. 87–99.

[53]Michael D. Mumford, Samuel T. Hunter, and Katrina E. Bedell-Avers, eds., *Multi-Level Issues in Creativity and Innovation,* Vol. 7 (Stamford, CT: JAI Press, 2008).

[54]Heinz Co., *Annual Report 2005.*

Chapter 4

[1]Dennis Coon, *Introduction to Psychology* (Belmont, CA: Wadsworth, 2001), pp. 200–1.

[2]J. Andre, D.A. Owens, and L.O. Harvey Jr., *Visual Perception* (Washington, DC: American Psychological Association, 2003).

[3]Antonella Sciangula and Marian M. Morry, "Self-Esteem and Perceived Regard: How I See Myself Affects My Relationship Satisfaction," *Journal of Social Psychology* 149, no. 2 (2009), pp. 143–58; and Jane E. Myers and Thomas J. Sweeney, "The Indivisible Self: An Evidence-Based Model of Wellness," *Journal of Individual Psychology,* Fall 2005, pp. 269–79.

[4]A.G. Lafley, "What Only the CEO Can Do," *Harvard Business Review* 87, no. 5 (May 2009), pp. 54–62; and Julian Birkinshaw and Jules Goddard, "What Is Your Management Model?" *MIT Sloan Management Review* 50, no. 2 (Winter 2009), pp. 81–90.

[5]Lin Choon-Hwa, R. Winter, and C.A. Christopher, "Cross-Culture Interviewing in the Hiring Process: Challenges and Strategies," *Career Development Quarterly,* March 2006, pp. 265–68.

[6]Ibid.

[7]Greg L. Stewart and Susan L. Dustin, "Exploring the Handshake in Employment Interviews," *Journal of Applied Psychology* 93, no. 5 (September 2008), pp. 1139–46.

[8]Andre et al., *Visual Perception.*

[9]Ibid.

[10]Tracy N. Anderson-Clark, Raymond J. Green, and Tracy Henley, "The Relationship between First Names and Teacher Expectations for Achievement Motivation," *Journal of Language and Social Psychology* 27, no. 1 (March 2008), pp. 94–99.

[11]Howard Markel and Sam Potts, "American Epidemics, a Brief History," *The New York Times,* May 3, 2009, p. 12, *Newspaper Source Plus,* EBSCO*host* (accessed May 6, 2009).

[12]C.R. Kaiser, S. Brook Vick, and B. Major, "Prejudice Expectations Moderate Preconscious Attention to Cues That Are Threatening to Social Identity," *Psychological Science,* April 2006, pp. 332–38.

[13]G. Allport, *The Nature of Prejudice* (Garden City, NY: Anchor Books, 1958).

[14]Duane T. Wegener, Jason K. Clark, and R.E. Petty, "Not All Stereotyping Is Created Equal: Differential Consequences of Thoughtful versus Nonthoughtful Stereotyping," *Journal of Personality and Social Psychology,* January 2006, pp. 42–59.

[15]Ibid.

[16]S.K. Reed, *Cognition: Theory and Applications* (Pacific Grove, CA: Brooks/Cole, 1996).

[17]N. London-Vargas, *Faces of Diversity* (New York: Vantage Press, 1999).

[18]H.L. Swanson, "What Develops in a Working Memory? A Lifetime Perspective," *Development and Psychology* 35 (1999), pp. 986–1000.

[19]Michael J. Marks, "Evaluations of Sexually Active Men and Women under Divided Attention: A Social Cognitive Approach to the Sexual Double Standard," *Basic & Applied Social Psychology* 30, no. 1 (March 2008), pp. 84–91.

[20]Ibid.

[21]T. Moore, "The Neurobiology of Visual Attention: Finding Sources," Current Opinion, *Neurobiology*, April 2006, pp. 159–65.

[22]S.A. Carless, "Applicant Reactions to Multiple Selection Procedures for the Police Force," *Applied Psychology: An International Review,* April 2006, pp. 145–67; and M.E. Heilman and M.H. Stopeck, "Being Attractive: Advantage or Disadvantage?" *Journal of Applied Psychology* 70 (1985), pp. 379–88.

[23]Phil Rosenzweig, "Common Errors in Marketing Research—and How to Fix Them," *Marketing Research* 20, no. 3 (Fall 2008), pp. 6–12.

[24]J.S. Boroman, "Performance Appraisal: Verisimilitude Trumps Veracity," *Public Personnel Management* 28 (Winter 1999), pp. 557–76.

[25]J.A. Deutsch, W.G. Young, and T.J. Kalogeris, "The Stomach Signals Satiety," *Science,* April 1978, pp. 23–33.

[26]H.H. Kelly, "Attribution Theory in Social Psychology," in *Nebraska Symposium on Motivation,* ed. D. Levine (Lincoln: University of Nebraska Press, 1967).

[27]J.K. Swim and L.J. Sanna, "He's Skilled, She's Lucky: A Meta-Analysis of Observers' Attributions for Women's and Men's Successes and Failures," *Personality and Social Psychology Bulletin* 22 (1996), pp. 507–19.

[28]B. Thornton, R.J. Audesse, R.M. Ryckman, and M.J. Burckle, "Playing Dumb and Knowing It All: Two Sides of an Impression Management Coin," *Individual Differences Research,* March 2006, pp. 37–45; M.C. Bolino, "More than One Way to Make an Impression: Exploring Profiles of Impression Management," *Journal of Management* 29 (2002), pp. 141–60.

[29]Corey E. Miller and Gerald V. Barrett, "The Coachability and Fakability of Personality-Based Selection Tests Used for Police Selection," *Public Personnel Management* 37, no. 3 (Fall 2008), pp. 339–51.

[30]E. Goffman, *The Presentation of Self in Everyday Life* (New York: Doubleday, 1959).

[31]K. Greene and R. Greene, "Inside the Dream: The Personal Story of Walt Disney," www.corporate.disney. com/corporate/cr_business_standards.html (accessed May 8, 2006).

[32]E.E. Jones and T.S. Pittman, "Toward a General Theory of Strategic Self-Presentation" in *Psychological Perspective on the Self,* Vol. 1, ed. J. Suls (Hillsdale, NJ: Lawrence Erlbaum, 1982), pp. 231–62.

[33]J. Tatu, "The Influence of Gender on the Use and Effectiveness of Managerial Accounts," *Group Organization Management* (1998), pp. 267–88.

[34]T.E. Becker and S.L. Martin, "Trying to Look Bad at Work: Methods and Motives for Poor Impressions in Organizations," *Academy of Management Journal* (1995), p. 145.

[35]Kevin P. Scheibe, James C. McElroy, and Paula C. Morrow, "Object Language and Impression Management," *Communications of the ACM* 52, no. 4 (April 2009), pp. 129–31.

[36]N.E. Rosenthal, *The Emotional Revolution* (New York: Kensington, 2002).

[37]R. Brown and I. Brooks, "Emotions at Work," *Journal of Management in Medicine* 16 (2002), pp. 327–44.

[38]Ibid.

[39]J. Burgdorf and J. Panksepp, "The Neurobiology of Positive Emotions," *Neuroscience and Biobehavioral Review*, April 2006, pp. 173–87.

[40]J. LeDoux, *The Emotional Brain: The Mysterious Underpinnings of Emotional Life* (New York: Simon & Schuster, 1998).

[41]R. Plutchik, *The Psychology and Biology of Emotion* (New York: HarperCollins, 1994).

[42]G. Kirchsteiger, L. Rigotti, and A. Rustichini, "Your Morals Might Be Your Moods," *Journal of Economic Behavior and Organization,* February 2006, pp. 155–72.

[43]D. Galete, K.R. Scherer, and P.E. Ricci-Bitti, "Voluntary Facial Expression of Emotions: Comparing Congenitally Blind with Normally Sighted Encoders," *Journal of Personality and Social Psychology* 73 (1997), pp. 1363–79.

[44]J.M. Carroll and J.A. Russell, "Do Facial Expressions Signal Specific Emotions? Judging Emotion from the Face in Context," *Journal of Personality and Social Psychology* 70 (1996), pp. 205–18.

[45]H.A. Elfenbein, "Learning in Emotion Judgments: Training and the Cross-Cultural Understanding of Facial Expressions," *Journal of Nonverbal Behavior,* March 2006, pp. 21–36.

[46]H. Markus, S. Kitayama, and G.R. Vanden Bos, "The Mutual Interactions of Culture and Emotion," *Psychiatric Services* 47 (1996), pp. 225–26.

[47]A.M. Kring and A.H. Gordon, "Sex Differences in Emotion: Expression, Experience, and Physiology" *Journal of Personality and Social Psychology* 74 (1998), pp. 686–703.

[48]Kathryn Lively, "Emotional Segues and the Management of Emotion by Women and Men," *Social Forces* 87, no. 2 (December 2008), pp. 911–36.

[49]G. Newton, "Body Language," *Southern Review,* Winter 2006, pp. 18–24.

[50]T.L. Chartrand and J.A. Bargh, "The Chameleon Effect: The Perception–Behavior Link and Social Interaction," *Journal of Personality and Social Psychology* 76 (June 1999), pp. 893–911.

[51]Marielle Stel, Rick B. van Baaren, and Roos Vonk, "Effects of Mimicking: Acting Prosocially by Being Emotionally Moved," *European Journal of Social Psychology* 38, no. 6 (October 2008), pp. 965–76.

[52] Sungsoo Park and Daijin Kim, "Subtle Facial Expression Recognition Using Motion Magnification," *Pattern Recognition Letters* 30, no. 7 (May 2009), pp. 708–16.

[53]P.K. Adelman and R.B. Zagone, "Facial Differences in the Experience of Emotion," *Annual Review of Psychology* 40 (1989), pp. 249–80.

[54]P. Ekman, "Facial Expression and Emotion," *American Psychologist* 48 (1993), pp. 384–92.

[55]Ibid.

[56]A.Q. Mears and W. Finlay, "Not Just a Paper Doll: How Models Manage Bodily Capital and Why They Perform Emotional Labor," *Journal of Contemporary Ethnography,* June 2005, pp. 317–43.

[57]A. Grandey, "Emotion Regulation in the Workplace: A New Way to Conceptualize Emotional Labor," *Journal of Occupational Health Psychology* 5 (2000), pp. 95–110.

[58]Sharmin Spencer and Deborah E. Rupp, "Angry, Guilty, and Conflicted: Injustice toward Coworkers Heightens Emotional Labor through Cognitive and Emotional Mechanisms," *Journal of Applied Psychology* 94, no. 2 (March 2009), pp. 429–44.

[59]P. Smith and M. Lorentzon, "Is Emotional Labour Ethical?" *Nursing Ethics,* November 2005, pp. 638–42.

[60]Mears and Finlay, "Not Just a Paper Doll."

[61]Ibid.

[62]P. Salovey and J.D. Mayer, "Emotional Intelligence," *Imagination, Cognition, and Personality* 9 (1990), pp. 185–211.

[63]Diane Coutu, "Leadership Lessons from Abraham Lincoln," *Harvard Business Review* 87, no. 4 (April 2009), pp. 43–47.

[64]V. Dulewicz, M. Higgs, and M. Slaski, "Measuring Emotional Intelligence: Content, Construct, and Criterion-Related Validity," *Journal of Managerial Psychology* 18 (2003), pp. 405–50.

[65]D.R. Caruso, J.D. Mayer, and P. Salovey, "Relation of an Ability Measure of Emotional Intelligence to Personality," *Journal of Personality Assessment* 79 (October 2002), pp. 81–108.

[66]R.D. Roberts, M. Zeidner, and G. Matthews, "Does Emotional Intelligence Meet Traditional Standards for Intelligence? Some New Data and Conclusions," *Emotion* (2001), pp. 196–231.

[67]H. Gardner, *Frames of Mind: The Theory of Multiple Intelligences* (New York: Basic Books, 1983).

[68]S.I. Pfeiffer, "Emotional Intelligence: Popular but Elusive Construct," *Roeper Review* 23 (April 2001), pp. 18–39.

[69]D. Goleman, *Emotional Intelligence* (New York: Bantam Books, 1995).

[70]Ibid.

[71]Salovey and Mayer, "Emotional Intelligence."

[72]J.D. Mayer, P. Salovey, and D.R. Caruso, *Mayer-Salovey-Caruso Emotional Intelligence Test (MSCEIT): Manual* (Toronto: Multi-Health Systems, 2002).

[73]R. Bar-On, *Bar-On Emotional Quotient Inventory: Technical Manual* (Toronto: Multi-Health Systems, 1997).

[74]M. Bernet, "Emotional Intelligence Components and Correlates," Toronto, Annual Convention of the American Psychological Association, 1996.

[75]D. Roger and B. Najarian, "The Construction and Validation of a New Scale for Measuring Emotion Control," *Personality and Individual Differences* 10 (1989), pp. 845–53.

[76]J.D. Mayer, P. Salovey, and D.R. Caruso, "Emotional Intelligence as Zeitgeist, as Personality, and as a Mental Ability," in *The Handbook of Emotional Intelligence,* ed. R. Bar-On and J.D.A. Parker (San Francisco: Jossey-Bass, 2000), pp. 92–117.

[77]Nick Tasler, and Lac D. Su, "The Emotional Ignorance Trap," *BusinessWeek Online,* January 19, 2009, p. 6. *Business Source Premier,* EBSCO*host* (accessed May 9, 2009).

[78]Gardner, *Frames of Mind.*

Chapter 5

[1]Story still related by executive level and operating manager level at IBM, October 2000.

[2]Oliver Gottschalg and Maurizio Zollo, "Interest Alignment and Competitive Advantage," *Academy of Management Review* 32, no. 2 (April 2007), pp. 418–37; Bard Kuvaas, "Work Performance, Affective Commitment, and Work Motivation: The Roles of Pay Administration and Pay Level," *Journal of Organizational Behavior* 27, no. 3 (May 2006), pp. 365–85; Naomi Ellemers, Dick de Gilder, S. Alexander Haslam, "Motivating Individuals

and Groups at Work: A Social Identity Perspective on Leadership and Group Performance," *Academy of Management Review* 29, no. 3 (July 2004), pp. 459–78; M.L. Ambrose and C.T. Kulik, "Old Friends, New Faces: Motivation Research in the 1990s," *Journal of Management,* Summer 1999, pp. 231–37.

³Craig R. Taylor, "The Tides of Talent," *Training and Development* 57, no. 4 (April 2003), pp. 34–39.

⁴A.H. Maslow and A.R. Kaplan, *Maslow on Management* (New York: John Wiley & Sons, 1998).

⁵"Wal-Mart's New Technology Eases Use of FSA Debit Cards," *Employee Benefit Plan Review* 61, no. 10 (April 2007), p. 25.

⁶Laverne Hadaway, "Market Trends: Flexible Benefits for SMEs," *Employee Benefits,* April 2008, p. 65.

⁷Sarah Rubenstein, "Buying Health Insurance, Cafeteria Style: Some Employers Offer a Menu of Deductibles, Co-Payments, Networks, and Prescription Plans," *The Wall Street Journal,* October 19, 2004, p. D4; and Jennifer Hutchins, "How to Make the Right Voluntary Benefit Choices," *Workforce* 81, no. 3 (March 2002), pp. 42–45.

⁸See www.marykay.com (accessed April 14, 2009).

⁹Lyman W. Porter, "A Study of Perceived Need Satisfaction in Bottom and Middle-Management Jobs," *Journal of Applied Psychology,* February 1961, pp. 1–10.

¹⁰Lyman W. Porter, *Organizational Patterns of Managerial Job Attitudes* (New York: American Foundation for Management Research, 1964).

¹¹Lyman W. Porter, "Job Attitudes in Management: Perceived Deficiencies in Need Fulfillment as a Function of Size of the Company," *Journal of Applied Psychology,* December 1963, pp. 386–97.

¹²John M. Ivancevich, "Perceived Need Satisfaction of Domestic versus Overseas Managers," *Journal of Applied Psychology,* August 1969, pp. 274–78.

¹³Edward E. Lawler, III, and J.L. Suttle, "A Causal Correlation Test of the Need Hierarchy Concept," *Organizational Behavior and Human Performance,* April 1972, pp. 265–87.

¹⁴Douglas T. Hall and K.E. Nougaim, "An Examination of Maslow's Need Hierarchy in an Organizational Setting," *Organizational Behavior and Human Performance,* February 1968, pp. 12–35.

¹⁵Clayton P. Alderfer, *Existence, Relatedness, and Growth: Human Needs in Organizational Settings* (New York: Free Press, 1972).

¹⁶Gerald R. Salancik and Jeffrey Pfeffer, "An Examination of Need-Satisfaction Models of Job Attitudes,"

Administrative Science Quarterly, September 1977, pp. 427–56.

¹⁷Frederick Herzberg, B. Mausner, and B. Snyderman, *The Motivation to Work* (New York: John Wiley & Sons, 1959).

¹⁸Cindy P. Zapata-Phelan, Jason A. Colquitt, Brent A. Scott, and Beth Livingston, "Procedural Justice, Interactional Justice, and Task Performance: The Mediating Role of Intrinsic Motivation," *Organizational Behavior and Human Decision Processes* 108, no. 1 (January 2009), pp. 93–105; Nigel Bassett-Jones and Geoffrey C. Lloyd, "Does Herzberg's Motivation Theory Have Staying Power?" *Journal of Management Development,* 24, no. 10 (2005), pp. 929–44; and Thad Green, *Motivation Management: Fueling Performance by Discovering What People Believe about Themselves and Their Organizations* (Palo Alto, CA: Davies-Black, 2000).

¹⁹Frederick Herzberg, "Workers' Needs: The Same around the World," *Industry Week* 234, no. 6 (September 21, 1987), pp. 29–32.

²⁰Isaac O. Adigun, "Cross-National Differences in Work Motivation: A Four Nation Comparison," *International Journal of Management* 17, no. 3 (September 2000), pp. 372–78.

²¹Sally Sledge, Angela K. Miles, and Samuel Coppage, "What Role Does Culture Play? A Look at Motivation and Job Satisfaction among Hotel Workers in Brazil," *The International Journal of Human Resource Management* 19, no. 9 (September 2008), pp. 1667–82; and Richard W. Brislin, Brent MacNab, Reginald Worthley, Florencio Kabigting, Jr., and Bob Zukis, "Evolving Perceptions of Japanese Workplace Motivation: An Employee-Manager Comparison," *International Journal of Cross Cultural Management* 5, no. 1 (April 2005), pp. 87–104.

²²David C. McClelland and David H. Burnham, "Power Is the Great Motivator," *Harvard Business Review* 81, no. 1 (January 2003), pp. 117–26; and David C. McClelland, "Business Drive and National Achievement," *Harvard Business Review,* July–August 1962, pp. 99–112.

²³Victor H. Vroom, *Work and Motivation* (New York: John Wiley & Sons, 1964). For earlier work, see Kurt Lewin, *The Conceptual Representation and the Measurement of Psychological Forces* (Durham, NC: Duke University Press, 1938), and E.C. Tolman, *Purposive Behavior in Animals and Men* (New York: Appleton-Century-Crofts, 1932).

²⁴Yei-Yi Chen and Wen Chang Fang, "The Moderating Effect of Impression Management on the Organizational Politics-Performance Relationship," *Journal of Business Ethics* 79, no. 3 (May 2008), pp. 263–78; William H. Murphy, Peter A. Dacin, and Neil M. Ford, "Sales Contest Effectiveness: An Examination of Sales Contest

Design Preferences of Field Sales Forces," *Journal of the Academy of Marketing Science* 32, no. 2 (Spring 2004), pp. 127–44; and R.M. Lynd-Stevenson, "Expectancy Theory and Predicting Future Employment Status in the Young Unemployed," *Journal of Occupational and Organizational Psychology,* March 1999, pp. 101–6.

[25]John B. Miner, "The Rated Importance, Scientific Validity, and Practical Usefulness of Organizational Behavior Theories: A Quantitative Review," *Academy of Management Learning and Education* 2, no. 3 (September 2003), pp. 250–69.

[26]Frito-Lay, *Annual Report,* 2000.

[27]J. Stacey Adams, "Toward an Understanding of Equity," *Journal of Abnormal and Social Psychology,* November 1963, pp. 422–36.

[28]Mark P. Brown, Michael C. Sturman, and Marcia J. Simmering, "Compensation Policy and Organizational Performance: The Efficiency, Operational, and Financial Implications of Pay Levels and Pay Structure," *Academy of Management Journal* 46, no. 6 (2003), pp. 752–62; Steve Werner and Neal P. Mero, "Fair or Foul?: The Effects of External, Internal, and Employee Equity on Changes in Performance of Major League Baseball Players," *Human Relations* 52, no. 10 (1999), pp. 1291–1311; and Larry Howard and Janis Miller, "Fair Pay for Fair Play: Estimating Pay Equity in Professional Baseball with Data Envelopment Analysis," *Academy of Management Journal,* August 1993, pp. 882–94.

[29]Edwin Locke, "The Nature and Causes of Job Satisfaction," in *Handbook of Industrial and Organizational Psychology,* ed. M.D. Dunnette (Skokie, IL: Rand McNally, 1976), pp. 1297–1349.

[30]J.P. Campbell and R.D. Pritchard, "Motivational Theories in Industrial and Organizational Psychology," in *Handbook of Industrial and Organizational Psychology,* ed. M.D. Dunnette (Skokie, IL: Rand McNally, 1976).

[31]J.E. Martin and M.M. Peterson, "Two-Tier Wage Structures: Implications for Equity Theory," *Academy of Management Journal,* June 1987, pp. 286–315.

[32]Russell Cropanzano, David E. Bowen, and Stephen W. Gilliland, "The Management of Organizations," *Academy of Management Perspectives* 21, no. 4 (2007), pp. 34–48; and Richard M. Steers, Richard T. Mowday, and Debra L. Shapiro, "The Future of Work Motivation Theory," *Academy of Management Review* 29, no. 3 (July 2004), pp. 379–87.

[33]Jason A Colquitt, "On the Dimensionality of Organizational Justice: A Construct Validation of a Measure," *Journal of Applied Psychology* 86, no. 3 (2001), pp. 386–400.

[34]Martin J. Lecker, "The Smoking Penalty: Distributive Justice or Smokism?" *Journal of Business Ethics* 84 (2009), pp. 47–64; Quinetta M. Roberson, "Shared and Configural Justice: A Social Network Model of Justice in Teams," *Academy of Management Review* 30, no. 3 (July 2005), pp. 595–607; Maureen L. Ambrose and Russell Cropanzano, "A Longitudinal Analysis of Organizational Fairness: An Examination of Reactions to Tenure and Promotion Decisions," *Journal of Applied Psychology* 88, no. 2 (2003), pp. 266–75; Margaret L. Williams, Stanley B. Malos, and David K. Palmer, "Benefit System and Benefit Level Satisfaction: An Expanded Model of Antecedents and Consequences," *Journal of Management* 28, no. 2, pp. 195–215; and Martha C. Andrews and K. Michele Kacmar, "Discrimination among Organizational Politics, Justice, and Support," *Journal of Organizational Behavior* 22, no. 4 (2001), pp. 347–59.

[35]Yadong Luo, "How Important Are Shared Perceptions of Procedural Justice in Cooperative Alliances?" *Academy of Management Journal* 48, no. 4 (August 2005), pp. 695–709; E.A. Lund and T.R. Tyler, *The Social Psychology of Procedural Justice* (New York: Plenum Press, 1988) p. 188.

[36]Cindy P. Zapata-Phelan, Jason A. Colquitt, Brent A. Scott, and Beth Livingston, "Procedural Justice, Interactional Justice, and Task Performance: The Mediating Role of Intrinsic Motivation," *Organizational Behavior and Human Decision Processes* 108 (2009), pp. 93–105; Joerg Dietz, Sandra L. Robinson, Robert Folger, Robert A. Baron, and Martin Schultz, "The Impact of Community Violence and an Organization's Procedural Justice Climate on Workplace Aggression," *Academy of Management Journal* 46, no. 3 (2003), pp. 317–26; and D.P. Skarlicki and R. Folger, "Retaliation in the Workplace: The Roles of Distributive, Procedural, and Interactional Justice," *Journal of Applied Psychology,* August 1997, pp. 434–43.

[37]Daniel P. Skarlicki, John H. Ellard, and Brad R.C. Kelln, "Third-Party Perceptions of a Layoff: Procedural, Derogation and Retributive Aspects of Justice," *Journal of Applied Psychology,* February 1998, pp. 119–27.

[38]Silvia Bagdadli, Quinetta Roberson, and Francesco Paoletti, "The Mediating Role of Procedural Justice in Responses to Promotion Decisions," *Journal of Business and Psychology* 21, no. 1 (2006), pp. 83–102.

[39]Stefanie E. Naumann and Nathan Bennett, "A Case for Procedural Justice Climate: Development and Test of a Multilevel Model," *Academy of Management Journal,* October 2000, pp. 881–89.

[40]R.J. Bies and J.F. Moag, "Interactional Justice: Communication Criteria of Fairness," in *Research on Negotiations in Organizations,* eds. R.J. Lewicki, B.H. Sheppard,

and M.H. Bazerman (Greenwich, CT: JAI Press, 1986); and J. Greenberg, "The Social Side of Fairness: Interpersonal and Informational Classes of Organizational Justice," in *Justice in the Workplace: Approaching Fairness in Human Resource Management,* ed. R. Cropanzano (Hillsdale, NJ: Erlbaum, 1993).

[41]R.J. Bies, "Interactional (In)justice: The Sacred and the Profane," in *Advances in Organizational Justice,* ed. J. Greenberg and R. Cropanzano (Stanford, CA: Stanford University Press, 2001).

[42]Bill Leonard, "Study: Bully Bosses Prevalent in U.S.," *HR Magazine,* May 2007, pp. 22–24.

[43]Rita Zeidner, "Bullying Worse than Sexual Harassment?" *HR Magazine,* May 2008, pp. 28–29.

[44]Bennett J. Tepper, "Consequences of Abusive Supervision," *Academy of Management Journal* 43, no. 2 (April 2000), pp. 178–90.

[45]Bies and Moag, "Interactional Justice"; and Greenberg, "The Social Side of Fairness."

[46]Susan J. Wells, "Layoff Aftermath," *HR Magazine* 53, no. 11 (November 2008), pp. 37–42.

[47]T.R. Tyler and R.J. Bies, "Beyond Formal Procedures: the Interpersonal Context of Procedural Justice," in *Applied Social Psychology and Organizational Settings,* ed. J.S. Carroll (Hillsdale, NJ: Lawrence Erlbaum Associates, 1990), pp. 77–98.

[48]Edwin A. Locke, "Toward a Theory of Task Motivation and Incentives," *Organizational Behavior and Human Performance,* May 1968, pp. 157–89.

[49]Gary P. Latham, "The Motivational Benefits of Goal-Setting," *Academy of Management Executive* 18, no. 4 (November 2004), pp. 126–29; and Gary P. Latham, "The Reciprocal Effects of Science on Practice: Insights from the Practice and Science of Goal Setting," *Canadian Psychology,* October 2000, pp. 1–33.

[50]Thomas A. Ryan, *Intentional Behavior* (New York: Ronald Press, 1970), p. 95.

[51]E.A. Locke and G.P. Latham, *A Theory of Goal Setting and Task Performance* (Englewood Cliffs, NJ: Prentice Hall, 1990).

[52]Edwin A. Locke and Gary P. Latham, "Has Goal Setting Gone Wild, or Have Its Attackers Abandoned Good Scholarship?" *Academy of Management Perspectives,* 2009 (in press).

[53]John M. Ivancevich, "Different Goal-Setting Treatments and Their Effects on Performance and Job Satisfaction," *Academy of Management Journal,* September 1977, pp. 406–19.

[54]C. Shalley, G. Oldham, and J. Porac, "Effects of Goal Difficulty, Goal-Setting Method, and Expected External Evaluation on Intrinsic Motivation," *Academy of Management Journal,* September 1987, pp. 553–63.

[55]P. Ekeh, *Social Exchange Theory* (Cambridge, MA: Harvard University Press, 1974).

[56]H. Schein, *Organizational Psychology,* 2nd ed. (Englewood Cliffs, NJ: Prentice Hall, 1980).

[57]Amanuel G. Tekleab, Riki Takeuchi, and M. Susan Taylor, "Extending the Chain of Relationships among Organizational Justice, Social Exchange, and Employee Reactions: The Role of Contract Violations," *Academy of Management Journal* 48, no. 1 (February 2005), pp. 146–57; Jeffery A. Thompson and J. Stuart Bunderson, "Violations of Principle: Ideological Currency in the Psychological Contract," *Academy of Management Review* 28, no. 4 (2003), pp. 571–85; Amanuel G. Tekleab and M. Susan Taylor, "Aren't There Two Parties in an Employment Relationship? Antecedents and Consequences of Organization–Employee Agreement on Contract Obligations and Violations," *Journal of Organizational Behavior* 24, no. 5 (2003), pp. 585–99; and Sandra Robinson, Matthew Kraatz, and Denise Rousseau, "Changing Obligations and the Psychological Contract: A Longitudinal Study," *Academy of Management Journal,* February 1994, pp. 137–52.

[58]Christopher C. Rosen, Chu-Hsiang Chang, Russell E. Johnson, and Paul E. Levy, "Perceptions of the Organizational Context and Psychological Contract Breach: Assessing Competing Perspectives," *Organizational Behavior and Human Decision Processes* 108 (2009), pp. 202–17.

[59]Thomas O. Davenport, *Human Capital: What It Is and Why People Invest in It* (San Francisco: Jossey-Bass, 1999).

Chapter 6

[1]Vicente Royuela, Jordi López-Tamayo, Jordi Suriñach, "The Institutional vs. the Academic Definition of the Quality of Work Life. What Is the Focus of the European Commission?" *Social Indicators Research* 86, no. 3 (2008), pp. 401–15; and Richard E. Kopelman, "Job Redesign and Productivity: A Review of the Evidence," *National Productivity Review,* Summer 1985, p. 239.

[2]Simone Grebner, Achim Elfering, Norbert K. Semmer, Claudia-Kaiser Probst, and Marie-Louise Schlapbach, "Stressful Situations at Work and in Private among Young Workers: An Event Sampling Approach," *Social Indicators Research* 67, no. 1/2 (June 2004), pp. 11–49; and Blake E. Ashforth, Glen E. Kreiner, and Mel Fugate, "All in a

Day's Work: Boundaries and Micro Role Transitions," *Academy of Management Review,* July 2000, pp. 472–91.

[3]Paul Osterman, "How Common Is Workplace Transformation and Who Adopts It?" *Industrial and Labor Relations Review,* January 1994, pp. 173–88; and Harry C. Katz, Thomas A. Kochan, and Mark R. Weber, "Assessing the Effects of Industrial Relations Systems and Efforts to Improve the Quality of Working Life on Organizational Effectiveness," *Academy of Management Journal,* September 1985, pp. 514–15.

[4]Remus Ilies, Kelly Schwind Wilson, and David T. Wagner, "The Spillover of Daily Job Satisfaction onto Employees' Family Lives: The Facilitating Role of Work-Family Integration," *Academy of Management Journal* 52, no. 1 (February 2009), pp. 87–102; Jeffrey H. Greenhaus and Gary N. Powell, "When Work and Family Are Allies: A Theory of Work–Family Enrichment," *Academy of Management Review* 31, no. 1 (January 2006), pp. 72–92; Michael G. Pratt and Jose Antonio Rosa, "Transforming Work–Family Conflict into Commitment in Network Marketing Organizations," *Academy of Management Journal* 46, no. 4 (August 2003), pp. 395–417; and Luis L. Martins, Kimberly A. Eddleston, and John F. Veiga, "Moderators of the Relationship between Work–Family Conflict and Career Satisfaction," *Academy of Management Journal* 45, no. 2 (April 2002), pp. 399–410.

[5]Ed Diener and Don R. Rahtz, eds., *Advances in Quality of Life Theory and Research* (Boston: Kluwer, 2000).

[6]Tarek M. Khalil, *Management of Technology: The Key to Competitiveness and Wealth Creation* (New York: McGraw-Hill, 2000).

[7]Charles Glisson and Lawrence R. James, "The Cross-Level Effects of Culture and Climate in Human Service Teams," *Journal of Organizational Behavior* 23, no. 6 (September 2002), pp. 767–94; Vishwanath V. Baba and Muhammad Jamal, "Routinization of Job Context and Job Content as Related to Employees' Quality of Working Life: A Study of Canadian Nurses," *Journal of Organizational Behavior,* September 1991, pp. 379–86; and Barry M. Staw, Robert I. Sutton, and Lisa H. Pelled, "Employee Positive Emotion and Favorable Outcomes at the Workplace," *Organization Science,* February 1994, pp. 51–71.

[8]Josette M.P. Gevers, Miranda A.G. Peeters, "A Pleasure Working Together? The Effects of Dissimilarity in Team Member Conscientiousness on Team Temporal Processes and Individual Satisfaction," *Journal of Organizational Behavior* 30, no. 3 (2009), pp. 379–400; Robert T. Golembiewski and Ben-Chu Sun, "QWL Applications in Public Agencies: Do Success Rates Reflect a Positive-Findings Bias?" *International Journal of Public Administration* 15, no. 6 (1992), pp. 1263–79; and

Robert T. Golembiewski and Ben-Chu Sun, "Positive-Findings Bias in QWL Studies: Rigor and Outcomes in a Large Sample," *Journal of Management,* September 1990, pp. 665–74.

[9]Scott E. Seibert, Seth R. Silver, and W. Alan Randolf, "Taking Empowerment to the Next Level: A Multiple-Level Model of Empowerment, Performance, and Satisfaction," *Academy of Management Journal* 47, no. 3 (June 2004), pp. 332–49; Amy Wrzesniewski and Jane E. Dutton, "Crafting a Job: Revisioning Employees as Active Crafters of Their Work," *Academy of Management Review* 26, no. 2 (April 2001), pp. 179–202; David J. Jalajas and Michael Bommer, "The Influence of Job Motivation versus Downsizing on Individual Behavior," *Human Resource Development Quarterly* 10, no. 4 (Winter 1999), pp. 329–42; and Kenneth W. Thomas and Betty A. Velthouse, "Cognitive Elements of Empowerment: An 'Interpretive' Model of Intrinsic Task Motivation," *Academy of Management Review,* October 1990, pp. 666–81.

[10]Hugo M. Kehr, "Integrating Implicit Motives, Explicit Motives, and Perceived Abilities: The Compensatory Model of Work Motivation and Volition," *Academy of Management Review* 29, no. 3 (July 2004), pp. 479–99; Aaron A. Buchko, "Effects of Employee Ownership on Employee Attitudes: A Test of Three Theoretical Perspectives," *Work and Occupations,* February 1992, pp. 59–78.

[11]Jon R. Katzenbach, *Peak Performance: Aligning the Hearts and Minds of Your Employees* (Boston: Harvard Business School Press, 2000).

[12]Michael A. Campion, Troy V. Mumford, Frederick P. Morgeson, and Jennifer D. Nahrgang, "Work Redesign: Eight Obstacles and Opportunities," *Human Resource Management* 44, no. 4 (2005), pp. 367–90; and Joan Magretta, ed., *Managing in the New Economy* (Cambridge, MA: Harvard Business Review Book, 1999).

[13]Michael Weinreb, "Power to the People," *Sales and Marketing Management* 155, no. 4 (April 2003), pp. 30–36; and Frank Shipper and Charles C. Manz, "Employee Self-Management without Formally Designated Teams: An Alternative Road to Empowerment," *Organizational Dynamics,* Winter 1992, pp. 48–61.

[14]Deborah Ancona, Elaine Backman, and Henrik Bresman, "X-Teams: New Ways of Leading in a New World," *Ivey Business Journal Online* 72, no. 3 (2008),

[15]Aaron Cohen, *Multiple Commitments in the Workplace: An Integrative Approach* (Mahwah, NJ: Lawrence Erlbaum, 2003); Kibeom Lee, Julie J. Carswell, and Natalie J. Allen, "A Meta-Analytic Review of Occupational Commitment: Relations with Person- and Work-Related Variables," *Journal of Applied Psychology* 85, no. 5

(October 2000), pp. 799–811; S.D. Saleh and James Hosek, "Job Involvement: Concepts and Measurements," *Academy of Management Journal,* June 1976, pp. 213–24; and Robert J. Vandenberg and Charles E. Lance, "Examining the Causal Order of Job Satisfaction and Organizational Commitment," *Journal of Management,* March 1992, pp. 153–67.

[16]Glenn Bassett, "The Case against Job Satisfaction," *Business Horizons,* May/June 1994, pp. 61–68; Jill Kanin-Lovers and Gordon Spunich, "Compensation and the Job Satisfaction Equation," *Journal of Compensation and Benefits,* January–February 1992, pp. 54–57.

[17]Stephen Bach and Keith Sisson, eds., *Personnel Management: A Comprehensive Guide to Theory and Practice* (Malden, MA: Blackwell, 2000).

[18]Michael T. Brannick, Edward L. Levine, and Frederick P. Morgeson, *Job and Work Analysis: Methods, Research, and Applications for Human Resource Management* (Thousand Oaks, CA: Sage Publications, 2007).

[19]Christelle C. LaPolice, Gary W. Carter, and Jeff W. Johnson, "Linking O*NET Descriptors to Occupational Literacy Requirements Using Job Component Validation," *Personnel Psychology* 61, no. 2 (2008), pp. 405–41; www.onetcenter.org (accessed May 18, 2009).

[20]Michael A. Campion and Paul W. Thayer, "Job Design: Approaches, Outcomes, and Trade-offs," *Organizational Dynamics,* Winter 1987, pp. 66–79; and Michael A. Campion, "Interdisciplinary Approaches to Job Design: A Constructive Replication with Extensions," *Journal of Applied Psychology,* August 1988, pp. 467–81.

[21]Michael T. Brannick and Edward Levine, *Job Analysis: Methods, Research, and Applications for Human Resource Management in the New Millennium* (Thousand Oaks, CA: Sage Publications, 2002); and Frank Ostroff, *The Horizontal Organization: What the Organization of the Future Actually Looks Like and How It Delivers Value to Customers* (London: Oxford University Press, 1999).

[22]Steven F. Cronshaw and Amanda J. Alfieri. "The Impact of Sociotechnical Task Demands on Use of Worker Discretion and Functional Skill," *Human Relations* 56, no. 9 (2003), pp. 1107–30.

[23]P. Richard Jeanneret and Mark H. Strong, "Linking O*Net Job Analysis Information to Job Requirements Predictors: An O*Net Application," *Personnel Psychology* 56, no. 2 (Summer 2003), pp. 465–78; E.J. McCormick, *Job Analysis: Methods and Applications* (New York: AMACOM, 1979); and E.J. McCormick, P.R. Jeanneret, and R.C. Mecham, "A Study of Job Characteristics and Job Dimensions as Based on the Position Analysis Questionnaire (PAQ)," *Journal of Applied Psychology,* August 1972, pp. 347–68.

[24]James Sparrow, "The Utility of PAQ in Relating Job Behaviours to Traits," *Journal of Occupational Psychology* (UK), June 1989, pp. 151–62; and Angelo S. DeNisi, Edwin T. Cornelius, III, and Allyn G. Blencoe, "Further Investigation of Common Knowledge Effects on Job Analysis Ratings," *Journal of Applied Psychology,* May 1987, pp. 262–68.

[25]LaPolice, Carter, and Johnson, "Linking O*NET Descriptors to Occupational Literacy Requirements Using Job Component Validation"; Brannick and Levine, *Job Analysis: Methods, Research, and Applications for Human Resource Management in the New Millennium;* Robert M. Madigan and David J. Hoover, "Effects of Alternative Job Evaluation Methods on Decisions Involving Pay Equity," *Academy of Management Journal,* March 1986, pp. 84–100; and Edward H. Lawler, III, "What's Wrong with Point-Factor Job Evaluation," *Personnel,* January 1987, pp. 38–44.

[26]Herbert G. Heneman, III, and Timothy A. Judge, *Staffing Organizations,* 4th ed. (New York: McGraw-Hill/Irwin, July 2002); and Philip C. Grant, "What Use Is a Job Description?" *Personnel Journal,* February 1988, pp. 44–65.

[27]Jai V. Ghorpade, *Job Analysis: A Handbook for the Human Resource Director* (Englewood Cliffs, NJ: Prentice Hall, 1988); and Edward L. Levine, Ronald A. Ash, Hardy Hall, and Frank Sistrunk, "Evaluation of Job Analysis Methods by Experienced Job Analysts," *Academy of Management Journal,* June 1983, pp. 339–48.

[28]The literature of scientific management is voluminous. The original works and the subsequent criticisms and interpretations would make a large volume. Of special significance are the works of the principal authors including Frederick W. Taylor, *Principles of Scientific Management* (New York: Harper & Row, 1911); Harrington Emerson, *The Twelve Principles of Efficiency* (New York: Engineering Magazine, 1913); Henry L. Gantt, *Industrial Leadership* (New Haven, CT: Yale University Press, 1916); Frank B. Gilbreth, *Motion Study* (New York: D. Van Nostrand, 1911); and Lillian M. Gilbreth, *The Psychology of Management* (New York: Sturgis & Walton, 1914).

[29]Taylor, *Principles of Scientific Management,* pp. 36–37.

[30]Donald Vincent, "Robots: Flexible Automation for a Strong Economy," *Robotics World* 23, no. 1 (January/February 2005), pp. 8–10; Steven J. Kass, Stephen J. Vodanovich, and Anne Callender, "State-Trait Boredom: Relationships to Absenteeism, Tenure, and Job Satisfaction," *Journal of Business and Psychology* 16, no. 2 (Winter 2001), pp. 317–27; and Larry D. Grieshaber, Patricia Parker, and Judy Deering, "Job Satisfaction of Nursing Assistants in Long-Term Care," *Health Care Supervisor,* June 1995, pp. 18–28.

[31]U.S. Bureau of Labor Statistics Economic News Release Table 1 at www.bls.gov/news.release/ecopro.t01.htm (accessed May 14, 2009).

[32]U.S. Bureau of Labor Statistics Economic New Release at www.bls.gov/news.release/ecopro.t05.htm (accessed May 14, 2009).

[33]Kevin Butler, "Graying Matters," *Occupational Health & Safety* 77, no. 12 (December 2008), pp. 14–15; Douglas R. May and Catherine E. Schwoerer, "Employee Health by Design: Using Employee Involvement Teams in Ergonomic Job Redesign," *Personnel Psychology,* Winter 1994, pp. 861–76; and Larry Reynolds, "Ergonomic Concerns Stiffen Rules Regarding VDT Use," *Personnel,* April 1991, pp. 1–2.

[34]Marjorie L. Baldwin and Richard J. Butler, "Upper Extremity Disorders in the Workplace: Costs and Outcomes Beyond the First Return to Work," *Journal of Occupational Rehabilitation* 16, no. 3 (2006), pp. 303–23; Bill Fine, "All for One and One for All?" *Occupational Health,* September 2005, pp. 15–18; Connie Vaughn-Miller, "Haven't Got Time for the Pain," *Occupational Health & Safety* 72, no. 6 (June 2003), pp. 112–16; and Judith N. Mottle, "Computer-Related Injuries: IT Helps Ease the Pain," *InformationWeek* 791 (June 19, 2000), pp. 120–24.

[35]Rob Cross and Lloyd Baird, "Technology Is Not Enough: Improving Performance by Building Organizational Memory," *Sloan Management Review,* Spring 2000, pp. 69–78.

[36]Kimberly D. Elsbach and Andrew B. Hargadon, "Enhancing Creativity through 'Mindless' Work: A Framework of Workday Design," *Organization Science* 17, no. 4 (July/August 2006), pp. 470–85; and Sharon Leonard, "The Demise of Job Descriptions," *HR Magazine,* August 2000, pp. 184–85.

[37]William Bridges, *Job Shift* (Reading, MA: Addison-Wesley, 1994).

[38]Carla Joinson, "Refocusing Job Descriptions," *HR Magazine* 46, no. 1 (January 2001), pp. 66–72; and Caitlin P. Williams, "The End of the Job as We Know It," *Training & Development,* January 1999, pp. 52–54.

[39]Kent W. Seibert, "Reflection-in-Action: Tools for Cultivating On-the-Job Learning Conditions," *Organizational Dynamics,* Winter 1999, pp. 54–65.

[40]Murray R. Barrick and Ryan D. Zimmerman, "Hiring for Retention and Performance," *Human Resource Management* 48, no. 2 (2009), pp. 183–206; Murray R. Barrick, Greg L. Steward, and Mike Piotrowski, "Personality and Job Performance: Test of the Mediating Effect of Motivation among Sales Representatives," *Journal of Applied Psychology* 87, no. 1 (February 2002), pp. 43–51; and Brett M. Wright and John L. Cordey, "Production

Uncertainty as a Contextual Moderator of Employee Reactions to Job Design," *Journal of Applied Psychology,* June 1999, pp. 456–63.

[41]Gary Johns, "The Essential Impact of Context on Organizational Behavior," *Academy of Management Review* 31, no. 2 (April 2006), pp. 386–408; Terry A. Beehr, Steve M. Jex, Beth A. Stacy, and Marshall A. Murray, "Work Stressors and Coworker Support as Predictors of Individual Strain and Job Performance," *Journal of Organizational Behavior* 21, no. 4 (June 2000), pp. 391–405; and William H. Turnley and Daniel C. Feldman, "The Impact of Psychological Contract Violations on Exit, Voice, Loyalty, and Neglect," *Human Relations,* July 1999, pp. 895–922.

[42]Marianne van Woerkom and Marcel Croon, "Operationalising Critically Reflective Work Behavior," *Personnel Review* 37, no. 3 (2008), pp. 317–31; Pere Joan Ferrando, "Likert Scaling Using Continuous, Censored, and Graded Response Models: Effects on Criterion-Rated Validity," *Applied Psychological Measurement,* June 1999, pp. 161–75.

[43]Eugene F. Stone and Hal G. Gueutal, "An Empirical Derivation of the Dimensions along Which Characteristics of Jobs Are Perceived," *Academy of Management Journal,* June 1985, pp. 376–96; and Arthur N. Turner and Paul R. Lawrence, *Industrial Jobs and the Worker: An Investigation of Response to Task Attributes* (Cambridge, MA: Harvard University Press, 1965).

[44]J. Richard Hackman and Edward W. Lawler, III, "Employee Reactions to Job Characteristics," *Journal of Applied Psychology,* June 1971, pp. 259–86; and J. Richard Hackman and Greg R. Oldham, "Development of the Job Diagnostic Survey," *Journal of Applied Psychology,* April 1975, pp. 159–70.

[45]Randall B. Dunham, Ramon J. Aldag, and Arthur P. Brief, "Dimensionality of Task Design as Measured by the Job Diagnostic Survey," *Academy of Management Journal,* June 1977, p. 222.

[46]Joseph E. Champoux, "A Three Sample Test of Some Extensions to the Job Characteristics Model of Work Motivation," *Academy of Management Journal,* September 1980, pp. 466–78.

[47]Jay P. Mulki, Jorge Fernando Jaramillo, and William B. Locander, "Critical Role of Leadership on Ethical Climate and Salesperson Behaviors," *Journal of Business Ethics* 86, no. 2 (2009), pp. 125–41; and Ricky W. Griffin, "Supervisory Behavior as a Source of Perceived Task Scope," *Journal of Occupational Psychology,* September 1981, pp. 175–82.

[48]Joe Thomas and Ricky W. Griffin, "The Social Information Processing Model of Task Design: A Review of

the Literature," *Academy of Management Review,* October 1983, pp. 672–82; Ricky W. Griffin, "Objective and Subjective Sources of Information in Task Redesign: A Field Experiment," *Administrative Science Quarterly,* June 1983, pp. 184–200; and Jeffrey Pfeffer, "A Partial Test of the Social Information-Processing Model of Job Attitudes," *Human Relations,* July 1980, pp. 457–76.

[49]A.G. Lafley, "What Only the CEO Can Do," *Harvard Business Review* 87, no. 5 (May 2009), pp. 54–62; "More Power for P&G's Innovator," *Marketing Week,* February 3, 2005, p. 3; and Katrina Brooker, "The un-CEO," *Fortune* 146, no. 5 (September 16, 2002), pp. 88–96.

[50]Bridges, *Job Shift.*

[51]Robert J. Grossman, "Putting HR in Rotation," *HR Magazine* 48, no. 3 (March 2003), pp. 50–58; and Gregory B. Northcraft, Terri L. Griffith, and Christina E. Shalley, "Building Top Management Muscle in a Slow Growth Environment," *Academy of Management Executive,* February 1992, pp. 32–41.

[52]Margery Weinstein, "Foreign but Familiar," *Training* 46, no. 1 (January 2009), pp. 20, 22–23.

[53]Judy Orr, "Job Rotations Give Future Leaders the Depth They Need," *Canadian HR Reporter* 19, no. 2 (January 30, 2006), pp. 17–19; Jaime Ortega, "Job Rotation as a Learning Machine," *Management Science* 47, no. 10 (October 21, 2001), pp. 1361–70; Michael A. Campion, Lisa Cheraskin, and Michael J. Stevens, "Career-Related Antecedents and Outcomes of Job Rotation," *Academy of Management Journal,* December 1994, pp. 1518–42; and Allan W. Farrant, "Job Rotation Is Important," *Supervision,* August 1987, pp. 14–16.

[54]Sandra E. Black, Lisa M. Lynch, and Anya Krivelyova, "How Workers Fare When Employers Innovate," *Industrial Relations* 43, no. 1 (January 2004), pp. 44–67; Michael A. Campion and Carol L. McClelland, "Follow-Up and Extension of the Interdisciplinary Costs and Benefits of Enlarged Jobs," *Journal of Applied Psychology,* June 1993, pp. 339–51; and Michael A. Campion and Carol L. McClelland, "Interdisciplinary Examination of the Costs and Benefits of Enlarged Jobs: A Job Design Quasi-Experiment," *Journal of Applied Psychology,* April 1991, pp. 186–98.

[55]Lance Hazzard, Joe Mautz, and Denver Wrightsman, "Job Rotation Cuts Cumulative Trauma Cases," *Personnel Journal,* February 1992, pp. 29–32.

[56]Charles R. Walker and Robert H. Guest, *The Man on the Assembly Line* (Cambridge, MA: Harvard University Press, 1952).

[57]Jeffrey R. Edwards, Mary D. Brtek, and Judith A. Scully, "The Nature and Outcomes of Work: A Replication and Extension of Interdisciplinary Work-Design Research," *Journal of Applied Psychology* 85, no. 6 (December 2000), pp. 860–68; and Jeffrey R. Edwards, Judith A. Scully, and Mary D. Brtek, "The Measurement of Work: Hierarchical Representation of the Multimethod Job Design Questionnaire," *Personnel Psychology,* Summer 1999, pp. 305–34.

[58]http://www.zao.com/aboutus.htm (accessed May 15, 2009); Anat Drach-Zahavy, "The Proficiency Trap: How to Balance Enriched Job Designs and the Team's Need for Support," *Journal of Organizational Behavior* 25, no. 8 (December 2004), pp. 979–97; and Alan J. Liddle, "Zao Executives Use Their Noodles to Keep Concept Exotic, Accessible, and Growing," *Nation's Restaurant News* 35, no. 16 (April 16, 2001), pp. 24–25.

[59]Stephen J. Wood and Toby D. Wall, "Work Enrichment and Employee Voice in Human Resource Management-Performance Studies," *International Journal of Human Resource Management* 18, no. 7 (July 2007), pp. 1335–72; and Blake E. Ashforth, Glen E. Kreiner, and Mel Fugate, "All in a Day's Work: Boundaries and Micro Role Transitions," *Academy of Management Review,* July 2000, pp. 472–91.

[60]M. Scott Myers, *Every Employee a Manager* (New York: McGraw-Hill, 1970), p. xii.

[61]Russ S. Moxley, *Leadership and Spirit: Breathing New Vitality into Individuals and Organizations* (San Francisco: Jossey-Bass, 2000).

[62]Gerald R. Ferris and David C. Gilmore, "The Moderating Role of Work Context in Job Design Research: A Test of Competing Models," *Academy of Management Journal,* December 1984, pp. 885–92.

[63]J. Richard Hackman, Greg Oldham, Robert Janson, and Kenneth Purdy, "New Strategy for Job Enrichment," *California Management Review,* Summer 1975, pp. 57–71; and J. Richard Hackman and Greg Oldham, "Development of the Job Diagnostic Survey," *Journal of Applied Psychology,* April 1975, pp. 159–70.

[64]J. Richard Hackman and Greg Oldham, *Work Redesign* (Reading, MA: Addison-Wesley, 1980).

[65]Tom D. Taber and Elisabeth Taylor, "A Review and Evaluation of the Psychometric Properties of the Job Diagnostic Survey," *Personnel Psychology,* Autumn 1990, pp. 467–500.

[66]Gary Johns, Jia L. Xie, and Yongqing Fang, "Mediating and Moderating Effects in Job Design," *Journal of Management,* December 1992, pp. 657–76.

[67]Richard E. Kopelman, "Job Redesign and Productivity: A Review of the Evidence," *National Productivity Review* 4, no. 3, pp. 237–55; and Kopelman, "Job Redesign and Productivity."

[68]Gardiner Morse, "Why We Misread Motives," *Harvard Business Review* 81, no. 1 (January 2003), p. 18; and William E. Zierden, "Congruence in the Work Situation: Effects of Growth Needs, Management Style, and Job Structure on Job-Related Satisfactions," *Journal of Occupational Behavior,* October 1980, pp. 297–310.

[69]Ricky W. Griffin, "Effects of Work Redesign on Employee Perceptions, Attitudes, and Behaviors: A Long-Term Investigation," *Academy of Management Journal,* June 1991, pp. 425–35.

[70]Kopelman, "Job Design and Productivity," p. 253.

[71]Jose R. Goris, "Effects of Satisfaction with Communication on the Relationship between Individual-Job Congruence and Job Performance/Satisfaction," *Journal of Management Development* 26, no. 8, pp. 737–52; Scott A. Snell and James W. Dean, Jr., "Strategic Compensation for Integrated Manufacturing: The Moderating Effects of Jobs and Organizational Inertia," *Academy of Management Journal,* October 1994, pp. 1109–40; and James W. Dean, Jr., and Scott A. Snell, "Integrated Manufacturing and Job Design: Moderating Effects of Organizational Inertia," *Academy of Management Journal,* December 1991, pp. 776–804.

[72]Campion, Mumford, Morgeson, and Nahrgang, "Work Redesign: Eight Obstacles and Opportunities"; Gerard Farias and Arup Varma, "Integrating Job Characteristics, Sociotechnical Systems and Reengineering: Presenting a Unified Approach to Work and Organizational Design," *Organization Development Journal* 18, no. 3 (Fall 2000), pp. 11–25; and Howard W. Oden, *Transforming the Organization: A Social-Technical Approach* (Westport, CT: Quorum, 1999).

[73]Stephanie T. Solansky, "Leadership Style and Team Processes in Self-Managed Teams," *Journal of Leadership & Organizational Studies* 14, no. 4 (May 2008), pp. 332–41; Senthil K. Muthusamy, Jane V. Wheeler, and Bret L. Simmons, "Self-Managing Work Teams: Enhancing Organizational Innovativeness," *Organization Development Journal* 23, no. 3 (Fall 2005), pp. 53–67; and David Barry, "Managing the Bossless Team: Lessons in Distributed Leadership," *Organizational Dynamics,* Summer 1991, pp. 31–47.

[74]Bernard Simon, "GM in Talks to Sell Saturn Brand," *Financial Times,* April 16, 2009, p. 17.

[75]S.C. Gwynne, "The Right Stuff," *Time,* October 29, 1990, pp. 74–84.

[76]Ceasar Douglas and William L. Gardner, "Transition to Self-Directed Work Teams: Implications of Transition Time and Self-Monitoring for Managers' Use of Influence Tactics," *Journal of Organizational Behavior* 25, no. 1 (February 2004), pp. 47–65; Roy A. Cook and J. Larry Goff, "Coming of Age with Self-Managed Teams: Dealing with a Problem Employee," *Journal of Business and Psychology* 16, no. 3 (Spring 2002), pp. 485–96; and Milam Moravec, "Self-Managed Teams," *Executive Excellence,* October 1999, p. 78.

[77]Frank Giancola, "Flexible Schedules: A Win–Win Reward," *Workspan* 48, no. 7 (July 2005), pp. 52–59.

[78]Cali Ressler and Jody Thompson, "Count Results, Not Hours," *BusinessWeek,* August 14, 2008, pp. 39–40.

[79]Sarah Boehle, David Stamps, and Jeremy Stratton, "The Increasing Value of Flexible Time," *Training,* July 2000, p. 32.

[80]Alan Deutschman, "Pioneers of the New Balance," *Fortune,* May 20, 1991, pp. 60–68.

[81]Jennifer Schramm, "Work Turns Flexible," *HR Magazine* 54, no. 3 (March 2009), p. 88.

[82]Sue Shellenbarger, "Does Avoiding a 9-to-5 Grind Make You a Target for Layoffs?" *The Wall Street Journal* (Eastern Edition), April 22, 2009, p. D1.

[83]Petru L. Curseu, Rene Schalk, and Inge Wessel, "How Do Virtual Teams Process Information? A Literature Review and Implications for Management," *Journal of Managerial Psychology* 23, no. 6 (2008), pp. 628–52; Michael Harvey, Milorad M. Novicevic, and Garry Garrison, "Global Virtual Teams: A Human Resource Capital Architecture," *The International Journal of Human Resource Management* 16, no. 9 (September 2005), pp. 1583–99; and Charlene M. Solomon, "Managing Virtual Teams," *Workforce,* June 2001, pp. 60–65.

[84]Luis Gomez-Mejia, David B. Balkin, and Robert L. Cardy, *Managing Human Resources,* 3rd ed. (Upper Saddle River, NJ: Prentice Hall, 2000).

[85]Eva Kaplan-Leiserson, "Virtual Work," *T+D* 59, no. 8 (August 2005), pp. 12–14; and Solomon, "Managing Virtual Teams."

[86]Blaise J. Bergiel, Erich B. Bergiel, and Phillip W. Balsmeier, "Nature of Virtual Teams: A Summary of Their Advantages and Disadvantages," *Management Research News* 31, no. 2 (2008), p. 99.

[87]David Drucker, "Virtual Teams Light Up GE—Customers, Suppliers Linked in Real Time with Collaboration Apps," *Internet Week,* April 2000, pp. 16–20.

[88]Ibid.

[89]Solomon, "Managing Virtual Teams."

[90]J. Webster and W.K.P. Wong, "Comparing Traditional and Virtual Group Forms: Identity, Communication and Trust in Naturally Occurring Project Teams," *The International Journal of Human Resource Management* 19, no. 1 (2008), pp. 41–62; Norhayati Zakaria, Andrea Amelinckx, and David Wilemon, "Working Together Apart? Building a Knowledge-Sharing Culture for Global Virtual Teams," *Creativity and Innovation Management* 13, no. 1 (March 2004), pp. 15–29; and Richard Benson-Armer and Tsun-yan Hsieh, "Teamwork across Time and Space," *The McKinsey Quarterly,* 1997, pp. 18–27.

[91]Julekah Dash, "Think of People When Planning Virtual Teams," *Computerworld,* February 2001, pp. 34–36.

[92]Jon Brodkin and Denise Dubie, "Collaborative Tools All the Rage at DEMO," *Network World* 25, no. 4 (January 28, 2008), p. 10.

[93]Thomas W. Lee, Terence R. Mitchell, Chris J. Sablynski, James P. Burton, and Brooks C. Holtom, "The Effects of Job Embeddedness on Organizational Citizenship, Job Performance, Volitional Absences, and Voluntary Turnover," *Academy of Management Journal* 47, no. 5 (October 2004), pp. 711–22; and Terence R. Mitchell, Brooks C. Holtom, Thomas W. Lee, Chris J. Sablynski, and Miriam Erez, "Why People Stay: Using Job Embeddedness to Predict Voluntary Turnover," *Academy of Management Journal* 44, no. 6 (December 2001), pp. 1102–22.

[94]James R. Detert, "A Framework for Linking Culture and Improvement Initiatives in Organizations," *Academy of Management Review* 25, no. 4 (October 2000), pp. 850–64.

[95]Kostas N. Dervitsiotis, "Guiding Human Organisations to Climb the Spiral Stages of Performance Improvements," *Total Quality Management & Business Excellence* 19, nos. 7/8 (2008), pp. 709–18; Anthony L. Patti, Sandra J. Hartmann, Lillian Fok, and Wing M. Fok, "Jobs and People in a Total Quality Management Environment: A Survey of Academicians and Practitioners," *International Journal of Management* 18, no. 3 (September 2001), pp. 359–70.

[96]Cynthia K. West, *Techno-Human Mesh* (Westport, CT: Quorum, 2001).

[97]Russ S. Moxley, *Leadership and Spirit: Breathing New Vitality and Energy into Individuals and Organizations* (San Francisco: Jossey-Bass, 2000).

[98]Eric Trist, "The Evolution of Sociotechnical Systems," *Occasional Paper* (Toronto: Ontario Quality of Working Life Centre, June 1981); and William M. Fox, "Sociotechnical System Principles and Guidelines," *Journal of Applied Behavioral Science,* March 1995, pp. 91–105.

[99]Fred Emery, "Participative Design: Effective, Flexible and Successful," *Journal of Quality and Participation,* January/February 1995, pp. 6–9.

[100]Elisabeth Davenport, "Social Informatics and Sociotechnical Research—A View from the U.K.," *Journal of Information Science* 34, no. 4 (2008), pp. 519–30; A.B. Shani and James A. Sena, "Information Technology and the Integration of Change: Sociotechnical System Approach," *Journal of Applied Behavioral Science,* June 1994, pp. 247–70; and Louis E. Davis and James C. Taylor, eds., *Design of Jobs* (Santa Monica, CA: Goodyear, 1979).

Chapter 7

[1]Diane Cadrain, "Put Success in Sight," *HR Magazine* 48, no. 5 (May 2003), pp. 84–90; and Shari Caudron, "Spreading Out the Carrots," *Industry Week,* May 19, 1997, pp. 20–25.

[2]Adrienne Fox, "Curing What Ails Performance Reviews," *HR Magazine* 54, no. 1 (January 2009), pp. 52–56; Mark D. Cannon and Robert Witherspoon, "Actionable Feedback: Unlocking the Power of Learning and Performance," *Academy of Management Executive* 19, no. 2 (May 2005), pp. 120–34; and Roger E. Herman and Joyce L. Gioia, *How to Become an Employer of Choice* (Winchester, VA: Oakhill Press, 2000).

[3]David D. Van Fleet, Tim O. Peterson, and Ella W. Van Fleet, "Closing the Performance Feedback Gap with Expert Systems," *Academy of Management Executive* 19, no. 3 (2005), pp. 38–53; Robert D. Behn, "Why Measure Performance? Different Purposes Require Different Measures," *Public Administration Review* 63, no. 5 (September/October 2003), pp. 586–606; and Jonathan A. Segal, "86 Your Appraisal Process," *HR Magazine,* October 2000, pp. 199–206.

[4]Mary Jo Ducharme, Parbudyal Singh, and Mark Podolsky, "Exploring the Links between Performance Appraisals and Pay Satisfaction," *Compensation and Benefits Review* 37, no. 5 (September/October 2005), pp. 46–63; I.M. Jawahar and Gary Salegna, "Adapting Performance Appraisal Systems for a Quality-Driven Environment," *Compensation and Benefits Review* 35, no. 1 (January/February 2003), pp. 64–71; and Dick Grote, "Performance Appraisals: Solving Tough Challenges," *HR Magazine,* July 2000, pp. 145–50.

[5]Liam O'Brian, "Improving Performance Appraisal Interviews," *Supply Management,* May 2000, pp. 36–37.

[6]A.N. Kluger and A. DeNisi, "The Effects of Feedback Interventions on Performance: A Historical Review, a Meta-Analysis, and a Preliminary Feedback Intervention Theory," *Psychological Bulletin,* March 1996, pp. 254–84.

[7]Van Fleet, et al., "Closing the Performance Feedback Gap with Expert Systems"; D.M. Herold, C.K. Parsons, and R.B. Rensvold, "Individual Differences in the Generation and Processing of Performance Feedback," *Educational and Psychological Measurement,* February 1996, pp. 5–25.

[8]Shari Caudron, "And the Point Is?" *Workforce* 79, no. 4 (April 2000), pp. 20–22; and M. Hequet, "Giving Good Feedback," *Training,* September 1994, pp. 72–77.

[9]Aliah D. Wright, "At Google, It Takes a Village to Hire an Employee," *HR Magazine: SHRM's 2009 HR Trendbook,* January 2009, pp. 56–57.

[10]John W. Fleenor, Sylvester Taylor, and Craig Chappelow, *Leveraging the Impact of 360-Degree Feedback* (San Francisco, CA: Pfeiffer Publishing, 2008); "360-Degree Feedback," *T + D* 58, no. 9 (September 2004), pp. 14–15; and Evelyn Rogers, Charles W. Rogers, and William Metlay, "Improving the Payoff from 360-Degree Feedback," *Human Resource Planning* 25, no. 3 (2002), pp. 44–55.

[11]J.W. Smither, M. London, and R.R. Reilly, "Does Performance Improve following Multi-Source Feedback? A Theoretical Model, Meta-Analysis, and Review of Empirical Findings," *Personnel Psychology* 58 (2005), pp. 33–66.

[12]Christine M. Hagan, Robert Konopaske, H. John Bernardin, Catherine L. Tyler, "Predicting Assessment Center Performance with 360-Degree, Top-Down, and Customer-Based Competency Assessments," *Human Resource Management* 45, no. 3 (2006), pp. 357–90.

[13]Leanne E. Atwater, Joan F. Brett, and Atira Cherise Charles, "Multisource Feedback: Lessons Learned and Implications for Practice," *Human Resource Management* 46, no. 2 (Summer 2007), pp. 285–307; and James W. Smither, Manuel London, Raymond Flautt, Yvette Vargas, and Ivy Kucine, "Can Working with an Executive Coach Improve Multisource Feedback Ratings over Time? A Quasi-Experimental Field Study," *Personnel Psychology* 56, no. 1 (Spring 2003), pp. 23–45.

[14]David Antonioni and Heejoon Park, "The Relationship between Rater Affect and Three Sources of 360-Degree Feedback Ratings," *Journal of Management* 27, no. 4 (2001), pp. 479–95; and Mark R. Edwards and Ann J. Ewen, *360-Degree Feedback* (New York: AMACOM, 1996).

[15]Darren Good and Duncan Coombe, "Giving Multisource Feedback a Facelift," *Journal of Change Management* 9, no. 1 (2009), pp. 109–26; Ginka Toegel and Jay A. Conger, "360-Degree Feedback: Time for Reinvention," *Academy of Management Learning and Education* 2,

no. 3 (September 2003), pp. 297–311; and Mary N. Vinson, "The Pros and Cons of 360-Degree Feedback: Making It Work," *Training and Development,* April 1996, pp. 11–12.

[16]John Day, "Simple Strong Team Ratings," *HR Magazine,* September 2000, pp. 159–61.

[17]James B. DeConinck, "The Effect of Punishment on Sales Managers' Outcome Expectancies and Responses to Unethical Sales Force Behavior," *American Business Review* 21, no. 2 (June 2003), pp. 135–47; and Gail Ball, Linda Trevino, and Henry Sims, Jr., "Just and Unjust Punishment: Influences on Subordinate Performance and Citizenship," *Academy of Management Journal,* April 1994, pp. 299–322.

[18]C.B. Ferster and B.F. Skinner, *Schedules of Reinforcement* (New York: Appleton-Century-Crofts, 1957).

[19]Edward E. Lawler, III, *Rewarding Excellence: Pay Strategies for the New Economy* (San Francisco: Jossey-Bass, 2000).

[20]Jon R. Katzenbach, *Peak Performance: Aligning the Hearts and Minds of Your Employees* (Boston: Harvard Business School Press, 2000).

[21]Karen Renk, "I Want My TV," *HR Magazine,* October 2000, pp. 153–63.

[22]Susan Ladika, "Take the Tax Sting out of Bonuses," *HR Magazine* 50, no. 7 (July 2005), pp. 85–89; and Lin Grensing-Pophal, "Rewards That Don't Penalize Your Employees," *HR Magazine,* November 1999, pp. 98–104.

[23]R.L. Opsahl and M.D. Dunnette, "The Role of Financial Compensation in Industrial Motivation," *Psychological Bulletin,* August 1966, p. 114.

[24]Edward E. Lawler, III, *Pay and Organizational Effects* (New York: McGraw-Hill, 1971), pp. 164–70.

[25]www.marykay.com/sellmarykay/rewardrecognition/default.aspx (accessed May 22, 2009).

[26]Michael Zwell, *Creating a Culture of Competence* (New York: John Wiley & Sons, 2000).

[27]U.S. Department of Labor, Bureau of Labor Statistics, "Employer Costs for Employee Compensation–December 2008," March 12, 2009.

[28]"Business: Doing Well by Being Rather Nice," *The Economist* 385, no. 8557 (December 2007), p. 82; Susan Ladika, "Adoption's Multiple Benefits," *HR Magazine* 50, no. 10 (October 2005), pp. 60–66; and Jennifer Schu, "Even in Hard Times, SAS Keeps Its Culture Intact," *Workforce* 80, no. 10 (October 2001), pp. 21–22.

[29]Bill Leonard, "The Key to Unlocking an Inexpensive Recognition Program," *HR Magazine,* October 1999, p. 26.

[30]David C. McClelland, *The Achieving Society* (New York: D. Van Nostrand, 1961).

[31]Edward L. Deci, Richard Koestner, and Richard M. Ryan, "A Meta-Analytic Review of Experiments Examining the Effects of Extrinsic Rewards on Intrinsic Motivation," *Psychological Bulletin* 125, no. 6 (1999), pp. 627–68; and E.L. Deci, "The Effects of Externally Mediated Rewards on Intrinsic Motivation," *Journal of Personality and Social Psychology,* 1971, pp. 105–15. Also see, E.L. Deci, *Intrinsic Motivation* (New York: Plenum Press, 1975).

[32]Hugo M. Kehr, "Integrating Implicit Motives, Explicit Motives, and Perceived Abilities: The Compensatory Model of Work Motivation and Volition," *Academy of Management Review* 29, no. 3 (July 2004), pp. 479–99; Mark R. Lepper, Jennifer Henderlong, and Isabelle Gingras, "Understanding the Effects of Extrinsic Rewards on Intrinsic Motivation—Uses and Abuses of Meta-Analysis: Comments on Deci, Koestner, and Ryan," *Psychological Bulletin* 125, no. 6 (1999), pp. 669–76.

[33]B.M. Staw, "The Attitudinal and Behavioral Consequences of Changing a Major Organizational Reward," *Journal of Personality and Social Psychology,* June 1974, pp. 742–51.

[34]C.D. Fisher, "The Effects of Personal Control, Competence, and Extrinsic Reward Systems on Intrinsic Motivation," *Organizational Behavior and Human Performance,* June 1978, pp. 273–87. Also see, J.S. Phillips and R.G. Lord, "Determinants of Intrinsic Motivation: Locus of Control and Competence Information as Components of Deci's Cognitive Evaluation Theory," *Journal of Applied Psychology,* April 1980, pp. 211–18.

[35]K.B. Boone and L.L. Cummings, "Cognitive Evaluation Theory: An Experimental Test of Processes and Outcomes," *Organizational Behavior and Human Performance,* December 1981, pp. 289–310.

[36]E.M. Lopez, "A Test of Deci's Cognitive Evaluation Theory in an Organizational Setting," presented at the 39th annual convention of the Academy of Management, Atlanta, Georgia, August 1979.

[37]Glenn Parker, Jerry McAdams, and David Zielinski, *Rewarding Teams: Lessons from the Trenches* (San Francisco: Jossey-Bass, 2000).

[38]Richard M. Steers, Richard T. Mowday, and Debra L. Shapiro, "The Future of Work Motivation Theory," *Academy of Management Review* 29, no. 3 (July 2004), pp. 379–87; R. Kanungo and J. Hartwick, "An Alternative to the Intrinsic-Extrinsic Dichotomy of Work Rewards," *Journal of Management,* Fall 1987, pp. 751–66; and V.H. Vroon, *Work and Motivation* (New York: John Wiley & Sons, 1964).

[39]Alain Salamin and Peter W. Hom, "In Search of the Elusive U-Shaped Performance–Turnover Relationship: Are High Performing Swiss Bankers More Liable to Quit?" *Journal of Applied Psychology* 90, no. 6 (November 2005), pp. 1204–16; and Carla Johnson, "Capturing Turnover Costs," *HR Magazine,* July 2000, pp. 107–19.

[40]Tom Washington, "Absence Management: Missing Links", *Employee Benefits,* April 2009, p. 31; and Julie Britt, "Workplace No-Shows' Costs to Employers Rise Again," *HR Magazine* 47, no. 12 (December 2002), pp. 26–27.

[41]Paul Falcone, "Tackling Excessive Absenteeism," *HR Magazine,* April 2000, pp. 138–44.

[42]Michelle Conlin, "Shirking Working: The War on Hooky," *BusinessWeek,* November 12, 2007, p. 72.

[43]K.R. Moore, "Trust and Relationship Commitment in Logistics Alliances: A Buyer Perspective," *Journal of Purchasing and Materials Management,* February 1998, pp. 24–37.

[44]S. Chow and R. Holden, "Toward an Understanding of Loyalty: The Moderating Role of Trust," *Journal of Management Issues*, Spring 1997, pp. 275–98.

[45]Charlie O. Trevor and Anthony J. Nyberg, "Keeping Your Headcount When All about You Are Losing Theirs: Downsizing, Voluntary Turnover Rates, and the Moderating Role of HR Practices," *Academy of Management Journal* 51, no. 2 (2008), pp. 259–76; Anat Freund, "Commitment and Job Satisfaction as Predictors of Turnover Intentions among Welfare Workers," *Administration in Social Work* 29, no. 2 (2005), pp. 5–21; and S. Arzu Wasti, "Organizational Commitment, Turnover Intentions and the Influence of Cultural Values," *Journal of Occupational and Organizational Psychology* 76, no. 3 (September 2003), pp. 303–15.

[46]Erich C. Dierdorff and Eric A. Surface, "If You Pay for Skills, Will They Learn? Skill Change and Maintenance Under a Skill-Based Pay System," *Journal of Management* 34, no. 4 (2008), pp. 721–43.

[47]Richard Long, "Paying for Knowledge: Does It Pay?" *Canadian HR Reporter* 18, no. 6 (March 28, 2005), pp. 12–14; James R. Thompson and Charles W. LeHew, "Skill-Based Pay as an Organizational Innovation," *Review of Public Personnel Administration* 20, no. 1 (Winter 2000), pp. 20–41; and Frederick Hills, Thomas Bergmann, and Vida Scarpello, *Compensation Decision Making* (New York: The Dryden Press, 1994).

[48]D.K. Denton, "Multi-Skilled Teams Replace Old Work Systems," *HR Magazine,* September 1992, pp. 55–56.

[49]Thomas P. Flannery, David A. Hofrichter, and Paul E. Platten, *People, Performance, and Pay* (New York: Free Press, 1996), pp. 98–99.

[50]Ibid.

[51]Duncan Brown, "Broadbanding: A Study of Company Practices in the United Kingdom," *Compensation & Benefits Review,* November–December 1996, pp. 41–49.

[52]"Hospitals Offering Concierge Service to Staff to Keep Workers Happy, Productive—and Loyal," *Health Care Strategic Management* 21, no. 11 (November 2003), p. 5.

[53]Stacey Hirsh, "Concierge Services Target Busy Working Professionals," *Knight Ridder Tribune Business News,* October 5, 2005, p. 1; "Work–Life Balance: Staff Pay Concierge Services Bill When Firms Bail Out," *Employee Benefits,* August 2003, pp. 12–14; and Karla Taylor, "May I Help You, Please?" *HR Magazine,* August 2000, pp. 90–96.

[54]Simon Taggar and Mitchell J. Neubert, "A Cognitive (Attributions)-Emotion Model of Observer Reactions to Free-Riding Poor Performers," *Journal of Business and Psychology* 22, no. 3 (2008), pp. 167–77; and Peter Richardson and D. Keith Denton, "How to Create a High-Performance Team," *Human Resource Development Quarterly* 16, no. 3 (Fall 2005), pp. 417–23.

[55]Edward E. Lawler, III, *From the Ground Up:* Six Principles for Building the New Logic Corporation (San Francisco: Jossey-Bass, 1996), pp. 211–13.

[56]Kimberly Merriman, "Low-Trust Teams Prefer Individualized Pay," *Harvard Business Review* 86, no. 11 (November 2008), pp. 32–36.

[57]Matt Bolch, "Rewarding the Team," *HR Magazine* 52, no. 2 (February 2007), pp. 91–94.

[58]Kimberly K. Merriman, "On the Folly of Rewarding Team Performance, While Hoping for Teamwork," *Compensation and Benefits Review* 41, no. 1, (January/ February 2009), pp. 61–66.

[59]Mohammed Shahedul Quader and Mohammed Rashedul Quader, "A Critical Analysis of High Performing Teams: A Case Study Based on the British Telecommunication (BT) PLC," *Journal of Services Research* 8, no. 2 (2008), pp. 175–216.

[60]Ron Cacioppe, "Using Team–Individual Reward and Recognition Strategies to Drive Organizational Success," *Leadership & Organization Development Journal* 20, no. 6 (1999), pp. 322–31.

[61]C. James Novak, "Proceed with Caution When Paying Teams," *HR Magazine,* April 1997, pp. 73–78.

[62]U.S. Department of Labor, "Employed Persons by Class of Worker and Part-Time Status: Household Data," Bureau of Labor Statistics, Table A-5, www.bls. gov/news.release/empsit.t05.htm (accessed May 22, 2009).

[63] Bill Leonard, "Recipes for Part-Time Benefits," *HR Magazine,* April 2000, pp. 56–62.

[64]Dinah Wisenberg Brin, "Hospitals Look to Pare Costs, Share Savings with Physicians," *The Wall Street Journal,* March 29, 2005, p. D4; Jeffrey B. Arthur and Lynda Aiman-Smith, "Gainsharing and Organizational Learning: An Analysis of Employee Suggestions over Time," *Academy of Management Journal* 44, no. 4 (August 2001), pp. 737–55; and Richard Blackburn and Benson Rosen, "Total Quality and Human Resources Management: Lessons Learned from Baldrige Award–Winning Companies," *Academy of Management Executive,* August 1993, pp. 49–66.

[65]Daniel Wren, "Joseph N. Scanlon: The Man and the Plan," *Journal of Management History* 15, no. 1 (2009), pp. 20–37.

[66]Luis R. Gomez-Mejia, "The Role of Risk Sharing and Risk Taking under Gainsharing," *Academy of Management Review* 25, no. 3 (July 2000), pp. 492–508.

[67]E.E. Lawler, S.A. Mohrman, and G.E. Ledford, *Creating High Performance Organizations: Practices and Results of Employee Involvement and Quality Management in Fortune 1000 Companies* (San Francisco: Jossey-Bass, 1995).

[68]"These Bonuses Are a Safe Bet," *Business Ethics,* March–April 1994, p. 31.

[69]John Stark, Glenn L. Dalton, and Donncha Carroll, "Goalsharing Plans Help Stillwater Mining Company through Tough Times," *Journal of Organizational Excellence* 23, no. 1 (Winter 2003), pp. 11–22; and Charlotte Garvey, "Goalsharing Scores," *HR Magazine,* April 2000, pp. 99–106.

[70]Edward J. Schnee, "Deduction Denied for ESOP Stock Redemption," *Journal of Accountancy* 207, no. 5 (2009), p. 65.

[71]Shari Caudron, "Employee, Cover Thyself," *Workforce,* April 2000, pp. 34–42.

[72]Lawler, *Pay and Organizational Effectiveness,* pp. 214–16.

[73]Ibid., p. 128.

Chapter 8

[1]Yoav Vardi and Ely Weitz, *Misbehavior in Organizations* (Mahwah, NJ: Lawrence Erlbaum, 2004).

[2]Vita Bekker, Joanna Chung, Brooke Masters, Megan Murphy, and Alan Rappeport, "Ponzi Victims Find Little Solace in Guilty Plea of a 'Con-Man,'" *Financial Times,* March 13, 2009, p. 16; Paul Betts and Andrew Hill, "Parmalat Scandal Rumbles on amid Subprime Debris," *Financial Times,* July 3, 2008, p. 14; "Former National Century Executives Are Sentenced in Fraud Case," *The Wall Street Journal,* August 7, 2008, p. B10; "News Corp," *The Wall Street Journal,* August 1, 2005, p. B12; and Robert Frank and Casell Bryan-Low et al., "Scandal Scorecard," *The Wall Street Journal,* October 3, 2003, pp. B-1, B-4.

[3]R.T. Mowday and R.I. Sutton, "Organizational Behavior: Linking Individuals and Groups to Organizational Contexts," *Annual Review of Psychology* 44 (1993), pp. 195–229; and C.A. O'Reilly, III, "Organizational Behavior: Where We've Been, Where We're Going," *Annual Review of Psychology* 78 (1991), pp. 679–703.

[4]For a review of the organizational misbehavior literature, see: James Richards "The Many Approaches to Organisational Misbehaviour: A Review, Map and Research Agenda," *Employee Relations* 30, no. 6 (2008), pp. 653–78.

[5]Julie Horney, "An Alternative Psychology of Criminal Behavior," *Criminology,* February 2006, pp. 1–16.

[6]E.H. Sutherland, "White-Collar Criminality," *American Sociological Review* 5 (1940), pp. 1–12.

[7]J.W. Coleman, "Toward an Integrated Theory of White-Collar Crime," *American Journal of Sociology* 93 (1987), pp. 406–39.

[8]Vardi and Weitz, *Misbehavior in Organizations.*

[9]Ibid.

[10]Jill Kickul, "When Organizations Break Their Promises: Employee Reactions to Unfair Processes and Treatment," *Journal of Business Ethics* 29, no. 4 (2001), pp. 289–307.

[11]R.D. Hackett, "Work Attitudes and Employee Absenteeism: A Synthesis of the Literature," *Journal of Psychology* 62 (1989), pp. 235–48.

[12]Danielle W. Warren, "Constructive and Destructive Deviance in Organizations," *Academy of Management Review* 28 (October 2003), pp. 622–32.

[13]Vardi and Weitz, *Misbehavior in Organizations.*

[14]R.A. Giacalone and J. Greenberg, eds., *Antisocial Behavior in Organizations* (Thousand Oaks, CA: Sage Publications, 1997).

[15]Edgar Schein, *Organizational Culture and Leadership* (San Francisco: Jossey-Bass, 2004).

[16]For a review of research on sexual harassment, see: A. O'Leary-Kelly, L. Bowes-Sperry, C. Bates, and E. Lean, "Sexual Harassment at Work: A Decade (Plus) of Progress," *Journal of Management* 35, no. 3 (2009), p. 503.

[17]J.N. Cleveland, M. Stockdale, and K.R. Murphy, *Women and Men in Organizations: Sex and Gender Issues* (Mahwah, NJ: Lawrence Erlbaum, 2000).

[18]O'Leary-Kelly et al., "Sexual Harassment at Work: A Decade (Plus) of Progress."

[19]J. Cogin and A. Fish, "An Empirical Investigation of Sexual Harassment and Work Engagement: Surprising Differences between Men and Women," *Journal of Management and Organization* 15, no. 1 (2009), pp. 47–61; S. Welsh, "Gender and Sexual Harassment," *Annual Review of Sociology* 25 (1999), pp. 169–90.

[20]Kathryn Tyler, "Sign in the Name of Love," *HR Magazine* 53, no. 2 (February 2008), pp. 41–44.

[21]Ibid.

[22]O'Leary-Kelly et al., "Sexual Harassment at Work: A Decade (Plus) of Progress."

[23]Ibid.

[24]J.B. Pryor and L.M. Stoller, "Sexual Cognition Processes in Men High in the Likelihood to Sexually Harass," *Personality and Social Psychology Bulletin* 20 (1994), pp. 163–69.

[25]J. Lee, J. Welbourne, W. Hoke, and J. Beggs, "Examining the Interaction among Likelihood to Sexually Harass, Ratee Attractiveness, and Job Performance," *Journal of Management* 35, no. 2 (2009), p. 445.

[26]Anne M. O'Leary-Kelly, "Sexual Harassment as Aggressive Behavior: An Actor-Based Perspective," *Academy of Management Review* 25 (April 2000), pp. 372–86.

[27]Anne C. Levy and Michele A. Paludi, *Workplace Sexual Harassment* (Upper Saddle River, NJ: Prentice Hall, 2002).

[28]See www.osha.gov/OshDoc/data_General_Facts/factsheet-workplace-violence.pdf (accessed July 16, 2009).

[29]A.H. Buss, *The Psychology of Aggression* (New York: John Wiley & Sons, 1961).

[30]A.M. O'Leary-Kelly, R.W. Griffin, and D.J. Glew, "Organization-Motivated Aggression: A Research

Framework," *Academy of Management Review* 21 (1996), pp. 225–53.

[31]Mark J. Martinko, Michael J. Gundlach, and Scott C. Douglas, "Toward an Integrative Theory of Counterproductive Workplace Behavior: A Causal Reasoning Perspective," *International Journal of Selection and Assessment* 10 (March–June 2002), pp. 36–50.

[32]See www.cdc.gov/niosh/topics/violence/ (accessed July 16, 2009).

[33]S. Smith, "Census of Fatal Occupational Injuries Shows a Decline in Worker Deaths," *Occupational Hazards* 70, no. 8 (September 2008), pp. 14–15.

[34]Joel H. Neuman and Robert A. Baron, "Aggression in the Workplace," in *Antisocial Behavior in Organizations*, eds. R.A. Giacalone and J. Greenberg (Thousand Oaks, CA: Sage Publications, 1997), pp. 37–67.

[35]M. Harvey, D. Treadway, J. Heames, and A. Duke, "Bullying in the 21st Century Global Organization: An Ethical Perspective," *Journal of Business Ethics* 85, no. 1 (2009), pp. 27–40.

[36]Dawn Jennifer, Helen Cowie, and Katerina Ananiadou, "Perceptions and Experience of Workplace Bullying in Five Different Work Populations," *Aggressive Behavior* 29 (2003), pp. 489–96; and Denise Salin, "Ways of Explaining Workplace Bullying: A Review of Enabling, Motivating and Precipitating Structures and Processes in the Work Environment," *Human Relations* 56, no. 10 (2003), pp. 1213–32.

[37]Jane L. Ireland and Rachel Monaghan, "Behaviors Indicative of Bullying among Young and Juvenile Male Offenders: A Study of Perpetrator and Victim Characteristics," *Aggressive Behavior*, May 2006, pp. 172–80.

[38]Harvey et al., "Bullying in the 21st Century Global Organization: An Ethical Perspective."

[39]John M. Ivancevich, Thomas N. Duening, Jacqueline A. Gilbert, and Robert Konopaske, "Deterring White-Collar Crime," *The Academy of Management Executive* 17, no. 2 (2003), pp. 114–27.

[40]S. Einarsen, "The Nature and Causes of Bullying at Work," *International Journal of Manpower* 20 (1999), pp. 16–27.

[41]Jennifer, Cowie, and Ananiadou, "Perceptions and Experience of Workplace Bullying," p. 495.

[42]Lilia M. Cortina, "Unseen Injustice: Incivility as Modern Discrimination in Organizations," *Academy of Management Review* 33, no. 1 (2008), pp. 55–75; and Lynne M. Anderson and Christine M. Pearson,

"Tit for Tat? The Spiraling Effect of Incivility in the Workplace," *Academy of Management Review* 24 (1999), pp. 452–71.

[43]Marilyn J. Davidson and Sandra L. Fielden, eds., *Individual Diversity and Psychology in Organizations* (San Francisco, Jossey-Bass, 2003).

[44]P.R. Johnson and J. Indvik, "Rudeness at Work: Impulse over Restraint," *Public Personnel Management* 30 (Winter 2001), pp. 457–65.

[45]Cortina, "Unseen Injustice: Incivility as Modern Discrimination in Organizations."

[46]Johnson and Indvik, "Rudeness at Work: Impulse over Restraint."

[47]B. Estes and J. Wang, "Workplace Incivility: Impacts on Individual and Organizational Performance," *Human Resource Development Review* 7, no. 2 (2008), pp. 218–40.

[48]C.C. Chen and W. Eastman, "Toward a Civic Culture for Multicultural Organizations," *Journal of Applied Behavioral Science* 33 (1997), pp. 454–70.

[49]Claire Lawrence, "Measuring Individual Responses to Aggression-Triggering Events: Development of the Situational Triggers of Aggressive Response (STAR) Scale," *Aggressive Behavior*, February 2006, pp. 241–52.

[50]Estes and Wang, "Workplace Incivility: Impacts on Individual and Organizational Performance."

[51]S.L. Carter, *Civility: Manners, Morals, and Etiquette of Democracy* (New York: Basic Books, 1998).

[52]Robert J. Grossman, "The Five-Finger Bonus," *HR Magazine*, October 2003, pp. 38–44.

[53]Joseph T. Wells, "Why Employees Commit Fraud," *Journal of Accountancy*, February 2001, pp. 89–92.

[54]Ibid.

[55]Ibid.

[56]Brent Kendall and Sarah N. Lynch, "Corporate News: Beazer to Pay as Much as $53 Million in Fraud Case," *The Wall Street Journal*, July 2, 2009, p. B3.

[57]John Gapper, "A Sentence Both Necessary and Rare," *Financial Times*, July 2, 2009, p. 9.

[58]William Greider, "Is This America's Top Corporate Crime Fighter?" *Nation*, August 2002, pp. 11–15.

[59]T. Buckhoff, J. Clifton, and R.H. Colson, "Exotic Embezzling: Investigating Off-Book Fraud Schemes," *CPA Journal* 73 (September 2003), pp. 56–58.

[60]M. Frone, "Are Work Stressors Related to Employee Substance Use? The Importance of Temporal Context Assessments of Alcohol and Illicit Drug Use," *Journal of Applied Psychology* 93, no. 1 (2008), pp. 199–206; and Michael R. Frone, "Prevalence and Distribution of Illicit Drug Use in the Workforce and in the Workplace: Findings and Implications from a U.S. National Survey," *Journal of Applied Psychology* 91, no. 4 (2006), pp. 856–69.

[61]S.B. Bacharach, P. Bamberger, and W.J. Sonnenstul, "Driven to Drink: Managerial Control, Work-Related Risk Factors, and Employee Problem Drinking," *Academy of Management Journal* 45 (2002), pp. 637–58.

[62]Timothy DeGroot and D. Scott Kiker, "A Meta-Analysis of the Non-Monetary Effects of Employee Health Programs," *Human Resource Management,* Spring 2003, pp. 53–65.

[63]Frone, "Are Work Stressors Related to Employee Substance Use?"

[64]Bacharach et al., "Driven to Drink."

[65]D.A. Dabney and R.C. Hollinger, "Illicit Prescription Drug Use among Pharmacists," *Work and Occupation* 26 (1999), pp. 77–106.

[66]J. Hoffman and C. Larison, "Drug Use, Workplace Accidents, and Employee Turnover," *Journal of Drug Use* 99 (Spring 1999), pp. 341–64.

[67]Ibid.

[68]Paulo Prada and Andy Pasztor, "American Airlines Hit by $7.1 Million in Fines," *The Wall Street Journal,* August 15, 2008, p. B1.

[69]K. Naughton, J. Raymond, K. Shulman, and D. Struzzi, "Cyberslacking," *Newsweek,* November 29, 1999, pp. 62–65.

[70]Patricia Borstorff and Glenn Graham, "E-Harassment: Employee Perceptions of E-Technology as a Source of Harassment," *Journal of Applied Management and Entrepreneurship* 11, no. 3 (2006), pp. 51–67.

[71]Barbara Kate Repa, *Your Rights in the Workplace* (Berkeley, CA: Nolo Press, 2006).

[72]A. Nancherla, "Surveillance Increases in Workplace," *T + D* 62, no. 5 (May 2008), p. 12.

[73]E. Doss and M. Loui, "Ethics and the Privacy of Electronic Mail," *Information Society* 11 (1995), pp. 223–35.

[74]Haughton et al., "Cyberslacking."

[75]M.P. McQueen, "Workers' Terminations for Computer Misuse Rise," *The Wall Street Journal,* July 15, 2006, p. B4.

[76]Ibid.

[77]J. Laabs, "Employee Sabotage: Don't Be a Target," www.workforceonline.com/future/00/03/17.

[78]K. Wehrum, "When IT Workers Attack," *Inc* 31, no. 3 (April 2009), pp. 132–34.

[79]R.A. Giacalone, C.A. Riordan, and P. Rosenfeld, "Employee Sabotage: Toward a Practitioner–Scholar Understanding," in Antisocial Behavior in Organizations, eds. R.A. Giacalone and J. Greenberg (Thousand Oaks, CA: Sage Publications, 1997), pp. 109–29.

[80]Ibid.

[81]Laabs, "Employee Sabotage."

[82]Michelle Conlin, "To Catch a Corporate Thief," *BusinessWeek,* February 16, 2009, p. 52.

[83] L. Ramos, "Combating Theft in Tough Economic Times," *Stores* 91, no. 3 (March 2009), p. 84.

[84]Conlin, "To Catch a Corporate Thief."

[85]J. Greenberg, "Who Stole the Money? Individual and Situational Determinants of Employee Theft," *Organizational Behavior and Human Decision Processes* 89 (2002), pp. 985–1003.

[86]Wells, "Why Employees Commit Fraud."

[87]Laura Heller, "The High Price of Crime," *DSN Retailing Today*, January 9, 2006, pp. 11–13.

[88]Berkeley Rice, "10 Ways to Foil an Embezzler," *Medical Economics,* March 17, 2006, p. 50.

[89]D.S. Ones, C. Viswesvaran, and F.L. Schmidt, "Comprehensive Meta-Analysis of Integrity Test Validities: Findings and Implications for Personnel Selection and Theories of Job Performance," *Journal of Applied Psychology* 78 (1993), pp. 679–703.

[90]Christopher M. Berry, Paul R. Sackett, and Shelly Wiemann, "A Review of Recent Developments in Integrity Test Research," *Personnel Psychology* 60, no. 2 (2007), pp. 271–301.

[91]Greenberg, "The STEAL Motive," offers an excellent presentation of the STEAL model.

[92]Ibid.

[93]G.E. Mautner, N.W. Anderson, and S.E. Haushield, "Privacy in the Workplace," manuscript of Lane, Powell, Spears, Lubersky, LLP, 2001.

[94]Richard A. Spinello, "The Case for E-Mail Privacy," unpublished paper (Boston, MA: Boston College, 2004).

[95]Naughton et al., "Cyberslacking."

[96]Spinello, "The Case for E-Mail Privacy."

[97]Ibid.

[98]Ken Liska, *Drugs and the Human Body with Implications for Society* (Upper Saddle River, NJ: Prentice Hall, 2004).

Chapter 9

[1]"Employee Well-being," www.ibm.com/ibm/responsibility/people/wellbeing/promoting-health.shtml (accessed May 14, 2006).

[2]Justin Fox, "We Can Beat This," *Fortune,* October 27, 2008, p. 96.

[3]Ibid.

[4]Kelly Evans, Joann S. Lublin, Timothy Aeppel, and Jonathan D. Rockoff, "Broader, Deeper Job Cuts Risk Steepening Slump," *The Wall Street Journal,* October 24, 2008, p. B.1.

[5]Mortimer B. Zuckerman, "Is Obama's Big Start Too Big?" *U.S. News & World Report,* 146, no. 5 (June 2009), p. 80.

[6]Michael T. Matteson and John M. Ivancevich, *Controlling Work Stress* (San Francisco: Jossey-Bass, 1987).

[7]Cary Cooper, "Future Research in Occupational Stress," *Stress Medicine,* March 2000, pp. 63–65.

[8]S. Gilboa, A. Shirom, Y. Fried, and C. Cooper, "A Meta-Analysis of Work Demand Stressors and Job Performance: Examining Main and Moderating Effects," *Personnel Psychology* 61, no. 2 (2008), pp. 227–71.

[9]R.L. Kahan, D.M. Wolfe, R.P. Quinn, J.D. Snoek, and R.A. Rosenthal, *Organizational Stress: Studies in Role Conflict and Ambiguity* (New York: John Wiley, 1964), p. 94.

[10]For a review, see J. Michel, J. Mitchelson, L. Kotrba, J. LeBreton, & B. Baltes, "A Comparative Test of Work-Family Conflict Models and Critical Examination of Work-Family Linkages." *Journal of Vocational Behavior* 74, no. 2 (2009), p. 199.

[11]S. MacDermid and A. Wittenborn, "Lessons from Work-Life Research for Developing Human Resources," *Advances in Developing Human Resources* 9, no. 4 (2007), pp. 556–68; and P. Cramer, "Defense Mechanisms in Psychology Today: Further Processes for Adaptation," *American Psychologist,* June 2000, pp. 637–46.

[12]Carol Hymowitz and Rachel Emma Silverman, "Stressed Out: Can Workplace Stress Get Worse?—In Soft Economy, Workplace Stress May Get Worse—In This Economy—You Bet; Add Financial Uncertainty to General Job Overload." *The Wall Street Journal,* January 16, 2001, p. B1.

[13]A. Stevens, "Suit over Suicide Raises Issue: Do Associates Work Too Hard?" *The Wall Street Journal,* April 15, 1994, pp. B1, B7.

[14]Clinton Weiman, "A Study of Occupational Stressors and the Incidence of Disease/Risk," *Journal of Occupational Medicine,* February 1977, pp. 119–22.

[15]Toby Wall, Paul Jackson, Sean Mullarkey, and Sharon K. Parker, "The Demands-Control Model of Job Strain: A More Specific Test," *Journal of Occupational and Organizational Psychology,* June 1996, pp. 153–66.

[16]R.L. Franche, A. Williams, S. Ibrahim, S. Grace, C. Mustard, B. Minore, and D.E. Stewart, "Path Analysis of Work Conditions and Work-Family Spillover as Modifiable Workplace Factors Associated with Depressive Symptomology," *Stress and Health,* April 2006, pp. 91–103.

[17]S.R. Maddi and S.C. Kobasa, *The Hardy Executive: Health under Stress* (Homewood, IL: Dow Jones/Irwin, 1984).

[18]Jarle Eid, Bjorn Helge Johnsen, Paul T. Bartone, and Odd Arne Nissestad, "Growing Transformational Leaders: Exploring the Role of Personality Hardiness," *Leadership & Organization Development Journal* 29, no. 1 (2008), pp. 4–23.

[19]M.V. Brooks, "Health-Related Hardiness and Chronic Illness: A Synthesis of Current Research," *Nursing Forum* 38 (July–September 2003), pp. 11–20.

[20]Matteson and Ivancevich, *Controlling Work Stress,* p. 48.

[21]M. Kivimaki, J. Vahtera, M. Elovainio, J. Pentti, and M. Virtanen, "Human Costs of Organizational Downsizing: Comparing Health Trends between Leavers and Stayers," *American Journal of Community Psychology* 32 (September 2003), pp. 57–67.

[22] M. Schwartz, "Return to Work in Progress," *Benefits Canada,* 33, no. 3 (March 2009), pp. 31–36; and Martha H. Peak, "Cutting Jobs? Watch Your Disability Expenses Grow," *Management Review,* March 1997, p. 9.

[23]A. Rafaeli and M. Worline, "Individual Emotions in Work Organizations," *Social Science Information* 40 (2001), pp. 95–124.

[24]K.J. Maier, S.R. Waldstein, and S.J. Synowski, "Relation of Cognitive Appraisal to Cardiovascular Reactivity, Affect, and Task Engagement," *Annals of Behavioral Medicine* 26 (August 2003), pp. 32–41.

[25]J. French, W. Rogers, and S. Cobb, "A Model of Person–Environment Fit," in *Coping and Adaptation,*

eds., G. Coehlo, D. Hamburgh, and J. Adams (New York: Basic Books, 1974).

[26]C. Maslaach, W.B. Schaufeli, and M.P. Leiter, *Job Burnout: Annual Review of Psychology* 52 (2001), pp. 397–422.

[27]L. Goldman and J. Lewis, "The Invisible Illness," *Occupational Health* 60, no. 6 (2008), pp. 20–21; and "Depression's Toll on U.S. Companies," www.prnewsservice.com (accessed May 14, 2006).

[28]Sharon Johnson, "Depression: Dragging Millions Down," *New York Times Magazine,* October 29, 2000, pp. 39, 47.

[29]Wayne N. Burton, Alyssa B. Schultz, Chin-Yu Chen, and Dee W. Edington, "The Association of Worker Productivity and Mental Health: A Review of the Literature," *International Journal of Workplace Health Management* 1, no. 2 (2008), pp. 78–94.

[30]Dwayne Runke, "Fighting Depression at Work," *Canadian HR Reporter* 20, no. 13 (July 2007), p. 22.

[31]Y. Raj, "How Primary Care Doctors Can Screen for Depression," *Medical Economics* 85, no. 14 (July 2008), pp. 28–33; K.B. Wells, R. Sturm, C.D. Sherbourne, and L.S. Meredith, *Caring for Depression: A Rand Study* (Cambridge, MA: Harvard University Press, 1996).

[32]M. Dewan, "Are Psychiatrists Cost-Effective? An Analysis of Integrated versus Split Treatment," *American Journal of Psychiatry,* Summer 1999, pp. 224–36.

[33]M. Gleimer and P. Purham, "Stress Management: MHC Class I and Class I–Like Molecules as Reporters of Cellular Stress," *Immunity* 19 (October 2003), pp. 469–77.

[34]M.L. Peters, G.L. Godaert, R.E. Ballieux, and C.J. Heijnen, "Moderation of Physiological Stress Reponses by Personality Traits and Daily Hassles: Less Flexibility of Immune System Responses," *Biological Psychology* 65 (December 2003), pp. 21–48.

[35]For a review, see: Jonathon R.B. Halbesleben, and M. Ronald Buckley, "Burnout in Organizational Life," *Journal of Management* 30, no. 6 (2004), pp. 859–79.

[36]Samuel Melamed, Arie Shirom, Sharon Toker, Shlomo Berliner, and Itzhak Shapira, "Burnout and Risk of Cardiovascular Disease: Evidence, Possible Causal Paths, and Promising Research Directions," *Psychological Bulletin* 132, no. 3 (2006), p. 327.

[37]R.J. Burke, "Workaholism in Organizations: Psychological and Physical Well-Being Consequences," *Stress Medicine,* January 2000, pp. 11–16.

[38]S.L. Langelaan, A.B. Bakker, L. Van Doornen, and W.B. Schaufeli, "Burnout and Work Engagement: Do Individual Differences Make a Difference?" *Personality and Individual Differences,* February 2006, pp. 521–32.

[39]D.L. Jones, T. Tanigawa, and S.M. Weiss, "Stress Management and Workplace Disability in the U.S., Europe, and Japan," *Journal of Occupational Health* 45 (January 2003), pp. 1–7.

[40]"Stress: It Is Deadly," *Holistic Online,* www.holisticonline.com/stress/stressintroduction.htm (accessed May 14, 2006).

[41]Burke, "Workaholism in Organizations: Psychological and Physical Well-Being Consequences."

[42]"Stress: It Is Deadly."

[43]Susan Seitel, "Work-Life Experts Launch New Web-Based Training to Help Employees Battle the Costs of Stress and Build a Resilient Workforce," *PRWeb,* www.prwebdirect.com/releases/2006/2/prweb340379.htm (accessed May 14, 2006).

[44]See facts about costs of stress at The American Institute of Stress at http://www.stress.org/job.htm?AIS=27d046 caf2a76185d8c703a31eea29b5 (accessed July 18, 2009).

[45]Meyer Friedman and Diane Ulmer, *Treating Type A Behavior and Your Heart* (New York: Alfred A. Knopf, 1984).

[46]Y. Chida and M. Hamer, "Chronic Psychosocial Factors and Acute Physiological Responses to Laboratory-Induced Stress in Healthy Populations: A Quantitative Review of 30 Years of Investigations," *Psychological Bulletin* 134, no. 6 (2008), pp. 829–85.

[47]R.S. Wilson, J.L. Bienars, C.F. Mendes de Leon, D.A. Evans, and D.A. Bennett, "Negative Affect and Mortality in Older Persons," *American Journal of Epidemiology* 158 (November 2003), pp. 827–35.

[48]R.B. Williams, J.C. Barefoot, and N. Schneiderman, "Psychosocial Risk Factors for Cardiovascular Disease: More Than One Culprit at Work," *Journal of American Medical Association* 290 (October 2003), pp. 2190–92.

[49]C. Thomas and M. Lankau, "Preventing Burnout: The Effects of LMX and Mentoring on Socialization, Role Stress, and Burnout," *Human Resource Management* 48, no. 3 (2009), p. 417; H.S. Lett, J.A. Blumenthal, M.A. Babyak, T.J. Strauman, C. Robins, and A. Sherwood, "Social Support and Coronary Heart Disease: Epidemiologic Evidence and Implications for Treatment," *Psychosomatic Medicine* 67 (2005), pp. 869–78.

[50]G. Luria and A. Torjman, "Resources and Coping with Stressful Events," *Journal of Organizational Behavior* 30, no. 6 (2009), pp. 685–707; and C.R. Synder, "Coping: Where Are You Going?" in Coping: The Psychology of What Works, ed. C.R. Snyder (New York: Oxford University Press, 1999), pp. 324–33.

[51]See, for example, Jeffrey R. Edwards, "An Examination of Competing Versions of the Person–Environment Fit Approach to Stress," *Academy of Management Journal,* April 1996, pp. 292–339.

[52]Karen J. Jansen, and Amy Kristof-Brown, "Toward a Multidimensional Theory of Person-Environment Fit," *Journal of Managerial Issues* 18, no. 2 (2006), pp. 193–212.

[53]Ibid.

[54]Terence F. Shea, "Employees First," *HR Magazine,* 53, no. 7 (July 2008), pp. 36–38.

[55]Matt Bolch, "Time to Refocus," *HR Magazine,* 51, no. 5 (May 2006), pp. 89–93.

[56]Sarah E. Needleman, "New Career, Same Employer: Companies Offer Staff Counseling, Assistance to Help with Change," *The Wall Street Journal,* April 21, 2008, p. B9.

[57]Iris C. Mushin, Michael T. Matteson, and Edward C. Lynch, "Developing a Resident Assistance Program," *Archives of Internal Medicine,* March 1993, pp. 729–34.

[58]Vijai P. Shaimi, "Take Advantage of Employee Assistance Programs," *Mindpub,* October 2000, p. 225.

[59]Pamela Babcock, "Workplace Stress? Deal with It!" *HR Magazine,* 54, no. 5 (May 2009), pp. 67–71.

[60]Ibid.

[61]K. Danna and R.W. Griffin, "Health and Well-Being in the Workplace: A Review and Synthesis of the Literature," *Journal of Management* 25 (1999), pp. 357–84.

[62]Tracey Walker, "Workplace Wellness," *Managed Healthcare Executive* 19, no. 2 (February 2009), pp. 16–19.

[63]See http://promisingpractices.fightchronicdisease.org/ programs/detail/johnson_johnson_health_wellness_ program_formerly_known_as_live_for_life (accessed July 21, 2009).

[64]Kelly Dunn, "Roche Chooses Health by Promoting Prevention," *Workforce,* April 2000, pp. 82–84.

[65]S. Musich, T. McDonald, D. Hirschland, and D.W. Edington, "Examination of Risk Status Transitions among Active Employees in a Comprehensive Worksite Health Downtown Program," *Journal of Occupational Environment Medicine* 45 (April 2003), pp. 393–99.

[66]D. Coglan and T. Brennick, *Doing Action Research in Your Own Organization* (Thousand Oaks, CA: Sage, 2002).

[67]Julia von Onciul, "Stress at Work," *British Medical Journal,* September 1996, pp. 745–48.

[68]E.E. Solberg, R. Halvorsen, and H.H. Holen, "Effect of Meditation on Immune Cells," *Stress Medicine,* April 2000, pp. 185–200.

[69]Ibid.

[70]A. Parente and R. Parente, "Mind-Operated Devices: Mental Control of a Computer Using Biofeedback," *CyberPsychology and Behavior,* February 2006, pp. 1–4.

Chapter 10

[1]David A. Price, "How Pixar Cheated Death," *Inc.* 28, no. 6 (June 2006), p. 34.

[2]Ibid.

[3]See http://www.pixar.com/featurefilms/index.html (accessed May 27, 2009); Richard Corliss, "Up, Up and Away: Another New High for Pixar," *Time,* May 28, 2009, p. 57; and Matthew Garrahan, "Pixar Excites Memory of Old-Time Disney," *Financial Times,* April 10, 2008, p. 19.

[4]An excellent example of trauma teams that triggered the use of Ben Taub's world-renowned emergency room is found in Afsaneh Nahavandi and Ali R. Malekzadeh *Organizational Behavior* (Englewood Cliffs, NJ: Prentice Hall, 1999), pp. 267–68.

[5]Jon R. Katzenbach and Jason A. Santamaria, "Firing Up the Front Line," *Harvard Business Review,* May–June 1999, pp. 107, 117.

[6]Richard J. Hackman and Ruth Wageman, "A Theory of Team Coaching," *Academy of Management Review* 30, no. 2 (April 2005), pp. 269–87; and Bill Parcells, "The Tough Work of Turning Around a Team," *Harvard Business Review,* November–December 2000, pp. 179–86.

[7]Susan Nash, *Turning Team Performance Inside Out* (Palo Alto, CA: Davies-Black, 2000).

[8]Jack K. Ito, Céleste M. Brotheridge, "Do Teams Grow Up One Stage at a Time? Exploring the Complexity of Group Development Models," *Team Performance Management* 14, no. 5/6 (2008), pp. 214–32; and K.L. Bettenhausen, "Five Years of Group Research: What We Have Learned and What Needs to Be Addressed," *Journal of Management,* June 1991, pp. 345–81.

[9]B.W. Tuckman, "Developmental Sequence in Small Groups," *Psychological Bulletin,* November 1965, pp. 384–99; and B.W. Tuckman and M. Jensen, "Stages of Small Group Development Revisited," *Groups and Organization Studies,* 1977, pp. 419–27.

[10]Rolf van Dick, Daan van Knippenberg, Silvia Hägele, Yves R.F. Guillaume, and Felix C. Brodbeck, "Group Diversity and Group Identification: The Moderating Role of Diversity Beliefs," *Human Relations* 61, no. 10 (2008), pp. 1463–92; Keith M. Hmieleski and Michael D. Ensley, "A Contextual Examination of New Venture Performance: Entrepreneur Leadership Behavior, Top Management Team Heterogeneity, and Environmental

Dynamism," *Journal of Organizational Behavior* 28, no. 7 (2007), pp. 865–89; and Jennifer A. Chatman and Francis J. Flynn, "The Influence of Demographic Heterogeneity on the Emergence and Consequences of Cooperative Norms in Work Teams," *Academy of Management Journal* 44, no. 5 (2001), pp. 956–75.

[11]Erica Gabrielle Foldy, "Learning from Diversity: A Theoretical Exploration," *Public Administration Review* 64, no. 5 (September–October 2004), pp. 529–39; and Margaret M. Gootnick and David Gootnick, *Action Tools for Effective Managers* (New York: AMACOM, 2000).

[12]Douglas B. Feaver, "Pilots Learn to Handle Crises—and Themselves," *Washington Post,* September 12, 1982, p. A6.

[13]Ramon Rico, Miriam Sánchez-Manzanares, Francisco Gil, and Cristina Gibson, "Team Implicit Coordination Processes: A Team Knowledge-Based Approach," *Academy of Management Review* 33, no. 1 (January 2008), pp. 163–84; and Dennis Organ, *Organizational Citizenship Behavior: The Good Citizen Syndrome* (Lexington, MA: Lexington Books, 1988).

[14]Peter Bamberger and Michal Biron, "Group Norms and Excessive Absenteeism: The Role of Peer Referent Others," *Organizational Behavior and Human Decision Processes* 103, no. 2 (2007), pp. 179–96.

[15]Kristina B. Dahlin, Laurie R. Weingart, and Pamela J. Hinds, "Team Diversity and Information Use," *Academy of Management Journal* 48, no. 6 (December 2005), pp. 1107–23; Chatman and Flynn, "The Influence of Demographic Heterogeneity on the Emergence and Consequences of Cooperative Norms in Work Teams"; and K.L. Bettenhausen and J.K. Murnighan, "The Development and Stability of Norms in Groups Facing Interpersonal and Structural Change," *Administrative Science Quarterly,* 1991, pp. 20–35.

[16]Frank Walter and Heike Bruch, "The Positive Group Affect Spiral: A Dynamic Model of the Emergence of Positive Affective Similarity in Work Groups," *Journal of Organizational Behavior* 29, no. 2 (2008), pp. 239–61.

[17]J.M. George, "Personality, Affect, and Behavior in Groups," *Journal of Applied Psychology* 75 (1990), pp. 107–16.

[18]Barrie E. Litzky, Kimberly A. Eddleston, and Deborah L. Kidder, "The Good, the Bad, and the Misguided: How Managers Inadvertently Encourage Deviant Behavior," *Academy of Management Perspectives* 20, no. 1 (February 2006), pp. 91–103; Christian S. Crandall, Amy Eshelman, and Laurie O'Brien, "Social Norms and the Expression and Suppression of Prejudice: The Struggle for Internalization," *Journal of Personality and Social Psychology* 82, no. 3

(2002), pp. 359–78; and Daniel C. Feldman, "The Development and Enforcement of Group Norms," *Academy of Management Review,* January 1984, pp. 47–53.

[19]Salvatore R. Maddi, *Personality Theories: A Comparative Analysis* (Homewood, IL: Dorsey Press, 1980), chap. 7.

[20]David J. Henderson, Sandy J. Wayne, Lynn M. Shore, William H. Bommer, and Lois E. Tetrick, "Leader-Member Exchange, Differentiation, and Psychological Contract Fulfillment: A Multilevel Examination," *Journal of Applied Psychology* 93, no. 6 (2008), pp. 1208–19; Prasad Balkundi and David A. Harrison, "Ties, Leaders, and Time in Teams: Strong Inference about Network Structure's Effects on Team Viability and Performance," *Academy of Management Journal* 49, no. 1 (February 2006), pp. 49–68; and The Arbinger Institute, *Leadership and Self-Deception* (San Francisco, Berrett–Koehher, 2000).

[21]C. Cartwright and A. Zander, *Group Dynamics: Research and Theory* (New York: Harper & Row, 1968).

[22]Peggy M. Beranek and Ben Martz, "Making Virtual Teams More Effective: Improving Relational Links," *Team Performance Management* 11, no. 5/6 (2005), pp. 200–14; and Richard A. Guzzo and Marcus W. Dickson, "Teams in Organizations: Recent Research on Performance and Effectiveness," *Annual Review of Psychology,* 1996, pp. 307–38.

[23]Cohesiveness is not the only factor that may influence performance. For just one example, see Glenn Littlepage, William Robison, and Kelly Reddington, "Effects of Task Experience and Group Experience on Group Performance," *Organizational Behavior and Human Decision Processes,* February 1997, pp. 133–47. Also see Claus W. Langfred, "The Paradox of Self-Management: Individual and Group Autonomy in Work Groups," *Journal of Organizational Behavior* 21, no. 5 (2000), pp. 563–85.

[24]Paul J.H. Schoemaker and George S. Day, "How to Make Sense of Weak Signals," *MIT Sloan Management Review* 50, no. 3 (Spring 2009), pp. 81–89.

[25]Ibid.

[26]Irving Janis, *Victims of Groupthink: A Psychological Study of Foreign Policy Decisions and Fiascos,* 2nd ed. (Boston: Houghton Mifflin, 1982).

[27]Ibid., p. 9. For a review, see James K. Esser, "Alive and Well after 25 Years: A Review of Groupthink Research," *Organizational Behavior and Human Decision Processes* 73, no. 2/3 (1998), pp. 116–41.

[28]Robert D. Dimitroff, Lu Ann Schmidt, and Timothy D. Bond, "Organizational Behavior and Disaster: A Study of Conflict at NASA," *Project Management Journal* 36,

no. 2 (June 2005), pp. 28–39; and Gregory Moorhead, Richard J. Ference, Chris P. Neck, "Group Decision Fiascoes Continue: Space Shuttle Challenger and a Revised Groupthink Framework," *Human Relations* 44, no. 6 (1991), pp. 539–51.

²⁹Mark Maier, "Ten Years after a Major Malfunction: Reflections on 'The Challenger Syndrome,'" *Journal of Management Inquiry* 11, no. 3 (2002), pp. 282–96.

³⁰Group performance is frequently, but not always, better than individual performance. See Daniel Gigone and Reid Hastie, "Proper Analysis of the Accuracy of Group Judgments," *Psychological Bulletin,* January 1997, pp. 149–67.

³¹Michael Callaway, Richard Marriott, and James Esser, "Effects of Dominance on Group Decision Making: Toward a Stress-Reduction Explanation of Groupthink," *Journal of Personality and Social Psychology,* October 1985, pp. 949–52. For further discussion of the relationship between cohesiveness and groupthink, see P.R. Bernthal and C.A. Insko, "Cohesiveness without Groupthink," *Group and Organizational Management,* March 1993, pp. 66–87.

³²J. Richard Hackman, ed., *Groups That Work (and Those That Don't)* (San Francisco: Jossey-Bass, 1990), pp. 6–7.

³³Low Sui-Pheng and Sarah Danielle Khoo, "Team Performance Management Enhancement through Japanese 5-S Principles," *Team Performance Management* 7, no. 5 (2001), pp. 105–12; and Afsaneh Nahavandi, *The Art and Science of Leadership* (Upper Saddle River, NJ: Prentice Hall, 1997).

³⁴Guzzo and Dickson, "Teams in Organizations," p. 325.

³⁵Gloria M. Pereira and H.G. Osburn, "Effects of Participation in Decision Making on Performance and Employee Attitudes: A Quality Circles Meta-Analysis," *Journal of Business and Psychology* 22, no. 2 (2007), pp. 145–53.

³⁶Jeffrey Pfeffer, "Fighting the War for Talent Is Hazardous to Your Organization's Health," *Organizational Dynamics* 29, no. 4 (2001), pp. 248–59; and J.R. Katzenbach and D.K. Smith, *The Wisdom of Teams* (Boston: Harvard Business School Press, 1993).

³⁷Discussion with human resources representative in Peoria, Illinois, October 23, 2000; and G. Taninecz, "Team Players," *Industry Week,* July 15, 1996, pp. 28–32.

³⁸Michael Mecham and Guy Norris. "Picture This," *Aviation Week & Space Technology* 170, no. 20 (May 18, 2009), p. 56.

³⁹Thomas H. Davenport and Keri Pearlson, "Two Cheers for the Virtual Office," *Sloan Management Review,* Summer 1998, pp. 51–65.

⁴⁰Benson Rosen, Stacie Furst, and Richard Blackburn, "Overcoming Barriers to Knowledge Sharing in Virtual Teams," *Organizational Dynamics* 36, no. 3 (2007), 259–73.

⁴¹Amy Oringel, "John Patrick Reinventing Big Blue," Developer.com, www.developer.com/news/profiles/022598-patrick, March 2, 1998.

⁴²Phillip L. Hunsaker and Johanna S. Hunsaker, "Virtual Teams: a Leader's Guide," *Team Performance Management* 14, nos. 1/2 (2008), pp. 86–101; Jenny Goodbody, "Critical Success Factors for Global Virtual Teams," *Strategic Communication Management* 9, no. 2 (February–March 2005), pp. 18–21; and Bradley L. Kirkman, Benson Rosen, Cristina Gibson, Paul E. Tesluk, and Simon O. McPherson, "Five Challenges to Virtual Team Success: Lessons from Sabre, Inc.," *Academy of Management Executive* 16, no. 3 (August 2002), pp. 67–80.

⁴³Charlene M. Solomon, "Managing Virtual Teams," *Workforce,* June 2001, pp. 60–65; and Deborah L. Duarte and Nancy Tennant, *Mastering Virtual Teams* (San Francisco: Jossey-Bass, 1999).

⁴⁴Arvind Malhotra, Ann Majchrzak, and Benson Rosen, "Leading Virtual Teams," *Academy of Management Perspectives* 21, no. 1 (2007), pp. 60–69; Cristina B. Gibson and Susan G. Cohen, *Virtual Teams That Work* (San Francisco: Jossey-Bass, 2003); Wayne F. Cascio and Stan Shurygailo, "E-Leadership and Virtual Teams," *Organizational Dynamics* 31, no. 4 (January 2003), pp. 362–76; and Wayne F. Cascio, "Managing a Virtual Workplace," *Academy of Management Executive,* August 2000, pp. 81–90.

⁴⁵Stephen J. Zaccaro and Paige Bader, "E-Leadership and the Challenges of Leading E-Teams: Minimizing the Bad and Maximizing the Good," *Organizational Dynamics* 31 no. 4 (January 2003), pp. 377–88; and S.L. Jarvenpaa, K. Knoll, and D.E. Leidner, "Is Anybody Out There? Antecedents of Trust in Global Virtual Teams," *Journal of Management Information Systems,* 1998, pp. 29–64.

⁴⁶John Sullivan, "Time to Telecommute," *Workforce Management* 87, no. 11 (June 23, 2008), p. 66.

⁴⁷Kathy Gurchiek, "Telecommuting Could Hold Back Career," *HR Magazine* 52, no. 3 (March 2007), pp. 34–39; and Anne Fisher, "How Telecommuters Can Stay Connected," *Fortune,* May 30, 2005, pp. 142–43.

⁴⁸"The New World of Work: Flexibility Is the Watchword" *BusinessWeek,* January 10, 2000, p. 36; and L. Rivenbark, "Employees Want More Opportunities to Telecommunicate," *HR News,* April 2000, pp. 14–16.

⁴⁹Jonathan Karp, "One Small Step for Drones: Legendary 'Skunk Works' Helps Lockheed Martin Jump into Unmanned-Plane Market," *The Wall Street Journal,*

February 7, 2006, p. B1; and Tim Carvell, "Lockheed Raises Stink over 'Skunkworks.' " *Fortune,* March 6, 2000, pp. 80–81.

[50]Aaron Ricadela, "Trouble on the Horizon for Vista," *BusinessWeek,* September 22, 2008, p. 84.

[51]J.B. White and O. Suris, "How a 'Skunk Works' Kept Mustang Alive—On a Tight Budget," *The Wall Street Journal,* September 21, 1993, pp. A1, A12; and Bradley L. Kirkman and Debra L. Shapiro, "The Impact of Cultural Values on Employee Resistance to Teams: Toward a Model of Globalized Self-Managing Work Team Effectiveness," *Academy of Management Review,* July 1997, pp. 730–57.

[52]Alan W. Randolf and Marshall Sashkin, "Can Organizational Empowerment Work in Multinational Settings?" *Academy of Management Executive* 16, no. 1 (February 2002), pp. 102–16.

[53]Brian Dumaine, "The Trouble with Teams," *Fortune,* September 5, 1994, pp. 86–92.

[54]Edward Ward, "Autonomous Work Groups: A Field Study of Correlates of Satisfaction," *Psychological Reports,* February 1997, pp. 60–62.

[55]Roy A. Cook and J. Larry Goff, "Coming of Age with Self-Managed Teams: Dealing with a Problem Employee," *Journal of Business and Psychology* 16, no. 3 (Spring 2002), pp. 485–96.

Chapter 11

[1]J. Dreyfuss, "TechSpin: Did the Ballmer-Gates Clash Hurt Microsoft?" *Red Herring* [serial online], June 5, 2008, pp. 1–2, available from Business Source Complete, Ipswich, MA (accessed June 9, 2009); Steve Janss, "Staying Connected Anytime Anywhere," *Network World* 19, no. 37 (September 16, 2002), pp. 44–46; Don Clark, "Microsoft Forms Team to Build Subscriber Unit," *The Wall Street Journal,* April 6, 2001, p. B5; Rebecca Buckman, "Microsoft Makes Changes to Focus on Internet," *The Wall Street Journal,* August 10, 2000, p. B6; and Rebecca Buckman, "Microsoft Readies a New 'Office' While Renovating the Old Standby," *The Wall Street Journal,* July 27, 2000, p. B1.

[2]Franz W. Kellermanns, Steven W. Floyd, Allison W. Pearson, and Barbara Spencer, "The Contingent Effect of Constructive Confrontation on the Relationship between Shared Mental Models and Decision Quality," *Journal of Organizational Behavior* 29, no. 1 (2008), pp. 119–37; Greg Roper, "Managing Employee Relations," *HR Magazine,* May 2005, pp. 101–5; Karen A. Jehn and Elizabeth A. Mannix, "The Dynamic Nature of Conflict: A Longitudinal Study of Intragroup Conflict and Group

Performance," *Academy of Management Journal* 44, no. 2 (April 2001), pp. 238–52; and Donald E. Conlon and Daniel P. Sullivan, "Examining the Actions of Organizations in Conflict: Evidence from the Delaware Court of Chancery," *Academy of Management Journal,* June 1999, pp. 319–29.

[3]Roger Bennett and Shamila Savair, "Managing Conflict between Marketing and Other Functions within Charitable Organizations," *Leadership and Organization Development Journal* 25, no. 1/2 (2004), pp. 180–200; and Allen C. Amason, "Distinguishing the Effects of Functional and Dysfunctional Conflict on Strategic Decision Making," *Academy of Management Journal* 39, no. 1 (February 1996), pp. 123–49.

[4]C. Marlene Fiol, Michael G. Pratt, and Edward J. O'Connor, "Managing Intractable Identity Conflicts," *Academy of Management Review* 34, no. 1 (2009), pp. 32–55.

[5]Ibid.

[6]J. Thompson, *Organizations in Action* (New York: McGraw-Hill, 1967).

[7]Zohar Laslo and Albert I. Goldberg, "Resource Allocation under Uncertainty in a Multi-Project Matrix Environment: Is Organizational Conflict Inevitable?" *International Journal of Project Management* 26, no. 8 (2008), pp. 773–90; Donald E. Conlon, Christopher O.L.H. Porter, and Judi McLean Parks, "The Fairness of Decision Rules," *Journal of Management* 30, no. 3 (2004), pp. 329–49; and B. Kabanoff, "Equity, Equality, Power, and Conflict," *Academy of Management Review,* April 1991, pp. 416–41.

[8]M.J. Gelfand and S. Christakopoulon, "Culture and Negotiator Cognition: Judgment Accuracy and Negotiation Processes in Individualistic and Collectivistic Cultures," *Organizational Behavior and Human Decision Processes,* April 1999, pp. 248–69.

[9]The classic work is M. Sherif and C. Sherif, *Groups in Harmony and Tension* (New York: Harper & Row, 1953). Their study was conducted among groups in a boys' camp. They stimulated conflict between the groups and observed the changes that occurred in group behavior. Also see their "Experiments in Group Conflict," *Scientific American,* March 1956, pp. 54–58.

[10]Allen Barra, "For A-Rod, Placebos Might've Worked Better," *The Wall Street Journal,* February 12, 2009, p. D7.

[11]Suzy Wetlaufer, "Common Sense and Conflict," *Harvard Business Review,* January–February 2000, pp. 114–24.

[12]Christopher Parkes, "Eisner to Sever All Ties with Walt Disney," *Financial Times,* September 21, 2004, p. 33.

[13]Mary Ann Von Glinow, Debra L. Shapiro, and Jeanne M. Brett, "Can We Talk, and Should We? Managing Emotional Conflict in Multicultural Teams," *Academy of Management Review* 29, no. 4 (October 2004), pp. 578–92. For an examination of specific devices for assessing how managers manage conflict, see John R. Darling and W. Earl Walker, "Effective Conflict Management: Use of the Behavioral Style Model," *Leadership and Organization Development Journal* 22, no. 5/6 (2001), pp. 230–43; and E. van de Vlert and B. Kabanoff, "Toward Theory-Based Measures of Conflict Management," *Academy of Management Journal,* March 1990, pp. 199–209.

[14]The conflict-resolution grid represents a melding of conflict-management concepts found in R.R. Blake and J.S. Mouton, *The Managerial Grid* (Houston, TX: Gulf Publishing, 1964); K.W. Thomas, "Conflict and Conflict Management," in *Handbook of Industrial and Organizational Psychology,* ed. M.D. Dunnette (Chicago: Rand McNally, 1976), pp. 889–935; and M.A. Rahim, *Managing Conflict in Organizations* (New York: Praeger, 1986).

[15]Matthew Dolan, "Corporate News: UAW Says Ford Workers Ratified Concessions," *The Wall Street Journal* (Eastern Edition), March 10, 2009, p. B3.

[16]Corinne Bendersky, "Organizational Dispute Resolution Systems: A Complementarities Model," *Academy of Management Review* 28, no. 4 (October 2003), pp. 643–56; and Rupert Brown and Samuel L. Gaertner, eds., *Blackwell Handbook of Social Psychology Intergroup Processes* (New York: Blackwell, 2001).

[17]M.A. Neale and M.H. Bazerman, "The Effects of Framing and Negotiator Overconfidence on Bargaining Behavior and Outcomes," *Academy of Management Journal,* March 1985, pp. 34–49.

[18]R.M. Marsh, "The Difference between Participation and Power in Japanese Factories," *Industrial and Labor Relations Review,* January 1992, pp. 250–57.

[19]Joel Lefowitz, "Sex-Related Differences in Job Attitudes and Dispositional Variables: Now You See Them, . . . ," *Academy of Management Journal,* April 1994, pp. 323–49.

[20]Roy J. Lewicki, David M. Saunders, John W. Minton, and Bruce Barry, *Negotiations* (New York: McGraw-Hill, 2003).

[21]Roy J. Lewicki, Bruce Barry, and David M. Saunders, *Essentials of Negotiation,* 4th ed. (New York: McGraw-Hill/Irwin, 2003); and M. Zetlin, "The Art of Negotiating," *Success!* June 1986, pp. 34–39.

[22]G.T. Savage, J.D. Blair, and R.L. Sorenson, "Consider Both Relationships and Substance When Negotiating Strategically," *Academy of Management Executive,* February 1989, pp. 37–48.

[23]W. Mastenbroek, *Negotiate* (Oxford, United Kingdom: Basil Blackwell, 1989).

[24]R.J. Fisher, *The Social Psychology of Intergroup and International Conflict Resolution* (New York: Springer-Verlag, 1990).

[25]M.H. Bazerman and M.A. Neale, *Negotiating Rationally* (New York: The Free Press, 1992).

[26]Steve Adams, "The Four Stages of Effective Team-Building," *Training & Management Development Methods* 23, no. 1 (2009), pp. 317–21.

[27]Gayle Lantz, "Team Building Blocks and Break-throughs," *Human Resource Planning* 30, no. 2 (2007), pp. 12–14.

[28]Ian MacDuff, "Your Pace or Mine? Culture, Time and Negotiation," *Negotiation Journal* 22, no. 1 (January 2006), pp. 31–46; Aahad M. Osman-Gani and Joo-Seng Tan, "Influence of Culture on Negotiation Styles of Asian Managers: An Empirical Study of Major Cultural/Ethnic Groups in Singapore," *Thunderbird International Business Review* 44, no. 6 (November–December 2002), pp. 819–39.

[29]T.T.B. Koh, "American Strengths and Weaknesses," *Negotiation Journal,* August 1996, pp. 313–17.

[30]J.W. Salacuse, "Ten Ways That Culture Affects Negotiating Style: Some Survey Results," *Negotiation Journal,* July 1998, pp. 221–40.

[31]Lynn E. Metcalf, Allan Bird, Mark F. Peterson, Mahesh Shankarmahesh, and Terri R. Lituchy, "Cultural Influences in Negotiations: A Four Country Comparative Analysis," *International Journal of Cross Cultural Management* 7, no. 2 (2007), pp. 147–68.

[32]M.J. Gelfand and A. Realo, "Individualism–Collectivism and Accountability in Intergroup Negotiations," *Journal of Applied Psychology,* October 1999, pp. 721–36.

[33]J.A. Wall and M.W. Blum, "Negotiations," *Journal of Management,* June 1991, p. 296.

Chapter 12

[1]Darrell Rigby and Barbara Bilodeau, "Selecting Management Tools Wisely," *Harvard Business Review* 85, no. 12 (December 2007), pp. 20–22; Peter H. Kim, Robin L. Pinkley, and Alison R. Fragale, "Power Dynamics in Negotiation," *Academy of Management Review* 30, no. 4

(October 2005), pp. 799–822; M. Kramer Roderick and Margaret A. Neale, eds., *Power and Influence in Organizations* (Thousand Oaks, CA: Sage Publications, 1998); and Jeffrey Pfeffer, *Managing with Power: Politics and Influence in Organizations* (Boston: Harvard Business School Press, 1992).

[2]Rosabeth Moss Kanter, "A Culture of Innovation," *Executive Excellence,* August 2000, pp. 10–11.

[3]Janet O. Hagberg, *Real Power: Stages of Personal Power in Organizations,* 3rd ed. (Salem, WI: Sheffield, 2002); and Tom Duffy, "Power Up!" *Network World,* January 3, 2000, pp. 97–98.

[4]Robert Dahl, "The Concept of Power," *Behavioral Science,* July 1957, pp. 202–3.

[5]Theresa M. Welborne and Charlie O. Trevor, "The Roles of Departmental and Position Power in Job Evaluation," *Academy of Management Journal* 43, no. 4 (August 2000), pp. 761–72; and Belle Rose Ragins, "Diversified Mentoring Relationships in Organizations: A Power Perspective," *Academy of Management Review,* April 1997, pp. 482–521.

[6]John R.P. French and Bertram Raven, "The Basis of Social Power," in *Studies in Social Power,* ed. D. Cartwright (Ann Arbor: Institute for Social Research, University of Michigan, 1959), pp. 150–67.

[7]Allan R. Cohen and David L. Bradford, "Exercising Power," *Executive Excellence* 19, no. 12 (December 2002), pp. 14–16; C. Marlene Fiol, "All for One and One for All? The Development and Transfer of Power across Organization Levels," *Academy of Management Review* 26, no. 2 (April 2001), pp. 224–43; and Daniel J. Brass and Marlene E. Burkhardt, "Potential Power and Power Use: An Investigation of Structure and Behavior," *Academy of Management Journal,* June 1993, pp. 441–70.

[8]Jeffrey Pfeffer, "Understanding Power in Organizations," *California Management Review,* Winter 1992, pp. 29–50.

[9]Kanter, "A Culture of Innovation."

[10]For an excellent discussion of structural and situationally oriented sources of power, see Don Hellriegel, John W. Slocum, Jr., and Richard W. Woodman, *Organizational Behavior,* 9th ed. (Cincinnati, OH: South-Western, 2001), pp. 465–68.

[11]Doris Kearns Goodwin, *No Ordinary Time: Franklin and Eleanor Roosevelt: The Home Front in World War II* (New York: Simon & Schuster, 1995); and Thomas A. Stewart, *Intellectual Capital* (New York: Doubleday, 1997).

[12]John Van Beveren, "A Model of Knowledge Acquisition That Refocuses Knowledge Management," *Journal of Knowledge Management* 6, no. 1 (2002), pp. 18–23.

[13]Stewart, *Intellectual Capital.*

[14]Anthony T. Cobb, "An Episodic Model of Power: Toward an Integration of Theory and Research," *Academy of Management Review,* July 1984, pp. 482–93.

[15]See www.lapdonline.org/lapd_command_staff/comm_bio_view/7574 (accessed June 15, 2009).

[16]Heather MacDonald, "How to Fight and Win," *The Wall Street Journal,* July 20, 1999, p. A20.

[17]Thomas A. Stewart, "Get with the New Power Game," *Fortune,* January 13, 1997, pp. 58–62.

[18]J.A. Conger and R.N. Kanungo, "The Empowerment Process: Integrating Theory and Practice," *Academy of Management Review,* July 1988, p. 474.

[19]Eileen Brownell, "Empowerment, the Key to Exceptional Service," *American Salesman,* August 2000, pp. 20–24.

[20]Kenneth J. Harris, Anthony R. Wheeler, K. Michele Kacmar, "Leader-Member Exchange and Empowerment: Direct and Interactive Effects on Job Satisfaction, Turnover Intentions, and Performance," *Leadership Quarterly* 20, no. 3 (2009), pp. 371–82; Peter K. Mills and Gerardo R. Ungson, "Reassessing the Limits of Structural Empowerment: Organizational Constitution and Trust as Controls," *Academy of Management Review* 28, no. 1 (January 2003), pp. 143–53; Brook Manville and Josiah Ober, "Beyond Empowerment: Building a Company of Citizens," *Harvard Business Review* 81, no. 1 (January 2003), p. 48; and Russ Forrester, "Empowerment: Rejuvenating a Potent Idea," *Academy of Management Executive* 14, no. 3 (August 2000), pp. 67–81.

[21]James R. Fisher, Jr., "A Culture of Contribution," *Executive Excellence,* January 1997, p. 16.

[22]See www.newfld.com/performance.aspx (accessed June 18, 2009).

[23]Gilad Chen, Bradley L. Kirkman, Ruth Kanfer, Don Allen, and Benson Rosen, "A Multilevel Study of Leadership, Empowerment, and Performance in Teams," *Journal of Applied Psychology* 92, no. 2 (2007), pp. 331–46; Scott E. Seibert, Seth R. Silver, and W. Alan Randolph, "Taking Empowerment to the Next Level: A Multiple-Level Model of Empowerment, Performance, and Satisfaction," *Academy of Management Journal* 47, no. 3 (June 2004), pp. 332–49; and W. Alan Randolph and Marshall Sashkin, "Can Organizational Empowerment Work in Multinational Settings?" *Academy of Management Executive* 16, no. 1 (February 2002), pp. 102–15.

[24]Thomas W. Malone, "Is 'Empowerment' Just a Fad? Control, Decision Making, and IT," *Sloan Management Review,* Winter 1997, pp. 23–35.

[25]Michael Crozier, *The Bureaucratic Phenomenon* (Chicago: University of Chicago Press, 1964).

[26]The strategic contingency theory was developed by D.J. Hickson and his colleagues. Other theorists and researchers have modified and discussed this approach. However, the reader is urged to use the original sources for a discussion of the complete and unmodified theory. See D.J. Hickson, C.R. Hinnings, C.A. Lee, R.E. Schneck, and J.M. Pennings, "A Strategic Contingency Theory of Intraorganizational Power," *Administrative Science Quarterly,* June 1971, pp. 216–29; and C.R. Hinnings, D.J. Hickson, J.M. Pennings, and R.E. Schneck, "Structural Conditions of Intraorganizational Power," *Administrative Science Quarterly,* March 1974, pp. 22–44.

[27]Hickson et al., "Strategic Contingency Theory."

[28]Herminia Ibarra, "Network Centrality, Power, and Innovation Involvement: Determinants of Technical and Administrative Roles," *Academy of Management Journal,* June 1993, pp. 471–501.

[29]Hickson et al., "Strategic Contingency Theory."

[30]S. Milgram, "Behavioral Study of Obedience," *Journal of Abnormal and Social Psychology*, October 1963, pp. 371–78; and S. Milgram, *Obedience to Authority* (New York: Harper & Row, 1974).

[31]Milgram, "Behavioral Study of Obedience," p. 377.

[32]Herb Greenberg, "Shutterfly's Shipping Revenue May Airbrush Profit Picture," *The Wall Street Journal* (Eastern Edition), September 29, 2007, p. B3; Steve Hamm and Ira Sager, "From Netscape to Seascape," *BusinessWeek,* September 8, 2003, p. 10; and Ralph King, "Do You Believe in Jim Clark?" www.ecompany.com, December 2000, pp. 123–30.

[33]Hamm and Sager, "From Netscape to Seascape," p. 10; Paul Saffo, "Failure Is the Best Medicine," *Newsweek,* March 25, 2002, p. 53; and Lisa Bransten, "E-Business: Starting Gate," *The Wall Street Journal,* November 5, 2001, p. B6.

[34]L.A. Witt, K. Michelle Kacmar, Dawn S. Carlson, and Suzanne Zivnuska, "Interactive Effects of Personality and Organizational Politics on Contextual Performance," *Journal of Organizational Behavior* 23, no. 8 (December 2002), pp. 911–26; and Russell Cropanzano, John Hughes, Alicia Grandey, and Paul Toth, "The Relationship of Organizational Politics and Support to Work Behaviors, Attitudes, and Stress," *Journal of Organizational Behavior,* March 1997, pp. 159–80.

[35]Gerald R. Ferris, Gerhard Blickle, Paula B. Schneider, Jochen Kramer, Ingo Zettler, Jutta Solga, Daniela Noethen, and James A. Meurs, "Political Skill Construct and Criterion-Related Validation: A Two-Study Investigation," *Journal of Managerial Psychology* 23, no. 7 (2008), pp. 744–71.

[36]G.R. Ferris, S. Davidson, and P. Perrewé, "Developing Political Skill at Work," *Training* 42 (2005), pp. 40–45; G.R. Ferris, D.C. Treadway, R.W. Kolodinsky, W.A. Hochwarter, C.J. Kacmar, C. Douglas, and D.D. Frink, "Development and Validation of the Political Skill Inventory," *Journal of Management* 31, no. 1 (2005), pp. 126–52.

[37]George Strauss, "Tactics of the Lateral Relationship: The Purchasing Agent," *Administrative Science Quarterly,* 1962, pp. 161–86.

[38]Robert W. Allen, Dan L. Madison, Lyman W. Porter, Patricia A. Renwick, and Bronston T. Mayes, "Organizational Politics: Tactics and Characteristics of Its Actors," *California Management Review* 22 (December 1979), pp. 77–83.

[39]This discussion of games relies on the presentation in Henry Mintzberg, *Power In and Around Organizations* (Englewood Cliffs, NJ: Prentice Hall, 1983), chap. 13, pp. 171–271. Please refer to this source for a complete and interesting discussion of political games.

[40]See, for example, Stacie A. Furst and Daniel M. Cable, "Employee Resistance to Organizational Change: Managerial Influence Tactics and Leader-Member Exchange," *Journal of Applied Psychology* 93, no. 2 (2008), pp. 453–62; Chad Higgins, Timothy A. Judge, and Gerald Ferris, "Influence Tactics and Work Outcomes: A Meta-Analysis," *Journal of Organizational Behavior* 24, no. 1 (February 2003), pp. 89–106; David Kipnis, Stuart Schmidt, and Ian Wilkinson, "Interorganizational Influence Tactics: Explorations in Getting One's Way," *Journal of Applied Psychology,* August 1980, pp. 440–52; Gary Yukl and Cecilia Falbe, "Influence Tactics and Objectives in Upward, Downward, and Lateral Influence Attempts," *Journal of Applied Psychology,* April 1990, pp. 132–40; Cecilia Falbe and Gary Yukl, "Consequences for Managers of Using Single Influence Tactics and Combinations of Tactics," *Academy of Management Journal,* August 1992, pp. 638–52; and Gary Yukl, Patricia Guinan, and Debra Sottolano, "Influence Tactics Used for Different Objectives with Subordinates, Peers, and Superiors," *Group and Organizational Management,* September 1995, pp. 272–96.

[41]Falbe and Yukl, "Consequences for Managers," pp. 645–46.

[42]For additional discussion of the effectiveness of various tactics, see Steven M. Farmer, John M. Maslyn, Donald

B. Dedor, and Jodi S. Goodman, "Putting Upward Influence Strategies in Context," *Journal of Organizational Behavior,* January 1997, pp. 17–42.

[43]Higgins, Judge, and Ferris, "Influence Tactics and Work Outcomes."

[44]Laura Morgan Roberts, "Changing Faces: Professional Image Construction in Diverse Organizational Settings," *Academy of Management Review* 30, no. 4 (October 2005), pp. 685–711; M.R. Leary and R.M. Kowalski, "Impression Management: A Literature Review and Two-Component Model," *Psychological Bulletin,* January 1990, pp. 34–47.

[45]Laura Morgan Roberts, Jane E. Dutton, Gretchen M. Spreitzer, Emily D. Heaphy, and Robert E. Quinn, "Composing the Reflected Best-Self Portrait: Building Pathways for Becoming Extraordinary in Work Organizations," *Academy of Management Review* 30, no. 4 (October 2005), pp. 712–36; Dennis P. Bozeman and K. Michele Kacmar, "A Cybernetic Model of Impression Management Processes in Organizations," *Organizational Behavior & Human Decision Processes,* January 1997, pp. 9–30.

[46]Wei-Chi Tsai, Chien-Cheng Chen, and Su-Fen Chiu, "Exploring Boundaries of the Effects of Applicant Impression Management Tactics in Job Interviews," *Journal of Management* 31, no. 1 (2004), pp. 108–25. For additional information on the use of impression management tactics within the interview context, see Lynn A. McFarland, Ann Marie Ryan, and S. David Kriska, "Impression Management Use and Effectiveness across Assessment Methods," *Journal of Management* 29, no. 5 (2003), pp. 641–61; Aleksander P.J. Ellis, Bradley J. West, Ann Marie Ryan, and Richard P. DeShon, "The Use of Impression Management Tactics in Structured Interviews: A Function of Question Type?" *Journal of Applied Psychology* 87, no. 6 (December 2002), pp. 1200–8.

[47]For a review of impression motives and behaviors, see: Mark C. Bolino, K. Michele Kacmar, William H. Turnley, and J. Bruce Gilstrap, "A Multi-Level Review of Impression Management Motives and Behaviors," *Journal of Management* 34, no. 6 (2008), pp. 1080–1109.

[48]Ibid.

[49]J. Michael Crant and Thomas S. Bateman, "Assignment of Credit and Blame for Performance Outcomes," *Academy of Management Journal,* February 1993, pp. 7–27.

[50]G.E. Cavanagh, D.J. Moberg, and M. Velasquez, "The Ethics of Organizational Politics," *Academy of Management Review,* July 1981, pp. 363–74; and M. Velasquez, D.J. Moberg, and G.F. Cavanagh, "Organizational Statesmanship and Dirty Politics: Ethical Guidelines for the Organizational Politician," *Organizational Dynamics,* Autumn 1983, pp. 65–79.

[51]Alan Stainer and Lorice Stainer, "Empowerment and Strategic Change—An Ethical Perspective," *Strategic Change* 9, no. 5 (August 2000), pp. 287–96; and Suzy Wetlaufer, "Organizing for Empowerment: An Interview with AES's Roger Sant and Dennis Bakke," *Harvard Business Review,* January–February 1999, pp. 110–23.

[52]Jean Thilmany, "Supporting Ethical Employees," *HR Magazine* 52, no. 9 (September 2007), pp. 105–6.

[53]Christopher L. Tyner, "Technitrol's James Papada," *Investor's Business Daily,* September 7, 2000, p. A4.

[54]Pfeffer, *Managing with Power.* This section is based primarily on pp. 337–45.

[55]John C. Bogle, "A Crisis of Ethic Proportions," *The Wall Street Journal* (Eastern Edition), April 21, 2009, p. A19.

[56]Michael Jacobs, "It's about Getting a Better Job: Students Say Their Motivation for Taking an MBA Has Stayed Consistent for the Best Part of a Decade," *Financial Times,* June 8, 2009, p. 13.

[57]Pfeffer, Managing with Power.

Chapter 13

[1]Bill Roberts, "Stay Ahead of the Technology Use Curve," *HR Magazine* 53, no. 10 (October 2008), pp. 57–58; Jonathan A. Segal, "Resolve or Report?" *HR Magazine,* October 2005, pp. 125–30; Lorrie Faith Cranor and Shane Greenstein, eds., *Communications Policy and Information Technology: Promises, Problems, and Prospects* (Cambridge, MA: MIT Press, 2002); and James M. Kouzes, "Link Me to Your Leader," *Business 2.0,* October 10, 2000, pp. 292–95.

[2]These five questions were first suggested in H.D. Lasswell, *Power and Personality* (New York: W. W. Norton, 1948), pp. 37–51.

[3]Claude Shannon and Warren Weaver, *The Mathematical Theory of Communication* (Urbana: University of Illinois Press, 1948); and Wilbur Schramm; "How Communication Works," in *The Process and Effects of Mass Communication,* ed. Wilbur Schramm, (Urbana: University of Illinois Press, 1953), pp. 3–26.

[4]www.nestle.com/AllAbout/AtGlance/MainBrands/MainBrands.htm (accessed June 25, 2009).

[5]William Echikson, "Nestlé: An Elephant Dances," *BusinessWeek,* December 11, 2000, pp. EB44–48.

[6]Patricia Wallace, *The Internet in the Workplace: How New Technology Is Transforming Work* (Cambridge, UK: Cambridge University Press, 2004); Bruce Barry and Ingrid Smithey Fulmer, "The Medium and the Message: The Adaptive Use of Communication Media in Dyadic Influence," *Academy of Management Review* 29, no. 2, pp. 272–92; and Boris B. Baltes, Marcus W. Dickson, Michael P. Sherman, Cara C. Bauer, and Jacqueline S. LaGanke, "Computer-Mediated Communication and Group Decision Making: A Meta-Analysis," *Organizational Behavior and Human Decision Processes* 87, no. 1 (2002), pp. 156–79.

[7]Mark D. Cannon and Robert Witherspoon, "Actionable Feedback: Unlocking the Power of Learning and Performance Improvement," *Academy of Management Executive* 19, no. 2 (May 2005), pp. 120–34; and Thad B. Green and Jay T. Knippen, *Breaking the Barrier to Upward Communication* (Westport, CT: Quorim, 1999).

[8]Carolyn Hirschman, "Giving Voice to Employee Concerns," *HR Magazine* 53, no. 8 (August 2008), pp. 51–54.

[9]Ibid.

[10]Greg L. Stewart, Susan L. Dustin, Murray R. Barrick, and Todd C. Darnold, "Exploring the Handshake in Employment Interviews," *Journal of Applied Psychology* 93, no. 5 (2008), pp. 1139–46; Judith A. Hall, Erik J. Coats, and Lavonia Smith LeBeau, "Nonverbal Behavior and the Vertical Dimension of Social Relations," *Psychological Bulletin* 131, no. 6 (November 2005), pp. 898–924; and Stanley E. Jones and Curtis D. LeBaron, "Research on the Relationship between Verbal and Nonverbal Communication: Emerging Integrations," *Journal of Communication* 52, no. 3 (September 1, 2002), pp. 499–521.

[11]Felecia F. Jordan-Jackson and Kimberly A. Davis, "Men Talk: An Exploratory Study of Communication Patterns and Communication Apprehension of Black and White Males," *Journal of Men's Studies* 13, no. 3 (Spring 2005), pp. 347–68; and Dorothy Leeds, "Body Language: Actions Speak Louder than Words," *National Underwriter,* May 1995, pp. 18–19.

[12]G. Hofstede, "The Universal and the Specific in 21st Century Management," *Organizational Dynamics,* Summer 1999, pp. 34–44.

[13]Leeds, "Body Language."

[14]J.R. Carlson and R.W. Zmud, "Channel Expansion Theory and the Experimental Nature of Media Richness Perceptions," *Academy of Management Journal,* 1999, pp. 153–70.

[15]Phillip G. Clampitt and M. Lee Williams, "Decision Downloading," *MIT Sloan Management Review* 48, no. 2 (2007), pp. 77–82.

[16]Gary L. Kreps, *Organizational Communication* (New York: Longman, 1990), p. 203.

[17]Richard Ettenson, Jonathan Knowles, "Don't Confuse Reputation with Brand," *MIT Sloan Management Review* 49, no. 2 (2008), pp. 19–21; Frank Korver and Betteke van Ruler, "The Relationship between Corporate Identity Structures and Communication Structures," *Journal of Communication Management* 7, no. 3 (2003), pp. 197–209; and Ale Smidts, Ad Th.H. Pruyn, and Cees B.M. van Riel, "The Impact of Employee Communication and Perceived External Prestige on Organizational Identification," *Academy of Management Journal* 44, no. 5 (October 2001), pp. 1051–62.

[18]Robert F. Otondo, James R. Van Scotter, David G. Allen, and Prashant Palvia, "The Complexity of Richness: Media, Message, and Communication Outcomes," *Information & Management* 45, no. 1 (2008), pp. 21–30; Vivian C. Sheer and Ling Chen, "Improving Media Richness Theory: A Study of Interaction Goals, Message Valence, and Task Complexity in Manager-Subordinate Communication," *Management Communication Quarterly* 18, no. 1 (August 2004), pp. 76–93; and G.S. Russ, R.L. Deft, and R.H. Lengel, "Media Selection and Managerial Characteristics in Organizational Communications," *Management Communication Quarterly,* 1990, pp. 151–75.

[19]Preston Gralla, *How the Internet Works,* 6th ed. (Indianapolis, IN: Que—A Division of Macmillan Computer Publishing, 2001).

[20]"AOL, Startups Vie for MySpace Magic," www.cnn.com (accessed May 22, 2006); and CIA World Factbook, www.cia.gov/cia/publications/factbook/rankorder/2153.htm (accessed May 15, 2006).

[21]www.internetworldstats.com/stats.htm (accessed June 27, 2009).

[22]Bill Roberts, "Portal Takes Off," *HR Magazine* 48, no. 2 (February 2003), pp. 95–99.

[23]Mary Hayes, "Hungry for Bottom-Line Results," *InformationWeek,* September 22, 2003, pp. 107–8.

[24]"Gambits & Gadgets in the World of Technology," *The Wall Street Journal,* June 5, 2003, p. B4.

[25]"Number of E-Mail Users Worldwide to Reach 1.6 Billion in 2011," *The Radicati Group Report,* http://software.tekrati.com/research/9512/ (accessed June 28, 2009).

[26]Tim Paradis, "Message to Wall Street: Save E-Mail," *The Wall Street Journal,* December 4, 2002, p. C5.

[27]Michelle Conlin, "Workers, Surf at Your Own Risk," *BusinessWeek,* June 12, 2000, pp. 105–6.

[28]Roger Cheng, "Corporate News: Yahoo-Google Messaging May Drive Growth," *The Wall Street Journal,* June 17, 2008, p. B4; D. Greenfield, "Permission to Speak Freely," *Information Week,* March 2008, pp. 56–60; and William M. Bulkeley, "Instant Message Goes Corporate; 'You Can't Hide,'" *The Wall Street Journal,* September 4, 2002, p. B1.

[29]David Strom, "Managing Your Instant Messaging Frontier," *Business Communications Review* 36, no. 4 (April 2006), pp. 62–65; and Michael D. Osterman, "Instant Messaging in the Enterprise," *Business Communications Review* 33, no. 1 (January 2003), pp. 59–63.

[30]Mary Hayes Weier, "Business Gone Mobile," *InformationWeek,* March 30, 2009, pp. 23–27.

[31]Bart Perkins, "Texting Rules!" *Computerworld* 43, no. 18 (May 11, 2009), p. 26.

[32]Ibid.

[33]Daniel Dombey and Chris Nattall, "Twitter Delays Service Break after State Department Talks," *Financial Times,* June 17, 2009, p. 2.

[34]Jack and Suzy Welch, "Why We Tweet," *BusinessWeek,* June 15, 2009, p. 76.

[35]Jena McGregor, "Job Review in 140 Keystrokes," *BusinessWeek,* March 23, 2009, p. 58.

[36]Michelle Conlin and Douglas MacMillan, "Managing the Tweets," *BusinessWeek,* June 1, 2009, p. 20.

[37]Bill Roberts, "Stay Ahead of the Technology Use Curve," *HR Magazine* 53, no. 10 (October 2008), pp. 57–61.

[38]Conlin and MacMillan, "Managing the Tweets."

[39]Maggie Jackson, "May We Have Your Attention, Please? With the Workplace Ever More Full of Distractions, Reseachers Are Developing Tools to Keep Us on Task," *BusinessWeek,* June 12, 2008, p. 55.

[40]Perkins, "Texting Rules!"

[41]Stephen Manes, "The Sound of One Hand E-Mailing," *Forbes* 172, no. 9 (October 27, 2003), p. 216; and "Business: PDA, RIP; Handheld Computers," *The Economist* 369, no. 8346 (October 18, 2003), p. 87.

[42]Reena Jana and Peter Burrows, "An All-Out Online Assault on the iPhone," *BusinessWeek,* April 6, 2009, p. 74.

[43]Adapted from Elizabeth Guilday, "Voicemail Like a Pro," *Training & Development,* October 2000, pp. 68–69.

[44]Tony Kontzer, "Victory for Videoconferencing," *InformationWeek,* December 15, 2003, p. 58.

[45]Paul Taylor, "Seats at the Virtual Table; Personal Technology," *Financial Times,* April 24, 2009, p. 16.

[46]Ibid.

[47]See www.hp.com and Hewlett-Packard, Annual Report 2002.

[48]J.M. Putti, S. Aryee, and J. Phua, "Communication Relationship Satisfaction and Organizational Commitment," *Group and Organizational Studies,* March 1990, pp. 44–52.

[49]Mary Ellen Guffey, *Business Communication* (Cincinnati, OH: South-Western, 2000), p. 50.

[50]Edward T. Hall and Mildred R. Hall, *Understanding Cultural Differences: Germans, French, and Americans* (Yarmouth, ME: Intercultural Press, 1989).

[51]Philip Harris and Robert Moran, *Managing Cultural Differences,* 4th ed. (Newton, MA: Butterworth-Heinemann Publishing, 2000).

[52]Hall and Hall, *Understanding Cultural Differences.*

[53]Ibid.

[54]See www.fourseasons.com.

[55]M.P. Nichols, *The Lost Art of Listening* (New York: Guilford, 1995).

[56]John Macaskill, "Dismissal of Worst Performers Should Be Part of Sound Management Policy," *Financial Times,* January 17, 2007, p. 14; and Amy Barrett, "Jack's Risky Last Act," *BusinessWeek,* November 6, 2000, pp. 40–45.

[57]Kim S. Nash, "Tech Jargon to Heavily Affect Microsoft Fate," *Computerworld,* November 30, 1998, pp. 1–2.

[58]Taylor Clark, "Starb*#!ked," *Psychology Today* 40, no. 5 (September 2007), pp. 99–108.

[59]For a complete ordering guide, see www.wikihow.com/Order-at-Starbucks.

[60]Clark, "Starb*#!ked."

[61]For a review of developments in decision making and communication, see Janet Fulk and Brian Boyd, "Emerging Theories of Communication in Organizations," *Journal of Management,* June 1991, pp. 407–46.

[62]Calvin Sun, "Spam Filters: Making Them Work," *Computerworld,* September 22, 2008, pp. 36–37.

[63]William Powell, "The Web," *Training and Development* 57, no. 4 (April 2003), pp. 22–25.

[64]G. Pike, "Anti-Spam Legislation Setbacks," *Information Today* 25, no. 11 (December 2008), pp. 17–20; and Yochi J. Dreazen, "Why Some Big Spammers Are Backing Spam-Control Laws," *The Wall Street Journal,* July 18, 2003, p. B1.

[65]Avi Baumstein, "New Tools Close Holes in Can-Spam," *InformationWeek,* February 23, 2009, pp. 42–44.

[66]Alison Overholt, "If You Have Received This by Mistake," *Fast Company* 66 (January 2003), p. 52.

[67]Eric Chabrow, "In the Fight against Spam, a Few Knockouts," *InformationWeek,* August 15, 2005, p. 34.

[68]C.D. Mortenson, *Miscommunication* (Thousand Oaks, CA: Sage Publications, 1997).

[69]Jean-Francois Manzoni, "A Better Way to Deliver Bad News," *Harvard Business Review* 80, no. 9 (September 2002), pp. 114–22.

[70]D.T. Hall, K.L. Otazo, and G.P. Hollenbeck, "Behind Closed Doors: What Really Happens in Executive Coaching," *Organizational Dynamics,* Winter 1999, pp. 39–53.

[71]Kreps, *Organizational Communication,* pp. 250–51.

[72]Mary Brandel, "How to Spot a Spy," *Computerworld,* April 14, 2008, pp. 36–38.

[73]A. Stanley and C. Crabb, "Corporate Espionage: No Longer a Hidden Threat," *Chemical Engineering* 105, no. 13 (1998), p. 82.

[74]ASIS/PricewaterhouseCoopers, *Trends in Proprietary Information Loss* (Alexandria, VA: American Society of Industrial Security, 1999).

[75]Carole Ashkinaze, "Spies Like Us," *BusinessWeek,* June 12, 2000, pp. F24–F32.

[76]Ibid.

[77]Eric R. Chabrow, "A Corporate Spy Story," *CIO Insight,* June 2008, pp. 13–14.

Chapter 14

[1]J. Keith Murnighan and John C. Mowen, *The Art of High-Stakes Decision-Making: Tough Calls in a Speed-Driven World* (New York: John Wiley & Sons, 2002); and Ralph Sanders, *The Executive Decisionmaking Process: Identifying Problems and Assessing Outcomes* (Westport, CT: Quorum, 1999).

[2]John R. Danley, "Polishing Up the Pinto: Legal Liability, Moral Blame, and Risk," *Business Ethics Quarterly* 15, no. 2 (April 2005), pp. 205–36; Mark Dowie, "Pinto Madness," *Mother Jones,* October 1977, http://www.motherjones.com/politics/1977/09/pinto-madness; Jerry Useem, "20 That Made History—June 27, 2005," *CNN Money.com,* http://money.cnn.com/magazines/fortune/fortune_archive/2005/06/27/8263412/index.htm.

[3]Herbert A. Simon, *The New Science of Management Decision* (New York: Harper & Row, 1960), pp. 5–6.

[4]"Amazon.com: Help Returns," www.amazon.com/gp/help/customer/display.html/180-3194073-5687307?ie=UTF8&nodeId=901888 (accessed April 30, 2009).

[5]Lane Harvey Brown, "Storming Back: Disaster Plan Helps I.H. Caffey Rebound," *The Business Journal,* May 16, 2008, www.bizjournals.com/triad/stories/2008/05/19/story2.html (accessed April 30, 2009).

[6]Sanders, *The Executive Decisionmaking Process.*

[7]John P. Kotter, *What Leaders Really Do* (Boston: Oxford University Press, 1999).

[8]Sanders, *The Executive Decisionmaking Process.*

[9]Zaneta Loh, "University of Houston: The Doughnut King of Texas—Danny Klam—Simply Splendid Doughnuts," *Inc.,* March 2009, www.inc.com/magazine/20090301/university-of-houston-the-doughnut-king-of-texas.html (accessed April 30, 2009); Casey Wooten, "Going with the Dough: Simply Splendid Donuts and Ice Cream," *Houston Business Journal,* March 30, 2009, http://houston.bizjournals.com/houston/stories/2009/03/30/smallb1.html (accessed May 1, 2009).

[10]David A. Cowan, "Developing a Classification Structure of Organizational Problems: An Empirical Investigation," *Academy of Management Journal,* June 1990, pp. 366–90.

[11]See G.P. Huber, *Managerial Decision Making* (Glenview, IL: Scott, Foresman, 1980).

[12]Ian Palmer and Cynthia Hardy, *Thinking about Management* (Thousand Oaks, CA: Sage Publications, 2000).

[13]"Facebook Gets Down to Business," *BusinessWeek,* April 20, 2009, pp. 30–33; and Jessica E. Vascellaro and Emily Steel, "Facebook Performs About-Face on Data," *The Wall Street Journal,* February 19, 2009, p. B8.

[14]J.M. Dukerich and M.L. Nichols, "Causal Information Search in Managerial Decision Making," *Organizational Behavior and Human Decision Processes,* October 1991, pp. 106–22.

[15]Joan Adams, "The Five Whys," *Supply House Times* 51, no. 10 (December 2008), pp. 16–18; and Joel Sutherland and Bob Bennett, "The Seven Deadly Supply Chain Wastes," *Supply Chain Management Review* 12, no. 5 (August 2008), pp. 38–44.

[16]Paul C. Nutt, "Expanding the Search for Alternatives during Strategic Decision-Making," *Academy of Management Executive* 18, no. 4 (November 2004), pp. 13–28; and David B. Jemison, "The Importance of Boundary Spanning Roles in Strategic Decision Making," *Journal of Management Studies,* April 1984, pp. 131–52.

[17]Michael Sivy, "Spending Spree," *Money* 31, no. 3 (March 2002), pp. 45–47.

[18]"Amazon.com Announces Fourth Quarter Sales Up 18% to $6.70 Billion," http://media.corporate-ir.net/media_files/irol/97/97664/consolidated_pressrelease_Q408.pdf (accessed May 2, 2009); Mylene Mangalindan, "Amazon Net Falls: Revenue Rises 20%," *The Wall Street Journal,* April 26, 2006, p. B3; Nick Wingfield, "Amazon Lures Stars—Gratis—to Promote Holiday Gifts," *The Wall Street Journal,* November 11, 2003, p. B1; and Fred Vogelstein, "Mighty Amazon," *Fortune* 147, no. 10 (May 26, 2003), p. 6.

[19]Katsuhiko Shimizu and Michael A. Hitt, "Strategic Flexibility: Organizational Preparedness to Reverse Ineffective Strategic Decisions," *Academy of Management Executive* 18, no. 4 (November 2004), pp. 44–59; Joseph S. Valacich and Charles Schwenk, "Devil's Advocacy and Dialectical Inquiry Effects on Face-to-Face and Computer-Mediated Group Decision Making," *Organizational Behavior and Human Decision Processes* 63, no. 2 (1995), pp. 158–74; and R.A. Cosier and C.R. Schwenk, "Agreement and Thinking Alike: Ingredients for Poor Decisions," *Academy of Management Executive,* February 1990, pp. 69–74.

[20]"JP Morgan Told to Explain India Outsourcing Plan," *The Economic Times,* March 20, 2009, http://economictimes.indiatimes.com/articleshow/4289770.cms (accessed May 2, 2009).

[21]Paul Shrivastava and I.I. Mitroff, "Enhancing Organizational Research Utilization: The Role of Decision Makers' Assumptions," *Academy of Management Review,* January 1984, pp. 18–26.

[22]Kimberly D. Elsbach and Greg Elofson, "How the Packaging of Decision Explanations Affects Perceptions of Trustworthiness," *Academy of Management Journal* 43, no. 1 (February 2000), pp. 80–90; and E.F. Harrison, *The Managerial Decision-Making Process* (Boston: Houghton-Mifflin, 1999).

[23]James G. March and Herbert A. Simon, *Organizations* (New York: John Wiley & Sons, 1958).

[24]C. Chet Miller and Duane R. Ireland, "Intuition in Strategic Decision Making: Friend or Foe in the Fast-Paced 21st Century?" *Academy of Management Executive* 19, no. 1 (February 2005), pp. 19–30; Stephen Turner,

Intuition at Work: Why Developing Your Gut Instincts Will Make You Better at What You Do (New York: Doubleday Business, 2002); and Alden M. Hayashi, "When to Trust Your Gut," *Harvard Business Review* 79, no. 2 (February 2001), pp. 59–69.

[25]Orlando Behling and N.L. Ecker, "Making Sense out of Intuition," *Academy of Management Executive,* February 1991, pp. 46–47; and S. Shapiro and M.T. Spence, "Managerial Intuition: A Conceptual and Operational Framework," *Business Horizons,* January–February 1997, pp. 63–68.

[26]Eric Bonabeau, "Don't Trust Your Gut," *Harvard Business Review* 81, no. 5 (May 2003), pp. 116–22.

[27]T.M. Jones, "Ethical Decision Making by Individuals in Organizations: An Issue-Contingent Model," *Academy of Management Review,* April 1991, pp. 366–95.

[28]Jesse Eisinger, "Year-End Review of Markets and Finance 2003," *The Wall Street Journal,* January 2, 2004, p. R3.

[29]Peter S. Goodman, "From Hometown Success to Global Scandal: Parmalat's Tangle of Financial Fraud Is Being Called Europe's Enron," *Washington Post,* January 10, 2004, p. A1; and R.T. DeGeorge, *Business Ethics* (Old Tappan, NJ: Prentice Hall, 1999).

[30]Gedeon J. Rossouw and Leon J. van Vuuren, "Modes of Managing Morality: A Descriptive Model of Strategies for Managing Ethics," *Journal of Business Ethics* 46, no. 4 (September 2003), pp. 389–402; and Linda K. Trevino, G.P. Weaver, D.G. Gibson, and B.L. Toffler, "Managing Ethics and Legal Compliance: What Works and What Hurts," *California Management Review,* Winter 1999, pp. 131–51.

[31]Dawn-Marie Driscoll and W. Michael Hoffman, *Ethics Matters: How to Implement Values-Driven Management* (Waltham, MA: Bentley College Press, 2000).

[32]Glen Whyte, "Decision Failures: Why They Occur and How to Prevent Them," *Academy of Management Executive,* August 1991, pp. 23–31.

[33]Leon Festinger, *A Theory of Cognitive Dissonance* (New York: Harper & Row, 1957), chap. 1.

[34]Richard Harrison and James G. March, "Decision Making and Post-Decision Surprises," *Administrative Science Quarterly,* March 1984, pp. 26–42.

[35]Kenneth T. Walsh, "The First 100 Days: Harry Truman Showed Decisiveness and Intelligence," *U.S. News and World Report,* February 26, 2009, www.usnews.com/articles/news/history/2009/02/26/the-first-100-days-harry-truman-showed-decisiveness-and-intelligence.html?PageNr=2 (accessed May 4, 2009).

[36]Barry Staw and his associates have done much of the work in this area. See, for example, Barry M. Staw, "The Escalation of Commitment to a Course of Action," *Academy of Management Review,* October 1981, pp. 577–87.

[37]"The Stupidest Business Decisions in History," *Neatorama,* April 15, 2008, www.neatorama. com/2008/04/15/the-stupidest-business-decisions-in-history/ (accessed May 2, 2009); Emily Fredrix, "U.S. Beer Schlitz Returns, Drums Up Nostalgic Drinkers," *The Canadian Press,* August 1, 2008; "No Foolin, It's Back," *Sauce Magazine,* April 1, 2009, www.saucemagazine.com/blog/?tag=schlitz-brewing-co (accessed May 2, 2009); and "Bottling Nostalgia," *Beverage World* 127, no. 12 (December 15, 2008), p. 45.

[38]John R. Hollenbeck, Daniel R. Ilgen, Jeffrey A. LePine, Jason A. Colquitt, and Jennifer Hedlund, "Extending the Multilevel Theory of Team Decision Making: Effects of Feedback and Experience in Hierarchical Teams," *Academy of Management Journal* 41, no. 3 (1998), pp. 269–83; and H.W. Crott, K. Szilvas, and J.A. Zuber, "Group Decision, Choice Shift, and Polarization in Consulting, Political, and Local Political Scenarios: An Experimental Investigation and Theoretical Analysis," *Organizational Behavior and Human Decision Processes,* June 1991, pp. 22–41.

[39]"The Special Forces Soldier," *Department of Military Affairs,* www.dma.state.fl.us/read3.asp?did=1643 (accessed May 4, 2009).

[40]Richard A. Guzzo and James A. Waters, "The Expression of Affect and the Performance of Decision-Making Groups," *Journal of Applied Psychology,* February 1982, pp. 67–74; D. Tjosvold and R.H.G. Field, "Effects of Social Context on Consensus and Majority Vote Decision Making," *Academy of Management Journal,* September 1983, pp. 500–6; and Frederick C. Miner, Jr., "Group versus Individual Decision Making: An Investigation of Performance Measures, Decision Strategies and Process Losses/Gains," *Organizational Behavior and Human Decision Processes,* Winter 1984, pp. 112–24.

[41]X.T. Wang, Frederic Simons, and Serge Bredart, "Social Cues and Verbal Framing in Risky Choice," *Journal of Behavioral Decision Making* 14, no. 1 (2001), pp. 1–15; and Glen Whyte, "Escalating Commitment in Individual and Group Decision Making: A Prospect Theory Approach," *Organizational Behavior and Human Decision Processes,* April 1993, pp. 430–55.

[42]S. Plous, *The Psychology of Judgment and Decision Making* (New York: McGraw-Hill, 1993).

[43]Patricia Sellers, "These Women Rule," *Fortune,* October 25, 1999, pp. 94–134.

[44]Patricia Sellers, Ann Harrington, and Melanie Shanley, "The 50 Most Powerful Women in American Business," *Fortune,* October 13, 2003, pp. 103–9; and Rochelle Sharpe, "As Leaders, Women Rule," *BusinessWeek,* November 30, 2000, pp. 75–84.

[45]Ming-Huei Chen, "Understanding the Benefits and Detriments of Conflict on Team Creativity Process," *Creativity and Innovation Management* 15, no. 1 (March 2006), pp. 105–16; Rajesh Sethi, Daniel C. Smith, and C. Whan Park, "How to Kill a Team's Creativity," *Harvard Business Review* 80, no. 8 (August 2002), pp. 16–18.

[46]Leigh Thompson and Leo F. Brajkovich, "Improving the Creativity of Organizational Work Groups," *Academy of Management Executive* 17, no. 1 (February 2003), pp. 96–110.

[47]Norman Dalkey, *The Delphi Method: An Experimental Study of Group Opinion* (Santa Monica, CA: Rand Corporation, 1969). This is a classic work on the Delphi methods.

[48]See Andre L. Delbecq, Andrew H. Van de Ven, and David H. Gustafson, *Group Techniques for Program Running* (Glenview, IL: Scott, Foresman, 1975). The discussion here is based on this work.

[49]Ibid., p. 18.

Chapter 15

[1]J.G. March and T. Weil, *On Leadership* (Malden, MA: Blackwell Publishing, 2005).

[2]"100 Leaders & Revolutionaries, Builders & Titans, Artists & Entertainers, Heroes & Icons, Scientists & Thinkers," *Time,* May 11, 2009.

[3]Jeffrey Pfeffer and Robert I. Sutton, *Hard Facts, Dangerous Half-Truths, and Total Nonsense* (Boston, MA: Harvard Business School Press, 2006).

[4]P.G. Northouse, *Leadership: Theory and Practice* (Thousand Oaks, CA: Sage Publications, 2004).

[5]M. Elaine Heard, "IV. New Formats: Reflections on Leadership: Conversations with Warren Bennis and Richard Kilburg," *Psychologist-Manager Journal* 10, no. 2 (2007), pp. 157–79.

[6]Warren Bennis, *Organizing Genius: The Secrets of Creative Collaboration* (Reading, MA: Addison-Wesley, 1997).

[7]R.S. Peterson and E.A., Mannix, eds., *Leading and Managing People in the Dynamic Organization* (Mahwah, NJ: Erlbaum, 2003).

[8]Northouse, *Leadership,* p. 3.

[9]Ibid.

[10]Charles C. Manz and Henry P. Sims, Jr., *Business Without Bosses* (New York: Berkley Books, 1990).

[11]Cheryl Dahl, "Natural Leader," *Fast Company,* December 2000, pp. 268–80.

[12]Ralph M. Stogdill, *Handbook of Leadership* (New York: Free Press, 1974), pp. 43–44.

[13]John Hawkins and Victor Dulewicz, "The Relationship between Performance as a Leader and Emotional Intelligence, Intellectual and Managerial Competences," *Journal of General Management* 33, no. 2 (Winter 2008), pp. 57–78.

[14]Edwin E. Ghiselli, "The Validity of Management Traits in Relation to Occupational Level," *Personnel Psychology,* Summer 1963, pp. 109–13.

[15]Kok-Yee Ng, Ang Soon, and Kim-Yin Chan, "Personality and Leader Effectiveness: A Moderated Mediation Model of Leadership Self-Efficacy, Job Demands and Job Security," *Journal of Applied Psychology* 93, no. 4 (July 2008), pp. 733–43.

[16]J.L. Rosenstein, *The Scientific Selection of Salesmen* (New York: McGraw-Hill, 1944).

[17]Nicholas O. Rule and Nalini Ambady, "The Face of Success: Inferences from Chief Executive Officers' Appearance Predict Company Profits," *Psychological Science* 19, no. 2 (February 2008), pp. 109–11.

[18]Edwin E. Ghiselli, *Explorations in Managerial Talent* (Santa Monica, CA: Goodyear, 1971).

[19]Ibid., p. 19.

[20]Shelley A. Kirkpatrick and Edwin A. Locke, "Leadership: Do Traits Matter?" *Academy of Management Executive,* May 1991, pp. 48–60.

[21]For a review of the studies, see Stogdill, *Handbook of Leadership,* chap. 11; also see E.A. Fleishman, "The Measurement of Leadership Attitudes in Industry," *Journal of Applied Psychology,* June 1953, pp. 153–58; C.L. Shartle, *Executive Performance and Leadership* (Englewood Cliffs, NJ: Prentice Hall, 1956); E.A. Fleishman, E.F. Harris, and H.E. Burtt, *Leadership and Supervision in Industry* (Columbus: Bureau of Educational Research, Ohio State University, 1955).

[22]Fleishman, "Measurement of Leadership Attitudes."

[23]Timothy A. Judge, Ronald F. Piccolo, and Remus Ilies, "The Forgotten Ones? The Validity of Consideration and Initiating Structure in Leadership Research," *Journal of Applied Psychology* 89, no. 1 (February 2004), pp. 36–51.

[24]R. Goffee and G. Jones, *Why Should Anyone Be Led by You?* (Boston, MA: Harvard Business School Press, 2006).

[25]Fred E. Fiedler, *A Theory of Leadership Effectiveness* (New York: McGraw-Hill, 1967).

[26]Fred E. Fiedler, "How Do You Make Leaders More Effective? New Answers to an Old Puzzle," *Organizational Dynamics,* Autumn 1972, pp. 3–8.

[27]See, for example, L.H. Peters, D.D. Hartke, and J.J. Pohlmann, "Fiedler's Contingency Theory of Leadership: An Application of the Meta-Analysis Procedures of Schmidt and Hunter," *Psychological Bulletin,* March 1985, pp. 274–85; C.A. Schriesheim, B.J. Tepper, and L.A. Tetrault, "Least Preferred Co-Worker Score, Situational Control, and Leadership Effectiveness: A Meta-Analysis of Contingency Model Performance Predictions," *Journal of Applied Psychology,* August 1994, pp. 561–73; and R. Ayman, M.M. Chemers, and F. Fiedler, "The Contingency Model of Leadership Effectiveness: Its Levels of Analysis," *Leadership Quarterly,* Summer 1995, pp. 147–67.

[28]Victor Vroom and Philip Yetton, *Leadership and Decision Making* (Pittsburgh: University of Pittsburgh Press, 1973).

[29]Victor Vroom and Arthur Jago, *The New Leadership: Managing Participation in Organizations* (Englewood Cliffs, NJ: Prentice Hall, 1988).

[30]V.H. Vroom, "Leadership and the Decision Process," *Organizational Dynamics,* Spring 2000, pp. 82–94.

[31]Victor H. Vroom and Arthur G. Jago, "Situation Effects and Levels of Analysis in the Study of Leader Participation," *Leadership Quarterly,* Spring 1995, pp. 45–52.

[32]Robert J. House, "A Path–Goal Theory of Leadership Effectiveness," *Administrative Science Quarterly,* September 1971, pp. 32–39. Also see Robert J. House and Terence R. Mitchell, "Path–Goal Theory of Leadership," *Journal of Contemporary Business,* Autumn 1974, pp. 81–98, which is the basis for the discussion.

[33]Robert J. House and Gary Dessler, "The Path–Goal Theory of Leadership: Some Post Hoc and A Priori Tests," in *Contingency Approaches to Leadership,* ed. James G. Hunt, (Carbondale: Southern Illinois University Press, 1974).

[34]Gary A. Yukl, *Leadership in Organizations* (Englewood Cliffs, NJ: Prentice Hall, 1998).

[35]James R. Detert, Roger G. Schroeder, and John J. Mauriel, "A Framework for Linking Culture and

Improvement Initiatives in Organizations," *Academy of Management Review,* October 2000, pp. 850–63.

[36]Robert J. House, "Path–Goal Theory of Leadership: Lessons, Legacy, and a Reformulated Theory," *Leadership Quarterly,* Autumn 1996, pp. 1–27.

[37]C.A. Schriesheim and L.L. Neider, "Path–Goal Theory: The Long and Winding Road," *Leadership Quarterly,* Summer 1996, pp. 317–21.

[38]Originally published in Paul Hersey and Kenneth H. Blanchard, *Management of Organizational Behavior in Utilizing Human Resources* (Englewood Cliffs, NJ: Prentice Hall, 1969), now in 7th edition, which first introduced the concept of "readiness." See also, Kenneth H. Blanchard and Robert Nelson, "Recognition and Reward," *Executive Excellence,* April 1997, pp. 15–16.

[39]Paul Hersey, "Situational Leaders," *Leadership Excellence* 26, no. 2 (February 2009), p. 12.

[40]Gary Yukl and Cecilia M. Falbe, "Importance of Different Power Sources in Downward and Lateral Relations," *Journal of Applied Psychology,* June 1991, pp. 416–23.

[41]Kenneth H. Blanchard, P. Zigarmi, and D. Zigarmi, *Leadership and the One-Minute Manager* (New York: William Morrow, 1985).

[42]Marshall Sashkin and Molly G. Sashkin, *Leadership That Matters: The Critical Factors for Making a Difference in People's Lives and Organizations' Success* (San Francisco: Berrett-Koehler, 2003).

[43]Max Weber, *The Theory of Social and Economic Organization,* trans. A.M. Henderson and T. Parsons (New York: Free Press, 1947; originally published 1924).

[44]John Sculley, "Sculley's Lessons from Inside Apple," *Fortune,* September 14, 1987, pp. 108–11.

[45]J. Adair, *How to Grow Leaders* (New York: Kogan Page, 2005).

[46]A.H.B. De Hoogh, D. Den Hartog, P. Koopman, H. Thierry, P.T. Van den Berg, J.G. Van der Weide, and C. Wilderom, "Leader Motives, Charismatic Leadership and Subordinates' Work Attitudes in the Profit and Voluntary Sector," *The Leadership Quarterly,* February 2005, pp. 17–38.

[47]Bradley R. Agle et al., "Does CEO Charisma Matter? An Empirical Analysis of the Relationships among Organizational Performance, Environmental Uncertainty, and Top Management Perceptions of CEO Charisma," *Academy of Management Journal* 49, no. 1 (February 2006), pp. 161–74.

[48]Ibid.

[49]Michael Marquardt and Nancy O. Berger, *Global Leaders for the 21st Century* (Albany: State University of New York Press, 2000), pp. 99–109.

[50]Ian I. Mitroff, *Crisis in Leadership* (New York: John Wiley & Sons, 2004).

[51]Robert F. Hartley, *Management Mistakes and Successes* (New York: John Wiley & Sons, 2000), pp. 312–26.

[52]R.J. House, P.J. Hanges, M. Javidan, P.W. Dorfman, and V. Gupta, eds., *Culture, Leadership, and Organizations: The GLOBE Study of 62 Societies* (Thousand Oaks, CA: Sage Publications, 2004).

[53]D. Yankelovich and J. Immerwahr, *Putting the Work Ethic to Work* (New York: Public Agenda Foundation, 1983).

[54]C.A. Schreisheim, S.L. Castro, X. Zhou, and L.A. DeChurch, "An Investigation of Path–Goal and Transformational Leadership Theory Predictions at the Individual Level of Analysis," *The Leadership Quarterly,* February 2006, pp. 21–38; Yankelovich and Immerwahr, *Putting the Work Ethic to Work.*

[55]Bernard M. Bass, *Leadership Performance beyond Expectations* (New York: Free Press, 1985).

[56]Ibid., p. 31.

[57]Silke A. Eisenbeiss, Daan van Knippenberg, and Sabine Boerner, "Transformational Leadership and Team Innovation: Integrating Team Climate Principles," *Journal of Applied Psychology* 93, no. 6 (November 2008), pp. 1438–46.

[58]David A. Waldman, Donald S. Siegel, and Mansour Javidan, "Components of CEO Transformational Leadership and Corporate Social Responsibility," *Journal of Management Studies* 43, no. 8 (December 2006), pp. 1703–25.

[59]"Newman's Own—Common Good," www.newmansown.com/commongood.aspx.

[60]"Ben & Jerry's Ice Cream, Ben & Jerry's Foundation, About," www.benjerry.com/company/foundation/about/.

[61]Waldman, Siegel, and Javidan, "Components of CEO Transformational Leadership."

[62]For a review, see Daniel C. Feldman and Melenie J. Lankau, "Executive Coaching: A Review and Agenda for Future Research," *Journal of Management* 31, no. 6 (December 2005), pp. 829–848.

[63]See "Doug Blevins Kicking & Punting," www.dougblevinskicking.com (accessed May 28, 2006);

and Dorothy Leonard and Walter Swap, "Gurus in the Garage," *Harvard Business Review,* November–December 2000, pp. 71–82.

[64]"Doug Blevins Kicking & Punting, Home Page," www. dougblevinskicking.com/.

[65]Peter B. Smith, Mark F. Peterson, and Zhong Ming Wang, "The Manager as Mediator of Alternative Meanings: A Pilot Study from China, the U.S.A. and U.K.," *Journal of International Business Studies,* January 1996, pp. 115–37.

[66]Sen Sendjaya, James C. Sarros, and Joseph C. Santora, "Defining and Measuring Servant Leadership Behaviour in Organizations," *Journal of Management Studies* 45, no. 2 (March 2008), pp. 402–24.

[67]"Dan Warmenhoven, Chairman and Chief Executive Officer," www.netapp.com/us/company/news/press-room/ warmenhoven_d_bio.html.

[68]M. Javidan and R.J. House, "Cultural Acumen for the Global Manager: Lessons from Project GLOBE," *Organizational Dynamics,* Spring 2001.

[69]Geert Hofstede, *Cultures and Organizations* (New York: McGraw-Hill, 1991).

[70]Gebert and Steinkamp, "Leadership Style and Economic Success in Nigeria and Taiwan."

[71]Smith, Peterson, and Wang, "The Manager as Mediator of Alternative Meanings."

[72]M.C. Walker, "Morality, Self-Interest, and Leaders in International Affairs," *The Leadership Quarterly,* April 2006, pp. 135–43.

[73]Richard M. Bass and P.C. Burger, *Assessment of Managers: An International Comparison* (New York: Free Press, 1979).

[74]D. Collinson, "Rethinking Followership: A Post-Structuralist Analysis of Follower Identities," *The Leadership Quarterly,* April 2006, pp. 174–89.

[75]Smith, Peterson, and Wang, "The Manager as Mediator of Alternative Meanings."

[76]Robert Keller, "Transformational Leadership, Initiating Structure, and Substitutes for Leadership: A Longitudinal Study of Research and Development Project Team Performance," *Journal of Applied Psychology* 91, no. 1 (January 2006), pp. 202–10.

[77]Ann S. Davis, "Handling Uncertainty: Do Managers in the People's Republic of China, the US, and the UK Differ?" *Academy of Management Executive,* February 1997, pp. 121–22.

Chapter 16

[1]Danny Miller, "Advantage by Design: Competing with Opportunity-Based Organizations," *Business Horizons* 48, no. 5 (September–October 2005), pp. 393–407; and William McKinley and Andreas Georg Scherer, "Some Unanticipated Consequences of Organizational Restructuring," *Academy of Management Review,* October 2000, pp. 735–52.

[2]Julia Balogun and Gerry Johnson, "Organizational Restructuring and Middle Manager Sensemaking," *Academy of Management Journal* 47, no. 4 (August 2004), pp. 523–49; John Child and Rita Gunther, "Organizations Unfettered: Organizational Form in an Information-Intensive Economy," *Academy of Management Journal* 44, no. 6 (2001), pp. 1135–49; and Wouter H.F.M. Cortenraad, *The Corporate Paradox: Economic Realities of the Corporate Form of Organizations* (Boston: Kluwer, 2000).

[3]John Hagel, III, and Marc Singer, "Unbundling the Corporation," *Harvard Business Review,* March–April 1999, pp. 133–41.

[4]Dan R. Dalton, William D. Todor, Michael J. Spendolina, Gordon J. Fielding, and Lyman W. Porter, "Organization Structure and Performance: A Critical Review," *Academy of Management Review,* January 1980, p. 49.

[5]Stewart Ranson, Bob Hinings, and Royston Greenwood, "The Structuring of Organizational Structures," *Administrative Science Quarterly,* March 1980, p. 2.

[6]David A. Nadler and Michael L. Tushman, "The Organization of the Future: Principles of Design for the 21st Century," *Organizational Dynamics,* Summer 1999, pp. 45–60.

[7]B.B. Lichtenstein, "Self-Organized Transitions: A Pattern amidst the Chaos of Transformative Change," *Academy of Management Executive,* November 2000, pp. 128–41.

[8]W.F. Joyce, *Megachange* (New York: Free Press, 1999).

[9]Wesley D. Sine, Hitoshi Mitsuhashi, and David A Kirsch, "Revisiting Burns and Stalker: Formal Structure and New Venture Performance in Emerging Economic Sectors," *Academy of Management Journal* 49, no. 1 (February 2006), pp. 121–32.

[10]Arthur Fishman and Avi Simhon, "The Division of Labor, Inequality and Growth," *Journal of Economic Growth* 7, no. 2 (2002), pp. 117–36; and Richard E. Kopelman, "Job Redesign and Productivity: A Review of the Literature," *National Productivity Review,* Summer 1985, p. 239.

[11]Lex Borghans and Bas ter Weel, "The Division of Labour, Worker Organisation, and Technological Change," *The Economic Journal* 116, no. 509 (February 2006), pp. F45–F72; and Donald J. Campbell, "Task Complexity: A Review and Analysis," *Academy of Management Review,* January 1988, pp. 40–52.

[12]Paul S. Adler, "Building Better Bureaucracies," *Academy of Management Executive,* November 1999, pp. 36–49.

[13]"No More Mr. Nice Guy at P&G—Not by a Long Shot," *BusinessWeek*, February 3, 1992, pp. 54–55.

[14]"Procter & Gamble's Innovation Success," *Strategic Direction* 21, no. 7 (July 2005), pp. 11–14; and "A.G. Lafley: Procter & Gamble," *BusinessWeek,* January 13, 2003, p. 67.

[15]Jeffrey A. Alexander, "Adaptive Change in Corporate Control Practices," *Academy of Management Journal,* March 1991, pp. 162–93.

[16]Jay Greene, "Gates and Ballmer on 'Making the Transition,'" *BusinessWeek,* April 19, 2004, p. 96; and Rebecca Buckman, "Soft Spot at Microsoft: System Still Revolves around Gates, Ballmer," *The Wall Street Journal,* April 8, 2002, p. A1.

[17]Jay Greene and Judith Nemes, "To Centralize or Not to Centralize: Centralization Paying Off at Not-for-Profits, For-Profits Cut Back at Corporate," *Modern Healthcare,* October 8, 1990, pp. 30–36.

[18]Chester A. Schriesheim, Linda L. Neider, and Terri A. Scandura, "Delegation and Leader–Member Exchange: Main Effects, Moderators, and Measurement Issues," *Academy of Management Journal* 41, no. 3 (1998), pp. 298–319; and Richard S. Blackburn, "Dimensions of Structure: A Review and Reappraisal," *Academy of Management Review,* January 1982, pp. 59–66.

[19]Marianne Jelinek, "Organization Structure: The Basic Conformations," in *Organization by Design,* eds. Marianne Jelinek, Joseph A. Litterer, and Raymond E. Miles, (Plano, TX: Business Publications, 1981), pp. 293–302.

[20]Peggy Leatt and Rodney Schneck, "Criteria for Grouping Nursing Subunits in Hospitals," *Academy of Management Journal,* March 1984, pp. 150–64.

[21]"Frito-Lay: Leadership," *Frito-Lay About Us,* www.fritolay.com/about-us/leadership.html.

[22]Gregory J. Wilcox, "GM Hits Target with Car Bargain," *Knight Ridder/Tribune Business News,* June 28, 2005, p. 1; and Joseph T. Mahoney, "The Adoption of the Multidivisional Form of Organization: A Contingency Approach," *Journal of Management,* January 1992, pp. 49–72.

[23]"10-K: Wind River Systems Inc.—MarketWatch," *MarketWatch,* April 1, 2009, www.marketwatch.com/news/story/10-k-wind-river-systems-inc/story.aspx?guid= %7B0E5D6C4E-5A35-44B4-A633-9AD5F06BF5CD%7D&dist= msr_1.

[24]Jay R. Galbraith, *Designing the Customer-Centric Organization: A Guide to Strategy, Structure and Process* (San Francisco: Jossey-Bass, 2005); and Alf H. Walle, III, *Rethinking Marketing* (Westport, CT: Quorum, 2001).

[25]Michael Maccoby, "Transforming R&D Services at Bell Labs," *Research-Technology Management,* January–February 1992, pp. 46–49.

[26]Jay R. Galbraith and Robert K. Kazanjian, "Organizing to Implement Strategies of Diversity and Globalization: The Role of Matrix Organizations," *Human Resource Management,* Spring 1986, pp. 37–54.

[27]Robert S. Kaplan and David P. Norton, "How to Implement a New Strategy without Disrupting Your Organization," *Harvard Business Review,* March 2006, pp. 100–10; and David Lei, John W. Slocum, Jr., and Robert A. Pitts, "Designing Organizations for Competitive Advantage: The Power of Unlearning and Learning," *Organizational Dynamics,* Winter 1999, pp. 24–38.

[28]Lei, Slocum, and Pitts, "Designing Organizations."

[29]Milton Harris and Artur Raviv, "Organization Design," *Management Science* 48, no. 7 (2002), pp. 852–66; Paul R. Lawrence, Harvey F. Kolodny, and Stanley M. Davis, "The Human Side of the Matrix," *Organizational Dynamics,* September 1977, p. 47; and George J. Chambers, "The Individual in a Matrix Organization," *Project Management Journal,* December 1989, pp. 37–42, 50.

[30]Michael Goold and Andrew Campbell, "Making Matrix Structures Work: Creating Clarity on Unit Roles and Responsibility," *European Management Journal* 21, no. 3 (2003), pp. 351–65; and Paul B. de Laat, "Matrix Management of Projects and Power Struggles: A Case Study of an R&D Laboratory," *Human Relations,* September 1994, pp. 1089–19.

[31]Lei, Slocum, and Pitts, "Designing Organizations."

[32]Christopher A. Bartlett and Sumantra Ghosal, "Organizing for Worldwide Effectiveness: The Transnational Solution," *California Management Review,* Fall 1988, pp. 54–74; and James K. McCollum and J. Daniel Sherman, "The Effects of Matrix Organization Size and Number of Project Assignments on Performance," *IEEE Transactions on Engineering Management,* February 1991, pp. 75–78.

[33]Christopher K. Best, "Organizing for New Development," *Journal of Business Strategy,* July–August 1988, pp. 34–39.

[34]V. Nilakant, "Dynamics of Middle Managerial Roles: A Study in Four Indian Organizations," *Journal of Managerial Psychology* (UK) 6, no. 1 (1991), pp. 17–24.

[35]Ronald J. Burke and Esther R. Greenglass, "Work Status Congruence, Work Outcomes and Psychological Well-Being," *Stress Medicine,* March 2000, pp. 91–99.

[36]Robin Bellis-Jones and Max Hand, "Improving Managerial Spans of Control," *Management Accounting* (UK), October 1989, pp. 20–21; and John S. McClenahen, "Managing More People in the '90s," *Industry Week,* March 20, 1989, pp. 30–38.

[37]"Wal-Mart to Cut Jobs at Sam's Club," *Los Angeles Times,* April 27, 2007, http://articles.latimes.com/2007/apr/27/business/fi-briefs27.3.

[38]E. Rupp, "Organization Structure and Fairness Perceptions: The Moderating Effects of Organizational Level," *Organizational Behavior and Human Decision Processes* 89, no. 1 (2002), pp. 881–905; and James P. Walsh and Robert D. Dewar, "Formalization and the Organizational Life-Cycle," *Journal of Management Studies,* March 1991, pp. 103–41.

[39]Michael V. Russo and Niran S. Harrison, "Organizational Design and Environmental Performance: Clues from the Electronics Industry," *Academy of Management Journal* 48, no. 4 (August 2005), pp. 582–93; and Robert W. Hetherington, "The Effects of Formalization on Departments of a Multi-Hospital System," *Journal of Management Studies,* March 1991, pp. 103–41.

[40]Peter H. Grinyer and Masoud Yasai-Ardekani, "Dimensions of Organizational Structure: A Critical Replication," *Academy of Management Journal,* September 1980, pp. 405–21, discusses formalization in relation to centralization.

[41]Eric J. Walton, "The Comparison of Measures of Organization Structure," *Academy of Management Review,* January 1981, pp. 155–60.

[42]Jeffrey D. Ford, "Institutional versus Questionnaire Measures of Organizational Structure," *Academy of Management Journal,* September 1979, pp. 601–10.

[43]Brian C. Robertson, *There's No Place Like Work* (Dallas: Spence, 2000).

[44]Richard L. Priem and Joseph Rosenstein, "Is Organization Theory Obvious to Practitioners? A Test of One Established Theory," *Organization Science,* September–October 2000, pp. 509–24.

[45]Phillip G. Clampitt, Robert J. DeKoch, and Thomas Cashman, "A Strategy for Communicating about Uncertainty," *Academy of Management Executive,* November 2000, pp. 41–57.

[46]Henri Fayol, *General and Industrial Management,* trans. J.A. Conbrough (Geneva: International Management Institute, 1929). The more widely circulated translation is that of Constance Storrs (London: Pitman, 1949).

[47]James D. Mooney and Alan C. Reilly, *Onward Industry!* (New York: Harper & Row, 1939). Revised in James D. Mooney, *The Principles of Organization* (New York: Harper & Row, 1947).

[48]Henry C. Metcalf and Lyndall Urwick, eds., *Dynamic Administration: The Collected Papers of Mary Parker Follett* (New York: Harper & Row, 1940).

[49]Lyndall Urwick, *The Elements of Administration* (New York: Harper & Row, 1944).

[50]Michael Crozier, *The Bureaucratic Phenomenon* (Chicago: University of Chicago Press, 1964), p. 3.

[51]Max Weber, *The Theory of Social and Economic Organization,* trans. A.M. Henderson and Talcott Parsons (New York: Oxford University Press, 1947).

[52]Richard M. Weiss, "Weber on Bureaucracy: Management Consultant or Political Theorist?" *Academy of Management Review,* April 1983, pp. 242–48.

[53]Weber, *The Theory of Social and Economic Organization,* p. 334.

[54]*From Max Weber: Essays in Sociology,* trans. H.H. Gerth and C.W. Mills (New York: Oxford University Press, 1946), p. 214.

[55]Beth Bacheldor, "Breakthrough," *InformationWeek,* February 9, 2004, p. 34; Paul Lukas and Maggie Overfelt, "United Parcel Service," *Fortune Small Business* 13, no. 3 (2003), p. 24; Kent C. Nelson, "Efficiency Wasn't Enough, So We Learned How to Dance," *Computerworld,* March 23, 1992, p. 33; and Richard B. Chase and Nicholas J. Aquilano, *Operations Management* (Homewood, IL: Richard D. Irwin, 1992), p. 533.

[56]Rensis Likert, *New Patterns of Management* (New York: McGraw-Hill, 1961); and Rensis Likert, *The Human Organization: Its Management and Value* (New York: McGraw-Hill, 1967).

[57]Likert, *The Human Organization.*

[58]Maureen L. Ambrose and Marshall Schminke, "Organization Structure as a Moderator of the Relationship between Procedural Justice, Interactional Justice, Perceived Organizational Support, and Supervisory Trust," *Journal of Applied Psychology,* 88, no. 2 (April 2003), pp. 295–305; and Joanne B. Ciulla, *The Working Life* (New York: Times Books, 2000).

[59]Likert, *New Patterns of Management* and *The Human Organization.*

[60]"About Us—Thrivent Financial for Lutherans," *Thrivent Financial for Lutherans,* April 29, 2009, www.thrivent.com/aboutus/; "Thrivent to Expand Sales Force by 675 Jobs," *Knight Ridder/Tribune Business News,* March 2, 2006, p. 1; and Kathy Chu, "Investors Put Faith in Funds Tied to Religion," *The Wall Street Journal,* December 19, 2002, p. D2.

[61]Donald J. McNerney, "Compensation Case Study: Rewarding Team Performance and Individual Skillbuilding," *HR Focus,* January 1995, pp. 1, 4; Dennis H. Pillsbury, "Team Concept Makes Vorpagel #1 for AAL," *Life & Health Insurance Sales,* October 1993, pp. 10–11; and Fred Luthans, "A Conversation with Charles Dull," *Organizational Dynamics,* Summer 1993, pp. 57–70.

[62]S. Ghoshal and C.A. Bartlett, "The Multinational Corporation as an Interorganizational Network," *Academy of Management Review,* October 1990, pp. 603–25.

[63]C.A. Bartlett and S. Ghoshal, *Managing across Borders: The Transnational Solution* (Boston: Harvard Business School Press, 1989), p. 38.

[64]Roger (Rongxin) Chen and Mark V. Cannice, "Global Integration and the Performance of Multinationals' Subsidiaries in Emerging Markets," *Ivey Business Journal,* January–February 2006, pp. 1–9; and D.A. Ricks, B. Toyne, and Z. Martinez, "Recent Developments in International Management Research," *Journal of Management,* June 1990, pp. 219–53.

[65]Mohammed M. Habib and Bart Victor, "Strategy, Structure, and Performance of U.S. Manufacturing and Service MNCs: A Comparative Analysis," *Strategic Management Journal,* November 1991, pp. 589–606.

[66]David J. Lemak and Jeffrey A. Bracker, "A Strategic Contingency Model of Multinational Corporate Structure," *Strategic Management Journal,* September–October 1988, pp. 521–26.

[67]John Hechinger, "Kodak to Reorganize Its Business Again," *The Wall Street Journal,* November 15, 2001, p. B12.

[68]Alexandra Jardine, "Is This a Kodak Moment?" *Marketing,* October 13, 2004, pp. 28–31.

[69]Christopher A. Bartlett, "How Multinational Organizations Evolve," *Journal of Business Strategy,* Winter 1982, pp. 20–32.

[70]J. Stewart Black and Hal B. Gregersen, "The Right Way to Manage Expats," *Harvard Business Review,* March–April 1999, pp. 52–64.

[71]Johna Till Johnson, "The Virtual Workplace: The Price Is Right," *Network World* 22, no. 36 (September 12, 2005), pp. 37–38; *Virtual Teams That Work: Creating Conditions for Virtual Team Effectiveness,* Cristina B. Gibson and Susan G. Cohen, eds. (San Francisco: Jossey-Bass, 2003); and Mangu K. Ahuja and Kathleen M. Carley, "Network Structure in Virtual Organizations," *Organization Science,* November–December 1999, pp. 741–57.

[72]Wayne F. Cascio, "Managing a Virtual Workplace," *Academy of Management Executive* 14, no. 3 (2000), pp. 81–91; and Geraldine DeSanctis and Peter Monge, "Communication Processes for Virtual Organizations," *Organizational Science,* November–December 1999, pp. 693–703.

[73]P.R. Monge and Janet R. Fulk, "Communication Technology for Global Network Organizations," in *Shaping Organization Form: Communication, Connection, and Community,* eds. Geraldine DeSanctis and Janet Fulk (Newbury Park, CA: Sage Publications, 1999), pp. 81–110.

[74]Paul R. Sparrow, "New Employee Behaviours, Work Designs, and Forms of Work Organization: What Is in Store for Future Work?" *Journal of Managerial Psychology* 15, no. 3 (2000), pp. 202–18; and Robert Kraut, Charles Steinfield, Alice P. Chin, Brian Butler, and Anne Hoag, "Coordination and Virtualization: The Role of Electronic Networks and Personal Relationships," *Organization Science,* November–December 1999, pp. 722–40.

[75]Kraut et al., "Coordination and Virtualization."

[76]Ron Ashkenas, Dave Ulrich, Todd Jick, and Steve Kerr, *The Boundaryless Organization: Breaking the Chains of Organization Structure* (San Francisco: Jossey-Bass, 2002); Abbe Mowshowitz, "Virtual Organization: A Vision of Management in the Information Age," *The Information Society,* October–December 1994, pp. 267–88; Heather Ogilvie, "At the Core, It's the Virtual Organization," *Journal of Business Strategy,* September/October 1994, p. 29; and "Learning from Japan," *BusinessWeek,* January 27, 1992, pp. 52–55, 58–59.

[77]Larry L. Cummings and P. Bromiley, "The Organizational Trust Inventory (OTI): Development and Validation," in *Trust in Organizations: Frontiers of Theory and Research,* eds. R.M. Kramer and T.R. Tyler (Thousand Oaks, CA: Sage Publications, 1996), pp. 302–30.

Chapter 17

[1]D. Lewis, J. Medland, S. Malone, and M. Murphy, "Appreciative Leadership: Defining Effective Leadership Methods," *Organizational Development Journal,* Spring 2006, pp. 87–100.

[2]John Hayes, *The Theory and Practice of Change Management* (London: Palgrave, 2003).

[3]Ralph Jacobson, "Sustainable Communities," *Leadership Excellence* 26, no. 5 (May 2009), p. 17.

[4]R. Garud, A. Kumaraswamy, and V. Sambamurthy, "Emergent by Design: Performance and Transformation at Infosys Technologies," *Organization Science,* March–April 2006, pp. 277–89.

[5]K. Harigopal, *Management of Organizational Change: Leveraging Transformation* (San Francisco: Sage Publications, 2006).

[6]Rosabeth Moss Kanter, "Transforming Giants," *Harvard Business Review,* January 2008, pp. 43–52.

[7]Rosabeth Moss Kanter, "Transcending Business Boundaries: 12,000 World Managers View Change," *Harvard Business Review,* May–June 1991, pp. 151–64.

[8]Viktor Jakupec and John Garrick, eds., *Flexible Learning, Human Resource and Organisational Development: Putting Theory to Work* (New York: Routledge, 2000).

[9]Patricia A. McLagan, "The Change-Capable Organization," *Training & Development,* January 2003, pp. 50–60.

[10]Rune Lines, "Using Power to Install Strategy: The Relationships between Expert Power, Position Power, Influence Tactics and Implementation Success," *Journal of Change Management* 7, no. 2 (June 2007), pp. 143–70.

[11]Susan A. Mohrman, Allan M. Mohrman, Jr., and Gerald E. Ledford, Jr., "Interventions That Change Organizations," in *Large-Scale Organizational Change,* ed. Allan M. Mohrman, Jr., Susan A. Mohrman, Gerald E. Ledford, Jr., Thomas G. Cummings, Edward E. Lawler, III, et al. (San Francisco: Jossey-Bass, 1989), p. 146.

[12]Elizabeth Wolfe Morrison and Frances J. Milliken, "Organizational Silence: A Barrier to Change and Development in a Pluralistic World," *Academy of Management Review,* October 2000, pp. 706–25.

[13]Louis V. Gerstner, Jr., *Who Says Elephants Can't Dance? Inside IBM's Historic Turnaround* (New York: Harper Business, 2002).

[14]Kurt Lewin, "Group Decisions and Social Change," in *Readings in Social Psychology,* ed. Eleanor E. Maccoby, Theodore M. Newcomb, and Eugene L. Hartley (New York: Holt, Rinehart & Winston, 1958).

[15]Rex Davenport, "Eliminate the Skills Gap," *Training & Development,* February 2006, pp. 26–34.

[16]Bas Verplanken et al., "Mental Habits: Metacognitive Reflection on Negative Self-Thinking," *Journal of Personality and Social Psychology* 92, no. 3 (March 2007), pp. 526–41.

[17]Tony Bingham and Pat Galagan, "You Won," *Training & Development,* April 2006, pp. 34–41.

[18]S. Cook, S. Macaulay, and H. Coldicott, "Using a Vision," *Training Journal,* April 2006, pp. 26–29.

[19]Rosabeth Moss Kanter, "Championing Change: An Interview with Bell Atlantic's CEO Raymond Smith," *Harvard Business Review,* January–February 1991, pp. 119–30.

[20]Jack Welch and Suzy Welch, "What Change Agents Are Made Of," *BusinessWeek,* October 20, 2008.

[21]Warner W. Burke and W. Trahant, *Business Climate Shifts: Profiles of Change Makers* (Boston: Butterworth/Heinemann, 2000).

[22]Léon de Caluwé and Hans Vermaak, *Learning to Change: A Guide for Organization Change Agents* (Thousand Oaks, CA: Sage Publications, 2003).

[23]Patrick E. Connor, Linda K. Lake, and Richard W. Stackman, *Managing Organizational Change* (Westport, CT: Praeger, 2003).

[24]Jeffrey D. Ford and Laurie W. Ford, "Resistance to Change: The Rest of the Story," *Academy of Management Review* 33, no. 2 (April 2008), pp. 362–77.

[25]A.P. Goldstein, *Reducing Resistance: Methods for Enhancing Openness to Change* (Champaign, IL: Research Press, 2001).

[26]Denise M. Rousseau and S.A. Tijoriwala, "What's a Good Reason to Change? Motivated Reasoning and Social Accounts in Promoting Organizational Change," *Journal of Applied Psychology,* August 1999, pp. 514–28.

[27]Sarah Cook, "Learning Needs Analysis Part 4: Planning the Learning Needs Analysis Project," *Training Journal,* April 2005, pp. 54–58.

[28]D. Jones, "Driving Change—Too Fast?" *USA Today,* August 11, 1999, p. 6B.

[29]David Fine, Maia A. Hansen, and Stefan Roggenhofer, "From Lean to Lasting: Making Operational Improvements Stick," *McKinsey Quarterly,* March 2009, pp. 109–17.

[30]Rousseau and Tijoriwala, "What's a Good Reason to Change?"

[31]David A. Garvin, Amy C. Edmondson, and Francesca Gino, "Is Yours a Learning Organization?" *Harvard Business Review,* March 2008, pp. 109–16.

[32]Peter Senge, *The Dance of Change: The Challenges to Sustaining Momentum in Learning Organizations* (New York: Doubleday, 1999).

[33]Satu Lahteenmaki, Jouko Toivonen, and Merja Mattila, "Critical Aspects of Organizational Learning Research and Proposals for Its Measurement," *British Journal of Management* 12, no. 2 (2001), pp. 113–29.

[34]Deborah Davis and Barbara J. Daley, "The Learning Organization and Its Dimensions as Key Factors in Firms' Performance," *Human Resource Development International* 11, no. 1 (February 2008), pp. 51–66.

[35]Donald L. Kirkpatrick, *Evaluating Training Programs: The Four Levels* (San Francisco: Berrett-Koehler, 2005).

[36]John P. Kotter, "Leading Change: The Eight Steps to Transformation," in *The Leader's Change Handbook,* ed. J.A. Conger, G.M. Spreitzer, and E.E. Lawler, III (San Francisco: Jossey-Bass, 1999), pp. 87–99.

[37]Pat McLagan, *Change Is Everybody's Business* (San Francisco: Berrett-Koehler, 2002).

[38]Michael E. Porter, "The Five Competitive Forces That Shape Strategy," *Harvard Business Review,* January 2008, pp. 78–93.

[39]T. Oppenheimer, *The Flickering Mind: The False Promise of Technology in the Classroom and How Learning Can Be Saved* (New York: Random House, 2003).

[40]Carol J. Haddal, *Managing Technological Change* (Thousand Oaks, CA: Sage Publications, 2002).

[41]S. Sundaramurthy and M. Lewis, "Control and Collaboration: Paradoxes of Governance," *Academy of Management Review* 28 (July 2003), pp. 397–415.

[42]Mark L. Lengnick-Hall and Cynthia A. Lengnick-Hall, *Human Resource Management in the Knowledge Economy: New Challenges, New Roles, New Capabilities* (San Francisco: Berrett-Koehler, 2002).

[43]T.L. Goldstein and J.K. Ford, *Training in Organizations: Needs Assessment, Development, and Evaluation* (Belmont, CA: Wadsworth, 2002).

[44]W. van Eerde, K.C. Simon Tang, and Graeme Talbot, "The Mediating Role of Training Utility in the Relationship between Training Needs Assessment and Organizational Effectiveness," *International Journal of Human Resource Management* 19, no. 1 (January 2008), pp. 63–73.

[45]Original statements regarding MBO may be found in Peter Drucker, *The Practice of Management* (New York: Harper & Row, 1954); George Odiorne, *Management by Objectives* (New York: Pitman Publishing, 1965); and W.J. Reddin, *Effective Management by Objectives* (New York: McGraw-Hill, 1970).

[46]See Ronald G. Greenwood, "Management by Objectives: As Developed by Peter Drucker, Assisted by Harold Smiddy," *Academy of Management Review,* April 1981, pp. 225–30.

[47]Jan P. Muczyk and Bernard Reimann, "MBO as a Complement to Effective Leadership," *Academy of Management Executive,* May 1989, pp. 131–38.

[48]Lisa D. Ordóñez, Maurice E. Schweitzer, Adam D. Galinsky, and Max H. Bazerman, "Goals Gone Wild: The Systematic Side Effects of Overprescribing Goal Setting," *Academy of Management Perspectives* 23, no. 1 (February 2009), pp. 6–16.

[49]M. Hammer and J. Champy, *Reengineering the Corporation* (New York: HarperCollins, 1993).

[50]J. Fong, *Information Systems Reengineering and Integration* (New York: Springer, 2005).

[51]Ric Merrifield, Jack Calhoun, and Dennis Stevens, "The Next Revolution in Productivity," *Harvard Business Review* 86, no. 6 (June 2008), pp. 72–80.

[52]Ralph Katz, ed., *The Human Side of Managing Technological Innovation: A Collection of Readings* (New York: Oxford University Press, 2003).

[53]Fredrick Tell, *Organizational Capabilities and Technological Change* (New York: Edward Elgar, 2006).

[54]Jeanne C. Meister, "Training Workers in the Three C's," *Nation's Business,* September 1994, pp. 51–53.

[55]Peter Senge, *The Fifth Discipline* (New York: Doubleday, 1990).

[56]Ibid.

[57]G.L. Stewart, Charles C. Manz, and H.P. Sims, Jr., *Team Work and Group Dynamics* (New York: John Wiley & Sons, 1999).

[58]J. Lipman-Blumen and Harold J. Leavitt, "Hot Groups 'With Attitude': A New Organizational State of Mind," *Organizational Dynamics,* Spring 1999, pp. 63–73.

[59]Muel Kaptein and Johan Wempe, *The Balanced Company: A Theory of Corporate Integrity* (Oxford, UK: Oxford University Press, 2002).

[60]Melenie J. Lankau and Terri A. Scandura, "An Investigation of Personal Learning in Mentoring Relationships: Content, Antecedents, and Consequences," *Academy of Management Journal* 45 (August 2002), pp. 779–90.

[61]Monica C. Higgins, and Kathy E. Kram, "Reconceptualizing Mentoring at Work: A Developmental Network Perspective," *Academy of Management Review* 26 (April 2001), pp. 264–88.

[62]Jeffrey Pfeffer and Robert I. Sutton, *Hard Facts, Dangerous Half-Truths and Total Nonsense: Profiting from Evidence-Based Management* (Boston: Harvard Business School Press, 2006).

[63]Paul F. Buller and Cecil H. Bell, "Effects of Team Building and Goal Setting on Productivity: A Field Experiment," *Academy of Management Journal,* June 1986, pp. 305–28.

[64] Barrie Dale, *Managing Quality* (Oxford, UK: Blackwell, 2003).

[65]Robert J. Marshak and David Grant, "Organizational Discourse and New Organization Development Practices," *British Journal of Management* 19, Supplement 1 (March 2008), pp. S7–S19.

[66]David L. Cooperrider and Diana Whitney, *A Positive Revolution in Change: Appreciative Inquiry, Draft Paper* (Cleveland, OH: Case Western Reserve University, 1997).

[67]Diana Whitney and Amanda Trosten-Bloom, *The Power of Appreciative Inquiring: A Practical Guide to Positive Change* (San Francisco: Berrett-Koehler, 2002).

[68]J.M. Watkins and B.J. Mohr, *Appreciative Inquiry: Change at the Speed of Imagination* (New York: John Wiley & Sons, 2001).

[69]Monty G. Miller, Stephen P. Fitzgerald, Joanne C. Preston, and Kenneth L. Murrell, "The Efficacy of Appreciative Inquiry in Building Relational Capital in a Transnational Strategic Alliance," *Academy of Management Proceedings,* 2002, pp. E1–E5.

[70]Watkins and Mohr, *Appreciative Inquiry,* pp. 123–26.

[71]J.E. Loehr and T. Schwartz, *The Power of Full Engagement* (New York: Free Press, 2003).

[72]J.R. Evans and J.W. Dean, *Total Quality Management* (Cincinnati, OH: South-Western, 2002).

[73]Jeffrey M. Hiatt and Timothy J. Creasey, *Change Management* (Loveland, CO: Prosci Research, 2003).

[74]J. McGregor, M. Arndt, R. Berner, I. Rowley, and K. Hall, "The World's Most Innovative Companies," *BusinessWeek,* April 24, 2006, pp. 62–65.

[75]Mary F. Sully de Luque and Stephen M. Sommer, "The Impact of Culture on Feedback-Seeking Behavior: An Integrated Model and Propositions," *Academy of Management Review,* October 2000, pp. 829–49.

[76]Winfred Arthur, Jr., Winston Bennett, Jr., Pamela S. Edens, and Suzanne T. Bell, "Effectiveness of Training in Organizations: A Meta-Analysis of Design and Evaluation, Features," *Journal of Applied Psychology* 88 (April 2003), pp. 234–45.

[77]Jerry Flint, "The Myth of the Electric Car," *Forbes. com,* www.forbes.com/2009/03/18/ford-electric-cars-business-autos-jerry-flint.html (accessed April 2, 2009).

[78]"Timeline: Space Flight," *BBC News,* July 29, 2008, http://news.bbc.co.uk/2/hi/science/nature/6996121.stm.

[79]Katz, *The Human Side.*

[80]Pfeffer and Sutton, *Hard Facts.*

[81]Donald F. Van Eynde and Julie A. Bledsoe, "The Changing Practice of Organisation Development," *Leadership and Organization Development Journal* (UK) 11, no. 2 (1990), pp. 25–30.

[82]Mark Wilson and George Engelhard, *Objective Measurement: Theory into Practice* (Stamford, CT: Ablex, 2000).

[83]John B. Nicholas, "The Comparative Impact of Organization Development Interventions on Hard Criteria Measures," *Academy of Management Review,* October 1982, pp. 531–42.

[84]Mark Ackerman, Volkmar Pipek, and Volker Wulf, eds., *Sharing Expertise: Beyond Knowledge Management* (Cambridge, MA: MIT Press, 2003).

Appendix A

[1]For an excellent discussion of organizations in ancient societies, see Claude S. George, Jr., *The History of Management Thought* (Englewood Cliffs, NJ: Prentice Hall, 1968), pp. 3–26.

[2]James D. Mooney, *The Principles of Organization* (New York: Harper & Row, 1939), p. 63.

[3]Ian I. Mitroff, "Why Our Old Pictures of the World Do Not Work Anymore," in *Doing Research That Is Useful for Theory and Research,* ed. E.E. Lawler, III, et al. (San Francisco: Jossey-Bass, 1985), pp. 18–44.

[4]R. Richard Ritter and Stephen Levy, *The Ropes to Know: Studies in Organizational Behavior* (Belmont, CA: Wadsworth, 2006).

[5]A. Tashakkori and C. Teddlie, eds., *Handbook of Mixed Methods in Social and Behavioral Research* (Thousand Oaks, CA: Sage Publications, 2003).

[6]F.J. Gravetter and L.B. Wallnau, *Statistics in the Behavioral Sciences* (Belmont, CA: Wadsworth, 2006).

[7]Harold Kerzner, *Project Management Case Studies* (New York: John Wiley & Sons, 2006).

[8]Ibid.

[9]See G.R. Salancik, "Field Stimulations for Organizational Behavior Research," *Administrative Science Quarterly,* December 1979, pp. 638–49, for an interesting approach to field studies.

[10]Donald Hedeker and Robert D. Gibbons, *Longitudinal Data Analysis* (New York: John Wiley-Interscience, 2006).

[11]James G. Hunt and A. Ropa, "Longitudinal Organizational Research and the Third Scientific Discipline," *Group and Organizational Management* 28 (2003), pp. 315–40.

[12]Linda Bergmann, *Academic Research: Fields of Study and Inquiry* (New York: Longman, 2006).

[13]See an account of the classic Hawthorne studies in Fritz J. Roethlisberger and W.J. Dickson, *Management and the Worker* (Boston: Division of Research, Harvard Business School, 1939). The original purpose of the studies, which were conducted at the Chicago Hawthorne Plant of Western Electric, was to investigate the relationship between productivity and physical working conditions.

[14]For a discussion of this problem, see K.W. Weick, "Laboratory Experimentation with Organizations: A Reappraisal," *Academy of Management Review,* January 1977, pp. 123–27.

[15]John E. Hunter and Frank L. Schmidt, *Methods of Meta-Analysis: Correcting Error and Bias in Research Findings* (San Francisco: Sage Publications, 2006).

[16]D. Ones, C. Viswesvaran, and F.L. Schmidt, "Comprehensive Meta-Analysis of Integrity Test Validities: Findings and Implications for Personnel Selection and Theories of Job Performance," *Journal of Applied Psychology,* December 1993, pp. 679–703.

[17]Bruce Mullen, *Enhanced Basic Meta-Analysis* (Mahwah, NJ: Lawrence Erlbaum, 2006).

[18]R. Sherman, "The Subjective Experience of Race and Gender in Quantitative Research," *American Behavioral Scientist* 45 (April 2002), pp. 1247–53.

[19]Somali Shah, "Sharing the World: The Researcher and the Researched," *Qualitative Research,* May 2006, pp. 207–20.

[20]A. Mulhall, "In the Field: Notes on Observation in Qualitative Research, "*Journal of Advanced Nursing,* February 2003, pp. 306–13.

[21]A. Tashakkori and C.B. Teddlie, *Mixed Methodology: Combining Qualitative and Quantitative Approaches* (San Francisco: Sage Publications, 2006).

[22]D.N. Gellner and E. Hirsch, *Inside Organizations: Anthropologists at Work* (London: Oxford Press, 2001).

[23]John Van Maanen, J.M. Dobbs, Jr., and R.R. Faulkner, *Varieties of Qualitative Research* (Beverly Hills, CA: Sage Publications, 1982).

[24]Tashakkori and Teddlie, *Mixed Methodology.*

Name Index

Company Index

Subject Index